Notes on the New Testament

Albert Barnes

Edited by

Robert Frew

ACTS

BAKER BOOK HOUSE

Grand Rapids, Michigan 49506

Heritage Edition

Fourteen Volumes 0834-4

When ordering by ISBN (International Standard Book Number), numbers listed above should be preceded by 0-8010-.

Reprinted from the 1884-85 edition published by Blackie & Son, London, edited by Robert Frew

Reprinted 1987 by Baker Book House Company

ISBN: 0-8010-0844-1

Printed and bound in the United States of America

INTRODUCTION

THERE is no evidence that the title, "The Acts of the Apostles," affixed to this book, was given by divine authority or by the writer himself. It is a title, however, which, with a little variation, has been given to it by the Christian church at all times. The term "Acts" is not used, as it is sometimes with us, to denote *decrees* or *laws*, but it denotes the *doings* of the apostles. It is a record of what the apostles *did* in founding and establishing the Christian church. It is worthy of remark, however, that it contains chiefly a record of the *doings* of Peter and Paul. Peter was commissioned to open the doors of the Christian church to both Jews and Gentiles (see Note on Mat. xvi. 18, 19); and Paul was chosen to bear the gospel especially to the pagan world. As these two apostles were the most prominent and distinguished in founding and organizing the Christian church, it was deemed proper that a special and permanent record should be made of their labours. At the same time occasional notices are given of the other apostles; but of their labours elsewhere than in Judea, and of their death, except that of James (Ac. xii. 2), the sacred writers have given no information.

All antiquity is unanimous in ascribing this book to Luke as its author. It is repeatedly mentioned and quoted by the early Christian writers, and without a dissenting voice is mentioned as his work. The same thing is clear from the book itself. It professes to have been written by the same person who wrote a former treatise, addressed to the same person (comp. ver. 1 with Lu. i. 3), and it bears manifest marks of being from the same pen. It is designed evidently as a continuation of that Gospel, as in this book the author has taken up the history at the very time where he left it in the Gospel (ver. 1, 2).

Where, or at what time, this book was written, is not certainly known. As the history, however, is continued to the second year of the residence of Paul at Rome (Ac. xxviii. 31), it was evidently written about as late as the year 62; and as it makes no mention of the subsequent facts in the life of Paul, or of any other event of history, it seems clear that it was not written much *after* that time. It has been common, therefore, to fix the date of the book at about A.D. 63. It is also probable that it was written at Rome. In ch. xxviii. 16 Luke mentions *his* arrival at Rome with Paul. As he does not mention his departure from that city, it is to be presumed that it was written there. Some have supposed that it was written at Alexandria in Egypt, but of that there is no sufficient evidence.

The canonical authority of this book rests on the same foundation as that of the Gospel by the same author. Its authenticity has not been called in question at any time in the church.

This book has commonly been regarded as a history of the Christian church, and of course the first ecclesiastical history that was written. But it cannot have been designed as a general history of the church. Many important transactions have been omitted. It gives no account of the church at Jerusalem after the conversion of Paul; it omits his journey into Arabia (Ga. i. 17); it gives no account of the propagation of the gospel in Egypt or in Babylon (1 Pe. v. 13), or of the foundation of the church at Rome, or of many of Paul's voyages and shipwrecks (2 Co. xi. 25); and it omits to record the labours of most of the apostles, and confines the narrative chiefly to the transactions of Peter and Paul.

The design and importance of this history may be learned from the following particulars:

1. It contains *a record of the promised descent and operations of the Holy Spirit.* The Lord Jesus promised that after he had departed to heaven he would send the Holy Ghost to carry forward the great work of redemption, Jn. xiv. 16, 17; xv. 26; xvi. 7–14. The apostles were directed to tarry in Jerusalem until they were endued with power from on high, Lu. xxiv. 49. The four Gospels contained a record of the life, instructions, death, and resurrection of the Lord Jesus. But it is clear that he contemplated that the most signal triumphs of his gospel should take place after his ascension to heaven, and under the influence of the Holy Spirit. The descent of the Spirit, and his influence on the souls of men, was therefore a most important part of the work of redemption. Without an authentic, an inspired record of that, the account of the operations of God the Father, Son, and Spirit in the work of redemption would not have been complete. The purposes of *the Father* in regard to that plan were made known clearly in the Old Testament; the record of what *the Son* did in accomplishing it was contained in the Gospels; and some book was needful that should contain a record of the *doings* of the Holy Spirit. As the Gospels, therefore, may be regarded as a record of the work of Christ to save men, so may the Acts of the Apostles be considered as a record of the doings of the Holy Spirit in the same great work. Without that, the

way in which the Spirit operates to renew and save would have been very imperfectly known.

2. This book is *an inspired account of the character of true revivals of religion.* It records the first revivals that occurred in the Christian church. The scene on the day of Pentecost was one of the most remarkable displays of divine power and mercy that the world has ever known. It was the commencement of a series of stupendous movements on the earth to recover men. It was the true model of a revival of religion, and it is a demonstration that such scenes as have characterized our own age and nation especially are strictly in accordance with the spirit of the New Testament. The entire book of the Acts of the Apostles records the effect of the gospel when it comes fairly in contact with the minds of men. The gospel was addressed to every class. It met the Jew and the Gentile, the bond and the free, the learned and the ignorant, the rich and the poor, and it showed its power everywhere in subduing the mind to itself. It was proper that some record should be preserved of the displays of that power, and that record we have in this book. And it was especially proper that there should be given by an inspired man an account of the descent of the Holy Spirit, *a record of a true revival of religion.* It was certain that the gospel would produce excitement. The human mind, as all experience shows, is prone to enthusiasm and fanaticism; and men might be disposed to pervert the gospel to scenes of wild-fire, disorder, and tumult. That the gospel *would* produce excitement was well known to its Author. It was well, therefore, that there should be some record to which the church might always appeal as an infallible account of the proper effects of the gospel, some inspired standard to which might be brought all excitements on the subject of religion. If they are in accordance with the first triumphs of the gospel, they are genuine; if not, they are false.

3. This book shows that *revivals of religion are to be expected in the church.* If they existed in the best and purest days of Christianity, they are to be expected now. If, by means of revivals, the Holy Spirit chose at first to bless the preaching of the truth, the same thing is to be expected still. If in this way the gospel was at first spread among the nations, then we are to infer that this will be the mode in which it will finally spread and triumph in the world.

4. The Acts of the Apostles contains a record of the organization of the Christian church. That church was founded simply by the preaching of the truth, and chiefly by a simple statement of the death and resurrection of Jesus Christ. The "Acts of the Apostles" contains the highest models of preaching, and the purest specimens of that simple, direct, and pungent manner of addressing men, which may be

expected to be attended with the influences of the Holy Spirit. It contains some of the most tender, powerful, and eloquent appeals to be found in any language. If a man wishes to learn how to preach well he can probably acquire it nowhere else so readily as by giving himself to the prayerful and profound study of the specimens of preaching contained in this book. At the same time we have here a view of the *character* of the true church of Christ. The *simplicity* of this church must strike every reader of "the Acts." Religion is represented as a work of the heart, the pure and proper effect of *truth* on the mind. It is free from pomp and splendour, and from costly and magnificent ceremonies. There is no apparatus to impress the senses, no splendour to dazzle, no external rite or parade adapted to draw the affections from the pure and spiritual worship of God. How unlike to the pomp and parade of pagan worship! How unlike the vain and pompous ceremonies which have since, alas! crept into no small part of the Christian church!

5. In this book we have many striking and impressive illustrations of what the gospel is fitted to produce, to make men self-denying and benevolent. The apostles engaged in the great enterprise of converting the world. To secure that they cheerfully forsook all. Paul became a convert to the Christian faith, and cheerfully for that gave up all his hopes of preferment and honour, and welcomed toil and privation in foreign lands. Comp. Phi. iii. 4–11, 2 Co. xi. 24–27. The early converts had all things in common, ch. ii. 44; those "which used curious arts," and were gaining property by a course of iniquity, forsook their schemes of ill-gotten gain, and burned their books publicly, ch. xix. 19; Ananias and Sapphira were punished for attempting to impose on the apostles by hypocritical professed self-denials, ch. v. 1–10; and throughout the book there occur constant instances of sacrifices and toil to spread the gospel around the globe. Indeed, these great truths had manifestly seized upon the minds of the early Christians: *that the gospel was to be preached to all nations; that whatever stood in the way of that was to be sacrificed; that whatever toils and dangers were necessary were to be borne; and that even death itself was cheerfully to be met if it would promote the spread of true religion.* This was *then* genuine Christianity; this is *still* the spirit of the gospel of Christ.

6. This book throws important light on *the Epistles.* It is a connecting link between the Gospels and the other parts of the New Testament. Instances of this will be noticed in the Notes. One of the most clear and satisfactory evidences of the genuineness of the books of the New Testament is to be found in the *undesigned coincidences* between the Acts and the Epistles. This argument was first

clearly stated and illustrated by Dr. Paley. His little work illustrating it, the *Horæ Paulinæ*, is one of the most unanswerable proofs which have yet been furnished of the truth of the Christian religion.

7. This book contains unanswerable evidence of the truth of Christianity. It is a record of its early triumphs. Within the space of *thirty years* after the death of Christ the gospel had been carried to all parts of the civilized and to no small portion of the uncivilized world. Its progress and its triumphs were not concealed. Its great transactions were not "done in a corner." It had been preached in the most splendid, powerful, and enlightened cities; churches were already founded in Jerusalem, Antioch, Corinth, Ephesus, Philippi, and at Rome. The gospel had spread in Arabia, Asia Minor, Greece, Macedon, Italy, and Africa. It had assailed the most mighty existing institutions; it had made its way over the most formidable barriers; it had encountered the most deadly and malignant opposition; it had travelled to the capital, and had secured such a hold even in the imperial city as to make it certain that it would finally overturn the established religion and seat itself on the ruins of paganism. Within thirty years it had settled the point that it would overturn every bloody altar, close every pagan temple, bring under its influence everywhere the men of office, rank, and power, and that "the banners of the faith would soon stream from the palaces of the Cæsars." All this would be accomplished by the instrumentality of Jews—of fishermen—of Nazarenes. They had neither wealth, armies, nor allies. With the exception of Paul, they were men without learning. They were taught only by the Holy Ghost, armed only with the power of God, victorious only because Christ was their captain, and the world acknowledged the presence of the messengers of the Highest and the power of the Christian religion. Its success never has been, and never can be accounted for by any other supposition than that God attended it. And if the Christian religion be not true the change wrought by the twelve apostles is the most inexplicable, mysterious, and wonderful event that has ever been witnessed in this world. Their success will stand to the end of time as an argument of the truth of the scheme, will ever onward confound the infidel, and will sustain the Christian with the assured belief that *this* is a religion which has proceeded from the almighty and the infinitely benevolent God.

THE
ACTS OF THE APOSTLES.

CHAPTER I.

THE[a] former treatise have I made, O Theophilus, of all that Jesus began both to do and to teach,

2 Until[b] the day in which he was

a Lu.1.1-4,&c. *b* Lu.24.51; ver.9; 1 Ti.3.16.

---

1. *The former treatise.* The former *book.* The gospel by Luke is here evidently intended. Greek, "the former *logos*," meaning a *discourse*, or a narrative. ¶ *O Theophilus.* See Notes on Lu. i. 3. As this book was written to the same individual as the former, it was evidently written with the same design—to furnish an authentic and full narrative of events concerning which there would be many imperfect and exaggerated accounts. See Lu. i. 1–4. As these events pertained to the descent of the Spirit, to the spread of the gospel, to the organization of the church, to the kind of preaching by which the church was to be collected and organized, and as the facts in the case constituted a full proof of the truth of the Christian religion, and the conduct of the apostles would be a model for ministers and the church in all future times, it was of great importance that a fair and full narrative of these things should be preserved. Luke was the companion of Paul in his travels, and was an eye-witness of no small part of the transactions recorded in this book. See Ac. xvi. 10, 17; xx. 1–6; xxvii.; xxviii. As an eye-witness, he was well qualified to make a record of the leading events of the primitive church. And as he was the companion of Paul, he had every opportunity of obtaining information about the great events of the gospel of Christ. ¶ *Of all.* That is, of the principal, or most important parts of the life and doctrines of Christ. It cannot mean that he recorded *all* that Jesus did, as he had omitted many things that have been preserved by the other evangelists. The word *all* is frequently thus used to denote the most important or material facts. See Ac. xiii. 10; 1 Ti. i. 16; Ja. i. 2; Mat. ii. 3; iii. 5; Ac. ii. 5; Ro. xi. 26; Col. i. 6. In each of these places the word here translated "all" occurs in the original, and means *many*, *a large part, the principal portion.* It has the same use in all languages. "This word often signifies, indefinitely, a large portion or number, or a great part" (Webster). ¶ *That Jesus.* The Syriac version adds, "Jesus our Messiah." This version was probably made in the second century. ¶ *Began to do,* &c. This is a Hebrew form of expression, meaning the same thing as that Jesus *did* and *taught.* See Ge. ix. 20, "Noah *began* to be an husbandman," that is, *was* an husbandman. Ge. ii. 3, in the Septuagint: "Which God *began* to create and make;" in the Hebrew, "which God created and made." Mar. iv. 7, "*Began* to send them forth by two and two," that is, *sent* them forth. See also Mar. x. 32; xiv. 65, "And some *began* to spit on him;" in the parallel place in Mat. xxvi. 67, "they *did* spit in his face." ¶ *To do.* This refers to his miracles and his acts of benevolence, including all that he *did* for man's salvation. It probably includes, therefore, his sufferings, death, and resurrection, as a part of what he has *done* to save men. ¶ *To teach.* His doctrines. As the writer had given an account of what the Lord Jesus did, so he was now about to give a narrative of what his apostles did in the same cause, that thus the world might be in possession of an inspired record respecting the establishment of the Christian church. The record of these events preserved in the sacred narrative is one of the greatest blessings that God has conferred on mankind; and one of the highest privileges which men can enjoy is that which has been conferred so abundantly on this age in the possession of the word of God.

2. *Until the day.* The fortieth day after the resurrection, ver. 3. See Lu. xxiv. 51. ¶ *In which he was taken up.* In which he ascended to heaven. He was taken up into a cloud, and is repre-

taken up, after that he through the Holy Ghost had given [c]commandments unto the apostles whom he had chosen:

3 To whom also he showed himself alive after his passion, [d]by many infallible proofs, being seen of them forty days, and speaking

c Mat.28.19; Mar.16.15–19.

d Lu. 24.; Jn. 20. & 21.

sented as having been *borne* or carried to heaven, ver. 9. ¶ *After that,* &c. This passage has been variously rendered. The Syriac translates it, "After he had given commandment unto the apostles whom he had chosen by the Holy Spirit." So also the Ethiopic version. Others have joined the words "through the Holy Ghost" to the phrase "was taken up," making it mean that he was taken up by the Holy Ghost. But the most natural and correct translation seems to be that which is in our version. ¶ *Through the Holy Ghost.* To understand this, it is necessary to call to mind the promise that Jesus made before his death, that after his departure, the Holy Ghost would descend to be a guide to his apostles. See Jn. xvi. 7–11, and the Notes on that place. It was to be *his* office to carry forward the work of redemption in applying it to the hearts of men. Whatever was done, therefore, *after* the death and resurrection of Jesus, was to be regarded as under the peculiar influence and direction of the Holy Ghost. Even the instructions of Jesus, and his commission to the apostles, were to be regarded as coming within the department of the sacred Spirit, or within the province of *his* peculiar work. The instructions were given by divine authority, by infallible guidance, and as a part of the work which the Holy Spirit was sent down to accomplish. Under the direction and guidance of that Spirit the apostles were to go forth; by *his* aid they were to preach the gospel, to organize the church, to establish its order and its doctrines; and hence the entire work was declared to be by his direction. Though in his larger and more mighty influences the Spirit did not descend until the day of Pentecost (Lu. xxiv. 49; comp. Ac. ii.), yet *in some measure* his influence was imparted to the apostles before the ascension of Christ, Jn. xx. 22. ¶ *Had given commandments.* Particularly the command to preach the gospel to all nations, Mat. xxviii. 19; Mar. xvi. 15–19. It may be worthy of remark, that the word *commandments,* as a noun in the plural number, does not occur in the original. The single word which is translated, "had given commandments" is a *participle,* and means simply *having commanded.* There is no need, therefore, of supposing that there is reference here to any other command than to that great and glorious injunction to preach the gospel to every creature. That was a command of so much importance as to be worthy of a distinct record, as constituting the sum of all that the Saviour taught them after his resurrection. ¶ *The apostles.* The eleven that remained after the treason and death of Judas. ¶ *Whom he had chosen.* Mat. x. 1–4; Lu. vi. 12–16.

3. *He showed himself.* The *resurrection* of Jesus was the great fact on which the truth of the gospel was to be established. Hence the sacred writers so often refer to it, and establish it by so many arguments. As the fact of his resurrection lay at the foundation of all that Luke was about to record in his history, it was of importance that he should state clearly the sum of the evidence of it in the beginning of his work. ¶ *After his passion.* After he *suffered,* referring particularly to his death as the consummation of his sufferings. The word *passion* with us means commonly excitement or agitation of mind, as love, hope, fear, anger, &c. The original means *after he suffered.* The word *passion,* applied to the Saviour, denotes his last sufferings. Thus, in the Litany of the Episcopal Church, it is beautifully said, "By thine agony and bloody sweat; by thy cross and *passion,* good Lord, deliver us." The Greek word of the same derivation is rendered *sufferings* in 1 Pe. i. 11; iv. 13; Col. i. 24. ¶ *By many infallible proofs.* The word rendered here *infallible proofs* does not occur elsewhere in the New Testament. In Greek authors it denotes an infallible sign or argument by which anything can be certainly known (Schleusner). Here it means the same—evidence that he was alive which could not deceive, or in which they could not be mistaken. That evidence consisted in his eating with them, conversing with them, meeting them at various times and places, working miracles (Jn. xxi. 6, 7), and

of the things pertaining to the kingdom of God;

4 And [1]being assembled together with *them*, [e]commanded them that they should not depart from Jerusalem, but wait for the promise of

[1] or, *eating together*.

e Lu.24.49.

uniformly showing himself to be the same friend with whom they had been familiar for more than three years. This evidence was infallible—(1) Because it was to them unexpected. They had manifestly not believed that he would rise again, Jn. xx. 25; Lu. xxiv. 19–24. There was, therefore, no *delusion* resulting from any *expectation* of seeing him, or from a *design* to impose on men. (2) It was impossible that they could have been *deceived* in relation to one with whom they had been familiar for more than three years. No men in the possession of reason could be made to believe that they really saw, talked with, and ate with, a friend whom they had known so long and familiarly, unless it was real. (3) There were *enough* of them to avoid the possibility of deception. Though it might be pretended that *one* man could be imposed on, yet it could not be that an imposition could be practised for forty days on eleven men, who were all at first incredulous. (4) He was with them sufficient *time* to give evidence of his personal identity. It might be pretended, if they had seen him but *once*, that they were deceived. But they saw him often, and for the space of more than a month. (5) They saw him in *various places* and at *times* in which there could be no deception. If they had pretended that they saw him *rise*, or saw him at twilight in the morning *when* he rose, it might have been said that they were deluded by something that was merely the result of imagination. It might have been said that, *expecting* to see him rise, their hopes, in the agitated state of their minds, deceived them, and that they only *fancied* that they saw him. But it is not pretended by the sacred writers that *they saw him rise*. An impostor *would have affirmed this, and would not have omitted it*. But the sacred writers affirmed that they saw him *after* he was risen; when they were free from agitation; when they could judge coolly; in Jerusalem; in their own company when at worship; when journeying to Emmaus; when in Galilee; when he went with them to Mount Olivet; and when he ascended to heaven: and how could they have been deceived in this? (6) He appeared to them as he had always done, as a friend, companion, and benefactor; he ate with them, wrought a miracle before them, was engaged in the same work as he was before he suffered, renewed the same promise of the Holy Spirit, and gave them his commands respecting the work which he had died to establish, and the work which he required them to do—carrying out the same purposes and plans which he had before he died. In all these circumstances it was impossible that they should be deceived. ¶ *Being seen of them forty days.* There are no less than THIRTEEN different appearances of Jesus to his disciples recorded. For an account of them, see the Notes at the end of the gospel of Matthew. ¶ *Speaking to them*, &c. He was not only *seen* by them, but he *continued the same topics of discourse* as before his sufferings; thus showing that he was the *same* person that had suffered, and that his heart was still intent on the same great work. And as his heart was occupied with the same purposes which engaged his attention before he suffered, we are taught by this that we should aim at the same great work in all the circumstances of our being. Afflictions, persecutions, and the prospect of death never turned *him* from *his* great plan; nor should they be allowed to divert *our* minds from the great work which God has given us to do. ¶ *The things pertaining to the kingdom of God.* For an explanation of this phrase, *the kingdom of God*, see the Notes on Mat. iii. 2. The meaning is, Jesus gave them instructions about the organization, spread, and edification of his church.

4. *And being assembled together.* Margin, "or, *eating together*." This sense is given to this place in the Latin Vulgate, the Ethiopic, and the Syriac versions. But the Greek word has not properly this signification. It has the meaning of *congregating*, or *assembling*. It should have been, however, translated in the *active* sense, "and *having assembled* them together." The apostles were scattered after his death. But this passage denotes that *he* had assembled them together by his authority, for the purpose of giving them a charge

the Father, which, *saith he*, [f] ye have heard of me:

5 For [g] John truly baptized with water; but ye shall be [h] baptized with the Holy Ghost, not many days hence.

6 When they therefore were come together, they asked of him, saying,

f Jn. 14. 15. & 16. *g* Mat.3.11. *h* ch.2.4; 10.45; 11.15.

respecting their conduct when he should have left them. *When* this occurred does not appear from the narrative; but it is probable that it was not long before his ascension; and it is clear that the *place* where they were assembled was Jerusalem. ¶ *But wait for the promise of the Father.* For the *fulfilment* of the promise respecting the descent of the Holy Spirit made by the Father. ¶ *Which ye have heard of me.* Which I have made to you. See Jn. xiv. 16, 26; xv. 26; xvi. 7–13.

5. *For John truly baptized*, &c. These are the words of Jesus to his apostles, and he evidently has reference to what was said of John's baptism compared with his own in Mat. iii. 11; Jn. i. 33. In those verses John is represented as baptizing with water, but the Messiah who was to come, as baptizing with the Holy Ghost and with fire. This promise was now about to be fulfilled in a remarkable manner. See Ac. ii. ¶ *Not many days hence.* This was probably spoken not long before his ascension, and of course not many days before the day of Pentecost.

6. *When they therefore were come together.* At the Mount of Olives. See ver. 9, 12. ¶ *Wilt thou at this time*, &c. The apostles had entertained the common opinions of the Jews about the *temporal* dominion of the Messiah. They expected that he would reign as a prince and conqueror, and would free them from the bondage of the Romans. Many instances where this expectation is referred to occur in the gospels, notwithstanding all the efforts which the Lord Jesus made to explain to them the true nature of his kingdom. This expectation was checked, and almost destroyed by his death (Lu. xxiv. 21), and it is clear that *his death* was the only means which could effectually change their opinions on this subject. Even his own instructions would not do it; and nothing but his being taken from them could direct their minds effectually to the true nature of his kingdom. Yet, though his death checked their expectations, and appeared to thwart their plans, his return to life excited them again. They beheld him with them; they were assured that it was the same Saviour; they saw now that his enemies had no power over him; they could not doubt that a being who could rise from the dead could easily accomplish all his plans. And as they did not doubt now that he *would* restore the kingdom to Israel, they asked whether he would do it *at that time?* They did not ask whether he would do it at all, or whether they had correct views of his kingdom; but, taking that for granted, they asked him whether *that was the time* in which he would do it. The emphasis of the inquiry lies in the expression, "*at this time*," and hence the answer of the Saviour refers solely *to the point of their inquiry*, and not to the correctness or incorrectness of their opinions. From these expectations of the apostles we may learn, (1) That there is nothing so difficult to be removed from the mind as *prejudice in favour of erroneous opinions.* (2) That such prejudice will survive the plainest proofs to the contrary. (3) That it will often manifest itself even after all proper means have been taken to subdue it. Erroneous opinions thus maintain a secret ascendency in a man's mind, and are revived by the slightest circumstances, even long after it was supposed that they were overcome, and in the face of the plainest proofs of reason or of Scripture. ¶ *Restore.* Bring back; put into its former situation. Judea was formerly governed by its own kings and laws; now, it was subject to the Romans. This bondage was grievous, and the nation sighed for deliverance. The inquiry of the apostles evidently was, whether he would now free them from the bondage of the Romans, and restore them to their former state of freedom and prosperity, as in the times of David and Solomon. See Is. i. 26. The word "restore" also may include more than a reducing it to its former state. It may mean, wilt thou now *bestow* the kingdom and dominion to Israel, according to the prediction in Da. vii. 27? ¶ *The kingdom.* The dominion; the empire; the reign. The expectation was that the Messiah—the king of Israel—would *reign* over men, and that thus the na-

Lord, [i]wilt thou at this time [k]restore again the kingdom to Israel?
7 And he said unto them, [l]It is not for you to know the times or the seasons which the Father hath put in his own power.
8 But ye shall receive [2]power, after that the Holy Ghost is come

i Mat.24.3,4. *k* Is.1.26; Da.7.27. *l* Mat.24.36; 1 Th.5.1,2.

2 or, *the power of the Holy Ghost coming upon you.*

---

tion of the Jews would extend their empire over all the earth. ¶ *To Israel.* To the Jews, and particularly to the *Jewish* followers of the Messiah. Lightfoot thinks that this question was asked in indignation against the Jews. "Wilt thou confer dominion on a nation which has just put thee to death?" But the answer of the Saviour shows that this was not the design of the question.

7. *It is not for you to know.* The question of the apostles respected the *time* of the restoration; it was not whether he *would* do it. Accordingly, his answer meets precisely their inquiry; and he tells them *in general* that the *time* of the great events of God's kingdom was not to be understood by them. They had asked a similar question on a former occasion, Mat. xxiv. 3, "Tell us when shall these things be?" Jesus had answered them *then* by showing them that certain signs would precede his coming, and then by saying (ver. 36), "But of that day and that hour knoweth no man, no, not the angels of heaven, but my Father only." God has uniformly reproved a vain curiosity on such points, 1 Th. v. 1, 2; 2 Pe. iii. 10; Lu. xii. 39, 40. ¶ *The times, or the seasons.* The difference between these words is, that the former denotes any time or period that is indefinite or uncertain; the latter denotes a fixed, definite, or appropriate time. They seem to be used here to denote the periods that would mark or determine all future events. ¶ *The Father hath put,* &c. So entirely had the Father reserved the knowledge of these to himself, that it is said that even the Son did not know them. See Mar. iii. 32, and the Notes on that place. ¶ *In his own power.* That is, he has fixed them by his own authority, he will bring them about in his own time and way; and therefore it is not proper for men anxiously to inquire into them. All prophecy is remarkably *obscure* in regard to the *time* of its fulfilment. The reasons why it is so are such as the following: (1) To excite men to watch for the events that are to come, as the time is uncertain, and they will come "like a thief in the night." (2) As they are to be brought about by human agency, they are so arranged as to call forth that agency. If men knew *just when* an event was to come to pass, they might be remiss, and feel that their own efforts were not needed. (3) The knowledge of future scenes—of the exact *time*, might alarm men, and absorb their thoughts so entirely as to prevent a proper attention to the present duties of life. Duty is ours now; God will provide for future scenes. (4) Promises sufficiently clear and full are therefore given us to encourage us, but not so full as to excite a vain and idle curiosity. All this is eminently true of our own death, one of the most important future scenes through which *we* are to pass. It is *certainly* before us; it is *near;* it *cannot* be long delayed; it *may come* at any moment. God has fixed the time, but will not inform us when it shall be. He does not gratify a vain curiosity; nor does he terrify us by announcing to us the day or the hour when we are to die, as we do a man that is to be executed. This would be to make our lives like that of a criminal sentenced to die, and we should through all our life, through fear of death, be subject to bondage, He. ii. 15. He has made *enough* known to excite us to make preparation, and to be always ready, having our loins girt about and our lamps trimmed and burning, Lu. xii. 35.

8. *But ye shall receive power,* &c. Literally, as it is translated in the margin, "Ye shall receive the power of the Holy Ghost coming upon you." This was said to them to console them. Though they could not know the *times* which God reserved in his own appointment, yet they should receive the promised Guide and Comforter. The word *power* here refers to the help or aid which the Holy Spirit would grant; the power of speaking with new tongues; of preaching the gospel with great effect; of enduring great trials, &c. See Mar. xvi. 17, 18. The apostles had *impatiently* asked him if he was *then* about to restore the kingdom to Israel. Jesus by this answer rebuked their impatience, taught them to repress their ill-timed ardour; and assured them again of the coming

upon you: and [m] ye shall be witnesses unto me, both in Jerusalem, and in all Judea, and in Samaria, and unto the uttermost part of the earth.

9 And when he had spoken these

m Lu.24.47-49; Mat.28.19.

---

of the Holy Ghost. ¶ *Ye shall be witnesses.* For this purpose they were appointed; and to prepare them for this they had been with him for more than three years. They had seen his manner of life, his miracles, his meekness, his sufferings; they had listened to his instructions, and had conversed and eaten with him as a friend; they had seen him after he was risen, and were about to see him ascend to heaven; and they were thus *qualified* to bear witness to these things in all parts of the earth. Their number was so great that it could not be pretended that they were deceived; they had been so intimate with him and his plans that they were qualified to state what his doctrines and purposes were; and there was no motive but conviction of the truth that could induce them to make the sacrifices which they would be required to make in communicating these things to the world. In every respect, therefore, they were qualified to be impartial and competent witnesses. The original word here is μάρτυρες, *martyrs.* From this word the name *martyrs* has been given to those who suffered in times of persecution. The reason why this name was given to them was that they *bore witness* to the life, instructions, death, and resurrection of the Lord Jesus, even in the midst of persecution and death. It is commonly supposed that nearly all of the apostles bore witness as *martyrs* in this sense to the truths of the Christian religion, but of this there is not clear proof. See Mosheim's *Ecclesiastical History*, vol. i. p. 55, 56. Still the word here does not necessarily mean that they to whom this was addressed would be *martyrs*, or would be put to death in bearing witness to the Lord Jesus; but that they were everywhere to testify to what they knew of him. The fact that this was the design of their appointment, and that they actually bore such testimony, is abundantly confirmed in the Acts of the Apostles, ch. i. 22; v. 32; x. 39, 42; xxii. 15. ¶ *In Jerusalem.* In the capital of the nation. See Ac. ii. The great work of the Spirit on the day of Pentecost occurred there. Most of the disciples remained in Jerusalem until the persecution that arose about the death of Stephen, Ac. viii. 1, 4. The apostles remained there till Herod put James to death. Comp. Ac. viii. 1, with xii. 1, 2. This was about eight years. During this time, however, Paul was called to the apostleship, and Peter had preached the gospel to Cornelius, Philip to the eunuch, &c. ¶ *In all Judea.* Judea was the southern division of the Holy Land, and included Jerusalem as the capital. See Notes on Mat. ii. 22. ¶ *And in Samaria.* This was the *middle* portion of Palestine. Notes, Mat. ii. 22. This was fulfilled by the disciples. See ch. viii. 1, "And they were all scattered abroad throughout the regions of Judea and Samaria;" comp. ver. 4, 5, "They that were scattered abroad went every where preaching the word. Then Philip went down to the city of Samaria, and preached Christ unto them." See also ver. 14; ch. ix. 31. ¶ *And unto the uttermost parts of the earth.* The word *earth*, or *land*, is sometimes taken to denote only the land of Palestine. But here there does not seem to be a necessity for limiting it thus. If Christ had intended that, he would have mentioned *Galilee*, as being the only remaining division of the country. But as he had expressly directed them to preach the gospel to all nations, the expression here is clearly to be considered as including the Gentile lands as well as the Jewish. The evidence that they did this is found in the subsequent parts of this book, and in the history of the church. It was in this way that Jesus replied to their question. Though he did not tell them the *time* when it was to be done, nor affirm that he would restore the kingdom to *Israel*, yet he gave them an answer that *implied* that the work should advance—should advance much farther than the land of Israel; and that *they* would have *much to do* in promoting it. All the commands of God, and all his communications, are such as to call up *our* energy, and teach us that *we* have much to do. The uttermost parts of the earth have been given to the Saviour (Ps. ii. 8), and the church should not rest until he whose right it is shall come and reign, Eze. xxi. 27.

9. *While they beheld.* While they *saw* him. It was of importance to state that circumstance, and to state it distinctly.

things, while they beheld, he was taken up; and a cloud received him out of their sight.

10 And while they looked stedfastly toward heaven, as he went

---

It is not affirmed in the New Testament that they *saw him rise* from the dead, because the evidence of that fact could be better established by their seeing him *after* he was risen. But the truth of his *ascension to heaven* could not be confirmed in that manner. Hence it was so arranged that he should ascend in open day, and in the presence of his apostles; and that not when they were asleep, or were inattentive to what was occurring, but when they were engaged in a conversation that would fix the attention, and even when they were looking upon him. Had Jesus vanished secretly, or had he disappeared in the night, the apostles would have been amazed and confounded; perhaps they would even have doubted whether they had not been deceived. But when they *saw* him leave them in this manner, they could not doubt that he had ascended to heaven, and that God approved his work, and would carry it forward. This event was exceedingly important. (1) It was a confirmation of the truth of the Christian religion. (2) It enabled the apostles to state distinctly *where* the Lord Jesus was, and *at once* directed their affections and their thoughts away from the earth, and opened their eyes on the glory of the scheme of religion they were to establish. If their Saviour was *in heaven*, it settled the question about the *nature* of his kingdom. It was clear that it was not designed to be a temporal kingdom. The *reasons* why it was proper that the Lord Jesus should ascend to heaven rather than remain on earth were: (1) That he had *finished* the work which God gave him to do *on the earth* (Jn. xvii. 4; xix. 30), and it was *proper* that he should be received back to the glory which he had with the Father before the world was, Jn. xvii. 4, 5; Phi. ii. 6, 9, 10. (2) It was proper that *he* should ascend in order that the Holy Spirit might come down and perform *his* part of the work of redemption. Jesus, by his *personal* ministry, as a man, could be but in one place; the Holy Spirit could be in all places, and could apply the work to all men. See Note on Jn. xvi. 7. (3) A *part* of the work of Christ was yet to be performed in heaven. That was the work of *intercession*. The high-priest of the Jews not only made an *atonement*, but also presented the blood of sacrifice before the mercy-seat, as the priest of the people, Le. xvi. 11–14. This was done to typify the entrance of the great High-priest of our profession into the heavens, He. ix. 7, 8, 11, 12. The work which he performs there is the work of *intercession*, He. vii. 25. This is properly the work which an advocate performs in a court for his client. As applicable to Christ, the meaning is, that he, as our great High-priest, still manages our cause in heaven; secures our interests; obtains for us grace and mercy. His work, in this respect, consists in his appearing in the presence of God for us (He. ix. 24); in his presenting the merits of his blood (He. ix. 12, 14); and in securing the continuance of the mercy which has been bestowed on us, and which is still needful for our welfare. The Lord Jesus also ascended that he might assume and exercise the office of *King* in the immediate seat of power. All worlds were made subject to him for the welfare of the church; and it was needful that he should be solemnly invested with that power in the presence of God as the reward of his earthly toils. 1 Co. xv. 25, "He must reign till he hath put all enemies under his feet." Comp. Ep. i. 20–22; Phi. ii. 6–11. ¶ *A cloud received him.* He entered into the region of the clouds, and was hid from their view. But *two* others of our race have been taken bodily from earth to heaven. Enoch was translated (Ge. v. 24; comp. He. xi. 5); and Elijah was taken up by a whirlwind, 2 Ki. ii. 11. It is remarkable that when the *return* of the Saviour is mentioned, it is uniformly said that he will return *in the clouds*, ver. 11; Mat. xxiv. 30; xxvi. 64; Mar. xiii. 26; Re. i. 7; Da. vii. 13. The clouds are an emblem of sublimity and grandeur, and perhaps this is all that is intended by these expressions, De. iv. 11; 2 Sa. xxii. 12; Ps. xcvii. 2; civ. 3.

10. *Looked stedfastly.* They fixed their eyes, or gazed intently toward heaven. Lu. iv. 20, "And the eyes of all them in the synagogue *were fastened* (Greek, the same word as here) on him." It denotes the intense gaze when we are deeply interested, and wish to see clearly and distinctly. They were

up, behold, [n]two men stood by
them in white apparel;
11 Which also said, [o]Ye men of
Galilee, why stand ye gazing up into
heaven? This same Jesus, which
is taken up from you into heaven,

n Jn.20.12. *o* ch.2.7; 13.31.

---

amazed and confounded; what had occurred was unlooked for; for they had just been inquiring whether he would not, *at that time*, restore the kingdom to Israel. With this mingled amazement, disappointment, and curiosity, and with an earnest desire to catch the last glimpse of their beloved master, they naturally continued to gaze on the distant clouds where he had mysteriously disappeared from their view. Never was a scene more impressive, grand, and solemn than this. ¶ *Toward heaven.* Toward the distant clouds or sky which had received him. ¶ *As he went up.* Literally *upon him going up;* that is, they gazed on him as he ascended, and doubtless they continued to gaze after he had disappeared from their view. ¶ *Two men.* From the *raiment* of these "men," and the nature of their message, it seems clear that they were angelic beings, who were sent to meet and comfort the disciples on this occasion. They appeared in *human form*, and Luke describes them as they appeared. Angels are not unfrequently called *men.* Lu. xxiv. 4, "Two *men* stood by them in shining garments," &c. Comp. Jn. xx. 12; Mat. xxviii. 5. As *two* angels are mentioned only as addressing the apostles after the resurrection of Jesus (Jn. xx. 12; Lu. xxiv. 4), it is no unnatural supposition that these were the same who had been designated to the honourable office of bearing witness to his resurrection, and of giving them all the information about that resurrection, and of his ascension, which their circumstances needed. ¶ *In white apparel.* Angels are commonly represented as clothed in white. See Notes on Jn. xx. 12; Mat. xxviii. 3; Mar. xvi. 5. It is an emblem of purity; and the worshippers of heaven are represented as clothed in this manner. Re. iii. 4, "They shall walk with me in white;" ver. 5, "He that overcometh shall be clothed in white raiment;" iv. 4; vii. 9, 13, 14.

11. *Ye men of Galilee.* Galilee was the place of their former residence, and they were commonly known by the name of Galileans. ¶ *Why stand ye,* &c. There is doubtless a *slight* degree of censure implied in this, as well as a design to call their attention away from a vain attempt to see the departed Saviour. The impropriety *may* have been (1) In the feeling of disappointment, as if he would *not* restore the kingdom to Israel. (2) Possibly they were expecting that he would again *soon* appear, though he had often foretold them that he would ascend to heaven. (3) There might have been an impropriety in their earnest desire for the mere *bodily presence* of the Lord Jesus, when it was more important that he should be in heaven. We may see here also that it is our duty not to stand in idleness, and to gaze *even toward heaven.* We, as well as the apostles, have a great work to do, and we should actively engage in it without delay. ¶ *Gazing up.* Looking up. ¶ *This same Jesus.* This was said to comfort them. The *same* tried friend who had been so faithful to them would return. They ought not, therefore, to look with despondency at his departure. ¶ *Into heaven.* This expression denotes into the immediate presence of God; or into the place of perpetual purity and happiness, where God peculiarly manifests his favour. The same thing is frequently designated by his sitting on the right hand of God, as emblematic of power, honour, and favour. See Notes on Mar. xvi. 19; xiv. 62; He. i. 3; viii. 1; Ac. vii. 55; Ro. viii. 34; Ep. i. 20. ¶ *Shall so come.* At the day of judgment. Jn. xiv. 3, "If I go and prepare a place for you, I will come again," &c. ¶ *In like manner,* &c. In clouds, as he ascended. See Notes on ver. 9; 1 Th. iv. 16. This address was designed to comfort the disciples. Though their master and friend was taken from them, yet he was not removed for ever. He would come again with similar majesty and glory to vindicate his people, and to tread his enemies under his feet. The *design* for which he will come will be to judge the world, Mat. xxv. There will be an evident fitness and propriety in his coming for such reasons as the following: (1) Because his appropriate work in heaven as mediator will have been accomplished; his people will have been saved; the great enemy of God and man will have been subdued; death will have been conquered; and the gospel will have

shall [p]so come in like manner as ye have seen him go into heaven.

12 Then[q] returned they unto Jerusalem, from the mount called Olivet, which is from Jerusalem a sabbath-day's journey.

13 And when they were come in, they went up into an upper room,

p Jn.14.3; 1 Th.4.16. q Lu.24.52.

shown its power in subduing *all forms* of wickedness; in removing the effects of sin; in establishing the law, and in vindicating the honour of God; and all will have been done that is necessary to establish the authority of God throughout the universe. It will be proper, therefore, that this mysterious order of things shall be *wound up*, and the *results* become a matter of record in the history of the universe. This will be better than it would be to suffer an *eternal millennium* on the earth, while the saints should many of them slumber, and the wicked still be in their graves. (2) It is proper that he should come to vindicate his people, and raise them up to glory. Here they have been persecuted, oppressed, put to death. Their character is assailed; they are poor; and the world despises them. It is fit that God should show himself to be their friend; that he should do justice to their injured names and motives; that he should bring out hidden and obscure virtue, and vindicate it; that he should enter every grave and bring forth his friends to life. (3) It is proper that he should show his hatred of sin. Here it triumphs. The wicked are rich, and honoured, and mighty, and say, Where is the promise of his coming? 2 Pe. iii. 4. It is right that he should defend his cause. Hence the Lord Jesus will come to guard the avenues to heaven, and to see *that the universe suffers no wrong* by the admission of an improper person to the skies. (4) The great transactions of redemption have been public, open, often grand. The apostasy was public, in the face of angels and of the universe. Sin has been open, public high-handed. Misery has been public, and has rolled its deep and turbid waves in the face of the universe. Death has been public; all worlds have seen the race cut down and moulder. The death of Jesus was public: the angels saw it; the heavens were clothed with mourning; the earth shook, and the dead arose. Jesus was publicly whipped, cursed, crucified; and it is proper that he should publicly triumph—that all heaven rejoicing, and all hell at length humbled, should *see* his public victory. Hence he will come with clouds—with angels—with fire—and will raise the dead, and exhibit to all the universe the amazing close of the scheme of redemption. (5) We have in these verses a description of the most grand and wonderful events that this world has ever known—the ascension and return of the Lord Jesus. Here is consolation for the Christian; and here is a source of ceaseless alarm to the sinner.

12. *Then they returned to Jerusalem.* In Lu. xxiv. 52, we are told that they *worshipped* Jesus before they returned, and it is probable that the *act* of worship to which he refers was that which is mentioned in this chapter—their gazing intently on their departing Lord. ¶ *From the mount called Olivet.* From the Mount of Olives. See Notes on Mat. xxi. 1. The *part* of the mountain from which he ascended was the eastern declivity, where stood the little village of Bethany, Lu. xxiv. 50. ¶ *A sabbath-day's journey.* As far as might be lawfully travelled by a Jew on the Sabbath. This was 2000 paces or cubits, or seven furlongs and a half—not quite one mile. See Notes on Mat. xxiv. 20. The distance of a lawful journey on the Sabbath was not fixed by the laws of Moses, but the Jewish teachers had fixed it at 2000 paces. This measure was determined on because it was a tradition that in the camp of the Israelites, when coming from Egypt, no part of the camp was more than 2000 paces from the tabernacle, and over this space, therefore, they were permitted to travel for worship. Perhaps, also, some countenance was given to this from the fact that this was the extent of the suburbs of the Levitical cities, Nu. xxxv. 5. Mount Olivet was but *five* furlongs from Jerusalem, and Bethany was fifteen furlongs. But on the eastern declivity of the mountain the *tract* of country was called, for a considerable space, the region of Bethany; and it was from this place that the Lord Jesus ascended.

13. *Were come in.* To Jerusalem. ¶ *They went up into an upper room.* The word ὑπερῷον, here translated *upper room*, occurs but four times in the New Testament: Ac. ix. 37, "She (Dorcas)

where abode both [r]Peter, and James, and John, and Andrew, Philip, and Thomas, Bartholomew, and Matthew, James *the son* of Alpheus, and Simon Zelotes, and Judas *the brother* of James.

14 These all continued with one accord in prayer and supplication, with [s]the women, and Mary the mother of Jesus, and with his brethren.

15 And in those days Peter stood up in the midst of the disciples, and said, (the number of the names

r Lu.6.13-16.

s Lu.23.49,55; 24.10.

---

was sick and died; whom when they had washed, they laid her in *an upper chamber*" (see also ver. 39); xx. 8, "And there were many lights in the *upper chamber* where they were gathered together." The room so designated was an upper chamber used for devotion, or as a place where to lay the dead before burial, or occasionally for conversation, &c. Here it evidently means the place where they were assembled for devotion. Luke (xxiv. 53) says they were continually *in the temple* praising and blessing God; and some have supposed that the upper room here designated was one of the rooms in the temple. But there is no evidence of that, and it is not very probable. Such a room as that here referred to was a part of every house, especially in Jerusalem; and the disciples probably selected one where they might be together, and yet so retired that they might be safe from the Jews. The expression used in Lu. xxiv. 53, "They were *continually*—διαπαντὸς—in the temple," signifies no more than that this was a frequent or customary resort; they were *always* in the temple at the usual seasons of devotion, or they were in the constant *habit* of resorting thither. "Even De Wette allows that there is no discrepancy." ¶ *Where abode.* Where were remaining. This does not mean that this was their *permanent* habitation; but they remained there waiting for the descent of the Holy Spirit. ¶ *Peter,* &c. All the apostles were there which Jesus had at first chosen except Judas, Lu. vi. 13–16.

14. *These all continued,* &c. The word *continued* denotes persevering and constant attention. The main business was devotion. Ac. vi. 4, "*We* will give ourselves continually to the ministry of the word." Ro. xii. 12, "Continuing instant in prayer;" xiii. 6, "Attending continually upon this very thing." It is their *main* and *constant* employment. Comp. Col. iv. 2. ¶ *With one accord.* Greek, ὁμοθυμαδὸν—*with one mind.* The word denotes the entire harmony of their views and feelings. There were no schisms, no divided interests, no discordant purposes. This is a beautiful picture of devotion, and a specimen of what social worship ought now to be, and a beautiful illustration of Ps. cxxxiii. The apostles felt that they had *one* great object; and their deep grief at the loss of their master, and their doubts and perplexities, led them, as all afflictions ought to lead us, to the throne of grace. ¶ *In prayer and supplication.* These words are nearly synonymous, and are often interchanged. They express here petitions to God for blessings, and prayer to avert impending evils. ¶ *With the women.* The women that had followed the Lord Jesus from Galilee, Lu. viii. 2, 3; xxiii. 49, 55; xxiv. 10; Mat. xxvii. 55. The women particularly mentioned are Mary Magdalene, Mary the mother of James and Joses, the mother of Zebedee's children, Joanna the wife of Chuza, and Susanna. Besides these, there were others whose names are not mentioned. Most of them were relatives of the apostles or of the Saviour; and it is not improbable that some of them were wives of the apostles. Peter is known to have been married (Mat. viii. 14), and had his wife in attendance with him in his travels (1 Co. ix. 5); and the same was doubtless true of some of the other apostles, 1 Co. ix. 5. Mary, the mother of Jesus, is here particularly mentioned, showing that she now cast in her lot with the apostles. She had, besides, been specially intrusted to the care of John (Jn. xix. 26, 27), and had no other home. This is the last time that she is mentioned in the New Testament. ¶ *And with his brethren.* See Notes on Mat. xii. 46. At first they had been unbelieving about the claims of Jesus (Jn. vii. 5); but it seems that they had been subsequently converted.

15. *In those days.* On one of the days intervening between the ascension of Jesus and the day of Pentecost. ¶ *Peter*

together were about an hundred and twenty,)

16 Men *and* brethren, this scripture must needs have been fulfilled, [t]which the Holy Ghost by the mouth of David spake before concerning Judas, which was [u]guide to them that took Jesus.

17 For [v]he was numbered with us, and had obtained part of this ministry.

t Ps.41.9; Jn.13.18. *u* Mat.26.47; Jn.18.3. *v* Lu.6.16.

---

stood up. Peter *standing up*, or rising. This is a customary expression in the Scriptures when one begins to do a thing, Lu. xv. 18. The reason why *Peter* did this may be seen in the Notes on Mat. xvi. 16, 17. It is not improbable, besides, that Peter was the most aged of the apostles; and from his uniform conduct we know that he was the most ardent. It was perfectly characteristic, therefore, for him to introduce the business of the election of a new apostle. ¶ *The disciples.* This was the name which was given to them as being *learners* in the school of Christ. See Notes on Mat. v. 1. ¶ *The number of the names.* The number of the *persons*, or *individuals.* The word *name* is often used to denote the person, Re. iii. 4; Ac. iv. 12; xviii. 15; Ep. i. 21. In Syriac it is, "The assembly of men was about an hundred and twenty." This was the first assembly convened to transact the business of the church; and it is not a little remarkable that the vote in so important a matter as electing an apostle was by the entire church. It settles the question that the election of a minister and pastor should be by the church, and that a pastor should not be placed over a church by a patron, or by an ecclesiastical body. If a case could ever occur where it would be right and proper that one should be selected to exercise the office of a minister of Christ by the ministry only, the election of one to fill the office of an apostle was such a case. And yet in this the entire church had a voice. Whether this was *all* the true church at this time does not appear from the history. This expression cannot mean that there were no more Christians, but that these were all that had convened in the upper room. It is certain that our Saviour had, by his own ministry, brought many others to be his true followers. Comp. 1 Co. xv. 6.

16. *Men* and *brethren.* This is a customary mode of address, implying affection and respect, Ac. xiii. 26. The Syriac renders it more appropriately than by the introduction of the conjunction "*and*"—"Men, *our* brethren." ¶ *This scripture.* This prediction contained in the writings of the Old Testament. Comp. Notes on Jn. v. 39. The passage to which Peter refers is commonly supposed to be that recorded in Ps. xli. 9, "Yea, mine own familiar friend . . . hath lifted up his heel against me." This is expressly applied to Judas by our Saviour, in Jn. xiii. 18. But it seems clear that the reference is not to the 41st Psalm, but to the passage in the 69th Psalm which Peter proceeds to quote in ver. 20. ¶ *Must needs be fulfilled.* It would certainly be fulfilled. Not that there was any physical necessity or any compulsion; but it could not but occur that a prediction of God would be fulfilled. This makes no affirmation about the *freedom* of Judas in doing it. A man will be just as free in wickedness if it be *foretold* that he will be wicked, as if it had never been known to any other being but himself. ¶ *The Holy Ghost*, &c. This is a strong attestation to the inspiration of David, and accords with the uniform testimony of the New Testament, that the sacred writers spake as they were moved by the Holy Ghost, 2 Pe. i. 21. ¶ *Concerning Judas.* In what respect this was concerning Judas, see ver. 20. ¶ *Which was guide*, &c., Mat. xxvi. 47; Jn. xviii. 3.

17. *He was numbered with us.* He was chosen as an apostle by the Lord Jesus, Lu. vi. 13–16. This does not mean that he was a true Christian, but that he was reckoned among the apostles. Long before he betrayed him, Jesus declared that he was a devil, Jn. vi. 70. He knew his whole character when he chose him, Jn. ii. 25. If it be asked why he chose *such* a man to be an apostle; why he was made the *treasurer* of the apostles, and was admitted to the fullest confidence; we may reply, that a most important object was gained in having such a man—*a spy*—among them. It might be pretended, when the apostles bore testimony to the purity of life, of doctrine, and of

18 Now[w] this man purchased a
field with [x]the reward of iniquity;
and falling headlong, he burst
asunder in the midst, and all his
bowels gushed out.

w Mat.27.5-10. x 2 Pe.2.15.

19 And it was known unto all
the dwellers at Jerusalem; insomuch as that field is called in their
proper tongue, Aceldama, that is
to say, The field of blood.
20 For it is written in the book

---

purpose of the Lord Jesus, that they were interested and partial friends; that they might be disposed to *suppress* some of his real sentiments, and represent him in a light more favourable than the truth. Hence the testimony of such a man as Judas, if favourable, must be invaluable. It would be free from the charge of partiality. If Judas *knew* anything unfavourable to the character of Jesus, he would have communicated it to the Sanhedrim. If he knew of any secret plot against the government, or seditious purpose, he had every inducement to declare it. He had every opportunity to know it; he was with him; heard him converse; was a member of his family, and admitted to terms of familiarity. Yet even Judas could not be *bought* or *bribed*, to testify against the moral character of the Saviour. If he *had* done it, or *could* have done it, it would have preserved him from the charge of treason; would have entitled him to the reputation of a public benefactor in discovering secret sedition; and would have saved him from the pangs of remorse, and from self-murder. Judas *would* have done it if he could. But he alleged no such charge; he did not even dare to lisp a word against the pure designs of the Lord Jesus; and his own reproofs of conscience (Mat. xxvii. 4), and his voluntary death (Mat. xxvii. 5), furnish the highest proof that can be desired of *his* conviction that the betrayed Redeemer was innocent. Judas would have been just the witness which the Jews desired of the treasonable purposes of Jesus. But *that* could not be procured, even by gold; and they were compelled to *suborn* other men to testify against the Son of God, Mat. xxvi. 60. We may add here, that the introduction of such a character as that of Judas Iscariot into the number of the apostles, and the *use* to be made of his testimony, would never have occurred to the author of a *forged* book. *He* would have said that they were *all* the true friends of the Lord Jesus. To have *invented* such a character as that of Judas, and to make him perform such a part in the plan as the sacred writers do, would have required too much art and cunning—was too refined and subtle a device, to have been thought of unless it had actually occurred.

18. *Now this man*, &c. The money which was given for betraying the Lord Jesus was thrown down in the temple, and the field was purchased with it by the Jewish priests. See Mat. xxvii. 5, 10, and the Notes on that place. A man is said often to do a thing when he furnishes *means* for doing it. Comp. Mat. xxvii. 60, "And laid it [the body of Jesus] in his own new tomb, which *he had hewn out* in the rock." That is, had caused to be hewn out. Jn. iv. 1, "When, therefore, the Lord knew how the Pharisees had heard that Jesus *made and baptized* more disciples than John." Through his disciples, for Jesus himself baptized not, ver. 2. The same principle is recognized in law in the well-known maxim, *Qui facit per alium, facit per se.* ¶ *The reward of iniquity.* The price which he had for that deed of stupendous wickedness—the betraying of the Lord Jesus. ¶ *And falling headlong.* The word here rendered *headlong*. —πρηνὴς (Latin *pronus*, whence the English word *prone*)—means properly *bent forward, head-foremost;* and the idea is, that his position in hanging himself was such that when the cord broke he fell headlong, or fell forward on his face. This can easily be supposed if he *threw himself* from a rock or elevated place. He first hanged himself, and then fell and was burst asunder. See Notes on Mat. xxvii. 5.

19. *It was known*, &c., Mat. xxvii. 8. The scene in the temple; the acts of the priests in purchasing the field, &c., would make it known; and the *name* of the field would preserve the memory of the guilt of Judas. ¶ *Their proper tongue.* The language spoken by the Jews—the *Syro-Chaldaic.* ¶ *Aceldama.* This is composed of two Syro-Chaldaic words, and means literally, the field of blood.

20. *For it is written*, &c. See Ps. lxix.

of Psalms, [y]Let his habitation be desolate, and let no man dwell therein; and, [z]His [3]bishopric let another take.

y Ps.69.25. *z* Ps.109.8. [3] or, *office;* or, *charge.*

---

25. This is the prediction doubtless to which Peter refers in ver. 16. The intermediate passage in ver. 18, 19, is probably a parenthesis; the words of Luke, not of Peter. So Calvin, Kuinoel, Olshausen, De Wette, and Hackett understand it. It is not probable that Peter would introduce a narrative like this, with which they were all familiar, in an address to the disciples. The Hebrew in the Psalm is, "Let their habitation (Heb. *fold, inclosure for cattle; tower*, or *palace*) be desolate, and let none dwell in their tents." This quotation is not made literally from the Hebrew, nor from the Septuagint. The *plural* is changed to the *singular*, and there are some other slight variations. The Hebrew is, "Let there be no one dwelling in their *tents.*" The reference to the *tents* is omitted in the quotation. The term *habitation*, in the Psalm, means evidently the dwelling-place of the enemies of the writer of the Psalm. It is an image expressive of their overthrow and defeat by a just God: "Let their families be scattered, and the places where they have dwelt be without an inhabitant, as a reward for their crimes." If the Psalm was originally composed with reference to the Messiah and his sufferings, the expression here was not intended to denote Judas *in particular*, but *one* of his foes who was to meet the just punishment of rejecting, betraying, and murdering him. The change, therefore, which Peter made from the plural to the singular, and the application to Judas especially *as one of those enemies*, accords with the design of the Psalm, and is such a change as the circumstances of the case justified and required. It is an image, therefore, expressive of judgment and desolation coming upon his betrayer—an image to be literally fulfilled in relation to his habitation, drawn from the desolation when a man is driven from his home, and when his dwelling-place becomes tenantless. It is not a little remarkable that this Psalm is repeatedly quoted as referring to the Messiah: ver. 9, "The zeal of thine house hath eaten me up," expressly applied to Christ in Jn. ii. 17; ver. 21, "They gave me also gall for my meat; and in my thirst they gave me vinegar to drink"—the thing which was done to Jesus on the cross, Mat. xxvii. 34. The whole Psalm is expressive of deep sorrow—of persecution, contempt, weeping, being forsaken, and is throughout applicable to the Messiah; with what is remarkable, not a single expression necessarily limited to David. It is not easy to ascertain whether the ancient Jews referred this Psalm to the Messiah. A part of the *title* to the Psalm in the *Syriac* version is, "It is called a prophecy concerning those things which Christ suffered, and concerning the casting away of the Jews." The prophecy in ver. 25 is not to be understood of *Judas alone, but of the enemies of the Messiah in general, of which Judas was one.* On this principle the application to Judas of the passage by Peter is to be defended. ¶ *And his bishopric let another take.* This is quoted from Ps. cix. 8, "Let his days be few, and let another take his office." This is called "a Psalm of David," and is of the same class as Ps. vi., xxii., xxv., xxxviii., xlii. This *class* of Psalms is commonly supposed to have expressed David's feelings in the calamitous times of the persecution by Saul, the rebellion of Absalom, &c. They are *all also* expressive of the condition of a suffering and persecuted Messiah, and many of them are applied to him in the New Testament. The *general principle* on which most of them are applicable is, not that David *personated* or *typified* the Messiah—which is nowhere affirmed, and which can be true in no intelligible sense—but that he was placed in circumstances similar to the Messiah; was encompassed with like enemies; was persecuted in the same manner. They are expressive of high rank, office, dignity, and piety, cast down, waylaid, and encompassed with enemies. In this way they express *general sentiments* as really applicable to the case of the Messiah as to David. They were placed in similar circumstances. The same help was needed. The same expressions would convey their feelings. The same treatment was proper for their enemies. On this principle it was that *David* deemed his enemy, whoever he was, unworthy of his office, and desired that it should be given to another. In like manner, Judas

21 Wherefore of [a]these men
which have companied with us all
the time that the Lord Jesus went
in and out among us,
22 Beginning from the baptism

a Lu.10.1,2; Jn.15.27.

had rendered *himself* unworthy of his office, and there was the *same propriety* that it should be given to another. And as the office had now become vacant by the death of Judas, and according to *one* declaration in the Psalms, so, according to another, it was proper that it should be conferred on some other person. The word rendered "office" in the Psalm means the *care, charge, business, oversight* of anything. It is a word applicable to *magistrates,* whose care it is to see that the laws are executed; and to military men who have charge of an army, or a part of an army. In Job x. 12 it is rendered "thy visitation." In Nu. iv. 16, "and to the office of Eleazar," &c. In the case of David it refers to those who were intrusted with military or other offices who had treacherously perverted them to persecute and oppose him, and who had thus shown themselves unworthy of the office. The Greek word which is used here, ἐπισκοπὴν, is taken from the Septuagint, and means the same thing as the Hebrew. It is well rendered in the margin "office, or charge." It means charge or office in general, without in itself specifying of what kind. It is the *concrete* of the noun ἐπισκόπος, commonly translated "bishop," and means *his* office, charge, or duty. That word means simply *having the oversight of anything,* and as applied to the officers of the New Testament, it denotes merely *their having charge of the affairs of the church,* without specifying the *nature* or the *extent* of their jurisdiction. Hence it is often interchanged with presbyter or elder, and denotes the discharge of the duties of the same office: Ac. xx. 28, "Take heed (presbyters or elders, ver. 17) to yourselves, and to all the flock over the which the Holy Ghost hath made *you overseers*"—ἐπισκόπους—*bishops;* He. xii. 15, "Looking diligently," &c. —ἐπισκοποῦντες; Phi. i. 1, "with the bishops and deacons;" "Paul called presbyters bishops, for they had at that time the same name" (Theodoret, as quoted by Schleusner); 1 Pe. v. 2, "Feed the flock of God (that is, you who are elders, or presbyters, v. 1), *taking the oversight thereof*"—ἐπισκοποῦντες. These passages show that the term in the New Testament designates the supervision or care which was exercised over the church, by whomsoever performed, without specifying the nature or extent of the jurisdiction. It is scarcely necessary to add that Peter here did not intend to affirm that Judas sustained any office corresponding to what is now commonly understood by the term "*bishop.*"

21, 22. *Wherefore of these men.* Of those who had witnessed the life and works of Christ, and who were therefore qualified to discharge the duties of the office from which Judas fell. Probably Peter refers to the seventy disciples, Lu. x. 1, 2. ¶ *Went in and out.* A phrase signifying that he was their constant companion. It expresses in general all the actions of the life, Ps. cxxi. 8; De. xxviii. 19; xxxi. 2. ¶ *Beginning from the baptism of John.* The words "beginning from" in the original refer to the Lord Jesus. The meaning may be thus expressed, "during all the time in which the Lord Jesus, beginning (his ministry) at the time when he was baptized by John, went in and out among us, until the time when he was taken up," &c. From those who had during that time been the constant companions of the Lord Jesus must one be taken, who would thus be a witness of *his whole ministry.* ¶ *Must one be ordained.* It is *fit* or *proper* that one should be ordained. The reason of this was, that Jesus had originally chosen the number twelve for this work, and as *one* of them had fallen, it was proper that the vacancy should be filled by some person equally qualified for the office. The reason why it was proper that he should be taken from the seventy disciples was, that *they* had been particularly distinguished by Jesus himself, and had been witnesses of most of his public life, Lu. x. 1-16. The word *ordained* with us has a fixed and definite signification. It means to set apart to a sacred office with proper forms and solemnities, commonly by the imposition of hands. But this is not, of necessity, the meaning of this passage. The Greek word usually denoting *ordination* is not used here. The expression is literally, "must one *be,* or *become,* γενέσθαι, a witness with us of his resurrection." The expression does not imof John, unto that same day that he was taken up from us, must one be ordained to be a witness with us of his resurrection.

23 And they appointed two, Joseph called [b]Barsabas, who was surnamed Justus, and Matthias.

24 And they prayed, and said, Thou, Lord, [c]which knowest the

b ch.15.22. *c* Je.17.10; Re.2.23.

---

ply that he must be set apart in any particular manner, but simply that one should be designated or appointed for this specific purpose, *to be a witness* of the resurrection of Christ.

23. *And they appointed two.* They *proposed*, or, as we should say, *nominated* two. Literally, they *placed* two, or made them to stand forth, as persons do who are candidates for office. These two were probably more distinguished by prudence, wisdom, piety, and age than the others, and they were so nearly equal in qualifications that they could not determine which was the best fitted for the office. ¶ *Joseph called Barsabas,* &c. It is not certainly known what the name *Barsabas* denotes. The Syriac word *Bar* means *son,* and the word *Sabas* has been translated *an oath, rest, quiet,* or *captivity.* Why the name was given to Joseph is not known; but probably it was the family name—*Joseph son of Sabas.* Some have conjectured that this was the same man who, in ch. iv. 36, is called Barnabas. But of this there is no proof. Lightfoot supposes that he was the son of Alpheus and brother of James the Less, and that he was chosen on account of his relationship to the family of the Lord Jesus. ¶ *Was surnamed Justus.* Who was *called* Justus. This is a Latin name, meaning *just,* and was probably given him on account of his distinguished integrity. It was not uncommon among the Jews for a man to have several names, Mat. x. 3. ¶ *And Matthias.* Nothing is known of the family of this man, or of his character, further than that he was numbered with the apostles, and shared their lot in the toils, the persecutions, and the honours of preaching the gospel to mankind.

24. *And they prayed.* As they could not *agree* on the individual, they invoked the direction of God in their choice—an example which should be followed in every selection of an individual to exercise the duties of the sacred office of the ministry. ¶ *Which knowest the hearts of all* men. This is often declared to be the peculiar prerogative of God, Je. xvii. 10, "*I, Jehovah, search the heart,*" &c.; Ps. cxxxix. 1, 23; 1 Ch. xxviii. 9. Yet this attribute is also expressly ascribed to Jesus Christ, Re. ii. 18; comp. 23, "These things saith the Son of God—I am he which searcheth the reins and the hearts;" Jn. ii. 25; vi. 64; xvi. 19. There are strong reasons for supposing that the apostles on this occasion addressed this prayer to the Lord Jesus Christ. (1) The name *Lord*—Κύριος—is the common appellation which they gave to him, Ac. ii. 36; vii. 59, 60; x. 36; 1 Co. ii. 8; Phi. ii. 11; Re. xi. 8, *et al.* (2) We are told that they *worshipped* him, or rendered him divine honours after his ascension, Lu. xxiv. 52. (3) The disciples were accustomed to address him after his crucifixion by the names Lord or God indifferently, Ac. i. 6; Jn. xx. 28; Ac. vii. 59. (4) This was a matter pertaining especially to the church which the Lord Jesus had redeemed, and *to his own arrangement* in regard to it. *He* had chosen the apostles; *he* had given them their commission; *he* had fixed their number; and, what is worthy of special remark here, *he* had been the companion of the very men here designated as candidates for the office, and knew their qualifications for this work. If the apostles *ever* called on the Lord Jesus after his ascension, this was a case in which they would be likely to do it. That it *was* done is clear from the account of the death of Stephen, Ac. vii. 59, 60. And in this important matter of ordaining a new apostle to be a witness for Jesus Christ, nothing was more natural than that they should address *him,* though bodily absent, as they would assuredly have done if he were present. But if on this occasion they *did* actually address Christ, then two things clearly follow. First, that it is proper to render him divine homage, agreeably to the uniform declarations of the Scripture: Jn. v. 23, "That all men should honour the Son even as they honour the Father;" He. i. 6, "And let all the angels of God worship him;" Phi. ii. 10, 11; Re. v. 8-14; 1 Th. iii. 11, 12. Secondly, he must be divine. To none other but God can religious homage be rendered; and none other

hearts of all *men*, show whether of
these two thou hast chosen,
25 That he may take part of this
ministry and apostleship, from
which Judas by transgression fell,
that he might go to his own place.

---

can be described as *knowing the hearts of all men.* The reason why they appealed to him on this occasion *as the searcher of the heart* was doubtless the great importance of the work to which the successor of Judas was to be called. One apostle of fair external character had proved a traitor; and, with this fact before them, they appealed to the Saviour himself to select one who would be true to him, and not bring dishonour on his cause. ¶ *Show whether*, &c. Show *which* of them. ¶ *Thou hast chosen.* Which of the two thou hast judged to be best qualified for the work.

25. *That he may take part of this ministry.* The word rendered *part*—κλῆρον—is the same which in the next verse is rendered *lots.* It properly means a lot or portion—the portion divided to a man, or assigned to him by casting lots; and also the instrument or means by which the lot is determined. The former is its meaning here; the *office*, or portion of apostolic work, which would fall to him by taking the place of Judas. ¶ *Ministry and apostleship.* This is an instance of the figure of speech *hendiadys*, when two words are used to express one thing. It means *the apostolic ministry.* See instances in Ge. i. 14, "Let them be for signs *and* for seasons," that is, signs *of* seasons; Ac. xxiii. 6, "Hope *and* resurrection of the dead," that is, hope *of the* resurrection of the dead. ¶ *From which Judas by transgression fell.* Literally, *went aside*—παρέβη—"as opposed to the idea of adhering faithfully to the character and service which his apostleship required of him" (Prof. Hackett). The *transgression* referred to was his treason and suicide. ¶ *That he might go to his own place.* These words by different interpreters have been referred both to Matthias and Judas. Those who refer them to Matthias say that they mean that Judas fell that Matthias might go to his own place, that is, to a place for which he was fitted, or well qualified. But to this there are many objections. 1. The apostolic office could with no propriety be called, in reference to Matthias, *his own place*, until it was actually conferred on him. 2. There is no instance in which the expression *to go to his own place* is applied to a successor in office. 3. It is not true that the design or reason why Judas fell was to make way for another. He fell by his crimes; his avarice, his voluntary and enormous wickedness. 4. The former part of the sentence contains this sentiment: "Another must be appointed to this office which the death of Judas has made vacant." If this expression, "that he might go," &c., refers to the successor of Judas, it expresses the same sentiment, but more obscurely. 5. The obvious and natural meaning of the phrase is to refer it to Judas. But those who suppose that it refers to Judas differ greatly about its meaning. Some suppose that it refers to his own house, and that the meaning is, that he left the apostolic office to return to his own house; and they appeal to Nu. xxiv. 25. But it is not true that Judas did this; nor is there the least proof that it was his design. Others refer it to the grave, as the *place* of man, where all must lie; and particularly as an ignominious place where it was proper that a traitor like Judas should lie. But there is no example where the word *place* is used in this sense, nor is there an instance where a man, by being buried, is said to return to his own or proper place. Others have supposed that the manner of his death by hanging is referred to as his own or his proper place. But this interpretation is evidently an unnatural and forced one. The word *place* cannot be applied to an *act* of self-murder. It denotes habitation, abode, situation in which to remain; not an *act.* These are the only interpretations of the passage which can be suggested, except the common one of referring it to the abode of Judas in the world of woe. This might be said to be his *own*, as he had prepared himself for it, and as it was proper that he who betrayed his Lord should dwell there. This interpretation may be defended by the following considerations: 1. It is the obvious and natural meaning of the words. It commends itself by its simplicity and its evident connection with the context. It has in all ages been the common interpretation; nor has any other been adopted, except in cases where there was a theory to be defended about future punishment.

Unless men had previously made up their minds *not to believe in future punishment*, no one would ever have thought of any other interpretation. This fact alone throws strong light on the meaning of the passage. 2. It accords with the crimes of Judas, and with all that we know of him. What the future doom of Judas would be was not unknown to the apostles. Jesus Christ had expressly declared this—"it had been good for that man if he had not been born;" a declaration which *could* not be true if, after *any* limited period of suffering, he were at last admitted to eternal happiness. See Mat. xxvi. 24, and the Notes on that place. This declaration was made in the presence of the eleven apostles, at the institution of the Lord's supper, and at a time when their attention was absorbed with deep interest in what Christ said; and it was therefore a declaration which they would not be likely to forget. As they *knew* the fate of Judas beforehand, nothing was more natural for them than to speak of it familiarly as a thing which *had* actually occurred when he betrayed his Lord and hung himself. 3. The expression "to go to his own place" is one which is used by the ancient writers to denote going to an eternal destiny. Thus the Jewish Tract, *Baal Turim*, on Nu. xxiv. 25, says, "Balaam went to his own place, that is, to Gehenna," to hell. Thus the Targum, or Chaldee Paraphrase on Ec. vi. 6, says, "Although the days of a man's life were two thousand years, and he did not study the law, and do justice, in the day of his death his soul shall descend to hell, to the one place where all sinners go." Thus Ignatius in the *Epistle to the Magnesians* says, "Because all things have an end, the two things death and life shall lie down together, *and each one shall go to his own place.*" The phrase *his own* place means the place or abode which was fitted for him, which was his appropriate home. Judas was not in a place which befitted his character when he was an apostle; he was not in such a place in the church; he would not be in heaven. Hell was the only place which was fitted to the man of avarice and of treason. And if this be the true interpretation of this passage, then it follows, 1. That there will be such a thing as future, eternal punishment. There is certainly one man in hell, and ever will be. If there is *one* there, for the same reason there may be others. All objections to the doctrine are removed by this single fact; and it cannot be true that *all* men will be saved. 2. Each individual in eternity will find his own proper place. The punishment of hell is not an arbitrary appointment. Every man will go to the place for which his character is fitted. The hypocrite is not fitted for heaven. The man of pride, and avarice, and pollution, and falsehood, is not fitted for heaven. The place *adapted* to such men is hell; and the design of the judgment will be to assign to each individual *his proper abode* in the eternal world. It would not be fit that the holy and pure should dwell for ever in the same place with the unholy and impure; and the Lord Jesus will come to assign to each his appropriate eternal habitation. 3. The sinner will have no cause of complaint. If he is assigned to his *proper place*, he cannot complain. If he is *unfit* for heaven, he cannot complain that he is excluded. And if his character and feelings are such as make it *proper* that he should find his eternal abode among the enemies of God, then he must expect that a God of justice and equity will assign him such a doom. But, 4. This will not alleviate his pain; it will *deepen* his woe. He will have the eternal consciousness that that, and that only, is *his* place—the abode for which he is fitted. The prison is no less dreadful because a man is conscious that he deserves it. The gallows is not the less terrible because the man knows that he *deserves* to die. And the consciousness of the sinner that he is *unfit* for heaven; that there is not a solitary soul there with whom he could have sympathy or friendship; that he is fit for hell, and hell only, will be an ingredient of eternal bitterness in the cup of woe that awaits him. Let not the sinner then hope to escape; for God will assuredly appoint his residence in that world to which his character here is adapted.

The character and end of Judas is one of the most important and instructive things in history. It teaches us, 1. That Christ may employ wicked men for important purposes in his kingdom. See Notes on ver. 17. He does no violence to their freedom; suffers them to act as they please, but brings important ends out of their conduct. One of the most conclusive arguments for the pure character of Jesus Christ is drawn from the silent testimony of Judas. 2. The character of Judas was eminently base

26 And they gave forth their lots: and the lot fell upon Matthias; and he was numbered with the eleven apostles.

---

and wicked. He was influenced by one of the worst human passions; and yet he concealed it from all the apostles. It was remarkable that any man should have *thought* of making money in such a band of men; but avarice will show itself everywhere. 3. We see the effects of covetousness in the church. It led to the betraying of Jesus Christ, and to his death; and it has often betrayed the cause of pure religion since. There is no single human passion that has done so much evil in the church of God as this. It *may be* consistent with external decency and order, and in accordance with the principles on which the world acts, and which it approves, and it may therefore be indulged without disgrace, while open and acknowledged vices would expose their possessors to shame and ruin. And yet it paralyses and betrays religion probably more than any single propensity of man. 4. The character of an avaricious man in the church will be developed. Opportunities will occur when it will be seen and known by what principle he is influenced. So it was with Achan (Jos. vii. 21); so it was with Judas; and so it will be with all. Occasions will occur which will *test* the character, and show what manner of spirit a man is of. Every appeal to a man's benevolence, every call upon his charity, shows what spirit influences him—whether he is actuated by the love of gold, or by the love of Christ and his cause.

26. *And they gave forth their lots.* Some have supposed that this means they *voted.* But to this interpretation there are insuperable objections. 1. The word *lots*, κλήρους, is not used to express *votes*, or *suffrage.* 2. The expression "the lot fell upon" is not consistent with the notion of voting. It is commonly expressive of casting lots. 3. Casting lots was common among the Jews on important and difficult occasions, and it was natural that the apostles should resort to it in this. Thus David divided the priests by lot, 1 Ch. xxiv. 5. The land of Canaan was divided by lot, Nu. xxvi. 55; Jos. xv., xvi., xvii., &c. Jonathan, son of Saul, was detected as having violated his father's command and as bringing calamity on the Israelites by lot, 1 Sa. xiv. 41, 42. Achan was detected by lot, Jos. vii. 16–18. In these instances the use of the lot was regarded as a solemn appeal to God for his direct interference in cases which they could not themselves decide. Pr. xvi. 33, "The lot is cast into the lap, but the whole disposing thereof is of the Lord." The choice of an apostle was an event of the same kind, and was regarded as a solemn appeal to God for his direction and guidance in a case which the apostles could not determine. The *manner* in which this was done is not certainly known. The common mode of casting lots was to write the names of the *persons* on pieces of stone, wood, &c., and put them in one urn, and the name of the office, portion, &c., on others. These were then placed in an urn with other pieces of stone, &c., which were blank. The names were then drawn at random, and also the other pieces, and this settled the case. The casting of a lot is determined by laws of nature as regularly as anything else. There is properly no *chance* in it. We do not know how a die may turn up; but this does not imply that it will turn up without any regard to rule, or at hap-hazard. We cannot trace the influences which may determine either this or that side to come up; but it is done by regular and proper laws, and according to the circumstances of position, force, &c., in which it is cast. Still, although it does not imply any *special* or miraculous interposition of Providence; though it may not be absolutely wrong, in cases which cannot otherwise be determined, to use the lot, yet it does not follow that it is proper often to make this appeal. Almost all cases of doubt can be determined more satisfactorily in some other way than by the lot. The habit of appealing to it engenders the love of hazards and of games; leads to heart-burnings, to jealousies, to envy, to strife, and to dishonesty. Still less does the example of the apostles authorize *games* of hazard, or lotteries, which are positively evil, and attended with ruinous consequences, apart from any inquiry about the lawfulness of the lot. They either originate in, or promote covetousness, neglect of regular industry, envy, jealousy, disappointment, dissipation, bankruptcy, falsehood, and despair. What is gained by one is lost by another, and both the

CHAPTER II.

AND when the day of [a] Pentecost was fully come, [b] they
were all with one accord in one place.
2 And suddenly there came a

a Le.23.15. *b* ch.1.14.

---

gain and the loss promote some of the worst passions of man—boasting, triumph, self-confidence, indolence, dissipation, on the one hand; and envy, disappointment, sullenness, desire of revenge, remorse, and ruin on the other. God intended that man should live by sober toil. All departures from this great law of our social existence lead to ruin. ¶ *Their lots.* The lots which were to decide *their* case. They are called *theirs*, because they were to determine which of them should be called to the apostolic office. ¶ *The lot fell.* This is an expression applicable to casting lots, not to voting. ¶ *He was numbered.* By the casting of the lot, συγκατεψηφίσθη. This word is from ψῆφος—*a calculus*, or *pebble*, by which votes were given or lots were cast. It means, that *by the result of the lot* he was reckoned as an apostle. Nothing farther is related of Matthias in the New Testament. Where he laboured, and when and where he died, is unknown; nor is there any tradition on which reliance is to be placed. The election of Matthias, however, throws some light on the organization of the church. 1. He was chosen to fill the place vacated by Judas, and for a specific purpose, to be *a witness* of the resurrection of Christ. There is no mention of any other design. It was not to ordain men exclusively, or to rule over the churches, but to be a witness to an important fact. 2. There is no intimation that it was designed that there should be *successors* to the apostles in the *peculiar* duties of the apostolic office. The election was for a definite object, and was therefore temporary. It was to fill up the *number* originally appointed by Christ. When the purpose for which he was appointed was accomplished, the *peculiar* part of the apostolic work ceased of course. 3. There *could be* no succession in future ages to the peculiar apostolic office. They were to be *witnesses* of the work of Christ, and when the desired effect resulting from such a witnessing was accomplished, the office itself would cease. Hence there is no record that after this the church even pretended to appoint successors to the apostles, and hence no ministers of the gospel can now pretend to be their successors in the *peculiar* and *original* design of the appointment of the apostles. 4. The only other apostle mentioned in the New Testament is the apostle Paul, not appointed as the successor of the others, not with any peculiar design except to be an apostle to the Gentiles, as the others were to the Jews, and appointed for the same end, to testify that Jesus Christ was alive, and that *he had seen him* after he rose, 1 Co. xv. 8; ix. 1, 15; Ac. xxii. 8, 9, 14, 15; xxvi. 17, 18. The ministers of religion, therefore, are successors of the apostles, not in their peculiar office as witnesses, but as preachers of the word, and as appointed to establish, to organize, to edify, and to rule the churches. The *peculiar* work of the apostleship ceased with their death. The ordinary work of the ministry, which they held in common with all others who preach the gospel, will continue to the end of time.

CHAPTER II.

1. *And when the day of Pentecost.* The word *Pentecost* is a Greek word signifying *the fiftieth* part of a thing, or the fiftieth in order. Among the Jews it was applied to one of their three great feasts which began on *the fiftieth* day after the Passover. This feast was reckoned from the sixteenth day of the month ABIB, or April, or the *second day* of the Passover. The paschal lamb was slain on the fourteenth of the month at even, Le. xxiii. 5; on the fifteenth of the month was a holy convocation—the proper beginning of the feast; on the sixteenth was the offering of the first-fruits of harvest, and *from that day* they were to reckon *seven weeks*, that is, forty-nine days, to the feast called the feast of Pentecost, so that it occurred *fifty* days after the first day of the feast of the Passover. This feast was also called *the feast of weeks*, from the circumstance that it followed a succession of weeks, Ex. xxxiv. 22; Nu. xxviii. 26; De. xvi. 10. It was also *a harvest festival*, and was accordingly called *the feast of harvest;* and it was for this reason that two loaves made of new meal were offered on this occasion as first-fruits, Le. xxiii. 17, 20; Nu. xxviii. 27-31. ¶ *Was fully come.* When the day had arrived. The

word here used means literally *to be completed*, and as employed here refers, not to the day itself, but to the completion of the interval which was to pass before its arrival (Olshausen). See Lu. ix. 51. Comp. Mar. i. 15; Lu. i. 57. This fact is mentioned, that the time of the Pentecost had come, or fully arrived, to account for what is related afterward, that there were so many strangers and foreigners present. The promised influences of the Spirit were withheld until the greatest possible number of Jews should be present at Jerusalem at the same time, and thus an opportunity be afforded of preaching the gospel to vast multitudes in the very place where the Lord Jesus was crucified, and also an opportunity be afforded of sending the gospel by them into distant parts of the earth. ¶ *They were all.* Probably not only the apostles, but also the one hundred and twenty mentioned in ch. i. 15. ¶ *With one accord.* See ch. i. 14. It is probable that they had *continued* together until this time, and given themselves entirely to the business of devotion. ¶ *In one place.* Where this was cannot be known. Commentators have been much divided in their conjectures about it. Some have supposed that it was in the upper room mentioned in ch. i. 13; others that it was a room in the temple; others that it was in a synagogue; others that it was among the promiscuous multitude that assembled for devotion in the courts of the temple. See ver. 2. It has been supposed by many that this took place on the first day of the week; that is, on the Christian Sabbath. But there is a difficulty in establishing this. There was probably a difference among the Jews themselves as to the time of observing this festival. The law said that they should reckon seven Sabbaths; that is seven weeks, "*from the morrow after the sabbath*," Le. xxiii. 15. By this Sabbath the Pharisees understood the *second day* of the Passover, on whatever day of the week it occurred, which was kept as a day of holy convocation, and which might be called a Sabbath. But the Caraite Jews, or those who insisted on a *literal* interpretation of the Scriptures, maintained that by the *Sabbath* here was meant the *usual Sabbath*, the seventh day of the week. Consequently *with them* the day of Pentecost *always* occurred on the *first day* of the week; and if the apostles fell in with their views, the day was fully come on what is now the Christian Sabbath. But if the views of the Pharisees were followed, and the Lord Jesus had with them kept the Passover on *Thursday*, as many have supposed, then the day of Pentecost would have occurred on the Jewish Sabbath, that is, on *Saturday* (Kuinoel; Lightfoot). It is impossible to determine the truth on this subject. Nor is it of much importance. According to the later Jews, the day of Pentecost was kept also as a festival to commemorate the giving of the law on Mount Sinai; but no trace of this custom is to be found in the Old Testament.

2. *And suddenly.* It burst upon them at once. Though they were waiting for the descent of the Spirit, yet it is not probable that they expected it in this manner. As this was an important event, and one on which the welfare of the church depended, it was proper that the gift of the Holy Spirit should take place in some *striking* and *sensible* manner, so as to convince their own minds that the promise was fulfilled, and so as deeply to impress others with the greatness and importance of the event. ¶ *There came a sound*—ἦχος. This word is applied to any noise or report. He. xii. 19, "The *sound* of a trumpet;" Lu. iv. 37, "The *fame* of him," &c. Comp. Mar. i. 28. ¶ *From heaven.* Appearing to rush down from the sky. It was fitted, therefore, to attract their attention no less from the *direction* from which it came, than on account of its *suddenness* and *violence*. Tempests blow commonly horizontally. This appeared to come *from above;* and this is all that is meant by the expression "from heaven." ¶ *As of a rushing mighty wind.* Literally, "*as of a violent blast borne along*"—φερομένης—*rushing along like a tempest.* Such a wind is sometimes borne along so violently, and with such a noise, as to make it difficult even to hear the thunder in the gale. Such appears to have been the sound of this remarkable phenomenon. It does not appear that there was any wind, but the sudden sound was *like* such a sweeping tempest. It may be remarked, however, that the *wind* in the sacred Scriptures is often put as an emblem of a divine influence. See Jn. iii. 8. It is *invisible*, yet *mighty*, and thus represents the agency of the Holy Spirit. The same word in Hebrew (רוּח) and in Greek (πνεῦμα) is used to denote both. The mighty power of God may be de-

sound from heaven, as of a rushing mighty wind, and [c]it filled all the house where they were sitting.

c ch.4.31.

3 And there appeared unto them cloven tongues like as of fire, and it sat upon each of them:

---

noted also by the violence of a tempest, 1 Ki. xix. 11; Ps. xxix.; civ. 3; xviii. 10. In this place *the sound* as of a gale was emblematic of the mighty *power* of the Spirit, and of the *effects* which his coming would accomplish among men. ¶ *And it filled.* Not the *wind* filled, but the *sound.* This is evident (1) Because there is no affirmation that there *was* any wind. (2) The grammatical structure of the sentence will admit no other construction. The word "filled" has no nominative case but the word *sound:* "and suddenly there was a sound as *of* a wind, and (the sound) filled the house." In the Greek, the word "wind" is in the genitive or possessive case. It may be remarked here that this miracle was *really* far more striking than the common supposition makes it to have been. A *tempest* would have been terrific. A mighty wind might have alarmed them. But there would have been nothing unusual or remarkable in this. Such things often happened; and the thoughts would have been directed of course to the *storm* as an ordinary, though perhaps alarming occurrence. But when all was still; when there was no storm, no wind, no rain, no thunder, such a rushing sound must have arrested their attention, and directed all minds to a phenomenon so unusual and unaccountable. ¶ *All the house.* Some have supposed that this was a room in or near the temple. But as the *temple* is not expressly mentioned, this is improbable. It was probably the private dwelling mentioned in ch. i. 13. If it be said that such a dwelling could not contain so large a multitude as soon assembled, it may be replied that their houses had large central courts (See Notes on Mat. ix. 2), and that it is not affirmed that the transactions recorded in this chapter occurred *in* the room which they occupied. It is probable that it took place in the court and around the house.

3. *And there appeared unto them.* There were *seen by them,* or they saw. The fire was first seen by them in the room before it rested in the form of tongues on the heads of the disciples. Perhaps the fire appeared at first as scintillations or coruscations, until it became fixed on their heads. ¶ *Tongues*—γλῶσσαι. The word *tongue* occurs often in the Scriptures to denote the member which is the instrument of taste and speech, and also to denote *language* or speech itself. It is also used, as with us, to denote that which *in shape* resembles the tongue. Thus Jos. vii. 21, 24 (in Hebrew), "a tongue of gold," that is, a *wedge* of gold; Jos. xv. 5; xviii. 19; Is. xi. 15, "The tongue of the sea," that is, a bay or gulf. Thus also we say a tongue of land. The phrase "tongue of fire" occurs once, and once only, in the Old Testament (Is. v. 24), "Therefore as the fire devoureth the stubble (Heb. *tongue of fire*), and the flame consumeth," &c. In this place the name tongue is given from the resemblance of a pointed flame to the human tongue. Anything long, narrow, and tending to a point is thus in the Hebrew called a *tongue.* The word here means, therefore, slender and pointed appearances of flame, perhaps at first moving irregularly around the room. ¶ *Cloven.* Divided, separated—διαμεριζόμεναι—from the verb διαμερίζω, to *divide,* or *distribute into parts.* Mat. xxvii. 35, "They *parted* his garments;" Lu. xxii. 17, "Take this (the cup) and *divide* it among yourselves." Probably the common opinion is, that these *tongues* or flames were, *each one* of them, split, or forked, or cloven. But this is not the meaning of the expression. The idea is that they were separated or divided *one from another;* it was not *one great flame,* but was broken up, or *cloven* into many parts, and probably these parts were moving without order in the room. In the Syriac it is, "And there appeared unto them tongues which divided themselves like fire, and sat upon each of them." The old Ethiopic version reads it, "And *fire,* as it were, appeared to them and sat on them." ¶ *And sat upon each of them.* Or rested, in the form of a lambent or gentle flame, upon the head of each one. This showed that the prodigy was directed to *them,* and was a very significant emblem of the promised descent of the Holy Spirit. After the rushing sound and the appearance of the flames, they could not doubt that here was some remarkable interposition of God. The appearance of *fire,* or

4 And they were all [d] filled with the Holy Ghost, and [e] began to speak with other tongues, as the Spirit gave them utterance.

d ch.1.5. e Mar.16.17; ch.10.46.

---

flame, has always been regarded as a most striking emblem of the Divinity. Thus, Ex. iii. 2, 3, God is said to have manifested himself to Moses in a bush which was *burning*, yet not consumed. Thus, Ex. xix. 16–20, God descended on Mount Sinai in the midst of thunders, and lightnings, and smoke, and *fire*, striking emblems of his presence and power. See also Ge. xv. 17. Thus De. iv. 24, God is said to be "a consuming fire." Comp. He. xii. 29. See Eze. i. 4; Ps. xviii. 12–14. The classic reader will also instantly recall the beautiful description in Virgil (*Æneid*, b. ii. 680–691). Other instances of a similar prodigy are also recorded in profane writers (Pliny, *H. N.*, ii. 37; Livy, i. 39). These appearances to the apostles were emblematic, doubtless, (1) Of the promised Holy Spirit, as a Spirit of *purity* and of *power*. The prediction of John the Baptist, "He shall baptize with the Holy Ghost and *with fire*" (Mat. iii. 11) would probably be recalled at once to their memory. (2) The peculiar appearance, that of *tongues*, was an emblem of the diversity of languages which they were about to be able to utter. Any *form* of fire would have denoted the presence and power of God; but a *form* was adopted expressive of *what was to occur*. Thus *any divine appearance* or *manifestation* at the baptism of Jesus might have denoted the presence and approbation of God; but the form chosen was that of *a dove* descending—expressive of the mild and gentle virtues with which he was to be imbued. So in Eze. i. 4, any form of flame might have denoted the presence of God; but the appearance *actually* chosen was one that was strikingly emblematical of his providence. In the same way, the appearance here symbolized their peculiar endowments for entering on their great work—the ability to speak with new tongues.

4. *Were all filled with the Holy Ghost.* Were entirely under his sacred influence and power. See Notes on Lu. i. 41, 67. To be *filled* with anything is a phrase denoting that all the faculties are pervaded by it, engaged in it, or under its influence, Ac. iii. 10, "Were *filled* with wonder and amazement;" v. 17, "Filled with indignation;" xiii. 45, "Filled with envy;" ver. 52, "Filled with joy and the Holy Ghost." ¶ *Began to speak with other tongues.* In other languages than their native tongue. The languages which they spoke are specified in ver. 9–11. ¶ *As the Spirit gave them utterance.* As the Holy Spirit gave them power to speak. This language implies plainly that they were now endued with a faculty of speaking languages which they had not before learned. Their native tongue was that of Galilee, a somewhat barbarous dialect of the common language used in Judea—*the Syro-Chaldaic.* It is possible that some of them might have been partially acquainted with the Greek and Latin, as each of those languages was spoken among the Jews to some extent; but there is not the slightest evidence that they were acquainted with the languages of the different nations afterward specified. Various attempts have been made to account for this remarkable phenomenon without supposing it to be a miracle. But the natural and obvious meaning of the passage is, that they were endowed by the supernatural power of the Holy Ghost with ability to speak foreign languages, and languages to them before unknown. It does not appear that *each one* had the power of speaking *all* the languages which are specified (ver. 9–11), but that this ability was among them, and that together they could speak these languages, probably some one and some another. The following remarks may perhaps throw some light on this remarkable occurrence. (1) It was predicted in the Old Testament that what is here stated would occur in the times of the Messiah. Thus, in Is. xxviii. 11, "With . . . another tongue will he speak unto this people." Comp. 1 Co. xiv. 21, where this passage is expressly applied to the power of speaking foreign languages under the gospel. (2) It was promised by the Lord Jesus that they should have this power, Mar. xvi. 17, "These signs shall follow them that believe . . . they shall speak with *new tongues.*" (3) The ability to do it existed extensively and long in the church, 1 Co. xii. 10, 11, "To another *divers* kinds of tongues; to another the interpretation of tongues: all these worketh that one and the self-same Spirit;" ver.

5 And there were dwelling at
Jerusalem, Jews, devout men, out
of every nation under heaven.

6 Now [1]when this was noised
abroad, the multitude came to-

[1] *when this voice was made.*

28, "God hath set in the church . . . diversities of tongues." Comp. also ver. 30, and ch. xiv. 2, 4, 5, 6, 9, 13, 14, 18, 19, 22, 23, 27, 39. From this it appears that the power was well known in the church, and was not confined to the apostles. This also may show that in the case in the Acts, the ability to do this was conferred on other members of the church as well as the apostles. (4) It was very important that they should be endowed with this power in their great work. They were going forth to preach to all nations; and though the Greek and Roman tongues were extensively spoken, yet their use was not universal, nor is it known that the apostles were skilled in those languages. To preach to all nations, it was indispensable that they should be able to understand their language. And in order that the gospel might be rapidly propagated through the earth, it was necessary that they should be endowed with ability to do this without the slow process of being compelled to learn them. It will contribute to illustrate this to remark that one of the principal hindrances in the spread of the gospel now arises from the inability to speak the languages of the nations of the earth, and that among missionaries of modern times a long time is necessarily spent in acquiring the language of a people before they are prepared to preach to them. (5) One design was to establish the gospel by means of miracles. Yet no miracle could be more impressive than the power of conveying their sentiments at once in all the languages of the earth. When it is remembered what a slow and toilsome process it is to learn a foreign tongue, this would be regarded by the heathen as one of the most striking miracles which could be wrought, 1 Co. xiv. 22, 24, 25. (6) The *reality* and *certainty* of this miracle is strongly attested by the early triumphs of the gospel. That the gospel was early spread over all the world, and that, too, by the apostles of Jesus Christ, is the clear testimony of all history. They preached it in Arabia, Greece, Syria, Asia, Persia, Africa, and Rome. Yet how *could* this have been effected without a miraculous power of speaking the languages used in all those places? *Now*, it requires the toil of many years to speak in foreign languages; and the *recorded success* of the gospel is one of the most striking attestations to the fact of the miracle that could be conceived. (7) The *corruption* of language was one of the most decided effects of *sin*, and the source of endless embarrassments and difficulties, Gen. xi. It is not to be regarded as wonderful that *one* of the effects of the plan of recovering men should be to show the power of God over *all* evil, and thus to furnish striking evidence that the gospel could meet all the crimes and calamities of men. And we may add, (8) That from this we see the necessity now of *training* men who are to be missionaries to other lands. The gift of miracles is withdrawn. The apostles, by that miracle, simply were *empowered* to speak other languages. That power must still be had if the gospel is to be preached. But it is now to be obtained, not by miracle, but by slow and careful study and toil. If possessed, men must be taught it. And as the church is bound (Mat. xxviii. 19) to send the gospel to all nations, so it is bound to provide that the *teachers* who shall be sent forth shall be qualified for their work. Hence *one* of the reasons of the importance of training men for the holy ministry.

5. *There were dwelling at Jerusalem.* The word rendered *dwelling*—κατοικοῦντες—properly means to have a *fixed* and permanent habitation, in distinction from another word—παροικοῦντες—which means to have a *temporary* and *transient* residence in a place. But it is not always confined to this signification; and it is not improbable that many wealthy foreign Jews had a permanent residence in Jerusalem for the convenience of being near the temple. This was the more probable, as about that time the Messiah was expected to appear, Mat. ii. ¶ *Jews.* Jews by birth; of Jewish descent and religion. ¶ *Devout men*—ἄνδρες εὐλαβεῖς. Literally, men of cautious and circumspect lives, or who lived in a prudent manner. The term is then applied to men who were cautious about offending God; who were careful to observe his commandments. It is hence a general expression to denote *pious* or *religious* men, Ac. viii. 2,

gether, and were [2]confounded, because that every man heard them speak in his own language.

[2] or, *troubled in mind.*

"And *devout* men carried Stephen to his burial;" Lu. ii. 25, "And the same man (Simeon) was just, and *devout.*" The word *devout* means "yielding a solemn and reverential attention to God in religious exercises, particularly in prayer, pious, sincere, solemn" (Webster), and very well expresses the force of the original. ¶ *Out of every nation under heaven.* A general expression meaning from all parts of the earth. The countries from which they came are more particularly specified in ver. 9–11. The Jews at that time were scattered into almost all nations, and in all places had synagogues. See Notes on Jn. vii. 35; Ja. i. 1; 1 Pe. i. 1. Still they would naturally desire to be present as often as possible at the great feasts of the nation in Jerusalem. Many would seek a residence there for the convenience of being present at the religious solemnities. Many who came up to the feast of the Passover would remain to the feast of the Pentecost. The consequence of this would be, that on such occasions the city would be full of strangers. We are told that when Titus besieged Jerusalem, an event which occurred at about the time of the feast of the Passover, there were no less than three millions of people in the city. Josephus also mentions an instance in which great multitudes of Jews from other nations were present at the feast of Pentecost (*Jewish Wars*, b. ii. ch. iii. § 1). What is here stated as occurring at that time is true of the inhabitants of Jerusalem—four or five thousand in number—who reside there now. A large portion of them are from abroad. Prof. Hackett (*Illustrations of Scripture*, p. 228, 229) says of them, "Few of them, comparatively, are natives of the country. The majority of them are aged persons, who repair to the holy city to spend the remainder of their days and secure the privilege of being buried in the valley of the Kedron, which, as their traditions assert, is to be the scene of the last judgment. At the Jews' Wailing Place I met one day a venerable man, bowed with age, apparently beyond fourscore, who told me that, in obedience to his sense of duty, he had forsaken his children and home in England, and had come, unattended by any friend, to die and make his grave at Jerusalem. Others of them are those who come hither to fulfil a vow, or acquire the merit of a pilgrimage, and then return to the countries where they reside. Among them may be found representatives from almost every land, though the Spanish, Polish, and German Jews compose the greater number. Like their brethren in other parts of Palestine, except a few in some commercial places, they are wretchedly poor, and live chiefly on alms contributed by their countrymen in Europe and America. They devote most of their time to holy employments, as they are called; they frequent the synagogues, roam over the country to visit places memorable in their ancient history, and read assiduously the Old Testament and the writings of their Rabbis. Those of them who make any pretensions to learning understand the Hebrew and Rabbinic, and speak as their vernacular tongue the language of the country where they formerly lived, or whence their fathers emigrated."

6. *When this was noised abroad.* When the rumour of this remarkable transaction was spread, as it naturally would be. ¶ *Were confounded*—συνεχύθη. The word here used means literally to *pour together*, hence to *confound, confuse.* It is used (*a*) of an assembly or multitude thrown into confusion, Ac. xxi. 27; (*b*) of the mind as perplexed or confounded, as in disputation, Ac. ix. 22; and (*c*) of persons in amazement or consternation, as in this place. They did not understand this; they could not account for it. ¶ *Every man heard them speak*, &c. Though the multitude spoke different tongues, yet they now heard *Galileans* use the language which *they* had learned in foreign nations. ¶ *His own language.* His own *dialect*—διαλέκτῳ. His own *idiom,* whether it was a foreign language, or whether it was a modification of the Hebrew. The word may mean either; but it is probable that the foreign Jews would greatly modify the Hebrew, or conform almost entirely to the language spoken in the country where they lived. We may remark here that *this* effect of the descent of the Holy Ghost was not peculiar to that time. A work of grace on the hearts of men in a revival of religion

7 And they were all amazed, and marvelled, saying one to another, Behold, are not all these which speak [f] Galileans?

[f] ch.1.11.

8 And how hear we every man in our own tongue, wherein we were born?

9 Parthians, and Medes, and Elamites, and the dwellers in

---

will always *be noised abroad*. A multitude will come together, and God often, as he did here, makes use of this motive to bring them under the influence of religion. *Curiosity* was the motive here, and it was the *occasion* of their being brought under the power of truth, and of their conversion. In thousands of cases this has occurred since. The *effect* of what they saw was to *confound* them, to *astonish* them, and to throw them into deep perplexity. They made no complaint at first of the *irregularity* of what was done, but were all amazed and overwhelmed. So the effect of a revival of religion is often to convince the multitude that it is indeed a work of the Holy One; to amaze them by the display of his power; and to silence opposition and cavil by the manifest presence and the power of God. A *few* afterward began to cavil (ver. 13), as some will always do in a revival; but the mass were convinced, as will be the case always, that this was a mighty display of the power of God.

7. *Galileans.* Inhabitants of Galilee. It was remarkable that *they* should speak in this manner, because, (1) They were ignorant, rude, and uncivilized, Jn. i. 46. Hence the term *Galilean* was used as an expression of the deepest reproach and contempt, Mar. xiv. 70; Jn. vii. 52. (2) Their dialect was proverbially barbarous and corrupt, Mar. xiv. 70; Mat. xxvi. 73. They were regarded as an outlandish people, unacquainted with other nations and languages, and hence the amazement that they could address them in the refined language of other people. Their native *ignorance* was the occasion of making the miracle more striking. The native *weakness* of Christian ministers makes the grace and glory of God more remarkable in the success of the gospel. "We have this treasure in earthen vessels, that the excellency of the power may be of God, and not of us," 2 Co. iv. 7. The *success* which God often grants to those who are of slender endowments and of little learning, though blessed with an humble and pious heart, is often amazing to the men of the world. God has "chosen the foolish things of the world to confound the wise," 1 Co. i. 27. This should teach us that no talent or attainment *is too humble* to be employed for mighty purposes, in its proper sphere, in the kingdom of Christ; and that pious effort may accomplish much, and then burn in heaven with increasing lustre for ever, while pride, and learning, and talent may blaze uselessly among men, and then be extinguished in eternal night.

8. *Wherein we were born.* That is, as we say, in our *native* language; that which is spoken where we were born.

9. *Parthians,* &c. To show the surprising extent and power of this miracle, Luke enumerates the different nations that were represented then at Jerusalem. In this way the number of *languages* which the apostles spoke, and the extent of the miracle, can be ascertained. The enumeration of these nations begins at the east and proceeds to the west. *Parthians* mean those Jews or proselytes who dwelt in *Parthia.* This country was a part of Persia, and was situated between the Persian Gulf and the Tigris on the west, and the river Indus on the east. The term *Parthia* originally referred to a small mountainous district lying to the northeast of Media. Afterward it came to be applied to the great Parthian kingdom into which this province expanded. Parthia proper, or Ancient Parthia, lying between Asia and Hyrcania, the residence of a rude and poor tribe, and traversed by bare mountains, woods, and sandy steppes, formed a part of the great Persian monarchy. Its inhabitants were of Scythian origin. About 256 years before Christ, Arsaces rose against the Syro-Macedonian power, and commenced a new dynasty in her own person, designated by the title of Arsacidæ. This was the beginning of the great Parthian empire, which extended itself in the early days of Christianity over all the provinces of what had been the Persian kingdom, having the Euphrates for its western boundary, by which it was separated from the dominions of Rome (Kitto's *Encyclop.*). Their empire lasted about four hundred years. The Parthians were much dis-

Mesopotamia, and in Judea, and Cappadocia, in Pontus, and Asia,
10 Phrygia, and Pamphylia, in Egypt, and in the parts of Libya about Cyrene, and strangers of Rome, Jews and proselytes,

---

tinguished for their manner of fighting. They usually fought on horseback, and when appearing to retreat, discharged their arrows with great execution behind them. They long disputed the empire of the East with the Romans. The language spoken there was that of *Persia*, and in ancient writers *Parthia* and *Persia* often mean the same country. ¶ *Medes.* Inhabitants of *Media.* This country was situated westward and southward of the Caspian Sea, between 35° and 40° of north latitude. It had Persia on the south and Armenia on the west. It was about the size of Spain, and was one of the richest parts of Asia. In the Scriptures it is called *Madai*, Ge. x. 2. The *Medes* are often mentioned, frequently in connection with the *Persians*, with whom they were often connected under the same government, 2 Ki. xvii. 6; xviii. 11; Es. i. 3, 14, 18, 19; Je. xxv. 25; Da. v. 28; vi. 8; viii. 20; ix. 1. The language spoken here was also that of Persia. ¶ *Elamites. Elam* is often mentioned in the Old Testament. The nation was descended from *Elam*, the son of Shem, Ge. x. 22. It is mentioned as being in alliance with Amraphel, the king of Shinar, and Arioch, king of Ellasar, and Tidal, king of nations, Ge. xiv. 1. Of these nations in alliance, Chedorlaomer, king of Elam, was the chief, Ge. xiv. 4. See also Ezr. ii. 7; viii. 7; Ne. vii. 12, 34; Is. xi. 11; xxi. 2; xxii. 6, &c. They are mentioned as a part of the Persian empire, and Daniel is said to have resided *at Shushan, which is in the province of Elam*, Da. viii. 2. The Greeks and Romans gave to this country the name of *Elymais.* It is now called *Kusistan.* It was bounded by Persia on the east, by Media on the north, by Babylonia on the west, and by the Persian Gulf on the south. The Elamites were a warlike people, and celebrated for the use of the bow, Is. xxii. 6; Je. xlix. 35. The language of this people was of course the Persian. Its capital, *Shusan*, called by the Greeks *Susa*, was much celebrated. It is said to have been fifteen miles in circumference, and was adorned with the celebrated palace of Ahasuerus. The inhabitants still pretend to show there the tomb of the prophet Daniel. ¶ *Mesopotamia.* This name, which is Greek, signifies *between the rivers;* that is, the region lying between the rivers *Euphrates* and *Tigris.* In Hebrew it was called *Aram-Naharaim;* that is, Aram, or Syria, *of the two rivers.* It was also called Padan Aram, the plain of Syria. In this region were situated some important places mentioned in the Bible: *Ur of the Chaldees*, the birthplace of Abraham (Ge. xi. 27, 28); *Haran*, where *Terah* stopped on his journey and died (Ge. xi. 31, 32); *Charchemish* (2 Ch. xxxv. 20); *Hena* (2 Ki. xix. 13); *Sepharvaim* (2 Ki. xvii. 24). This region, known as Mesopotamia, extended between the two rivers from their sources to Babylon on the south. It had on the north Armenia, on the west Syria, on the east Persia, and on the south Babylonia. It was an extensive, level, and fertile country. The language spoken here was probably the *Syriac*, with perhaps a mixture of the *Chaldee.* ¶ *In Judea.* This expression has greatly perplexed commentators. It has been thought difficult to see why *Judea* should be mentioned, as if it were a matter of surprise that they could speak in this language. Some have supposed that there is an error in the manuscripts, and have proposed to read *Armenia*, or *India*, or *Lydia*, or *Idumea*, &c. But all this has been without any authority. Others have supposed that the language of Galilee was so different from that of the other parts of Judea as to render it remarkable that they could speak that dialect. But this is an idle supposition. This is one of the many instances in which commentators have perplexed themselves to very little purpose. Luke recorded this as any other historian would have done. In running over the languages which they spoke, he enumerated this as a matter of course; not that it was remarkable simply that they should speak the language of *Judea*, but that they should *speak so many*, meaning about the same by it as if he had said *they spoke every language in the world.* It is as if a similar miracle were to occur at this time among an assembly of native Englishmen and foreigners. In describing it, nothing would be more natural than to say they spoke French, and German, and Spanish, and *English*, and Italian, &c. In this there would be nothing remarkable except that they spoke *so many languages*. ¶ *Cappadocia.* This was a region of Asia Minor, and was bounded on the east by the Euphrates and Armenia, on the north by Pontus, west by Phrygia and Galatia, and south by Mount Taurus, beyond which are Cilicia and Syria. The language which was spoken here is not certainly known. It was probably, however, a mixed dialect, made up of Greek and Syriac, perhaps the same as that of their neighbours, the Lycaonians, Ac. xiv. 11. This place was formerly celebrated for iniquity, and is mentioned in Greek writers as one of the three eminently wicked places whose name began with C. The others were Crete (comp. Tit. i. 12) and Cilicia. After its conversion to the Christian religion, however, it produced many eminent men, among whom were Gregory Nyssen and Basil the Great. It was one of the places to which Peter directed an epistle, 1 Pe. i. 1. ¶ *In Pontus.* This was another province of Asia Minor, and was situated north of Cappadocia, and was bounded west by Paphlagonia. Pontus and Cappadocia under the Romans constituted one province. This was one of the places to which the apostle Peter directed his epistle, 1 Pe. i. 1. This was the birthplace of Aquila, one of the companions of Paul, Ac. xviii. 2, 18, 26; Ro. xvi. 3; 1 Co. xvi. 19; 2 Ti. iv. 19. ¶ *And Asia.* Pontus and Cappadocia, &c., were *parts* of Asia. But the word *Asia* is doubtless used here to denote the regions or provinces *west* of these, which are not particularly enumerated. Thus it is used Ac. vi. 9; xvi. 6; xx. 16. It probably embraced Mysia, Æolis, Ionia, Caria, and Lydia. "The term probably denoted not so much a definite region as a jurisdiction, the limits of which varied from time to time, according to the plan of government which the Romans adopted for their Asiatic provinces" (Prof. Hackett, *in loco*). The capital of this region was Ephesus. See also 1 Pe. i. 1. This region was frequently called *Ionia*, and was afterward the seat of the seven churches in Asia, Re. i. 4.

10. *Phrygia, and Pamphylia.* These were also two provinces of Asia Minor. Phrygia was surrounded by Galatia, Cappadocia, and Pisidia. Pamphylia was on the Mediterranean, and was bounded north by Pisidia. The language of all these places was doubtless the *Greek*, more or less pure. ¶ *In Egypt.* This was that extensive country, well known, on the south of the Mediterranean, watered by the Nile. It extends 600 miles from north to south, and from 100 to 120 east and west. The language used there was the *Coptic.* At present the Arabic is spoken. Vast numbers of Jews dwelt in Egypt, and many from that country would be present at the great feasts at Jerusalem. In this country the first translation of the Old Testament was made, which is now called the Septuagint. ¶ *In the parts of Libya.* Libya is a general name for Africa. It *properly* denoted the region which was near to Egypt; but the Greeks gave the name to all Africa. ¶ *About Cyrene.* This was a region about 500 miles west of Alexandria in Egypt. It was also called *Pentapolis*, because there were in it five celebrated cities. This country now belongs to *Tripoli.* Great numbers of Jews resided here. A Jew of this place, Simon by name, was compelled to bear our Saviour's cross after him to the place of crucifixion, Mat. xxvii. 32; Lu. xxiii. 26. Some of the Cyrenians are mentioned among the earliest Christians, Ac. xi. 20; xiii. 1. The language which they spoke is not certainly known. ¶ *Strangers of Rome.* This literally means "Romans dwelling or tarrying," that is, at Jerusalem. It may mean either that they were *permanently* fixed, or only *tarrying* at Jerusalem—οἱ ἐπιδημοῦντες Ῥωμαῖοι. They were doubtless Jews who had taken up their residence in Italy, and had come to Jerusalem to attend the great feasts. The language which they spoke was the Latin. Great numbers of Jews were at that time dwelling at Rome. Josephus says that there were eight synagogues there. The Jews are often mentioned by the Roman writers. There was a Jewish colony across the Tiber from Rome. When Judea was conquered, about sixty years before Christ, vast numbers of Jews were taken captive and carried to Rome. But they had much difficulty in managing them as slaves. They pertinaciously adhered to their religion, observed the Sabbath, and refused to join in the idolatrous rites of the Romans. Hence they were freed, and lived by themselves across the Tiber. ¶ *Jews.* Native-born Jews, or descendants of Jewish families. ¶ *Proselytes.* Those who had been converted to the Jewish religion from among the Gentiles. The great zeal of the Jews to

11 Cretes and Arabians, we do hear them [g]speak in our tongues the wonderful works of God.
12 And they were all amazed, and were in doubt, saying one to another, [h]What meaneth this?
13 Others, mocking, said, These men are full of new wine.

g 1 Co.12.10,28.

h ch.17.20.

make proselytes is mentioned by our Saviour as one of the peculiar characteristics of the Pharisees, Mat. xxiii. 15. Some have supposed that the expression *Jews and proselytes* refers to the Romans only. But it is more probable that reference is made to *all* those that are mentioned. It has the appearance of a hurried enumeration; and the writer evidently mentioned them as they occurred to his mind, just as we would in giving a rapid account of so many different nations.

11. *Cretes. Crete,* now called *Candia,* is an island in the Mediterranean, about 200 miles in length and 50 in breadth, about 500 miles south-west of Constantinople, and about the same distance west of Syria or Palestine. The climate is mild and delightful, the sky unclouded and serene. By some this island is supposed to be the *Caphtor* of the Hebrews, Ge. x. 14. It is mentioned in the Acts as the place touched at by Paul, Ac. xxvii. 7, 8, 13. This was the residence of Titus, who was left there by Paul *to set in order the things that were wanting,* &c., Tit. i. 5. The Cretans among the Greeks were famous for deceit and falsehood. See Notes on Tit. i. 12, 13. The language spoken there was probably the Greek. ¶ *Arabians.* Arabia is the great peninsula which is bounded north by part of Syria, east by the Euphrates and the Persian Gulf, south by the Indian Ocean, and west by the Red Sea. It is often mentioned in the Scriptures; and there were doubtless there many Jews. The language spoken there was the *Arabic.* ¶ *In our tongues.* The languages spoken by the apostles could not have been less than seven or eight, besides different dialects of the same languages. It is not certain that the Jews present from foreign nations spoke those languages perfectly, but they had doubtless so used them as to make them the common tongue in which they conversed. No miracle could be more decided than this. There was no way in which the apostles could *impose* on them, and make them *suppose* they spoke foreign languages, if they really did not; for these foreigners were abundantly able to determine that. It may be remarked that this miracle had most important effects besides that witnessed on the day of Pentecost. The gospel would be carried by those who were converted to all these places, and the way would be prepared for the labours of the apostles there. Accordingly, most of these places became afterward celebrated by the establishment of Christian churches and the conversion of great multitudes to the Christian faith. ¶ *The wonderful works of God*—τὰ μεγαλεῖα τοῦ Θεοῦ. The *great things* of God; that is, the great things that God had done in the gift of his Son; in raising him from the dead; in his miracles, ascension, &c. Comp. Lu. i. 49; Ps. lxxi. 19; xxvi. 7; lxvi. 3; xcii. 5; civ. 24; &c.

12. *Were in doubt.* This expression, διηπόρουν, denotes a state of *hesitancy* or *anxiety* about an event. It is applied to those who are travelling, and are ignorant of the way, or who hesitate about the road. They were *all* astonished at this; they did not know how to understand it or explain it, until some of them supposed that it was merely the effect of new wine.

13. *Others, mocking, said.* The word rendered "mocking" means *to cavil, to deride.* It occurs in the New Testament but in one other place: Ac. xvii. 32, "And when they heard of the resurrection of the dead, some mocked." This was an effect that was not confined to the day of Pentecost. There has seldom been a revival of religion, a remarkable manifestation of the power of the Holy Spirit, that has not given occasion for profane mockery and merriment. One characteristic of wicked men is to deride those things which are done to promote their own welfare. Hence the Saviour himself was mocked; and the efforts of Christians to save others have been the subject of derision. *Derision,* and *mockery,* and *a jeer,* have been far more effectual in deterring men from becoming Christians than any attempts at sober argument. God will treat men as they treat him, Ps. xviii. 26. And hence he says to the wicked, "Because I have called and ye refused . . . but ye have set at naught my counsel; I

14 But Peter, standing up with the eleven, lifted up his voice, and said unto them, Ye men of Judea, and all *ye* that dwell at Jerusalem,

---

also will laugh at your calamity, I will *mock* when your fear cometh," Pr. i. 24–26. ¶ *These men are full of new wine.* These men are drunk. In times of a revival of religion men will have some way of accounting for the effects of the gospel, and the way is commonly about as wise and rational as the one adopted on this occasion. "To escape the absurdity of acknowledging their own ignorance, they adopted the theory *that strong drink can teach languages*" (Dr. M'Lelland). In modern times it has been usual to denominate such scenes fanaticism, or wildfire, or enthusiasm. When men fail in argument, it is common to attempt to confute a doctrine or bring reproach upon a transaction by "giving it an ill name." Hence the names Puritan, Quaker, Methodist, &c., were at first given in derision, to account for some remarkable effect of religion on the world. Comp. Mat. xi. 19; Jn. vii. 20; viii. 48. And thus men endeavour to trace revivals to ungoverned and heated passions, and they are regarded as the mere offspring of fanaticism. The friends of revivals should not be discouraged by this; but they should remember that the very first revival of religion was by many supposed to be *the effect of a drunken frolic.* ¶ *New wine*—γλεύκους. This word properly means the juice of the grape which distils before a pressure is applied, and called *must.* It was *sweet* wine, and hence the word in Greek meaning *sweet* was given to it. The ancients, it is said, had the art of preserving their new wine with the peculiar flavour before fermentation for a considerable time, and were in the habit of drinking it in the morning. See Hor. *Sat.*, b. ii. iv. One of the methods in use among the Greeks and Romans of doing this was the following: An amphora or jar was taken and coated with pitch within and without, and was then filled with the juice which flowed from the grapes before they had been fully trodden, and was then corked so as to be air-tight. It was then immersed in a tank of cold water or buried in the sand, and allowed to remain six weeks or two months. The contents after this process were found to remain unchanged for a year, and hence the name ἀει γλεῦκος—*always sweet.* The process was not much unlike that which is so common now of preserving fruits and vegetables. *Sweet wine*, which was probably the same as that mentioned here, is also mentioned in the Old Testament, Is. xlix. 26; Am. ix. 13.

14. *But Peter.* This was in accordance with the natural temperament of Peter. He was bold, forward, ardent; and he rose now to defend the apostles of Jesus Christ, and Christ himself, from an injurious charge. Not daunted by ridicule or opposition, he felt that now was the time for preaching the gospel to the crowd that had been assembled by curiosity. No ridicule should deter Christians from an honest avowal of their opinions, and a defence of the operations of the Holy Spirit. ¶ *With the eleven.* Matthias was now one of the apostles, and now appeared as one of the witnesses for the truth. They probably all arose, and took part in the discourse. Possibly Peter *began* to discourse, and either all spoke together in different languages, or one succeeded another. ¶ *Ye men of Judea.* Men who are Jews; that is, Jews by birth. The original does not mean that they were permanent dwellers *in Judea*, but that they were *Jews*, of Jewish families. Literally, "men, Jews." ¶ *And all* ye *that dwell*, &c. All others besides native-born Jews, whether proselytes or strangers, who were abiding at Jerusalem. This comprised, of course, the whole assembly, and was a respectful and conciliatory introduction to his discourse. Though they had mocked them, yet he treated them with respect, and did not render railing for railing (1 Pe. iii. 9), but sought to *convince* them of their error. ¶ *Be this known*, &c. Peter did not intimate that this was a doubtful matter, or one that could not be explained. His address was respectful, yet firm. He proceeded calmly to *show* them their error. When the enemies of religion deride us or the gospel, we should answer them kindly and respectfully, yet firmly. We should *reason* with them coolly, and convince them of their error, Pr. xv. 1. In this case Peter acted on the principle which he afterward enjoined on all, 1 Pe. iii. 15, "Be ready always to give an answer to every man that asketh you a reason of the hope that is in you, with meekness

be this known unto you, and hearken to my words:

15 For these are not drunken, as ye suppose, [i]seeing it is *but* the third hour of the day.

16 But this is that which was spoken by the prophet [k]Joel:

17 And it shall come to pass in the last days, (saith God,) [l]I will pour out of my Spirit upon all

i 1 Th.5.7. *k* Joel 2.28-32. *l* Is.44.3; Eze.36.27.

and fear." The design of Peter was to *vindicate* the conduct of the apostles from the reproach of intoxication; to show that this could be no other than the work of God; and to make an application of the truth to his hearers. This he did, (1) By showing that this could not be reasonably supposed to be the effect of new wine, ver. 15. (2) By showing that what had occurred had been expressly predicted in the writings of the Jewish prophets, ver. 16–21. (3) By a calm argument, proving the resurrection and ascension of Christ, and showing that this also was in accordance with the Jewish Scriptures, ver. 22–35. We are not to suppose that this was the *whole* of Peter's discourse, but that these were the topics on which he insisted, and the main points of his argument.

15. *For these are not drunken*, &c. The word *these* here includes Peter himself, as well as the others. The charge doubtless extended to all. ¶ *The third hour of the day*. The Jews divided their day into *twelve* equal parts, reckoning from sunrise to sunset. Of course the hours were longer in summer than in winter. The *third* hour would answer to our nine o'clock in the morning. The reasons why it was so improbable that they would be drunk at that time were the following: (1) It was the hour of morning worship, or sacrifice. It was highly improbable that, at an hour usually devoted to public worship, they would be intoxicated. (2) It was not usual for even drunkards to become drunk in the daytime, 1 Th. v. 7, "They that be drunken are drunken in the night." (3) The charge was, that they had become drunk with wine. Ardent spirits, or alcohol, that curse of *our* times, was unknown. It was very improbable that so much of the weak wine commonly used in Judea should have been taken at that early hour as to produce intoxication. (4) It was a regular practice with the Jews not to eat or drink *anything* until after the third hour of the day, especially on the Sabbath, and on all festival occasions. Sometimes this abstinence was maintained until noon. So universal was this custom, that the apostle could appeal to it with confidence, as a full refutation of the charge of drunkenness at that hour. Even the intemperate were not accustomed to drink before that hour. The following testimonies on this subject from Jewish writers are from Lightfoot: "This was the custom of pious people in ancient times, that each one should offer his morning prayers with additions in the synagogue, and then return home and take refreshment" (Maimonides, *Shabb.*, ch. 10). "They remained in the synagogue until the sixth hour and a half, and then each one offered the prayer of the Mincha before he returned home, and then he ate." "The fourth is the hour of repast, when all eat." One of the Jewish writers says that the difference between thieves and honest men might be known by the fact that the *former* might be seen in the morning at the fourth hour eating and sleeping, and holding a cup in his hand. But for those who made pretensions to religion, as the apostles did, such a thing was altogether improbable.

16. *This is that.* This is the *fulfilment* of that, or this was predicted. This was the *second* part of Peter's argument, to show that this was in accordance with the predictions in their own Scriptures. ¶ *By the prophet Joel.* Joel ii. 28–32. This is not quoted *literally*, either from the Hebrew or the Septuagint. The substance, however, is preserved.

17. *It shall come to pass.* It shall happen, or shall occur. ¶ *In the last days.* Hebrew, Chaldee, Syriac, and Arabic, *after these things*, or *afterward.* The expression *the last days*, however, occurs frequently in the Old Testament: Ge. xlix. 1, Jacob called his sons, that he might tell them what should happen to them *in the last days*, that is, in future times—Heb. *in after times*; Mi. iv. 1, "*In the last days* (Heb. in after times) the mountain of the Lord's house," &c.; Is. ii. 2, "*In the last days* the mountain of the Lord's house shall be established in the tops of the mountains," &c. The

flesh: and your sons and your daughters shall prophesy, and your young men shall see visions, and your old men shall dream dreams;

expression then properly denoted *the future times* in general. But, as the coming of the Messiah was to the eye of a Jew the most important event in the coming ages—the great, glorious, and crowning scene in all the vast futurity, the phrase came to be regarded as properly expressive of that. It stood in opposition to the usual denomination of earlier times. It was a phrase in contrast with the days of the patriarchs, the kings, the prophets, &c. The *last days*, or the closing period of the world, were the days of the Messiah. It does not appear from this, and it certainly is not implied in the expression, that they supposed the world would then come to an end. Their views were just the contrary. They anticipated a long and glorious time under the dominion of the Messiah, and to this expectation they were led by the promise that his kingdom should be for ever; that of the increase of his government there should be no end, &c. This expression was understood by the writers of the New Testament as referring undoubtedly to the times of the gospel. And hence they often used it as denoting that the time of the expected Messiah had come, but *not* to imply that the world was drawing near to an end: He. i. 2, "God hath spoken in these last days by his Son;" 1 Pe. i. 20, "Was manifested in these last times for you;" 2 Pe. iii. 3; 1 Pe. i. 5; 1 Jn. ii. 18, "Little children, it is the last time," &c.; Jude 18. The expression *the last day* is applied by our Saviour to the resurrection and the day of judgment, Jn. vi. 39, 40, 44, 45; xi. 24; xii. 48. Here the expression means simply *in those future times, when the Messiah shall have come.* ¶ *I will pour out of my Spirit.* The expression in Hebrew is, "I will pour out my Spirit." The word *pour* is commonly applied to *water* or to *blood*, to pour it out, or to shed it, Is. lvii. 6; to *tears*, to pour them out, that is, to weep, &c., Ps. xlii. 4; 1 Sa. i. 15. It is applied to water, to wine, or to blood, in the New Testament, Mat. ix. 17; Re. xvi. 1; Ac. xxii. 20, "The blood of thy martyr Stephen *was shed.*" It conveys also the idea of *communicating largely* or *freely*, as water is poured freely from a fountain, Tit. iii. 5, 6, "The renewing of the Holy Ghost, which he *shed on us abundantly.*" Thus Job xxxvi. 27, "They (the clouds) pour down rain according to the vapour thereof;" Is. xliv. 3, "I will pour water on him that is thirsty;" xlv. 8, "Let the skies pour down righteousness;" Mal. iii. 10, "I will pour you out a blessing." It is also applied to *fury* and *anger*, when God intends to say that he will not spare, but will signally punish, Ps. lxix. 24; Je. x. 25. It is not unfrequently applied *to the Spirit*, Pr. i. 23; Is. xliv. 3; Zec. xii. 10. As thus used it means that he will bestow large measures of spiritual influences. As the *Spirit* renews and sanctifies men, so to pour out the Spirit is to grant freely his influences to renew and sanctify the soul. ¶ *My Spirit.* The *Spirit* here denotes the third person of the Trinity, promised by the Saviour, and sent to finish his work, and apply it to men. The Holy Spirit is regarded as the source or *conveyer* of all the blessings which Christians experience. Hence he renews the heart, Jn. iii. 5, 6. He is the source of all proper feelings and principles in Christians, or he produces the Christian graces, Ga. v. 22–25; Tit. iii. 5–7. The spread and success of the gospel is attributed to him, Is. xxxii. 15, 16. Miraculous gifts are traced to him, especially the various gifts with which the early Christians were endowed, 1 Co. xii. 4–10. The promise that he would pour out his Spirit means that he would, in the time of the Messiah, impart a large measure of those influences which it was his peculiar province to communicate to men. A *part* of them were communicated on the day of Pentecost, in the miraculous endowment of the power of speaking foreign languages, in the wisdom of the apostles, and in the conversion of the three thousand. ¶ *Upon all flesh.* The word *flesh* here means *persons*, or *men*. See Notes on Ro. i. 3. The word *all* here does not mean every individual, but every *class* or *rank* of men. It is to be limited to the cases specified immediately. The influences were not to be confined to any one class, but were to be communicated to all *kinds* of persons—old men, youth, servants, &c. Comp. 1 Ti. ii. 1–4. ¶ *And your sons and your daughters.* Your children.

It would seem that females shared in the remarkable influences of the Holy Spirit. Philip the Evangelist had four daughters which did prophesy, Ac. xxi. 9. It is probable also that the females of the church of Corinth partook of this gift, though they were forbidden to exercise it in public, 1 Co. xiv. 34. The office of prophesying, whatever was meant by that, was not confined to the *men* among the Jews: Ex. xv. 20, "Miriam, the prophetess, took a timbrel," &c.; Ju. iv. 4, "Deborah, a prophetess, judged Israel;" 2 Ki. xxii. 14. See also Lu. ii. 36, "There was one Anna, a prophetess," &c. ¶ *Shall prophesy.* The word *prophesy* is used in a great variety of senses. (1) It means to *predict* or *foretell* future events, Mat. xi. 13; xv. 7. (2) To divine, to conjecture, to declare as a prophet might, Mat. xxvi. 68, "Prophesy who smote thee." (3) To celebrate the praises of God, being under a divine influence, Lu. i. 67. This seems to have been a considerable part of the employment in the ancient schools of the prophets, 1 Sa. x. 5; xix. 20; xxx. 15. (4) To *teach*—as no small part of the office of the prophets was to teach the doctrines of religion, Mat. vii. 22, "Have we not prophesied in thy name?" (5) It denotes, then, in general, *to speak under a divine influence,* whether in foretelling future events, in celebrating the praises of God, in instructing others in the duties of religion, or *in speaking foreign languages under that influence.* In this last sense the word is used in the New Testament, to denote those who were miraculously endowed with the power of speaking foreign languages, Ac. xix. 6. The word is also used to denote *teaching,* or speaking in intelligible language, in *opposition* to speaking a foreign tongue, 1 Co. xiv. 1–5. In this place it means that they would speak under a divine influence, and is *specially* applied to the power of speaking in a foreign tongue. ¶ *Your young men shall see visions.* The will of God in former times was communicated to the prophets in various ways. One was by *visions,* and hence one of the most usual names of the prophets was *seers.* The name *seer* was first given to that class of men, and was superseded by the name *prophet,* 1 Sa. ix. 9, "He that is now called a prophet was beforetime called a *seer;*" ix. 11, 18, 19; 2 Sa. xxiv. 11; xxix. 29, &c. This name was given from the *manner* in which the divine will was communicated, which seems to have been by throwing the prophet into an ecstasy, and then by causing the *vision,* or the *appearance* of the objects or events to pass before the mind. The prophet looked upon the passing scene, the often splendid diorama as it actually occurred, and recorded it as it appeared to his mind. Hence he recorded rather the *succession* of images than the *times* in which they would occur. These visions occurred sometimes when they were *asleep,* and sometimes during a prophetic ecstasy, Da. ii. 28; vii. 1, 2, 15; viii. 2; Eze. xi. 24; Ge. xv. 1; Nu. xii. 6; Job iv. 13; vii. 14; Eze. i. 1; viii. 3. Often the prophet seemed to be transferred or translated to another place from where he was, and the scene in a distant *land* or *age* passed before the mind, Eze. viii. 3; xl. 2; xi. 24; Da. viii. 2. In this case the distant scene or time passed before the prophet, and he recorded it as it appeared to him. That this did not cease before the times of the gospel is evident: Ac. ix. 10, "To Ananias said the Lord *in a vision,*" &c.; 12, "And hath seen *in a vision* a man named Ananias," &c.; that is, Paul hath seen Ananias represented to him, though absent; he has had an image of him coming in to him; Ac. x. 3, Cornelius "saw in a vision evidently an angel of God coming to him," &c. This was one of the modes by which in former times God made known his will; and the language of the Jews came to express a revelation in this manner. Though there were strictly no *visions* on the day of Pentecost, yet that was one scene under the great economy of the Messiah under which God would make known his will in a manner as clear as he did to the ancient Jews. ¶ *Your old men shall dream dreams.* The will of God in former times was made known often in this manner; and there are several instances recorded in which it was done under the gospel. God informed Abimelech in a dream that Sarah was the wife of Abraham, Ge. xx. 3. He spoke to Jacob in a dream, Ge. xxxi. 11; to Laban, xxxi. 24; to Joseph, xxxvii. 5; to the butler and baker, xl. 5; to Pharaoh, xli. 1–7; to Solomon, 1 Ki. iii. 5; to Daniel, Da. ii. 3; vii. 1. It was prophesied by Moses that in this way God would make known his will, Nu. xii. 6. It occurred even in the times of the gospel. Joseph was warned in a dream, Mat. i. 20; ii. 12, 13, 19, 22. Pilate's wife was also

18 And on my servants and on my handmaidens I will pour out, in those days, of my Spirit; [m]and they shall prophesy:

19 And I will show wonders in heaven above, and signs in the earth beneath; blood, and fire, and vapour of smoke:

m ch.21.4,9,10; 1 Co.12.10.

troubled in this manner about the conduct of the Jews to Christ, Mat. xxvii. 19. As this was one way in which the will of God was made known formerly to men, so the expression here denotes simply that his will would be made known; that it would be one characteristic of the times of the gospel that God would reveal himself to man. The ancients probably had some mode of determining whether their *dreams* were divine communications, or whether they were, as they are now, the mere erratic wanderings of the mind when unrestrained and unchecked by the will. At present no confidence is to be put in dreams. Comp. Introd. to Is. § 7, 12.

18. *And on my servants.* The Hebrew in Joel is "upon *the* servants." The Septuagint and the Latin Vulgate, however, render it "on *my* servants." In Joel, the prophet would seem to be enumerating the different conditions and ranks of society. The influences of the Spirit would be confined to no class; they would descend on old and young, and even on servants and handmaids. So the Chaldee Paraphrase understood it. But the Septuagint and Peter evidently understood it in the sense of *servants of God*, as the worshippers of God are often called *servants* in the Scriptures. See Ro. i. 1. It is possible, however, that Joel intended to refer to the servants of God. It is not "upon *your* servants," &c., as in the former expression, "*your* sons," &c.; but the form is changed, "upon *servants* and handmaids." The language, therefore, will admit the construction of the Septuagint and of Peter; and it was this variation in the original Hebrew which suggested, doubtless, the mention of "*my* servants," &c., instead of *your* servants. ¶ *And handmaids.* Female servants. The name is several times given to pious women, Ps. lxxxvi. 16; cxvi. 16; Lu. i. 38, 48. The meaning of this verse does not materially differ from the former. In the times of the gospel, those who were brought under its influence would be remarkably endowed with ability to declare the will of God.

19, 20. *I will show wonders.* Literally, "I will give signs"—δώσωτέρατα. The word in the Hebrew, מופתים, *mophethim*, means properly *prodigies;* wonderful occurrences; miracles wrought by God or his messengers, Ex. iv. 21; vii. 3, 9; xi. 9; De. iv. 34, &c. It is the common word to denote a *miracle* in the Old Testament. Here it means, however, *a portentous appearance, a prodigy, a remarkable occurrence.* It is commonly joined in the New Testament with the word *signs*—"signs and wonders," Mat. xxiv. 24; Mar. xiii. 22; Jn. iv. 48. In these places it does not of necessity mean *miracles*, but unusual and remarkable appearances. Here it is used to mean great and striking changes in the sky, the sun, moon, &c. The Hebrew is, "I will give signs in the heaven and upon the earth." Peter has quoted it according to the sense, and not according to the letter. The Septuagint is here a literal translation of the Hebrew; and this is one of the instances where the New Testament writers did not quote from either.

Much of the difficulty of interpreting these verses consists in affixing the proper meaning to the expression "that great and notable *day* of the Lord." If it be limited to the day of Pentecost, it is certain that no such events occurred at that time. But there is, it is believed, no propriety in confining it to that time. The description here pertains to "the last days" (ver. 17); that is, to the *whole* of that period of duration, however long, which was known by the prophets as *the last times.* That period might be extended through many centuries; and *during* that period *all* these events would take place. The *day of the Lord* is the day when God will *manifest himself* in a peculiar manner; a day when *he* will so strikingly be seen in his wonders and his judgments that it may be called *his* day. Thus it is applied to the day of judgment as the *day of the Son of man;* the day in which *he* will be the great attractive object, and will be signally glorified, Lu. xvii. 24; 1 Th. v. 2; Phi. i. 6; 2 Pe. iii. 12. If, as I suppose, "that notable day of the Lord" here refers to that future time when God will manifest himself in judgment, then we are not to suppose

20 The[n] sun shall be turned into darkness, and the moon into blood, before that great and notable day of the Lord come:
21 And it shall come to pass, *that*

n Mar.13.24; 2 Pe.3.7,10.

---

that Peter meant to say that these "wonders" would take place on the day of Pentecost, or had their fulfilment then, *but would occur under that indefinite period called "the last days," the days of the Messiah, and* BEFORE *that period was closed by the great day of the Lord.* The gift of tongues was a *partial* fulfilment of the *general* prophecy pertaining to those times. And as the prophecy was thus *partially* fulfilled, it was a pledge that it would be *entirely;* and thus there was laid a foundation for the necessity of repentance, and for calling on the Lord in order to be saved. ¶ *Blood. Blood* is commonly used as an emblem of slaughter or of battle. ¶ *Fire. Fire* is also an image of war, or the conflagration of towns and dwellings in time of war. ¶ *Vapour of smoke.* The word *vapour*, ἀτμὶς, means commonly an exhalation from the earth, &c., easily moved from one place to another. Here it means (Heb. Joel) *rising columns* or *pillars of smoke*, and is another image of the calamities of war—the smoke rising from burning towns. It has always been customary in war to burn the towns of an enemy, and to render him as helpless as possible. Hence the calamities denoted here are those *represented* by such scenes. To what *particular* scenes there is reference here it is impossible now to say. It may be remarked, however, that scenes of this kind occurred before the destruction of Jerusalem, and there is a striking resemblance between the description in Joel and that by which our Saviour foretells the destruction of Jerusalem. See Notes on Mat. xxiv. 21–24. Dr. Thomson (*Land and the Book*, vol. ii. p. 311) supposes that the reference in Joel may have been to the usual appearances of the sirocco, or that they may have suggested the image used here. He says: "We have two kinds of sirocco, one accompanied with vehement wind, which fills the air with dust and fine sand. I have often seen the whole heavens veiled in gloom with this sort of sand-cloud, through which the sun, shorn of his beams, looked like a globe of dull smouldering fire. It may have been this phenomenon which suggested that strong prophetic figure of Joel, quoted by Peter on the day of Pentecost. Wonders in the heaven and in the earth; blood, and fire, and pillars of smoke; the sun shall be turned into darkness, and the moon into blood. The pillars of smoke are probably those columns of sand and dust raised high in the air by local whirlwinds, which often accompany the sirocco. On the great desert of the Hauran I have seen a score of them marching with great rapidity over the plain, and they closely resemble 'pillars of smoke.'"

20. *The sun shall be turned into darkness.* See Notes on Mat. xxiv. 29. The same images used here with reference to the sun and moon are used also there. They occur not unfrequently, Mar. xiii. 24; 2 Pe. iii. 7–10. The shining of the sun is an emblem of prosperity; the withdrawing, the eclipse, or the setting of the sun is an emblem of calamity, and is often thus used in the Scriptures, Is. lx. 20; Je. xv. 9; Eze. xxxii. 7; Am. viii. 9; Re. vi. 12; viii. 12; ix. 2; xvi. 8. To say that the sun is darkened, or turned into darkness, is an image of calamity, and especially of the calamities of war, when the smoke of burning cities rises to heaven and obscures his light. This is not, therefore, to be taken literally, nor does it afford any indication of what will be at the end of the world in regard to the sun. ¶ *The moon into blood.* The word *blood* here means that obscure, sanguinary colour which the moon has when the atmosphere is filled with smoke and vapour, and especially the lurid and alarming appearance which it assumes when smoke and flames are thrown up by earthquakes and fiery eruptions, Re. vi. 12, "And I beheld when he had opened the sixth seal, and lo, there was a great earthquake, and the sun became black as sackcloth of hair, and the moon became as blood," Re. viii. 8. In this place it denotes great calamities. The figures used are indicative of wars, and conflagrations, and earthquakes. As these things are (Mat. xxiv.) applied to the destruction of Jerusalem; as they actually occurred previous to that event (see Notes on Mat. xxiv.), it may be supposed that the prophecy in Joel had an immediate reference to that. The meaning of the

whosoever[o] shall call on the name of the Lord shall be saved.

o Ps.86.5; Ro.10.13; 1 Co.1.2; He.4.16.

22 Ye men of Israel, hear these words; Jesus of Nazareth, a man

quotation by Peter in this place therefore is, that what occurred on the day of Pentecost *was the beginning of the series of wonders that was to take place during the times of the Messiah.* It is not intimated that those scenes were to close or to be exhausted in that age. They may precede that great day of the Lord which is yet to come in view of the whole earth. ¶ *That great and notable day of the Lord.* This is called the *great* day of the Lord, because on that day he will be signally manifested, more impressively and strikingly than on other times. The word *notable,* ἐπιφανῆ, means signal, illustrious, distinguished. In Joel the word is *terrible* or *fearful;* a word applicable to days of calamity, and trial, and judgment. The Greek word here rendered *notable* is also in the Septuagint frequently used to denote calamity or times of judgment, De. x. 21; 2 Sa. vii. 23. This will apply to *any* day in which God signally manifests himself, but particularly to a day when he shall come forth to punish men, as at the destruction of Jerusalem, or at the day of judgment. The meaning is, that those wonders would take place *before* that distinguished day should arrive when God would come forth in judgment.

21. *Whosoever shall call.* In the midst of these wonders and dangers, whosoever should call on the Lord should be delivered (Joel). The *name* of the Lord is the same as the Lord himself. It is a Hebraism, signifying to call on the Lord, Ps. lxxix. 6; Zec. xiii. 9. ¶ *Shall be saved.* In Hebrew, shall be *delivered,* that is, from impending calamities. When they threaten, and God is coming forth to judge them, it shall be that those who are characterized as those who call on the Lord shall be delivered. This is equally true at all times. It is remarkable that no Christians perished in the siege of Jerusalem. Though more than a million of Jews perished, yet the followers of Christ who were there, having been warned by him, when they saw the signs of the Romans approaching, withdrew to *Ælia,* and were preserved. So it shall be in the day of judgment. All whose character it has been that *they called on God* will then be saved. While the wicked will then call on the rocks and the mountains to shelter them *from* the Lord, those who *have* invoked his *favour* and *mercy* will find deliverance. The use which Peter makes of this passage is this: Calamities were about to come; the day of judgment was approaching; they were passing through *the last days* of the earth's history, and therefore it became them to call on the name of the Lord, and to obtain deliverance from the dangers which impended over the guilty. There can be little doubt that Peter intended to apply this to the Messiah, and that by the name of the Lord he meant the Lord Jesus. See 1 Co. i. 2. Paul makes the same use of the passage, expressly applying it to the Lord Jesus Christ, Ro. x. 13, 14. In Joel, the word translated *Lord* is JEHOVAH, the incommunicable and peculiar name of God; and the use of the passage before us in the New Testament shows how the apostles regarded the Lord Jesus Christ, and proves that they had no hesitation in applying to him names and attributes which could belong to no one but God.

This verse teaches us, 1. That in prospect of the judgments of God which are to come, we should make preparation. We shall be called to pass through the closing scenes of this earth; the time when the sun shall be turned into darkness, and the moon into blood, and when the great day of the Lord shall come. 2. It is easy to be saved. All that God requires of us is to call upon him, to pray to him, and he will answer and save. If men will not do so easy a thing as to call on God, and *ask* him for salvation, it is obviously proper that they should be cast off. The terms of salvation could not be made plainer or easier. The offer is wide, free, universal, and there is no obstacle but what exists in the heart of the sinner. And from this part of Peter's vindication of the scene on the day of Pentecost we may learn also, 1. That revivals of religion are to be expected as a part of the history of the Christian church. He speaks of God's pouring out his Spirit, &c., as what was to take place *in the last days,* that is, in the indefinite and large tract of time which was to come, under the administration of the Messiah. His remarks are by no means

approved of God among you [p]by miracles, and wonders, and signs, which God did, by him, in the midst of you, [q]as ye yourselves also know:

23 Him, [r]being delivered by

p Jn.14.10,11; He.2.4. q Jn.15.24. r Lu.22.22; 24.44; ch.3.18.

limited to the day of Pentecost. They are as applicable to future periods as to that time; and we are to expect it *as a part of Christian history*, that the Holy Spirit will be sent down to awaken and convert men. 2. This will also vindicate revivals from all the charges which have ever been brought against them. All the objections of irregularity, extravagance, wildfire, enthusiasm, disorder, &c., which have been alleged against revivals in modern times, *might* have been brought with equal propriety against the scene on the day of Pentecost. Yet an apostle showed that that was in accordance with the predictions of the Old Testament, and was an undoubted work of the Holy Spirit. If *that* work could be vindicated, then modern revivals may be. If that was really liable to no objections on these accounts, then modern works of grace should not be objected to for the same things. And if that excited deep interest in the apostles; if they felt deep concern to vindicate it from the charge brought against it, then Christians and Christian ministers now should feel similar solicitude to defend revivals, and not be found among their revilers, their calumniators, or their foes. There will be enemies enough of the work of the Holy Spirit without the aid of professed Christians, and that man possesses no enviable feelings or character who is found with the enemies of God and his Christ in opposing the mighty work of the Holy Spirit on the human heart.

22. *Ye men of Israel.* Descendants of Israel or Jacob, that is, Jews. Peter proceeds now to the third part of his argument, to show that Jesus Christ had been raised up; that the scene which had occurred was in accordance with his promise, was proof of his resurrection, and of his exaltation to be the Messiah; and that, therefore, they should repent for their great sin in having put their own Messiah to death. ¶ *A man approved of God.* A man who was *shown* or *demonstrated* to have the approbation of God, or to have been sent by him. ¶ *By miracles, and wonders, and signs.* The first of these words properly means the displays of *power* which Jesus made; the second, the unusual or remarkable events which attended him, as fitted to excite *wonder* or *amazement;* the third, the *signs* or *proofs* that he was from God. Together, they denote the *array* or *series* of remarkable works—raising the dead, healing the sick, &c., which showed that Jesus was sent from God. The *proof* which they furnished that he was from God was this, that He would not confer such power on an impostor, and that therefore Jesus was what he pretended to be. ¶ *Which God did by him.* The Lord Jesus himself often traced his power to do these things to his commission from the Father, but he did it in such a way as to show that he was closely united to him, Jn. v. 19, 30. Peter here says that God did these works *by* Jesus Christ, to show that Jesus was truly *sent* by him, and that therefore he had the seal and attestation of God. The same thing Jesus himself said, Jn. v. 36, "The work which the Father hath given me to finish, the same works that I do, bear witness of me, that the Father hath sent me." The great works which God has wrought in creation, as well as in redemption, he is represented as having done by his Son, He. i. 2, "By whom also he made the worlds," Jn. i. 3; Col. i. 15–19. ¶ *In the midst of you.* In your own land. It is also probable that many of the persons present had been witnesses of his miracles. ¶ *As ye yourselves also know.* They knew it either by having witnessed them, or by the evidence which everywhere abounded of the truth that he had wrought them. The Jews, even in the time of Christ, did not dare to call his miracles in question, Jn. xv. 24. While they admitted the miracle, they attempted to trace it to the influence of Beelzebub, Mat. ix. 34; Mar. iii. 22. So decided and numerous were the miracles of Jesus, that Peter here appeals to them as having been known by the Jews themselves to have been performed, and with a confidence that even *they* could not deny it. On this he proceeds to rear his argument for the truth of his Messiahship.

23. *Him, being delivered*—ἔκδοτον. This word, *delivered*, is used commonly of

the determinate counsel and foreknowledge of God, [s]ye have taken, and [t]by wicked hands have crucified and slain:

s ch.5.30.

t Mat.27.1.

those who are *surrendered* or delivered into the hands of enemies or adversaries. It means that Jesus was surrendered, or given up to his enemies by those who should have been his protectors. Thus he was delivered to the chief priests, Mar. x. 33. Pilate released Barabbas, and *delivered* Jesus to their will, Mar. xv. 15; Lu. xxiii. 25. He was delivered unto the Gentiles, Lu. xviii. 32; the chief priests delivered him to Pilate, Mat. xxvii. 2; and Pilate delivered him to be crucified, Mat. xxvii. 26; Jn. xix. 16. In this manner was the death of Jesus accomplished, by being *surrendered* from one tribunal to another, and one demand of his countrymen to another, until they succeeded in procuring his death. It may also be implied here that he was given or surrendered *by God himself* to the hands of men. Thus he is represented to have been *given* by God, Jn. iii. 16; 1 Jn. iv. 9, 10. The Syriac translates this, "Him, who was destined to this by the foreknowledge and will of God, *you delivered* into the hands of wicked men," &c. The Arabic, "Him, delivered *to you* by the hands of the wicked, you received, and after you had mocked him you slew him." ¶ *By the determinate counsel.* The word translated *determinate*—τῇ ὡρισμένῃ—means, properly, that which is *defined*, *marked out*, or *bounded;* as, to mark out or define the boundary of a field, &c. See Ro. i. 1, 4. In Ac. x. 42, it is translated *ordained* of God; denoting *his purpose that it should be so*, that is, that Jesus should be the judge of quick and dead; Lu. xxii. 22, "The Son of man goeth as it is *determined* of him," that is, as God has purposed or determined beforehand that he should go; Ac. xi. 29, "The disciples . . . *determined* to send relief unto the brethren which dwelt in Judea," that is, they *resolved* or *purposed* beforehand to do it; Ac. xvii. 26, "God . . . *hath determined* the times before appointed and fixed," &c. In all these places there is the idea of a *purpose*, *intention*, or *plan* implying *intention*, and marking out or fixing the boundaries to some future action or event. The word implies that the death of Jesus was *resolved on* by God before it took place. And this truth is established by all the predictions made in the Old Testament, and by the Saviour himself. God was not *compelled* to give up his Son. There was no *claim* on him for it. He had a right, therefore, to determine when and how it should be done. The fact, moreover, that this was *predicted*, shows that it was fixed or resolved on. No event can be *foretold*, evidently, unless it be *certain* that it will take place. The event, therefore, must in some way be fixed or resolved on beforehand. ¶ *Counsel*—βουλῇ. This word properly denotes *purpose*, *decree*, *will.* It expresses the act of the mind in *willing*, or the purpose or design which is formed. Here it means the purpose or will of God; it was his plan or decree that Jesus should be delivered: Ac. iv. 28, "For to do whatsoever thy hand and *thy counsel* (ἡ βουλή σου) determined before to be done;" Ep. i. 11, "Who worketh all things after *the counsel* of his own will;" He. vi. 17, "God willing . . . to show . . . the immutability of *his counsel.*" See Ac. xx. 27; 1 Co. iv. 5; Lu. xxiii. 51. The word here, therefore, proves that Jesus was delivered by the deliberate purpose of God; that it was according to his previous intention and design. The reason why this was insisted on by Peter was that he might convince the Jews that Jesus was not delivered by *weakness*, or because he was unable to rescue himself. Such an opinion would have been inconsistent with the belief that he was the Messiah. It was important, then, to assert the *dignity* of Jesus, and to show that his death was in accordance with the fixed design of God, and therefore that it did not interfere in the least with his claims to be the Messiah. The same thing our Saviour has himself expressly affirmed, Jn. xix. 10, 11; x. 18; Mat. xxvi. 53. ¶ *Foreknowledge.* This word denotes the seeing beforehand of an event yet to take place. It implies, 1. Omniscience; and, 2. That the event is fixed and certain. To foresee a contingent event, that is, to foresee that an event will take place when it may or may not take place, is an absurdity. Foreknowledge, therefore, implies that for some reason the event *will certainly* take place. What that reason is the word itself does not determine.

As, however, *God* is represented in the Scriptures as purposing or determining future events; as they could not be *foreseen* by him unless he had so determined, so the word sometimes is used in the sense of determining beforehand, or as synonymous with decreeing, Ro. viii. 29; xi. 2. In this place the word is used to denote that the delivering up of Jesus was something more than a bare or naked decree. It implies that God did it according to his *foresight* of what would be the best time, place, and manner of its being done. It was not the result merely of *will;* it was will directed by a wise foreknowledge of what would be best. And this is the case with all the decrees of God. It follows from this that the conduct of the Jews was foreknown. God was not disappointed in anything respecting their treatment of his Son, nor will he be disappointed in any of the doings of men. Notwithstanding the wickedness of the world, his counsel shall stand, and he will do all his pleasure, Is. xlvi. 10. ¶ *Ye have taken.* See Mat. xxvi. 57. Ye *Jews* have taken. It is possible that some were present on this occasion who had been personally concerned in taking Jesus, and many who had joined in the cry, "Crucify him," Lu. xxiii. 18–21. It was, at any-rate, the act *of the Jewish people* by which this had been done. This was a striking instance of the fidelity of that preaching which says, as Nathan did to David, "Thou art the man!" Peter, once so timid that he denied his Lord, now charged this atrocious crime on his countrymen, regardless of their anger and his own danger. He did not deal in *general* accusations, but brought the charges home, and declared that *they* were the men who had been concerned in this amazing crime. No preaching can be successful that does not charge on men their personal guilt, and that does not fearlessly proclaim their ruin and danger. ¶ *With wicked hands.* Greek, "through or by the hands of the lawless or wicked." This refers, doubtless, to Pilate and the Roman soldiers, through whose instrumentality this had been done. The reasons for supposing that this is the true interpretation of the passage are these: (1) The Jews had not the power of inflicting death themselves. (2) The term used here, *wicked*, ἀνόμων, is not applicable to the *Jews*, but to the Romans. It properly means *lawless*, or those who had not the law, and is often applied to the heathen, Ro. ii. 12, 14; 1 Co. ix. 21. (3) The punishment which was inflicted was a Roman punishment. (4) It was a matter of fact that the Jews, though they had *condemned* him, yet had not put him to death themselves, but had demanded it of the Romans. But, though they had employed the Romans to do it, still they were the prime movers in the deed; they had plotted, and compassed, and demanded his death, and they were, therefore, not the less guilty. The maxim of the common law and of common sense is, "He who does a deed by the instrumentality of another is responsible for it." It was from no merit of the Jews that *they* had not put him to death themselves. It was simply because the power was taken away from them. ¶ *Have crucified.* Greek, "Having affixed him to the cross, ye have put him to death." Peter here charges the crime fully on them. Their guilt was not diminished because they had employed others to do it. From this we may remark, 1. That this was one of the most amazing and awful crimes that could be charged on any men. It was malice, and treason, and hatred, and murder combined. Nor was it any common murder. It was *their own Messiah* whom they had put to death; the hope of their fathers; he who had been long promised by God, and the prospect of whose coming had so long cheered and animated the nation. They had now imbrued their hands in his blood, and stood charged with the awful crime of having murdered the Prince of Peace. 2. It is no mitigation of guilt that we do it by the instrumentality of others. It is often, if not always, a deepening and extending of the crime. 3. We have here a striking and clear instance of the doctrine that the decrees of God do not interfere with the free agency of men. This event was certainly *determined* beforehand. Nothing is clearer than this. It is here expressly asserted; and it had been foretold with undeviating certainty by the prophets. God had, for wise and gracious purposes, purposed or decreed in his own mind that his Son should die at the time and in the manner in which he did; for all the circumstances of his *death*, as well as of his birth and his life, were foretold; and yet in this the Jews and the Romans never supposed or alleged that they were compelled or cramped in what they did. They *did what they chose.* If in this case the decrees of God were not

24 Whom [u]God hath raised up, having loosed the pains of death: because [v]it was not possible that he should be holden of it.

u Lu.24.; ch.13.30,34; 1 Co.6.14; Ep.1.20; Col.2.12; 1 Th.1.10; He.13.20; 1 Pe.1.21.

v Jn.10.18.

inconsistent with human freedom, neither can they be in any case. Between those decrees and the freedom of man there *is* no inconsistency, unless it could be shown—what never can be—that God *compels* men to act contrary to their own will. In such a case there could be no freedom. But that is *not* the case with regard to the decrees of God. An act is what it is *in itself;* it it can be contemplated and measured by itself. That it was *foreseen, foreknown,* or *purposed* does not alter its nature, any more than it does that it be *remembered* after it is performed. The *memory* of what we have done does not destroy our freedom. *Our own purposes* in relation to our conduct do not destroy our freedom; nor can the purposes or designs of any other being violate one free moral action, unless he *compels* us to do a thing against our will. 4. We have here a proof that the decrees of God do not take away *the moral character* of an action. It does not prove that an action is *innocent* if it is shown that it is a part of the wise plan of God to permit it. Never was there a more atrocious *crime* than the crucifixion of the Son of God; and yet it was determined on in the divine counsels. So with all the deeds of human guilt. The purpose of God to *permit* them does not destroy their nature or make them innocent. They are what they are in themselves. The purpose of God does not change their character; and if it is *right* to punish them *in fact,* they will be punished. If it is right for God to punish them, it was right to *resolve* to do it. The sinner must answer for *his sins,* not for the plans of his Maker; nor can he take shelter in the day of wrath against *what he deserves* in the plea that God has determined future events. If any men could have done it, it would have been those whom Peter addressed; yet neither he nor they felt that their guilt was in the least diminished by the fact that Jesus was "delivered by the determinate counsel and foreknowledge of God." 5. If this event was predetermined; if that act of amazing wickedness, when the Son of God was put to death, was fixed by the determinate counsel of God, then all the events leading to it, and the circumstances attending it, were also a part of the decree. The one could not be determined without the other. 6. If *that* event was determined, then others may also be consistently with human freedom and responsibility. There can be no deed of wickedness that will surpass that of crucifying the Son of God, and if the acts of his murderers were a part of the wise counsel of God, then on the same principle are we to suppose that all events are under his direction, and ordered by a purpose infinitely wise and good. 7. If the Jews could not take shelter from the charge of wickedness under the plea that it was foreordained, then no sinners can do it. This was as clear a case as can ever occur; and yet the apostle did not intimate that an excuse or mitigation for their sin could be pled from this cause. This case, therefore, meets *all* the excuses of sinners from this plea, and *proves* that those excuses will not avail them or save them in the day of judgment.

24. *Whom God hath raised up.* This was the main point, in this part of his argument, which Peter wished to establish. He could not but admit that the Messiah had been in an ignominious manner put to death. But he now shows them that *God* had also raised him up; had thus given his attestation to his doctrine; and had sent down his Spirit according to the promise which the Lord Jesus made before his death. ¶ *Having loosed the pains of death.* The word *loosed,* λύσας, is opposed to *bind,* and is properly applied to a *cord,* or to anything which is *bound.* See Mat. xxi. 2; Mar. i. 7. Hence it means to *free* or to *liberate,* Lu. xiii. 16; 1 Co. vii. 27. It is used in this sense here; though the idea of *untying* or loosing a band is retained, because the word translated *pains* often means a *cord* or *band.* ¶ *The pains of death*—ὠδῖνας τοῦ θανάτου. The word translated *pains* denotes properly the extreme sufferings of parturition, and then any *severe* or excruciating pangs. Hence it is applied also to *death,* as being a state of extreme suffering. A very frequent meaning of the Hebrew word of which this is the translation is *cord* or *band.* This, perhaps, was the *original* idea of the word;

25 For David speaketh concerning him, [w]I foresaw the Lord always before my face; for he is on my right hand, that I should not be moved:
26 Therefore did my heart rejoice, and my tongue was glad;

w Ps.16.8-11.

and the Hebrews expressed any extreme agony under the idea of *bands* or *cords* closely drawn, binding and constricting the limbs, and producing severe pain. Thus death was represented under this image of *a band* that confined men, that pressed closely on them, that prevented escape, and produced severe suffering. For this use of the word חבל, see Ps. cxix. 61; Is. lxvi. 7; Je. xxii. 23; Ho. xiii. 13. It is applied to death, Ps. xviii. 5, "The *snares* of death prevented me;" answering to the word *sorrows* in the previous part of the verse; Ps. cxvi. 3, "The sorrows of death compassed me, and the *pains* of hell (*Hades* or *Sheol*, the cords or pains that were *binding me down* to the grave) gat hold on me." We are not to infer from this that our Lord suffered anything *after* death. It means simply that he could not be held by the grave, but that God loosed the *bonds* which *had* held him there; that he now set him free who had been encompassed by these pains or bonds until they had brought him down to the grave. Pain, mighty pain, will encompass us all like the constrictions and bindings of a cord which we cannot loose, and will fasten our limbs and bodies in the grave. Those bands begin to be thrown around us in early life, and they are drawn closer and closer, until we lie panting under the stricture on a bed of pain, and then are still and immovable in the grave—subdued in a manner not a little resembling the mortal agonies of the tiger in the convolutions of the boa constrictor, or like Laocoon and his sons in the folds of the serpents from the island of Tenedos. ¶ *It was not possible.* This does not refer to any *natural* impossibility, or to any inherent efficacy or power in the *body* of Jesus itself, but simply means that *in the circumstances of the case such an event could not be. Why* it could not be he proceeds at once to show. It could not be consistently with the promises of the Scriptures. Jesus was the *Prince of life* (Ac. iii. 15); he had life in himself (Jn. i. 4; v. 26); he had power to lay down his life and to take it again (Jn. x. 18); and it was indispensable that he should rise. He came, also, that through death he might destroy him that had the power of death—that is, the devil (He. ii. 14); and as it was his purpose to gain this victory, he could not be defeated in it by being confined to the grave.

25–28. *For Daniel speaketh*, &c. This doctrine that the Messiah must rise from the dead Peter proceeds to prove by a quotation from the Old Testament. This passage is taken from Ps. xvi. 8–11. It is made from the Greek version of the Septuagint, with only one slight and unimportant change. Nor is there any material change, as will be seen, from the Hebrew. In what sense this Psalm can be applied to Christ will be seen after we have examined the expressions which Peter alleges. ¶ *I foresaw the Lord.* This is an unhappy translation. To *foresee* the Lord always *before* us conveys no idea, though it may be a *literal* translation of the passage. The word means to *foresee*, and then to *see before us*, that is, as *present* with us, to *regard* as being near. It thus implies to put *confidence* in one; to rely on him, or expect assistance from him. This is its meaning here. The Hebrew is, *I expected*, or *waited for*. It thus expresses the petition of one who is helpless and dependent, who *waits* for help from God. It is often thus used in the Old Testament. ¶ *Always before my face.* As being always present to help me, and to deliver me out of all my troubles. ¶ *He is on my right hand.* To be *at hand* is to be *near* to afford help. The *right* hand is mentioned because that was the place of dignity and honour. David did not design simply to say that he was *near* to help him, but that he had the place of honour, the highest place in his affections, Ps. cix. 31. In our dependence on God we should *exalt* him. We should not merely regard him as our *help*, but should at the same time give him the highest place in our affections. ¶ *That I should not be moved.* That is, that no great evil or calamity should happen to me; that I may stand firm. The phrase denotes to sink into calamities, or to fall into the power of enemies, Ps. lxii. 2, 6; xlvi. 6. This expresses the confidence of one who is in danger of great

moreover also my flesh shall rest in hope:
27 Because thou wilt not leave my soul in hell, neither wilt thou suffer thine Holy One to see corruption.

---

calamities, and who puts his trust in the help of God alone.

26. *Therefore.* Peter ascribes these expressions to the Messiah. The *reason* why he would exult or rejoice was, that he would be preserved amidst the sorrows that were coming on him, and could look forward to the triumph that awaited him. Thus Paul says (He. xii. 2) that "Jesus . . . . *for the joy that was set before him*, endured the cross, despising the shame," &c. Throughout the New Testament, the shame and sorrow of his sufferings were regarded as connected with his glory and his triumph, Lu. xxiv. 26; Phi. ii. 6–9; Ep. i. 20, 21. In this our Saviour has left us an example that we should walk in his steps. The prospect of future glory and triumph should sustain us amidst all afflictions, and make us ready, like him, to lie down in even the corruptions of the grave. ¶ *Did my heart rejoice.* In the Hebrew this is in the *present* tense, "my heart rejoices." The word *heart* here expresses the *person*, and is the same as saying *I* rejoice. The Hebrews used the different *members* to express the person. And thus *we* say, "every *soul* perished; the vessel had forty *hands;* wise *heads* do not think so; *hearts* of steel will not flinch," &c. (Prof. Stuart on Ps. xvi.). The meaning is, because God is near me in time of calamity, and will support and deliver me, I will not be agitated or fear, but will exult in the prospect of the future, in view of the "joy that is set before me." ¶ *My tongue was glad.* Hebrew, My *glory* or my *honour* exults. The word is used to denote majesty, splendour, dignity, honour. It is also used to express the *heart* or *soul*, either because that is the chief source of man's dignity, or because the word is also expressive of the *liver*, regarded by the Hebrews as the seat of the affections, Ge. xlix. 6, "Unto their assembly, *mine honour*," that is, my soul, or myself, "be not thou united;" Ps. lvii. 8, "Awake up, my glory," &c.; Ps. cviii. 1, "I will sing . . . . even with *my glory*." This word the Septuagint translated *tongue.* The Arabic and Latin Vulgate have also done the same. Why they thus use the word is not clear. It may be because the tongue, or the gift of speech, was that which chiefly contributes to the honour of man, or distinguishes him from the brutal creation. The word *glory* is used expressly for tongue in Ps. xxx. 12: "To the end that my *glory* may sing praise to thee, and not be silent." ¶ *Moreover also.* Truly; in addition to this. ¶ *My flesh.* My body. See ver. 31; 1 Co. v. 5. It means here properly the body separate from the soul; the dead body. ¶ *Shall rest.* Shall rest or repose in the grave, free from corruption. ¶ *In hope.* In confident expectation of a resurrection. The Hebrew word rather expresses *confidence* than *hope.* The passage means, "My body will I commit to the grave, with a confident expectation of the future, that is, with a firm belief that it will not see corruption, but will be raised up." It thus expresses the feelings of the dying Messiah; the assured confidence which he had that his repose in the grave would not be long, and would certainly come to an end. The death of Christians is also in the New Testament represented as a *sleep*, and as *repose* (Ac. vii. 60; 1 Co. xv. 6, 18; 1 Th. iv. 13, 15; 2 Pe. iii. 4); and they may also, after the example of their Lord, commit their bodies to the dust, *in hope*. They will lie in the grave under the assurance of a happy resurrection; and though their bodies, unlike his, will moulder to their native dust, yet this corruptible will put on incorruption, and this mortal will put on immortality, 1 Co. xv. 53.

27. *Thou wilt not leave my soul.* The word *soul*, with us, means the *thinking*, the *immortal* part of man, and is applied to it whether existing in connection with the body or separate from it. The Hebrew word translated *soul* here, נפש, *nephesh*, however, may mean spirit, mind, life, and may denote here nothing more than *me* or *myself.* It means, properly, breath; then life, or the vital principle, a living being; then the soul, the spirit, the thinking part. Instances where it is put for the individual himself, meaning "me" or "myself," may be seen in Ps. xi. 1; xxxv. 3, 7; Job ix. 21. There is no clear instance in which it is applied to the soul in its *separate* state, or disjoined from the body. In this place it must be explained in part

by the meaning of the word *hell.* If that means *grave*, then this word probably means "me;" thou wilt not leave *me in the grave.* The meaning probably is, "Thou wilt not leave *me* in *Sheol*, neither," &c. The word *leave* here means, "Thou wilt not *resign me* to, or wilt not give me over to it, to be held under its power." ¶ *In hell*—εἰς ᾅδου. The word *hell*, in English, now commonly denotes the place of the future eternal punishment of the wicked. This sense it has acquired by long usage. It is a Saxon word, derived from *helan*, to cover, and denotes literally a covered or deep place (Webster); then the dark and dismal abode of departed spirits; and then the place of torment. As the word is used *now* by us, it by no means expresses the force of the original; and if with *this* idea we read a passage like the one before us, it would convey an erroneous meaning altogether, although *formerly* the English word perhaps expressed no more than the original. The Greek word *Hades* means literally a place devoid of light; a dark, obscure abode; and in Greek writers was applied to the dark and obscure regions where disembodied spirits were supposed to dwell. It occurs but eleven times in the New Testament. In this place it is the translation of the Hebrew *Sheol.* In Re. xx. 13, 14, it is connected with *death:* "And death and hell (*Hades*) delivered up the dead which were in them;" "And death and hell (*Hades*) were cast into the lake of fire." See also Re. vi. 8; Re. i. 18, "I have the keys of hell and death." In 1 Co. xv. 55 it means the grave: "O *grave* (*Hades*), where is thy victory?" In Mat. xi. 23 it means a deep, profound place, opposed to an exalted one; a condition of calamity and degradation, opposed to former great prosperity: "Thou, Capernaum, which art exalted to heaven, shalt be thrust down to *hell*" (*Hades*). In Lu. xvi. 23 it is applied to the place where the rich man was after death, in a state of punishment: "In hell (*Hades*) he lifted up his eyes, being *in torments.*" In this place it is connected with the idea of suffering, and undoubtedly denotes a place of punishment. The Septuagint has used this word commonly to translate the word *Sheol.* Once it is used as a translation of the phrase "the stones of the pit" (Is. xiv. 19); twice to express *silence*, particularly the silence of the grave (Ps. xciv. 17; cxv. 17); once to express the Hebrew for "the shadow of death" (Job xxxviii. 17); and *sixty* times to translate the word *Sheol.* It is remarkable that it is *never* used in the Old Testament to denote the word *kēber*, קבר, which properly denotes *a grave* or *sepulchre.* The idea which was conveyed by the word *Sheol*, or *Hades*, was not properly *a grave* or *sepulchre*, but that dark, unknown state, *including the grave*, which constituted the dominions of the dead. What idea the Hebrews had of the future world it is now difficult to explain, and is not necessary in the case before us. The word originally denoting simply the state of the dead, the insatiable demands of the grave, came at last to be extended in its meaning, in proportion as they received new revelations or formed new opinions about the future world. Perhaps the following may be the process of thought by which the word came to have the peculiar meanings which it is found to have in the Old Testament. (1) The word *death* and the *grave* (*kēber*) would express the abode of a deceased *body* in the earth. (2) Man has a soul, a thinking principle, and the inquiry *must* arise, What will be its state? Will it die also? The Hebrews never appear to have believed that. Will it ascend to heaven at once? On that subject they had at first no knowledge. Will it go at once to a place of happiness or of torment? Of that, also, they had no information at first. Yet they supposed it would live; and the word *Sheol* expressed just this state—the dark, unknown regions of the dead; the abode of spirits, whether good or bad; the residence of departed men, whether fixed in a permanent habitation, or whether wandering about. As they were ignorant of the size and spherical structure of the earth, they seem to have supposed this region to be situated *in the earth*, far below us, and hence it is put in opposition to heaven, Ps. cxxxix. 8, "If I ascend up into heaven, thou art there; if I make my bed in hell (*Sheol*), behold, thou art there;" Am. ix. 2. The most *common* use of the word is, therefore, to express those dark regions, *the lower world*, the region of ghosts, &c. Instances of this, almost without number, might be given. See a most striking and sublime instance of this in Is. xiv. 9: "Hell from beneath is moved to meet thee," &c.; where the assembled dead are represented as being agitated in all their vast regions at the death of

28 Thou hast made known to me the ways of life; thou shalt make me full of joy with thy countenance.

---

the King of Babylon. (3) The inquiry could not but arise whether all these beings were happy. This point revelation decided; and it was decided in the Old Testament. Yet this word would better express the state of the *wicked dead* than the righteous. It conveyed the idea of darkness, gloom, wandering; the idea of a sad and unfixed abode, unlike heaven. Hence the word *sometimes* expresses the idea of a place of punishment: Ps. ix. 17, "The wicked shall be turned into *hell*," &c.; Pr. xv. 11; xxiii. 14; xxvii. 20; Job xxvi. 6. While, therefore, the word does not mean properly *a grave* or a sepulchre, it does mean often *the state of the dead*, without designating whether in happiness or woe, but implying the continued existence of the soul. In this sense it is often used in the Old Testament, where the Hebrew word is *Sheol*, and the Greek *Hades:* Ge. xxxvii. 35, "I will go down into the grave, *unto my son*, mourning"—I will go down to the dead, to *death*, to my son, still there existing; xlii. 38; xliv. 29, "He shall bring down my gray hairs with sorrow to the grave;" Nu. xvi. 30, 33; 1 Ki. ii. 6, 9; &c. &c. In the place before us, therefore, the meaning is simply, *thou wilt not leave me* AMONG THE DEAD. This conveys *all* the idea. It does not mean literally the *grave* or the *sepulchre;* that relates only to *the body*. This expression refers to the *deceased Messiah*. Thou wilt not leave *him* among the dead; thou wilt raise him up. It is from this passage, perhaps, aided by two others (Ro. x. 7, and 1 Pe. iii. 19), that the doctrine originated that Christ "descended," as it is expressed in the Creed, "*into hell;*" and many have invented strange opinions about his going among lost spirits. The doctrine of the Roman Catholic Church has been that he went to *purgatory*, to deliver the spirits confined there. But if the interpretation now given be correct, then it will follow, (1) That nothing is affirmed here about the destination of the human *soul* of Christ after his death. That he went to the region of the dead is implied, but nothing further. (2) It may be remarked that the Scriptures affirm nothing about the state of his *soul* in that time which intervened between his death and resurrection. The only intimation which occurs on the subject is such as to leave us to suppose that he was in a state of happiness. To the dying thief he said, "*This day* shalt thou be with me in paradise." When Jesus died, he said, "It is finished;" and he doubtless meant by that that his sufferings and toils for man's redemption were at an end. All suppositions of any toils or pains after his death are fables, and without the slightest warrant in the New Testament. ¶ *Thine Holy One.* The word in the Hebrew which is translated here *Holy One* properly denotes one who is tenderly and piously devoted to another, and answers to the expression used in the New Testament, "my *beloved* Son." It is also used, as it is here by the Septuagint and by Peter, to denote one that is *holy*, that is set apart to God. In this sense it is applied to Christ, either as being set apart to this office, or as so pure as to make it proper to designate him by way of eminence *the Holy One*, or the *Holy One of God.* It is several times used as the well-known designation of the Messiah: Mar. i. 24, "I know thee who thou art, *the Holy One* of God;" Lu. iv. 34; Ac. iii. 14, "But ye denied *the Holy One*, and the just," &c. See also Lu. i. 35, "That *holy thing* that is born of thee shall be called the Son of God." ¶ *To see corruption.* To *see* corruption is to experience it, to be made partakers of it. The Hebrews often expressed the idea of experiencing anything by the use of words pertaining to the senses, as, to *taste* of death, to *see* death, &c. *Corruption* here means putrefaction in the grave. The word which is used in the Psalm, שחת, *shahath*, is thus used in Job xvii. 14, "I have said to corruption, thou art my father," &c. The Greek word here used properly denotes this. Thus it is used in Ac. xiii. 34–37. This meaning would be properly suggested by the Hebrew word, and thus the ancient versions understood it. The meaning *implied* in the expression is, that he of whom the Psalm was written should be restored to life again; and this meaning Peter proceeds to show that the words *must have.*

28. *Thou hast made known*, &c. The Hebrew is, "Thou *wilt* make known to me," &c. In relation to the Messiah, it means, Thou wilt *restore* me to life.

29 Men *and* brethren, [3]let me freely speak unto you of the patriarch David, that he is both dead and buried, and his sepulchre is with us unto this day.

[3] or, *I may.*

¶ *The way of life.* This properly means the path to life; as we say, the *road* to preferment or honour; the *path* to happiness; the *highway* to ruin, &c. See Pr. vii. 26, 27. It means, thou wilt make known to me *life itself*, that is, thou wilt restore me to life. The expressions in the Psalm are capable of this interpretation without doing any violence to the text; and if the preceding verses refer to the death and burial of the Messiah, then the natural and proper meaning of this is, that he would be restored to life again. ¶ *Thou hast made me full of joy.* This expresses the feelings of the Messiah in view of the favour that would thus be showed him; the resurrection from the dead, and the elevation to the right hand of God. It was this which is represented as sustaining him—the prospect of the joy that was before him, in heaven, He. xii. 2; Ep. i. 20–22. ¶ *With thy countenance.* Literally, "with thy face," that is, in thy presence. The words *countenance* and *presence* mean the same thing, and denote *favour*, or the honour and happiness provided by being admitted to the presence of God. The prospect of the honour that would be bestowed on the Messiah was that which sustained him. And this proves that the person contemplated in the Psalm *expected* to be raised from the dead, and exalted to the *presence* of God. That expectation is now fulfilled, and the Messiah is now filled with joy in his exaltation to the throne of the universe. He has "ascended to his Father and our Father;" he is "seated at the right hand of God;" he has entered on that "joy which was set before him;" he is "crowned with glory and honour;" and "all things are put under his feet." In view of this, we may remark, (1) That the Messiah had full and confident expectation that he would rise from the dead. This the Lord Jesus always evinced, and often declared it to his disciples. (2) If the Saviour *rejoiced* in view of the glories before him, we should also. We should anticipate with joy an everlasting dwelling in the presence of God, and the high honour of sitting "with him on *his* throne, as he overcame, and is set down with the Father on his throne." (3) The prospect of this should sustain us, as it did him, in the midst of persecution, calamity, and trials. Thy will soon be ended; and if we are his friends, we shall "overcome," as he did, and be admitted to "the fulness of joy" above, and to the "right hand" of God, "where are pleasures for evermore."

29. *Men* and *brethren.* This passage of the Psalms Peter now proves could not relate to David, but must have reference to the Messiah. He begins his argument in a respectful manner, addressing them as his *brethren*, though they had just charged him and the others with intoxication. Christians should use the usual respectful forms of salutation, whatever contempt and reproaches they may meet with from opposers. ¶ *Let me freely speak.* That is, "It is lawful or proper to speak with boldness, or openly, respecting David." Though he was eminently a pious man, though venerated by us all as a king, yet it is proper to say of him that *he* is dead, and has returned to corruption. This was a delicate way of expressing high respect for the monarch whom they all honoured, and yet evinced boldness in examining a passage of Scripture which probably many supposed to have reference solely to him. ¶ *Of the patriarch David.* The word *patriarch* properly means the head or ruler of a family; and then the *founder* of a family, or an illustrious ancestor. It was commonly applied to Abraham, Isaac, and Jacob by way of eminence, the illustrious founders of the Jewish nation, He. vii. 4; Ac. vii. 8, 9. It was also applied to the heads of the families, or the chief men of the tribes of Israel, 1 Ch. xxiv. 31; 2 Ch. xix. 8, &c. It was thus a title of honour, denoting high respect. Applied to David, it means that he was the illustrious head or founder of the royal family, and the word is expressive of Peter's intention not to say anything disrespectful of such a king, at the same time that he freely canvassed a passage of Scripture which had been supposed to refer to him. ¶ *Dead and buried.* The record of that fact they had in the Old Testament. There had been no pretence that he had risen, and therefore the Psalm could not apply to him. ¶ *His*

sepulchre is with us. Is *in* the city of Jerusalem. Sepulchres were commonly situated *without* the walls of cities and the limits of villages. The custom of burying *in* towns was not commonly practised. This was true of other ancient nations as well as the Hebrews, and is still in Eastern countries, except in the case of kings and very distinguished men, whose ashes are permitted to rest within the walls of a city: 1 Sa. xxviii. 3, "Samuel was dead . . . and Israel . . . buried him in Ramah, in his own city;" 2 Ki. xxi. 18, "Manasseh . . . was buried in the garden of his own house;" 2 Ch. xvi. 14, Asa was buried in the city of David; 2 Ki. xiv. 20. David was buried in the city of David (1 Ki. ii. 10), with his fathers; that is, on Mount Zion, where he built a city called after his name, 2 Sa. v. 7. Of what form the tombs of the kings were is not certainly known. It is almost certain, however, that they would be constructed in a magnificent manner. The tombs were commonly excavations from rocks, or natural caves; and sepulchres cut out of the solid rock, of vast extent, are known to have existed. The following account of the tomb called "the sepulchre of the kings" is abridged from Maundrell: "The approach is through an entrance cut out of a solid rock, which admits you into an open court about forty paces square, cut down into the rock. On the south side is a portico nine paces long and four broad, hewn likewise out of the solid rock. At the end of the portico is the descent to the sepulchres. The descent is into a room about 7 or 8 yards square, cut out of the natural rock. From this room there are passages into six more, all of the same fabric with the first. In every one of these rooms, except the first, were coffins placed in niches in the sides of the chamber," &c. (Maundrell's *Travels*). If the tombs of the kings were of this form, it is clear that they were works of great labour and expense. Probably, also, there were, as there are now, costly and splendid monuments erected to the memory of the mighty dead. The following extract from *The Land and the Book*, and cut on the next page (from Williams's *Holy City*), will illustrate the usual construction of tombs: "The entire system of rooms, niches, and passages may be comprehended at once by an inspection of the plan of the Tombs of the Judges near Jerusalem. The entrance faces the west, and has a vestibule (A) 13 feet by 9. Chamber (B), nearly 20 feet square, and 8 high. The north side is seen in elevation in Fig. 2, and shows two tiers of niches, one over the other, not often met with in tombs. There are seven in the lower tier, each 7 feet long, 20 inches wide, and nearly 3 feet high. The upper tier has three arched recesses, and each recess has two niches. From this room (B) doors lead out into chambers (C and D), which have their own peculiar system of niches, or loculi, for the reception of the bodies, as appears on the plan. I have explored scores of sepulchres at Ladakîyeh closely resembling this at Jerusalem, and there are many in the plain and on the hillsides above us here at Sidon of the same general form—chambers within chambers, and each with niches for the dead, variously arranged according to taste or necessity." These tombs are about a mile north-west of Jerusalem. "The tombs which are commonly called the 'Tombs of the Kings' are in an olive-grove about half a mile north of the Damascus Gate, and a few rods east of the great road to Nablûs. A court is sunk in the solid rock about 90 feet square and 20 deep. On the west side of this court is a sort of portico, 39 feet long, 17 deep, and 15 high. It was originally ornamented with grapes, garlands, and festoons, beautifully wrought on the cornice; and the columns in the centre, and the pilasters at the corners, appear to have resembled the Corinthian order. A *very low* door in the south end of the portico opens into the ante-chamber—19 feet square, and 7 or 8 high. From this three passages conduct into other rooms, two of them, to the south, having five or six crypts. A passage also leads from the west room down several steps into a large vault running north, where are crypts parallel to the sides. These rooms are all cut in rock intensely hard, and the entrances were originally closed with stone doors, wrought with panels and hung on stone hinges, which are now all broken. The whole series of tombs indicates the hand of royalty and the leisure of years, but by whom and for whom they were made is a mere matter of conjecture. I know no good reason for ascribing them to Helena of Adiabene. Most travellers and writers are inclined to make them the sepulchres of the Asmonean kings" (*The Land and the Book*, vol. ii. p. 487, 488). The site of the tomb of David is no longer known.

30 Therefore[x] being a prophet, and knowing that [y]God had sworn

x 2 Sa.23.2. y 2 Sa.7.12,13; Ps.132.11.

¶ *Unto this day.* That the sepulchre of David was well known and honoured is clear from Josephus (*Antiq.*, b. vii. ch. xv. § 3): "He (David) was buried by his son Solomon *in Jerusalem* with great magnificence, and with all the other funeral pomps with which kings used to be buried. Moreover, he had

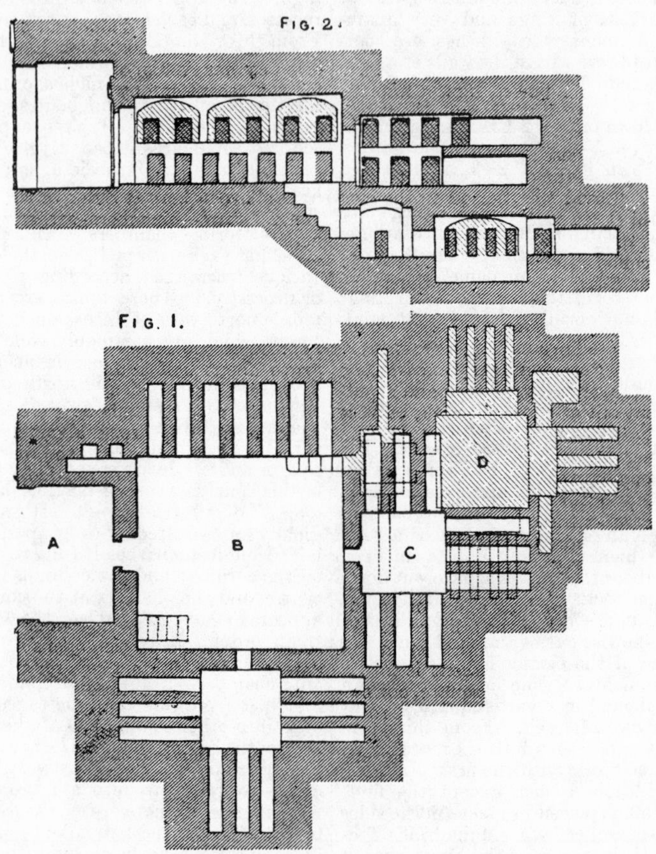

immense wealth buried with him: for a thousand and three hundred years afterward Hyrcanus the high-priest, when he was besieged by Antiochus, and was desirous of giving him money to raise the siege, opened one room of David's sepulchre and took out three thousand talents. Herod, many years afterward, opened another room, and took away a great deal of money," &c. See also *Antiq.*, b. xiii. ch. viii. § 4. The tomb of a monarch like David would be well known and had in reverence. Peter might, then, confidently appeal to *their own belief* and knowledge that David had not been raised from the dead. No Jew *believed* or *supposed* it. All, by their care of his sepulchre, and by the honour with which they regarded his grave, *believed* that he had returned to corruption. The Psalm, therefore, *could* not apply to him.

30. *Therefore.* As David was dead and buried, it was clear that he could not have referred to himself in this remarkable declaration. It followed that

with[z] an oath to him, that of the fruit of his loins, according to the flesh, he would raise up Christ to sit on his throne;

z He.6.17.

he must have had reference to some other one. ¶ *Being a prophet.* One who foretold future events. That David was inspired is clear, 2 Sa. xxiii. 2. Many of the prophecies relating to the Messiah are found in the Psalms of David: Ps. xxii. 1, comp. Mat. xxvii. 46; Lu. xxiv. 44.—Ps. xxii. 18, comp. Mat. xxvii. 35.—Ps. lxix. 21, comp. Mat. xxvii. 34, 48.—Ps. lxix. 25, comp. Ac. i. 20. ¶ *And knowing.* Knowing by what God had said to him respecting his posterity. ¶ *Had sworn with an oath.* The places which speak of God as having sworn to David are found in Ps. lxxxix. 3, 4, "I have made a covenant with my chosen, I have sworn unto David my servant, Thy seed will I establish," &c.; and Ps. cxxxii. 11, "The Lord hath sworn in truth unto David, he will not turn from it, Of the fruit of thy body will I set upon my throne;" Ps. lxxxix. 35, 36. The promise to which reference is made in all these places is in 2 Sa. vii. 11–16. ¶ *Of the fruit of his loins.* Of his descendants. See 2 Sa. vii. 12; Ge. xxxv. 11; xlvi. 26; 1 Ki. viii. 19, &c. ¶ *According to the flesh.* That is, so far as the human nature of the Messiah was concerned, he would be descended from David. Expressions like these are very remarkable. If the Messiah was only a *man*, they would be unmeaning. They are *never* used in relation to a mere man; and they imply that the speaker or writer supposed that there pertained to the Messiah a nature which was *not* according to the flesh. See Ro. i. 3, 4. ¶ *He would raise up Christ.* That is, the Messiah. To *raise up* seed, or descendants, is to give them to him. The promises made to David in all these places had immediate reference to Solomon and to his descendants. But it is clear that the New Testament writers understood them as referring also to the Messiah. And it is no less clear that the Jews understood that the Messiah was to be descended from David, Mat. xii. 23; xxi. 9; xxii. 42, 45; Mar. xi. 10; Jn. vii. 42, &c. In what way these promises that were made to David were understood as applying to the Messiah, it may not be easy to determine. The *fact*, however, is clear. The following remarks may throw some light on the subject: (*a*) The kingdom which was promised to David was to have no end; it was to be established for ever. Yet his descendants died, and all other kingdoms changed. (*b*) The promise likewise stood *by itself;* it was not made to any other of the Jewish kings; nor were similar declarations made of surrounding kingdoms and nations. It came, therefore, gradually to be applied to that future king and kingdom which was the hope of the nation; and their eyes were anxiously fixed on the long-expected Messiah. (*c*) At the time that he came it had become the settled doctrine of the Jews that he was to descend from David, and that his kingdom was to be perpetual. On this belief of the prophecy the apostles argued; and the opinions of the Jews furnished a strong point by which they could convince them that Jesus was the Messiah. Peter affirms that David was *aware* of this, and that he so understood the promise as referring not only to Solomon, but in a far more important sense to the Messiah. Happily we have a commentary of David himself as expressing his own views of that promise. That commentary is found particularly in Ps. ii., xxii., lxix., and xvi. In these Psalms there can be no doubt that David looked forward to the coming of the Messiah; and there can be as little that he regarded the promise made to him as extending to his coming and his reign.

It may be remarked that there are some important variations in the manuscripts in regard to this verse. The expression "according to the flesh" is omitted in many MSS., and is now left out by Griesbach in his New Testament. It is omitted also by the ancient Syriac and Ethiopic versions, and by the Latin Vulgate. ¶ *To sit on his throne.* To be his successor in his kingdom. Saul was the first of the kings of Israel. The kingdom was taken away from him and his posterity, and conferred on David and his descendants. It was determined that it should be continued *in the family* of David, and no more go out of his family, as it had from the family of Saul. The peculiar characteristic of David as king, or that which distinguished him from the other kings of the earth, was that *he reigned over the people*

31 He, seeing this before, [a]spake of the resurrection of Christ, that his soul was not left in hell, neither his flesh did see corruption.

32 This[b] Jesus hath God raised up, [c]whereof we all are witnesses.

33 Therefore, [d]being by the right hand of God exalted, and [e]having

a 1 Pe.1.11,12.

b ver.24. c Lu.24.48. d ch.5.31; Phi.2.9. e Jn.16.7,13; ch.1.4.

of God. Israel was his chosen people, and the kingdom was over that nation. Hence he that should reign *over the people of God*, though in a manner somewhat different from David, would be regarded as occupying *his throne*, and as being his successor. The form of the administration might be varied, but it would still retain its prime characteristic as being a reign *over the people of God.* In this sense the Messiah sits on the throne of David. He is his descendant and successor. He has an empire *over all the friends of the Most High.* And as that kingdom is destined to fill the earth, and to be eternal in the heavens, so it may be said that it is a kingdom which shall have no end. It is spiritual, but not the less real; defended not with carnal weapons, but not the less really defended; advanced not by the sword and the din of arms, but not the less *really* advanced against principalities, and powers, and spiritual wickedness in high places; not under a *visible* head and earthly monarch, but not less really under the Captain of salvation and the King of kings.

31. *He, seeing this before*, &c. By the spirit of prophecy. From this it appears that David had distinct views of the great doctrines pertaining to the Messiah. ¶ *Spake*, &c. See Ps. xvi. ¶ *That his soul*, &c. See Notes on ver. 27.

32. *This Jesus.* Peter, having shown that it was *predicted* that the Messiah would rise, now affirms that such a resurrection occurred in the case of Jesus. If it was a matter of prophecy, all objection to the truth of the doctrine was taken away, and the only question was whether there was *evidence* that this had been done. The proof of this Peter now alleges, and offers his own testimony, and that of his brethren, to the truth of this great and glorious fact. ¶ *We are all witnesses.* It seems probable that Peter refers here to the whole hundred and twenty who were present, and who were ready to attest it in any manner. The matter which was to be proved was that Jesus was seen alive after he had been put to death. The apostles were appointed to bear witness of this. We are told by Paul (1 Co. xv. 6) that he was seen by more than five hundred brethren, that is, Christians, at one time. The hundred and twenty assembled on this occasion were doubtless part of the number, and were ready to attest this. This was the proof that Peter alleged; and the strength of this proof was, and should have been, perfectly irresistible. (1) They had *seen* him themselves. They did not conjecture it or reason about it; but they had the evidence on which men act every day, and which must be regarded as satisfactory—the evidence of their own senses. (2) The *number* was such they could not be imposed on. If one hundred and twenty persons could not prove a plain matter of fact, nothing could be established by testimony; there could be no way of arriving at any facts. (3) The thing to be established was a plain matter. It was not that they *saw him rise.* That they never pretended. Impostors *would* have done this. But it was that they saw him, talked, walked, ate, drank with him, *being alive*, AFTER he had been crucified. The fact of his death was matter of Jewish record, and no one called it in question. The only fact for Christianity to make out was that he was seen *alive* afterward, and this was attested by many witnesses. (4) They had no interest in deceiving the world in this thing. There was no prospect of pleasure, wealth, or honour in doing it. (5) They offered themselves now as ready to endure any sufferings, or to die, in attestation of the truth of this event.

33. *Therefore being by the right hand.* The *right hand* among the Hebrews was often used to denote *power;* and the expression here means, not that he was exalted *to* the right hand of God, but *by* his power. He was raised from the dead by his power, and borne to heaven, triumphant over all his enemies. The use of the word right hand to denote *power* is common in the Scriptures: Job xl. 14, "Thine own right hand can save thee;" Ps. xvii. 7, "Thou savest by thy right hand them that trust in thee;"

received of the Father the promise of the Holy Ghost, [f]he hath shed forth this, which ye now see and hear.

34 For David is not ascended into the heavens: but he saith himself, [g]The LORD said unto my Lord, Sit thou on my right hand,

35 Until I make thy foes thy footstool.

36 Therefore let all [h]the house of Israel know assuredly [i]that God

f ch.10.45; Ep.4.8. g Ps.110.1; Mat.22.44. h Zec.13.1. i ch.5.31.

Ps. xviii. 35; xx. 6; xxi. 8; xliv. 3; lx. 5, &c. ¶ *Exalted.* Constituted King and Messiah in heaven. Raised up from his condition of humiliation to the glory which he had with the Father before the world was, Jn. xvii. 5. ¶ *And having received,* &c. The Holy Ghost was promised to the disciples before his death, Jn. xiv. 26; xv. 26; xvi. 13–15. It was expressly declared, (1) That the Holy Ghost would not be given except the Lord Jesus should return to heaven (Jn. xvi. 7); and (2) That this gift was in the power of the Father, and that *he* would send him, Jn. xiv. 26; xv. 26. This promise was now fulfilled, and those who witnessed the extraordinary scene before them could not doubt that it was the effect of divine power. ¶ *Hath shed forth this,* &c. This power of speaking different languages and declaring the truth of the gospel. In this way Peter accounts for the remarkable events before them. What had occurred could not be produced by new wine, ver. 15. It was expressly foretold, ver. 16–21. It was predicted that Jesus would rise, ver. 22–31. The apostles were witnesses that he *had* risen, and that he had promised that the Holy Spirit would descend; and the fulfilment of this promise was a rational way of accounting for the scene before them. It was unanswerable; and the effect on those who witnessed it was such as might be expected.

34, 35. *For David is not ascended into the heavens.* That is, David has not risen from the dead and ascended to heaven. This further shows that Ps. xvi. could not refer to David, but must refer to the Messiah. Great as they esteemed David, and much as they were accustomed to apply these expressions of the Scripture to him, yet they could not be applicable to him. They *must* refer to some other being; and especially that passage which Peter now proceeds to quote. It was of great importance to show that these expressions could not apply to David, and also that David bore testimony to the exalted character and dignity of the Messiah. Hence Peter here adduces David himself as affirming that the Messiah was to be exalted to a dignity far above his own. This does not affirm that David was not saved, or that his spirit had not ascended to heaven, but that he had not been *exalted* in the heavens in the sense in which Peter was speaking of the Messiah. ¶ *But he saith himself.* Ps. cx. 1. ¶ *The* LORD. The small capitals used in translating the word LORD in the Bible denote that the original word is *Jehovah.* The Hebrews regarded this as the *peculiar* name of God, a name incommunicable to any other being. It is not applied to any being but God in the Scriptures. The Jews had such a reverence for it that they never pronounced it; but when it occurred in the Scriptures they pronounced another name, *Adoni.* Here it means, *Jehovah* said, &c. ¶ *My Lord.* This is a different word in the Hebrew—it is *Adoni,* אדני. It properly is applied by a servant to his master, or a subject to his sovereign, or is used as a title of respect by an inferior to a superior. It means here, "Jehovah said to him whom I, David, acknowledge to be *my* superior and sovereign." Thus, though he regarded him as his descendant according to the flesh, yet he regarded him also as his superior and Lord. By reference to this passage our Saviour confounded the Pharisees, Mat. xxii. 42–46. That the passage in this Psalm refers to the Messiah is clear. Our Saviour, in Mat. xxii. 42, expressly applied it thus, and in such a manner as to show that this was the well-understood doctrine of the Jews. See Notes on Mat. xxii. 42, &c.

36. *Therefore let all,* &c. "Convinced by the prophecies, by our testimony, and by the remarkable scenes exhibited on the day of Pentecost, let all be convinced that the true Messiah has come and has been exalted to heaven." ¶ *House of Israel.* The word *house* often means *family:* "let all the family

hath made that same Jesus, whom
ye have crucified, both [k]Lord and
Christ.[l]
37 Now when they heard *this*,
they were [m]pricked in their heart,
and said unto Peter and to the rest
of the apostles, Men *and* brethren,
[n]what shall we do?

k Jn.3.35. *l* Ps.2.2,6-8. *m* Eze.7.16; Zec.12.10. *n* ch.9.6; 16.30.

---

of Israel, that is, all the nation of the Jews, know this." ¶ *Know assuredly.* Be assured, or know without any hesitation or possibility of mistake. This is the sum of his argument or his discourse. He had established the points which he purposed to prove, and he now applies it to his hearers. ¶ *God hath made.* God hath appointed or constituted. See ch. v. 31. ¶ *That same Jesus.* The very person who had suffered. He was raised with the same body, and had the same soul; he was the same being, as distinguished from all others. So Christians, in the resurrection, will be the *same* beings that they were before they died. ¶ *Whom ye crucified.* See ver. 23. There was nothing better fitted to show them the guilt of having done this than the argument which Peter used. He showed them that God had sent him as the Messiah, and that he had showed his love for him in raising him from the dead. The Son of God, and the hope of their nation, they had put to death. He was not an impostor, nor a man sowing sedition, nor a blasphemer, but the Messiah of God; and they had imbrued their hands in his blood. There is nothing better fitted to make sinners fear and tremble than to show them that, in rejecting Christ, they have rejected God; in refusing to serve him they have refused to serve God. The crime of sinners has a double malignity, as committed against a kind and lovely Saviour, and against the God who loved *him*, and appointed him to save men. Comp. ch. iii. 14, 15. ¶ *Both Lord.* The word *lord* properly denotes *proprietor*, *master*, or *sovereign*. Here it means clearly that God had exalted him to be the *king* so long expected; and that he had given him dominion in the heavens, or, as we should say, made him ruler of all things. The extent of this dominion may be seen in Jn. xvii. 2; Ep. i. 21, &c. In the exercise of this office, he now rules in heaven and on earth, and will yet come to judge the world. This truth was particularly fitted to excite their fear. They had murdered their sovereign, now shown to be raised from the dead, and intrusted with infinite power. They had reason, therefore, to fear that he would come forth in vengeance, and punish them for their crimes. Sinners, in opposing the Saviour, are at war with their living and mighty sovereign and Lord. He has all power, and it is not safe to contend against the judge of the living and the dead. ¶ *And Christ.* Messiah. They had thus crucified the hope of their nation; imbrued their hands in the blood of him to whom the prophets had looked; and put to death that Holy One, the prospect of whose coming had sustained the most holy men of the world in affliction, and cheered them when they looked on to future years. He who was the hope of their fathers had come, and they had put him to death; and it is no wonder that the consciousness of this—that a sense of guilt, and shame, and confusion should overwhelm their minds, and lead them to ask, in deep distress, what they should do.

37. *Now when they heard* this. When they heard this declaration of Peter, and this *proof* that Jesus was the Messiah. There was no fanaticism in his discourse; it was cool, close, pungent reasoning. He *proved* to them the truth of what he was saying, and thus prepared the way for this effect. ¶ *They were pricked in their heart.* The word translated *were pricked*, κατενύγησαν, is not used elsewhere in the New Testament. It properly denotes to *pierce* or *penetrate* with a needle, lancet, or sharp instrument; and then to pierce with grief, or acute pain of any kind. It answers precisely to our word *compunction.* It implies also the idea of *sudden* as well as *acute* grief. In this case it means that they were *suddenly* and *deeply* affected with anguish and alarm at what Peter had said. The causes of their grief may have been these: (1) Their *sorrow* that the Messiah had been put to death by his own countrymen. (2) Their deep sense of guilt in having done this. There would be mingled here a remembrance of ingratitude, and a consciousness that they had been guilty of *murder* of the most aggravated and horrid kind, that

of having killed their own Messiah. (3) The fear of his wrath. He was still alive; exalted to be their *Lord;* and intrusted with all power. They were afraid of his vengeance; they were conscious that they deserved it; and they supposed that they were exposed to it. (4) What they had done could not be undone. The guilt remained; they could not wash it out. They had imbrued their hands in the blood of innocence, and the guilt of that oppressed their souls. This expresses the usual feelings which sinners have when they are convicted of sin. ¶ *Men* and *brethren.* This was an expression denoting affectionate earnestness. Just before this they mocked the disciples, and charged them with being filled with new wine, ver. 13. They now treated them with respect and confidence. The views which sinners have of Christians and Christian ministers are greatly changed when they are under conviction for sin. Before that they may deride and oppose them; then, they are glad to be taught by the obscurest Christian, and even cling to a minister of the gospel as if he could save them by his own power. ¶ *What shall we do?* What shall we do to avoid the wrath of this crucified and exalted Messiah? They were apprehensive of his vengeance, and they wished to know how to avoid it. Never was a more important question asked than this. It is the question which all convicted sinners ask. It implies an apprehension of danger, a sense of guilt, and a readiness to *yield the will* to the claims of God. This was the same question asked by Paul (Ac. ix. 6), "Lord, what wilt thou have me to do?" and by the jailer (Ac. xvi. 30), "He . . . came, trembling, . . . and said, Sirs, what must I do to be saved?" The state of mind in this case—the case of a convicted sinner—consists in, (1) A deep sense of the evil of the past life; remembrance of a thousand crimes perhaps before forgotten; a pervading and deepening conviction that the heart, and conversation, and life have been evil, and deserve condemnation. (2) Apprehension about the justice of God; alarm when the mind looks upward to him, or onward to the day of death and judgment. (3) An earnest wish, amounting sometimes to agony, to be delivered from this sense of condemnation and this apprehension of the future. (4) A readiness to sacrifice all to the will of God; to surrender the governing purpose of the mind, and to do what he requires. In this state the soul is prepared to receive the offers of eternal life; and *when* the sinner comes to this, the offers of mercy meet his case, and he yields himself to the Lord Jesus, and finds peace.

In regard to this discourse of Peter, and this remarkable result, we may observe, (1) That this is the first discourse which was preached after the ascension of Christ, and is a model which the ministers of religion should imitate. (2) It is a clear and close argument. There is no ranting, no declamation, nothing but *truth* presented in a clear and striking manner. It abounds with *proof* of his main point, and supposes that his hearers were rational beings, and capable of being influenced by truth. Ministers have no right to address men as incapable of reason and thought, nor to imagine, because they are speaking on religious subjects, that therefore they are at liberty to speak nonsense. (3) Though these were eminent sinners, and had added to the crime of murdering the Messiah that of deriding the Holy Ghost and the ministers of the gospel, yet Peter *reasoned* with them coolly, and endeavoured to *convince* them of their guilt. Men should be treated as endowed with *reason*, and as capable of seeing the force and beauty of the great truths of religion. (4) The arguments of Peter were *adapted* to produce this effect on their minds, and to impress them deeply with the sense of their guilt. He *proved* to them that they had been guilty of putting the Messiah to death; that God had raised him up, and that they were now in the midst of the scenes which established one strong proof of the truth of what he was saying. No class of truths could have been so well adapted to make an impression of their guilt as these. (5) Conviction for sin is a rational process on a sinner's mind. It is the *proper* state produced by a view of past sins. It is suffering *truth* to make an appropriate impression; suffering the mind to feel as it *ought* to feel. The man who *is* guilty ought to be willing to see and confess it. It is no disgrace to confess an error, or to feel deeply when we know we are guilty. Disgrace consists in a hypocritical desire to conceal crime; in the *pride* that is unwilling to avow it; in the *falsehood* which denies it. To feel

38 Then Peter said unto them, Repent,[o] and be baptized, every one of you, in the name of Jesus Christ, for the remission of sins; and ye shall receive the gift of the Holy Ghost.

o Lu.24.47; ch.3.19.

---

it and to acknowledge it is the mark of an open and ingenuous mind. (6) These same truths are adapted still to produce conviction for sin. The sinner's treatment of the Messiah should produce grief and alarm. He did not murder him, but he has rejected him; he did not crown him with thorns, but he has despised him; he did not insult him when hanging on the cross, but he has a thousand times insulted him since; he did not pierce his side with the spear, but he has pierced his heart by rejecting him and contemning his mercy. *For these things he should weep.* In the Saviour's resurrection he has also a deep interest. He rose as the pledge that we may rise; and when the sinner looks forward, he should remember that he *must* meet the ascended Son of God. The Saviour reigns; he lives, Lord of all. The sinner's deeds now are aimed at his throne, and his heart, and his crown. All his crimes are seen by his sovereign, and it is not safe to mock the Son of God on his throne, or to despise him who will soon come to judgment. When the sinner feels these truths he *should* tremble and cry out, What shall I do? (7) We see here *how* the Spirit operates in producing conviction of sin. It is not in an arbitrary manner; it is in accordance with *truth*, and by the *truth*. Nor have we a right to expect that he will convict and convert men except as the *truth* is presented to their minds. They who desire success in the gospel should present clear, striking, and impressive truth, for such only God is accustomed to bless. (8) We have in the conduct of Peter and the other apostles a striking instance of the *power* of the gospel. Just before, Peter, trembling and afraid, had denied his Master with an oath; now, in the presence of the murderers of the Son of God, he boldly charged them with their crime, and dared their fury. Just before, all the disciples forsook the Lord Jesus and fled; now, in the presence of his murderers, they lifted their voice and proclaimed their guilt and danger, even in the city where he had been just arraigned and put to death. What could have produced this change but the power of God? And is there not proof here that a religion which produces such changes came from heaven?

38. *Then Peter said unto them.* Peter had been the chief speaker, though others had also addressed them. He now, in the name of all, directed the multitude what to do. ¶ *Repent.* See Notes on Mat. iii. 2. Repentance implies sorrow for sin as committed against God, with a purpose to forsake it. It is not merely a fear of the *consequences of sin*, or of the wrath of God in hell. It is such a view of *sin*, as evil in itself, as to lead the mind to hate it and forsake it. Laying aside all view of the *punishment* of sin, the true penitent hates it. Even if sin were the means of procuring him happiness; if it would promote his gratification and be unattended with any future punishment, he would hate it and turn from it. The mere fact that it is *evil*, and that *God* hates it, is a sufficient reason why those who are truly penitent hate it and forsake it. False repentance dreads the *consequences* of sin; true repentance dreads *sin itself*. These persons whom Peter addressed had been merely *alarmed;* they were afraid of wrath, and especially of the wrath of the Messiah. They had no true sense of sin as an evil, but were simply afraid of punishment. This *alarm* Peter did not regard as by any means genuine repentance. Such conviction for sin would soon wear off, unless their *repentance* became thorough and complete. Hence he told them to *repent*, to turn from sin, to exercise sorrow for it as an evil and bitter thing, and to *express* their sorrow in the proper manner. We may learn here, (1) That there is no safety in *mere conviction* for sin: it may soon pass off, and leave the soul as thoughtless as before. (2) There is no *goodness* or *holiness* in mere alarm or conviction. The devils . . . tremble. A man may fear who yet has a firm purpose to do evil, if he can do it with impunity. (3) Many are greatly troubled and alarmed who never repent. There is no situation where souls are so easily deceived as here. Alarm is taken for repentance; trembling for godly sorrow; and the fear of wrath is taken to be the true fear of God. (4) True repentance is

the only thing in such a state of mind that can give any relief. An ingenuous confession of sin, a solemn purpose to forsake it, and a true *hatred* of it, is the only thing that can give the mind composure. Such is the constitution of the mind that nothing else will furnish relief. But the moment we are willing to make an open confession of guilt, the mind is delivered of its burden, and the convicted soul finds peace. Till this is done, and the *hold on sin* is broken, there *can be* no peace. (5) We see here what direction is to be given to a convicted sinner. We are not to direct him to wait; nor to lead him to suppose that he is in a good way; nor to tell him to continue to seek; nor to call him a mourner; nor to take sides with him, as if God were wrong and harsh; nor to advise him to read, and search, and postpone the subject to a future time. We are to direct him to *repent;* to mourn over his sins, and to forsake them. Religion demands that he should *at once* surrender himself to God by genuine repentance; by confession that God is right and that *he* is wrong; and by a firm purpose to live a life of holiness. ¶ *Be baptized.* See Notes on Mat. iii. 6. The direction which Christ gave to his apostles was that they should baptize all who believed, Mat. xxviii. 19; Mar. xvi. 16. The Jews had not been baptized; and a baptism now would be a profession of the religion of Christ, or a declaration made before the world that they embraced Jesus as their Messiah. It was equivalent to saying that they should *publicly* and *professedly* embrace Jesus Christ as their Saviour. The gospel requires such a profession, and no one is at liberty to withhold it. A similar declaration is to be made to all who are inquiring the way to life. They are to exercise repentance; and then, without any unnecessary delay, to evince it by partaking of the ordinances of the gospel. If men are unwilling to profess religion they have none. If they will not, in the proper way, show that they are truly attached to Christ, it is proof that they have no such attachment. Baptism is the application of water, as expressive of the need of purification, and as emblematic of the influences from God that can alone cleanse the soul. It is also a form of dedication to the service of God. ¶ *In the name of Jesus Christ.* Not εἰς, *into*, but ἐπί, *upon.* The usual form of baptism is *into* the name of the Father, &c.—εἰς. Here it does not mean to be baptized *by the authority* of Jesus Christ, but it means to be baptized *for* him and his service; to be consecrated in this way, and by this public profession, *to* him and to his cause. The expression is literally *upon the name of Jesus Christ:* that is, as the foundation of the baptism, or as that on which its propriety rested or was based. In other words, it is with an acknowledgment of him in that act as being what his name imports—the Sinner's only Hope, his Redeemer, Lord, Justifier, King (Prof. Hackett, *in loco*). The *name* of Jesus Christ means the same as Jesus Christ himself. To be baptized to his *name* is to be devoted *to him.* The word *name* is often thus used. The profession which they were to make amounted to this: a confession of sins; a hearty purpose to turn from them; a reception of Jesus as the Messiah and as a Saviour; and a determination to become *his followers* and to be devoted to his service. Thus (1 Co. x. 2), to be *baptized unto Moses* means to take him as a leader and guide. It does not follow that, in administering the ordinance of baptism, they used only the name of Jesus Christ. It is much more probable that they used the form prescribed by the Saviour himself (Mat. xxviii. 19); though, as the peculiar mark of a *Christian* is that he receives and honours Jesus Christ, this name is used here as implying the whole. The same thing occurs in Ac. xix. 5. ¶ *For the remission of sins.* Not merely the sin of crucifying the Messiah, but of *all* sins. There is nothing in *baptism itself* that can wash away sin. That can be done only by the pardoning mercy of God through the atonement of Christ. But baptism is expressive of a willingness to be pardoned in that way, and is a solemn declaration of our conviction that there is no other way of remission. He who comes to be baptized, comes with a *professed* conviction that he is a sinner; that there is no other way of mercy but in the gospel, and with a professed willingness to comply with the terms of salvation, and to receive it as it is offered through Jesus Christ. ¶ *And ye shall receive*, &c. The gift of the Holy Ghost here does not mean his *extraordinary gifts*, or the power of working miracles, but it simply means, you shall partake of the influences of the Holy Ghost *as far as they may be*

39 For the [p]promise is unto you, and to your children, and [q]to all that are afar off, *even* as many as the Lord our God shall call.

p Joel 2.28. q Ep.2.13,17.

adapted to your case—as far as may be needful for your comfort, peace, and sanctification. There is no evidence that they were all endowed with the power of working miracles, nor does the connection of the passage require us thus to understand it. Nor does it mean that they had not been awakened *by his influences.* All true conviction is from him, Jn. xvi. 8–10. But it is also the office of the Spirit to comfort, to enlighten, to give peace, and thus to give evidence that the soul is born again. To this, probably, Peter refers; and this all who are born again and profess faith in Christ possess. There is peace, calmness, joy; there is *evidence* of piety, and that evidence is the product of the influences of the Spirit. "The fruit of the Spirit is love, joy, peace," &c., Ga. v. 22, 24.

39. *For the promise.* That is, the promise respecting the particular thing of which he was speaking—the influences of the Holy Ghost. This promise he had adduced in the beginning of his discourse (ver. 17), and he now applies it to them. As the Spirit was promised to descend on Jews and their sons and daughters, it was applicable to them in the circumstances in which they then were. The only hope of lost sinners is in the promises of God, and the only thing that can give comfort to a soul that is convicted of sin is the hope that *God* will pardon and save. ¶ *To you.* To you Jews, even though you have crucified the Messiah. The promise had especial reference to the Jewish people. ¶ *To your children.* In Joel, to their sons and daughters, who would, nevertheless, be old enough to prophesy. Similar promises occur in Is. xliv. 3, "I will pour my Spirit on thy seed, and my blessing on thine offspring;" and in Is. lix. 21, "My Spirit that is upon thee, and my words which I have put in thy mouth, shall not depart out of thy mouth, nor out of the mouth of thy seed, nor out of the mouth of thy seed's seed, saith the Lord, from henceforth and for ever." In these and similar places their *descendants* or *posterity* are denoted. It does not refer merely to children *as children*, and should not be adduced as applicable exclusively to infants. It is a promise to parents that the blessings of salvation shall not be confined to parents, but shall be extended also to their posterity. Under this promise parents may be encouraged to train up their children for God; they are authorized to devote them to him in the ordinance of Christian baptism, and they may trust in his gracious purpose thus to perpetuate the blessings of salvation from age to age. ¶ *To all.* To the whole race; not limited to Jews. ¶ *Afar off.* To those in other lands. It is probable that *Peter* here referred to *the Jews* who were scattered in other nations; for he does not seem yet to have understood that the gospel was to be preached to the Gentiles. See ch. x. Yet the promise was equally applicable to the Gentiles as the Jews, and the apostles were afterward brought so to understand it, Ac. x.; Ro. x. 12, 14–20; xi. The Gentiles are sometimes clearly indicated by the expression "afar off" (Ep. ii. 13, 17); and they are represented as having been brought *nigh* by the blood of Christ. The phrase is equally applicable to those who have been far off from God *by their sins* and their *evil affections.* To them also the promise is extended if they will return. ¶ Even *as many*, &c. The promise is not to those who do not *hear* the gospel, nor to those who do not *obey* it; but it is to those to whom God in his gracious providence shall send it. He has the power and right to pardon. The meaning of Peter is, that the promise is ample, full, free; that it is fitted to all, and may be applied to all; that there is no defect or want in the provisions or promises, but that God *may* extend it to whomsoever he pleases. We see here how ample and full are the offers of mercy. God is not limited in the provisions of his grace; but the plan is *applicable* to all mankind. It is also the purpose of God to send it to all men, and he has given a solemn charge to his church to do it. We cannot reflect but with deep pain on the fact that, although these provisions have been made—fully made; that they are adapted to all men; but that yet they have been extended by his people to so small a portion of the human family. If the promise of life is to all, it is the duty of the church to send to all the message of mercy.

40 And with many other words did he testify and exhort, saying, Save yourselves from this untoward generation.

---

40. *Many other words.* This discourse, though one of the longest in the New Testament, is but an outline. It contains, however, the substance of the plan of salvation, and is admirably arranged to attain its object. ¶ *Testify.* Bear witness to. He bore witness to the promises of Christianity; to the truths pertaining to the danger of sinners; and to the truth respecting the character of that generation. ¶ *Exhort.* He entreated them by arguments and promises. ¶ *Save yourselves.* This expression here denotes, preserve yourselves from the *influence*, opinions, and fate of this generation. It implies that they were to use diligence and effort to deliver themselves. God deals with men as free agents. He calls upon them to put forth their own power and effort to be saved. Unless they put forth their own strength, they will never be saved. When they *are* saved, they will ascribe to God the praise for having inclined them to seek him, and for the grace whereby they are saved. ¶ *This generation.* This age or race of men; the Jews then living. They were not to apprehend danger *from* them from which they were to deliver themselves; but they were to apprehend danger from being *with* them, united in their plans, designs, and feelings. From the influence of their opinions, &c., they were to escape. That generation was signally corrupt and wicked. See Mat. xxiii.; xii. 39; xvi. 4; Mar. viii. 38. They had crucified the Messiah; and they were, for their sins, soon to be destroyed. ¶ *Untoward.* "Perverse, refractory, not easily guided or taught" (Webster). The same character our Saviour had given of that generation in Mat. xi. 16–19. This character they had shown uniformly. They were smooth, cunning, plausible; but they were corrupt in principle, and wicked in conduct. The Pharisees had a vast hold on the people. To break away from them was to set at defiance all their power and doctrines; to alienate themselves from their teachers and friends; to brave the authority of those in office, and those who had long claimed the right of teaching and guiding the nation. The chief danger of those who were now awakened was from that generation; that they would deride, or denounce, or persecute them, and induce them to abandon their seriousness, and turn back to their sins. And hence Peter exhorted them at once to break off from them, and give themselves to Christ. We may hence learn, (1) That if sinners will be saved they must make an effort. There is no promise to any unless they will exert themselves. (2) The principal danger which besets those who are awakened arises from their former companions. They are often wicked, cunning, rich, mighty. They may be their kindred, and will seek to drive off their serious impressions by derision, or argument, or persecution. They have a powerful hold on the affections, and they will seek to use it to prevent those who are awakened from becoming Christians. (3) Those who are awakened should resolve at once to break off from their evil companions, and unite themselves to Christ and his people. There may be no other way in which this can be done than by resolving to forsake altogether the society of those who are infidels, and scoffers, and profane. They should forsake the world, and give themselves up to God, and resolve to have only so much intercourse with the world, in any respect, as may be required by duty, and as may be consistent with a supreme purpose to live to the honour of God.

41. *They that gladly received.* The word rendered *gladly* means *freely*, cheerfully, joyfully. It implies that they did it without compulsion, and with joy. Religion is not compulsion. They who become Christians do it cheerfully; they do it rejoicing in the *privilege* of becoming reconciled to God through Jesus Christ. Though so many received his word and were baptized, yet it is implied that there were others who did not. It is probable that there were multitudes assembled who were alarmed, but who did *not* receive the word with joy. In all revivals there are many who become alarmed, and who are anxious about their souls, but who refuse to embrace the gospel, and again become thoughtless, and are ruined. ¶ *His word.* The message which Peter had spoken respecting the pardon of sin through Jesus Christ. ¶ *Were baptized.* That is, those who professed a readiness to embrace the offers of salvation. The narrative plainly

41 Then they that gladly received his word were baptized: and the same day there were added *unto them* about three thousand souls.

42 And[r] they continued stedfastly in the apostles' doctrine and fellowship, and in breaking of bread, and in prayers.

r 1 Co.11.2; He.10.25.

implies that this was done the same day. Their conversion was instantaneous. The demand on them was to yield themselves at once to God. And their profession was made, and the ordinance which sealed their profession administered without delay. ¶ *And the same day.* The discourse of Peter commenced at nine o'clock in the morning, ver. 15. How long it continued it is not said; but the ceremony of admitting them to the church and of baptizing them was evidently performed on the same day. The mode in which this is done is not mentioned; but it is highly improbable that *in* the midst of the city of Jerusalem three thousand persons were wholly immersed in one day. The whole narrative supposes that it was all done *in* the city; and yet there is no probability that there were conveniences there for *immersing* so many persons in a single day. Besides, in the ordinary way of administering baptism by immersion, it is difficult to conceive that *so many persons* could have been immersed in so short a time. There is, indeed, here no positive *proof* that they were not immersed; but the narrative is one of those incidental circumstances often much more satisfactory than philological discussion, that show the extreme improbability that all this was done by wholly immersing them in water. It may be further remarked that here is an example of very quick admission to the church. It was the first great work of grace under the gospel. It was the model of all revivals of religion. And it was doubtless intended that this should be a specimen of the manner in which the ministers of religion should act in regard to admissions to the Christian church. Prudence is indeed required; but this example furnishes no warrant for advising those who profess their willingness to obey Jesus Christ, to delay uniting with the church. If persons give evidence of piety, of true hatred of sin, and of attachment to the Lord Jesus, they should unite themselves to his people without delay. ¶ *There were added.* To the company of disciples, or to the followers of Christ. ¶ *Souls.* Persons. Comp. 1 Pe. iii. 20; Ge. xii. 5. It is not affirmed that all this took place in one part of Jerusalem, or that it was all done at once; but it is probable that this was what was afterward ascertained to be the fruit of this day's labour, the result of this revival of religion. This was the first effusion of the Holy Spirit under the preaching of the gospel; and it shows that such scenes are to be expected in the church, and that the gospel is fitted to work a rapid and mighty change in the hearts of men.

42. *And they continued stedfastly.* They persevered in, or they adhered to. This is the inspired record of the result. That any of these apostatized is nowhere recorded, and is not to be presumed. Though they had been suddenly converted; though they were suddenly admitted to the church; though they were exposed to much persecution and contempt, and to many trials, yet the record is that they adhered to the doctrines and duties of the Christian religion. The word rendered *continued stedfastly*—προσκαρτεροῦντες—means attending one, remaining by his side, not leaving or forsaking him. ¶ *The apostles' doctrine.* This does not mean that they held or believed the *doctrines* of the apostles, though that was true; but it means that they adhered to, or attended on, their *teaching* or *instruction.* The word *doctrine* has now a technical sense, and means a collection and arrangement of abstract views supposed to be contained in the Bible. In the Scriptures the word means simply *teaching;* and the expression here denotes that they continued to attend on their *instructions.* One evidence of conversion is a desire to be *instructed* in the doctrines and duties of religion, and a willingness to attend on the preaching of the gospel. ¶ *And fellowship.* The word rendered *fellowship,* κοινωνία, is often render *communion.* It properly denotes *having things in common,* or participation, society, friendship. It may apply to anything which may be possessed in common, or in which all may partake. Thus all Christians have the same hope of heaven; the same joys; the same hatred of sin; the same enemies to contend with. Thus they

43 And fear came upon every
soul: and [s]many wonders and
signs were done by the apostles.
44 And all that believed were together,[t]and had all things common;
45 And sold their possessions

s Mar.16.17.

t ch.4.32,34.

---

have the same subjects of conversation, of feeling, and of prayer; or they have communion in these things. And thus the early Christians had their property in common. The word here may apply to either or to all of these things—to their conversation, their prayers, their dangers, or their property; and means that they were *united* to the apostles, and participated with them in whatever befell them. It may be added that the effect of a revival of religion is to unite Christians more and more, and to bring those who were before separated to union and love. Christians feel that they are a band of brethren, and that, however much they were separated *before* they became Christians, now they have great and important interests in common; they are united in feelings, in interests, in dangers, in conflicts, in opinions, and in the hopes of a blessed immortality. ¶ *Breaking of bread.* The Syriac renders this "the eucharist," or the Lord's supper. It cannot, however, be determined whether this refers to their partaking of their ordinary food together, or to feasts of charity, or to the Lord's supper. The bread of the Hebrews was made commonly into cakes, thin, hard, and brittle, so that it was *broken* instead of being cut. Hence, to denote intimacy or friendship, the phrase to *break bread together* would be very expressive in the same way as the Greeks denoted it by *drinking together*, συμπόσιον. From the expression used in ver. 44, comp. with ver. 46, that they had all things common, it would rather seem to be implied that this referred to the participation of their ordinary meals. The action of *breaking bread* was commonly performed by the master or head of a family immediately after asking a blessing (Lightfoot). ¶ *In prayers.* This was one *effect* of the influence of the Spirit, and an evidence of their change. A genuine revival will be always followed by a love of prayer.

43. *And fear came.* That is, there was great reverence or awe. The multitude had just before derided them (ver. 13); but so striking and manifest was the power of God on this occasion, that it silenced all clamours, and produced a general veneration and awe. The effect of a great work of God's grace is commonly to produce an unusual seriousness and solemnity in a community, even among those who are not converted. It restrains, subdues, and silences opposition. ¶ *Every soul.* Every person or individual; that is, upon the people generally; not only on those who became Christians, but upon the multitudes who witnessed these things. All things were fitted to produce this fear: the recent crucifixion of Jesus of Nazareth; the wonders that attended that event; the events of the day of Pentecost; and the miracles performed by the apostles, were all fitted to diffuse solemnity, thought, anxiety through the community. ¶ *Many wonders and signs.* See Notes on ver. 22. This was promised by the Saviour, Mar. xvi. 17. Some of the miracles which they wrought are specified in the following chapters.

44. *All that believed.* That is, that believed that Jesus was the Messiah; for that was the distinguishing point by which they were known from others. ¶ *Were together.* Were united; were joined in the same thing. It does not mean that they *lived* in the same house, but they were *united in the same community*, or engaged in the same thing. They were doubtless *often* together in the same place for prayer and praise. One of the best means for strengthening the faith of young converts is for them *often* to meet together for prayer, conversation, and praise. ¶ *Had all things common.* That is, all their *property* or *possessions.* See ch. iv. 32–37; v. 1–10. The apostles, in the time of the Saviour, evidently had all their property in common stock, and Judas was made their treasurer. They regarded themselves as one family, having common wants, and there was no use or propriety in their possessing extensive property by themselves. Yet even then it is probable that *some* of them retained an interest in their property which was not supposed to be necessary to be devoted to the common use. It is evident that *John* thus possessed property which he retained, Jn. xix. 27. And it is clear that the Saviour did not *command*

and goods, and [u]parted them to all *men*, as every man had need.

46 And they, continuing daily with one accord in the temple,

u Is.58.7; 2 Co.9.1,9; 1 Jn.3.17.

them to give up their property into a common stock, nor did the apostles enjoin it: Ac. v. 4, "While it remained, was it not thine own? and after it was sold was it not in thine own power?" It was, therefore, perfectly voluntary, and was evidently adapted to the peculiar circumstances of the early converts. Many of them came from abroad. They were from Parthia, and Media, and Arabia, and Rome, and Africa, &c. It is probable, also, that they now remained longer in Jerusalem than they had at first proposed; and it is not at all improbable that they would be denied now the usual hospitalities of the Jews, and excluded from their customary kindness, because they had embraced Jesus of Nazareth, who had been just put to death. In these circumstances, it was natural and proper that they should share their property while they remained together.

45. *And sold.* That is, they sold as much as was necessary in order to procure the means of providing for the wants of each other. ¶ *Possessions.* Property, particularly *real* estate. This word, κτήματα, refers properly to their *fixed* property, as lands, houses, vineyards, &c. The word rendered *goods*, ὑπάρξεις, refers to their *personal* or movable property. ¶ *And parted them to all.* They *distributed* them to supply the wants of their poorer brethren, according to their necessities. ¶ *As every man had need.* This expression *limits* and fixes the meaning of what is said before. The passage does not mean that they sold *all* their possessions, or that they relinquished their title to *all* their property, but that they so far regarded all as common as to be willing to part with it IF it was needful to supply the wants of the others. Hence the property was laid at the disposal of the apostles, and they were desired to distribute it freely to meet the wants of the poor, ch. iv. 34, 35.

This was an important incident in the early propagation of religion, and it may suggest many useful reflections.

1. We see the effect of religion. The love of property is one of the strongest affections which men have. There is nothing that will overcome it but religion. That will; and one of the *first* effects of the gospel was to loosen the hold of Christians on property.

2. It is the duty of the church to provide for the wants of its poor and needy members. There can be no doubt that property should now be regarded as *so far* common as that the wants of the poor should be supplied by those who are rich. Comp. Mat. xxvi. 11.

3. If it be asked *why* the early disciples evinced this readiness to part with their property in this manner, it may be replied, (1) That the apostles had done it before them. The family of the Saviour had all things common. (2) It was the nature of religion to do it. (3) The circumstances of the persons assembled on this occasion were such as to require it. They were many of them from distant regions, and probably many of them of the poorer class of the people in Jerusalem. In this they evinced what *should* be done in behalf of the poor in the church at all times.

4. If it be asked whether this was done *commonly* among the early Christians, it may be replied that there is no evidence that it was. It is mentioned here, and in ch. iv. 32–37, and ch. v. 1–7. It does not appear that it was done even by *all* who were afterward converted in Judea; and there is no evidence that it was done in Antioch, Ephesus, Corinth, Philippi, Rome, &c. That the effect of religion was to make men *liberal* and willing to provide for the poor there can be no doubt. See 2 Co. viii. 19; ix. 2; 1 Co. xvi. 2; Ga. ii. 10. But there is no proof that it was *common* to part with their possessions and to lay them at the feet of the apostles. Religion does not contemplate, evidently, that men should break up all the arrangements in society, but it contemplates that those who *have* property should be ready and willing to part with it for the help of the poor and needy.

5. If it be asked, then, whether all the arrangements of property should be broken up now, and believers have all things in common, we are prepared to answer *No.* For, (1) This was an extraordinary case. (2) It was not even enjoined by the apostles on them. (3) It was practised nowhere else. (4) It would be impracticable. No community

and breaking bread [4]from house to house, did eat their meat with gladness and singleness of heart,

47 Praising God, and [v]having favour with all the people. [w]And the Lord added to the church daily such as should be saved.

[4] or, *at home*.

v Lu.2.52; Ro.14.18. *w* ch.5.14; 11.24.

---

where all things were held in common has long prospered. It has been attempted often, by pagans, by infidels, and by fanatical sects of Christians. It ends soon in anarchy, licentiousness, idleness, and profligacy; or the more cunning secure the mass of the property, and control the whole. Till all men are *made alike*, there could be no hope of such a community; and if there could be, it would not be desirable. God evidently intended that men should be excited to industry by the hope of gain; and *then* he demands that their gains shall be devoted to *his* service. Still, this was a noble instance of Christian generosity, and evinced the power of religion in loosing the hold which men commonly have on the world. It rebukes also those professors of religion, of whom, alas! there are many, who *give* nothing to benefit either the souls or bodies of their fellow-men.

46. *With one accord.* Comp. ch. i. 14; ii. 1. ¶ *In the temple.* This was the public place of worship; and the disciples were not disposed to leave the place where their fathers had so long worshipped God. This does not mean that they were *constantly* in the temple, but only at the customary hours of prayer—at nine o'clock in the morning, and at three in the afternoon. ¶ *And breaking bread.* See Notes on ver. 42. ¶ *From house to house.* In the margin, "at home." So the Syriac and Arabic. The common interpretation, however, is, that they did it in their various houses, now in this and now in that, as might be convenient. If it refers to their ordinary meals, then it means that they partook *in common* of what they possessed, and the expression "did eat their meat" seems to imply that this refers to their common meals, and not to the Lord's supper. ¶ *Did eat their meat.* Did partake of their food. The word *meat* with us is applied to *flesh.* In the Bible, and in old English authors, it is applied to provisions of any kind. Here it means all kinds of sustenance; that which nourished them—τροφῆς—and the use of this word *proves* that it does not refer to the Lord's supper; for that ordinance is nowhere represented as designed for an ordinary meal, or to nourish the *body.* Comp. 1 Co. xi. 33, 34. ¶ *With gladness.* With rejoicing. This is one of the effects of religion. It is far from gloom; it diffuses happiness over the mind; it bestows additional joy in the participation of even our ordinary pleasures. ¶ *Singleness of heart.* This means with a *sincere* and pure heart. They were satisfied and thankful. They were not perplexed or anxious; nor were they solicitous for the luxurious living, or aspiring after the vain objects of the men of the world. Comp. Ro. xii. 8; 2 Co. i. 12; Col. iii. 22; Ep. vi. 5.

47. *Praising God.* See Lu. xxiv. 53. ¶ *And having favour.* See Lu. ii. 52. ¶ *With all the people.* That is, with the great mass of the people; with the people generally. It does not mean that all the people had become reconciled to Christianity; but their humble, serious, and devoted lives won the favour of the great mass of the community, and silenced opposition and cavil. This was a remarkable effect, but God has power to silence opposition; and there it nothing so well fitted to do this as the humble and consistent lives of his friends. ¶ *And the Lord added.* See ch. v. 14; xi. 24, &c. It was *the Lord* who did this. There was no power in man to do it; and the Christian loves to trace *all* increase of the church to the grace of God. ¶ *Added.* Caused, or inclined them to be joined to the church. ¶ *The church.* To the *assembly* of the followers of Christ—τῇ ἐκκλησίᾳ. The word rendered *church* properly means those who are *called out,* and is applied to Christians as being *called out,* or separated from the world. It is used but three times in the gospels, Mat. xvi. 18; xviii. 17, *twice.* It occurs frequently in other parts of the New Testament, and usually as applied to the followers of Christ. Comp. Ac. v. 11; vii. 38; viii. 1, 3; ix. 31; xi. 22, 26; xii. 1, 5, &c. It is used in classic writers to denote an *assembly* of any kind, and is twice thus used in the New Testament (Ac. xix. 39, 41), where it is translated "assembly." ¶ *Such as should be saved.* This whole phrase is a translation of a participle—τοὺς σωζομένους. It does not express any *purpose* that they

CHAPTER III.

NOW Peter and John went up together into the temple [a] at the hour of prayer, *being* the ninth *hour*.

2 And a certain man, lame from his mother's womb, was carried,

a Ps.55.17; Da.6.10.

should be saved, but simply *the fact* that they were those who *would be*, or who were about to be saved. It is clear, however, from this expression, that those who became members of the church were those who continued to adorn their profession, or who gave proof that they were sincere Christians. It is implied here, also, that those who are to be saved will join themselves to the church of God. This is everywhere required; and it constitutes *one* evidence of piety when they are willing to face the world, and give themselves at once to the service of the Lord Jesus. Two remarks may be made on the last verse of this chapter; one is, that the effect of a consistent Christian life will be to command the *respect* of the world; and the other is, that the effect will be continually to increase the number of those who shall be saved. In this case they were *daily* added to it; the church was constantly increasing; and the same result may be expected in all cases where there is similar zeal, self-denial, consistency, and prayer.

We have now contemplated the foundation of the Christian church, and the first glorious revival of religion. This chapter deserves to be profoundly studied by all ministers of the gospel, and by all who pray for the prosperity of the kingdom of God. It should excite our fervent gratitude that God has left this record of the first great work of grace, and our earnest prayers that he would multiply and extend such scenes until the earth shall be filled with his glory.

CHAPTER III.

1. *Peter and John went up*, &c. In Lu. xxiv. 53, it is said that the apostles were continually in the temple, praising and blessing God. From Ac. ii. 46, it is clear that all the disciples were accustomed daily to resort to the temple for devotion. Whether they joined in the *sacrifices* of the temple-service is not said; but the thing is not improbable. This was the place and the manner in which they and their fathers had worshipped. They came slowly to the conclusion that they were to leave the *temple*, and they would naturally resort there with their countrymen to worship the God of their fathers. In the previous chapter (ii. 43) we are told *in general* that many wonders and signs were done by the hands of the apostles. From the many miracles which were performed, Luke selects one of which he gives a more full account, and especially as it gives him occasion to record another of the addresses of Peter to the Jews. An impostor would have been satisfied with the *general* statement that many miracles *were* performed. The sacred writers descend to particulars, and tell us where, and in relation to whom, they were performed. This is a proof that they were honest men, and did not intend to deceive. ¶ *Into the temple.* Not into the edifice properly called the temple, but into the *court* of the temple, where prayer was accustomed to be made. See Notes on Mat. xxi. 12. ¶ *At the hour of prayer*, &c. The Jewish day was divided into twelve equal parts; of course, the ninth hour would be about three o'clock P.M. This was the hour of evening prayer. Morning prayer was offered at nine o'clock. Comp. Ps. lv. 17; Da. vi. 10.

2. *Lame from his mother's womb.* The mention of this shows that there was no deception in the case. The man had been always lame; he was obliged to be carried; and he was well known to the Jews. ¶ *Whom they laid daily.* That is, his friends laid him there *daily*. He would therefore be well known to those who were in the habit of entering the temple. Among the ancients there were no hospitals for the sick, and no alms-houses for the poor. The poor were dependent, therefore, on the charity of those who were in better circumstances. It became an important matter for them to be placed where they would see many people. Hence it was customary to place them at the gates of rich men (Lu. xvi. 20); and they also sat by the highway to beg where many persons would pass, Mar. x. 46; Lu. xviii. 35; Jn. ix. 1–8. The entrance to the *temple* would be a favourable place for begging; for (1) great multitudes were accustomed to enter there; and (2) when going up for the purposes of religion, they would be

whom they laid daily at [b]the gate of the temple which is called Beautiful, to ask alms of them that entered into the temple;
3 Who, seeing Peter and John about to go into the temple, asked an alms.
4 And Peter, fastening his eyes
upon him, with John, said, Look on us.
5 And he gave heed unto them, expecting to receive something of them.
6 Then Peter said, Silver and gold have I none; but such as I have give I thee: [c]In the name

b Jn.9.8.

c ch.4.10.

---

more inclined to give alms than at other times; and especially was this true of the Pharisees, who were particularly desirous of *publicity* in bestowing charity. It is recorded by Martial (i. 112) that the custom prevailed among the Romans of placing the poor by the gates of the temples; and the custom was also observed a long time in the Christian churches. ¶ *At the gate of the temple which is called Beautiful.* In regard to this gate there have been two opinions, one of which supposes that it was the gate commonly called *Nicanor*, which led from the court of the Gentiles to the court of the women (see Plan in Notes on Mat. xxi. 12), and the other that it was the gate at the eastern entrance of the temple, commonly called *Susan.* It is not easy to determine which is intended; though from the fact that what is here recorded occurred near Solomon's porch (ver. 11; comp. Plan of the Temple, Mat. xxi. 12), it seems probable that the latter was intended. This gate was large and splendid. It was made of Corinthian brass, a most valuable metal, and made a magnificent appearance (Josephus, *Jewish Wars*, b. v. ch. v. § 3). ¶ *To ask alms.* Charity.

3. *Who, seeing Peter*, &c. There is no evidence that he was acquainted with them or knew who they were. He asked of them as he was accustomed to do of the multitude that entered the temple.

4. *Fastening his eyes.* The word used here denotes to look *intently*, or with fixed attention. It is one of the peculiar words which *Luke* uses, Lu. iv. 20; xxii. 56; Ac. i. 10; iii. 12; vi. 15; vii. 55; x. 4; &c.—in all twelve times. It is used by no other writer in the New Testament, except by Paul twice, 2 Co. iii. 7, 13. ¶ *Look on us.* All this was done to fix the attention. He wished to call the attention of the man distinctly to himself, and to what he was about to do. It was also done that the man might be fully apprised that his restoration to health came from him.

6. *Silver and gold have I none.* The man had asked for money; Peter assures him that he had not that to give; what he did was done, however, in such a way as to show his *willingness* to aid him if he *had* possessed money. ¶ *Such as I have.* Such as is in my power. It is not to be supposed that he meant to say that he originated this power himself, but only that it was *intrusted* to him. He immediately adds that it was derived solely from the Lord Jesus Christ. ¶ *In the name.* Comp. ch. iv. 10. In Mar. xvi. 17, 18, it is said, "These signs shall follow them that believe; *in my name* shall they cast out devils . . . . they shall lay hands on the sick, and they shall recover." The expression means *by his authority*, or *in virtue of power derived from him.* We are here struck with a remarkable difference between the manner in which the Lord Jesus wrought miracles and that in which it was done by his apostles. *He* did it in his *own name* and by virtue of his own power. The apostles never attempted to perform a miracle by their *own power.* It was only in the name of Jesus; and this circumstance alone shows that there was a radical difference between Christ and all other prophets and teachers. ¶ *Of Nazareth.* This was the name by which he was commonly known. By this name he had been designated among the Jews and on the cross. It is by no means improbable that the man had heard of him by this name, and it was important that he should understand that it was by the authority of him who had been crucified as an impostor. ¶ *Rise and walk.* To do this would be evidence of signal power. It is remarkable that in cases like this they were commanded to do the thing at once. See similar cases in Jn. v. 8; Mat. ix. 6; xii. 13. It would have been easy to allege that they had *no power;* that they were lame, or sick,

of Jesus Christ of Nazareth, rise up and walk.

7 And he took him by the right hand, and lifted *him* up; and immediately his feet and ankle-bones received strength.

8 And he, [d]leaping up, stood, and walked, and entered with them into the temple, walking, and leaping, and praising God.

9 And all the people saw him walking and praising God:

d Is.35.6.

---

or palsied, and could do nothing until God should give them strength. But the command was *to do the thing;* nor did the Saviour or the apostles stop to convince them that they *could* do nothing. They did not doubt that if it were done they would ascribe the power to God. Precisely like this is the condition of the sinner. God commands him *to do the thing;* to repent, and believe, and lead a holy life. It is not merely to *attempt* to do it, to make use of means, or to wait on him, but it is *actually to repent and believe* the gospel. Where he may obtain power to do it is another question. It is easy for him to involve himself in difficulty, as it would have been in these cases. But the command of God is positive, and must be obeyed. If not obeyed, men must perish, just as this man would have been always lame if he had put forth no effort of his own. When done, a convicted sinner will do just as this man did, *instinctively give all the praise to God*, ver. 8.

7. *And he took him.* He took hold of his hand. To take hold of the hand in such a case was an offer of aid, an indication that Peter was sincere, and was an inducement to him to make an effort. This may be employed as a beautiful illustration of the manner of God when he commands men to repent and believe. He does not leave them alone; he extends help, and aids their efforts. If they tremble, and feel that they are weak, and needy, and helpless, his hand is stretched out and his power exerted to impart strength and grace. ¶ *His feet and ankle-bones.* The fact that strength was immediately imparted; that the feet, long lame, were now made strong, was a full and clear proof of miraculous power.

8. *And he, leaping up.* This was a natural expression of joy, and it was a striking fulfilment of the prophecy in Is. xxxv. 6: "Then shall the lame man leap as an hart." The account here given is one that is perfectly natural. The man would be filled with joy, and would express it in this manner. He had been lame from a child; he had never walked; and there was more in the miracle than merely giving *strength.* The art of *walking* is one that is acquired by long practice. Children learn slowly. *Caspar Hauser*, discovered in one of the cities of Germany, who had been confined in prison from a child, was unable to walk in an easy way when released, but stumbled in a very awkward manner (see his Life). When, therefore, this man was able at once to walk, it was clear proof of a miracle. ¶ *Praising God.* This was the natural and appropriate expression of his feelings on this occasion. His heart would be full; and he could have no doubt that this blessing had come from God alone. It is remarkable that he did not even express his gratitude to Peter and John. They had not pretended to restore him in their own name, and he would feel that man could not do it. It is remarkable that he praised God without being *taught* or entreated to do it. It was instinctive—the natural feeling of the heart. So a sinner. His first feelings, when he is converted, will be to ascribe the praise to God. While he may and will feel regard for the ministry by whose instrumentality he has received the blessing, yet his main expression of gratitude will be to God. And this he will do instinctively. He needs no prompter; he knows that no power of man is equal to the work of converting the soul, and will rejoice, and give all the praise to the God of grace.

9, 10. *And all the people*, &c. The people who had been accustomed to see him sit in a public place. ¶ *And they knew*, &c. In this they could not be deceived; they had seen him a long time, and now they saw the same man expressing his praise to God for complete recovery. The particulars in this miracle are the following, and they are as far as possible from any appearance of imposture: 1. The man had been afflicted from a child. This was known to all the people. At this time he was

10 And they knew that it was he
which sat for alms at the Beautiful
gate of the temple: and they were
filled with wonder and amazement
at that which had happened unto
him.
11 And, as the lame man which
was healed held Peter and John,
all the people ran together unto
them in [e]the porch that is called
Solomon's, greatly wondering.
12 And when Peter saw *it*, he
answered unto the people, Ye men
of Israel, why marvel ye at this?
or why look ye so earnestly on us,

e Jn.10.23; ch.5.12.

forty years of age, ch. iv. 22. 2. He was not an impostor. If he had *pretended* lameness, it is wonderful that he had not been detected before, and not have been suffered to occupy a place thus in the temple. 3. The apostles had no agency in placing him there. They had not seen him before. There was manifestly no *collusion* or *agreement* with him to attempt to impose on the people. 4. The man himself was convinced of the miracle, and did not doubt that the power by which he had been healed was of God. 5. The *people* were convinced of the same thing. They saw the effects; they had known him well; they had had every opportunity to know that he was diseased, and they were now satisfied that he was restored. There was no possibility of deception in the case. It was not merely the *friends* of Jesus that saw this; not those who had an *interest* in the miracle, but those who had been his enemies, and who had just before been engaged in putting him to death. Let this miracle be compared, in these particulars, with those *pretended* miracles which have been affirmed to have been wrought in defence of other systems of religion, and it will be seen at once that in these there is every appearance of sincerity, honesty, and truth; in them, every mark of deception, fraud, and imposition. (See Paley's *Evidences of Christianity*, proposition ii. ch. ii.)

11. *Held Peter and John.* The word *held* means that he *adhered* to them; he joined himself to them; he was desirous of remaining with them and participating with them. "He clung to his benefactors, and would not be separated from them" (Prof. Hackett). ¶ *All the people*, &c. Excited by curiosity, they came together. The fact of the cure and the conduct of the man would soon draw together a crowd, and thus furnish a favourable opportunity for preaching to them the gospel. ¶ *In the porch*, &c. This *porch* was a covered way or passage on the east side of the temple. It was distinguished for its magnificence. See the plan and description of the temple, Notes on Mat. xxi. 12.

12. *When Peter saw* it. Saw the people assembling in such multitudes and wondering at the miracle. ¶ *He answered.* The word *answer*, with us, implies that a question had been asked, or that some subject had been proposed for consideration. But the word is used in a different sense in the Bible. It is often used when no question was asked, but when *an occasion* was offered for remarks, or when an opportunity was presented to make a statement. It is the same as replying *to a thing*, or making *a statement* in regard to some subject, Da. ii. 26; Ac. v. 8. ¶ *Ye men of Israel.* Jews. Comp. ch. ii. 14. ¶ *Why marvel ye at this?* The particular thing which he intended to reprove here was not that they *wondered*, for that was proper; but that they *looked on himself and John* as if they had been the authors of this healing. They ought to have understood it. The Jews were sufficiently acquainted with miracles to interpret them and to know whence they proceeded; and they ought not, therefore, to ascribe them to *man*, but to inquire *why* they had been wrought *by God.* ¶ *Why look ye*, &c. Why do ye fix the eyes with amazement *on us*, as though *we* could do this? Why not look at once to God? ¶ *By our own power.* By any *art of healing* or by any medicine we had done this. ¶ *Or holiness.* Piety. As if God had bestowed this on us on account of our personal and eminent piety. It may be remarked that here was ample opportunity for them to establish a reputation of their own. The people were disposed to pay them honour; they *might* at once have laid claim to vast authority over them; but they refused all such personal honour, and ascribed all to the Lord Jesus. Whatever success may attend the ministers of the gospel, or however much the world may be disposed to do them hon-

as though [f]by our own power or
holiness we had made this man to
walk?

13 The[g] God of Abraham, and
of Isaac, and of Jacob, [h]the God of
our fathers, [i]hath glorified his
Son Jesus; whom ye delivered up,
and [k]denied him in the presence
of Pilate, [l]when he was determined
to let *him* go.

14 But ye denied [m]the Holy
One and [n]the Just, and desired a
murderer to be granted unto you;

15 And killed the [1]Prince of life,

f 2 Co.3.5. *g* Mat.22.32. *h* ch.5.30,31. *i* Jn.17.1; Ep.1.20-22; Phi.2.9-11; He.2.9; Re.1.5,18. *k* Jn.19.15. *l* Mat.27.17-25; Lu.23.16-23. *m* Ps.16.10; Lu.1.35. *n* ch.7.52; 22.14. [1] or, *Author*, Jn.1.4; 1 Jn.5.11.

our, they should disclaim all power in themselves, and ascribe it to the Lord Jesus Christ. It is not by the talents or personal holiness of ministers, valuable as these are, that men are saved; it is only by the power of God, designed to honour his Son. See 2 Co. iii. 5, 6.

13. *The God of Abraham.* He is called the God of Abraham because Abraham *acknowledged* him as his God, and because God showed himself to be his friend. Comp. Mat. xxii. 32; Ex. iii. 6, 15; Ge. xxviii. 13; xxvi. 24. It was important to show that it was the *same* God who had done this that had been acknowledged by their fathers, and that they were not about to introduce the worship of any other God. And it was especially important, because the promise had been made to Abraham that in his seed all the families of the earth would be blessed, Ge. xii. 3. Comp. Ga. iii. 16. ¶ *Hath glorified.* Has honoured. *You* denied, despised, and murdered him, but God has exalted and honoured him. This miracle was done in the *name* of Jesus, ver. 6. It was the *power of God* that had restored the man; and by putting forth this power, God had shown that he approved the work of his Son, and was disposed to honour him in the view of men. Comp. Jn. xvii. 1; Ep. i. 20–22; Phi. ii. 9–11; He. ii. 9; Re. i. 5–18. ¶ *Ye delivered up.* That is, you delivered him to the Romans to be put to death. See Notes on ch. ii. 23. ¶ *And denied him in the presence of Pilate.* Denied that he was the Messiah. Were unwilling to own him as your long-expected King, Jn. xix. 15. ¶ *When he was determined*, &c. Mat. xxvii. 17–25; Lu. xxiii. 16–23. Pilate was satisfied of his innocence; but he was weak, timid, and irresolute, and he yielded to their wishes. The fact that *Pilate* regarded him as innocent was a strong aggravation of their crime. They should have regarded him as innocent; but they urged on his condemnation against the deliberate judgment of him before whom they had arraigned him, and thus showed how obstinately they were resolved on his death.

14. *The Holy One*, &c. See Ps. xvi. 10. Comp. Notes on Ac. ii. 27. ¶ *And the Just.* The word *just* here denotes *innocent*, or one who was free from crime. It properly is used in reference to *law*, and denotes one who stands upright in the view of the law, or who is not chargeable with crime. In this sense the Lord Jesus was not only *personally* innocent, but even before his judges he stood unconvicted of any crime. The crime charged on him at first was *blasphemy* (Mat. xxvi. 65), and on *this* charge the Sanhedrim had condemned him without proof. But of *this* charge Pilate would not take cognizance, and hence *before him* they charged him with sedition, Lu. xxiii. 2. Neither of these charges were made out, and of course, in the eye of the law, he was innocent and just. It greatly aggravated their crime that they demanded his death still, even *after* it was ascertained that they could prove nothing against him, thus showing that it was mere hatred and malice that led them to seek his death. ¶ *And desired a murderer*, Mat. xxvii. 21.

15. *And killed the Prince of life.* The word rendered *prince* denotes properly a *military leader* or commander. Hence, in He. ii. 10, it is translated *captain:* "It became him . . . to make the *Captain of their salvation* perfect through sufferings." As a captain or commander leads on to victory and is said to obtain it, so the word comes to denote one who is the *cause*, the *author*, the *procurer*, &c. In this sense it is used, Ac. v. 31, "Him hath God exalted to be a *Prince* and a Saviour, *for to give* repentance to Israel," &c. In He. xii. 2 it is properly rendered *author*, "Looking unto Jesus, the *author* and finisher of our faith." The word *author*, or giver, would express the meaning of the word here. It also implies that he

whom God [o]hath raised from the
dead; [p]whereof we are witnesses.
16 And his name, through faith
in his name, hath made this man
strong, whom ye see and know;
yea, the faith which is by him hath
given him this perfect soundness
in the presence of you all.
17 And now, brethren, I wot

o Mat.28.2-6; Ep.1.20. *p* ch.2.32.

---

has *dominion* over life; an idea, indeed, which is essentially connected with that of his being the author of it. The word *life* here is used in a large sense, as denoting *all* manner of life. In this sense it is used in reference to Christ in Jn. i. 4, "In him was *life.*" Comp. Jn. v. 26; 1 Jn. v. 11; 1 Co. xv. 45. Jesus is here called the *Prince of life* in contrast with him whom the Jews demanded in his place, Barabbas. He was a *murderer* (Lu. xxiii. 19; Mar. xv. 7), one who had *destroyed life*, and yet they demanded that he whose character it was *to destroy life* should be released, and *the Author of life* be put to death. ¶ *Whom God hath raised*, &c. Ch. ii. 24, 32.

16. *And his name.* The *name* of Jesus is here put for Jesus himself, and it is the same as saying "and *he*," &c. In this way the word *name* is often used by the Hebrews, especially when speaking of God, Ac. i. 15; iv. 12; Ep. i. 21; Re. iii. 4. It does not mean that there was any efficacy in the mere *name* of Jesus that would heal the man, but that it was done by his authority and power. ¶ *Through faith in his name.* By means of faith in him; that is, by the faith which Peter and John had in Jesus. It does not refer to any faith that the man had himself, for there is no evidence that he believed in him. But it was by means of the faith which the apostles exercised in him that the miracle was wrought, and was thus a fulfilment of the declaration in Mat. xvii. 20, "If ye have faith . . . ye shall say to this mountain, remove hence," &c. This truth Peter repeats two or three times in the verse to impress it more distinctly on the minds of his hearers. ¶ *Whom ye see and know.* There could, therefore, be no mistake. He was well known to them. There was no doubt about the truth of the miracle (ch. iv. 16), and the only inquiry was in what way it had been done. This Peter affirms to have been accomplished *only* by the power of the Lord Jesus. ¶ *Perfect soundness*—ὁλοκληρίαν. This word is not used elsewhere in the New Testament. It denotes *integrity of parts, freedom from any defect;* and it here means that the cure was perfect and entire, or that he was *completely* restored to the use of his limbs. ¶ *In the presence of you all.* You are all witnesses of it, and can judge for yourselves. This shows how confident the apostles were that a *real* miracle had been performed. They were willing that it should be examined; and this is conclusive proof that there was no attempt at imposture. A deceiver, or one who *pretended* to work miracles, would have been *cautious* of exposing the subject to the danger of detection.

17. *And now, brethren.* Though they had been guilty of a crime so enormous, yet Peter shows the tenderness of his heart in addressing them still as his *brethren.* He regarded them as of the same nation with himself; as having the same hopes, and as being entitled to the same privileges. The expression also shows that he was not disposed to exalt himself as being by nature more holy than they. This verse is a remarkable instance of *tenderness* in appealing to sinners. It would have been easy to have reproached them for their enormous crimes; but that was not the way to reach the heart. He had indeed stated and *proved* their wickedness. The object now was to bring them to repentance for it; and this was to be done by *tenderness, kindness,* and *love.* Men are melted to contrition, not by *reproaches*, but by *love.* ¶ *I wot.* I know; I am well apprised of it. I know you will affirm it, and I admit that it was so. Still the enormous deed *has been done.* It cannot be recalled, and it cannot be innocent. It remains, therefore, that you should repent of it, and seek for pardon. ¶ *That through ignorance*, &c. Peter does not mean to affirm that they were *innocent* in having put him to death, for he had just proved the contrary, and he immediately proceeds to exhort them to repentance. But he means to say that their offence was *mitigated* by the fact that they were ignorant that he was the Messiah. The same thing the Saviour himself affirmed when dying, Lu. xxiii. 34: "Father, forgive them, for they know not what they do." Comp. Ac. xiii. 27; 1 Co.

that through [q] ignorance ye did *it*, as *did* also your rulers.

18 But [r] those things, which God before had showed by the mouth of

q Lu.23.34; Jn.16.3; 1 Co.2.8.

r Lu.24.44; ch.26.22,23.

ii. 8. The same thing the apostle Paul affirmed in relation to himself, as one of the reasons why he obtained pardon from the enormous crime of persecution, 1 Ti. i. 13. In cases like these, though crime might be *mitigated*, yet it was not taken entirely away. They were guilty of demanding that a man should be put to death who was declared innocent; they were urged on with ungovernable fury; they did it from contempt and malice; and the crime of *murder* remained, though they were ignorant that he was the Messiah. It is plainly implied that if they had put him to death *knowing* that he was the Messiah, and *as the Messiah*, there would have been no forgiveness. Comp. He. x. 26–29. Ignorance, therefore, is a circumstance which must always be taken into view in an estimate of crime. It is at the same time true that they had opportunity to know that he was the Messiah, but the *mere fact* that they were ignorant of it was still a mitigating circumstance in the estimate of their crime. There can be no doubt that the *mass* of the people had no fixed belief that he was the Messiah. ¶ *As* did *also your rulers.* Comp. 1 Co. ii. 8, where the apostle says that none of the princes of this world knew the wisdom of the gospel, for had they known it, they would not have crucified the Lord of glory. It is certain that the *leading* scribes and Pharisees were urged on by the most ungovernable fury and rage to put Jesus to death, even when they had abundant opportunity to know his true character. This was particularly the case with the high-priest. But yet it was true that they did not *believe* that he was the Messiah. Their minds had been prejudiced. They had expected a prince and a conqueror. All their views of the Messiah were different from the character which Jesus manifested. And though they *might* have known that he was the Messiah; though he had given abundant proof of the fact, yet it is clear that they did not believe it. It is not credible that they *would* have put to death one whom they *really* believed to be the Christ. He was the hope, the only hope of their nation; and they would not have dared to imbrue their hands in the blood of him whom they really believed to be the illustrious personage so long promised and expected by their fathers. It was also probably true that no small part of the Sanhedrim was urged on by the zeal and fury of the chief priests. They had not courage to resist them; and yet they *might* not have entered heartily into this work of persecution and death. Comp. Jn. vii. 50–53. The speech of Peter, however, is not intended to free them entirely from blame; nor should it be pressed to show that they were innocent. It is a mitigating circumstance thrown in to show them that there was still *hope of mercy*.

18. *But those things.* To wit, those things that *did* actually occur, pertaining to the life and death of the Messiah. ¶ *Had showed.* Had announced, or foretold. ¶ *By the mouth of all his prophets.* That is, by the prophets in general, without affirming that *each* individual prophet had uttered a distinct prediction respecting this. The prophets *taken together*, or the prophecies *as a whole*, had declared this. The word *all* is not unfrequently used in this somewhat limited sense, Mar. i. 37; Jn. iii. 26. In regard to the prophecies respecting Christ, see Notes on Lu. xxiv. 27. ¶ *Hath so fulfilled.* He has caused to be fulfilled *in this manner;* that is, by the rejection, the denial, and the wickedness of the rulers. It has *turned out* to be in strict accordance with the prophecy. This fact Peter uses in exhorting them to repentance; but it is not to be regarded as an *excuse* for their sins. The mere fact that all this was foretold; that it was in accordance with the purposes and predictions of God, does not take away the *guilt* of it, or constitute an excuse for it. In regard to this, we may remark, (1) The prediction did not change the *nature* of the act. The mere fact that it was *foretold*, or foreknown, did not change its character. See Notes on ch. i. 23. (2) Peter still regarded them as guilty. He did not urge the fact that this was foreknown as an excuse for their sin, but to show them that *since* all this happened according to the prediction and the purpose of God, they might hope in his mercy. The plan was that the Messiah should die to make a way for pardon, and,

all his prophets, that Christ should suffer, he hath so fulfilled.

19 Repent[s] ye, therefore, and be[t] converted, [u]that your sins may be blotted out, when [v]the times of refreshing shall come from the presence of the Lord;

s ch.2.38. *t* Is.1.16-20; Joel 2.13. *u* Is.43.25. *v* Je.31.23-25; Zep.3.14-20; Re.21.4.

therefore, *they* might hope in his mercy. (3) This was a signal instance of the power and mercy of God in overruling the wicked conduct of men to further his own purposes and plans. (4) All the other sins of men *may* thus be overruled, and thus the wrath of man may be made to praise him. But, (5) This will constitute no excuse for the sinner. It is no part of his *intention* to honour God, or to advance his purposes; and there is no direct *tendency* in his crimes to advance his glory. The direct tendency of his deeds is counteracted and overruled, and God brings good out of the evil. But this surely constitutes no excuse for the sinner.

If it be asked why Peter insisted on this if he did not mean that it should be regarded as an *excuse* for their sin, I reply, that it was his design to prove *that Jesus was the Messiah*, and having proved this, he could assure them that there was mercy. Not that they had not been guilty; not that they *deserved* favour; but that *the fact* that the Messiah had come was an argument which proved that *any* sinners might obtain mercy, as he immediately proceeds to show them.

19. *Repent ye.* See Notes on Mat. iii. 2. ¶ *Therefore. Because* of your sin in putting Jesus to death, and *because* he is the Messiah, and God through him is willing to show mercy to the chief of sinners. ¶ *And be converted.* This expression conveys an idea not at all to be found in the original. It conveys the idea of *passivity*, BE *converted*, as if they were to yield to some foreign influence that they were now resisting. But the idea of being *passive* in this is not conveyed by the original word. The word means properly to *turn;* to return to a path from which one has gone astray; and then to turn away from sins, or to forsake them. It is a word used in a general sense to denote the whole *turning* to God. That the form of the word here (ἐπιστρέψατε) does not denote *passivity* may be clearly seen by referring to the following places where the same form of the word is used: Mat. xxiv. 18; Mar. xiii. 16; Lu. xvii. 31; 1 Th. i. 9. The expression, therefore, would have been more appropriately rendered "*repent*, and *turn*, that your sins," &c. *To be converted* cannot be a matter of obligation, but *to turn to God* is the duty of every sinner. The crimes of which he exhorted them to repent were those pertaining to the death of the Lord Jesus, as well as all the past sins of their lives. They were to turn from the course of wickedness in which they and the nation had been so long walking. *That your sins,* &c. *In order* that your sins *may be* forgiven. Sin cannot be pardoned *before* man repents of it. In the order of the work of grace, repentance must always precede pardon. Of course, no man can have evidence that his sin is pardoned until he repents. Comp. Is. i. 16–20; Joel ii. 13. ¶ *May be blotted out.* May be forgiven, or pardoned. The expression *to blot out sins* occurs also in Is. xliii. 25; Ps. li. 1, 9; Je. xviii. 23; Ne. iv. 5; Is. xliv. 22. The expression *to blot out a name* is applied to expunging it from a *roll*, or *catalogue*, or *list*, as of an army, &c., Ex. xxxii. 32, 33; De. ix. 14; xxv. 19; xxix. 29, &c. The expression *to blot out sins* is taken from the practice of creditors charging their debtors, and when the debt is paid, cancelling it, or wholly removing the record. The word used here *properly* refers to the practice of writing on tables covered with wax, and then by inverting the stylus, or instrument of writing, smoothing the wax again, and thus removing *every trace* of the record. This more entirely expresses the idea of *pardoning* than *blotting* does. It means wholly *to remove* the record, the charge, and every *trace* of the account against us. In this way *God* forgives sins. ¶ *When the times,* &c. The word ὅπως, rendered "when," is commonly rendered *that*, and denotes the *final cause*, or the *reason* why a thing is done, Mat. ii. 23; v. 16, 45, &c. By many it has been supposed to have this sense here, and to mean, "repent . . . *in order that* the times of refreshing may come," &c. Thus Kuinoel, Grotius, Lightfoot, the Syriac version, &c. If used in this sense, it means that their repentance and forgiveness would be the *means* of introducing peace and joy. Others have rendered it, in accordance with our

translation, "when," meaning that they might find peace in the day when Christ should return to judgment, which return would be to them a day of *rest*, though of terror to the wicked. Thus Calvin, Beza, the Latin Vulgate, Schleusner, &c. The *grammatical* construction will admit of either, though the former is more in accordance with the usual use of the word. The objection to the former is, that it is not easy to see how their repenting, &c., would be the *means* of introducing the times of refreshing. And this, also, corresponds very little with the *design* of Peter in this discourse. That was to *encourage them* to repentance; to adduce arguments why they should repent, and why they might hope in his mercy. To do this, it was needful only to assure them that they were living under the times graciously promised by God—the times of refreshing, when pardon might be obtained. The main inquiry, therefore, is, What did Peter refer to by *the times of refreshing*, and by the *restitution of all things?* Did he refer to any particular manifestation to be made then, or to the influence of the gospel on the earth, or to the future state, when the Lord Jesus shall come to judgment? The idea which I suppose Peter intended to convey was this: "Repent, and be converted. You have been great sinners, and are in danger. Turn from your ways, that your sins may be forgiven." But then, what encouragement would there be for this? or why should it be done? Answer: "You are living under the times of the gospel, the reign of the Messiah, the times of refreshing. This happy, glorious period has been long anticipated, and is to continue to the close of the world. The period which will *include* the restitution of all things, and the return of Christ to judgment, has come, and is, therefore, the period when you *may* find mercy, and when you *should* seek it, to be prepared for his return." In this sense the passage refers to the fact that this time, this dispensation, this economy, *including all this*, had come, and they were living under it, and *might* and *should* seek for mercy. It expresses, therefore, the *common belief of the Jews* that such a time *would* come, and the comment of *Peter* about its nature and continuance. The belief of the Jews was that such times *would* come. Peter affirms that the belief of such a period was well founded—a time when mercy may be obtained. That time *has come*. The doctrine that it *would* come was *well founded*, and has been fulfilled. This was a reason why they should repent, and hope in the mercy of God. Peter goes on, then, to state further *characteristics* of that period. It would include the restitution of all things, the return of Christ to judgment, &c. And *all this* was an additional consideration why they should repent, and turn from their sins, and seek for forgiveness. The meaning of the passage may therefore be thus summed up: "Repent, *since* it is a true doctrine that such times *would* come: they are clearly predicted; they were to be expected; and you are now living under them. *In these times;* in this dispensation, also, God shall send his Son again to judge the world, and all things shall be closed and settled for ever. Since you live under this period, you *may* seek for mercy, and you *should* seek to avoid the vengeance due to the wicked, and to be admitted to heaven when the Lord Jesus shall return." ¶ *Times of refreshing.* The word rendered *refreshing*, ἀνάψυξις, means properly *breathing*, or *refreshment*, after being *heated* with *labour*, *running*, &c. It hence denotes any kind of refreshment, as rest, or deliverance from evils of any kind. It is used nowhere else in the New Testament, except that the *verb* is used in 2 Ti. i. 16, "Onesiphorus . . . . oft *refreshed* me, and was not ashamed of my chain." He administered comfort to me in my trials. It is used by the LXX. in the Old Testament nine times: Ex. viii. 15, "But when Pharaoh saw that there was *respite;*" that is, cessation or rest from the plagues, Ho. xii. 8; Je. xlix. 31; Ps. lxix. 11, &c. In no place in the Old Testament is the *word* applied to the terms of the gospel. The *idea*, however, that the times of the Messiah would be times of *rest*, *ease*, and *prosperity*, was a favourite one among the Jews, and was countenanced in the Old Testament. See Is. xxviii. 12, "To whom he said, This is the rest wherewith ye may cause the weary to rest; and this is the refreshing," &c. They anticipated the times of the gospel as a period when they would have rest from their enemies, a respite from the evils of oppression and war, and great national prosperity and peace. Under the idea that the *happy times of the Messiah* had come, Peter now addresses them, and assures them that they might

20 And[w] he shall send Jesus Christ, which before was preached unto you:

w ch.1.11; He.9.28.

21 Whom the heavens must receive until [x]the times of restitution of all things, which [y]God

x Mat.17.11. *y* Lu.1.70.

---

obtain pardon and peace. ¶ *Shall come.* This does not mean that this period was *still future*, for it had come; but that the expectation of the Jews that such a Messiah would come was well founded. A remarkably similar construction we have concerning Elijah (Mat. xvii. 11), "And Jesus answered and said, Elias truly *shall first come*, and restore," &c.; that is, the doctrine that Elijah would come was true, though he immediately adds that it *had already* taken place, ver. 12. See Notes on that place. ¶ *From the presence of the Lord.* Greek, "From *the face* of the Lord." The expression means that God was *its author*. From the face of the Lord means from *the Lord himself:* Mar. i. 2, "I send thy messenger *before thy face*," that is, before *thee*. Comp. Mal. iii. 1; Lu. i. 76; ii. 31.

20. *And he shall send*, &c. Ch. i. 11. *Under this economy of things*, he shall send Jesus Christ, that is, the Messiah, to teach men; to redeem them; to save them; to judge the world; to gather his people to himself; and to condemn the wicked. Under *this* economy they were then. *This*, therefore, was an argument why they should repent and turn to God, that they might escape in the day of judgment. ¶ *Which before was preached*, &c. Who has been proclaimed as the Messiah. The name *Jesus Christ* is equivalent here to *the Messiah*. The *Messiah* had been proclaimed to the Jews as about to come. In his time was to be the period of refreshing. He *had* come; and they were under the economy in which the blessings of the Messiah were to be enjoyed. This does not refer to his personal ministry, or to the preaching of the apostles, but to the fact that the Messiah had been a long time *announced* to them by the prophets as about to come. All the prophets had *preached* him as the hope of the nation. It may be remarked, however, that there is here a difference in the manuscripts. A large majority of them read προκεχειρισμενον, who was *designated* or *appointed*, instead of who was *preached*. This reading is approved by Griesbach, Knapp, Bengel, &c. It was followed in the ancient Syriac, the Arabic, &c., and is undoubtedly the true reading.

21. *Whom the heavens must receive.* The common belief of the Jews was, that the Messiah would reign on the earth for ever, Jn. xii. 34. On this account they would object that Jesus could not be the Messiah, and hence it became so important for the apostles to establish the fact that he had ascended to heaven. The evidence which they adduced was the fact that they *saw* him ascend, Ac. i. 9. The meaning of the expression "whom the heavens MUST receive," is that it was *fit* or *proper* (δεῖ) that he should ascend. *One* reason of that fitness or propriety he himself stated in Jn. xvi. 7; comp. xvii. 2. It was also *fit* or expedient that he should do it, to direct the affairs of the universe for the welfare of the church (Ep. i. 20–22), and that he should exercise there his office as a priest in interceding for his people, 1 Jn. ii. 1, 2; He. vii. 25; ix. 24; Ro. viii. 34, &c. It is remarkable that Peter did not adduce any passage of Scripture on this subject; but it was one of the points on which there was no clear revelation. Obscure intimations of it might be found in Ps. cx., xvi., &c., but the fact that he would *ascend* to heaven was not made prominent in the Old Testament. The words "whom the heaven must receive" also convey the idea of *exaltation* and *power;* and Peter doubtless intended to say that he was clothed with power, and exalted to honour in the presence of God. See Ps. cxv. 3. Comp. 1 Pe. iii. 22, "Who is gone into heaven, and is on the right hand of God; angels, and authorities, and powers being made subject unto him." See Notes on Ac. ii. 33. ¶ *Until.* This word implies that he would then *return* to the earth, but it does not imply that he would not again ascend to heaven. ¶ *The times of the restitution of all things.* The *noun* rendered *restitution* (ἀποκαταστάσεως) does not elsewhere occur in the New Testament. The *verb* from which it is derived occurs eight times. It means properly to *restore a thing to its former situation*, as restoring a *sprained* or *dislocated* limb to its former soundness. Hence it is used to restore, or to *heal*, in the New Testament: Mat. xii. 13, "And it (the hand) was *restored whole* as the

hath spoken by the mouth of all
his holy prophets since the world
began.
22 For Moses truly said unto
the fathers, [z]A Prophet shall the
Lord your God raise up unto you
of your brethren, like unto me;

z De.18.15-19.

other;" Mar. iii. 5; Lu. vi. 10. And hence it is applied to the *preparation* or *fitness* for the coming of the Messiah which was to attend the preaching of John in the character of Elias, Mat. xvii. 11; Mar. ix. 12. Thus, in Josephus (*Antiq.*, ii. 3, 8), the word is used to denote the return of the Jews from the captivity of Babylon, and their restoration to their former state and privileges. The word has also the idea of *consummation*, *completion*, or *filling up*. Thus it is used in Philo, Hesychius, Phavorinus, and by the Greek classics. (See Lightfoot and Kuinoel.) Thus it it is used here by the Syriac: "Until the *complement* or *filling up* of the times;" that is, of all the events foretold by the prophets, &c. Thus the Arabic: "Until the times which shall establish the perfection or completion of all the predictions of the prophets," &c. In this sense the passage means that the heavens must receive the Lord Jesus until all things spoken by the prophets in relation to his work, his reign, the spread of the gospel, the triumph of religion, &c., shall have been fulfilled. It also conveys the idea of the predicted recovery of the world from sin, and the restoration of peace and order; the *consummation* of the work of the Messiah, now begun, but not yet complete; slow it may be in its advances, but triumphant and certain in its progress and its close. ¶ *All things.* All things which *have been foretold by the prophets.* The expression is limited by the connection to this; and of course it does not mean that all men will be saved, or that all the evils of sin can be repaired or remedied. This can never be, for the mischief is done and cannot be undone; but everything which the prophets have foretold shall receive their completion and fulfilment. ¶ *Which God hath spoken.* Which have been revealed, and are recorded in the Old Testament. ¶ *Of all his holy prophets.* This does not mean that *each* one of the prophets had spoken of these things, but that all which *had been spoken* would be fulfilled. ¶ *Since the world began.* This is an expression denoting the same as *from the beginning*, meaning to affirm with emphasis that *all* the prophecies would be fulfilled. The apostles were desirous to show that they, as well as the Jews, held entirely to the prophets, and taught no doctrine which they had not taught before them.

22. *For Moses truly said.* The authority of Moses among the Jews was absolute and final. It was of great importance, therefore, to show not only that they were not *departing* from his law, but that he had actually *foretold* these very things. The object of the passage is not to prove that the heavens must receive him, but that he was truly the Messiah. ¶ *Unto the fathers.* To their ancestors, or the founders of the nation. See De. xviii. 15–19. ¶ *A Prophet.* Literally, one who foretells future events. But it is also used to denote a religious teacher in general. See Ro. xii. 6. In the passage in Deuteronomy it is evidently used in a large sense, to denote one who would infallibly guide and direct the nation in its religious affairs; one who would be commissioned by *God* to do this, in opposition to *the diviners* (ver. 14) on which other nations relied. The meaning of this passage in Deuteronomy is apparent from the connection. Moses is stating to the Hebrews (ver. 1–8) the duty and office of the priests and Levites. He then cautions them against conforming to the surrounding nations, particularly on the subject of religious instruction and guidance. They, said he, consult, in times of perplexity, with enchanters, and charmers, and necromancers, and wizards, &c. (ver. 11–14), but it shall not be so with you. You shall not be *left* to this false and uncertain guidance in times of perplexity and danger, for the Lord will raise up, from time to time, a *prophet*, a man directly commissioned in an extraordinary manner from heaven, like me, who shall direct and counsel you. The promise, therefore, pertains to *the series of prophets* which God would raise up; or it is a promise that God would send his prophets, as occasion might demand, to instruct and counsel the nation. The *design* was to keep them from consulting with diviners, &c., and to preserve them from following the pretended and false religious teachers of surrounding idolatrous people. In

him shall ye hear in all things, whatsoever he shall say unto you.

23 And it shall come to pass, *that* every soul which will not hear that

this interpretation most commentators agree. See particularly *Calvin* on this place. Thus explained, the prophecy had no *exclusive* or even *direct* reference to the Messiah, and there is no evidence that the Jews understood it to have any such reference, except as *one of the series* of prophets that God would raise up and send to instruct the nation. If, then, it be asked *on what principle* Peter appealed to this, we may reply, (1) That the Messiah was to sustain the character of a prophet, and the prophecy had reference to him as *one* of the teachers that God would raise up to instruct the nation. (2) It would apply to him *by way of eminence*, as *the greatest* of the messengers that God would send to instruct the people. In this sense it is probable that the Jews would understand it. (3) This was one of those *emergencies* in the history of the nation when they might expect such an intervention. The prophecy implied that in times of perplexity and danger God would raise up such a prophet. Such a time then existed. The nation was corrupt, distracted, subjected to a foreign power, and *needed* such a teacher and guide. If it be asked *why* Peter appealed to this rather than to *explicit* prophecies of the Messiah, we may remark, (1) That his main object was to show their *guilt* in having rejected him and put him to death, ver. 14, 15. (2) That in order to do this, he sets before them clearly the *obligation* to *obey* him; and in doing this, appeals to the express command of Moses. He shows them that, according to Moses, whoever would not obey such a prophet should be cut off from among the people. In refusing, therefore, to hear this great prophet, and putting him to death, they had violated the express command of their own lawgiver. But it was possible *still* to obey him, for he still *lived* in heaven; and all the authority of *Moses*, therefore, made it a matter of obligation for them still to hear and obey him. The Jews were accustomed to apply the name *prophet* to the Messiah (Jn. i. 21; vi. 14; vii. 40; Mat. xxi. 11; Lu. iv. 24), and it has been shown from the writings of the Jewish Rabbins that they believed the Messiah would be the greatest of the prophets, even greater than Moses. See Notes on Jn. i. 21. ¶ *The Lord your God.* In the Hebrew, "Jehovah, thy God." ¶ *Raise up unto you.* Appoint, or commission to come to you. ¶ *Of your brethren.* Among yourselves; of your own countrymen; so that you shall not be dependent on foreigners, or on teachers of other nations. All the prophets were native-born Jews. And it was particularly true of the Messiah that he was to be a Jew, descended from Abraham, and raised up from the midst of his brethren, He. ii. 11, 16, 17. On this account it was to be presumed that they would feel a deeper interest in him, and listen more attentively to his instructions. ¶ *Like unto me.* Not in all things, but only in the point which was under discussion. He was to resemble him in being able to make known to them the will of God, and thus preventing the necessity of looking to other teachers. The idea of *resemblance* between Moses and the prophet is not very strictly expressed in the Greek, except in the mere circumstance of being *raised up*. God shall raise up to you a prophet *as he has raised up me* —ὡς ἐμέ. The resemblance between Moses and the Messiah should not be pressed too far. The Scriptures have not traced it farther than to the fact that *both* were raised up by God to communicate his will to the Jewish people, and therefore one should be heard as well as the other. ¶ *Him shall ye hear.* That is, him shall you *obey*, or you shall receive his instructions as a communication from God. ¶ *In all things whatsoever*, &c. These words are not quoted *literally* from the Hebrew, but they express the *sense* of what is said in De. xviii. 15, 18.

23. *And it shall come to pass.* It shall be, or shall occur. This is not the usual word rendered "it shall come to pass." It is a word commonly expressing *futurity*, but here it conveys the notion of *obligation*. In this verse Peter has not quoted the passage in Deuteronomy *literally*, but he has given the *sense.* ¶ *Every soul.* Every *person* or *individual*. Soul is often put for the whole man by the Hebrews, Ac. vii. 14; Jos. x. 28. ¶ *Hear that Prophet.* That is, *obey* his instructions. He shall have *authority* to declare the will of God; and he that does not obey him refuses

Prophet shall be destroyed from among the people.

24 Yea, and all the prophets from Samuel, and those that follow after, as many as have spoken, have likewise foretold of these days.

25 Ye[a] are the children of the

[a] Ro.9.4; 15.8.

to obey God. Comp. Lu. x. 16; Jn. xiii. 20. ¶ *Shall be destroyed.* This quotation is made according to the *sense*, and not *literally*. In the Hebrew the expression is (De. xviii. 19), "I will require it of him," that is, I will hold him *answerable* or *responsible* for it; I will *punish* him. This expression the LXX. have rendered by "I will take vengeance on him." The idea of the passage is, therefore, that God would *punish* the man that would not hear the prophet, without specifying the particular way in which it should be done. The *usual mode* of punishing such offences was by *cutting the offender off from among the people*, Ex. xxx. 33; xii. 15; xix. 31; Nu. xv. 31; xix. 13; Le. vii. 20, 21, 25, 27, &c. The sense is, that he should be punished in the usual manner; that is, by *excision*, or by being *destroyed* from among the people. The word translated *shall be destroyed* means properly to *exterminate*, wholly to devote to ruin, as of a wicked people, a wicked man whose life is taken, &c. To be destroyed *from among the people* means, however, to be excommunicated, or to be deprived of the *privileges* of a people. Among the Jews this was probably the most severe punishment that could be inflicted. It involved the idea of being cut off from the privileges of sacrifice and worship in the temple and in the synagogue, &c., and of being regarded as a *heathen* and an outcast. The idea which Peter expressed here was, that the Jews had exposed themselves to the severest punishment in rejecting and crucifying the Lord Jesus, and that they should, therefore, repent of this great sin, and seek for mercy. The same remark is applicable still to men. The Scriptures abundantly declare the truth, that if sinners will not hear the Lord Jesus, they shall be destroyed. And it becomes each individual to inquire with honesty whether he listens to *his* instructions and obeys his law, or whether he is rejecting him and following the devices and desires of his own heart. It will be a solemn day when the sinner shall be called to *render a reason* why he has rejected the teachings and laws of the Son of God!

24. *All the prophets.* That is, the prophets in general. It may be said of the prophets *generally*, or of all of them, that they have foretold these things. This expression is not to be pressed as if we were to look for distinct predictions of the Messiah in *each one* of the prophets. The use of language does not require so strict an interpretation. ¶ *From Samuel.* In the previous verse (22) *Moses* was mentioned as the *first* in order. The next in order was *Samuel.* The same mention of *Moses* and *Samuel* occurs in Ps. xcix. 6. The reason why *Samuel* is mentioned here is probably that he was the first prophet after Moses who recorded a prediction respecting the times of the Messiah. The Jews, in their divisions of the books of the Old Testament, reckoned the book of Joshua as the first of *the prophets.* But in Joshua and Judges there does not occur any distinct prediction of the Messiah. The prophecy in Samuel, to which Peter probably had reference, is in 2 Sa. vii. 16. From the time of Moses to Samuel, also, it is probable that no prophet arose. God was consulted by *Urim* and *Thummim* (Ex. xxviii. 30; Nu. xxvii. 21), and consequently no extraordinary messenger was sent to instruct the nation. ¶ *As many as have spoken.* Whosoever has declared the will of God. This is to be taken in a *general* sense. The meaning is, that the prophets had *concurred* in foretelling these days. They not merely concurred in foretelling a happy future period, but they foretold *distinctly* the very things which had actually occurred respecting Jesus of Nazareth; and the Jews, therefore, should listen to the voice of their own prophets.

25. *Ye are the children of the prophets.* Greek, "Ye are the *sons* of the prophets." The meaning is, not that they were literally the *descendants* of the prophets, but that they were their *disciples*, *pupils*, *followers.* They professed to follow the prophets as their *teachers* and *guides.* Teachers among the Jews were often spoken of under the appellation of *fathers*, and disciples as *sons*, Mat. xii. 27. See Notes on Mat. i. 1. As

prophets, and of the covenant which God made with our fathers, saying unto Abraham, [b]And in thy seed shall all the kindreds of the earth be blessed.

26 Unto[c] you first, God, having raised up his Son Jesus, sent him to bless you, in [d]turning away every one of you from his iniquities.

CHAPTER IV.

AND as they spake unto the people, the priests, and the

b Ge.22.18. c Mat.10.5; Lu.24.47. d Is.59.20; Mat.1.21; Tit.2.11-14.

they were the professed disciples of the prophets, they should listen to them. As they lived among the people to whom the prophets were sent, and to whom the promises were made, they should avail themselves of the offer of mercy, and embrace the Messiah. ¶ *And of the covenant.* Ye are the *sons* of the covenant; that is, you are of the posterity of Abraham, with whom the covenant was made. The word "sons" was often thus used to denote those to whom any favour appertained, whether by inheritance or in any other way. Thus Mat. viii. 12, "The children (sons) of the kingdom;" Jn. xvii. 12, "the son of perdition." The word *covenant* denotes properly a compact or agreement between equals, or those who have a right to make such a compact, and to choose or refuse the terms. When applied to God and man, it denotes a *firm promise* on the part of God; a pledge to be regarded with all the sacredness of a compact, that he will do certain things on certain conditions. It is called a *covenant* only to designate its sacredness and the certainty of its fulfilment, not that *man* had any *right to reject* any of the terms or stipulations. As man has no such right, as he is bound to receive all that his Maker proposes, so, strictly and literally, there has been no *compact* or *covenant* between God and man. The *promise* to which Peter refers in the passage before us is in Ge. xxii. 18; xii. 3. ¶ *In thy seed.* Thy posterity. See Ro. iv. 13, 16. This promise the apostle Paul affirms had express reference to the Messiah, Ga. iii. 16. The word *seed* is used sometimes to denote an individual (Ge. iv. 25); and the apostle (Ga. iii. 16) affirms that there was special reference to Christ in the promise made to Abraham. ¶ *All the kindreds.* The word translated *kindreds* (πατριαὶ) denotes those who have a common *father* or *ancestor*, and is applied to *families.* It is also referred to those larger communities which were descended from the same ancestor, and thus refers to *nations*, Ep. iii. 15. Here it evidently refers to *all nations.* ¶ *Be blessed.* Be made happy.

26. *Unto you first.* To you who are Jews. This was the direction, that the gospel should be first preached to the Jews, beginning at Jerusalem, Lu. xxiv. 47. Jesus himself also confined his ministry entirely to the Jews. ¶ *Having raised up.* This expression does not refer to his having raised him from the dead, but is used in the same sense as in ver. 22, where God promised that he would *raise up* a prophet, and send him to teach the people. Peter means that God had *appointed* his Son Jesus, or had commissioned him to go and preach to the people to turn them away from their sins. ¶ *To bless you.* To make you happy; to fulfil the promise made to Abraham. ¶ *In turning away.* That is, by his preaching, example, death, &c. The highest blessing that can be conferred on men is to be turned from sin. Sin is the source of all woes, and if men are turned from that, they will be happy. Christ blesses no one *in* sin, or while *loving* sin, but by turning them *from* sin. This was the object which he had in view in coming, Is. lix. 20; Mat. i. 21. The design of Peter in these remarks was to show them that the Messiah had come, and that now they might look for happiness, pardon, and mercy through him. As the Jews might, so may all; and as Jesus, while living, sought to turn away men from their sins, so he does still, and still designs to bless *all nations* by the gospel which he had himself preached, and to establish which he died. All may therefore come and be blessed; and all may rejoice in the prospect that these blessings will yet be bestowed on all the kindreds of the earth. May the happy day soon come!

CHAPTER IV.

1. *The priests.* It is probable that these *priests* were a part of the Sanhe-

captain[1] of the temple, and [a] the Sadducees came upon them,

2 Being grieved that they taught the people, and preached through Jesus the resurrection from the dead.

[1] or, *ruler*. [a] Mat.22.23; ch.23.8.

drim, or great council of the nation. It is evident that they claimed some authority for preventing the preaching of the apostles. ¶ *The captain of the temple.* See Notes on Mat. xxvi. 47; Lu. xxii. 4. This was the commander of the guard stationed chiefly in the tower *Antonia*, especially during the great feasts; and it was his duty to preserve order and prevent any tumult. He came at this time to prevent a tumult or suppress a riot, as it was supposed that the teaching of the apostles and the crowd collected by the healing of the lame man would lead to a tumult. ¶ *And the Sadducees.* See Notes on Mat. iii. 7. One of the doctrines which the Sadducees maintained was, that there was no resurrection of the dead. Hence they were particularly opposed to the apostles for preaching it, because they gave so clear proof that Jesus had risen, and were thus spreading the doctrine of the resurrection among the people. ¶ *Came upon them.* This expression implies that they came in a *sudden* and *violent* manner. See Lu. xx. 1.

2. *Being grieved.* The word thus translated occurs but in one other place in the New Testament: Ac. xvi. 18. It implies more than simple *sorrow;* it was a mingled emotion of *indignation* and *anger*. They did not *grieve* because they thought it a public *calamity*, but because it interfered with their authority and opposed their doctrine. It means that it was *painful* to them, or they could *not bear it.* It is often the case that bigots, and men in authority, have this kind of *grief* at the zeal of men in spreading the truth, and thus undermining their influence and authority. ¶ *That they taught the people.* The ground of their grief was as much the fact that *they* should presume to instruct the people as the *matter* which they taught them. They were offended that unlearned Galileans, in no way connected with the priestly office, and unauthorized by *them*, should presume to set themselves up as religious teachers. *They* claimed the right to watch over the interests of the people, and to declare who was authorized to instruct the nation. It has been no unusual thing for men in ecclesiastical stations to take exceptions to the ministry of those who have not been commissioned by themselves. Such men easily fancy that all power to instruct others is lodged in their hands, and they oppose others simply from the fact that they have not derived their authority from *them.* The true question in this case was whether these Galileans gave proof that they were sent by God. The working of the miracle in this case should have been satisfactory. We have here, also, a striking instance of the fact that men may turn away from evidence, and from most important points, and fix their attention on something that opposes their prejudices, and which may be a matter of very little moment. No inquiry was made whether the *miracle* had been really wrought; but the only inquiry was whether they had conformed to *their* views of doctrine and order. ¶ *And preached through Jesus*, &c. The Sadducees would be particularly opposed to this. They denied the doctrine of the resurrection, and they were troubled that the apostles adduced proof of it so strong as the resurrection of Jesus. It was perceived that this doctrine was becoming established among the people; multitudes believed that he had risen; and if he *had* been raised up, it followed also that others would rise. The Sadducees, therefore, felt that their cause was in danger, and they joined with the priests in endeavouring to arrest its spread among the people. This is the account of the first opposition that was made to the gospel as it was preached by the apostles. It is worthy of remark that it excited so much and so speedily the enmity of those in power, and that the apostles were so soon called to test the sincerity of their attachment to their Master. They who but a few days before had fled at the approach of danger, were now called to meet this opposition, and to show their attachment to a risen Redeemer; and they did it without shrinking. They showed *now* that they were indeed the true friends of the crucified Saviour, and this remarkable change in their conduct is one of the many proofs that they were influenced from above.

3 And they laid hands on them, and put *them* in hold unto the next day: for it was now eventide.

4 Howbeit [b]many of them which heard the word believed; and the number of the men was about five thousand.

5 And it came to pass on the morrow that their rulers, and elders, and scribes,

6 And [c]Annas the high-priest, and Caiaphas, and John, and Alexander, and as many as were of the kindred of the high-priest, were gathered together at Jerusalem.

b ch.28.24. *c* Jn.18.13.

---

3. *Put* them *in hold.* That is, they took them into *custody*, or into safekeeping. Probably they committed them to the care of a guard. ¶ *Eventide.* Evening. It was not convenient to assemble the council at night. This was, moreover, the time for the evening prayer or sacrifice, and it was not usual to assemble the Sanhedrim at that hour.

4. *Howbeit.* But; notwithstanding. ¶ *Many of them*, &c. This was one of the instances, which has since been so often repeated, in which *persecution* is seen to have a tendency to extend and establish the faith which it was designed to destroy. It finally came to be a proverb that "the blood of the martyrs is the seed of the church;" and there is no lesson which men have been so slow to learn as that to *oppose* and *persecute* men is the very way to *confirm* them in their opinions and to spread their doctrines. It was supposed here that the disciples were few; that they were without power, wealth, and influence; and that it was easy to crush them at once. But God made their persecution the means of extending, in a signal manner, the truths of the gospel and the triumphs of his word. And so in all ages it has been, and so it ever will be. ¶ *And the number*, &c. It seems probable that in this number of five thousand there were included the one hundred and twenty who are mentioned in ch. i. 15, and the three thousand who were converted on the day of Pentecost, ch. ii. 41. It does not appear probable that five thousand would have been assembled and converted in *Solomon's porch* (ch. iii. 11) on occasion of the cure of the lame man. Luke doubtless means to say that, up to this time, the number of persons who had joined themselves to the apostles was about five thousand. On this supposition, the work of religion must have made a very rapid advance. How long this was after the day of Pentecost is not mentioned, but it is clear that it was at no very distant period; and the accession of near *two thousand* to the number of believers was a very striking proof of the power and presence of the Holy Spirit. ¶ *Of the men.* Of the *persons.* The word *men* is often used without reference to sex, Lu. xi. 31; Ro. iv. 8; xi. 4.

5, 6. *Their rulers.* The rulers of the Jews; doubtless the members of the *Sanhedrim*, or *great council of the nation.* Comp. ver. 15. See Notes on Mat. ii. 4; v. 22. The expression *their* rulers looks as if this book was written for the Gentiles, or Luke would have said *our* rulers. ¶ *Elders.* Presbyters, or those who were *chosen* from among the people to sit in the Sanhedrim. It is probable that the *rulers* were those who held also some other office, but were also authorized to sit in the great council. ¶ *Scribes.* See Notes on Mat. ii. 4. ¶ *And Annas*, &c. See Notes on Jn. xviii. 13. It is by no means certain that *Annas* was *at that time* the high-priest, but he *had been*, and doubtless retained the *title.* He was father-in-law to Caiaphas, the high-priest; and from this fact, together with his former dignity, he is mentioned first. ¶ *Caiaphas.* Son-in-law of Annas, and now exercising the office of the high-priest, Jn. xviii. 13. ¶ *John and Alexander*, &c. Of these persons nothing more is known. It is clear that they were members of the great council, and the mention of their names shows that the men of chief authority and influence were assembled to silence the apostles. Annas and Caiaphas had been concerned in the condemnation of Jesus, and they would now feel a special interest in arresting the progress of the gospel among the people. All the success of the gospel reflected back light upon the wickedness of the act of condemning the Lord Jesus. And this fact may serve, in part, to account for their strong desire to silence the apostles. ¶ *At Jerusalem*—εἰς. This was the usual place of assem-

7 And when they had set them in the midst, they asked, [d]By what power, or by what name, have ye done this?

8 Then Peter, [e]filled with the Holy Ghost, said unto them, Ye rulers of the people, and elders of Israel,

d Mat.21.23.

e ch.7.55.

bling the Sanhedrim. But the Jewish writers (see Lightfoot on this place) say that forty years before the destruction of the city, on account of the great increase of crime, &c., the Sanhedrim was removed from place to place. The declaration of Luke that they were now assembled *in Jerusalem*, seems to imply that they sometimes met in other places. It is probable that the members of the Sanhedrim were not in the city at the time mentioned in ver. 3, and this was the reason why the trial was deferred to the next day,

7. *In the midst.* In the presence of the great council. ¶ *By what power*, &c. A similar question was put to Christ in the temple, Mat. xxi. 23. ¶ *By what name.* That is, by whose authority. It is very probable that they expected to intimidate the apostles by this question. *They* claimed the right of regulating the religious affairs of the nation. They had vast power with the people. They assumed that all power to instruct the people should originate with them; and they expected that the apostles would be confounded, as having violated the established usage of the nation. It did not seem to occur to them to enter into an investigation of the question whether this *acknowledged* miracle did not prove that they were sent by God, but they *assumed* that they were impostors, and attempted to silence them by authority. It has been usual with the enemies of religion to attempt to *intimidate* its friends, and when *argument* fails, to attempt to *silence* Christians by appealing to their fears.

8. *Filled with the Holy Ghost.* See Notes on ch. ii. 4. ¶ *Ye rulers*, &c. Peter addressed the Sanhedrim with perfect respect. He did not call in question their authority to propose this question. He seemed to regard this as a favourable opportunity to declare the truth and state the evidence of the Christian religion. In this he acted on the principle of the injunction which he himself afterward gave (1 Pe. iii. 15), "Be ready always to give an answer to every man that asketh you a reason of the hope that is in you, with meekness and fear." Innocence is willing to be questioned; and a believer in the truth will rejoice in *any* opportunity to state the evidence of what is believed. It is remarkable, also, that this was before the great council of the nation—the body that was clothed with the highest authority. Peter could not have forgotten that before this very council, and these very men, his Master had been arraigned and condemned; nor could he have forgotten that in the very room where this same council was convened to try his Lord, *he had himself* shrunk from an honest avowal of attachment to him, and shamefully and profanely denied him. That he was now able to stand boldly before this same tribunal evinced a remarkable *change* in his feelings, and was a most clear and impressive proof of the genuineness of his repentance when he went out and wept bitterly. Comp. Lu. xxii. 54–62. And we may remark here, that one of the most clear evidences of the sincerity of repentance is when it leads to a result like this. So deeply was the heart of Peter affected by his sin (Lu. xxii. 62), and so genuine was his sorrow, that he doubtless remembered his crime on this occasion, and the memory of it inspired him with boldness. It may be further remarked, that *one* evidence of the genuineness of repentance is a desire to *repair* the evil which is done by crime. Peter had done dishonour to his Master and his cause in the presence of the great council of the nation. Nothing, on such an occasion, would be more likely to do injury to the cause than for one of the disciples of the Saviour to deny him—one of his followers to be guilty of *profaneness* and *falsehood*. But here was an opportunity, in some degree, at least, to repair the evil. Before the same council, in the same city, and in the presence of the same people, it is not an unnatural supposition that Peter rejoiced that he might have opportunity to bear *his* testimony to the divine mission of the Saviour whom he had before denied. By using the customary language of respect applied to the great council, Peter also has shown us that it is proper to evince respect for office and for those in power.

9 If we this day be examined of the good deed done to the impotent man, by what means he is made whole;

10 Be it known unto you all, and to all the people of Israel, that [f] by the name of Jesus Christ of Nazareth, whom ye crucified, whom God raised from the dead,

f ch.3.6,16.

Religion requires us to render this homage, and to treat men in office with deference, Mat. xxii. 21; Ro. xiii. 7; 1 Pe. ii. 13–17.

9. *If we this day.* If as is the fact; or since we *are* thus examined. ¶ *Examined.* Questioned; if the purpose is to institute an inquiry into this case, or since it *is* the purpose to institute such an inquiry. ¶ *The good deed.* The act of benevolence; the benefit conferred on an infirm man. He assumes that it was undeniable that the deed had been done. ¶ *To the impotent man.* To *this* man who was infirm or lame. The man was then present, ver. 10, 14. He may have been arrested with the apostles; or he may have been present as a spectator; or, as Neander supposes, he may have been summoned as a witness. ¶ *By what means.* This was the real point of the inquiry. The *fact* that he had been made whole was not denied. The only question was whether it had been done by the authority and power of Jesus of Nazareth, as Peter declared it to be, ch. iii. 6, 16.

10. *Be it known,* &c. Peter might have evaded the question, or he might have resorted to many excuses and subterfuges (Calvin), if he had been desirous of avoiding this inquiry. But it was a noble opportunity for vindicating the honour of his Lord and Master. It was a noble opportunity also for repairing the evil which he had done by his guilty denial of his Lord. Although, therefore, this frank and open avowal was attended with danger, and although it was in the presence of the great and the mighty, yet he chose to state fully and clearly his conviction of the truth. Never was there an instance of greater boldness, and never could there be a more striking illustration of the fitness of the name which the Lord Jesus gave him, that of a *rock*, Jn. i. 42; Mat. xvi. 17, 18. The timid, trembling, yielding, and vacillating Simon; he who just before was terrified by a servant-girl, and who on the lake was afraid of sinking, is now transformed into the manly, decided, and firm *Cephas*, fearless before the great council of the nation, and in an unwavering tone asserting the authority of him whom *he* had just before denied, and whom *they* had just before put to death. It is not possible to account for this change except on the supposition that this religion is true. Peter had no worldly motive to actuate him. He had no prospect of wealth or fame by this. Even the hopes of honour and preferment which the apostles had cherished before the death of Jesus, and which *might* have been supposed to influence them then, were now abandoned by them. Their Master had died, and all their hopes of human honour and power had been buried in his grave. Nothing but the conviction of the *truth* could have wrought this change, and transformed this timid disciple to a bold and uncompromising apostle. ¶ *By the name.* By the authority or power, ch. iii. 6. ¶ *Of Jesus Christ.* The union of these two names would be particularly offensive to the Sanhedrim. They *denied* that Jesus was the Christ, or the Messiah; Peter, by the use of the word *Christ,* affirmed that he was. In the language then used, it would be, "By the name of Jesus, *the Messiah.*" ¶ *Of Nazareth.* Lest there should be any mistake about his meaning, he specified that he referred to the despised *Nazarene;* to him who had just been put to death, as they supposed, covered with infamy. Christians little regard the epithets of opprobrium which may be affixed to themselves or to their religion. ¶ *Whom ye crucified.* There is emphasis in all the expressions that Peter uses. He had before charged the *people* with the crime of having put him to death, ch. ii. 23; iii. 14, 15. But he now had the opportunity, contrary to all expectation, of urging the charge with still greater force on the *rulers themselves,* on the very council which had condemned him and delivered him to Pilate. It was a remarkable providence that an opportunity was thus afforded of urging this charge in the presence of the Sanhedrim, and of proclaiming *to them* the necessity of repentance. Little did *they* imagine, when they condemned the Lord Jesus, that this charge would be so soon urged. This

even by him doth this man stand
here before you whole.
11 This is the [g] stone which
was set at nought of you builders,
which is become the head of the
corner.
12 Neither is there salvation
in any other: [h] for there is none

g Ps.118.22; Is.28.16; Mat.21.42.

h ch.10.43; 1 Ti.2.5,6.

---

is one of the instances in which God takes the wise in their own craftiness, Job v. 13. *They* had arraigned the apostles; they demanded their authority for what they had done; and thus they had directly opened the way, and invited them to the serious and solemn charge which Peter here urges against them.

11. *This is the stone.* This passage is found in Ps. cxviii. 22. It is quoted, also, by our Saviour as applicable to himself. See Notes on Mat. xxi. 42. The ancient Jews applied this to David. In the Targum on Ps. cxviii. 22, this passage is rendered, "The child who was among the sons of Jesse, and was worthy to be constituted king, the builders rejected." The New Testament writers, however, apply it without any doubt to the Messiah. Comp. Is. xxviii. 16; Ro. ix. 33; Ep. ii. 20. And from this passage we may learn that God will overrule the devices and plans of wicked men to accomplish his own purposes. What men despise and set at naught, *he* esteems of inestimable value in his kingdom. What the great and the mighty contemn, he regards as the very foundation and corner-stone of the edifice which he designs to rear. Nothing has been more remarkable than this in the history of man; and in nothing is more contempt thrown on the proud projects of men, than that what *they* have rejected God has made the very basis of his schemes.

12. *Neither is there salvation.* The word *salvation* properly denotes any *preservation*, or keeping anything in a *safe* state; a preserving from harm. It signifies, also, deliverance from *any* evil of body or mind; from pain, sickness, danger, &c., Ac. vii. 25. But it is in the New Testament applied particularly to the work which the Messiah came to do, "to seek and to *save* that which was lost," Lu. xix. 10. This work refers primarily to a deliverance of the soul *from* sin, Mat. i. 21; Ac. v. 31; Lu. iv. 18; Ro. viii. 21; Ga. v. 1. It then denotes, *as a consequence* of freedom from sin, freedom from all the ills to which sin exposes man, and the attainment of that perfect peace and joy which will be bestowed on the children of God in the heavens. The reasons why Peter introduces this subject here seem to be these: (1) He was discoursing on the *deliverance* of the man that was healed—his *salvation* from a long and painful calamity. This deliverance had been accomplished by the power of Jesus. The mention of this suggested that greater and more important *salvation* from sin and death which it was the object of the Lord Jesus to effect. As it was by *his* power that this man had been healed, so it was by *his* power only that men could be saved from death and hell. Deliverance from any temporal calamity should lead the thoughts to that higher redemption which the Lord Jesus contemplates in regard to the soul. (2) This was a favourable opportunity to introduce the doctrines of the gospel to the notice of the great council of the nation. The occasion invited to it; the mention of a *part* of the work of Jesus invited to a contemplation of his *whole* work. Peter would not have done justice to the character and work of Christ if he had not introduced that great design which he had in view to save men from death and hell. It is probable, also, that he advanced a sentiment in which he expected they would immediately *concur*, and which accorded with their well-known opinions, that salvation was to be obtained only by the Messiah. Thus Paul (Ac. xxvi. 22, 23) says that he taught nothing else than what was delivered by Moses and the prophets, &c. Comp. Ac. xxiii. 6; xxvi. 6. The apostles did not *pretend* to proclaim any doctrine which was not delivered by Moses and the prophets, and which did not, in fact, constitute a part of the *creed* of the Jewish nation. ¶ *In any other.* Any other person. He does not mean to say that *God* is not able to save, but that the salvation of the human family is intrusted to the hands of Jesus the Messiah. ¶ *For there is none other name.* This is an explanation of what he had said in the previous part of the verse. The word *name* here is used to denote the person himself—there is no other *being* or *person*. As

other [i]name under heaven given among men whereby we must be saved.

i Ps.45.17.

we would say, there is *no one* who can save but Jesus Christ. The word *name* is often used in this sense. See Notes on iii. 6, 16. That there is no *other* Saviour, or mediator between God and man, is abundantly taught in the New Testament; and it is, indeed, the main design of revelation to prove this. See 1 Ti. ii. 5, 6; Ac. x. 43. ¶ *Under heaven.* This expression does not materially differ from the one immediately following, "among men." They are designed to express with emphasis the sentiment that salvation is to be obtained in *Christ alone*, and not in any patriarch, or prophet, or teacher, or king, or in any false Messiah. ¶ *Given.* In this word it is implied that *salvation* has its origin in God; that a Saviour for men must be *given* by him; and that salvation cannot be originated by any power among men. The Lord Jesus is thus uniformly represented as *given* or *appointed* by God for this great purpose (Jn. iii. 16; xvii. 4; 1 Co. iii. 5; Ga. i. 4; ii. 20; Ep. i. 22; v. 25; 1 Ti. ii. 6; Ro. v. 15–18, 23); and hence Christ is called the "unspeakable gift" of God, 2 Co. ix. 15. ¶ *Whereby we must be saved.* By which it is *fit*, or proper (δεῖ), that we should be saved. There is no other way of salvation that is *adapted* to the great object contemplated, and therefore, if saved, it must be in this way and by this plan. The schemes of men's own devices are *not adapted* to the purpose, and therefore cannot save. The doctrine that men can be saved *only* by Jesus Christ is abundantly taught in the Scriptures. To show the failure of all other schemes of religion was the great design of the first part of the epistle to the Romans. By a laboured argument Paul there shows (ch. i.) that the *Gentiles* had failed in their attempt to justify themselves; and in ch. ii. iii. that the same thing was true also of the Jews. If *both* these schemes failed, then there was need of some *other* plan, and that plan was that by Jesus Christ. If it be asked, then, whether this affirmation of Peter is to be understood as having respect to *infants* and *the heathen*, we may remark, (1) That his design was primarily to address the Jews, "Whereby *we* must be saved." But, (2) The same thing is doubtless true of others. If, as Christians generally believe, infants are saved, there is no absurdity in supposing that it is by the merits of the atonement. *But* for that there would have been no promise of salvation to any of the human race. No offer *has* been made except by the Mediator; and to him, doubtless, is to be ascribed all the glory of raising up even those in infancy to eternal life. If any of the heathen are to be saved, as most Christians suppose, and as seems in accordance with the mercy of God, it is no less certain that it will be in consequence of the intervention of Christ. Those who will be brought to heaven will sing one song (Re. v. 9), and will be prepared for eternal union in the service of God in the skies. Still, the Scriptures have *not* declared that *great numbers* of the heathen will be saved who have not the gospel. The contrary is more than implied in the New Testament, Ro. ii. 12. Neither has the Scripture affirmed that *all* the heathen will certainly be cut off. It has been discovered by missionaries among the heathen that individuals have, in a remarkable way, been convinced of the folly of idolatry, and were seeking a better religion; that their minds were in a serious, thoughtful, inquiring state; and that they *at once* embraced the gospel when it was offered to them as *exactly* adapted to their state of mind, and as meeting their inquiries. Such was extensively the case in the Sandwich Islands; and the following instance recently occurred in this country: "The Flathead Indians, living west of the Rocky Mountains, recently sent a deputation to the white settlements to inquire after the Bible. The circumstance that led to this singular movement is as follows: It appears that a white man (Mr. Catlin) had penetrated into their country, and happened to be a spectator at one of their religious ceremonies. He informed them that their mode of worshipping the Supreme Being was radically wrong, and that the people away towards the rising of the sun had been put in possession of the true mode of worshipping the Great Spirit. On receiving this information, they called a national council to take this subject into consideration. Some said, if this be true, it is certainly high time we were put in possession of this

13 Now when they saw the boldness of Peter and John, and perceived that they were [k] unlearned and ignorant men, they

k Mat.11.25; 1 Co.1.27.

mode. They accordingly deputed four of the chiefs to proceed to St. Louis to see their great father, General Clark, to inquire of him the truth of this matter. They were cordially received by the general, who gave them a succinct history of revelation, and the necessary instruction relative to their important mission. Two of them sunk under the severe toils attending a journey of 3000 miles. The remaining two, after acquiring what knowledge they could of the Bible, its institutions and precepts, returned, to carry back those few rays of divine light to their benighted countrymen." In *what way* their minds were led to this state we cannot say, or how this *preparation* for the gospel was connected with the *agency* and *merits* of Christ we perhaps cannot understand; but we know that the affairs of *this entire world* are placed under the control of Christ (Jn. xvii. 2; Ep. i. 21, 22), and that the arrangements of events by which such men were brought to this state of mind are in his hands. Another remark may here be made. It is, that it often occurs that blessings come upon us *from benefactors whom we do not see, and from sources which we cannot trace.* On this principle we receive *many* of the mercies of life; and from anything that appears, in this way many blessings of salvation may be conferred on the world, and possibly many of the heathen be saved. Still, this view does not interfere with the command of Christ to preach the gospel, Mar. xvi. 15. *The great mass of the heathen* are not in this state; but the fact here adverted to, so far as it goes, is an encouragement to preach the gospel to the entire world. If *Christ* thus prepares the way; if he extensively fits the minds of the heathen for the reception of the gospel; if he shows them the evil and folly of their own system, and leads them to desire a better, then this should operate not to produce indolence, but activity, and zeal, and encouragement to enter into the field white for the harvest, and to toil that *all* who seek the truth, and are *prepared* to embrace the gospel, may be brought to the light of the Sun of righteousness.

13. *Boldness.* This word properly denotes *openness* or *confidence in speaking.* It stands opposed to *hesitancy*, and to *equivocation* in declaring our sentiments. Here it means that, in spite of danger and opposition, they avowed their doctrines without any attempt to conceal or disguise them. ¶ *Peter and John.* It was they only who had been concerned in the healing of the lame man, ch. iii. 1. ¶ *And perceived.* When they knew that they were unlearned. This might have been ascertained either by report or by the manner of their speaking. ¶ *Unlearned.* This word properly denotes those who were not acquainted with *letters*, or who had not had the benefit of an education. ¶ *Ignorant men*—ἰδιῶται. This word properly denotes those who live in private, in contradistinction from those who are engaged in *public* life or in office. As this class of persons is commonly also supposed to be less learned, talented, and refined than those in office, it comes to denote those who are rude and illiterate. The idea intended to be conveyed here is, that these men had not had opportunities of education (comp. Mat. iv. 18–21), and had not been accustomed to public speaking, and hence they were surprised at their boldness. This same character is uniformly attributed to the early preachers of Christianity. Comp. 1 Co. i. 27; Mat. xi. 25. The Galileans were regarded by the Jews as particularly rude and uncultivated, Mat. xxvi. 73; Mar. xiv. 17. ¶ *They marvelled.* They *wondered* that men who had not been educated in the schools of the Rabbins, and accustomed to speak in public, should declare their sentiments with so much boldness. ¶ *And they took knowledge.* This expression means simply that *they knew*, or that they obtained evidence that they had been with Jesus. It is not said *in what way* they obtained this evidence, but the connection leads us to suppose it was by the *miracle* which they had wrought, by their firm and bold declaration of the doctrines of Jesus, and perhaps by the irresistible conviction that none *would* be thus bold who had not been personally with him, and who had not the firmest conviction that he was the Messiah. They had not been trained in their schools, and their boldness could not be attributed to the arts

marvelled; and they took knowledge of them that they had been with Jesus.

14 And beholding the man which was healed standing with them, they [l]could say nothing against it.

15 But when they had com-

[l] ch.19.36.

of rhetoric, but was the native, ingenuous, and manly exhibition of a deep conviction of the truth of what they spoke, and that conviction could have been obtained only by their having been *with* him, and having been satisfied that he was the Messiah. Such conviction is of far more value in preaching than all the mere teachings of the schools; and *without* such a conviction, all preaching will be frigid, hypocritical, and useless. ¶ *Had been with Jesus.* Had been his followers, and had attended personally on his ministry. They gave evidence that they had *seen* him, been with him, heard him, and were convinced that he was the Messiah. We may learn here, (1) That if men wish to be successful in preaching, it must be based on deep and thorough conviction of the truth of that which they deliver. (2) They who preach should give evidence that they are acquainted with the Lord Jesus Christ; that they have imbibed his spirit, pondered his instructions, studied the evidences of his divine mission, and are thoroughly convinced that he was from God. (3) Boldness and success in the ministry, as well as in everything else, will depend far more on honest, genuine, thorough conviction of the truth than on the endowments of talent and learning, and the arts and skill of eloquence. No man should attempt to preach without such a thorough conviction of truth; and no man who has it will preach in vain. (4) God often employs the ignorant and unlearned to confound the wise, 1 Co. i. 27, 28. But it is not *by* their ignorance. It was not the ignorance of Peter and John that convinced the Sanhedrim. It was done *in spite* of their ignorance. It was their *boldness* and their honest conviction of truth. Besides, though not learned in the schools of the Jews, they had been under a far more important training, under the personal direction of Christ himself, for three years; and now they were directly endowed by the Holy Ghost with the power of speaking with tongues. Though not taught in the schools, yet there was an important sense in which they were *not* unlearned and ignorant men. Their example should not, therefore, be pled in favour of an unlearned ministry. Christ himself expressed his opposition to an unlearned ministry by *teaching them himself*, and then by bestowing on them miraculous endowments which no learning at present can furnish. It may be remarked, further, that in the single selection which *he* made of an apostle after his ascension to heaven, when he came to choose one who had *not* been under his personal teaching, he chose *a learned man*, the apostle Paul, and thus evinced his purpose that there should be *training* or *education* in those who are invested with the sacred office. (5) Yet in the case before us there is a striking proof of the truth and power of religion. These men had not acquired their boldness in the schools; they were not trained for argument among the Jews; they did not meet them by cunning sophistry; but they came with the honest conviction that what they were saying was true. Were they deceived? Were they not competent to bear witness? Had they any motive to attempt to palm a falsehood on men? Infidelity must answer *many* such questions as these before the apostles can be convicted of imposture.

14. *They could say nothing*, &c. The presence of the man that was healed was an unanswerable fact in proof of the truth of what the apostles alleged. The miracle was so public, clear, and decisive; the man that was healed was so well known, that there was no evasion or subterfuge by which they could escape the conclusion to which the apostles were conducting them. It evinced no little gratitude in the man that was healed that he was present on this occasion, and showed that he was deeply interested in what befell his benefactors. The miracles of Jesus and his apostles were such that they could not be denied, and hence the Jews did not *attempt* to deny that they wrought them. Comp. Mat. xii. 24; Jn. xi. 45, 46; Ac. xix. 36.

15–18. *What shall we do to these men?* The object which they had in view was evidently to prevent their preaching. The miracle was wrought, and it was believed by the people to have been

manded them to go aside out of the council, they conferred among themselves,

16 Saying, [m] What shall we do to these men? for that indeed a notable miracle hath been done by them *is* manifest to all them that dwell at Jerusalem; and we cannot deny *it*.

17 But that it spread no further among the people, let us straitly threaten them, [n] that they speak henceforth to no man in this name.

18 And they called them, and commanded them not to speak at all nor teach in the name of Jesus.

19 But Peter and John answered and said unto them, Whether it be right in the sight of God [o] to

m Jn.11.47. n ch.5.40. o ch.5.29.

wrought. This they could not expect to be able successfully to deny. Their only object, therefore, was to prevent the apostles from making the use which they saw they would to convince the people that Jesus was the Messiah. The question was, in what way they should *prevent* this; whether by putting them to death, by imprisoning them, or by scourging them; or whether by simply exerting their *authority* and forbidding them. From the former they were deterred, doubtless, by fear of the multitude; and they therefore adopted the latter, and seemed to suppose that the mere exertion of their authority would be sufficient to deter them from this in future. ¶ *The council.* Greek, The *Sanhedrim.* This body was composed of seventy-one or seventy-two persons, and was intrusted with the principal affairs of the nation. It was a body of vast influence and power, and hence they supposed that their command might be sufficient to restrain ignorant Galileans from speaking. Before this same body, and probably the same men, our Saviour was arraigned, and by them condemned before he was delivered to the Roman governor, Mat. xxvi. 59, &c. And before this same body, and in the presence of the same men, Peter had just before denied his Lord, Mat. xxvi. 70, &c. The fact that the disciples had fled on a former occasion, and that Peter had denied his Saviour, may have operated to induce them to believe that they would be terrified by their threats, and deterred from preaching publicly in the name of Jesus. ¶ *A notable miracle.* A known, undeniable miracle. ¶ *That it spread.* That the *knowledge* of it may not spread among them any farther. ¶ *Let us straitly threaten them.* Greek, *Let us threaten them with a threat.* This is a *Hebraism* expressing *intensity*, *certainty*, &c. The *threat* was a *command* (ver. 18) not to teach, implying their displeasure if they did do it. This threat, however, was not effectual. On the next occasion, which occurred soon after (ch. v. 40), they added *beating* to their threats in order to deter them from preaching in the name of Jesus.

19. *Whether it be right*, &c. The apostles abated nothing of their boldness when threatened. They openly appealed to their judges whether their command could be right. And in doing this, they expressed their full conviction of the truth of what they had said, and their deliberate purpose not to regard their command, but still to proclaim to the people the truth that Jesus was the Messiah. ¶ *In the sight of God.* That is, whether *God* will judge this to be right. The grand question was how *God* would regard it. If *he* disapproved it, it was wrong. It was not merely a question pertaining to their reputation, safety, or life; it was a question of conscience before God. We have here a striking instance of the principle on which Christians act. It is, to lay their safety, reputation, and life out of view, and bring everything to the test WHETHER IT WILL PLEASE GOD. If it will, it is right; if it will not, it is wrong. ¶ *To hearken.* To *hear* and to *hearken* are often used to denote *to obey*, Jn. v. 24; viii. 47, &c. ¶ *Judge ye.* This was an appeal to them directly as judges and as men. And it may be presumed that it was an appeal which they could not resist. The Sanhedrim acknowledged itself to have been appointed by God, and to have no authority which was not derived from his appointment. Of course, God could modify, supersede, or repeal their authority; and the abstract principle that it was better to obey God than man they could not call in question. The only inquiry was whether they had *evidence* that God had issued any command in the case. Of

hearken unto you more than unto God, judge ye.

20 For[p] we cannot but speak

p Je.20.9.

that the apostles were satisfied, and that the rulers could not deny. It may be remarked that this is one of the first and most bold appeals on record in favour of the right of private judgment and the liberty of conscience. That liberty was supposed in all the Jewish religion. It was admitted that the authority of God in all matters was superior to that of man. And the same spirit manifested itself thus early in the Christian church against all dominion over the conscience, and in favour of the right to follow the dictates of the conscience and the will of God. As a mere historical fact, therefore, it is interesting to contemplate this, and still more interesting in its important bearings on human liberty and human happiness. The doctrine is still more explicitly stated in ch. v. 29, "We ought to obey God rather than man."

20. *For*, &c. This is given as a reason why they should obey God rather than man. They had had so clear evidence that God had sent the Messiah, and they had received a direct and solemn command (Mar. xvi. 15) to preach the gospel, that they could not be restrained. There was a necessity laid on them to preach. See 1 Co. ix. 16. Comp. Je. xx. 9; Ac. xviii. 5; Job xxxii. 18, 19; Ps. xxxix. 1–3.

It has already been remarked that these two verses contain an important *principle* in favour of religious *liberty*—the liberty of conscience and of private judgment. They contain the *great principle* of Christianity and of the *Protestant* religion, that the responsibility of men for their religious opinions is direct to God, and that other men have no power of control. The opposite of this is tyranny and oppression. It may be proper, in addition, to present some further remarks, involved in the principle here stated. (1) Religion, from the beginning, has been favourable to *liberty*. There was no principle more sacred among the Jews than that they were to be independent of other nations. Perhaps no people have ever been so restive under a foreign yoke, so prone to rebel, and so difficult to be broken down by oppression and by arms, as were the Jews. So true was this, that it appeared to other nations to be mere obstinacy. They were often subdued, but they rose against their oppressors and threw off the yoke. No people have been found who were so difficult to be reduced to slavery. It is well known that the Romans were accustomed to subject the captives taken in war to perpetual servitude; and *commonly* the spirit of the captive was broken, and he remained quietly in bondage. But not so the Jew. Nothing ever tamed his spirit. No bribes, or threats, or chains could induce him to violate the laws of his religion. Even in captivity, we are told that the Jewish slaves at Rome *would* observe the Sabbath; would keep the feasts of their nation, and would never conform to the customs of an idolatrous people. To the Romans this appeared to be mere obstinacy. But it was the genius of their religion. The right of liberty of thought was one which they would not surrender. The spirit of the patriarchs was favourable to liberty, and implied responsibility only to God. Familiarity with the sacred books had taught them these lessons, and neither time nor distance could obliterate them. In the time of Christ, the great mass of the nation were evidently *opposed* to the tax paid to the Roman nation, and sighed under this burden, until they rose and attempted to assert their rights; and their city, and temple, and land were sacrificed rather than *yield* this great principle. (2) This same principle was evinced by the apostles and by the early Christians. With this doctrine fresh upon their hearts, they went forth to other lands. They maintained it at the expense of their blood, and thousands fell as martyrs in the cause of liberty and of private judgment in religion. No men ever more firmly defended liberty than the early martyrs; and each one that died, died in defence of a principle which is now the acknowledged right of all men. (3) The designs of tyranny and superstition have been to destroy this principle. This was the aim of the Sanhedrim; and yet, when Peter and John appealed to their *consciences*, they did not dare to avow their purpose. This has been the aim of all tyrants, and this the effect of all superstition. Hence the Church of Rome has taken away the Scriptures from the people, and has thus furnished incontestable evidence that in its view the Bible

the things [q] which we have seen
and heard.
21 So when they had further
threatened them, they let them go,
finding nothing how they might
punish them, [r] because of the people:
for all men glorified God for that
which was done.

q ch.22.15; 1 Jn.1.1,3.

r Mat.21.26; ch.5.26.

---

is favourable to liberty. For centuries tyranny reigned in one black night over Europe; nor was the darkness dispelled until the Bible, that taught men the principles of freedom, was restored to them. (4) The effect of the principle avowed by the apostles had been uniform. Luther began the Reformation by finding in a monastery a copy of the Bible, a book which till that time—when more than twenty years of age—he had never seen. The effect on the liberties of Europe was immediately seen. Hume admitted that whatever liberty England possessed was to be traced to the Puritans. Our own land (America) is a striking instance of the effect of this great principle, and of its influence on the rights of man. And just in proportion as the New Testament is spread abroad will men seek for freedom and break the chains of oppression. The best way to promote universal liberty is to spread the Bible to the ends of the earth. There is not a precept in it that is not favourable to freedom. It tends to enlarge and liberalize the mind; to teach men their rights; to put an end to *ignorance*, the universal stronghold of superstition and tyranny; and to diffuse the love of justice, truth, and order. It shows man that he is responsible to God, and that no one has a right to ordain anything which contravenes the liberty of his fellow.

If it be asked here what the principle is, I answer, (1) That men have a right to their private judgment in matters of religion, subject only to God. The *only* restraint which, it is now settled, can be imposed on this, is, that no man has a right, under pretence of conscience, to injure or molest his fellow-men, or to disturb the peace and harmony of society. (2) No magistrate, church, council, or parent, has a right to *impose* a creed on others, and to demand subscription to it by mere authority. (3) No magistrate, church, or parent, has a right to *control* the free exercise of private judgment in this case. The power of a *parent* is to teach, advise, and entreat. The duty of a child is to listen with respect; to examine with candour; to pray over the subject, and to be deliberate and calm, not rash, hasty, impetuous, and self-willed. But when the child is thus convinced that his duty to God requires a particular course, then here is a *higher* obligation than any earthly law, and he must obey God rather than man, even a father or a mother, Mat. x. 37, 38. (4) Every man *is* responsible to God for his opinions and his conduct. Man may not control him, but God may and will. The great question before every man is, *What is right in the sight of God?* It is not, What is expedient, or safe, or pleasurable, or honourable among men? but, What is right in the sight of God? Neither in their opinions nor their conduct are men free from responsibility. From this whole subject we see the duty of spreading the Bible. If we love liberty; if we hate tyranny and superstition; if we wish to extend the knowledge of the rights of man, and break every arm of oppression, let us spread far and wide the Book of God, and place in every palace and every cottage on the globe a copy of the sacred Scriptures.

21. *Finding nothing*, &c. That is, not being able to devise any way of punishing them without exciting a tumult among the people, and endangering their own authority. The Sanhedrim was frequently influenced by this fear; and it shows that their own authority was much dependent on the caprice of the multitude. Comp. Mat. xxi. 26. ¶ *All men.* That is, the great mass or body of the people. ¶ *Glorified God. Praised* God for the miracle. This implies, (1) That they believed that the miracle was genuine. (2) That they were grateful to God for so signal a mercy in conferring health and comfort on a man who had been long afflicted. We may add further, that here is the highest evidence of the reality of the miracle. Even the Sanhedrim, with all their prejudice and opposition, did not call it in question; and the common people, who had doubtless been acquainted with this man for years, were convinced that it was real. It would have been impossible to *impose* on keen-sighted and jealous adversaries in this manner if this had been an imposture.

22. *For the man*, &c. The *age* of the

22 For the man was above forty years old on whom this miracle of healing was showed.
23 And being let go, [s]they went to their own company, and reported all that the chief priests and elders had said unto them.

24 And when they heard that, they lifted up their voice to God with one accord, and said, [t]Lord, thou *art* God, which hast made heaven and earth, and the sea, and all that in them is;
25 Who by the mouth of thy

s ch.2.44–46.

t 2 Ki.19.15.

man is mentioned to show the certainty and greatness of the miracle. If it had been a man who had been lame but a few years, or if it had been a child or a very young man, the case would not been so remarkable. But after a continuance of forty years, all hope of healing him by any ordinary means must have been abandoned, and all pretence that this was jugglery or deception must have been absurd.

23. *Their own company.* They joined the other apostles and Christians, ch. ii. 44, 45. ¶ *And reported,* &c. It doubtless became a subject of interesting inquiry what they should do in this case. They had been *threatened* by the highest authority of the nation, and *commanded* not to preach again in the name of Jesus. Whether they should obey them and be silent, or whether they should leave Jerusalem and preach elsewhere, could not but be an interesting subject of inquiry, and they very properly sought the counsel of their brethren, and looked to God for direction, an example which all should follow who are exposed to persecution, or who are in any perplexity about the path of duty.

24. *They lifted up their voice.* To lift up the voice, among the Hebrews, was a phrase denoting either an address to the people (Ju. ix. 7), or a phrase expressive of *weeping* (Ge. xxix. 11; Ju. ii. 4; Ru. i. 9; 1 Sa. xxiv. 16), or of *prayer.* To lift up the voice *to God* means simply they *prayed* to him. ¶ *With one accord.* Unitedly. Properly, with one *mind* or purpose. See Notes on ch. i. 14. The *union* of the early Christians is often noticed in the Acts of the Apostles. Thus far there was no jar or dissension in their society, and everything has the appearance of the most entire affection and confidence. ¶ *Lord.* Greek, Δέσποτα — *Despota.* From this word is derived the word *despot.* This is not the usual word employed by which to address God. The word commonly translated *Lord* is Κυρίος—*Kurios.* The word here used denotes one who rules over others, and was applied to the highest magistrate or officer. It denotes authority; power; *absoluteness* in ruling. It is a word denoting more authority in *ruling* than the other. That more commonly denotes a *property* in a thing; this denotes absolute *rule.* It is applied *to God* in Lu. ii. 29; Re. vi. 10; Jude 4; *to Jesus Christ,* 2 Pe. ii. 1; *to masters,* 1 Ti. vi. 1; Tit. ii. 9; 1 Pe. ii. 18; *to husbands,* 1 Pe. iii. 6; and *to a possessor* or *owner,* 2 Ti. ii. 21. ¶ *Thou* art *God.* This ascription of praise seems to have been designed to denote their sense of his *power* to deliver them, and of his *right* to dispose of them. They were employed in his service; they were encompassed with dangers; and they acknowledged him as *their* God, who had made all things, and who had an entire right to direct, and to dispose of them for his own glory. In times of danger and perplexity we should remember that God has a right to do with us as he pleases; and we should go cheerfully, and commit ourselves into his hands. ¶ *Which hast made,* &c., Ge. i. This passage is taken directly from Ps. cxlvi. 6. Comp. Re. xiv. 7.

25. *Who by the mouth,* &c., Ps. ii. 1, 2. This is a strong, solemn testimony to the inspiration of David. It is a declaration of the apostles, made in solemn prayer, that *God* himself spake by the mouth of David. This is the *second* part of their prayer. In the first, they acknowledge the right of God to rule; in this, they appeal to a prophecy; they plead that this was a thing foretold; and as *God* had foreseen it and foretold it, they appealed to him to protect them. The times of tumult and opposition which had been foreseen, as about to attend the introduction of the gospel, had now come. They inferred, therefore, that Jesus was the Messiah; and as God had designed to establish *his* kingdom, they appealed to him to aid and protect them in this great work.

servant David hast said, [u] Why did the heathen rage, and the people imagine vain things?

u Ps.2.1,2.

26 The kings of the earth stood up, and the rulers were gathered together, against the Lord, and against his Christ.

This passage is taken from Ps. ii. 1, 2, and is an exact quotation from the Septuagint. This proves that the Psalm had reference to the *Messiah*. Thus it was manifestly understood by the Jews; and the authority of the apostles settles the question. The Psalm was composed by David, but on what occasion is not known; nor is it material to our present purpose. It has been a matter of inquiry whether it referred to the Messiah *primarily*, or only in a *secondary* sense. Grotius supposes that it was composed by David when exposed to the hostility of the Assyrians, the Moabites, Philistines, Amalekites, &c.; and that, in the midst of his dangers, he sought consolation in the *purpose* of God to establish him and his kingdom. But the more probable opinion is, that it referred *directly* and *solely* to the Messiah. ¶ *Why did the heathen.* The nations which were not Jews. This refers, doubtless, to the opposition which would be made to the spread of Christianity, and not *merely* to the opposition made to the Messiah himself, and to the act of putting him to death. ¶ *Rage.* This word refers to the excitement and tumult of a *multitude;* not a settled *plan*, but rather the heated and disorderly conduct of a *mob*. It means that the progress of the gospel would encounter tumultuous opposition, and that the excited nations would rush violently to put it down and destroy it. ¶ *And the people.* The expression "the people" does not refer to a class of men different essentially from the heathen. The "heathen," Heb. and Greek, "*the nations*," refer to men as *organized* into communities; the expression *the people* is used to denote the same persons without respect to their being so organized. The Hebrews were in the habit, in their poetry, of expressing the same idea essentially in parallel members of a sentence; that is, the last member of a sentence or verse expressed the same idea, with some slight variation, as the former. (See Lowth on the sacred poetry of the Hebrews.) ¶ *Imagine.* The word *imagine* does not quite express the force of the original. The Hebrew and the Greek both convey the idea of *meditating, thinking, purposing.* It means that they employed *thought, plan, purpose*, in opposing the Messiah. ¶ *Vain things.* The word here used (κενά) is a literal translation of the Hebrew (ריק), and means usually *empty*, as a vessel which is not filled; then *useless*, or that which amounts to nothing, &c. Here it means that they devised a plan which *turned out* to be vain or ineffectual. They attempted an opposition to the Messiah which could not succeed. God would establish his kingdom in spite of their plans to oppose it. *Their* efforts were vain because they were not strong enough to oppose God; because he had purposed to establish the kingdom of his Son; and because he could overrule even their opposition to advance his cause.

26. *The kings of the earth.* The Psalmist specifies more particularly that *kings* and *rulers* would be opposed to the Messiah. This had occurred already by the opposition made to the Messiah by the rulers of the Jewish people, and it would be still more evinced by the opposition of princes and kings as the gospel spread among the nations. ¶ *Stood up.* The word here used (παρίστημι) commonly means to present one's self, or to stand forth, for the purpose of aiding, counselling, &c. But here it means that they *rose*, or *presented themselves*, to evince their opposition. They stood opposed to the Messiah, and offered resistance to him. ¶ *The rulers.* This is another instance of the Hebrew *parallelism*. The word does not denote another class of men from kings, but expresses the same idea in another form, or in a more general manner, meaning that all classes of persons in authority would be opposed to the gospel. ¶ *Were gathered together.* Hebrew, *consulted together;* were *united* in a consultation. The Greek implies that they were *assembled* for the purpose of consultation. ¶ *Against the Lord.* In the Hebrew, "against *Jehovah*." This is the peculiar name which is given in the Scriptures to God. They rose against his plan of appointing a Messiah, and against the Messiah whom he had chosen. ¶ *Against his Christ.* Hebrew, against his *Messiah*, or his Anointed. See Notes on Mat. i. 1. This

27 For of a truth against thy holy child Jesus, whom thou hast anointed, both [v]Herod and Pontius Pilate, with the Gentiles and the people of Israel, were gathered together,

28 For[w] to do whatsoever thy

v Lu.23.1-8,&c.

w ch.3.18.

is one of the places where the word *Messiah* is used in the Old Testament. The word occurs in about forty places, and is commonly translated *his anointed*, and is applied to kings. The *direct* reference of the word to the Messiah in the Old Testament is not frequent. This passage implies that opposition to the *Messiah* is opposition to *Jehovah*. And this is uniformly supposed in the sacred Scriptures. He that is opposed to Christ is opposed to God. He that neglects him neglects God. He that despises him despises God, Mat. x. 40; xviii. 5; Jn. xii. 44, 45; Lu. x. 16, "He that despiseth me, despiseth him that sent me." The reasons of this are: (1) That the Messiah is "the brightness of the Father's glory, and the express image of his person," He. i. 3. (2) He is equal with the Father, possessing the same attributes and the same power, Jn. i. 1; Phi. ii. 6. (3) He is *appointed* by God to this great work of saving men. To despise him, or to oppose him, is to despise and oppose him who appointed him to this work, to contemn his counsels, and to set him at naught. (4) His work is dear to God. It has engaged his thoughts. It has been approved by him. His mission has been confirmed by the miraculous power of the Father, and by every possible manifestation of his approbation and love. To oppose the Messiah is, therefore, to oppose that which is dear to the heart of God, and which has long been the object of his tender solicitude. It follows from this, that they who *neglect* the Christian religion are exposing themselves to the displeasure of God, and endangering their everlasting interests. No man is safe who opposes God; and no man can have evidence that God will approve him who does not embrace the Messiah, whom He has appointed to redeem the world.

27. *For of a truth.* Truly; in reality. ¶ *Thy holy child Jesus.* The word *child* is commonly applied to *infants*, or to sons and daughters in very early life. The word which is used here (παῖς) is different from that which is commonly applied to the Lord Jesus (υἱός). The latter expresses sonship without respect to age. The word which is here used also sometimes expresses sonship without any regard to age, and the word *son* would have been a more happy translation. Thus the same word is translated in Ac. iii. 13, 26. In Ac. xx. 12, it is translated "young man." ¶ *Both Herod,* &c. Lu. xxiii. 1–12. ¶ *With the Gentiles.* The Romans, to whom he was delivered to be crucified. ¶ *The people of Israel.* The Jews, who were excited to this by the rulers, Mat. xxvii. 20.

28. *For to do,* &c. See Notes on ch. ii. 23; iii. 18. The *facts* which are brought to view in these verses are among the most remarkable on record. They are briefly these: (1) That the Jewish rulers were opposed to the Messiah, and slew him. (2) That the very people to whom he came, and for whose benefit he laboured, joined in the opposition, so that it became the act of a united people. (3) That the Romans, who were there as a sort of representation of all pagan nations, were easily prevailed on to join in the persecution, and to become the executioners. (4) That thus opposite factions, and dissimilar and prejudiced people, became united in opposing the Messiah. (5) That the rulers of the Roman people, the emperors, the statesmen, the philosophers, and the rulers of other nations, united to oppose the gospel, and brought all the power of persecution to stay its progress. (6) That the *people* of the empire, the *mass* of men, were easily prevailed upon to join in the persecution, and to endeavour to arrest its progress. It may be added, (7) That the gospel has encountered similar difficulties and opposition wherever it has been faithfully presented to the attention of men. It has become a very serious question *why* this has been; on what pretence this opposition has been vindicated, or how it can be accounted for—a question which it is of as much importance for the infidel as for the Christian to settle. We know that accusations of the corrupt lives of the early Christians were freely circulated, and that most gross accounts of their scandalous conduct were propagated by those who chose to persecute them. (See Lardner's *Credibility.*) But such

hand and thy counsel [x]determined before to be done.

29 And now, Lord, behold their threatenings: and grant unto thy

x Pr.21.30; Is.46.10; 53.10.

accounts are not now believed, and it is not certain that they were *ever* seriously believed by the rulers of the pagan people. It is certain that it was not on *this* account that the first opposition arose to Christ and his religion.

It is not proper here to enter into an examination of the causes of this opposition. We may state the outlines, however, in few words. (1) The Jewish *rulers* were mortified, humbled, and moved with envy, that one so poor and despised should claim to be the Messiah. They had expected a Messiah of a different rank and character; and all their prejudices rose at once against *his* claims to this high office, Mat. xxvii. 18; Mar. xv. 10. (2) The common people, disposed extensively to acknowledge his claims, were urged on by the enraged and vindictive priests to demand his death, Mat. xxvii. 20. (3) Pilate was pressed on against his will by the impetuous and enraged multitude to deliver one whom he regarded as innocent. (4) The Christian religion, in its advances, struck at once at the whole fabric of superstition in the Roman empire and throughout the world. It did not, like other religions, ask a place *amidst* the religions already existing. It was *exclusive* in its claims. It denounced *all* other systems as idolatry or superstition, and sought to overthrow them. Those religions were interwoven with all the habits of the people; they were connected with all the departments of the state; they gave occupation to a vast number of priests and other officers who obtained their livelihood by the existing superstitions, and who brought, of course, all the supposed sacredness of their character to support them. A religion which attempted to overthrow the whole fabric, therefore, at once excited all their malice. The monarchs whose thrones were based on the existing state of things, and the people who venerated the religion of their ancestors, would be opposed to the new system. (5) Christianity was despised. It was regarded as one form of the superstition of the Jews, and there were no people who were regarded with so much contempt by other nations as the Jews. The writings of the Romans on this point are full proof. (6) The new religion was opposed to all the *crimes* of the world. It began its career in a time of eminent wickedness. It plunged at once into the midst of that wickedness; sought the great cities where crimes and pollutions were concentrated, and boldly reproved every form of prevailing impiety. At Athens, at Corinth, at Ephesus, at Rome itself, it denounced the judgment of God against every form of guilt. Whatever may be charged on the apostles, it will *not* be alleged that they were *timid* in denouncing the sins of the world. From all these causes it is not wonderful that the early Christians were persecuted. If it be asked (7) Why the same religion meets with opposition now in lands that are nominally Christian, it may be remarked, (*a*) that the human heart is the same that it always was, opposed to truth and righteousness; (*b*) that religion encounters still a host of sins that are opposed to it—pride, envy, malice, passion, and the love of the world; (*c*) that there has always been a peculiar opposition in the human heart to receiving salvation as the gift of God through a crucified Redeemer; and (*d*) that all the forms of vice, and lust, and profaneness that exist in the world, are opposed, and ever will be, to a religion of purity, self-denial, and love.

On the whole, we may remark here, (1) That the fact that Christianity has been thus opposed, and has triumphed, is no small proof of its divine origin. It has been *fairly tried*, and still survives. It was well to put it to the *test*, and to bring to bear on it everything which had a tendency to crush it, and thus to furnish the highest proof that it is from God. (2) This religion cannot be destroyed; it will triumph; opposition to it is vain; it will make its way throughout the world; and the path of safety is *not* to oppose that which God is intending to establish in the earth. Sinners who stand opposed to the gospel should tremble and be afraid, for sooner or later they *must* fall before its triumphant advances. It is not SAFE to oppose that which has already been opposed by kings and rulers in every form, and yet has triumphed. It is not WISE to risk one's eternal welfare on the question of suc-

servants, that [y]with all boldness
they may speak thy word,
30 By stretching forth thine
hand to heal: and that [z]signs
and wonders may be done by
the name of thy holy child Jesus.
31 And when they had [a]prayed,
the place was shaken where they
were assembled together; and they
were all filled with the Holy Ghost,
and [b]they spake the word of God
with boldness.
32 And the multitude of them
that believed were [c]of one heart

y ver.13,31; ch.14 3; 28.31; Ep.6.19. z ch.2.43; 5.12. a ch.2.2,4; 16.26.

b ver.29. c Ro.15.5,6; 2 Co.13.11; Phi.2.2; 1 Pe.3.8.

cessful opposition to that which God has, in so many ages and ways, pledged himself to protect; and when God has solemnly declared that the Son, the Messiah, whom he would set on his holy hill of Zion, should "break" his enemies "with a rod of iron, and dash them in pieces like a potter's vessel," Ps. ii. 9.

29. *Behold their threatenings.* So look upon them as to grant us deliverance. They did not purpose to abandon their undertaking; they resolved to persevere; and they expected that this purpose would involve them in danger. With this purpose they implored the protection of God; they asked that he would not suffer them to be deterred from speaking boldly; and they sought that constant additional proof might be granted of the presence and power of God to confirm the truth of their message. ¶ *And grant*, &c. This is an instance of heroic boldness, and a determination to persevere in doing their duty to God. When we are assailed by those in power; when we are persecuted and in danger, we should commit our way unto God, and seek his aid, that we may not be deterred from the path of duty.

30. *By stretching forth thine hand*, &c. The apostles not only desired *boldness* to speak, but they asked that God would continue to work miracles, and thus furnish to them, and to the people, evidence of the truth of what they delivered. They did not even ask that he would preserve their lives, or keep them from danger. They were intent on their work, and they confidently committed their way to God, making it their great object to promote the knowledge of the truth, and seeking that God would glorify himself by establishing his kingdom among men. ¶ *Signs and wonders.* Miracles. See Notes on ch. ii. 43.

31. *And when they had prayed.* The event which followed was regarded by them as an evidence that God heard their prayer. ¶ *The place was shaken.* The word which is translated "was shaken" commonly denotes violent agitation, as the raging of the sea, the convulsion of an earthquake, or trees shaken by the wind, Mat. xi. 7; Ac. xvi. 26; He. xii. 26. The language here is fitted to express the idea of an earthquake. Whether the motion was confined to the house where they were is not said. They probably regarded this as an answer to their prayer, or as an evidence that God would be with them, (1) Because it was sudden and violent, and was not produced by any natural causes; (2) Because it occurred *immediately*, while they were seeking divine direction; (3) Because it was an exhibition of great *power*, and was an evidence that God could protect them; and (4) Because a convulsion so great, sudden, and mighty was fitted at that time to awe them with a proof of the presence and power of God. A similar instance of an answer to prayer by an earthquake is recorded in Ac. xvi. 25, 26. Comp. ch. ii. 1, 2. It may be added, that among the Jews an *earthquake* was very properly regarded as a striking and impressive proof of the presence of Jehovah, Is. xxix. 6; Ps. lxviii. 8, "The earth shook, the heavens also dropped at the presence of God; even Sinai itself was moved at the presence of God, the God of Israel." See also the sublime description in Hab. iii., particularly ver. 6–11. Comp. Mat. xxvii. 54. Among the heathen, an earthquake was regarded as proof of the presence and *favour* of the Deity. (See Virgil, *Æneid*, iii. 89.) ¶ *They were all filled*, &c. See Notes on ch. ii. 4. Their being filled with the Holy Ghost here rather denotes their being inspired with *confidence* or *boldness* than being endowed with new powers, as in Ac. ii. 4.

32. *And the multitude.* The number of believers at this time had become large. In ch. iv. 4, it is said that it

and of one soul: neither said any *of them* that aught of the things which he possessed was his own; but [d]they had all things common.

d ch.2.44.

33 And [e]with great power gave the apostles [f]witness of the resurrection of the Lord Jesus: and [g]great grace was upon them all.

e ch.1.8. f Lu.11.48,49; ch.1.22. g Jn.1.16.

was five thousand, and the number was constantly increasing. ¶ *One heart.* This expression denotes tender union. They *felt* alike, or were attached to the same things, and this preserved them from jars and dissensions. ¶ *One soul.* This phrase also denotes close and tender union. No expression could denote it more strikingly than to say of friends they have *one soul.* Plutarch cites an ancient verse in his life of Cato of Utica with this very expression—"Two friends, one soul" (Grotius). Thus Diogenes Laertius also (5, i. 11) says respecting Aristotle, that "being asked what was a friend, answered that it was *one soul* dwelling in two bodies" (Kuinoel). The Hebrews spake of two friends as being "one man." There can be no more striking demonstration of *union* and *love* than to say of more than five thousand suddenly drawn together that they had one soul! And this union they evinced in every way possible—in their conduct, in their prayers, and in their property. How different would have been the aspect of the church if the union had continued to the present time! ¶ *Neither said,* &c. That is, they did not *regard* it as their own, but to be used for the benefit of the whole society. See Notes on ch. ii. 44.

33. *And with great power.* See ch. i. 8. The word *power* here denotes *efficacy*, and means that they had *ability* given them to bear witness of the resurrection of the Saviour. It refers, therefore, rather to their *preaching* than to their *miracles.* ¶ *Gave the apostles witness.* The apostles bore testimony to. ¶ *The resurrection of the Lord Jesus.* This was the main point to be established. If it proved that the Lord Jesus *came to life again* after having been put to death, it established all that he taught, and was a demonstration that he was sent from God. They exerted, therefore, all their powers to prove this, and their success was such as might have been expected. Multitudes were converted to the Christian faith. ¶ *And great grace,* &c. The word *grace* means *favour.* See Notes on Jn. i. 16. The expression here may mean either that the favour *of God* was remarkably shown to them, or that they had great favour in the sight of the people. It does not refer, as the expression now does commonly, to the internal blessings of religion on a man's own soul, to their personal advancement in the Christian *graces*, but to the *favour* or success that attended their preaching. The meaning probably is, that the *favour* of the *people* toward them was great, or that great success attended their ministry among them. Thus the same word *grace* (Greek) is used in ch. ii. 47. If this is its meaning, then here is an instance of the power of the testimony of the resurrection of the Lord Jesus to impress the minds of men. But this is not all, nor probably is it the main idea. It is that their union, their benevolence, their liberality in supplying the wants of the needy, was a means of opening the hearts of the people, and of winning them to the Saviour. If we wish to incline others to our opinions, nothing is better adapted to it than to show them kindness, and even to minister to their temporal wants. Benevolence toward them softens the heart, and inclines them to listen to us. It disarms their prejudices, and disposes them to the exercise of the mild and amiable feelings of religion. Hence our Saviour was engaged in healing the diseases and supplying the wants of the people. He drew around him the poor, the needy, and the diseased, and supplied their necessities, and *thus* prepared them to receive his message of truth. Thus God is love, and is constantly doing good, that his *goodness* may lead men to repentance, Ro. ii. 4. And hence no persons have better opportunities to spread the true sentiments of religion, or are clothed with higher responsibilities, than those who have it in their *power* to do good, or than those who are habitually engaged in bestowing favours. Thus physicians have access to the hearts of men which other persons have not. Thus parents have an easy access to the minds of children, for they are constantly doing them good. And thus Sunday-school teachers, whose whole work is a work of benevolence, have direct and most

34 Neither was there any among
them that lacked: for as many as
were possessors of lands or houses,
sold them, and brought the prices
of the things that were sold,
35 And[h] laid *them* down at the
apostles' feet; [i]and distribution
was made unto every man according as he had need.
36 And Joses, who by the apostles
was surnamed Barnabas, (which is,
being interpreted, The son of conso-

h ver.37; ch.5.2.

i ch.2.45; 6.1.

---

efficient access to the hearts of the children committed to their care.

34. *That lacked.* That was in want, or whose wants were not supplied by the others. ¶ *As many as,* &c. The word used here is employed in a large, indefinite sense; but it would be improper to press it so as to suppose that every individual that became a Christian sold at once all his property. The sense doubtless is, that this was done *when it was necessary:* they parted with whatever property was needful to supply the wants of their poor brethren. That it was by no means considered a matter of *obligation*, or enjoined by the apostles, is apparent from the case of Ananias, ch. v. 4. The fact that *Joses* is particularly mentioned (ver. 36) shows that it was by no means a universal practice thus to part with all their possessions. He was *one* instance in which it was done. Perhaps there were many other similar instances; but all that the passage requires us to believe is, that they parted with whatever was *needful* to supply the wants of the poor. This was an eminent and instructive instance of Christian liberality, and of the power of the gospel in overcoming one of the strongest passions that ever exist in the human bosom—the love of money. Many of the early Christians were poor. They were collected from the lower orders of the people. But *all* were not so. Some of them, it seems, were men of affluence; but the effect of religion was to bring them all, in regard to feeling, at least, on a level. They felt that they were members of one family, and they therefore imparted their property cheerfully to their brethren. Besides this, they were about to go to other lands to preach the gospel, and they cheerfully parted with their property that they might go and proclaim the unsearchable riches of Christ. See Notes on ch. ii. 44.

35. *And laid* them *down,* &c. That is, they committed the money received for their property to the disposal of the apostles, to distribute it as was necessary among the poor. This soon became a burdensome and inconvenient office, and they therefore appointed men who had especial charge of it, ch. vi. 1, 2, &c.

36. *And Joses.* Many manuscripts, instead of *Joses,* here read *Joseph.* The reasons why this individual is selected and specified particularly were, doubtless, because he was a foreigner; because it was a remarkable instance of liberality; and because he subsequently distinguished himself in the work of the ministry. He gave himself, his property, his all, to the service of the Lord Jesus, and went forth to the self-denying labours of the gospel. He is elsewhere mentioned with honour in the New Testament (Ac. xi. 24, 30), and usually as the companion of the apostle Paul. The occasion on which he became connected with Paul in the ministry was when he himself was sent forth by the church at Jerusalem to Antioch. There, it seems, he heard of the fame of Paul and went to Tarsus to seek him, and brought him with him to Antioch, Ac. xi. 22–26. Before this he had been acquainted with him, and had introduced him to the other apostles at a time when they were afraid of Paul, and unwilling to acknowledge him as an apostle, Ac. ix. 26, 27. At Antioch, Barnabas was led into dissimulation by Peter in regard to the Gentiles, and was reproved by his friend and companion, Paul, Ga. ii. 13. He and Paul continued to travel in fellowship until a dispute arose at Antioch about Mark, and they separated, Paul going with Silas through Syria and Cilicia, and Barnabas, with Mark, sailing for his native place, Cyprus, Ac. xv. 35–41. See the following places for particulars of his history: Ac. xi. 22, 25, 30; xii. 25; xiii. 1, 2, 50; xiv. 12; xv. 12; 1 Co. ix. 6; Ga. ii. 1, 9. ¶ *Who by the apostles was surnamed,* &c. The practice of giving surnames, as expressive of character, was not uncommon. Thus Simon was called Peter, or Cephas, Jn. i. 44; and thus James and

lation,) a Levite, *and* of the country of Cyprus,

37 Having land, sold *it*, and brought the money, and laid *it* at the apostles' feet.

CHAPTER V.

BUT a certain man named Ananias, with Sapphira his wife, sold a possession,

2 And kept back *part* of the

John were surnamed Boanerges, Mar. iii. 17. ¶ *Barnabas, which is*, &c. This word properly denotes *the son of prophecy.* It is compounded of two Syriac words, the one meaning *son*, and the other *prophecy.* The Greek word which is used to interpret this (παρακλήσις), translated *consolation*, means properly exhortation, entreaty, petition, or advocacy. It also means *consolation* or *solace;* and from *this* meaning the interpretation has been given to the word *Barnabas*, but with evident impropriety. It does not appear that the name was bestowed on account of this, though it is probable that he possessed the qualification for administering comfort or consolation in an eminent degree, but on account of his talent for *speaking*, or *exhorting* the people to holiness, and his success in preaching. Comp. Ac. xi. 23. ¶ *A Levite.* One of the descendants of Levi employed in the lower services of the temple. The whole tribe of Levi was set apart to the service of religion. It was divided into priests and Levites. The three sons of Levi were Gershon, Kohath, and Merari. Of the family of *Kohath* Aaron was descended, who was the first high-priest. His eldest son succeeded him, and the remainder of his sons were *priests.* All the others of the tribe of Levi were called *Levites*, and were employed in the work of the temple, in assisting the priests in performing sacred music, &c., Nu. iii.; De. xii. 18, 19; xviii. 6–8; 1 Ch. xxiii. 24. ¶ *Of the country of Cyprus.* Cyprus is the largest island in the Mediterranean; an island extremely fertile, abounding in wine, honey, oil, wool, &c. It is mentioned in Ac. xiii. 4; xv. 39. The island is near to Cilicia, and is not far from the Jewish coast. It is said by Dion Cassius (lib. 68, 69) that the Jews were very numerous in that island.—Clark.

Barnabas afterward became, with Paul, a distinguished preacher to the Gentiles. It is worthy of remark, that *both* were born in heathen countries, though by descent Jews; and as they were trained in heathen lands, they were better fitted for their peculiar work. The case of Barnabas is that of a man who had property when he entered the ministry, and who gave up all for the Lord Jesus. The great mass of ministers, like very many who have been distinguished in other professions, have been taken from among the poor, and from humble ranks in life. But all have not been. Many have been wealthy, and have devoted all to Christ; and in regard to others, it is to be remarked, that a very considerable proportion of them could have gained more *wealth* in some other profession than they do in the ministry. The ministry is a work of self-denial, and none should enter it who are not prepared to devote all to the service of the Lord Jesus Christ.

CHAPTER V.

1. *But a certain man.* In the previous chapter the historian had given an account of the eminent liberality and sincerity of the mass of early Christians, in being willing to give up their property to provide for the poor, and had mentioned the case of Barnabas as worthy of special attention. In this chapter he proceeds to mention a case, quite as striking, of insincerity, and hypocrisy, and of the just judgment of God on those who were guilty of it. The case is a remarkable instance of the nature of *hypocrisy*, and goes to illustrate the art and cunning of the enemy of souls in attempting to corrupt the church, and to pervert the religion of the gospel. Hypocrisy consists in an attempt to *imitate* the people of God, or to assume the *appearance* of religion, in whatever form it may be manifested. In this case religion had been manifested by great self-denial and benevolence. The hypocrisy of Ananias consisted in *attempting* to imitate this in appearance, and to impose in this way on the early Christians and on God. ¶ *With Sapphira his wife.* With her concurrence or consent. It was a matter of *agreement* between them, ver. 2, 9. ¶ *Sold a possession.* The word here used (κτῆμα) does not indicate whether this was *land* or some other property. In ver. 3, however, we learn that it was *land* that was sold; and the word here translated *pos-*

price, his wife also being privy *to it*, and [a]brought a certain part, and laid *it* at the apostles' feet.

a ch.4.34,37.

3 But Peter said, Ananias, why hath [b]Satan filled thine heart [1]to [c]lie to the Holy Ghost, and [d]to

b Lu.22.3. *c* ver.9. 1 or, *to deceive*. *d* Nu.30.2; De.23.21; Ec.5.4.

session is translated in the Syriac, Arabic, and the Latin Vulgate, *land*. The *pretence* for which this was sold was doubtless to have the appearance of religion. That it was *sold* could be easily known by the Christian society, but it might not be so easily known for *how much* it was sold. Hence the attempt to impose on the apostles. It is clear that they were not under obligation to sell their property. But, *having* sold it for the purposes of religion, it became their duty, if they professed to devote the avails of it to God, to do it entirely, and without any reservation.

2. *And kept back*. The word here used means properly *to separate, to part:* and then it means to *separate surreptitiously or clandestinely for our own use* a part of public property, as taxes, &c. It is used but three times in the New Testament, ver. 3, and in Tit. ii. 10, where it is rendered *purloining*. Here it means that they *secretly* kept back a part, while *professedly* devoting all to God. ¶ *His wife being privy to it*. His wife *knowing it*, and evidently concurring in it. ¶ *And laid it at the apostles' feet*. This was evidently an act *professedly* of devoting all to God. Comp. ch. iv. 37; also ver. 8, 9. That this was his *profession*, or *pretence*, is further implied in the fact that Peter charges him with having *lied* unto God, ver. 3, 4.

3. *But Peter said*, &c. Peter could have known this only by *revelation*. It was the manifest design of Ananias to deceive; nor was there any way of detecting him but by its being revealed to him by the Spirit of God. As it was an instance of enormous wickedness, and as it was very important to detect and punish the crime, it was made known to Peter directly by God. ¶ *Why hath Satan*. Great deeds of wickedness in the Scripture are traced to the influence of Satan. Comp. Lu. xxiii. 3; Jn. xiii. 27. Especially is Satan called the *father of lies*, Jn. viii. 44, 45. Comp. Ge. iii. 1–5. As this was an act of *falsehood*, or an attempt to deceive, it is with great propriety traced to the influence of Satan. The sin of Ananias consisted in his *yielding* to the temptation. Nowhere in the Bible are men supposed to be free from guilt from the mere fact that they have been *tempted* to commit it. God requires them to *resist* temptation; and if they *yield* to it, they must be punished. ¶ *Filled thine heart*. A man's *heart* or *mind* is *full* of a thing when he is *intent on it;* when he is strongly *impelled* to it; or when he is fully occupied with it. The expression here means that he was *strongly impelled* or *excited* by Satan to this crime. ¶ *To lie to*. To attempt to deceive. The deception which he meant to practise was to keep back a *part* of the price, while he *pretended* to bring the whole of it; thus *tempting* God, and supposing that he could not detect the fraud. ¶ *The Holy Ghost*—τὸ πνεῦμα τὸ ἅγιον. The main inquiry here is, whether the apostle Peter intended to designate in this place the *third person* of the Trinity; or whether he meant to speak of God *as God*, without any reference to the distinction of persons; or whether he referred to the *divine influence* which inspired the apostles, without reference to the peculiar offices which are commonly ascribed to the Holy Spirit. Or, in other words, is there a *distinction* here recognized between the *Father* and the *Holy Ghost?* That there *is*, will be apparent from the following considerations: (1) If no such distinction is *intended*, it is remarkable that Peter did not use the usual and customary *name* of God. It does not appear why he guarded it so carefully as to denote that this offence was committed against the *Holy Ghost*, and *the Spirit of the Lord*, ver. 9. (2) The name here used is the one employed in the Scriptures to designate the third person of the Trinity, as implying a distinction from the Father. See Mat. iii. 16; i. 18, 20; iii. 11; xii. 32; xxviii. 19; Mar. i. 8; iii. 29; xii. 36; Lu. xii. 10; Jn. xiv. 26; vii. 39; xx. 22; Ac. iv. 8; v. 32, &c. (3) Peter intended, doubtless, to designate an offence as committed particularly against the person, or influence, by which he and the other apostles were inspired. Ananias supposed that he could escape detection, and the offence was one, therefore, against the Inspirer of the apostles. Yet that was the Holy Ghost as *distinct*

keep back *part* of the price of the land?

4 Whiles it remained, was it not thine own? and after it was sold, was it not in thine own power? Why hast thou conceived this thing

---

from the Father. See Jn. xiv. 16, 17, 26; xv. 26; xvi. 7-11; xx. 22. Comp. Ac. v. 32. The offence, therefore, being against him who was *sent* by the Father, and who was appointed to a particular work, clearly supposes that the Holy Spirit is distinct from the Father. (4) A further incidental proof of this may be found in the fact that the sin here committed was one of peculiar magnitude—so great as to be deemed worthy of the immediate and signal vengeance of God. Yet the sin against the Holy Ghost is uniformly represented to be of this description. Comp. Mat. xii. 31, 32; Mar. iii. 28, 29. As these sins evidently coincide in enormity, it is clear that the same class of sins is referred to in both places; or, in other words, the sin of Ananias was against the third person of the Trinity. Two remarks may be made here: (1) The Holy Ghost is a distinct person from the Father and the Son; or, in other words, there is a distinction of some kind in the divine nature that may be designated by the word *person*. This is clear from the fact that *sin* is said to have been committed against him—a sin which it was supposed could not be detected. *Sin* cannot be committed against an *attribute* of God, or an *influence* from God. We cannot *lie unto* an attribute, or against wisdom, or power, or goodness; nor can we *lie unto* an *influence*, merely, of the Most High. Sin is committed against a *Being*, not against an *attribute;* and as a sin is here charged on Ananias against *the Holy Ghost*, it follows that the Holy Ghost has a *personal* existence, or that there is such a distinction in the divine essence that it may be proper to *specify* a sin as committed peculiarly against him. In the same way sin may be represented as committed peculiarly against the *Father* when his *name* is blasphemed; when his *dominion* is denied; when his mercy in sending his Son is called in question. Sin may be represented as committed against *the Son* when his atonement is denied; his divinity assailed; his character derided, or his invitations slighted. And thus sin may be represented as committed against *the Holy Ghost* when his office of renewing the heart, or sanctifying the soul, is called in question, or when *his* work is ascribed to some malign or other influence. See Mar. iii. 22-30. And as sin against the Son proves that he is in some sense distinct from the Father, so does sin against the Holy Ghost prove that in some sense he is distinct from the Father and the Son. (2) The Holy Ghost is divine. This is proved, because he is represented here as being able to search the heart, and to detect insincerity and hypocrisy. Comp. Je. xvii. 10; 1 Ch. xxviii. 9; 1 Co. ii. 10, "The Spirit searcheth all things, yea, the deep things of God;" Re. ii. 23. And he is expressly *called* God. See Notes on ver. 4.

4. *Whiles it remained*. As long as it remained unsold. This place proves that there was no *obligation* imposed on the disciples to sell their property. They who did it, did it voluntarily; and it does not appear that it was done by all, or expected to be done by all. ¶ *And after it was sold*, &c. Even after the property was *sold*, and Ananias had the money, still there was no obligation on him to devote it in this way. He had the disposal of it still. The apostle mentions this to show him that his offence was peculiarly aggravated. He was not *compelled* to sell his property—he had not even the poor pretence that he was *obliged* to dispose of it, and was *tempted* to withhold it for his own use. It was *all* his, and might have been retained if he had chosen. ¶ *Thou hast not lied unto men*. Unto men *only*, or, it is not your *main* and *chief* offence that you have attempted to deceive men. It is true that Ananias *had* attempted to deceive the apostles, and it is true, also, that this was a crime; but still, the principal magnitude of the offence was that he had attempted to deceive *God*. So small was his crime as committed against *men* that it was lost sight of by the apostles, and the great, crowning sin of attempting to deceive *God* was brought fully into view. Thus David also saw his sin as committed against *God* to be so enormous that he lost sight of it as an offence to man, and said, "Against thee, *thee* ONLY, have I sinned, and done this evil in *thy* sight," Ps. li. 4. ¶ *But unto God*. It has been *particularly* and *eminently* against God. This is true,

in thine heart? thou hast not lied unto men, but [e]unto God.
5 And Ananias, hearing these words, [f]fell down, and gave up the ghost: and [g]great fear came on all them that heard these things.
6 And the young men arose,

e Ps.139.4. f ver.10,11. g Ps.64.9.

---

because, (1) He had professedly *devoted* it to God. The act, therefore, had express and direct reference to him. (2) It was an attempt to deceive him. It implied the belief of Ananias that God would not detect the crime, or see the motives of the heart. (3) It is the prerogative of God to judge of sincerity and hypocrisy; and this was a case, therefore, which came under his special notice. Comp. Ps. cxxxix. 1-4. The word *God* here is evidently used in its plain and obvious sense as denoting the *supreme divinity*, and the use of the word here shows that the Holy Ghost is *divine*. The whole passage demonstrates, therefore, one of the important doctrines of the Christian religion, that the Holy Ghost is distinct from the Father and the Son, and yet is divine.

5. *And Ananias, hearing these words*, &c. Seeing that his guilt was known, and being charged with the enormous crime of attempting to deceive God. He had not expected to be thus exposed; and it is clear that the exposure and the charge came upon him unexpectedly and terribly, like a bolt of thunder. ¶ *Fell down*. Greek, Having fallen down. ¶ *Gave up the ghost*. This is an unhappy translation. The original means simply *he expired*, or *he died*. Comp. Notes on Mat. xxvii. 50. This remarkable fact may be accounted for in this way: (1) It is evidently to be regarded as a *judgment* of God for the sin of Ananias and his wife. It was not the act of Peter, but of God, and was clearly designed to show his abhorrence of this sin. See remarks on ver. 11. (2) Though it was the act of God, yet it does not follow that it was not in connection with the usual laws by which he governs men, or that he did not make use of natural means to do it. The sin was one of great aggravation. It was suddenly and unexpectedly detected. The fact that it was known, and the solemn charge that he had *lied unto God*, struck him with horror. His conscience would reprove him for the enormity of his crime, and overwhelm him at the memory of his wickedness. These circumstances may be sufficient to account for this remarkable event. It has occurred in other cases that the consciousness of crime, or the fact of being suddenly detected, has given such a shock to the frame that it has never recovered from it. The effect *commonly* is that the memory of guilt preys secretly and silently upon the frame, until, worn out with the want of rest and peace, it sinks exhausted into the grave. But there have not been wanting instances where the shock has been so great as to destroy the vital powers at once, and plunge the wretched man, like Ananias, into eternity. It is not at all improbable that the shock in the case of Ananias was so great as at once to take his life. ¶ *Great fear came*, &c. Such a striking and awful judgment on insincerity and hypocrisy was fitted to excite awful emotions among the people. Sudden death always does it; but sudden death in immediate connection with crime is fitted much more deeply to affect the mind.

6. *And the young men*. The youth of the congregation; very probably young men who were in attendance as *servants*, or those whose business it was to attend on the congregation, and perform various offices when Christians celebrated their worship (Mosheim). The word used here sometimes denotes a *servant*. It is used also, ver. 10, to denote *soldiers*, as they were commonly enlisted of the vigorous and young. The fact that they took up Ananias voluntarily implies that they were accustomed to perform offices of servitude to the congregation. ¶ *Wound him up*. It was the usual custom with the Jews to wind the body in many folds of linen before it was buried; commonly also with spices, to preserve it from putrefaction. See Notes on Jn. xi. 44. It may be asked *why* he was so soon buried; and especially why he was hurried away without giving information to his wife. In reply to this, it may be remarked, 1. That it does not appear from the narrative that it was *known* that Sapphira was privy to the transaction, or was near at hand, or even that he had a wife. Ananias came *himself* and offered the money, and the judgment fell at once on him. 2. It was customary among the ancient Persians to bury the body almost im-

wound[h] him up, and carried *him* out, and buried *him*.

7 And it was about the space of three hours after, when his wife, not knowing what was done, came in.

8 And Peter answered unto her, Tell me whether ye sold the land for so much? And she said, Yea, for so much.

9 Then Peter said unto her, How is it that ye have [i]agreed together to tempt the Spirit of the Lord?

h Jn.19.40.

i Ps.50.18; ver.2.

mediately after death (Jahn); and it seems probable that the Jews, when the body was not embalmed, imitated the custom. It would also appear that this was an ancient custom among the Jews. See Ge. xxiii. 19; xxv. 9; xxxv. 29; xlviii. 7; 1 Ki. xiii. 30. Different nations differ in their customs in burying the dead; and there is no impropriety in committing a body soon after death to the tomb. 3. There might have been some danger of an excitement and tumult in regard to this scene if the corpse had not soon been removed; and as no valuable purpose could be answered by delaying the burial, the body was decently committed to the dust.

7. *And it was about the space*, &c. As Sapphira had been no less guilty than her husband, so it was ordered in the providence of God that the same judgment should come upon both.

8. *For so much.* That is, for the sum which Ananias had presented. This was true, that this sum had been received for it; but it was also true that a larger sum had been received. It is as really a falsehood to deceive in this manner, as it would have been to have affirmed that they received much *more* than they actually did for the land. Falsehood consists in making an erroneous representation of a thing in any way for the purpose of deceiving. And *this* species is much more common than an open and bold lie, affirming what is in no sense true.

9. *Agreed together.* Conspired, or laid a plan. From this it seems that Sapphira was as guilty as her husband. ¶ *To tempt.* To try; to endeavour to impose on, or to deceive; that is, to act as if the Spirit of the Lord could not detect the crime. They did this by trying to see whether the Spirit of God could detect hypocrisy. ¶ *At the door.* Are near at hand. They had not yet returned. The dead were buried without the walls of cities; and the space of three hours, it seems, had elapsed before they returned from the burial. ¶ *Shall carry thee out.* This passage shows that it was by divine interposition or judgment that their lives were taken. The judgment was in immediate connection with the crime, and was designed as an expression of the divine displeasure.

If it be asked here *why* Ananias and Sapphira were punished in this severe and awful manner, an answer may be found in the following considerations: (1) This was an atrocious crime—a deep and dreadful act of iniquity. It was committed knowingly, and without excuse, ver. 4. It was important that sudden and exemplary punishment should follow it, because the society of Christians was just then organized, and it was designed that it should be a *pure* society, and should be regarded as a body of holy men. Much depended on making an *impression* on the people that sin could not be allowed in this new community, but would be detected and punished. (2) God has often, in a most solemn manner, shown his abhorrence of hypocrisy and insincerity. By awful declarations and fearful judgments he has declared his displeasure at it. In a particular manner, no small part of the preaching of the Saviour was employed in detecting the hypocrisy of the scribes and Pharisees, and denouncing heavy judgments on them. See Mat. xxiii. throughout for the most sublime and awful denunciation of hypocrisy anywhere to be found. Comp. Mar. xii. 15; Lu. xii. 1; 1 Ti. iv. 2; Job viii. 13; xiii. 16; xv. 34; xx. 5; xxxvi. 13; Mat. vii. 5; Lu. xi. 44. In the very beginning of the Christian church it was important, by a decided and awful act, to *impress* upon the church and the world the danger and guilt of hypocrisy. Well did the Saviour know that it would be one of the most insidious and deadly foes to the purity of the church; and at its very *threshold*, therefore, he set up this solemn warning to guard it, and laid the bodies of Ananias and Sapphira in the path of every hypocrite that would enter the church. If they enter and are destroyed, they

Behold, the feet of them which
have buried thy husband *are* at
the door, and shall carry thee out.
10 Then[k] fell she down straightway at his feet, and yielded up
the ghost: and the young men
came in and found her dead, and,
carrying *her* forth, buried *her* by
her husband.
11 And[l] great fear came upon
all the church, and upon as many
as heard these things.

k ver.5.

l ch.2.43.

cannot plead that they were not fully warned. If they practise iniquity *in* the church, they cannot plead ignorance of the fact that God intends to detect and punish them. (3) The apostles were just then establishing their authority. They claimed to be under the influence of inspiration. To establish that, it was necessary to show that they could know the views and motives of those who became connected with the church. If easily imposed on, it would go far to destroy their authority and their claim to infallibility. If they showed that they could detect hypocrisy, even where most artfully concealed, it would establish the divine authority of their message. At the *commencement* of their work, therefore, they gave this decisive and most awful proof that they were under the guidance of an infallible Teacher. (4) This case does not stand alone in the New Testament. It is clear from other instances that the apostles had the power of punishing sinners, and that a violation of the commands of Christ was attended by sudden and fearful judgments. See 1 Co. xi. 30, and the case of Elymas the sorcerer in Ac. xiii. 8-11. (5) Neither does this event stand alone in the history of the world. Acts of judgment sometimes occur as sudden and decided, in the providence of God, as in this case. The profane man, the drunkard, the profligate offender is sometimes suddenly stricken down, as in this instance. Cases have not been uncommon where the blasphemer has been smitten in death with the curse on his lips; and God often thus comes forth in judgment to slay the wicked, and to show that there is a God that reigns in the earth. This narrative cannot be objected to as improbable until *all* such cases are disposed of, nor can this infliction be regarded as unjust until all the instances where men die by remorse of conscience, or by the direct judgment of heaven, are *proved* to be unjust also.

In view of this narrative, we may remark, (1) That God searches the heart, and knows the purposes of the soul. Comp. Ps. cxxxix. (2) God judges the *motives* of men. It is not so much the *external* act, as it is the views and feelings by which it is prompted, that determines the character of the act. (3) God will bring forth sin which man may not be able to detect, or which may elude human justice. The day is coming when the secrets of all hearts shall be revealed, and God will reward every man according as his works shall be. (4) Fraud and hypocrisy will be detected. They are often detected in this life. The providence of God often lays them open to human view, and overwhelms the soul in shame at the guilt which was long concealed. But if not in this life, yet the day is coming when they will be disclosed, and the sinner shall stand *revealed* to an assembled universe. (5) We have here an illustration of the power of conscience. If *such* was its overwhelming effect *here*, what will it be when *all* the crimes of the life shall be disclosed in the day of judgment, and when the soul shall sink to the woes of hell? Through *eternity* the conscience will do its office; and these terrible inflictions will go on from age to age, for ever and ever, in the dark world of hell. (6) We see here the guilt of attempting to impose on God in regard to *property*. There is no subject in which men are more liable to hypocrisy; none in which they are more apt to keep back a *part*. Christians professedly devote ALL that they have to God. They profess to believe that he has a *right* to the silver and the gold, and the cattle on a thousand hills, Ps. l. 10. Their *property*, as well as their bodies and their spirits, they have devoted to him, and they profess to desire to employ it as *he* shall direct and please. And yet, is it not clear that the sin of Ananias has not ceased in the church? How many professing Christians there are who give *nothing* really to God; who contribute nothing for the poor and needy; who devote nothing, or next to nothing, to any purposes of benevolence; who

12 And by the hands of the apostles were [m]many signs and wonders wrought among the people; (and they were all with one accord in Solomon's porch.

13 And[n] of the rest durst no

m ch.4.30; Ro.15.19; He.2.4.

n Jn.12.42.

would employ "millions" for their own gratification, and their families, "but not a cent for *tribute*" to God. The case of Ananias is, to all such, a case of most fearful warning. And on no point should Christians more faithfully examine themselves than in regard to the professed devotion of their *property* to God. If God punished this sin in the beginning of the Christian church, he will do it still in its progress; and in nothing have professed Christians more to fear his wrath than on this very subject. (7) Sinners should fear and tremble before God. He holds their breath in his hands. He can cut them down in an instant. The bold blasphemer, the unjust man, the liar, the scoffer, he can destroy in a moment, and sink them in all the woes of hell. Nor have they any security that he will not do it. The profane man has no evidence that he will live to finish the curse which he has begun; nor the drunkard that he will again become sober; nor the seducer that God will not arrest him in his act of wickedness and send him down to hell! The sinner walks over the grave, and over hell! In an instant he may die, and be summoned to the judgment-seat of God! How awful it is to sin in a world like this; and how fearful the doom which *must* soon overtake the ungodly!

12. *And by the hands*, &c. By the apostles. This verse should be read in connection with the 15th, to which it belongs. ¶ *Signs and wonders.* Miracles. See Notes on Ac. ii. 43. ¶ *With one accord.* With one *mind*, or intention. See Notes on ch. i. 14. ¶ *In Solomon's porch.* See Notes on Mat. xxi. 12; Jn. x. 23. They were doubtless there for the purpose of worship. It does not mean that they were there constantly, but at the regular periods of worship. Probably they had two designs in this; one was, to join in the public worship of God in the usual manner with the people, for they did not design to leave the temple service; the other, that they might have opportunity to preach to the people assembled there. In the presence of the great multitudes who came up to worship, they had an opportunity of making known the doctrines of Jesus, and of confirming them by miracles, the reality of which could not be denied, and which could not be resisted, as proofs that Jesus was the Messiah.

13. *And of the rest.* Different interpretations have been given of this expression. Lightfoot supposes that by *the rest* are meant the remainder of the one hundred and twenty disciples of whom Ananias had been one; and that they feared to put themselves on an equality with the apostles. But this interpretation seems to be far-fetched. Kuinoel supposes that by *the rest* are meant those who had not already joined with the apostles, whether Christians or Jews, and that they were deterred by the fate of Ananias. Pricæus, Morus, Rosenmueller, Schleusner, and others, suppose that by *the rest* are meant the *rich* men, or the men of authority and influence among the Jews, of whom Ananias was one, and that they were deterred from it by the fate of Ananias. This is by far the most probable opinion, because, (1) There is an evident contrast between them and the people; *the rest*, that is, the others of the rich and great, feared to join with them; but *the people*, the common people, magnified them. (2) The fate of Ananias was fitted to have this effect on the rich and great. (3) Similar instances had occurred before, that the great, though they believed on Jesus, were afraid to come forth publicly and profess him before men. See Jn. xii. 42, 43; v. 44. (4) The phrase *the rest* denotes sometimes that which is more excellent, or which is superior in value or importance to something else. See Lu. xii. 26. ¶ *Join himself.* Become united to, or associated with. The rich and the great then, as now, stood aloof from them, and were deterred by fear or shame from professing attachment to the Lord Jesus. ¶ *But the people.* The mass of the people; the body of the nation. ¶ *Magnified them.* Honoured them; regarded them with reverence and fear.

14. *And believers.* This is the name by which Christians were designated, because one of the main things that distinguished them was that they *believed* that Jesus was the Christ. It is also an

man join himself to them, [o]but the
people magnified them.
14 And believers were the more
added to the Lord, [p]multitudes
both of men and women;)
15 Insomuch that they brought
forth the sick [2]into the streets,
and laid *them* on beds and couches,
that at the least the shadow of
Peter passing by might overshadow
some of them.
16 There came also a multitude
out of the cities round about unto
Jerusalem, bringing [q]sick folks,
and them which were vexed with
unclean spirits: and [r]they were
healed every one.
17 Then the high-priest rose up,

o ch.4.21. *p* ch.2.47. 2 or, *in every street.* *q* Mar.16.17,18; Jn.14.12. *r* Ja.5.16.

incidental proof that none should join themselves to the church who are not *believers;* that is, who do not profess to be Christians in heart and in life. ¶ *Were the more added.* The effect of all these things was to increase the number of converts. Their persecutions, their preaching, and the judgment of God, *all* tended to impress the minds of the people, and to lead them to the Lord Jesus Christ. Comp. ch. iv. 4. Though the judgment of God had the effect of deterring hypocrites from entering the church—though it produced awe and caution, yet still the number of true converts was increased. An effort to keep the church pure by wholesome discipline, and by cutting off unworthy members, however rich or honoured, so far from weakening its true strength, has a tendency greatly to increase its numbers as well as its purity. Men will not seek to enter a corrupt church, or regard it as worth any effort to be connected with a society that does not endeavour to be pure. ¶ *Multitudes.* Comp. ch. iv. 4.

15. *Insomuch.* So that. This should be connected with ver. 12. Many miracles were wrought by the apostles, *insomuch,* &c. ¶ *They brought forth.* The people, or the friends of the sick, brought them forth. ¶ *Beds*—κλινῶν. This word denotes usually the *soft* and *valuable* beds on which the rich commonly lay. And it means that the rich, as well as the poor, were laid in the path of Peter and the other apostles. ¶ *Couches*—κραββάτων. The coarse and hard couches on which the poor used to lie, Mar. ii. 4, 9, 11, 12; vi. 55; Jn. v. 8–12; Ac. ix. 33. ¶ *The shadow of Peter.* That is, they were laid in the path so that the shadow of Peter, as he walked, might pass over them. Perhaps the sun was near setting, and the lengthened shadow of Peter might be thrown afar across the way. They were not able to approach him on account of the crowd, and they *imagined* that if they could *anyhow* come under his influence they might be healed. The sacred writer does not say, however, that any *were* healed in this way, nor that they were commanded to do this. He simply states the *impression* which was on the minds of the people that it *might be.* Whether they were healed by this, it is left for us merely to conjecture. An instance somewhat similar is recorded in Ac. xix. 12, where it is expressly said, however, that the sick were healed by contact with *handkerchiefs* and *aprons* that were brought from the body of Paul. Comp. also Mat. ix. 21, 22, where the woman said respecting Jesus, "If I may but touch his garment I shall be whole." ¶ *Might overshadow.* That his shadow might pass over them. Though there is no certain evidence that any were healed in this way, yet it shows the full belief of the people that Peter had the power of working miracles. *Peter* was supposed by them to be eminently endowed with this power, because it was by him that the lame man in the temple had been healed (ch. iii. 4–6), and because he had been most prominent in his addresses to the people. The persons who are specified in this verse were those who dwelt at Jerusalem.

16. *There came also,* &c. Attracted by the fame of Peter's miracles, as the people formerly had been by the miracles of the Lord Jesus. ¶ *Vexed.* Troubled, afflicted, or tormented. ¶ *Unclean spirits.* Possessed with devils; called *unclean* because they prompted to sin and impurity of life. See Notes on Mat. iv. 23, 24. ¶ *And they were healed.* Of these persons it is expressly affirmed that they were healed. Of those who were so laid as that the shadow of Peter might pass over them, there is no such direct affirmation.

17. *Then the high-priest.* Probably *Caiaphas.* Comp. Jn. xi. 49. It seems from this place that he belonged to the

and all they that were with him, (which is [s]the sect of the Sadducees,) and were filled with [3]indignation,

18 And laid their hands on the apostles, and put them in [t]the common prison.

19 But the angel of the Lord by night opened the prison doors, and brought them forth, and said,

s ch.4.1,2. 3 or, *envy*. t ch.12 5-7; 16.23-27.

---

sect of the Sadducees. It is certain that he had signalized himself by opposition to the Lord Jesus and to his cause constantly. ¶ *Rose up.* This expression is sometimes *redundant*, and at others it means simply to *begin* to do a thing, or to resolve to do it. Comp. Lu. xv. 18. ¶ *And all they that were with him.* That is, all they that coincided with him in doctrine or opinion; or, in other words, that portion of the Sanhedrim that was composed of *Sadducees.* There was a strong party of Sadducees in the Sanhedrim; and perhaps at this time it was so strong a majority as to be able to control its decisions. Comp. Ac. xxiii. 6. ¶ *Which is the sect.* The word translated *sect* here is that from which we have derived our word *heresy*. It means simply *sect* or *party*, and is not used in a bad sense as implying reproach, or even error. The idea which *we* attach to it of error, and of denying fundamental doctrines in religion, is one that does not occur in the New Testament. ¶ *Sadducees.* See Notes on Mat. iii. 7. The main doctrine of this sect was the denial of the resurrection of the dead. The reason why *they* were particularly opposed to the apostles rather than the Pharisees was that the apostles dwelt much on the *resurrection of the Lord Jesus*, which, if true, completely overthrew their doctrine. All the converts, therefore, that were made to Christianity, tended to diminish their numbers and influence, and also to establish the belief of the *Pharisees* in the doctrine of the resurrection. So long, therefore, as the effect of the labours of the apostles was to establish one of the main doctrines of the *Pharisees*, and to confute the *Sadducees*, so long we may suppose that the *Pharisees* would either favour them or be silent; and so long the *Sadducees* would be opposed to them, and enraged against them. One sect will often see with composure the progress of another that it really hates, if it will humble a rival. Even opposition to the gospel will sometimes be silent provided the spread of religion will tend to humble and mortify those against whom we may be opposed. ¶ *Were filled with indignation.* Greek, *zeal.* The word denotes any kind of *fervour* or *warmth*, and may be applied to *any* warm or violent affection of the mind, either *envy*, *wrath*, *zeal*, or *love*, Ac. xiii. 45; Jn. ii. 17; Ro. x. 2; 2 Co. vii. 7; xi. 2. Here it probably *includes envy* and *wrath.* They were *envious* at the success of the apostles—at the number of converts that were made to a doctrine that they hated, and they were envious that the *Pharisees* were deriving such an accession of strength to their doctrine of the resurrection; and they were *indignant* that the apostles regarded so little their authority, and disobeyed the solemn injunction of the Sanhedrim. Comp. ch. iv. 18-21.

18. *The common prison.* The public prison; or the prison for the keeping of common and notorious offenders.

19. *But the angel of the Lord.* This does not denote any *particular* angel, but simply *an* angel. The *article* is not used in the original. The word *angel* denotes properly a *messenger*, and particularly it is applied to the pure spirits that are sent to this world on errands of mercy. See Notes on Mat. i. 20. The case here was evidently *a miracle.* An angel was employed for this special purpose, and the design might have been, (1) To reprove the Jewish rulers, and to convince them of their guilt in resisting the gospel of God; (2) To convince the apostles more firmly of the protection and approbation of God; (3) To encourage them more and more in their work, and in the faithful discharge of their high duty; and (4) To give the people a new and impressive proof of the truth of the message which they bore. That they were *imprisoned* would be known to the people. That they were made as secure as possible was also known. When, therefore, the next morning, before they could have been tried or acquitted, they were found again in the temple, delivering the same message still, it was a new and striking proof that they were sent by God.

20. *In the temple.* In a public and conspicuous place. In this way there

20 Go, stand and speak in the temple to the people [u] all the words[v] of this life.

21 And when they heard *that*, they entered into the temple early in the morning, and taught. [w] But the high-priest came, and they that were with him, and called the council together, and all the senate of the children of Israel, and sent to the prison to have them brought.

22 But when the officers came, and found them not in the prison, they returned and told,

23 Saying, The prison truly found we shut with all safety, and the keepers standing without before the doors; but when we had opened, we found no man within.

24 Now when the high-priest, and [x] the captain of the temple, and the chief priests heard these things, they doubted of them whereunto this would grow.

25 Then came one and told them, saying, Behold, the men whom ye put in prison are standing in the temple, and teaching the people.

26 Then went the captain with the officers, and brought them with-

u Ex.24.3. *v* Jn.6.63,68; 17.8. *w* ch.4.5,6. *x* ch.4.1.

would be a most striking exhibition of their boldness; a proof that *God* had delivered them, and a manifestation of their purpose to obey God rather than man. ¶ *All the words.* All the *doctrines.* Comp. Jn. vi. 68, "Thou hast *the words* of eternal life." ¶ *Of this life.* Pertaining to life, to the eternal life which they taught through the resurrection of Jesus. The word *life* is used sometimes to express the whole of religion, as opposed to the spiritual *death* of sin. See Jn. i. 4; iii. 36. Their deliverance from prison was not that they might be idle, and escape to a place of safety. Again they were to engage in the toils and perils which they had just before encountered. God delivers us from dangers sometimes that we may plunge into *new* dangers; he preserves us from one form of calamity that we may be tried in some new furnace of affliction; he calls us to encounter trials simply *because* he demands it, and as an expression of gratitude to him for his gracious interposition.

21. *Early in the morning.* Greek, at the break of day. Comp. Lu. xxiv. 1; Jn. viii. 2. ¶ *Called the council together.* The Sanhedrim, or the great council of the nation. This was clearly for the purpose of *trying* the apostles for disregarding their commandments. ¶ *And all the senate.* Greek, *eldership.* Probably these were not a part of the Sanhedrim, but were men of age and experience, who in ch. iv. 8, xxv. 15, are called *elders of the Jews,* and who were present for the sake of counsel and advice in a case of emergency.

23. *Found we shut.* It had not been broken open; and there was therefore clear proof that they had been delivered by the interposition of God. Nor could they have been released by the guard, for they were keeping watch, as if unconscious that anything had happened, and the officers had the only means of entering the prison.

24. *The captain of the temple.* See Notes on ch. iv. 1. ¶ *Doubted of them.* They were in *perplexity* about these things. The word rendered *doubted* denotes that state of anxiety which arises when a man *has lost his way,* or when he does not know what to do to escape from a difficulty. See Lu. ix. 7. ¶ *Whereunto this would grow.* What this *would be;* or, what would be the result or end of these events. For, (1) Their authority was disregarded. (2) God had opposed them by a miracle. (3) The doctrines of the apostles were gaining ground. (4) Their efforts to resist them had been in vain. They need *not* have doubted; but sinners are not disposed to be convinced of the truth of religion.

26. *Without violence.* Not by force; not by *binding* them. Comp. Mat. xxvii. 2. The command of the Sanhedrim was sufficient to secure their presence, as they did not intend to refuse to answer for any alleged violation of the laws. Besides, their going before the council would give them another noble opportunity to bear witness to the truth of the gospel. Christians, when charged with a violation of the laws of the land, should not refuse to answer, Ac. xxv. 11, "If I be an offender, or have committed anything worthy of death, I refuse not to die." It is a part of our religion to yield

out violence; for [y] they feared the people, lest they should have been stoned.

27 And when they had brought them, they set *them* before the council; and the high-priest asked them,

28 Saying, Did not we [z] straitly command you that ye should not teach in this name? and, behold, ye have filled Jerusalem with your doctrine, and intend to bring this man's [a] blood upon us.

29 Then Peter and the *other* apostles answered and said, [b] We ought to obey God rather than men.

30 The God of our fathers raised

y Mat.21.26. z ch.4.18. a Mat.27.25; ch.2.23,36; 3.15; 7.52. b ch.4.19.

---

obedience to all the just laws of the land, and to evince respect for all that are in authority, Ro. xiii. 1–7. ¶ *For they feared the people.* The people were favourable to the apostles. If violence had been attempted, or they had been taken in a cruel and forcible manner, the consequence would have been tumults and bloodshed. In this way, also, the apostles showed that they were not disposed to excite tumult. Opposition by them would have excited commotion; and though *they* would have been rescued, yet they resolved to show that they were not obstinate, contumacious, or rebellious, but were disposed, as far as it could be done with a clear conscience, to yield obedience to the laws of the land.

28. *Straitly command you.* Did we not command you with *a threat?* ch. iv. 17, 18, 21. ¶ *In this name.* In the name of Jesus. ¶ *Ye have filled Jerusalem.* This, though not so designed, was an honourable tribute to the zeal and fidelity of the apostles. When Christians are arraigned or persecuted, it is well if the only charge which their enemies can bring against them is that they have been distinguished for zeal and success in propagating their religion. See 1 Pe. iv. 16, "If any man suffer as a Christian, let him not be ashamed, but let him glorify God on this behalf;" also ver. 13–15. ¶ *Intend to bring this man's blood upon us.* To bring *one's blood* upon another is a phrase signifying to hold or to prove him guilty of murdering the innocent. The expression here charges them with designing to prove that they had put Jesus to death when he was innocent; to convince *the people* of this, and thus to enrage them against the Sanhedrim; and also to prove that they were guilty, and were exposed to the divine vengeance for having put the Messiah to death. Comp. ch. ii. 23, 36; iii. 15; vii. 52. That the apostles *did* intend to charge them with being guilty of murder is clear; but it is observable that on *this occasion* they had said nothing of this, and it is further observable that they did not charge it on them *except in their presence.* See the places just referred to. They took no pains to spread this among the people, *except as the people were accessory to the crime of the rulers,* ch. ii. 23, 36. Their consciences were not at ease, and the remembrance of the death of Jesus would occur to them at once at the sight of the apostles.

29. *We ought to obey,* &c. See Notes on ch. iv. 19.

30. *Raised up Jesus.* This refers to his resurrection. ¶ *Hanged on a tree.* That is, on the *cross,* Ga. iii. 13; 1 Pe. ii. 24; Ac. x. 39; xiii. 29. This is the amount of Peter's defence. He begins with the great principle (ver. 29), which they could not gainsay, that God ought to be obeyed rather than man. He then proceeds to state that they were convinced that God had raised up Jesus from the dead, and as they had such decisive evidence of that, and were commanded by the authority of the Lord Jesus to be *witnesses of that,* they were not *at liberty* to be silent. They were bound to obey God rather than the Sanhedrim, and to make known everywhere the fact that the Lord Jesus was risen. The remark that God had raised up Jesus whom they had *slain,* does not seem to have been made to irritate or to reproach them, but merely to *identify* him as the person that had been raised. It was also a confirmation of the truth and reality of the miracle. Of his *death* they had no doubt, for they had been at pains to certify it, Jn. xix. 31–34. It is certain, however, that Peter did not shrink from charging on them their guilt; nor was he at any pains to *soften* or *mitigate* the severe charge that they had murdered their own Messiah.

up Jesus, whom ye slew and [c]hanged on a tree.

31 Him[d] hath God exalted with his right hand *to be* a [e]Prince and a [f]Saviour, for to give repentance to Israel, and forgiveness of sins.

c Ga.3.13; 1 Pe.2.24. d Phi.2.9. e Is.9.6. f Mat.1.21.

---

31. *Him hath God exalted.* See Notes on ch. ii. 33. ¶ To be *a Prince*—ἀρχηγὸν. See Notes on Ac. iii. 15. In that place he is called *the Prince of life.* Here it means that he is actually in the *exercise* of the office of a prince or a king, at the right hand of his Father. The title *Prince*, or *King*, was one which was well known as applied to the Messiah. It denotes that he has *dominion* and *power*, especially the power which is needful to give repentance and the pardon of sins. ¶ *A Saviour.* See Notes on Mat. i. 21. ¶ *To give repentance.* The word *repentance* here is equivalent to *reformation* and a change of life. The sentiment does not differ from what is said in ch. iii. 26. ¶ *To Israel.* This word properly denotes the *Jews;* but his office was not to be confined to the Jews. Other passages show that it would be also extended to the *Gentiles.* The reasons why the *Jews* are particularly specified here are, probably, (1) Because the Messiah was long promised to the Jewish people, and his first work was there; and (2) Because Peter was addressing Jews, and was particularly desirous of leading *them* to repentance. ¶ *Forgiveness of sins.* Pardon of sin; the act which can be performed by God only, Mar. ii. 7.

If it be asked in what sense the Lord Jesus *gives repentance*, or how his *exaltation* is connected with it, we may answer, (1) His exaltation is evidence that his work was accepted, and that thus a foundation is laid by which repentance is available, and may be connected with pardon. Unless there was some way of *forgiveness*, sorrow for sin would be of no value, even if exercised. The relentings of a culprit condemned for murder will be of no avail unless the executive can *consistently* pardon him; nor would relentings in hell be of avail, for there is no promise of forgiveness. But Jesus Christ by his death has laid a foundation by which repentance *may be* accepted. (2) He is intrusted with all power in heaven and earth with *reference* to this, to apply his work to men; or, in other words, to bring them to repentance. See Jn. xvii. 2; Mat. xxviii. 18. (3) His exaltation is immediately connected with the bestowment of the Holy Spirit, by whose influence men are brought to repentance, Jn. xvi. 7-11. The Spirit is represented as being *sent* by him as well as by the Father, Jn. xv. 26; xvi. 7. (4) Jesus has power in this state of exaltation over all things that can affect the mind. He sends his ministers; he directs the events of sickness or disappointment, of health or prosperity, that will influence the heart. There is no doubt that he can so recall the sins of the past life, and refresh the memory, as to overwhelm the soul in the consciousness of guilt. Thus also he can appeal to man by his *goodness*, and by a sense of his mercies; and especially he can so present a view of *his own* life and death as to affect the heart, and show the evil of the past life of the sinner. Knowing the heart, he knows all the avenues by which it can be approached, and in an instant he can overwhelm the soul with the remembrance of crime.

It was *proper* that the power of pardon should be lodged with the same being that has the power of producing repentance, because, 1. The one appropriately follows the other. 2. They are parts of the same great work—the work which the Saviour came to do; *to remove sin, with all its effects, from the human soul.* This power of *pardon* Jesus exercised when he was on the earth, and this he can now dispense in the heavens, Mar. ii. 9-11.

And from this we may learn, (1) That Christ is *divine.* It is a dictate of natural religion that none can forgive sins against God but God himself. None can pardon but the Being who has been offended. And this is also the dictate of the Bible. The power of *pardoning* sin is one that God claims as *his* prerogative, and it is clear that it can appertain to no other. See Is. xliii. 25; Da. ix. 9; Ps. cxxx. 4. Yet Jesus Christ exercised this power when on earth; gave *evidence* that the exercise of that power was one that was acceptable to God by working a miracle, and removing the *consequences* of sin with which *God* had visited the sinner (Mat. ix. 6); and exercises it still in heaven. He must, therefore, be divine. (2) The

32 And[g] we are his witnesses of these things; and [h]*so is* also the Holy Ghost, whom God hath given to them that obey him.

33 When they heard *that,* [i]they were cut *to the heart,* and took counsel to slay them.

34 Then stood there up one in the council, a Pharisee, named [k]Gamaliel, a doctor of the law,

g Lu.24.48. h ch.2.4. i ch.7.54. k ch.22.3.

sinner is dependent on him for the exercise of repentance, and for forgiveness. (3) The proud sinner must be humbled at his feet. He must be willing to come and receive eternal life at *his* hands. No step is more humiliating than this for proud and hardened men; and there is none which they are more reluctant to do. We always shrink from coming into the presence of one whom we have offended; we are extremely reluctant to confess a fault; but it *must be done*, or the soul must be lost for ever. (4) Christ has power to pardon the greatest offender. He is exalted for this purpose; and he is fitted to his work. Even his murderers he could pardon; and no sinner need fear that he who is *a Prince and a Saviour at the right hand of God* is unable to pardon his sins. To him we may come with confidence; and when pressed with the consciousness of the blackest crimes, and when we feel that we deserve eternal death, we may confidently roll all on his arm.

32. *And we are witnesses.* For this purpose they had been appointed, ch. i. 8, 21, 22; ii. 32; iii. 15; Lu. xxiv. 48. ¶ *Of these things.* Particularly of the resurrection of the Lord Jesus, and of the events which had followed it. Perhaps, however, he meant to include everything pertaining to the life, teachings, and death of the Lord Jesus. ¶ *And* so is *also*, &c. The descent of the Holy Ghost to endow them with remarkable gifts (ch. ii. 1–4), to awaken and convert such a multitude (ch. ii. 41; iv. 4; v. 14), was an unanswerable attestation of the truth of these doctrines and of the Christian religion. So manifest and decided was the presence of God attending them, that *they* could have no doubt that what they said was true; and so open and public was this attestation, that it was an evidence to all the people of the truth of their doctrine.

33. *When they heard* that. That which the apostle Peter had said, to wit, that they were guilty of murder; that Jesus was raised up; and that he still lived as the Messiah. ¶ *They were cut* to the heart. The word used here properly denotes *to cut with a saw;* and as applied to the *mind*, it means to be agitated with *rage* and *indignation*, as if wrath should seize upon the mind as a saw does upon wood, and tear it violently, or agitate it severely. When used in connection with *the heart*, it means that the heart is violently agitated and rent with rage. See ch. vii. 54. It is not used elsewhere in the New Testament. The *reasons* why they were thus indignant were doubtless, (1) Because the apostles had disregarded their command; (2) Because they charged them with murder; (3) Because they affirmed the doctrine of the resurrection of Jesus, and thus tended to overthrow the sect of the Sadducees. The effect of the doctrines of the gospel is often to make men enraged. ¶ *Took counsel.* The word rendered *took counsel* denotes commonly *to will;* then, *to deliberate;* and sometimes *to decree* or *to determine.* It doubtless implies here that *their minds were made up* to do it; but probably the formal decree was not passed to put them to death.

34. *There stood up one.* He *rose*, as is usual in deliberative assemblies, to speak. ¶ *In the council.* In the Sanhedrim, ch. iv. 15. ¶ *A Pharisee.* The high-priest and those who had been most active in opposing the apostles were Sadducees. The Pharisees were opposed to them, particularly on the doctrine in regard to which the apostles were so strenuous, the resurrection of the dead. See Notes on Mat. iii. 7. Comp. Ac. xxiii. 6. ¶ *Gamaliel.* This name was very common among the Jews. Dr. Lightfoot says that this man was the teacher of Paul (Ac. xxii. 3), the son of the *Simon* who took the Saviour in his arms (Lu. ii.), and the grandson of the famous *Hillel*, and was known among the Jews by the title of *Rabban Gamaliel the elder*. There were other men of this name, who were also eminent among the Jews. This man is said to have died eighteen years after the destruction of Jerusalem, and he died as he had lived, a Pharisee. There is not the least evidence that he was a friend of the Christian religion; but he was evi-

had in reputation among all the
people, and commanded to put
the apostles forth a little space;
35 And said unto them, Ye
men of Israel, take heed to yourselves
what ye intend to do as
touching these men.
36 For before these days[4] rose
up Theudas, boasting himself to be
somebody; to whom a number of
men, about four hundred, joined
themselves: who was slain; and all,
as many as [5]obeyed him, were scattered,
and brought to nought.
37 After this man rose up Judas
of Galilee, in the days of the tax-

[4] In the third year before the account called A.D.

[5] or, *believed*.

---

dently a man of far more liberal views than the other members of the Sanhedrim. ¶ *A doctor of the law.* That is, a *teacher* of the Jewish law; one whose province it was to *interpret* the laws of Moses, and probably to preserve and transmit the *traditional* laws of the Jews. See Notes on Mat. xv. 3. So celebrated was he, that Saul of Tarsus went to Jerusalem to receive the benefit of his instructions, Ac. xxii. 3. ¶ *Had in reputation among all the people. Honoured* by all the people. His advice was likely, therefore, to be respected. ¶ *To put the apostles forth.* This was done, doubtless, because, if the apostles had been suffered to remain, it was apprehended that they would take fresh courage, and be confirmed in their purposes. It was customary, besides, when they deliberated, to command those accused to retire, ch. iv. 15. ¶ *A little space.* A little *time*, Lu. xxii. 58.

36. *For before those days.* The *advice* of Gamaliel was to suffer these men to go on. The *arguments* by which he enforced his advice were: (1) That there were *cases* or *precedents* in point (ver. 36, 37); and (2) That *if* it should turn out *to be* of God, it would be a solemn affair to be involved in the consequences of opposing him. How long before *these days* this transaction occurred, cannot now be determined, as it is not certain to what case Gamaliel refers. ¶ *Rose up.* That is, commenced or excited an insurrection. ¶ *Theudas.* This was a name quite common among the Jews. Of this man nothing more is known than is here recorded. Josephus (*Antiq.*, b. xx. ch. v.) mentions one *Theudas*, in the time of *Fadus*, the procurator of Judea, in the reign of the Emperor Claudius (A.D. 45 or 46), who persuaded a great part of the people to take their effects with them and follow him to the river Jordan. He told them he was a prophet, and that he would divide the river and lead them over. Fadus, however, came suddenly upon them, and slew many of them. Theudas was taken alive and conveyed to Jerusalem, and there beheaded. But this occurred at least ten or fifteen years after this discourse of Gamaliel. Many efforts have been made to reconcile Luke and Josephus, on the supposition that they refer to the same man. Lightfoot supposed that Josephus had made an error in chronology. But there is no reason to suppose that there is reference to the same event; and the fact that Josephus has not recorded the insurrection referred to by Gamaliel does not militate at all against the account in the Acts. For, (1) Luke, for anything that appears to the contrary, is quite as credible an historian as Josephus. (2) The name *Theudas* was a common name among the Jews; and there is no improbability that there were *two* leaders of an insurrection of this name. If it *is* improbable, the improbability would affect Josephus's credit as much as that of Luke. (3) It is altogether improbable that *Gamaliel* should refer to a case which was not well authenticated, and that Luke should record a speech of this kind unless it was delivered, when it would be so easy to detect the error. (4) Josephus has recorded many instances of insurrection and revolt. He has represented the country as in an unsettled state, and by no means professes to give an account of *all* that occurred. Thus he says (*Antiq.*, xvii. x. § 4) that there were "at this time *ten thousand* other disorders in Judea;" and (§ 8) that "Judea was full of robberies." When this *Theudas* lived cannot be ascertained; but as Gamaliel mentions him before Judas of Galilee, it is probable that he lived not far from the time that our Saviour was born; at a time when many false prophets appeared, claiming to be the Messiah. ¶ *Boasting himself to be somebody.* Claiming to be an eminent prophet probably, or the Messiah. ¶ *Obeyed him.* The word used here is the one commonly

ing, and drew away much people after him: [l]he also perished; and all, *even* as many as obeyed him, were dispersed.

38 And now I say unto you, Refrain from these men, and let them alone: [m]for if this counsel or this work be of men, it will come to nought;

l Lu.13.1,2.

m Pr.21.30; Is.8.10; Mat.15.13.

used to denote *belief*. As many as *believed* on him, or gave credit to his pretensions.

37. *Judas of Galilee*. Josephus has given an account of this man (*Antiq*., b. xvii. ch. x. § 5), and calls him a *Galilean*. He afterwards calls him a *Gaulonite*, and says he was of the city of *Gamala* (*Antiq*., xviii. i. 1). He says that the revolt took place under *Cyrenius*, a Roman senator, who came into "Syria to be judge of that nation, and to take account of their substance." "Moreover," says he, "Cyrenius came himself into Judea, which was now added to the province of Syria, to take an account of their substance, and to dispose of Archelaus's money." "Yet Judas, taking with him Saddouk, a Pharisee, became zealous to draw them to a revolt, who both said that this taxation was no better than an introduction to slavery, and exhorted the nation to assert their liberty," &c. *This* revolt, he says, was the commencement of the series of revolts and calamities that terminated in the destruction of the city, temple, and nation. ¶ *In the days of the taxing*. Or, rather, the *enrolling*, or *the census*. Josephus says it was designed to take an account of their substance. Comp. Lu. ii. 1, 2.

38. *Refrain from these men*. Cease to oppose them or to threaten them. The *reason* why he advised this he immediately adds, that if it were of men, it would come to nought; if of God, they could not overthrow it. ¶ *This counsel or this work be of men*. This plan or purpose. If the apostles had originated it for the purposes of imposture. ¶ *It will come to nought*. Gamaliel *inferred* that from the two instances which he specified. They had been suppressed without the interference of the Sanhedrim; and he inferred that *this* would also die away if it was a human device. It will be remembered that this is the mere advice of Gamaliel, who was not inspired, and that this opinion should not be adduced to guide us, except as it was an instance of great shrewdness and prudence. It is doubtless right to oppose *error* in the proper way and with the proper temper, not with arms, or vituperation, or with the civil power, but with argument and kind entreaty. But the sentiment of Gamaliel is full of wisdom in regard to error. For, (1) The very way to exalt error into notice, and to confirm men in it, is to oppose it in a harsh, authoritative, and unkind manner. (2) Error, if left alone, will often die away itself. The interest of men in it will often cease as soon as it ceases to be opposed; and, having nothing to fan the flame, it will expire. It is not so with truth. (3) In this respect the remark may be applied to the Christian religion. It has stood too long, and in too many circumstances of prosperity and adversity, to be of men. It has been subjected to all trials from its pretended friends and real foes; and it still lives as vigorous and flourishing as ever. Kingdoms have changed; empires have risen and fallen since Gamaliel spoke this; systems of opinion and belief have had their day, and expired; but the preservation of the Christian religion, unchanged through so many revolutions, and in so many fiery trials, shows that it is not of men, but of God. The argument for the divine origin of the Christian religion from its perpetuity is one that can be applied to no other system that has been, or that now exists. For Christianity has been opposed in every form. It confers no temporal conquests, and appeals to no base and strong native passions. Mohammedanism is supported by the sword and the state; paganism relies on the arm of the civil power and the terrors of superstition, and is sustained by all the corrupt passions of men; atheism and infidelity have been short-lived, varying in their forms, dying to-day, and to-morrow starting up in a new form; never organized, consolidated, or pure; and never tending to promote the peace or happiness of men. Christianity, without arms or human power, has lived, keeping on its steady and triumphant movement among men, regardless alike of the opposition of its foes, and of the treachery of its pretended friends. If the opinion of Gamaliel was just, it is from God; and the

39 But[n] if it be of God, ye cannot overthrow it: lest haply ye be found even to [o]fight against God.

n Job 34.29; 1 Co.1.25. o ch.9.5; 23.9.

Jews particularly should regard as important an argument derived from the opinion of one of the wisest of their ancient Rabbins.

39. *But if it be of God.* If God is the *author* of this religion. From this it seems that Gamaliel supposed that it was at least possible that this religion was divine. He evinced a far more candid mind than did the rest of the Jews; but still it does not appear that he was entirely convinced. The arguments which could not but stagger the Jewish Sanhedrim were those drawn from the resurrection of Jesus, the miracle on the day of Pentecost, the healing of the lame man in the temple, and the release of the apostles from the prison. ¶ *Ye cannot overthrow it.* Because, (1) God has almighty power, and can execute his purposes; (2) Because he is unchanging, and will not be diverted from his plans, Job xxiii. 13, 14. The plan which God forms *must* be accomplished. All the devices of man are feebleness when opposed to him, and he can dash them in pieces in an instant. The prediction of Gamaliel has been fulfilled. Men have opposed Christianity in every way, but in vain. They have reviled it; have persecuted it; have resorted to argument and to ridicule; to fire, and faggot, and sword; they have called in the aid of science; but all has been in vain. The more it has been crushed, the more it has risen, and it still exists with as much life and power as ever. The *preservation* of this religion amidst so much and so varied opposition proves that it is of God. No severer trial *can* await it than it has already experienced; and as it has survived so many storms and trials, we have every evidence that, according to the predictions, it is destined to live and to fill the world. See Notes on Mat. xvi. 18; Is. liv. 17; lv. 11; Da. iv. 35. ¶ *Lest.* That is, if you continue to oppose it, you may be found to have been opposing God. ¶ *Haply.* Perhaps. In the Greek this is *lest at any time;* that is, at some *future* time, when too late to retract your doings, &c. ¶ *Ye be found.* It shall appear that you have been opposing God. ¶ *Even to fight against God.* Greek θεομάχοι, *those who contend with God.* The word occurs nowhere else in the New Testament. To fight against God is to oppose him, or to maintain an attitude of hostility against him. It is an attitude that is most fearful in its character, and will most certainly be attended with an overthrow. No condition can be more awful than such an opposition to the Almighty; no overthrow more terrible than that which must follow such opposition. Comp. Ac. ix. 5; xxiii. 9. Opposition to the *gospel* in the Scriptures is uniformly regarded as opposition to God, Mat. xii. 30; Lu. xi. 23. Men may be said to *fight against* God in the following ways, or on the following subjects: (1) When they oppose his *gospel*, its preaching, its plans, its influence among men; when they endeavour to prevent its diffusion, or to withdraw their families and friends from its influence. (2) When they oppose the *doctrines* of the Bible. When they become angry that the real truths of religion are preached, and suffer themselves to be irritated and excited by an *unwillingness* that those doctrines should be true, and should be presented to men. Yet this is no uncommon thing. Men by nature do not love those doctrines, and they are often indignant that they are preached. Some of the most angry feelings which men ever have arise from this source; and man can never find peace until he is *willing* that God's truth should exert its influence on his own soul, and rejoice that it is believed and loved by others. (3) Men oppose the *law* of God. It seems to them too *stern* and *harsh.* It condemns them; and they are unwilling that it should be applied to them. There is nothing which a sinner likes *less* than he does the pure and holy law of God. (4) Sinners fight against the *providence* of God. When he afflicts them they rebel. When he takes away their health, or property, or friends, they murmur. They esteem him harsh and cruel; and instead of finding peace by *submission*, they greatly aggravate their sufferings, and infuse a mixture of wormwood and gall into the cup by murmuring and repining. There is no peace in affliction but in the feeling that God is *right.* And until this belief is cherished, the wicked will be like the troubled sea which cannot rest, whose waters cast up mire and dirt, Is. lvii. 20. Such opposition

40 And to him they agreed: and when they had called the apostles, and [p]beaten *them*, [q]they commanded that they should not

p Mat.10.17. q ch.4.18.

to God is as wicked as it is foolish. The Lord gave, and has a right to remove our comforts; and we should be still, and know that he is God. (5) Sinners fight against God when they resist the influences of his Spirit; when they *oppose* serious thoughts; when they seek evil or gay companions and pleasures rather than submit to God; and when they spurn all the entreaties of their friends to become Christians. All these may be the appeals which God is making to men to be prepared to meet him. And yet it is common for sinners thus to stifle conviction, and refuse even to think of their eternal welfare. Nothing can be an act of more direct and deliberate wickedness and folly than this. Without the aid of the Holy Spirit none can be saved; and to resist his influences is to put away the only prospect of eternal life. To do it is to do it over the grave; not knowing that another hour of life may be granted; and not knowing that *if* life is prolonged, the Spirit will ever strive again with the heart.

In view of this verse, we may remark, 1. That the path of wisdom is to submit at once to the requirements of God. Without this, we must expect conflicts with him, and peril and ruin. No man can be *opposed* to God without endangering himself every minute. 2. Submission to God should be entire. It should extend to every doctrine and demand; every law, and every act of the Almighty. In all his requirements, and in all afflictions, we should submit to him, for thus only shall we find peace. 3. Infidels and scoffers will gain nothing by opposing God. They have thus far been thwarted, and unsuccessful; and they will be still. None of their plans have succeeded; and the hope of destroying the Christian religion, after the efforts of almost two thousand years, must be vain, and will recoil with tremendous vengeance on those who make them.

40. *And to him they agreed.* Greek, They *were persuaded* by him; or they *trusted* to him. They agreed only so far as their design of putting them to death was concerned. They abandoned *that* design. But they did *not* comply with his advice to let them entirely alone. ¶ *And beaten* them. The usual amount of *lashes* which were inflicted on offenders was thirty-nine, 2 Co. xi. 24. *Beating*, or *whipping*, was a common mode of punishing minor offences among the Jews. It was expressly foretold by the Saviour that the apostles would be subjected to this, Mat. x. 17. The reason why they did not adopt the advice of Gamaliel altogether doubtless was, that if they did, they feared that their *authority* would be despised by the people. They had commanded them not to preach; they had threatened them (ch. iv. 18; v. 28); they had imprisoned them (ch. v. 18); and now, if they suffered them to go without even the *appearance* of punishment, their authority, they feared, would be despised by the nation, and it would be supposed that the apostles had triumphed over the Sanhedrim. It is probable, also, that they were so indignant, that they could not suffer them to go without the gratification of subjecting them to the public odium of a *whipping*. Men, if they cannot accomplish their *full* purposes of malignity against the gospel, will take up with even some petty annoyance and malignity rather than let it alone.

41. *Rejoicing.* Nothing to most men would seem more disgraceful than a public whipping. It is a punishment inflicted usually not so much because it gives *pain*, as because it is esteemed to be attended with disgrace. The Jewish rulers doubtless desired that the apostles might be so affected with the sense of this disgrace as to be unwilling to appear again in public, or to preach the gospel any more. Yet in this they were disappointed. The effect was just the reverse. If it be asked *why* they *rejoiced* in this manner, we may reply, (1) Because they were permitted thus to imitate the example of the Lord Jesus. He had been scourged and reviled, and they were glad that they were permitted to be treated as he was. Comp. Phi. iii. 10; Col. i. 24; 1 Pe. iv. 13, "Rejoice inasmuch as ye are partakers of Christ's sufferings." (2) Because, by this, they had evidence that they were the friends and followers of Christ. It was clear they were engaged in the same cause that he was. They were enduring the same sufferings, and striv-

speak in the name of Jesus, and let them go.

41 And they departed from the presence of the council, [r]rejoicing that they were counted worthy to suffer shame for his name.

42 And[s] daily in the temple, and in every house, they ceased not to teach and preach Jesus Christ.

r Mat.5.12; 2 Co.12.10; Phi.1.29; Ja.1.2; 1 Pe.4. 13-16.

s 2 Ti.4.2.

---

ing to advance the same interests. As they loved the *cause*, they would rejoice in enduring even the shame and sufferings which the cause, of necessity, involved. The kingdom of the Redeemer was an object so transcendently important, that *for* it they were willing to endure *all* the afflictions and disgrace which it might involve. (3) They had been told to *expect* this, and they now rejoiced that they had *this* evidence that they were engaged in the cause of truth, Mat. v. 11, 12; x. 17, 22; 2 Co. xii. 10; Phi. i. 29; Ja. i. 2. (4) Religion appears to a Christian so excellent and lovely, that he is willing, for its sake, to endure trial, persecution, and death. With *all* this, it is infinite gain; and we should be willing to endure these trials, if, by them, we may gain a crown of glory. Comp. Mar. x. 30. (5) Christians are the professed friends of Christ. We show attachment for friends by being willing to suffer for them; to bear contempt and reproach on their account; and to share *their* persecutions, sorrows, and calamities. (6) The apostles were engaged in a cause of innocence, truth, and benevolence. They had *done* nothing of which to be ashamed; and they rejoiced, therefore, in a conscience void of offence, and in the consciousness of integrity and benevolence. When other men *disgrace themselves* by harsh, or vile, or opprobrious language or conduct toward *us*, we should not feel that the disgrace belongs to *us*. It is *theirs;* and we should not be ashamed or distressed, though their rage should fall on us. See 1 Pe. iv. 14–16. ¶ *Counted worthy.* Esteemed to be deserving. That is, esteemed *fit* for it *by the Sanhedrim.* It does not mean that *God* esteemed them worthy, but that the Jewish council judged them fit to suffer shame in this cause. They evinced so much zeal and determination of purpose that they were judged fit objects to be treated as the Lord Jesus had himself been. ¶ *To suffer shame.* To be *dishonoured* or *disgraced* in the estimation of the Jewish rulers. The *particular* disgrace to which reference is made here was *whipping.* To various other kinds of shame they were also exposed. They were persecuted, reviled, and finally put to death. Here we may remark that a profession of the Christian religion has been in all ages esteemed by many to be a *disgrace.* The *reasons* are, (1) That Jesus is himself despised; (2) That his precepts are opposed to the gaiety and follies of the world; (3) That it attacks that on which the men of the world pride themselves; (4) That it requires a *spirit* which the world esteems mean and grovelling—meekness, humility, self-denial, patience, forgiveness of injuries; and (5) That it requires *duties*—prayer, praise, seriousness, benevolence. All these things the men of the world esteem degrading and mean, and hence they endeavour to subject those who practise them to disgrace. The *kinds* of disgrace to which Christians have been subjected are too numerous to be mentioned here. In former times they were subjected to the loss of property, of reputation, and to all the shame of public punishment, and to the terrors of the dungeon, the stake, or the rack. One main design of persecution was, to select a kind of punishment so *disgraceful* as to deter others from professing religion. Disgrace even yet may attend it. It may subject one to the ridicule of friends—of even a father, mother, or brother. Christians hear their opinions abused; their names vilified; their Bible travestied; the name of their God profaned, and of their Redeemer blasphemed. Their feelings are often wantonly and rudely torn by the cutting sarcasm or the bitter sneer. Books and songs revile them; their peculiarities are made the occasion of indecent merriment on the stage and in novels; and in this way they are still subjected to shame for the name of Jesus. Every one who becomes a Christian should remember that this is a part of his inheritance, and should not esteem it dishonourable to be treated as his Master was before him, Jn. xv. 18–20; Mat. x. 25. ¶ *For his name.* For attachment to him.

42. *And daily,* &c. Comp. 2 Ti. iv. 2. See also Notes on Ac. ii. 46.

CHAPTER VI.

AND in those days, when the number of the disciples was multiplied, there arose a murmuring of the [a]Grecians against the Hebrews, because their widows were neglected in [b]the daily ministration.

a ch.9.29; 11.20. b ch.4.35.

CHAPTER VI.

1. *In those days*, &c. The first part of this chapter contains an account of the appointment of *deacons.* It may be asked, perhaps, why the apostles did not appoint these officers at the first organization of the church? To this question we may reply, that it was better to defer the appointment until an occasion should occur when it would appear to be manifestly necessary and proper. When the church was small, its alms could be distributed by the apostles themselves without difficulty. But when it was greatly increased; when its charities were multiplied; and when the distribution might give rise to contentions, it was necessary that this matter should be intrusted to the hands of *laymen*, and that the *ministry* should be freed from all embarrassment, and all suspicions of dishonesty and unfairness in regard to pecuniary matters. It has never been found to be wise that the temporal affairs of the church should be intrusted in any considerable degree to the clergy, and they should be freed from such sources of difficulty and embarrassment. ¶ *Was multiplied.* By the accession of the three thousand on the day of Pentecost, and of those who were subsequently added, ch. iv. 4; v. 14. ¶ *A murmuring.* A *complaint*—as if there had been partiality in the distribution. ¶ *Of the Grecians.* There has been much diversity of opinion in regard to these persons, whether they were *Jews* who had lived among the Gentiles, and who spoke the Greek language, or whether they were proselytes from the Gentiles. The former is probably the correct opinion. The word here used is not that which is commonly employed to designate the inhabitants of Greece, but it properly denotes those who *imitate* the customs and habits of the Greeks, who use the Greek language, &c. In the time when the gospel was first preached, there were two classes of Jews—those who remained in Palestine, who used the Hebrew language, and who were appropriately called *Hebrews;* and those who were scattered among the Gentiles, who spoke the Greek language, and who used in their synagogues the Greek translation of the Old Testament, called the Septuagint. These were called *Hellenists*, or, as it is in our translation, *Grecians.* See Notes on Jn. vii. 35. These were doubtless the persons mentioned here—not those who were proselyted from Gentiles, but those of Jewish origin who were not natives of Judea, who had come up to Jerusalem to attend the great festivals. See ch. ii. 5, 9–11. Dissensions would be very likely to arise between these two classes of persons. The Jews of Palestine would pride themselves much on the fact that they dwelt in the land of the patriarchs and the land of promise; that they used the language which their fathers spoke, and in which the oracles of God were given; and that they were constantly near the temple, and regularly engaged in its solemnities. On the other hand, the Jews from other parts of the world would be suspicious, jealous, and envious of their brethren, and would be likely to charge them with partiality, or of taking advantage in their intercourse with them. These occasions of strife would not be destroyed by their conversion to Christianity, and one of them is furnished on this occasion. ¶ *Because their widows*, &c. The property which had been contributed, or thrown into common stock, was understood to be designed for the equal benefit of *all* the poor, and particularly, it would seem, for the poor widows. The distribution before this seems to have been made by the apostles themselves—or possibly, as Mosheim conjectures (*Comm. de rebus Christianorum ante Constantinum*, p. 139, 118), the apostles committed the distribution of these funds to the Hebrews, and hence the Grecians are represented as murmuring against them, and not against the apostles. ¶ *In the daily ministration.* In the daily distribution which was made for their wants. Comp. ch. iv. 35. The property was contributed doubtless with an understanding that it should be *equally* distributed to all classes of Christians that had need. It is clear from the Epistles that *widows* were objects of special attention in the

2 Then the twelve called the multitude of the disciples *unto them*, and said, [c]It is not reason that we should leave the word of God, and serve tables.

c Ex.18.17-26.

3 Wherefore, brethren, [d]look ye out among you seven men [e]of honest report, full of the Holy Ghost and wisdom, whom we may appoint over this business.

d De.1.13. e ch.16.2; 1 Ti.3.7,8,10.

---

primitive church, and that the first Christians regarded it as a matter of indispensable obligation to provide for their wants, 1 Ti. v. 3, 9, 10, 16; Ja. i. 27.

2. *Then the twelve.* That is, the apostles. Matthias had been added to them after the apostasy of Judas, which had completed the original number. ¶ *The multitude of the disciples.* It is not necessary to suppose that *all* the disciples were convened, which amounted to many thousands, but that the business was laid before a large number; or perhaps *the multitude* here means those merely who were more particularly interested in the matter, and who had been engaged in the complaint. ¶ *It is not reason.* The original words used here properly denote *it is not pleasing* or *agreeable;* but the meaning evidently is, it is not *fit* or *proper.* It would be a departure from the design of their appointment, which was to preach the gospel, and not to attend to the pecuniary affairs of the church. ¶ *Leave the word of God.* That we should neglect or abandon the preaching of the gospel so much as would be necessary if we attended personally to the distribution of the alms of the church. The *gospel* is here called the *word of God*, because it is *his* message; it is that which he has *spoken*, or which he has commanded to be proclaimed to men. ¶ *Serve tables.* This expression properly denotes to take care of, or provide for the table, or for the daily wants of a family. It is an expression that properly applies to a steward or a servant. The word *tables* is, however, sometimes used with reference to *money*, as being the place where money was kept for the purpose of *exchange*, &c., Mat. xxi. 12; xxv. 27. Here the expression means, therefore, to attend to the pecuniary transactions of the church, and to make the proper distribution for the wants of the poor.

3. *Look ye out.* Select, or choose. As this was a matter pertaining to their own pecuniary affairs, it was proper that *they* should be permitted to choose such men as they could confide in. By this means the apostles would be free from all suspicions. It could not be pretended that *they* were partial, nor could it ever be charged on them that they wished to embezzle the funds by managing them themselves, or by intrusting them to men of their own selection. It follows from this, also, that the right of selecting *deacons* resides *in* the church, and does not pertain to the ministry. It is evidently proper that men who are to be intrusted with the alms of the church should be selected by the church itself. ¶ *Among you.* That is, from among the Grecians and Hebrews, that there may be justice done, and no farther cause of complaint. ¶ *Seven men.* Seven was a sacred number among the Hebrews, but there does not appear to have been any *mystery* in choosing this number. It was a convenient number, sufficiently large to secure the faithful performance of the duty, and not so large as to cause confusion and embarrassment. It does not follow, however, that the same number is now to be chosen as deacons in a church, for the precise number is not commanded. ¶ *Of honest report.* Of fair reputation; regarded as men of integrity. Greek, *testified of*, or *borne witness to;* that is, whose characters were well known and fair. ¶ *Full of the Holy Ghost.* This evidently does not mean endowed with miraculous gifts, or the power of speaking foreign languages, for such gifts were not necessary to the discharge of their office, but it means men who were eminently under the influence of the Holy Ghost, or who were of distinguished piety. This was all that was necessary in the case, and this is all that the words fairly imply. ¶ *And wisdom.* Prudençe, or skill, to make a wise and equable distribution. The qualifications of deacons are still further stated and illustrated in 1 Ti. iii. 8–10. In this place it is seen that they must be men of eminent piety and fair character, and that they must possess *prudence*, or wisdom, to manage the affairs connected with their office. These qualifications are indispensable to a faithful discharge of the duty intrusted

4 But we will [f]give ourselves continually to prayer, and to the ministry of the word.

5 And the saying pleased the whole multitude; and they chose Stephen, a man [g]full of faith and

f 1 Ti.4.15.

g ch.11.24.

to the officers of the church. ¶ *Whom we may appoint.* Whom we may *constitute*, or *set* over this business. The way in which this was done was by prayer and the imposition of hands, ver. 6. Though they were *selected* by the church, yet the power of ordaining them, or setting them apart, was retained by the apostles. Thus the rights of *both* were preserved—the right of the church to designate those who should serve them in the office of deacon, and the right of the apostles to organize and establish the church with its appropriate officers; on the one hand, a due regard to the liberty and privileges of the Christian community, and, on the other, the security of proper respect for the office as being of apostolic appointment and authority. ¶ *Over this business.* That is, over the distribution of the alms of the church—not to preach, or to govern the church, but solely to take care of the sacred funds of charity, and distribute them to supply the wants of the poor. The office is distinguished from that of *preaching* the gospel. To that the apostles were to attend. The deacons were expressly set apart to a different work, and to that work they should be confined. In this account of their original appointment, there is not the slightest intimation that they were to *preach*, but the contrary is supposed in the whole transaction. Nor is there here the slightest intimation that they were regarded as an order of *clergy*, or as in any way connected with the clerical office. In the ancient synagogues of the Jews there were three men to whom was intrusted the care of the poor. They were called by the Hebrews *parnasin* or *pastors* (Lightfoot, *Hor. Heb. et Talm.;* Mat. iv. 23). From these officers the apostles took the idea probably of appointing deacons in the Christian church, and doubtless intended that their duties should be the same.

4. *But we will give ourselves continually.* The original expression here used denotes *intense and persevering* application to a thing, or unwearied effort in it. See Notes on Ac. i. 14. It means that the apostles designed to make this their constant and main object, undistracted by the cares of life, and even by attention to the temporal wants of the church. ¶ *To prayer.* Whether this means *private* or *public* prayer cannot be certainly determined. The passage, however, would rather incline us to suppose that the *latter* was meant, as it is immediately connected with preaching. If so, then the phrase denotes that they would give themselves to the duties of their office, one part of which was public prayer, and another preaching. Still it is to be believed that the apostles felt the need of secret prayer, and practised it, as preparatory to their public preaching. ¶ *And to the ministry of the word.* To preaching the gospel, or communicating the message of eternal life to the world. The word ministry (διακονία) properly denotes the employment of a *servant*, and is given to the preachers of the gospel because they are employed in this as the *servants* of God and of the church. We have here a view of what the apostles thought to be the proper work of the ministry. They were set apart to this work. It was their main, their only employment. To this their lives were to be devoted, and both by their example and their writings they have shown that it was on this principle they acted. Comp. 1 Ti. iv. 15, 16; 2 Ti. iv. 2. It follows also that if their time and talents were to be wholly devoted to this work, it was reasonable that they should receive competent support from the churches, and this reasonable claim is often urged. See Notes on 1 Co. ix. 7-14; Ga. vi. 6.

5. *And the saying.* The *word*—the counsel, or command. ¶ *And they chose Stephen*, &c. A man who soon showed (ch. vii.) that he was every way qualified for his office, and fitted to defend also the cause of the Lord Jesus. This man had the distinguished honour of being the first Christian martyr. ¶ *And Nicolas.* From this man some of the fathers (Iren., lib. i. 27; Epiphanius, 1; Hæres., 5) says that the sect of the *Nicolaitanes*, mentioned with so much disapprobation (Re. ii. 6, 15), took their rise. But the evidence of this is not clear. ¶ *A proselyte.* A *proselyte* is one

of the Holy Ghost, and [h]Philip, and Prochorus, and Nicanor, and Timon, and Parmenas, and [i]Nicolas a proselyte of Antioch:

6 Whom they set before the apostles: and [k]when they had prayed, [l]they laid *their* hands on them.

7 And [m] the word of God increased; and the number of the disciples multiplied in Jerusalem

h ch.8.5,26; 21.8. i Re.2.6,15. k ch.1.24. l ch.9.17; 13.3; 1 Ti.4.14; 5.22; 2 Ti.1.6. m Is.55.11; ch.12.24; 19.20.

who is converted from one religion to another. See Notes on Mat. xxiii. 15. The word does not mean here that he was a convert to *Christianity*—which was true—but that he had been converted at Antioch from paganism to the Jewish religion. As this is the only proselyte mentioned among the seven deacons, it is evident that the others were native-born Jews, though a part of them might have been born out of Palestine, and have been of the denomination of *Grecians*, or *Hellenists.* ¶ *Of Antioch.* This city, often mentioned in the New Testament (Ac. xi. 19, 20, 26; xv. 22, 35; Ga. ii. 11, &c.), was situated in Syria, on the river Orontes, and was formerly called *Riblath.* It is not mentioned in the Old Testament, but is frequently mentioned in the Apocrypha. It was built by Seleucus Nicanor, A.C. 301, and was named *Antioch*, in honour of his father Antiochus. It became the seat of empire of the Syrian kings of the Macedonian race, and afterward of the Roman governors of the eastern provinces. In this place the disciples of Christ were first called *Christians*, Ac. xi. 26. Josephus says it was the third city in size of the Roman provinces, being inferior only to Seleucia and Alexandria. It was long, indeed, the most powerful city of the East. The city was almost square, had many gates, was adorned with fine fountains, and possessed great fertility of soil and commercial opulence. It was subject to earthquakes, and was often almost destroyed by them. In A.D. 588 above sixty thousand persons perished in it in this manner. In A.D. 970 an army of one hundred thousand Saracens besieged it, and took it. In 1268 it was taken possession of by the Sultan of Egypt, who demolished it, and placed it under the dominion of the Turk. It is now called *Antakia*, and till the year 1822 it occupied a remote corner of the ancient inclosure of its walls, its splendid buildings being reduced to hovels, and its population living in Turkish debasement. It contains now about ten thousand inhabitants (Robinson's Calmet). This city should be distinguished from Antioch in Pisidia, also mentioned in the New Testament, Ac. xiii. 14.

6. *And when they had prayed.* Invoking in this manner the blessing of God to attend them in the discharge of the duties of their office. ¶ *They laid* their *hands*, &c. Among the Jews it was customary to lay hands on the head of a person who was set apart to any particular office, Nu. xxvii. 18; Comp. Ac. viii. 19. This was done, not to impart any power or ability, but to *designate* that they received their authority or commission from those who thus laid their hands on them, as the act of laying hands on the sick by the Saviour was an act signifying that the power of healing came from him, Mat. ix. 18; comp. Mar. xvi. 18. In such cases the laying on of the hands conveyed of itself no healing power, but was a sign or token that the power came from the Lord Jesus. Ordination has been uniformly performed in this way. See 1 Ti. v. 22. Though the seven deacons had been chosen by the church to this work, yet they derived their immediate commission and authority from the apostles.

7. *And the word of God increased.* That is, the gospel was more and more successful, or became more mighty and extensive in its influence. An instance of this success is immediately added. ¶ *And a great company of the priests.* A great *multitude.* This is recorded justly as a remarkable instance of the power of the gospel. How great this *company* was is not mentioned. But the number of the priests in Jerusalem was very great; and their conversion was a striking proof of the power of truth. It is probable that they had been opposed to the gospel with quite as much hostility as any other class of the Jews. And it is now mentioned, as worthy of special record, that the gospel was sufficiently mighty to humble even the proud, and haughty, and self-

greatly; [n]and a great company of the priests were obedient to the faith.

8 And Stephen, full of faith and power, did great wonders and miracles among the people.

9 Then there arose certain of the synagogue, which is called *the synagogue* of the Libertines,

n Ps.132.9,16; Jn.12.42.

---

ish, and envious priests to the foot of the cross. One design of the gospel is to evince the power of truth in subduing all classes of men; and hence in the New Testament we have the record of its having actually subdued every class to the obedience of faith. Some MSS., however, here instead of *priests* read *Jews*. This reading is followed in the Syriac version. ¶ *Were obedient to the faith.* The word *faith* here is evidently put for the *Christian religion*. Faith is one of the main requirements of the gospel (Mar. xvi. 16), and by a figure of speech is put for the gospel itself. To become *obedient to the faith*, therefore, is to obey the requirements of the gospel, particularly that which requires us to *believe*. Comp. Ro. x. 16. By the accession of the *priests* also no small part of the reproach would be taken away from the gospel, that it made converts only among the lower classes of the people. Comp. Jn. vii. 48.

8. *And Stephen.* The remarkable death of this first Christian martyr, which soon occurred, gave occasion to the sacred writer to give a detailed account of his character, and of the causes which led to his death. Hitherto the opposition of the Jews had been confined to threats and imprisonment; but it was now to burst forth with furious rage and madness, that could be satisfied only with blood. This was the first in a series of persecutions against Christians which filled the church with blood, and which closed the lives of thousands, perhaps millions, in the great work of establishing the gospel on the earth. ¶ *Full of faith.* Full of *confidence* in God, or trusting entirely to his promises. See Notes on Mar. xvi. 16. ¶ *And power.* The power which was evinced in working miracles. ¶ *Wonders.* This is one of the words commonly used in the New Testament to denote miracles.

9. *Then there arose.* That is, they stood up against him, or they opposed him. ¶ *Of the synagogue.* See Notes on Mat. iv. 23. The Jews were scattered in all parts of the world. In every place they would have synagogues. But it is also probable that there would be enough foreign Jews residing at Jerusalem from each of those places to maintain the worship of the synagogue; and at the great feasts, those synagogues adapted to Jewish people of different nations would be attended by those who came up to attend the great feasts. It is certain that there was a large number of synagogues in Jerusalem. The common estimate is, that there were four hundred and eighty in the city (Lightfoot; Vitringa). ¶ *Of the Libertines.* There has been very great difference of opinion about the meaning of this word. The chief opinions may be reduced to three: 1. The word is Latin, and means properly a *freedman*, a man who had been a slave and was set at liberty. Many have supposed that these persons were manumitted slaves of Roman origin, but who had become proselyted to the Jewish religion, and who had a synagogue in Jerusalem. This opinion is not very probable; though it is certain, from Tacitus (*Ann.*, lib. ii. c. 85), that there were many persons of this description at Rome. He says that four thousand Jewish proselytes of Roman slaves made free were sent at one time to Sardinia. 2. A second opinion is, that these persons were Jews by birth, and had been taken captives by the Romans, and then set at liberty, and were thus called *freedmen* or *libertines*. That there *were* many Jews of this description there can be no doubt. Pompey the Great, when he subjugated Judea, sent large numbers of the Jews to Rome (Philo, *In Legat. ad Caium*). These Jews were set at liberty at Rome, and assigned a place beyond the Tiber for a residence. See Introduction to the Epistle to the Romans. These persons are by Philo called *libertines*, or *freedmen* (Kuinoel, *in loco*). Many Jews were also conveyed as captives by Ptolemy I. to Egypt, and obtained a residence in that country and the vicinity. 3. Another opinion is, that they took their name from some *place* which they occupied. This opinion is more probable from the fact that all the *other* persons mentioned here are named from the countries which they occupied. Suidas says that this is the name of a place. And

and Cyrenians, and Alexandrians, and of them of Cilicia and of Asia, disputing with Stephen.
10 And they [o]were not able to
resist the wisdom and the spirit by which he spake.
11 Then they [p]suborned men, which said, We have heard him

o Lu.21.15.

p 1 Ki.21.10,13; Mat.26.59,60.

in one of the fathers this passage occurs: "Victor, bishop of the Catholic Church at *Libertina*, says, unity is there," &c. From this passage it is plain that there was a place called *Libertina*. That place was in Africa, not far from ancient Carthage. See Bishop Pearce's *Comment.* on this place. ¶ *Cyrenians.* Jews who dwelt at *Cyrene* in Africa. See Notes on Mat. xxvii. 32. ¶ *Alexandrians.* Inhabitants of Alexandria in Egypt. That city was founded by Alexander the Great, B.C. 332, and was peopled by colonies of Greeks and Jews. It was much celebrated, and contained not less than three hundred thousand free citizens, and as many slaves. The city was the residence of many Jews. Josephus says that Alexander himself assigned to them a particular quarter of the city, and allowed them equal privileges with the Greeks (*Antiq.*, xiv. 7, 2; *Against Apion*, ii. 4). Philo affirms that of five parts of the city, the Jews inhabited two. According to his statement, there dwelt in his time at Alexandria and the other Egyptian cities not less than *ten hundred thousand Jews.* Amron, the general of Omar, when he took the city, said that it contained 40,000 tributary Jews. At this place the famous version of the Old Testament called the *Septuagint*, or the Alexandrian version, was made. See Robinson's Calmet. ¶ *Cilicia.* This was a province of Asia Minor, on the sea-coast, at the north of Cyprus. The capital of this province was Tarsus, the native place of Paul, ch. ix. 11. As Paul was of this place, and belonged doubtless to this synagogue, it is probable that he was one who was engaged in this dispute with Stephen. Comp. ch. vii. 58. ¶ *Of Asia.* See Notes on ch. ii. 9. ¶ *Disputing with Stephen.* Doubtless on the question whether Jesus was the Messiah. This word does not denote *angry disputing*, but is commonly used to denote fair and impartial inquiry; and it is probable that the discussion began in this way, and when they were overcome by *argument*, they resorted, as disputants are apt to do, to angry criminations and violence.

10. *To resist.* That is, they were not able to *answer* his arguments. ¶ *The wisdom.* This properly refers to his knowledge of the Scriptures; his skill in what *the Jews* esteemed to be wisdom—acquaintance with their sacred writings, opinions, &c. ¶ *And the spirit.* This has been commonly understood of the Holy Spirit, by which he was aided; but it rather means the *energy*, *power*, or *ardour* of Stephen. He *evinced* a spirit of zeal and sincerity which they could not withstand; which served, more than mere argument could have done, to convince them that he was right. The evidence of sincerity, honesty, and zeal in a public speaker will often go farther to convince the great mass of mankind, than the most able argument if delivered in a cold and indifferent manner.

11. *Then they suborned men.* To *suborn* in law means to procure a person to take such a false oath as constitutes perjury (Webster). It has substantially this sense here. It means that they induced them to declare that which was false, or to bring a false accusation against him. This was done, not by declaring a palpable and open falsehood, but by *perverting* his doctrines, and by stating their own *inferences* as what he had actually maintained—the common way in which men oppose doctrines from which they differ. The Syriac reads this place, "Then they sent certain men, and instructed them that they should say," &c. This was repeating an artifice which they had before practised so successfully in relation to the Lord Jesus Christ. See Mat. xxvi. 60, 61. ¶ *We have heard*, &c. *When* they alleged that they had heard this is not said. Probably, however, they referred to some of his discourses with the people when he wrought miracles and wonders among them, ver. 8. ¶ *Blasphemous words.* See Notes on Mat. ix. 3. Moses was regarded with profound reverence. His laws they held to be unchangeable. Any intimation, therefore, that there was a greater lawgiver than he, or that his institutions were mere shadows and types, and were no longer binding, would be regarded as blasphemy, even though it should be

speak blasphemous words against
Moses, and *against* God.
12 And they stirred up the
people, and the elders, and the
scribes, and came upon *him*, and
caught him, and brought *him* to
the council,
13 And set up false witnesses,
which said, This man ceaseth not to
speak blasphemous words against
this holy place, and the law:
14 For[q] we have heard him say,
that this Jesus of Nazareth [r]shall
destroy this place, and shall change
the [1]customs which Moses delivered us.
15 And all that sat in the coun-

q ch.25.8. r Da.9.26. 1 or, *rites*.

---

spoken with the highest professed respect for Moses. That the Mosaic institutions were to be changed, and give place to another and a better dispensation, all the Christian teachers would affirm; but this was not said with a design to blaspheme or revile Moses. *In the view of the Jews*, to say that was to speak blasphemy; and hence, instead of reporting what he actually *did* say, they accused him of *saying* what *they* regarded as blasphemy. If reports are made of what men say, their very *words* should be reported; and we should not report *our* inferences or impressions as what they said. ¶ *And against God.* God was justly regarded by the Jews as the giver of their law and the author of their institutions. But the Jews, either wilfully or involuntarily, not knowing that they were a shadow of good things to come, and were therefore to pass away, regarded all intimations of such a change as blasphemy against God. God had a right to change or abolish those ceremonial observances, and it was *not* blasphemy in Stephen to declare it.

12. *And they stirred up the people.* They *excited* the people, or alarmed their fears, as had been done before when they sought to put the Lord Jesus to death, Mat. xxvii. 20. ¶ *The elders.* The members of the Sanhedrim, or great council. ¶ *Scribes.* See Notes on Mat. ii. 4. ¶ *To the council.* To the Sanhedrim, or the great council of the nation, which claimed jurisdiction in the matters of religion. See Notes on Mat. ii. 4.

13. *And set up false witnesses.* It has been made a question why these persons are called *false* witnesses, since it is supposed by many that they reported merely the *words* of Stephen. It may be replied that *if* they did report merely his *words;* if Stephen had actually said what they affirmed, yet they perverted his meaning. They accused him of *blasphemy;* that is, of calumnious and reproachful words against Moses and against God. That Stephen had spoken in such a manner, or had designed to *reproach* Moses, there is no evidence. What was said in the mildest manner, and in the way of cool argument, might easily be perverted so as in *their view* to amount to blasphemy. But there is no evidence whatever that Stephen had ever *used* these words on any occasion, and it is altogether improbable that he ever did, for the following reasons: (1) Jesus himself never affirmed that *he* would destroy that place. He uniformly taught that it would be done by the *Gentiles*, Mat. xxiv. It is altogether improbable, therefore, that Stephen should declare any such thing. (2) It is equally improbable that he taught that Jesus would abolish the peculiar customs and rites of the Jews. It was long, and after much discussion, before the apostles themselves were convinced that they were to be changed, and when they were changed it was done gradually. See Ac. x. 14, &c.; xi. 2, &c.; xv. 20; xxi. 20, &c. The probability therefore is, that the whole testimony was *false*, and was artfully invented to produce the utmost exasperation among the people, and yet was at the same time so plausible as to be easily believed. For on this point the Jews were particularly sensitive; and it is clear that they had some expectations that the Messiah *would* produce some such changes. Comp. Mat. xxvi. 61 with Da. ix. 26, 27. The same charge was afterward brought against Paul, which he promptly denied. See Ac. xxv. 8. ¶ *This holy place.* The temple. ¶ *The law.* The law of Moses.

14. *Shall change.* Shall abolish them, or shall introduce others in their place. ¶ *The customs.* The ceremonial rites and observances of sacrifices, festivals, &c., appointed by Moses.

15. *Looking stedfastly on him.* Fixing the eyes intently on him. Probably they were attracted by the unusual

cil, looking stedfastly on him, [s]saw his face as it had been the face of an angel.

s Ex.34.30,35

CHAPTER VII.

THEN said the high-priest, Are these things so?

---

appearance of the man, his meekness, his calm and collected fearlessness, and the proofs of conscious innocence and sincerity. ¶ *The face of an angel.* This expression is one evidently denoting that he manifested evidence of sincerity, gravity, fearlessness, confidence in God. It is used in the Old Testament to denote peculiar wisdom, 2 Sa. xiv. 17; xix. 27. In Ge. xxxiii. 10, it is used to denote peculiar majesty and glory, as if it were the face of God. When Moses came down from Mount Sinai, it is said that the skin of his face shone so that the children of Israel were afraid to come nigh to him, Ex. xxxiv. 29, 30; 2 Co. iii. 7, 13. Comp. Re. i. 16; Mat. xvii. 2. The expression is used to denote the impression produced on the countenance by communion with God; the calm serenity and composure which follow a confident committing of all into his hands. It is not meant that there was anything *miraculous* in the case of Stephen, but it is language that denotes calmness, dignity, and confidence in God, all of which were so marked on his countenance that it impressed them with clear proofs of his innocence and piety. The language is very common in the Jewish writings. It is not unusual for deep feeling, sincerity, and confidence in God, to impress themselves on the countenance. Any deep emotion will do this; and it is to be expected that religious feeling, the most tender and solemn of all feeling, will diffuse seriousness, serenity, calmness, and peace, not affected sanctimoniousness, over the countenance.

In this chapter we have another specimen of the manner in which the church of the Lord Jesus was established. It was from the beginning amidst scenes of persecution, encountering opposition adapted to try the nature and power of religion. If Christianity was an imposture, it had enemies acute and malignant enough to detect the imposition. The learned, the cunning, and the mighty rose up in opposition, and by all the arts of sophistry, all the force of authority, and all the fearfulness of power, attempted to destroy it in the commencement. Yet it lived; it gained new accessions of strength from every new form of opposition; it evinced its genuineness more and more by showing that it was superior to the arts and malice of earth and of hell.

CHAPTER VII.

This chapter contains the defence of Stephen before the Sanhedrim, or great council of the Jews. There has been great diversity of opinion about the *object* which Stephen had in view in this defence, and about the reason why he introduced at such length the history of the Jewish people. But a few remarks may perhaps show his design. He was accused of *blasphemy in speaking against the institutions of Moses and the temple, that is, against everything held sacred among the Jews.* To meet this charge, he gives a statement, at length, of his belief in the Mosaic religion, in the great points of their history, and in the fact that God had interposed in a remarkable manner in defending them from dangers. By this historical statement he avows his full belief in the divine origin of the Jewish religion, and thus *indirectly* repels the charge of blasphemy. It is further to be remembered that this was the best way of securing the *attention* of the council. Had he entered on an abstract defence, he might expect to be stopped by their cavils or their clamour. But the history of their own nation was a favourite topic among the Jews. They were always ready to listen to an account of their ancestors; and to secure their attention, nothing more was necessary than to refer to their illustrious lives and deeds. Comp. Ps. lxxviii., cv., cvi., cxxxv.; Eze. xx. In this way Stephen secured their attention, and practically repelled the charge of speaking reproachfully of Moses and the temple. He showed them that *he* had as firm a belief as *they* in the great historical facts of their nation. It is to be remembered, also, that this speech was broken off in the midst (ver. 53, 54), and it is therefore difficult to state fully what the design of Stephen was. It seems clear, however, that he intended to convict *them* of guilt, by showing that *they* sustained the same character as their fathers had manifested (ver. 51, 52); and there is some probability that he intended to

2 And he said, [a]Men, brethren, and fathers, hearken: The God of glory appeared unto our father Abraham, when he was in Mesopotamia, before he dwelt in Charran,

a ch.22.1.

show that the acceptable worship of God was not to be confined to any place particularly, from the fact that the worship of Abraham, and the patriarchs, and Moses, was acceptable *before* the temple was reared (ver. 2, &c.), and from the declaration in ver. 48, that God dwells not in temples made with hands. All that can be said here is, (1) That Stephen showed his full belief in the divine appointment of Moses and the historical facts of their religion; (2) That he laid *the foundation* of an argument to show that those things were not perpetually binding, and that acceptable worship *might* be offered in other places and in another manner than at the temple.

It has been asked in what way Luke became acquainted with this speech so as to repeat it. The Scripture has not informed us. But we may remark, (1) That Stephen was the first martyr. His death, and the incidents connected with it, could not but be a matter of interest to the first Christians, and the *substance* of his defence, at least, would be familiar to them. There is no improbability in supposing that imperfect copies might be preserved by writing, and circulated among them. (2) Luke was the companion of Paul. (See Introduction to the Gospel by Luke.) Paul was present when this defence was delivered, and was a man who would be likely to *remember* what was said on such an occasion. From him Luke might have derived the account of this defence. In regard to this discourse, it may be further remarked, that it is not necessary to suppose that Stephen was inspired. Even if there should be found inaccuracies, as some critics have pretended, in the address, it would not militate against its genuineness. It is the defence of a man on trial under a serious charge; not a man of whom there is evidence that he was *inspired*, but a pious, devoted, heavenly-minded man. All that the sacred narrative is responsible for is the *correctness of the report.* Luke alleges only that *such a speech was in fact delivered,* without affirming that every particular in it is correct.

1. *Then said the high-priest.* See Notes on Mat. ii. 4. In this case the high-priest seems to have presided in the council. ¶ *Are these things so?* To wit, the charge alleged against him of blasphemy against Moses and the temple, ch. vi. 13, 14.

2. *Men, brethren, and fathers.* These were the usual titles by which the Sanhedrim was addressed. In all this Stephen was perfectly respectful, and showed that he was disposed to render due honour to the institutions of the nation. ¶ *The God of glory.* This is a Hebrew form of expression denoting *the glorious God.* It properly denotes his majesty, or splendour, or magnificence; and the word *glory* is often applied to the splendid appearances in which God has manifested himself to men, De. v. 24; Ex. xxxiii. 18; xvi. 7, 10; Le. ix. 23; Nu. xiv. 10. Perhaps Stephen meant to affirm that God appeared to Abraham in some such glorious or splendid manifestation, by which he would know that he was addressed by God. Stephen, moreover, evidently uses the word *glory* to repel the charge of *blasphemy* against God, and to show that he regarded him as worthy of honour and praise. ¶ *Appeared,* &c. In what *manner* he appeared is not said. In Ge. xii. 1, it is simply recorded that God *had said* unto Abraham, &c. ¶ *To our father.* The Jews valued themselves much on being the children of Abraham. See Notes on Mat. iii. 9. The expression was therefore well calculated to conciliate their minds. ¶ *When he was in Mesopotamia.* In Ge. xi. 31, it is said that Abraham dwelt *in Ur of the Chaldees.* The word Mesopotamia properly denotes the region between the two rivers, the Euphrates and the Tigris. See Notes on Ac. ii. 9. The name is Greek, and the region had also other names before the Greek name was given to it. In Ge. xi. 31; xv. 7, it is called Ur of the Chaldees. Mesopotamia and Chaldea might not exactly coincide; but it is evident that Stephen meant to say that *Ur* was in the country afterward called Mesopotamia. Its precise situation is unknown. A Persian fortress of this name is mentioned by Ammianus (xxv. 8) between Nisibis and the Tigris. ¶ *Before he dwelt in Charran.* From Ge. xi. 31, it would seem that Terah took his son Abraham of his own accord, and removed to Haran. But from Ge.

3 And said unto him, [b]Get thee out of thy country, and from thy kindred, and come into the land which I shall show thee.

4 Then[c] came he out of the land of the Chaldeans, and dwelt in Charran; and from thence, when his father was dead, he re-

b Ge.12.1.

c Ge.12.5.

xii. 1; xv. 7, it appears that God had commanded *Abraham* to remove, and so he ordered it in his providence that *Terah* was disposed to remove his family with an intention of going into the land of Canaan. The word *Charran* is the Greek form of the Hebrew *Haran*, Ge. xi. 31. This place was also in Mesopotamia, in 36° 52′ N. lat. and 39° 5′ E. long. Here Terah died (Ge. xi. 32); and to this place Jacob retired when he fled from his brother Esau, Ge. xxvii. 43. It is situated "in a flat and sandy plain, and is inhabited by a few wandering Arabs, who select it for the delicious water which it contains" (Robinson's Calmet).

3. *And said unto him.* How long this was said before he went is not recorded. Moses simply says that God *had* commanded him to go, Ge. xii. 1. ¶ *Thy kindred.* Thy relatives, or family connections. It seems that *Terah* went with him as far as to Haran; but Abraham was apprised that he was to leave his family, and to go almost alone. ¶ *Into the land*, &c. The country was yet unknown. The place was to be shown him. This is presented in the New Testament as a strong instance of faith, He. xi. 8, 9. It was an act of *simple confidence* in God. And to leave his country and home; to go into a land of strangers, not knowing whither he went, required strong confidence in God. It is a simple illustration of what man is always required to do at the command of God. Thus the gospel requires him to commit all to God; to yield body and soul to his disposal; to be ready at his command to forsake father, and mother, and friends, and houses, and lands, for the sake of the Lord Jesus, Lu. xiv. 33; Mat. xix. 27, 29. The trials which Abraham might have anticipated may be readily conceived. He was going, in a rude and barbarous age of the world, into a land of strangers. He was without arms or armies, and almost alone. He did not even know the nature or situation of the land, or the character of its inhabitants. He had no title to it; no claim to urge; and he went depending on the simple promise of God that he would give it to him. He went, therefore, trusting simply to the promise of God. Thus his conduct illustrated precisely what *we* are to do in reference to all our coming life, and to the eternity before us: we are to trust simply to the promise of God, and *do* that which he requires. This is faith. In Abraham it was as simple and intelligible an operation of mind as ever occurs in any instance. Nor is faith in the Scriptures regarded as more mysterious than any other mental operation. Had Abraham *seen* all that was to result from his going into that land, it would have been a sufficient *reason* to induce him to do as he did. But *God* saw it; and Abraham was required to act just *as if* he had seen it all, and all the reasons why he was called. On the strength of God's promises he was called to act. This was *faith*. It did not require him to act where there was *no reason* for his so acting, but where he did not *see* the reason. So in all cases of faith. If man could see all that God sees, he would *perceive* reasons for acting as God requires. But the reasons of things are often concealed, and man is required to act on the *belief* that *God* sees reasons why he should so act. To act under the proper impression of that truth which God presents is faith; as simple and intelligible as any other act or operation of the mind. See Notes on Mar. xvi. 16.

4. *Land of the Chaldeans.* From Ur of the Chaldees, Ge. xi. 31. ¶ *When his father was dead.* This passage has given rise to no small difficulty in the interpretation. The difficulty is this: From Ge. xi. 26, it would seem that Abraham was born when Terah was seventy years of age. "And Terah lived seventy years, and begat Abram, Nahor, and Haran." From Ge. xii. 4, it seems that Abraham was seventy-five years of age when he departed from Haran to Canaan. The age of Terah was therefore but one hundred and forty-five years. Yet in Ge. xi. 32, it is said that Terah was two hundred and five years old when he died, thus leaving sixty years of Terah's life beyond the time when Abraham left Haran.

moved him into this land, wherein
ye now dwell.
5 And he gave him none inheritance in it, no, not *so much as* to set his foot on: yet [d]he promised that he would give it to him for a possession, and to his seed after him, when *as yet* he had no child.
6 And God spake on this wise, [e]That his seed should sojourn in a strange land; and that they should

d Ge.13.15. e Ge.15.13,16.

Various modes have been proposed of meeting this difficulty. (1) Errors in *numbers* are more likely to occur than any other. In the *Samaritan* copy of the Pentateuch, it is said that Terah died in Haran at the age of one hundred and five years, which would suppose that his death occurred forty years before Abraham left Haran. But the Hebrew, Latin, Vulgate, Septuagint, Syriac, and Arabic read it two hundred and five years. (2) It is not affirmed that Abraham was born just at the time when Terah was seventy years of age. All that the passage in Ge. xi. 26 proves, according to the usual meaning of similar expressions, is, that Terah was seventy years old *before* he had any sons, and that the three were born subsequently to that. But which was born first, or what intervals intervened between their birth, does not appear. Assuredly it does not mean that all were born precisely at the time when Terah was seventy years of age. Neither does it appear that Abraham was the oldest of the three. The sons of Noah are said to have been Shem, Ham, and Japheth (Ge. v. 32); yet Japheth, though mentioned last, was the eldest, Ge. x. 21. As Abraham afterward became much the most distinguished, and as he was the father of the Jewish people, of whom Moses was writing, it was natural that he should be mentioned first. If it cannot be *proved* that Abraham was the eldest, as assuredly it cannot be, then there is no improbability in supposing that his birth might have occurred many years after Terah was seventy years of age. (3) The Jews unanimously affirm that Terah relapsed into idolatry before Abraham left Haran; and this they denominate *death*, or a moral death (Kuinoel). It is certain, therefore, that, from some cause, they were accustomed to speak of Terah as *dead* before Abraham left him. Stephen only used language which was customary among the Jews, and would employ it, doubtless, correctly, though *we* may not be able to see precisely how it can be reconciled with the account in Genesis.

5. *And he gave him none inheritance.* Abraham led a wandering life; and this passage means that he did not himself receive a permanent possession or residence in that land. The only land which he owned was the field which he *purchased* of the children of Heth for a burial place, Ge. xxiii. As this was obtained by *purchase*, and not by the direct gift of God, and as it was not designed for a *residence*, it is said that God gave him no *inheritance*. It is mentioned as a strong instance of his faith that he should remain there without a permanent residence himself, with only the prospect that his children, at some distant period, would inherit it. ¶ *Not* so much as *to set his foot on.* This is a proverbial expression, denoting in an emphatic manner that he had *no land*, De. ii. 5. ¶ *Would give it to him.* Ge. xiii. 15. Abraham did not himself possess all that land; and the promise is evidently equivalent to saying that it would be conferred on the family of Abraham, or the family of which he was the father, without affirming that *he* would himself personally possess it. It is true, however, that Abraham himself afterward dwelt many years in that land as his home, Ge. xiii., &c. ¶ *For a possession.* To be held as his own property. ¶ *When* as yet *he had no child.* When there was no human probability that he would have any posterity. Comp. Ge. xv. 2, 3; xviii. 11, 12. This is mentioned as a strong instance of his faith; "who against hope believed in hope," Ro. iv. 18.

6. *And God spake on this wise.* In this manner, Ge. xv. 13, 14. ¶ *His seed.* His posterity; his descendants. ¶ *Should sojourn.* This means that they would have a *temporary residence* there. The word is used in opposition to a fixed, permanent home, and is applied to travellers, or foreigners. ¶ *In a strange land.* In the Hebrew (Ge. xv. 13), "Shall be a stranger in a land that is not theirs." The land of Canaan and the

bring them into bondage, and entreat *them* evil [f] four hundred years.

7 And the nation to whom they shall be in bondage will I judge,

f Ex.12.40,41.

land of Egypt were to them strange lands, though the obvious reference here is to the latter. ¶ *Should bring them into bondage.* Or, would make them slaves, Ex. i. 11. ¶ *And entreat* them *evil.* Would *oppress* or *afflict* them. ¶ *Four hundred years.* This is the precise time which is mentioned by Moses, Ge. xv. 13. Great perplexity has been experienced in explaining this passage, or reconciling it with other statements. In Ex. xii. 40, it is said that their sojourning in Egypt was four hundred and thirty years. Josephus (*Antiq.*, b. ii. ch. ix. § 1) also says that the time in which they were in Egypt was four hundred years; though in another place (*Antiq.*, b. ii. ch. xv. § 2) he says that they left Egypt four hundred and thirty years after their forefather Abraham came to *Canaan*, but two hundred and fifteen years after Jacob removed to Egypt. Paul also (Ga. iii. 17) says that it was four hundred and thirty years from the time when the promise was given to Abraham to the time when the law was given on Mount Sinai. The Samaritan Pentateuch says also (Ex. xii. 40) that the "dwelling of the sons of Israel, and of their fathers, which they dwelt *in the land of Canaan*, and in the land of Egypt, was four hundred and thirty years." The same is the version of the Septuagint. A *part* of this perplexity is removed by the fact that Stephen and Moses use, in accordance with a very common custom, *round numbers* in speaking of it, and thus speak of four hundred years when the *literal* time was four hundred and thirty. The other perplexities are not so easily removed. From the account which Moses has given of the lives of certain persons, it would seem clear that the time which they spent in *Egypt* was *not* four hundred years. From Ge. xlvi. 8, 11, it appears that *Kohath* was born when Jacob went into Egypt. He lived one hundred and thirty-three years, Ex. vi. 18. Amram, his son, and the father of Moses lived one hundred and thirty-seven years, Ex. vi. 20. Moses was eighty years old when he was sent to Pharaoh, Ex. vii. 7. The *whole* time thus mentioned, including the time in which the father lived *after* his son was born, was only three hundred and fifty years. Exclusive of that, it is reasonable to suppose that the actual time of their being in Egypt could not have been but about two hundred years, according to one account of Josephus. The question then is, how can these accounts be reconciled? The only satisfactory way is by supposing that the four hundred and thirty years includes the whole time from the calling of Abraham to the departure from Egypt. And that this was the fact is probable from the following circumstances. (1) The purpose of *all* the narratives on this subject is to trace the period *before* they became finally settled in the land of Canaan. During *all* this period from the calling of Abraham, they were in a wandering, unfixed situation. This constituted substantially *one* period, including *all* their oppressions, hardships, and dangers; and it was natural to have reference to this *entire* period in any account which was given. (2) All this period was properly the period of *promise*, not of *possession.* In this respect the wanderings of Abraham and the oppressions of Egypt came under the same general description. (3) Abraham was himself occasionally in Egypt. He was unsettled; and since Egypt was so *pre-eminent* in all their troubles, it was natural to speak of *all* their oppressions as having occurred in that country. The phrase "residence in Egypt," or "in a strange land," would come to be synonymous, and would denote *all* their oppressions and trials. They would speak of their sufferings as having been endured in Egypt, because their afflictions *there* were so much more prominent than before. (4) All this receives countenance from the version of the LXX., and from the Samaritan text, showing the manner in which the ancient Jews were accustomed to understand it. (5) It should be added, that difficulties of chronology are more likely to occur than any others; and it should not be deemed strange if there are perplexities of this kind found in ancient writings which we cannot explain. It is so in *all* ancient records; and all that is usually expected in relation to such difficulties is that we should be able to present a *probable* explanation.

7. *And the nation*, &c. Referring

said God: and after that shall they come forth, and [g]serve me in this place.

8 And[h] he gave him the covenant of circumcision: [i]and so *Abraham* begat Isaac, and circumcised him the eighth day; and [k]Isaac *begat* Jacob; and [l]Jacob *begat* the twelve patriarchs,

9 And the patriarchs, [m]moved with envy, sold Joseph into Egypt; [n]but God was with him,

10 And delivered him out of

g Ex.3.12. h Ge.17.9-11. i Ge.21.1-4. k Ge.25.26. l Ge.29.32,&c. m Ge.37.28; Ps.105.17. n Ge.39.2,21.

particularly to the Egyptians. ¶ *Will I judge.* The word *judge*, in the Bible, often means to *execute judgment* as well as to pronounce it; that is, *to punish.* See Jn. xviii. 31; iii. 17; viii. 50; xii. 47; Ac. xxiv. 6; 1 Co. v. 13, &c. It has this meaning here. God regarded their oppressive acts as *deserving* his indignation, and he evinced it in the *plagues* with which he visited them, and in their overthrow in the Red Sea. ¶ *Shall serve me.* Shall worship me, or be regarded as my people. ¶ *In this place.* That is, in the place where God made this promise to Abraham. These words are not found in Genesis, but similar words are found in Ex. iii. 12, and it was a practice, in making quotations, to quote the sense only, or to connect two or more promises having relation to the same thing.

8. *And he gave him.* That is, God appointed or commanded this, Ge. xvii. 9–13. ¶ *The covenant.* The word *covenant* denotes properly a compact or agreement between two or more persons, usually attended with seals, pledges, or sanctions. In Ge. xvii. 7, and elsewhere, it is said that God would establish his *covenant* with Abraham; that is, he made him certain definite promises, attended with pledges and seals, &c. The idea of a strict *compact* or *agreement* between God and man, as between *equal parties*, is not found in the Bible. The word is commonly used, as here, to denote a promise on the part of God, attended with pledges, and demanding, on the part of man, in order to avail himself of its benefits, a specified course of conduct. The *covenant* is therefore another name for denoting two things on the part of God: (1) A *command*, which man is not at liberty to reject, as he *would be* if it were a literal covenant; and, (2) A *promise*, which is to be fulfilled only on the condition of obedience. The covenant with Abraham was simply a *promise* to give him the land, and to make him a great nation, &c. It was *never* proposed to Abraham with the supposition that he was at liberty to *reject* it, or to *refuse* to comply with its conditions. Circumcision was appointed as the *mark* or *indication* that Abraham and those thus designated were the persons included in the gracious purpose and promise. It served to *separate* them as a peculiar people; a people whose peculiar characteristic it was that they obeyed and served the God who had made the promise to Abraham. The phrase "covenant of circumcision" means, therefore, the covenant or promise which God made to Abraham, of which circumcision was the distinguishing *mark* or *sign*. ¶ *The twelve patriarchs.* The word *patriarch* properly denotes the father and ruler of a family. But it is commonly applied, by way of eminence, to the progenitors of the Jewish race, particularly to the twelve sons of Jacob. See Notes on Ac. ii. 29.

9. *Moved with envy.* That is, dissatisfied with the favour which their father Jacob showed Joseph, and envious at the dreams which indicated that he was to be raised to remarkable honour above his parents and brethren, Ge. xxxvii. 3–11. ¶ *Sold Joseph into Egypt.* Sold him, that he might be taken to Egypt. This was done at the suggestion of *Judah*, who advised it that Joseph might not be put to death by his brethren, Ge. xxxvii. 28. It is possible that Stephen, by this fact, might have designed to prepare the way for a severe rebuke of the Jews for having dealt in a similar manner with their Messiah. ¶ *But God was with him.* God protected him, and overruled all these wicked doings, so that he was raised to extraordinary honours.

10. *And delivered him*, &c. That is, restored him to liberty from his servitude and humiliation, and raised him up to high honours and offices in Egypt. ¶ *Favour and wisdom.* The favour was the result of his wisdom. His wisdom was particularly evinced in interpreting the dreams of Pharaoh, Ge. xli. ¶ *And made him governor*, &c. Ge. xli. 40.

all his afflictions, and gave him
favour and wisdom in the sight
of Pharaoh, king of Egypt; and
he[o] made him governor over
Egypt and all his house.
11 Now[p] there came a dearth
over all the land of Egypt and
Chanaan, and great affliction; and
our fathers found no sustenance.
12 But[q] when Jacob heard that
there was corn in Egypt, he sent
out our fathers first.
13 And at the second *time*
[r]Joseph was made known to his
brethren; and Joseph's kindred
was made known unto Pharaoh.
14 Then sent Joseph, and called
his father Jacob to *him*, and [s]all
his kindred, threescore and fifteen
souls.
15 So Jacob went down into

o Ge.41.40. *p* Ge.41.54. *q* Ge.42.1,2. *r* Ge.45.4,16. *s* Ge.46.27; De.10.22.

¶ *All his house.* All the family, or all the court and government of the nation.

11. *Now there came a dearth.* A famine, Ge. xli. 54. ¶ *And Chanaan.* Jacob was living at that time in Canaan. ¶ *Found no sustenance.* No food; no means of living.

12. *Was corn in Egypt.* The word *corn* here rather denotes *wheat.* See Notes on Mat. xii. 1. ¶ *Our fathers.* His ten sons; all his sons except Joseph and Benjamin, Ge. xlii. Stephen here *refers* only to the history, without entering into details. By this general reference he sufficiently showed that he *believed* what Moses had spoken, and did not intend to show him disrespect.

13. *Joseph was made known,* Ge. xlv. 4. ¶ *Joseph's kindred,* &c. His relatives; his family, Ge. xlv. 16.

14. *All his kindred.* His father and family, Ge. xlv. 17–28; xlvi. 1–26. ¶ *Threescore and fifteen souls.* Seventy-five persons. There has been much perplexity felt in the explanation of this passage. In Ge. xlvi. 26, Ex. i. 5, and De. x. 22, it is expressly said that the number which went down to Egypt consisted of seventy persons. The question is, in what way these accounts can be reconciled? It is evident that Stephen has followed the account which is given by the Septuagint. In Ge. xlvi. 27, that version reads, "But the sons of Joseph who were with him in Egypt were nine souls; all the souls of the house of Jacob which came with Jacob into Egypt were seventy-five souls." This number is made out by adding these *nine* souls to the sixty-six mentioned in ver. 26. The difference between the Septuagint and Moses is, that the former mentions five descendants of Joseph who are not recorded by the latter. The *names* of the sons of Ephraim and Manasseh are recorded in 1 Ch. vii. 14–21. Their names were Ashriel, Machir, Zelophehad, Peresh, sons of Manasseh; and Shuthelah, son of Ephraim. Why the Septuagint inserted these, it may not be easy to see. But such was evidently the fact; and the fact accords accurately with the historic record, though Moses did not insert their names. The solution of difficulties in regard to chronology is always difficult; and what might be entirely apparent to a Jew in the time of Stephen, may be wholly inexplicable to us.

15, 16. *And died.* Ge. xlix. 33. ¶ *He and our fathers.* The time which the Israelites remained in Egypt was two hundred and fifteen years, so that all the sons of Jacob were deceased before the Jews went out to go to the land of Canaan. ¶ *And were carried over.* Jacob himself was buried in the field of Macpelah by Joseph and his brethren, Ge. l. 13. It is expressly said that the bones of Joseph were carried by the Israelites when they went into the land of Canaan, and buried in Shechem, Jos. xxiv. 32; comp. Ge. l. 25. No mention is made in the Old Testament of their carrying the bones of any of the other patriarchs, but the thing is highly probable in itself. If the descendants of Joseph carried *his* bones, it would naturally occur to them to take also the bones of each of the patriarchs, and give them an honourable sepulchre together in the land of promise. Josephus (*Antiq.*, b. ii. ch. viii. § 2) says that "the posterity and sons of these men (of the brethren of Joseph), after some time, carried their bodies and buried them in Hebron; but as to the bones of Joseph, they carried them into the land of Canaan afterward, when the Hebrews went out of Egypt." This is in accordance with the common opinion of the Jewish writers, that they were buried in Hebron. Yet

Egypt, and died, he, and our fathers,

16 And[t] were carried over into Sychem, and laid in the sepulchre that Abraham bought for a sum of money of the sons of Emmor *the father* of Sychem.

17 But when the time of the promise drew nigh, which God had sworn to Abraham, [u]the people grew and multiplied in Egypt,

18 Till another king arose, which knew not Joseph.

19 The same dealt subtilly with

t Jos.24.32.

u Ex.1.7-9.

the tradition is not uniform. Some of the Jews affirm that they were buried in Sychem (Kuinoel). As the Scriptures do not anywhere deny that the patriarchs were buried in Sychem, it cannot be proved that Stephen was in error. There is one circumstance of strong probability to show that he was correct. At the time when this defence was delivered, *Sychem* was in the hands of the Samaritans, between whom and the Jews there was a violent hostility. Of course the Jews would not be willing to concede that the Samaritans had the bones of their ancestors, and hence perhaps the opinion had been maintained that they were buried in Hebron. ¶ *Into Sychem.* This was a town or village near to Samaria. It was called *Sichar* (see Notes on Jn. iv. 5), *Shechem*, and *Sychem.* It is now called *Naplous* or *Napolose*, and is ten miles from Shiloh, and about forty from Jerusalem, toward the north. ¶ *That Abraham bought.* The word *Abraham* here has given rise to considerable perplexity, and it is now pretty generally conceded that it is a mistake. It is certain, from Ge. xxxiii. 19 and Jos. xxiv. 32, that this piece of land was bought, not by Abraham, but by *Jacob*, of the sons of Hamor, the father of Shechem. The land which *Abraham* purchased was the cave of Macpelah, of the sons of Heth, in Hebron, Ge. xxiii. Various solutions have been proposed of this difficulty, which it is not necessary to detail. It may be remarked, however, (1) That as the text now stands, it is an evident error. This is clear from the passages cited from the Old Testament above. (2) It is not at all probable that either Stephen or Luke would have committed such an error. Every consideration must lead us to the conclusion that they were too well acquainted with such prominent points of the Jewish history to commit an error like this. (3) The *probability*, therefore, is, that the error has arisen since; but *how*, is not known, nor is there any way of ascertaining. All the ancient versions agree in reading *Abraham.* One MS. only reads "*Abraham our father.*" Some have supposed, therefore, that it was written "which our father bought," and that some early transcriber inserted the name of Abraham. Others, that the name was omitted entirely by Stephen; and then the antecedent to the verb "bought" will be "Jacob," in ver. 15, according with the fact. Other modes have been proposed also, but none are entirely satisfactory. If there was positive proof of Stephen's inspiration, or if it were necessary to make that out, the difficulty would be much greater. But it has already been remarked that there is no decisive evidence of that, and it is not necessary to make out that point to defend the Scriptures. All that can be demanded of the historian is, that he should give a fair account of the defence as it was delivered; and though the *probability* is that Stephen would not commit such an error, yet, admitting that he did, it by no means proves that *Luke* was not inspired, or that Luke has committed any error in recording *what was actually said.* ¶ *Of the sons of Emmor.* In the Hebrew (Ge. xxxiii. 19), "the children of Hamor"—but different ways of rendering the same word.

17. *The time of the promise.* The time of the *fulfilment* of the promise. ¶ *The people grew*, &c. Ex. i. 7-9.

18. *Till another king arose.* This is quoted from Ex. i. 8. What was the *name* of this king is not certainly known. The *common* name of all the kings of Egypt was *Pharaoh*, as *Cæsar* became the common name of the emperors of Rome after the time of Julius Cæsar: thus we say, Augustus Cæsar, Tiberius Cæsar, &c. It has commonly been supposed to have been the celebrated Rameses, the sixth king of the eighteenth dynasty, and the event is supposed to have occurred about 1559 years before the Christian era. M. Champollion supposes that his name was Mandonei, whose reign commenced 1585, and ended

our kindred, and evil-entreated
our fathers, [v]so that they cast out
their young children, to the end
they might not live.
20 In which time [w]Moses was
born, and was [1]exceeding fair, and
nourished up in his father's house
three months:
21 And when he was cast out,
Pharaoh's daughter took him up,
and [x]nourished him for her own
son.
22 And Moses was learned in
all the wisdom of the Egyptians,
and was [y]mighty in words and in
deeds.

v Ex.1.22. w Ex.2.2,&c. 1 or, *fair to God.* x Ex.2.10. y Lu.24.19.

1565 years before Christ (*Essay on the Hieroglyphic System*, p. 94, 95). Sir Jas. G. Wilkinson supposes that it was Amosis, or Ames, the *first* king of the eighteenth dynasty (*Manners and Customs of the Ancient Egyptians*, vol. i. p. 42, 2d ed.). "The present knowledge of Egyptian history is too imperfect to enable us to determine this point" (Prof. Hackett). ¶ *That knew not Joseph.* It can hardly be supposed that he would be ignorant of the name and deeds of Joseph; and this expression, therefore, probably means that he did not *favour* the designs of Joseph; he did not remember the benefits which he had conferred on the nation; or furnish the patronage for the kindred of Joseph which had been secured for them by Joseph under a former reign. National ingratitude has not been uncommon in the world, and a change of dynasty has often obliterated all memory of former obligations and compacts.

19. *Dealt subtilly.* He acted deceitfully; he used fraud. The cunning or deceitful attempt which is referred to, is his endeavour to weaken and destroy the Jewish people by causing their male children to be put to death, Ex. i. 22. ¶ *Our kindred.* Our nation, or our ancestors. ¶ *And evil-entreated.* Was unjust and cruel toward them. ¶ *So that,* &c. For that purpose, or to *cause* them to cast them out. He dealt with them in this cruel manner, hoping that the Israelites themselves would destroy their own sons, that they might not grow up to experience the same sufferings as their fathers had. The cunning or subtilty of Pharaoh extended to everything that he did to oppress, to keep under, and to destroy the children of Israel.

20. *In which time,* &c. During this period of oppression. See Ex. ii. 2, &c. ¶ *Was exceeding fair.* Greek, "was fair *to God;*" properly rendered, *was very handsome.* The word *God* in the Greek here in accordance with the Hebrew usage, by which anything that is very handsome, lofty, or grand is thus designated. Thus, Ps. xxxvi. 7, *mountains of God*, mean lofty mountains; Ps. lxxx. 11, *cedars of God*, mean lofty, beautiful cedars. Thus Nineveh is called "a great city *to God*" (Jonah iii. 3, Greek), meaning a very great city. The expression here simply means that Moses was *very fair*, or handsome. Comp. He. xi. 23, where he is called "a *proper* child;" that is, a *handsome* child. It would seem from this that Moses was preserved by his mother on account of his *beauty;* and this is hinted at in Ex. ii. 2. And it would also seem from this that Pharaoh had succeeded by his oppressions in what he had attempted; and that it was not unusual for parents among the Jews to *expose* their children, or to put them to death.

21. *Was cast out.* When he was exposed on the banks of the Nile, Ex. ii. 3. ¶ *And nourished him.* Adopted him, and treated him as her own son, Ex. ii. 10. It is implied in this that he was *educated* by her. An adopted son in the family of Pharaoh would be favoured with all the advantages which the land could furnish for an education.

22. *Moses was learned.* Or, was *instructed.* It does not mean that he *had* that learning, but that he was carefully *trained* or educated in that wisdom. The passage does not express the fact that Moses was distinguished for *learning*, but that he was carefully *educated*, or that pains were taken to *make* him learned. ¶ *In all the wisdom,* &c. The learning of the Egyptians was confined chiefly to astrology, to the interpretation of dreams, to medicine, to mathematics, and to their sacred science or traditionary doctrines about religion, which were concealed chiefly under their hieroglyphics. Their learning is not unfrequently spoken of in the Scriptures, 1 Ki. iv. 30; comp. Is. xix. 11, 12. Their knowledge is equally celebrated

23 And[z] when he was full forty years old, it came into his heart to visit his brethren the children of Israel.

24 And seeing one *of them* suffer wrong, he defended *him*, and avenged him that was oppressed, and smote the Egyptian:

25 For[2] he supposed his brethren would have understood how that God by his hand would deliver them: but they understood not.

26 And the next day he showed himself unto them as they strove, and would have set them at one again, saying, Sirs, ye are brethren; why do ye wrong one to another?

27 But he that did his neighbour wrong thrust him away, saying,

z Ex.2.11,&c. 2 or, *Now*.

---

in the heathen world. It is known that science was carried from Egypt to Phenicia, and thence to Greece; and not a few of the Grecian philosophers travelled to Egypt in pursuit of knowledge. Herodotus himself frankly concedes that the Greeks derived very much of their knowledge from Egypt. (See Rawlinson's Herodotus, vol. ii. p. 80, 81; Herodotus, bk. ii. p. 50, 51.) ¶ *And was mighty.* Was powerful, or was distinguished. This means that he was eminent *in* Egypt before he conducted the children of Israel forth. It refers to his addresses to Pharaoh, and to the miracles which he wrought *before* their departure. ¶ *In words.* From Ex. iv. 10, it seems that Moses was "slow of speech, and of a slow tongue." When it is said that he was mighty in words, it means that he was mighty in his communications to Pharaoh, though they were spoken by his brother Aaron. Aaron was in his place, and *Moses* addressed Pharaoh through him, who was appointed to deliver the message, Ex. iv. 11-16. ¶ *Deeds.* Miracles, Ex. vii. &c.

23. *Full forty years of age.* This is not recorded in the Old Testament; but it is a constant tradition of the Jews that Moses was forty years of age when he undertook to deliver them. Thus it is said, "Moses lived in the palace of Pharaoh forty years; he was forty years in Midian; and he ministered to Israel forty years" (Kuinoel). ¶ *To visit,* &c. Probably with a view of delivering them from their oppressive bondage. Comp. ver. 25.

24. *Suffer wrong.* The wrong or injury was, that the Egyptian was smiting the Hebrew, Ex. ii. 11, 12. ¶ *Smote the Egyptian.* He slew him, and buried him in the sand.

25. *For he supposed.* This is not mentioned by Moses; but it is not at all improbable. When they saw him *alone* contending with the Egyptian; when it was understood that he had come and taken vengeance on one of their oppressors, it might have been presumed that he regarded himself as directed by God to interpose, and save the people.

26. *And the next day.* Ex. ii. 13. ¶ *He showed himself.* He appeared in a sudden and unexpected manner to them. ¶ *Unto them.* That is, to *two* of the Hebrews, Ex. ii. 13. ¶ *As they strove.* As they were engaged in a quarrel. ¶ *Have set them at one.* Greek, "would have urged them to peace." This he did by remonstrating with the man that did the wrong. ¶ *Saying.* What follows is not quoted literally from the account which Moses gives, but it is substantially the same. ¶ *Sirs.* Greek, "Men." ¶ *Ye are brethren.* You belong not only to the same nation, but you are brethren and companions in affliction, and should not, therefore, contend with each other. One of the most melancholy scenes in the world is that, where those who are poor, and afflicted, and oppressed, add to all their other calamities altercations and strifes among themselves. Yet it is from this class that contentions and law-suits usually arise. The address which Moses here makes to the contending Jews might be applied to the whole human family in view of the contentions and wars of nations: "Ye are *brethren*, members of the same great family, and why do you contend with each other?"

27. *But he that did,* &c. Intent on his purpose, filled with rage and passion, he rejected all interference, and all attempts at peace. It is usually the man that *does* the injury that is unwilling to be reconciled; and when we find a man that regards the entreaties of his friends as improper interference, when he becomes increasingly angry when we exhort him to peace, it is usually a strong evidence that he is conscious that he has been at fault. If we

Who made thee a ruler and a judge over us?
28 Wilt thou kill me as thou didst the Egyptian yesterday?
29 Then fled Moses at this saying;
and was a stranger in the land of Madian, where he begat two sons.
30 And[a] when forty years were expired, there appeared to him

a Ex.3.2,&c.

wish to reconcile parties, we should go first to the man that has been injured. In the controversy between God and man, it is the *sinner* who has done the wrong that is unwilling to be reconciled, and not God. ¶ *His neighbour.* The Jew with whom he was contending. ¶ *Who made thee*, &c. What right have you to interfere in this matter? The usual salutation with which a man is greeted who attempts to prevent quarrels.

28. *Wilt thou kill me*, &c. How it was known that he had killed the Egyptian does not appear. It was probably communicated by the man who was rescued from the hands of the Egyptian, Ex. ii. 11, 12.

29. *Then fled Moses*, &c. Moses fled because he now ascertained that what he had done was known. He supposed that it had been unobserved, Ex. ii. 12. But he now thought that the knowledge of it might reach Pharaoh, and that his life might thus be endangered. Nor did he judge incorrectly; for as soon as Pharaoh heard of it, he sought to take his life, Ex. ii. 15. ¶ *Was a stranger.* Or became a *sojourner* (πάροικος), one who had a temporary abode in the land. The use of this word implies that he did not expect to make that his permanent dwelling. ¶ *In the land of Madian.* This was a part of Arabia. "This would seem," says Gesenius, "to have been a tract of country extending from the eastern shore of the Elanitic Gulf to the region of Moab on the one hand, and to the vicinity of Mount Sinai on the other. The people were nomadic in their habits, and moved often from place to place." This was extensively a desert region, an unknown land; and Moses expected there to be safe from Pharaoh. ¶ *Where he begat two sons.* He married Zipporah, the daughter of *Reuel* (Ex. ii. 18), or *Jethro* (Nu. x. 29; Ex. iii. 1), a *priest* of Midian. The names of the two sons were Gershom and Eliezer, Ex. xviii. 3, 4.

30. *And when forty years*, &c. At the age of eighty years. This, however, was known by tradition. It is not expressly mentioned by Moses. It is said, however, to have been after the king of Egypt had died (Ex. ii. 23); and the tradition is not improbable. ¶ *In the wilderness of mount Sina.* In the desert adjacent to, or that surrounded Mount Sinai. In Ex. iii. 1, it is said that this occurred at Mount *Horeb.* But there is no contradiction; Horeb and Sinai are different peaks or elevations of the same mountain. They are represented as springing from the same base, and branching out in different elevations. The mountains, according to Burckhardt, are a prodigious pile, comprehending many peaks, and about thirty miles in diameter. From one part of this mountain, *Sinai*, the law was given to the children of Israel. ¶ *An angel of the Lord.* The word *angel* means properly a *messenger* (see Notes on Mat. i. 20), and is applied to the invisible spirits in heaven, to men, to the winds, to the pestilence, or to whatever is appointed as a messenger *to make known* or to *execute* the will of God. The mere *name*, therefore, can determine nothing about the *nature* of the messenger. That *name* might be applied to *any* messenger, even an inanimate object. The nature and character of this messenger are to be determined by other considerations. The word *may* denote that the *bush on fire* was the messenger. But a comparison with the other places where this occurs will show that it was a celestial messenger, and perhaps that it was the Messiah who was yet to come, appearing to take the people of Israel under his own charge and direction. Comp. Jn. i. 11, where the Jews are called "his own." In Ex. iii. 2, it is said that the angel of the Lord appeared IN a flame of fire; in ver. 4 it is said that Jehovah spake to him out of the midst of the bush; language which implies that God was there, and which is strongly expressive of the doctrine that the angel was Jehovah. In Ex. xxiii. 20, 21, God says, "I send an angel before thee, to keep thee in the way, and to bring thee into the place which I have prepared. Beware of *him*, and obey *his* voice," &c., ver. 23; xxxii. 34; xxxiii. 2. In all these places this angel is mentioned as an extraordinary messenger sent to conduct them to the land

in the wilderness of mount Sina
an angel of the Lord, in a flame
of fire in a bush.
31 When Moses saw *it*, he wondered at the sight; and as he drew near to behold *it*, the voice of the Lord came unto him,
32 *Saying*, I *am* the [b]God of thy fathers, the God of Abraham, and the God of Isaac, and the God of Jacob. Then Moses trembled, and durst not behold.
33 Then said the Lord to him, [c]Put off thy shoes from thy feet; for the place where thou standest is holy ground.
34 I have seen, I have seen the affliction of my people which is in Egypt, and I have heard their groaning, and am come down to deliver them. And now come, I will send thee into Egypt.
35 This Moses, whom they refused, (saying, Who made thee

b Mat.22.32; He.11.16.

c Jos.5.15; Ec.5.1.

---

of Canaan. He was to guide them, to defend them, and to drive out the nations before them. All these circumstances seem to point to the conclusion that this was no other than the future deliverer of the world, who came then to take his people under his own guidance, as emblematic of the redemption of his people. ¶ *In a flame of fire.* That is, in what *appeared* to be a flame of fire. The *bush* or clump of trees seemed to be on fire, or to be illuminated with a peculiar splendour. God is often represented as encompassed with this splendour, or glory, Lu. ii. 9; Mat. xvii. 1-5; Ac. ix. 3; xii. 7. ¶ *In a bush.* In a grove, or clump of trees. Probably the light was seen issuing from the *midst* of such a grove.

31. *He wondered*, &c. What particularly attracted his attention was the fact that the bush was not consumed, Ex. iii. 2, 3. ¶ *The voice of the Lord.* Jehovah spake to him from the midst of the bush. He did not see him. He merely heard a voice.

32. Saying, *I* am *the God*, &c. See this explained in the Notes on Mat. xxii. 32. ¶ *Then Moses trembled.* Ex. iii. 6.

33. *Then said the Lord*, &c. In Ex. iii. this is introduced in a different order, as being spoken *before* God said "I am the God," &c. ¶ *Put off thy shoes*, &c., Ex. iii. 5. To put off the shoes, or sandals, was an act of reverence. Especially the ancients were not permitted to enter a temple or holy place with their shoes on. Indeed, it was customary for the Jews to remove their shoes whenever they entered *any* house as a mere matter of civility. Comp. Notes on Jn. xiii. 5. See Jos. v. 15. "The same custom, growing out of the same feeling," says Professor Hackett (*Illustrations of Scripture*, p. 74, 75), "is observed among the Eastern nations at the present day. The Arabs and Turks never enter the mosques without putting off their shoes. They exact a compliance with this rule from those of a different faith who visit these sacred places. Though, until a recent period, the Mohammedans excluded Christians entirely from the mosques, they now permit foreigners to enter some of them, provided they leave their shoes at the door, or exchange them for others which have not been defiled by common use.

"A Samaritan from Nablus, who conducted Messrs. Robinson and Smith to the summit of Gerizim, when he came within a certain distance of the spot, took off his shoes, saying it was unlawful for his people to tread with shoes upon this ground, it being holy." ¶ *Is holy ground.* Is rendered sacred by the symbol of the divine presence. We should enter the sanctuary, the place set apart for divine worship, not only with reverence in our hearts, but with every *external* indication of veneration. Solemn awe and deep seriousness become the place set apart to the service of God. Comp. Ec. v. 1.

34. *I have seen*, &c. The repetition of this word is in accordance with the usage of the Hebrew writers when they wish to represent anything emphatically. ¶ *Their groaning.* Under their oppressions. ¶ *Am come down.* This is spoken in accordance with human conceptions. It means that God was about to deliver them. ¶ *I will send thee*, &c. This is a mere *summary* of what is expressed at much greater length in Ex. iii. 7-10.

35. *Whom they refused.* That is, when he *first* presented himself to them, Ex. ii. 13, 14. Stephen introduces and dwells

a ruler and a judge?) the same did God send *to be* a ruler and a deliverer, by the hand of [d]the angel which appeared to him in the bush.

36 He brought them out, [e]after that he had showed wonders and signs in the land of Egypt, and in the Red sea, and in the wilderness, forty[f] years.

37 This is that Moses which said unto the children of Israel, [g]A prophet shall the Lord your God raise up unto you of your brethren, [3]like unto me; [h]him shall ye hear.

38 This[i] is he that was in the church in the wilderness, with [k]the angel which [l]spake to him in the mount Sina, and *with* our fathers; [m]who [n]received the lively oracles to give unto us:

39 To whom our fathers would

d Ex.14.19; Nu.20.16.
e Ex. 7. 8. 9. 10. 11. & 14. *f* Ex.16.35.
g De.18.15,18; ch.3.22. [3] or, *as myself.*
h Mat.17.5. *i* He.2.2.
k Is.63.9; Ga.3.19. *l* Ex.19.3,17.
m De.5.27,31; Jn.1.17. *n* Ro.3.2.

upon this refusal in order, perhaps, to remind them that this had been the character of their nation, and to prepare the way for the charge which he intended to bring against those whom he addressed, as being stiff-necked and rebellious. See ver. 51, 52, &c. ¶ *A ruler.* A military leader, or a governor in civil matters. ¶ *A deliverer.* A Redeemer—λυτρωτὴν. It properly means one who redeems a captive or a prisoner by paying a *price* or *ransom.* It is applied thus to the Lord Jesus, as having redeemed or purchased sinners by his blood as a price, Tit. ii. 14; 1 Pe. i. 18; He. ix. 12. It is used here, however, in a more *general* sense to denote *the deliverance*, without specifying the manner. Comp. Ex. vi. 6; Lu. xxiv. 21; i. 68; ii. 38. ¶ *By the hand of the angel.* Under the *direction* and by the *help* of the angel, Nu. xx. 16. See on ver. 30.

36. *Wonders and signs.* Miracles, and remarkable interpositions of God. See Notes on Ac. ii. 22. ¶ *In the land of Egypt.* By the ten plagues. Ex. iv.–xii. ¶ *In the Red sea.* Dividing it, and conducting the Israelites in safety, and overthrowing the Egyptians, Ex. xiv. ¶ *In the wilderness.* During their forty years' journey to the promised land. The wonders or miracles were, providing them with manna daily; with flesh in a miraculous manner; with water from the rock, &c., Ex. xvi., xvii., &c.

37. *Which said*, &c. De. xviii. 15, 18. See this explained, Ac. iii. 22. Stephen introduced this to remind them of the promise of a Messiah; to show his faith in that promise; and *particularly* to remind them of their obligation to hear and obey him.

38. *In the church.* The word *church* means literally *the people called out*, and is applied with great propriety to the assembly or multitude called out of Egypt, and separated from the world. It has not, however, of necessity our idea of a church, but means the *assembly*, or people called out of Egypt and placed under the conduct of Moses. ¶ *With the angel.* In this place there is undoubted reference to the giving of the law on Mount Sinai. Yet that was done by God himself, Ex. xx. It is clear, therefore, that by *the angel* here, Stephen intends to designate him who was God. It may be observed, however, that *the law* is represented as having been given by the ministry of an angel (in this place) and by the ministry of *angels*, Ac. vii. 53; He. ii. 2. The essential idea is, that God did it by a messenger, or by mediators. The *character* and *rank* of the messengers, or of the *principal* messenger, must be learned by looking at all the circumstances of the case. ¶ *The lively oracles.* See Ro. iii. 2. The word *oracles* here means *commands* or *laws* of God. The word *lively*, or *living* (ζῶντα), stands in opposition to that which is dead, or useless, and means that which is vigorous, efficacious; and in this place it means that the commands were of such a nature, and given in such circumstances, as to secure attention; to produce obedience; to excite them to act for God—in opposition to laws which would fall powerless, and produce no effect.

39. *Would not obey*, &c. This refers to what they said of him when he was in the mount, Ex. xxxii. 1, 23. ¶ *In their hearts turned*, &c. They wished to return to Egypt. They regretted that they had come out of Egypt, and desired again the things which they had there, as preferable to what they had

not obey, but thrust *him* from them, and in their hearts turned back again into Egypt,

40 Saying[o] unto Aaron, Make us gods to go before us; for *as for* this Moses, which brought us out of the land of Egypt, we wot not what is become of him.

41 And they [p]made a calf in those days, and offered sacrifice unto the idol, and rejoiced in the works of their own hands.

42 Then God turned and [q]gave them up to worship [r]the host of heaven: as it is written in the book of the prophets, [s]O ye house of Israel, have ye offered to me slain beasts, and sacrifices, *by the space of* forty years in the wilderness?

43 Yea, ye took up the tabernacle of Moloch, and the star of your god Remphan, figures which ye made, to worship them: and I will carry you away beyond Babylon.

o Ex.32.1. *p* De.9.16; Ps.106.19,20. *q* Ps.81.12. *r* De.4.19; 2 Ki.17.16; Je.19.13. *s* Am.5.25,26.

in the desert, Nu. xi. 5. Perhaps, however, the expression means, not that they desired literally to *return* to Egypt, but that *their hearts inclined to the habits and morals of the Egyptians.* They forsook God, and imitated the idolatries of the Egyptians.

40. *Saying unto Aaron.* Ex. xxxii. 1. ¶ *Make us gods.* That is, idols.

41. *And they made a calf.* This was made of the ear-rings and ornaments which they had brought from Egypt, Ex. xxxii. 2–4. Stephen introduces this to remind them how prone the nation had been to reject God, and to walk in the ways of sin.

42. *Then God turned.* That is, turned away from them; abandoned them to their own desires. ¶ *The host of heaven.* The stars, or heavenly bodies. The word *host* means *armies.* It is applied to the heavenly bodies because they are very numerous, and appear to be *marshalled* or arrayed in military order. It is from this that God is called JEHOVAH *of hosts*, as being the ruler of these well-arranged heavenly bodies. See Notes on Is. i. 9. The proof that they did this Stephen proceeds to allege by a quotation from the prophets. ¶ *In the book of the prophets.* Am. v. 25, 26. The twelve minor prophets were commonly written in one volume, and were called the Book of the Prophets; that is, the book containing these several prophecies, Daniel, Hosea, Micah, &c. They were small *tracts* separately, and were bound up together to preserve them from being lost. This passage is not quoted literally; it is evidently made from memory; and though in its main spirit it coincides with the passage in Amos, yet in some important respects it varies from it. ¶ *O ye house of Israel.* Ye people of Israel. ¶ *Have ye offered,* &c. That is, ye have *not* offered. The interrogative form is often an emphatic way of saying that the thing had *not* been done. But it is certain that the Jews *did* offer sacrifices to God in the wilderness, though it is also certain that they did not do it with a pure and upright heart. They kept up the *form* of worship generally, but they frequently forsook God, and offered worship to idols. *Through* the continuous space of forty years they did *not* honour God, but often departed from him, and worshipped idols.

43. *Yea, ye took up.* That is, you *bore*, or you carried with you, for purposes of idolatrous worship. ¶ *The tabernacle.* This word properly means a *tent;* but it is also applied to the small tent or house in which was contained the image of the god; the shrine, box, or tent in which the idol was placed. It is customary for idolatrous nations to bear their idols about with them, inclosed in *cases* or boxes of various sizes, usually very small, as their idols are commonly small. Probably they were made in the shape of small *temples* or tabernacles; and such appear to have been the *silver shrines* for Diana, made at Ephesus, Ac. xix. 24. These shrines, or images, were borne with them as a species of *amulet, charm,* or *talisman,* to defend them from evil. Such images the Jews seem to have borne with them. ¶ *Moloch.* This word comes from the Hebrew word signifying *king.* This was a god of the Ammonites, to whom human sacrifices were offered. Moses in several places forbids the Israelites, under penalty of death, to dedicate their children to Moloch, by making them pass through the fire, Le. xviii. 21; xx. 2–5. There

44 Our fathers had the tabernacle of witness in the wilderness, as he had appointed, [4]speaking unto Moses, [t]that he should make it according to the fashion that he had seen.

45 Which[u] also our fathers [5]that came after brought in with Jesus

[4] or, *who spake*. *t* Ex.25.40; 26.30; He.8.5. *u* Jos.3.14. [5] or, *having received*.

is great probability that the Hebrews were addicted to the worship of this deity after they entered the land of Canaan. Solomon built a temple to Moloch on the Mount of Olives (1 Ki. xi. 7); and Manasseh made his son pass through the fire in honour of this idol, 2 Ki. xxi. 3, 6. The image of this idol was made of brass, and his arms extended so as to embrace anyone; and when they offered children to him, they heated the statue, and when it was burning hot, they placed the child in his arms, where it was soon destroyed by heat. It is not certain what this god was supposed to represent. Some suppose it was in honour of the planet Saturn; others, the sun; others, Mercury, Venus, &c. What particular god it was is not material. It was the most cutting reproof that could be made to the Jews, that their fathers had been guilty of worshipping this idol. ¶ *And the star*. The Hebrew in this place is, "Chiun your images, the star of your god." The expression here used leads us to suppose that this was a *star* which was worshipped, but *what* star it is not easy to ascertain; nor is it easy to determine why it is called both *Chiun* and *Remphan*. Stephen quotes from the Septuagint translation. In that translation the word *Chiun* is rendered by the word *Raiphan*, or *Rephan*, easily changed into *Remphan*. Why the authors of that version adopted this is not known. It was probably, however, from one of two causes. (1) Either because the word *Chiun* in Hebrew meant the same as *Remphan* in the language of Egypt, where the translation was made; or, (2) Because the *object* of worship called *Chiun* in Hebrew was called *Remphan* in the language of Egypt. It is generally agreed that the *object* of their worship was the planet *Saturn*, or *Mars*, both of which planets were worshipped as gods of evil influence. In Arabic, the word *Chevân* denotes the planet Saturn. Probably *Rephan*, or *Remphan*, is the Coptic name for the same planet, and the Septuagint adopted this because that translation was made in Egypt, where the Coptic language was spoken. ¶ *Figures which ye made*. Images of the god which they made. See the article "Chiun" in Robinson's Calmet. ¶ *And I will carry you away*, &c. This is simply expressing in few words what is stated at greater length in Am. v. 27. In Hebrew it is *Damascus;* but this evidently denotes the eastern region, in which also Babylon was situated.

44. *The tabernacle of witness*. The *tent* or *tabernacle* which Moses was commanded to make. It was called a tabernacle of *witness*, or of *testimony*, because it was the visible witness or proof of God's presence with them; the evidence that he to whom it was devoted was their protector and guide. The name is given either to the *tent*, to the two tables of stone, or to the ark; all of which were *witnesses*, or *evidences* of God's relation to them as their lawgiver and guide, Ex. xvi. 34; xxv. 16, 21; xxvii. 21; xxx. 6, 36; xxxi. 18, &c.; Nu. i. 50, 53. The two charges against Stephen were, that he had spoken blasphemy against Moses, or his law, and against the temple, ch. vi. 13, 14. In the previous part of this defence he had shown his respect for Moses and his law. He now proceeds to show that he did not design to speak with disrespect of the temple, or the holy places of their worship. He therefore expresses his belief in the divine appointment of both the tabernacle (ver. 44–46) and of the temple (ver. 47). ¶ *According to the fashion*, &c. According to the *pattern* that was shown to him, by which it was to be made, Ex. xxv. 9, 40; xxvi. 30. As God showed him *a pattern*, it proved that the tabernacle had his sanction. Against that Stephen did not intend to speak.

45. *Our fathers that came after*. None of the generation that came out of Egypt were permitted to enter into the land of Canaan except Caleb and Joshua, Nu. xiv. 22–24; xxxii. 11, 12. Hence it is said that their fathers *who came after*, that is, after the generation when the tabernacle was built. The Greek, however, here means, properly, "which also our fathers, having *received*, brought," &c. The sense is not materially different. Stephen means

into the possession of the Gentiles,
whom[v] God drave out before the
face of our fathers, unto the days
of David;

46 Who[w] found favour before
God, and [x]desired to find a tabernacle for the God of Jacob.

47 But [y]Solomon built him an
house.

48 Howbeit, [z]the Most High
dwelleth not in temples made with
hands; as saith the prophet,

49 Heaven[a] *is* my throne, and
earth *is* my footstool: what house
will ye build me? saith the Lord:
or what *is* the place of my rest?

50 Hath not my hand made all
these things?

51 Ye [b]stiff-necked, and [c]uncir-
cumcised in heart and ears, ye do

v Ne.9.24; Ps.44.2; 78.55. w 1 Sa.16.1. x 1 Ch.22.7. y 1 Ki.6.1,&c.; 8.20. z 1 Ki.8.27; ch.17.24.

a Is.66.1,2. b Ex.32.9; Is.48.4. c Le.26.41; Je.9.26; Ro.2.28,29.

---

that it was not brought in by that generation, but by the next. ¶ *With Jesus.* This should have been rendered "with *Joshua.*" *Jesus* is the Greek mode of writing the name *Joshua.* But the Hebrew name should by all means have been retained here, as also in He. iv. 8. ¶ *Into the possession of the Gentiles.* Into the land possessed *by* the Gentiles, that is, into the promised land then occupied by the Canaanites, &c. ¶ *Whom God,* &c. That is, he continued to drive them out until the time of David, when they were completely expelled. Or it may mean that the tabernacle was in the possession of the Jews, and was the appointed place of worship, until the time of David, who desired to build him a temple. The Greek is ambiguous. The *connection* favours the latter interpretation.

46. *Who found favour,* &c. That is, God granted him great prosperity, and delivered him from his enemies. ¶ *To find a tabernacle.* To prepare a permanent dwelling-place for the *ark,* and for the visible symbols of the divine presence. Hitherto the ark had been kept in the tabernacle, and had been borne about from place to place. David sought to build a house that would be permanent, where the ark might be deposited, 2 Sa. vii.; 1 Ch. xxii. 7.

47. *But Solomon,* &c. Built the temple. David was not permitted to do it because he had been a man of war, 1 Ch. xxii. 8. He prepared the principal materials for the temple, but Solomon built it, 1 Ch. xxii. Comp. 1 Ki. vi.

48. *Howbeit.* But. Stephen was charged with speaking against the temple. He had now shown that he had due veneration for it, by his declaring that it had been built by the command of God. But he *now* adds that God does not need such a temple. Heaven is his throne; the universe his dwelling-place; and *therefore* this temple might be destroyed. A new, glorious truth was to be revealed to mankind, that God was not *confined* in his worship to any age, or people, or nation. In entire consistency, therefore, with all proper respect for the temple at Jerusalem, it might be maintained that the time would come when that temple would be destroyed, and when God might be worshipped by all nations. ¶ *The Most High.* God. This sentiment was expressed by Solomon when the temple was dedicated, 1 Ki. viii. 27. ¶ *As saith the prophet.* Is. lxvi. 1, 2. The place is not literally quoted, but the sense is given.

49. *Heaven* is *my throne.* See Notes on Mat. v. 34. ¶ *Earth* is *my footstool.* See Notes on Mat. v. 35. ¶ *What house,* &c. What house or temple can be large or magnificent enough for the dwelling of Him who made all things? ¶ *The place of my rest.* My home, my abode, my fixed seat or habitation. Comp. Ps. xcv. 11.

51. *Ye stiff-necked.* The discourse of Stephen has every appearance of having been interrupted by the clamours and opposition of the Sanhedrim. This verse has no immediate connection with that which precedes, and *appears* to have been spoken in the midst of opposition and clamour. If we may conjecture in this case, it would seem that the Jews saw the drift of his argument; that they interrupted him; and that when the tumult had somewhat subsided, he addressed them in the language of this verse, showing them that they sustained a character precisely similar to their rebellious fathers. The word *stiff-necked* is often used in the Old Testament, Ex. xxxii. 9; xxxiii. 3, 5; xxxiv. 9; De. ix. 6, 13; x. 16, &c. It is a figurative expression taken from oxen that are refractory, and that will

always resist the Holy Ghost: as
your fathers *did*, so *do* ye.
52 Which[d] of the prophets have
not your fathers persecuted? And
they have slain them which showed
before of the coming of [e]the Just
One, of whom ye have been now
the betrayers and murderers.
53 Who have [f]received the law
by the disposition of angels, and
have not kept *it*.
54 When[g] they heard these things,

d 2 Ch.36.16; 1 Th.2.15. e ch.3.14. f Ga.3.19. g ch.5.33.

not submit to be yoked. Applied to men, it means that they are stubborn, contumacious, and unwilling to submit to the restraints of law. ¶ *Uncircumcised in heart. Circumcision* was a sign of being a Jew—of acknowledging the authority of the laws of Moses. It was also emblematic of purity, and of submission to the law of God. The expression *uncircumcised in heart* denotes those who were not willing to acknowledge that law, and submit to it. They had hearts filled with vicious and unsubdued affections and desires. ¶ *And ears.* That is, who are unwilling to *hear* what God says. Comp. Le. xxvi. 41; Je. ix. 26. Notes on Ro. ii. 28, 29. ¶ *Resist the Holy Ghost.* You oppose the message which is brought to you by the authority of God and the inspiration of his Spirit. The message brought by Moses; by the prophets; by the Saviour; and by the apostles—all by the infallible direction of the Holy Ghost—they and their fathers opposed. ¶ *As your fathers* did, &c. As he had specified in ver. 27, 35, 39–43.

52. *Which of the prophets*, &c. The interrogative form here is a strong mode of saying that they had persecuted *all* the prophets. It was *the characteristic of the nation* to persecute the messengers of God. This is not to be taken as literally and universally true; but it was a general truth; it was the national characteristic. See Notes on Mat. xxi. 33–40; xxiii. 29–35. ¶ *And they have slain them*, &c. That is, they have slain the prophets, whose main message was that the Messiah was to come. It was a great aggravation of their offence that they put to death the messengers which foretold the greatest blessing that the nation could receive. ¶ *The Just One.* The Messiah. See Notes on ch. iii. 14. ¶ *Of whom ye*, &c. You thus show that you resemble those who rejected and put to death the prophets. You have even gone beyond them in guilt, because you have put the Messiah himself to death. ¶ *The betrayers.* They are called *betrayers* here because they employed Judas to betray him—agreeable to the maxim in law, *He who does anything by another is held to have done it himself.*

53. *Who have received the law.* The law of Moses, given on Mount Sinai. ¶ *By the disposition of angels.* There has been much diversity of opinion in regard to this phrase, εἰς διαταγὰς ἀγγέλων. The word translated *disposition* does not elsewhere occur in the New Testament. It properly means the *constituting* or *arranging* of an army; disposing it into ranks and proper divisions. Hence it has been supposed to mean that the law was given *amidst* the various ranks of angels, being present to witness its promulgation. Others suppose that the angels were employed as agents or instruments to communicate the law. All that the expression fairly implies is the former; that the law was given amidst the attending ranks of angels, as if they were summoned to witness the pomp and ceremony of giving *law* to an entire people, and through them to an entire world. It should be added, moreover, that the Jews applied the word *angels* to any messengers of God; to fire, and tempest, and wind, &c. And all that Stephen means here may be to express the common Jewish opinion that God was attended on this occasion by the heavenly hosts, and by the symbols of his presence, fire, and smoke, and tempest. Comp. Ps. civ. 4; lxviii. 17. Other places declare that the law was spoken by *an angel*, one eminent above all attending angels, the peculiar messenger of God. See Notes on ver. 38. It is plain that Stephen spoke only the common sentiment of the Jews. Thus Herod is introduced by Josephus (*Antiq.*, b. xv. ch. v. § 3) as saying, "We have learned from God the most excellent of our doctrines, and the most holy part of our law *by angels*," &c. In the eyes of the Jews, it justly gave increased majesty and solemnity to the law, that it had been given in so grand and imposing circumstances. It greatly aggravated

they were cut to the heart, and they
gnashed on him with *their* teeth.
55 But he, [h]being full of the
Holy Ghost, looked up stedfastly
into heaven, and saw the glory of
God, and Jesus standing on the
right hand of God,
56 And said, Behold, I see [i]the
heavens opened, and [k]the Son of
man standing on the right hand
of God.
57 Then they cried out with
a loud voice, and stopped their
ears, and ran upon him with one
accord,
58 And [l]cast *him* out of the

h ch.6.5. *i* Eze.1.1. *k* Da.7.13. *l* Lu.4.29; He.13.12,13.

their guilt that, notwithstanding this, they had not kept it.

54. *They were cut to the heart.* They were exceedingly enraged and indignant. The whole course of the speech had been such as to excite their anger, and now they could restrain themselves no longer. ¶ *They gnashed on him,* &c. Expressive of the bitterness and malignity of their feeling.

55. *Full of the Holy Ghost.* See Notes on ch. ii. 4. ¶ *Looked up stedfastly.* Fixed his eyes intently on heaven. Foreseeing his danger, and the effect his speech had produced; seeing that there was no safety in the great council of the nation, and no prospect of justice at their hands, he cast his eyes to heaven and sought protection there. When dangers threaten us, our hope of safety lies in heaven. When men threaten our persons, reputation, or lives, it becomes us to fix our eyes on the heavenly world; and we shall not look in vain. ¶ *And saw the glory of God.* This phrase is commonly used to denote the visible symbols of God. It means some magnificent representation; a splendour, or light, that is the appropriate exhibition of the presence of God, Mat. xvi. 27; xxiv. 30. See Notes on Lu. ii. 9. In the case of Stephen there is every indication of a vision or supernatural representation of the heavenly objects; something in advance of mere *faith* such as dying Christians now have. What was its precise nature we have no means of ascertaining. Objects were often represented to prophets by *visions;* and probably something similar is intended here. It was such an elevation of view—such a representation of truth and of the glory of God, as to be denoted by the word *see;* though it is not to be maintained that Stephen really saw the Saviour with the bodily eye. ¶ *On the right hand of God.* That is, exalted to a place of honour and power in the heavens. See Notes on Mar. xxvi. 64; Ac. ii. 25.

56. *I see the heavens opened.* A figurative expression, denoting that he was permitted to see *into* heaven, or to see what was there, *as if* the firmament was divided, and the eye was permitted to penetrate the eternal world. Comp. Eze. i. 1.

57. *Then they cried out.* That is, probably, *the people,* not the members of the council. It is evident he was put to death in a popular tumult. They had charged him with blasphemy; and they regarded what he had now said as full proof of it. ¶ *And stopped their ears.* That they might hear no more blasphemy. ¶ *With one accord.* In a tumult; unitedly.

58. *And cast* him *out of the city.* This was in accordance with the usual custom. In Le. xxiv. 14, it was directed to bring forth him that had cursed without the camp; and it was not usual, the Jewish writers inform us, to stone in the presence of the Sanhedrim. Though this was a popular tumult, and Stephen was condemned without the regular process of trial, yet some of the *forms* of law were observed, and he was stoned in the manner directed in the case of blasphemers. ¶ *And stoned* him. This was the punishment appointed in the case of blasphemy, Le. xxiv. 16. See Notes on Jn. x. 31. ¶ *And the witnesses.* That is, the false witnesses who bore testimony against him, ch. vi. 13. It was directed in the law (De. xvii. 7) that the *witnesses* in the case should be first in executing the sentence of the law. This was done to prevent false accusations by the prospect that *they* must be employed as executioners. After *they* had commenced the process of execution, all the people joined in it, De. xvii. 7; Le. xxiv. 16. ¶ *Laid down their clothes.* Their *outer garments.* They were accustomed to lay these aside when they ran or worked. See Notes on Mat. v. 40. ¶ *At a young man's feet,* &c. That is, they procured him to take care of their

city, and stoned *him:* and [m]the witnesses laid down their clothes at a young man's feet, whose name was [n]Saul.

59 And they stoned Stephen, calling upon *God*, and saying, Lord Jesus, [o]receive my spirit!

60 And he kneeled down, and

m ch.6.13. *n* ch.8.1,3; 22.20. *o* Ps.31.5; Lu.23.46.

garments. This is mentioned solely because Saul, or Paul, afterward became so celebrated, first as a persecutor, and then an apostle. His whole heart was in this persecution of Stephen; and he himself afterward alluded to this circumstance as an evidence of his sinfulness in persecuting the Lord Jesus, Ac. xxii. 20.

59. *Calling upon* God. The word *God* is not in the original, and should not have been in the translation. It is in none of the ancient MSS. or versions. It should have been rendered, They stoned Stephen, invoking, or calling upon, and saying, Lord Jesus, &c. That is, he was engaged *in prayer* to the Lord Jesus. The word is used to express *prayer* in the following, among other places: 2 Co. i. 23, "I call God to witness;" 1 Pe. i. 17, "And if ye call on the Father," &c.; Ac. ii. 21, "Whosoever shall call on the name of the Lord," &c.; ix. 14; xxii. 16; Ro. x. 12-14. This was, therefore, an act of worship; a solemn invocation of the Lord Jesus, in the most interesting circumstances in which a man can be placed—in his dying moments. And this shows that it is *right* to worship the Lord Jesus, and to pray to him. For if Stephen was *inspired*, it settles the question. The example of an inspired man in such circumstances is a safe and correct example. If it should be said that the inspiration of *Stephen* cannot be made out, yet the inspiration of *Luke*, who has recorded it, will not be called in question. Then the following circumstances show that *he*, an inspired man, regarded it as right, and as a proper example to be followed. (1) He has recorded it without the slightest expression of an opinion that it was improper. On the contrary, there is every evidence that he regarded the conduct of Stephen in this case as right and praiseworthy. There is, therefore, this attestation to its propriety. (2) The spirit that inspired Luke knew what use would be made of this case. He knew that it would be used as an *example*, and as an evidence that it was *right* to worship the Lord Jesus. It is one of the cases which has been used to perpetuate the worship of the Lord Jesus in every age. If it was wrong, it is inconceivable that it should be recorded without some expression of disapprobation. (3) The case is strikingly similar to that recorded in Jn. xx. 28, where Thomas offered worship to the Lord Jesus *as his God*, without reproof. If Thomas did it in the presence of the Saviour without reproof, it was right. If Stephen did it without any expression of disapprobation from the inspired historian, it was right. (4) These examples were used to encourage Christians and Christian martyrs to offer homage to Jesus Christ. Thus Pliny, writing to the Emperor Trajan, and giving an account of the Christians in Bithynia, says that they were accustomed to meet and *sing hymns to Christ as to God* (Lardner). (5) It is worthy of remark that Stephen, in his death, offered the same act of homage to Christ that Christ himself did to the Father when he died, Lu. xxiii. 46. From all these considerations, it follows that the Lord Jesus is a proper object of worship; that in most solemn circumstances it is right to call upon him, to worship him, and to commit our dearest interests to his hands. If this may be done, he is divine. ¶ *Receive my spirit.* That is, receive it to thyself; take it to thine abode in heaven.

60. *And he kneeled down.* This seems to have been a *voluntary* kneeling; a placing himself in this position for the purpose of *prayer*, choosing to die in this attitude. ¶ *Lord.* That is, Lord *Jesus.* See Notes on ch. i. 24. ¶ *Lay not*, &c. Forgive them. This passage strikingly resembles the dying prayer of the Lord Jesus, Lu. xxiii. 34. Nothing but the Christian religion will enable a man to utter such sentiments in his dying moments. ¶ *He fell asleep.* This is the usual mode of describing the death of saints in the Bible. It is an expression indicating, (1) The *peacefulness* of their death, compared with the alarm of sinners; (2) The hope of a resurrection; as we retire to sleep with the hope of again awaking to the

cried with a loud voice, Lord, [p]lay
not this sin to their charge! And
when he had said this, he fell asleep.

CHAPTER VIII.

AND[a] Saul was consenting unto
his death. And at that
time there was a great persecution against the church which was
at Jerusalem; and [b]they were all
scattered abroad throughout the
regions of Judea and Samaria, except the apostles.
2 And devout men carried Ste-

p Mat.5.44; Lu.23.34. a ch.7.58. b ch.11.19.

---

duties and enjoyments of life. See Jn. xi. 11, 12; 1 Co. xi. 30; xv. 51; 1 Th. iv. 14; v. 10; Mat. ix. 24.

In view of the death of this first Christian martyr, we may remark:

1. That it is right to address to the Lord Jesus the language of prayer.

2. It is peculiarly proper to do it in afflictions, and in the prospect of death, He. iv. 15.

3. Sustaining grace will be derived in trials chiefly from a view of the Lord Jesus. If we can look to him as *our* Saviour; see him to be exalted to deliver us; and truly commit our souls to him, we shall find the grace which we need in our afflictions.

4. We should have such confidence in him as to enable us to commit ourselves to him at any time. To do this, we should live a life of faith. In health, and youth, and strength, we should seek him *as our first and best friend.*

5. While we are in health we should prepare to die. What an unfit place for preparation for death would have been the situation of Stephen! How impossible then would it have been to have made preparation! Yet the dying bed is often a place as unfit to prepare as were the circumstances of Stephen. When racked with pain; when faint and feeble; when the mind is indisposed to thought, or when it raves in the wildness of delirium, what an unfit place is this to prepare to die! I have seen many dying beds; I have seen many persons in all stages of their last sickness; but never have I yet seen a dying bed which seemed to me to be a proper place to make preparation for eternity.

6. How peaceful and calm is a death like that of Stephen, when compared with the alarms and anguish of a sinner! One moment of such peace in that trying time is better than all the pleasures and honours which the world can bestow; and to *obtain* such peace then, the dying sinner would be willing to give all the wealth of the Indies, and all the crowns of the earth. So may I die—and so may all my readers—enabled, like this dying martyr, to commit my departing spirit to the sure keeping of the great Redeemer! When we take a parting view of the world; when our eyes shall be turned for the last time to take a look of friends and relatives; when the darkness of death shall begin to come around us, then may we be enabled to cast the eye of faith to the heavens, and say, "Lord Jesus, receive our spirits." Thus may we fall asleep, peaceful in death, in the hope of the resurrection of the just.

CHAPTER VIII.

1. *And Saul was consenting,* &c. Was pleased with his being put to death, and approved it. Comp. ch. xxii. 20. This part of the verse should have been connected with the previous chapter. ¶ *And at that time.* That is, immediately following the death of Stephen. The persecution arose on account of Stephen, ch. xi. 19. The tumult did not subside when Stephen was killed. The anger of his persecutors continued to be excited against *all* Christians. They had become so embittered by the zeal and success of the apostles, and by their frequent charges of *murder* in putting the Son of God to death, that they resolved at once to put a period to their progress and success. This was the *first* persecution against Christians; the first in a series that terminated only when the religion which they wished to destroy was fully established on the ruins of both Judaism and paganism. ¶ *The church.* The collection of Christians which were now organized into a church. The church at Jerusalem was the *first* that was collected. ¶ *All scattered.* That is, the great mass of Christians. ¶ *The regions of Judea,* &c. See Notes on Mat. ii. 22. ¶ *Except the apostles.* Probably the other Christians fled from fear. Why the apostles, who were particularly in danger, did not flee also, is not stated by the historian. Having been, however, more fully in-

phen *to his burial*, and made great
lamentation over him.
3 As for Saul, [c]he made havoc
of the church, entering into every
house; and haling men and women,
committed *them* to prison.
4 Therefore they that were scat-

c ch.26.10,11; Ga.1.13.

structed than the others, and having been taught their duty by the example and teaching of the Saviour, they resolved, it seems, to remain and brave the fury of the persecutors. For *them* to have fled then would have exposed them, as leaders and founders of the new religion, to the charge of timidity and weakness. They therefore resolved to remain in the midst of their persecutors; and a merciful Providence watched over them, and defended them from harm. The dispersion extended not only to Judea and Samaria, but those who fled carried the gospel also to Phenice, Cyprus, and Antioch, ch. xi. 19. There was a *reason* why this was permitted. The early converts were Jews. They had strong feelings of attachment to the city of Jerusalem, to the temple, and to the land of their fathers. Yet it was the design of the Lord Jesus that the gospel should be preached everywhere. To accomplish this, he suffered a persecution to rage; and they were scattered abroad, and bore his gospel to other cities and lands. Good thus came out of evil; and the first persecution resulted, as all others have done, in advancing the cause which was intended to be destroyed.

2. *And devout men*. Religious men. The word used here does not imply of necessity that they were Christians. There might have been Jews who did not approve of the popular tumult, and the murder of Stephen, who gave him a decent burial. Joseph of Arimathea, and Nicodemus, both Jews, thus gave to the Lord Jesus a decent burial, Jn. xix. 38, 39. ¶ *Carried Stephen*. The word translated *carried* means properly to *collect*, as fruits, &c. Then it is applied to all the preparations necessary for fitting a dead body for burial, as *collecting*, or confining it by bandages, with spices, &c. ¶ *And made great lamentation*. This was usual among the Jews at a funeral. See Notes on Mat. ix. 23.

3. *As for Saul*. But Saul. He took no interest or part in the pious attentions shown to Stephen, but engaged with zeal in the work of persecution. ¶ *He made havoc*—ἐλυμαίνετο. This word is commonly applied to wild beasts, to lions, wolves, &c., and denotes the devastations which they commit. Saul raged against the church like a wild beast—a strong expression, denoting the zeal and fury with which he engaged in persecution. ¶ *Entering into every house*. To search for those who were suspected of being Christians. ¶ *Haling*. Dragging, or compelling them. ¶ *Committed* them *to prison*. The Sanhedrim had no power to put them to death, Jn. xviii. 31. But they had power to imprison; and they resolved, it seems, to exercise this power to the utmost. Paul frequently refers to his zeal in persecuting the church, Ac. xxvi. 10, 11; Ga. i. 13. It may be remarked here that there never was a persecution commenced with more flattering prospects to the persecutors. Saul, the principal agent, was young, zealous, learned, and clothed with power. He showed afterward that he had talents fitted for any station, and zeal that tired with no exertion, and that was appalled by no obstacle. With this talent and this zeal he entered on his work. The Christians were few and feeble. They were scattered and unarmed. They were unprotected by any civil power, and exposed, therefore, to the full blaze and rage of persecution. That the church was not destroyed was owing to the protection of God—a protection which not only secured its existence, but which extended its influence and power by means of this very persecution far abroad on the earth.

4. *Went every where*. That is, they travelled through the various regions where they were scattered. In all places to which they came, they preached the word. ¶ *Preaching the word*. Greek, *evangelizing*, or announcing the good news of the message of mercy, or the word of God. This is not the usual word which is rendered *preach*, but it means simply announcing the good news of salvation. There is no evidence, nor is there any probability, that all these persons were *ordained* to preach. They were manifestly common Christians who were scattered by the persecution; and the meaning is, that they communicated to their fellow-men in conversation wherever they met them, and probably

tered abroad went every where preaching the word.

5 Then[d] Philip went down to the city of Samaria, and preached Christ unto them.

6 And the people [e] with one ac-

d ch.6.5.

e 2 Ch.30.12.

in the synagogues, where all Jews had a right to speak, the glad tidings that the Messiah had come. It is not said that they set themselves up for public teachers, or that they administered baptism, or that they founded churches, but they proclaimed everywhere the news that a Saviour had come. Their hearts were full of it. Out of the abundance of the heart the mouth speaks; and they made the truth known to *all* whom they met. We may learn from this, (1) That persecution tends to promote the very thing which it would destroy. (2) That one of the best means to make Christians active and zealous is to persecute them. (3) That it is right for *all* Christians to make known the truths of the gospel. When the heart is full the lips will speak, and there is no more impropriety in their speaking of redemption than of anything else. (4) It should be the great object of all Christians to make the Saviour known *everywhere*. By their lives, their conversation, and their pious exhortations and entreaties, they should beseech dying sinners to be reconciled to God. And especially should this be done when they are *travelling*. Christians when away from home seem almost to imagine that they lay aside the obligations of religion. But the example of Christ and his early disciples has taught us that this is the very time to attempt to do good.

5. *Then Philip*. One of the seven deacons, ch. vi. 5. He is afterward called *the evangelist*, Ac. xxi. 8. ¶ *The city of Samaria*. This does not mean a city whose *name* was Samaria, for no such city at that time existed. Samaria was a *region*, Mat. ii. 22. The ancient city Samaria, the capital of that region, had been destroyed by *Hyrcanus*, so completely as to leave no vestige of it remaining; and he "took away," says Josephus, "the very marks that there had ever been such a city there" (*Antiq.*, b. xiii. ch. x. § 3). Herod the Great afterward built a city on this site, and called it *Sebaste;* that is, *Augusta*, in honour of the Emperor Augustus (Jos. *Antiq.*, b. xv. ch. viii. § 5). Perhaps this city is intended, as being the principal city of Samaria; or possibly *Sychar*, another city where the gospel had been before preached by the Saviour himself, Jn. iv. ¶ *And preached Christ*. Preached that the Messiah had come, and made known his doctrines. The same truths had been before stated in Samaria by the Saviour himself (Jn. iv.); and this was doubtless one of the reasons why they so gladly now received the word of God. The field had been prepared by the Lord Jesus. He had said that it was white for the harvest (Jn. iv. 35), and into that field Philip now entered, and was signally blessed. His coming was attended with a remarkable *revival of religion*. The word translated *preach* here is not that which is used in the previous verse. This denotes to *proclaim as a crier*, and is commonly employed to denote the preaching of the gospel, so called, Mar. v. 20; vii. 36; Lu. viii. 39; Mat. xxiv. 14; Ac. x. 42; Ro. x. 15; 1 Co. ix. 27; xv. 12; 2 Ti. iv. 2. It has been argued that because *Philip* is said thus to have preached to the Samaritans, that *therefore* all *deacons* have a right to preach, or that they are, under the New Testament economy, an *order* of ministers. But this is by no means clear. For, (1) It is not evident, nor can it be shown, that the *other* deacons (ch. vi.) ever preached. There is no record of their doing so; and the narrative would lead us to suppose that they did not. (2) They were *appointed* for a very different purpose (ch. vi. 1-5); and it is fair to suppose that, *as deacons*, they confined themselves to the design of their appointment. (3) It is not said that *Philip* preached in virtue of his being *a deacon*. From anything in *this* place, it would seem that he preached as the other Christians did—wherever he was. (4) But *elsewhere* an express distinction is made between Philip and the others. A new appellation is given him, and he is expressly called the *evangelist*, Ac. xxi. 8. From *this*, it seems that he preached, not *because* he was a *deacon*, but because he had received a special *appointment* to this business as an evangelist. (5) This same office, or rank of Christian teachers, is expressly recognized elsewhere, Ep. iv. 11. All these considerations show that there is *not* in the sacred Scriptures an order

cord gave heed unto those things which Philip spake, [f]hearing, and seeing the miracles which he did.

7 For[g] unclean spirits, crying with loud voice, came out of many that were possessed *with them;* [h]and many taken with palsies, [i]and that were lame, were healed.

8 And there was great joy in that city.

9 But there was a certain man called Simon, which beforetime in the same city used [k]sorcery, and bewitched the people of Samaria, [l]giving out that himself was some great one:

f Jn.4.41,42. g Mar.16.17. h Mar.2.3-11; ch.9.33,34. i Mat.11.5.

k ch.13.6; Re.22.15. l ch.5.36; 2 Ti.3.2,5.

of ministers appointed to preach *as deacons.*

6. *With one accord.* Unitedly, or with one mind. Great multitudes of them did it. ¶ *Gave heed.* Paid attention to; embraced. ¶ *Hearing.* Hearing what he said.

7. *For unclean spirits.* See Notes on Mat. iv. 24. ¶ *Crying with loud voice.* See Notes on Mar. i. 26. ¶ *Palsies.* See Notes on Mat. iv. 24.

8. *And there was great joy.* This joy arose (1) From the fact that so many persons, before sick and afflicted, were restored to health. (2) From the conversion of individuals to Christ. (3) From the mutual joy of *families* and *friends* that their friends were converted. The tendency of a revival of religion is thus to produce great joy.

9. *But there was a certain man called Simon.* The fathers have written much respecting this man, and have given strange accounts of him; but nothing more is certainly known of him than is stated in this place. Rosenmüller and Kuinoel suppose him to have been a Simon mentioned by Josephus (*Antiq.*, b. xx. ch. vii. § 2), who was born in Cyprus. He was a magician, and was employed by Felix to persuade Drusilla to forsake her husband Azizus, and to marry Felix. But it is not very probable that this was the same person. (See Note in Whiston's Josephus.) Simon Magus was probably a *Jew* or a *Samaritan,* who had addicted himself to the arts of magic, and who was much celebrated for it. He had studied philosophy in Alexandria in Egypt (Mosheim, i. p. 113, 114, Murdock's translation), and then lived in Samaria. After he was cut off from the hope of adding to his other powers the power of working miracles, the *fathers* say that he fell into many errors, and became the founder of the sect of the Simonians. They accused him of affirming that he came down as the *Father* in respect to the Samaritans, the *Son* in respect to the Jews, and the *Holy Spirit* in respect to the Gentiles. He did not acknowledge Christ to be the Son of God, but a rival, and pretended himself to be Christ. He rejected the law of Moses. Many other things are affirmed of him which rest on doubtful authority. He seems to have become an enemy to Christianity, though he was willing *then* to avail himself of some of its doctrines in order to advance his own interests. The account that he came to a tragical death in Rome; that he was honoured as a deity by the Roman senate; and that a statue was erected to his memory in the isle of Tiber, is now generally rejected. His end is not known. (See Calmet, art. "Simon Magus," and Mosheim, i. p. 114, note.) ¶ *Beforetime.* The practice of magic, or sorcery, was common at that time, and in all the ancient nations. ¶ *Used sorcery.* Greek, μαγεύων. Exercising the arts of the *Magi,* or *magicians;* hence the name Simon *Magus.* See Notes on Mat. ii. 1. The ancient *Magi* had their rise in Persia, and were at first addicted to the study of philosophy, astronomy, medicine, &c. This name came afterward to signify those who made use of the knowledge of these arts for the purpose of imposing on mankind—astrologers, soothsayers, necromancers, fortune-tellers, &c. Such persons pretended to predict future events by the positions of the stars, and to cure diseases by incantations, &c. See Is. ii. 6. See also Da. i. 20; ii. 2. It was expressly forbidden the Jews to consult such persons on pain of death, Le. xix. 31; xx. 6. In these arts Simon had been eminently successful. ¶ *And bewitched.* This is an unhappy translation. The Greek means merely that he *astonished* or *amazed* the people, or *confounded* their judgment. The idea of *bewitching* them is not in the original. ¶ *Giving out,* &c. *Saying;* that is, boasting. It was in this way, partly, that he so confounded

10 To[m] whom they all gave heed,
from the least to the greatest, saying,
This man is the great power of
God.

11 And to him they had regard,
because that of long time [n]he had
bewitched them with sorceries.

12 But when they [o]believed
Philip preaching [p]the things concerning
the kingdom of God, and
the name of Jesus Christ, they were
baptized, both men and women.

13 Then Simon himself believed
also; and when he was baptized,
he continued with Philip, and wondered,
beholding the [1]miracles and
signs which were done.

14 Now when the apostles which
were at Jerusalem heard that Samaria
had received the word of

m 2 Co.11.19. *n* Ga.3.1. *o* ch.2.41; ver.37. *p* ch.1.3.

1 *signs and great miracles.*

them. Jugglers generally impose on people just in proportion to the *extravagance* and *folly* of their pretensions. The same remark may be made of *quack doctors*, and of all persons who attempt to delude and impose on mankind.

10. *The great power of God.* Probably this means only that they believed that he was *invested with* the power of God, not that they supposed he was really the Great God.

13. *Then Simon himself believed also.* That is, he believed that Jesus had wrought miracles, and was raised from the dead, &c. All this he could believe in entire consistency with his own notions of the power of magic; and all that the connection requires us to suppose is that he believed this Jesus had the power of working miracles; and as he purposed to turn this to his own account, he was willing to profess himself to be his follower. It might have injured his popularity, moreover, if he had taken a stand in opposition when so many were professing to become Christians. Men often profess religion because, if they do not, they fear that they will lose their influence, and be left with the ungodly. That Simon was not a real Christian is apparent from the whole narrative, ver. 18, 21–23. ¶ *And when he was baptized.* He was admitted to a *profession* of religion in the same way as others. Philip did not pretend to know the heart; and Simon was admitted because he *professed* his belief. This is all the evidence that ministers of the gospel can now have, and it is no wonder that they, as well Philip, are often deceived. The reasons which influenced Simon to make a profession of religion seem to have been these: (1) An impression that Christianity was *true*. He seems to have been convinced of this by the miracles of Philip. (2) The fact that many others were becoming Christians; and *he* went in with the multitude. This is often the case in revivals of religion. (3) He was willing to make use of Christianity to advance his own power, influence, and popularity—a thing which multitudes of men of the same mind with Simon Magus have been willing since to do. ¶ *And continued*, &c. It was customary and natural for the disciples to remain with their teachers. See ch. ii. 42. ¶ *And wondered.* This is the same word that is translated *bewitched* in ver. 9, 11. It means that he was amazed that Philip could *really* perform so much greater miracles than *he* had even pretended to. Hypocrites will sometimes be greatly attentive to the external duties of religion, and will be greatly surprised at what is done by God for the salvation of sinners. ¶ *Miracles and signs.* Greek, signs and *great powers*, or great miracles. That is, so much greater than he *pretended* to be able to perform.

14. *They sent.* That is, the apostles *deputed* two of their number. This shows conclusively that there was no *chief* or *ruler* among them. They acted as being equal in authority. The reason why they sent Peter and John was probably that there would be a demand for more labour than Philip could render; a church was to be founded, and it was important that persons of experience and wisdom should be present to organize it, and to build it up. The *harvest* had occurred in Samaria, of which the Saviour spoke (Jn. iv. 35), and it was proper that they should enter into it. In times of revival there is often more to be done than can be done by the regular pastor of a people, and it is proper that he should be aided from abroad. ¶ *Peter.* This shows that *Peter* had no such authority and primacy as the Roman Catholics claim for him. He exercised no authority in *sending* others, but was himself *sent*. He was

God, they sent unto them Peter and John;

15 Who, when they were come down, prayed for them, that they might receive the Holy Ghost:

16 (For[q] as yet he was fallen upon none of them; [r]only they were baptized in the name of the Lord Jesus.)

17 Then [s]laid they *their* hands on them, and they received the Holy Ghost.

q ch.19.2.

r ch.2.38; 10.48; 19.5,6; 1 Co.1.13. s ch.6.6; He.6.2.

---

appointed by *their* united voice, instead of claiming the power himself of directing *them*. ¶ *And John.* Peter was ardent, bold, zealous, rash; John was mild, gentle, tender, persuasive. There was wisdom in uniting them in this work, as the talents of both were needed; and the excellencies in the character of the one would compensate for the defects of the other. It is observable that the apostles sent *two* together, as the Saviour had himself done. See Notes on Mar. vi. 7.

15. *Were come down.* To Samaria. Jerusalem was generally represented as *up*, or *higher* than the rest of the land, Mat. xx. 18; Jn. vii. 8. ¶ *Prayed for them.* They sought at the hand of God the extraordinary communications of the Holy Spirit. They did not even pretend to have the power of doing it without the aid of God. ¶ *That they might receive the Holy Ghost.* The main question here is, what was *meant* by the Holy Ghost? In ver. 20, it is called "the gift of God." The following remarks may make this plain. (1) It was not that gift of the Holy Ghost by which *the soul is converted*, for they had this when they believed, ver. 6. Everywhere the conversion of the sinner is traced to his influence. Comp. Jn. i. 13. (2) It was not the ordinary influences of the Spirit by which *the soul is sanctified;* for sanctification is a progressive work, and this was sudden. (3) It was something that was discernible by *external effects;* for Simon *saw* (ver. 18) that this was done by the laying on of hands. (4) The phrase "the gift of the Holy Ghost," and "the descent of the Holy Ghost," signified not merely his *ordinary* influences in converting sinners, but those *extraordinary* influences that attended the first preaching of the gospel—the power of speaking with new tongues (ch. ii.), the power of working miracles, &c., Ac. xix. 6. (5) This is further clear from the fact that Simon wished to *purchase* this power, evidently to keep up his influence among the people, and to retain his ascendency as a juggler and sorcerer. But surely Simon would not wish to *purchase* the converting and sanctifying influences of the Holy Spirit; it was the power of working miracles. These things made it clear that by the gift of the Holy Spirit here is meant the power of speaking with new tongues (comp. 1 Co. xiv.) and the power of working miracles. And it is further clear that *this* passage should not be adduced in favour of "the rite of confirmation" in the Christian church. For, besides the fact that there are now no *apostles*, the thing spoken of here is entirely different from the rite of confirmation. *This* was to confer the extraordinary power of working miracles; *that* is for a different purpose.

If it be asked *why* this power was conferred on the early Christians, it may be replied that it was to furnish striking proof of the truth of the Christian religion; to impress the people, and thus to win them to embrace the gospel. The early church was thus armed with the power of the Holy Spirit; and this extraordinary attestation of God to his message was one cause of the rapid propagation and permanent establishment of the gospel.

16. *He was fallen.* This expression is several times applied to the Holy Spirit, ch. x. 44; xi. 15. It does not differ materially from the common expression, "The Holy Ghost *descended.*" It means that he came from heaven; and the expression *to fall*, applied to his influences, denotes the *rapidity* and *suddenness* of his coming. Comp. ch. xix. 2. ¶ *In the name of the Lord Jesus.* See Notes on ch. ii. 38. See also ch. x. 48; xix. 5, 6.

17. *Then laid they* their *hands*, &c. This was an act of *prayer*, expressing an invocation to God that he would impart the blessing to *them*. On *how many* they laid their hands is not said. It is evident that it was not on *all*, for they did not thus lay hands on Simon. Perhaps it was done on a few of the more prominent and leading persons, who were to be employed particularly

18 And when Simon saw that through laying on of the apostles' hands the Holy Ghost was given, he [t]offered them money,

19 Saying, Give me also this power, that on whomsoever I lay hands, he may receive the Holy Ghost.

20 But Peter said unto him, Thy money perish with thee, [u]because thou hast thought that [v]the gift of God may be purchased with money.

21 Thou hast [w]neither part nor lot in this matter; for [x]thy heart is not right in the sight of God.

t 1 Ti.6.5.

u 2 Ki.5.15,16; Mat.10.8. *v* ch.10.45; 11.17. *w* Jos.22.25. *x* Ps.78.36,37; Eze.14.3.

---

in bearing witness to the truth of the gospel. It was customary to lay the hands on any person when a *favour* was to be conferred or a blessing imparted. See Notes on Mat. ix. 18.

18. *Simon saw*, &c. That is, he witnessed the extraordinary effects, the power of speaking in a miraculous manner, &c. See Notes on ver. 15. ¶ *He offered them money.* He had had a remarkable influence over the Samaritans, and he saw that the possession of this power would perpetuate and increase his influence. Men commonly employ the tricks of legerdemain for the purpose of making money, and it seems probable that such had been the design of Simon. He saw that if he could communicate to *others* this power; if he could confer on *them* the talent of speaking other languages, it might be turned to vast account, and he sought, therefore, to purchase it of the apostles. From this act of Simon we have derived our word *simony*, to denote the buying and selling of ecclesiastical preferment, or church offices, where religion is supported by the state. This act of Simon shows conclusively that he was influenced by improper motives in becoming connected with the church.

20. *Thy money perish with thee.* This is expressive of the horror and indignation of Peter at the base offer of Simon. It is not to be understood as an imprecation on Simon. The main idea is the apostle's contempt for the *money*, as if he regarded it as of no value. "Let your money go to destruction. We abhor your impious offer. We can freely see *any* amount of money destroyed before we will be tempted to *sell* the gift of the Holy Ghost." But there was here also an expression of his belief that *Simon* also would perish. It was a declaration that he was hastening to ruin, and *as if* this was certain, Peter says, let your money *perish too.* ¶ *The gift of God.* That which he has *given*, or conferred as a favour. The idea was *absurd* that that which God himself *gave* as a sovereign could be purchased. It was *impious* to think of attempting to buy with worthless gold that which was of so inestimable value. The *gift of God* here means the extraordinary influences of the Holy Ghost, ch. x. 45; xi. 17. How can we pay a *price* to God? All that *we* can give, the silver, and the gold, and the cattle on a thousand hills, belong to him already. We have *nothing* which we can present for his favours. And yet there are many who seek to *purchase* the favour of God. Some do it by alms and prayers; some by penance and fasting; some by attempting to make their own hearts better, and by self-righteousness; and some by penitence and tears. All these will not *purchase* his favour. Salvation, like every other blessing, will be *his gift;* and if ever received, we must be willing to accept it on his own terms; at his own time; in his own way. We are without merit; and if saved, it will be by the sovereign grace of God.

21. *Neither part.* You have no *portion* of the grace of God; that is, you are destitute of it altogether. This word commonly denotes the *part* of an inheritance which falls to one when it is divided. ¶ *Nor lot.* This word means properly a portion which *falls* to one when an estate, or when spoil in war is divided into portions, according to the number of those who are to be partakers, and the part of each one is determined by *lot.* The two words denote *emphatically* that he was in no sense a partaker of the favour of God. ¶ *In this matter.* Greek, in this *word;* that is, thing. That which is referred to here is the religion of Christ. Simon was not a Christian. It is remarkable that Peter judged him so soon, and when he had seen but *one* act of his. But it was an act which satisfied him that he was a stranger to religion. One act may sometimes bring out the

22 Repent, therefore, of this thy wickedness; and pray God, [y]if perhaps the thought of thine heart may be forgiven thee:
23 For I perceive that thou art

y Da.4.27; 2 Ti.2.25.

whole character; it may evince the *governing* motives; it may show traits of character utterly *inconsistent* with true religion; and then it is as certain a criterion as any long series of acts. ¶ *Thy heart.* Your *affections*, or *governing motives;* your principle of conduct. Comp. 2 Ki. x. 15. You love gold and popularity, and not the gospel for what it is. There is no evidence here that Peter saw this in a miraculous manner, or by any supernatural influence. It was apparent and plain that Simon was not influenced by the pure, disinterested motives of the gospel, but by the love of power and of the world. ¶ *In the sight of God.* That is, God *sees* or judges that your heart is not sincere and pure. No external profession is acceptable without the heart. Reader, is *your* heart right with God? Are your motives pure; and does *God* see there the exercise of holy, sincere, and benevolent affections toward him? God *knows* the motives; and with unerring certainty he will judge, and with unerring justice he will fix our doom according to the affections of the heart.

22. *Repent, therefore.* Here we may remark, (1) That Simon was at this time an unconverted sinner. (2) That the command was given to him *as such.* (3) That he was required to *do the thing;* not to wait or seek merely, but actually to repent. (4) That this was to be the *first step* in his conversion. He was not even directed to *pray* first, but his first indispensable work was to *repent;* that is, to exercise proper sorrow for this sin, and to *abandon* his plan or principle of action. And this shows, (1) That *all* sinners are to be exhorted to *repent*, as their first work. They are not to be told to *wait*, and *read*, and *pray*, in the expectation that repentance will be *given* them. With such helps as they can obtain, they are to *do the thing.* (2) Prayer will not be acceptable or heard unless the sinner comes *repenting;* that is, unless he regrets his sin, and *desires* to forsake it. Then, and then only, will he be heard. When he comes *loving* his sins, and resolving still to practise them, God will not hear him. When he comes *desirous* of forsaking them, grieved that he is guilty, and *feeling* his need of help, God will hear his prayer. See Is. i. 15; Mi. iii. 4; Pr. i. 28; Ps. lxvi. 18. ¶ *And pray God.* Having a *desire* to forsake the sin, and to be pardoned, *then* pray to God to forgive. It would be absurd to ask forgiveness until a man felt his need of it. This shows that a sinner *ought* to pray, and *how* he ought to do it. It should be with a desire and purpose to forsake sin, and in that state of mind God will hear the prayer. Comp. Da. iv. 27. ¶ *If perhaps.* There was no certainty that God would forgive him; nor is there any evidence either that Simon prayed, or that he was forgiven. This direction of Peter presents *another* important principle in regard to the conduct of sinners. They are to be directed to repent; not because they have the *promise* of forgiveness, and not because they *hope* to be forgiven, but because sin *is a great evil*, and because it is *right* and *proper* that they should repent, whether they are forgiven or not. That is to be left to the sovereign mercy of God. *They* are to repent of sin, and then they are to feel, not that they have any *claim* on God, but that they are dependent on him, and must be saved or lost at his will. They are not to suppose that their tears will *purchase* forgiveness, but that they lie at the footstool of mercy, and that there is *hope*—not certainty—that *God* will forgive. The language of the humbled sinner is,

"Perhaps he will admit my plea,
Perhaps will hear my prayer;
But if I perish I will pray,
And perish only there.

"I can but perish if I go;
I am resolved to try;
For if I stay away, I know
I shall for ever die."

¶ *The thought*, &c. Your *purpose*, or *wish.* *Thoughts* may be, therefore, evil, and need forgiveness. It is not open sin only that needs to be pardoned; it is the secret purpose of the soul.

23. *For I perceive.* That is, by the act which he had done. His offer had shown a state of mind that was wholly inconsistent with true religion. One single sin *may* as certainly show that there is no true piety as *many* acts of iniquity. It may be so decided, so malignant, so utterly inconsistent with just views as at once to determine what

in the [z]gall of bitterness, and *in* the
bond[a] of iniquity.
24 Then answered Simon, and
said, [b]Pray ye to the Lord for me,
that none of these things which ye
have spoken come upon me.
25 And they, when they had
testified and preached the word of
the Lord, returned to Jerusalem,
and preached the gospel in many
villages of the Samaritans.
26 And the angel of the Lord
spake unto Philip, saying, Arise,

z Je.4.18; He.12.15. a Ps.116.16; Pr.5.22; Is.28.22.
b Ex.8.8; Nu.21.7; 1 Ki.13.6; Job 42.8; Ja.5.16.

the character is. The sin of Simon was of this character. Peter here does not appear to have claimed the power of judging the *heart;* but he judged, as all other men would, by the act. ¶ *In the gall.* This word denotes properly *bile*, or that bitter, yellowish-green fluid that is secreted in the liver. Hence it means anything very bitter; and also any bad passion of the mind, as anger, malice, &c. We speak of *bitterness* of mind, &c. ¶ *Of bitterness.* This is a Hebraism; the usual mode of expressing the *superlative*, and means *excessive bitterness.* The phrase is used respecting *idolatry* (De. xxix. 18), "Lest there should be among you a root that beareth gall and wormwood." A similar expression occurs in He. xii. 15, "Lest any root of bitterness springing up, trouble you." *Sin* is thus represented as a *bitter* or poisonous thing; a thing not only *unpleasant* in its consequences, but ruinous in its character, as a poisonous plant would be in the midst of other plants, Je. ii. 19, "It is an evil and *bitter* thing that thou hast forsaken the Lord thy God;" Je. iv. 18; Ro. iii. 14, "Whose mouth is full of cursing and bitterness;" Ep. iv. 31. The meaning here is, that the heart of Simon was full of dreadful, malignant sin. ¶ *Bond of iniquity.* Or, that thou art *bound by* iniquity. That is, that it has the *rule* over you, and *binds* you as a captive. Sin is often thus represented as *bondage* and *captivity*, Ps. cxvi. 16; Pr. v. 22, "He shall be holden with the cords of his sins;" Ro. vii. 23, 24. These expressions prove conclusively that Simon was a stranger to religion.

24. *Pray ye*, &c. Here remark, (1) That Simon was directed to pray for himself (ver. 22), but he had no disposition to do it, but was willing to ask others to do it for him. Sinners will often ask others to pray for them, when they are too proud, or too much in love with sin, to pray for themselves. (2) The main thing that Peter wished to impress on him was a sense of his *sin*. Simon did not regard this, but looked only to the *punishment.* He was terrified and alarmed; he sought to avoid future punishment, but he had no alarm about his *sins.* So it is often with sinners. So it was with Pharaoh (Ex. viii. 28, 32), and with Jeroboam (1 Ki. xiii. 6). Sinners often quiet their own consciences by asking ministers and Christian friends to pray for them, while *they* still purpose to persevere in iniquity. If men expect to be saved, they must pray *for themselves;* and pray not chiefly to be freed from *punishment*, but from the *sin which deserves hell.* This is all that we hear of Simon in the New Testament; and the probability is, that, like many other sinners, he did *not* pray for himself, but continued to live in the gall of bitterness, and died in the bond of iniquity. The testimony of antiquity is decided on that point. See Notes on ver. 9.

25. *In many villages*, &c. They went at first directly to the *city* of Samaria. On their return to Jerusalem they travelled more at leisure, and preached in the villages also—a good example for the ministers of the gospel, and for all Christians, when travelling from place to place. The reason why they returned to Jerusalem, and made that their permanent abode, might have been, that it was important to bear witness to the resurrection of Christ in the very city where he had been crucified, and where his resurrection had occurred. If the doctrine was established *there*, it would be more easy to establish it elsewhere.

26. *And the angel of the Lord.* The word *angel* is used in the Scriptures in a great variety of significations. See Notes on Mat. i. 20. Here it has been supposed by some to mean literally a celestial messenger sent from God; others have supposed that it means *a dream;* others *a vision*, &c. The word properly means *a messenger;* and all that it can be shown to signify here is, that the Lord sent a *message* to Philip of this kind. It is most probable, I think, that the passage means that God communi-

and go toward the south, unto the way that goeth down from Jerusalem unto [c]Gaza, which is desert.

27 And he arose and went: and, behold, a man of [d]Ethiopia, an [e]eunuch of great authority under

c Jos.15.47. d Zep.3.10. e Is.56.3-5.

cated the message by his Spirit; for in ver. 29, 39, it is expressly said that *the Spirit* spake to Philip, &c. Thus, in Ac. xvi. 7, the *Spirit* is said to have forbidden Paul to preach in Bithynia; and in ver. 9, the message on the subject is said to have been conveyed in *a vision.* There is no absurdity, however, in supposing that an *angel* literally was employed to communicate this message to Philip. See He. i. 14; Ge. xix. 1; xxii. 11; Ju. vi. 12. ¶ *Spake unto Philip.* Comp. Mat. ii. 13. ¶ *Arise.* See Notes on Lu. xv. 18. ¶ *And go*, &c. Philip had been employed in Samaria. As God now intended to send the gospel to another place, he gave a special direction to him to go and convey it. It is evident that God designed the *conversion* of this eunuch, and the direction to Philip shows *how* he accomplishes his designs. It is not by miracle, but by the use of means. It is not by direct power without *truth*, but it is by a message fitted to the end. The salvation of a single sinner is an object worthy the attention of God. When such a sinner *is* converted, it is because God forms a *plan* or *purpose* to do it. *When* it is done, he inclines his servants to labour; he directs their labours; he leads his ministers; and he prepares the way (ver. 28) for the reception of the truth. ¶ *Toward the south.* That is, south of Samaria, where Philip was then labouring. ¶ *Unto Gaza.* Gaza, or AZZAH (Ge. x. 19), was a city of the Philistines, given by Joshua to Judah (Jos. xv. 47; 1 Sa. vi. 17). It was one of the *five* principal cities of the Philistines. It was formerly a large place; was situated on an eminence, and commanded a beautiful prospect. It was in this place that Samson took away the gates of the city, and bore them off, Ju. xvi. 2, 3. It was near Askelon, about 60 miles south-west from Jerusalem. ¶ *Which is desert.* This may refer either to the *way* or to the *place.* The natural construction is the latter. In explanation of this, it is to be observed that there were *two* towns of that name, Old and New Gaza. The prophet Zephaniah (ii. 4) said that *Gaza* should be *forsaken*, that is, destroyed. "This was partly accomplished by Alexander the Great (Jos. *Antiq.*, b. xi. ch. viii. § 3, 4; b. xiii. ch. xiii. § 3). Another town was afterward built of the same name, but at some distance from the former, and Old Gaza was abandoned to desolation. Strabo mentions 'Gaza the desert,' and Diodorus Siculus speaks of 'Old Gaza'" (Robinson's Calmet). Some have supposed, however, that Luke refers here to the *road* leading to Gaza, as being desolate and uninhabited. Dr. Robinson (*Biblical Res.*, ii. 640) remarks: "There were several ways leading from Jerusalem to Gaza. The most frequented at the present day, although the longest, is the way by Ramleh. Anciently there appear to have been two more direct roads. Both these roads exist at the present day, and the one actually passes through the desert, that is, through a tract of country without villages, inhabited only by nomadic tribes." "In this place, in 1823, the American missionaries, Messrs. Fisk and King, found Gaza, a town built of stone, making a very mean appearance, and containing about five thousand inhabitants" (Hall on the Acts).

27. *A man of Ethiopia.* Gaza was near the confines between Palestine and Egypt. It was in the direct road from Jerusalem to Egypt. *Ethiopia* was one of the great kingdoms of Africa, part of which is now called Abyssinia. It is frequently mentioned in Scripture under the name of *Cush.* But *Cush* comprehended a much larger region, including the southern part of Arabia, and even sometimes the countries adjacent to the Tigris and Euphrates. Ethiopia proper lay south of Egypt, on the Nile, and was bounded north by Egypt, that is, by the cataracts near Syene; east by the Red Sea, and perhaps part by the Indian Ocean; south by unknown regions in the interior of Africa; and west by Libya and the deserts. It comprehended the modern kingdoms of Nubia or Sennaar, and Abyssinia. The chief city in it was the ancient Meroë, situated on the island or tract of the same name, between the Nile and Ashtaboras, not far from the modern Shendi (Robinson's Calmet). ¶ *An eunuch*, &c. See Notes on Mat.

Candace, queen of the Ethiopians, who had the charge of all her treasure, and had [f]come to Jerusalem for to worship,

28 Was returning; and, sitting in his chariot, read Esaias the prophet.

29 Then[g] the Spirit said unto Philip, Go near, and join thyself to this chariot.

f 2 Ch.6.32,33.

g Is.65.24; Ho.6.3.

---

xix. 12. Eunuchs were commonly employed in attendance on the females of the harem; but the word is often used to denote any confidential officer, or counsellor of state. It is evidently so used here. ¶ *Of great authority.* Of high rank; an officer of the court. It is clear from what follows that this man was a Jew. But it is known that Jews were often raised to posts of high honour and distinction in foreign courts, as in the case of Joseph in Egypt, and of Daniel in Babylon. ¶ *Under Candace*, &c. Candace is said to have been the common name of the queens of Ethiopia, as *Pharaoh* was of the sovereigns of Egypt. This is expressly stated by Pliny (*Nat. History*, vii. 29). His words are: "The edifices of the city were few; a woman reigned there of the name of CANDACE, which name had been transmitted to these queens for many years." Strabo mentions also a queen of Ethiopia of the name of Candace. Speaking of an insurrection against the Romans, he says, "Among these were the officers of queen CANDACE, who in our days reigned over the Ethiopians." As this could not have been the Candace mentioned here, it is plain that the name was common to these queens—a sort of royal title. She was probably queen of Meroë, an important part of Ethiopia (Bruce's *Travels*, vol. ii. p. 431; Clarke). ¶ *Who had the charge*, &c. The treasurer was an officer of high trust and responsibility. ¶ *And had come*, &c. This proves that he was a *Jew*, or at least a Jewish proselyte. It was customary for the Jews in foreign lands, as far as practicable, to attend the great feasts at Jerusalem. He had gone up to attend the Passover, &c. See Notes on ch. ii. 5.

28. *And sitting in his chariot.* His carriage; his vehicle. The form of the carriage is not known. In some instances the carriages of the ancients were placed on wheels; in others were borne on poles, in the form of a *litter* or palanquin, by men, mules, or horses. See Calmet, article "Chariot." ¶ *Reading Esaias*, &c. Isaiah. Reading doubtless the translation of Isaiah called the Septuagint. This translation was made in Egypt for the special use of the Jews in Alexandria and throughout Egypt, and was that which was commonly used. *Why* he was reading the Scriptures, and especially this prophet, is not certainly known. It is morally certain, however, that he was in Judea at the time of the crucifixion and resurrection of Jesus; that he had heard much of him; that this would be a subject of discussion; and it was natural for him, in returning, to look at the prophecies respecting the Messiah, either to meditate on them as a suitable subject of inquiry and thought, or to examine the claims of Jesus of Nazareth to this office. The prophecy in Is. liii. was so striking, and coincided so clearly with the character of Jesus, that it was natural for a candid mind to examine whether *he* might not be the person intended by the prophet. On this narrative we may remark, (1) It is a proper and profitable employment, on returning from *worship*, to examine the sacred Scriptures. (2) It is well to be in the habit of reading the Scriptures when we are on a journey. It may serve to keep the heart from worldly objects, and secure the affections for God. (3) It is well at *all* times to read the Bible. It is one of the means of grace. And it is when we are searching his will that we obtain light and comfort. The sinner should examine with a candid mind the sacred volume. It may be the means of conducting him in the true path of salvation. (4) God often gives us light in regard to the meaning of the Bible in unexpected modes. How little did this eunuch *expect* to be enlightened in the manner in which he actually was. Yet God, who intended to instruct and save him, sent the living teacher, and opened to him the Scriptures, and led him to the Saviour.

29. *The Spirit.* See Notes on ver. 26. The Holy Spirit is here evidently intended. The thought in Philip's mind is here traced to his suggestion. All good thoughts and designs have the same origin. ¶ *Join thyself.* Join him in his chariot. Go and sit with him.

30 And Philip ran thither to
him, and heard him read the prophet Esaias, and said, [h]Under-
standest thou what thou readest?
31 And he said, [i]How can I, except some man should [k]guide me?
And he desired Philip that he would
come up and sit with him.
32 The place of the scripture
which he read was this, [l]He was

h Mat.13.23,51; Ep.5.17. *i* Ro.10.14. *k* Ps.25.9. *l* Is.53.7,8.

---

30. *And Philip ran*, &c. Indicating his haste and his desire to obey the suggestions of the Spirit. A thousand difficulties might have been started in the mind of Philip if he had reflected a little. The eunuch was a stranger; he had the appearance of a man of rank; he was engaged in reading; he might be indisposed to be interrupted or to converse, &c. But Philip obeyed without any hesitation the monitions of the Spirit, and *ran* to him. It is well to follow the *first* suggestions of the Spirit; to yield to the clear indications of duty, and to perform it *at once*. Especially in a deed of benevolence, and in conversing with others on the subject of religion, our *first* thoughts are commonly safest and best. If we do not follow them, the calculations of avarice, or fear, or of worldly prudence are very apt to come in. We become alarmed; we are afraid of the rich and the great; we suppose that our conversation and admonitions will be unacceptable. We may learn from this case, (1) To do our duty at once, without hesitation or debate. (2) We shall often be disappointed in regard to subjects of this kind. We shall find candid, humble, Christian conversation far more acceptable to strangers, to the rich, and to the great, than we commonly suppose. If, as in this case, they are *alone;* if we approach them kindly; if we do not rudely and harshly address them, we shall find most men willing to talk on the subject of religion. I have conversed with some hundreds of persons on the subject of religion, and do not now recollect but *two* instances in which I was rudely treated, and in which it was not easy to gain a respectful and kind attention to Christian conversation. ¶ *And heard him read.* He was reading *loud*—sometimes the best way of impressing truth on the mind in our private reading the Scriptures. ¶ *And said*, &c. This question, there might have been reason to fear, would not be kindly received. But the eunuch's mind was in such a state that he took no offence from such an inquiry, though made by a footman and a stranger. He doubtless recognized him as a brother Jew. It is an important question to ask ourselves when we read the sacred Scriptures.

31. *And he said*, &c. This was a *general* acknowledgment of his need of direction. It evinced a humble state of mind. It was an acknowledgment, also, originating probably from this particular passage which he was reading. He did not understand how it could be applied to the Messiah; how the description of his humiliation and condemnation (ver. 33) could be reconciled to the prevalent ideas of his being a prince and a conqueror. The same sentiment is expressed by Paul in Ro. x. 14. The circumstance, the state of mind in the eunuch, and the result, strongly remind one of the declaration in Ps. xxv. 9, "The meek will he guide in judgment, and the meek will he teach his way." ¶ *And he desired*, &c. He was willing to receive instruction even from a stranger. The rich and the great may often receive valuable instruction from a stranger, and from a poor, unknown man.

32. *The place*, &c. Is. liii. 7, 8. ¶ *He was led*, &c. This quotation is taken literally from the Septuagint. It varies very little from the Hebrew. It has been almost universally understood that this place refers to the Messiah; and Philip expressly applies it to him. The word "was led" (ἤχθη) implies that he was conducted by others; that he was led as a sheep is led to be killed. The general idea is that of *meekness* and *submission* when he was led to be put to death; a description that applies in a very striking manner to the Lord Jesus. ¶ *To the slaughter*. To be killed. The characteristic here recorded is more remarkable in sheep than in any other animals. ¶ *And like a lamb dumb*, &c. Still, patient, unresisting. ¶ *So he opened not his mouth.* He did not *complain* or murmur; he offered no resistance, but yielded patiently to what was done by others. Comp. Notes on Isa. liii.

led as a sheep to the slaughter; and like a lamb dumb before his shearer, so opened he not his mouth:
33 In his humiliation his judgment was taken away: and who shall declare his generation? for his life is taken from the earth.
34 And the eunuch answered

33. *In his humiliation.* This varies from the Hebrew, but is copied exactly from the Septuagint, showing that he was reading the Septuagint. The Hebrew is, "He was taken from prison and from judgment." The word rendered "prison" denotes any kind of *detention*, or even oppression. It does not mean, as with us, to be confined *in* a prison or jail, but may mean *custody*, and be applied to the detention or custody of the Saviour when his hands were bound, and he was led to be tried. See Notes on Mat. xxvii. 2. It is not known why the LXX. thus translated the expression "he was taken from prison," &c., by "in his humiliation," &c. The word "from prison" may mean, as has been remarked, however, from *oppression*, and this does not differ materially from *humiliation;* and in this sense the LXX. understood it. The *meaning* of the expression in the Septuagint and the Acts is clear. It denotes that in his state of oppression and calamity; when he was destitute of protectors and friends; when at the *lowest* state of humiliation, and therefore most the object of pity, *in addition to that,* justice was denied him; his judgment—a just sentence—was taken away, or withheld, and he was delivered to be put to death. His deep humiliation and friendless state was *followed* by an unjust and cruel condemnation, when no one would stand forth to plead his cause. Every circumstance thus goes to deepen the view of his sufferings. ¶ *His judgment.* Justice, a just sentence, was denied him, and he was cruelly condemned. ¶ *And who shall declare his generation?* The word *generation* used here properly denotes *posterity;* then *an age* of mankind, comprehending about thirty years, as we speak of this and the next generation; then it denotes *the men* of a particular age or time. Very various interpretations have been given of this expression. Lowth translates it, "His manner of life who would declare?" referring, as he supposes, to the fact that when a prisoner was condemned and led to execution, it was customary for a proclamation to be made by a crier in these words, "Whoever knows anything about his innocence, let him come and declare it." This passage is taken from the Gemara of Babylon (Kennicott, as quoted by Lowth). The same Gemara of Babylon on this passage adds, "that before the death of Jesus, this proclamation was made forty days; but no defence could be found"—a manifest falsehood, and a story strikingly illustrative of the character of the Jewish writings. The Gemara was written some time after Christ, perhaps not far from the year 180 (Lardner), and is a collection of commentaries on the traditional laws of the Jews. That this custom existed is very probable; but it is certain that no such thing was done on the trial of the Saviour. The Chaldee paraphrase translates the passage in Isaiah, "He shall collect our captivity from infirmities and vengeance; and who can declare what wonderful things shall be done for us in his days?" Others have referred this question to his Deity, or his divine *generation;* intimating that no one could explain the mystery of his eternal generation. But the word in the Scriptures has no such signification; and such a sense would not suit the connection. (See Calvin *in loco.*) Others have referred it to *his own spiritual posterity,* his disciples, his family; "the number of his friends and followers who could enumerate?" (Calvin, Beza, &c.) Another sense which the word has is to denote *the men* of any particular age or time (Mat. xi. 16; xxiii. 36; Lu. xvi. 8, &c.); and it has been supposed that the question here means, "Who can describe the character and wickedness of the generation when he shall live—the enormous crime of that age, in putting him to death?" On this passage, see Notes on Is. liii. 8. Perhaps, after all that has been written on this passage, the simple idea is, "Who shall stand up for him, declaring who he is? Who will appear for him? Who will vindicate him?" meaning that all would forsake him, and that there would be none *to declare really who he was.* ¶ *For his life,* &c. The Hebrew is, "For he was cut off from the land of the living;" that is he was put to death. The expression used in the Acts was taken from the Septua-

Philip, and said, I pray thee, of whom speaketh the prophet this? of himself, or of some other man?

35 Then Philip opened his mouth, and [m]began at the same scripture, and [n]preached unto him Jesus.

36 And as they went on *their* way, they came unto a certain water: and the eunuch said, See, *here is* water; [o]what doth hinder me to be baptized?

37 And Philip said, [p]If thou believest with all thine heart, thou mayest. And he answered and

m Lu.24.27. n ch.18.28. o ch.10.47. p Mar.16.16; ver.12.

---

gint, and means substantially the same as the Hebrew.

34. *Answered Philip.* That is, *addressed* Philip. The Hebrews often use the word *answer* as synonymous with addressing one, whether he had spoken or not. ¶ *Of himself*, &c. This was a natural inquiry, for there was nothing in the text itself that would determine to whom the reference was. The ancient Jews expressly applied the passage to the Messiah. Thus the Targum of Jonathan on Is. lii. 13, "Behold, my servant shall deal prudently," &c., renders it, "Behold, my servant, *the Messiah*, shall be prospered," &c. But we should remember that the eunuch was probably not deeply versed in the Scriptures. We should remember, further, that he had just been at Jerusalem, and that the public mind was agitated about the proceedings of the Sanhedrim in putting Jesus of Nazareth, who claimed to be the Messiah, to death. It is by no means improbable that *this* passage had been urged as a proof that he was the Messiah; and that the Jews, to evade the force of it, had maintained that it referred to Isaiah or Jeremiah—as they have since done. Yet the subject was so important and so difficult that it had occupied the attention of the traveller during his journey; and his question shows that he had been deeply pondering the inquiry whether it *could* refer to Isaiah himself or any of the prophets, or whether it must have reference to the Messiah. In this state of suspense and agitation, when his mind was just fitted to receive instruction, God sent a messenger to guide him. He often thus prepares, by his providence, or by a train of affecting and solemn events, the minds of men for a reception of the truth; and *then* he sends his messengers to guide the thoughtful and the anxious in the way of peace and salvation.

35. *Opened his mouth.* See Mat. v. 2. ¶ *At the same scripture.* Taking this as a *text* to be illustrated. ¶ *Preached unto him Jesus.* Showed him that Jesus of Nazareth exactly answered to the description of the prophet, and that therefore he referred to the Messiah, and that the Messiah was Jesus of Nazareth. How far Philip detailed the circumstances of the life and death of Christ is unknown. What follows shows also that he stated the design of baptism, and the duty of being baptized.

36. *As they went on* their *way.* In their journey. ¶ *A certain water.* The expression used here does not determine whether this was a river, a brook, or a standing pool. And there are no circumstances to determine that. It is well known, however, that there is no large river or very considerable stream in this vicinity. All that is intimated is that there was water enough to perform the rite of baptism, whether that was by sprinkling, pouring, or immersion. It must be admitted, I think, that there might have been water enough for either. Grotius says they came "*to a fountain* which was in the neighbourhood of *Bethsora*, in the tribe of Juda, at the twentieth milestone from Ælia (*Jerusalem*) to Hebron." This is, however, a tradition taken from Eusebius. The place is still shown (Pococke). ¶ *What doth hinder me*, &c. This shows that he had been instructed by Philip in the nature and design of baptism. It evinces also a purpose *at once* to give himself to Christ, to profess his name, and to be dedicated to his service. ¶ *To be baptized.* On the meaning of the word *baptize*, see Notes on Mat. iii. 6.

37. *And Philip said*, &c. This was stated by Philip as the proper qualification for making a profession of religion. The terms are, (1) *Faith;* that is, a reception of Jesus as a Saviour; yielding the mind to the proper influences of the truths of redemption. See Notes on Mar. xvi. 16. (2) There is required not merely the assent of the understanding, but a surrender of *the heart*, *the will*, *the*

said, [q] I believe that Jesus Christ is the Son of God.

38 And he commanded the chariot to stand still: and they went down both into the water, both Philip and the eunuch; and he baptized him.

q Jn.11.27; 1 Co.12.3; 1 Jn.4.15.

---

affections, to the truth of the gospel. As these were the proper qualifications then, so they are now. Nothing less is required; and nothing but this can constitute a proper qualification for the Lord's supper. ¶ *I believe*, &c. This profession is more than a professed belief that Jesus was *the Messiah*. The name *Christ* implies that. "I believe that *Jesus the Messiah* is the Son of God." He professed his belief that he was *the Son of God*—showing either that he had before supposed that the Messiah *would be* the Son of God, or that Philip had instructed him on that point. It was natural for Philip, in discoursing on the humiliation and poverty of Jesus, to add also that he sustained a higher rank of being than a man, and was the Son of God. What precise ideas the eunuch attached to this expression cannot be now determined. This verse is wanting in a very large number of manuscripts (Mill), and has been rejected by many of the ablest critics. It is also omitted in the Syriac and Ethiopic versions. It is not easy to conceive why it has been omitted in almost all the Greek MSS. unless it is spurious. If it was not in the original copy of the Acts, it was probably inserted by some early transcriber, and was deemed so important to the connection, to show that the eunuch was not admitted hastily to baptism, that it was afterward retained. It contains, however, an important truth, elsewhere abundantly taught in the Scriptures, that *faith* is necessary to a proper profession of religion.

38. *And they went down both into the water*. This passage has been made the subject of much discussion on the subject of baptism. It has been adduced in proof of the necessity of immersion. It is not proposed to enter into that subject here. It may be remarked here that the preposition εἰς, translated "into," does not of necessity mean that they went *into* the water. Its meaning would be as well expressed by "to" or "unto," or as we should say, "they went *to* the water," without meaning to determine whether they went *into* it or not. Out of *twenty-six* significations which Schleusner has given the word, this is one, and one which frequently occurs: Jn. xi. 38, "Jesus, therefore, groaning in himself, cometh *to* (εἰς) the grave"—assuredly not *into* the grave; Lu. xi. 49, "I send them prophets," Greek, "I send *to* (εἰς) them prophets"—*to* them, not *into* them, comp. Ro. ii. 4, 1 Co. xiv. 36; Mat. xii. 41, "They repented *at* (εἰς) the preaching of Jonas"—not *into* his preaching; Jn. iv. 5, "Then cometh he *to* (εἰς) a city of Samaria," that is, *near to it*, for the context shows that he had not yet entered *into* it, comp. ver. 6, 8; Jn. xxi. 4, "Jesus stood *on* (εἰς) the shore," that is, not *in*, but *near* the shore. These passages show, (1) That the word does not necessarily mean that they entered *into* the water. But, (2) If it did, it does not necessarily follow that the eunuch was immersed. There might be various ways of baptizing, even after they were *in* the water, besides immersing. Sprinkling or pouring might be performed there as well as elsewhere. The most solemn act of baptism that I ever saw performed was, when I was a boy, in the river on the banks of which I was born, where the minister and the candidate went both of them *into* the river, and, when near to the middle of the river, the candidate kneeled down in the water, and the minister with a bowl *poured* water on his head. Yet if the fact had been stated, in reference to this case, that "they went both down *into* the water, and came up out of the water," and it had been hence inferred that the man was *immersed*, it would have been wholly a false inference. No such immersion occurred, and there is, from the narrative here, no more evidence that it occurred in the case of the eunuch. (3) It is incumbent on those who maintain that *immersion* is the *only* valid mode of baptism, to prove that this passage cannot *possibly* mean anything else, and that there *was* no other mode practised by the apostles. (4) It would be still incumbent to show that *if* this were the common and even the only mode then, in a warm climate, that it is indispensable that this mode should be practised everywhere else. No such positive command can be adduced. And it follows, therefore, that it cannot be proved that immersion is the only

39 And when they were come up
out of the water, [r]the Spirit of the
Lord caught away Philip, that the
eunuch saw him no more: and he
went on his way [s]rejoicing.
40 But Philip was found at

r 1 Ki.18.12; Eze.3.12,14.

s Ps.119.14,111.

---

lawful mode of baptism. See Notes on Mat. iii. 6.

39. *Out of the water* (ἐκ). This preposition stands opposed to εἰς, "into;" and as that may mean *to*, so this may mean *from;* if that means *into*, this means here *out of*. ¶ *The Spirit of the Lord.* See ver. 29. The *Spirit* had suggested to Philip to go to meet the eunuch, and the same Spirit, now that he had fulfilled the design of his going there, directed his departure. ¶ *Caught away.* This phrase has been usually understood of a *forcible* or *miraculous* removal of Philip to some other place. Some have even supposed that he was borne through the air by an angel (see even Doddridge). To such foolish interpretations have many expositors been led. The meaning is, clearly, that the Spirit, who had directed Philip to go near the eunuch, now removed him in a similar manner. That this is the meaning is clear, (1) Because it accounts for all that occurred. It is not wise to suppose the existence of a miracle except where the effect cannot otherwise be accounted for, and except where there is a plain statement that there was a miracle. (2) The word "caught away" (ἥρπασε) does not imply that there was a miracle. The word properly means to seize and bear away anything violently, without the consent of the owner, as robbers and plunderers do. Then it signifies to remove anything in a *forcible* manner; to make use of strength or power to remove it, Ac. xxiii. 10; Mat. xiii. 19; Jn. x. 28; 2 Co. xii. 2, 4, &c. In *no case* does it ever denote that a *miracle* is performed. And all that can be signified here is, that the Spirit *strongly admonished* Philip to go to some other place; that he so *forcibly* or *vividly suggested* the duty to his mind as to *tear him away*, as it were, from the society of the eunuch. He had been deeply interested in the case. He would have found pleasure in continuing the journey with him. But the strong convictions of duty urged by the Holy Spirit impelled him, as it were, to break off this new and interesting acquaintanceship, and to go to some other place. The purpose for which he was sent, to instruct and baptize the eunuch, was accomplished, and now he was called to some other field of labour. A similar instance of interpretation has been considered in the Notes on Mat. iv. 5. ¶ *And he went on his way rejoicing.* His mind was enlightened on a perplexing passage of Scripture. He was satisfied respecting the Messiah. He was baptized; and he experienced that which all feel who embrace the Saviour and are baptized—*joy.* It was joy resulting from the fact that he was reconciled to God; and a joy the natural effect of having done his duty *promptly* in making a profession of religion. If we wish happiness—if we would avoid clouds and gloom, we should *do our duty at once.* If we delay till to-morrow what we *ought* to do to-day, we may expect to be troubled with melancholy thoughts. If we find peace, it will be in doing promptly *just that* which God requires at our hands. This is the last that we hear of this man. Some have supposed that he carried the gospel to Ethiopia, and preached it there. But there is strong evidence to believe that the gospel was not preached there successfully until about the year 330, when it was introduced by *Frumentius*, sent to Abyssinia for that purpose by Athanasius, bishop of Alexandria. From this narrative we may learn, (1) That God often prepares the mind to receive the truth. (2) That this takes place sometimes with the great and the noble, as well as the poor and obscure. (3) That we should study the Scriptures. This is the way in which God usually directs the mind in the truths of religion. (4) That they who read the Bible with candour and care may expect that God will, in some mode, guide them into the truth. It will often be in a way which they least expect; but they need not be afraid of being left to darkness or error. (5) That we should be ready at all times to speak to sinners. God often prepares their minds, as he did that of the eunuch, to receive the truth. (6) That we should not be afraid of the great, the rich, or of strangers. God often prepares *their* minds to receive the truth; and we may find a man willing to hear of the Saviour where we least expected it. (7) That we should do our duty in this respect, as Philip did,

Azotus: and passing through, he preached in all the cities till he came to Cesarea.

CHAPTER IX.

AND Saul, yet [a]breathing out threatenings and slaughter

a ch.8.3; Ga.1.13.

promptly. We should not delay or hesitate, but should *at once* do that which we believe to be in accordance with the will of God. See Ps. cxix. 60.

40. *But Philip was found.* That is, he came to Azotus, or he was not heard of until he reached Azotus. The word is often used in this sense. See 1 Ch. xxix. 17, margin; 2 Ch. xxix. 29, margin; Ge. ii. 20; see also Lu. xvii. 18; Ro. vii. 10. In all these places the word is used in the sense of *to be*, or *to be present.* It does not mean here that there was any *miracle* in the case, but that Philip, after leaving the eunuch, *came to* or was *in* Azotus. ¶ *Azotus.* This is the Greek name of the city which by the Hebrews was called *Ashdod.* It was one of the cities which were *not* taken by Joshua, and which remained in the possession of the Philistines. It was to this place that the ark of God was sent when it was taken by the Philistines from the Israelites; and here Dagon was cast down before it, 1 Sa. v. 2, 3. Uzziah, king of Judah, broke down its wall, and built cities or watch-towers around it, 2 Ch. xxvi. 6. It was a place of great strength and consequence. It was distant about thirty miles from Gaza. It was situated on the coast of the Mediterranean, and had a seaport, which has now entirely disappeared. The sea is now some two miles distant, and the intervening space is a desert of moving sand, which has reached the outskirts of the town (*Land and the Book*, Dr. Thomson, vol. ii. p. 320). Prof. Hackett (*Illustrations of Scripture*, p. 142, 143) says of this place: "A little village called Esdud perpetuates the ancient name. Ashdod was one of the chief cities of the Philistines, but is now utterly forsaken. The prophet's sentence has been executed upon it to the letter: 'I will cut off the inhabitant from Ashdod' (Am. i. 8). The only marks of antiquity which I could discover were a high mound, where the old city stood, covered now with fragments of pottery; two or three cellars or cisterns that seemed to have been recently laid open; two marble columns, one prostrate in the court of a neighbouring khan, and the other wrought into a drinking-trough; several broken pieces of columns or tablets, mostly built into a sakieh, or watering machine; and a few traces of masonry near the Jaffa road, which may have belonged to the city walls. These last are so concealed as to be found only with special pains." ¶ *He preached in all the cities.* Joppa, Lydda, Askelon, Arimathea, &c., lying along the coast of the Mediterranean. ¶ *Cesarea.* This city was formerly called *Strato's Tower.* It is situated on the coast of the Mediterranean, at the mouth of a small river, and has a fine harbour. It is thirty-six miles south of Acre, and about sixty-two north-west of Jerusalem, and about the same distance north-east of Azotus. The city is supposed by some to be the Hazor mentioned in Jos. xi. 1. It was rebuilt by Herod the Great, and named *Cæsarea* in honour of Augustus Cæsar. The city was dedicated to him, and was called *Sebaste*, the Greek word for Augustus. It was adorned with most splendid houses; and the Temple of Cæsar was erected by Herod over against the mouth of the haven, in which was placed the statue of the Roman emperor. It became the seat of the Roman governor while Judea was a Roman province, Ac. xxiii. 33; xxv. 6, 13. Philip afterward resided at this place. See Ac. xxi. 8, 9. Cesarea at present is inhabited only by jackals and beasts of prey. "Perhaps," says Dr. Clarke, "there has not been in the history of the world an example of any city that in so short a space of time rose to such an extraordinary height of splendour as did this of Cesarea, or that exhibits a more awful contrast to its former magnificence by the present desolate appearance of its ruins. Not a single inhabitant remains. Of its gorgeous palaces and temples, enriched with the choicest works of art, scarcely a trace can be discerned. Within the space of ten years after laying the foundation, from an obscure fortress, it became the most flourishing and celebrated city of all Syria." Now it is in utter desolation. See Robinson's Calmet, art. "Cæsarea."

CHAPTER IX.

This chapter commences a very important part of the Acts of the Apostles—the conversion and labours of Saul of

against the disciples of the Lord, went unto the high-priest,

2 And desired of him letters to Damascus to the synagogues, that,

---

Tarsus. The remainder of the book is chiefly occupied with an account of his labours and trials in the establishment of churches, and in spreading the gospel through the Gentile world. As the fact that the gospel was to be thus preached to the Gentiles was a very important fact, and as the toils of the apostle Paul and his fellow-labourers for this purpose were of an exceedingly interesting character, it was desirable to preserve an authentic record of those labours; and that record we have in the remainder of this book.

1. *And Saul.* See Notes on ch. vii. 58; viii. 3. He had been engaged before in persecuting the Christians, but he now sought opportunity to gratify his insatiable desire on a larger scale. ¶ *Yet breathing out.* Not satisfied with what he had done, ch. viii. 3. The word *breathing out* is expressive often of *any* deep, agitating emotion, as we then *breathe* rapidly and violently. It is thus expressive of violent *anger.* The emotion is absorbing, agitating, exhausting, and demands a more rapid circulation of blood to supply the exhausted vitality; and this demands an increased supply of oxygen, or vital air, which leads to the increased action of the lungs. The word is often used in this sense in the classics (Schleusner). It is a favourite expression with Homer. Euripides has the same expression: "Breathing out fire and slaughter." So Theocritus: "They came unto the assembly breathing mutual slaughter" (*Idyll.* xxii. 82). ¶ *Threatening.* Denunciation; threatening them with every breath—the action of a man violently enraged, and who was bent on vengeance. It denotes also intense activity and energy in persecution. ¶ *Slaughter.* Murder. Intensely desiring to put to death as many Christians as possible. He rejoiced in their death, and joined in condemning them, Ac. xxvi. 10, 11. From this latter place it seems that he had been concerned in putting many of them to death. ¶ *The disciples of the Lord.* Against Christians. ¶ *Went unto the high-priest.* See Notes on Mat. ii. 4. The letters were written and signed in the name and by the authority of the Sanhedrim, or great council of the nation. The high-priest did it as president of that council. See ver. 14, and ch. xxii. 5. The high-priest at that time was Theophilus, son of Ananus, who had been appointed at the feast of Pentecost, A.D. 37, by Vitellius, the Roman governor. His brother Jonathan had been removed from that office the same year (Kuinoel).

2. *And desired of him.* This shows the intensity of his wish to persecute the Christians, that he was willing to *ask* for such an employment. ¶ *Letters.* Epistles, implying a *commission* to bring them to Jerusalem for trial and punishment. From this it seems that the Sanhedrim at Jerusalem claimed jurisdiction over *all* synagogues everywhere. ¶ *To Damascus.* This was a celebrated city of Syria, and long the capital of a kingdom of that name. It is situated in a delightful region about one hundred and twenty miles north-east of Jerusalem, and about one hundred and ninety miles south-east of Antioch. It is in the midst of an extensive plain, abounding with cypress and palm-trees, and extremely fertile. It is watered by the river Barrady, anciently called *Abana,* 2 Ki. v. 12. About five miles from the city is a place called the "meeting of the waters," where the Barrady is joined by another river, and thence is divided by art into several streams that flow through the plain. These streams, six or seven in number, are conveyed to water the orchards, farms, &c., and give to the whole scene a very picturesque appearance. The city, situated in a delightful climate, in a fertile country, is perhaps among the most pleasant in the world. It is called by the Orientals themselves the *paradise on earth.* It is mentioned often in the Old Testament. It was a city in the time of Abraham, Ge. xv. 2. By whom it was founded is unknown. It was taken and garrisoned by David A.M. 2992, 2 Sa. viii. 6; 1 Ch. xviii. 6. It is subsequently mentioned as sustaining very important parts in the conflicts of the Jews with Syria, 2 Ki. xiv. 25; xvi. 5; Is. ix. 11. It was taken by the Romans A.M. 3939, or about sixty years before Christ, in whose possession it was when Saul went there. It was conquered by the Saracens A.D. 713. About the year 1250 it was taken by the Christians in the Crusades, and was captured A.D. 1517 by Selim, and

if he found any of [1]this way, whether they were men or women, he might bring them bound unto Jerusalem.

3 And[b] as he journeyed he came near Damascus; and suddenly there

1 *the way.*

b 1 Co.15.8.

has been since under the Ottoman emperors.

The Arabians call this city *Damasch*, or *Demesch*, or *Schams*. It is one of the most commercial cities in the Ottoman empire, and is distinguished also for manufactures, particularly for *steel*, hence called Damascus steel. The population is estimated by Ali Bey at two hundred thousand; Volney states it at eighty thousand; Hassel at one hundred thousand. About twenty thousand are Maronites of the Catholic church, five thousand Greeks, and one thousand are Jews. The road from Jerusalem to Damascus lies between two mountains, not above one hundred paces distant from each other; both are round at the bottom, and terminate in a point. That nearest the great road is called *Cocab, the star*, in memory of the dazzling light which is here said to have appeared to Saul. ¶ *To the synagogues.* See Notes on Mat. iv. 23. The Jews were scattered into nearly all the regions surrounding Judea, and it is natural to suppose that many of them would be found in Damascus. Josephus assures us that ten thousand were massacred there in one hour; and at another time eighteen thousand, with their wives and children (*Jewish Wars*, b. ii. ch. xx. § 2; b. vii. ch. viii. § 7). By whom the gospel was preached there, or how they had been converted to Christianity, is unknown. The presumption is, that some of those who had been converted on the day of Pentecost had carried the gospel to Syria. See Notes on Ac. ii. 9–11. ¶ *That if*, &c. It would seem that it was not certainly *known* that there were any Christians there. It was presumed that there were, and probably there was a report of that kind. ¶ *Of this way.* Of this *way* or *mode* of life; of this kind of opinions and conduct; that is, any Christians. ¶ *He might bring them*, &c. To be tried. The Sanhedrim at Jerusalem claimed jurisdiction over religious opinions, and their authority would naturally be respected by foreign Jews.

3. *And as he journeyed.* On his way, or while he was travelling. The *place* where this occurred is not known. Irby and Mangles say it is "outside the eastern gate." In the *Boat and Caravan* it is described as about a mile from the town, and near the Christian burying-ground which belongs to the Armenians. All that we know of it is that it was near to Damascus. ¶ *And suddenly.* Like a flash of lightning. ¶ *There shined round about him*, &c. The *language* which is expressed here would be used in describing a flash of lightning. Many critics have supposed that God made use of a sudden flash to arrest Paul, and that he was thus alarmed and brought to reflection. That God *might* make use of such means cannot be denied. But to this supposition in this case there are some unanswerable objections. (1) It was declared to be the appearance of the Lord Jesus: ver. 27, "Barnabas declared unto them how that he had *seen the Lord in the way;*" 1 Co. xv. 8, "And last of all he was seen of me also;" 1 Co. ix. 1, "Have I not seen Jesus Christ our Lord?" (2) Those who were *with* Saul saw the light, but did not hear the voice, Ac. xxii. 9. This is incredible on the supposition that it was a flash of lightning near them. (3) It was manifestly regarded as a message to *Saul*. The light appeared, and the voice spake to him. The others did not even *hear* the address. Besides, (4) It was as easy for Jesus to appear in a supernatural manner as to appear amidst thunder and lightning. That the Lord Jesus appeared is distinctly affirmed, and we shall see that it is probable that he would appear in a supernatural manner.

In order to understand this, it may be necessary to make the following remarks: (1) God was accustomed to appear to the Jews in a cloud; in a pillar of smoke, or of fire; in that peculiar splendour which they denominated the *Shechinah*. In this way he went before them into the land of Canaan, Ex. xiii. 21, 22; comp. Is. iv. 5, 6. This appearance or visible manifestation they called the *glory of* JEHOVAH, Is. vi. 1–4; Ex. xvi. 7, "In the morning ye shall see the glory of the Lord;" ver. 10; Le. ix. 23; Nu. xiv. 10; xvi. 19, 42; xxiv. 16; 1 Ki. viii. 11; Eze. x. 4. See Notes on Lu. ii. 9, "The glory of the Lord shone round about them." (2) The Lord Jesus, in his transfiguration on the mount,

shined round about him a light from heaven:

4 And he fell to the earth, and heard a voice saying unto him, Saul, Saul, [c] why persecutest thou me?

5 And he said, Who art thou,

c Mat.25.40,45.

---

had been encompassed with that glory. See Notes on Mat. xvii. 1-5. (3) He had spoken of similar glory as pertaining to him; as that with which he had been invested before his incarnation, and to which he would return; Jn. xvii. 5, "And now, Father, glorify thou me with the glory which I had with thee before the world was;" Mat. xxv. 31, "The Son of Man shall come in his glory." Comp. Mat. xvi. 27; xix. 28. To *this glory* he had returned *when* he left the earth. (4) It is a sentiment which cannot be shown to be incorrect, that the various appearances of "the angel of Jehovah," and of Jehovah, mentioned in the Old Testament, were appearances of the Messiah—the God who would be incarnate—the peculiar protector of his people. See Is. vi.; comp. with Jn. xii. 41. (5) *If* the Lord Jesus appeared to Saul, it would be in his appropriate glory and honour as the ascended Messiah. That he *did* appear is expressly affirmed. (6) This was *an occasion* when, if ever, such an appearance was proper. The design was to convert an infuriated persecutor, and to make him an *apostle.* To do this, it was necessary that he should *see* the Lord Jesus, 1 Co. ix. 1, 2. The design was further to make him an eminent instrument in carrying the gospel to the Gentiles. A signal miracle; a demonstration that he was invested with his appropriate glory (Jn. xvii. 5); a calling up a new *witness* to the fact of his resurrection, and of his solemn investment with glory in the heavens, seemed to be required in thus calling a violent persecutor to be an apostle and friend. (7) We are to regard this appearance, therefore, as the reappearance of the Shechinah, the Son of God invested with appropriate glory, appearing to convince an enemy of his ascension, and to change him from a foe to a friend.

It has been objected that as the Lord Jesus had ascended to heaven, it cannot be presumed that his body would return to the earth again. To this we may reply, that the New Testament has thrown no light on this. Perhaps it is not necessary to suppose that his body returned, but that he made such a visible manifestation of himself as to convince Saul that he was the Messiah. ¶ *From heaven.* From above; from the sky. In Ac. xxvi. 13, Paul says that the light was above the brightness of the sun at mid-day.

4. *And he fell to the earth.* He was astonished and overcome by the sudden flash of light. There is a remarkable similarity between what occurred here, and what is recorded of *Daniel* in regard to the visions which he saw, Da. viii. 17. Also Da. x. 8, "Therefore I was left alone, and saw this great vision; and there remained no strength in me, for my comeliness (vigour) was turned into corruption, and I retained no strength." The effect was such as to overpower the body. ¶ *And heard a voice.* The whole company heard a voice (ver. 7), but did not distinguish it as addressed particularly to Saul. *He* heard it speaking to himself. ¶ *Saying unto him,* &c. This shows that it was not *thunder*, as many have supposed. It was a distinct articulation or utterance, addressing him by name. ¶ *Saul, Saul.* A mode of address that is emphatic. The repetition of the name would fix his attention. Thus Jesus addresses Martha (Lu. x. 41), and Simon (Lu. xxii. 31), and Jerusalem (Mat. xxiii. 37). ¶ *Why.* For what reason. Jesus had done him no injury; had given him no provocation. All the opposition of sinners to the Lord Jesus and his church is without cause. See Notes on Jn. xv. 25, "They hated me without a cause." ¶ *Persecutest.* See Notes on Mat. v. 11. ¶ *Thou me?* Christ and his people are one, Jn. xv. 1-6. To persecute *them*, therefore, was to persecute *him*, Mat. xxv. 40, 45.

5. *And he said, Who art thou, Lord?* The word *Lord* here, as is frequently the case in the New Testament, means no more than *sir*, Jn. iv. 19. It is evident that Saul did not as yet know that this was the Lord Jesus. He heard a voice as of a *man;* he heard himself addressed, but by whom the words were spoken was to him unknown. In his amazement and confusion, he naturally asked who it was that was thus addressing him. ¶ *And the Lord said.* In this place the word *Lord* is used in a higher

Lord? And the Lord said, I am Jesus, whom thou persecutest: *it is* hard for thee to [d]kick against the pricks.

6 And he, trembling and astonished, said, Lord, [e]what wilt thou have me to do? And the Lord *said* unto him, Arise, and go into the

d ch.5.39.

e ch.16.30.

sense, to denote the Saviour. It is his usual appellation. See Notes on Ac. i. 24. ¶ *I am Jesus.* It is clear, from this, that there was a personal appearance of the Saviour; that he was present to Saul; but in what particular *form*—whether *seen* as a man, or only appearing by the manifestation of his glory, is not affirmed. Though it was a personal appearance, however, of the Lord Jesus, designed to take the work of converting such a persecutor into his own hands, yet he designed to convert him in a natural way. He *arrested* his attention; he filled him with alarm at his guilt; and then he presented the *truth* respecting himself. In ch. xxii. 8, the expression is thus recorded: "I am Jesus of Nazareth," &c. There is no contradiction, as Luke here records only a *part* of what was said; Paul afterward stated the whole. This declaration was fitted peculiarly to humble and mortify Saul. There can be no doubt that he had often blasphemed his name, and profanely derided the notion that the Messiah could come out of Nazareth. Jesus here uses, however, that very designation. "I am Jesus *the Nazarene*, the object of your contempt and scorn." Yet Saul saw him now invested with peculiar glory. ¶ It is *hard*, &c. This is evidently a proverbial expression. Kuinoel has quoted numerous places in which a similar mode of expression occurs in Greek writers. Thus Euripides, *Bacch.*, 791, "I, who am a frail mortal, should rather sacrifice to him who is a god, than, by giving place to anger, *kick against the goads.*" So Pindar, *Pyth.*, ii. 173, "It is profitable to bear willingly the assumed yoke. To kick against the goad is pernicious conduct." So Terence, *Phome.*, 1, 2, 27, "It is foolishness for thee to kick against a goad." Ovid has the same idea, *Trist.*, b. ii. 15. The word translated "pricks" here (κέντρον) means properly any sharp point which will pierce or perforate, as the sting of a bee, &c. But it commonly means an ox-goad, a sharp piece of iron stuck into the end of a stick, with which the ox is urged on. These goads among the Hebrews were made very large. Thus Shamgar slew six hundred men with one of them, Ju. iii. 31. Comp. 1 Sa. xiii. 21. The expression "to kick against the prick" is derived from the action of a stubborn and unyielding ox kicking against the goad. And as the ox would injure no one by it but himself; as he would gain nothing, it comes to denote an obstinate and refractory disposition and course of conduct, resisting the authority of him who has a right to command, and opposing the leadings of Providence, to the injury of him who makes the resistance. It denotes rebellion against lawful authority, and thus getting into greater difficulty by attempting to oppose the commands to duty. This is the condition of every sinner. If men wish to be happy, they should cheerfully submit to the authority of God. They should not rebel against his dealings. They should not murmur against their Creator. They should not resist the claims of their consciences. By all this they only injure themselves. No man can resist God or his own conscience and be happy. Men evince this temper in the following ways: (1) By violating plain laws of God. (2) By attempting to resist his claims. (3) By refusing to do what their conscience requires. (4) By attempting to free themselves from serious impressions and alarms. (5) By pursuing a course of vice and wickedness against what they know to be right. (6) By refusing to submit to the dealings of Providence. And (7) In any way by opposing God, and refusing to submit to his authority, and to do what is right.

6. *And he, trembling.* Alarmed at what he saw and heard, and at the consciousness of his own evil course. It is not remarkable that a sinner trembles when he sees his guilt and danger. ¶ *And astonished.* At what he saw. ¶ *Lord, what wilt thou have me to do?* This indicates a subdued soul, a humbled spirit. Just before, he had sought only to do his own will; now he inquired what was the will of the Saviour. Just before he was acting under a commission from the Sanhedrim; now he renounced their authority, and asked what the Lord Jesus would have him

city, and it shall be told thee what
thou must do.
7 And the men which journeyed
with him stood speechless, hearing
a voice, [f] but seeing no man.

f Da.10.7.

to do. Just before he had been engaged in a career of opposition to the Lord Jesus; now he sought at once to do his will. This indicates the usual change in the mind of the sinner when he is converted. The great controversy between him and God is, *whose will* shall be followed. The sinner follows his own; the first act of the Christian is to surrender his own will to that of God, and to resolve to do that which he requires. We may further remark here that this indicates the true nature of conversion. It is decided, prompt, immediate. Paul did not *debate* the matter (Gal. i. 16); he did not inquire what the scribes and Pharisees would say; he did not consult his own reputation; he did not ask what the world would think. With characteristic promptness--with a readiness which showed what he *would* yet be, he gave himself up *at once*, and *entirely*, to the Lord Jesus, evidently with a purpose to do *his* will alone. This was the case also with the jailer at Philippi, Ac. xvi. 30. Nor can there be any real conversion where the *heart* and *will* are not given to the Lord Jesus, to be directed and moulded by him at his pleasure. We may test our conversion then by the example of the apostle Paul. If our hearts have been given up as his was, we are true friends of Christ. ¶ *Go into the city*. Damascus. They were near it, ver. 3. ¶ *And it shall be told thee.* It is remarkable that he was thus directed. But we may learn from it, (1) That even in the most striking and remarkable cases of conversion, there is not *at once* a clear view of duty. What course of life should be followed; what should be done; nay, what should be *believed*, is not at once apparent. (2) The aid of others, and especially ministers, and of experienced Christians, is often very desirable to aid even those who are converted in the most remarkable manner. Saul was converted by a miracle; the Saviour appeared to him in his glory; of the truth of his Messiahship he had no doubt, but still he was dependent on an humble disciple in Damascus to be instructed in what he should do. (3) Those who are converted, in however striking a manner it may be, should be *willing* to seek the counsel of those who are in the church before them. The most striking evidence of their conversion will not prevent their deriving important direction and benefit from the aged, the experienced, and the wise in the Christian church. (4) Such remarkable conversions are fitted to *induce* the subjects of the change to seek counsel and direction. They produce humility; a deep sense of sin and of unworthiness; and a willingness to be taught and directed by any one who *can* point out the way of duty and of life.

7. *And the men which journeyed with him.* *Why* these men attended him is unknown. They might have been appointed to aid him, or they may have been travellers with whom Saul had accidentally fallen in. ¶ *Stood speechless.* In Ac. xxvi. 14, it is said that they all fell to the earth at the appearance of the light. But there is no contradiction. The narrative in that place refers to the *immediate* effect of the appearance of the light. They were *immediately* smitten to the ground together. This was *before* the voice spake to Saul, Ac. xxvi. 14. In *this* place (ix. 7) the historian is speaking of what occurred *after* the first alarm. There is no improbability that they rose from the ground immediately, and surveyed the scene with silent amazement and alarm. The word *speechless* (ἐννεοὶ) properly denotes those who are so astonished or stupefied as to be unable to speak. In the Greek writers it means those who are deaf and dumb. ¶ *Hearing a voice.* Hearing a *sound* or *noise.* The word here rendered voice is thus frequently used, as in Ge. iii. 8; 1 Sa. xii. 18; Ps. xxix. 3, 4; Mat. xxiv. 31 (Greek); 1 Th. iv. 16. In Ac. xxii. 9, it is said, "They which were with me (Paul) saw indeed the light, and were afraid, but they *heard not the voice* of him that spake to me." In this place, the words "heard not the voice" must be understood in the sense of *understanding the words*, of hearing the address, the distinct articulation, which Paul heard. They heard a *noise;* they were amazed and alarmed, but they did not hear the distinct words addressed to Saul. A similar instance occurs in Jn. xii. 28, 29, when the voice of God came from heaven to Jesus, "The people who stood by and heard

8 And Saul arose from the earth; and when his eyes were opened, he saw no man: but they led him by the hand, and brought *him* into Damascus.

9 And he was three days without sight, and neither did eat nor drink.

10 And there was a certain disciple at Damascus, named [g] Ananias;

[g] ch.22.12.

it said it thundered." They heard the *sound*, the *noise;* they did *not* distinguish the *words* addressed to him. See also Da. x. 7, and 1 Ki. xix. 11-13.

8. *When his eyes were opened.* He naturally closed them at the appearance of the light, and in his fright kept them closed for some time. ¶ *He saw no man.* This darkness continued three days, ver. 9. There is no reason to suppose that there was a *miracle* in this blindness, for in ch. xxii. 11, it is expressly said to have been caused by the intense light. "And when I could not see for the glory of that light," &c. The intense, sudden light had so affected the optic nerve of the eye as to cause a temporary blindness. This effect is not uncommon. The disease of the eye which is thus produced is called *amaurosis*, or more commonly *gutta serena*. It consists in a loss of sight without any apparent defect of the eye. Sometimes the disease is periodical, coming on suddenly, continuing for three or four days, and then disappearing (Webster). A disease of this kind is often caused by excessive light. When we look at the sun, into a furnace, or into a crucible with fused metal, we are conscious of a temporary pain in the eye, and of a momentary blindness. "In northern and tropical climates, from the glare of the sun or snow, a variety of amaurosis (gutta serena) occurs, which, if it produces blindness during the day, is named nyctalopia; if during the night, hemeralopia. Another variety exists in which the individual is blind all day, until a certain hour, when he sees distinctly, or he sees and is blind every alternate day, or is only blind one day in the week, fortnight, or month" (*Edinb. Encyc.*, art. "Surgery"). A total loss of sight has been the consequence of looking at the sun during an eclipse, or of watching it as it sets in the west. This effect is caused by the intense action of the light on the optic nerve, or sometimes from a disorder of the brain. A case is mentioned by Michaelis (Kuinoel *in loco*) of a man who was made blind by a bright flash of lightning, and who continued so for four weeks, who was again restored to sight in a tempest by a similar flash of lightning. Electricity has been found one of the best remedies for restoring sight in such cases.

9. *And neither did eat nor drink.* Probably because he was overwhelmed with a view of his sins, and was thus indisposed to eat. All the circumstances would contribute to this. His past life; his great sins; the sudden change in his views; his total absorption in the vision; perhaps also his grief at the loss of his sight, would all fill his mind, and indispose him to partake of food. Great grief always produces this effect. And it is not uncommon now for an awakened and convicted sinner, in view of his past sins and danger, to be so pained as to destroy his inclination for food, and to produce involuntary fasting. We are to remember also that Paul had yet no assurance of forgiveness. He was arrested, alarmed, convinced that Jesus was the Messiah, and humbled, but he had not found comfort. He was brought to the dust, and left to three painful days of darkness and suspense, before it was told him what he was to do. In this painful and perplexing state, it was natural that he should abstain from food. This case should not be brought now, however, to prove that convicted sinners *must* remain in darkness and under conviction. Saul's case was extraordinary. His blindness was literal. This state of darkness was necessary to humble him and fit him for his work. But the moment a sinner will give his heart to Christ, he may find peace. If he resists, and rebels longer, it will be his own fault. By the nature of the case, as well as by the promises of the Bible, if a sinner will yield himself at once to the Lord Jesus, he will obtain peace. That sinners do not sooner obtain peace is because they do not sooner submit themselves to God.

10. *A certain disciple.* A Christian. Many have supposed that he was one of the seventy disciples. But nothing more is certainly known of him than is related here. He had very probably been some time a Christian (ver. 13), and had heard of Saul, but was personally a stranger to him. In ch. xxii. 12,

and to him said the Lord in a vision, Ananias. And he said, Behold, I *am here*, Lord.

11 And the Lord *said* unto him, Arise, and go into the street which is called Straight, and inquire in

---

it is said that he was a devout man according to the law, having a good report of all the Jews which dwelt there. There was wisdom in sending such a Christian to Saul, as it might do much to conciliate the minds of the Jews there toward him. ¶ *Said the Lord.* The Lord *Jesus* is alone mentioned in all this transaction. And as he had commenced the work of converting Saul, it is evident that he is intended here. See Notes on ch. i. 24. ¶ *In a vision.* Perhaps by a dream. The main idea is, that he *revealed* his will to him in the case. The word *vision* is often used in speaking of the communications made to the prophets, and commonly means that future events were made to pass in review before the mind, as we look upon a landscape. See Notes on Is. i. 1; comp. Ge. xv. 1; Nu. xii. 6; Eze. xi. 24; Ac. x. 3; xi. 5; xvi. 9; Da. ii. 19; vii. 2; viii. 1, 2, 26; x. 7. Notes on Mat. xvii. 9.

11. *Into the street which is called Straight.* This street extends now from the eastern to the western gate, about three miles, crossing the whole city and suburbs in a direct line. Near the eastern gate is a house, said to be that of Judah, in which Paul lodged. There is in it a very small closet, where tradition reports that the apostle passed three days without food, till Ananias restored him to sight. Tradition also says that he had here the vision recorded in 2 Co. xii. 2. There is also in this street a fountain whose water is drunk by Christians, in remembrance of that which, they suppose, the same fountain produced for the baptism of Paul (Rob. Calmet). ¶ *Of Tarsus.* This city was the capital of Cilicia, a province of Asia Minor. It was situated on the banks of the river Cydnus. It was distinguished for the culture of Greek philosophy and literature, so that at one time in its schools, and in the number of its learned men, it was the rival of Athens and Alexandria. In allusion to this, perhaps, Paul says that he was "born in Tarsus, a citizen of no mean city," Ac. xxi. 39. In reward for its exertions and sacrifices during the civil wars of Rome, Tarsus was made a free city by Augustus. See Notes on Ac. xvi. 37; xxi. 39; xxii. 28. It still exists as Tersous, with a population of about 20,000, but is described as filthy and ruinous. ¶ *Behold, he prayeth.* This gives us a full indication of the manner in which Saul passed the three days mentioned in ver. 9. It is plain, from what follows, that Ananias regarded Saul as an enemy to Christianity, and that he would have been apprehensive of danger if he were with him, ver. 13, 14. This remark, "Behold, he prayeth," is made to him to silence his fears, and to indicate the change in the feelings and views of Saul. Before, he was a persecutor; now, his change is indicated by his giving himself to prayer. That Saul did not *pray* before is not implied by this; for he fully accorded with the customs of the Jews, Phi. iii. 4–6. But his prayers were not the prayers of a saint. They were the prayers of a Pharisee (comp. Lu. xviii. 10, &c.), now they were the prayers of a broken-hearted sinner; then he prayed depending on his own righteousness, now depending on the mercy of God in the Messiah. We may learn here, (1) That one indication of conversion to God is real prayer. A Christian may as well be characterized by that as by any single appellation—"a man of prayer." (2) It is always the attendant of true conviction for sin that we pray. The convicted sinner feels his danger, and his need of forgiveness. Conscious that he has no righteousness himself, he now seeks that of another, and depends on the mercy of God. Before, he was too proud to pray; now, he is willing to humble himself and to ask for mercy. (3) It is a sufficient indication of the character of *any* man to say, "Behold, he prays." It at once tells us, better than volumes would without this, what is his *real* character. Knowing this, we know all about him. We at once confide in his piety, his honesty, his humility, his willingness to do good. It is at the same time the indication of his state with God, and the pledge that he will do his duty to men. We mean, of course, *real* prayer. Knowing that a man is sincere, and humble, and faithful in his private devotions, and in the devotions of his family, we confide in him; and are willing to trust to his readiness to do all that he is convinced that he *ought* to do. Ananias, apprised

the house of Judas for *one* called
called Saul of Tarsus; for, behold,
he prayeth,
12 And hath seen in a vision a
man named Ananias coming in, and
putting *his* hand on him, that he
might receive his sight.
13 Then Ananias answered, Lord,
I have heard by many of [h]this man
how much evil he hath done to thy
saints at Jerusalem:
14 And here [i]he hath authority
from the chief priests to bind all
that [k]call on thy name.
15 But the Lord said unto him,
Go thy way: for [l]he is a chosen
vessel unto me, to bear my name
before [m]the Gentiles, and [n]kings,
and [o]the children of Israel.
16 For I will show him how

h 1 Ti.1.13.
i ver.21. *k* 1 Co.1.2; 2 Ti.2.22.
l ch.13.2; Ro.1.1; 1 Co.15.10; Ga.1.15; Ep.3.7,8.
m Ro.11.13; Ga.2.7,8. *n* ch.25.23,&c.
o ch.28.17,&c.

---

of this in Saul, had full evidence of the change of his character, and was convinced that he ought to lay aside all his former prejudices, and to seek him, and to acknowledge him as a brother.

12. *And he hath seen in a vision*, &c. *When* this was shown to Saul, or how, is not recorded. The vision was shown to Saul to assure him when Ananias came that he was no impostor. He was thus *prepared* to receive consolation from this disciple. He was even apprised of his *name*, that he might be the more confirmed.

13, 14. *I have heard by many*, &c. This was in the *vision*, ver. 10. The passage of such a train of thoughts through the mind was perfectly natural at the command to go and search out Saul. There would instantly occur all that had been heard of his fury in persecution; and the expression here may indicate the state of a mind *amazed* that such a one should need his counsel, and *afraid*, perhaps, of intrusting himself to one thus bent on persecution. All this evidently passed in the *dream* or *vision* of Ananias, and perhaps cannot be considered as any *deliberate* unwillingness to go to him. It is clear, however, that *such* thoughts should have been banished, and that he should have gone *at once* to the praying Saul. When Christ commands, we should suffer no suggestion of our own thoughts, and no apprehension of our own danger, to interfere. ¶ *By many.* Probably many who had fled from persecution, and had taken refuge in Damascus. It is also evident (ver. 14) that Ananias had been *apprised*, perhaps by letters from the Christians at Jerusalem, of the purpose which Saul had in view in now going to Damascus. ¶ *To thy saints.* Christians; called saints (ἅγιοι) because they are holy, or consecrated to God.

15. *Go thy way.* This is often the only answer that we obtain to the suggestion of our doubts and hesitations about duty. God tells us still to *do* what he requires, with an assurance only that his commands are just, and that there are good reasons for them. ¶ *A chosen vessel.* The usual meaning of the word *vessel* is well known. It commonly denotes a *cup* or *basin*, such as is used in a house. It then denotes *any* instrument which may be used to accomplish a purpose, perhaps particularly with the notion of *conveying* or communicating. In the Scriptures it is used to denote the *instrument* or *agent* which God employs to convey his favours to mankind, and is thus employed to represent the ministers of the gospel, 2 Co. iv. 7; 1 Th. iv. 4. Comp. Is. x. 5–7. Paul is called *chosen* because Christ had *selected* him, as he did his other apostles, for this service. See Notes on Jn. xv. 16. ¶ *To bear my name.* To communicate the knowledge of me. ¶ *Before the Gentiles.* The nations; all who were not Jews. This was the *principal* employment of Paul. He spent his life in this, and regarded himself as peculiarly called to be the apostle of the Gentiles, Ro. xi. 13; xv. 16; Ga. ii. 8. ¶ *And kings.* This was fulfilled, Ac. xxv. 23, &c.; xxvi. 32; xxvii. 24. ¶ *And the children of Israel.* The Jews. This was done. He *immediately* began to preach to them, ver. 20–22. Wherever he went, he preached the gospel first to them, and then to the Gentiles, Ac. xiii. 46; xxviii. 17.

16. *For I will show him*, &c. This seems to be added to encourage Ananias. He had feared Saul. The Lord now informs him that Saul, hitherto his enemy, would ever after be his friend. He would not merely *profess* repentance, but would *manifest* the sincerity of it by encountering trials

great things he must [p]suffer for
my name's sake.
17 And Ananias went his way,
and entered into the house; [q]and
putting his hands on him, said,
Brother Saul, the Lord, *even* Jesus,
that appeared unto thee in the way
as thou camest, hath sent me, that
thou mightest receive thy sight, [r]and
be filled with the Holy Ghost.
18 And immediately there fell
from his eyes as it had been scales;
and he received sight forthwith,
and arose, and was baptized.
19 And when he had received
meat, he was strengthened. Then

p ch.20.23; 2 Co.11.23-27; 2 Ti.1.11,12. *q* ch.8.17. *r* ch.2.4.

and reproaches for his sake. The prediction here was fully accomplished, ch. xx. 23; 2 Co. xi. 23–27; 2 Ti. i. 11, 12.

17. *Putting his hands on him.* This was not *ordination*, but was the usual mode of imparting or communicating blessings. See Notes on Mat. xix. 13; ix. 18. ¶ *Brother Saul.* An expression recognizing him as a fellow-Christian. ¶ *Be filled with the Holy Ghost.* See Notes on Ac. ii. 4.

18. *As it had been scales—ὡσεὶ λεπίδες.* The word ὡσεὶ, "as it had been," is designed to *qualify* the following word. It is not said that scales *literally* fell from his eyes, but that an effect followed *as if* scales had been suddenly taken off. Evidently the expression is designed to mean no more than this. The effect was such as would take place if some dark, impervious substance had been placed before the eyes, and had been suddenly removed. The cure was as sudden, the restoration to sight was as immediate, *as if* such an interposing substance had been suddenly removed. This is all that the expression fairly implies, and this is all that the nature of the case demands. As the blindness had been caused by the natural effect of the light, probably on the optic nerve (ver. 8, 9, Note), it is manifest that no *literal* removing of scales would restore the vision. We are therefore to lay aside the idea of *literal* scales falling to the earth. No such thing is affirmed, and no such thing would have met the case. The word translated *scales* is used nowhere else in the New Testament. It means properly the small crust or layer which composes a part of the covering of a fish, and also any thin layer or leaf exfoliated or separated, as scales of iron, bone, or a piece of bark, &c. (Webster). An effect similar to this is described in Tobit xi. 8, 13. It is evident that there was a miracle in the *healing* of Saul. The *blindness* was the natural effect of the light. The *cure* was by miraculous power. This is evident, (1) Because there were no means used that would naturally restore the sight. It may be remarked here that *gutta serena* has been regarded by physicians as one of the most incurable of diseases. Few cases are restored, and few remedies are efficacious. (See *Edinb. Encyc.*, art. "Surgery," on Amaurosis.) (2) Ananias was *sent* for this very purpose to heal him, ver. 17. (3) The *immediate* effect shows that this was miraculous. Had it been a *slow* recovery, it might have been doubtful; but here it was instantaneous, and it was thus put beyond a question that it was a miracle. ¶ *And was baptized.* In this he followed the example of all the early converts to Christianity. They were baptized immediately. See Ac. ii. 41; viii. 12, 36–39.

19. *Had received meat.* Food. The word *meat* has undergone a change since our translation was made. It then meant, as the original does, food of all kinds. ¶ *With the disciples.* With Christians, comp. Ac. ii. 42. ¶ *Certain days.* How long is not known. It was long enough, however, to preach the gospel, ver. 22; ch. xxvi. 20. It might have been for some months, as he did not go to Jerusalem under three years from that time. He remained some time at Damascus, and then went to Arabia, and returned again to Damascus, and then went to Jerusalem, Ga. i. 17. This visit to *Arabia* Luke has omitted, but there is no contradiction. He does not affirm that he did *not* go to Arabia.

We have now passed through the account of one of the most remarkable conversions to Christianity that has ever occurred—that of the apostle Paul. His conversion has always been justly considered as a strong proof of the Christian religion. For, (1) This change could not have occurred by any want of fair prospects of honour. He was distinguished already as a Jew. He

was Saul certain days [s]with the disciples which were at Damascus.

20 And straightway he preached Christ in the synagogues, that he is the Son of God.

21 But all that [t]heard *him* were amazed, and said, Is not this [u]he that destroyed them which called on this name in Jerusalem, and came hither for that intent, that

s ch.26.20; Ga.1.17. t Ga.1.13,23. u ch.8.3.

had had the best opportunities for education that the nation afforded. He had every prospect of rising to distinction and office. (2) It could not have been produced by any prospect of wealth or fame by becoming a Christian. Christians were poor; and to be a Christian then was to be exposed to contempt, to persecution, and to death. Saul had no reason to suppose that *he* would escape the common lot of Christians. (3) He was as firmly opposed to Christianity before his conversion as possible. He had already distinguished himself for his hostility. Infidels often say that Christians are prejudiced in favour of their religion. But here was a man, at first a bitter infidel, and a deadly foe to Christianity. All the prejudices of his education, all his prospects, all his former views and feelings, were opposed to the gospel of Christ. He became, however, one of its most firm advocates and friends, and it is for infidels to account for this change. There must have been *some* cause, some motive for it; and is there anything more rational than the supposition that Saul was convinced in a most striking and wonderful manner of the truth of Christianity? (4) His subsequent life showed that the change was sincere and real. He encountered danger and persecution to evince his attachment to Christ; he went from land to land, and exposed himself to every peril and every form of obloquy and scorn, always rejoicing that he was a Christian, and was permitted to suffer *as* a Christian, and has thus given the highest proofs of his sincerity. If such sufferings and such a life were not evidences of sincerity, then it would be impossible to fix on any circumstances of a man's life that would furnish proof that he was not a deceiver. (5) If Paul was sincere; if his conversion was genuine, the Christian religion is true. Nothing else *but* a religion from heaven could produce this change. There is here, therefore, the independent testimony of a man who was once a persecutor; converted in a wonderful manner; his whole life, views, and feelings revolutionized, and all his subsequent career evincing the sincerity of his feelings and the reality of the change. He is just such a *witness* as infidels ought to be satisfied with; a man once an enemy; a man whose testimony cannot be impeached; a man who had no interested motives, and who was willing to stand forth anywhere, and avow his change of feeling and purpose. We adduce him as such a witness; and infidels are *bound* to dispose of his testimony, or to embrace the religion which *he* embraced. (6) The example of Saul does not stand alone. Hundreds and thousands of enemies, persecutors, and slanderers have been changed, and every such one becomes a living witness of the power and truth of the Christian religion. The scoffer becomes reverent; the profane man learns to speak the praise of God; the sullen, bitter foe of Christ becomes his friend, and lives and dies under the influence of his religion. Could better proof be asked that this religion is from God?

20. *And straightway.* Immediately. It was an evidence of the genuineness of his conversion that he was willing at once to avow himself to be the friend of the Lord Jesus. ¶ *He preached Christ.* He proclaimed that Jesus was the Christ. See ver. 22. Many manuscripts read here *Jesus* instead of *Christ.* Griesbach has adopted this reading. Such is also the Syriac, the Vulgate, and the Ethiopic. The reading accords much better with the subject than the common reading. That *Christ,* or the *Messiah,* was the Son of God, all admitted. In the New Testament the names *Christ* and *Son of God* are used as synonymous. But the question was whether *Jesus* was the Christ, and was therefore the Son of God, and this Paul showed to the Jews. Paul continued the practice of attending the synagogues; and in the synagogues anyone had a right to speak who was invited by the officiating minister. See ch. xiii. 15. ¶ *That he is the Son of God.* That he is the Messiah.

21. *Were amazed.* Amazed at his sudden and remarkable change. ¶ *That destroyed.* That opposed; laid waste;

he might bring them bound unto the chief priests?

22 But Saul [v]increased the more in strength, and confounded [w]the Jews which dwelt at Damascus, proving that this is very Christ.

23 And after that many days were fulfilled, [x]the Jews took counsel to kill him.

v Ps.84.7. w ch.18.28. x ch.23.12; 25.3.

persecuted. Comp. Ga. i. 13. ¶ *For that intent.* With that design, that he might destroy the church at Damascus.

22. *Increased the more in strength.* His conviction of the truth of the Christian religion became stronger every day, and hence his *moral* strength or boldness increased. ¶ *And confounded.* See Ac. ii. 6. The word here means *confuted.* It means also occasionally to produce a *tumult* or *excitement*, Ac. xix. 32; xxi. 31. Perhaps the idea of producing such a tumult is intended to be conveyed here. Paul confuted the Jews, and by so doing he was the occasion of their tumultuous proceedings, or he so enraged them as to lead to great agitation and excitement—a very common effect of close and conclusive argumentation. ¶ *Proving that this.* This Jesus. ¶ *Is very Christ.* Greek, that this is *the* Christ. The word *very* means here simply *the.* Greek, ὁ Χριστός. It means that Paul showed by strong and satisfactory arguments that Jesus of Nazareth was the true Messiah. The arguments which he would use may be easily conceived, but the evangelist has not seen fit to record them.

23. *And after that many days*, &c. How long a time elapsed before this is not recorded in this place, but it is evident that the writer means to signify that a *considerable* time intervened. There is, therefore, an *interval* here which Luke has not filled up; and if this were the only narrative which we had, we should be at a loss how to understand this. From all that we know now of the usual conduct of the Jews toward the apostles, and especially toward Paul, it would seem highly improbable that this interval would be passed peaceably or quietly. Nay, it would be highly improbable that he would be allowed to remain in Damascus *many days* without violent persecution. Now it so happens that by turning to another part of the New Testament, we are enabled to ascertain the manner in which this interval was filled up. Turn then to Ga. i. 17, and we learn from Paul himself that he went into Arabia, and spent some time there, and then returned again to Damascus. The precise *time* which would be occupied in such a journey is not specified, but it would not be performed under a period of some months. In Ga. i. 18, we are informed that he did not go to Jerusalem until *three years* after his conversion; and as there is reason to believe that he went up to Jerusalem *directly* after escaping from Damascus the second time (Ac. ix. 25, 26), it seems probable that the three years were spent chiefly in Arabia. We have thus an account of the "*many days*" here referred to by Luke. And in this instance we have a striking example of the truth and honesty of the sacred writers. By comparing these *two* accounts together, we arrive at the whole state of the case. Neither seems to be complete without the other. Luke has left a chasm which he has nowhere else supplied. But that chasm we are enabled to fill up from the apostle himself, in a letter written long after, and without any *design* to amend or complete the history of Luke—for the introduction of this history into the epistle to the Galatians was for a very different purpose—to show that he received his commission directly from the Lord Jesus, and in a manner independent of the other apostles. The two accounts, therefore, are like the two parts of a *tally;* neither is complete without the other; and yet, being brought together, they so exactly fit as to show that the one is precisely adjusted to the other. And as the two parts were made by different individuals, and without design of adapting them to each other, they show that the writers had formed no collusion or agreement to impose on the world; that they are separate and independent witnesses; that they are honest men; that their narratives are true records of what actually occurred; and the two narratives constitute, therefore, a strong and very valuable proof of the correctness of the sacred narrative. If asked why *Luke* has not recorded a full account of this in the Acts, it may be replied that there are many circumstances and facts omitted in all histories from the necessity of the

24 But their laying await was known of Saul. And they[y] watched the gates day and night to kill him.
25 Then the disciples took him by night, and[z] let *him* down by the wall in a basket.
26 And when Saul was[a] come to Jerusalem, he assayed to join

y 2 Co.11.26,&c.; Ps.21.11; 37.32,33. *z* Jos.2.15. *a* Ga.1.18.

case. Comp. Jn. xxi. 25. It is remarkable here, not that he has not *recorded* this, but that he has left a *chasm* in his own history which can be so readily filled up. ¶ *Were fulfilled.* Had elapsed. ¶ *Took counsel,* &c. Laid a scheme, or designed to kill him. Comp. ch. xxiii. 12; xxv. 3. His zeal and success would enrage them, and they knew of no other way in which they could free themselves from the effects of his arguments and influence.

24. *But their laying await.* Their counsel; their design. ¶ *Was known of Saul.* Was made known to him. In what way this was communicated we do not know. This design of the Jews against Saul is referred to in 2 Co. xi. 32, 33, where it is said, "In Damascus, the governor under Aretas the king kept the Damascenes with a garrison, desirous to apprehend me; and through a window in a basket was I let down by the wall, and escaped his hands." ¶ *And they watched the gates.* Cities were surrounded by high walls, and of course the *gates* were presumed to be the only places of escape. As they supposed that Saul, apprised of their designs, would make an attempt to escape, they stationed guards at the gates to intercept him. In 2 Co. xi. 32, it is said that the *governor* kept the city for the purpose of apprehending him. It is possible that the governor might have been a Jew, and one, therefore, who would enter into their views. Or if not a Jew, the Jews who were there might easily represent Saul as an offender, and demand his being secured, and thus a garrison or guard might be furnished them for their purpose. See a similar attempt made by the Jews recorded in Mat. xxviii. 14.

25. *Took him by night,* &c. This was done through a window in the wall, 2 Co. xi. 33. ¶ *In a basket.* This word is used to denote commonly the basket in which food was carried, Mat. xv. 37; Mar. viii. 8, 20. It was in this way that Rahab let down the spies (Jos. ii. 15), and so David escaped from Saul, 1 Sa. xix. 12. Probably this occurred in an unguarded part of the wall, where some overhanging houses, as is usual in Eastern cities, opened into the outer country. This conduct of Saul was in accordance with the direction of the Lord Jesus (Mat. x. 23), "When they persecute you in one city, flee ye into another," &c. Saul was certain of death if he remained; and as he could secure his life by flight without abandoning any principle of religion, or denying his Lord, it was his duty to do so. Christianity requires us to sacrifice our lives only when we cannot avoid it without denying the Saviour, or abandoning the principles of our religion.

26. *Was come to Jerusalem.* He did not go to Jerusalem immediately after he escaped from Damascus. He first went into Arabia, where he spent a considerable part, or the whole of three years. For the reasons why he went there, and why this fact is omitted by Luke in the Acts, see Notes on Ga. i. 18. ¶ *He assayed.* He attempted; he endeavoured. ¶ *To join himself.* To become connected with them as a fellow-Christian. ¶ *But they were all afraid of him.* Their fear, or suspicion, was excited probably on these grounds: (1) They remembered his former violence against Christians. They had an instinctive shrinking from him, and suspicion of the man that had been so violent a persecutor. (2) He had been absent three years. If they had *not* heard of him during that time, they would naturally retain much of their old feelings toward him. If they *had*, they might suspect the man who had not returned to Jerusalem; who had not before sought the society of other Christians; and who had spent that time in a distant country, and among strangers. It would seem remarkable that he had not at once returned to Jerusalem and connected himself with the apostles. But the sacred writer does not justify the fears of the apostles. He simply records the *fact* of their apprehension. It is not unnatural, however, to have doubts respecting an open and virulent enemy of the gospel who suddenly professes a change in favour of it. The human mind does not easily cast off suspicion of some unworthy motive, and open itself at once to entire

himself to the disciples; but they
were all afraid of him, and believed
not that he was a disciple.
27 But [b]Barnabas took him, and
brought *him* to the apostles, and
declared unto them how he had
seen the Lord in the way, and that
he had spoken to him, and how he
had [c]preached boldly at Damascus
in the name of Jesus.
28 And he was with them coming
in and going out at Jerusalem.
29 And he spake boldly in the
name of the Lord Jesus, and disputed against the Grecians: [d]but
they went about to slay him.
30 *Which* when the brethren knew,
they brought him down to Cesarea,
and sent him forth to Tarsus.
31 Then [e]had the churches [f]rest

b ch.4.36. *c* ver.20-22. *d* ver.23. *e* Zec.9.1; ch.8.1. *f* Ps.94.13.

---

confidence. When great and notorious sinners profess to be converted—men who have been violent, artful, or malignant—it is natural to ask whether they have not some unworthy motive still in their professed change. Confidence is a plant of slow growth, and starts up, not by a sudden profession, but is the result of a course of life which is *worthy* of affection and of trust. ¶ *A disciple.* A sincere Christian.

27. *But Barnabas.* See Notes on ch. iv. 36. Barnabas was of Cyprus, not far from Tarsus, and it is not improbable that he had been before acquainted with Saul. ¶ *To the apostles.* To Peter and James, Ga. i. 18, 19. Probably the other apostles were at that time absent from Jerusalem. ¶ *And declared unto them*, &c. It may seem remarkable that the apostles at Jerusalem had not before heard of the conversion of Saul. The following considerations may serve in some degree to explain this. (1) It is certain that intercourse between different countries was then much more difficult than it is now. There were no posts; no public conveyances; no mails; no telegraphs; nothing that corresponded with our modes of intercourse between one part of the world and another. (2) There was at this time a state of animosity amounting to hostility subsisting between Herod and Aretas. Herod the tetrarch had married the daughter of Aretas, king of Arabia, and had put her away (Josephus, *Antiq.*, b. xviii. ch. v. § 1, 2). The result of this was a long misunderstanding between them, and a war; and the effects of that war might have been to interrupt the communication very much throughout all that country. (3) Though the *Jews* at Jerusalem *might* have heard of the conversion of Saul, yet it was for their interest to keep it a secret, and not to mention it to Christians. But, (4) Though the Christians who were there *had* heard of it, yet it is probable that they were not fully informed on the subject; that they had not had all the evidence of his conversion which they desired; and that they looked with suspicion on him. It was therefore proper that they should have a *full* statement of the evidence of his conversion; and this was made by Barnabas.

28. *And he was with them*, &c. That is, he was admitted to their friendship, and recognized as a Christian and an apostle. The *time* during which he then remained at Jerusalem was, however, only fifteen days, Ga. i. 18.

29. *And spake boldly.* He openly defended the doctrine that Jesus was the Messiah. ¶ *In the name*, &c. By the authority of the Lord Jesus. ¶ *Against the Grecians.* See the word *Grecians* explained in the Notes on Ac. vi. 1. It means that he not only maintained that Jesus was the Christ in the presence of those Jews who resided at Jerusalem, and who spoke the Hebrew language, but also before those *foreign* Jews who spoke the Greek language, and who had come up to Jerusalem. They would be as much opposed to the doctrine that Jesus was the Christ as those who resided in Jerusalem. ¶ *They went about.* They *sought* to slay him; or they formed a purpose to put him to death as an apostate. See ver. 23.

30. *To Cesarea.* See Notes on ch. viii. 40. ¶ *And sent him forth to Tarsus.* This was his native city. See Notes on ver. 11. It was in Cilicia, where Paul doubtless preached the gospel, Ga. i. 21, "Afterward I came into the regions of Syria and Cilicia."

31. *Then had the churches rest.* That is, the persecutions against Christians ceased. Those persecutions had been excited by the opposition made to Ste-

throughout all Judea, and Galilee, and Samaria, and [g]were edified; and [h]walking in the fear of the Lord, and [i]in the comfort of the Holy Ghost, [k]were multiplied.

32 And it came to pass, as Peter

g Ro.14.19. h Ps.86.11; Col.1.10. i Jn.14.16,17. k Zec.8.20–22.

phen (Ac. xi. 19); they had been greatly promoted by Saul (Ac. viii. 3); and they had extended doubtless throughout the whole land of Palestine. The precise causes of this cessation of the persecution are not known. Probably they were the following: (1) It is not improbable that the great mass of Christians had been driven into other regions by these persecutions. (2) He who had been most active in exciting the persecution; who was, in a sort, its leader, and who was best adapted to carry it on, had been converted. He had ceased his opposition; and even he was now removed from Judea. All this would have some effect in causing the persecution to subside. (3) But it is not improbable that the state of things in Judea contributed much to turn the attention of the Jews to other matters. Dr. Lardner accounts for this in the following manner: "Soon after Caligula's accession, the Jews at Alexandria suffered very much from the Egyptians in that city, and at length their oratories there were all destroyed. In the third year of Caligula, A.D. 39, Petronius was sent into Syria, with orders to set up the emperor's statue in the temple at Jerusalem. This order from Caligula was, to the Jews, a thunderstroke. The Jews must have been too much engaged after this to mind anything else, as may appear from the accounts which Philo and Josephus have given us of this affair. Josephus says 'that Caligula ordered Petronius to go with an army to Jerusalem, to set up his statue in the temple there; enjoining him, if the Jews opposed it, to put to death all who made any resistance, and to make all the rest of the nation slaves. Petronius therefore marched from Antioch into Judea with three legions and a large body of auxiliaries raised in Syria. *All were hereupon filled with consternation*, the army being come as far as Ptolemais.'" See Lardner's *Works*, vol. i. p. 101, 102, London edit. 1829. Philo gives the same account of the consternation as Josephus (Philo, *De Legat. ad Cai.*, p. 1024, 1025). He describes the Jews "as abandoning their cities, villages, and open country; as going to Petronius in Phenicia, both men and women, the old, the young, the middle-aged; as throwing themselves on the ground before Petronius with weeping and lamentation," &c. The effect of this consternation in diverting their minds from the Christians can be easily conceived. The prospect that the images of the Roman emperor were about to be set up by violence in the temple, or, that in case of resistance, death or slavery was to be their portion, and the advance of a large army to execute that purpose, all tended to throw the nation into alarm. By the providence of God, therefore, this event was permitted to occur to divert the attention of bloody-minded persecutors from a feeble and bleeding church. Anxious for their own safety, the Jews would cease to persecute the Christians, and thus, by the conversion of the main instrument in persecution, and by the universal alarm for the welfare of the nation, the trembling and enfeebled church was permitted to obtain repose. Thus ended the *first* general persecution against Christians, and thus effectually did God show that he had power to guard and protect his chosen people. ¶ *All Judea, and Galilee, and Samaria.* These three places included the land of Palestine. See Notes on Mat. ii. 22. The formation of churches in Galilee is not expressly mentioned before this; but there is no improbability in supposing that Christians had travelled there, and had preached the gospel. Comp. Ac. xi. 19. The formation of churches in Samaria is expressly mentioned, ch. viii. ¶ *Were edified.* Were built up, increased, and strengthened. See Ro. xiv. 19; xv. 2; 1 Co. viii. 1. ¶ *And walking.* Living. The word is often used to denote Christian conduct, or manner of life, Col. i. 10; Lu. i. 6; 1 Th. iv. 1; 1 Jn. ii. 6. The idea is that of *travellers* who are going to any place, and who walk in the right path. Christians are thus travellers to another country, an heavenly. ¶ *In the fear of the Lord.* Fearing the Lord; with reverence for him and his commandments. This expression is often used to denote piety in general, 2 Ch. xix. 7; Job xxviii. 28; Ps. xix. 9; cxi. 10; Pr. i. 7; ix. 10; xiii. 13. ¶ *In the comfort of the Holy*

passed throughout all *quarters*, he came down also to the saints which dwelt at Lydda.

33 And there he found a certain man named Eneas, which had kept his bed eight years, and was sick of the palsy.

34 And Peter said unto him, Eneas, [l]Jesus Christ maketh thee whole; arise, and make thy bed. And he arose immediately.

35 And all that dwelt in Lydda and [m]Saron saw him, and [n]turned to the Lord.

36 Now there was at Joppa a certain disciple named Tabitha, which by interpretation is called [2]Dorcas: this woman was [o]full of

l ch.3.6,16; 4.10.

m 1 Ch.5.16. *n* ch.11.21; 2 Co.3.16.
2 or, *Doe*; or, *Roe*. *o* 1 Ti.2.10; Tit.2.7,14.

Ghost. In the consolations which the Holy Ghost produced, Jn. xiv. 16, 17; Ro. v. 1-5. ¶ *Were multiplied.* Were increased.

32. *To the saints.* To the Christians. ¶ *Which dwelt at Lydda.* This town was situated on the road from Jerusalem to Cesarea Philippi. It was about 10 or 12 miles south-east from Joppa, and belonged to the tribe of Ephraim. It was called by the Greeks Diospolis, or city of Jupiter, probably because a temple was at some period erected to Jupiter in that city. It is now so entirely ruined as to be a miserable village. Since the Crusades, it has been called by the Christians St. George, on account of its having been the scene of the martyrdom of a saint of that name. Tradition says that in this city the Emperor Justinian erected a church.

33. *Eneas.* This is a Greek name; and probably he was a Hellenist. See Notes on ch. vi. 1. ¶ *Sick of the palsy.* See Notes on Mat. iv. 24.

34. *Maketh thee whole.* Cures thee. Peter claimed no power to do it himself. Comp. ch. iii. 6, 16; iv. 10. ¶ *Make thy bed.* This would show that he was truly healed. Comp. Mat. ix. 6; Mar. ii. 9, 11; Jn. v. 11, 12.

35. *And all.* The mass, or body of the people. The affliction of the man had been long, and was probably well known; the miracle would be celebrated, and the effect was an extensive revival of religion. ¶ *Saron.* This was the *champaign*, or open country, usually mentioned by the name of *Sharon* in the Old Testament, 1 Ch. v. 16; xxvii. 29; Ca. ii. 1; Is. xxxiii. 9. It was a region of extraordinary fertility, and the name was almost proverbial to denote any country of great beauty and fertility. Comp. Is. xxxiii. 9; xxxv. 2; lxv. 10. It was situated south of Mount Carmel, along the coast of the Mediterranean, extending to Cesarea and Joppa. Lydda was situated in this region. ¶ *Turned to the Lord.* Were converted; or received the Lord Jesus as the Messiah, ch. xi. 21; 2 Co. iii. 16.

36. *At Joppa.* This was a seaport town situated on the Mediterranean, in the tribe of Dan, about 30 miles south of Cesarea, and 45 north-west of Jerusalem. It was the principal seaport of Palestine; and hence, though the harbour was poor, it had considerable celebrity. It was occupied by Solomon to receive the timber brought for the building of the temple from Tyre (2 Ch. ii 16), and was used for a similar purpose in the time of Ezra, Ezr. iii. 7. The present name of the town is *Jaffa.* It is situated on a promontory jutting out into the sea, rising to the height of about 150 feet above its level, and offering on all sides picturesque and varied prospects. "It owes its existence to the low ledge of rocks which extends into the sea from the extremity of the little cape on which the city stands, and forms a small harbour. Insignificant as it is, and insecure, yet there being no other on all this coast, it was sufficient to cause a city to spring up around it even in the earliest times, and to sustain its life through numberless changes of dynasties, races, and religions down to the present hour. It was, in fact, the only harbour of any notoriety possessed by the Jews throughout the greater part of their national existence. To it the timber for both the temples of Jerusalem was brought from Lebanon, and no doubt a lucrative trade in cedar and pine was always carried on through it with the nations who had possession of the forests of Lebanon. Through it also nearly all the foreign commerce of the Jews was conducted until the artificial port of Cesarea was built by Herod. Hither Jonah came to find a ship in which to flee from the presence of the Lord, and from it he sailed for Tarshish.

"Twenty-five years ago the inhabi-

good works and almsdeeds which she did.

37 And it came to pass in those days that she was sick, and died: whom, when they had washed, they laid *her* in an upper chamber.

38 And forasmuch as Lydda was nigh to Joppa, and the disciples

---

tants of city and gardens were about 6000; now there must be 15,000 at least, and commerce has increased at even a greater ratio. Several sources of prosperity account for the existence and rapid increase of Jaffa. It is the natural landing-place of pilgrims to Jerusalem, both Christians and Jews, and they have created a considerable trade. The Holy City itself has also been constantly rising in importance during the present generation. Then there are extensive soap factories, not only here, but in Ramleh, Lydd, Nablûs, and Jerusalem, much of which is exported from this port to all the cities along the coast, to Egypt, and even to Asia Minor through Tarsus. The fruit trade from Jaffa is likewise quite considerable, and lately there have been large shipments of corn to Europe. Add to this that silk is now being cultivated extensively along the river 'Aujeh, and in the gardens about the city, and the present prosperity of Jaffa is fully explained.

"Jaffa is celebrated in modern times for her gardens and orchards of delicious fruit more than for anything else. They are very extensive, flourishing, and profitable, but their very existence depends upon the fact that water to any amount can be procured in every garden, and at a moderate depth. The entire plain seems to cover a river of vast breadth, percolating through the sand en route to the sea. A thousand Persian wheels working night and day produce no sensible diminution, and this inexhaustible source of wealth underlies the whole territory of the Philistines down to Gaza at least, and probably much farther south.

"The fruits of Jaffa are the same as those of Sidon, but with certain variations in their character. Sidon has the best bananas, Jaffa furnishes the best pomegranates. The oranges of Sidon are more juicy and of a richer flavour than those of Jaffa; but the latter hang on the trees much later, and will bear to be shipped to distant regions. They are therefore more valuable to the producer. It is here only that you see in perfection fragrant blossoms encircling golden fruit. In March and April these Jaffa gardens are indeed enchanting. The air is overloaded with the mingled spicery of orange, lemon, apple, apricot, quince, plum, and china trees in blossom. The people then frequent the groves, sit on mats beneath their grateful shade, sip coffee, smoke the argela, sing, converse, or sleep, as best suits their individual idiosyncrasies, till evening, when they slowly return to their homes in the city. To us of the restless West, this way of making *kaif* soon wearies by its slumberous monotony, but it is Elysium to the Arabs.

"I have been strolling along the streets, or rather *street* of Jaffa, for there seems to be but one, and a more crowded thoroughfare I never saw. I had to force my way through the motley crowd of busy citizens, wild Arabs, foreign pilgrims, camels, mules, horses, and donkeys. Then what a strange rabble outside the gate, noisy, quarrelsome, ragged, and filthy! Many are blind, or at least have some painful defect about their eyes, and some are leprous. The peasants hereabout must be very poor, to judge by their rags and squalid appearance. I was reminded of Dorcas and the widows around Peter exhibiting the *coats* and garments which that benevolent lady had made, and I devoutly hoped she might be raised again, at least in spirit, for there is need of a dozen Dorcas societies in Jaffa at the present time."—*The Land and the Book* (Thomson), vol. ii. p. 271-281. ¶ *Tabitha.* This word is properly Syriac, and means literally the *gazelle* or *antelope.* The name became an appellation of a female, probably on account of the beauty of its form. "It is not unusual in the East to give the names of beautiful animals to young women" (Clark). Comp. Cant. ii. 9; iv. 5. ¶ *Dorcas.* A Greek word signifying the same as Tabitha. Our word *doe* or *roe* answers to it in signification. ¶ *Full of good works.* Distinguished for good works. Comp. 1 Ti. ii. 10; Tit. ii. 7. ¶ *And almsdeeds.* Acts of kindness to the poor.

37. *Whom, when they had washed.* Among most people it has been customary to wash the body before it is buried or burned. They prepared her in the usual manner for interment. ¶ *In an upper chamber.* See Notes on

had heard that Peter was there, they sent unto him two men, desiring *him* that he would not [3]delay to come to them.

39 Then Peter arose, and went with them. When he was come, they brought him into the upper chamber: and all the widows stood by him weeping, and showing the coats and garments which Dorcas made [p]while she was with them.

40 But Peter [q]put them all forth, and kneeled down, and prayed: and turning *him* to the body, said, Tabitha, [r]arise. And she opened her eyes; and when she saw Peter, she sat up.

41 And he gave her *his* hand, and lifted her up; and when he had called the saints and widows, [s]he presented her alive.

42 And it was known throughout all Joppa; [t]and many believed in the Lord.

43 And it came to pass that he tarried many days in Joppa with one Simon, a tanner.

CHAPTER X.

THERE was a certain man in Cesarea called Cornelius, a

3 or, *be grieved*. *p* Ec.9.10. *q* Mat.9.25. *r* Mar.5.41,42; Jn.11.43.

s 1 Ki.17.23. *t* Jn.12.11.

Ac. i. 13. There is no evidence that they expected that Peter would raise her up to life.

38. *Was nigh unto Joppa.* See Notes on ver. 32. ¶ *They sent unto him*, &c. Why they sent is not affirmed. It is probable that they desired his presence to comfort and sustain them in their affliction. It is certainly *possible* that they expected he would restore her to life; but as this is not mentioned; as the apostles had as yet raised up no one from the dead; as even Stephen had not been restored to life, we have no authority for assuming, or supposing, that they had formed any such expectation.

39. *Then Peter arose.* See Notes on Lu. xv. 18. ¶ *And all the widows.* Whom Dorcas had benefited by her kindness. They had lost a benefactress; and it was natural that they should recall her kindness, and express their gratitude, by enumerating the proofs of her beneficence. Each one would therefore naturally dwell on the kindness which had been shown to herself.

40. *But Peter put them all forth.* From the room. See a similar case in Mat. ix. 25. *Why* this was done is not said. Perhaps it was because he did not wish to appear as if seeking publicity. If done in the presence of many persons, it might seem like ostentation. Others suppose it was that he might offer more fervent prayer to God than he would be willing they should witness. Comp. 2 Ki. iv. 33. ¶ *Tabitha, arise.* Comp. Mar. v. 41, 42.

41. *He presented her alive.* He exhibited, or showed her to them alive. Comp. 1 Ki. xvii. 23.

42. *And many believed*, &c. A similar effect followed when Jesus raised up Lazarus. See Jn. xii. 11.

This was the first miracle of this kind that was performed by the apostles. The effect was that many believed. It was not merely a work of benevolence, in restoring to life one who contributed largely to the comfort of the poor, but it was a means of extending and establishing, as it was designed doubtless to do, the kingdom of the Saviour.

CHAPTER X.

This chapter commences a very important part of the history of the transactions of the apostles. Before this, they had preached the gospel to the Jews only. They seemed to have retained the feelings of their countrymen on this subject, that the Jews were to be regarded as the peculiarly favoured people, and that salvation was not to be offered beyond the limits of their nation. It was important, indeed, that the gospel should be offered to them first; but the whole tendency of the Christian religion was to enlarge and liberalize the mind; to overcome the narrow policy and prejudices of the Jewish people; and to diffuse itself over all the nations of the earth. In various ways, and by various parables, the Saviour had taught the apostles, indeed, that his gospel should be spread among the Gentiles. He had commanded them to go and preach it to every creature, Mar. xvi. 15. But he had told them

centurion of the band called the Italian *band*,

2 A[a] devout *man*, and [b]one that feared God [c]with all his house, which [d]gave much alms to the people, and [e]prayed to God alway.

a ch.8.2; 22.12. b Ec.7.18. c Ge.18.19; Ps.101.2-7; ch.18.8. d Ps.41.1. e Ps.119.2; Pr.2.3-5.

---

to tarry in Jerusalem until they were endued with power from on high, Lu. xxiv. 49. It was natural, therefore, that they should receive *special* instructions and divine revelation on a point so important as this; and God selected the case of Cornelius as the instance by which he would fully establish his purpose of conveying the gospel to the Gentile world. It is worthy of observation, also, that he selected *Peter* for the purpose of conveying the gospel first to the Gentiles. The Saviour had told him that on him he would build his church; that he would give to him first the keys of the kingdom of heaven; that is, that he should be the agent in opening the doors of the church to both Jews and Gentiles. See Notes on Mat. xvi. 18, 19. Peter had, in accordance with these predictions, been the agent in first presenting the gospel to the Jews (Ac. ii.); and the prediction was now to be *completely* fulfilled in extending the same gospel to the Gentile world. The transaction recorded in this chapter is one, therefore, that is exceedingly important in the history of the church, and we are not to be surprised that it is recorded at length. It should be remembered, also, that this point became afterward the source of incessant controversy in the early church. The converts from Judaism insisted on the observance of the whole of the rites of their religion; the converts from among the Gentiles claimed exemption from them all. To settle these disputes; to secure the reception of the gospel among the Gentiles, and to introduce them to the church with all the privileges of the Jews, required all the wisdom, talent, and address of the apostles. See Ac. xi. 1-18; xv.; Ro. xiv., xv.; Ga. ii.11-16.

1. *In Cesarea.* See Notes on ch. viii. 40. ¶ *Cornelius.* This is a Latin name, and shows that the man was doubtless a Roman. It has been supposed by many interpreters that he was "a proselyte of the gate;" that is, one who had renounced idolatry, and who observed some of the Jewish rites, though not circumcised, and not called a Jew. But there is no sufficient evidence of this. The reception of the narrative of Peter (ch. xi. 1-3) shows that the other apostles regarded him as a Gentile. In ch. x. 28, Peter evidently regards him as a foreigner—one who did not in any sense esteem himself to be a Jew. In ch. xi. 1, it is expressly said that "*the Gentiles*" had received the word of God, evidently alluding to Cornelius and to those who were with him. ¶ *A centurion.* One who was the commander of a division in the Roman army, consisting of a hundred men. A captain of a hundred. See Notes on Mat. viii. 5. ¶ *Of the band.* A division of the Roman army, consisting of from four hundred to six hundred men. See Notes on Mat. xxvii. 27. ¶ *The Italian* band. Probably a band or regiment that was composed of soldiers from *Italy*, in distinction from those which were composed of soldiers born in provinces. It is evident that many of the soldiers in the Roman army would be those who were born in other parts of the world; and it is altogether probable that those who were born in Rome or Italy would claim pre-eminence over those enlisted in other places.

2. A *devout* man. Pious, or one who maintained the worship of God. See Notes on Lu. ii. 25. Comp. Ac. ii. 5; viii. 2. ¶ *And one that feared God.* This is often a designation of piety. See Notes on ch. ix. 31. It has been supposed by many that the expressions here used denote that Cornelius was a Jew, or was instructed in the Jewish religion, and was a proselyte. But this by no means follows. It is probable that there might have been among the Gentiles a few at least who were fearers of God, and who maintained his worship according to the light which they had. So there may be now persons found in pagan lands who in some unknown way have been taught the evils of idolatry and the necessity of a purer religion, and who may be *prepared* to receive the gospel. The Sandwich Islands were very much in this state when the American missionaries first visited them. They had thrown away their idols, and seemed to be *waiting* for the message of mercy and the word of eternal life, as Cornelius was. A few other instances have been found by missionaries in heathen

3 He saw in a vision evidently, about the ninth hour of the day, an [f] angel of God coming in to him, and saying unto him, Cornelius.
4 And when he looked on him, he was afraid, and said, What is it, Lord? And he said unto him, Thy prayers and thine alms are come up for a [g] memorial before God.

f He.1.14.

g Is.45.19.

lands of those who have thus been prepared by a train of providential events, or by the teaching of the Spirit, for the gospel of Christ. ¶ *With all his house.* With all his family. It is evident here that Cornelius instructed his family, and exerted his influence to train them in the fear of God. True piety will always lead a man to seek the salvation of his family. ¶ *Much alms.* Large and liberal charity. This is always an effect of piety. See Ja. i. 27; Ps. xli. 1. ¶ *Prayed to God alway.* Constantly; meaning that he was in the regular habit of prayer. Comp. Ro. xii. 12; Lu. xviii. 1; Ps. cxix. 2; Pr. ii. 2–5. As no particular *kind* of prayer is mentioned except secret prayer, we are not authorized to affirm that he offered prayer in any other manner. It may be observed, however, that he who prays in secret will usually pray in his family; and as the *family* of Cornelius is mentioned as being also under the influence of religion, it is, perhaps, not a forced inference that he observed family worship.

3. *He saw in a vision.* See Notes on ch. ix. 10. ¶ *Evidently.* Openly; manifestly. ¶ *About the ninth hour.* About 3 o'clock P.M. This was the usual hour of evening worship among the Jews. ¶ *An angel of God.* See Notes on Mat. i. 20. Comp. He. i. 14. This angel was sent to signify to Cornelius that his alms were accepted by God as an evidence of his piety, and to direct him to send for Peter to instruct him in the way of salvation. The importance of the occasion—the introduction of the gospel to a *Gentile*, and hence to the entire Gentile world—was probably the chief reason why an angel was commissioned to visit the Roman centurion. Comp. ch. xvi. 9, 10.

4. *And when he looked on him.* Greek, Having fixed his eyes attentively on him. ¶ *He was afraid.* At the suddenness and unexpected character of the vision. ¶ *What is it, Lord?* This is the expression of surprise and alarm. The word *Lord* should have been translated *sir*, as there is no evidence that this is an address to *God*, and still less that he regarded the personage present as *the Lord.* Comp. Notes on ch. ix. 5. It is such language as a man would naturally use who was suddenly surprised; who should witness a strange form appearing unexpectedly before him; and who should exclaim, "Sir, what is the matter?" ¶ *Are come up for a memorial.* Are remembered before God. Comp. Is. xlv. 19. They were an evidence of piety toward God, and were accepted as such. Though he had not offered sacrifice according to the Jewish laws; though he had not been circumcised; yet, having acted according to the light which he had, his prayers were heard, and his alms were accepted. This was done in accordance with the general principle of the divine administration, that God prefers the offering of the *heart* to external forms; the expressions of *love* to sacrifice without it. This he had often declared, Is. i. 11–15; Am. v. 21, 22; 1 Sa. xv. 22, "To obey is better than sacrifice, and to hearken than the fat of rams," Ho. vi. 6; Ec. v. 1. It should be remembered, however, that Cornelius was not depending on external morality. His *heart* was in the work of *religion.* It should be remembered, further, that he was ready to receive *the gospel* when it was offered to him, and to become a Christian. In this there was an important difference between him and those who are depending for salvation on their morality in Christian lands. Such men are inclined to defend themselves by the example of Cornelius, and to suppose that as he was accepted *before* he embraced the gospel, so they may be *without* embracing it. But there is an important difference in the two cases. For, (1) There is no evidence that Cornelius was depending on *external morality* for salvation. His offering was that of the *heart*, and not merely an external offering. (2) Cornelius did not rely on his *morality* at all. His was a work of *religion.* He feared God; he prayed to him; he exerted his influence to bring his *family* to the same state.

5 And now send men to Joppa,
and call for *one* Simon, whose surname is Peter.

6 He lodgeth with one [h]Simon,
a tanner, whose house is by the
sea-side: [i]he shall tell thee what
thou oughtest to do.

7 And when the angel which
spake unto Cornelius was departed,
he called two of his household
servants, and a devout soldier of
them that waited on him continually:

8 And when he had declared all
these things unto them, he sent them
to Joppa.

9 On the morrow, as they went
on their journey, and drew nigh

h ch.9.43. *i* ch.11.14.

Moral men do neither. "All their works they do to be seen of men;" and in their heart there is "no good thing toward the Lord God of Israel." Comp. 1 Ki. xiv. 13; 2 Ch. xix. 3. Who ever hears of a man that "fears God," and that prays, and that instructs his household in *religion*, that *depends* on *morality* for salvation? (3) Cornelius was disposed to do the will of God as far as it was made known to him. Where this exists there is religion. The moral man is not. (4) Cornelius was willing to embrace a Saviour when he was made known to him. The moral man is not. He hears of a Saviour with unconcern; he listens to the message of God's mercy from year to year without embracing it. In all this there is an important difference between him and the Roman centurion; and while we hope that there may be many in pagan lands who are in the same state of mind that he was—disposed to do the will of God as far as made known, and therefore accepted and saved by his mercy in the Lord Jesus, yet this cannot be adduced to encourage the hope of salvation in those who *do* know his will, and yet will not do it.

6. *He lodgeth.* He remains as a guest at his house. See ch. ix. 43. ¶ *By the sea-side.* Joppa was a seaport on the Mediterranean. Tanneries are erected on the margin of streams, or of any body of water, to convey away the filth produced in the operation of dressing skins.

7. *A devout soldier.* A pious man. This is an instance of the effect of piety in a military officer. Few men have more influence; and in this case the effect was seen not only in the piety of his family, but of this attending soldier. Such men have usually been supposed to be far from the influence of religion; but this instance shows that even the disadvantages of a camp are not necessarily hostile to the existence of piety. Comp. Lu. iii. 14.

8. *And when*, &c. "It has been remarked that from Joppa, Jonah was sent to preach to the Gentiles at Nineveh, and that from the same place Peter was sent to preach to the Gentiles at Cesarea" (Clarke).

9. *Peter went up*, &c. The small room in the second story, or on the roof of the house, was the usual place for retirement and prayer. See Notes on Mat. vi. 6; ix. 2. Even when there was no *room* constructed on the roof, the roof was a common resort for retirement and prayer. Around the edge a battlement or parapet was commonly made, within which a person could be quite retired from public view. "At Jaffa, the ancient Joppa," says Prof. Hackett (*Illustrations of Scripture*, p. 81), "where Peter was residing at the time of his vision on the house-top, I observed houses furnished with a wall around the roof, within which a person could sit or kneel without any exposure to the view of others, whether on the adjacent houses or in the streets. At Jerusalem I entered the house of a Jew early one morning, and found a member of the family, sitting secluded and alone on one of the lower roofs, engaged in reading the Scriptures and offering his prayers."

Dr. Thomson (*Land and the Book*, vol. i. p. 52) says of these roofs, "When surrounded with battlements, and shaded by vines trained over them, they afford a very agreeable retreat, even at the sixth hour of the day — the time when Peter was favoured with that singular vision, by which the kingdom of heaven was thrown open to the Gentile world." ¶ *About the sixth hour.* About twelve o'clock, or at noon. The Jews had two stated seasons of prayer, morning and evening. But it is evident that the more pious of the Jews frequently added a *third* season of devotion, probably at noon. Thus David says (Ps. lv.

unto the city, [k]Peter went up upon the house-top to pray, about the sixth hour:

10 And he became very hungry, and would have eaten; but while they made ready, he fell into a trance,

11 And [l]saw heaven opened, and a certain vessel descending unto him, as it had been a great sheet, knit at the four corners, and let down to the earth;

12 Wherein were all manner of four-footed beasts of the earth, and wild beasts, and creeping things, and fowls of the air.

13 And there came a voice to him, Rise, Peter; kill, and eat.

14 But Peter said, Not so, Lord;

k ch.11.5,&c. *l* ch.7.56; Re.19.11.

17), "Evening and morning, and *at noon*, will I pray, and cry aloud." Thus Daniel "kneeled upon his knees three times a day and prayed," Da. vi. 10, 13. It was also customary in the early Christian church to offer prayer at the third, sixth, and ninth hours (Clem. Alex. as quoted by Doddridge). Christians will, however, have not merely *stated* seasons for prayer, but they will seize upon moments of leisure, and when their feelings strongly incline them to it, to pray.

10. *And he became very hungry.* From the connection, where it is said that they were making ready, that is, preparing a meal, it would seem that this was the customary hour of dining. The Hebrews, Greeks, and Romans, however, had but two meals, and the first was usually taken about ten or eleven o'clock. This meal usually consisted of fruit, milk, cheese, &c. Their principal meal was about six or seven in the afternoon, at which time they observed their feasts. See Jahn's *Bibl. Archæol.* § 145. ¶ *He fell into a trance.* Greek, an ecstasy, ἔκστασις, fell upon him. In ch. xi. 5, Peter says that *in* a trance he saw a vision. The word *trance*, or *ecstasy*, denotes a state of mind when the attention is absorbed in a particular train of thought, so that the external senses are partially or entirely suspended. It is a high species of abstraction from external objects, when the mind becomes forgetful of surrounding things, and is fixed solely on its own thoughts, so that appeals to the external senses do not readily rouse it. The soul seems to have passed out of the body, and to be conversant only with spiritual essences. Thus Balaam is said to have seen the vision of the Almighty, falling into a trance (Nu. xxiv. 4, 16); thus Paul, in praying in the temple, fell into a trance (Ac. xxii. 17); and perhaps a similar state is described in 2 Co. xii. 2. This effect seems to be caused by so intense and absorbing a train of thought as to overcome the senses of the body, or wholly to withdraw the mind from their influence, and to fix it on the unseen object that engrosses it. It is often a high state of *reverie*, or absence of mind, which Dr. Rush describes as "induced by the stimulus of ideas of absent subjects, being so powerful as to destroy the perception of present objects" (*Diseases of the Mind*, p. 310, ed. Philada. 1812). In the case of Peter, however, there was a supernatural influence that drew his attention away from present objects.

11. *And saw heaven opened.* Ch. vii. 56. See Notes on Mat. iii. 16. This *language* is derived from a common mode of speaking in the Hebrew Scriptures, as if the sky above us was a solid, vast expanse, and as if it were *opened* to present an opportunity for anything to descend. It is language that is highly figurative. ¶ *And a certain vessel.* See Notes on ch. ix. 15. ¶ *As it had been.* It is important to mark this expression. The sacred writer does not say that Peter literally saw such an object descending; but he uses this as an imperfect description of the vision. It was not a literal descent of a vessel, but it was such a kind of representation to him, producing the same impression, and the same effect, *as if* such a vessel had descended. ¶ *Knit at the four corners.* Bound, united, or *tied.* The corners were collected, as would be natural in putting anything into a great sheet.

12. *Wherein,* &c. This particular vision was suggested by Peter's hunger, ver. 10. It was designed, however, to teach him an important lesson in regard to the introduction of all nations to the gospel. Its descending from heaven may have been an intimation that that religion which was about to abolish the distinction between the Jews and other nations was of divine origin. See Re. xxi. 2.

for I have never eaten [m]any thing
that is common or unclean.
15 And the voice *spake* unto
him again the second time, [n]What
God hath cleansed, *that* call not
thou common.
16 This was done thrice; and
the vessel was received up again
into heaven.
17 Now while Peter doubted in
himself what this vision which he
had seen should mean, behold, the
men which were sent from Cornelius had [o]made inquiry for Simon's
house, and stood before the gate.

m Le.11.2,&c.; 20.25; De.14.3,&c.; Eze.4.14.
n Mat.15.11; ver.28; Ro.14.14,&c.; 1 Co.10.25; 1 Ti. 4.4.
o ch.9.43.

---

14. *I have never eaten*, &c. In the Old Testament God had made a distinction between clean and unclean animals. See Le. xi. 2-27; De. xiv. 3–20. This law remained in the Scriptures, and Peter pled that he *had* never violated it, implying that he could not now violate it, as it was a law of God, and that, as it was unrepealed, he did not dare to act in a different manner from what it required. Between that law and the command which he now received in the vision there was an apparent variation, and Peter naturally referred to the well-known and admitted written law. One design of the vision was to show him that that law was now to pass away. ¶ *That is common.* This word properly denotes *that which pertains to all*, but among the Jews, who were bound by special laws, and who were prohibited from many things that were freely indulged in by other nations, the word *common* came to be opposed to the word *sacred*, and to denote that which was in common use among the heathens, hence that which was *profane*, or *polluted*. Here it means the same as *profane*, or *forbidden*. ¶ *Unclean.* Ceremonially unclean; that is, that which is forbidden by the ceremonial law of Moses.

15. *What God hath cleansed.* What God has pronounced or declared pure. If God has commanded you to do a thing, it is not impure or wrong. Perhaps Peter would suppose that the design of this vision was to instruct him that the distinction between clean and unclean food, as recognized by the Jews, was about to be abolished, ver. 17. But the result showed that it had a higher and more important design. It was to show him that they who had been esteemed by the Jews as unclean or profane—the entire Gentile world—might now be admitted to similar privileges with the Jews. That barrier was to be broken down, and the whole world was to be admitted to the same fellowship and privileges in the gospel. See Ep. ii. 14; Ga. iii. 28. It was also true that the ceremonial laws of the Jews in regard to clean and unclean beasts was to pass away, though this was not directly taught in this vision. But when once the barrier was removed that separated the Jews and Gentiles, all the laws which *were founded* on such a distinction, and which were framed to *keep up* such a distinction, passed away of course. The ceremonial laws of the Jews were designed *solely* to keep up the distinction between them and other nations. When the distinction was abolished; when other nations were to be admitted to the same privileges, the laws which were made to keep up such a difference received their death-blow, and expired of course. For it is a maxim of all law, that when the *reason* why a law was made ceases to exist, the law becomes obsolete. Yet it was not easy to convince the Jews that their laws ceased to be binding. This point the apostles laboured to establish; and from this point arose most of the difficulties between the Jewish and Gentile converts to Christianity. See Ac. xv., and Ro. xiv., xv.

16. *This was done thrice.* Three times, doubtless to impress the mind of Peter with the certainty and importance of the vision. Comp. Ge. xli. 32.

17. *Doubted in himself.* Doubted in his own mind. He was perplexed, and did not know how to understand it. ¶ *Behold, the men*, &c. We see here an admirable arrangement of the events of Providence to fit each other. Every part of this transaction is made to harmonize with every other part; and it was so arranged that just in the moment when the mind of Peter was filled with perplexity, the very event should occur which would relieve him of his embarrassment. Such a coincidence is not uncommon. An event of divine Providence may be as clear an expression of his will, and may as certainly serve to indicate our duty, as the most

18 And called, and asked whether
Simon, which was surnamed Peter,
were lodged there.
19 While Peter thought on the
vision, [p]the Spirit said unto him,
Behold, three men seek thee.
20 Arise, [q]therefore, and get thee
down, and go with them, doubting
nothing; for I have sent them.
21 Then Peter went down to
the men which were sent unto him
from Cornelius, and said, Behold,
I am he whom ye seek; what *is*
the cause wherefore ye are come?
22 And they said, [r]Cornelius, the
centurion, a just man, and one that
feareth God, and [s]of good report
among all the nation of the Jews,
was warned from God by an holy
angel to send for thee into his
house, and to hear words of thee.
23 Then called he them in, and
lodged *them*. And on the morrow
Peter went away with them, [t]and
certain brethren from Joppa accompanied him.
24 And the morrow after they
entered into Cesarea. And Cornelius waited for them, and had
called together his kinsmen and
near friends.
25 And as Peter was coming in
Cornelius met him, and fell down
at his feet and worshipped *him*.
26 But Peter took him up, saying, [u]Stand up; I myself also am
a man.
27 And as he talked with him,

p ch.11.12. *q* ch.15.7. *r* ver.1,&c. *s* ch.22.12; He.11.2. *t* ver.45. *u* ch.14.14,15; Re.19.10; 22.9.

---

manifest revelation would do, and a state of mind may, by an arrangement of circumstances, be produced that will be extremely perplexing until some event shall occur, or some field of usefulness shall open, that will exactly correspond to it, and indicate to us the will of God. We should then carefully mark the events of God's providence. We should observe and record the train of our own thoughts, and should watch with interest any event that occurs, when we are perplexed and embarrassed, to obtain, if possible, an expression of the will of God. ¶ *Before the gate.* The word here rendered "gate," πυλῶνα, refers properly to *the porch* or principal entrance to an Eastern house. See Notes on Mat. ix. 2; xxvi. 71. It does not mean, as with us, a *gate*, but rather a *door*. See Ac. xii. 13.

19. *The Spirit.* See Notes on Ac. viii. 29. Comp. Is. lxv. 24, "And it shall come to pass, that before they call I will answer," &c.

22. *To hear words of thee.* To be instructed by thee.

23. *And lodged* them. They remained with him through the night. Four days were occupied before Peter met Cornelius at Cesarea. On the first the angel appeared to Cornelius. On the second the messengers arrived at Joppa, ver. 9. On the third, Peter returned with them, ver. 23; and on the fourth they arrived at Cesarea, ver. 24, 30. ¶ *And certain brethren.* Some Christians. They were six in number, ch. xi. 12. It was usual for the early Christians to accompany the apostles in their journeys. See Ro. xv. 24; Ac. xv. 3; 3 Jn. 6; 1 Co. xvi. 6, 11. As this was an important event in the history of the church—the bearing of the gospel to a Gentile—it was more natural and proper that Peter should be attended with others.

24. *His kinsmen.* His relatives, or the connections of his family. A man may often do vast good by calling his kindred and friends to hear the gospel.

25. *Fell down at his feet.* This was an act of profound regard for him as an ambassador of God. In Oriential countries it was usual for persons to prostrate themselves at length on the ground before men of rank and honour. ¶ *Worshipped* him. This does not mean religious *homage*, but civil respect—the homage, or profound regard which was due to one in honour. See Notes on Mat. ii. 2.

26. *Stand up*, &c. This does not imply that Peter supposed that Cornelius intended to do him *religious* reverence. It was practically saying to him, "I am nothing more than a man as thou art, and pretend to no right to such profound respects as these, but am ready in civil life to show thee all the respect that is due" (Doddridge).

27. *And as he talked with him.* He probably met him at the door, or at a small distance from the house. It was

he went in, and found many that
were come together.
28 And he said unto them, Ye
know how that [v]it is an unlawful
thing for a man that is a Jew to
keep company, or come unto one
of another nation; but [w]God hath
showed me that I should not call
any man common or unclean.
29 Therefore came I *unto you*
without gainsaying, as soon as I
was sent for. I ask, therefore, for
what intent ye have sent for me?
30 And Cornelius said, Four
days ago I was fasting until this
hour; and at the ninth hour I
prayed in my house; and, behold,
a man [x]stood before me in bright
clothing,

v Jn.4.9. w ch.15.8,9; Ep.3.6. x Mat.28.3; ch.1.10.

31 And said, Cornelius, [y]thy
prayer is heard, and thine alms
are had in remembrance in the
sight of God.
32 Send therefore to Joppa, and
call hither Simon, whose surname
is Peter: he is lodged in the house
of *one* Simon, a tanner, by the sea-
side; who, when he cometh, shall
speak unto thee.
33 Immediately therefore I sent
to thee; and thou hast well done
that thou art come. Now[z] therefore are we all here present before
God, to hear all things that are
commanded thee of God.
34 Then Peter opened *his* mouth,
and said, Of a truth, I perceive

y ver.4,&c.; Da.10.12; He.6.10. z De.5.27.

---

an expression of joy thus to go out to meet him.

28. *It is an unlawful thing.* This was not explicitly enjoined by Moses, but it seemed to be implied in his institutions, and was, at anyrate, the common understanding of the Jews. The design was to keep them a separate people. To do this, Moses forbade alliances by contract, or marriage, with the surrounding nations, which were idolatrous. See Le. xviii. 24–30; De. vii. 3–12; comp. Ezr. ix. 11, 12. This command the Jews perverted, and explained it as referring to intercourse of all kinds, even to the exercise of friendly offices and commercial transactions. Comp. Jn. iv. 9. ¶ *Of another nation.* Greek, another *tribe.* It refers here to all who were not Jews. ¶ *God hath showed me.* Comp. ch. xv. 8, 9. He had showed him by the vision, ver. 11, 12. ¶ *Any man common or unclean.* See Notes on ver. 14. That no man was to be regarded as excluded from the opportunity of salvation, or was to be despised and abhorred. The gospel was to be preached to all; the barrier between Jews and Gentiles was broken down, and all were to be regarded as capable of being saved.

29. *Without gainsaying.* Without *saying anything against it;* without hesitation or reluctance. ¶ *I ask, therefore,* &c. The main design for which Cornelius had sent for him had been mentioned to Peter by the messenger, ver. 22. But Peter now desired from his own lips a more particular statement of the considerations which had induced him to send for him. ¶ *For what intent.* For what purpose or design.

30. *Four days ago.* See Notes on ver. 23. ¶ *Until this hour.* The ninth hour, or three o'clock, P.M. See ver. 3. ¶ *A man.* Called, in ver. 3, an angel. He had the *appearance* of a man. Comp. Mar. xvi. 5. ¶ *In bright clothing.* See Notes on Mat. xxviii. 3.

33. *Thou hast well done.* This is an expression of grateful feeling. ¶ *Before God.* In the presence of God. It is implied that they believed that God saw them; that they were assembled at his command, and that they were disposed to listen to his instructions.

34. *Then Peter opened* his *mouth.* Began to speak, Mat. v. 2. ¶ *Of a truth.* Truly, evidently. That is, I have *evidence here* that God is no respecter of persons. ¶ *Is no respecter of persons.* The word used here denotes the act of showing favour to one on account of rank, family, wealth, or partiality arising from any cause. It is explained in Ja. ii. 1–4. A judge is a respecter of persons when he favours one of the parties on account of private friendship, or because he is a man of rank, influence, or power, or because he belongs to the same political party, &c. The Jews supposed that they were peculiarly favoured by God, and that salvation was not extended to other nations, and that the fact of *being a Jew* entitled

that [a]God is no respecter of persons:

a De.10.17; 2 Ch.19.7; Job 34.19; Ro.2.11; Ga.2.6; 1 Pe.1.17.

35 But[b] in every nation he that feareth him, and worketh righteousness, is accepted with him.

b Ro.2.13,27; 3.22,29; 10.12,13; Ep.2.13-18.

---

them to this favour. Peter here says that he had learned the error of this doctrine, and that a man is not to be *accepted* because he is a *Jew*, nor to be *excluded* because he is a *Gentile*. The barrier is broken down; the offer is made to all; God will save all on the same principle; not by external privileges or rank, but according to their character. The same doctrine is elsewhere explicitly stated in the New Testament, Ro. ii. 11; Ep. vi. 9; Col. iii. 25. It may be observed here that this does not refer to the doctrine of divine sovereignty or election. It simply affirms that God will not save a man because he is a Jew, or because he is rich, or learned, or of elevated rank, or on account of external privileges; nor will he exclude a man because he is destitute of these privileges. But this does not affirm that he will not make a difference *in their character*, and then treat them *according* to their character, nor that he will not pardon whom he pleases. That is a different question. The interpretation of this passage should be limited strictly to the case in hand—to mean that God will not accept and save a man on account of external national rank and privileges. That he will not make a difference *on other grounds* is not affirmed here, nor anywhere in the Bible. Comp. 1 Co. iv. 7; Ro. xii. 6. It is worthy of remark further, that the most strenuous advocate for the doctrines of sovereignty and election—the apostle Paul—is also the one that laboured most to establish the doctrine that God is no respecter of persons—that is, that there is no difference between the Jews and Gentiles in regard to the way of salvation; that God would not *save* a man because he was a Jew, nor *destroy* a man because he was a Gentile. Yet in regard to *the whole race viewed as lying on a level*, he maintained that God has a right to exercise the prerogatives of a sovereign, and to have mercy on whom he will have mercy. The doctrine may be thus stated. (1) The barrier between the Jews and Gentiles was broken down. (2) All men thus were placed on a level—none to be saved by external privileges, none to be lost by the want of them. (3) *All* were guilty (Ro. i., ii., iii.), and none had a claim on God. (4) If any were saved, it would be by God's showing mercy on such of this *common mass* as he chose. See Ro. iii. 22; x. 12; ii. 11; Ga. ii. 6; comp. with Ro. ix. and Ep. i.

35. *But in every nation*, &c. This is given as a reason for what Peter had just said, that God was no respecter of persons. The sense is, that he now perceived that the favours of God were not confined to the *Jew*, but might be extended to all others on the same principle. The remarkable circumstances here—the vision to him, and to Cornelius, and the declaration that the alms of Cornelius were accepted—now convinced him that the favours of God were no longer to be confined to the Jewish people, but might be extended to all. This was what the vision was designed to teach, and to communicate this knowledge to the apostles was an important step in their work of spreading the gospel. ¶ *In every nation.* Among all people. Jews or Gentiles. Acceptance with God does not depend on the fact of being descended from Abraham, or of possessing external privileges, but on the state of the heart. ¶ *He that feareth him.* This is put for piety toward God in general. See Notes on ch. ix. 31. It means that he who honours God and keeps his law; he who is a true worshipper of God, according to the light and privileges which he has, is approved by him, as giving evidence that he is his friend. ¶ *And worketh righteousness.* Does that which is right and just. This refers to his conduct toward man. He that discharges conscientiously his duty to his fellow-men, and evinces by his conduct that he is a righteous man. These *two* things comprehend the whole of religion, the sum of all the requirements of God—piety toward God, and justice toward men; and as Cornelius had showed these, he showed that, though a Gentile, he was actuated by true religion. We may observe here, (1) That it is not said that Cornelius was accepted *on account* of his good works. Those works were simply an evidence of true piety in the heart; a proof that he feared and loved God, and not a meritorious ground of accept-

36 The word which *God* sent
unto the children of Israel, [c]preach-
ing peace by Jesus Christ; ([d]he is
Lord of all;)

37 That word, *I say*, ye know,
which was published throughout
all Judea, and began from Galilee, after the baptism which John
preached:
38 How God [e]anointed Jesus

c Is.57.19; Col.1.20.
d Ps.24.7-10; Mat.28.18; He.14.9; 1 Co.15.27; Ep.1.20-22; 1 Pe.3.22; Re.17.14.
e Lu.4.18; He.1.9.

ance. (2) He improved the light which he had. (3) *He embraced the Saviour when he was offered to him.* This circumstance makes an essential difference between Cornelius and those who depend on their morality in Christian lands. They do *not* embrace the Lord Jesus, and they are, therefore, totally unlike the Roman centurion. His example should not be pled, therefore, by those who *neglect* the Saviour, for it furnishes no evidences that *they* will be accepted when they are totally unlike him.

36. *The word.* That is, this is the word, or the doctrine. Few passages in the New Testament have perplexed critics more than this. It has been difficult to ascertain to what the term "word" in the accusative case (τὸν λόγον) here refers. Our translation would lead us to suppose that it is synonymous with what is said in the following verse. But it should be remarked that the term used there, and translated "word," as if it were a repetition of what is said here, is a different term. It is not λόγον, *logon*, but ῥῆμα, *rhema*—a word, a thing; not a doctrine. I understand the first term "word" to be an introduction of the doctrine which Peter set forth, and to be governed by a preposition understood. The whole passage may be thus expressed: Peter had been asked to *teach* Cornelius and his assembled friends. It was expected, of course, that he would instruct him in regard to the true doctrines of religion—the doctrine which had been communicated to the Jews. He commences, therefore, with a statement respecting the true doctrine of the Messiah, or the way of salvation which was now made known to the Jews. "In regard to the *word*, or the doctrine which God sent to the children of Israel, proclaiming peace through Jesus Christ (who is Lord of all), you know already that which was done, or the transactions which occurred throughout all Judea, from Galilee, where he commenced his ministry after John had preached, that this was by Jesus Christ, since God had anointed him," &c. Peter here assumes that Cornelius had *some* knowledge of the principal events of the life of the Saviour, though it was obscure and imperfect; and his discourse professes only to state this more *fully and clearly*. ¶ *Unto the children of Israel.* To the *Jews.* The Messiah was promised to them, and spent his life among them. ¶ *Preaching.* That is, proclaiming, or announcing. God did this by Jesus Christ. ¶ *Peace.* This word sometimes refers to the *peace* or union which was made between Jews and Gentiles, by breaking down the wall of division between them. But it is here used in a wider sense, to denote peace or reconciliation with God. He announced the way by which man might be reconciled to God, and might find peace. ¶ *He is Lord of all.* That is, Jesus Christ. He is sovereign, or ruler of both Jews and Gentiles, and hence Peter saw the propriety of preaching the gospel to one as to the other. See Jn. xvii. 2; Mat. xxviii. 18; Ep. i. 20–22. The word *Lord* here used does not necessarily imply divinity, but only that the Lord Jesus, as Mediator, had been constituted or appointed lord or ruler over all nations. It is true, however, that this is a power which we cannot conceive to have been delegated to one that was not divine. Comp. Ro. ix. 5.

37. *That word.* Greek, ῥῆμα—a different word from that in the previous verse. It may be translated *thing* as well as *word.* ¶ *Which was published.* Greek, which was *done.* "You know, though it may be imperfectly, what was *done* or accomplished in Judea," &c. ¶ *Throughout all Judea.* The miracles of Christ were not confined to any place, but were wrought in every part of the land. For an account of the divisions of Palestine, see Notes on Mat. ii. 22. ¶ *And began*, &c. Greek, having been begun in Galilee. Galilee was not far from Cesarea. There was, therefore, the more probability that Cornelius had heard of what had occurred there. Indeed, the gospels themselves furnish the highest evidence that

of Nazareth with the Holy Ghost
and with power, [f]who went about
doing good, and [g]healing all that
were oppressed of the devil: [h]for
God was with him.
39 And[i] we are witnesses of all
things which he did, both in the
land of the Jews and in Jerusalem;
whom they slew and hanged on
a tree.
40 Him[k] God raised up the third
day, and showed him openly;

f Mat.12.15. *g* 1 Jn.3.8. *h* Jn.3.2.
i Lu.24.48; ch.2.32. *k* Mat.28.1,2.

41 Not[l] to all the people, but
unto [m]witnesses chosen before of
God, *even* to us, who did eat and
drink with him after he rose from
the dead.
42 And he [n]commanded us to
preach unto the people, and to
[o]testify that it is he which was
ordained of God *to be* the Judge
of quick and dead.
43 To [p]him give all the prophets

l Jn.14.22; 20. & 21. *m* Jn.15.16. *n* Mat.28.19,20.
o Jn.5.22,27; ch.17.31; 2 Co.5.10; 1 Pe.4.5.
p Lu.24.27,44; Jn.5.39.

---

the fame of the miracles of Christ spread into all the surrounding regions.

38. *How God anointed*, &c. That is, set him apart to this work, and was with him, acknowledging him as the Messiah. See Notes on Mat. i. 1. ¶ *With the Holy Ghost.* See Notes on Lu. iv. 19. The act of anointing kings and priests seems to have been emblematic of the influences of the Holy Ghost. Here it means that God imparted to him the influences of the Holy Spirit, thus consecrating him for the work of the Messiah. See Mat. iii. 16, 17; Jn. iii. 34, "God giveth not the Holy Spirit by measure unto him." ¶ *And with power.* The power of healing the sick, raising the dead, &c. ¶ *Who went about doing good.* Whose main business it was to travel from place to place to do good. He did not go for applause, or wealth, or comfort, or ease, but to diffuse happiness as far as possible. This is the simple but sublime record of his life. It gives us a distinct portrait of his character, as he is distinguished from conquerors and kings, from false prophets and from the mass of men. ¶ *And healing*, &c. Restoring to health. ¶ *All that were oppressed of the devil.* All that were possessed by him. See Notes on Mat. iv. 23, 24. ¶ *God was with him.* God appointed him, and furnished by his miracles the highest evidence that *he* had sent him. His miracles were such that they could be wrought only by God.

39. *And we are witnesses.* We who are apostles. See Notes on Lu. xxiv. 48. ¶ *In the land of the Jews.* In the country of Judea. ¶ *Whom they slew*, &c. Our translation would seem to imply that there were two separate acts—first slaying him, and *then* suspending him. But this is neither according to truth nor to the Greek text. The original is simply, "whom they put to death, *suspending him* on a tree." ¶ *On a tree.* On a cross. See Notes on ch. v. 30.

40. *Showed him openly.* Manifestly; so that there could be no deception, no doubt of his resurrection.

41. *Not to all the people.* Not to the nation at large, for this was not necessary in order to establish the truth of his resurrection. He, however, showed himself to *many* persons. See the Harmony of the Accounts of the Resurrection of Jesus at the close of the Notes on Matthew. ¶ *Chosen of God.* Appointed *by* God, or set apart by his authority through Jesus Christ. ¶ *Who did eat and drink*, &c. And by doing this he furnished the clearest possible proof that he was truly risen; that they were not deceived by an illusion of the imagination or by a phantasm. Comp. Jn. xxi. 12, 13.

42. *And he commanded us*, &c.; Mat. xxviii. 19, 20; Mar. xvi. 15, 16. ¶ *And to testify.* To bear witness. ¶ *That it is he*, &c. See Notes on Jn. v. 22–27. Comp. the references in the margin. ¶ *Of quick.* The *living.* The doctrine of the New Testament is, that those who are alive when the Lord Jesus shall return to judge the world, will be caught up in vast numbers like clouds, to meet him in the air, without seeing death, 1 Th. iv. 16, 17. Yet before this they will experience such a *change* in their bodies as shall fit them for the judgment and for their eternal residence —a change which will liken them to those who have died, and have risen from the dead. What this change will be, speculation may fancy, but the Bible has not revealed. See 1 Co. xv.

witness, that through his name
whosoever[q] believeth in him shall
receive remission of sins.
44 While Peter yet spake these
words, [r]the Holy Ghost fell on all
them which heard the word.
45 And [s]they of the circumcision
which believed were astonished, as
many as came with Peter, because
that on the Gentiles also was poured
out the gift of the Holy Ghost;
46 For they heard them [t]speak
with tongues, and magnify God.
Then answered Peter,
47 Can[u] any man forbid water,
that these should not be baptized
which have received the Holy Ghost
as well as we?
48 And he commanded them to
be baptized in the name of the Lord.
Then prayed they him to tarry
certain days.

CHAPTER XI.

AND the apostles and brethren
that were in Judea heard
that the Gentiles had also received
the word of God.
2 And when Peter was come up

q Jn.3.14-17; Ro.10.11. r ch.4.31. s ver.23. t ch.2.4. u ch.8.12.

52, "The dead shall be raised, and we shall be changed."

43. *To him give*, &c. See Notes on Lu. xxiv. 27, 44. ¶ *That through his name*, &c. This was *implied* in what the prophets said. See Ro. x. 11. It was not, indeed, expressly affirmed that they who believed in him should be pardoned, but this was *implied* in what they said. They promised a Messiah, and their religion consisted mainly in believing in a Messiah to come. See the reasoning of the apostle Paul in Ro. iv.

44. *The Holy Ghost fell*, &c. Endowing them with the power of speaking with other tongues, ver. 46. Of this the apostle Peter makes much in his argument in ch. xi. 17. By this, God showed that the *Gentiles* were to be admitted to the same privileges with the Jews, and to the blessings of salvation in the same manner. Comp. ch. ii. 1-4. ¶ *Which heard the word*. The word of God; the message of the gospel.

45. *And they of the circumcision*. Who had been Jews. ¶ *Were astonished*. Were amazed that *Gentiles* should be admitted to the same favour as themselves.

46. *Speak with tongues*. In other languages than their own native tongue, ch. ii. 4. ¶ *And magnify God*. And praise God.

47. *Can any man forbid water*, &c. They have shown that they are favoured in the same way as the Jewish converts. God has manifested himself to them as he did to the Jews on the day of Pentecost. Is it not clear, therefore, that they are entitled to the privilege of Christian baptism? The expression here used is one that would *naturally* refer to water as being *brought;* that is, to a small quantity; and would seem to imply that they were baptized, not by immersion, but by pouring or sprinkling.

48. *And he commanded them*, &c. Why Peter did not himself baptize them is unknown. It *might* be, perhaps, because he chose to make use of the ministry of the brethren who were with him, to prevent the possibility of future cavil. If *they* did it themselves, they could not so easily be led by the Jews to find fault with it. It may be added, also, that it seems not to have been the practice of the apostles themselves to baptize very extensively. See 1 Co. i. 14-17, "Christ sent me not to baptize, but to preach the gospel."

CHAPTER XI.

1. *And the apostles and brethren*. The Christians who were in Judea. ¶ *Heard*, &c. So extraordinary an occurrence as that at Cesarea, the descent of the Holy Spirit on the Gentiles, and their reception into the church, would excite attention, and be likely to produce much sensitiveness in regard to the conduct of Peter and those with him. It was so contrary to all the ideas of the Jews, that it is not to be wondered at that it led to contention.

2. *They that were of the circumcision*. The Christians who had been converted from among the Jews. ¶ *Contended with him*. Disputed; reproved him; charged him with being in fault. This is one of the circumstances which show conclusively that the apostles and early Christians did not regard Peter as having any particular *supremacy* over the church, or

to Jerusalem, [a]they that were of the circumcision contended with him,

3 Saying, Thou wentest in to men uncircumcised, and didst eat with them.

4 But Peter rehearsed *the matter* from the beginning, and expounded *it* by order unto them, saying,

5 I[b] was in the city of Joppa, praying; and in a trance I saw a vision, A certain vessel descend, as it had been a great sheet let down from heaven by four corners; and it came even to me:

6 Upon the which when I had fastened mine eyes, I considered, and saw four-footed beasts of the earth, and wild beasts, and creeping things, and fowls of the air.

7 And I heard a voice saying unto me, Arise, Peter; slay, and eat.

8 But I said, Not so, Lord; for nothing common or unclean hath at any time entered into my mouth.

9 But the voice answered me again from heaven, What God hath cleansed, *that* call not thou common.

10 And this was done three times: and all were drawn up again into heaven.

11 And, behold, immediately there were three men already come unto the house where I was, sent from Cesarea unto me.

12 And[c] the Spirit bade me go with them, nothing doubting. Moreover, these six brethren accompanied me; and we entered into the man's house:

13 And he showed us how he had seen an angel in his house, which stood and said unto him, Send men to Joppa, and call for Simon, whose surname is Peter;

14 Who shall tell thee [d]words, whereby thou and all thy house shall be saved.

15 And as I began to speak, the

a ch.10.23,28; Ga.2.12. *b* ch.10.9,&c. *c* Jn.16.13. *d* Ps.19.7-11; Jn.6.63,68.

as being in any peculiar sense the *vicar* of Christ upon earth. If he had been regarded as having the authority which the Roman Catholics claim for him, they would have submitted at once to what he had thought proper to do. But the primitive Christians had no such idea of his authority. This claim for Peter is not only opposed to this place, but to every part of the New Testament.

3. *And didst eat with them.* See Notes on ch. x. 13, 14.

4. *But Peter rehearsed.* Greek, Peter beginning, explained it to them in order; that is, he began with the vision which he saw, and gave a narrative of the various events in order, as they actually occurred. A simple and unvarnished statement of *facts* is usually the best way of disarming prejudice and silencing opposition. Opposition most commonly arises from prejudice, or from false and exaggerated statements, and such opposition can be best removed, not by angry contention, but by an unvarnished relation of facts. In most cases prejudice will thus be disarmed, and opposition will die away, as was the case in regard to the admission of the Gentiles to the church. ¶ *And expounded* it. Explained it; stated it as it actually occurred. ¶ *In order.* One event after another, as they happened. He thus showed that *his own mind* had been as much biased as theirs, and stated in what manner his prejudices had been removed. It often happens that those who become most zealous and devoted in any new measures for the advancement of religion were as much opposed to them at first as others. They are led from one circumstance to another, until their prejudices die away, and the providence and Spirit of God indicate clearly their duty.

5–14. See ch. x. 9–33.

14. *And all thy house.* Thy family. This is a circumstance which is omitted in the account in ch. x. It is said, however, in ch. x. 2, that Cornelius feared God *with all his house.* It is evident from ch. x. 48 that the family also received the ordinance of baptism, and was received into the church.

15. *And as I began to speak.* Or, while I was speaking. ¶ *The Holy Ghost,* &c. Ch. x. 44.

16. *The word of the Lord.* See Notes on ch. i. 5.

Holy Ghost fell on them, [e]as on
us at the beginning.

16 Then remembered I the word
of the Lord, how that he said,
John[f] indeed baptized with water;
but [g]ye shall be baptized with the
Holy Ghost.

17 Forasmuch then as [h]God gave
them the like gift as *he did* unto
us, who believed on the Lord Jesus
Christ, [i]what was I, that I could
withstand God?

18 When they heard these things
they held their peace, and glorified
God, saying, [k]Then hath God also
to the Gentiles granted repentance
unto life.

19 Now[l] they which were scattered abroad upon the persecution
that arose about Stephen, travelled
as far as Phenice, and Cyprus, and

e ch.2.4. f Mat.3.11; Jn.1.26,33; ch.1.5. g Is.44.3; Joel 2.28. h ch.15.8,9. i Ro.9.21-26. k Ro.10.12,13; 15.9,16. l ch.8.1.

17. *What was I.* What power or right had I to oppose the manifest will of God that the Gentiles should be received into the Christian church. ¶ *Withstand God.* Oppose or resist God. He had indicated his will; he had showed his intention to save the Gentiles; and the prejudices of Peter were all overcome. One of the best means of destroying prejudice and false opinions is a powerful revival of religion. More erroneous doctrines and unholy feelings are overcome in such scenes than in all the bigoted and fierce contentions that have ever taken place. If men wish to root error out of the church, they should strive by all means to promote everywhere revivals of pure and undefiled religion. The Holy Spirit more easily and effectually silences false doctrine, and destroys heresy, than all the denunciations of fierce theologians; all the alarms of heated zealots for orthodoxy; and all the anathemas which professed love for the purity of the church ever utters from the icebergs on which such champions usually seek their repose and their home.

18. *They held their peace.* They were convinced, as Peter had been, by the manifest indications of the will of God. ¶ *Then hath God*, &c. The great truth is in this manner established that the doors of the church are opened to the entire Gentile world—a truth that was worthy of this remarkable interposition. It at once changed the views of the apostles and of the early Christians; gave them new, large, and liberal conceptions of the gospel; broke down their long-cherished prejudices; taught them to look upon all men as their brethren; impressed their hearts with the truth, never after to be eradicated, that the Christian church was founded for the wide world, and that it opened the same glorious pathway to life wherever man might be found, whether with the narrow prejudice of the Jew, or amidst the degradations of the pagan world. To this truth we owe our hopes; for this, we should thank the God of heaven; and, impressed with it, we should seek to invite the entire world to partake with us of the rich provisions of the gospel of the blessed God.

19. *Now they*, &c. This verse introduces a new train of historical remark; and from this point the course of the history of the Acts of the Apostles takes a new direction. Thus far, the history had recorded chiefly the preaching of the gospel to the Jews. From this point the history records the efforts made to convert the Gentiles. It begins with the labours put forth in the important city of Antioch (ver. 19, 20); and as, during the work of grace that occurred in that city, the labours of the apostle Paul were especially sought (ver. 25, 26), the sacred writer thenceforth confines the history mainly to his travels and labours. ¶ *Which were scattered abroad.* See ch. viii. 1. ¶ *As far as Phenice.* Phœnice, or Phœnicia, was a province of Syria, which in its largest sense comprehended a narrow strip of country lying on the eastern coast of the Mediterranean, and extending from Antioch to the borders of Egypt. But Phenice Proper extended only from the cities of Laodicea to Tyre, and included only the territories of Tyre and Sidon. This country was called sometimes simply *Canaan.* See Notes on Mat. xv. 22. ¶ *And Cyprus.* An island off the coast of Asia Minor, in the Mediterranean Sea. See Notes on Ac. iv. 36. ¶ *And Antioch.* There were two cities of this name, one situated in Pisidia in Asia Minor (see ch. xiii. 14); the other, referred to here, was situated on the river Orontes, and was long the capital

Antioch, [m]preaching the word to
none but unto the Jews only.

m Mat.10.6.

20 And some of them were men of
Cyprus and Cyrene, which, when
they were come to Antioch, spake

---

of Syria. It was built by Seleucus Nicanor, and was called Antioch in honour of his father Antiochus. It was founded three hundred and one years before Christ. It is not mentioned in the Old Testament, but is several times mentioned in the Apocrypha and in the New Testament. It was long the most powerful city of the East, and was inferior only to Seleucia and Alexandria. It was famous for the fact that the right of citizenship was conferred by Seleucus on the Jews as well as the Greeks and Macedonians, so that here they had the privilege of worship in their own way without molestation. It is probable that the Christians would be regarded merely as a sect of Jews, and would be here suffered to celebrate their worship without interruption. On this account it may have been that the early Christians regarded this city as of such particular importance, because here they could find a refuge from persecution, and be permitted to worship God without molestation. This city was honoured as a Roman colony, a metropolis, and an asylum. It was large; was almost square; had many gates; was adorned with fine fountains; and was a city of great opulence. It was, however, subject to earthquakes, and was several times nearly destroyed. In the year 588 it experienced an earthquake in which 60,000 persons were destroyed. It was conquered by the Saracens in A.D. 638, and, after some changes and revolutions, was taken during the Crusades, after a long and bloody siege, by Godfrey of Bouillon, June 3, A.D. 1098. In 1268 it was taken by the Sultan of Egypt, who demolished it, and placed it under the dominion of the Turk. Antioch is now called Antakia, and contains about 10,000 inhabitants (Robinson's Calmet). "There was everything in the situation and circumstances of the city," say Conybeare and Howson (*Life and Epistles of St. Paul*, vol. i. p. 121), "to make it a place of concourse for all classes and kinds of people. By its harbour of Seleucia it was in communication with all the trade of the Mediterranean; and, through the open country behind the Lebanon, it was conveniently approached by the caravans from Mesopotamia and Arabia. It united the inland advantages of Aleppo with the maritime opportunities of Smyrna. It was almost an Oriental Rome, in which all the forms of the civilized life of the empire found some representative. Through the first two centuries of the Christian era it was what Constantinople became afterward, 'the Gate of the East.'" "If any city in the first century was worthy to be called the Heathen Queen and Metropolis of the East, that city was Antioch. She was represented, in a famous allegorical statue, as a female figure, seated on a rock and crowned, with the river Orontes at her feet" (Conybeare and Howson, vol. i. p. 125). ¶ *Preaching the word.* The word of God, the gospel. ¶ *To none but unto the Jews only.* They had the common prejudices of the Jews, that the offers of salvation were to be made only to Jews.

20. *Were men of Cyprus and Cyrene.* Were natives of Cyprus and Cyrene. Cyrene was a province and city of Libya in Africa. It is at present called Cairoan, and is situated in the kingdom of Barca. In Cyprus the Greek language was spoken; and from the vicinity of Cyrene to Alexandria, it is probable that the Greek language was spoken there also. From this circumstance it might have happened that they were led more particularly to address the *Grecians* who were in Antioch. It is possible, however, that they might have heard of the vision which Peter saw, and felt themselves called on to preach the gospel to the Gentiles. ¶ *Spake unto the Grecians*—πρὸς τοὺς Ἑλληνιστάς. To the Hellenists. This word usually denotes in the New Testament those Jews residing in foreign lands, who spoke the Greek language. See Notes on ch. vi. 1. But to them the gospel had been already preached; and yet in this place it is evidently the intention of Luke to affirm that the men of Cyprus and Cyrene preached to those who were *not* Jews, and that thus their conduct was distinguished from those (ver. 19) who preached to the Jews only. It is thus manifest that we are here required to understand the *Gentiles* as those who were addressed by the men of Cyprus and Cyrene. In many MSS. the word used here is Ἕλληνας, *Greeks*, instead

unto the [n]Grecians, preaching the Lord Jesus.

21 And[o] the hand of the Lord was with them; and a great number believed, [p]and turned unto the Lord.

22 Then tidings of these things came unto the ears of the church which was in Jerusalem; and they sent forth [q]Barnabas, that he should go as far as Antioch.

23 Who, when he came, and had seen the grace of God, [r]was glad, and [s]exhorted them all, that [t]with purpose [u]of heart they would cleave unto the Lord.

24 For he was a good man, [v]and full of the Holy Ghost, and of faith;

n ch.6.1; 9.29. *o* Lu.1.66. *p* ch.15.19; 1 Th.1.9. *q* ch.9.27. *r* 3 Jn.4. *s* ch.13.43; 14.22. *t* Ps.17.3; 2 Co.1.17. *u* Pr.23.15,26. *v* ch.6.5.

---

of *Hellenists*. This reading has been adopted by Griesbach, and is found in the Syriac, the Arabic, the Vulgate, and in many of the fathers. The Æthiopic version reads "to the Gentiles." There is no doubt that this is the true reading; and that the sacred writer means to say that the gospel was here preached to those who were not Jews, for all were called *Greeks* by them who were not Jews, Ro. i. 16. The connection would lead us to suppose that they had heard of what had been done by Peter, and that, imitating his example, they preached the gospel now to the Gentiles also.

21. *And the hand of the Lord.* See Notes on Lu. i. 66. Comp. Ps. lxxx. 17. The meaning is, that God showed them favour, and evinced his power in the conversion of their hearers.

22. *Then tidings*, &c. The church at Jerusalem heard of this. It was natural that so remarkable an occurrence as the conversion of the Gentiles, and the extraordinary success of the gospel in a splendid and mighty city, should be reported at Jerusalem, and excite deep interest there. ¶ *And they sent forth.* To aid the disciples there, and to give them their sanction. They had done a similar thing in the revival which occurred in Samaria. See Notes on ch. viii. 14. ¶ *Barnabas.* See ch. iv. 36, 37. He was a native of Cyprus, and was probably well acquainted with Antioch. He was, therefore, peculiarly qualified for the work on which they sent him.

23. *Had seen the grace of God.* The *favour*, or *mercy* of God, in converting sinners to himself. ¶ *Was glad.* Approved of what had been done in preaching the gospel to the Gentiles, and rejoiced that God had poured down his Spirit on them. The effect of a revival is to produce joy in the hearts of all those who love the Saviour. ¶ *And exhorted them all.* Entreated them. They would be exposed to many trials and temptations, and he sought to secure their firm adherence to the cause of religion. ¶ *That with purpose of heart.* With a firm mind; with a fixed, settled resolution that they would make this their settled plan of life, their main object. A *purpose*, πρόθεσις, is a resolution of the mind, a plan, or intention, Ro. viii. 28; Ep. i. 11; iii. 11; 2 Ti. i. 9; iii. 10. It is especially a resolution of the mind in regard to future conduct, and the doctrine of Barnabas here was, undoubtedly, that it should be a regular, fixed, determined *plan* or *design* in their minds that they *would* henceforward adhere to God. Such a plan should be formed by all Christians in the beginning of their Christian life, and without such a plan there can be no evidence of piety. We may also remark that such a plan is one of the *heart*. It is not simply of the *understanding*, but is of the entire mind, including the will and affections. It is the leading principle; the strongest affection; the guiding purpose of the *will* to adhere to God, and, unless this is the prevalent, governing desire of the heart, there can be no evidence of conversion. ¶ *That they would cleave.* Greek, that they would *remain;* that is, that they would *adhere* constantly and faithfully attached to the Lord.

24. *For he was a good man.* This is given as a reason why he was so eminently successful. It is not said that he was a man of distinguished talents or learning; that he was a splendid or an imposing preacher; but simply that he was a man of an amiable, kind, and benevolent disposition—a pious, humble man of God. We should not undervalue talent, eloquence, or learning in the ministry, but we may remark that humble piety will often do more in the conversion of souls than the most splendid talents. No endowments can be a substitute for this. The real power of

and [w]much people was added unto the Lord.

25 Then[x] departed Barnabas to Tarsus for to seek Saul:

26 And when he had found him, he brought him unto Antioch. And it came to pass, that a whole year they assembled themselves

w ver.21. x ch.9.27,30.

a minister is concentrated in this, and without this his ministry will be barrenness and a curse. There is nothing on the earth so mighty as *goodness.* If a man wished to make the most of his powers, the true secret would be found in employing them for a good object, and suffering them to be wholly under the direction of benevolence. John Howard's purpose *to do good* has made a more permanent impression on the interests of the world than the talents of Alexander or Cæsar. ¶ *Full of the Holy Ghost.* Was entirely under the influence of the Holy Spirit. This is the *second* qualification here mentioned of a good minister. He was not merely exemplary for mildness and kindness of temper, but he was eminently a man of God. He was filled with the influences of the sacred Spirit, producing zeal, love, peace, joy, &c. See Ga. v. 22, 23. Comp. Notes on Ac. ii. 4. ¶ *And of faith.* Confidence in the truth and promises of God. This is the *third* qualification mentioned; and this was another cause of his success. He confided in God. He depended, not on his own strength, but on the strength of the arm of God. With these qualifications he engaged in his work, and he was successful. These qualifications should be sought by the ministry of the gospel. Others should not indeed be neglected, but a man's ministry will usually be successful only as he seeks to possess those endowments which distinguished Barnabas—a kind, tender, benevolent heart; devoted piety; the fulness of the Spirit's influence; and strong, unwavering confidence in the promises and power of God. ¶ *And much people.* Many people. ¶ *Was added unto the Lord.* Became Christians.

25. *Then departed,* &c. *Why* Barnabas sought Saul is not known. It is probable, however, that it was owing to the remarkable success which he had in Antioch. There was a great revival of religion, and there was need of additional labour. In such times the ministers of the gospel need additional help, as men in harvest-time need the aid of others. Saul was in this vicinity (ch. ix. 30), and he was eminently fitted to assist in this work. With him Barnabas was well acquainted (Ac. ix. 27), and probably there was no other one in that vicinity whose help he could obtain. ¶ *To Tarsus.* See Notes on Ac. ix. 11.

26. *That a whole year.* Antioch was a city exceedingly important in its numbers, wealth, and influence. It was for this reason, probably, that they spent so long a time there, instead of travelling in other places. The attention of the apostles was early and chiefly directed to *cities,* as being places of influence and centres of power. Thus Paul passed three years in the city of Ephesus, Ac. xx. 31. And thus he continued a year and a half at Corinth, Ac. xviii. 11. It may be added that the first churches were founded in cities; and the most remarkable success attended the preaching of the gospel in large towns. ¶ *They assembled themselves,* &c. They came together for worship. ¶ *With the church.* Margin, *in* the church. The Greek (ἐν) will bear this construction; but there is no instance in the New Testament where the word *church* refers to the *edifice* in which a congregation worships. It evidently here means that Barnabas and Saul convened *with* the Christian assembly at proper times, through the space of a year, for the purposes of public worship. ¶ *And the disciples were called Christians,* &c. As this became the distinguishing name of the followers of Christ, it was worthy of record. The name was evidently given because they were the followers of *Christ.* But by whom, or with what views it was given, is not certainly known. Whether it was given by their enemies in *derision,* as the names *Puritan, Quaker, Methodist,* &c., have been; or whether the disciples assumed it themselves, or whether it was given by divine intimation, has been a matter of debate. That it was given in derision is not probable, for in the name *Christian* there was nothing dishonourable. To be the professed friends of *the Messiah,* or *the Christ,* was not with Jews a matter of reproach, for they *all* professed to be the friends of the Messiah. The cause of reproach with the disciples was that they regarded *Jesus of Nazar-*

with[1] the church, [y]and taught much people. And the disciples were called Christians first in Antioch.

[1] or, *in*. *y* Mat.28.19.

27 And in these days [z]came prophets from Jerusalem unto Antioch.

z ch.2.17; 13.1; Ep.4.11.

---

eth as the Messiah; and hence, when their enemies wished to speak of them with contempt, they would speak of them as *Galileans* (Ac. ii. 7), or as *Nazarenes* (Ac. xxiv. 5), "And a ringleader of the sect *of the Nazarenes.*" It is possible that the name might have been given to them as a mere *appellation*, without intending to convey by it any reproach. The *Gentiles* would probably use this name to distinguish them, and it might have become thus the common appellation. It is evident from the New Testament, I think, that it was not designed as a term of reproach. It occurs but twice elsewhere: Ac. xxvi. 28, "Agrippa said unto Paul, Almost thou persuadest me to be *a Christian;*" 1 Pe. iv. 16, "Yet if any man suffer as *a Christian*, let him not be ashamed." No certain argument can be drawn in regard to the source of the name from the word which is used here. The word used here, and translated *were called*—χρηματίζω—means, (1) To transact any business; to be employed in accomplishing anything, &c. This is its usual signification in the Greek writers. (2) To be divinely admonished, to be instructed by a divine communication, &c., Mat. ii. 12; Lu. ii. 26; Ac. x. 22; He. viii. 5; xi. 7; xii. 25. (3) To be named, or called, in any way, without a divine communication, Ro. vii. 3, "She shall be *called* an adulteress." It cannot be denied, however, that the most usual signification in the New Testament is that of a *divine monition*, or *communication;* and it is certainly *possible* that the name was given by Barnabas and Saul. I incline to the opinion, however, that it was given to them by the Gentiles who were there, simply as an appellation, without intending it as a name of reproach; and that it was readily assumed by the disciples as a name that would fitly designate them. If it had been assumed by them, or if Barnabas and Saul had conferred the name, the record would probably have been to this effect; not simply that they "*were called,*" but that they took this name, or that it was given by the apostles. It is, however, of little consequence whence the name originated. It soon became a name of reproach, and has usually been in all ages since, by the wicked, the gay, the licentious, and the ungodly. It is, however, an honoured name—the *most* honourable appellation that can be conferred on a mortal. It suggests at once to a Christian the name of his great Redeemer; the idea of our intimate relation to him; and the thought that we receive him as our chosen Leader, the source of our blessings, the author of our salvation, the fountain of our joys. It is the *distinguishing* name of all the redeemed. It is not that we belong to this or that denomination; it is not that our names are connected with high and illustrious ancestors; it is not that they are recorded in the books of heraldry; it is not that they stand high in courts, and among the gay, the fashionable, and the rich, that true honour is conferred on men. These are not the things that give *distinction* and *peculiarity* to the followers of the Redeemer. It is that they are *Christians*. This is their peculiar name; by this they are known; this at once suggests their character, their feelings, their doctrines, their hopes, their joys. This binds them all together—a name which rises above every other appellation; which unites in one the inhabitants of distant nations and tribes of men; which connects the extremes of society, and places them in most important respects on a common level; and which is a bond to unite in one family all those who love the Lord Jesus, though dwelling in different climes, speaking different languages, engaged in different pursuits of life, and occupying distant graves at death. He who lives according to the import of this name is the most blessed and eminent of mortals. This name shall be had in remembrance when the names of royalty shall be remembered no more, and when the appellations of nobility shall cease to amuse or to dazzle the world.

27. *And in those days.* While Barnabas and Saul were at Antioch. ¶ *Came prophets.* The word prophet denotes properly one who foretells future events. See Notes on Mat. vii. 15. It is sometimes used in the New Testament to denote simply *religious teachers, instruct-*

28 And there stood up one of
them, named [a]Agabus, and signified by the Spirit that there should
be great dearth throughout all the
world; which came to pass in the
days of Claudius Cæsar.
29 Then the disciples, every

a ch.21.10.

---

ors sent from God, without particular reference to future events. To teach the people in the doctrines of religion was a part of the prophetic office, and this idea was only sometimes denoted by the use of the word. See Ro. xii. 6; 1 Co. xii. 10, 28; xiii. 2, 8; xiv. 3, 5, 24. These *prophets* seem to have been endowed in a remarkable manner with the knowledge of future events; with the power of explaining mysteries; and in some cases with the power of speaking foreign languages. In this case, it seems that one of them at least had the power of foretelling future events.

28. *Named Agabus.* This man is mentioned but in one other place in the New Testament. In Ac. xxi. 10, 11, he is referred to as having foretold that Paul would be delivered into the hands of the Gentiles. It is not expressly said that he was a Christian, but the connection seems to imply that he was. ¶ *And signified.* See Jn. xii. 33. The word usually denotes *to indicate by signs*, or with a degree of obscurity and uncertainty, not to declare in explicit language. But here it seems to denote simply to foretell, to predict. ¶ *By the Spirit.* Under the influence of the Spirit. He was inspired. ¶ *A great dearth.* A great famine. ¶ *Throughout all the world.* The word here used (οἰκουμένην) usually denotes the inhabitable world, the parts of the earth which are cultivated and occupied. It is sometimes used, however, to denote an *entire land* or *country*, in contradistinction from *the parts* of it: thus, to denote *the whole* of the land of Palestine in distinction from its parts; or to denote that an event would have reference to *all* the land, and not be confined to one or more parts, as Galilee, Samaria, &c. See Notes on Lu. ii. 1. The meaning of this prophecy evidently is, that the famine would be extensive; that it would not be confined to a single province or region, but that it would extend so far as that it might be called *general*. In fact, though the famine was particularly severe in Judea, it extended much farther. This prediction was uttered not long after the conversion of Saul, and probably, therefore, about the year A.D. 38 or A.D. 40. Dr. Lardner has attempted to show that the prophecy had reference *only* to the land of Judea, though in fact there were famines in other places (Lardner's *Works*, vol. i. p. 253, 254, edit. London, 1829). ¶ *Which came to pass*, &c. This is one of the few instances in which the sacred writers in the New Testament affirm the fulfilment of a prophecy. The history having been written after the event, it was natural to give a passing notice of the fulfilment. ¶ *In the days of Claudius Cæsar.* The Roman emperor. He began his reign A.D. 41, and reigned thirteen years. He was at last poisoned by one of his wives, Agrippina, who wished to raise her son Nero to the throne. During his reign no less than *four* different famines are mentioned by ancient writers, one of which was particularly severe in Judea, and was the one, doubtless, to which the sacred writer here refers. (1) The first happened at Rome, and occurred in the first or second year of the reign of Claudius. It arose from the difficulties of importing provisions from abroad. It is mentioned by Dio, whose words are these: "There being a great famine, he (Claudius) not only took care for a present supply, but provided also for the time to come." He then proceeds to state the great expense which Claudius was at in making a good port at the mouth of the Tiber, and a convenient passage from thence up to the city (Dio, lib. lx. p. 671, 672; see also Suetonius, Claudius, cap. 20). (2) A second famine is mentioned as having been particularly severe in Greece. Of this famine Eusebius speaks in his *Chronicon*, p. 204: "There was a great famine in Greece, in which a modius of wheat (about half a bushel) was sold for six drachms." This famine is said by Eusebius to have occurred in the ninth year of the reign of Claudius. (3) In the latter part of his reign, A.D. 51, there was another famine at Rome, mentioned by Suetonius (Claud., cap. 18), and by Tacitus (*Ann.*, xii. 43). Of this Tacitus says that it was so severe that it was deemed to be a divine judgment. (4) A *fourth* famine is mentioned as having occurred particularly in Judea. This is described by Josephus

man according to his ability, determined to [b]send relief unto the brethren which dwelt in Judea:

30 Which also they did, [c]and sent it to the elders by the hands of Barnabas and Saul.

b Ro.15.26; 1 Co.16.1; 2 Co.9.1,2. c ch.12.25.

CHAPTER XII.

NOW about that time, Herod the king [1]stretched forth *his* hands to vex certain of the church.

1 or, *began*.

(*Antiq.*, b. xx. ch. 2, § 5). "A famine," says he, "did oppress them at the time (in the time of Claudius); and many people died for the want of what was necessary to procure food withal. Queen Helena sent some of her servants to Alexandria with money to buy a great quantity of corn, and others of them to Cyprus to bring a cargo of dried figs." This famine is described as having continued under the two procurators of Judea, Tiberius Alexander and Cassius Fadus. Fadus was sent into Judea, on the death of Agrippa, about the fourth year of the reign of Claudius, and the famine, therefore, continued probably during the fifth, sixth, and seventh years of the reign of Claudius. See Note in Whiston's Josephus, *Antiq.*, b. xx. ch. 2, § 5; also Lardner as quoted above. Of this famine, or of the want consequent on the famine, repeated mention is made in the New Testament.

29. *Then the disciples.* The Christians at Antioch. ¶ *According to his ability.* According as they had prospered. It does not imply that they were rich, but that they rendered such aid as they could afford. ¶ *Determined to send relief.* This arose not merely from their general sense of obligation to aid the poor, but they felt themselves particularly bound to assist their Jewish brethren. The obligation to relieve the *temporal* wants of those from whom important spiritual mercies are received is repeatedly enforced in the New Testament. Comp. Ro. xv. 25-27; 1 Co. xvi. 1, 2; 2 Cor. ix. 1, 2; Ga. ii. 10.

30. *Sent it to the elders.* Greek, to the presbyters. This is the first mention which we have in the New Testament of *elders*, or *presbyters*, in the Christian church. The word literally denotes *aged men*, but in the Jewish synagogue it was a name of office merely. It is clear, however, I think, that the elders of the Jewish synagogue here are not included, for the relief was intended for the "brethren" (ver. 29); that is, the Christians who were at Jerusalem, and it is not probable that a charity like this would have been intrusted to the hands of Jewish elders. The connection here does not enable us to determine anything about the sense in which the word was used. I think it probable that it does not refer to *officers* in the church, but that it means simply that the charity was intrusted to the *aged*, prudent, and experienced men in the church, for distribution among the members. Calvin supposes that the apostles were particularly intended. But this is not probable. It is possible that the *deacons*, who were probably aged men, may be here particularly referred to, but it seems more probable that the charity was sent to the aged members of the church without respect to their office, to be distributed according to their discretion.

CHAPTER XII.

1. *Now about that time.* That is, during the time that the famine existed, or the time when Barnabas and Saul went up to Jerusalem. This was probably about the fifth or sixth year of the reign of Claudius, not far from A.D. 47. ¶ *Herod the king.* This was Herod Agrippa. The Syriac so renders it expressly, and the chronology requires us so to understand it. He was a grandson of Herod the Great, and one of the sons of Aristobulus, whom Herod put to death (Josephus, *Antiq.*, b. xviii. 5). Herod the Great left three sons, between whom his kingdom was divided—Archelaus, Philip, and Antipas. See Notes on Mat. ii. 19. To Philip was left Iturea and Trachonitis. See Lu. iii. 1. To Antipas, Galilee and Perea; and to Archelaus, Judea, Idumea, and Samaria. Archelaus, being accused of cruelty, was banished by Augustus to Vienna in Gaul, and Judea was reduced to a province, and united with Syria. When Philip died, this region was granted by the Emperor Caligula to Herod Agrippa. Herod Antipas was driven as an exile also into Gaul, and then into Spain, and Herod Agrippa received also *his* tetrarchy. In the reign of Claudius also, the dominions of Herod Agrippa were still farther enlarged. When Caligula

2 And he killed [a]James, the
brother of John, with the sword.
3 And because he saw it [b]pleased
the Jews, he proceeded further to
take [c]Peter also. (Then were the
[d]days of unleavened bread.)
4 And when he had apprehended
him, he put *him* in prison, and

a Mat.4.21; 20.23. b ch.24.27. c Jn.21.18. d Ex.12.14,15.

---

was slain, he was at Rome, and having ingratiated himself into the favour of Claudius, he conferred on him also Judea and Samaria, so that his dominions were equal in extent to those of his grandfather, Herod the Great. See Josephus, *Antiq.*, b. xix. ch. 5, § 1. ¶ *Stretched forth* his *hands.* A figurative expression, denoting that he laid his hands on them, or that he endeavoured violently to oppress the church. ¶ *To vex.* To injure, to do *evil to—κακῶσαί.* ¶ *Certain.* Some of the church. Who they were the writer immediately specifies.

2. *And he killed*, &c. He caused to be put to death with a sword, either by beheading, or piercing him through. The Roman procurators were intrusted with authority over life, though in the time of Pilate the Jews had not this authority. ¶ *James, the brother of John.* This was the son of Zebedee, Mat. iv. 21. He is commonly called James the Greater, in contradistinction from James, the son of Alpheus, who is called James the Less, Mat. x. 3. In this manner were the predictions of our Saviour respecting him fulfilled, Mat. xx. 23, "Ye shall indeed drink of my cup, and be baptized with the baptism that I am baptized with."

3. *And because he saw that it pleased the Jews.* This was the principle on which he acted. It was not from a sense of right; it was not to do justice, and to protect the innocent; it was not to discharge the appropriate duties of a magistrate and a king, but it was to promote his own popularity. It is probable that Agrippa would have acted in this way in any circumstances. He was ambitious, vain, and fawning; he sought, as his great principle, popularity, and he was willing to sacrifice, like many others, truth and justice to obtain this end. But there was also a particular reason for this in his case. He held his appointment under the Roman emperor. This foreign rule was always unpopular among the Jews. In order, therefore, to secure a peaceful reign, and to prevent insurrection and tumult, it was necessary for him to court their favour; to indulge their wishes, and to fall in with their prejudices. Alas! how many monarchs and rulers there have been who were governed by no better principle, and whose sole aim has been to secure popularity, even at the expense of law, truth, and justice. That this was the character of Herod is attested by Josephus (*Antiq.*, xix. ch. 8, § 3): "This king (Herod Agrippa) was by nature very beneficent, and liberal in his gifts, *and very ambitious to please the people* with such large donations; and he made himself very illustrious by the many expensive presents he made them. He took delight in giving, and rejoiced in living *with good reputation.*" ¶ *To take Peter also.* Peter was one of the most conspicuous men in the church. He had made himself particularly obnoxious by his severe and pungent discourses, and by his success in winning men to Christ. It was natural, therefore, that he should be the next object of attack. ¶ *The days of unleavened bread.* The Passover, or the seven days immediately succeeding the Passover, during which the Jews were required to eat bread without leaven, Ex. xii. 15–18. It was some time during this period that Herod chose to apprehend Peter. *Why* this time was selected is not known. As it was, however, a season of religious solemnity, and as Herod was desirous of showing his attachment to the *religious* rites of the nation (Jos. *Antiq.*, xix. 7, 3), it is probable that he chose *this* period to show to them more impressively his purpose to oppose all false religions, and to maintain the existing establishments of the nation.

4. *And when he had apprehended him.* When he had *taken* or *arrested* him. ¶ *He put* him *in prison.* During the solemnities of this religious festival, it would have been deemed improper to have engaged in the trial of a supposed criminal. The minds of the people were expected to be devoted solely to the services of religion; and hence Herod chose to retain him in custody until the Passover had ended. ¶ *To four quaternions of soldiers.* A *quaternion* was a company of *four;* consequently the whole number employed here was sixteen. The Romans divided the night

delivered *him* to four quaternions of soldiers, to keep him; intending after Easter to bring him forth to the people.

5 Peter therefore was kept in prison; but [2]prayer was made without ceasing of the church unto God for him.

6 And when Herod would have brought him forth, the same night Peter was sleeping between two soldiers, bound with two chains; and the keepers before the door kept the prison.

2 or, *instant and earnest prayer was made,* 2 Co. 1.11; Ep.6.18,19; 1 Th.5.17; Ja.5.16.

---

into four watches so that the guards could be relieved; those who were on guard occupying three hours, and being then relieved. Of the *four* who were on guard, two were with Peter in the prison (ver. 6), and two kept watch before the door of the prison. The utmost precaution was taken that he should not escape; and Herod thus gave the most ample assurance to the Jews of his intention to secure Peter, and to bring him to trial. ¶ *Intending after Easter.* There never was a more absurd or unhappy translation than this. The original is simply *after the Passover* (μετὰ τὸ πάσχα). The word *Easter* now denotes the festival observed by many Christian churches in honour of the resurrection of the Saviour. But the original has no reference to that, nor is there the slightest evidence that any such festival was observed at the time when this book was written. The translation is not only unhappy, as it does not convey at all the meaning of the original, but because it may contribute to foster an opinion that such a festival was observed in the time of the apostles. The word *Easter* is of Saxon origin, and is supposed to be derived from *Eostre*, the goddess of Love, or the Venus of the North, in honour of whom a festival was celebrated by our pagan ancestors in the month of April (Webster). As this festival coincided with the Passover of the Jews, and with the feast observed by Christians in honour of the resurrection of Christ, the name came to be used to denote the latter. In the old Anglo-Saxon service-books the term *Easter* is used frequently to translate the word Passover. In the translation by Wickliffe, the word *paske*, that is, *passover*, is used. But Tindal and Coverdale used the word *Easter*, and hence it has very improperly crept into our translation. ¶ *To bring him forth to the people.* That is, evidently, to put him publicly to death to gratify them. The providence of God in regard to Peter is thus remarkable. Instead of his being put suddenly to death, as was James, he was reserved for *future* trial; and thus an opportunity was given for the prayers of the church, and for his consequent release.

5. *But prayer was made.* The church was apprised of his imprisonment and danger, and had no resource but to apply to God by prayer. In scenes of danger there is no other refuge; and the result shows that even in most discouraging circumstances God can hear prayer. Nothing scarcely could appear more hopeless than the idea of rescuing Peter out of the hands of Herod, and out of the prison, and out of the custody of sixteen men, by prayer. But the prayer of faith was prevalent with God. ¶ *Without ceasing.* Intense, steady, ardent prayer. The word here used (ἐκτενὴς) is found in but one other place in the New Testament, 1 Pe. iv. 8, "Have *fervent* charity among yourselves." The word has rather the idea that their prayer was *earnest* and *fervent* than that it was *constant.* ¶ *Of the church.* By the church.

6. *And when Herod would have brought him forth.* When he was about to bring him to be put to death. ¶ *The same night.* That is, the night *preceding.* The intention of Herod was to bring him out as soon as the Passover was over; but during the night which immediately *preceded* the day in which he intended to bring him to punishment, Peter was rescued. ¶ *Peter was sleeping.* Here is an instance of remarkable composure, and an illustration of the effects of peace of conscience and of confidence in God. It was doubtless known to Peter what the intention of Herod was. James had just been put to death, and Peter had no reason to expect a better fate. And yet in this state he slept as quietly as if there had been no danger, and it was necessary that he should be roused even by an *angel* to contemplate his condition and to make his escape. There is nothing that will give quiet rest and gentle sleep so certainly as a conscience void of offence; and in the midst of

7 And, behold, [e]the angel of
the Lord came upon *him*, and a
light shined in the prison; and he
smote Peter on the side, and raised
him up, saying, Arise up quickly.
And[f] his chains fell off from *his*
hands.
8 And the angel said unto him,
Gird thyself, and bind on thy sandals: and so he did. And he saith
unto him, Cast thy garment about
thee, and follow me.
9 And he went out, and followed
him; [g]and wist not that it was
true which was done by the angel;
but [h]thought he saw a vision.
10 When they were past the first
and the second ward, they came
unto the iron gate that leadeth
unto the city, which opened to

e Ps.37.32,33; ch.5.19. f ch.16.26. g Ps.126.1. h ch.10.3,17.

imminent dangers, he who confides in God may rest securely and calmly. Comp. Ps. iii. 5; iv. 8. ¶ *Between two soldiers.* See Notes on ver. 4. Peter was bound to the two. His left hand was chained to the right hand of one of the soldiers, and his right hand to the left hand of the other. This was a common mode of securing prisoners among the Romans. See abundant authorities for this quoted in Lardner's *Credibility*, part i. ch. x. § 9, Lond. edit. 1829, vol. i. p. 242, 243, &c. ¶ *And the keeper*, &c. See ver. 4. Two soldiers were stationed at the door. We may see now that every possible precaution was used to ensure the safe custody of Peter. (1) He was in prison. (2) He was under the charge of sixteen men, who could relieve each other when weary, and thus every security was given that he could not escape by inattention on their part. (3) He was bound fast between two men. And (4) He was further guarded by two others, whose business it was to watch the door of the prison. It is to be remembered, also, that it was death for a Roman soldier to be found sleeping at his post. But God can deliver in spite of all the precautions of men; and it is easy for him to overcome the most cunning devices of his enemies.

7. *And, behold, the angel of the Lord.* See Notes on ch. v. 19. ¶ *Came upon him.* Greek, was present with him; stood near him (ἐπέστη). ¶ *And a light shined in the prison.* Many have supposed that this was lightning. But *light*, and *splendour*, and *shining apparel* are commonly represented as the accompaniments of the heavenly beings when they visit the earth, Lu. ii. 9; xxiv. 4; comp. Mar. ix. 3. It is highly probable that this light was discerned only by Peter; and it would be to him an undoubted proof of the divine interposition in his behalf. ¶ *And he smote Peter on the side.* This was, doubtless, a gentle blow or stroke to arouse him from sleep. ¶ *And his chains*, &c. This could have been only by divine power. No natural means were used, or could have been used without arousing the guard. It is a sublime expression of the *ease* with which God can deliver from danger, and rescue his friends. Comp. ch. xvi. 26.

8. *Gird thyself.* When they slept the outer garment was thrown off, and the *girdle* with which they bound their inner garment, or tunic, was loosed. He was directed now to gird up that inner garment as they usually wore it; that is, to *dress himself*, and prepare to follow him. ¶ *Bind on thy sandals.* Put on thy sandals; prepare to walk. See Notes on Mat. iii. 11. ¶ *Cast thy garment about thee.* The *outer* garment, that was thrown loosely around the shoulders. It was nearly square, and was laid aside when they slept, or worked, or ran. The direction was that he should dress himself in his usual apparel. See Notes on Mat. v. 38–42.

9. *And wist not.* Knew not. ¶ *That it was true.* That it was real. ¶ *But thought he saw a vision.* He supposed that it was a representation made to his mind similar to that which he had seen before. Comp. ch. x. 11, 12. It was so astonishing, so unexpected, so wonderful, that he could not realize that it was true.

10. *The first and second ward.* The word which is here rendered *ward* (φυλακήν) properly denotes the act of guarding; but it is most commonly used to denote a prison, or place of confinement. In this place it seems to denote the *guard* itself—the soldiers stationed at intervals in the entrance into the prison. These were passed silently, probably a deep sleep having been sent on them to facilitate the escape of Peter. ¶ *The iron gate.* The outer gate, secured

them of his own accord : and they
went out, and passed on through
one street; and forthwith the angel
departed from him.
11 And when Peter was come
to himself, he said, Now I know
of a surety that the Lord hath [i]sent
his angel, and [k]hath delivered me
out of the hand of Herod, and *from*
all the expectation of the people of
the Jews.
12 And when he had considered
the thing, he came to the house of
Mary, the mother of John, whose
surname was Mark; where [l]many
were gathered together, praying.
13 And as Peter knocked at the
door of the gate, a damsel came [3]to
hearken, named Rhoda.

i 2 Ch.16.9; Ps.34.7; Da.3.28; 6.22; He.1.14.
k Ps.33.18,19; 97.10; 2 Co.1.10; 2 Pe.2.9.

l ver.5. 3 or, *to ask who was there.*

---

with iron, as the doors of prisons are now. ¶ *That leadeth unto the city.* Or rather *into* (εἰς) the city. The precise situation of the prison is unknown. It is supposed by some (comp. Lightfoot on this place) that the prison was *between* two walls of the city, and that the *entrance* to the prison was immediately from the inner wall, so that the gate opened directly into the city. ¶ *Of his own accord.* Itself. It opened spontaneously, without the application of any force or key, thus showing conclusively that Peter was delivered by miraculous interposition. ¶ *And passed on through one street.* Till Peter was entirely safe from any danger of pursuit, and then the angel left him. God had effected his complete rescue, and now left him to his own efforts as usual.

11. *And when Peter was come to himself.* This expression naturally means, when he had overcome his amazement and astonishment at the unexpected deliverance, so as to be capable of reflection. He had been amazed by the whole transaction. He thought it was a vision; and in the suddenness and rapidity with which it was done, he had no time for cool reflection. The events of divine providence often overwhelm and confound us; and such are their suddenness, and rapidity, and unexpected character in their development as to prevent calm and collected reflection. ¶ *Of a surety.* Certainly, surely. He considered all the circumstances; he saw that he was actually at liberty, and he was satisfied that it could have been effected only by divine interposition. ¶ *The expectation of the people.* From this it appears that the people earnestly desired his death; and it was to gratify that desire that Herod had imprisoned him.

12. *And when he had considered,* &c. Thinking on the subject; considering what he should do in these circumstances. ¶ *He came to the house of Mary,* &c. Probably this house was near him; and he would naturally seek the dwelling of a Christian friend. ¶ *The mother of John,* &c. Probably this was the John *Mark* who wrote the gospel. But this is not certain. ¶ *Whose surname.* Greek, who was *called* Mark. It does not mean that he had two names conferred, as with us, *both* of which were used at the same time, but he was called by either, the Greeks probably using the name *Mark*, and the Jews the name *John*. He is frequently mentioned afterward as having been the attendant of Paul and Barnabas in their travels, ver. 25; xv. 39; 2 Ti. iv. 11. He was a nephew of Barnabas, Col. iv. 10. ¶ *Where many were gathered together, praying.* This was in the *night*, and it shows the propriety of observing extraordinary seasons of prayer, even in the night. Peter was to have been put to death the next day; and they assembled to pray for his release, and did not intermit their prayers. When dangers increase around us and our friends, we should become more fervent in prayer. While life remains we may pray; and even when there is no human hope, and we have no power to heal or deliver, still God may interpose, as he did here, in answer to prayer.

13. *At the door of the gate.* Rather the door of the *vestibule*, or principal entrance into the house. The house was entered through such a *porch* or *vestibule*, and it was the *door* opening into this which is here intended. See Notes on Mat. ix. 2. ¶ *A damsel.* A girl. ¶ *Came to hearken.* To hear who was there. ¶ *Named Rhoda.* This is a Greek name signifying *a rose*. It was not unusual for the Hebrews to give the names of flowers, &c., to their daughters. Thus *Susanna*, a lily; *Hadessa*, a myrtle; *Tamar*, a palm-tree, &c. (Grotius).

14. *She opened not the gate.* At this time of night, and in these circum-

14 And when she knew Peter's
voice, she opened not the gate for
gladness, but ran in, and told how
Peter stood before the gate.
15 And they said unto her, Thou
art mad. But she constantly affirmed
that it was even so. Then
said they, It is [m]his angel.
16 But Peter continued knocking:
and when they had opened
the door, and saw him, they were
astonished.
17 But he, [n]beckoning unto them
with the hand to hold their peace,
[o]declared unto them how the Lord
had brought him out of the prison.
And he said, Go, show these things
unto James, and to the brethren.

m Mat.18.10. *n* ch.13.16. *o* Ps.66.16.

---

stances, the door would be fastened. Christians were doubtless alarmed by the death of James and the imprisonment of Peter, and they would take all possible precautions for their own safety. ¶ *For gladness.* In her joy she hastened to inform those who were assembled of the safety of Peter.

15. *Thou art mad.* Thou art insane. They seemed to have regarded his rescue as so difficult and so hopeless, that they deemed it proof of derangement that she now affirmed it. And yet this was the very thing for which they had been so earnestly praying. When it was now announced to them that the object of their prayers was granted, they deemed the messenger that announced it insane. Christians are often surprised even when their prayers are answered. They are overwhelmed and amazed at the success of their own petitions, and are slow to believe that the very thing for which they have sought could be granted. It shows, perhaps, with how *little faith*, after all, they pray, and how slow they are to believe that God can hear and answer prayer. In a revival of religion in answer to prayer, Christians are often overwhelmed and astonished when even their own petitions are granted, and when God manifests his own power in his own way and time. Prayer should be persevered in, and we should place ourselves in a waiting posture to catch the first indications that God has heard us. ¶ *But she constantly affirmed it.* She insisted on it. How much better it would have been to have hastened at once to the gate, than thus to have engaged in a controversy on the subject. Peter was suffered to remain knocking while they debated the matter. Christians are often engaged in some unprofitable controversy when they should hasten to catch the first tokens of divine favour, and open their arms to welcome the proofs that God has heard their prayers. ¶ *Then said they.* Still resolved not to be convinced. ¶ *It is his angel.* Any way of accounting for it rather than to admit the simple fact, or to ascertain the simple truth. All this was caused by the *little hope* which they had of his release, and their earnest desire that it should be so. It was just such a state of mind as is indicated when we say, "The news is too good to be believed." The expression *It is his angel* may mean that they supposed that the *tutelary guardian*, or angel appointed to attend Peter, had come to announce something respecting him, and that he had assumed the voice and form of Peter in order to make them certain that he came from him. This notion arose from the common belief of the Jews that each individual had assigned to him, at birth, a celestial spirit, whose office it was to guard and defend him through life. See Notes on Mat. xviii. 10. That the Jews entertained this opinion is clear from their writings. See Kuinoel. Lightfoot thinks that they who were assembled supposed that the angel had assumed the voice and manner of Peter in order to intimate to them that he was about to die, and to excite them to earnest prayer that he might die with constancy and firmness. Whatever their opinions were, however, it *proves* nothing on these points. There is no evidence that they were inspired in these opinions, nor are their notions countenanced by the Scriptures. They were the mere common traditions of the Jews, and prove nothing in regard to the truth of the opinion one way or the other.

16. *Were astonished.* They were now convinced that it was Peter, and they were amazed that he had been rescued. As yet they were of course ignorant of the manner in which it was done.

17. *But he, beckoning,* &c. To prevent the noise, and tumult, and transport which was likely to be produced. His

And he departed, and went into
another place.
18 Now as soon as it was day,
there was no small stir among the
soldiers, what was become of Peter.
19 And when Herod had sought
for him, and found him not, he
examined the keepers, and commanded that *they* should be put
to death. And he went down
from Judea to Cesarea, and *there*
abode.
20 And Herod [4]was highly displeased with them of Tyre and
Sidon; but they came with one

[4] or, *bare an hostile mind, intending war.*

---

wish was, not that there should be clamorous joy, but that they should listen in silence to what God had done. It was sufficient to awe the soul, and produce deep, grateful feeling. A noise might excite the neighbouring Jews, and produce danger. Religion is calm and peaceful; and its great scenes and surprising deliverances are rather fitted to awe the soul, to produce calm, sober, and grateful contemplation, than the noise of rejoicing, and the shoutings of exultation. The consciousness of the presence of God, and of his mighty power, does not produce rapturous disorder and tumult, but holy, solemn, calm, grateful emotion. ¶ *Go, show these things*, &c. Acquaint them that their prayer is heard, and that they may rejoice also at the mercy of God. ¶ *Unto James.* James, the son of Alpheus, commonly called the Less. See Notes on ver. 2; Ac. i. 13; Mat. x. 2. ¶ *And to the brethren.* Particularly to the other apostles. ¶ *And went into another place.* Probably a place of greater safety. Where he went is not known. The Papists pretend that he went to Rome. But of this there is no evidence. He is mentioned as in Jerusalem again in ch. xv. The meaning is evidently that he went into some place of retirement till the danger was past.

18. *No small stir.* Amazement that he had escaped, and apprehension of the consequences. The punishment which they had reason to expect, for having suffered his escape, was death.

19. *He examined the keepers.* The soldiers who were intrusted with his custody. Probably only those who had the special care of him at that watch of the night. The word *examine* here means to inquire diligently, to make investigation. He subjected them to a rigid scrutiny to ascertain the manner of his escape; for it is evident that Herod did not mean to admit the possibility of a miraculous interposition. ¶ *Should be put to death.* For having failed to keep Peter. This punishment they had a right to expect for having suffered his escape. ¶ *And he went down*, &c. How soon after the escape of Peter he went down to Cesarea, or how long he abode there, is not known. Cesarea was rising into magnificence, and the Roman governors made it often their abode. See Notes on Ac. viii. 40. Comp. Ac. xxv. 1, 4. This journey of Herod is related by Josephus (*Antiq.*, b. xix. ch. viii. § 2). He says that it was after he had reigned over all Judea three years. ¶ *And* there *abode.* That is, till his death, which occurred shortly after. We do not learn that he made any further inquiry after Peter, or that he attempted any further persecutions of the Christians. The men on guard were undoubtedly put to death; and thus Herod used all his power to create the impression that Peter had escaped by their negligence; and this would undoubtedly be believed by the Jews. See Mat. xxviii. 15. He might *himself*, perhaps, have been convinced, however, that the escape was by miracle, and afraid to attempt any further persecutions; or the affairs of his government might have called off his attention to other things; and thus, as in the case of the "persecution that arose about Stephen," the political changes and dangers might divert the attention from putting Christians to death. See Notes on ch. ix. 31. Thus, by the providence of God, *this* persecution, that had been commenced, not by popular tumult, but by royal authority and power, and that was aimed at the very pillars of the church, ceased. The prayers of the church prevailed; and the monarch was overcome, disappointed, humbled, and, by divine judgment, soon put to death.

20. *And Herod was highly displeased*, &c. Greek, *bare an hostile mind, intending war.* See the margin. The Greek word (θυμομαχῶν) does not occur elsewhere in the New Testament. It means to meditate war; to purpose war in the mind; or here, probably, to be

accord to him, and, having made Blastus, [5]the king's chamberlain, their friend, desired peace; because their[p] country was nourished by the king's *country*.

21 And upon a set day, Herod, arrayed in royal apparel, sat upon his throne, and made an oration unto them.

22 And the people gave a shout,

[5] *that was over the king's bed-chamber.* p Eze.27.17.

enraged or *angry* at them. What was the cause of this hostility to the people of Tyre and Sidon is not mentioned, and conjecture is useless. It is not at all inconsistent, however, with the well-known character of Herod. It was probably from some cause relating to commerce. Tyre and Sidon were under the Roman power, and had some shadow of liberty (Grotius), and it is probable that they might have embarrassed Herod in some of his regulations respecting commerce. ¶ *Tyre and Sidon.* See Notes on Mat. xi. 21. They were *north* of Cesarea. ¶ *They came with one accord.* Fearing the effects of his anger, they united in sending an embassage to him to make peace. ¶ *Blastus, the king's chamberlain.* See Ro. xvi. 23. The word *chamberlain* denotes an officer who is charged with the direction and management of a chamber or chambers, particularly a bed-chamber. It denotes here a man who had charge of the bed-chamber of Herod. ¶ *Because their country was nourished*, &c. Was supplied by the territories of Herod. The country of Tyre and Sidon included a narrow strip of land on the coast of the Mediterranean. Of course they were dependent for provisions, and for articles of commerce, on the interior country; but this belonged to the kingdom of Herod; and as they were entirely dependent on his country, as he had power to dry up the sources of their support and commerce, they were the more urgent to secure his favour.

21. *And upon a set day.* An *appointed, public* day. This was the second day of the sports and games which Herod celebrated in Cesarea in honour of Claudius Cæsar. Josephus has given an account of this occurrence, which coincides remarkably with the narrative here. The account is contained in his *Antiquities of the Jews*, b. xix. ch. viii. § 2, and is as follows: "Now when Agrippa had reigned three years over all Judea, he came to the city Cesarea, which was formerly called Strato's Tower; and there he exhibited shows in honour of Cæsar, upon his being informed that there was a certain festival celebrated to make vows for his safety. At which festival a great multitude was gotten together of the principal persons, and such as were of dignity throughout his province. On the second day of which shows he put on a garment made wholly of silver," &c. ¶ *Arrayed in royal apparel.* In the apparel of a king. Josephus thus describes the dress which Herod wore on that occasion. "He put on a garment made wholly of silver, and of wonderful contexture, and early in the morning came into the theatre [place of the shows and games], at which time the silver of his garment, being illuminated by the first reflection of the sun's rays upon it, shone after a surprising manner, and was so resplendent as to spread a horror over those that looked intently on him." ¶ *Sat upon his throne.* This does not denote a *throne* in the usual sense of that word, but a high seat in the theatre, where he sat, and from whence he could have a full view of the games and sports. From this place he made his speech. ¶ *Made an oration.* Addressed the people. What was the subject of this speech is not intimated by Luke or Josephus.

22. *And the people gave a shout.* A loud applause. ¶ It is *the voice of a god*, &c. It is not probable that the *Jews* joined in this acclamation, but that it was made by the idolatrous Gentiles. Josephus gives a similar account of their feelings and conduct. He says, "And presently his flatterers cried out, one from one place, and another from another (though not for his good), that he was a god; and they added, 'Be thou merciful unto us; for although we have hitherto reverenced thee only as a king, yet shall we henceforth own thee as a superior to mortal nature.'" It is true that Josephus says that this was done when they saw his splendid apparel, and that he gives no account of his addressing the people, while Luke describes it as the effect of his speech. But the discrepancy is of no consequence. Luke is as credible an historian as Josephus, and his account is more consistent than that of the Jewish

saying, [q] *It is* the voice of a god, and not of a man.

23 And immediately the angel of the Lord smote him, because he gave not God the glory: and he was eaten of worms, and gave up the ghost.

24 But the word of God [r] grew and multiplied.

25 And Barnabas and Saul re-

q Jude 16.

r Col.1.6.

historian. It is far more probable that this applause and adoration would be excited by a speech than simply by beholding his apparel.

23. *And immediately the angel of the Lord.* Diseases and death are in the Scriptures often attributed to an angel. See 2 Sa. xxiv. 16; 1 Ch. xxi. 12, 15, 20, 27; 2 Ch. xxxii. 21. It is not intended that there was a *miracle* in this case, but it certainly *is* intended by the sacred writer that his death was a divine judgment on him for his receiving homage as a god. Josephus says of him that he "did neither rebuke them [the people] nor reject their impious flattery. A severe pain arose in his belly, and began in a most violent manner. And when he was quite worn out by the pain in his belly for five days, he departed this life, in the fifty-fourth year of his age, and the seventh of his reign." Josephus does not mention that it was done by *an angel*, but says that when he looked up, he saw an owl sitting on a rope over his head, and judging it to be an evil omen, he immediately became melancholy, and was seized with the pain. ¶ *Because he gave not God the glory.* Because he was willing to receive the worship due to God. It was the more sinful in him as he was a Jew, and was acquainted with the true God, and with the evils of idolatry. He was proud, and willing to be flattered, and even adored. He had *sought* their applause; he had arrayed himself in this splendid manner to excite admiration; and when they carried it even so far as to offer *divine homage*, he did not reject the impious flattery, but listened still to their praises. Hence he was judged; and God vindicated his own insulted honour by inflicting severe pains on him, and by a most awful death. ¶ *And he was eaten of worms.* The word used here is not elsewhere found in the New Testament. A similar disease is recorded of Antiochus Epiphanes, in the Apocrypha, 2 Mac. ix. 5, "But the Lord Almighty, the God of Israel, smote him with an invisible and incurable plague; for a pain in the bowels that was remediless came upon him, and sore torments of the inner parts (ver. 9), so that worms rose up out of the body of this wicked man," &c. Probably this was the disease known as *morbus pedicularis.* It is loathsome, offensive, and most painful. See the death of Antiochus Epiphanes described in 2 Mac. ix. With this disease also Herod the Great, grandfather of Herod Agrippa, died (Josephus, *Antiq.*, b. xvii. ch. vi. § 5). Such a death, so painful, so sudden, and so loathsome, was an appropriate judgment on the pride of Herod. We may here learn, (1) That sudden and violent deaths are often acts of direct divine judgment on wicked men. (2) That men, when they seek praise and flattery, expose themselves to the displeasure of God. His glory he will not give to another, Is. xlii. 8. (3) That the most proud, and mighty, and magnificent princes have no security of their lives. God can in a moment—even when they are surrounded by their worshippers and flatterers—touch the seat of life, and turn them to loathsomeness and putrefaction. What a pitiable being is a man of pride receiving from his fellow-men that homage which is due to God alone! See Is. xiv. (4) Pride and vanity, in any station of life, are hateful in the sight of God. Nothing is more inappropriate to our situation as lost, dying sinners, and nothing will more certainly meet the wrath of heaven. (5) We have here a strong confirmation of the truth of the sacred narrative. In all essential particulars Luke coincides in his account of the death of Herod with Josephus. This is one of the many circumstances which show that the sacred Scriptures were written at the time when they professed to be, and that they accord with the truth. See Lardner's *Credibility*, part i. ch. i. § 6.

24. *But the word of God grew*, &c. Great success attended it. The persecutions had now ceased; and notwithstanding all the attempts which had been made to crush it, still the church increased and flourished. The liberation of Peter and the death of Herod would contribute to extend it. It was

turned from Jerusalem when they had fulfilled *their* [6]ministry, and took with them John, whose surname was Mark.

CHAPTER XIII.

NOW there were in the church that was at Antioch certain prophets and teachers, as Barnabas, and Simeon that was called Niger, and Lucius of Cyrene, and Manaen, [1]which had been brought up with Herod the tetrarch, and Saul.

2 As they ministered to the Lord, and fasted, the Holy Ghost said, [a]Separate me Barnabas and

6 or, *charge*, ch.11.29,30.

1 or, *Herod's foster-brother*. a Ga.1.15.

---

a new evidence of divine interposition in behalf of the church; it would augment the zeal of Christians; it would humble their enemies, and would fill those with fear who had attempted to oppose and crush the church of God.

25. *Returned from Jerusalem.* They had gone to Jerusalem to carry alms, and they now returned to Antioch, ch. xi. 30. ¶ *When they had fulfilled* their *ministry.* When they had accomplished the purpose for which they had been sent there; that is, to deposit the alms of the church at Antioch in the hands of the elders of the churches, ch. xi. 30. ¶ *John, whose surname was Mark.* See Notes on ver. 12. From this period the sacred historian records chiefly the labours of Paul. The labours of the other apostles are, after this, seldom referred to in this book, and the attention is fixed almost entirely on the trials and travels of the great apostle of the Gentiles. His important services, his unwearied efforts, his eminent success, and the fact that *Luke* was his companion, may be the reasons why *his* labours are made so prominent in the history. Through the previous chapters we have seen the church rise from small beginnings, until it was even now spreading into surrounding regions. We have seen it survive two persecutions, commenced and conducted with all the power and malice of Jewish rulers. We have seen the most zealous of the persecutors converted to the faith which he once destroyed, and the royal persecutor put to death by the divine judgment. And we have thus seen that God was the protector of the church; that no weapon formed against it could prosper; that, according to the promise of the Redeemer, the gates of hell could not prevail against it. In that God and Saviour who *then* defended the church, we may still confide, and may be assured that he who was then its friend has it still "engraved on the palms of his hands," and designs that it shall extend until it fills the earth with light and salvation.

CHAPTER XIII.

1. *The church that was at Antioch.* See Notes on ch. xi. 20. ¶ *Certain prophets.* See Notes on ch. xi. 27. ¶ *And teachers.* Teachers are several times mentioned in the New Testament as an order of ministers, 1 Co. xii. 28, 29; Ep. iv. 11; 2 Pe. ii. 1. Their precise rank and duty are not known. It is probable that those here mentioned as prophets were the same persons as the teachers. They might discharge *both* offices, predicting future events, and instructing the people. ¶ *As Barnabas.* Barnabas was a *preacher* (ch. iv. 35, 36; ix. 27; xi. 22, 26); and it is not improbable that the names "prophets and teachers" here simply designate the preachers of the gospel. ¶ *Simeon that was called Niger. Niger* is a Latin name meaning black. Why the name was given is not known. Nothing more is known of him than is here mentioned. ¶ *Lucius of Cyrene.* Cyrene was in Africa. See Notes on Mat. xxvii. 32. Lucius is afterward mentioned as with the apostle Paul when he wrote the Epistle to the Romans, Ro. xvi. 21. ¶ *And Manaen.* He is not elsewhere mentioned in the New Testament. ¶ *Which had been brought up with Herod the tetrarch.* Herod Antipas, not Herod Agrippa. Herod was *tetrarch* of Galilee, Lu. iii. 1. The word here translated "which had been brought up," σύντροφος, denotes one who is educated or nourished at the same time with another. It is not elsewhere used in the New Testament. He might have been connected with the royal family, and, being nearly of the same age, was educated by the father of Herod Antipas with him. He was, therefore, a man of rank and education, and his conversion shows that the gospel was not confined entirely in its influence to the poor. ¶ *And Saul.* Saul was an

Saul for [b]the work whereunto I have called them.

b 1 Ti.2.7.

3 And when they had fasted and prayed, and laid *their* hands on them, they sent *them* away.

---

apostle; and yet he is here mentioned among the "prophets and teachers," showing that these words denote ministers of the gospel in general, without reference to any particular order or rank.

2. *As they ministered to the Lord.* It is probable that this took place on some day set apart for fasting and prayer. The expression "ministered to the Lord" means as they were engaged in prayer to the Lord, or as they were engaged in divine service. The Syriac thus renders the passage. ¶ *The Holy Ghost said.* Evidently by direct revelation. ¶ *Separate me.* Set apart to me, or for my service. It does not mean to *ordain*, but simply to designate, or appoint to this specific work. ¶ *For the work whereunto I have called them.* Not the apostolic office, for Saul was called to that by the express revelation of Jesus Christ (Ga. i. 12), and Barnabas was not an apostle. The "work" to which they were now set apart was that of preaching the gospel in the regions round about Antioch. It was not any *permanent* office in the church, but was a temporary designation to a *missionary enterprise* in extending the gospel, especially through Asia Minor, and the adjacent regions. Accordingly, when, in the fulfilment of this appointment, they had travelled through Seleucia, Cyprus, Paphos, Pamphylia, Pisidia, &c., they returned to Antioch, having fulfilled the work to which they were separated. See Ac. xiv. 26, 27. ¶ *Whereunto I have called them.* This proves that they received their commission to this work directly from God the Holy Spirit. Paul and Barnabas had been influenced by the Spirit to engage in this work, but they were to be sent forth by the concurrence and designation of the church.

3. *And when they had fasted.* They were *fasting* when they were commanded to set them apart. Yet this probably refers to an appointed day of prayer, with reference to this very purpose. The first formal *mission* to the Gentiles was an important event in the church, and they engaged in this appointment with deep solemnity and with humbling themselves before God. ¶ *And prayed.* This enterprise was a new one. The gospel had been preached to the Jews, to Cornelius, and to the Gentiles at Antioch. But there had been no solemn, public, and concerted plan of sending it to the Gentiles, or of appointing a mission to the heathen. It was a new event, and was full of danger and hardships. The primitive church felt the need of divine direction and aid in the great work. Two missionaries were to be sent forth among strangers, to be exposed to perils by sea and land; and the commencement of the enterprise demanded *prayer*. The church humbled itself, and this primitive missionary society sought, as all others should do, the divine blessing to attend the labours of those employed in this work. The result showed that the prayer was heard. ¶ *And laid* their *hands on them.* That is, those who are mentioned in ver. 1. This was not to set them apart to the apostolic office. Saul was chosen by Christ himself, and there is no evidence that any of the apostles were ordained by the imposition of hands (see Notes on Ac. i. 26; Mat. x. 1–5; Lu. vi. 12–16), and Barnabas was not an apostle in the original and peculiar sense of the word. Nor is it meant that this was an *ordination* to the *ministry*, to the office of preaching the gospel, for both had been engaged in this before. Saul received his commission directly from the Saviour, and began at once to preach, Ac. ix. 20; Ga. i. 11–17. Barnabas had preached at Antioch, and was evidently recognized as a preacher by the apostles, Ac. ix. 27; xi. 22, 23. It follows, therefore, that this was not an *ordination* in the doctrinal sense of this term, either Episcopal or Presbyterian, but was a designation to a particular work—a work of vast importance; strictly a *missionary appointment* by the church, under the authority of the Holy Ghost. The act of laying hands on any person was practised not only in ordination, but in conferring a favour, and in setting apart *for any purpose.* See Le. iii. 2, 8, 13; iv. 4, 29; xvi. 21; Nu. viii. 12; Mar. v. 23; xvi. 18; Mat. xxi. 46. It means in this case that they appointed *them* to a particular field of labour, and by laying hands on them they implored the blessing of God to attend them. ¶ *They sent them away.* The church by its teachers

4 So they, being sent forth by the Holy Ghost, departed unto Seleucia; and from thence they sailed to Cyprus.

5 And when they were at Salamis, they preached the word of God in the synagogues of the Jews: and they had also John to *their* minister.

6 And when they had gone through the isle unto Paphos, they

---

sent them forth under the direction of the Holy Ghost. All missionaries are thus sent by the church; and the church should not forget its ambassadors in their great and perilous work.

4. *Being sent forth by the Holy Ghost.* Having been called to this work by the Holy Spirit, and being under his direction. ¶ *Departed unto Seleucia.* This city was situated at the mouth of the river Orontes, where it falls into the Mediterranean. Antioch was connected with the sea by the river Orontes. Strabo says that in his time they sailed up the river in one day. The distance from Antioch to Seleucia by water is about 41 miles, while the journey by land is only 16½ miles (*Life and Epistles of St. Paul*, vol. i. p. 135). "Seleucia united the two characters of a fortress and a seaport. It was situated on a rocky eminence, which is the southern extremity of an elevated range of hills projecting from Mount Amanus. From the south-east, where the ruins of the Antioch gate are still conspicuous, the ground rose toward the north-east into high and craggy summits; and round the greater part of the circumference of 4 miles the city was protected by its natural position. The harbour and mercantile suburb were on level ground toward the west; but here, as on the only weak point at Gibraltar, strong artificial defences had made compensation for the weakness of nature. Seleucus, who had named his metropolis in his father's honour (p. 122), gave his own name to this maritime fortress; and here, around his tomb, his successors contended for the key of Syria. 'Seleucia by the sea' was a place of great importance under the Seleucidæ and the Ptolemies, and so it remained under the sway of the Romans. In consequence of its bold resistance to Tigranes when he was in possession of all the neighbouring country, Pompey gave it the privileges of a 'free city;' and a contemporary of St. Paul speaks of it as having those privileges still. Here, in the midst of unsympathizing sailors, the two missionary apostles, with their younger companion, stepped on board the vessel which was to convey them to Salamis. As they cleared the port, the whole sweep of the bay of Antioch opened on their left—the low ground by the mouth of the Orontes; the wild and woody country beyond it; and then the peak of Mount Casius, rising symmetrically from the very edge of the sea to a height of 5000 feet. On the right, in the south-west horizon, if the day was clear, they saw the island of Cyprus from the first. The current sets northerly and north-east between the island and the Syrian coast. But with a fair wind, a few hours would enable them to run down from Seleucia to Salamis, and the land would rapidly rise in forms well known and familiar to Barnabas and Mark" (*Life and Epistles of St. Paul*, vol. i. p. 135, 138). ¶ *They sailed to Cyprus.* An island in the Mediterranean, not far from Seleucia. See Notes on ch. iv. 36.

5. *And when they were at Salamis.* This was the principal city and seaport of Cyprus. It was situated on the south-east part of the island, and was afterward called Constantia. ¶ *In the synagogues of the Jews.* Jews were living in all the countries adjacent to Judea, and in those countries they had synagogues. The apostles uniformly preached *first* to them. ¶ *And they had also John to* their *minister.* John Mark, Ac. xii. 12. He was their *attendant*, yet not pretending to be equal to them in office. They had been specifically designated to this work. He was with them as their friend and travelling companion; perhaps also employed in making the needful arrangements for their comfort, and for the supply of their wants in their travels.

6. *And when they had gone through the isle.* The length of the island, according to Strabo, was one thousand and four hundred stadia, or nearly one hundred and seventy miles. ¶ *Unto Paphos.* Paphos was a city at the western extremity of the island. It was the residence of the proconsul, and was distinguished for a splendid temple erected to *Venus*, who was worshipped throughout the island. Cyprus was fabled to be the place of the birth of this goddess. It had, besides Paphos

found a certain sorcerer, a false
prophet, a Jew, whose name *was*
Bar-jesus:
7 Which was with the deputy
of the country, Sergius Paulus, a
prudent man; who called for Barnabas and Saul, and desired to hear
the word of God.
8 But Elymas the sorcerer (for
so is his name by interpretation)

---

and Salamis, several towns of note—Citium, the birthplace of Zeno, Amathus, sacred to Venus, &c. Its present capital is Nicosia. Whether Paul preached at any of these places is not recorded. The island is supposed formerly to have had a million of inhabitants. ¶ *A certain sorcerer.* Greek, magus, or magician. See Notes on ch. viii. 9. ¶ *A false prophet.* Pretending to be endowed with the gift of prophecy; or a man, probably, who pretended to be inspired. ¶ *Bar-jesus.* The word *Bar* is Syriac, and means *son.* Jesus, or Joshua, was not an uncommon name among the Jews. The name was given from his father—son of Jesus, or Joshua; as Bar-Jonas, son of Jonas.

7. *Which was with the deputy.* Or with the proconsul. The exact accuracy of Luke in this statement is worthy of special remark. In the time when Augustus united the world under his own power, the provinces were divided into two classes. Augustus found two names which were applied to public officers in existence, one of which was henceforward inseparably blended with the imperial dignity and with military command, and the other with the authority of the senate and its civil administration. The first of these names was "*Prætor;*" the other was "*Consul.*" What is to be accounted for here is that the *latter* is the name given by Luke to Sergius Paulus, *as* if he derived his authority from the *senate.* The difficulty in the case is this: that Augustus told the senate and the people of Rome that he would resign to them those provinces where soldiers were unnecessary to secure a peaceful administration, and that he would himself take the care and risk of the other provinces where the presence of the Roman legions would be necessary. Hence, in the time of Augustus, and in the subsequent reigns of the emperors, the provinces were divided into these two classes; the one governed by men who went forth *from the senate,* and who would be styled *Proconsul,* 'Ανθύπατος—the term used here; and the other those sent forth by *the emperor,* and who would be styled *Procurator,* 'Επίτροπος, or *Proprætor,* 'Αντιστράτηγος. Both these kind of officers are referred to in the New Testament. Now we are told by Strabo and Dio Cassius that "Asaia" and "Achaia" were assigned to the senate, and the title, therefore, of the governor would be *Proconsul,* as we find in Ac. xviii. 12; xix. 38. At the same time Dio Cassius informs us that *Cyprus was retained by the emperor for himself,* and the title of the governor, therefore, *would* naturally have been, not "*Proconsul,*" as here, but "*Procurator.*" Yet it so happens that Dio Cassius has stated the reason *why* the title "*Proconsul*" was given to the governor of Cyprus, in the fact which he mentions that "*Augustus restored Cyprus to the senate in exchange for another district of the empire.*" It is this statement which vindicates the strict accuracy of Luke in the passage before us. See *Life and Epistles of St. Paul,* vol. i. p. 142–144, and also Lardner's *Credibility,* part i. ch. i. § 11, where he has fully vindicated the accuracy of the appellation which is here given to Sergius by Luke. ¶ *Sergius Paulus, a prudent man.* The word here rendered *prudent* means *intelligent, wise, learned.* It also may have the sense of *candid,* and may have been given to this man because he was of large and liberal views; of a philosophic and inquiring turn of mind; and was willing to obtain knowledge from any source. Hence he had entertained the Jews; and hence he was willing also to listen to Barnabas and Saul. It is not often that men of rank are thus willing to listen to the instructions of the professed ministers of God. ¶ *Who called for Barnabas and Saul.* It is probable that they had preached in Paphos, and Sergius was desirous himself of hearing the import of their new doctrine. ¶ *And desired to hear,* &c. There is no evidence that he then wished to listen to this as divine truth, or that he was anxious about his own salvation, but it was rather as a speculative inquiry. It was a professed characteristic of many ancient philosophers that they were willing to receive instruction from any quarter. Comp. Ac. xvii. 19, 20.

8. *But Elymas the sorcerer, for so is his*

withstood[c] them, seeking to turn
away the deputy from the faith.
9 Then Saul, (who also *is called*
Paul,) filled with the Holy Ghost,
set his eyes on him,
10 And said, O full of all subtilty
and all mischief, *thou* child of the

c 2 Ti.3.8.

---

name by interpretation. Elymas the magician. Elymas is the interpretation, not of the name Bar-jesus, but of the word rendered *the sorcerer.* It is an Arabic word, and means the same as *Magus.* It seems that he was better known by this foreign name than by his own. ¶ *Withstood them.* Resisted them. He was sensible that if the influence of Saul and Barnabas should be extended over the proconsul, that *he* would be seen to be an impostor, and his power be at an end. His *interest,* therefore, led him to oppose the gospel. His own popularity was at stake; and being governed by this, he opposed the gospel of God. The love of popularity and power, the desire of retaining some *political* influence, is often a strong reason why men oppose the gospel. ¶ *To turn away the deputy from the faith.* To prevent the influence of the truth on his mind; or to prevent his becoming the friend and patron of the Christians.

9. *Then Saul (who is also called Paul).* This is the last time that this apostle is called *Saul.* Henceforward he is designated by the title by which he is usually known, as *Paul.* When, or why, this change occurred in the name, has been a subject on which commentators are not agreed. From the fact that the change in the name is here first intimated, it would seem probable that it was first used in relation to him at this time. *By whom* the name was given him—whether he assumed it himself, or whether it was first given him by Christians or by Romans—is not intimated. The name is of Roman origin. In the Latin language the name *Paulus* signifies *little, dwarfish;* and some have conjectured that it was given by his parents to denote that he was small when born; others, that it was assumed or conferred in subsequent years because he was little in stature. The name is not of the same signification as the name *Saul.* This signifies one that is asked, or desired. After all the conjectures on this subject, it is probable, (1) That this name was first used here; for before this, even after his conversion, he is uniformly called *Saul.* (2) That it was given by the Romans, as being a name with which they were more familiar, and one that was more consonant with their language and pronunciation. It was made by the change of a single letter; and probably because the name Paul was common among them, and pronounced, perhaps, with greater facility. (3) Paul suffered himself to be called by this name, as he was employed chiefly among the Gentiles. It was common for names to undergo changes quite as great as this, without our being able to specify any particular cause, in passing from one language to another. Thus the Hebrew name Jochanan among the Greeks and Latins was Johannes, with the French it is Jean, with the Dutch Hans, and with us John (Doddridge). Thus Onias becomes Menelaus; Hillel, Pollio; Jakim, Alcimus; Silas, Silvanus, &c. (Grotius). ¶ *Filled with the Holy Ghost.* Inspired to detect his sin; to denounce divine judgment; and to inflict punishment on him. See Notes on ch. ii. 4. ¶ *Set his eyes on him.* Looked at him intently.

10. *O full of all subtilty and mischief.* The word *subtilty* denotes deceit and fraud, and implies that he was practising an imposition, and that he knew it. The word rendered *mischief* (ῥᾳδιουργίας) denotes properly *facility of acting,* and then *sleight of hand;* sly, cunning arts, by which one imposes on another, and deceives him with a fraudulent intention. It is not elsewhere used in the New Testament. The art of Elymas consisted probably in sleight of hand, legerdemain, or trick, aided by skill in the abstruse sciences, by which the ignorant might be easily imposed on. See Notes on ch. viii. 9. ¶ *Child of the devil.* Under his influence; practising his arts; promoting his designs by deceit and imposture, so that *he* may be called your father. See Notes on Jn. viii. 44. Satan is here represented as the author of deceit and the father of lies. ¶ *Enemy of all righteousness.* Practising deceit and iniquity, and thus opposed to righteousness and honesty. A man who lives by wickedness will, of course, be the foe of every form of integrity. A man who lives by fraud will be opposed to the truth; a pander to the vices of men will hate the rules of

devil, *thou* enemy of all righteousness, wilt thou not cease to pervert the right ways of the Lord?

11 And now, behold, the hand of the Lord *is* upon thee, and thou shalt be blind, not seeing the sun for a season. And immediately there fell on him a mist and a darkness; and he went about, seeking some to lead him by the hand.

12 Then the deputy, when he saw what was done, believed, being

---

chastity and purity; a manufacturer or vender of ardent spirits will be the enemy of temperance societies. ¶ *Wilt thou not cease to pervert.* In what way he had opposed Paul and Barnabas is not known. It may have been either by misrepresenting their doctrines, or by representing them as apostate Jews —thus retarding or hindering the progress of the gospel. The expression "wilt thou *not cease*" implies that he had been engaged sedulously in doing this, probably from the commencement of their work in the city. ¶ *The right ways of the Lord.* The straight paths or doctrines of the Christian religion, in opposition to the *crooked* and *perverse* arts of deceivers and impostors. Straight paths denote integrity, sincerity, truth, Je. xxxi. 9; He. xii. 13; comp. Is. xl. 3, 4; xlii. 16; Lu. iii. 5. *Crooked* ways denote the ways of the sinner, the deceiver, the impostor, De. xxxii. 5; Ps. cxxv.; Pr. ii. 15; Is. lix. 8; Phi. ii. 15.

11. *The hand of the Lord* is *upon thee.* God shall punish thee. By this sudden and miraculous punishment he would be awed and humbled, and the proconsul and others would be convinced that he was an impostor, and that the gospel was true. His *wickedness* deserved such a punishment; and at the same time that due punishment was inflicted, it was designed that the gospel should be extended by this means. In all this there was the highest evidence that Paul was under the inspiration of God. He was full of the Holy Ghost; he detected the secret feelings and desires of the heart of Elymas; and he inflicted on him a punishment that could have proceeded from none but God. That the apostles had the power of inflicting *punishment* is apparent from various places in the New Testament, 1 Co. v. 5; 1 Ti. i. 20. The punishment inflicted on Elymas, also, would be highly emblematic of the *darkness* and *perverseness* of his conduct. ¶ *Not seeing the sun for a season.* For how long a time this blindness was to continue is nowhere specified. It was, however, in mercy ordained that the blindness should not be permanent and final; and though it was a *punishment*, it was at the same time *benevolent*, for nothing would be more likely to lead him to reflection and repentance than such a state of blindness. It was such a manifest proof that God was opposed to him; it was such a sudden divine judgment; it so completely cut him off from all possibility of practising his arts of deception, that it was adapted to bring him to repentance. Accordingly there is a tradition in the early church that he became a Christian. Origen says that "Paul, by a word striking him blind, by anguish converted him to godliness" (Clark). ¶ *A mist.* The word here used properly denotes a darkness or obscurity of the air; a cloud, &c. But it also denotes an extinction of sight by the drying up or disturbance of the humours of the eye (Hippocrates, as quoted by Schleusner). ¶ *And darkness.* Blindness, night. What was the precise cause or character of this miracle is not specified. ¶ *And he went about,* &c. This is a striking account of the effect of the miracle. The change was so sudden that he knew not where to go. He sought some one to guide him in the paths with which he had before been familiar. How soon can God bring down the pride of man, and make him helpless as an infant! How easily can he touch our senses, the organs of our most exquisite pleasures, and wither all our enjoyments! How dependent are we on him for the inestimable blessing of sight! And how easily can he annihilate all the sinner's pleasures, break up all his plans, and humble him in the dust! Sight is his gift; and it is a mercy unspeakably great that he does not whelm us in thick darkness, and destroy for ever all the pleasure that through this organ is conveyed to the soul.

12. *Then the deputy . . . believed.* Was convinced that Elymas was an impostor, and that the doctrine of Paul was true. There seems no reason to doubt that his faith was that which is connected

astonished at the doctrine of the
Lord.
13 Now when Paul and his company loosed from Paphos, they came
to Perga in Pamphylia; and John,
departing[d] from them, returned to
Jerusalem.
14 But when they departed from
Perga, they came to Antioch in Pisidia, and went into [e]the synagogue
on the sabbath-day, and sat down.
15 And after the [f]reading of the
law and the prophets, the rulers of
the synagogue sent unto them, saying, *Ye* men *and* brethren, if ye have
any [g]word of exhortation for the
people, say on.
16 Then Paul stood up, and

d ch.15.38. e ch.18.4. f ver.27. g He.13.22.

with eternal life; and if so, it is an evidence that the gospel was not always confined to the poor, and to those in obscure ranks of life. ¶ *At the doctrine of the Lord.* The word *doctrine* here seems to denote, not the *teaching* or *instruction*, but the wonderful effects which were connected with the doctrine. It was particularly *the miracle* with which he was astonished; but he might have been also deeply impressed and amazed at the purity and sublimity of the truths which were now expanded to his view. We learn nothing further respecting him in the New Testament.

13. *Paul and his company.* Those with him—Barnabas and John—and perhaps others who had been converted at Paphos; for it was common for many of the converts to Christianity to attend on the apostles in their travels. See ch. ix. 30. ¶ *Loosed from Paphos.* Departed from Paphos. See Notes on ver. 6. ¶ *They came to Perga in Pamphylia.* Pamphylia was a province of Asia Minor, lying over against Cyprus, having Cilicia east, Lycia west, Pisidia north, and the Mediterranean south. Perga was the metropolis of Pamphylia, and was situated, not on the sea-coast, but on the river Cestus, at some distance from its mouth. There was on a mountain near it a celebrated temple of Diana. ¶ *And John, departing from them,* &c. Why he departed from them is unknown. It might have been from fear of danger; or from alarm in travelling so far into unknown regions. But it is plain from ch. xv. 38, that it was from some cause which was deemed blameworthy, and that his conduct now was such as to make Paul unwilling again to have him as a companion.

14. *They came to Antioch in Pisidia.* Pisidia was a province of Asia Minor, and was situated north of Pamphylia. Antioch was not *in* Pisidia, but within the limits of Phrygia; but it belonged to Pisidia, and was called Antioch of Pisidia to distinguish it from Antioch in Syria.—Pliny, *Nat. Hist.*, 5, 27; Strabo, 12, p. 577 (Kuinoel; Robinson's Calmet). The city was built by Seleucus, the founder of the Antioch in Syria, and was called after the name of his father, *Antiochus.* He is said to have built *sixteen* cities of that name (*Life and Epistles of St. Paul*, vol. i. p. 122). ¶ *Went into the synagogue.* Though Paul and Barnabas were on a special mission to the Gentiles, yet they availed themselves of every opportunity to offer the gospel to the Jews first.

15. *And after the reading of the law and the prophets.* See Notes on Lu. iv. 16. ¶ *The rulers of the synagogue.* Those were persons who had the general charge of the synagogue and its service, to keep everything in order, and to direct the affairs of public worship. They designated the individuals who were to read the law; and called on those whom they pleased to address the people, and had the power also of inflicting punishment, and of excommunicating, &c. (Schleusner), Mar. v. 22, 35, 36, 38; Lu. viii. 49; xiii. 14; Ac. xviii. 8, 17. Seeing that Paul and Barnabas were Jews, though strangers, they sent to them, supposing it probable that they would wish to address their brethren. ¶ *Men* and *brethren.* An affectionate manner of commencing a discourse, recognizing them as their own countrymen, and as originally of the same religion. ¶ *Say on.* Greek, *speak.*

16. *Men of Israel.* Jews. The design of this discourse of Paul was to introduce to them the doctrine that Jesus was the Messiah. To do this, he evinced his usual wisdom and address. To have commenced at once on this would have probably excited their prejudice and rage. He therefore pursued a train of argument which showed that he was a firm believer in the Scriptures; that he was acquainted with the history and

beckoning with *his* hand, said, Men of Israel, and ye that fear God, give audience.

17 The God of this people of Israel [h]chose our fathers, and exalted the people when they [i]dwelt as strangers in the land of Egypt, and [k]with an high arm brought he them out of it.

18 And about the time of [l]forty years [2]suffered he their manners in the wilderness.

h De.7.6,7. *i* Ps.105.23. *k* Ex.13.14.16. *l* Ex.16.35.

2 ἐτροποφόρησεν, perhaps for ἐτροφοφόρησεν, *bore*, or, *fed them, as a nurse beareth*, or, *feedeth her child*, De.1.31, according to the LXX.; and so Chrysostom.

---

promises of the Old Testament; and that he was not disposed to call in question the doctrines of their fathers. The passage which had been read had probably given occasion for him to pursue this train of thought. By going over, in a summary way, their history, and recounting the former dealings of God with them, he showed them that he believed the Scriptures; that a promise had been given of a Messiah; and that he had actually come according to the promise. ¶ *Ye that fear God.* Probably *proselytes of the gate*, who had not yet been circumcised, but who had renounced idolatry, and were accustomed to worship with them in their synagogues. ¶ *Give audience.* Hear.

17. *The God of this people.* Who has manifested himself as the peculiar friend and protector of this nation. This implied a belief that he had been particularly *their* God; a favourite doctrine of the Jews, and one that would conciliate their favour toward Paul. ¶ *Of Israel.* The Jews. ¶ *Chose our fathers.* Selected the nation to be a chosen and peculiar people to himself, De. vii. 6, 7. ¶ *And exalted the people.* Raised them up from a low and depressed state of bondage, to freedom, and to peculiar privileges as a nation. ¶ *When they dwelt as strangers in Egypt*—ἐν τῇ παροικίᾳ. This properly refers to their dwelling there as foreigners. They were always strangers there in a strange land. It was not their home. They never mingled with the people; never became constituent parts of the government; never used their language; never united with their usages and laws. They were a strange, separate, depressed people there; not less so than Africans are strangers and foreigners—a depressed and degraded people in this land (America), Ge. xxxvi. 7; Ex. vi. 4; xxii. 21; xxiii. 9; Le. xix. 34; De. x. 19. ¶ *And with an high arm.* This expression denotes great power. The *arm* denotes strength, as that by which we perform anything. A *high* arm, an arm lifted up, or stretched out, denotes that strength exerted to the utmost. The children of Israel are represented as having been delivered with an "outstretched arm," De. xxvi. 8; Ex. vi. 6. "With a strong hand," Ex. vi. 1. Reference is made in these places to the plagues inflicted on Egypt, by which the Israelites were delivered; to their passage through the Red Sea; to their victories over their enemies, &c.

18. *And about the time of forty years.* They were this time going from Egypt to the land of Canaan, Ex. xvi. 35; Nu. xxxiii. 38. ¶ *Suffered he their manners.* This passage has been very variously rendered. See the margin. Syriac, "He *nourished* them," &c. Arabic, "He blessed them, and nourished them," &c. The Greek word is not elsewhere used in the New Testament. It properly means to *tolerate*, or *endure the conduct* of any one, implying that that conduct is evil, and tends to provoke to punishment. This is doubtless its meaning here. Probably Paul referred to the passage in De. i. 31, "The Lord thy God bare thee." But instead of this word, ἐτροποφόρησεν, *to bear with*, many MSS. read ἐτροφοφόρησεν, *he sustained* or *nourished*. This reading was followed by the Syriac, Arabic, and has been admitted by Griesbach into the text. This is also found in the Septuagint, in De. i. 31, which place Paul doubtless referred to. This would well suit the connection of the passage; and a change of a single letter might easily have occurred in a MS. It adds to the probability that this is the true reading, that it accords with De. i. 31; Nu. xi. 12; De. xxxii. 10. It is furthermore not probable that Paul would have commenced a discourse by reminding them of the obstinacy and wickedness of the nation. Such a course would rather tend to exasperate than to conciliate; but by reminding them of the *mercies* of God to them, and showing them that He had been their protector, he was better fitting them for his main purpose

19 And when he had [m]destroyed seven nations in the land of Chanaan he [n]divided their land to them by lot.

m De.7.1. *n* Jos.14.1,&c.

20 And after that, he gave *unto them* [o]judges about the space of four hundred and fifty years, until Samuel the prophet.

o Ju.2.16.

—that of showing them the kindness of the God of their fathers in sending to them a Saviour. ¶ *In the wilderness.* The desert through which they passed in going from Egypt to Canaan.

19. *And when he had destroyed.* Subdued, cast out, or extirpated them *as nations.* It does not mean that all were put to death, for many of them were left in the land; but that they were subdued as nations, they were broken up and overcome, De. vii. 1, "And hath *cast out* many nations before them," &c. ¶ *Seven nations.* The Hittites, the Girgashites, the Amorites, the Canaanites, the Perizzites, the Hivites, and the Jebusites, De. vii. 1; Jos. iii. 10; Ne. ix. 8. ¶ *In the land of Canaan.* The whole land was called by the name of one of the principal nations. This was the promised land; the holy land, &c. ¶ *He divided,* &c. See an account of this in Jos. xiv., xv. The *lot* was often used among the Jews to determine important questions. See Note on ch. i. 26.

20. *He gave* unto them *judges.* Men who were raised up in an extraordinary manner to administer the affairs of the nation, to defend it from enemies, &c. See Ju. ii. 16. ¶ *About the space of four hundred and fifty years.* This is a most difficult passage, and has exercised all the ingenuity of chronologists. The ancient versions agree with the present Greek text. The *difficulty* has been to reconcile it with what is said in 1 Ki. vi. 1, "And it came to pass in the four hundred and eightieth year after the children of Israel were come out of the land of Egypt, in the fourth year of Solomon's reign over Israel . . . he began to build the house of the Lord." Now if to the forty years that the children of Israel were in the wilderness there be added the four hundred and fifty said in Acts to have been passed under the administration of the judges, and about seventeen years of the time of Joshua, forty for Samuel and the reign of Saul together, and forty for the reign of David, and three of Solomon before he began to build the temple, the sum will be five hundred and ninety years, a period greater by one hundred and ten years than that mentioned in 1 Ki. vi. 1. Various ways have been proposed to meet the difficulty. Doddridge renders it, "After these transactions, [which lasted] four hundred and fifty years, he gave them a series of judges," &c., reckoning from the birth of Isaac, and supposing that Paul meant to refer to this whole time. But to this there are serious objections. (1) It is a forced and constrained interpretation, and one manifestly made to meet a difficulty. (2) There is no propriety in commencing this period at the birth of *Isaac.* That was in no manner remarkable, so far as Paul's narrative was concerned; and Paul had not even referred to it. This same solution is offered also by Calovius, Mill, and De Dieu. Luther and Beza think it should be read *three* hundred instead of *four* hundred. But this is a mere conjecture, without any authority from MSS. Vitringa and some others suppose that the text has been corrupted by some transcriber, who has inserted this without authority. But there is no evidence of this; and the MSS. and ancient versions are uniform. None of these explanations are satisfactory. In the solution of the difficulty we may remark, (1) That nothing is more perplexing than the chronology of ancient facts. The difficulty is found in all writings; in profane as well as sacred. Mistakes are so easily made in transcribing numbers, where *letters* are used instead of writing the words at length, that we are not to wonder at such errors. (2) Paul would naturally use the chronology which was in current, common use among the Jews. It was not his business to *settle* such points; but he would speak of them as they were usually spoken of, and refer to them as others did. (3) There is reason to believe that that which is here mentioned was the *common* chronology of his time. It accords remarkably with that which is used by Josephus. Thus (*Antiq.*, b. vii. ch. iii. § 1), Josephus says expressly that Solomon "began to build the temple in the fourth year of his reign, *five hundred and ninety-two years* after the exodus out of Egypt," &c. This would allow forty years for

21 And afterward [p] they desired a king; and God gave unto them Saul,[q] the son of Cis, a man of the tribe of Benjamin, by the space of forty years.

22 And when [r] he had removed him, he raised up unto them [s] David to be their king; to whom also he gave testimony, and said, I have found David, the *son* of Jesse, [t] a man after mine own heart, which shall fulfil all my will.

p 1 Sa.8.5. *q* 1 Sa.10.1. *r* 1 Sa.31.6. *s* 2 Sa.5.3. *t* 1 Sa.13.14.

---

their being in the wilderness, seventeen for Joshua, forty for Samuel and Saul, forty for the reign of David, and *four hundred and fifty-two* years for the time of the judges and the times of anarchy that intervened. This remarkable coincidence shows that this was the chronology which was then used, and which Paul had in view. (4) This chronology has the authority, also, of many eminent names. See Lightfoot and Boyle's *Lectures*, ch. xx. In what way this computation of Josephus and the Jews originated, it is not necessary here to inquire. It is a sufficient solution of the difficulty that *Paul spake in their usual manner*, without departing from his regular object by settling a point of chronology.

21. *And afterward they desired a king.* See 1 Sa. viii. 5; Ho. xiii. 10. It was predicted that they would have a king, De. xvii. 14, 15. ¶ *Saul, the son of Cis*, is the Greek mode of writing the Hebrew name *Kish.* In the Old Testament it is uniformly written *Kish*, and it is to be regretted that this has not been retained in the New Testament. See 1 Sa. ix. 1. ¶ *By the space of forty years.* During forty years. The Old Testament has not mentioned the time during which Saul reigned. Josephus says (*Antiq.*, b. vi. ch. xiv. § 9) that he reigned eighteen years while Samuel was alive, and twenty-two years after his death. But Dr. Doddridge (note *in loco*) has shown that this cannot be correct, and that he probably reigned, as some copies of Josephus have it, but two years after the death of Samuel. Many critics suppose that the term of forty years here mentioned includes also the time in which Samuel judged the people. This supposition does not violate the text in this place, and may be probable. See Doddridge and Grotius on the place.

22. *And when he had removed him.* This was done because he rebelled against God in sparing the sheep and oxen and valuable property of Amalek, together with Agag the king, when he was commanded to destroy all, 1 Sa. xv. 8–23. He was put to death in a battle with the Philistines, 1 Sa. xxxi. 1–6. The phrase "when he removed him" refers probably to his *rejection* as a king, and not to his death; for David was anointed king before the death of Saul, and almost immediately after the rejection of Saul on account of his rebellion in the business of Amalek. See 1 Sa. xvi. 12, 13. ¶ *He gave testimony.* He bore witness, 1 Sa. xiii. 14. ¶ *I have found David*, &c. This is not quoted *literally*, but contains the *substance* of what is expressed in various places. Comp. 1 Sa. xiii. 14, with Ps. lxxxix. 20, and 1 Sa. xvi. 1, 12. ¶ *A man after mine own heart.* This expression is found in 1 Sa. xiii. 14. The connection shows that it means simply a man who would not be rebellious and disobedient as Saul was, but would do the will of God and keep his commandments. This refers, doubtless, rather to the public than to the private character of David; to his character *as a king.* It means that he would make the will of God the great rule and law of his reign, in contradistinction from Saul, who, *as a king*, had disobeyed God. At the same time it is true that the *prevailing* character of David, as a pious, humble, devoted man, was that he was a man after God's own heart, and was beloved by him as a holy man. He had faults; he committed sin; but who is free from it? He was guilty of great offences; but he also evinced, in a degree equally eminent, *repentance* (see Ps. li.); and not less in his private than his public character did he evince those traits which were *prevailingly* such as accorded with *the heart*, that is, the earnest desires, of God. ¶ *Which shall fulfil all my will.* Saul had not done it. He had disobeyed God in a case where he had received an express command. The characteristic of David would be that he would *obey* the commands of God. That David *did* this — that he maintained the worship of God, opposed idolatry, and sought to promote universal obe-

23 Of this man's seed hath God,
according to *his* promise, [u]raised
unto Israel [v]a Saviour, Jesus:
24 When [w]John had first preached,
before his coming, the baptism of
repentance to all the people of
Israel.
25 And as John fulfilled his
course, he said, Whom think ye
that I am? I am not *he:* but,
behold, there cometh one after me,
whose shoes of *his* feet I am not
worthy to loose.
26 Men *and* brethren, children
of the stock of Abraham, and whosoever among you feareth God, [x]to
you is the word of this salvation
sent.
27 For they that dwell at Jerusalem, and their rulers, because
they knew him not, nor yet the
voices of the prophets which are
read every sabbath-day, [y]they have
fulfilled *them* in condemning *him.*
28 And though they found no
cause of death in *him,* yet desired

u Ps.132.11. *v* Mat.1.21. *w* Mat.3.1-11. *x* Mat.10.6. *y* Lu.24.20,44.

dience to God among the people—is expressly recorded of him, 1 Ki. xiv. 8, 9, "And thou [Jeroboam] hast not been as my servant David, *who kept my commandments, and who followed me with all his heart, to do that only which was right in mine eyes,*" &c., 1 Ki. xv. 3, 5.

23. *Of this man's seed.* Of his posterity. ¶ *According to* his *promise.* See Notes on Ac. ii. 30. ¶ *Raised unto Israel.* See Notes on Ac. ii. 30. ¶ *A Saviour, Jesus.* See Notes on Mat. i. 21.

24. *When John had first preached,* &c. After John had preached and prepared the way, Mat. iii.

25. *And as John fulfilled his course.* As he was engaged in completing his work. His ministry is called a *course* or *race,* that which was to be *run,* or completed. ¶ *He said,* &c. These are not the precise words which the evangelists have recorded, but the sense is the same. See Notes on Jn. i. 20; Mat. iii. 11.

26. *Men* and *brethren.* Paul now exhorts them to embrace the Lord Jesus as the Messiah. He uses, therefore, the most respectful and fraternal language. ¶ *Children of the stock of Abraham.* Descendants of Abraham; you who regard Abraham as your ancestor. He means here to address particularly the native-born Jews; and this appellation is used because they valued themselves highly on account of their descent from Abraham (see Notes on Mat. iii. 9); and because the promise of the Messiah had been specially given to him. ¶ *And whosoever,* &c. Proselytes. See Notes on ver. 16. ¶ *Is the word of this salvation sent.* This message of salvation. It was sent *particularly* to the Jewish people. The Saviour was sent to that nation (Mat. xv. 24); and the design was to offer to them first the message of life. See Notes on ver. 46.

27. *Because they knew him not.* The statement in this verse is designed, not to reproach the Jews at Jerusalem, but to introduce the fact that Jesus had died, and had risen again. With great wisdom and tenderness, Paul speaks of the murderers of the Saviour in such a manner as not to exasperate, but, as far as possible, to mitigate their crime. There was sufficient guilt in the murder of the Son of God to fill the nation with alarm, even after all that could be said to mitigate the deed. See Ac. ii. 23, 36, 37. When Paul says, "They knew him not," he means that they did not know him to be the Messiah (see 1 Co. ii. 8); they were ignorant of the true meaning of the prophecies of the Old Testament; they regarded him as an impostor. See Notes on Ac. iii. 17. ¶ *Nor yet the voices of the prophets.* The meaning of the predictions of the Old Testament respecting the Messiah. They expected a prince and a conqueror, but did not expect a Messiah that was poor and despised; that was a man of sorrows and that was to die on a cross. ¶ *Which are read every sabbath-day.* In the synagogues. Though the Scriptures were read so constantly, yet they were ignorant of their true meaning. They were blinded by pride, and prejudice, and preconceived opinions. Men may often in this way read the Bible a good part of their lives and never understand it. ¶ *They have fulfilled* them, &c. By putting him to death they have accomplished what was foretold.

28. *And though they found,* &c. They found no crime which deserved death.

they Pilate that he should be
slain.

29 And when they had fulfilled
all that was written of him, they
took *him* down from the tree, and
laid *him* in a sepulchre.

30 But God raised him from
the dead:

31 And[z] he was seen many days
of them which came up with him
from Galilee to Jerusalem, who are
his witnesses unto the people.

32 And we declare unto you glad
tidings, how that [a] the promise
which was made unto the fathers,

33 God hath fulfilled the same
unto us their children, in that he
hath raised up Jesus again; as it

z ch.1.3.

a Ro.4.13.

This is conclusively shown by the trial itself. After all their efforts; after the treason of Judas; after their employing false witnesses; still no crime was laid to his charge. The Sanhedrim condemned him for blasphemy; and yet they knew that they could not substantiate the charge before Pilate, and they therefore endeavoured to procure his condemnation on the ground of sedition. Comp. Lu. xxii. 70, 71, with xxiii. 1, 2. ¶ *Yet desired they Pilate*, &c. Mat. xxvii. 1, 2; Lu. xxiii. 4, 5.

29. *They took* him *down*, &c. That is, it was done by the Jews. Not that it was done by those who put him to death, but by Joseph of Arimathea, and by Nicodemus, who were Jews. Paul is speaking of what was done to Jesus by *the Jews* at Jerusalem; and he does not affirm that the *same* persons put him to death and laid him in a tomb, but that all this was done *by Jews*. See Jn. xix. 38, 39.

30. *But God raised him*, &c. See Notes on ch. ii. 23, 24.

31. *And he was seen*. See Notes at the end of Matthew. ¶ *Many days*. Forty days, ch. i. 3. ¶ *Of them which came up*. By the apostles particularly. He was seen by others; but they are especially mentioned as having been chosen for this object, to bear witness to him, and as having been particularly qualified for it.

32. *And we*. We who are here present. Paul and Barnabas. ¶ *Declare unto you glad tidings*. We preach the gospel—the good news. To a Jew, nothing could be more grateful intelligence than that the Messiah had come; to a sinner convinced of his sins nothing can be more cheering than to hear of a Saviour. ¶ *The promise*, &c. The *promise* here refers to *all* that had been spoken in the Old Testament respecting the advent, sufferings, death, and resurrection of Christ.

33. *God hath fulfilled*. God has *completed* or *carried into effect* by the resurrection of Jesus. He does not say that every part of the promise had reference to *his resurrection;* but his being raised up *completed* or *perfected* the fulfilment of the promises which had been made respecting him. ¶ *In the second psalm*, ver. 7. ¶ *Thou art my Son*. This psalm has been usually understood as referring to the Messiah. See Notes on ch. iv. 25. ¶ *This day have I begotten thee*. It is evident that Paul uses the expression here as implying that the Lord Jesus is called the Son of God because he raised him up from the dead, and that he means to imply that it was for *this* reason that he is so called. This interpretation of an inspired apostle fixes the meaning of this passage in the psalm, and proves that it is not there used with reference to the doctrine of eternal generation, or to his incarnation, but that he is called his *Son* because he was raised from the dead. And this interpretation accords with the scope of the psalm. In ver. 1–3 the psalmist records the combination of the rulers of the earth against the Messiah, and their efforts to cast off his reign. This was done, and the Messiah was rejected. All this pertains, not to his previous existence, but to the Messiah on the earth. In ver. 4, 5, the psalmist shows that their efforts would not be successful; that God would laugh at their designs; that is, that their plans should not succeed. In ver. 6, 7, he shows that the Messiah would be established as a king; that this was the fixed decree, and that he had been *begotten* for this. All this is represented as *subsequent* to the raging of the heathen, and to the counsel of the kings against him, and *must*, therefore, refer, not to his eternal generation or his incarnation, but to something succeeding his death; that is, to his resurrection, and his establishment as King at the right hand of God. This interpretation by the apostle Paul

is also written in the second psalm, Thou[b] art my Son, this day have I begotten thee.

34 And as concerning that he raised him up from the dead, *now* no more to return to corruption, he said on this wise, I will give you the sure [3]mercies of David.

b Ps.2.7.

3 τὰ ὅσια, *holy*, or, *just things;* which word the LXX., both in the place of Is.55.3, and in many others, use for that which is in the Hebrew, *mercies*.

---

proves, therefore, that this passage is not to be used to establish the doctrine of the eternal generation of Christ. Christ is called the Son of God for various reasons. In Lu. i. 35, because he was begotten by the Holy Ghost. In this place, on account of his resurrection. In Ro. i. 4 it is also said that he was declared to be the Son of God by the resurrection from the dead. See Notes on that place. The resurrection from the dead is represented as in some sense *the beginning* of life, and it is with reference to this that the terms *Son*, and *begotten from the dead*, are used, as the birth of a child is the beginning of life. Thus Christ is said, Col. i. 18, to be "the *first-born* from the dead;" and thus, in Re. i. 5, he is called "the *first-begotten* of the dead;" and with reference to this *renewal* or beginning of life he is called *a Son*. In whatever other senses he is called *a Son* in the New Testament, yet it is here proved, (1) That he is called a Son from his resurrection; and (2) That this is the sense in which the expression in the psalm is to be used. ¶ *This day.* The words "this day" would naturally, in the connection in which they are found, refer to the time when the "decree" was made. The purpose was formed before Christ came into the world; it was executed or carried into effect by the resurrection from the dead. See Notes on Ps. ii. 7. ¶ *Have I begotten thee.* This evidently cannot be understood in a *literal* sense. It *literally* refers to the relation of an earthly father to his children; but in no such sense can it be applied to the relation of God the Father to the Son. It *must*, therefore, be figurative. The word sometimes figuratively means to produce, to cause to exist in any way: 2 Ti. ii. 23, "Unlearned questions avoid, knowing that they do *gender* [beget] strifes." It refers also to the labours of the apostles in securing the conversion of sinners to the gospel: 1 Co. iv. 15, "In Christ Jesus I have *begotten* you through the gospel;" Phile. ver. 10, "Whom [Onesimus] I have *begotten* in my bonds." It is applied to Christians: Jn. i. 13, "Which were born [begotten], not of blood, &c., but of God;" iii. 3, "Except a man be born [begotten] again," &c. In all these places it is used in a figurative sense to denote the commencement of spiritual life by the power of God; so raising up sinners from the death of sin, or so producing spiritual life that they should sustain to him the relation of sons. Thus he raised up Christ from the dead, and imparted life to his body; and hence he is said figuratively to have *begotten* him from the dead, and thus sustains toward the risen Saviour the relation of father. Comp. Col. i. 18; Re. i. 5; He. i. 5.

34. *And as concerning.* In further proof of this. To show that he actually did it, he proceeds to quote another passage of Scripture. ¶ *No more to return to corruption.* The word *corruption* is usually employed to denote putrefaction, or the mouldering away of a body in the grave; its returning to its native dust. But it is certain (ver. 35. See Notes on ch. ii. 27) that the body of Christ never in this sense saw corruption. The word is therefore used to denote *death*, or *the grave*, the cause and place of corruption. The word is thus used in the Septuagint. It means here simply that he should not again *die.* ¶ *He said on this wise.* He said thus (οὕτως). ¶ *I will give you.* This quotation is made from Is. lv. 3. It is quoted from the Septuagint, with a change of but one word, not affecting the sense. In Isaiah the passage does not refer particularly to the *resurrection* of the Messiah, nor is it the design of Paul to affirm that it does. His object in this verse is not to prove that he would *rise from the dead*, but that, *being* risen, he would *not again die.* That the passage in Isaiah refers to the Messiah there can be no doubt, ver. 1, 4. The passage here quoted is an address to the people, an assurance to them that the promise made to David would be performed, a solemn declaration that he would make an everlasting covenant with them through the Messiah, the promised descendant of David. ¶ *The*

35 Wherefore he saith also [c] in another *psalm*, Thou shalt not suffer thine Holy One to see corruption.

36 For David, [4] after he had served his own generation by the will of God, [d] fell on sleep, and was laid unto his fathers, and saw corruption:

37 But he, whom [e] God raised again, saw no corruption.

38 Be it known unto you, therefore, men *and* brethren, [f] that through this man is preached unto you the forgiveness of sins:

39 And [g] by him, all that believe are justified from all things, from

c Ps.16.10.
4 or, *after he had in his own age served the will of God.* d 1 Ki.2.10.
e ch.2.24. f Da.9.24; Lu.24.47; 1 Jn.2.12. g Is.53.11; Hab.2.4; Ro.3.28; 8.1.

---

sure mercies of David. The word *mercies* here refers to the *promise* made to David; the *mercy* or *favour* shown to him by promising to him a successor that should not fail to sit on his throne, 2 Sa. vii. 16; Ps. lxxxix. 4, 5; cxxxii. 11, 12. These mercies and promises are called "sure," as being true or unfailing; they would certainly be accomplished. Comp. 2 Co. i. 20. The word *David* here does not refer, as many have supposed, to the Messiah, but to the King of Israel. God made to David a promise, a certain pledge; he bestowed on him this special *mercy*, in promising that he should have a successor who should sit for ever on his throne. This promise was understood by the Jews, and is often referred to in the New Testament, as relating to the Messiah. Paul here says that that promise is fulfilled. The only question is how it refers to the subject on which he was discoursing. The point was not mainly to prove his *resurrection*, but to show particularly that he would *never die* again, or that he would for ever live and reign. And the argument is, that as God had promised that David should have a successor who should sit for ever on his throne, and as this prediction now terminated in the Messiah, the Lord Jesus, it followed that, as that promise was sure and certain, he would never die again. He must live if the promise was fulfilled. And though he had been put to death, yet under that general promise there was a certainty that he would live again. It was impossible, the meaning is, that the Messiah, the promised successor of David, the perpetual occupier of his throne, should remain under the power of death. Under this assurance the church now reposes its hopes. Zion's King now lives, ever able to vindicate and save his people.

35. *Wherefore*—Διὸ. To the same intent or end. In proof of the same thing—that he must rise and live for ever. ¶ *He saith.* God says by David, or David spake the promises made by God. ¶ *In another* psalm. Ps. xvi. 10. ¶ *Thou wilt not suffer*, &c. See this explained in the Notes on ch. ii. 27.

36. *For David*, &c. This verse is designed to show that the passage in Ps. xvi. could not refer to David, and must therefore relate to some other person. In ver. 37 it is affirmed that this *could* refer to no one, in fact, but to the Lord Jesus. ¶ *After he had served his generation.* See the margin. Syriac, "David in his own generation having served the will of God, and slept," &c. Arabic, "David served in his own age, and saw God." The margin probably most correctly expresses the sense of the passage. To serve a generation, or an age, is an unusual and almost unintelligible expression. ¶ *Fell on sleep.* Greek, slept, that is, *died.* This is the usual word to denote the death of saints. It is used of David in 1 Ki. ii. 10. See Notes on Mat. xxvii. 52. ¶ *And was laid unto*, &c. And was buried with his fathers, &c., 1 Ki. ii. 10. ¶ *And saw corruption.* Remained in the grave, and returned to his native dust. See this point argued more at length by Peter in Ac. ii. 29–31, and explained in the Notes on that place.

37. *But he, whom God raised again.* The Lord Jesus. ¶ *Saw no corruption.* Was raised without undergoing the usual change that succeeds death. As David *had* returned to corruption, and the Lord Jesus had *not*, it followed that this passage in Ps. xvi. referred to the Messiah.

38. *Be it known*, &c. Paul, having proved his resurrection, and shown that he was the Messiah, now states the *benefits* that were to be derived from his death. ¶ *Through this man.* See Notes on Lu. xxiv. 47.

39. *And by him.* By means of him; by his sufferings and death. ¶ *All that*

which ye could not be justified by
the law of Moses.
40 Beware, therefore, lest that
come upon you [h] which is spoken
of in the prophets;

h Is.29.14; Hab.1.5.

41 Behold, ye despisers, and
wonder, and perish; for I work a
work in your days, a work which
ye shall in no wise believe, though
a man declare it unto you.

---

believe. See Notes on Mar. xvi. 16. ¶ *Are justified.* Are regarded and treated as if they were righteous. They are pardoned, and admitted to the favour of God, and treated as if they had not offended. See this point explained in the Notes on Ro. i. 17; iii. 24, 25; iv. 1-8. ¶ *From all things.* From the guilt of all offences. ¶ *From which ye could not,* &c. The law of Moses commanded what was to be done. It appointed sacrifices and offerings as typical of a greater sacrifice. But those sacrifices could not take away sin. See Notes on He. ix. 7-14; x. 1-4, 11. The design of the *law* was not to reveal a way of pardon. That was reserved to be the peculiar purpose of the gospel. ¶ *The law of Moses.* The commands and institutions which he, under the direction of God, established.

40. *Beware, therefore.* Avoid that which is threatened. It will come on *some;* and Paul exhorted his hearers to beware lest it should come on *them.* It was the more important to caution them against this danger, as the Jews held that *they* were safe. ¶ *Lest that come.* That calamity; that threatened punishment. ¶ *In the prophets.* In that part of the Scriptures called "the Prophets." The Jews divided the Old Testament into three parts, of which "the Book of the Prophets" was one. See Notes on Lu. xxiv. 44. The place where this is recorded is Hab. i. 5. It is not taken from the Hebrew, but substantially from the Septuagint. The original design of the threatening was to announce the destruction that would come upon the nation by the Chaldeans. The original threatening was fulfilled. But it was as *applicable* to the Jews in the time of Paul as in the time of Habakkuk. The *principle* of the passage is, that if they held in contempt the doings of God, they would perish. The work which God was to do by means of the Chaldeans was so fearful, so unusual, and so remarkable, that they would not believe it in time to avoid the calamity. In the same way, the manner in which God gave the Messiah was so little in accordance with their expectation, that they might see it, yet disbelieve it; that they might have the fullest proof, and yet despise it; that they might wonder, and be amazed and astonished, and yet refuse to believe it, and be destroyed.

41. *Behold, ye despisers.* Hebrew, "Behold, ye among the heathen." The change from this expression to "ye despisers" was made by the Septuagint translators by a very slight alteration in the Hebrew word—probably from a variation in the copy which they used. It arose from reading בוגדים instead of בגוים, *bogedim* instead of *baggoim.* The Syriac, the Arabic, as well as the LXX., follow this reading. ¶ *And wonder.* Hebrew, "And regard, and wonder marvellously." ¶ *And perish.* This is not in the Hebrew, but is in the Septuagint and the Arabic. The word means literally to be removed from the sight; to disappear; and then to corrupt, defile, destroy, Mat. vi. 16, 19. The word, however, may mean *to be suffused with shame;* to be overwhelmed and confounded (Schleusner); and it may perhaps have this meaning here, answering to the Hebrew. The word used here is not that which is commonly employed to denote eternal perdition, though Paul seems to use it with reference to their destruction for rejecting the gospel. ¶ *For I work a work.* I do a thing. The thing to which the prophet Habakkuk referred was, that God would bring upon them the Chaldeans, that would destroy the temple and nation. In like manner Paul says that God in *that* time might bring upon the nation similar calamities. By rejecting the Messiah and his gospel, and by persevering in wickedness, they would bring upon themselves the destruction of the temple, the city, and the nation. It was this threatened destruction doubtless to which the apostle referred. ¶ *Which ye shall in no wise believe.* Which you will not believe. So remarkable, so unusual, so surpassing anything which had occurred. The original reference in Habakkuk is to the destruction of the temple by the Chaldeans; a thing which the Jews would not suppose *could* happen. The temple

42 And when the Jews were gone out of the synagogue, the Gentiles besought that these words might be preached to them [5]the next sabbath.

43 Now when the congregation was broken up, many of the Jews and religious proselytes followed Paul and Barnabas; who, speaking

[5] *in the week between*, or, *in the sabbath between.*

---

was so splendid; it had been so manifestly built by the direction of God; it had been so long under his protection, that they would suppose that it *could not* be given into the hands of their enemies to be demolished; and even though it were predicted by a prophet of God, still they would not believe it. The same feelings the Jews would have respecting the temple and city in the time of Paul. Though it was foretold by the Messiah, yet they were so confident that it was protected by God, that they would not believe that it could *possibly* be destroyed. The same infatuation seems to have possessed them during the siege of the city by the Romans. ¶ *Though a man*, &c. Though it be plainly predicted. We may learn, (1) That men may be greatly amazed and impressed by the doings or works of God, and yet be destroyed. (2) There may be a prejudice so obstinate that even a divine revelation will not remove it. (3) The fancied security of sinners will not save them. (4) There are men who will not believe in the possibility of their being lost, though it be declared by prophets, by apostles, by the Saviour, and by God. They will still remain in fancied security, and suffer nothing to alarm or rouse them. But, (5) As the fancied security of the Jews furnished no safety against the Babylonians or the Romans, so it is true that the indifference and unconcern of sinners will not furnish any security against the dreadful wrath of God. Yet there are multitudes who live amidst the displays of God's power and mercy in the redemption of sinners, and who witness the effects of his goodness and truth in revivals of religion, who live to *despise* it all; who are amazed and confounded by it; and who perish.

42. *And when the Jews*, &c. There is a great variety in the MSS. on this verse, and in the ancient versions. Griesbach and Knapp read it, "And when they were gone out, they besought them that these words might be spoken," &c. The Syriac reads it, "When they departed from them, they sought from them that these words might be spoken to them on another Sabbath." The Arabic, "Some of the synagogue of the Jews asked of them that they would exhort the Gentiles with them," &c. If these readings be correct, then the meaning is, that some of the Jews exhorted the apostles to proclaim these truths at some other time, particularly to the Gentiles. The MSS. greatly vary in regard to the passage, and it is, perhaps, impossible to determine the true reading. If the present reading in the English translation is to be regarded as genuine—of which, however, there is very little evidence—the meaning is, that a *part* of the Jews, perhaps a majority of them, rejected the message, and went out, though many of them followed Paul and Barnabas, ver. 43. ¶ *The Gentiles besought.* This expression is wanting in the Vulgate, Coptic, Arabic, and Syriac versions, and in a great many MSS. (Mill). It is omitted by Griesbach, Knapp, and others, and is probably spurious. Among other reasons which may be suggested why it is not genuine, this is one, that it is not probable that the *Gentiles* were in the habit of attending the synagogue. Those who attended there were called *proselytes.* The expression, if genuine, might mean either that the *Gentiles* besought, or that *they* besought the Gentiles. The latter would be the more probable meaning. ¶ *The next sabbath.* The *margin* has probably the correct rendering of the passage. The meaning of the verse is, that a wish was expressed that these doctrines might be repeated to them in the intermediate time before the next Sabbath.

43. *When the congregation.* Greek, when *the synagogue* was dissolved. ¶ *Broken up.* Dismissed. It does not mean that it was broken up by violence or disorder. It was dismissed in the usual way. ¶ *Many of the Jews.* Probably the majority of them rejected the message. See ver. 45. Still a deep impression was made on many of them. ¶ *And religious proselytes.* See ver. 16. Comp. Notes on Mat. xxiii. 15. Greek, *proselytes worshipping.* ¶ *Persuaded them to continue*, &c. It would appear from

to them, persuaded them to [i]continue in the grace of God.

44 And the next sabbath-day came almost the whole city together, to hear the word of God.

45 But when the Jews saw the multitudes, they were filled with envy, and spake against those things which were spoken by Paul, [k]contradicting and blaspheming.

46 Then Paul and Barnabas waxed bold, and said, It was necessary that the word of God should [l]first have been spoken to you; but seeing ye put it from you, and judge yourselves un-

i ch.14.22; He.6.11,12; 12.15. k ch.18.6. l Mat.10.6; Lu.24.47; Ro.1.16.

---

this that they professedly received the truth and embraced the Lord Jesus. This success was remarkable, and shows the power of the gospel when it is preached faithfully to men. ¶ *In the grace of God.* In *his favour*—in the faith, and prayer, and obedience which would be connected with his favour. The *gospel* is called the *grace* or *favour* of God, and they were exhorted to persevere in their attachment to it.

44. *And the next sabbath-day.* This was the *regular* day for worship, and it was natural that a greater multitude should convene on that day than on the other days of the week. ¶ *Came almost the whole city.* Whether this was in the synagogue is not affirmed; but it is probable that that was the place where the multitude convened. The news of the presence of the apostles, and of their doctrines, had been circulated, doubtless, by the Gentiles who had heard them, and curiosity attracted the multitude to hear them. Comp. Notes on ver. 7.

45. *They were filled with envy.* Greek, *zeal.* The word here denotes *wrath, indignation,* that such multitudes should be disposed to hear a message which they rejected, and which threatened to overthrow their religion. ¶ *Spake against.* Opposed the doctrine that Jesus was the Messiah; that the Messiah would be humble, lowly, despised, and put to death. ¶ *Contradicting.* Contradicting the apostles. This was evidently done in their presence, ver. 46, and would cause great tumult and disorder. ¶ *And blaspheming.* See Notes on Mat. ix. 3. The sense evidently is, that they *reproached* and *vilified* Jesus of Nazareth; they spake of him with contempt and scorn. To speak thus of him is denominated *blasphemy*, Lu. xxii. 65. When men are enraged they little regard the words which they utter, and little care how they may be estimated by God. When men attached to sect and party, in religion or politics, have no good *arguments* to employ, they attempt to overwhelm their adversaries by bitter and reproachful words. Men in the heat of strife, and in professed zeal for peculiar doctrines, more frequently utter *blasphemy* than they are aware. Precious and pure doctrines are often thus vilified because *we* do not believe them; and the heart of the Saviour is pierced anew, and his cause bleeds, by the wrath and wickedness of his professed friends. Comp. ch. xviii. 6.

46. *Waxed bold.* Became bold; spake boldly and openly. They were not terrified by their strife, or alarmed by their opposition. The contradictions and blasphemies of sinners often show that their consciences are alarmed; that the truth has taken effect; and then is not the time to shrink, but to declare more fearlessly the truth. ¶ *It was necessary.* It was so designed; so commanded. They regarded it as their duty to offer the gospel *first* to their own countrymen. See Notes on Lu. xxiv. 47. ¶ *Ye put it from you.* You reject it. ¶ *And judge yourselves.* By your conduct, by your rejecting it, you declare this. The word *judge* here does not mean *they expressed such an opinion*, or that *they regarded themselves* as unworthy of eternal life—for they thought just the reverse; but that by their conduct they CONDEMNED *themselves.* By such conduct they did, in fact, *pass sentence* on themselves, and show that they were unworthy of eternal life, and of having the offer of salvation any farther made to them. Sinners by their conduct do, in fact, condemn themselves, and show that they are not only unfit to be saved, but that they have advanced so far in wickedness that there is no *hope* of their salvation, and no propriety in offering them, any farther, eternal life. See Notes on Mat. vii. 6. ¶ *Unworthy*, &c. Unfit to be saved. They had *deliberately* and *solemnly* rejected the gospel, and thus

worthy of everlasting life, lo, [m]we turn to the Gentiles.

47 For so hath the Lord commanded us, *saying*, [n]I have set thee to be a light of the Gentiles,

m De.32.21; Mat.21.43; Ro.10.19. n Is.49.6.

that thou shouldest be for salvation unto the ends of the earth.

48 And when the Gentiles heard this, they were glad, and glorified the word of the Lord; and [o]as many

o ch.2.47; Ro.8.30.

---

shown that they were not fitted to enter into everlasting life. We may remark here, (1) When men, even but *once*, deliberately and solemnly *reject* the offers of God's mercy, it greatly endangers their salvation. The *probability* is, that they then put the cup of salvation for ever away from themselves. (2) The gospel produces an effect wherever it is preached. (3) When sinners are hardened, and spurn the gospel, it may often be the duty of ministers to turn their efforts toward others where they may have more prospect of success. A man will not long labour on a rocky, barren, sterile soil, when there is near him a rich and fertile valley that will abundantly reward the pains of cultivation. ¶ *Lo, we turn*, &c. We shall offer the gospel to them, and devote ourselves to seeking their salvation.

47. *For so*, &c. Paul, as usual, appeals to the Scriptures to justify his course. He here appeals to the *Old Testament* rather than to the command of the Saviour, because the Jews recognized the authority of their own Scriptures, while they would have turned in scorn from the command of Jesus of Nazareth. ¶ *I have set thee*, &c. I have constituted or appointed thee. This passage is found in Is. xlix. 6. See Notes on Is. xlix. 1–6. ¶ *To be a light.* See Notes on Jn. i. 4. ¶ *To the Gentiles.* This was in accordance with the uniform doctrines of Isaiah, Is. xlii. 1; liv. 3; lx. 3, 5, 16; lxi. 6, 9; lxii. 2; lxvi. 12; comp. Ro. xv. 9–12. ¶ *For salvation.* To save sinners. ¶ *Unto the ends of the earth.* To all lands; in all nations. See Notes on ch. i. 8.

48. *When the Gentiles heard this.* Heard that the gospel was to be preached to them. The doctrine of the Jews had been that salvation was confined to themselves. The Gentiles rejoiced that from the mouths of Jews themselves they now heard a different doctrine. ¶ *They glorified the word of the Lord.* They *honoured* it as a message from God; they recognized and received it as the word of God. The expression conveys the idea of *praise* on account of it, and of *reverence* for the message as the word of God. ¶ *And as many as were ordained* — ὅσοι ἦσαν τεταγμένοι. Syriac, "Who were *destined*," or constituted. Vulgate, "As many as were foreordained (quotquot erant præordinati) to eternal life believed." There has been much difference of opinion in regard to this expression. One class of commentators has supposed that it refers to the doctrine of election—to *God's ordaining* men to eternal life, and another class to their being *disposed themselves* to embrace the gospel—to those among them who did not reject and despise the gospel, but who were *disposed* and *inclined* to embrace it. The main inquiry is, what is the meaning of the word rendered *ordained?* The word is used but eight times in the New Testament: Mat. xxviii. 16, "Into a mountain where Jesus *had appointed* them;" that is, *previously* appointed—before his death; Lu. vii. 8, "For I also am a man *set under authority;*" appointed, or designated as a soldier, to be under the authority of another; Ac. xv. 2, "They *determined* that Paul and Barnabas, &c., should go to Jerusalem;" Ac. xxii. 10, "It shall be told thee of all things which *are appointed* for thee to do;" Ac. xxviii. 23, "And when they *had appointed* him a day,"&c.; Ro. xiii. 1, "The powers that be *are ordained* of God;" 1 Co. xvi. 15, "They *have addicted* themselves to the ministry of saints." The word τάσσω, *tasso*, or τάττω, *tatto*, properly means *to place—to place in a certain rank or order.* Its meaning is derived from arranging or disposing a body of soldiers in regular military order. In the places which have been mentioned above, the word is used to denote the following things: (1) *To command*, or to designate, Mat. xxviii. 16; Ac. xxii. 10; xxviii. 23. (2) To institute, constitute, or appoint, Ro. xiii. 1; comp. 2 Sa. vii. 11; 1 Sa. xxii. 7. (3) To determine, to take counsel, to resolve, Ac. xv. 2. (4) To subject to the anthority of another, Lu. vii. 8. (5) To addict to; to devote to, 1 Co. xvi. 15. The meaning may be thus expressed: (1) The word is *never* used to

as were ordained to eternal life,
believed.
49 And the word of the Lord
was published throughout all the
region.
50 But the Jews stirred up the
devout and honourable women,
and the chief men of the city,
[p]and raised persecution against
Paul and Barnabas, and expelled
them out of their coasts.
51 But they [q]shook off the dust
of their feet against them, and
came unto Iconium.
52 And the disciples were [r]filled
with joy, and with the Holy Ghost.

p 2 Ti.3.11. q Mar.6.11; Lu.9.5; ch.18.6. r Mat.5.12; 1 Th.1.6.

denote an internal *disposition* or *inclination* arising from one's own self. It does *not* mean that they *disposed themselves* to embrace eternal life. (2) It has uniformly the notion of an *ordering*, *disposing*, or *arranging from without;* that is, from some other source than the individual himself; as of a soldier, who is arranged or classified according to the will of the proper officer. In relation to these persons it means, therefore, that they were *disposed* or *inclined* to this from some other source than themselves. (3) It does not properly refer to an eternal decree, or directly to the doctrine of election—though that may be *inferred* from it; but it refers to their being THEN IN FACT *disposed* to embrace eternal life. They were *then inclined* by an influence from without themselves, or so *disposed* as to embrace eternal life. That this was done by the influence of the Holy Spirit is clear from all parts of the New Testament, Tit. iii. 5, 6; Jn. i. 13. It was not a disposition or *arrangement* originating with themselves, but with God. (4) This *implies* the doctrine of election. It was, *in fact*, that doctrine expressed *in an act*. It was nothing but God's disposing them to embrace eternal life. And that he does this according to a plan in his own mind—a plan which is unchangeable as he himself is unchangeable—is clear from the Scriptures. Comp. Ac. xviii. 10; Ro. viii. 28-30; ix. 15, 16, 21, 23; Ep. i. 4, 5, 11. The meaning may be expressed in few words—*who were* THEN *disposed, and in good earnest determined, to embrace eternal life, by the operation of the grace of God on their hearts.* ¶ *Eternal life.* Salvation. See Notes on Jn. iii. 36.

50. *But the Jews stirred up.* Excited opposition. ¶ *Honourable women.* See Notes on Mar. xv. 43. Women of influence, and connected with families of rank. Perhaps they were proselytes, and were connected with the magistrates of the city. ¶ *And raised persecution.* Probably on the ground that they produced disorder. The aid of "*chief men*" has often been called in to oppose revivals of religion, and to put a period, if possible, to the spread of the gospel. ¶ *Out of their coasts.* Out of the regions of their country; out of their province.

51. *But they shook off the dust*, &c. See Notes on Mat. x. 14. ¶ *And came unto Iconium.* This was the capital of Lycaonia. It is now called Konieh, and is the capital of Caramania. "Konieh extends to the east and south over the plain far beyond the walls, which are about two miles in circumference. . . . Mountains covered with snow rise on every side, excepting toward the east, where a plain, as flat as the desert of Arabia, extends far beyond the reach of the eye" (Capt. Kinneir). "Little, if anything, remains of Greek or Roman Iconium, if we except the ancient inscriptions and the fragments of sculptures which are built into the Turkish walls." "The city wall is said to have been erected by the Seljukian sultans: it seems to have been built from the ruins of more ancient buildings, as broken columns, capitals, pedestals, bas-reliefs, and other pieces of sculpture contribute toward its construction. It has eighty gates, of a square form, each known by a separate name, and, as well as most of the towers, embellished with Arabic inscriptions. . . . I observed a few Greek characters on the walls, but they were in so elevated a situation that I could not decipher them" (Capt. Kinneir). See Colonel Leake's description; and also the work of Col. Chesney (1850) on the Euphrates Expedition, vol. i. p. 348, 349.

52. *And the disciples.* The disciples in Antioch. ¶ *Were filled with joy.* This happened even in the midst of persecution, and is one of the many evidences that the gospel is able to fill the soul with joy even in the severest trials.

CHAPTER XIV.

AND it came to pass in Iconium that they went both together into the synagogue of the Jews, and so spake that a great multitude, both of the Jews and also of the Greeks, believed.

2 But the unbelieving Jews stirred up the Gentiles, and made their minds evil-affected against the brethren.

3 Long time therefore abode they speaking boldly in the Lord, which [a]gave testimony unto the word of his grace, and granted signs and wonders to be done by their hands.

4 But the multitude of the city was divided; and [b]part held with the Jews, and part with the apostles.

5 And when there was an assault made, both of the Gentiles and also of the Jews, with their rulers, to use *them* despitefully, and to stone them,

6 They were ware of *it*, [c]and fled unto Lystra and Derbe, cities of

a Mar.16.20; He.2.4. b ch.28.24. c Mat.10.23.

CHAPTER XIV.

1. *In Iconium.* See Notes on ch. xiii. 51. In this place, and in Antioch and Lystra, Timothy became acquainted with Paul and his manner of life, 2 Ti. iii. 10, 11. ¶ *So spake.* Spake with such power—their preaching was attended so much with the influence of the Spirit. ¶ *And of the Greeks.* Probably *proselytes* from the Greeks, who were in the habit of attending the synagogue.

2. *But the unbelieving Jews,* &c. See Notes on ch. xiii. 50. ¶ *And made their minds evil-affected.* Irritated, or exasperated them. ¶ *Against the brethren.* One of the common appellations by which Christians were known.

3. *Long time therefore.* It seems probable that there were here no forcible or public measures to expel them, as there had been at Antioch (ch. xiii. 50), and they therefore regarded it as their duty to remain. God granted them here also great success, which was the main reason for their continuing a long time. Persecution and opposition may be attended often with signal success to the gospel. ¶ *Spake boldly in the Lord.* In the *cause* of the Lord Jesus, or in his name and by his authority. Perhaps, also, the expression includes the idea of their *trusting* in the Lord. ¶ *Which gave testimony.* Bore witness to the truth of their message by working miracles, &c. Comp. Mar. xvi. 20. This was evidently *the Lord Jesus* to whom reference is here made, and it shows that he was still, though bodily absent from them, clothed with power, and still displayed that power in the advancement of his cause. The conversion of sinners accomplished by him is always a *testimony* as decided as it is cheering to the labours and messages of his servants. ¶ *Unto the word of his grace.* His gracious word, or message. ¶ *And granted signs,* &c. Miracles. See Notes on Ac. ii. 22.

4. *Was divided.* Into parties. Greek, there was a schism—'Εσχίσθη. ¶ *A part held with the Jews.* Held to the doctrines of the Jews, in opposition to the apostles. A revival of religion often produces excitement by the bad passions of opposers. The enemies of the truth form parties, and organize opposition. It is no uncommon thing even now for such parties to be formed; but the fault is not in Christianity. It lies with those who form a party *against* religion, and who confederate themselves, as was done here, to oppose it.

5. *An assault made.* Greek, a *rush*—ὁρμὴ. It denotes an impetuous excitement and aggression; a *rush* to put them to death. It rather describes a popular tumult than a calm and deliberate purpose. There was a violent, tumultuous excitement. ¶ *Both of the Gentiles,* &c. Of that part of them which was opposed to the apostles. ¶ *To use* them *despitefully.* See Notes on Mat. v. 44. To *reproach* them; to bring contempt upon them; to injure them. ¶ *And to stone them.* To put them to death by stoning; probably as blasphemers, Ac. vii. 57–59.

6. *They were ware of* it. They were in some way informed of the excitement and of their danger. ¶ *And fled unto Lystra and Derbe, cities of Lycaonia.* Lycaonia was one of the provinces of Asia Minor. It had Galatia north, Pisidia south, Cappadocia east, and Phrygia west. It was formerly within the limits of Phrygia, but was erected into a separate province by Augustus. "The district of Lycaonia extends from the ridges of Mount Taurus and the borders of Cilicia on the south,

Lycaonia, and unto the region that lieth round about:

7 And there they preached the gospel.

8 And there sat a certain man at Lystra, impotent in his feet, being a [d]cripple from his mother's womb, who never had walked.

9 The same heard Paul speak; who stedfastly beholding him, and perceiving that he [e]had faith to be healed,

10 Said with a loud voice, Stand upright on thy feet. And he [f]leaped and walked.

11 And when the people saw

d ch.3.2. e Mat.9.28,29. f Is.35.6.

---

to the Cappadocian hills on the north. It is a bare and dreary region, unwatered by streams, though in parts liable to occasional inundations. Strabo mentions one place where water was even sold for money. Across some portion of this plain Paul and Barnabas travelled both before and after their residence in Iconium. After leaving the high land to the north-west, during a journey of several hours before arriving at the city, the eye ranges freely over a vast expanse of level ground to the south and the east. The two most eminent objects in the view are the snowy summits of Mount Argæus, rising high above all the intervening hills in the direction of Armenia, and the singular mountain mass called the 'Kara-Dagh,' or 'Black Mount,' south-eastward in the direction of Cilicia. And still these features continue to be conspicuous after Iconium is left behind, and the traveller moves on over the plain toward Lystra and Derbe. Mount Argæus still rises far to the north-east, at the distance of 150 miles. The Black Mountain is gradually approached, and discovered to be an isolated mass, with reaches of the plain extending round it like channels of the sea. The cities of Lystra and Derbe were somewhere about the bases of the Black Mountain." The exact position of Lystra and Derbe is still subject to some uncertainty. In 1824 Col. Leake wrote thus: "Nothing can more strongly show the little progress that has hitherto been made in a knowledge of the ancient geography of Asia Minor, than that, of the cities which the journey of St. Paul has made so interesting to us, the site of one only (Iconium) is yet certainly known. Perga, Antioch of Pisidia, Lystra, and Derbe, remain to be discovered." The situation of the first two of these towns has been since that fully identified, and some ruins have been found which have been supposed to mark the place of Lystra and Derbe, though not with entire certainty. ¶ *And unto the region*, &c. The adjacent country. Though persecuted, they still preached; and though driven from one city, they fled into another. This was the direction of the Saviour, Mat. x. 23.

8. *And there sat.* There dwelt, Mat. ix. 16; Ac. xviii. 11 (margin). The word *sat*, however, indicates his usual posture, his helpless condition. Such persons commonly sat by the wayside, or in some public place, to ask for alms, Mar. x. 46. ¶ *Impotent in his feet*—ἀδύνατος. Without any power. Entirely deprived of the use of his feet. ¶ *Being a cripple.* Lame. ¶ *Who never had walked.* The miracle, therefore, would be more remarkable, as the man would be well known. As they were persecuted from place to place, and opposed in every manner, it was desirable that a signal miracle should be performed to carry forward and establish the work of the gospel.

9. *Who stedfastly beholding him.* Fixing his eyes intently on him. See Notes on Ac. i. 10. ¶ *And perceiving.* How he perceived this is not said. Perhaps it was indicated by the ardour, humility, and strong desire depicted in his countenance. He had heard Paul, and perhaps the apostle had dwelt particularly on the *miracles* with which the gospel had been attested. The miracles wrought also in Iconium had doubtless also been heard of in Lystra. ¶ *Had faith to be healed.* Comp. Mat. ix. 21, 22, 28, 29; Lu. vii. 50; xvii. 19; xviii. 42.

10. *Said with a loud voice.* See Notes on Jn. xi. 43. ¶ *And he leaped.* See Notes on Ac. iii. 8. Comp. Is. xxxv. 6.

11. *They lifted up their voices.* They spoke with astonishment, such as might be expected when it was supposed that the gods had come down. ¶ *In the speech of Lycaonia.* What this language was has much perplexed commentators. It was probably a mixture of the Greek and Syriac. In that region generally the Greek was usually

what Paul had done, they lifted up their voices, saying in the speech of Lycaonia, [g]The gods are come down to us in the likeness of men.

12 And they called Barnabas, Jupiter; and Paul, Mercurius, because he was the chief speaker.

13 Then the priest of Jupiter, which was before their city, brought

g ch.28.6.

spoken with more or less purity; and from the fact that it was not far from the regions of Syria, it is probable that the Greek language was corrupted with this foreign admixture. ¶ *The gods*, &c. All the region was idolatrous. The gods which were worshipped there were those which were worshipped throughout Greece. ¶ *Are come down.* The miracle which Paul had wrought led them to suppose this. It was evidently beyond human ability, and they had no other way of accounting for it than by supposing that their gods had personally appeared. ¶ *In the likeness of men.* Many of their gods were heroes, whom they worshipped after they were dead. It was a common belief among them that the gods appeared to men in human form. The poems of Homer, of Virgil, &c., are filled with accounts of such appearances, and the only way in which they supposed the gods to take knowledge of human affairs, and to aid men, was by their personally appearing in this form. See Homer's *Odyssey*, xvii. 485; Catullus, 64, 384; Ovid's *Metamorph.*, i. 212 (Kuinoel). Thus Homer says:

> "For in similitude of strangers oft
> The gods, who can with ease all shapes assume,
> Repair to populous cities, where they mark
> Th' outrageous and the righteous deeds of men."
> COWPER.

12. *And they called Barnabas, Jupiter.* Jupiter was the most powerful of all the gods of the ancients. He was represented as the son of Saturn and Ops, and was educated in a cave on Mount Ida, in the island of Crete. The worship of Jupiter was almost universal. He was the Ammon of Africa, the Belus of Babylon, the Osiris of Egypt. His common appellation was, The Father of gods and men. He was usually represented as sitting upon a golden or an ivory throne, holding in one hand a thunderbolt, and in the other a sceptre of cypress. His power was supposed to extend over other gods; and everything was subservient to his will except the Fates. There is the most abundant proof that he was worshipped in the region of Lycaonia and throughout Asia Minor. There was, besides, a fable among the inhabitants of Lycaonia that Jupiter and Mercury had once visited that place, and had been received by Philemon. The whole fable is related by Ovid, *Metam.*, 8, 611, &c. ¶ *And Paul, Mercurius.* Mercury, called by the Greeks *Hermes*, was a celebrated god of antiquity. No less than five of this name are mentioned by Cicero. The most celebrated was the son of Jupiter and Maia. He was the messenger of the gods, and of Jupiter in particular; he was the patron of travellers and shepherds; he conducted the souls of the dead into the infernal regions; he *presided over orators, and declaimers*, and merchants; and he was also the god of thieves, pickpockets, and all dishonest persons. He was regarded as *the god of eloquence;* and as light, rapid, and quick in his movements. The conjecture of Chrysostom is, that Barnabas was a large, athletic man, and was hence taken for Jupiter; and that Paul was small in his person, and was hence supposed to be Mercury. ¶ *Because he was the chief speaker.* The office of Mercury was to deliver the messages of the gods; and as Paul only had been discoursing, he was supposed to be Mercury.

13. *Then the priest of Jupiter.* He whose office it was to conduct the worship of Jupiter by offering sacrifices, &c. ¶ *Which was before their city.* The word "which" here refers not to *the priest*, but to *Jupiter*. The temple or image of Jupiter was in front of their city, or near the gates. Ancient cities were supposed to be under the protection of particular gods; and their *image*, or a temple for their worship, was placed commonly in a conspicuous place at the entrance of the city. ¶ *Brought oxen.* Probably brought two—one to be sacrificed to each. It was common to sacrifice bullocks to Jupiter. ¶ *And garlands.* The victims of sacrifice were usually decorated with ribbons and chaplets of flowers. See Kuinoel. ¶ *Unto the gates.* The gates of the city, where were the images or temple of the gods. ¶ *Would have done sacrifice.* Would have offered sacrifice to Barnabas and Paul. This the priest deemed a part of his office. And here we have

oxen and garlands unto the gates,
and [h] would have done sacrifice with
the people.
14 *Which*, when the apostles,
Barnabas and Paul, heard *of*, [i] they
rent their clothes, and ran in among
the people, crying out,
15 And saying, Sirs, why do ye
these things? We [k] also are men
of like passions with you, and preach
unto you, that ye should turn from
[l] these vanities [m] unto the living God,
[n] which made heaven and earth, and
the sea, and all things that are
therein:
16 Who [o] in times past suffered all
nations to walk in their own ways.

h Da.2.46. *i* Mat.26.65. *k* ch.10.26; Ja.5.17; Re.19.10.
l 1 Sa.12.21; 1 Ki.16.13; Je.14.22; Jn.2.8; 1 Co.8.4. *m* 1 Th.1.9. *n* Ge.1.1; Ps.33.6; 146.6; Re.14.7. *o* Ps.81.12; ch.17.30.

---

a remarkable and most affecting instance of the folly and stupidity of idolatry.

14. Which, *when the apostles.* Barnabas is called an apostle because he was *sent forth* by the church on a particular message (ch. xiii. 3; comp. ch. xiv. 26), not because he had been chosen to the peculiar work of the apostleship—to bear witness to the life and resurrection of Christ. See Notes on ch. i. 22. ¶ *They rent their clothes.* As an expression of their abhorrence of what the people were doing, and of their deep grief that they should thus debase themselves by offering worship to men. See Notes on Mat. xxvi. 65.

15. *And saying, Sirs.* Greek, *Men.* ¶ *Why do ye these things?* This is an expression of solemn remonstrance at the folly of their conduct in worshipping those who were *men.* The *abhorrence* which they evinced at this may throw strong light on the rank and character of the Lord Jesus Christ. When an offer was made to worship Paul and Barnabas, they shrank from it with strong expressions of aversion and indignation. Yet when similar worship was offered to the Lord Jesus; when he was addressed by Thomas in the language of worship, "My Lord and my God" (Jn. xx. 28), he uttered not the slightest reproof. Nay, he approved it, and expressed his approbation of others who should also do it, ver. 29. Comp. Jn. v. 23. How can this difference be accounted for except on the supposition that the Lord Jesus was divine? Would he, if a mere man, receive homage as God, when his disciples rejected it with horror? ¶ *Of like passions with you.* We are *men* like yourselves. We have no claim, no pretensions to anything more. The word "passions" here means simply that they had the common feelings and propensities of men—the *nature* of men; the *affections* of men. It does not mean that they were subject to any improper *passions*, to ill temper, &c., as some have supposed; but that they did not pretend to be gods. "We need food and drink; we are exposed to pain, and sickness, and death." The Latin Vulgate renders it, "We are *mortal* like yourselves." The expression stands opposed to the proper conception of God, who is not subject to these affections, who is most blessed and immortal. Such a Being *only* is to be worshipped; and the apostles remonstrated strongly with them on the folly of paying religious homage to beings like themselves. Comp. Ja. v. 17, "Elias [Elijah] was a man subject to like passions as we are," &c. ¶ *That ye should turn from these vanities.* That you should cease to worship idols. Idols are often called vanities, or vain things, De. xxxii. 21; 2 Ki. xvii. 15; 1 Ki. xvi. 13, 26; Je. ii. 5; viii. 19; x. 8; Jonah ii. 8. They are called *vanities*, a *lie*, or lying vanities, as opposed to the living and true God, because they are *unreal;* because they have no power to help; because confidence in them is vain. ¶ *Unto the living God.* 1 Th. i. 9. He is called the *living* God to distinguish him from idols. See Notes on Mat. xvi. 16. ¶ *Which made heaven,* &c. Who thus showed that he was the only proper object of worship. This doctrine, that there is *one* God who has made all things, was new to them. They worshipped multitudes of divinities; and though they regarded Jupiter as the father of gods and men, yet they had no conception that all things had been created by the will of one Infinite Being.

16. *Who in times past.* Previous to the gospel; in past ages. ¶ *Suffered all nations.* Permitted all nations; that is, all Gentiles, Ac. xvii. 30, "And the times of this ignorance God winked at." ¶ *To walk in their own ways.* To conduct themselves without the restraints and instructions of a written law. They

17 Nevertheless, [p] he left not himself without witness, in that he did good, and [q] gave us rain from heaven, and fruitful seasons, filling our hearts with food and gladness.

18 And with these sayings scarce restrained they the people, that they had not done sacrifice unto them.

19 And there came thither *certain* Jews from Antioch and Iconium, who persuaded the people, and, having [r] stoned Paul, drew

p Ro.1.20. q Job 5.10; Ps.147.8; Mat.5.45. r 2 Co.11.25.

were permitted to follow their own reason and passions, and their own system of religion. God gave them no written laws, and sent to them no messengers. *Why* he did this we cannot determine. It might have been, among other reasons, to show to the world conclusively: (1) The insufficiency of *reason* to guide men in the matters of religion. The experiment was made under the most favourable circumstances. The most enlightened nations, the Greeks and Romans, were left to pursue the inquiry, and failed no less than the most degraded tribes of men. The trial was made for four thousand years, and attended with the same results everywhere. (2) It showed the need of revelation to guide man. (3) It evinced, beyond the possibility of mistake, the depravity of man. In all nations, in all circumstances, men had shown the same alienation from God. By suffering them to walk in their *own* ways, it was seen that those ways were sin, and that some power more than human was necessary to bring men back to God.

17. *Nevertheless.* Though he gave them no revelation. ¶ *He left not himself without witness.* He gave demonstration of his existence and of his moral character. ¶ *In that he did good.* By doing good. The manner in which he did it, Paul immediately specifies. Idols did *not* do good; they conferred no favours, and were, therefore, unworthy of confidence. ¶ *And gave us rain from heaven.* Rain from above—from the clouds, Mar. viii. 11; Lu. ix. 54; xvii. 29; xxi. 11; Jn. vi. 31, 32. Rain is one of the evidences of the goodness of God. Man could not cause it; and without it, regulated at proper intervals of time and in proper quantities, the earth would soon be one wide scene of desolation. There is scarcely anything which more certainly indicates unceasing care and wisdom than the needful and refreshing showers of rain. The sun and stars move by fixed laws, whose operation we can see and anticipate. The falling of rain is regulated by laws which we cannot trace, and it *seems*, therefore, to be poured, as it were, directly from God's hollow hand, Ps. cxlvii. 8, "Who covereth the heaven with clouds; who prepareth rain for the earth." ¶ *And fruitful seasons.* Seasons when the earth produces abundance. It is remarkable, and a striking proof of the divine goodness, that so few seasons are unfruitful. The earth yields her increase; the labours of the husbandman are crowned with success; and the goodness of God demands the expressions of praise. God does not forget his ancient covenant (Ge. viii. 22), though *man* forgets it, and disregards his great Benefactor. ¶ *Filling our hearts with food.* The word *hearts* is here used as a Hebraism, to denote *persons themselves;* filling *us* with food, &c. Comp. Mat. xii. 40. ¶ *Gladness.* Joy; comfort—the comfort arising from the supply of our constantly returning wants. This is proof of ever-watchful goodness. It is a demonstration at once that there *is* a God, and that he is good. It would be easy for God to withdraw these blessings, and leave us to want. A single word, or a single deviation from the fulness of benevolence, would blast all these comforts, and leave us to lamentation, woe, and death, Ps. civ. 27-29; cxlv. 15, 16.

18. *And with these sayings.* With these arguments. ¶ *Scarce restrained they the people.* They were so fully satisfied that the gods had appeared, and were so full of zeal to do them honour.

19. *And there came thither* certain *Jews.* Not satisfied with having expelled them from Antioch and Iconium, they still pursued them. Persecutors often exhibit a zeal and perseverance in a bad cause which it would be well if Christians evinced in a holy cause. Bad men will often travel farther to do evil than good men will to do good; and wicked men often show more zeal in opposing the gospel than professed Christians do in advancing it. ¶ *Antioch and Iconium.* See Notes on ch. xiii. 14, 51. ¶ *Who persuaded the people.* That they were

him out of the city, supposing he had been dead.

20 Howbeit, as the disciples stood round about him, he rose up, and came into the city; and the next day he departed with Barnabas to Derbe.

21 And when they had preached the gospel to that city, and [1]had

[1] had many disciples.

impostors; and who excited their rage against them. ¶ *And having stoned Paul.* Whom they were just before ready to worship as a god! What a striking instance of the fickleness and instability of idolaters! and what a striking instance of the instability and uselessness of mere *popularity!* Just before they were ready to adore him; now they sought to put him to death. Nothing is more fickle than popular favour. The unbounded admiration of a man may soon be changed into unbounded indignation and contempt. It was well for Paul that he was not *seeking* this popularity, and that he did not depend on it for happiness. He had a good conscience; he was engaged in a good cause; he was under the protection of God; and his happiness was to be sought from a higher source than the applause of men, fluctuating and uncertain as the waves of the sea. To this transaction Paul referred when he enumerated his trials in 2 Co. xi. 25, "Once was I stoned." ¶ *Drew* him *out of the city.* Probably in haste, and in popular rage, as if he was unfit to be *in* the city, and was unworthy of a decent burial; for it does not appear that they contemplated an interment, but indignantly dragged him beyond the walls of the city to leave him there. Such sufferings and trials it cost to establish that religion in the world which has shed so many blessings on man; which now crowns us with comfort; which saves us from the abominations and degradations of idolatry here, and from the pains of hell hereafter. ¶ *Supposing he had been dead.* The next verse shows that he was really *not* dead, though many commentators, as well as the Jews, have supposed that he was, and was miraculously restored to life. It is remarkable that Barnabas was not exposed to this popular fury. But it is to be remembered that Paul was the chief speaker, and it was his peculiar zeal that exposed him to this tumult.

20. *Howbeit.* Notwithstanding the supposition that he was dead. ¶ *As the disciples stood round about him.* It would seem that *they* did not suppose that he was dead; but might be expecting that he would revive. ¶ *He rose up,* &c. Most commentators have supposed that this was the effect of a miracle. They have maintained that he could not have risen so soon, and entered into the city, without the interposition of miraculous power (Calvin, Doddridge, Clarke, &c.). But the commentators have asserted that which is not intimated by the sacred penman. The probability is that he was *stunned* by a blow—perhaps a single blow—and after a short time recovered from it. Nothing is more common than thus by a violent blow on the head to be rendered apparently lifeless, the effect of which soon is over, and the person restored to strength. Pricæus and Wetstein suppose that Paul *feigned* himself to be dead, and when out of danger rose and returned to the city. But this is wholly improbable. ¶ *And came into the city.* It is remarkable that he should have returned again into the same city. But probably it was only among the new converts that he showed himself. The Jews supposed that he was dead; and it does not appear that he again exposed himself to their rage. ¶ *And the next day,* &c. The opposition here was such that it was vain to attempt to preach there any longer. Having been seen by the disciples after his supposed death, their faith was confirmed, and he departed to preach in another place. ¶ *To Derbe,* ver. 6.

21. *Had taught many.* Or, rather, had made many disciples (margin). ¶ *To Lystra,* ver. 6. ¶ *And* to *Iconium,* ver. 1. We have here a remarkable instance of the *courage* of the apostles. In these very places they had been persecuted and stoned, and yet in the face of danger they ventured to return. The welfare of the infant churches they deemed of more consequence than their own safety; and they threw themselves again into the midst of danger, to comfort and strengthen those just converted to God. There are times when ministers should not count their own lives dear to them (Ac. xx. 24), but when they should fearlessly throw themselves into the midst of danger, confid-

taught many, they returned again
to Lystra, and *to* Iconium, and
Antioch,
22 Confirming the souls of the
disciples, *and* exhorting them [s]to
continue in the faith, [t]and that
we must through much tribulation
enter into the kingdom of God.
23 And when they had ordained
them elders in every church, and

s ch.13.43.

t Ro.8.17; 2 Ti.3.12.

ing only in the protecting care of their God and Saviour.

22. *Confirming, strengthening*—ἐπιστηρίζοντες. The expression "to confirm" has in some churches a technical signification, denoting "to admit to the full privileges of a Christian by the imposition of hands" (Johnson). It is scarcely necessary to say that the word here refers to no such rite. It has no relation to an imposition of hands, or to the thing which is usually supposed to be denoted by the rite of "confirmation." It means simply that they *established*, *strengthened*, made firm, or encouraged by the presentation of truth and by the motives of the gospel. Whether the rite of confirmation, as practised by some churches, be founded on the authority of the New Testament or not, it is certain that it can receive no support from this passage. The truth was, that these were young converts; that they were surrounded by enemies, and exposed to temptations and to dangers; that they had as yet but a slight acquaintance with the truths of the gospel, and that it was therefore important that they should be further instructed in the truth, and established in the faith of the gospel. This was what Paul and Barnabas returned to accomplish. There is not the slightest evidence that they had not been admitted to the full privileges of the church before, or that any *ceremony* was now performed in confirming or strengthening them. ¶ *The souls.* The minds, the hearts, or *the disciples themselves.* ¶ *Disciples.* They were as yet *scholars*, or *learners*, and the apostles returned to instruct them further in the doctrines of Christ. ¶ And *exhorting them*, &c. Ch. xiii. 43. ¶ *In the faith.* In the belief of the gospel. ¶ *And that we must*—καὶ ὅτι δεῖ. That it is fit or proper that we should. Not that it is fixed by any fatal necessity, but that we are not to expect that it will be otherwise. We are to calculate on it when we become Christians. *Why* it is proper, or fit, the apostle did not state. But we may remark that it is proper, (1) Because such is the opposition of the world to pure religion that it cannot be avoided. Of this they had had striking demonstration in Lystra and Iconium. (2) It is necessary to reclaim us from wandering, and to keep us in the path of duty, Ps. cxix. 67, 71. (3) It is necessary to wean us from the world; to keep before our minds the great truth that we have here "no continuing city and no abiding place." Trial here makes us pant for a world of rest. The opposition of sinners makes us desire that world where "the wicked shall cease from troubling," and where there shall be eternal friendship and peace. (4) When we are persecuted and afflicted, we may remember that it has been the lot of Christians from the beginning. We tread a path that has been watered by the tears of the saints, and rendered sacred by the shedding of the best blood on the earth. The Saviour trod that path; and it is enough that the "disciple be as his master, and the servant as his lord," Mat. x. 24, 25. ¶ *Through much tribulation.* Through many afflictions. ¶ *Enter into the kingdom of God.* Be saved. Enter into heaven. See Notes on Mat. iii. 2.

23. *And when they had ordained*—χειροτονήσαντες. The word *ordain* we now use in an ecclesiastical sense, to denote a setting apart to an office by the imposition of hands. But it is evident that the word here is not employed in that sense. That imposition of hands *might* have occurred in setting apart afterwards to this office is certainly possible, but it is not implied in the word employed here, and did not take place in the transaction to which this word refers. The word occurs but in one other place in the New Testament, 2 Co. viii. 19, where it is applied to Luke, and translated, "who was also chosen of the church (that is, appointed or elected by suffrage by the churches) to travel with us," &c. The verb properly denotes *to stretch out the hand;* and as it was customary to elect to office, or to vote, by stretching out or elevating the hand, so the word simply

had prayed with fasting, they commended them to the Lord, on whom they believed.

means to elect, appoint, or designate to any office. The word here refers simply to an *election* or *appointment* of the elders. It is said, indeed, that Paul and Barnabas did this. But probably all that is meant by it is that they presided in the assembly when the choice was made. It does not mean that they appointed them without consulting the church; but it evidently means that they appointed them in the usual way of appointing officers, by the suffrages of the people. See Schleusner, and the notes of Doddridge and Calvin. ¶ *Ordained them.* Appointed for *the disciples*, or for the church. It is not meant that the elders were ordained for the apostles. ¶ *Elders.* Greek, *presbyters.* Literally this word refers to the aged. See Notes on ch. xi. 30. But it may also be a word relating to office, denoting those who were more experienced than others, and who were chosen to preside over and to instruct the rest. What was the nature of this office, and what was the design of the appointment, is not intimated in this word. All that seems to be implied is, that they were to take the charge of the churches during the absence of the apostles. The apostles were about to leave them. They were just organized into churches; they were inexperienced; they needed counsel and direction; they were exposed to dangers; and it was necessary, therefore, that persons should be designated to watch over the spiritual interests of the brethren. The probability is, that they performed all the functions that were required in the infant and feeble churches; in exhorting, instructing, governing, &c. The more experienced and able would be most likely to be active in exhorting and instructing the brethren; and all would be useful in counselling and guiding the flock. The same thing occurred in the church at Ephesus. See Notes on Ac. xx. 17–28. It is not improbable that the business of instructing, or teaching, would be gradually confined to the more talented and able of the elders, and that the others would be concerned mainly in governing and directing the general affairs of the church. ¶ *In every church.* It is implied here that there were *elders in each church;* that is, that in each

24 And after they had passed throughout Pisidia, they came to Pamphylia.

25 And when they had preach-

church there was more than one. See ch. xv. 21, where a similar phraseology occurs, and where it is evident that there was more than one reader of the law of Moses in each city. Comp. Tit. i. 5, "I left thee in Crete, that thou shouldst . . . ordain *elders in every city;*" Ac. xx. 17, "And from Miletus he sent to Ephesus, and called *the elders of the church.*" It could not mean, therefore, that they appointed a *single* minister or pastor to each church, but they committed the whole affairs of the church to a bench of elders. ¶ *And had prayed with fasting.* With the church. They were about to leave them. They had intrusted the interests of the church to a body of men chosen for this purpose; and they now commended the church and its elders together to God. Probably they had no prospect of seeing them again, and they parted as ministers and people should part, and as Christian friends should part, with humble prayer, commending themselves to the protecting care of God. ¶ *They commended them,* &c. They *committed* the infant church to the guardianship of the Lord. They were feeble, inexperienced, and exposed to dangers; but in his hands they were safe. ¶ *To the Lord,* &c. The Lord Jesus. The connection shows that he is particularly referred to. In his hands the redeemed are secure. When we part with Christian friends, we may, with confidence, leave them in his holy care and keeping.

24. *Throughout Pisidia.* Note, ch. xiii. 14. ¶ *They came to Pamphylia.* See Notes on ch. xiii. 13. These places they had visited before.

25. *In Perga.* See Notes on ch. xiii. 13. ¶ *They went down into Attalia.* "Attalia had something of the same relation to Perga which Cadiz has to Seville. In each case the latter city is approached by a river voyage, and the former is more conveniently placed on the open sea. Attalus Philadelphus, king of Pergamus, whose dominions extended from the north-western corner of Asia Minor to the Sea of Pamphylia, had built this city in a convenient position for commanding the trade of Syria or Egypt. When Alexander the Great passed this way, no such city was in

ed the word in Perga, they went down into Attalia:

26 And thence sailed to Antioch, from[u] whence they had been [v]recommended to the grace of God for the work which they fulfilled.

27 And when they were come, and had gathered the church together, [w]they rehearsed all that God had done with them, and how he had [x]opened the door of faith unto the Gentiles.

28 And there they abode long time with the disciples.

u ch.13.1,3. v ch.15.40. w ch.15.4. x 1 Co.16.9; 2 Co.2.12; Re.3.8.

---

existence; but since the days of the kings of Pergamus, who inherited a fragment of his vast empire, Attalia has always existed and flourished, retaining the name of the monarch who built it. Its ancient site is not now certainly known" (*Life and Epistles of St. Paul*, vol. i. p. 200, 201). It is probable that it is the modern *Satalia*.

26. *And thence sailed to Antioch.* Note, ch. xi. 19. ¶ *From whence they had been recommended*, &c. Where they had been appointed to this missionary tour by the church, ch. xiii. 1–4. ¶ *To the grace of God.* His favour and protection had been implored for them in their perilous undertaking. ¶ *For the work which they fulfilled.* This shows conclusively, (1) That they had accomplished fully the work which was originally contemplated. It was strictly a *missionary tour* among the Gentiles. It was an important and hazardous enterprise, and was the first in which the church formally engaged. Hence so much importance is attached to it, and so faithful a record of it is preserved. (2) It shows that the act by which they were set apart to this (Ac. xiii. 1–3) was not an ordination to the ministerial office. It was an appointment to a missionary tour. (3) It shows that the act was not an appointment to *the apostleship.* Paul was an apostle before by the express appointment of the Saviour; and Barnabas was never an apostle in the original and proper sense of the term. It was a designation to a temporary work, which was now fulfilled.

We may remark, also, in regard to this *missionary tour*, (1) That the work of *missions* is one which early engaged the attention of Christians. (2) It entered into their *plans*, and was one in which the church was deeply interested. (3) The work of missions is attended with danger. Men are now no less hostile to the gospel than they were in Lystra and Iconium. (4) Missionaries should be sustained by the prayers of the church. And, (5) In the conduct of Paul and Barnabas we have an example for missionaries in founding churches, and in regard to their own trials and persecutions. If they were persecuted, missionaries may be now; and if the grace of Christ was sufficient to sustain them, it is not the less sufficient to sustain those of our own times amidst all the dangers attending the preaching of the cross in pagan lands.

27. *They rehearsed*, &c. Ch. xi. 4. They related what had happened; their dangers and their success. This they did because they had been sent out by the church, and it was proper that they should give an account of their work; and because it furnished a suitable occasion of gratitude to God for his mercy. ¶ *All that God had done*, &c. In protecting, guarding them, &c. All was traced to God. ¶ *Had opened the door of faith.* Had furnished an opportunity of preaching the gospel to the Gentiles, 1 Co. xvi. 9; 2 Co. ii. 12.

28. *And there they abode.* At Antioch. ¶ *Long time.* How long is not intimated; but we hear no more of them until the council at Jerusalem, mentioned in the next chapter. If the transactions recorded in this chapter occurred, as is supposed, about A.D. 45 or 46, and the council at Jerusalem assembled A.D. 51 or 53, as is supposed, then here is an interval of from five to eight years in which we have no account of them. Where they were, or what was their employment in this interval, the sacred historian has not informed us. It is certain, however, that Paul made several journeys of which we have no particular record in the New Testament, and it is possible that some of those journeys occurred during this interval. Thus he preached the gospel as far as Illyricum, Ro. xv. 19. And in 2 Co. xi. 23–27, there is an account of trials and persecutions, of many of which we have no distinct record, and which might have occurred during this interval. We may be certain that these holy men were not idle. From the example of Paul and

CHAPTER XV.

AND[a] certain men which came down from Judea taught the brethren, *and said*, [b]Except ye be circumcised [c]after the manner of Moses, ye cannot be saved.

a Ga.2.12. b Jn.7.22. c Le.12.3.

Barnabas as recorded in this chapter, we may learn to bear all persecutions and trials without a murmur, and to acknowledge the good hand of God in our preservation in our travels; in our defence when we are persecuted; in all the opportunities which may be open before us to do-good; and in all the success which may attend our efforts. Christians should remember that it is *God* who opens doors of usefulness; and they should regard it as a matter of thanksgiving that such doors *are* opened, and that they are permitted to spread the gospel, whatever toil it may cost, whatever persecution they may endure, whatever perils they may encounter.

CHAPTER XV.

1. *And certain men.* These were undoubtedly men who had been Jews, but who were now converted to Christianity. The fact that they were willing to refer the matter in dispute to the apostles and elders (ver. 2) shows that they had professedly embraced the Christian religion. The account which follows is a record of the first internal dissension which occurred in the Christian church. Hitherto the church had been struggling against external foes. Violent persecutions had raged, and had fully occupied the attention of Christians. But now the churches were at peace. They enjoyed great external prosperity in Antioch, and the great enemy of souls took occasion then, as he has often done in similar circumstances since, to excite contentions in the church itself, so that when external violence could not destroy it, an effort was made to secure the same object by internal dissension and strife. This history, therefore, is particularly important, as it is the record of the first unhappy debate which arose in the bosom of the church. It is further important, as it shows the manner in which such controversies were settled in apostolic times, and as it established some very important principles respecting the perpetuity of the religious rites of the Jews. ¶ *Came down from Judea.* To Antioch, and to the regions adjacent, which had been visited by the apostles, ver. 23. Judea was a high and hilly region, and going from that toward the level countries adjacent to the sea was represented to be descending, or going down. ¶ *Taught the brethren.* That is, Christians. They endeavoured to *convince* them of the necessity of keeping the laws of Moses. ¶ *Except ye be circumcised.* This was the leading or principal rite of the Jewish religion. It was indispensable to the name and privileges of a Jew. Proselytes to their religion were circumcised as well as native-born Jews, and they held it to be indispensable to salvation. It is evident from this that Paul and Barnabas had dispensed with this rite in regard to the Gentile converts, and that they intended to found the Christian church on the principle that the Jewish ceremonies were to cease. When, however, it was necessary to conciliate the minds of the Jews and to prevent contention, Paul did not hesitate to practise circumcision, ch. xvi. 3. ¶ *After the manner of Moses.* According to the custom which Moses commanded; according to the Mosaic ritual. ¶ *Ye cannot be saved.* The Jews regarded this as indispensable to salvation. The grounds on which they would press it on the attention of Gentile converts would be very plausible, and such as would produce much embarrassment. For, (1) It would be maintained that the laws of Moses were the laws of God, and were therefore unchangeable; and, (2) It would doubtless be maintained that the religion of the Messiah was only a completing and perfecting of the Jewish religion—that it was designed simply to carry out its principles according to the promises, and not to subvert and destroy anything that had been established by divine authority. It is usually not difficult to perplex and embarrass young converts with questions of modes, and rites, and forms of religion; and it is not uncommon that a revival is followed by some contention just like this. Opposing sects urge the claims of their peculiar rites, and seek to make proselytes, and introduce contention and strife into an otherwise peaceful and happy Christian community.

2 When, therefore, Paul and Barnabas had no small dissension and disputation with them, they determined that [d]Paul and Barnabas, and certain other of them, should go up to Jerusalem, unto the apostles and elders, about this question.

d Ga.2.1.

2. *Had no small dissension and disputation.* The word rendered *dissension* (στάσις) denotes sometimes sedition or intestine war, and sometimes earnest and violent disputation or controversy, Ac. xxiii. 7, 10. In this place it clearly denotes that there was earnest and warm discussion; but it is *not* implied that there was any improper heat or temper on the part of Paul and Barnabas. Important principles were to be settled in regard to the organization of the church. Doctrines were advanced by the Judaizing teachers which were false, and which tended to produce great disorder in the church. Those doctrines were urged with zeal, were declared to be essential to salvation, and would therefore tend to distract the minds of Christians, and to produce great anxiety. It became, therefore, necessary to meet them with a determined purpose, and to establish the truth on an immovable basis. And the case shows that it is right to "contend earnestly for the faith" (Jude 3); and, when similar cases occur, that it is proper to resist the approach of error with all the arguments which may be at our command, and with all the weapons which truth can furnish. It is further implied here that it is the duty of the ministers of the gospel to defend the truth and to oppose error. Paul and Barnabas regarded themselves as set for this purpose (comp. Phi. i. 17, "Knowing that I am set for the *defence* of the gospel"); and Christian ministers should be *qualified* to defend the truth, and should be willing with a proper spirit and with great earnestness to maintain the doctrines revealed. ¶ *They determined.* There was no prospect that the controversy would be settled by contention and argument. It would seem, from this statement, that those who came down from Judea were also willing that the whole matter should be referred to the apostles at Jerusalem. The reason for this may have been, (1) That Jerusalem would be regarded by them as the source of authority in the Christian church, as it had been among the Jews. (2) Most of the apostles and the most experienced Christians were there. They had listened to the instructions of Christ himself; had been long in the church; and were supposed to be better acquainted with its design and its laws. (3) Those who came from Judea would not be likely to acknowledge the authority of Paul as an apostle: the authority of those at Jerusalem they would recognize. (4) They might have had a very confident expectation that the decision there would be in their favour. The question had not been agitated there. They had all been Jews, and it is certain that they continued as yet to attend in the temple service, and to conform to the Jewish customs. They might have expected, therefore, with great confidence, that the decision would be in their favour, and they were willing to refer it to those who resided at Jerusalem. ¶ *Certain other of them.* Of the brethren; probably of each party. They did not go to debate, or to give their opinion, or to vote in the case themselves, but to lay the question fairly before the apostles and elders. ¶ *Unto the apostles.* The authority of the apostles in such a case would be acknowledged by all. They had been immediately instructed by the Saviour, and had the promise of infallible guidance in the organization of the church. See Notes on Mat. xvi. 19; xviii. 18. ¶ *And elders.* Note, ch. xi. 30. Greek, presbyters. See Notes on ch. xiv. 23. Who these were, or what was their office and authority, is not easy now to determine. It may refer either to the *aged* men in the church at Jerusalem, or to those who were appointed to rule and to preach in connection with the apostles. As in the synagogue it was customary to determine questions by the advice of a bench of elders, there is no improbability in the supposition that the apostles would imitate that custom, and appoint a similar arrangement in the Christian church (Grotius). It is generally agreed that this is the journey to which Paul refers in Ga. ii. 1–10. If so, it happened fourteen years after his conversion, Ga. ii. 1. It was done in accordance with the divine command, "by revelation," Ga. ii. 2. Among those who went with him was Titus,

3 And[e] being brought on their way by the church, they passed through Phenice and Samaria, [f]declaring the conversion of the Gentiles; and they caused [g]great joy unto all the brethren.

4 And when they were come to Jerusalem, they were received of the church, and *of* the apostles and elders; and [h]they declared all things that God had done with them.

5 But there [1]rose up certain of the sect of the Pharisees which believed, saying, [i]That it was needful to circumcise them, and to command *them* to keep the law of Moses.

6 And[k] the apostles and elders came together for to consider of this matter.

e Ro.15.24; 1 Co.16.6,11; 3 Jn.6. f ch.14.27. g Lu.15.7,10. h ch.21.19.

1 or, *rose up*, said they, *certain*. i ver.1. k Mat.18.20.

who was afterwards so much distinguished as his companion, Ga. ii. 3. ¶ *About this question.* The question whether the ceremonial laws of Moses were binding on Christian converts. In regard to the nature and design of this council at Jerusalem, see Notes on ver. 30, 31.

3. *And being brought on their way by the church.* Being attended and conducted by the Christian brethren. See Notes on Ro. xv. 24. It was customary for the Christians to attend the apostles in their travels. Comp. 1 Co. xvi. 6, 11; 3 Jn. 6. ¶ *Through Phenice.* Note, ch. xi. 19. ¶ *And Samaria.* These places were directly on their route to Jerusalem. ¶ *Declaring the conversion*, &c. Of the Gentiles in Antioch, and in the regions in Asia Minor through which they had travelled. These remarkable events they would naturally communicate with joy to the Christians with whom they would have intercourse in their journey. ¶ *Caused great joy.* At the news of the extensive spread of the gospel. It was an indication of their deep feeling in the interests of religion that they thus rejoiced. Where Christians are themselves awake, and engaged in the service of Christ, they rejoice at the news of the conversion of sinners. Where they are cold, they hear such news with indifference, or with the utmost unconcern. One way of testing our feelings on the subject of religion is by the emotions which we have when we hear of extensive and glorious revivals of religion. Comp. Notes on Ac. viii. 8.

4. *They were received of the church.* By the church, in a hospitable and friendly manner. They were acknowledged as Christian brethren, and received with Christian kindness. See Ga. ii. 9. ¶ *And they declared.* Paul and Barnabas, and those with them. That is, they stated the case; the remarkable conversion of the Gentiles, the evidence of their piety, and the origin of the present dispute.

5. *But there rose up*, &c. It has been doubted whether these are the words of Paul and Barnabas, relating what occurred at Antioch, or whether they are the words of Luke recording what took place at Jerusalem. The correct exposition is probably that which refers it to the latter. For, (1) This seems to be the most obvious interpretation. (2) The use of the words "rose up" implies that. Those who disturbed the church at Antioch are said to have come down from Judea (ver. 1), and if this place referred to that occurrence, the same words would have been retained. (3) The particular specification here of "the sect of the Pharisees" looks as if this was an occurrence taking place at Jerusalem. No such specification exists respecting those who came down to Antioch; but it would seem here as if this party in Jerusalem resolved still to abide by the law, and to impose those rites on the Christian converts. However, this interpretation is by no means certain. ¶ *Which believed.* Who maintained or taught. ¶ *That it was needful*, &c. See Notes on ver. 1.

6. *And the apostles and elders*, &c. They came together in accordance with the authority in Mat. xviii. 19, 20. It would seem, also, that the whole church was convened on this occasion, and that the church concurred, at least, in the judgment expressed in this case. See ver. 12, 22, 23. ¶ *For to consider this matter.* Not to decide it arbitrarily, or even by authority, without deliberation; but to compare their views, and to express the result of the whole to the church at Antioch. It was a grave

7 And when there had been
much disputing, Peter rose up and
said unto them, Men *and* brethren,
ye[l] know how that a good while
ago God made choice among us,
that the Gentiles by my mouth
should hear the word of the gospel, and believe.
8 And God, [m]which knoweth
the hearts, bare them witness, giving them the Holy Ghost, even as
he did unto us;
9 And put no difference between
us and them, [n]purifying their
hearts by faith.
10 Now, therefore, why tempt
ye God, to put a [o]yoke upon the
neck of the disciples, which neither

l Mat.16.18,19; ch.10.20. *m* ch.1.24. *n* He.9.13,14; 1 Pe.1.22. *o* Ga.5.1.

---

and difficult question, deeply affecting the entire constitution of the Christian church, and they therefore solemnly engaged in deliberation on the subject.

7. *Much disputing.* Or rather, much *inquiry* or *deliberation.* With our word *disputing* we commonly connect the idea of heat and anger. This is not necessarily implied in the word used here. It might have been calm, solemn, deliberate inquiry; and there is no evidence that it was conducted with undue warmth or anger. ¶ *Peter rose up and said.* Peter was probably the most aged, and was most accustomed to speak, ch. ii. 14, &c.; iii. 6, 12. Besides, there was a particular reason for his speaking here, as he had been engaged in similar scenes, and understood the case, and had had evidence that God had converted sinners *without* the Mosaic rites, and knew that it would have been inexpedient to have imposed these rites on those who had thus been converted. ¶ *A good while ago.* See ch. x. Some time since. So long since that there had been opportunity to ascertain whether it was necessary to observe the laws of Moses in order to the edification of the church. ¶ *God made choice,* &c. That is, of all the apostles, he designated me to engage in this work. Comp. Notes on Mat. xvi. 18, with Ac. x. ¶ *That the Gentiles.* Cornelius, and those who were assembled with him at Cesarea. This was the first case that had occurred, and therefore it was important to appeal to it.

8. *And God, which knoweth the hearts.* Ch. i. 24. God thus knew whether they were *true* converts or not, and gave a demonstration that he acknowledged them as his. ¶ *Giving them the Holy Ghost,* &c. Ch. x. 45, 46.

9. *And put no difference,* &c. Though they had not been circumcised, and though they did not conform to the law of Moses. Thus God showed that the observance of these rites was not necessary in order to the true conversion of men, and to acceptance with him. He did not give us, who are Jews, any advantage over them, but justified and purified all in the same manner. ¶ *Purifying their hearts.* Thus giving the best evidence that he had renewed them, and admitted them to favour with him. ¶ *By faith.* By believing on the Lord Jesus Christ. This demonstrated that the plan on which God was now about to show favour to men was not by external rites and ceremonies, but by a scheme which required faith as the only condition of acceptance. It is further implied here that there is no true faith which does not purify the heart.

10. *Why tempt ye God?* Why provoke him to displeasure? Why, since he has shown his determination to accept them *without* such rites, do you provoke him by attempting to impose on his own people rites without his authority, and against his manifest will? The *argument* is, that God had already accepted them. To attempt to impose these rites would be to provoke him to anger; to introduce observances which he had shown it was his purpose should now be abolished. ¶ *To put a yoke.* That which would be burdensome and oppressive, or which would infringe on their just freedom as the children of God. It is called in Ga. v. 1, "a yoke of bondage." Comp. Notes on Mat. xxiii. 4. A *yoke* is an emblem of slavery or bondage (1 Ti. vi. 1); or of affliction (La. iii. 27); or of punishment (La. i. 14); or of oppressive and burdensome ceremonies, as in this place, or of the restraints of Christianity, Mat. xi. 29, 30. In this place those rites are called *a yoke,* because (1) They were burdensome and oppressive; and (2) Because they would be an infringement of Christian freedom. One design of the

our fathers nor we were able to bear?

11 But we believe that [p]through the grace of the Lord Jesus Christ we shall be saved, even as they.

12 Then all the multitude kept silence, and gave audience to Barnabas and Paul, declaring what miracles and wonders [q]God had wrought among the Gentiles by them.

13 And after they had held their peace, James answered, saying, Men *and* brethren, hearken unto me:

14 Simeon[r] hath declared how God at the first did visit the Gentiles, to take out of them a people for his name.

15 And to this agree the words of the prophets; as it is written,

16 After[s] this I will return, and

p Ro.3.24; Ep.2.8; Tit.3.4,5. *q* ch.14.27. *r* Lu.2.31,32. *s* Am.9.11,12.

---

gospel was to set men free from such rites and ceremonies. ¶ *Which neither our fathers,* &c. Which have been found burdensome at all times. They were expensive, and painful, and oppressive; and as they had been found to be so, it was not proper to impose them on the Gentile converts, but should rather rejoice at any evidence that the people of God might be delivered from them. ¶ *Were able to bear.* Which are found to be oppressive and burdensome. They were attended with great inconvenience and many transgressions, as the consequence.

11. *But we believe.* We apostles, who have been with them, and have seen the evidences of their acceptance with God. ¶ *Through the grace,* &c. By the grace or mercy of Christ alone, without any of the rites and ceremonies of the Jews. ¶ *We shall be saved, even as they.* In the same manner, by the mere grace of Christ. So far from being necessary to *their* salvation, they are really of no use in *ours.* We are to be saved, not by these ceremonies, but by the mere mercy of God in the Redeemer. They should not, therefore, be imposed on others.

12. *Then all the multitude.* Evidently the multitude of private Christians who were assembled on this occasion. That it does not refer to a synod of ministers and elders merely is apparent, (1) Because the church, the brethren, are represented as having been present, and as concurring in the final opinion (ver. 22, 23); and (2) Because the word *multitude* (τὸ πλῆθος) would not have been used in describing the collection of apostles and elders merely. Comp. Lu. i. 10, 11, 13; v. 6; vi. 17; xix. 37; Jn. v. 3; xxi. 6; Ac. iv. 32; vi. 2; Mat. iii. 7. ¶ *Gave audience.* Heard, listened attentively to. ¶ *Barnabas and Paul.* They were deeply interested in it, and they were qualified to give a fair statement of the facts as they had occurred. ¶ *Declaring what miracles and wonders,* &c. The argument here evidently is, that God had approved their work by miracles; that he gave evidence that what they did had his approbation; and that as all this was done without imposing on them the rites of the Jews, so it would follow that those were not now to be commanded.

13. *James answered.* James the Less, son of Alpheus. See Notes on ch. xii. 1. ¶ *Hearken unto me.* This whole transaction shows that *Peter* had no such authority in the church as the Papists pretend, for otherwise his opinion would have been followed without debate. James had an authority not less than that of Peter. It is possible that he might have been next in age (comp. 1 Co. xv. 7); and it seems morally certain that he remained for a considerable part of his life in Jerusalem, Ac. xii. 17; xxi. 18; Ga. i. 19; ii. 9, 12.

14. *Simeon.* This is a Hebrew name. The Greek mode of writing it commonly was *Simon.* It was one of the names of Peter, Mat. iv. 18. ¶ *To take out of them a people.* To choose from among the Gentiles those who should be his friends.

15. *The words of the prophets.* Am. ix. 11, 12. It was a very material point with them, as Jews, to inquire whether this was in accordance with the predictions of the Scriptures. The most powerful revivals of religion, and the most striking demonstrations of the divine presence, will be in accordance with the Bible, and should be tested by them. This habit was always manifested by the apostles and early Christians, and should be followed by Christians at all times. Unless a supposed work of grace accords with the Bible,

will build again the tabernacle of David, which is fallen down; and I will build again the ruins thereof, and I will set it up:

17 That the residue of men might seek after the Lord, and all the Gentiles, upon whom my name is called, saith the Lord, who doeth all these things.

---

and can be defended by it, it must be false, and should be opposed. Comp. Is. viii. 20.

16. *After this.* This quotation is not made literally either from the Hebrew or the Septuagint, which differs also from the Hebrew. The 17th verse is quoted literally from the Septuagint, but in the 16th the general sense only of the passage is retained. The *main point* of the quotation, as made by James, was to show that, according to the prophets, it was contemplated that *the Gentiles* should be introduced to the privileges of the children of God; and on this point the passage has a direct bearing. The prophet Amos (ix. 8–10) had described the calamities which would come upon the nation of the Jews by their being scattered and driven away. This implied that the city of Jerusalem, the temple, and the walls of the city would be destroyed. But *after that* (Heb. "on that day," ver. 11, that is, the day when he should revisit them and recover them) he would restore them to their former privileges —would rebuild their temple, their city, and their walls, ver. 11. And not only so, not only would the blessing descend on the Jews, but it would also be extended to others. The "remnant of Edom," "the heathen upon whom" his "name would be called" (Am. ix. 12), would also partake of the mercy of God, and be subject to the Jewish people, and a time of general prosperity and of permanent blessings would follow, Am. ix. 13–15. James understands this as referring to the times of the Messiah, and to the introduction of the gospel to the Gentiles. And so the passage (Am. ix. 12) is rendered in the Septuagint. See ver. 17. ¶ *I will return.* When the people of God are subjected to calamities and trials, it is often represented as if God had *departed* from them. His *returning*, therefore, is an image of their restoration to his favour and to prosperity. This is not, however, in the Hebrew, in Am. ix. 11. ¶ *I will build again.* In the calamities that would come upon the nation (Am. ix. 8), it is implied that the temple and the city would be destroyed. To build them again would be a proof of his returning favour. ¶ *The tabernacle of David.* The *tent* of David. Here it means the house or royal residence of David and the kings of Israel. That is, he would restore them to their former glory and splendour as his people. The reference here is not to the *temple*, which was the work of Solomon, but to the magnificence and splendour of the dwelling-place of David; that is, to the full enjoyment of their former high privileges and blessings. ¶ *Which is fallen down.* Which would be destroyed by the King of Babylon, and by the long neglect and decay resulting from their being carried to a distant land. ¶ *The ruins thereof.* Heb. "close up the breaches thereof." That is, it would be restored to its former prosperity and magnificence; an emblem of the favour of God, and of the spiritual blessings that would in future times descend on the Jewish people.

17. *That the residue of men.* This verse is quoted literally from the Septuagint, and differs in some respects from the Hebrew. The phrase, "the residue of men," here is evidently understood, both by the LXX. and by James, as referring to others than Jews, to the Gentiles—the *rest* of the world—implying that many of them would be admitted to the friendship and favour of God. The Hebrew is, "that they may possess the remnant of Edom." This change is made in the Septuagint by a slight difference in the reading of two Hebrew words. The LXX., instead of the Hebrew וירשו, *shall inherit*, read ידרשו, *shall seek of thee;* and instead of אדום, *Edom*, they read אדם, *man*, or *mankind;* that is, men. Why this variation occurred cannot be explained; but the *sense* is not materially different. In the Hebrew the word *Edom* has undoubted reference to another nation than the Jewish; and the expression means that, in the great prosperity of the Jews after their return, they would extend the influence of their religion to other nations; that is, as James applies it, the *Gentiles* might be brought to the privileges of the children of God. ¶ *And also the Gentiles.* Heb. all the heathen; that

18 Known[t] unto God are all his works, from the beginning of the world.

19 Wherefore my sentence is, that we trouble not them, which from among the Gentiles are [u]turned to God:

20 But that we write unto them,

t Nu.23.19; Is.46.10. *u* 1 Th.1.9.

is, all who were not Jews. This was a clear prediction that other nations were to be favoured with the true religion, and that without any mention of their conforming to the rites of the Jewish people. ¶ *Upon whom my name is called.* Who are called by my name, or who are regarded as my people. ¶ *Who doeth all these things.* That is, who will certainly accomplish this in its time.

18. *Known unto God*, &c. See Notes on ch. i. 24. The meaning of this verse, in this connection, is this. God sees everything future; he knows what he will accomplish; he has a plan; all his works are so arranged in his mind that he sees everything distinctly and clearly. As he foretold these, it was a part of his plan; and as it was a part of his plan long since foretold, it should not be opposed and resisted by us.

19. *My sentence.* Greek, I judge (κρίνω); that is, I give my opinion. It is the usual language in which a judge delivers his opinion; but it does not imply here that James assumed authority to settle the case, but merely that he gave his opinion, or counsel. ¶ *That we trouble not them.* That we do not molest, disturb, or oppress them by imposing on them unnecessary rites and ceremonies.

20. *That we write unto them.* Expressing our judgment, or our views of the case. ¶ *That they abstain.* That they refrain from these things, or wholly avoid them. ¶ *Pollutions of idols.* The word rendered *pollutions* means any kind of defilement. But here it is evidently used to denote the flesh of those animals that were offered in sacrifice to idols. See ver. 29. That flesh, after being offered in sacrifice, was often exposed for sale in the markets, or was served up at feasts, 1 Co. x. 25–29. It became a very important question whether it was *right* for Christians to partake of it. The Jews would contend that it was, in fact, partaking of idolatry. The Gentile converts would allege that they did not eat it *as a sacrifice* to idols, or lend their countenance in any way to the idolatrous worship where it had been offered. See this subject discussed at length in 1 Co. viii. 4–13. As idolatry was forbidden to the Jews in every form, and as partaking even of the sacrifices of idols in their feasts might seem to countenance idolatry, the Jews would be utterly opposed to it; and for the sake of peace, James advised that the Christians at Antioch be recommended to abstain from this. To partake of that food might not be *morally* wrong (1 Co. viii. 4), but it would give occasion for scandal and offence; and, therefore, as a matter of *expediency*, it was advised that they should abstain from it. ¶ *And from fornication.* The word used here (πορνεία) is applicable to all illicit intercourse, and may refer to adultery, incest, or licentiousness in any form. There has been much diversity of opinion in regard to this expression. Interpreters have been greatly perplexed to understand why this violation of the *moral* law has been introduced amidst the violations of the *ceremonial* law, and the question is naturally asked whether this was a sin about which there could be any debate between the Jewish and Gentile converts? Were there any who would practise it, or plead that it was lawful? If not, why is it prohibited here? Various explanations of this have been proposed. Some have supposed that James refers here to the *offerings* which harlots would make of their gains to the service of religion, and that James would prohibit the reception of it. Beza, Selden, and Schleusner suppose the word is taken for *idolatry*, as it is often represented in the Scriptures as consisting in unfaithfulness to God, and as it is often called adultery. Heringius supposes that marriage between idolaters and Christians is here intended. But, after all, the usual interpretation of the word, as referring to illicit intercourse of the sexes of any kind, is undoubtedly here to be retained. If it be asked, then, why *this* was particularly forbidden, and was introduced in this connection, we may reply, (1) That this vice prevailed everywhere among the Gentiles, and was that to which all were particularly exposed. (2) That it was not deemed by the Gentiles disgraceful. It was practised without shame and

that they abstain from [v]pollutions of idols, and *from* [w]fornication, and *from* things strangled, and *from* [x]blood.

21 For Moses of old time hath in every city them that preach him, [y]being read in the synagogues every sabbath-day:

22 Then pleased it the apostles

v Ex.20.4,5; 1 Co.8.1,&c.; 10.28; Re.2.14,20; 9.20.
w 1 Co.6.9,18; Col.3.5. 1 Th.4.3.
x Le.17.14; De.12.16,23.
y ch.13 15,27.

without remorse. (Terence, *Adelphi*, 1, 2, 21. See Grotius.) It was important, therefore, that the pure laws of Christianity on this subject should be known, and that special pains should be taken to instruct the early converts from paganism in those laws. The same thing is necessary still in heathen lands. (3) This crime was connected with religion. It was the practice not only to introduce indecent pictures and emblems into their worship, but also for females to devote themselves to the service of particular temples, and to devote the avails of indiscriminate prostitution to the service of the god, or the goddess. The vice was connected with no small part of the pagan worship; and the images, the emblems, and the customs of idolatry everywhere tended to sanction and promote it. A mass of evidence on this subject which sickens the heart, and which would be too long and too indelicate to introduce here, may be seen in Tholuck's *Nature and Moral Influence of Heathenism*, in the *Biblical Repository* for July, 1832, p. 441–464. As this vice was almost universal; as it was practised without shame or disgrace; as there were no laws among the heathen to prevent it; as it was connected with all their views of idol worship and of religion, it was important for the early Christians to frown upon and to oppose it, and to set a peculiar guard against it in all the churches. It was the sin to which, of all others, they were the most exposed, and which was most likely to bring scandal on the Christian religion. It is for this cause that it is so often and so pointedly forbidden in the New Testament, Ro. i. 29; 1 Co. vi. 13, 18; Ga. v. 19; Ep. v. 3; 1 Th. iv. 3. ¶ *And* from *things strangled*. That is, from animals or birds that were killed without shedding their blood. The reason why these were considered by the Jews unlawful to be eaten was, that thus they would be under a necessity of eating blood, which was positively forbidden by the law. Hence it was commanded in the law that when any beast or fowl was taken in a snare, the blood should be poured out before it was lawful to be eaten, Le. xvii. 13. ¶ *And* from *blood*. The eating of blood was strictly forbidden to the Jews. The reason of this was that it contained *the life*, Le. xvii. 11, 14. See Notes on Ro. iii. 25. The use of *blood* was common among the Gentiles. They *drank* it often at their sacrifices, and in making covenants or compacts. To separate the Jews from them in this respect was one design of the prohibition. See Spencer, *De Leg. Hebræ.*, p. 144, 145, 169, 235, 377, 381, 594, edit. 1732. See also this whole passage examined at length in Spencer, p. 588–626. The primary reason of the prohibition was, that it was thus used in the feasts and compacts of idolaters. That blood was thus drank by the heathens, particularly by the Sabians, in their sacrifices, is fully proved by Spencer, *De Leg.*, p. 377–380. But the prohibition specifies a *higher* reason, that the *life* is in the blood, and that *therefore* it should not be eaten. On this opinion see Notes on Ro. iii. 25. This reason existed before any ceremonial law; it is founded in the nature of things; it has no particular reference to any custom of the Jews; and it is as forcible in any other circumstances as in theirs. It was proper, therefore, to forbid it to the early Christian converts; and for the same reason, its use should be abstained from everywhere. It adds to the force of these remarks when we remember that the same principle was settled before the laws of Moses were given, and that God regarded the fact that the life was in the blood as of so much importance as to make the shedding of it worthy of death, Ge. ix. 4–6. It is supposed, therefore, that this law is still obligatory. Perhaps, also, there is no food more unwholesome than blood; and it is a further circumstance of some moment that all men naturally revolt from it as an article of food.

21. *For Moses*. The meaning of this verse is, that the law of Moses, prohibiting these things, was read in the synagogues constantly. As these com-

and elders, with the whole church,
to send chosen men of their own
company to Antioch, with Paul
and Barnabas; *namely*, Judas surnamed [z]Barsabas, and Silas, chief
men among the brethren:
23 And wrote *letters* by them
after this manner: The apostles

z ch.1.23.

and elders, and brethren, *send*
greeting unto the brethren which
are of the Gentiles in Antioch, and
Syria, and Cilicia:
24 Forasmuch as we have heard
that [a]certain which went out from
us [b]have troubled you with words,
[c]subverting your souls, saying, *Ye*

a ver.1. b Ga.5.12. c Ga.5.4.

---

mands were constantly read, and as the Jewish converts would not soon learn that their ceremonial law had ceased to be binding, it was deemed to be a matter of expediency that no needless offence should be given to them. For the sake of peace, it was better that they should abstain from meat offered to idols than to give offence to the Jewish converts. Comp. 1 Co. viii. 10–13. ¶ *Of old time.* Greek, from ancient generations. It is an established custom, and therefore his laws are well known, and have, in their view, not only the authority of revelation, but the venerableness of antiquity. ¶ *In every city.* Where there were Jews. This was the case in all the cities to which the discussion here had reference. ¶ *Them that preach him.* That is, by reading the law of Moses. But, in addition to *reading* the law, it was customary also to offer an *explanation* of its meaning. See Notes on Lu. iv. 16–22.

22. *Then it pleased.* It seemed fit and proper to them. ¶ *The apostles and elders.* To whom the business had been particularly referred, ver. 2. Comp. ch. xvi. 4. ¶ *With the whole church.* All the Christians who were there assembled together. They *concurred* in the sentiment, and expressed their approbation in the letter that was sent, ver. 23. Whether they were *consulted* does not particularly appear. But as it is not probable that they would volunteer an opinion unless they were consulted, it seems most reasonable to suppose that the apostles and elders submitted the case to them for their approbation. It would seem that the apostles and elders deliberated on it, and decided it; but still, for the sake of peace and unity, they also took measures to ascertain that their decision agreed with the sentiment of the church. ¶ *Chosen men.* Men chosen for this purpose. ¶ *Of their own company.* From among themselves. Greater weight and authority would thus be attached to their message. ¶ *Judas surnamed Barsabas.* Possibly the same who was nominated to the vacant place in the apostleship, ch. i. 23. But Grotius supposes that it was his brother. ¶ *And Silas.* He was afterward the travelling companion of Paul, ver. 40; ch. xvi. 25, 29; xvii. 4, 10, 15. He is also the same person, probably, who is mentioned by the name of *Silvanus*, 2 Co. i. 19; 1 Th. i. 1; 2 Th. i. 1; 1 Pe. v. 12. ¶ *Chief men among the brethren.* Greek, *leaders.* Comp. Lu. xxii. 26. Men of influence, experience, and authority in the church. Judas and Silas are said to have been *prophets*, ver. 32. They had, therefore, been engaged as preachers and rulers in the church at Jerusalem.

23. *And wrote* letters. Greek, *Having written.* It does not mean that they wrote more than one epistle. ¶ *By them.* Greek, by their hand. ¶ *After this manner.* Greek, these things. ¶ Send *greeting.* A word of salutation, expressing their desire of the happiness (χαίρειν) of the persons addressed. Comp. Mat. xxvi. 49; xxvii. 29; Lu. i. 28; Jn. xix. 3. ¶ *In Antioch.* Where the difficulty first arose. ¶ *And Syria.* Antioch was the capital of Syria, and it is probable that the dispute was not confined to the capital. ¶ *And Cilicia.* See Notes on Ac. vi. 9. Cilicia was adjacent to Syria. Paul and Barnabas had travelled through it, and it is probable that the same difficulty would exist there which had disturbed the churches in Syria.

24. *Forasmuch.* Since we have heard. ¶ *That certain.* That some, ver. 1. ¶ *Have troubled you with words.* With doctrines. They have disturbed your minds, and produced contentions. ¶ *Subverting your souls.* The word here used occurs nowhere else in the New Testament (ἀνασκευάζοντες). It properly means to collect together the vessels used in a house — the household furniture — for the purpose of removing it. It is applied to marauders, robbers, and ene-

must be circumcised, and keep the law: [d]to whom we gave no *such* commandment:

25 It seemed good unto us, being assembled with one accord, to send chosen men unto you, with our beloved Barnabas and Paul,

26 Men that have [e]hazarded their lives for the name of our Lord Jesus Christ.

27 We have sent, therefore, Judas and Silas, who shall also tell *you* the same things by [2]mouth.

28 For it seemed good to the Holy Ghost, and to us, to lay upon you [f]no greater burden than these necessary things;

29 That ye [g]abstain from meats offered to idols, and from blood, and from things strangled, and from fornication; from which if ye [h]keep yourselves, ye shall do well. Fare ye well.

30 So when they were dismissed they came to Antioch; and when they had gathered the multitude together, they delivered the epistle:

31 *Which*, when they had read, they rejoiced for the [3]consolation.

d Ga.2.4. *e* ch.13.50; 14.19. 2 *word*.

f Re.2.24. *g* ver.20.
h 2 Co.11.9; Ja.1.27; 1 Jn.5.21; Jude 20,21.
3 or, *exhortation*.

mies who remove and bear off property, thus producing distress, confusion, and disorder. It is thus used in the sense of disturbing or destroying, and here denotes that they unsettled their minds —that they produced anxiety, disturbance, and distress by these doctrines about Moses. ¶ *To whom we gave no* such *commandment*. They went, therefore, without authority. Self-constituted and self-sent teachers not unfrequently produce disturbance and distress. Had the apostles been consulted on this subject, the difficulty would have been avoided. By thus saying that they had not given them a command to teach these things, they practically assured the Gentile converts that they did not approve of the course which those who went from Judea had taken.

26. *Men that have hazarded their lives*, &c. See ch. xiv. This was a noble testimony to the character of Barnabas and Paul. It was a commendation of them to the confidence of the churches, and an implied expression that they wished their authority to be regarded in the establishment and organization of the church. ¶ *For the name*. In the cause of the Lord Jesus.

27. *The same things*. The same things that we wrote to you. They will confirm all by their own statements.

28. *For it seemed good to the Holy Ghost*. This is a strong and undoubted claim to inspiration. It was with special reference to the organization of the church that the Holy Spirit had been promised to them by the Lord Jesus, Mat. xviii. 18–20; Jn. xiv. 26. ¶ *No greater burden*. To impose no greater restraints· to enjoin no other observances. See Notes on ver. 10. ¶ *Than these necessary things*. Necessary, (1) In order to preserve the peace of the church. (2) To conciliate the minds of the Jewish converts, ver. 21. (3) In their circumstances particularly, because the crime which is specified—licentiousness — was one to which all early converts were especially exposed. See Notes on ver. 20.

29. *From meats offered to idols*. This explains what is meant by "pollutions of idols," ver. 20. ¶ *Ye shall do well*. You will do what ought to be done in regard to the subjects of dispute.

31. *They rejoiced for the consolation*. They acquiesced in the decision of the apostles and elders, and rejoiced that they were not to be subjected to the burdensome rites and ceremonies of the Jewish religion. This closes the account of the first Christian council. It was conducted throughout on Christian principles; in a mild, kind, conciliatory spirit, and is a model for all similar assemblages. It came together, not to promote, but to silence disputation; not to persecute the people of God, but to promote their peace; not to be a scene of harsh and angry recrimination, but to be an example of all that was mild, and tender, and kind. Those who composed it came together, not to carry a point, not to overreach their adversaries, not to be party men, but to mingle their sober counsels, to ininquire what was right, and to express, in a Christian manner, that which was proper to be done. Great and important principles were to be established in regard to the Christian church, and

32 And Judas and Silas, being prophets also themselves, exhorted the brethren with many words, and [i]confirmed *them*.

i ch.14.22.

they engaged in their work evidently with a deep sense of their responsibility, and with a just view of their dependence on the aid of the Holy Spirit. How happy would it have been if this spirit had been possessed by all professedly Christian councils; if all had really sought the peace and harmony of the churches; if none had ever been convened to kindle the fires of persecution, or to rend and destroy the church of God!

This council has been usually appealed to as the authority for councils in the church as a permanent arrangement, and especially as an authority for courts of appeal and control. But it establishes neither, and should be brought as authority for neither. For, (1) It was *not* a court of appeal in any intelligible sense. It was an assembly convened for a special purpose; designed to settle an inquiry which arose in a particular part of the church, and which required the collected wisdom of the apostles and elders. (2) It had none of the marks or appendages of a *court*. The term court, or judicature, is nowhere applied to it, nor to any assembly of Christian men in the New Testament. Nor should these terms be used now in the churches. Courts of judicature imply a degree of authority which cannot be proved from the New Testament to have been conceded to any ecclesiastical body of men. (3) There is not the slightest intimation that anything like permanency was to be attached to this council, or that it would be periodically or regularly repeated. It proves, indeed, that, when cases of difficulty occur—when Christians are perplexed and embarrassed, or when contentions arise—it is proper to refer to Christian men for advice and direction. Such was the case here, and such a course is obviously proper. If it should be maintained that it is well that Christian ministers and laymen should assemble periodically, at stated intervals, on the supposition that such cases may arise, this is conceded; but the example of the apostles and elders should not be pleaded as making such assemblies of divine right and authority, or as being essential to the existence of a church of God. Such an arrangement has been deemed to be so desirable by Christians, that it has been adopted by Episcopalians in their regular annual and triennial Conventions; by Methodists in their Conferences; by Presbyterians in their General Assembly; by Friends in their Yearly Meetings; by Baptists and Congregationalists in their Associations, &c.; but the example of the council *summoned on a special emergency* at Jerusalem should not be pleaded as giving divine authority to these periodical assemblages. They are wise and prudent arrangements, contributing to the peace of the church, and the example of the council at Jerusalem can be adduced as furnishing *as much* divine authority for one as for another; that is, it does not make all or either of them of divine authority, or obligatory on the church of God. (4) It should be added that a degree of authority (comp. ch. xvi. 4) would, of course, be attached to the decision of the apostles and elders at that time which cannot be to any body of ministers and laymen now. Besides, it should never be forgotten —what, alas! it seems to have been the pleasure and the interest of ecclesiastics to forget—that neither the apostles nor elders *asserted* any jurisdiction over the churches of Antioch, Syria, and Cilicia; that they did not claim a *right* to have these cases referred to them; that they did not attempt to "lord it" over their faith or their consciences. The case was a single, specific, definite question *referred to them*, and they decided it as such. They asserted no abstract right of such jurisdiction; they sought not to intermeddle with the case; they enjoined no future reference of such cases to them, to their successors, or to any ecclesiastical tribunal. They evidently regarded the churches as blessed with the most ample freedom, and contemplated no arrangement of a permanent character asserting a right to legislate on articles of faith, or to make laws for the direction of the Lord's freemen.

32. *Being prophets.* See Notes on ch. xi. 27. This evidently implies that they had been preachers before they went to Antioch. What was the precise nature of the office of a *prophet* in the Christian church it is not easy to ascertain. Possibly it may imply that they were *teachers* of unusual or remark-

33 And after they had tarried
there a space, [k]they were let go in
peace from the brethren unto the
apostles.
34 Notwithstanding, it pleased
Silas to abide there still.
35 Paul also, and Barnabas, continued in Antioch, teaching and
preaching the word of the Lord,
with many others also.
36 And some days after, Paul
said unto Barnabas, Let us go
again and visit our brethren [l]in
every city where we have preached
the word of the Lord, *and see* how
they do.

k 1 Co.16.11; 2 Jn.10. *l* ch.13.4,&c.

37 And Barnabas determined to
take with them [m]John, whose surname was Mark.
38 But Paul thought not good to
take him with them, [n]who departed
from them from Pamphylia, and
went not with them to the work.
39 And the contention was so
sharp between them, that they departed asunder one from the other;
and so Barnabas took Mark, and
sailed unto Cyprus:
40 And Paul chose Silas, and
departed, [o]being recommended by
the brethren unto the grace of
God.

m ch.12.12,25; Col.4.10. *n* ch.13.13. *o* ch.14.26; 20.32.

able ability. Comp. Notes on Ro. xii. 6. ¶ *Confirmed* them. Strengthened them; that is, by their instructions and exhortations. See Notes on ch. xiv. 22.

33. *A space.* For some time. ¶ *They were let go in peace.* An expression implying that they departed with the affectionate regard of the Christians to whom they had ministered, and with their highest wishes for their prosperity, 1 Co. xvi. 11; 2 Jn. 10. ¶ *Unto the apostles.* At Jerusalem. Many MSS., however, instead of "unto the *apostles*," read "unto those who had sent them." The sense is not materially different.

34. *Notwithstanding,* &c. This whole verse is wanting in many MSS.; in the Syriac, Arabic, and Coptic versions; and is regarded as spurious by Mill, Griesbach, and by other critics. It was probably introduced by some early transcriber, who judged it necessary to complete the narrative. The Latin Vulgate reads, "It seemed good to Silas to remain, but Judas went alone to Jerusalem."

35. *Paul also, and Barnabas, continued in Antioch.* How long a time is unknown. It is probable that at this time the unhappy incident occurred between Paul and Peter which is recorded in Ga. ii. 11–14.

36. *Let us go again and visit our brethren.* That is, in the churches which they had established in Asia Minor, ch. xiii. xiv. This was a natural wish, and was an enterprise that might be attended with important advantages to those feeble churches.

37. *But Barnabas determined.* Greek, willed, or was disposed to (ἐβουλεύσατο). ¶ *John,* &c. See Notes on ch. xii. 12. He had been with them before as a travelling companion, ch. xii. 25; xiii. 5. He was the son of a sister of Barnabas (Col. iv. 10), and it is probable that Barnabas's affection for his nephew was the main reason for inducing him to wish to take him with him in the journey.

38. *But Paul thought not good.* Did not think it proper. Because he could not confide in his perseverance with them in the toils and perils of their journey. ¶ *Who departed from them,* &c., ch. xiii. 13. Why he did this is not known. It was evidently, however, for some cause which Paul did not consider satisfactory, and which, in his view, disqualified him from being their attendant again. ¶ *To the work.* Of preaching the gospel.

39. *And the contention was so sharp.* The word used here (παροξυσμὸς) is that from which our word *paroxysm* is derived. It may denote any excitement of mind, and is used in a good sense in He. x. 24. It here means, however, a violent altercation that resulted in their separation for a time, and in their engaging in different spheres of labour. ¶ *And sailed unto Cyprus.* This was the native place of Barnabas. See Notes on ch. iv. 36.

40. *Being recommended.* Being commended by prayer to God. See Notes on ch. xiv. 26.

41. *Syria and Cilicia.* These were countries lying near to each other, which Paul, in company with Barnabas, had before visited. ¶ *Confirming the*

41 And he went through Syria and Cilicia, [p]confirming the churches.

CHAPTER XVI.

THEN came he to [a]Derbe and Lystra; and behold, a certain disciple was there, named [b]Timotheus, the son of [c]a certain woman, which was a Jewess, and believed; but his father *was* a Greek:

2 Which was [d]well reported of by the brethren that were at Lystra and Iconium.

p ch.16.5. *a* ch.14.6. *b* ch.19.22; Ro.16.21; 1 Co.4.17. *c* 2 Ti.1.5. *d* ch.6.3; 1 Ti.5.10; He.11.2.

---

churches. Strengthening them by instruction and exhortation. It has no reference to the rite of confirmation. See Notes on Ac. xiv. 22.

In regard to this unhappy contention between Paul and Barnabas, and their separation from each other, we may make the following remarks. (1) That no apology or vindication of it is offered by the sacred writer. It was undoubtedly improper and evil. It was a melancholy instance in which even apostles evinced an improper spirit, and engaged in improper strife. (2) In this contention it is probable that Paul was, in the main, right. Barnabas seems to have been influenced by attachment to a relative; Paul sought a helper who would not shrink from duty and danger. It is clear that Paul had the sympathies and prayers of the church in his favour (ver. 40), and it is more than probable that Barnabas departed without any such sympathy, ver. 39. (3) There is reason to think that this contention was overruled for the furtherance of the gospel. They went to different places, and preached to different people. It often happens that the unhappy and wicked strifes of Christians are the means of exciting their mutual zeal, and of extending the gospel, and of establishing churches. But no thanks to their contention; nor is the guilt of their anger and strife mitigated by this. (4) This difference was afterward reconciled, and Paul and Barnabas again became travelling companions, 1 Co. ix. 6; Gal. ii. 9. (5) There is evidence that Paul also became reconciled to John Mark, Col. iv. 10; Phile. 24; 2 Ti. iv. 11. How long this separation continued is not known; but perhaps in this journey with Barnabas John gave such evidence of his courage and zeal as induced Paul again to admit him to his confidence as a travelling companion, and as to become a profitable fellow-labourer. See 2 Ti. iv. 11, "Take Mark, and bring him with thee; for he is profitable to me for the ministry." (6) This account proves that there was no *collusion* or *agreement* among the apostles to impose upon mankind. Had there been such an agreement, and had the books of the New Testament been an imposture, the apostles would have been represented as *perfectly harmonious*, and as united in all their views and efforts. What impostor would have thought of the device of representing the early friends of the Christian religion as *divided*, and *contending*, and *separating* from each other? Such a statement has an air of candour and honesty, and at the same time is apparently so much *against* the truth of the system, that no impostor would have thought of resorting to it.

CHAPTER XVI.

1. *Then came he.* That is, Paul in company with Silas. Luke does not give us the history of Barnabas, but confines his narrative to the journey of Paul. ¶ *To Derbe and Lystra.* See Notes on ch. xiv. 6. ¶ *And, behold, a certain disciple named Timotheus.* It was to this disciple that Paul afterward addressed the two epistles which bear his name. It is evident that he was a native of one of these places, but whether of Derbe or Lystra it is impossible to determine. ¶ *The son of a certain woman,* &c. Her name was Eunice, 2 Ti. i. 5. ¶ *And believed.* And was a Christian. It is stated also that *her* mother was a woman of distinguished Christian piety, 2 Ti. i. 5. It was not lawful for a Jew to marry a woman of another nation, or to give his daughter in marriage to a Gentile, Ezr. ix. 12. But it is probable that this law was not regarded very strictly by the Jews who lived in the midst of heathen nations. It is evident that Timothy, at this time, was very young; for when Paul besought him to abide at Ephesus, to take charge of the church there (1 Ti. i. 3), he addressed him then as a young man, 1 Ti. iv. 12, "Let no man despise thy youth." ¶ *But his father* was *a Greek.* Evidently a man who had not been cir-

3 Him would Paul have to go forth with him; [e]and took and circumcised him, [f]because of the Jews which were in those quarters; for they knew all that his father was a Greek.

4 And as they went through the cities, they delivered them the decrees for to keep [g]that were ordained of the apostles and elders which were at Jerusalem.

5 And so were [h]the churches established in the faith, and increased in number daily.

6 Now when they had gone throughout Phrygia and [i]the re-

e Ga.2.3-8; 5.1-3. f 1 Co.9.20. g ch.15.28,29. h ch.15.41. i Ga.1.2; 1 Pe.1.1.

cumcised, for had he been Timothy would have been also.

2. *Which.* That is, *Timothy.* The connection requires us to understand this of him. Of the character of his father nothing is known. ¶ *Was well reported of.* Was esteemed highly as a young man of piety and promise. Comp. Notes on ch. vi. 3. Comp. 1 Ti. v. 10. Timothy had been religiously educated. He was carefully trained in the knowledge of the holy Scriptures, and was therefore the better qualified for his work, 2 Ti. iii. 15.

3. *Him would Paul have,* &c. This was an instance of Paul's selecting young men of piety for the holy ministry. It shows, (1) That he was disposed to look up and call forth the talent in the church that might be usefully employed. It is quite evident that Timothy would not have thought of this had it not been suggested by Paul. The same thing education societies are attempting now to accomplish. (2) That Paul sought proper qualifications, and valued them. Those were (*a*) That he had a good reputation for piety, &c., ver. 2. This he demanded as an indispensable qualification for a minister of the gospel, 1 Ti. iii. 7, "Moreover he (a bishop) must have a good report of them which are without." Comp. Ac. xxii. 12. (*b*) Paul esteemed him to be a young man of talents and prudence. His admitting him to a partnership in his labours, and his intrusting to him the affairs of the church at Ephesus, prove this. (*c*) He had been carefully trained in the holy Scriptures. A foundation was thus laid for usefulness. And this qualification seems to have been deemed by Paul of indispensable value for the right discharge of his duties in this holy office. ¶ *And he took and circumcised him.* This was evidently done to avoid the opposition and reproaches of the Jews. It was a measure not binding in itself (comp. ch. xv. 1, 28, 29), but the neglect of which would expose to contention and opposition among the Jews, and greatly retard or destroy his usefulness. It was an act of expediency for the sake of peace, and was in accordance with Paul's uniform and avowed principle of conduct, 1 Co. ix. 20, "And unto the Jews I became as a Jew, that I might gain the Jews." Comp. Ac. xxi. 23-26.

4. *And as they went through the cities.* The cities of Syria, Cilicia, &c. ¶ *They delivered them.* Paul and Silas delivered to the Christians in those cities. ¶ *The decrees*—τὰ δόγματα. The decrees in regard to the four things specified in ch. xv. 20, 29. The word translated *decrees* occurs in Lu. ii. 1, "*A decree* from Cæsar Augustus;" in Ac. xvii. 7, "The *decrees* of Cæsar;" in Ep. ii. 15; and in Col. ii. 14. It properly means a law or edict of a king or legislature. In this instance it was the decision of the council in a case submitted to it, and implied an obligation on the Christians to submit to that decision, since they had submitted the matter to them. The same *principles,* also, would be applicable everywhere, and the decision, therefore, at Jerusalem became conclusive. It is probable that a correct and attested copy of the letter (ch. xv. 23-29) would be sent to the various churches of the Gentiles. ¶ *To keep.* To obey, or to observe. ¶ *That were ordained.* Greek, that were adjudged or determined.

5. *Established in the faith.* Confirmed in the belief of the gospel. The effect of the wise and conciliatory measure was to increase and strengthen the churches.

6. *Throughout Phrygia.* This was the largest province of Asia Minor. It had Bithynia north; Pisidia and Lycia south; Galatia and Cappadocia east; and Lydia and Mysia west. ¶ *And the region of Galatia.* This province was directly east of Phrygia. The region was formerly conquered by the Gauls. They settled in it, and called it, after their

gion of Galatia, and were [k]forbid-
den of the Holy Ghost to preach
the word [l]in Asia,
7 After they were come to Mysia, they assayed to go into Bithynia; but the Spirit suffered them
not.

k Am.8.11,12; 1 Co.12.11. *l* Re.1.4,11.

8 And they, passing by Mysia,
came down to [m]Troas.
9 And a vision appeared to Paul
in the night: [n]There stood a man
of Macedonia, and prayed him,
saying, Come over into Macedonia,
and help us.

m 2 Co.2.12; 2 Ti.4.13. *n* ch.10.30.

---

own name, *Galatia.* The Gauls invaded the country at different times, and no less than three tribes or bodies of Gauls had possession of it. Many Jews were also settled there. It was from this cause that so many parties could be formed there, and that so much controversy would arise between the Jewish and Gentile converts. See the Epistle to the Galatians. ¶ *And were forbidden.* Probably by a direct revelation. The reason of this was, doubtless, that it was the intention of God to extend the gospel farther into the regions of Greece than would have been done if they had remained in Asia Minor. This prohibition was the means of the first introduction of the gospel into Europe. ¶ *In Asia.* See Notes on ch. ii. 9. This was doubtless the region of proconsular Asia. It was also called *Ionia.* Of this region Ephesus was the capital; and here were situated also the cities of Smyrna, Thyatira, Philadelphia, &c., within which the seven churches mentioned in Re. i. ii. iii. were established. Cicero speaks of proconsular Asia as containing the provinces of Phrygia, Mysia, Caria, and Lydia. In all this region the gospel was afterward preached with great success. But now a more important and a wider field was opened before Paul and Barnabas in the extensive country of Macedonia.

7. *Mysia.* This was a province of Asia Minor, having Propontis on the north, Bithynia on the east, Lydia on the south, and the Ægean Sea on the west. ¶ *They assayed.* They endeavoured; they attempted. ¶ *Into Bithynia.* A province of Asia Minor lying east of Mysia.

8. *Came down to Troas.* This was a city of Phrygia or Mysia, on the Hellespont, between Troy north, and Assos south. Sometimes the name *Troas*, or *Troad*, is used to denote the whole country of the Trojans, the province where the ancient city of Troy had stood. This region was much celebrated in the early periods of Grecian history. It was here that the events recorded in the Iliad of Homer are supposed to have occurred. The city of Troy has long since been completely destroyed. *Troas* is several times mentioned in the New Testament, 2 Co. ii. 12; 2 Ti. iv. 13; Ac. xx. 5.

9. *And a vision.* See Notes on ch. ix. 10. ¶ *There stood a man*, &c. The appearance of a man who was known to be of Macedonia, probably by his dress and language. Whether this was in a dream, or whether it was a representation made to the senses while awake, it is impossible to tell. The will of God was at different times made known in both these ways. Comp. Mat. ii. 12; Note, Ac. x. 3. Grotius supposes that this was the guardian angel of Macedonia, and refers for illustration to Da. x. 12, 13, 20, 21. But there seems to be no foundation for this opinion. ¶ *Of Macedonia.* This was an extensive country of Greece, having Thrace on the north, Thessaly south, Epirus west, and the Ægean Sea east. It is supposed that it was peopled by Kittim, son of Javan, Ge. x. 4. The kingdom rose into celebrity chiefly under the reign of Philip and his son, Alexander the Great. It was the first region in Europe in which we have any record that the gospel was preached. ¶ *And help us.* That is, by preaching the gospel. This was a call to preach the gospel in an extensive heathen land, amid many trials and dangers. To this call, notwithstanding all this prospect of danger, Paul and Silas cheerfully responded, and gave themselves to the work. Their conduct was thus an example to the church. From all portions of the earth a similar call is now coming to the churches. Openings of a similiar character for the introduction of the gospel are presented in all lands. Appeals are coming from every quarter, and all that seems now necessary for the speedy conversion of the world is for the church to enter into these vast

10 And after he had seen the vision, [o]immediately we endeavoured to go into Macedonia, assuredly gathering that the Lord had called us for to preach the gospel unto them.

11 Therefore loosing from Troas, we came with a straight course to Samothracia, and the next *day* to Neapolis;

12 And from thence to [p]Philippi, which is [1]the chief city of that part of Macedonia, *and* a colony. And we were in that city abiding certain days.

13 And on the [2]sabbath we went out of the city by a river side, [q]where prayer was wont to be made: and we sat down, and spake unto the women which resorted *thither*.

o 2 Co.2.13. p Phi.1.1. 1 or, *the first*. 2 *sabbath-day*. q ch.21.5.

fields with the self-denial, the spirit, and the zeal which characterized the apostle Paul.

10. *We endeavoured.* This is the first instance in which Luke refers to himself as being in company with Paul. It is hence probable that he joined Paul and Silas about this time, and it is evident that he attended Paul in his travels, as recorded throughout the remainder of the Acts. ¶ *Assuredly gathering.* Being certainly convinced.

11. *Loosing from Troas.* Setting sail from this place. ¶ *To Samothracia.* This was an island in the Ægean Sea not far from Thrace. It was peopled by inhabitants from Samos and from Thrace, and hence called *Samothracia.* It was about twenty miles in circumference, and was an asylum for fugitives and criminals. ¶ *And the next day to Neapolis.* This was a maritime city of Macedonia, near the borders of Thrace. It was about ten miles from Philippi.

12. *And from thence to Philippi.* The former name of this city was Dathos. It was repaired and adorned by Philip, the father of Alexander the Great, and after him was called Philippi. It was famous for having been the place where several battles were fought during the civil wars of the Romans, and, among others, for the decisive battle between Brutus and Antony. At this place Brutus killed himself. To the church in this place Paul afterward wrote the epistle which bears its name. ¶ *Which is the chief city of that part of Macedonia.* This whole region had been conquered by the Romans under Paulus Æmilius. By him it was divided into four parts or provinces (Livy). The Syriac version renders it "a city of the *first* part of Macedonia," and there is a medal extant which also describes this region by this name. It has been proposed, therefore, to alter the Greek text in accordance with this, since it is known that Amphipolis was made the chief city by Paulus Æmilius. But it may be remarked that, although Amphipolis was the chief city in the time of Paulus Æmilius, it may have happened that in the lapse of two hundred and twenty years from that time Philippi might have become the most extensive and splendid city. The Greek here may also mean simply that this was the *first* city to which they arrived in their travels. ¶ And *a colony.* This is a Latin word, and means that this was a Roman colony. The word denotes a city or province which was planted or occupied by Roman citizens. It is a strong confirmation of the fact here stated by Luke, that Philippi had the rank and dignity of a Roman colony, as coins are still extant, in which Philippi is distinctly referred to as a colony. Such coins exist from the reign of Augustus to the reign of Caracalla. ¶ *Certain days.* Some days.

13. *And on the sabbath.* There is no doubt that in this city there were Jews. In the time of the apostles they were scattered extensively throughout the known world. ¶ *By a river side.* What river this was is not known. It is known, however, that the Jews were accustomed to provide water, or to build their synagogues and oratories near water, for the convenience of the numerous washings before and during their religious services. ¶ *Where prayer.* Where there was a place of prayer, or where prayer was commonly offered. The Greek will bear either, but the sense is the same. Places for prayer were erected by the Jews in the vicinity of cities and towns, and particularly where there were not Jewish families enough, or where they were forbidden by the magistrate to erect a synagogue. These *proseuchæ*, or places of prayer, were simple inclosures made of stones, in a

14 And a certain woman named Lydia, a seller of purple, of the city of Thyatira, which worshipped God, heard *us:* [r] whose heart the Lord opened, that she attended unto the things which were spoken of Paul.
15 And when she was baptized, and her household, [s] she besought *us*, saying, If ye have judged me to be faithful to the Lord, come into my house, and abide *there*. And she constrained us.
16 And it came to pass, as we went to prayer, a certain damsel

r Lu.24.45.

s He.13.2.

---

grove or under a tree, where there would be a retired and convenient place for worship. ¶ *Was wont.* Was accustomed to be offered, or where it was established by custom. ¶ *And spake unto the women*, &c. This was probably before the regular service of the place commenced.

14. *A seller of purple.* Purple was a most valuable colour, obtained usually from shell-fish. It was chiefly worn by princes and by the rich, and the traffic in it might be very profitable. Comp. Notes on Is. i. 18; Lu. xvi. 19. ¶ *The city of Thyatira.* This was a city of Lydia, in Asia Minor, now called *Akhisar.* The art of dyeing was early cultivated in the neighbourhood of Thyatira, as we learn from Homer (*Iliad*, iv. 141), and as is confirmed by inscriptions found in that city—a circumstance which may be referred to as confirming the veracity of the statements of Luke even in his casual allusions. Several of these inscriptions have been published. See the *Life and Epistles of St. Paul*, i. 295. ¶ *Which worshipped God.* A religious woman, a proselyte. Note, ch. xiii. 16. ¶ *Whose heart the Lord opened.* See Note, Lu. xxiv. 45.

15. *And when she was baptized.* Apparently without any delay. Comp. Ac. ii. 41; viii. 38. It was usual to be baptized immediately on believing. ¶ *And her household.* Greek, her house (ὁ οἶκος αὐτῆς), her family. No mention is made of *their* having believed, and the case is one that affords a strong presumptive proof that this was an instance of *household* or infant baptism. For, (1) *Her* believing is particularly mentioned. (2) It is not intimated that *they* believed. (3) It is manifestly implied that *they* were baptized because *she* believed. It was the offering of her family to the Lord. It is just such an account as would now be given of a household or family that were baptized on the faith of the parent. ¶ *If ye have judged me to be faithful.* If you deem me a Christian or a believer. ¶ *And she constrained us.* She urged us. This was an instance of great hospitality, and also an evidence of her desire for farther instruction in the doctrines of religion.

16. *As we went to prayer.* Greek, as we were going to the *proseuche*, the place of prayer, ver. 13. Whether this was on the same day in which the conversion of Lydia occurred, or at another time, is not mentioned by the historian. ¶ *A certain damsel.* A maid, a young woman. ¶ *Possessed with a spirit of divination.* Greek, *Python.* See the margin. Python, or Pythios, was one of the names of Apollo, the Grecian god of the fine arts, of music, poetry, medicine, and eloquence. Of these he was esteemed to have been the inventor. He was reputed to be the third son of Jupiter and Latona. He had a celebrated temple and oracle at Delphi, which was resorted to from all parts of the world, and which was perhaps the only oracle that was in universal repute. The name *Python* is said to have been given him because, as soon as he was born, he destroyed with arrows a serpent of that name, that had been sent by Juno to persecute Latona; hence his common name was *the Pythian Apollo.* He had temples on Mount Parnassus, at Delphi, Delos, Claros, Tenedos, &c., and his worship was almost universal. In the celebrated oracle at Delphi, the priestess of Apollo pretended to be inspired; became violently agitated during the periods of pretended inspiration; and during those periods gave such responses to inquirers as were regarded as the oracles of the god. Others, it is probable, would also make pretensions to such inspiration; and the art of fortune-telling, or of jugglery, was extensively practised, and was the source of much gain. See Notes on ch. viii. 8-10. What was the cause of this extensive delusion in regard to the oracle at Delphi it is not necessary now to inquire. It is plain that Paul regarded this as a case of demoniacal possession,

possessed[t] with a spirit of [3]divina-
tion met us,[u]which brought her masters much gain by soothsaying:
17 The same followed Paul and
us, and cried, saying, These men
are the servants of [v]the most high
God, which show unto us [w]the way
of salvation.
18 And this she did many days.
But Paul, being grieved, turned and
[x]said to the spirit, I command thee,
in the name of Jesus Christ, to come
out of her. And[y] he came out the
same hour.
19 And when her masters saw
that [z]the hope of their gains was
gone, they caught Paul and Silas,

t 1 Sa.28.7. 3 or, *Python.* u ch.19.24. v Ge.14.18-22. w ch.18.26; He.10.20. x Mar.1.25,34. y Mar.16.17. z ch.19.24-27.

and treated it accordingly. ¶ *Her masters.* Those in whose employ she was. ¶ *By soothsaying.* Pretending to foretell future events.

17. *The same followed Paul*, &c. Why she did this, or under what pretence, the sacred writer has not informed us. It *may* have been, (1) That as she prophesied for gain, she supposed that Paul and Silas would reward her if she publicly proclaimed that they were the servants of God. Or, (2) Because she was conscious that an evil spirit possessed her, and she feared that Paul and Silas would expel that spirit, and by proclaiming them to be the servants of God she hoped to conciliate their favour. Or, (3) More probably it was because she saw evident tokens of their being sent from God, and that their doctrine would prevail; and by proclaiming this she hoped to acquire more authority, and a higher reputation for being herself inspired. Comp. Mar. v. 7.

18. *But Paul, being grieved.* Being molested, troubled, offended. Paul was grieved, probably, (1) Because her presence was troublesome to him; (2) Because it might be said that he was in alliance with her, and that his pretensions were just like hers; (3) Because what she did was for the sake of gain, and was a base imposition; (4) Because her state was one of bondage and delusion, and it was proper to free her from this demonaical possession; and (5) Because the system under which she was acting was a part of a scheme of delusion and imposture, which had spread over a large portion of the pagan world, and which was then holding it in bondage. Throughout the Roman empire the inspiration of the priestesses of Apollo was believed in, and temples were everywhere reared to perpetuate and celebrate the delusion. Against this extensive system of imposture and fraud Christianity must oppose itself; and this was a favourable instance to expose the delusion, and to show the power of the Christian religion over all the arts and powers of imposture. The mere fact that in a *very few* instances—of which this was one—they spoke the truth, did not make it improper for Paul to interpose. That fact would only tend to perpetuate the delusion, and to make his interposition more proper and necessary. The expulsion of the evil spirit would also afford a signal proof of the fact that the apostles were *really* from God—a far better proof than her noisy and troublesome proclamation of it would furnish. ¶ *In the name of Jesus Christ.* Or, by the authority of Jesus Christ. See Notes on ch. iii. 6.

19. *The hope of their gains was gone.* It was this that troubled and enraged them. Instead of regarding the act as proof of divine power, they were intent only on their profits. Their indignation furnishes a remarkable illustration of the fixedness with which men will regard wealth; of the fact that the love of it will blind them to all the truths of religion, and all the proofs of the power and presence of God; and of the fact that *any* interposition of divine power that destroys their hopes of gain, fills them with wrath, and hatred, and murmuring. Many a man has been opposed to God and his gospel because, if religion should be extensively prevalent, his hopes of gain would be gone. Many a slave-dealer, and many a trafficker in ardent spirits, and many a man engaged in other unlawful modes of gain, has been unwilling to abandon his employments simply because his hopes of gain would be destroyed. No small part of the opposition to the gospel arises from the fact that, if embraced, it would strike at so much of the dishonourable employments of men, and make them honest and conscientious. ¶ *The market-place.* The court

and drew *them* into the [4]market-
place, [a]unto the rulers,
20 And brought them to the
magistrates, saying, These men,
being Jews, do exceedingly [b]trouble
our city,
21 And teach customs which
are not lawful for us to receive,
neither to observe, being Romans.

[4] or, *court*. [a] Mat.10.18.

[b] 1 Ki.18.17; ch.17.6.

---

or forum. The market-place was a place of concourse, and the courts were often held in or near those places. ¶ *The rulers.* The term used here refers commonly to *civil magistrates.*

20. *And brought them to the magistrates.* To the *military rulers* (στρατηγοῖς) or prætors. Philippi was a Roman colony, and it is probable that the officers of the army exercised the double function of civil and military rulers. ¶ *Do exceedingly trouble our city.* In what way they did it they specify in the next verse. The charge which they wished to substantiate was that of being disturbers of the public peace. All at once they became conscientious. They forgot the subject of their gains, and were greatly distressed about the violation of the laws. There is nothing that will make men more hypocritically conscientious than to denounce, and detect, and destroy their unlawful and dishonest practices. Men who are thus exposed become suddenly filled with reverence for the law or for religion, and they who have heretofore cared nothing for either become greatly alarmed lest the public peace should be disturbed. Men slumber quietly in sin, and pursue their wicked gains; they hate or despise all law and all forms of religion; but the moment their course of life is attacked and exposed, they become full of zeal for laws that they would not themselves hesitate to violate, and for the customs of religion which in their hearts they thoroughly despise. Worldly-minded men often thus complain that their neighbourhoods are disturbed by revivals of religion; and the preaching of the truth, and the attacking of their vices, often arouses this hypocritical conscientiousness, and makes them alarmed for the laws, and for religion, and for order, which they at other times are the first to disturb and disregard.

21. *And teach customs.* The word *customs* here (ἔθη) refers to religious *rites* or forms of worship. See Notes on ch. vi. 14. They meant to charge the apostles with introducing a new religion which was unauthorized by the Roman laws. This was a cunning and artful accusation. It is perfectly evident that they cared nothing either for the religion of the Romans or of the Jews. Nor were they really concerned about any change of religion. Paul had destroyed their hopes of gain; and as they could not prevent that except by securing his punishment or expulsion, and as they had no way of revenge except by endeavouring to excite indignation against him and Silas for violating the laws, they endeavoured to convict them of such violation. This is one, among many instances, where wicked and unprincipled men will endeavour to make religion the means of promoting their own interest. If they can make money by it, they will become its professed friends; or if they can annoy Christians, they will at once have remarkable zeal for the laws and for the purity of religion. Many a man opposes revivals of religion, and the real progress of evangelical piety, from professed zeal for truth and order. ¶ *Which are not lawful for us to receive.* There were *laws* of the Roman empire under which they might shield themselves in this charge, though it is evident that their zeal was, not because they loved the laws *more*, but because they loved Christianity *less*. Thus Servius on Virgil, *Æneid,* viii. 187, says, "Care was taken among the Athenians and the Romans that no one should introduce new religions. It was on this account that Socrates was condemned, and the Chaldeans or Jews were banished from the city." Cicero (*De Legibus*, ii. 8) says, "No person shall have any separate gods, or new ones; nor shall he privately worship any strange gods, unless they be publicly allowed." Wetstein (*in loco*) says, "The Romans would indeed allow foreigners to worship their own gods, but not unless it were done secretly, so that the worship of foreign gods would not interfere with the allowed worship of the Romans, and so that occasion for dissension and controversy might be avoided. Neither was it lawful among the Romans to recommend a new religion to the citizens, contrary to that which was confirmed and established

22 And the multitude rose up together against them; and the magistrates rent off their clothes, and commanded to beat *them*.

23 And when they had [c]laid many stripes upon them, they cast *them* into prison, charging the jailer to keep them safely:

24 Who, having received such a charge, thrust them into the inner prison, and made their feet fast in the stocks.

25 And at midnight Paul and Silas [d]prayed, and [e]sang praises unto God; and the prisoners heard them.

c 2 Co.6.5; 11.23,25; 1 Th.2.2.

d Ja.5.13. e Ps.34.1.

---

by the public authority, and to call off the people from that. It was on this account that there was such a hatred of the Romans against the Jews" (Kuinoel). Tertullian says that "there was a decree that no god should be consecrated unless approved by the senate" (Grotius). See many other authorities quoted in Bishop Watson's *Apology for Christianity*. ¶ *To observe.* To do. ¶ *Being Romans.* Having the privileges of Roman citizens. See Notes on ver. 12.

22. *And the multitude*, &c. It is evident that this was done in a popular tumult, and without even the form of law. Of this Paul afterward justly complained, as it was a violation of the privileges of a Roman citizen, and contrary to the laws. See Notes on ver. 37. It was one instance in which men affect great zeal for the honour of the law, and yet are among the first to disregard it. ¶ *And the magistrates*, ver. 20. They who should have been their protectors until they had had a fair trial according to law. ¶ *Rent off their clothes.* This was always done when one was to be scourged or whipped. The criminal was usually stripped entirely naked. Livy says (ii. 5), "The lictors, being sent to inflict punishment, beat them with rods, *being naked*." Cicero, against Verres, says, "He commanded the man to be seized, and to be stripped naked in the midst of the forum, and to be bound, and rods to be brought." ¶ *And commanded to beat* them—ῥαβδίζειν. To beat them with rods. This was done by *lictors*, whose office it was, and was a common mode of punishment among the Romans. Probably Paul alludes to this as one of the instances which occurred in his life of his being publicly scourged, when he says (2 Co. xi. 25), "Thrice was I beaten with rods."

23. *And when they had laid many stripes on them.* The Jews were by law prohibited from inflicting more than forty stripes, and usually inflicted but thirty-nine, 2 Co. xi. 24. But there was no such law among the Romans. They were unrestricted in regard to the number of lashes, and probably inflicted many more. Perhaps Paul refers to this when he says (2 Co. xi. 23), "In stripes above measure," that is, beyond the usual measure among the Jews, or beyond moderation. ¶ *They cast* them *into prison.* The magistrates did this partly as a punishment, and partly with a view hereafter of taking vengeance on them more according to the forms of law.

24. *Thrust them into the inner prison.* Into the most retired and secure part of the prison. The cells in the interior of the prison would be regarded as more safe, being doubtless more protected, and the difficulty of escape would be greater. ¶ *And made their feet fast in the stocks.* Greek, and made their feet secure to wood. The word *stocks*, with us, denotes a machine made of two pieces of timber between which the feet of criminals are placed, and in which they are thus made secure. The account here does not imply necessarily that they were secured precisely in this way, but that they were fastened or secured by the feet, probably by cords, to a piece or beam of wood, so that they could not escape. It is probable that the legs of the prisoners were bound to large pieces of wood which not only encumbered them, but which were so placed as to extend their feet to a considerable distance. In this condition it might be necessary for them to lie on their backs; and if this, as is probable, was on the cold ground, after their severe scourging, their sufferings must have been very great. Yet in the midst of this they sang praises to God.

25. *And at midnight.* Probably their painful posture, and the sufferings of their recent scourging, prevented their sleeping. Yet, though they had no repose, they had a quiet conscience, and the supports of religion. ¶ *Prayed.*

26 And suddenly there was a
great earthquake, [f] so that the
foundations of the prison were
shaken; [g] and immediately all the
doors were opened, and every one's
bands were loosed.
27 And the keeper of the prison
awaking out of his sleep, and seeing the prison doors open, he drew

f ch.4.31. g Is.42.7; ch.5.19; 12.7,10.

Though they had suffered much, yet they had reason to apprehend more. They sought, therefore, the sustaining grace of God. ¶ *And sang praises.* Comp. Notes on Job xxxv. 10. Nothing but religion would have enabled them to do this. They had endured much, but they had cause still for gratitude. The Christian may find more true joy in a prison than the monarch on his throne. ¶ *And the prisoners heard them.* And doubtless with astonishment. Prayer and praise are not common in a prison. The song of rejoicing and the language of praise is not usual among men lying bound in a dungeon. From this narrative we may learn, (1) That the Christian has the sources of his happiness within him. External circumstances cannot destroy his peace and joy. In a dungeon he may find as real happiness as on a throne. On the cold earth, beaten and bruised, he may be as truly happy as on a bed of down. (2) The enemies of Christians cannot destroy their peace. They may incarcerate the body, but they cannot bind the spirit. They may exclude from earthly comforts, but they cannot shut them out from the presence and sustaining grace of God. (3) We see the value of a good conscience. Nothing else can give peace; and amidst the wakeful hours of the night, whether in a dungeon or on a bed of sickness, it is of more value than all the wealth of the world. (4) We see the inestimable worth of the religion of Christ. It fits for all scenes; supports in all trials; upholds by day or by night; inspires the soul with confidence in God; and puts into the lips the songs of praise and thanksgiving. (5) We have here a sublime and holy scene which sin and infidelity could never furnish. What more sublime spectacle has the earth witnessed than that of scourged and incarcerated men, suffering from unjust and cruel inflictions, and anticipating still greater sorrows; yet, with a calm mind, a pure conscience, a holy joy, pouring forth their desires and praises at midnight, into the ear of the God who always hears prayer! The darkness, the stillness, the loneliness, all give sublimity to the scene, and teach us how invaluable is the privilege of access to the throne of mercy in this suffering world.

26. *And suddenly.* While they were praying and singing. ¶ *A great earthquake,* Mat. xxviii. 2. An earthquake, in such circumstances, was regarded as a symbol of the presence of God, and as an answer to prayer. See Notes on ch. iv. 31. The *design* of this was, doubtless, to furnish them proof of the presence and protection of God, and to provide a way for them to escape. It was one among the series of wonders by which the gospel was established, and the early Christians protected amidst their dangers. ¶ *And immediately all the doors were opened.* An effect that would naturally follow from the violent concussion of the earthquake. Comp. ch. v. 19. ¶ *Every one's bands were loosed.* This was evidently a miracle. Some have supposed that their chains were dissolved by electric fluid; but the narrative gives no account of any such fluid, even supposing such an effect to be possible. It was evidently a direct interposition of divine power. But for what purpose it was done is not recorded. Grotius supposes that it was that they might know that the apostles might be useful to them and to others, and that by them their spiritual bonds might be loosed. Probably the design was to impress all the prisoners with the conviction of the presence and power of God, and thus to prepare them to receive the message of life from the lips of his servants Paul and Silas. They had just before heard them singing and praying; they were aware, doubtless, of the cause for which they were imprisoned; they saw evident tokens that they were the servants of the Most High, and under his protection; and their own minds were impressed and awed by the terrors of the earthquake, and by the fact of their own liberation. It renders this scene the more remarkable, that though the doors were opened, and the prisoners loosed, yet no one made any attempt to escape.

27. *Would have killed himself.* This

out his sword, and would have killed himself, supposing that the prisoners had been fled.

28 But[h] Paul cried with a loud voice, saying, [i]Do thyself no harm; for we are all here.

29 Then he called for a light, and sprang in,[k] and came trembling, and fell down before Paul and Silas,

30 And brought them out, and said, Sirs, [l]what must I do to be saved?

h Pr.24.11,12; 1 Th.5.15. i Ec.7.15-17. k Je.5.22. l ch.2.37; 9.6.

---

was done in the midst of agitation and alarm. He supposed that the prisoners had fled. He presumed that their escape would be charged on him. It was customary to hold a jailer responsible for the safe keeping of prisoners, and to subject him to the punishment due them if he suffered them to escape. See ch. xii. 19. It should be added that it was common and approved among the Greeks and Romans for a man to commit suicide when he was encompassed with dangers from which he could not escape. Thus Cato was guilty of self-murder in Utica; and thus, at this very place—Philippi—Brutus and Cassius, and many of their friends, fell on their own swords, and ended their lives by suicide. The custom was thus sanctioned by the authority and example of the great; and we are not to wonder that the jailer, in a moment of alarm, should also attempt to destroy his own life. It is not one of the least benefits of Christianity that it has proclaimed the evil of self-murder, and has done so much to drive it from the world.

28. *Do thyself no harm.* This is the solemn command of religion in his case, and in all others. It enjoins on men to do themselves no harm—by self-murder, whether by the sword, the pistol, the halter; by intemperance, by lust, or by dissipation. In all cases, Christianity seeks the true welfare of man. In all cases, if it were obeyed, men would do themselves no harm. They would promote their own best interests here, and their eternal welfare hereafter.

29. *Then he called for a light.* Greek, *lights*, in the plural. Probably several torches were brought by his attendants. ¶ *And came trembling.* Alarmed at the earthquake; amazed that the prisoners were still there; confounded at the calmness of Paul and Silas, and overwhelmed at the proof of the presence of God. Comp. Je. v. 22, "Fear ye not me, saith the Lord? will ye not tremble at my presence?" &c. ¶ *And fell down.* This was an act of profound reverence. See Notes on Mat. ii. 11. It is evident that he regarded them as the favourites of God, and was constrained to recognize them as religious teachers.

30. *And brought them out.* From the prison. ¶ *Sirs.* Greek, κύριοι, lords—an address of respect; a title usually given to masters or owners of slaves. ¶ *What must I do to be saved?* Never was a more important question asked than this. It is clear that by the question he did not refer to any danger to which he might be exposed from what had happened. For, (1) The apostles evidently understood him as referring to his eternal salvation, as is manifest from their answer, since to believe on the Lord Jesus Christ would have no effect in saving him from any danger of punishment to which he might be exposed from what had occurred. (2) He could scarcely now consider himself as exposed to punishment by the Romans. The prisoners were all safe; none had escaped, or showed any disposition to escape; and besides, for the earthquake and its effects he could not be held responsible. It is not improbable that there was much confusion in his mind. There would be a *rush* of many thoughts; a state of agitation, alarm, and fear; and in view of all, he would naturally ask those whom he now saw to be men sent by God, and under his protection, what he should do to obtain the favour of that great Being under whose protection he saw that they manifestly were. Perhaps the following thoughts might have tended to produce this state of agitation and alarm. (1) They had been designated by the Pythoness (ver. 17) as religious teachers sent from God, and appointed to "show *the way of salvation*," and in her testimony he might have been disposed to put confidence, or it might now be brought fresh to his recollection. (2) He manifestly saw that they were under the protection of God. A remarkable interposition—an earthquake—an event which all the heathen regarded as ominous of the presence of

31 And they said, [m]Believe on the Lord Jesus Christ, and thou shalt be saved, [n]and thy house.

m Hab.2.4; Jn.3.16,36; 6.47; ch.13.39. *n* ch.2.39.

32 And they spake unto him the word of the Lord, [o]and to all that were in his house.

o Ro.1.14,16.

the divinity—had showed this. (3) The guilt of their imprisonment might rush upon his mind; and he might suppose that he, the agent of the imprisonment of the servants of God, would be exposed to his displeasure. (4) His guilt in attempting his own life might overwhelm him with alarm. (5) The whole scene was fitted to show him the need of the protection and friendship of the God that had thus interposed. In this state of agitation and alarm, the apostles directed him to the only source of peace and safety—the blood of the atonement. The feelings of an awakened sinner are often strikingly similar to those of this jailer. He is agitated, alarmed, and fearful; he sees that he is a sinner, and trembles; the sins of his life rush over his memory, and fill him with deep anxiety, and he inquires what he must do to be saved. Often too, as here, the providence of God is the means of awakening the sinner, and of leading to this inquiry. Some alarming dispensation convinces him that God is near, and that the soul is in danger. The loss of health, or property, or of a friend, may thus alarm the soul; the ravages of the pestilence, or any fearful judgment, may arrest the attention, and lead to the inquiry, "What must I do to be saved?" Reader, have you ever made this inquiry? Have you ever, like the heathen jailer at Philippi, seen yourself to be a lost sinner, and been willing to ask the way to life?

In this narrative we see the *contrast* which exists in periods of distress and alarm between Christians and sinners. The guilty jailer was all agitation, fear, distress, and terror; the apostles, all peace, calmness, joy. The one was filled with thoughts of self-murder; the others, intent on saving life and doing good. This difference is to be traced to religion. It was confidence in God that gave peace to *them;* it was the want of that which led to agitation and alarm in *him.* It is so still. In the trying scenes of this life the same difference is seen. In bereavement, in sickness, in times of pestilence, in death, it is still so. The Christian is calm; the sinner is agitated and alarmed. The Christian can pass through such scenes with peace and joy; to the sinner, they are scenes of terror and of dread. And thus it will be beyond the grave. In the morning of the resurrection, the Christian will rise with joy and triumph; the sinner, with fear and horror. And thus at the judgment seat. Calm and serene, the saint shall witness the solemnities of that day, and triumphantly hail the Judge as his friend; fearful and trembling, the sinner shall look on these solemnities with a soul filled with horror as he listens to the sentence that consigns him to eternal woe! With what solicitude, then, should we seek, without delay, an interest in that religion which alone can give peace to the soul!

31. *Believe on the Lord Jesus Christ.* This was a simple, a plain, and an effectual direction. They did not direct him to use the means of grace, to pray, or to continue to seek for salvation. They did not advise him to delay, or to wait for the mercy of God. They told him to believe at once; to commit his agitated, and guilty, and troubled spirit to the Saviour, with the assurance that he should find peace. They presumed that he would understand what it was to believe, and they commanded him *to do the thing.* And this was the uniform direction which the early preachers gave to those inquiring the way to life. See Notes on Mat. xvi. 16. Comp. Notes on Ac. viii. 22. ¶ *And thy house.* And thy family. That is, the same salvation is equally adapted to, and offered to your family. It does not mean that his family would be saved simply by *his* believing, but that the offers had reference to them as well as to himself; that they might be saved as well as he. His attention was thus called at once, as every man's should be, to his family. He was reminded that they needed salvation, and he was presented with the assurance that they might unite with him in the peace and joy of redeeming mercy. Comp. Notes on ch. ii. 39. It *may be* implied here that the faith of a father may be expected to be the means of the salvation of his family. It often is so in fact; but the direct meaning is, that salvation was offered to his family as well as himself, implying that if they believed they should also be saved.

33 And he took them the same hour of the night, and washed *their* stripes; and was baptized, he, and all his, straightway.

34 And when he had brought them into his house, [p]he set meat before them, [q]and rejoiced, believing in God with all his house.

35 And when it was day, the

p Lu.5.29. q Ro.5.11.

---

32. *To all that were in his house.* Old and young. They instructed them in the doctrines of religion, and doubtless in the nature of the ordinances of the gospel, and then baptized the entire family.

33. *And he took them.* To a convenient place for washing. It is evident from this that, though the apostles had the gift of miracles, they did not exercise it in regard to their own sufferings or to heal their own wounds. They restored others to health, not themselves. ¶ *And washed* their *stripes.* The wounds which had been inflicted by the severe scourging which they had received the night before. We have here a remarkable instance of the effect of religion in producing humanity and tenderness. This same man, a few hours before, had thrust them into the inner prison, and made them fast in the stocks. He evidently had then no concern about their stripes or their wounds. But no sooner was he converted than one of his first acts was an act of humanity. He saw them suffering; he pitied them, and hastened to minister to them and to heal their wounds. Till the time of Christianity there never had been a hospital or an almshouse. Nearly all the hospitals for the sick since have been reared by Christians. They who are most ready to minister to the sick and dying are Christians. They who are most willing to encounter the pestilential damps of dungeons to aid the prisoner are, like Howard, Christians. Who ever saw an infidel attending a dying bed if he could help it? and where has infidelity ever reared a hospital or an almshouse, or made provision for the widow and the fatherless? Often one of the most striking changes that occurs in conversion is seen in the disposition to be kind and humane to the suffering. Comp. Ja. i. 27. ¶ *And was baptized.* This was done *straightway;* that is, immediately. As it is altogether improbable that either in his house or in the prison there would be water sufficient for *immersing* them, there is every reason to suppose that this was performed in some other mode. All the circumstances lead us to suppose that it was not by immersion. It was at the dead of night; in a prison; amidst much agitation; and was evidently performed in haste.

34. *He set meat before them.* Food. Greek, he placed a *table.* The word *meat* formerly meant food of all kinds. ¶ *And rejoiced.* This was the effect of believing. Religion produces joy. See Notes on ch. viii. 8. He was free from danger and alarm; he had evidence that his sins were forgiven, and that he was now the friend of God. The agitating and alarming scenes of the night had passed away; the prisoners were safe; and religion, with its peace, and pardon, and rejoicings, had visited himself and his family. What a change to be produced in one night! What a difference between the family when Paul was thrust into prison, and when he was brought out and received as an honoured guest at the very table of the renovated jailer! Such a change would Christianity produce in every family, and such joy would it diffuse through every household. ¶ *With all his house.* With all his family. Whether they believed *before* they were baptized or *after* is not declared. But the whole narrative would lead us to suppose that, as soon as the jailer believed, he and all his family were baptized. It is subsequently added that they believed also. The *joy* arose from the fact that they all believed the gospel; the *baptism* appears to have been performed on account of the faith of the head of the family.

35. *And when it was day,* &c. It is evident from the narrative that it was not contemplated at first to release them so soon, ver. 22-24. But it is not known what produced this change of purpose in the magistrates. It is probable, however, that they had been brought to reflection, somewhat as the jailer had, by the earthquake, and that their consciences had been troubled by the fact, that in order to please the multitude, they had caused strangers to be beaten and imprisoned without trial, and contrary to the Roman laws. An

magistrates sent the serjeants, saying, Let those men go.
36 And the keeper of the prison told this saying to Paul, The magistrates have sent to let you go; now therefore depart, and go in peace.
37 But Paul said unto them, They have beaten us openly [r]uncondemned, being Romans, and have cast *us* into prison; and now do they thrust us out privily? Nay, verily; but let them [s]come themselves, and fetch us out.

r ch.22.25. s Da.6.18,19; Mat.10.16.

earthquake is always fitted to alarm the guilty; and among the Romans it was regarded as an omen of the anger of the gods, and was therefore adapted to produce agitation and remorse. The agitation and alarm of the magistrates were shown by the fact that they sent the officers *as soon* as it was day. The judgments of God are eminently fitted to alarm sinners. Two ancient MSS. read this, "The magistrates *who were alarmed by the earthquake*, sent," &c. (Doddridge). Whether this reading be genuine or not, it doubtless expresses the true cause of their sending to release the apostles. ¶ *The serjeants*—ῥαβδούχους. Literally, those having rods; the lictors. These were public officers who walked before magistrates with the emblems of authority. In Rome they bore before the senators the *fasces;* that is, a bundle of rods with an axe in its centre, as a symbol of office. They performed somewhat the same office as a beadle in England, or as a constable in our courts (America).

37. *They have beaten us openly uncondemned.* There are three aggravating circumstances mentioned, of which Paul complains. (1) That they had been *beaten* contrary to the Roman laws. (2) That it had been *public;* the disgrace had been in the presence of the people, and the reparation ought to be as public. (3) That it had been done without a trial, and while they were uncondemned, and therefore the magistrates ought themselves to come and release them, and thus publicly acknowledge their error. Paul knew the privileges of a Roman citizen, and at proper times, when the interests of justice and religion required it, he did not hesitate to assert them. In all this, he understood and accorded with the Roman laws. The Valerian law declared that if a citizen appealed from the magistrate to the people, it should not be lawful for the magistrate to beat him with rods, or to behead him (Plutarch, Life of P. Valerius Publicola; Livy, ii. 8). By the Porcian law it was expressly forbidden that a citizen should be beaten (Livy, iv. 9). Cicero says that the body of every Roman citizen was inviolable. "The Porcian law," he adds, "has removed the rod from the body of every Roman citizen." And in his celebrated oration against Verres, he says, "A Roman citizen was beaten with rods in the forum, O judges; where, in the meantime, no groan, no other voice of this unhappy man, was heard except the cry, 'I am a Roman citizen!' Take away this hope," he says, "take away this defence from the Roman citizens, let there be no protection in the cry *I am a Roman citizen*, and the prætor can with impunity inflict any punishment on him who declares himself a citizen of Rome," &c. ¶ *Being Romans.* Being Romans, or having the privilege of Roman citizens. They were born Jews, but they claimed that they were Roman citizens, and had a right to the privileges of citizenship. On the ground of this claim, and the reason why Paul claimed to be a Roman citizen, see Notes on ch. xxii. 28. ¶ *Privily.* Privately. The release should be as public as the unjust act of imprisonment. As they have publicly attempted to disgrace us, so they should as publicly acquit us. This was a matter of mere justice; and as it was of great importance to their character and success, they insisted on it. ¶ *Nay, verily; but let them come*, &c. It was proper that they should be required to do this, (1) Because they had been illegally imprisoned, and the injustice of the magistrates should be acknowledged. (2) Because the Roman laws had been violated, and the majesty of the Roman people insulted, and honour should be done to the laws. (3) Because injustice had been done to Paul and Silas, and they had a right to demand just treatment and protection. (4) Because such a public act on the part of the magistrates would strengthen the young converts, and show them that the apostles were not guilty of a violation of the laws. (5) Because it

38 And the serjeants told these
words unto the magistrates; and
they feared when they heard that
they were Romans.
39 And they came and [t]besought
them, and brought *them* out, [u]and
desired *them* to depart out of the
city.
40 And they went out of the
prison, and entered into [v]*the house*

t Ex.11.8; Re.3.9. u Mat.8.34. v ver.14.

---

would tend to the honour and to the furtherance of religion. It would be a public acknowledgement of their innocence, and would go far toward lending to them the sanction of the laws as religious teachers. We may learn from this also, (1) That though Christianity requires meekness in the reception of injuries, yet that there are occasions on which Christians may insist on their rights according to the laws. Comp. Jn. xviii. 23. (2) That this is to be done particularly where the honour of religion is concerned, and where by it the gospel will be promoted. A Christian may bear much as a man in a private capacity, and may submit, without any effort to seek reparation; but where the honour of the gospel is concerned; where submission, without any effort to obtain justice, might be followed by disgrace to the cause of religion, a higher obligation may require him to seek a vindication of his character, and to claim the protection of the laws. His name, and character, and influence belong to the church. The laws are designed as a protection to an injured name, or of violated property and rights, and of an endangered life. And when that protection can be had only by an appeal to the laws, such an appeal, as in the case of Paul and Silas, is neither vindictive nor improper. My private interests I may sacrifice, if I choose; my public name, and character, and principles belong to the church and the world, and the laws, if necessary, may be called in for their protection.

38. *They feared when they heard*, &c. They were apprehensive of punishment for having imprisoned them in violation of the laws of the empire. To punish unjustly a Roman citizen was deemed an offence to the majesty of the Roman people, and was severely punished by the laws. Dionysius Hal. (*Ant. Rom.*, ii.) says, "The punishment appointed for those who abrogated or transgressed the Valerian law was death, and the confiscation of his property." The emperor Claudius deprived the inhabitants of Rhodes of freedom for having crucified some Roman citizens (Dio Cass., lib. 60). See Kuinoel and Grotius.

39. *And they came and besought them.* A most humiliating act for Roman magistrates, but in this case it was unavoidable. The apostles had them completely in their power, and could easily effect their disgrace and ruin. Probably they *besought* them by declaring them innocent; by affirming that they were ignorant that they were Roman citizens, &c. ¶ *And desired* them *to depart*, &c. Probably, (1) To save their own character, and be secure from their taking any further steps to convict the magistrates of violating the laws; and (2) To evade any further popular tumult on their account. This advice Paul and Silas saw fit to comply with, after they had seen and comforted the brethren, ver. 40. They had accomplished their main purpose in going to Philippi; they had preached the gospel; they had laid the foundation of a flourishing church (comp. the Epistle to the Philippians); and they were now prepared to prosecute the purpose of their agency into surrounding regions. Thus the opposition of the people and the magistrates at Philippi was the occasion of the founding of the church there, and thus their unkind and inhospitable request that they should leave them was the means of the extension of the gospel into adjacent regions.

40. *They comforted them.* They exhorted them, and encouraged them to persevere, notwithstanding the opposition and persecution which they might meet with. ¶ *And departed.* That is, Paul and Silas departed. It would appear probable that Luke and Timothy remained in Philippi, or, at least, did not attend Paul and Silas. For Luke, who, in ch. xvi. 10, uses the first person, and speaks of himself as with Paul and Silas, speaks of them now in the third person, implying that he was not with them until Paul had arrived at Troas, where Luke joined him from Philippi, ch. xx. 5, 6. In ch. xvii. 14, also, Timothy is mentioned as being at Berea in company with Silas, from which it

of Lydia: and when they had seen the brethren, they comforted them, and departed.

CHAPTER XVII.

NOW when they had passed
through Amphipolis and
Apollonia, they came to Thessalonica, where was a synagogue of
the Jews:
2 And Paul, [a]as his manner
was, went in unto them, and three
sabbath-days reasoned with them
out of the scriptures,
3 Opening and alleging [b]that

a Lu.4.16; ch.9.20; 13.5,14.
b Lu.24.26,46; ch.18.28; Ga.3.1.

---

appears that he did not accompany Paul and Silas to Thessalonica. Comp. ch. xvii. 1, 4. Paul and Silas, when they departed from Philippi, went to Thessalonica, ch. xvii. 1.

CHAPTER XVII.

1. *Amphipolis.* This was the capital of the eastern province of Macedonia. It was originally a colony of the Athenians, but under the Romans it was made the capital of that part of Macedonia. It was near to Thrace, and was situated not far from the mouth of the river Strymon, which flowed *around the city,* and thus occasioned its name, *around the city.* The *distances* laid down in the Itineraries in regard to these places are as follows: *Philippi to Amphipolis, thirty-three miles; Amphipolis to Apollonia, thirty miles; Apollonia to Thessalonica, thirty-seven miles.* "These distances are evidently such as might have been traversed each in one day; and since nothing is said of any delay on the road, but everything to imply that the journey was rapid, we conclude (unless, indeed, their recent sufferings made rapid travelling impossible) that Paul and Silas rested one night at each of the intermediate places, and thus our notice of their journey is divided into three parts. The position of Amphipolis is one of the most important in Greece. It stands in a pass which traverses the mountains bordering the Strymonic Gulf, and it commands the only easy communication from the coast of that gulf into the great Macedonian plains, which extend, for sixty miles, from beyond Meleniko to Philippi. The ancient name of the place was 'Nine Ways,' from the great number of Thracian and Macedonian roads which met at this point. The Athenians saw the importance of the position, and established a colony there, which they called Amphipolis, because the river surrounded it." ¶ *And Apollonia.* This city was situated between Amphipolis and Thessalonica, and was formerly much celebrated for its trade. ¶ *They came to Thessalonica.* This was a seaport of the second part of Macedonia. It is situated at the head of the Bay Thermaicus. It was made the capital of the second division of Macedonia by Æmilius Paulus, when he divided the country into four districts. It was formerly called Therma, but afterward received the name of Thessalonica, either from Cassander, in honour of his wife Thessalonica, the daughter of Philip, or in honour of a victory which Philip obtained over the armies of Thessaly. It was inhabited by Greeks, Romans, and Jews. It is now called *Saloniki,* and, from its situation, must always be a place of commercial importance. It is situated on the inner bend of the Thermaic Gulf, half-way between the Adriatic and the Hellespont, on the sea margin of a vast plain, watered by several rivers, and was evidently designed for a commercial emporium. It has a population at present of sixty or seventy thousand, about half of whom are Jews. They are said to have thirty-six synagogues, "none of them remarkable for their neatness or elegance of style." In this place a church was collected, to which Paul afterward addressed the two epistles to the Thessalonians. ¶ *Where was a synagogue.* Greek, where was THE synagogue (ἡ συναγωγὴ) of the Jews. It has been remarked by Grotius and Kuinoel that the article used here is emphatic, and denotes that there was probably no synagague at Amphipolis and Apollonia. This was the reason why they passed through those places without making any delay.

2. *His manner was.* His custom was to attend on the worship of the synagogue, and to preach the gospel to his countrymen first, ch. ix. 20; xiii. 5, 14. ¶ *Reasoned with them.* Discoursed to them, or attempted to prove that Jesus was the Messiah. The word used here (διελέγετο) means often no more than to make a public address or dis-

Christ must needs have suffered,
and risen again from the dead;
and that this Jesus, [1]whom I
preach unto you, is Christ.
4 And [c]some of them believed,
and [d]consorted with Paul and
Silas; and of the devout Greeks a
great multitude, and of the chief
women not a few.
5 But the Jews which believed
not, moved with envy, took unto
them certain lewd fellows of the
baser sort, and gathered a com-

[1] or, *whom*, said he, *I preach*. c ch.28.24. d 2 Co.8.5; 1 Th.1.5,6.

---

course. See Notes on ch. xxiv. 25. ¶ *Out of the scriptures.* By many critics this is connected with the following verse, "Opening and alleging from the scriptures that Christ must needs have suffered," &c. The sense is not varied materially by the change.

3. *Opening*—διανοίγων. See Lu. xxiv. 32. The word means to explain or to unfold. It is usually applied to that which is *shut*, as the eye, &c. Then it means to explain that which is concealed or obscure. It means here that he *explained* the Scriptures in their true sense. ¶ *And alleging*—παρατιθέμενος. Laying down the proposition; that is, maintaining that it must be so. ¶ *That Christ must needs have suffered.* That there was a fitness and necessity in his dying, as Jesus of Nazareth had done. The sense of this will be better seen by retaining the word Messiah. "That there was a fitness or necessity that the *Messiah* expected by the Jews, and predicted in their Scriptures, should suffer." This point the Jews were unwilling to admit; but it was essential to his argument in proving that Jesus was the Messiah to show that it was foretold that he should die for the sins of men. On the *necessity* of this, see Notes on Lu. xxiv. 26, 27. ¶ *Have suffered.* That he should die. ¶ *And that this Jesus.* And that this Jesus of Nazareth, who has thus suffered and risen, whom, said he, I preach to you, is the Messiah.

The arguments by which Paul probably proved that Jesus was the Messiah were, (1) That he corresponded with the *prophecies* respecting him in the following particulars. (*a*) He was born at Bethlehem, Mi. v. 2. (*b*) He was of the tribe of Judah, Ge. xlix. 10. (*c*) He was descended from Jesse, and of the royal line of David, Is. xi. 1, 10. (*d*) He came at the *time* predicted, Da. ix. 24–27. (*e*) His appearance, character, work, &c., corresponded with the predictions, Is. liii. (2) His miracles proved that he was the Messiah, for he *professed* to be, and God would not work a miracle to confirm the claims of an impostor. (3) For the same reason, his resurrection from the dead proved that he was the Messiah.

4. *And consorted.* Literally, had their lot with Paul and Silas; that is, they united themselves to them, and became their disciples. The word is commonly applied to those who are partakers of an inheritance. ¶ *And of the devout Greeks. Religious* Greeks; or, of those who worshipped God. Those are denoted who had renounced the worship of idols, and who attended on the worship of the synagogue, but who were not fully admitted to the privileges of Jewish proselytes. They were called, by the Jews, proselytes of the gate. ¶ *And of the chief women.* See Notes on ch. xiii. 50.

5. *Moved with envy.* That they made so many converts, and met with such success. ¶ *Certain lewd fellows of the baser sort.* This is an unhappy translation. The word *lewd* is not in the original. The Greek is, "And having taken certain wicked men of those who were about the forum," or market-place. The forum, or market-place, was the place where the idle assembled, and where those were gathered together that wished to be employed, Mat. xx. 3. Many of these would be of abandoned character—the idle, the dissipated, and the worthless, and, therefore, just the materials for a mob. It does not appear that they felt any particular interest in the subject; but they were, like other mobs, easily excited, and urged on to any acts of violence. The pretence on which the mob was excited was, that they had everywhere produced disturbance, and that they violated the laws of the Roman emperor, ver. 6, 7. It may be observed, however, that a mob usually regards very little the cause in which they are engaged. They may be roused either for or against religion, and become as full of zeal *for* the *insulted* honour of religion as *against* it. The profane, the worthless, and the abandoned thus often become violently

pany, and set all the city on an
uproar, and assaulted the house
of [e]Jason, and sought to bring
them out to the people.
6 And when they found them
not, they drew Jason and certain
brethren unto the rulers of the
city, crying, [f]These that have
turned the world upside down are
come hither also;
7 Whom Jason hath received;
and these all do [g]contrary to the
decrees of Cæsar, saying that there
is another king, *one* Jesus.
8 And they [h]troubled the people,
and the rulers of the city, when
they heard these things.
9 And when they had taken
security of Jason, and of the others,
they let them go.
10 And the brethren immediately [i]sent away Paul and Silas

e Ro.16.21. *f* Lu.23.5; ch.16.20.
g Lu.23.2; Jn.19.12.
h Mat.2.3; Jn.11.48. *i* ch.9.25; ver.14.

---

enraged for the *honour* of religion, and full of indignation and tumult against those who are accused of violating public peace and order. ¶ *The house of Jason.* Where Paul and Silas were, ver. 7. Jason appears to have been a relative of Paul, and for this reason it was probable that he lodged with him, Ro. xvi. 21.

6. *These that have turned the world upside down.* That have excited commotion and disturbance in other places. The charge has been often brought against the gospel that it has been the occasion of confusion and disorder.

7. *Whom Jason hath received.* Has received into his house, and entertained kindly. ¶ *These all do contrary to the decrees of Cæsar.* The charge against them was that of sedition and rebellion against the Roman emperor. Grotius on this verse remarks that the Roman people, and after them the emperors, would not permit the name of king to be mentioned in any of the vanquished provinces except by their permission. ¶ *Saying that there is another king.* This was probably a charge of mere malignity. They probably understood that when the apostles spoke of Jesus as a king, they did not do it as of a temporal prince. But it was easy to pervert their words, and to give plausibility to the accusation. The same thing had occurred in regard to the Lord Jesus himself, Lu. xxiii. 2.

8. *And they troubled the people.* They excited the people to commotion and alarm. The rulers feared the tumult that was excited, and the people feared the Romans, when they heard the charge that there were rebels against the government in their city. It does not appear that there was a disposition in the rulers or the people to persecute the apostles; but they were excited and alarmed by the representations of the Jews, and by the mob that they had collected.

9. *And when they had taken security of Jason.* This is an expression taken from courts, and means that Jason and the other gave satisfaction to the magistrates for the good conduct of Paul and Silas, or became responsible for it. Whether it was by depositing a sum of money, and by thus giving bail, is not quite clear. The sense is, that they did it in accordance with the Roman usages, and gave sufficient security for the good conduct of Paul and Silas. Heuman supposes that the pledge given was that they should leave the city. Michaelis thinks that they gave a pledge that they would no more harbour them; but if they returned again to them, they would deliver them to the magistrates. ¶ *And of the other.* The other brethren (ver. 6) who had been drawn to the rulers of the city.

10. *And the brethren immediately sent away Paul and Silas.* Comp. ch. ix. 25. They did this for their safety. Yet this was not done until the gospel had taken deep root in Thessalonica. Having preached there, and laid the foundation of a church; having thus accomplished the purpose for which they went there, they prepared to leave the city. ¶ *Unto Berea.* This was a city of Macedonia, near Mount Cithanes. "Berœa is on the eastern slope of the Olympian range, and commands an extensive view of the plain which is watered by the Haliacmon and Axius. It has many natural advantages, and is now considered one of the most agreeable towns in Rumili. Plane-trees spread a grateful shade over its gardens. Streams of water are in every street. Its ancient name is said to have been derived from the abundance of its waters; and the

by night into Berea; who coming
thither, went into the synagogue of
the Jews.
11 These were [k]more noble than
those in Thessalonica, in that they
received the word [l]with all readiness of mind, and [m]searched the
scriptures daily, whether those
things were so.
12 Therefore many of them be-

k Ps.119.99,100.

l Ja.1.21; 1 Pe.2.2.
m Is.34.16; Lu.16.29; 24.44; Jn.5.39.

name still survives in the modern Verria, or Kara-Verria. It is situated on the left of the Haliacmon, about 5 miles from the point where that river breaks through an immense rocky ravine from the mountains to the plain. A few insignificant ruins of the Greek and Roman periods may yet be noticed. It still boasts of eighteen or twenty thousand inhabitants, and is placed in the second rank of the cities of European Turkey."—*Life and Epistles of St. Paul.*

11. *These were more noble*—εὐγενέστεροι. This literally means more noble by birth; descended from more illustrious ancestors. But here the word is used to denote a quality of mind and heart. They were more generous, liberal, and noble in their feelings; more disposed to inquire candidly into the truth of the doctrines advanced by Paul and Silas. It is always proof of a noble, liberal, and ingenuous disposition to be willing to examine into the truth of any doctrine presented. The writer refers here particularly to the Jews. ¶ *In that.* Because. ¶ *They received the word*, &c. They listened attentively and respectfully to the gospel. They did not reject and spurn it as unworthy of examination. This is the first particular in which they were more noble than those in Thessalonica. ¶ *And searched the scriptures.* That is, the Old Testament. See Notes on Jn. v. 39. The apostles always affirmed that the doctrines which they maintained respecting the Messiah were in accordance with the Jewish scriptures. The Bereans made diligent and earnest inquiry in respect to this, and were willing to ascertain the truth. ¶ *Daily.* Not only on the Sabbath, and in the synagogue, but they made it a daily employment. It is evident from this that they *had* the Scriptures; and this is one proof that Jewish families would, if possible, obtain the oracles of God. ¶ *Whether these things were so.* Whether the doctrines stated by Paul and Silas were in accordance with the Scriptures. The Old Testament they received as the standard of truth, and whatever could be shown to be in accordance with that, they received. On this verse we may remark, (1) That it is proof of true nobleness and liberality of mind to be willing to examine the proofs of the truth of religion. What the friends of Christianity have had most cause to lament and regret is, that so many are unwilling to examine its claims; that they spurn it as unworthy of serious thought, and condemn it without hearing. (2) The Scriptures should be examined *daily.* If we wish to arrive at the truth, they should be the object of constant study. That man has very little reason to expect that he will grow in knowledge and grace who does not peruse, with candour and with prayer, a portion of the Bible every day. (3) The constant searching of the Scriptures is the best way to keep the mind from error. He who does not do it daily may expect to "be carried about with every wind of doctrine," and to have no settled opinions. (4) The preaching of ministers should be examined by the Scriptures. Their doctrines are of no value unless they accord with the Bible. Every preacher should expect his doctrines to be examined in this way, and to be rejected if they are not in accordance with the Word of God. The church, in proportion to its increase in purity and knowledge, will feel this more and more; and it is an indication of advance in piety when men are increasingly disposed to examine everything by the Bible. How immensely important, then, is it that the young should be trained up to diligent habits of searching the Word of God. And how momentous is the obligation of parents, and of Sabbath-school teachers, to inculcate just views of the interpretation of the Bible, and to form the habits of the rising generation, so that they shall be disposed and enabled to examine every doctrine by the sacred oracles. The purity of the church depends on the extension of the spirit of the noble-minded Bereans, and that spirit is to be extended in a very considerable degree by the instrumentality of Sabbath-schools.

'lieved; also of honourable women which were Greeks, and of men, not a few.

13 But when the Jews of Thessalonica had knowledge that the word of God was preached of Paul at Berea, they came thither also, and [n]stirred up the people.

14 And then immediately the brethren [o]sent away Paul to go as it were to the sea; but Silas and Timotheus abode there still.

15 And they that conducted Paul brought him unto Athens; and receiving a commandment unto [p]Silas and Timotheus for to come

n Lu.12.51. o Mat.10.23. p ch.18.5.

---

12. *Therefore many of them believed.* As the result of their examination. This result will commonly follow when people search the Scriptures. Much is gained when men can be induced to examine the Bible. We may commonly take it for granted that such an examination will result in their conviction of the truth. The most prominent and usual cause of infidelity is found in the fact that men will not investigate the Scriptures. Many infidels have confessed that they had never carefully read the New Testament. Thomas Paine confessed that he wrote the first part of the *Age of Reason* without having a Bible at hand, and without its being possible to procure one where he then was (in Paris). "I had," says he, "neither Bible nor Testament to refer to, though I was writing against both; nor could I procure any" (*Age of Reason*, p. 65, ed. 1831; also p. 33). None, it may safely be affirmed, have ever read the Scriptures with candour, and with the true spirit of prayer, who have not been convinced of the truth of Christianity, and been brought to submit their souls to its influence and its consolations. The great thing which Christians desire their fellow-men to do is candidly to search the Bible, and when this is done they confidently expect that they will be truly converted to God. ¶ *Of honourable women.* See Notes on ch. xiii. 50.

13. *Stirred up the people.* The word used here (σαλεύειν) denotes properly *to agitate* or *excite*, as the waves of the sea are agitated by the wind. It is with great beauty used to denote the agitation and excitement of a popular tumult, from its resemblance to the troubled waves of the ocean. The figure is often employed by the classic writers, and also occurs in the Scriptures. See Ps. lxv. 7; Is. xvii. 12, 13; Je. xlvi. 7, 8.

14. *The brethren.* Those who were Christians. ¶ *Sent away Paul.* In order to secure his safety. A similar thing had been done in Thessalonica, ver. 10. The tumult was great; and there was no doubt, such was the hostility of the Jews, that the life of Paul would be endangered, and they therefore resolved to secure his safety. ¶ *As it were.* Rather, "even to the sea," for that is its signification. It does not imply that there was any feint or sleight in the case, *as if* they intended to deceive their pursuers. They took him to the sea-coast, not far from Berea, and from that place he probably went by sea to Athens.

15. *Unto Athens.* This was the first visit of Paul to this celebrated city; and perhaps the first visit of a Christian minister. His success in this city, for some cause, was not great, but his preaching was attended with the conversion of some individuals. See ver. 34. Athens was the most celebrated city of Greece, and was distinguished for the military talents, the learning, the eloquence, and the politeness of its inhabitants. It was founded by Cecrops and an Egyptian colony about 1556 years before the Christian era. It was called *Athens* in honour of Minerva, who was chiefly worshipped there, and to whom the city was dedicated. The city, at first, was built on a rock in the midst of a spacious plain; but in process of time the whole plain was covered with buildings, which were called the lower city. No city of Greece, or of the ancient world, was so much distinguished for philosophy, learning, and the arts. The most celebrated warriors, poets, statesmen, and philosophers were either born or flourished there. The most celebrated models of architecture and statuary were there; and for ages it held its pre-eminence in civilization, arts, and arms. The city still exists, though it has been often subject to the calamities of war, to a change of masters, and to the mouldering hand of time. It was twice burnt by the Persians; destroyed by Philip II. of Mace-

to him with all speed, they departed.

16 Now while Paul waited for them at Athens, [q]his spirit was stirred in him when he saw the city [2]wholly given to idolatry.

17 Therefore disputed he in the synagogue with the Jews, and

q Ps.119.136; 2 Pe.2.8.

2 or, *full of idols.*

don; again by Sylla; was plundered by Tiberius; desolated by the Goths in the reign of Claudius; and the whole territory ravaged and ruined by Alaric. From the reign of Justinian to the thirteenth century the city remained in obscurity, though it continued to be a town at the head of a small state. It was seized by Omar, general of Mohammed the Great, in 1455; was sacked by the Venetians in 1464; and was taken by the Turks again in 1688. In 1812 the population was 12,000; but it has since been desolated by the sanguinary contests between the Turks and the Greeks, and left almost a mass of ruins. It is now free; and efforts are making by Christians to restore it to its former elevation in learning and importance, and to impart to it the blessings of the Christian religion. In the revolutions of ages it has been ordered that men should bear the torch of learning to Athens from a land unknown to its ancient philosophers, and convey the blessings of civilization to them by that gospel which in the time of Paul they rejected and despised. ¶ *And receiving a commandment.* They who accompanied Paul received his commands to Silas and Timothy. ¶ *With all speed.* As soon as possible. Perhaps Paul expected much labour and success in Athens, and was therefore desirous of securing their aid with him in his work.

16. *Now while Paul waited.* How long he was there is not intimated; but doubtless some time would elapse before they could arrive. In the meantime Paul had ample opportunity to observe the state of the city. ¶ *His spirit was stirred within him.* His mind was greatly excited. The word used here (παρωξύνετο) denotes any excitement, agitation, or *paroxysm* of mind, 1 Co. xiii. 5. It here means that the mind of Paul was greatly *concerned*, or agitated, doubtless with pity and distress at their folly and danger. ¶ *The city wholly given to idolatry.* Greek, κατείδωλον. It is well translated in the margin, "or full of idols." The word is not elsewhere used in the New Testament. That this was the condition of the city is abundantly testified by profane writers. Thus Pausanias (*in Attic.* i. 24) says, "the Athenians greatly surpassed others in their zeal for religion." Lucian (t. i. *Prometh.* p. 180) says of the city of Athens, "On every side there are altars, victims, temples, and festivals." Livy (45, 27) says that Athens "was full of the images of gods and men, adorned with every variety of material, and with all the skill of art." And Petronius (*Sat.* xvii.) says humorously of the city, that "it was easier to find a god than a man there." See Kuinoel. In this verse we may see how a splendid idolatrous city will strike a pious mind. Athens then had more that was splendid in architecture, more that was brilliant in science, and more that was beautiful in the arts, than any other city of the world; perhaps more than all the rest of the world united. Yet there is no account that the mind of Paul was filled with admiration; there is no record that he spent his time in examining the works of art; there is no evidence that he forgot his high purpose in an idle and useless contemplation of temples and statuary. His was a Christian mind; and he contemplated all this with a Christian heart. That heart was deeply affected in view of the amazing guilt of a people who were ignorant of the true God, who had filled their city with idols reared to the honour of imaginary divinities, and who, in the midst of all this splendour and luxury, were going down to destruction. So should every pious man feel who treads the streets of a splendid and guilty city. The Christian will not despise the productions of art, but he will feel, deeply feel, for the unhappy condition of those who, amidst wealth, and splendour, and outward adorning, are withholding their affections from the living God, and who are going unredeemed to eternal woe. Happy would it be if every Christian traveller who visits cities of wealth and splendour would, like Paul, be affected in view of their crimes and dangers; and happy if, like him, men could cease their unbounded admiration of magnificence and splendour in temples, and

with the [r]devout persons, and in the market daily with them that met with him.

18 Then certain [s]philosophers of the Epicureans, and of the Stoics, encountered him. And some said, What will this [3]babbler say? Other some, He seemeth to be a setter

r ch.8.2. s Col.2.8.

3 or, *base fellow*.

palaces, and statuary, to regard the condition of *mind*, not perishable like marble—of *the soul*, more magnificent even in its ruins than all the works of Phidias or Praxiteles.

17. *Therefore disputed he.* Or reasoned. He engaged in an argument with them. ¶ *With the devout persons.* Those worshipping God after the manner of the Jews. They were Jewish proselytes, who had renounced idolatry, but who had not been fully admitted to the privileges of the Jews. See Notes on ch. x. 2. ¶ *And in the market.* In the forum. It was not only the place where provisions were sold, but was also a place of great public concourse. In this place the philosophers were not unfrequently found engaged in public discussion.

18. *Then certain philosophers.* Athens was distinguished, among all the cities of Greece and the world, for the cultivation of a subtle and refined philosophy. This was their boast, and the object of their constant search and study, 1 Co. i. 22. ¶ *Of the Epicureans.* This sect of philosophers was so named from Epicúrus, who lived about 300 years before the Christian era. They denied that the world was created by God, and that the gods exercised any care or providence over human affairs, and also the immortality of the soul. Against these positions of the sect Paul directed his main argument in proving that the world was created and governed by God. One of the distinguishing doctrines of Epicurus was that pleasure was the *summum bonum*, or chief good, and that virtue was to be practised only as it contributed to pleasure. By pleasure, however, Epicurus did not mean sensual and grovelling appetites and degraded vices, but rational pleasure, properly regulated and governed. See Good's *Book of Nature.* But whatever *his* views were, it is certain that his followers had embraced the doctrine that the pleasures of sense were to be practised without restraint. Both in principle and practice, therefore, they devoted themselves to a life of gaiety and sensuality, and sought happiness only in indolence, effeminacy, and voluptuousness. Confident in the belief that the world was not under the administration of a God of justice, they gave themselves up to the indulgence of every passion—the infidels of their time, and the exact example of the gay and fashionable multitudes of all times, that live without God, and that seek *pleasure* as their chief good. ¶ *And of the Stoics.* This was a sect of philosophers, so named from the Greek *στοά*, *stoa*, a porch or portico, because Zeno, the founder of the sect, held his school and taught in a *porch*, in the city of Athens. Zeno was born in the island of Cyprus, but the greater part of his life was spent at Athens in teaching philosophy. After having taught publicly forty-eight years, he died at the age of ninety-six, two hundred and sixty-four years before Christ. The doctrines of the sect were, that the universe was created by God; that all things were fixed by Fate; that even God was under the dominion of fatal necessity; that the Fates were to be submitted to; that the passions and affections were to be suppressed and restrained; that happiness consisted in the insensibility of the soul to pain; and that a man should gain an absolute mastery over all the passions and affections of his nature. They were stern in their views of virtue, and, like the Pharisees, prided themselves on their own righteousness. They supposed that matter was eternal, and that God was either the animating principle or soul of the world, or that all things were a part of God. They fluctuated much in their views of a future state; some of them holding that the soul would exist only until the destruction of the universe, and others that it would finally be absorbed into the divine essence and become a part of God. It will be readily seen, therefore, with what pertinency Paul discoursed to them. The leading doctrines of both sects were met by him. ¶ *Encountered him.* Contended with him; opposed themselves to him. ¶ *And some said.* This was said in scorn and contempt. He had excited attention; but they scorned such doctrines as they supposed would be delivered by an unknown foreigner from

forth of strange gods: because he preached unto them Jesus, and the resurrection.

19 And they took him, and brought him unto [4] Areopagus,

[4] or, *Mars' hill.* It was the highest court in Athens.

Judea. ¶ *What will this babbler say?* Margin, *base fellow.* Greek, σπερμολόγος. The word occurs nowhere else in the New Testament. It properly means *one who collects seeds,* and was applied by the Greeks to the poor persons who collected the scattered grain in the fields after harvest, or to gleaners; and also to the poor who obtained a precarious subsistence around the markets and in the streets. It was also applied to birds that picked up the scattered seeds of grain in the field or in the markets. The word came hence to have a twofold signification: (1) It denoted the poor, the needy, and the vile—the refuse and offscouring of society; and (2) From the birds which were thus employed, and which were troublesome by their continual unmusical sounds, it came to denote those who were talkative, garrulous, and opinionated—those who collected the opinions of others, or scraps of knowledge, and retailed them fluently, without order or method. It was a word, therefore, expressive of their contempt for an unknown foreigner who should pretend to instruct the learned men and philosophers of Greece. Doddridge renders it "retailer of scraps." Syriac, "collector of words." ¶ *Other some.* Others. ¶ *He seemeth to be a setter forth.* He announces or declares the existence of strange gods. The reason why they supposed this was, that he made the capital points of his preaching to be Jesus and the resurrection, which they mistook for the names of divinities. ¶ *Of strange gods.* Of *foreign* gods, or demons. They worshipped many gods themselves, and as they believed that every country had its own peculiar divinities, they supposed that Paul had come to announce the existence of some such foreign, and to them unknown gods. The word translated *gods* (δαιμονίων) denotes properly the genii, or spirits who were superior to men, but inferior to the gods. It is, however, often employed to denote the gods themselves, and is evidently so used here. The *gods* among the Greeks were such as were supposed to have that rank by nature. The *demons* were such as had been exalted to divinity from being heroes and distinguished men. ¶ *He preached unto them Jesus.* He proclaimed him as the Messiah. The mistake which they made by supposing that Jesus was a foreign divinity was one which was perfectly natural for minds degraded like theirs by idolatry. They had no idea of a pure God; they knew nothing of the doctrine of the Messiah; and they naturally supposed, therefore, that he of whom Paul spoke so much must be a god of some other nation, of a rank similar to their own divinities. ¶ *And the resurrection.* The resurrection of Jesus, and through him the resurrection of the dead. It is evident, I think, that by the resurrection (τὴν ἀνάστασιν) they understood him to refer to the name of some goddess. Such was the interpretation of Chrysostom. The Greeks had erected altars to Shame, and Famine, and Desire (Paus., i. 17), and it is probable that they supposed "the resurrection," or *the Anastasis,* to be the name also of some unknown goddess who presided over the resurrection. Thus they regarded him as a setter forth of *two* foreign or strange gods, Jesus, and the Anastasis, or resurrection.

19. *And brought him unto Areopagus.* Margin, or *Mars' hill.* This was the place or court in which the Areopagites, the celebrated supreme judges of Athens, assembled. It was on a hill almost in the middle of the city; but nothing now remains by which we can determine the form or construction of the tribunal. The hill is almost entirely a mass of stone, and is not easily accessible, its sides being steep and abrupt. On many accounts this was the most celebrated tribunal in the world. Its decisions were distinguished for justice and correctness; nor was there any court in Greece in which so much confidence was placed. This court took cognizance of murders, impieties, and immoralities; they punished vices of all kinds, including idleness; they rewarded the virtuous; they were peculiarly attentive to blasphemies against the gods, and to the performance of the sacred mysteries of religion. It was, therefore, with the greatest propriety that Paul was brought before this tribunal, as being regarded as a setter forth of strange gods, and as being supposed to wish to introduce a

saying, May we know what
this [t]new doctrine whereof thou
speakest *is?*
20 For thou bringest [u]certain
strange things to our ears: we
would know, therefore, what these
things mean.
21 (For all the Athenians, and
strangers which were there, spent
their time in nothing else, but
either to tell or to hear some new
thing.)
22 Then Paul stood in the midst
of [5]Mars' hill, and said, *Ye* men of

t Jn.13.34; 1 Jn.2.7,8. u Ho.8.12.

5 or, *the court of the Areopagites.*

new mode of worship. See Potter's *Antiquities of Greece*, b. i. ch. xix.; and *Travels of Anacharsis*, vol. i. 136, 185; ii. 292–295. ¶ *May we know.* We would know. This seems to have been a respectful inquiry; and it does not appear that Paul was brought there for the sake of *trial.* There are no accusations; no witnesses; none of the forms of trial. They seem to have resorted thither because it was the place where the subject of religion was usually discussed, and because it was a place of confluence for the citizens, and judges, and wise men of Athens, and of foreigners. The design seems to have been, not to *try* him, but fairly to canvass the claims of his doctrines. See ver. 21. It was just an instance of the inquisitive spirit of the people of Athens, willing to hear before they condemned, and to examine before they approved.

20. *Certain strange things.* Literally, something pertaining to a *foreign* country or people. Here it means something unusual or remarkable—something different from what they had been accustomed to hear from their philosophers. ¶ *What these things mean.* We would understand more clearly what is affirmed respecting Jesus and the resurrection.

21. *For all the Athenians.* This was their *general* character. ¶ *And strangers which were there.* Athens was greatly distinguished for the celebrity of its schools of philosophy. It was at that time at the head of the literary world. Its arts and its learning were celebrated in all lands. It is known, therefore, that it was the favourite resort of men of other nations, who came there to become acquainted with its institutions and to listen to its sages. ¶ *Spent their time in nothing else.* The learned and subtle Athenians gave themselves much to speculation, and employed themselves in examining the various new systems of philosophy that were proposed. Strangers and foreigners who were there, having much leisure, would also give themselves to the same inquiries. ¶ *But either to tell or to hear some new thing.* Greek, *something newer*—καινότερον. The latest news; or the latest subject of inquiry proposed. This is well known to have been the character of the people of Athens at all times. "Many of the ancient writers bear witness to the garrulity, and curiosity, and intemperate desire of novelty among the Athenians, by which they inquired respecting all things, even those in which they had no interest, whether of a public or private nature (Kuinoel). Thus Thucyd. (3, 38) says of them, "You excel in suffering yourselves to be deceived with *novelty of speech.*" On which the old scholiast makes this remark, almost in the words of Luke: "He (Thucydides) here blames the Athenians, who care for nothing else but to tell or to hear something new." Thus Ælian (5, 13) says of the Athenians that they are versatile in novelties. Thus Demosthenes represents the Athenians "as inquiring in the place of public resort if there were any NEWS"—τι νεώτερον. Meursius has shown, also, that there were more than three hundred public places in Athens of public resort, where the principal youth and reputable citizens were accustomed to meet for the purpose of conversation and inquiry.

22. *Then Paul.* This commences Paul's explanation of the doctrines which he had stated. It is evident that Luke has recorded but a mere summary or outline of the discourse; but it is such as to enable us to see clearly his course of thought, and the manner in which he met the two principal sects of their philosophers. ¶ *In the midst of Mars' hill.* Greek, Areopagus. This should have been retained in the translation. ¶ Ye *men of Athens.* This language was perfectly respectful, notwithstanding his heart had been deeply affected by their idolatry. Everything about this discourse is calm, grave, cool, argumentative. Paul understood the

Athens, I perceive that in all things ye[v] are too superstitious.

v Je.50.38.

23 For as I passed by, and beheld your [6]devotions, I found an altar

6 or, *gods that ye worship*, Ga.4.8.

character of his auditors, and did not commence his discourse by denouncing them, nor did he suppose that they would be convinced by mere dogmatical assertion. No happier instance can be found of cool, collected argumentation than is furnished in this discourse. ¶ *I perceive.* He perceived this by his observations of their forms of worship in passing through their city, ver. 23. ¶ *In all things.* In respect to all events. ¶ *Ye are too superstitious*—δεισιδαιμονεστέρους. This is a most unhappy translation. We use the word *superstitious* always in a bad sense, to denote being over-scrupulous and rigid in religious observances, particularly in smaller matters, or a zealous devotion to rites and observances which are not commanded. But the word here is designed to convey no such idea. It properly means reverence for the gods. It is used in the classic writers in a *good* sense, to denote piety toward the gods, or suitable *fear* and reverence for them; and also in a *bad* sense, to denote improper fear or excessive dread of their anger; and in this sense it accords with our word superstitious. But it is altogether improbable that Paul would have used it in a bad sense. For, (1) It was not his custom needlessly to blame or offend his auditors. (2) It is not probable that he would commence his discourse in a manner that would only excite prejudice and opposition. (3) In the thing which he specifies (ver. 23) as proof on the subject, he does not introduce it as a matter of blame, but rather as a proof of their devotedness to the cause of religion and of their regard for God. (4) The whole speech is calm, dignified, and argumentative—such as became such a place, such a speaker, and such an audience. The meaning of the expression is, therefore, "I perceive that you are greatly devoted to reverence for religion; that it is a characteristic of the people to honour the gods, to rear altars to them, and to recognize the divine agency in times of trial." The *proof* of this was the altar reared to the unknown God; its *bearing* on his purpose was, that such a state of public sentiment must be favourable to an inquiry into the truth of what he was about to state.

23. *For as I passed by.* Greek, "For I, coming through, and seeing," &c. ¶ *And beheld.* Diligently contemplated; attentively considered (ἀναθεωρῶν). The worship of an idolatrous people will be an object of intense and painful interest to a Christian. ¶ *Your devotions*—τὰ σεβάσματα. Our word *devotions* refers to the *act of worship*—to prayers, praises, &c. The Greek word here used means properly any sacred *thing;* any *object* which is worshipped, or which is connected with the place or rites of worship. Thus it is applied either to the gods themselves, or to the temples, altars, shrines, sacrifices, statues, &c., connected with the worship of the gods. This is its meaning here. It does not denote that Paul saw them engaged in the *act* of worship, but that he was struck with the numerous temples, altars, statues, &c., which were reared to the gods, and which indicated the state of the people. Syriac, "the temple of your gods." Vulgate, "your images." Margin, "gods that ye worship." ¶ *I found an altar.* An altar usually denotes a place for sacrifice. Here, however, it does not appear that any sacrifice was offered; but it was probably a monument of stone, reared to commemorate a certain event, and dedicated to the unknown God. ¶ *To the unknown God*—ἀγνώστῳ Θεῷ. Where this altar was reared, or on what occasion, has been a subject of much debate with expositors. That there was such an altar in Athens, though it may not have been specifically mentioned by the Greek writers, is rendered probable by the following circumstances. (1) It was customary to rear such altars. Minutius Felix says of the Romans, "They build altars to unknown divinities." (2) The term *unknown God* was used in relation to the worship of the Athenians. Lucian, in his *Philopatris,* uses this form of an oath: "I swear by the *unknown God* at Athens," the very expression used by the apostle. And again he says (ch. xxix. 180), "We have found out the *unknown God* at Athens, and worshipped him with our hands stretched up to heaven," &c. (3) There were altars at Athens inscribed *to the unknown gods.* Philostratus says (*in Vita Apol.,* vi. 3), "And this at Athens, where

with this inscription, TO THE UN-
KNOWN GOD. Whom there-
fore ye ignorantly worship, him
declare I unto you.
24 God[w] that made the world,
and all things therein, seeing that
he is [x]Lord of heaven and earth,
[y]dwelleth not in temples made
with hands;
25 Neither is worshipped with

w ch.14.15. x Mat.11.25. y ch.7.48.

there are even altars to the *unknown gods*." Thus Pausanius (*in Attic.*, ch. i.) says, that "at Athens there are altars of gods which are called the UNKNOWN ones." Jerome, in his commentary (Tit. i. 12), says that the whole inscription was, "To the gods of Asia, Europe, and Africa; to *the unknown and strange gods.*" (4) There was a remarkable altar reared in Athens in a time of pestilence, in honour of the unknown god which had granted them deliverance. Diogenes Laertius says that Epimenides restrained the pestilence in the following manner: "Taking white and black sheep, he led them to the Areopagus, and there permitted them to go where they would, commanding those who followed them to sacrifice (τῷ προσήκοντι θεῷ) *to the god to whom these things pertained* [or who had the power of averting the plague, whoever he might be, without adding the name], and thus to allay the pestilence. From which it has arisen that at this day, through the villages of the Athenians, altars are found without any name" (Diog. Laert., b. i. § 10). This took place about 600 years before Christ, and it is not improbable that one or more of those altars remained until the time of Paul. It should be added that the natural inscription on those altars would be, "To the unknown God." None of the gods to whom they usually sacrificed could deliver them from the pestilence. They therefore reared them to some unknown Being who had the power to free them from the plague. ¶ *Whom therefore.* The true God, who had really delivered them from the plague. ¶ *Ye ignorantly worship.* Or worship without knowing his name. You have expressed your homage for him by rearing to him an altar. ¶ *Him declare I unto you.* I make known to you his name, attributes, &c. There is remarkable *tact* in Paul's seizing on this circumstance; and yet it was perfectly fair and honest. God only could deliver in the time of the pestilence. This altar had, therefore, been *really* reared to him, though his name was unknown. The same Being who had interposed at that time, and whose interposition was recorded by the building of this altar, was He who had made the heavens; who ruled over all; and whom Paul was now about to make known to them. There is another feature of skill in the allusion to this altar. In other circumstances it might seem to be presumptuous for an unknown Jew to attempt to instruct the sages of Athens. But here they had confessed and proclaimed their ignorance. By rearing this altar they acknowledged their need of instruction. The way was, therefore, fairly open for Paul to address even these philosophers, and to discourse to them on a point on which they acknowledged their ignorance.

24. *God that made the world.* The main object of this discourse of Paul is to convince them of the folly of idolatry (ver. 29), and thus to lead them to repentance. For this purpose he commences with a statement of the true doctrine respecting God as the Creator of all things. We may observe here, (1) That he speaks here of *God* as the Creator of the world, thus opposing *indirectly* their opinions that there were *many* gods. (2) He speaks of him as the *Creator* of the world, and thus opposes the opinion that matter was eternal; that all things were controlled by Fate; and that God could be confined to temples. The Epicureans held that matter was eternal, and that the world was formed by a fortuitous concourse of atoms. To this opinion Paul opposed the doctrine that all things were *made* by one God. Comp. ch. xiv. 15. ¶ *Seeing that*, &c. Greek, "He being Lord of heaven and earth." ¶ *Lord of heaven and earth.* Proprietor and Ruler of heaven and earth. It is highly absurd, therefore, to suppose that he who is present in heaven and in earth at the same time, and who rules over all, should be confined to a temple of an earthly structure, or dependent on man for anything. ¶ *Dwelleth not*, &c. See Notes on ch. vii. 48.

25. *Neither is worshipped with men's hands.* The word here rendered *wor-*

men's hands, [z]as though he needed any thing; seeing [a]he giveth to all life, and breath, [b]and all things;

26 And hath made of [c]one blood all nations of men, for to dwell on all the face of the earth; and hath

z Ps.50.8. a Job 12.10; Zec.12.1. b Ro.11.36. c Mal.2.10.

---

shipped (θεραπεύεται) denotes to *serve;* to wait upon; and then to render religious service or homage. There is reference here, undoubtedly, to a notion prevalent among the heathen, that the gods were fed or nourished by the offerings made to them. The idea is prevalent among the Hindoos that the sacrifices which are made, and which are offered in the temples, are consumed by the gods themselves. Perhaps, also, Paul had reference to the fact that so many persons were employed in their temples in serving them *with their hands;* that is, in preparing sacrifices and feasts in their honour. Paul affirms that the great Creator of all things cannot be thus dependent on his creatures for happiness, and consequently, that that mode of worship must be highly absurd. The same idea occurs in Ps. l. 10–12:

For every beast of the forest is mine;
And the cattle upon a thousand hills.
I know all the fowls of the mountain;
And the wild beasts of the field are mine.
If I were hungry, I would not tell thee;
For the world is mine, and the fulness thereof.

¶ *Seeing he giveth.* Greek, he having given to all, &c. ¶ *Life.* He is the source of life, and therefore he cannot be dependent on that life which he has himself imparted. ¶ *And breath.* The power of breathing, by which life is sustained. He not only originally gave life, but he gives it at each moment; he gives the power of drawing each breath by which life is supported. It is possible that the phrase "life and breath" may be the figure *hendyades*, by which one thing is expressed by two words. It is highly probable that Paul here had reference to Ge. ii. 7: "And the Lord God breathed into his nostrils the breath of life." The same idea occurs in Job xii. 10:

In whose hand is the life (*margin*) of every living thing;
And the breath of all mankind.

¶ *And all things.* All things necessary to sustain life. We may see here how dependent man is on God. There can be no more absolute dependence than that for every *breath.* How easy it would be for God to suspend our breathing! How incessant the care, how unceasing the providence, by which, whether we sleep or wake—whether we remember or forget him, he heaves our chest, fills our lungs, restores the vitality of our blood, and infuses vigour into our frame! Comp. Notes on Ro. xi. 36.

26. *And hath made of one blood.* All the families of men are descended from one origin or stock. However different their complexion, features, or language, yet they are derived from a common parent. The word *blood* is often used to denote *race, stock, kindred.* This passage affirms that all the human family are descended from the same ancestor; and that, consequently, all the variety of complexion, &c., is to be traced to some other cause than that they were originally different races created. See Ge. i.; comp. Mal. ii. 10. The *design* of the apostle in this affirmation was probably to convince the Greeks that he regarded them all as brethren; that, although he was a Jew, yet he was not enslaved to any narrow notions or prejudices in reference to other men. It follows from the truth here stated that no one nation, and no individual, can claim any pre-eminence over others in virtue of birth or blood. All are in this respect equal; and the whole human family, however they may differ in complexion, customs, and laws, are to be regarded and treated as brethren. It follows, also, that no one part of the race has a right to enslave or oppress any other part, on account of difference of complexion. No man has a right because

He finds his fellow guilty of a skin
Not coloured like his own; and having power
T' enforce the wrong, for such a worthy cause
to
Doom and devote him as his lawful prey.

¶ *For to dwell*, &c. To cultivate and till the earth. This was the original command (Ge. i. 28); and God, by his providence, has so ordered it that the descendants of one family have found their way to all lands, and have become adapted to the climate where he has placed them. ¶ *And hath determined.* Greek, ὁρίσας. Having fixed, or marked out a boundary. See Notes on Ro. i. 4. The word is usually applied to a *field.* It means here that God marked out, or designated in his purpose, their future abodes. ¶ *The*

determined [d]the times before appointed, and [e]the bounds of their habitation;
27 That they should seek the Lord, if haply they might feel after him, and find him, [f]though he be not far from every one of us:
28 For [g] in him we live, and

d Ps.31.15. e Is.45.21. f ch.14.17. g Col.1.17.

times before appointed. This evidently refers to the dispersion and migration of nations. And it means that God had, in his plan, fixed the times when each country should be settled, and the rise, the prosperity, and the fall of each nation. The different continents and islands have not, therefore, been settled by chance, but by a wise rule, and in accordance with God's arrangement and design. ¶ *And the bounds of their habitation.* Their limits and boundaries as a people. By customs, laws, inclinations, and habits he has fixed the boundaries of their habitations, and disposed them to dwell there. We may learn, (1) That the revolutions and changes of nations are under the direction of infinite wisdom; (2) That men should not be restless and dissatisfied with the place where God has located them; (3) That God has given sufficient limits to all, so that it is not needful to invade others; and, (4) That wars of conquest are evil. God has given to men their places of abode, and we have no right to disturb those abodes, or to attempt to displace them in a violent manner. This strain of remark by the apostle was also opposed to all the notions of the Epicurean philosophers, and yet so obviously true and just that they could not gainsay or resist it.

27. *That they should seek the Lord.* Greek, to seek the Lord. The design of thus placing them on the earth—of giving them their habitation among his works—was, that they should contemplate his wisdom in his works, and thus come to a knowledge of his existence and character. All nations, though living in different regions and climates, have thus the opportunity of becoming acquainted with God, Ro. i. 19, 20. The fact that the nations did *not* thus learn the character of the true God shows their great stupidity and wickedness. The design of Paul in this was doubtless to reprove the idolatry of the Athenians. The argument is this: "God has given to each nation its proper opportunity to learn his character. Idolatry, therefore, is folly and wickedness, since it is possible to find out the existence of the *one* God from his works." ¶ *If haply*—εἰ ἄρα γε. If perhaps—implying that it was *possible* to find God, though it might be attended with some difficulty. God has placed us here that we may make the trial, and has made it possible thus to find him. ¶ *They might feel after him.* The word used here (ψηλαφήσειαν) means properly *to touch, to handle* (Lu. xxiv. 39; He. xii. 18), and then to ascertain the qualities of an object by the sense of touch. And as the sense of touch is regarded as a certain way of ascertaining the existence and qualities of an object, the word means to search diligently, that we may know distinctly and certainly. The word has this sense here. It means to search diligently and accurately for God, to learn his existence and perfections. The Syriac renders it, "That they may seek for God, and find him from his creatures." ¶ *And find him.* Find the proofs of his existence. Become acquainted with his perfections and laws. ¶ *Though he be not far,* &c. This seems to be stated by the apostle to show that it was *possible* to find him; and that even those who were without a revelation need not despair of becoming acquainted with his existence and perfections. He is near to us, (1) Because the proofs of his existence and power are round about us everywhere, Ps. xix. 1–6. (2) Because he fills all things in heaven and earth by his essential presence, Ps. cxxxix. 7–10; Je. xxiii. 23, 24; Am. ix. 2–4; 1 Ki. viii. 27. We should learn then, (1) To be afraid of sin. God is present with us, and sees all. (2) He can protect the righteous. He is ever with them. (3) He can detect and punish the wicked. He sees all their plans and thoughts, and records all their doings. (4) We should seek him continually. It is the design for which he has made us; and he has given us abundant opportunities to learn his existence and perfections.

28. *For in him we live.* The expression "*in* him" evidently means *by* him; by his originally forming us, and continually sustaining us. No words can better express our constant dependence on God. He is the original fountain of life, and he upholds us each moment.

move, and have our being; [h]as certain also of your own poets have said, For we are also his offspring.

29 Forasmuch then as we are the offspring of God, [i]we ought not to think that the Godhead is like unto gold, or silver, or stone, graven by art and man's device.

30 And the times of this ignor-

h Tit.1.12.

i Is.40.18,&c.

A similar sentiment is found in Plautus (5. 4, 14): "O Jupiter, who dost cherish and nourish the race of man; by whom we live, and with whom is the hope of the life of all men" (Kuinoel). It does not appear, however, that Paul designed this as a quotation; yet he doubtless intended to state a sentiment with which they were familiar, and with which they would agree. ¶ *And move*—κινούμεθα. Doddridge translates this, "And are moved." It may, however, be in the middle voice, and be correctly rendered as in our version. It means that we derive strength to move from him; an expression denoting constant and absolute dependence. There is no idea of dependence more striking than that we owe to him the ability to perform the slightest motion. ¶ *And have our being*—καὶ ἐσμεν. *And are.* This denotes that our *continued* existence is owing to him. That we live at all is his gift; that we have power to move is his gift; and our *continued* and *prolonged* existence is his gift also. Thus Paul traces our dependence on him from the lowest pulsation of life to the highest powers of action and of continued existence. It would be impossible to express in more emphatic language our entire dependence on God. ¶ *As certain also.* As some. The sentiment which he quotes was found substantially in several Greek poets. ¶ *Of your own poets.* He does not refer particularly here to poets of Athens, but to Greek poets—poets who had written in their language. ¶ *For we are also his offspring.* This precise expression is found in Aratus (*Phænom.*, v. 5), and in Cleanthus in a hymn to Jupiter. Substantially the same sentiment is found in several other Greek poets. Aratus was a Greek poet of Cilicia, the native place of Paul, and flourished about 277 years before Christ. As Paul was a native of the same country it is highly probable he was acquainted with his writings. Aratus passed much of his time at the court of Antigonus Gonatas, king of Macedonia. His principal work was the *Phænomena*, which is here quoted, and was so highly esteemed in Greece that many learned men wrote commentaries on it. The sentiment here quoted was directly at variance with the views of the Epicureans; and it is proof of Paul's address and skill, as well as his acquaintance with his auditors and with the Greek poets, that he was able to adduce a sentiment so directly in point, and that had the concurrent testimony of so many of the Greeks themselves. It is *one* instance among thousands where an acquaintance with profane learning may be of use to a minister of the gospel.

29. *Forasmuch then.* Admitting or assuming this to be true. The argument which follows is drawn from the concessions of their own writers. ¶ *We ought not to think.* It is absurd to suppose. The argument of the apostle is this: "Since we are formed by God; since we are like him, living and intelligent beings; since we are more excellent in our nature than the most precious and ingenious works of art, it is absurd to suppose that the original source of our existence can be like gold, and silver, and stone. Man himself is far more excellent than an image of wood and stone; how much more excellent still must be the great Fountain and Source of all our wisdom and intelligence." See this thought pursued at length in Isa. xl. 18–23. ¶ *The Godhead.* The divinity (τὸ Θεῖον), the divine nature, or essence. The word used here is an adjective employed as a noun, and does not occur elsewhere in the New Testament. ¶ *Is like unto gold*, &c. All these things were used in making images or statues of the gods. It is absurd to think that the source of all life and intelligence resembles a lifeless block of wood or stone. Even degraded heathen, one would think, might see the force of an argument like this. ¶ *Graven.* Sculptured; wrought into an image.

30. *And the times of this ignorance.* The long period when men were ignorant of the true God, and when they worshipped stocks and stones. Paul here refers to the times preceding the

ance [k]God winked at, but [l]now commandeth all men every where to repent:

31 Because he hath [m]appointed a day in the which he will judge the world in righteousness, by *that* man whom he hath ordained; *whereof* he hath [7]given assurance unto all *men*, in that he hath raised him from the dead.

32 And when they heard of [n]the resurrection of the dead, some mocked; and others said, [o]We will hear thee again of this *matter*.

k Ro.3.25. *l* Lu.24.47; Tit.2.11,12. *m* Ro.2.16. [7] or, *offered faith.* *n* ch.26.8. *o* Lu.14.18; ch.24.25.

gospel. ¶ *God winked at*—ὑπεριδών. Overlooked; connived at; did not come forth to punish. In ch. xiv. 16 it is expressed thus: "Who in times past suffered all nations to walk in their own ways." The sense is, he passed over those times without punishing them, as if he did not see them. For wise purposes he suffered them to walk in ignorance that there might be a fair experiment to show what men would do, and how much necessity there was for a revelation to instruct them in the true knowledge of God. We are not to suppose that God regarded idolatry as innocent, or the crimes and vices to which idolatry led as of no importance; but their ignorance was a mitigating circumstance, and he suffered the nations to live without coming forth in direct judgment against them. Comp. Notes on ch. iii. 17; xiv. 16. ¶ *But now commandeth.* By the gospel, Lu. xxiv. 47. ¶ *All men.* Not Jews only, who had been favoured with peculiar privileges, but all nations. The barrier was broken down, and the call to repentance was sent abroad into all the earth. ¶ *To repent.* To exercise sorrow for their sins, and to forsake them. If God *commands* all men to repent, we may observe, (1) That it is their *duty* to do it. There is no higher obligation than to obey the command of God. (2) It *can* be done. God would not command an impossibility. (3) It is binding on *all*. The rich, the learned, the great, the gay, are as much bound as the beggar and the slave. (4) It *must* be done, or the soul lost. It is not safe to neglect a plain law of God. It will not be well to die reflecting that we have all our life despised his commands. (5) We should send the gospel to the heathen. God calls on the *nations* to repent, and to be saved. It is the duty of Christians to make known to them the command, and to invite them to the blessings of pardon and heaven.

31. *Because he hath appointed a day.* This is given as a reason why God commands men to repent. They must be judged; and if they are not penitent and pardoned, they must be condemned. See Notes on Ro. ii. 16. ¶ *Judge the world.* The whole world—Jews and Gentiles. ¶ *In righteousness.* According to the principles of strict justice. ¶ *Whom he hath ordained.* Or whom he has constituted or appointed as judge. See Notes on chap. x. 42; Jn. v. 25. ¶ *Hath given assurance.* Has afforded evidence of this. That evidence consists, (1) In the fact that Jesus *declared* that he would judge the nations (Jn. v. 25, 26; Mat. xxv.); and (2) God confirmed the truth of his declarations by raising him from the dead, or gave his sanction to what the Lord Jesus had said, for God would not work a miracle in favour of an impostor.

32. *Some mocked.* Some of the philosophers derided him. The doctrine of the resurrection of the dead was believed by none of the Greeks; it seemed incredible; and they regarded it as so absurd as not to admit of an argument. It has not been uncommon for even professed philosophers to mock at the doctrines of religion, and to meet the arguments of Christianity with a sneer. The Epicureans particularly would be likely to deride this, as they denied altogether any future state. It is not improbable that this derision by the Epicureans produced such a disturbance as to break off Paul's discourse, as that of Stephen had been by the clamour of the Jews, ch. vii. 54. ¶ *And others said.* Probably some of the Stoics. The doctrine of a future state was not denied by them; and the fact, affirmed by Paul, that one had been raised up from the dead, would appear more plausible to them, and it *might* be a matter worth inquiry to ascertain whether the alleged fact did not furnish a new argument for their views. They therefore proposed to examine this further at some future time. That the inquiry was

33 So Paul departed from among them.

34 Howbeit certain men clave unto him, and believed; among the which *was* Dionysius the Areopagite, and a woman named Damaris, and others with them.

CHAPTER XVIII.

AFTER these things Paul departed from Athens, and came to Corinth:

2 And found a certain Jew named [a]Aquila, born in Pontus,

a Ro.16.3.

---

prosecuted any further does not appear probable, for, (1) No church was organized at Athens. (2) There is no account of any future interview with Paul. (3) He departed almost immediately from them, ch. xviii. 1. Men who defer inquiry on the subject of religion seldom find the favourable period arrive. Those who propose to examine its doctrines at a future time often do it to avoid the *inconvenience* of becoming Christians now, and as a plausible and easy way of rejecting the gospel altogether, without appearing to be rude, or to give offence.

33. *So Paul departed.* Seeing there was little hope of saving them. It was not his custom to labour long in a barren field, or to preach where there was no prospect of success.

34. *Clave unto him.* Adhered to him firmly; embraced the Christian religion. ¶ *Dionysius.* Nothing more is certainly known of this man than is here stated. ¶ *The Areopagite.* Connected with the court of Areopagus, but in what way is not known. It is probable that he was one of the judges. The conversion of *one* man was worth the labour of Paul, and that conversion might have had an extensive influence on others.

In regard to this account of the visit of Paul to Athens—probably the only one which he made to that splendid capital—we may remark, (1) That he was indefatigable and constant in his great work. (2) Christians, amidst the splendour and gaieties of such cities, should have their hearts deeply affected in view of the moral desolations of the people. (3) They should be willing to do their duty, and to bear witness to the pure and simple gospel in the presence of the great and the noble. (4) They should not consider it their main business to admire splendid temples, statues, and paintings—the works of art; but their main business should be to do good as they may have opportunity. (5) A discourse, even in the midst of such wickedness and idolatry, may be calm and dignified; not an appeal merely to the passions, but to the understanding. Paul *reasoned* with the philosophers of Athens; he did not denounce them; he endeavoured calmly to convince them, not harshly to censure them. (6) The example of Paul is a good one for all Christians. In all places—cities, towns, or country; amidst all people—philosophers, the rich, the poor; among friends and countrymen, or among strangers and foreigners, the great object should be to do good, to instruct mankind, to seek to elevate the human character, and to promote human happiness by diffusing the pure precepts of the gospel of Christ.

CHAPTER XVIII.

1. *After these things.* After what occurred at Athens, as recorded in the previous chapter. ¶ *Came to Corinth.* Corinth was the capital of Achaia, called anciently Ephyra, and was seated on the isthmus which divides the Peloponnesus from Attica. The city itself stood on a little island; it had two ports, Lechæum on the west, and Cenchrea on the east. It was one of the most populous and wealthy cities of Greece, and at the same time one of the most luxurious, effeminate, ostentatious, and dissolute. Lasciviousness here was not only practised and allowed, but was consecrated by the worship of Venus; and no small part of the wealth and splendour of the city arose from the offerings made by licentious passion in the very temples of this goddess. No city of ancient times was more profligate. It was the *Paris* of antiquity; the seat of splendour, and show, and corruption. Yet even here, notwithstanding all the disadvantages of splendour, gaiety, and dissoluteness, Paul entered on the work of rearing a church; and here he was eminently successful. The two epistles which he afterwards wrote to this church show the extent of his success; and the well-known character and propensities of the people will account for the general drift of the admonitions and arguments in those epistles. Corinth was

lately come from Italy, with his wife Priscilla; (because that Claudius had commanded all Jews to depart from Rome;) and came unto them.

3 And because he was of the same craft, he abode with them, and [b]wrought: (for by their occupation they were tent-makers.)

b ch.20.34.

destroyed by the Romans 146 years before Christ; and during the conflagration several metals in a fused state, running together, produced the composition known as Corinthian brass. It was afterwards restored by Julius Cæsar, who planted in it a Roman colony. It soon regained its ancient splendour, and relapsed into its former dissipation and licentiousness. Paul arrived there A.D. 52 or 53.

2. *And found a certain Jew.* Aquila is elsewhere mentioned as the friend of Paul, Ro. xvi. 3; 2 Ti. iv. 19; 1 Co. xvi. 19. Though a Jew by birth, yet it is evident that he became a convert to the Christian faith. ¶ *Born in Pontus.* See Notes on ch. ii. 9. ¶ *Lately come from Italy.* Though the command of Claudius extended only to Rome, yet it was probably deemed not safe to remain, or it might have been difficult to procure occupation in any part of Italy. ¶ *Because that Claudius.* Claudius was the Roman emperor. He commenced his reign A.D. 41, and was poisoned A.D. 54. At what time in his reign this command was issued is not certainly known. ¶ *Had commanded,* &c. This command is not mentioned by Josephus, but it is recorded by Suetonius, a Roman historian (*Life of Claudius,* ch. 25), who says that "he expelled the Jews from Rome, who were constantly exciting tumults under their leader, Chrestus." Who this *Chrestus* was is not known. It *might* have been a foreign Jew, who raised tumults on some occasion of which we have no knowledge, as the Jews in all heathen cities were greatly prone to excitements and insurrections. Or it *may* be that Suetonius, little acquainted with Jewish affairs, mistook this for the name *Christ,* and supposed that he was the leader of the Jews. This explanation has much plausibility; for, (1) Suetonius could scarcely be supposed to be intimately acquainted with the affairs of the Jews. (2) There is every reason to believe that, before this, the Christian religion was preached at Rome. (3) It would produce there, as everywhere else, great tumult and contention among the Jews. (4) Claudius, the emperor, might suppose that such tumults endangered the peace of the city, and resolve to remove the cause at once by the dispersion of the Jews. (5) A Roman historian might easily mistake the true state of the case; and while they were contending *about* Christ, he might suppose that it was *under* him, as a leader, that these tumults were excited. All that is material, however, here, is *the fact,* in which Luke and Suetonius agree, that the Jews were expelled from Rome during his reign.

3. *The same craft.* Of the same *trade* or *occupation.* ¶ *And wrought.* And worked at that occupation. *Why* he did it the historian does not affirm; but it seems pretty evident that it was because he had no other means of maintenance. He also laboured for his own support in Ephesus (Ac. xx. 34) and at Thessalonica, 2 Th. iii. 9, 10. The apostle was not ashamed of honest industry for a livelihood; nor did he deem it any disparagement that a minister of the gospel should labour with his own hands. ¶ *For by their occupation.* By their trade; that is, they had been brought up to this business. Paul had been designed originally for a lawyer, and had been brought up at the feet of Gamaliel. But it was a regular custom among the Jews to train up their sons to some useful employment, that they might have the means of an honest livelihood. Even though they were instructed in the liberal sciences, yet they deemed a handicraft trade, or some honourable occupation, an indispensable part of education. Thus Maimonides (in the Tract Talm. Tora, ch. i. § 9) says, "the wise generally practise some of the arts, lest they should be dependent on the charity of others." See Grotius. The wisdom of this is obvious; and it is equally plain that a custom of this kind now might preserve the health and lives of many professional men, and save from ignoble dependence or vice, in future years, many who are trained up in the lap of indulgence and wealth. ¶ *They were tent-makers* — σκηνοποιοὶ. There have been various opinions about the meaning of this word. Many have supposed that it denotes a weaver of tapestry. Luther

4 And he [c]reasoned in the synagogue every sabbath, and persuaded the Jews and the Greeks.

5 And when [d]Silas and Timotheus were come from Macedonia, Paul was pressed in spirit, and testified to the Jews *that* Jesus *was*[1] Christ.

6 And when they [e]opposed themselves, and blasphemed, [f]he shook *his* raiment, and said unto them, [g]Your blood *be* upon your own heads; I *am* clean: from henceforth I will go unto the Gentiles.

7 And he departed thence, and entered into a certain *man's* house, named Justus, *one* that worshipped God, whose house joined hard to the synagogue.

8 And [h]Crispus, the chief ruler of the synagogue, believed on the Lord, with all his house; and many of the Corinthians hearing, believed, and were baptized.

9 Then spake the Lord to Paul in the night by a vision, Be not

c ch.17.2. d ch.17.14,15. 1 or, is *the Christ.* e 2 Ti.2.25. f Ne.5.13. g Eze.33.4. h 1 Co.1.14.

---

thus translated it. But it is probable that it denotes, as in our translation, a manufacturer of tents, made of skin or cloth. In Eastern countries, where there was much travel, where there were no inns, and where many were shepherds, such a business might be useful, and a profitable source of living. It was an honourable occupation, and Paul was not ashamed to be employed in it.

4. *And he reasoned*, &c. See Notes on ch. xvii. 2.

5. *And when Silas and Timotheus*, &c. They came to Paul according to the request which he had sent by the brethren who accompanied him from Thessalonica, ch. xvii. 15. ¶ *Paul was pressed.* Was urged; was borne away by an unusual impulse. It was deeply impressed on him as his duty. ¶ *In spirit.* In his mind; in his feelings. His love to Christ was so great, and his conviction of the truth so strong, that he laboured to make known to them the truth that Jesus was the Messiah. ¶ That *Jesus* was *Christ.* That Jesus of Nazareth was the Messiah. Comp. ch. xvii. 16. The presence of Silas and Timothy animated him; and the certainty of aid in his work urged him to zeal in making known the Saviour.

6. *And when they opposed themselves.* To him and his message. ¶ *And blasphemed.* See Notes on ch. xiii. 45. ¶ *He shook* his *raiment.* As an expressive act of shaking off the guilt of their condemnation. Comp. ch. xiii. 45. He shook his raiment to show that he was resolved henceforward to have nothing to do with them; perhaps, also, to express the fact that God would soon shake them off, or reject them (Doddridge). ¶ *Your blood*, &c. The guilt of your destruction is your own. You only are the cause of the destruction that is coming upon you. See Notes on Mat. xxvii. 25. ¶ *I* am *clean.* I am not to blame for your destruction. I have done my duty. The gospel had been fairly offered and deliberately rejected; and Paul was not to blame for their ruin, which he saw was coming upon them. ¶ *I will go*, &c. See ch. xiii. 46.

7. *A certain* man's *house.* Probably he had become a convert to the Christian faith. ¶ *Joined hard.* Was near to the synagogue.

8. *And Crispus.* He is mentioned in 1 Co. i. 14 as having been one of the few whom Paul baptized with his own hands. The conversion of such a man must have tended greatly to exasperate the other Jews, and to further the progress of the Christian faith among the Corinthians. ¶ *With all his house.* With all his family, ch. x. 2. ¶ *And many of the Corinthians.* Many even in this voluptuous and wicked city. Perhaps the power of the gospel was never more signal than in converting sinners in Corinth, and rearing a Christian church in a place so dissolute and abandoned. If it was adapted to such a place as *Corinth;* if a church, under the power of Christian truth, could be organized *there*, it is adapted to any city, and there is none so corrupt that the gospel cannot change and purify it.

9. *By a vision.* Comp. Notes on ch. ix. 10; xvi. 9. ¶ *Be not afraid. Perhaps* Paul might have been intimidated by the learning, refinement, and splendour of Corinth; *perhaps* embarrassed in view of his duty of addressing the rich, the

afraid, but speak, and hold not thy peace:
10 For [i]I am with thee, and no man shall set on thee to hurt thee; for I have much people in this city.
11 And he [2]continued *there* a year and six months, teaching the word of God among them.
12 And when Gallio was the deputy of Achaia, the Jews made

i Mat.28.20.

2 or, *sat there.*

polite, and the great. To this he may allude in 1 Co. ii. 3: "And I was with you in weakness, and in fear, and in much trembling." In such circumstances it pleased God to meet him, and disarm his fears. This he did by assuring him of success. The fact that God had much people in that city (ver. 10) was employed to remove his apprehensions. The prospect of success in the ministry, and the certainty of the presence of God, will take away the fear of the rich, the learned, and the great.

10. *For I am with thee.* I will attend, bless, and protect you. See Notes on Mat. xxviii. 20. ¶ *No man shall set on thee.* No one who shall rise up against thee will be able to hurt thee. His life was in God's hands, and he would preserve him in order that his people might be collected into the church. ¶ *For I have.* Greek, there is to me; that is, I possess, or there belongs to me. ¶ *Much people.* Many who should be regarded as his true friends, and who should be saved. ¶ *In this city.* In that very city that was so voluptuous, so rich, so effeminate, and where there had been already so decided opposition shown to the gospel. This passage evidently means that God had a design or purpose to save many of that people, for it was given to Paul as an encouragement to him to labour there, evidently meaning that God *would* grant him success in his work. It cannot mean that the Lord meant to say that the great mass of the people, or that the moral and virtuous part, if there were any such, was *then* regarded as *his* people; but that he *intended* to convert many of those guilty and profligate Corinthians to himself, and to gather a people for his own service there. We may learn from this, (1) That God has a *purpose* in regard to the salvation of sinners. (2) That that purpose is so fixed in the mind of God that *he* can say that those in relation to whom it is formed are *his.* (3) This is the ground of encouragement to the ministers of the gospel. Had God no purpose to save sinners, they could have no hope in their work. (4) This plan may have reference to the most gay, the most guilty, and the most abandoned, and ministers should not be deterred by the amount or the degree of wickedness from attempting to save them. (5) There may be more hope of success among a dissolute and profligate population, than among proud, cold, and sceptical philosophers. Paul had little success in philosophic Athens; he had great success in dissolute Corinth. There is often more hope of converting a man openly dissolute and abandoned, than one who prides himself on his philosophy, and is confident in his own wisdom.

11. *And he continued*, &c. Paul was not accustomed to remain long in a place. At Ephesus, indeed, he remained three years (Ac. xx. 31); and his stay at Corinth was caused by his success, and by the necessity of placing a church, collected out of such corrupt and dissolute materials, on a firm foundation.

12. *And Gallio.* After the Romans had conquered Greece they reduced it to two provinces, Macedonia and Achaia, which were each governed by a proconsul. Gallio was the brother of the celebrated philosopher Seneca, and was made proconsul of Achaia A.D. 53. His proper name was Marcus Annæus Novatus, but, having been adopted into the family of Gallio, a rhetorician, he took his name. He is mentioned by ancient writers as having been of a remarkably mild and amiable disposition. His brother Seneca (*Præf. Quest. Nat.* 4) describes him as being of the most lovely temper: "No mortal," says he, "was ever so mild to anyone as he was to all; and in him there was such a natural power of goodness, that there was no semblance of art or dissimulation." ¶ *Was deputy.* See this word explained in the Notes on Ac. xiii. 7. It means here proconsul. ¶ *Of Achaia.* This word, in its largest sense, comprehended the whole of Greece. Achaia proper, however, was a province of which Corinth was the capital. It embraced that part of Greece lying between Thessaly and the southern part of the Pelopon-

insurrection with one accord against
Paul, and [k]brought him to the
judgment seat,
13 Saying, This *fellow* persuadeth
men to worship God contrary to
the law.
14 And when Paul was now
about to open *his* mouth, Gallio
said unto the Jews, [l]If it were a
matter of wrong, or wicked lewdness, O *ye* Jews, reason would
that I should bear with you:
15 But if it be a question of
words and names, [m]and *of* your
law, look ye *to it;* for I will be no
judge of such *matters.*
16 And he drave them from the
judgment seat.
17 Then all the Greeks [n]took
Sosthenes, the chief ruler of the

k Ja.2.6. *l* Ro.13.3. *m* Jn.18.31; ch.23.29; 25.11,19. *n* 1 Co.1.1.

---

nesus. ¶ *The Jews made insurrection.* Excited a tumult, as they had in Philippi, Antioch, &c. ¶ *And brought him to the judgment seat.* The tribunal of Gallio; probably intending to arraign him as a disturber of the peace.

13. *Contrary to the law.* Evidently intending contrary to *all* law—the laws of the Romans and of the Jews. It was permitted to the Jews to worship God according to their own views in Greece; but they could easily pretend that Paul had departed from *that* mode of worshipping God. It was easy for them to maintain that he taught contrary to the laws of the Romans and their acknowledged religion; and their design seems to have been to accuse him of teaching men to worship God in an unlawful and irregular way, a way unknown to *any* of the laws of the empire.

14. *About to open* his *mouth.* In self-defence, ever ready to vindicate his conduct. ¶ *A matter of wrong.* Injustice, or crime, such as could be properly brought before a court of justice. ¶ *Or wicked lewdness.* Any flagrant and gross offence. The word used here occurs nowhere else in the New Testament. It denotes properly an act committed by him who is skilled, facile, or an adept in iniquity—an act of a veteran offender. Such crimes Gallio was willing to take cognizance of. ¶ *Reason would,* &c. Greek, "I would bear with you according to reason." There would be propriety or fitness in my hearing and trying the case. That is, it would fall within the sphere of my duty, as appointed to guard the peace, and to punish crimes.

15. *Of words.* A dispute about *words,* for such he would regard all their controversies about religion to be. ¶ *And names.* Probably he had heard something of the nature of the controversy, and understood it to be a dispute about *names;* that is, whether Jesus was to be called the Messiah or not. To him this would appear as a matter pertaining to the Jews alone, and to be ranked with their other disputes arising from the difference of sect and name. ¶ Of *your law.* A question respecting the proper interpretation of the law, or the rites and ceremonies which it commanded. The Jews had many such disputes, and Gallio did not regard them as coming under his cognizance as a magistrate. ¶ *Look ye* to it. Judge this among yourselves; settle the difficulty as you can. Comp. Jn. xviii. 31. ¶ *For I will be no judge,* &c. I do not regard such questions as pertaining to my office, or deem myself called on to settle them.

16. *And he drave them,* &c. He refused to hear and decide the controversy. The word used here does not denote that there was any violence used by Gallio, but merely that he dismissed them in an authoritative manner.

17. *Then all the Greeks.* The Greeks who had witnessed the persecution of Paul by the Jews, and who had seen the tumult which they had excited. ¶ *Took Sosthenes,* &c. As he was the chief ruler of the synagogue, he had probably been a leader in the opposition to Paul, and in the prosecution. Indignant at the Jews; at their bringing such questions before the tribunal; at their bigotry, and rage, and contentious spirit, they probably fell upon him in a tumultuous and disorderly manner as he was leaving the tribunal. The Greeks would feel no small measure of indignation at these disturbers of the public peace, and they took this opportunity to express their rage. ¶ *And beat* him—ἔτυπτον. This word is not that which is commonly used to denote a judicial act of scourging. It probably means that they fell upon him and beat

synagogue, and beat *him* before the judgment seat. And Gallio cared for none of those things.

18 And Paul *after this* tarried *there* yet a good while, and then took his leave of the brethren, and

---

him with their fists, or with whatever was at hand. ¶ *Before the judgment seat.* Probably while leaving the tribunal. Instead of "Greeks" in this verse, some MSS. read "Jews," but the former is probably the true reading. The Syriac, Arabic, and Coptic read it "the Gentiles." It is probable that this Sosthenes afterward became a convert to the Christian faith, and a preacher of the gospel. See 1 Co. i. 1, 2, "Paul, and *Sosthenes our brother*, unto the church of God which is at Corinth." ¶ *And Gallio cared*, &c. This has been usually charged on Gallio as a matter of reproach, as if he were wholly indifferent to religion. But the charge is unjustly made, and his name is often most improperly used to represent the indifferent, the worldly, the careless, and the sceptical. By the testimony of ancient writers he was a most mild and amiable man, and an upright and just judge. There is not the least evidence that he was indifferent to the religion of his country, or that he was of a thoughtless and sceptical turn of mind. All that this passage implies is, (1) That he did not deem it to be his duty, or a part of his office, to settle questions of a theological nature that were started among the Jews. (2) That he was unwilling to make this subject a matter of legal discussion and investigation. (3) That he would not interfere, either on one side or the other, in the question about proselytes either to or from Judaism. So far, certainly, his conduct was exemplary and proper. (4) That he did not choose to interpose, and rescue Sosthenes from the hands of the mob. From some cause he was willing that *he* should feel the effects of the public indignation. Perhaps it was not easy to quell the riot; perhaps he was not unwilling that he who had joined in a furious and unprovoked persecution should feel the effect of it in the excited passions of the people. At all events, he was but following the common practice among the Romans, which was to regard the Jews with contempt, and to care little how much they were exposed to popular fury and rage. In this he was wrong; and it is certain, also, that he was indifferent to the disputes between Jews and Christians; but there is no propriety in defaming his name, and making him the type and representative of all the thoughtless and indifferent on the subject of religion in subsequent times. Nor is there propriety in using this passage as a text as applicable to this class of men.

18. *And sailed thence into Syria.* Or set sail for Syria. His design was to go to Jerusalem to the festival which was soon to occur, ver. 21. ¶ *Having shorn* his *head.* Many interpreters have supposed that this refers to Aquila, and not to Paul. But the connection evidently requires us to understand it of Paul, though the Greek construction does not with certainty determine to which it refers. The Vulgate refers it to Aquila, the Syriac to Paul. ¶ *In Cenchrea.* Cenchrea was the eastern port of Corinth. A church was formed in that place, Ro. xvi. 1. ¶ *For he had a vow.* A *vow* is a solemn promise made to God respecting anything. The use of vows is observable throughout the Scripture. Jacob, going into Mesopotamia, vowed the tenth of his estate, and promised to offer it at Bethel to the honour of God, Ge. xxviii. 22. Moses made many regulations in regard to vows. A man might devote himself or his children to the Lord. He might devote any part of his time or property to his service. The vow they were required sacredly to observe (De. xxiii. 21, 22), except in certain specified cases they were permitted to redeem that which had been thus devoted. The most remarkable vow among the Jews was that of the Nazarite, by which a man made a solemn promise to God to abstain from wine, and from all intoxicating liquors, to let the hair grow, not to enter any house polluted by having a dead body in it, or to attend any funeral. This vow generally lasted eight days, sometimes a month, sometimes during a definite period fixed by themselves, and sometimes during their whole lives. When the vow expired, the priest made an offering of a he-lamb for a burnt-offering, a she-lamb for an expiatory sacrifice, and a ram for a peace-offering. The priest then, or some other person, shaved the head of the Nazarite at the door of the taber-

sailed thence into Syria, and with
him Priscilla and Aquila; [o]having
shorn *his* head in [p]Cenchrea; for
he had a vow.
19 And he came to Ephesus,
and left them there; but he himself entered into the synagogue,
and [q]reasoned with the Jews.
20 When they desired *him* to
tarry longer time with them, he
consented not;
21 But bade them farewell, saying, I must by all means keep [r]this
feast that cometh in Jerusalem;
but I will return again unto you,
[s]if God will. And he sailed from
Ephesus.
22 And when he had landed at

o Nu.6.18; ch.21.24. *p* Ro.16.1. *q* ch.17.2. *r* ch.19.21; 20.16. *s* 1 Co.4.19; Ja.4.15.

nacle, and burnt the hair on the fire of the altar. Those who made the vow out of Palestine, and who could not come to the temple when the vow was expired, contented themselves with observing the abstinence required by the law, and cutting off the hair where they were. This I suppose to have been the case with Paul. His hair he cut off at the expiration of the vow at Cenchrea, though he delayed to perfect the vow by the proper ceremonies until he reached Jerusalem, Ac. xxi. 23, 24. *Why* Paul made this vow, or on what occasion, the sacred historian has not informed us, and conjecture, perhaps, is useless. We may observe, however, (1) That it was common for the Jews to make such vows to God, as an expression of gratitude or of devotedness to his service, when they had been raised up from sickness, or delivered from danger or calamity. See Josephus, i. 2, 15. Vows of this nature were also made by the Gentiles on occasions of deliverance from any signal calamity (Juvenal, *Sat.*, 12, 81). It is *possible* that Paul may have made such a vow in consequence of signal deliverance from some of the numerous perils to which he was exposed. But, (2) There is reason to think that it was mainly with a design to convince the Jews that he did not despise their law, and was not its enemy. See ch. xxi. 22–24. In accordance with the custom of the nation, and in compliance with a law which was not wrong in itself, he might have made this vow, not for a time-serving purpose, but in order to conciliate them, and to mitigate their anger against the gospel. See 1 Co. ix. 19–21. But where nothing is recorded, conjecture is useless. Those who wish to see the subject discussed may consult Grotius and Kuinoel *in loco;* Spencer, *De Legibus Hebræ.*, p. 862; and Calmet's *Dict.*, art. "Nazarite."

19. *And he came to Ephesus.* See Notes on Re. ii. 1–5. This was a celebrated city in Ionia, in Asia Minor, about 40 miles south of Smyrna. It was chiefly famous for the Temple of Diana, usually reckoned one of the seven wonders of the world. Pliny styles this city the ornament of Asia. In the times of the Romans it was the metropolis of the province of Asia. This city is now under the dominion of the Turks, and is almost in a state of ruin. Dr. Chandler, in his *Travels in Asia Minor*, says: "The inhabitants are a few Greek peasants, living in extreme wretchedness, dependence, and insensibility; the representatives of an illustrious people, and inhabiting the wreck of their greatness; some in the substructions of the glorious edifices which they raised; some beneath the vaults of the stadium, once the crowded scene of their diversions; and some in the sepulchres which received their ashes" (*Travels*, p. 131, Oxford, 1775). The Jews, according to Josephus, were very numerous in Ephesus, and had obtained the privilege of citizenship. ¶ *Left them there.* That is, Aquila and Priscilla, ver. 24–26. ¶ *Reasoned with the Jews.* See Notes on ch. xvii. 2.

21. *Keep this feast.* Probably the Passover is here referred to. *Why* he was so anxious to celebrate that feast at Jerusalem, the historian has not informed us. It is probable, however, that he wished to meet as many of his countrymen as possible, and to remove, if practicable, the prejudices which had everywhere been raised against him, ch. xxi. 20, 21. Perhaps, also, he supposed that there would be many Christian converts present, whom he might meet also. ¶ *But I will return,* &c. This he did (ch. xix. 1), and remained there three years, ch. xx. 31.

22. *At Cesarea.* See Notes on ch. viii. 40. ¶ *And gone up.* From the ship. ¶ *And saluted the church.* The church at Jerusalem. This was Paul's

Cesarea, and gone up, and saluted the church, he went down to Antioch.

23 And after he had spent some time *there*, he departed, and went over *all* the country of [t]Galatia and Phrygia in order, [u]strengthening all the disciples.

24 And a certain Jew [v]named Apollos, born at Alexandria, an eloquent man, *and* mighty in the scriptures, came to Ephesus.

25 This man was instructed in the way of the Lord; and [w]being fervent in the spirit, he spake and taught diligently the things of the Lord, [x]knowing only the baptism of John.

26 And he began to speak boldly in the synagogue: whom when Aquila and Priscilla had heard,

t Ga.1.2. *u* ch.14.22; 15.32,41. *v* 1 Co.1.12; 3.5,6; Tit.3.13.

w Ro.12.11; Ja.5.16. *x* ch.19.3.

---

main design; and though it is not distinctly *specified*, yet the whole narrative implies that he went there before returning to Antioch. The word *saluted* implies that he expressed for them his tender affection and regard. ¶ *To Antioch.* In Syria. See Notes on ch. xi. 19.

23. *The country of Galatia and Phrygia.* He had been over these regions before, preaching the gospel, ch. xvi. 6. ¶ *Strengthening.* Establishing them by exhortation and counsel. See Notes on ch. xiv. 22.

24. *And a certain Jew named Apollos.* Apollos afterward became a distinguished and successful preacher of the gospel, 1 Co. i. 12; iii. 5, 6; iv. 6; Tit. iii. 13. Nothing more is known of him than is stated in these passages. ¶ *Born at Alexandria.* Alexandria was a celebrated city in Egypt, founded by Alexander the Great. There were large numbers of Jews resident there. See Notes on ch. vi. 9. ¶ *An eloquent man.* Alexandria was famous for its schools, and it is probable that Apollos, in addition to his natural endowments, had enjoyed the benefit of these schools. ¶ *Mighty in the scriptures.* Well instructed, or able in the Old Testament. The foundation was thus laid for future usefulness in the Christian church. See Notes on Lu. xxiv. 19.

25. *This man was instructed.* Greek, was *catechised.* He was instructed, in some degree, into the knowledge of the Christian religion. By whom this was done we have no information. ¶ *In the right way of the Lord.* The word *way* often refers to doctrine, Mat. xxi. 32. It means here that he had been correctly taught in regard to the Messiah, yet his knowledge was imperfect, ver. 26. The amount of his knowledge seems to have been, (1) He had correct views of the Messiah to come—views which he had derived from the study of the Old Testament. He was expecting a Saviour that would be humble, obscure, and a sacrifice, in opposition to the prevailing notions of the Jews. (2) He had heard of John; had embraced his doctrine; and probably had been baptized with reference to him that was to come. Comp. Mat. iii. 2; Ac. xix. 4. But it is clear that he had not heard that *Jesus* was the Messiah. With his correct views in regard to the coming of the Messiah he was endeavouring to instruct and reform his countrymen. He was just in the state of mind to welcome the announcement that the Messiah had come, and to embrace Jesus of Nazareth as the hope of the nation. ¶ *Being fervent in the spirit.* Being zealous and ardent. See Notes on Ro. xii. 11. ¶ *Taught diligently.* Defended with zeal and earnestness his views of the Messiah. ¶ *The things of the Lord.* The doctrines pertaining to the Messiah as far as he understood them. ¶ *Knowing only the baptism of John.* Whether he had himself heard John, and been baptized by him, has been made a question which cannot now be decided. It is not necessary, however, to suppose this, as it seems that the knowledge of John's preaching and baptism had been propagated extensively in other nations beside Judea, ch. xix. 1–3. The Messiah was expected about that time. The foreign Jews would be waiting for him; and the news of John's ministry, doctrine, and success would be rapidly propagated from synagogue to synagogue in the surrounding nations. John preached repentance, and baptized with reference to him that was to come after him (ch. xix. 4), and this doctrine Apollos seems to have embraced.

26. *And expounded.* Explained. ¶ *The*

they took him unto *them*, and expounded unto him [y] the way of God more perfectly.

27 And when he was disposed to pass into Achaia, the brethren wrote, exhorting the disciples to receive him; who, when he was come, [z] helped them much [a] which had believed through grace:

28 For he mightily convinced the Jews, *and that* publicly, [b] showing by the scriptures that Jesus [3] was Christ.

y He.6.1; 2 Pe.3.18. *z* 1 Co.3.6. *a* Ep.2.8. *b* Jn.5.39.

3 or, *is the Christ*, ver.5.

CHAPTER XIX.

AND it came to pass, that, while [a] Apollos was at Corinth, Paul, having passed through the upper coasts, came to Ephesus; and finding certain disciples,

2 He said unto them, have ye received the Holy Ghost since ye

a 1 Co.3.5,6.

---

way of God. Gave him full and ample instructions respecting the Messiah as having already come, and respecting the nature of his work.

27. *Into Achaia.* See Notes on ch. xviii. 12. ¶ *The brethren wrote.* The brethren at Ephesus. *Why* he was disposed to go into Achaia the historian does not inform us. But he had heard of the success of Paul there; of the church which he had established; of the opposition of the Jews; and it was doubtless with a desire to establish that church, and with a wish to convince his unbelieving countrymen that their views of the Messiah were erroneous, and that Jesus of Nazareth corresponded with the predictions of the prophets, that he went there. Many of the Greeks at Corinth were greatly captivated with his winning eloquence (1 Co. i. 12; iii. 4, 5), and his going there was the occasion of some unhappy divisions that sprung up in the church. But in all this he retained the confidence and love of Paul, 1 Co. i. iii. It was thus shown that Paul was superior to envy, and that great success by one minister need not excite the envy, or alienate the confidence and good-will of another. ¶ *Helped them much.* Strengthened them, and aided them in their controversies with the unbelieving Jews. ¶ *Which had believed through grace.* The words "through grace" may either refer to Apollos, or to the Christians who had believed. If to *him*, it means that he was enabled by grace to strengthen the brethren there; if to *them*, it means that they had been led to believe by the grace or favour of God. Either interpretation makes good sense. Our translation has adopted that which is most natural and obvious.

28. *For he mightily convinced the Jews.* He did it by strong arguments; he bore down all opposition, and effectually silenced them. ¶ And that *publicly.* In his public preaching in the synagogue and elsewhere. ¶ *Showing by the scriptures.* Proving from the Old Testament. Showing that Jesus of Nazareth corresponded with the account of the Messiah given by the prophets. See Notes on Jn. v. 39. ¶ *That Jesus was Christ.* See the margin. That Jesus of Nazareth was the Messiah.

CHAPTER XIX.

1. *While Apollos was at Corinth.* It is probable that he remained there a considerable time. ¶ *Paul, having passed through the upper coasts.* The upper, or more elevated regions of Asia Minor. The writer refers here particularly to the provinces of Phrygia and Galatia, ch. xviii. 23. These regions were called *upper*, because they were situated on the high table-land in the interior of Asia Minor, while Ephesus was in the low maritime regions, and called the *low* country. ¶ *Came to Ephesus.* Agreeably to his promise, ch. xviii. 21. ¶ *And finding certain disciples.* Certain persons who had been baptized into John's baptism, and who had embraced John's doctrine that the Messiah was soon to appear, ver. 3, 4. It is very clear that they had not yet heard that he had come, or that the Holy Ghost was given. They were evidently in the same situation as Apollos. See Notes on ch. xviii. 25.

2. *Have ye received the Holy Ghost?* Have ye received the extraordinary effusions and miraculous influences of the Holy Ghost? Paul would not doubt that, if they had "believed," they had received the ordinary converting influences of the Holy Spirit—for it was one of his favourite doctrines that the Holy Spirit renews the heart. But, besides this, the miraculous influences

believed? And they said unto
him, [b]We have not so much as
heard whether there be any Holy
Ghost.
3 And he said unto them, Unto
what then were ye baptized? And
they said, [c]Unto John's baptism.

b ch.8.16; 1 Sa.3.7. c ch.18.25.

4 Then said Paul, [d]John verily
baptized with [e]the baptism of repentance, saying unto the people
that they should believe on him
which should come after him, that
is, on Christ Jesus.
5 When they heard *this*, [f]they

d Mat.3.11. e Jn.1.15,27,30. f ch.8.16; 1 Co.1.13.

---

of the Spirit were conferred on many societies of believers. The power of speaking with tongues, or of working miracles, was imparted as an evidence of the presence of God, and of their acceptance with him, ch. x. 45, 46; 1 Co. xiv. It was natural for Paul to ask whether *this* evidence of the divine favour has been granted to them. ¶ *Since ye believed.* Since you embraced the doctrine of John that the Messiah was soon to come. ¶ *We have not so much as heard,* &c. This seems to be a very strange answer. Yet we are to remember, (1) That these were mere disciples of *John's* doctrine, and that *his* preaching related particularly to the Messiah, and not to the Holy Ghost. (2) It does not even appear that they had heard that the Messiah *had* come, or had heard of Jesus of Nazareth, ver. 4, 5. (3) It is not remarkable, therefore, that they had no clear conceptions of the character and operations of the Holy Ghost. Yet, (4) They were just in that state of mind that they were willing to embrace the doctrine when it was proclaimed to them, thus showing that they were *really* under the influence of the Holy Spirit. God may often produce important changes in the hearts and lives of sinners, even where they have no clear and systematic views of religious doctrines. In all such cases, however, there will be a readiness of heart to embrace the truth where it is made known.

3. *Unto what.* Unto what faith or doctrine. What did you profess to believe when you were baptized? ¶ *Unto John's baptism.* See Notes on ch. xviii. 25.

4. *John verily baptized.* John did indeed baptize. ¶ *With the baptism of repentance.* Having special reference to repentance, or as a profession that they *did* repent of their sins. See Notes on Mat. iii. 6. ¶ *Saying unto the people.* The design of his preaching was to turn the people from their sins, and to prepare them for the coming of the Messiah. He therefore directed their attention principally to him that was to come, Jn. i. 15, 22–27. ¶ *That is, on Christ Jesus.* These are the words of Paul, explaining what John taught. John taught them to believe in the Messiah, and Paul now showed them that the Messiah was Jesus of Nazareth. The argument of Paul is, that it was highly proper for them now to profess publicly that Saviour to whom John had borne such explicit testimony. "Jesus is the Messiah for whom John came to prepare the way; and as you have embraced John's doctrine, you ought now publicly to acknowledge that Redeemer by baptism in his name."

5. *When they heard* this. When they heard what Paul had said respecting the nature of John's baptism. ¶ *They were baptized,* &c. As there is no other instance in the New Testament of any persons having been rebaptized, it has been made a question by some critics whether it was done here; and they have supposed that all this is the narrative of Luke respecting what took place under the ministry of John: to wit, that he told them to believe on Christ Jesus, and then baptized them in his name. But this is a most forced construction; and it is evident that these persons were *rebaptized* by the direction of Paul. For, (1) This is the *obvious* interpretation of the passage—that which would strike all persons as correct, unless there were some previous theory to support. (2) It was not a matter of fact that John baptized in the name of Christ Jesus. His was the baptism of repentance; and there is not the slightest evidence that he ever used the name of Jesus in the form of baptism. (3) If it be the sense of the passage that John baptized them in the name of Jesus, then this verse is a mere repetition of ver. 4; a tautology of which the sacred writers would not be guilty. (4) It is evident that the persons on whom Paul laid his hands (ver. 6), and those who were baptized, were the same. But these were the persons who *heard* (ver. 5)

were baptized in the name of the Lord Jesus.

6 And when Paul had [g]laid *his* hands upon them, [h]the Holy Ghost came on them; [i]and they spake with tongues, and prophesied.

7 And all the men were about twelve.

8 And he went into the synagogue, and spake boldly for the space of three months, [k]disputing, and [l]persuading the things concerning the kingdom of God.

9 But when divers [m]were hardened, and believed not, but [n]spake evil of [o]that way before the multitude, [p]he departed from them, and separated the disciples, disputing daily in the school of one Tyrannus.

10 And this continued by [q]the space of two years; so that [r]all

g ch.8.17. h ch.2.4; 10.46. i 1 Co.14.1,&c. k ch.18.19.

l ch.28.23. m Ro.11.7; He.3.13. n 2 Ti.1.15; 2 Pe.2.2; Jude 10. o ver.23. p 1 Ti.6.5. q ch.20.31. r ch.20.18.

---

what was said. The narrative is *continuous*, all parts of it cohering together as relating to a transaction that occurred at the same time. If the *obvious* interpretation of the passage be the true one, it follows that the baptism of John was not strictly Christian baptism. It was the baptism of repentance; a baptism designed to prepare the way for the introduction of the kingdom of the Messiah. It will *not* follow, however, from this that Christian baptism is now ever to be repeated. For this there is no warrant in the New Testament. There is no command to repeat it, as in the case of the Lord's supper; and the nature and design of the ordinance evidently supposes that it is to be performed but once. The disciples of John were rebaptized, not because baptism is designed to be repeated, but because they never had been, in fact, baptized in the manner prescribed by the Lord Jesus. ¶ *In the name of the Lord Jesus.* See Notes on ch. ii. 38.

6. *And when Paul laid* his *hands*, &c. See Notes on ch. viii. 17. ¶ *And they spake with tongues.* See Notes on ch. ii. 4; x. 46. ¶ *And prophesied.* See Notes on ch. ii. 17; xi. 27.

7. *And all the men.* The whole number.

8. *Persuading the things.* Endeavouring to persuade them of the truth of what was affirmed respecting the kingdom of God.

9. *But when divers.* When *some* were hardened. ¶ *Were hardened.* When their hearts were hardened, and they became violently opposed to the gospel. When the truth made no *impression* on them. The word *harden*, as applied to the heart, is often used to denote insensibility, and opposition to the gospel. ¶ *But spake evil of that way.* Of the gospel—the *way*, path, or manner in which God saves men. See Acts xvi. 17; xviii. 26; Mat. vii. 13, 14. ¶ *Separated the disciples.* Removed them from the influence and society of those who were seeking to draw them away from the faith. This is often the best way to prevent the evil influence of others. Christians, if they wish to preserve their minds calm and peaceful; if they wish to avoid the agitations of conflict, and the temptations of those who would lead them astray, should withdraw from their society, and seek the fellowship of their Christian brethren. ¶ *Disputing daily.* This is not a happy translation. The word used here (διαλεγόμενος) does not of necessity denote *disputation* or *contention*, but is often used in a good sense of *reasoning* (Ac. xvii. 2; xviii. 4, 19; xxiv. 25), or of public *preaching*, Ac. xx. 7, 9. It is used in this sense here, and denotes that Paul taught publicly, or reasoned on the subject of religion in this place. ¶ *In the school of one Tyrannus.* Who this Tyrannus was is not known. It is probable that he was a Jew, who was engaged in this employment, and who might not be unfavourably disposed toward Christians. In his school, or in the room which he occupied for teaching, Paul instructed the people when he was driven from the synagogue. Christians at that time had no churches, and they were obliged to assemble in any place where it might be convenient to conduct public worship.

10. *This continued.* This public instruction. ¶ *By the space*, &c. For two whole years. ¶ *So that all.* That is, the great mass of the people. ¶ *That dwelt in Asia.* In that province of Asia Minor of which Ephesus was the principal city. The name *Asia* was used sometimes to denote that single pro-

they which dwelt in Asia heard the word of the Lord Jesus, both Jews and Greeks.

11 And God wrought [s]special miracles by the hands of Paul:

12 So that from his body were brought unto the sick [t]handkerchiefs or aprons, and the diseases departed from them, and the evil spirits went out of them.

13 Then certain of the vagabond Jews, exorcists, [u]took upon them to call over them which had evil spirits the name of the Lord Jesus,

s Mar.16.20. t ch.5.15. u Mar.9.38; Lu.9.49.

---

vince. See Notes on Ac. ii. 9. Ephesus was the capital; and there was, of course, a constant and large influx of people there for the purposes of commerce and worship. ¶ *Heard the word of the Lord Jesus.* Heard the doctrine respecting the Lord Jesus.

11. *Special miracles.* Miracles that were remarkable; that were not common, or that were very unusual (*οὐ τὰς τυχούσας*). This expression is classic Greek. Thus Longinus says of Moses that he was no common man—*ὀυχ' ὁ τύχων ἀνήρ*.

12. *So that from his body.* That is, those handkerchiefs which had been applied to his body, which he had used, or which he had touched. An instance somewhat similar to this occurs in the case of the woman who was healed by touching the hem of the Saviour's garment, Mat. ix. 20–22. ¶ *Unto the sick.* The sick who were at a distance, and who were unable to go where he was. If it be asked *why* this was done, it may be observed, (1) That the working of miracles in that region would greatly contribute to the spread of the gospel. (2) We are not to suppose that there was any *efficacy* in the aprons thus brought, or in the mere fact that they had touched the body of Paul, any more than there was in the hem of the Saviour's garment which the woman touched, or in the clay which he made use of to open the eyes of the blind man, Jn. viii. 6. (3) In this instance, the fact that the miracles were wrought in this manner by garments which had touched his body, was *a mere sign*, or *an evidence* to the persons concerned, that it was done by the instrumentality of Paul, as the fact that the Saviour put his fingers into the ears of a deaf man, and spit and touched his tongue (Mar. vii. 33), was an evidence to those who saw it that the power of healing came from him. The bearing of these aprons to the sick was, therefore, merely *evidence* to all concerned that miraculous power was given to *Paul.* ¶ *Handkerchiefs.* The word used here (*σουδάρια*) is of Latin origin, and properly denotes a piece of linen with which *sweat* was wiped from the face; and then any piece of linen used for tying up, or containing anything. In Lu. xix. 20, it denotes the "napkin" in which the talent of the unprofitable servant was concealed; in Jn. xi. 44; xx. 7, the "napkin" which was used to bind up the face of the dead applied to Lazarus and to our Saviour. ¶ *Or aprons*—*σιμικίνθια*. This is also a Latin word, and means literally a *half girdle*, or covering half the person—a piece of cloth which was girded round the waist to preserve the clothes of those who were engaged in any kind of work. The word *aprons* expresses the idea. ¶ *And the diseases departed.* The sick were healed. ¶ *And the evil spirits.* See Notes on Mat. iv. 24. It is evident that this power of working miracles would contribute greatly to Paul's success among the people.

13. *The vagabond Jews.* Greek, *Jews going about*—*περιερχομένων*. The word *vagabond* with us is now commonly used in a bad sense, to denote a vagrant; a man who has no home; an idle, worthless fellow. The word, however, properly means one wandering from place to place, without any settled habitation, from whatever cause it may be. Here it denotes those Jews who wandered from place to place, practising exorcism. ¶ *Exorcists*—*ἐξορκιστῶν*. This word properly denotes those who went about pretending to be able to expel evil spirits, or to cure diseases by charms, incantations, &c. The word is derived from *ὀρκίζω*, *orkizo*, to bind with an oath. It was applied in this sense, because those who pretended to be able to expel demons used the formula of an oath, or adjured them, to compel them to leave the possessed persons. Comp. Mat. xii. 27. They commonly used the name of God, or called on the demons in the name of God to leave the person. Here they used the name Jesus to command

saying, [v]We adjure you by Jesus, whom Paul preacheth.

14 And there were seven sons of *one* Sceva, a Jew, *and* chief of the priests, which did so.

15 And the evil spirit answered and said, Jesus I know, and Paul I know; but who are ye?

16 And the man in whom the evil spirit was [w]leaped on them, and overcame them, and prevailed against them, so that they fled out of that house naked and wounded.

17 And this was known to all the Jews and Greeks also dwelling at Ephesus; [x]and fear fell on them all, and the name of the Lord Jesus was magnified.

18 And many that believed came, and [y]confessed, and showed their deeds.

19 Many of them also which

v Jos.6.26. *w* Lu.8.29. *x* Lu.1.65; ch.2.43; 5.5,11. *y* Mat.3.6; Ro.10.10.

---

them to come out. Such wanderers and pretenders are common in Oriental countries now. See *Land and the Book*, vol. i. 224, 510. ¶ *To call over them.* To name, or to use his name as sufficient to expel the evil spirit. ¶ *The name of the Lord Jesus.* The reasons why they attempted this were, (1) That Jesus had expelled many evil spirits; and (2) That it was in his name that Paul had wrought his miracles. Perhaps they supposed there was some *charm* in this name to expel them. ¶ *We adjure you.* We bind you by an oath; we command you as under the solemnity of an oath, Mar. v. 7; 1 Th. v. 27. It is a form of putting one under oath, 1 Ki. ii. 43; Ge. xxiv. 37; 2 Ki. xi. 4; Ne. xiii. 25 (Septuagint). That this art was practised then, or attempted, is abundantly proved from Irenæus, Origen, and Josephus (*Antiq.*, b. viii. ch. 2, § 5). See Doddridge. The common name which was used was the incommunicable name of God, JEHOVAH, by pronouncing which, in a peculiar way, it was pretended they had the power of expelling demons.

14. One *Sceva.* Sceva is a Greek name, but nothing more is known of him. ¶ *Chief of the priests.* This cannot mean that he was high-priest among the Jews, as it is wholly improbable that his sons would be wandering exorcists. But it denotes that he was of the sacerdotal order. He was a Jewish chief priest; a priest of distinction, and had held the office of a ruler. The word *chief priest,* in the New Testament, usually refers to men of the sacerdotal order who were also rulers in the Sanhedrim.

15. *Jesus I know.* His power to cast out devils I know. Comp. Mat. viii. 29. ¶ *Paul I know.* Paul's power to cast out devils, ver. 12. ¶ *But who are ye?* What power have you over evil spirits? By what right do you attempt to expel them? The meaning is, "You belong neither to Jesus nor Paul, and you have no right or authority to attempt to work miracles in the name of either."

16. *Leaped on them.* Several such instances are recorded of the extraordinary power and rage of those who were possessed with evil spirits, Mar. v. 3; ix. 29; Lu. ix. 42.

17. *The name of the Lord Jesus was magnified.* Acquired increasing honour. The transaction showed that the miracles performed in the name of the Lord Jesus by Paul were real, and were wrought in attestation of the truth of the doctrine which he taught. Impostors could not work such miracles; and they who pretended to be able to do it only exposed themselves to the rage of evil spirits. It was thus shown that there was a real, vital difference between Paul and these impostors, and their failure only served to extend his reputation and the power of the gospel.

18. *Their deeds.* Their actions; their evil course of life. The direct reference here is to the magical arts which had been used, but the word may also be designed to denote iniquity in general. They who make a profession of religion will be willing to confess their transgressions, and no man can have evidence that he is truly renewed who is not willing to *confess* as well as to *forsake* his sins, Ro. x. 10; Pr. xxviii. 13, "He that covereth his sins shall not prosper; but whoso confesseth and forsaketh them shall find mercy."

19. *Curious arts.* Arts or practices requiring *skill, address, cunning.* The word used here (περίεργα) denotes properly those things that require care or

used curious arts brought their
books together, and burned them
before all *men;* and they counted
the price of them, and found *it*
fifty thousand *pieces* of silver.

20 So mightily [z]grew the word
of God, and prevailed.
21 After[a] these things were ended,
Paul purposed in the spirit, when

z ch.12.24. a Ga.2.1.

skill, and was thus applied to the arts of magic, jugglery, and sleight of hand, that were practised so extensively in Eastern countries. That such arts were practised at Ephesus is well known. The *Ephesian letters*, by which incantations and charms were supposed to be produced, were much celebrated. They seem to have consisted of certain combinations of letters or words, which, by being pronounced with certain intonations of voice, were believed to be effectual in expelling diseases, or evil spirits; or which, by being written on parchment and worn, were supposed to operate as *amulets*, or charms, to guard from evil spirits or from danger. Thus Plutarch (*Sympos.*, 7) says, "The magicians compel those who are possessed with a demon to recite and pronounce *the Ephesian letters*, in a certain order, by themselves." Thus Clemens Alex. (*Strom.* ii.) says, "Androcydes, a Pythagorean, says that the letters which are called Ephesian, and which are so celebrated, are symbols," &c. Erasmus says (*Adagg. Cent.*, 2) that there were certain marks and magical words among the Ephesians, by using which they succeeded in every undertaking. Eustath. ad Hom., *Odys.* τ, says "that those letters were incantations which Crœsus used when on the funeral pile, and which greatly befriended him." He adds that, in the war between the Milesians and Ephesians, the latter were thirteen times saved from ruin by the use of these letters. See Grotius and Kuinoel. ¶ *Brought their books.* Books which explained the arts, or which contained the magical forms and incantations—perhaps pieces of parchment, on which were written the letters which were to be used in the incantations and charms. ¶ *And burned them before all* men. Publicly. Their arts and offences had been public, and they sought now to *undo* the evil, as much as lay in their power, as extensively as they had done it. ¶ *And they counted.* The price was estimated. By whom this was done does not appear. Probably it was not done by those who had been engaged in this business, and who had suffered the loss, but by the people, who were amazed at the sacrifice, and who were astonished at their folly in thus destroying their own property. ¶ *Fifty thousand* pieces *of silver.* What coin the word (ἀργυρίου) here translated *silver* denotes, it is impossible to tell, and consequently the precise value of this sacrifice cannot be ascertained. If it refers to the Jewish *shekel*, the sum would be $25,000 (about £5420), as the shekel was worth about half a dollar. If it refers to Grecian or Roman coin—which is much more probable, as this was a heathen country, where the Jewish coin would not, probably, be much used—the value would be much less. Probably, however, it refers to the Attic *drachm*, which was a silver coin worth about 9*d.* sterling, or not far from 17 cents, and then the value would be about $8500 (£1875). The precise value is not material. It was a large sum; and it is recorded to show that Christianity had power to induce men to forsake arts that were most lucrative, and to destroy the means of extending and perpetuating those arts, however valuable in a pecuniary point of view they might be. We are to remember, however, that this was not the *intrinsic* value of these books, but only their value *as* books of incantation. In themselves they might have been of very little worth. *The universal prevalence of Christianity would make much that is now esteemed valuable property utterly worthless*, as, for example, all that is used in gambling, in fraud, in counterfeiting, in distilling ardent spirits for drink, in the slave-trade, and in attempts to impose on and defraud mankind.

20. *So mightily grew the word of God.* So powerfully. It had such efficacy and power in this wicked city. That power *must* have been mighty which would thus make them willing not only to cease to practise imposition, but to give up all hopes of future gains, and to destroy their property. On this instructive narrative we may remark, (1) That religion has power to break the hold of sinners on unjust and dishonest means of living. (2) That those who have been engaged in an unchris-

he had passed through Macedonia
and Achaia, to go to Jerusalem,
saying, After I have been there,
I[b] must also see Rome.
22 So he sent into Macedonia
two of them that ministered unto
him, Timotheus and [c]Erastus; but
he himself stayed in Asia for a
season.
23 And the same time [d]there
arose no small stir about that way.
24 For a certain *man* named

b Ro.15.23-28.

c Ro.16.23; 2 Ti.4.20. d 2 Co.1.8; 6.9.

tian and dishonourable practice will abandon it when they become Christians. (3) That their abhorrence of their former course will be, and ought to be, expressed as publicly as was the offence. (4) That the evil practice will be abandoned at any sacrifice, however great. The question will be, *what is right;* not *what will it cost.* Property, in the view of a converted man, is nothing when compared with a good conscience. (5) This conduct of those who had used curious arts shows us what ought to be done by those who have been engaged in any evil course of life, and who are then converted. If what they did when they were converted was right—and who can doubt it?—it settles a great principle on which young converts should act. If a man has been engaged in the slave-trade, he will abandon it, and his duty will *not* be to sell his ship to one who he knows will continue the traffic. His property should be withdrawn from the business publicly, either by being destroyed, or by being converted to a useful purpose. If a man has been a distiller of ardent spirits as a drink, his duty will be to forsake his evil course. Nor will it be his duty to sell his distillery to one who will continue the business, but to withdraw his property from it *publicly*, either by destroying it, or converting it to some useful purpose. If a man has been engaged in the *traffic* in ardent spirits, his duty is not to sell his stock to those who will continue the sale of the poison, but to withdraw it from public use—converting it to some useful purpose, if he can; if not, by destroying it. All that has ever been said by money-loving distillers, or venders of ardent spirits, about the loss which they would sustain by abandoning the business, might have been said by these practitioners of curious arts in Ephesus. And if the excuses of rum-selling men are valid, *their* conduct was folly; and they should either have continued the business of practising "curious arts" after they were converted, or should have sold their "books" to those who would have continued it. For assuredly it was not worse to practise jugglery and fortune-telling than it is to destroy the bodies and souls of men by the traffic in ardent spirits. And yet, how few men there are in Christian lands who practise on the principle of these honest, but comparatively unenlightened men at Ephesus.

21. *After these things were ended.* After the gospel was firmly established at Ephesus, so that his presence there was no longer necessary. ¶ *Purposed in the spirit.* Resolved in his mind. ¶ *When he had passed through Macedonia and Achaia.* In these places he had founded flourishing churches. It is probable that his main object in this visit was to take up a collection for the poor saints at Jerusalem. See Notes on Ro. xv. 25, 26. ¶ *To go to Jerusalem.* To bear the contribution of the Gentile churches to the poor and oppressed Christians in Judea. ¶ *I must also see Rome.* See Notes on Ro. xv. 24. He did go to Rome, but he went in chains, as a prisoner.

22. *Timotheus.* Timothy. He was a proper person to send there to visit the churches, as he had been there before with Paul, when they were established, ch. xvi. 3; xvii. 14. ¶ *And Erastus.* Erastus was chamberlain of Corinth (Ro. xvi. 23), or, more properly, the *treasurer* of the city (see Notes on that place), and he was, therefore, a very proper person to be sent with Timothy for the purpose of making the collection for the poor at Jerusalem. Paul had wisdom enough to employ a man accustomed to monied transactions in making a collection. On this collection his heart was intent, and he afterward went up with it to Jerusalem. See 2 Co. viii. ix., and Notes on Ro. xv. 25, 26. ¶ *Staid in Asia.* At Ephesus. ¶ *For a season.* How long is uncertain. He waited for a convenient opportunity to follow them, probably intending to do it as soon as they had fully prepared the way for the collection. See Paley's *Horæ Paulinæ*, p. 1, ch. ii.

Demetrius, a silversmith, which made silver shrines for Diana, brought [e]no small gain unto the craftsmen;

25 Whom[f] he called together with the workmen of like occupation, and said, Sirs, ye know that by this craft we have our wealth.

26 Moreover, ye see and hear, that not alone at Ephesus, but almost throughout all Asia, this Paul hath persuaded and turned away much people, [g]saying that they be no gods which are made with hands:

27 So that not only this our

e ch.16.16,19. f Re.18.11. g Ps.115.4; Is.44.10-20.

23. *No small stir.* No little excitement, disturbance, or tumult (τάραχος). Comp. ch. xvii. 4, 5. ¶ *About that way.* Respecting the doctrines of Christianity which Paul preached. See Notes on ch. ix. 2; xviii. 26; xix. 9.

24. *A silversmith.* The word used here denotes one who works in silver in any way, either in making money, in stamping silver, or in forming utensils of it. It is probable that the employment of this man was confined to the business here specified, that of making shrines, as his complaint (ver. 26, 27) implied that destroying this would be sufficient to throw them out of all employment. *Silver shrines*—ναοὺς. Temples. The word *shrine* properly means a case, small chest, or box; particularly applied to a box in which sacred things are deposited. Hence we hear of the *shrines* for relics (Webster). The word *shrines* here denotes small portable temples, or edifices, made of silver, so as to represent the temple of Diana, and probably containing a silver image of the góddess. Such shrines would be purchased by devotees and by worshippers of the goddess, and by strangers, who would be desirous of possessing a representation of one of the seven wonders of the world. See Notes on ver. 27. The great number of persons that came to Ephesus for her worship would constitute an ample sale for productions of this kind, and make the manufacture a profitable employment. It is well known that pagans everywhere are accustomed to carry with them small images, or representations of their gods, as an amulet or charm. The Romans had such images in all their houses, called *penates*, or household gods. A similar thing is mentioned as early as the time of Laban (Ge. xxxi. 19), whose *images* Rachel had stolen and taken with her. Comp. Ju. xvii. 5, "The man Micah had an house of gods;" 1 Sa. xix. 13; Ho. iii. 4. These images were usually inclosed in a box, case, or chest, made of wood, iron, or silver; and probably, as here, usually made to resemble the temple where the idol was worshipped. ¶ *Diana.* This was a celebrated goddess of the heathen, and one of the twelve superior deities. In the heavens she was Luna, or Meni (the moon); on earth, Diana; and in hell, Hecate. She was sometimes represented with a crescent on her head, a bow in her hand, and dressed in a hunting habit; at other times with a triple face, and with instruments of torture. She was commonly regarded as the goddess of hunting. She was also worshipped under the various names of Lucina, Proserpine, Trivia, &c. She was also represented with a great number of breasts, to denote her being the fountain of blessings, or as distributing her benefits to each in their proper station. She was worshipped in Egypt, Athens, Cilicia, and among heathen nations generally; but the most celebrated place of her worship was Ephesus, a city peculiarly dedicated to her. ¶ *To the craftsmen.* To the labourers employed under Demetrius in the manufacture of shrines.

25. *With the workmen of like occupation.* Those who were in his employ, and all others engaged in the same business. As they would be all affected in the same way, it was easy to produce an excitement among them all. ¶ *Sirs.* Greek, Men. ¶ *By this craft.* By this business or occupation. This is our *trade.* ¶ *Our wealth.* Greek, our acquisition; our property. We are dependent on it for a living. It does not mean that they were *rich*, but that they relied on this for a subsistence. That it was a lucrative business is apparent, but it is not affirmed that they were in fact rich.

26. *Ye see and hear.* You see at Ephesus, and you hear the same in other places. ¶ *Throughout all Asia.* All Asia Minor; or perhaps the province of which Ephesus was the capital. See Notes on ch. ii. 9. ¶ *This Paul hath persuaded.*

craft is in danger to be set at nought, but also that [h]the temple of the great goddess Diana should be despised, and her magnificence should be destroyed, whom all Asia and [i]the world worshippeth.

h Zep.2.11.

i 1 Jn.5.19; Re.13.8.

We have here the noble testimony of a heathen to the zeal and success of the ministry of Paul. It is an acknowledgment that his labours had been most strikingly successful in turning the people from idolatry. ¶ *Saying that they be no gods*, &c. See Notes on ch. xiv. 14, 15.

27. *So that not only*, &c. The grounds of the charge which Demetrius made against Paul were two: first, that the business of the craftsmen would be destroyed—usually the first thing that strikes the mind of a sinner who is influenced by self-interest alone; and, second, that the worship of Diana would cease if Paul and his fellow-labourers were suffered to continue their efforts. ¶ *This our craft*. This business in which we are engaged, and on which we are dependent. Greek, this part (τὸ μέρος) which pertains to us. ¶ *To be set at nought*. To be brought into contempt. It will become so much an object of ridicule and contempt that we shall have no further employment. Greek, "*Is in danger of coming into refutation*"—εἰς ἀπελεγμὸν. As that which is *refuted* by argument is deemed *useless*, so the word comes also to signify that which is useless, or which is an object of contempt or ridicule. We may here remark, (1) That the extensive prevalence of the Christian religion would *destroy* many kinds of business in which men now engage. It would put an end to all that now ministers to the pride, vanity, luxury, vice, and ambition of men. Let religion prevail, and wars would cease, and all the preparations for war which now employ so many hearts and hands would be useless. Let religion prevail, and temperance would prevail also; and consequently all the capital and labour now employed in distilling and vending ardent spirits would be withdrawn, and the business be broken up. Let religion prevail, and licentiousness would cease, and all the arts which minister to it would be useless. Let Christianity prevail, and all that goes now to minister to idolatry, and the corrupt passions of men, would be destroyed. No small part of the talent, also, that is now worse than wasted in corrupting others by ballads and songs, by fiction and licentious tales, would be withdrawn. A vast amount of capital and talent would thus be at once set at liberty, to be employed in nobler and better purposes. (2) The effect of religion is often to bring the employments of men into shame and contempt. A revival of religion often makes the business of distilling an object of abhorrence. It pours shame on those who are engaged in ministering to the vices and luxuries of the world. Religion reveals the evil of such a course of life, and those vices are banished by the mere prevalence of better principles. Yet, (3) The talent and capital thus disengaged is not rendered useless. It may be directed to other channels and other employments. Religion does not make men idle. It leads men to devote their talents to useful employments, and opens fields in which all may toil usefully to themselves and to their fellow-men. If all the capital, the genius, and the learning which are now wasted, and worse than wasted, were to be at once withdrawn from their present pursuits, they might be profitably employed. There is not now a useless man who might not be useful; there is not a cent wasted which might not be employed to advantage in the great work of making the world better and happier. ¶ *But also that the temple of the great goddess Diana should be despised*. This temple, so celebrated, was regarded as one of the seven wonders of the world. It was two hundred and twenty years in building before it was brought to perfection. It was built at the expense of all Asia Minor. The original object of worship among the Ephesians was a small statue of Diana, made of wood, but of what kind of wood is unknown. Pliny says that the temple was made of cedar, but that it was doubtful of what kind of wood the image was made. Some have said that it was of ebony. Mucian, who was three times consul, says that the image was made of vine, and was never changed, though the temple was rebuilt seven times (Pliny, xvi. 79). See Vitruvius, ii. 9. It was merely an Egyptian hieroglyphic, with many breasts, representing the goddess of Nature—under

28 And when they heard *these*
sayings, they were [k]full of wrath,
and cried out, saying, Great *is*
Diana of the Ephesians!
29 And the whole city was filled
with confusion; and having caught
[l]Gaius and [m]Aristarchus, men of
Macedonia, Paul's companions in
travel, they rushed with one accord
into the theatre.

k Je.50.38. *l* Ro.16.23; 1 Co.1.14. *m* Col.4.10.

---

which idea Diana was probably worshipped at Ephesus. As the original figure became decayed by age, it was propped up by two rods of iron like spits, which were carefully copied in the image which was afterward made in imitation of the first. A temple, most magnificent in structure, was built to contain the image of Diana, which was several times built and rebuilt. The first is said to have been completed in the reign of Servius Tullius, at least 570 years before Christ. Another temple is mentioned as having been designed by Ctesiphon, 540 years before the Christian era, and which was completed by Daphnis of Miletus and a citizen of Ephesus. This temple was partially destroyed by fire on the very day on which Socrates was poisoned, 400 years B.C., and again 356 years B.C., by the philosopher Herostratus, on the day on which Alexander the Great was born. He confessed, on being put to the torture, that the only motive he had was to immortalize his name. The four walls, and a few columns only, escaped the flames. The temple was repaired, and restored to more than its former magnificence, in which, says Pliny (lib. xxxvi. c. 14), 220 years were required to bring it to completion. It was 425 feet in length, 220 in breadth, and was supported by 127 pillars of Parian marble, each of which was 60 feet high. These pillars were furnished by as many princes, and 36 of them were curiously carved, and the rest were finely polished. Each pillar, it is supposed, with its base, contained 150 tons of marble. The doors and panelling were made of cypress wood, the roof of cedar, and the interior was rendered splendid by decorations of gold, and by the finest productions of ancient artists. This celebrated edifice, after suffering various partial demolitions, was finally burned by the Goths, in their third naval invasion, in A.D. 260. Travellers are now left to conjecture where its site was. Amidst the confused ruins of ancient Ephesus, it is now impossible to tell where was this celebrated temple, once one of the wonders of the world. "So passes away the glory of this world." See *Edinburgh Encycl.*, art. "Ephesus;" also Anacharsis's *Travels*, vol. vi. p. 188; *Ancient Universal Hist.*, vol. vii. p. 416; and Pococke's *Travels*. ¶ *And her magnificence.* Her majesty and glory; that is, the splendour of her temple and her worship. ¶ *Whom all Asia.* All Asia Minor. ¶ *And the world.* Other parts of the world. The temple had been built by contributions from a great number of princes, and doubtless multitudes from all parts of the earth came to Ephesus to pay their homage to Diana.

28. *Were full of wrath.* Were greatly enraged—probably at the prospect of losing their gains. ¶ *Great* is *Diana*, &c. The term *great* was often applied by the Greeks to Diana. Thus, in Xenophon (*Ephes.* i.), he says, "I adjure you by your own goddess, the great (τὴν μεγάλην) Diana of the Ephesians." The *design* of this clamour was doubtless to produce a persecution against Paul, and thus to secure a continuance of their employment. Often, when men have no arguments, they raise a clamour; when their employments are in danger of being ruined, they are filled with rage. We may learn, also, that when men's pecuniary interests are affected, they often show great zeal for religion, and expect by clamour in behalf of some doctrine to maintain their own interest, and to secure their own gains.

29. *Confusion.* Tumult; disorder. ¶ *Gaius.* He had lived at Corinth, and had kindly entertained Paul at his house, 1 Co. i. 14; Ro. xvi. 23. ¶ *Aristarchus.* He attended Paul to Rome, and was there a prisoner with him, Col. iv. 10. ¶ *With one accord.* Tumultuously; or with one mind or purpose. ¶ *Into the theatre.* The *theatres* of the Greeks were not only places for public exhibitions, but also for holding assemblies, and often for courts, elections, &c. The people, therefore, naturally rushed there, as being a suitable place to decide this matter.

30. *Would have entered in unto the*

30 And when Paul would have entered in unto the people, the disciples suffered him not.

31 And certain of the chief of Asia, which were his friends, sent unto him, [n]desiring *him* that he would not adventure himself into the theatre.

32 Some[o] therefore cried one thing, and some another; for the assembly was confused; and the more part knew not wherefore they were come together.

33 And they drew Alexander out of the multitude, the Jews putting him forward. And [p]Alexander beckoned with the hand, and would have made his defence unto the people.

34 But when they knew that he

n ch.21.12. *o* ch.21.34. *p* 1 Ti.1.20; 2 Ti.4.14.

---

people. Probably to have addressed them, and to defend his own cause.

31. *Certain of the chief of Asia*—τῶν Ἀσιαρχῶν. Of the *Asiarchs.* These were persons who presided over sacred things and over the public games. It was their business to see that the proper services of religion were observed, and that proper honour was rendered to the Roman emperor in the public festivals, at the games, &c. They were annually elected, and their election was confirmed at Rome before it was valid. They held a common council at the principal city within their province, as at Ephesus, Smyrna, Sardis, &c., to consult and deliberate about the interests committed to their charge in their various provinces (Kuinoel and Schleusner). Probably they were assembled on such an occasion now; and during their remaining there they had heard Paul preach, and were friendly to his views and doctrines. ¶ *Which were his friends.* It does not appear from this that they were Christian converts; but they probably had feelings of respect toward him, and were disposed to defend him and his cause. Perhaps, also, there might have existed a personal acquaintance and attachment. ¶ *Would not adventure.* Would not risk his life in the tumult, and under the excited feelings of the multitude.

32. *Some therefore cried one thing,* &c. This is an admirable description of a mob, assembled for what purpose they knew not; but agitated by passions, and strifes, and tumults. ¶ *And the most part knew not,* &c. The greater part did not know. They had been drawn together by the noise and excitement, and but a small part would know the real cause of the commotion. This is usually the case in tumultuous meetings.

33. *And they drew Alexander.* Who this Alexander was is not known. Grotius supposes that it was "Alexander the coppersmith," who had in some way done Paul much harm (2 Ti. iv. 14); and whom, with Philetus, Paul had excommunicated. He supposes that it was a device of the Jews to put forward one who had been of the Christian party, in order to accuse Paul, and to attempt to cast the odium of the tumult on him. But it is not clear that the Alexander whom Paul had excommunicated was the person concerned in this transaction. All that appears in this narrative is, that Alexander was one who was known to be a Jew, and who wished to defend the Jews from being regarded as the authors of this tumult. It would be supposed by the heathen that the Christians were only a sect of the Jews, and the Jews wished, doubtless, to show that *they* had not been concerned in giving occasion to this tumult, but that it was to be traced wholly to Paul and his friends. ¶ *The Jews putting him forward.* That he might have a convenient opportunity to speak to the people. ¶ *Would have made his defence.* Our translation, by the phrase "*his* defence," would seem to imply that he was personally accused. But it was not so. The Greek is simply, "was about to apologize to the people;" that is, to make a defence, not of himself particularly, but of the Jews in general. The translation should have been "*a defence.*"

34. *But when they knew.* When they perceived or ascertained. ¶ *That he was a Jew.* There was a general prejudice against the Jews. They were disposed to charge the whole difficulty on Jews—esteeming Christians to be but a sect of the Jews. They were, therefore, indiscriminate in their wrath, and unwilling to listen to any defence. ¶ *With one voice.* Unitedly, in one continued shout and clamour. ¶ *About the space of two hours.* The day, from sun-

was a Jew, all with one voice, about the space of two hours, cried out, Great *is* Diana of the Ephesians!

35 And when the town-clerk had appeased the people, he said, [q] Ye men of Ephesus, what man is there that knoweth not how that the city

q Ep.2.12.

---

rise to sunset, among the Greeks and Romans, was divided into twelve equal parts, Jn. xi. 9. An *hour*, therefore, did not differ materially from an hour with us. It is not at all improbable that the tumult would continue for so long a time, before it would be possible to allay the excitement. ¶ *Cried out*, &c. This they at first did to silence Alexander. The shouting, however, was continued in order to evince their attachment to Diana, as would be natural in an excited and tumultuous mob of heathen worshippers.

35. *And when the town-clerk*—ὁ γραμματεὺς. The scribe; the secretary. This word is often used in the Bible, and is commonly translated *scribe*, and is applied to public notaries in the synagogues; to clerks; to those who transcribed books, and hence to men skilled in the law or in any kind of learning. Comp. 2 Sa. viii. 17; 2 Ki. xii. 11; Ezr. vii. 6, 11, 12; Mat. v. 20; xii. 38; xiii. 52; xv. 1; xxiii. 34; 1 Co. i. 20. It is, however, nowhere else applied to a heathen magistrate. It probably denoted a recorder; or a transcriber of the laws; or a chancellor (Kuinoel, Doddridge). This officer had a seat in their deliberative assemblies, and on him it seems to have devolved to keep the peace. The Syriac, "Prince of the city." The Vulgate and Arabic, "Scribe." ¶ *Had appeased the people*—καταστείλας. Having restrained, quieted, tranquillized, so as to be able to address them. ¶ *What man is there.* Who is there that can deny this? It is universally known and admitted. This is the language of strong confidence, of reproof, and of indignation. It implied that the worship of Diana was so well established that there was no danger that it could be destroyed by a few Jews, and he therefore reproved them for what he deemed their unreasonable fears. But he little knew the power of that religion which had been the innocent cause of all this tumult; nor that, at no very distant period, this despised religion would overturn not only the worship of Diana at Ephesus, but the splendid idolatry of the mighty Roman empire. ¶ *Is a worshipper*—νεωκόρον. Margin, temple-keeper. The word here used does not occur elsewhere in the New Testament. It is derived from νεὼς, for ναὸς, a temple, and κορέω, to sweep, to cleanse. But among the ancients, the office of keeping their temples was by no means as humble as that of sexton is with us. It was regarded as an office of honour and dignity to have charge of the temples of the gods, and to keep them in order. The term was also given to the cities that were regarded as the peculiar patrons or worshippers of certain gods and goddesses. They esteemed it an honour to be regarded as the peculiar *keepers* of their temples and images, or as having adopted them as their tutelar divinities. Such was Ephesus in regard to Diana. It was considered to be a high honour that the city was everywhere regarded as being *intrusted* with the worship of Diana, or with keeping the temple regarded by the whole world as peculiarly her own. See Schleusner on this word. ¶ *And of the* image. A special guardian of the image, or statue of Diana. ¶ *Which fell down*, &c. Which was feigned or believed to have been sent down from heaven. See Notes on ver. 27. It is probable that the image was so ancient that the maker of it was unknown, and it was therefore feigned to have fallen from heaven. It was for the interest of the priest to keep up this impression. Many cities pretended to have been favoured in a similar manner with images or statues of the gods, sent directly from heaven. The safety of Troy was supposed to dedepend on the *Palladium*, or image of Pallas Minerva, which was believed to have fallen from heaven. Numa pretended that the *ancilia*, or sacred shields, had descended from heaven. Herodian expressly affirms that "the Phœnicians had no statue of the sun polished by the hand, but only a certain large stone, circular below, and terminated acutely above in the figure of a cone, of a black colour, and that they believed it to have fallen from heaven." The same thing was affirmed of the ancient Minerva of the Athenian Acropolis (Paus., *Att.* 26); of the Paphian Venus, and the Ceres of Sicily (Cic. *in Verr.*, v. 187). It has been supposed by some that this image at Ephe-

of the Ephesians is [1]a worshipper
of the great goddess Diana, and of
the *image* which fell down from
Jupiter?
36 Seeing then that these things
cannot be spoken against, ye ought
to be quiet, and to [r]do nothing
rashly.
37 For ye have brought hither
these men, which are neither [s]rob-
bers of churches, nor yet blasphemers of your goddess.
38 Wherefore if Demetrius, and
the craftsmen which are with him,
have a matter against any man,
[2]the law is open, and there are
deputies; let them implead one
another.

1 *the temple-keeper.* r Pr.14.29. s ch.25.8. 2 or, *the court-days are kept.*

sus was merely a conical or pyramidal stone which fell from the clouds—*a meteorite*—and that it was regarded with superstitious reverence, as having been sent from heaven. See the *Edinburgh Encycl.*, art. "Meteorites." ¶ *From Jupiter.* See Notes on ch. xiv. 12.

36. *Seeing then*, &c. Since no one can call in question the zeal of the Ephesians on this subject, or doubt the sincerity of their belief, and since there can be no danger that this well-established worship is to be destroyed by the efforts of a few evil-disposed Jews, there is no occasion for this tumult. ¶ *Be quiet.* Be appeased. The same Greek word which is used in ver. 35, "had *appeased* the people." ¶ *To do nothing rashly.* To do nothing in a heated, inconsiderate manner. There is no occasion for tumult and riot. The whole difficulty can be settled in perfect consistency with the maintenance of order.

37. *For ye*, &c. Demetrius and his friends. The blame was to be traced to them. ¶ *Which are neither robbers of churches.* The word *churches* we now apply to edifices reared for purposes of Christian worship. As no such churches had then been built, this translation is unhappy, and is not at all demanded by the original. The Greek word (ἱεροσύλους) is applied properly to those who *commit sacrilege;* who plunder temples of their sacred things. The meaning here is that Paul and his companions had not been guilty of robbing the temple of Diana, or any other temple. The charge of *sacrilege* could not be brought against them. Though they had preached against idols and idol worship, yet they had offered no violence to the temples of idolaters, nor had they attempted to strip them of the sacred utensils employed in their service. What they had done, they had done peaceably. ¶ *Nor yet blasphemers of your goddess.* They had not used harsh or reproachful language of Diana. This had not been charged on them, nor is there the least evidence that they had done it. They had opposed idolatry; had reasoned against it; and had endeavoured to turn the people from it. But there is not the least evidence that they had ever done it in harsh or reproachful language. This shows that men should employ *reason*, and not harsh or reproachful language against a pervading evil; and that the way to remove it is to *enlighten* the minds of men, and to *convince* them of the error of their ways. Men gain nothing by bitter and reviling words; and it is much to obtain the testimony of even the enemies of religion—as Paul did of the chancellor of Ephesus—that no such words had been used in describing their crimes and follies.

38. *Have a matter against any man.* Have a complaint of injury; if injustice has been done them by anyone. ¶ *The law is open.* See the margin. Ἀγόραιοι ἄγονται, *i.e.* ἡμέραι. There are *court-days;* days which are open, or appointed for judicial trials, where such matters can be determined in a proper manner. Perhaps the courts were then held, and the matter might be immediately determined. ¶ *And there are deputies.* Roman proconsuls. See Notes on ch. xiii. 7. The cause might be brought before them with the certainty that it would be heard and decided. The Syriac reads this in the singular number—"Lo, the proconsul is in the city." ¶ *Let them implead one another.* Let them *accuse* each other in the court. The laws are equal, and impartial justice will be done.

39. *But if we inquire.* If you seek to determine any other matters than that pertaining to the alleged wrong which Demetrius has suffered in his business. ¶ *Other matters.* Anything respecting public affairs; anything pertaining to the government and the worship of

39 But if ye inquire any thing
concerning other matters, it shall be
determined in a [3]lawful assembly.
40 For we are in danger to be
called in question for this day's
uproar, there being no cause
whereby we may give an account
of this concourse.
41 And[t] when he had thus
spoken he dismissed the assembly.

CHAPTER XX.

AND after [a]the uproar was
ceased, Paul called unto
him the disciples, and embraced
them, and departed [b]for to go into
Macedonia.
2 And when he had gone over
those parts, and had [c]given them
much exhortation, he came into
Greece,
3 And *there* abode three months.
And when [d]the Jews laid wait
for him, as he was about to sail
into Syria, he purposed to return
through Macedonia.
4 And there accompanied him

3 or, *ordinary*. *t* 2 Co.1.8-10. *a* ch.19.40.

b 1 Co.16.5; 1 Ti.1.3. *c* 1 Th.2.3,11. *d* ch.23.12; 25.3; 2 Co.11.26.

Diana. ¶ *In a lawful assembly.* In an assembly convened, not by tumult and riot, but in conformity to law. This was a tumultuous assemblage, and it was proper in the public officer to demand that they should disperse; and that, if there were any public grievances to be remedied, it should be done in an assembly properly convened. It may be remarked here that the original word rendered *assembly* is that which is usually in the New Testament rendered *church*—ἐκκλησία. It is properly rendered by the word *assembly*—not denoting here a *mixed* or *tumultuous* assemblage, but one *called out*, or convened in the legal manner. The proper meaning of the word is *that which is called out.* The *church*, the Christian *assembly* of the faithful, is made up of those who are *called out* from the world.

40. *To be called in question.* By the government; by the Roman authority. Such a tumult, continued for so long a time, would be likely to attract the attention of the magistrates, and expose them to their displeasure. Popular commotions were justly dreaded by the Roman government; and such an assembly as this, convened without any good cause, would not escape their notice. There was a Roman law which made it capital for anyone to be engaged in promoting a riot. *Sui cœtum, et concursum fecerit, capite puniatur:* "He who raises a mob, let him be punished with death."

41. *Dismissed the assembly*—τὴν ἐκκλησίαν. The word usually translated *church.* Here it is applied to the irregular and tumultuous assemblage which had convened in a riotous manner.

CHAPTER XX.

1. *The uproar.* The tumult excited by Demetrius and the workmen. After it had been quieted by the town-clerk, ch. xix. 40, 41. ¶ *Embraced* them. Saluted them; gave them parting expressions of kindness. Comp. Notes on Lu. vii. 45; Ro. xvi. 16; 1 Co. xvi. 20; 2 Co. xiii. 12; 1 Th. v. 26; 1 Pe. v. 14. The Syriac translates this, "Paul called the disciples, and consoled them, and kissed them." ¶ *To go to Macedonia.* On his way to Jerusalem, agreeably to his purpose, as recorded in ch. xix. 21.

2. *Over those parts.* The parts of country in and near Macedonia. He probably went to Macedonia by *Troas*, where he expected to find Titus (2 Co. ii. 12); but, not finding him there, he went by himself to Philippi, Thessalonica, &c., and then returned to Greece proper. ¶ *Into Greece.* Into Greece proper, of which Athens was the capital. While in Macedonia he had great anxiety and trouble, but was at length comforted by the coming of Titus, who brought him intelligence of the liberal disposition of the churches of Greece in regard to the collection for the poor saints at Jerusalem, 2 Co. vii. 5–7. It is probable that the second epistle to the Corinthians was written during this time in Macedonia, and sent to them by Titus.

3. *And* there *abode.* Why he remained here is unknown. It is probable that while in Greece he wrote the epistle to the Romans. Comp. Ro. xv. 25–27. ¶ *And when the Jews laid wait for him.* There was a design formed against him by the Jews, which they sought to execute. Why they formed this purpose the historian has not informed us. ¶ *As*

into Asia Sopater of Berea; and
of the Thessalonians, [e]Aristarchus
and Secundus; and Gaius of Derbe,
and [f]Timotheus; and of Asia,
Tychicus[g] and [h]Trophimus.
5 These going before tarried for
us at Troas.
6 And we sailed away from
Philippi after [i]the days of unleavened bread, and came unto them
[k]to Troas in five days; where we
abode seven days.
7 And upon [l]the first *day* of
the week, when the disciples came
together [m]to break bread, Paul
preached unto them, ready to depart
on the morrow; and continued his
speech until midnight.

e ch.19.29. *f* ch.16.1. *g* Ep.6.21; Col.4.7; 2 Ti.4.12; Tit.3.12. *h* ch.21.29; 2 Ti.4.20. *i* Ex.23.15.

k 2 Ti.4.13. *l* 1 Co.16.2; Re.1.10. *m* ch.2.42,46; 1 Co.10.16; 11.20-34.

---

he was about to sail. It would seem from this, that the design of the Jews was to attack the ship in which he was about to sail, or to arrest him on shipboard. This fact determined him to take a much more circuitous route by land, so that the churches of Macedonia were favoured with another visit from him. ¶ *Into Syria.* On his way to Jerusalem. ¶ *He purposed,* &c. He resolved to avoid the snare which they had laid for him, and to return by the same way in which he had come into Greece.

4. *And there accompanied him.* It was usual for some of the disciples to attend the apostles in their journeys. ¶ *Into Asia.* It is not meant that they attended him from Greece through Macedonia, but that they went with him to Asia, having gone before him, and joined him at Troas. ¶ *Sopater of Berea.* Perhaps the same person who, in Ro. xvi. 21, is called *Sosipater,* and who is there said to have been a kinsman of Paul. ¶ *Aristarchus.* Ch. xix. 29. ¶ *Gaius of Derbe.* See Notes on ch. xix. 29. ¶ *Tychicus.* This man was high in the confidence and affection of Paul. In Ep. vi. 21, 22 he styles him "a beloved brother, and faithful minister in the Lord." ¶ *And Trophimus.* Trophimus was from Ephesus, ch. xx. 29. When Paul wrote his second epistle to Timothy he was at Miletum, sick, 2 Ti. iv. 20.

5. *These going before.* Going before Paul and Luke. Dr. Doddridge supposes that only Tychicus and Trophimus went before the others. Perhaps the Greek most naturally demands this interpretation. ¶ *Tarried for us.* The word "us," here, shows that Luke had again joined Paul as his companion. In ch. xvi. 12 it appears that Luke was in Philippi, in the house of Lydia. Why he remained there, or why he did not attend Paul in his journey to Athens, Corinth, Ephesus, &c., is not known. It is evident, however, that he here joined him again. ¶ *At Troas.* See Notes on ch. xvi. 8.

6. *After the days of unleavened bread.* After the seven days of the Passover, during which they ate only unleavened bread. See Ex. xii. ¶ *In five days.* They crossed the Ægean Sea. Paul, when he crossed it on a former occasion, did it in two days (ch. xvi. 11, 12); but the navigation of the sea is uncertain, and they were now probably hindered by contrary winds.

7. *And upon the first* day *of the week.* Showing thus that this day was then observed by Christians as holy time. Comp. 1 Co. xvi. 2; Re. i. 10. ¶ *To break bread.* Evidently to celebrate the Lord's supper. Comp. ch. ii. 46. So the Syriac understands it, by translating it, "to break the eucharist;" that is, the eucharistic bread. It is probable that the apostles and early Christians celebrated the Lord's supper on every Lord's day. ¶ *And continued his speech until midnight.* The discourse of Paul continued until the breaking of day, ver. 11. But it was interrupted about midnight by the accident that occurred to Eutychus. The fact that Paul was about to leave them on the next day, probably to see them no more, was the principal reason why his discourse was so long continued. We are not to suppose, however, that it was one continued or set discourse. No small part of the time might have been passed in hearing and answering questions, though Paul was the chief speaker. The case proves that such seasons of extraordinary devotion may, in peculiar circumstances, be proper. Occasions may arise where it will be proper for Christians to spend a much longer time than usual in public worship. It is evident, however, that such seasons do not often occur.

8 And there were many lights in the [n]upper chamber where they were gathered together.

9 And there sat in a window a certain young man named Eutychus, being fallen into a deep sleep; and as Paul was long preaching, he sunk down with sleep, and fell down from the third loft, and was taken up dead.

10 And Paul went down, [o]and fell on him, and, embracing *him*, said, [p]Trouble not yourselves; for his life is in him.

11 When he therefore was come up again, and had broken bread, and eaten, and talked a long while, even till break of day, so he departed.

12 And they brought the young man alive, and were not a little comforted.

13 And we went before to ship, and sailed unto Assos, there intending to take in Paul; for so had he appointed, minding himself to go afoot.

14 And when he met with us at

n ch.1.13. *o* 1 Ki.17.21; 2 Ki.4.34. *p* Mat.9.24.

8. *And there were many lights.* Why this circumstance is mentioned is not apparent. It, however, meets one of the slanders of the early enemies of Christianity, that the Christians in their assemblies were accustomed to extinguish all the lights, and to commit every kind of abomination. Perhaps the mention of many lights here is designed to intimate that it was a place of public worship, as not only the Jews, but the Gentiles were accustomed to have many lights burning in such places. ¶ *In the upper chamber.* See Notes on ch. i. 13.

9. *And there sat in a window.* The window was left open, probably to avoid the malice of their enemies, who might be disposed otherwise to charge them with holding their assemblies in darkness for purposes of iniquity. The window was probably a mere opening in the wall to let in light, as *glass* was not common at that time. As the shutters of the window were not closed, there was nothing to prevent Eutychus from falling down. ¶ *The third loft.* The third story. ¶ *And was taken up dead.* Some have supposed that he was merely stunned with the fall, and that he was still alive. But the obvious meaning is, that he was actually killed by the fall, and was miraculously restored to life. This is an instance of sleeping in public worship that has some apology. The late hour of the night, and the length of the services, were the excuse. But, though the thing is often done now, yet how seldom is a sleeper in a church furnished with an excuse for it. No practice is more shameful, disrespectful, and abominable than that so common of sleeping in the house of God.

10. *And fell on him,* &c. Probably stretching himself on him as Elisha did on the Shunammite's son, 2 Ki. iv. 33–35. It was an act of tenderness and compassion, evincing a strong desire to restore him to life. ¶ *Trouble not yourselves.* They would doubtless be thrown into great consternation by such an event. Paul therefore endeavoured to compose their minds by the assurance that he would live. ¶ *For his life is in him.* He is restored to life. This has all the appearance of having been a miracle. Life was restored to him as Paul spoke.

11. *Come up again.* To the upper room, ver. 8. ¶ *And had broken bread, and eaten.* Had taken refreshment. As this is spoken of Paul only, it is evidently distinguished from the celebration of the Lord's supper.

12. *Not a little comforted.* By the fact that he was alive; perhaps also strengthened by the evidence that a miracle had been wrought.

13. *Sailed unto Assos.* There were several cities of this name. One was in Lycia; one in the territory of Eolis; one in Mysia; one in Lydia; and another in Epirus. The latter is the one intended here. It was between Troas and Mitylene. The distance to it from Troas by land was about 20 miles, while the voyage round Cape Lectum was nearly twice as far, and accordingly Paul chose to go to it on foot. ¶ *Minding himself.* Choosing or preferring to go on foot. Most of his journeys were probably performed in this way.

14. *Came to Mitylene.* This was the capital of the island of Lesbos. It was distinguished by the beauty of its situa-

Assos, we took him in, and came
to Mitylene.

15 And we sailed thence, and
came the next *day* over against
Chios; and the next *day* we arrived
at Samos, and tarried at Trogyllium;
and the next *day* we came to
Miletus.

16 For Paul had determined to
sail by Ephesus, because he would
not spend the time in Asia; for he
hasted, if it were possible for him,
to be [q]at Jerusalem the day of
[r]Pentecost.

17 And from Miletus he sent to
Ephesus, and called the elders of
the church.

18 And when they were come to
him, he said unto them, [s]Ye know,

q ch.18.21; 24.17. r ch.2.1; 1 Co.16.8. s ch.19.1,10.

tion, and the splendour and magnificence of its edifices. The island on which it stood, Lesbos, was one of the largest in the Ægean Sea, and the seventh in the Mediterranean. It is a few miles distant from the coast of Æolia, and is about 168 miles in circumference. The name of the city now is *Castro*.

15. *Over against Chios.* Opposite to. Into the neighbourhood of; or near to it. *Chios*, called also *Coos*, is an island in the Archipelago, between Lesbos and Samos. It is on the coast of Asia Minor, and is now called *Scio*. It will long be remembered as the seat of a dreadful massacre of almost all its inhabitants by the Turks in 1823. ¶ *At Samos.* This was also an island of the Archipelago, lying off the coast of Lydia, from which it is separated by a narrow strait. These islands were celebrated among the ancients for their extraordinary wines. ¶ *Trogyllium.* This was the name of a town and promontory of Ionia in Asia Minor, between Ephesus and the mouth of the river Meander, opposite to Samos. The promontory is a spur of Mount Mycale. ¶ *Miletus.* Called also Miletum. It was a city and seaport, and the ancient capital of Ionia. It was originally composed of a colony of Cretans. It became extremely powerful, and sent out colonies to a great number of cities on the Euxine Sea. It was distinguished for a magnificent temple dedicated to Apollo. It is now called by the Turks *Melas*. It was the birth-place of Thales, one of the seven wise men of Greece. It was about 40 or 50 miles from Ephesus.

16. *To sail by Ephesus.* The word *by* in our translation is ambiguous. We say to go *by* a place, meaning either to take it in our way and to go *to* it, or to go *past* it. Here it means the latter. He intended to sail *past* Ephesus without going *to* it. ¶ *For he hasted*, &c. Had he gone *to* Ephesus, he would probably have been so delayed in his journey that he could not reach Jerusalem at the time of Pentecost. ¶ *The day of Pentecost.* See Notes on ch. ii. 1.

17. *He sent to Ephesus.* Perhaps a distance of twenty or thirty miles. ¶ *The elders of the church.* Who had been appointed while he was there to take charge of the church. See Notes on ch. xv. 2.

18. *And when they were come unto him.* The discourse which follows is one of the most tender, affectionate, and eloquent which is any-where to be found. It is strikingly descriptive of the apostle's manner of life while with them; evinces his deep concern for their welfare; is full of tender and kind admonition; expresses the firm purpose of his soul to live to the glory of God, and his expectation to be persecuted still; and is a most affectionate and solemn farewell. No man can read it without being convinced that it came from a heart full of love and kindness; and that it evinces a great and noble purpose to be entirely employed in one great aim and object—the promotion of the glory of God, in the face of danger and of death. ¶ *Ye know.* From your own observation. He had been with them three years, and could make this solemn appeal to themselves that he had led a faithful and devoted life. How happy is it when a minister can thus appeal to those with whom he has laboured in proof of his own sincerity and fidelity! How comforting to himself, and how full of demonstration to a surrounding world, of the truth and power of the gospel which is preached! We may further remark that this appeal furnishes strong proof of the purity and holiness of Paul's life. The elders at Ephesus must have had abundant opportunity to know him. They had seen him, and heard him publicly, and in their private dwellings. A man does not make such an appeal unless he has

from the first day that I came into Asia, after what manner I have been with you at all seasons,
19 Serving the Lord [t] with all humility of mind, and [u] with many tears, and [v] temptations, which befell me by [w] the lying in wait of the Jews:
20 *And* how [x] I kept back nothing that was profitable *unto*

t 1 Co.15.9,10. *u* Phi.3.18. *v* 2 Co.4.8-11. *w* ver.3. *x* ver.27.

a consciousness of integrity, nor unless there is conclusive *proof* of his integrity. It is strong evidence of the holiness of the character of the apostles, and proof that they were not impostors, that they could thus appeal with the utmost assurance to those who had every opportunity of knowing them. ¶ *From the first day.* He was with *them* three years, ver. 31. ¶ *Into Asia.* Asia Minor. They would probably know not only how he had demeaned himself while with them, but also how he had conducted in other places near them. ¶ *After what manner I have been with you.* How I have lived and acted. What has been my manner of life. What *had* been his mode of life he specifies in the following verses. ¶ *At all seasons.* At all times.

19. *Serving the Lord.* In the discharge of the appropriate duties of his apostolic office, and in private life. To discharge aright our duties in any vocation is serving the Lord. Religion is often represented in the Bible as a *service* rendered to the Lord. ¶ *With all humility.* Without arrogance, pride, or a spirit of dictation; without a desire to "lord it over God's heritage;" without being elated with the authority of the apostolic office, the variety of the miracles which he was enabled to perform, or the success which attended his labours. What an admirable model for all who are in the ministry; for all who are endowed with talents and learning; for all who meet with remarkable success in their work! The proper effect of such success, and of such talent, will be to produce true humility. The greatest endowments are usually connected with the most simple and child-like humility. ¶ *And with many tears.* Paul not unfrequently gives evidence of the tenderness of his heart, of his regard for the souls of men, and of his deep solicitude for the salvation of sinners, ver. 31; Phi. iii. 18; 2 Co. ii. 4. The *particular* thing, however, here specified as producing weeping was the opposition of the Jews. But it cannot be supposed that those tears were shed from an apprehension of personal danger. It was rather because the opposition of the Jews impeded his work, and retarded his progress in winning souls to Christ. A minister of the gospel will, (1) Feel, and deeply feel for the salvation of his people. He will weep over their condition when he sees them going astray, and in danger of perishing. He will, (2) Be specially affected with opposition, because it will retard his work, and prevent the progress and the triumph of the gospel. It is not because it is a *personal* concern, but because it is the cause of his Master. ¶ *And temptations.* Trials arising from their opposition. We use the word *temptation* in a more limited sense, to denote inducements offered to one to lead him into sin. The word in the Scriptures most commonly denotes *trials* of any kind. ¶ *Which befell me.* Which happened to me; which I encountered. ¶ *By the lying in wait,* &c. By their snares and plots against my life. Comp. ver. 3. Those snares and plans were designed to blast his reputation and to destroy his usefulness.

20. *I kept back nothing,* &c. No doctrine, no admonition, no labour. Whatever he judged would promote their salvation, he faithfully and fearlessly delivered. A minister of the gospel must be the judge of what will be profitable to the people of his charge. His aim should be to promote their real welfare—to preach that which will be *profitable.* His object will not be to please their fancy, to gratify their taste, to flatter their pride, or to promote his own popularity. "All Scripture is *profitable*" (2 Ti. iii. 16); and it will be his aim to declare that only which will tend to promote their real welfare. Even if it be unpalatable; if it be the language of reproof and admonition; if it be doctrine to which the heart is by nature opposed; if it run counter to the native prejudices and passions of men; yet, by the grace of God, it should be, and will be delivered. No doctrine that will be profitable should be kept back; no labour that

you, but have showed you, and
have taught you publicly, [y]and
from house to house,
21 Testifying both to the Jews
and also to the Greeks, [z]repentance
toward God, and faith toward
our Lord Jesus Christ.
22 And now, behold, I go [a]bound

y 2 Ti.4.2.

z Mar.1.15; Lu.24.47. a ch.19.21.

---

may promote the welfare of the flock should be withheld. ¶ *But have showed you.* Have announced or declared to you. The word here used (ἀναγγεῖλαι) is most commonly applied to preaching in public assemblies, or in a public manner. ¶ *Have taught you publicly.* In the public assembly; by public preaching. ¶ *And from house to house.* Though Paul preached in public, and though his time was much occupied in manual labour for his own support (ver. 34), yet he did not esteem his *public* preaching to be all that was required of him, nor his daily occupation to be an excuse for not visiting from house to house. We may observe here, (1) That Paul's example is a warrant and an implied injunction for family visitation by a pastor. If proper in Ephesus, it is proper still. If practicable in that city, it is in other cities. If it was useful there, it will be elsewhere. If it furnished to him consolation in the retrospect when he came to look over his ministry, and if it was *one* of the things which enabled *him* to say, "I am pure from the blood of all men," it will be so in other cases. (2) The design for which ministers should visit should be a *religious* design. Paul did not visit for mere ceremony; for idle gossip, or chit-chat; or to converse on the news or politics of the day. His aim was to show the way of salvation, and to teach in private what he taught in public. (3) How much of this is to be done is, of course, to be left to the discretion of every minister. Paul, in private visiting, did not neglect public instruction. The latter he evidently considered to be his main or chief business. His high views of *preaching* are evinced in his life, and in his letters to Timothy and Titus. Yet, while public preaching is the main, the prime, the leading business of a minister, and while his first efforts should be directed to preparation for that, he may and should find time to enforce his public instructions by going from house to house; and often he will find that his most *immediate* and *apparent* success will result from such family instructions. (4) If it is his duty to visit, it is the duty of his people to receive him as becomes an ambassador of Christ. They should be willing to listen to his instructions; to treat him with kindness, and to aid his endeavours in bringing a family under the influence of religion.

21. *Testifying.* Bearing witness to the necessity of repentance toward God. Or *teaching* them the nature of repentance, and exhorting them to repent and believe. Perhaps the word *testifying* includes both ideas of giving evidence, and of urging with great earnestness and affection that repentance and faith were necessary. See 1 Ti. v. 21; 2 Ti. ii. 14; where the word here used, and here translated *testify*, is there translated, correctly, *charge*, in the sense of strongly *urging*, or entreating with great earnestness. ¶ *And to the Greeks.* To all who were not Jews. The *Greeks* properly denoted those who lived in Greece, and who spoke the Greek language. But the phrase, "Jews and Greeks," among the Hebrews, denoted the whole human race. He urged the necessity of repentance and faith in all. Religion makes no distinction, but regards all as sinners, and as needing salvation by the blood of the Redeemer. ¶ *Repentance toward God.* See Notes on Mat. iii. 2. Repentance is to be exercised "toward God," because, (1) Sin has been committed *against* him, and it is proper that we express our sorrow to the Being whom we have offended; and, (2) Because God only can pardon. Sincere repentance exists only where there is a willingness to make acknowledgment to the very Being whom we have offended or injured. ¶ *And faith.* See Notes on Mar. xvi. 16. ¶ *Toward*—εἰς. In regard to; in; confidence *in* the work and merits of the Lord Jesus. This is required, because there is no other one who can save from sin. See Notes on ch. iv. 12.

22. *Bound in the spirit.* Strongly urged or constrained by the influences of the Holy Spirit on my mind. Not by any desire to see the place where my fathers worshipped, and not urged merely by reason, but by the convictions and mighty promptings of the

in the spirit unto Jerusalem, [b]not
knowing the things that shall befall
me there:
23 Save that the Holy Ghost
witnesseth in every city, saying that
bonds[c] and afflictions [1]abide me.

b Ja.4.14. c ch.9.16; 21.11. 1 or, *wait for me*.

24 But [d]none of these things
move me, neither count I my life
dear unto myself, so that I might
[e]finish my course with joy, and [f]the
ministry which I have [g]received

d ch.21.13; Ro.8.35,37; 2 Co.4.16. e 2 Ti.4.7. f 2 Co.4.1. g Ga.1.1.

Holy Spirit to do my duty in this case. The expression "bound in the spirit" (δεδεμένος τῷ πνεύματι) is one of great strength and emphasis. The word δέω, *to bind*, is usually applied to confinement by cords, fetters, or bands (Mat. xiii. 30; xiv. 3; xxi. 2); and then it denotes any strong obligation (Ro. vii. 2), or anything that strongly urges or impels, Mat. xxi. 2. When we are strongly urged by the convictions of duty, by the influences of the Holy Spirit, we should not shrink from danger or from death. Duty is to be done at all hazards. It is ours to follow the directions of God; *results* we may safely and confidently leave with him. ¶ *Not knowing the things that shall befall me there.* He knew that calamities and trials of some kind awaited him (ver. 23), but he did not know, (1) Of what particular kind they would be; nor, (2) Their issue, whether it would be life or death. We should commit our way unto God, not knowing what trials may be before us in life; but knowing that, if we are found faithful at the post of duty, we have nothing to fear in the result.

23. *Save that.* Except that. This was all that he knew, that bonds and afflictions were to be his portion. ¶ *The Holy Ghost witnesseth.* Either by direct revelation to him, or by the predictions of inspired men whom Paul might meet. An instance of the latter mode occurs in ch. xxi. 11. It is probable that the meaning here is that the Holy Ghost had deeply impressed the mind of Paul by his direct influences, and by his experience in every city, that bonds and trials were to be his portion. Such had been his experience in every city where he had preached the gospel by the direction of the Holy Ghost, that he regarded it as his certain portion that he was thus to be afflicted. ¶ *In every city.* In almost every city where Paul had been, he had been subjected to these trials. He had been persecuted, stoned, and scourged. So uniform was this, so constant had been his experience in this way, that he regarded it as his certain portion to be thus afflicted, and he approached Jerusalem, and every other city, with a confident expectation that such trials awaited him there. ¶ *Saying.* In his experience, by direct revelation, and by the mouth of prophets, ch. xxi. 11. When Paul was called to the apostleship it was predicted that he would suffer much, ch. ix. 16. ¶ *Bonds.* Chains. That I would be bound, as prisoners are who are confined. ¶ *Abide me.* See the margin. They remain or wait for me; that is, I must expect to suffer them.

24. *Move me.* Alarm me, or deter me from my purpose. Greek, "I make an account of none of them." I do not regard them as of any moment, or as worth consideration in the great purpose to which I have devoted my life. ¶ *Neither count I my life.* I do not consider my life as so valuable as to be retained by turning away from bonds and persecutions. I am *certain* of bonds and afflictions; I am willing also, if it be necessary, to lay down my life in the prosecution of the same purpose. ¶ *Dear unto myself.* So precious or valuable as to be retained at the sacrifice of duty. I am willing to sacrifice it if it be necessary. This was the spirit of the Saviour, and of all the early Christians. Duty is of more importance than life; and when either duty or life is to be sacrificed, life is to be cheerfully surrendered. ¶ *So that.* This is my main object, to finish my course with joy. It is implied here, (1) That this was the great purpose which Paul had in view. (2) That if he should even lay down his life in this cause, it *would* be a finishing his course with joy. In the faithful discharge of duty, he had nothing to fear. Life would be ended with peace whenever God should require him to finish his course. ¶ *Finish my course.* Close my career as an apostle and a Christian. Life is thus represented as a *course*, or *race* that is to be run, 2 Ti. iv. 7; He. xii. 1; 1 Co. ix. 24; Ac. xiii. 25. ¶ *With joy.* With the approbation of conscience and of God, with peace in the recollection of the past.

of the Lord Jesus, to testify the gospel of the grace of God.

25 And now, behold, I know that ye all, among whom I have gone preaching the kingdom of God, shall see my face no more.

Man should strive so to live that he will have nothing to regret when he lies on a bed of death. It is a glorious privilege to finish life with joy. It is most sad when the last hours are embittered with the reflection that life has been wasted. The only way in which life may be finished with joy is by meeting faithfully every duty, and encountering, as Paul did, every trial, with a constant desire to glorify God. ¶ *And the ministry.* That I may fully discharge the duty of the apostolic office, the preaching of the gospel. In 2 Ti. iv. 5, he charges Timothy to *make full proof of his ministry*. He here shows that this was the ruling principle of his own life. ¶ *Which I have received of the Lord Jesus.* Which the Lord Jesus has committed to me, Ac. ix. 15-17. Paul regarded his ministry as an office intrusted to him by the Lord Jesus himself. On this account he deemed it to be peculiarly sacred, and of high authority, Ga. i. 12. Every minister has been intrusted with an office by the Lord Jesus. He is not his own; and his great aim should be to discharge fully and entirely the duties of that office. ¶ *To testify the gospel.* To bear witness to the good news of the favour of God. This is the great design of the ministry. It is to bear witness to a dying world of the good news that God is merciful, and that his favour may be made manifest to sinners. From this verse we may learn, (1) That we all have a course to run, a duty to perform. Ministers have an allotted duty; and so have men in all ranks and professions. (2) We should not be deterred by danger, or the fear of death, from the discharge of that duty. We are safe only when we are doing the will of God. We are really in danger only when we neglect our duty, and make the great God our enemy. (3) We should so live as that the end of our course may be joy. It is, at best, a solemn thing to die; but death may be a scene of triumph and of joy. (4) It matters little when, or where, or how we die, if we die in the discharge of our duty to God. He will order the circumstances of our departure, and He can sustain us in the last conflict. Happy is that life which is spent in doing the will of God, and peaceful that death which closes a life of toil and trial in the service of the Lord Jesus.

25. *I know that ye all.* Perhaps this means simply, "I have no expectation of seeing you again; I have every reason to suppose that this is my final interview with you." He expected to visit Ephesus no more. The journey to Jerusalem was dangerous. Trials and persecutions he knew awaited him. Besides, it is evident that he designed to turn his attention to other countries, and to visit Rome; and probably he had already formed the purpose of going into Spain. See Ac. xix. 21; comp. Ro. xv. 23-28. From all these considerations it is evident that he had no expectation of being again at Ephesus. It is probable, however, that he did again return to that city. See Notes on ch. xxviii. 31. ¶ *Among whom I have gone preaching.* Among whom I have preached. The parting of a minister and people is among the most tender and affecting of the separations that occur on earth. ¶ *The kingdom of God.* Making known the nature of the reign of God on earth by the Messiah. See Notes on Mat. iii. 2.

26. *Wherefore.* In view of the past, of my ministry and labours among you, I appeal to your own selves to testify that I have been faithful. ¶ *I take you to record.* Greek, I call you to witness. If any of you are lost; if you prove unfaithful to God, I appeal to yourselves that the fault is not mine. It is well when a minister can make this appeal, and call his hearers to bear testimony to his own faithfulness. Ministers who preach the gospel with fidelity *may* thus appeal to their hearers; and in the day of judgment may call on themselves to witness that the fault of the ruin of the soul is not to be charged to them. ¶ *That I am pure.* I am not to be charged with the guilt of your condemnation, as owing to my unfaithfulness. This does not mean that he set up a claim to absolute perfection; but that, in the matter under consideration, he had a conscience void of offence. ¶ *The blood of all men.* The word *blood* is used often in the sense of *death*, of blood *shed;* and hence of the

26 Wherefore I take you to record this day, that [h]I *am* pure from the blood of all *men*.

27 For I have not shunned to declare unto you all the [i]counsel of God.

28 Take[k] heed, therefore, unto yourselves, and to all the flock,

h 2 Co.7.2. i Ep.1.11. k Col.4.17; 1 Ti.4.16.

guilt or crime of putting one to death, Mat. xxiii. 35; xxvii. 25; Ac. v. 28; xviii. 6. It here means that if they should die the second death; if they should be lost for ever, *he* would not be to blame. He had discharged his duty in faithfully warning and teaching them; and now, if they were lost, the fault would be their own, not his. ¶ *All men.* All classes of men—Jews and Gentiles. He had warned and instructed all alike. Ministers may have many fears that their hearers will be lost. Their aim, however, should be, (1) To save them, if possible; and, (2) If they *are* lost, that it should be by no neglect or fault of theirs.

27. *For.* This verse contains a reason for what had been said in the previous verse. It shows *why* Paul regarded himself as innocent if they should be lost. ¶ *I have not shunned.* I have not kept back; I have not been deterred by fear, by the desire of popularity, by the fact that the doctrines of the gospel are unpalatable to men, from declaring them fully. The proper meaning of the word translated here, "I have not shunned" (ὑπεστειλάμην), is to *disguise* any important truth; to *withdraw* it from public view; to *decline* publishing it from fear, or an apprehension of the consequences. Paul means that he had not *disguised* any truth; he had not *withdrawn* or kept it from open view, by any apprehension of the effect which it might have on their minds. Truth may be disguised or kept back, (1) By avoiding the subject altogether from timidity, or from an apprehension of giving offence if it is openly proclaimed; or, (2) By giving it too little prominency, so that it shall be lost in the multitude of other truths; or, (3) By presenting it amidst a web of metaphysical speculations, and entangling it with other subjects; or, (4) By making use of other terms than the Bible does, for the purpose of involving it in a mist, so that it cannot be understood. Men may resort to this course, (1) Because the truth itself is unpalatable; (2) Because they may apprehend the loss of reputation or support; (3) Because they may not love the truth themselves, and choose to conceal its prominent and offensive points; (4) Because they may be afraid of the rich, the great, and the gay, and apprehend that they shall excite their indignation; and, (5) By a love of metaphysical philosophy, and a constant effort to bring everything to the test of their own reason. Men often preach a *philosophical explanation* of a doctrine instead of the *doctrine itself.* They deserve the credit of ingenuity, but not that of being open and bold proclaimers of the truth of God. ¶ *The whole counsel* — πᾶσαν τὴν βουλήν. The word counsel (βουλή) denotes properly consolation, deliberation, and then will or purpose, Lu. xxiii. 51; Ac. ii. 23. It means here the will or purpose of God, as revealed in regard to the salvation of men. Paul had made a full statement of that plan—of the guilt of men, of the claims of the law, of the need of a Saviour, of the provisions of mercy, and of the state of future rewards and punishments. Ministers ought to declare *all* that counsel, because God commands it; because it is needful for the salvation of men; and because the message is not theirs, but God's, and they have no right to change, to disguise, or to withhold it. And if it is the duty of ministers to *declare* that counsel, it is the duty of a people to *listen* to it with respect and candour, and with a desire to know the truth, and to be saved by it. *Declaring* the counsel of God will do no good unless it is *received* into honest and humble hearts, and with a disposition to know what God has revealed for salvation.

28. *Take heed, therefore.* Attend to; be on your guard against the dangers which beset you, and seek to discharge your duty with fidelity. ¶ *To yourselves.* To your own piety, opinions, and mode of life. This is the first duty of a minister; for without this all his preaching will be vain. Comp. Col. iv. 17; 1 Ti. iv. 14. Ministers are beset with peculiar dangers and temptations, and against them they should be on their guard. In addition to the temptations which they have in common with other men, they are exposed to those peculiar to their office—arising from

over the which the Holy Ghost hath [l] made you overseers, to feed the [m] church of God, [n] which he hath purchased with his own blood.

l He.13.17.

m Pr.10.21; Je.3.15; Jn.21.15-17; 1 Pe.5.2,3.
n Ep.1.14; Col.1.14; He.9.12,14; 1 Pe.1.18,19; Re.5.9.

---

flattery, and ambition, and despondency, and worldly-mindedness. And just in proportion to the importance of their office is the importance of the injunction of Paul, to take heed to themselves. ¶ *And to all the flock.* The church; the charge intrusted to them. The church of Christ is often compared *to a flock.* See Notes on Jn. x. 1–20; also Jn. xxi. 15–17. The word *flock* here refers particularly to *the church*, and not to the congregation in general, for it is represented to be that which was purchased with the blood of the atonement. The command here is, (1) To *take heed* to the church; that is, to instruct, teach, and guide it; to guard it from enemies (ver. 29), and to make it their special object to promote its welfare. (2) To take heed to ALL the flock—the rich and the poor, the bond and the free, the old and the young. It is the duty of ministers to seek to promote the welfare of each individual of their charge—not to pass by the poor because they are poor, and not to be afraid of the rich because they are rich. A shepherd regards the interest of the tenderest of the fold as much as the strongest; and a faithful minister will seek to advance the interest of *all.* To do this he should *know all* his people; should be acquainted, as far as possible, with their peculiar wants, character, and dangers, and should devote himself to their welfare as his first and main employment. ¶ *Over the which the Holy Ghost.* Though they had been appointed, doubtless, by the church, or by the apostles, yet it is here represented as having been done by the Holy Ghost. It was by him, (1) Because he had called and qualified them for their work; and, (2) Because they had been set apart in accordance with his direction and will. ¶ *Overseers* —ἐπισκόπους. Bishops. The word properly denotes those who are appointed to oversee or inspect anything. This passage proves that the name *bishop* was applicable to elders; that in the time of the apostles, the name *bishop* and *presbyter*, or *elder*, was given to the same class of officers, and, of course, that there was no distinction between them. One term was originally used to denote *office*, the other *age*, and both were applied to the same persons in the church. The same thing occurs in Tit. i. 5–7, where those who in ver. 5 are called *elders*, are in ver. 7 called *bishops.* See also 1 Ti. iii. 1–10; Phi. i. 1. ¶ *To feed*—ποιμαίνειν. This word is properly applied to the care which a shepherd exercises over his flock. See Notes on Jn. xxi. 15, 16. It is applicable not only to the act of *feeding* a flock, but also to that of protecting, guiding, and guarding it. It here denotes not merely the duty of *instructing* the church, but also of *governing* it; of securing it from enemies (ver. 29), and of directing its affairs so as to promote its edification and peace. ¶ *The church of God.* This is one of three passages in the New Testament in regard to which there has been a long controversy among critics, which is not yet determined. The controversy is, whether is this the correct and genuine reading. The other two passages are, 1 Ti. iii. 16, and 1 Jn. v. 7. The MSS. and versions here exhibit three readings: *the church* OF GOD (τοῦ Θεοῦ); *the church* OF THE LORD (τοῦ Κυρίου); and *the church of* THE LORD *and* GOD (Κυρίου καὶ Θεοῦ). The Latin Vulgate reads it *God.* The Syriac, *the Lord.* The Arabic, *the Lord God.* The Ethiopic, *the Christian family of God.* The reading which now occurs in our text is found in no ancient MSS. except the Vatican Codex, and occurs nowhere among the writings of the fathers except in Athanasius, in regard to whom also there is a various reading. It is retained, however, by Beza, Mill, and Whitby as the genuine reading. The most ancient MSS., and the best, read *the church of the Lord*, and this probably was the genuine text. It has been adopted by Griesbach and Wetstein; and many important reasons may be given why it should be retained. See those reasons stated at length in Kuinoel *in loco;* see also Griesbach and Wetstein. It may be remarked, that a change from *Lord* to *God* might easily be made in the transcribing, for in ancient MSS. the words are not written at length, but are abbreviated. Thus, the name *Christ* (Χριστός) is written ΧΟΣ; the name God (Θεός) is written ΘΟΣ; the name Lord (Κυρίος) is written ΚΟΣ; and a mistake, therefore, of a single letter would lead to the variations observable

29 For I know this, that after my departing shall [o]grievous wolves enter in among you, [p]not sparing the flock.

o Mat.7.15; 2 Pe.2.1.
p Je.13.20; 23.1; Eze.34.2,3; Zec.11.17.

30 Also [q] of your own selves shall men arise, speaking perverse things, to draw away disciples after them.

q 1 Jn.2.19; Jude 4,&c.

---

in the manuscripts. Comp. in this place the note of Mill in his Greek Testament. The authority for the name *God* is so doubtful that it should not be used as a proof text on the divinity of Christ, and is not necessary, as there are so many undisputed passages on that subject. ¶ *Which he hath purchased.* The word here used (περιεποιήσατο) occurs but in one other place in the New Testament: 1 Ti. iii. 13, "For they that have used the office of deacon well, *purchase* to themselves a good degree and great boldness in the faith." The word properly means to *acquire* or *gain* anything; to *make it ours.* This may be done by a price, or by labour, &c. The noun (περιποίησις) derived from this verb is several times used in the New Testament, and denotes *acquisition:* 1 Th. v. 9, "God hath appointed us *to obtain* [unto the obtaining or acquisition of] salvation;" 2 Th. ii. 14, "Whereunto he called you by our gospel to the *obtaining* of the glory of our Lord Jesus Christ;" 1 Pe. ii. 9; Tit. ii. 14; Ep. i. 14. In this place it means that Christ had *acquired, gained,* or *procured,* the church for himself by paying his own life as the price. The church is often represented as having thus been bought with a *price,* 1 Co. vi. 20; vii. 23; 2 Pe. ii. 1. ¶ *With his own blood.* With the sacrifice of his own life; for blood is often put for life, and to shed the blood is equivalent to taking the life. See Notes on Ro. iii. 25. The doctrines taught here are, (1) That the death of Christ was an atoning sacrifice; that he offered himself to purchase a people to his own service. (2) That the church is, therefore, of peculiar value—a value to be estimated by the price paid for it. Comp. 1 Pe. i. 18, 19. (3) That this fact should make the purity and salvation of the church an object of special solicitude with ministers of the gospel. They should be deeply affected in view of that blood which has been shed for the church; and they should guard and defend it as having been bought with the highest price in the universe. The chief consideration that will make ministers faithful and self-denying is, that the church has been bought with a price. If the Lord Jesus so loved it; if he gave himself for it, they should be willing to deny themselves; to watch, and toil, and pray, that the great object of his death—the purity and the salvation of that church—may be obtained.

29. *For I know this.* By what he had seen in other places; by his knowledge of human nature, and of the dangers to which they were exposed; and by the guidance of inspiration. ¶ *After my departure.* His presence had been the means of guarding the church, and preserving it from these dangers. Now that the founder and guide of the church was to be removed, they would be exposed to dissensions and dangers. ¶ *Grievous wolves.* Heavy (βαρεῖς), strong, mighty, dangerous wolves—so strong that the feeble flock would not be able to resist them. The term *wolves* is used to denote the enemies of the flock—false, and hypocritical, and dangerous teachers. Comp. Mat. x. 16. ¶ *Enter in among you.* From abroad; doubtless referring particularly to the *Jews,* who might be expected to distract and divide them. ¶ *Not sparing the flock.* Seeking to destroy the church. The Jews would regard it with peculiar hostility, and would seek to destroy it in every way. Probably they would approach them with great professed friendship for them, and expressing a desire only to defend the laws of Moses.

30. *Also of your own selves.* From your own church; from those who profess to be Christians. ¶ *Speaking perverse things.* Crooked, perverted, distracting doctrines (διεστραμμένα). Comp. Notes on Ac. xiii. 10. They would proclaim doctrines tending to distract and divide the church. The most dangerous enemies which the church has had have been nurtured in its own bosom, and have consisted of those who have perverted the true doctrines of the gospel. Among the Ephesians, as among the Corinthians (1 Co. i. 11–13), there might be parties formed; there might be men influenced by ambition, like Diotrephes (3 Jn. 9), or like Phygellus or Hermogenes (2 Ti. i. 15), or like Hymeneus and Alexander, 1 Ti. i. 20.

31 Therefore [r]watch, and remember that by the space of three years I ceased not to [s]warn every one night and day with tears.

r 2 Ti.4.5. *s* Col.1.28.

32 And now, brethren, I commend you to God, and to the word of his grace, [t]which is able to build you up, and to give you

t Jn.17.17.

Men under the influence of ambition, or from the love of power or popularity, form parties in the church, produce divisions and distractions, and greatly retard its internal prosperity, and mar its peace. The church of Christ would have little to fear from external enemies if it nurtured no foes in its own bosom; and all the power of persecutors is not so much to be dreaded as the plans, the parties, the strifes, the heart-burnings, and the contentions which are produced by those who love and seek power, among the professed friends of Christ.

31. *Therefore watch.* Mat. xxiv. 42. In view of the dangers which beset yourselves (ver. 28), the danger from men not connected with the church (ver. 29), and the danger which will arise from the love of power among yourselves (ver. 30), be on your guard. Observe the approach of danger, and set yourselves against it. ¶ *Remember.* Recall my counsels and admonitions in reference to these dangers. ¶ *By the space of three years.* In ch. xix. 10, we are told that Paul spent two years in the school of Tyrannus. In ch. xix. 8, it is said that he was teaching in the synagogue at Ephesus three months. In addition to this, it is not improbable that he spent some months more in Ephesus in instructing the church in other places. Perhaps, however, by the phrase three years, he meant to use merely a round number, denoting *about* three years; or, in accordance with the Jewish custom, part of each of the three years—one whole year, and a considerable portion of the two others. Comp. Notes on Mat. xii. 40. ¶ *I ceased not.* I continued to do it. ¶ *To warn.* To admonish; to place before the mind (νουθετῶν); setting the danger and duty of each individual before him. ¶ *Every one.* He had thus set them an example of what he had enjoined, ver. 28. He had admonished each individual, whatever was his rank or standing. It is well when a minister can refer to his own example as an illustration of what he meant by his precepts. ¶ *Night and day.* Continually; by every opportunity. ¶ *With tears.* Expressive of his deep feeling, and his deep interest in their welfare. See Notes on ver. 19.

32. *And now, brethren.* About to leave them, probably to see them no more, he committed them to the faithful care and keeping of God. Amidst all the dangers of the church, when human strength fails or is withdrawn, we may commit that church to the safe keeping and tender care of God. ¶ *I commend you.* I commit you; I *place you* (παρατίθεμαι) in his hands and under his protection. See Notes on Ac. xiv. 23. ¶ *And to the word of his grace.* That is, to his gracious word; to his merciful promise. Paul refers, doubtless, to the *gospel*, including its promises of support, its consoling truths, and its directions to seek all needful help and comfort in God. ¶ *Which is able.* Which has power. Τῷ δυναμένῳ. Which word, or gospel, has power to build you up, He. iv. 12, "For the word of God is quick [living, life-giving, ζῶν], and powerful, and sharper than any two-edged sword," &c. Comp. Is. xlix. 2; Je. xxiii. 29, "Is not my word like as a fire? saith the Lord; and like a hammer that breaketh the rock in pieces?" It is implied here that the gospel is not a dead letter; that it has *power* to accomplish a great work; that it is *adapted* to the end in view, the conversion and sanctification of the soul. There is no danger in representing the gospel as *mighty*, and as fitted by infinite wisdom to secure the renovation and salvation of man. Comp. Ro. i. 16; 1 Co. i. 18; 2 Co. x. 4. ¶ *To build you up.* The word used here is properly applied to a house which is reared and completed by slow degrees, and by toil. It here means to establish, make firm, or permanent, and hence to instruct, to establish in doctrine and in hope. The idea is, that the word of God was able to confirm and establish them, amidst the dangers to which they would be exposed. ¶ *And to give you an inheritance.* To make you heirs, or to make you joint partakers with the saints of the blessings in reserve for the children of God. Those blessings are often represented as an inheritance, or heirship, which God will confer on his

an [u]inheritance among all them which are sanctified.

33 I[v] have coveted no man's silver, or gold, or apparel.

34 Yea, [w]ye yourselves know that these hands have ministered unto my necessities, and to them that were with me.

35 I have showed you all things,

u ch.26.18; Col.1.12; He.9.15; 1 Pe.1.4.
v 1 Sa.12.3; 1 Co.9.12; 2 Co.7.2.
w ch.18.3; 1 Co.4.12; 1 Th.2.9; 2 Th.3.8.

---

adopted children, Mat. xix. 29; xxv. 34; Mar. x. 17; He. vi. 12; Re. xxi. 7; Ep. i. 11; v. 5; Col. i. 12; iii. 24; Ro. viii. 17; Ga. iii. 29. ¶ *Among all them which are sanctified.* With all who are holy; with all the saints. See Notes on Jn. x. 36. Those who shall be saved are made holy. They who receive a part in the inheritance beyond the grave will have it only among the sanctified and the pure. They must, therefore, be pure themselves, or they can have no part in the kingdom of Christ and of God.

33. *I have coveted.* I have not desired. I have not made it an object of my living among you to obtain your property. Thus (2 Co. xii. 14) he says, "I seek not yours, but you." Paul had power to demand support in the ministry as the reward of his labour, 1 Co. ix. 13, 14. Yet he did not choose to exercise it, lest it should bring the charge of avarice against the ministry, 1 Co. ix. 12, 15. He also had power in another respect. He had a vast influence over the people. The early Christians were disposed to commit their property to the disposal of the apostles. See Ac. iv. 34, 35, 37. The heathen had been accustomed to devote their property to the support of religion. Of this propensity, if the object of Paul had been to make money, he might have availed himself, and have become enriched. Deceivers often thus impose on people for the purpose of amassing wealth; and one of the incidental but striking proofs of the truth of the Christian religion is here furnished in the appeal which the apostle Paul made to his hearers, that this had *not* been his motive. If it had been, how easy would it have been for them to have contradicted him! and who, in such circumstances, would have dared to make such an appeal? The circumstances of the case, therefore, prove that the object of the apostle was *not* to amass wealth. And this fact is an important proof of the truth of the religion which he defended. What should have induced him to labour and toil in this manner but a conviction of the truth of Christianity? And if he really believed it was true, it is, in his circumstances, a strong proof that this religion is from heaven. See this proof stated in Faber's *Difficulties of Infidelity*, and in Lord Lyttleton's *Letter on the Conversion of St. Paul.* ¶ *Or apparel.* Raiment. Changes of raiment among the ancients, as at present among the Orientals, constituted an important part of their property. See Notes on Mat. vi. 19.

34. *Yea, ye yourselves know.* By your own acquaintance with my manner of life. In Corinth he had lived and laboured with Apollos (Note, ch. xviii. 3); and he refers elsewhere to the fact that he had supported himself, in part at least, by his own labour, 1 Co. iv. 12; 1 Th. ii. 9; 2 Th. iii. 8. We may hence learn that it is no discredit to a minister to labour. Whatever it may be to a people who put him under a necessity to toil for his support, yet the example of Paul shows that a man should rejoice in the privilege of preaching the gospel, even if it is done while he is obliged to resort to labour for his daily bread. It is well when a minister of the gospel can make an appeal to his people like this of Paul, and say, "I have coveted no man's gold, or silver, or apparel." Every minister should so live that he can make this appeal to their own consciences of the sincerity and disinterestedness of his labours from the pulpit; or when called to separate from them as Paul did; or when on a dying bed. Every minister of the gospel, when he comes to lie down to die, will desire to be able to make this appeal, and to leave a solemn testimony there, that it was not for gold, or ease, or fame, that he toiled in the ministerial office. How much more influence will such a man have than he who has been worldly-minded; he who has sought to become rich; and he, the only memorials of whose life is, that he has sought "the fleece, not the flock"—that he has gained the *property*, not the *souls* of men.

35. *I have showed you.* I have taught you by instruction and example. I

how that so labouring [x]ye ought to support the weak; and to remember the words of the Lord Jesus, how he said, [y]It is more blessed to give than to receive.

36 And when he had thus

x Ro.15.1; Ep.4.28; 1 Th.5.14.

y Lu.14.12-14.

have not merely *discoursed* about it, but have *showed* you how to do it. ¶ *All things.* Or, in respect to all things. In everything that respects preaching and the proper mode of life, I have for three years set you an example, illustrating the design, nature, and duties of the office by my own self-denials and toil. ¶ *How that.* Or, *that*—ὅτι. I have showed you *that* ye should by so labouring support the weak. ¶ *So labouring.* Labouring as I have done. Setting this example, and ministering in this way to the wants of others. ¶ *To support the weak.* To provide for the wants of the sick and feeble members of the flock, who are unable to labour for themselves. The *weak* here denote the poor, the needy, the infirm. ¶ *And to remember.* To call to mind for encouragement, and with the force of a command. ¶ *The words of the Lord Jesus.* These words are nowhere recorded by the evangelists. But they did not pretend to record *all* his sayings and instructions. Comp. Jn. xxi. 25. There is the highest reason to suppose that many of his sayings which are not recorded would be treasured up by those who heard them; would be transmitted to others; and would be regarded as a precious part of his instructions. Paul evidently addresses the elders of Ephesus as if they had heard this before, and were acquainted with it. Perhaps he had himself reminded them of it. This is one of the Redeemer's most precious sayings; and it seems even to have a peculiar value from the fact that it is *not* recorded in the regular and professed histories of his life. It comes to us *recovered*, as it were, from the great mass of his unrecorded sayings; *rescued* from that oblivion to which it was hastening if left to mere tradition, and placed in permanent form in the sacred writings by the act of an apostle who had never seen the Saviour before his crucifixion. It is a precious relic—a memento of the Saviour—and the effect of it is to make us regret that more of his words were not recovered from an uncertain tradition, and placed in a permanent form by an inspired penman. God, however, who knows what is requisite to guide us, has directed the words which are needful for the welfare of the church, and has preserved by inspiration the doctrines which are adapted to convert and bless man. ¶ *It is more blessed to give.* It is a higher privilege; it tends more to the happiness of the individual and of the world. The giver is more blessed or happy than the receiver. This appears, (1) Because it is a condition for which we should be thankful when we are in a situation to promote the happiness of others. (2) Because it tends to promote the happiness of the benefactor himself. There is pleasure in the act of giving when it is done with pure motives. It promotes our own peace; is followed by happiness in the recollection of it; and will be followed by happiness for ever. That is the most truly happy man who is most benevolent. He is the most miserable who has never known the luxury of doing good, but who lives to gain all he can, and to hoard all he gains. (3) It is blessed in the reward that shall result from it. Those who give from a pure motive God will bless. They will be rewarded, not only in the peace which they shall experience in this life, but in the higher bliss of heaven, Mat. xxv. 34–36. We may also remark that this is a sentiment truly great and noble. It is worthy of the Son of God. It is that on which he himself acted when he came to *give* pardon to the guilty, comfort to the disconsolate and the mourner, peace to the anxious sinner, sight to the blind, hearing to the deaf, life to the dead, and heaven to the guilty and the lost. Acting on this, he *gave* his own tears to weep over human sorrows and human guilt; his own labours and toils to instruct and save man; his own life a sacrifice for sin on the cross. Loving to give, he has freely given us all things. Loving to give, he delights in the same character in his followers, and seeks that they who have wealth, and strength, and influence, should be willing to give all to save the world. Imitating his great example, and complying with his command, the church shall yet learn more and more to *give* its wealth to bless the poor and needy; its sons and its daughters to bear the gospel to the

spoken, [z]he kneeled down, and prayed with them all.

37 And they all wept sore, [a]and fell on Paul's neck, and kissed him,

38 Sorrowing most of all for the[b] words which he spake, that they should see his face no more. And they accompanied him unto the ship.

z ch.21.5. a Ge.46.29. b ver.25.

CHAPTER XXI.

AND it came to pass, that after we were gotten from them, and had launched, we came with a straight course unto Coos, and

---

benighted heathen; its undivided and constant efforts to save a lost world. Here closes this speech of Paul; an address of inimitable tenderness and beauty. Happy would it be if every minister could bid *such* an adieu to his people, when called to part from them; and happy if, at the close of life, every Christian could leave the world with a like consciousness that he had been faithful in the discharge of his duty. Thus dying, it will be blessed to leave the world; and thus would the example of the saints live in the memory of survivors long after they themselves have ascended to their rest.

36. *He kneeled down.* The usual attitude of prayer. It is the proper posture of a suppliant. It indicates reverence and humility; and is represented in the Scriptures as the usual attitude of devotion, 2 Ch. vi. 13; Da. vi. 10; Lu. xxii. 41; Ac. vii. 60; ix. 40; xxi. 5; Ro. xi. 4; Phi. ii. 10; Ep. iii. 14; Mar. i. 40.

37. *Wept sore.* Wept much. Greek, "There was a great weeping of all." ¶ *And fell on Paul's neck.* Embraced him, as a token of tender affection. The same thing Joseph did when he met his aged father Jacob, Ge. xlvi. 29. ¶ *And kissed him.* This was the common token of affection. See Notes on Mat. xxvi. 48; Lu. xv. 20; Ro. xvi. 16; 1 Co. xvi. 20.

38. *Sorrowing most of all*, &c. This was a most tender and affectionate parting scene. It can be more easily imagined than described. We may learn from it, (1) That the parting of ministers and people is a most solemn event, and should be one of much tenderness and affection. (2) The effect of true religion is to make the heart more tender; to make friendship more affectionate and sacred; and to unite more closely the bonds of love. (3) Ministers of the gospel should be prepared to leave their people with the same consciousness of fidelity and the same kindness and love which Paul evinced. They should live such lives as to be able to look back upon their whole ministry as pure and disinterested, and as having been employed in guarding the flock, and in making known to them the whole counsel of God. So parting, they may separate in peace; and so living and acting, they will be prepared to give up their account with joy, and not with grief. May God grant to every minister the spirit which Paul evinced at Ephesus, and enable each one, when called to leave his people by death or otherwise, to do it with the same consciousness of fidelity which Paul evinced when he left his people to see their face no more.

CHAPTER XXI.

1. *After we were gotten from them.* After we had left the elders at Miletus, ch. xx. 38. They were on their way to Jerusalem. ¶ *Unto Coos.* This was a small island in the Grecian Archipelago, a short distance from the south-western point of Asia Minor. It is now called *Stan-co.* It was celebrated for its fertility, and for the wine and silk-worms which it produced. It was about 40 miles south of Miletus. ¶ *Unto Rhodes.* This was also an island in the Grecian Archipelago. On the island was a city of the same name, which was principally distinguished for its brazen Colossus, which was built by Chares of Lyndus. It stood across the mouth of the harbour, and was so high that vessels could pass between its legs. It stood fifty-six years, and was then thrown down by an earthquake. It was reckoned as one of the seven wonders of the world. When the Saracens took possession of this island they sold this prostrate image to a Jew, who loaded 900 camels with the brass of it. This was A.D. 600, about 900 years after it had been thrown down. The ancient name of the island was Asteria. Its name, *Rhodes*, was given from the great quantity of *roses* which it produced. ¶ *Unto Patara.*

the *day* following unto Rhodes, and from thence unto Patara:

2 And finding a ship sailing over unto Phenicia, we went aboard, and set forth.

3 Now when we had discovered Cyprus, we left it on the left hand, and sailed into Syria, and landed at Tyre; for there the ship was to unlade her burden.

4 And finding disciples, we tarried there seven days; [a]who said to Paul through the Spirit that he should not go up to Jerusalem.

5 And when we had accomplished those days, we departed and went our way; and they all brought us on our way with wives

a ver.12.

This was a maritime city of Lycia, in Asia Minor, over against Rhodes.

2. *Into Phenicia.* See Notes on ch. xi. 19. Phœnicia was on their way to Jerusalem. ¶ *Set forth.* Sailed.

3. *Had discovered Cyprus.* See Notes on ch. iv. 36. ¶ *Into Syria.* See Notes on Mat. iv. 24. ¶ *And landed at Tyre.* See Notes on Mat. xi. 21. ¶ *To unlade her burden.* Her cargo. Tyre was formerly one of the most commercial cities of the world; and it is probable that in the time of Paul its commercial importance had not entirely ceased.

4. *And finding disciples.* Christians. This is the first mention of there being Christians at Tyre, but there is no improbability in supposing that the gospel had been preached there, though it is not expressly recorded by Luke. ¶ *Who said to Paul.* Comp. ver. 12. Their deep interest in his welfare, and their apprehension of his danger, was the reason why they admonished him not to go. ¶ *Through the Spirit.* There is some difficulty in understanding this. In solving this difficulty, we may remark, (1) That it is evident that the Holy Spirit is meant, and that Luke means to say that this was spoken by his inspiration. The Holy Spirit was bestowed on Christians at that time in large measures, and many appear to have been under his inspiring guidance. (2) It was not understood by Paul as a positive *command* that he should not go up to Jerusalem; for had it been, it would not have been disobeyed. He evidently understood it as expressive of their earnest wish that he should not go, as apprising him of danger, and as a kind expression in regard to his own welfare and safety. Comp. ver. 13. Paul was in better circumstances to understand this than we are, and his interpretation was doubtless correct. (3) It is to be understood, therefore, simply as an *inspired prophetic warning*, that if he went, he went at the risk of his life—a prophetic warning, joined with their individual personal wishes that he would not expose himself to this danger. The meaning evidently is that they said by inspiration of the Spirit that he should not go unless he was willing to encounter danger, for they foresaw that the journey would be attended with the hazard of his life. Grotius renders it, "That he should not go *unless he was willing to be* bound." Michaelis and Stolzius, "They gave him prophetic warning that he should not go to Jerusalem." Doddridge, "If he tendered his own liberty and safety, not to go up to Jerusalem, since it would certainly expose him to very great hazard." The inspiration in the case was that of admonition and warning, not of positive command. Paul was simply apprised of the danger, and was then left to the free determination of his own will. He chose to encounter the danger of which he was thus apprised. He did not despise the intimations of the Spirit, but he judged that his duty to God called him thus to meet the perils of the journey. We may be apprised of danger in a certain course, either by our friends or by the word of God, and still it may be our duty to meet it. Our duty is not to be measured by the fact that we shall experience *danger*, in whatever way that may be made known to us. Duty consists in following the will of God, and *encountering* whatever trials may be in our way.

5. *Had accomplished those days.* When those days were passed. ¶ *They all brought us on our way.* They attended us. See Notes on ch. xv. 3; Ro. xv. 24; 1 Co. xvi. 6, 11; 3 Jn. 6. This was an expression of tender attachment, and of a deep interest in the welfare of Paul and his fellow-travellers. ¶ *We kneeled down.* See Notes on ch. xx. 36. ¶ *On the shore.* Any place may be proper for prayer. See Notes on Jn. iv. 21–24. God is everywhere, and can as easily hear

and children, till *we were* out of
the city; and we [b]kneeled down
on the shore, and prayed.
6 And when we had taken our
leave one of another, we took ship;
and they returned home again.
7 And when we had finished *our*
course from Tyre, we came to Ptolemais,
and saluted the brethren,
and abode with them one day.
8 And the next *day*, we that
were of Paul's company departed,
and came unto Cesarea; and we
entered into the house of [c]Philip
the [d]evangelist, which was [e]*one* of
the seven; and abode with him.
9 And the same man had four
daughters, virgins, [f]which did prophesy.
10 And as we tarried *there* many
days, there came down from Judea
a certain prophet named [g]Agabus.

b ch.20.36.

c ch.8.26-40. d Ep.4.11; 2 Ti.4.5. e ch.6.5. f Joel 2.28; ch.2.17. g ch.11.28.

prayer on the sea-shore as in the most magnificent temple. This is an instance, as well as that in ch. xx. 36, where the apostle evidently prayed with the church without a form of prayer. No man can believe that he thus poured forth the desires of his heart at parting, and commended them to God in a *prescribed form of words*. Scenes like this show more clearly than abstract arguments could do that such a form was not needed, and would not be used. Paul and his fellow-Christians, on the sand of the sea-shore, would pour forth the gushing emotions of their souls in language such as their circumstances would suggest, and no man can read this narrative in a dispassionate manner without believing that they offered an *extempore* prayer.

7. *We came to Ptolemais.* This was a city situated on the coast of the Mediterranean, on the north angle of a bay which extends, in a semicircle of three leagues, as far as the point of Mount Carmel. At the south and west sides the city was washed by the sea, and was surrounded by triple walls. It was in the tribe of Asher (Ju. i. 31), and was originally called ACCHO; but was called *Ptolemais* in honour of one of the *Ptolemies*, who beautified and adorned it. The Christian crusaders gave it the name of Acre, or St. John of Acre, from a magnificent church which was built in it, and which was dedicated to the apostle John. It is still called *Akha* by the Turks. The Syriac and Arabic render it *Accho* in this place. It sustained several sieges during the Crusades, and was the last fortified place wrested from the Christians by the Turks. It sustained a memorable siege under Bonaparte, and since then it has been much increased and strengthened. Its present population is estimated at from 18,000 to 20,000. ¶ *And saluted the brethren.* Embraced them; gave them expressions of affection and regard.

8. *We that were of Paul's company.* From this it would appear that they had been attended thus far by some persons who were going only to Ptolemais. This clause, however, is wanting in many MSS., and has been omitted by Bengel, Griesbach, Knapp, and others as spurious. It is also wanting in the Syriac and the Vulgate. ¶ *Unto Cesarea.* See Notes on ch. viii. 40. ¶ *Into the house of Philip.* One of the seven deacons, ch. vi. 5. After his conversation with the eunuch of Ethiopia, he went to Cesarea, and probably there abode. ¶ *The evangelist.* This word properly means one who announces good news. In the New Testament it is applied to a preacher of the gospel, or one who declares the glad tidings of salvation. It occurs only in two other places, Ep. iv. 11; 2 Ti. iv. 5. What was the precise rank of those who bore this title in the early Christian church cannot perhaps be determined. It is evident, however, that it is used to denote the office of preaching the gospel; and as this title is applied to *Philip*, and not to any other of the seven deacons, it would seem probable that he had been intrusted with a special commission to *preach*, and that *preaching* did not pertain to him *as a deacon*, and does not properly belong to that office. The business of a deacon was to take care of the poor members of the church, ch. vi. 1–6. The office of preaching was distinct from this, though, as in this case, it might be conferred on the same individual.

9. *Which did prophesy.* See Notes on ch. ii. 17; xi. 27. That females sometimes partook of the prophetic influence, and foretold future events, is evident

11 And when he was come unto
us, he took Paul's girdle, and bound
his own hands and feet, and said,
Thus saith the Holy Ghost, [h] So
shall the Jews at Jerusalem bind
the man that owneth this girdle,
and shall deliver *him* into the
hands of the Gentiles.
12 And when we heard these
things, both we, and they of that
place, [i] besought him not to go up
to Jerusalem.
13 Then Paul answered, What
mean ye to weep and to break mine
heart? for [k] I am ready not to be
bound only, but also to die at Jerusalem
for the name of the Lord
Jesus.

h ver.33; ch.20.23. *i* Mat.16.22,23. *k* 2 Ti.4.6.

from various places in the New Testament. See Notes on ch. ii. 17.

10. *There came down.* See Notes on ch. xv. 1. ¶ *Named Agabus.* See Notes on ch. xi. 28.

11. *He took Paul's girdle.* The loose, flowing robes, or outer garments, which were worn in Eastern countries, were bound by a *girdle*, or *sash*, around the body when they ran, or laboured, or walked. Such a girdle was therefore an indispensable part of dress. ¶ *And bound his own hands and feet.* As emblematic of what would be done by the Jews to Paul. It was common for the prophets to perform actions which were emblematic of the events which they predicted. The design was to make the prediction more forcible and impressive by representing it to the eye. Thus Jeremiah was directed to bury his girdle by the Euphrates, to denote the approaching captivity of the Jews, Je. xiii. 4. Thus he was directed to make bands and yokes, and to put them around his neck, as a sign to Edom and Moab, &c., Je. xxvii. 2, 3. Thus the act of the potter was emblematic of the destruction that was coming upon the nation of the Jews, Je. xviii. 4. So Isaiah walked naked and barefoot as a sign of the captivity of Egypt and Ethiopia, Is. xx. 3, 4. Comp. Eze. iv. xii. &c. ¶ *So shall the Jews,* &c. This was fulfilled. See ver. 33, and ch. xxiv. ¶ *Into the hands of the Gentiles.* To be tried; for the Romans then had jurisdiction over Judea.

13. *What mean ye.* Greek, What do ye. A tender and affectionate, but firm reproach. ¶ *To weep and to break mine heart?* To afflict me, and distract my mind by alarms, and by the expressions of tenderness. His mind was fixed on going to Jerusalem; and he felt that he was prepared for whatever awaited him. Expressions of tenderness among friends are proper. Tears may be inevitable at parting from those whom we love. But such expressions of love ought not to be allowed to interfere with the convictions of duty in their minds. If they have made up their minds that a certain course is proper, and have resolved to pursue it, we ought neither to attempt to divert them from it, nor to distract their minds by our remonstrances or our tears. We should resign them to *their* convictions of what is demanded of them with affection and prayer, but with cheerfulness. We should lend them all the aid in our power, and then commend them to the blessing and protection of God. These remarks apply especially to those who are engaged in the missionary enterprise. It is trying to part with a son, a daughter, or a beloved friend, in order that they may go to proclaim the gospel to the benighted and dying heathen. The act of parting—*for life*, and the apprehension of the perils which they may encounter on the ocean, and in heathen lands, may be painful; but if they, like Paul, have looked at it calmly, candidly, and with much prayer; if they have come to the deliberate conclusion that it is the will of God that they should devote their lives to this service, we ought not to weep and to break their hearts. We should cheerfully and confidently commit them to the protection of the God whom they serve, and remember that the parting of Christians, though for life, will be short. Soon, in a better world, they will be united again, to part no more; and the blessedness of that future meeting will be greatly heightened by all the sorrows and self-denials of separation here, and by all the benefits which such a separation may be the means of conveying to a dying world. That mother will meet, with joy, in heaven, the son from whom, with many tears, she was sundered when he entered on a missionary life; and, surrounded with many ransomed heathen, heaven will be made more blessed

14 And when he would not be persuaded, we ceased, saying, [l]The will of the Lord be done.

15 And after those days we took up our carriages, and went up to Jerusalem.

16 There went with us also *certain* of the disciples of Cesarea, and brought with them one Mnason of Cyprus, [m]an old disciple, with whom we should lodge.

17 And when we were come to Jerusalem, [n]the brethren received us gladly.

18 And the *day* following Paul went in with us unto [o]James; and all the elders were present.

19 And when he had saluted

l Mat.6.10; 26.42.

m Pr.16.31. *n* ch.15.4. *o* ch.15.13,&c.; Ga.1.19.

---

and eternity more happy. ¶ *But also to die.* This was the true spirit of a martyr. This spirit reigned in the hearts of all the early Christians. ¶ *For the name of the Lord Jesus.* For his sake; in making his name known.

14. *Would not be persuaded.* To remain. He was resolved to go. ¶ *We ceased.* We ceased remonstrating with him, and urging him to remain. ¶ *The will of the Lord be done.* They were now assured that it was the will of God that he should go, and they were now ready to submit to that will. This is an instance and an evidence of true piety. It was the expression of a wish that whatever God might judge to be necessary for the advancement of his cause might take place, even though it should be attended with many trials. They commended their friend to the protection of God, confident that whatever should occur would be right. Comp. Notes on Mat. vi. 10; xxvi. 42.

15. *After those days.* After what had occurred, as related in the previous verses. ¶ *We took up our carriages.* This is a most unhappy translation. The word *carriage* we apply now exclusively to a vehicle for conveying anything—as a coach, chariot, gig, cannon carriage, &c. The original word means simply that they prepared themselves; made themselves ready; put their baggage in order, &c.—ἀποσκευασάμενοι. They prepared for the journey. The English word *carriage* was formerly used in the sense of *that which is carried*, baggage, burden, vessels, furniture, &c. Thus it was used in the time that our translation was made; and in this sense it is to be understood in 1 Sa. xvii. 22, "And David left his *carriage* [baggage] in the hand of the keeper of the carriage," &c. See ver. 20, margin; Is. x. 28, "At Michmash he hath laid up his *carriages*" [his baggage, &c.].

16. *One Mnason of Cyprus.* The original in this place would be better translated, "And brought us *to* Mnason of Cyprus, an old disciple," &c. It is evident that, though Mnason was originally of Cyprus, yet he was now an inhabitant of Jerusalem, and was well known to the disciples at Cesarea. It is possible that he might have been at Cesarea, and accompanied Paul to Jerusalem; but the more correct interpretation of the passage is, that Paul and his fellow-travellers were conducted *to* his house in Jerusalem, and that he was not with them in the journey. ¶ *Of Cyprus.* See Notes on ch. iv. 36. ¶ *An old disciple.* An early convert to Christianity—perhaps one who was converted before the crucifixion of the Saviour. ¶ *With whom we should lodge.* In whose house we were to take up our abode. The rites of hospitality were shown in a distinguished manner by the early Christians.

17. *The brethren.* Christians. ¶ *Received us gladly.* They had been long absent. They had been into distant regions, and had encountered many dangers. It was a matter of joy that they had now returned in safety.

18. *Unto James.* James the Less. See Notes on ch. xv. 13. He resided at Jerusalem. Comp. Ga. i. 19. It is not improbable that he was the only one of the apostles then at Jerusalem; and there is reason to believe that the church at Jerusalem was left under his particular care. It was natural, therefore, that Paul and his companions should take an early opportunity to see him. James was the cousin of our Lord, and in Ga. i. 19 he is called the Lord's brother. On all accounts, therefore, he was entitled to, and would receive, particular respect from the early disciples.

19. *Had saluted them.* With the usual tokens of respect and affection. ¶ *He declared particularly*, &c. As an evidence that God had been with him. It is not improbable that there might have been some suspicion in regard to

them, he [p] declared particularly what things God had wrought among the Gentiles [q] by his ministry.

20 And when they heard *it*, they glorified the Lord; and said unto him, Thou seest, brother, how many thousands of Jews there are which believe; and [r] they are all zealous of the law:

21 And they are informed of thee, that thou teachest all the Jews which are among the Gentiles to forsake Moses, [s] saying that

p Ro.15.18,19. q ch.20.24; 2 Co.12.12. r ch.22.3; Ro.10.2. s Ga.5.3.

Paul among the disciples at Jerusalem, and he might have heard that they were prejudiced against him. This prejudice would be removed by his stating what had actually occurred under his ministry.

20. *They glorified the Lord.* They gave praise to the Lord for what he had done. They saw new proofs of his goodness and mercy, and they rendered him thanks for all that had been accomplished. There was no jealousy that it had been done by the instrumentality of Paul. True piety will rejoice in the spread of the gospel, and in the conversion of sinners, by whatever instrumentality it may be effected. ¶ *Thou seest, brother.* The language of tenderness in this address, recognizing Paul as a fellow-labourer and fellow-Christian, implies a wish that Paul would do all that could be done to avoid giving offence, and to conciliate the favour of his countrymen. ¶ *How many thousands.* The number of converts at this time must have been very great. Twenty-five years before this, three thousand had been converted at one time (ch. ii.), and afterward the number had swelled to some more thousands, ch. iv. 4. The assertion that there were then "many thousands," implies that the work so signally begun on the day of Pentecost in Jerusalem had not ceased, and that many more had been converted to the Christian faith. ¶ *Which believe.* Who are Christians. They are spoken of as *believers*, or as having faith in Christ, in contradistinction from those who rejected him, and whose characteristic trait it was that they were *unbelievers.* ¶ *And they are all zealous of the law.* They still observe the law of Moses. The reference here is to the law respecting circumcision, sacrifices, distinctions of meats and days, festivals, &c. It may seem remarkable that they should still continue to observe those rites, since it was the manifest design of Christianity to abolish them. But we are to remember, (1) That those rites had been appointed by God, and that they were trained to their observance. (2) That the apostles conformed to them while they remained at Jerusalem, and did not deem it best to set themselves violently against them, ch. iii. 1; Lu. xxiv. 53. (3) That the question about their observance had never been agitated at Jerusalem. It was only among the Gentile converts that the question had risen, and there it *must* arise, for if they were to be observed, they must have been *imposed* upon them by authority. (4) The decision of the council (ch. xv.) related only to the *Gentile* converts. It did not touch the question whether those rites were to be observed by the *Jewish* converts. (5) It was to be presumed that as the Christian religion became better understood—that as its large, free, and catholic nature became more and more developed, the peculiar institutions of Moses would be laid aside of course, without agitation and without tumult. Had the question been agitated at Jerusalem, it would have excited tenfold opposition to Christianity, and would have rent the Christian church into factions, and greatly retarded the advance of the Christian doctrine. We are to remember also, (6) That, in the arrangement of divine Providence, the time was drawing near which was to destroy the temple, the city, and the nation, which was to put an end to sacrifices, and *effectually* to close for ever the observance of the Mosaic rites. As this destruction was so near, and as it would be so effectual an *argument* against the observance of the Mosaic rites, the Great Head of the church did not suffer the question of their obligation to be needlessly agitated among the disciples at Jerusalem.

21. *And they are informed of thee.* Reports respecting the conduct of Paul would be likely to be in circulation among all at Jerusalem. His remarkable conversion, his distinguished zeal, his success among the Gentiles, would

they ought not to circumcise *their*
children, neither to walk after their
customs.
22 What is it therefore? the
multitude must needs [t]come to-

t ch.19.32.

gether; for they will hear that
thou art come.
23 Do therefore this that we
say to thee: We have four men
which have a vow on them;
24 Them take, and purify thy-

---

make his conduct a subject of special interest. Evil-minded men among the Jews, who came up to Jerusalem from different places where he had been, would be likely to represent him as the decided enemy of the laws of Moses, and these reports would be likely to reach the ears of the Jewish converts. The reports, as they gained ground, would be greatly magnified, until suspicion might be excited among the Christians at Jerusalem that he was, as he was reputed to be, the settled foe of the Jewish rites and customs. ¶ *That thou teachest all the Jews*, &c. From all the evidence which we have of his conduct, this report was incorrect and slanderous. The truth appears to have been, that he did not enjoin the observance of those laws on the Gentile converts; that the effect of his ministry on them was to lead them to suppose that their observance was not necessary — contrary to the doctrines of the Judaizing teachers (see ch. xv.); and that he argued with the Jews themselves, where it could be done, against the *obligation* of those laws and customs since the Messiah had come. The Jews depended on their observance for justification and salvation. This Paul strenuously opposed; and this view he defended at length in the epistles which he wrote. See the epistles to the Romans, the Galatians, and the Hebrews. Yet these facts might be easily misunderstood and perverted, so as to give rise to the slanderous report that he was the enemy of Moses and the law. ¶ *Which are among the Gentiles.* Who live in heathen countries. The Jews were extensively scattered and settled in all the large towns and cities of the Roman empire. ¶ *To forsake Moses.* The law and authority of Moses. That is, to regard his laws as no longer binding. ¶ *To walk after the customs.* To observe the institutions of the Mosaic ritual. See Notes on ch. vi. 14. The word *customs* denotes the *rites* of the Mosaic economy—the offering of sacrifices, incense, the oblations, anointings, festivals, &c., which the law of Moses prescribed.

22. *What is it therefore?* What is to be done? What is it proper to do to avoid the effects of the evil report which has been circulated? What they deemed it proper to do is suggested in the following verses. ¶ *The multitude.* The multitude of Jews. ¶ *Must needs come together.* There will be inevitably a tumultuous assemblage. It will be impossible to prevent that. The reasons were, because the minds of the Jews were exceedingly agitated that one of their own countrymen had, as they understood, been advising *apostasy* from the religion of their fathers; because this had been extensively done in many parts of the world, and with great success; and because Paul, having, as they believed, himself apostatized from the national religion, had become very conspicuous, and his very presence in Jerusalem, as in other places, would be likely to excite a tumult. It was, therefore, the part of friendship to him and to the cause to devise some proper plan to prevent, if possible, the anticipated excitement.

23. *We have four men.* There are with us four men. It is evident that James and the elders meant to say that these men were connected with them in the Christian church; and the fact shows that the Christians at Jerusalem did not disregard the institutions of Moses, and had not been so far enlightened in the doctrines of Christianity as to forsake yet the ceremonial rites of the Jews. ¶ *Which have a vow on them.* Which have made a vow. See Notes on ch. xviii. 18. From the mention of shaving the head (in ver. 24), it is evident that the vow which they had taken was that of the *Nazarite;* and that as the time of their vow was about expiring, they were about to be shaven, in accordance with the custom usual on such occasions. See Notes on ch. xviii. 18. These persons Paul could join, and thus show decisively that he did not intend to undervalue or disparage the laws of Moses when those laws were understood as mere ceremonial observances.

self with them, and be at charges with them, that they may [u]shave *their* heads; and all may know that those things whereof they were informed concerning thee are nothing, but *that* thou thyself also walkest orderly, and keepest the law.

25 As touching the Gentiles which believe, [v]we have written, *and* concluded that they observe no such thing, save only that they

u Nu.6.2,13,18; ch.18.18.

v ch.15.20,29.

24. *Them take.* Take with you. Join yourself with them. ¶ *And purify thyself with them.* Join them in observing the forms of purification prescribed by the law of Moses in the observance of the vow of the Nazarite. The *purifying* here refers to the vows of sanctity which the Nazarites were to observe. They were to abstain from wine and strong drink; they were to eat no grapes, moist or dried; they were to come near no dead body, nor to make themselves "unclean" for their father, mother, brother, or sister, when they died (Nu. vi. 3-7); and they were to present an offering when the days of the vow were completed, Nu. vi. 8. ¶ *And be at charges with them.* Share with them the expense of the offerings required when the vow is completed. Those offerings were a ram of a year old for a burnt-offering, a sheep of the same age for a sin-offering, a ram for a thank-offering, a basket of unleavened cakes, and a libation of wine. See Nu. vi. 13–20. ¶ *That they may shave their heads.* The shaving of the head, or the cutting off the hair which had been suffered to grow during the continuance of the vow (Nu. vi. 5), was an observance indicating that the vow had been performed. Paul was requested to join with them in the expense of the offerings, that thus, the whole of the ceremonies having been observed, their heads might be shaved as an indication that every part of the vow had been complied with. ¶ *And all may know.* By the fact of your observance of one of the rites of the Mosaic religion, all may have evidence that it is not your purpose or practice to speak contemptuously of those rites, or to undervalue the authority of Moses. ¶ *Are nothing.* Are untrue, or without any foundation. ¶ *Walkest orderly.* That you live in accordance with the real requirements of the law of Moses. To *walk*, in the Scriptures, often denotes *to live*, *to act*, *to conduct* in a certain manner. All, probably, that they wished Paul to show by this was, that he was not an enemy of Moses. They who gave this counsel were Christians, and they could not wish him to do anything which would imply that *he* was not a Christian.

25. *As touching the Gentiles.* In regard to the Gentile converts. It might be *expedient* for Paul to do what could not be *enjoined* on the Gentiles. They could not *command* the Gentile converts to observe those ceremonies, while yet it might be proper, for the sake of peace, that the converts to Christianity from among the Jews should regard them. The conduct of the Christians at Jerusalem in giving this advice, and of Paul in following it, may be easily vindicated. If it be objected, as it has been by infidels, that it looks like double-dealing; that it was designed to *deceive* the Jews in Jerusalem, and to make them believe that Paul actually conformed to the ceremonial law, when his conduct among the Gentiles showed that he did not, we may reply, (1) That the observance of that law was not necessary in order to salvation; (2) That it would have been improper to have enjoined its observance on the Gentile converts as necessary, and therefore it was never done; (3) That when the Jews urged its observance as necessary to justification and salvation, Paul strenuously *opposed* this view of it everywhere; (4) Yet that, as a matter of expediency, he did not oppose its being observed either by the Jews, or by the converts made among the Jews. In fact, there is other evidence besides the case before us that Paul himself continued to observe some, at least, of the Jewish rites, and his conduct in public at Jerusalem was in strict accordance with his conduct in other places. See ch. xviii. 18. The sum of the whole matter is this, that when the observance of the Jewish ceremonial law was urged as necessary to justification and acceptance with God, Paul resisted it; when it was demanded that its observance should be enjoined on the Gentiles, he opposed it; in all other cases he made *no* opposition to it, and was ready himself to comply

keep themselves from *things* offered
to idols, and from blood, and from
strangled, and from fornication.
26 Then Paul [w]took the men;
and the next day, purifying himself with them, [x]entered into the
temple, to signify [y]the accomplishment of the days of purification,
until that an offering should be
offered for every one of them.
27 And when the seven days
were almost ended, [z]the Jews
which were of Asia, when they
saw him in the temple, stirred up

w 1 Co.9.20. x ch.24.18. y Nu.6.13. z ch.24.18.

---

with it, and willing that others should also. ¶ *We have written.* Ch. xv. 20, 29.

26. *Then Paul took the men.* Took them to himself; united with them in observing the ceremonies connected with their vow. To transactions like this he refers in 1 Co. ix. 20: "And unto the Jews I became as a Jew, that I might gain the Jews; to them that are under the law, as under the law, that I might gain them that are under the law." Thus it has always been found necessary, in propagating the gospel among the heathen, not to offend them needlessly, but to conform to their innocent customs in regard to dress, language, modes of travelling, sitting, eating, &c. Paul did nothing more than this. He violated none of the dictates of honesty and truth. ¶ *Purifying himself with them.* Observing the ceremonies connected with the rite of purification. See Notes on ver. 24. This means evidently that he *entered* on the ceremonies of the separation according to the law of the Nazarite. ¶ *To signify.* Greek, signifying or making known. That is, he announced to the priests in the temple his purpose of observing this vow with the four men, according to the law respecting the Nazarite. It was proper that such an announcement should be made beforehand, in order that the priests might know that all the ceremonies required had been observed. ¶ *The accomplishment,* &c. The fulfilling, the completion. That is, he announced to them his purpose to observe all the days and all the rites of purification required in the law, in order that an offering might be properly made. It does not mean that the days *had been* accomplished, but that it was his intention to observe them, *so that* it would be proper to offer the usual sacrifice. Paul had not, indeed, engaged with them *in the beginning* of their vow of separation, but he might come in with hearty intention to share with them. It cannot be objected that he meant to impose on the priests, and to make them believe that he had observed the whole vow with them, for it appears from their own writings (*Bereshith Rabba*, 90, and *Koheleth Rabba*, 7) that in those instances where the Nazarites had not sufficient property to enable them to meet the whole expense of the offerings, other persons, who possessed more, might become sharers of it, and thus be made parties to the vow. See Jahn's *Archæology*, § 395. This circumstance will vindicate Paul from any intention to take an improper advantage, or to impose on the priests or the Jews. All that he announced was his intention to *share* with the four men in the offering which they were required to make, and thus to show his *approval* of the thing, and his accordance with the law which made such a vow proper. ¶ *Until that an offering,* &c. The sacrifices required of all those who had observed this vow. See Notes on ver. 24. Comp. Nu. vi. 13. It is a complete vindication of Paul in this case that he did no more here than he had done in a voluntary manner (ch. xviii. 18), and as appears then in a secret manner, showing that he was still in the practice of observing this rite of the Mosaic institution. Nor can it be proved that Paul ever, *in any way*, or *at any time*, spoke against the vow of the Nazarite, or that a vow of a similar kind in spirit would be improper for a Christian in any circumstances.

27. *And when the seven days were almost ended.* Greek, as the seven days were about to be fulfilled—ἔμελλον συντελεῖσθαι. The seven days which were to complete the observance of the vow, ver. 26. Perhaps the whole observance in this case was intended to be but seven days, as the *time* of such a vow was voluntary. The translation, "were almost ended," is not quite correct. The Greek implies no more than that the period of the seven days was *about to be accomplished*, without implying that it was near the close of them when he was seized. By

all the people, and [a]laid hands on him,

28 Crying out, Men of Israel, help; this is the man that [b]teacheth all *men* every where against the people, and the law, and this place; and further, brought Greeks also into the temple, and hath polluted this holy place.

29 (For they had seen before with him in the city [c]Trophimus an Ephesian, whom they supposed that Paul had brought into the temple.)

30 And all the city was moved, and the people ran together; and they took Paul, and drew him out of the temple; and forthwith the doors were shut.

31 And as they [d]went about to

a ch.26.21. *b* ch.6.13,14; 24.5,6. *c* ch.20.4. *d* 2 Co.11.23,&c.

comparing the following places, ch. xxi. 18, 26; xxii. 30; xxiii. 12, 32; xxiv. 1, 11, it appears that the time of his seizure must have been near the beginning of those days (Doddridge). ¶ *The Jews which were of Asia.* Who resided in Asia Minor, but who had come up to Jerusalem for purposes of worship. Comp. Notes on ch. ii.

28. *Men of Israel.* Jews. All who are the friends of the law of Moses. ¶ *This is the man,* &c. This implies that they had before given information to the Jews at Jerusalem that there was such a man, and they now exulted in the fact that they had found him. They therefore called on all these to aid in securing and punishing him. ¶ *That teacheth,* &c. See Notes on ch. vi. 13, 14. ¶ *Against the people.* The people of the Jews. That is, they pretended that he taught that the customs and laws of the Jewish nation were not binding, and endeavoured to prejudice all men against them. ¶ *And the law.* The law of Moses. ¶ *And this place.* The temple. Everything against the law would be interpreted also as being against the temple, as most of the ceremonies required in the law were celebrated there. It is possible also that Paul might have declared that the temple was to be destroyed. Comp. ch. vi. 13, 14. ¶ *And further, brought Greeks,* &c. The temple was surrounded by various areas called *courts.* See Notes on Mat. xxi. 12. The outermost of these courts was called the court of the Gentiles, and into that it was lawful for the Gentiles to enter. But the word "temple" here refers, doubtless, to the parts of the area appropriated especially to the Israelites, and which it was unlawful for a Gentile to enter. These parts are marked G G G G in the plan of the temple, Mat. xxi. 12. ¶ *And hath polluted,* &c. He has defiled the temple by thus introducing a Gentile. No greater defilement, in their view, could scarcely be conceived. No more effective appeal could be made to the passions of the people than this.

29. *In the city.* In Jerusalem. As he was with Paul, it was *inferred* that he would attend him everywhere. ¶ *Trophimus.* He had accompanied Paul on his way from Ephesus, ch. xx. 4. ¶ *Whom they supposed,* &c. This is a most striking illustration of the manner in which accusations are often brought against others. They had *seen* him with Paul in the city; they *inferred,* therefore, that he had been with him in the temple. They did not even pretend that they had *seen* him in the temple; but the inference was enough to inflame the angry and excitable passions of the multitude. So in the accusations which men now often make of others. They *see* one thing, they *infer* another; they could *testify* to one thing, but they *conclude* that another thing will also be true, and that *other thing* they charge on them as the truth. If men would state facts as they are, no small part of the slanderous accusations against others would cease. An end would be made of the most of the charges of falsehood, error, heresy, dishonesty, double-dealing, and immorality. If a statement is made, it should be of the thing as it was. If we attempt to say what a man has done, it should not be what we *suppose* he has done. If we attempt to state what he *believes,* it should not be what we *suppose* he believes.

30. *The city was moved.* Was agitated; was thrown into commotion. ¶ *Drew him out of the temple.* Under the pretence that he had defiled it. The evident design was to put him to death, ver. 31. ¶ *The doors were shut.* The doors leading into the courts of the temple.

31. *And as they went about to kill him.* Greek, they *seeking* to kill him. This

kill him, tidings came unto the
chief captain of the band that all
Jerusalem was in an uproar:
32 Who[e] immediately took soldiers and centurions, and ran down
unto them; and when they saw
the chief captain and the soldiers,
they left beating of Paul.
33 Then the chief captain came
near, and took him, and commanded
him to be [f] bound with two chains;
and demanded who he was, and
what he had done.
34 And some cried one thing,
some another, among the multitude; and when he could not
know the certainty for the tumult,
he commanded him to be carried
into [g] the castle.
35 And when he came upon the
stairs, so it was, that he was borne
of the soldiers [h] for the violence of
the people.
36 For the multitude of the people
followed after, crying, [i] Away with
him!
37 And as Paul was to be led

e ch.23.27; 24.7. f ver.11; ch.20.23; Ep.6.20.

g ch.23.10,16. h Ps.55.9; Hab.1.3. i Lu.23.18; Jn.19.15; ch.22.22; 1 Co.4.13.

---

was evidently done in a popular tumult, as had been done in the case of Stephen, ch. vii. They could not pretend that they had a right to do it by law. ¶ *Tidings came.* The news, or rumour came; he was told of it. ¶ *The chief captain of the band.* This band or body of Roman soldiers was stationed in the castle Antonia, on the north of the temple. This was built by John Hyrcanus, high-priest of the Jews, and was by him called *Baris.* It was beautified and strengthened by Herod the Great, and was called *Antonia* in honour of his friend, Mark Antony. Josephus describes this castle as consisting of four towers, one of which overlooked the temple, and which he says was 70 cubits high (*Jewish Wars*, b. v. ch. v. § 8). In this castle a guard of Roman soldiers was stationed to secure the temple and to maintain the peace. The commander of this cohort is here called "the chief captain." Reference is made to this guard several times in the New Testament, Mat. xxvii. 65, 66; Jn. xviii. 12; Ac. v. 26. The word translated "chief captain" denotes properly one who commanded a thousand men. The *band* (σπεῖρα) was the tenth part of a legion, and consisted sometimes of four hundred and twenty-five soldiers, at others of five hundred, and at others of six hundred, according to the size of the legion. The name of this captain was Claudius Lysias, ch. xxiii. 26. ¶ *In an uproar.* That the whole city was in commotion.

32. *Centurions.* Captains of a hundred men.

33. *To be bound with two chains.* To show to the enraged multitude that he did not intend to rescue anyone from justice, but to keep the peace. Paul's being thus bound would convince them of his determination that justice should be done in the case. Probably he was bound between two soldiers, his right arm to the left arm of the one, and his left arm to the right arm of the other. See Notes on ch. xii. 6. Or, if his hands and feet were bound, it is evident that it was so done that he was able still to walk, ver. 37, 38. This was in accordance with the prediction of Agabus, ch. xxi. 11.

34. *Into the castle.* The castle of Antonia, where the guard was kept. See Notes on ver. 31. Comp. ch. xxiii. 10, 16.

35. *Upon the stairs.* The stairs which led from the temple to the castle of Antonia. Josephus says (*Jewish Wars*, b. v. ch. v. § 8), that the castle of Antonia "was situated at the corner of two cloisters of the temple, of that on the west, and of that on the north; it was erected on a rock of 50 cubits [75 feet] in height, and was on a great precipice. On the corner where it joined to the two cloisters of the temple, *it had passages down to them both, through* which the guards went several ways among the cloisters with their arms, on the Jewish festivals, &c." It was on these stairs, as the soldiers were returning, that the tumult was so great, or the crowd so dense, that they were obliged to bear Paul along to rescue him from their violence. ¶ *The violence of the people.* The *rush* of the multitude.

36. *Away with him!* That is, to death. Comp. Lu. xxiii. 18.

37. *May I speak unto thee?* May I have the privilege of making my defence before thee; or of stating the

into the castle, he said unto the chief captain, May I speak unto thee? Who said, Canst thou speak Greek?

38 Art not thou that [1]Egyptian, which before these days madest an uproar, and leddest out into the

[1] This Egyptian rose A.D. 55, ch.5.36.

case truly; the cause of my accusation; of this tumult, &c. ¶ *Canst thou speak Greek?* Implying that if he could, he might be permitted to speak to him. The Greek language was that which was then almost universally spoken, and it is not improbable that it was the native tongue of the chief captain. It is evident that he was not a Roman by birth, for he says (ch. xxii. 28) that he had obtained the privilege of citizenship by paying a great sum. The language which the Jews spoke was the Syro-Chaldaic; and as he took Paul to be an Egyptian Jew (ver. 38), he supposed, from that circumstance also, that he was not able to speak the Greek language.

38. *Art not thou that Egyptian?* That Egyptian was probably a Jew who resided in Egypt. Josephus has given an account of this Egyptian which strikingly accords with the statement here recorded by Luke. See Josephus, *Antiq.*, b. xx. ch. viii. § 6, and *Jewish Wars*, b. ii. ch. xiii. § 5. The account which he gives is, that this Egyptian, whose name he does not mention, came from Egypt to Jerusalem, and said that he was a prophet, and advised the multitude of the common people to go with him to the Mount of Olives. He said further that he would show them from thence how the walls of Jerusalem would fall down; and he promised them that he would procure for them an entrance through those walls when they were fallen down. Josephus adds (*Jewish Wars*) that he got together thirty thousand men that were deluded by him; "these he led round about *from the wilderness* to the mount which was called the Mount of Olives, and was ready to break into Jerusalem by force from that place. But Felix, who was apprised of his movements, marched against him with the Roman soldiers, and discomfited him, and slew four hundred of them, and took two hundred alive. But the Egyptian escaped himself out of the fight, but did not appear any more." It was natural that the Roman tribune should suppose that Paul was this Egyptian, and that his return had produced this commotion and excitement among the people. ¶ *Madest an uproar.* Producing a sedition, or a *rising* among the people. Gr., "That Egyptian, who before these days having risen up." ¶ *Into the wilderness.* This corresponds remarkably with the account of Josephus. He indeed mentions that he led his followers to the Mount of Olives, but he expressly says that "he led them round about from the wilderness." This wilderness was the wild and uncultivated mountainous tract of country lying to the east of Jerusalem, and between it and the river Jordan. See Notes on Mat. iii. 1. It is also another striking coincidence showing the truth of the narrative, that neither Josephus nor Luke mention the *name* of this Egyptian, though he was so prominent and acted so distinguished a part. ¶ *Four thousand men.* There is here a remarkable discrepancy between the chief captain and Josephus. The latter says that there were thirty thousand men. In regard to this, the following remarks may be made. (1) This cannot be alleged to convict Luke of a false statement, for his record is, that the *chief captain* made the statement, and it cannot be proved that Luke has put into his mouth words which he did not utter. All that he is responsible for is a correct *report* of what the Roman tribune *said*, not the truth or falsehood of his statement. It is certainly *possible* that that might have been the common estimate of the number then, and that the account given by Josephus might have been made from more correct information. Or it is possible, certainly, that the statement by Josephus is incorrect. (2) If Luke *were* to be held responsible for the statement of the number, yet it remains to be shown that he is not as credible a historian as Josephus. Why should Josephus be esteemed infallible, and Luke false? Why should the accuracy of Luke be tested by Josephus, rather than the accuracy of Josephus by Luke? Infidels usually *assume* that profane historians are infallible, and *then* endeavour to convict the sacred writers of falsehood. (3) The narrative of Luke is the more probable of the two. It is more probable that the number was only four

wilderness four thousand men that
were murderers?
39 But Paul said, [k]I am a man
which am a Jew of Tarsus, *a city*
in Cilicia, [l]a citizen of no mean
city; and, I beseech thee, suffer
me to speak unto the people.
40 And when he had given him
licence, Paul stood on the stairs,
and [m]beckoned with the hand
unto the people; and when there
was made a great silence, he spake
unto *them* in the Hebrew tongue,
saying,

k ch.9.11; 22.3. l ch.22.25. m ch.12.17.

CHAPTER XXII.

MEN,[a] brethren, and fathers,
[b]hear ye my defence, *which*
I make now unto you.
2 (And when they heard that

a ch.7.2. b 1 Pe.3.15.

thousand than that it was thirty thousand; for Josephus says that four hundred were killed and two hundred taken prisoners, and that thus they were dispersed. Now, it is scarcely credible that an army of thirty thousand desperadoes and cut-throats would be dispersed by so small a slaughter and captivity. But if the number was originally but four thousand, it is entirely credible that the loss of six hundred would discourage and dissipate the remainder. (4) It is possible that the chief captain refers only to the *organized Sicarii*, or murderers that the Egyptian led with him, and Josephus to the *multitude* that afterward joined them—the rabble of the discontented and disorderly that followed them on their march. Or, (5) There may have been an error in transcribing Josephus. It has been supposed that he originally wrote four thousand, but that ancient copyists, mistaking the Δ delta, *four*, for Λ lambda, *thirty*, wrote thirty thousand instead of four thousand. Which of these solutions is adopted is not material. ¶ *Which were murderers.* Greek, men of the *Sicarii*—τῶν σικαρίων. This is originally a Latin word, and is derived from *sica*, a short sword, sabre, or crooked knife, which could be easily concealed under the garment. Hence it came to denote assassins, and to be applied to banditti, or robbers. It does not mean that they *had* actually committed murder, but that they were desperadoes and banditti, and were drawn together for purposes of plunder and of blood. This class of people was exceedingly numerous in Judea. See Notes on Lu. x. 30.

39. *A Jew of Tarsus.* A Jew by birth. ¶ *Of no mean city.* Not obscure, or undistinguished. He could claim an honourable birth, so far as the place of his nativity was concerned. See Notes on ch. ix. 11. Tarsus was much celebrated for its learning, and was at one time the rival of Alexandria and Athens. Xenophon calls it *a great and flourishing city.* Josephus (*Antiq.*, b. i. ch. vi. § 6) says that *it was the metropolis, and most renowned city among them* [*the Cilicians*].

40. *Licence.* Liberty; permission. ¶ *On the stairs.* See Notes on ver. 35. ¶ *Beckoned with the hand.* Waving the hand as a sign that he was about to address them, and to produce silence and attention. See ch. xii. 17. ¶ *In the Hebrew tongue.* The language which was spoken by the Jews, which was then a mixture of the Chaldee and Syriac, called *Syro-Chaldaic.* This language he doubtless used on this occasion in preference to the Greek, because it was understood better by the multitude, and would tend to conciliate them if they heard him address them in their own tongue. The following chapter should have been connected with this. The division here is unnatural.

CHAPTER XXII.

1. *Men, brethren, and fathers.* This defence was addressed to the Jews, and Paul commenced it with an expression of sincere respect for them. Stephen began his defence with the same form of address. See Notes on ch. vii. 2. ¶ *My defence.* Against the charges brought against me. Those charges were, that he had endeavoured to prejudice men everywhere against the Jews, the law, and the temple, ch. xxi. 28. In order to meet this charge, Paul stated (1) That he was a Jew by birth, and had enjoyed all the advantages of a Jewish education, ver. 3; (2) He recounted the circumstances of his conversion, and the reason why he believed that he was called to preach the gospel, ver. 4–16; (3) He proceeded

he spake in the Hebrew tongue to
them, they kept the more silence;
and he saith,)
3 I[c] am verily a man *which am*
a Jew, born in Tarsus, *a city* in
Cilicia, yet brought up in this
city, at the feet of [d]Gamaliel, *and*
taught[e] according to the perfect
manner of the law of the fathers,
and [f]was zealous toward God, [g]as
ye all are this day.
4 And[h] I persecuted this way

c ch.21.39; 2 Co.11.22; Phi.3.5. d ch.5.34. e ch.26.5. f Ga.1.14. g ch.21.20; Ro.10.2. h ch.8.3; 26.9-13; Phi.3.6; 1 Ti.1.13.

unto the death, binding and delivering into prisons both men and
women.
5 As also the high-priest doth
bear me witness, and all the estate
of the elders; from whom also I
received letters unto the brethren,
and [i]went to Damascus, to bring
them which were there bound
unto Jerusalem, for to be punished.
6 And it came to pass, that as I
made my journey, and was come
nigh unto Damascus about noon,

i ch.9.2,&c.

---

to state the reasons why he went among the Gentiles, and evidently intended to vindicate his conduct there, ver. 17–21; but at this point, at the name *Gentiles*, his defence was interrupted by the enraged multitude, and he was not permitted to proceed. What *would* have been his defence, therefore, had he been suffered to finish it, it is impossible to know with certainty. On another occasion, however, he was permitted to make a *similar* defence, and perhaps to complete the train of thought which he had purposed to pursue here. See ch. xxvi.

2. *The Hebrew tongue.* See Notes on ch. xxi. 40.

3. *Born in Tarsus.* See Notes on ch. ix. 11. ¶ *Brought up in this city.* In Jerusalem, sent there for the advantage of more perfect instruction in the law. ¶ *At the feet of Gamaliel.* As a scholar, or disciple of Gamaliel. The phrase *to sit at the feet of one* is expressive of the condition of a disciple or learner. Comp. De. xxxiii. 3; Lu. x. 39. It is probable that the expression arose from the fact that the learners occupied a lower place or seat than the teacher. On the character and rank of Gamaliel, see Notes on ch. v. 34. Paul mentions his having been instructed in this manner in order to show that he was entitled to the full privileges of a Jew, and that he had had every opportunity to become fully acquainted with the nature of the law. ¶ *According to the perfect manner*—κατὰ ἀκρίβειαν. By strict diligence or exact care; or in the utmost rigour and severity of that instruction. No pains were spared to make him understand and practise the law of Moses. ¶ *The law of the fathers.* The law of our fathers; that is, the law which they received and handed down to us. Paul was a Pharisee, and the law in which he had been taught was not only the *written* law of Moses, but the *traditional* law which had been handed down from former times. See Notes on Mat. iii. 6. ¶ *And was zealous toward God.* Ga. i. 14. He had a constant burning zeal for God and his law, which was expressed not only by scrupulous adherence to its forms, but by persecuting all who opposed it, ver. 4, 5.

4. *And I persecuted.* Ch. viii. 3. ¶ *This way.* Those who were of this mode of worshipping God; that is, Christians. See Notes on Ac. ix. 2. ¶ *Unto the death.* Intending to put them to death. He did not probably put any to death himself, but he committed them to prison; he sought their lives; he was the agent employed in arresting them; and when they were put to death, he tells us that he gave his voice against them (Ac. xxvi. 10); that is, he joined in, and approved of their condemnation. ¶ *Delivering into prisons*, &c. Ch. viii. 3.

5. *As also the high-priest*, &c. See Notes on ch. ix. 2. ¶ *All the estate of the elders.* Greek, *all the presbytery;* that is, the whole body of the Sanhedrim, or great council of the nation. ¶ *Unto the brethren.* The *Jewish* brethren who were at Damascus. Paul here speaks as a Jew, and regards his countrymen as his brethren.

6. *As I made my journey.* As I was on my journey. ¶ *About noon.* Ch. xxvi. 13, "at mid-day." This circumstance is omitted by Luke in his account in ch. ix. Paul mentions it as being the more remarkable since it occurred at mid-day, to show that he was not

suddenly there shone from heaven
a great light round about me.
7 And I fell unto the ground,
and heard a voice saying unto me,
Saul, Saul, why persecutest thou
me?
8 And I answered, Who art
thou, Lord? And he said unto
me, I am Jesus of Nazareth, whom
thou persecutest.
9 And[k] they that were with me
saw indeed the light, and were
afraid; but they heard not the
voice of him that spake to me.
10 And I said, What shall I do,
Lord? And the Lord said unto
me, Arise, and go into Damascus;
and there it shall be told thee of
all things which are appointed for
thee to do.
11 And when I could not see
for the glory of that light, being
led by the hand of them that were
with me, I came into Damascus.
12 And one [l]Ananias, a devout
man according to the law, [m]having a good report of all the Jews
which dwelt *there*,
13 Came unto me, and stood,
and said unto me, Brother Saul,
receive thy sight. And the same
hour I looked up upon him.
14 And he said, [n]The God of
our fathers [o]hath chosen thee,
that thou shouldest know his will,
[p]and see that [q]Just One, [r]and
shouldest hear the voice of his
mouth.
15 For[s] thou shalt be his witness
unto all men of what thou hast seen
and heard.
16 And now, why tarriest thou?

k Da.10.7.

l ch.9.17. m ch.10.22; 1 Ti.3.7; He.11.2. n ch.3.13; 5.30. o ch.9.15; Ga.1.15. p ver.18; 1 Co.9.1; 15.8. q ch.3.14; 7.52. r 1 Co.11.23; Ga.1.12. s ch.23.11; 26.16,&c.

---

deluded by any meteoric or natural appearances, which usually occur at night.

6-11. See Notes on ch. ix. 3-7.

11. *The glory of that light.* The splendour, the intense brilliancy of the light. See this and its effects explained in the Notes on ch. ix. 8.

12, 13. See Notes on ch. ix. 17, 18.

14. *Shouldest know his will.* His will in the plan of salvation, and in regard to your future life. ¶ *And see that Just One.* The Messiah. See Notes on ch. iii. 14. As Paul was to be an apostle, and as it was the peculiar office of an apostle to bear witness to the person and deeds of the Lord Jesus (see Notes on ch. i. 21, 22), it was necessary that he should *see* him, that thus he might be a competent witness of his resurrection. ¶ *Shouldest hear the voice of his mouth.* Shouldst hear and obey his commands.

15. *For thou shalt be his witness,* &c. As an *apostle*—to testify to all men that the Messiah has come, that he has died, that he has risen, and that he is the Saviour of the world. ¶ *Of what thou hast seen and heard.* Of the remarkable proof which has been furnished you of the divine mission and character of the Lord Jesus.

16. *And now why tarriest thou?* Why dost thou delay, or wait any longer? These words are not recorded by Luke in ch. ix., where he has given an account of the conversion of Paul; but there is nothing here contradictory to his statement. ¶ *And wash away thy sins.* Receive baptism as emblematic of the washing away of sins. It cannot be intended that the external rite of baptism was sufficient to make the soul pure, but that it was an ordinance divinely appointed as *expressive* of the washing away of sins, or of purifying the heart. Comp. He. x. 22. Sinners are represented in the Scriptures as *defiled* or *polluted* by sin. To *wash* away the sins denotes the purifying of the soul from this polluted influence, 1 Co. vi. 11; Re. i. 5; vii. 14; Is. i. 16; Ps. li. 2, 7. ¶ *Calling on the name of the Lord.* For pardon and sanctification, Ro. x. 13, "Whosoever shall call upon the name of the Lord shall be saved." It was proper that this calling on the name of the Lord should be connected with the ordinance of baptism. That ordinance was emblematic of a purifying which the Lord only could produce. It is proper that the rite of baptism should be attended with extraordinary prayer; that he who is to be baptized should make it the occasion of peculiar and very solemn religious exercises.

arise, and be baptized, and [t]wash away thy sins, [u]calling on the name of the Lord.

17 And it came to pass, that when I was come again to Jerusalem, even while I prayed in the temple, [v]I was in a trance;

18 And[w] saw him saying unto me, Make haste, and get thee quickly out of Jerusalem; for they will not receive thy testimony concerning me.

19 And I said, Lord, [x]they know that I imprisoned and beat in every synagogue them that believed on thee:

20 And when the blood of thy martyr Stephen was shed, [y]I also was standing by, and [z]consenting unto his death, and kept the raiment of them that slew him.

t He.10.22; 1 Pe.3.21. *u* Ro.10.13; 1 Co.1.2. *v* 2 Co.12.2. *w* ver.14.

x ver.4. *y* ch.7.58. *z* ch.8.1.

The external rite will avail nothing without the pardoning mercy of God.

17. *When I was come again to Jerusalem.* That is, three years after his conversion. See Ga. i. 17, 18. ¶ *While I prayed in the temple.* Paul, like other converts to Christianity from among the Jews, would naturally continue to offer his devotions in the temple. We meet with repeated instances of their continuing to comply with the customs of the Jewish people. ¶ *I was in a trance.* Greek, *ecstasy.* See Notes on ch. x. 10. It is possible that he may here refer to what he elsewhere mentions (2 Co. xii. 1–5) as "visions and revelations of the Lord." In that place he mentions his being "caught up to the third heaven" (ver. 2) and "into paradise," where he heard words which it was "not lawful (marg. *possible*) for a man to utter," ver. 4. It is not certain, however, that he alludes in this place to that remarkable occurrence. The narrative would rather imply that the Lord Jesus appeared to him in the temple in a remarkable manner, in a vision, and gave him a special command to go to the Gentiles. Paul had now stated the evidence of his conversion, which appears to have been satisfactory to them—at least they made no objection to his statement; he had shown, by his being in the temple, his respect for their institutions; and he *now* proceeds to show that in his other conduct he had been directed by the same high authority by which he had been called into the ministry, and that the command had been given to him in their own temple and in their own city.

18. *And saw him.* Evidently the Lord Jesus, ver. 14. He had received his commission from him, and he now received a distinct command to go to the Gentiles. ¶ *For they will not receive.* The inhabitants of Jerusalem, probably including both Jews and Christians. The *Jews* would not listen to him because he had become, in their view, an apostate, and they would hate and persecute him. The *Christians* would not be likely to receive him, for they would remember his former persecutions, and would be suspicious of him because he had been so long in Arabia, and had not sooner connected himself with them. See Notes on ch. ix. 26, "And when Saul was come to Jerusalem, he assayed to join himself to the disciples; but they were all afraid of him, and believed not that he was a disciple."

19. *And I said, Lord.* This shows that it was the Lord Jesus whom Paul saw in a trance in the temple. The term *Lord* is usually applied to him in the Acts. See Notes on ch. i. 24. ¶ *They know.* Christians know; and they will therefore be not likely to receive to their fellowship their former enemy and persecutor. ¶ *Beat in every synagogue.* Beating, or scourging, was often done in the synagogue. See Notes on Mat. x. 17. Comp. Ac. xxvi. 11. It was customary for those who were converted to Christianity still to meet with the Jews in their synagogues, and to join with them in their worship.

20. *The blood of thy martyr Stephen was shed.* See ch. vii. 58; viii. 1. ¶ *I was standing by.* Ch. vii. 58. ¶ *And consenting unto his death.* Ch. viii. 1. ¶ *And kept the raiment.* The outer robes or garments, which were usually laid aside when they engaged in running or labour. See ch. vii. 58. All this showed that, though Paul was not engaged in stoning Stephen, yet he was with them in spirit, and fully accorded with what they did. These circumstances are mentioned here by him as *reasons* why he knew that he would not be received by Christians as one of their number, and

21 And he said unto me, Depart;
for [a]I will send thee far hence
unto the Gentiles.
22 And they gave him audience
unto this word, and *then* lifted up
their voices, and said, Away with
such a *fellow* from the earth; [b]for
it is not fit that he should live.
23 And as they cried out, and
cast off *their* clothes, and threw
dust into the air,
24 The chief captain commanded
him to be brought into the castle,
and bade that he should be examined by scourging; that he might
know wherefore they cried so
against him.
25 And as they bound him with
thongs, Paul said unto the centurion that stood by, Is it lawful
for you to scourge a man that is
[c]a Roman, and uncondemned?
26 When the centurion heard
that, he went and told the chief
captain, saying, Take heed what
thou doest; for this man is a
Roman.
27 Then the chief captain came,

a ch.13.2,47; Ro.1.5; 11.13; 15.16; Ga.2.7,8; Ep.3.7,8; 1 Ti.2.7. *b* ch.25.24.

c ch.16.37; 25.16.

---

why it was necessary, therefore, for him to turn to the Gentile world.

21. *And he said unto me, Depart.* Because the Christians at Jerusalem would not receive him. ¶ *Far hence.* Paul travelled far in the heathen nations. A large part of his ministry was spent in remote countries, and in the most distant regions then known. See Ro. xv. 19.

22. *And they gave him audience.* They heard him patiently. ¶ *Unto this word.* The word *Gentiles.* ¶ *Away with such a* fellow. Greek, *take such a man from the earth;* that is, put him to death. It is language of strong indignation and abhorrence. The reasons of their indignation were, not that they supposed that the Gentiles could not be brought into covenant with God, for they would themselves compass sea and land to make one proselyte, but, (1) That they believed that Paul taught that they might be saved without conforming to the law of Moses; and, (2) His speech implied that the Jews were more hardened than the Gentiles, and that he had a greater prospect of success in bringing them to God than he had in regard to the Jews.

23. *Cast off* their *clothes.* Their outer garments. Probably they did it now intending to stone him, ch. vii. 58. ¶ *And threw dust into the air.* As expressive of their abhorrence and indignation. This was a striking exhibition of rage and malice. Paul was guarded by Roman soldiers so that they could not injure him; and their only way of expressing their wrath was by menaces and threats, and by these tokens of furious indignation. Thus Shimei expressed his indignation against David by cursing him, throwing stones at him, and casting dust, 2 Sa. xvi. 13.

24. *The castle.* The castle of Antonia. He would be there removed entirely from the wrath of the Jews. ¶ *Should be examined*—ἀνετάζεσθαι. The word *examine* with us commonly means to inquire, to question, to search for, to look carefully into a subject. The word here used is commonly applied to *metals* whose nature is tested, or *examined* by fire; and then it means to subject to torture or torments, in order to extort a confession where persons were accused of crime. It was often resorted to among the ancients. A common mode has been by the *rack*, but various kinds of torments have been invented in order to extort confessions of guilt from those who were accused. The whole practice has been one of the most flagrant violations of justice, and one of the foulest blots on human nature. In this case, the tribune saw that Paul was accused violently by the Jews; he was probably ignorant of the Hebrew language, and had not understood the address of Paul; he supposed from the extraordinary excitement that Paul must have been guilty of some flagrant offence, and he therefore resolved to subject him to torture to extort from him a confession. ¶ *By scourging.* By the scourge or whip. Comp. He. xi. 36. This was one mode of torture, in order to extort a secret from those who were accused.

25. *Bound him with thongs.* With cords, preparatory to scourging. ¶ *Is it lawful*, &c. It was directly contrary to the Roman law to bind and scourge a Roman citizen. See Notes on ch. xvi. 36, 37.

and said unto him, Tell me, art
thou a Roman? He said, Yea.
28 And the chief captain answered, With a great sum obtained I this freedom. And Paul said, But I was *free* born.
29 Then straightway they departed from him which should have [1]examined him; and the chief captain also was afraid, after he knew that he was a Roman, and because he had bound him.
30 On the morrow, [d]because he would have known the certainty wherefore he was accused of the Jews, he loosed him from *his* bands, and commanded the chief priests and all their council to appear, and brought Paul down, and set him before them.

1 or, *tortured him.*

d ch.23.28.

---

28. *With a great sum obtained I this freedom.* The freedom or privilege of Roman citizenship. From this it would seem that the privilege of being a Roman citizen might be purchased, unless perhaps he refers to the expenses which were necessarily attendant in passing through the proper *forms* of becoming a Roman citizen. The argument of the tribune in this case is this: "*I* obtained this privilege at a great price. Whence did you, Paul, thus poor and persecuted, obtain the means of becoming a Roman citizen?" Paul had informed him that he was a native of Tarsus (ch. xxi. 39); and the chief captain supposed that that was not a free city, and that Paul could not have derived the privilege of citizenship from his birth. ¶ *But I was* free *born.* I was born a Roman citizen, or I am such in virtue of my birth. Various opinions have been formed on the question in what way or for what reasons Paul was entitled to the privileges of a Roman citizen. Some have supposed that Tarsus was a Roman colony, and that he thus became a Roman citizen. But of this there does not appear to be sufficient proof. Pliny says (v. 27) that it was *a free city*. Appian says that it was endowed with the privileges of a free city by Augustus Cæsar after it had been greatly afflicted and oppressed by wars. Dio Chrysost. says to the people of Tarsus, "He (Augustus) has conferred on you everything which anyone could bestow on his friends and companions, a country (that is, a free country), laws, honour, authority over the river (Cydranus) and the neighbouring sea." Free cities were permitted in the Roman empire to use their own laws, customs, and magistrates, and they were free from being subject to Roman guards. They were required only to acknowledge the supremacy and authority of the Roman people, and to aid them in their wars. Such a city was Tarsus; and, having been born there, Paul was entitled to these privileges of a free man. Many critics have supposed that this privilege of Roman citizenship had been conferred on some of the ancestors of Paul in consequence of some distinguished military service. Such a conferring of the rights of citizenship was not unusual, and possibly might have occurred in this case. But there is no direct historical proof of it; and the former fact, that he was born in a free city, will amply account for his affirmation that he was free born. Comp. Notes on ch. xvi. 37.

29. *Then straightway.* Immediately. They saw that by scourging him they would have violated the Roman law, and exposed themselves to its penalty. ¶ *Which should have examined him.* Who were about to torture him by scourging him, ver. 24. ¶ *Because he had bound him.* Preparatory to scourging him. The act of *binding* a Roman citizen with such an intent, untried and uncondemned, was unlawful. Prisoners who were to be scourged were usually bound by the Romans to a pillar or post; and a similar custom prevailed among the Jews. That it was unlawful to bind a man with this intent, who was uncondemned, appears from an express declaration in Cicero (against Verres): "It is a heinous sin to *bind* a Roman citizen; it is wickedness to *beat* him; it is next to parricide to kill him, and what shall I say to crucify him?"

30. *On the morrow.* After he had arrested Paul. Paul was still a prisoner; and if suffered to go at liberty among the Jews, his life would have been in danger. ¶ *And commanded the chief priests*, &c. Summoned a meeting of the Sanhedrim, or great council of the nation. He did this, as he was prevented from scourging Paul, in order to know what he had done, and that he

CHAPTER XXIII.

AND Paul, earnestly beholding
the council, said, Men *and*
brethren, [a]I have lived in all good
conscience before God until this
day.
2 And the high-priest Ananias
commanded them that stood by
him to [b]smite him on the mouth.

a ch.24.16; 2 Co.1.12; He.13.18.
b Jn.18.22.

---

might learn from the Jews themselves the nature of the charge against him. This was necessary for the safety of Paul and for the ends of justice. This should have been done without any attempt to *torture* him in order to extort a confession. ¶ *And brought Paul down.* From the elevated castle of Antonia. The council assembled commonly in the house of the high-priest. ¶ *And set him before them.* He brought the prisoner to their bar, that they might have have an opportunity to accuse him, and that thus the chief captain might learn the real nature of the charge against him.

CHAPTER XXIII.

1. *And Paul, earnestly beholding*—ἀτενίσας. Fixing his eyes intently on the council. The word denotes a fixed and earnest gazing; a close observation. See Lu. iv. 20. Comp. Notes on Ac. iii. 4. Paul would naturally look with a keen and attentive observation on the council. He was arraigned before them, and he would naturally observe the appearance, and endeavour to ascertain the character of his judges. Besides, it was by this council that he had been formerly commissioned to persecute the Christians, ch. ix. 1, 2. He had not seen them since that commission was given. He would naturally, therefore, regard them with an attentive eye. The result shows, also, that he looked at them to see what was the character of the men there assembled, and what was the proportion of Pharisees and Sadducees, ver. 6. ¶ *The council.* Greek, the Sanhedrim, ch. xxii. 30. It was the great council, composed of seventy elders, to whom was intrusted the affairs of the nation. See Notes on Mat. i. 4. ¶ *Men* and *brethren.* Greek, "Men, brethren;" the usual form of beginning an address among the Jews. See ch. ii. 29. He addressed them still as his *brethren.* ¶ *I have lived in all good conscience.* I have conducted myself so as to maintain a good conscience. I have done what I believed to be right. This was a bold declaration, after the tumult, and charges, and accusations of the previous day (ch. xxii.); and yet it was strictly true. His persecutions of the Christians had been conducted *conscientiously,* Ac. xxvi. 9, "I verily thought with myself," says he, "that I *ought* to do many things contrary to the name of Jesus of Nazareth." Of his conscientiousness and fidelity in *their* service they could bear witness. Of his conscientiousness *since,* he could make a similar declaration. He doubtless meant to say that as he had been conscientious in persecution, so he had been in his conversion and in his subsequent course. And as they *knew* that his former life had been with a good conscience, they ought to *presume* that he had maintained the same character still. This was a remarkably bold appeal to be made by an accused man, and it shows the strong consciousness which Paul had of his innocence. What would have been the drift of his discourse in proving this we can only conjecture. He was interrupted (ver. 2); but there can be no doubt that he would have pursued such a course of argument as would tend to establish his innocence. ¶ *Before God.* Greek, to God—τῷ Θεῷ. He had lived *to* God, or with reference to his commands, so as to keep a conscience pure in his sight. The same principle of conduct he states more at length in ch. xxiv. 16: "And herein do I exercise myself, to have always a conscience void of offence toward God and toward men." ¶ *Until this day.* Including the time *before* his conversion to Christianity, and after. In both conditions he was conscientious; in one, conscientious in persecution and error, though he deemed it to be right; in the other, conscientious in the truth. The mere fact that a man is conscientious does not prove that he is right or innocent. See Note on Jn. xvi. 2.

2. *And the high-priest Ananias.* This Ananias was doubtless the son of Nebedinus (Jos. *Antiq.*, b. xx. ch. v. § 3), who was high-priest when Quadratus, who preceded Felix, was president of Syria. He was sent bound to Rome by Quadratus, at the same time with Ananias, the prefect of the temple, that they

3 Then said Paul unto him, God shall smite thee, *thou* whited wall; for sittest thou to judge me after the law, and [c]commandest me to be smitten contrary to the law?

c Le.19.35; De.25.1,2; Jn.7.51.

might give an account of their conduct to Claudius Cæsar (Josephus, *Antiq.*, b. xx. ch. vi. § 2). But in consequence of the intercession of Agrippa the younger, they were dismissed and returned to Jerusalem. Ananias, however, was not restored to the office of high-priest. For, when Felix was governor of Judea, this office was filled by Jonathan, who succeded Ananias (Josephus, *Antiq.*, b. xx. ch. x.). Jonathan was slain in the temple itself, by the instigation of Felix, by assassins who had been hired for the purpose. This murder is thus described by Josephus (*Antiq.*, b. xx. ch. viii. § 5): "Felix bore an ill-will to Jonathan, the high-priest, because he frequently gave him admonitions about governing the Jewish affairs better than he did, lest complaints should be made against him, since he had procured of Cæsar the appointment of Felix as procurator of Judea. Accordingly, Felix contrived a method by which he might get rid of Jonathan, whose admonitions had become troublesome to him. Felix persuaded one of Jonathan's most faithful friends, of the name Doras, to bring the robbers upon him, and to put him to death." This was done in Jerusalem. The robbers came into the city as if to worship God, and with daggers, which they had concealed under their garments, they put him to death. After the death of Jonathan, the office of high-priest remained vacant until King Agrippa appointed Ismael, the son of Fabi, to the office (Josephus, *Antiq.*, b. xx. ch. viii. § 8). It was during this interval, while the office of high-priest was vacant, that the events which are here recorded took place. Ananias was then at Jerusalem; and as the office of high-priest was vacant, and as he was the last person who had borne the office, it was natural that he should discharge, probably by common consent, its duties, so far, at least, as to preside in the Sanhedrim. Of these facts Paul would be doubtless apprised; and hence what he said (ver. 5) was strictly true, and is one of the evidences that Luke's history accords precisely with the peculiar circumstances which then existed. When Luke here calls Ananias "the high-priest," he evidently intends not to affirm that he was actually such, but to use the word, as the Jews did, as applicable to one who *had* been in that office, and who, on that occasion, when the office was vacant, performed its duties. ¶ *To smite him on the mouth.* To stop him from speaking; to express their indignation at what he had said. The anger of Ananias was aroused because Paul affirmed that all he had done had been with a good conscience. Their feelings had been excited to the utmost; they regarded him as certainly guilty; they regarded him as an apostate; and they could not bear it that he, with such coolness and firmness, declared that *all* his conduct had been under the direction of a good conscience. The injustice of the command of Ananias is apparent to all. A similar instance of violence occurred on the trial of the Saviour, Jn. xviii. 22.

3. *God shall smite thee.* God shall punish thee. God is just; and he will not suffer such a manifest violation of all the laws of a fair trial to pass unavenged. This was a remarkably bold and fearless declaration. Paul was surrounded by enemies. They were seeking his life. He must have known that such declarations would only excite their wrath and make them more thirsty for his blood. That he could thus address the president of the council was not only strongly characteristic of the man, but was also a strong proof that he was conscious of innocence, and that justice was on his side. This expression of Paul, "God shall smite thee," is not to be regarded in the light of an *imprecation*, or as an expression of angry feeling, but of a *prediction*, or of a strong conviction on the mind of Paul that a man so hypocritical and unjust as Ananias was could not escape the vengeance of God. Ananias was slain, with Hezekiah his brother, during the agitation that occurred in Jerusalem when the robbers, or *Sicarii*, under their leader, Manahem, had taken possession of the city. He attempted to conceal himself in an aqueduct, but was drawn forth and killed. See Josephus, *Jewish Wars*, b. ii. ch. xvii. § 8. Thus Paul's prediction was fulfilled. ¶ Thou *whited wall.* This is evidently a proverbial expression, meaning *thou*

4 And they that stood by said, Revilest thou God's high-priest?
5 Then said Paul, I wist not, brethren, that he was the high-priest; for it is written, [d]Thou shalt not speak evil of the ruler of thy people.

d Ex.22.28; Ec.10.20; 2 Pe.2.10; Jude 8.

hypocrite. His hypocrisy consisted in the fact that while he pretended to sit there to do justice, he commanded the accused to be smitten in direct violation of the law, thus showing that his character was not what he professed it to be, but that of one determined to carry the purposes of his party and of his own feelings. Our Saviour used a similar expression to describe the hypocritical character of the Pharisees (Mat. xxiii. 27), when he compares them to whited sepulchres. A whited wall is a wall or inclosure that is covered with lime or gypsum, and that thus appears to be different from what it is, and thus aptly describes the hypocrite. Seneca (*De Providentia*, ch. 6) uses a similar figure to describe hypocrites: "They are sordid, base, and like their walls adorned only externally." See also Seneca, *Epis.* 115. ¶ *For sittest thou*, &c. The law required that justice should be done, and in order to that, it gave every man an opportunity of defending himself. See Note, Jn. vii. 51. Comp. Pr. xviii. 13; Le. xix. 15, 16; Ex. xxiii. 1, 2; De. xix. 15, 18. ¶ *To judge me after the law.* As a judge, to hear and decide the case according to the rules of the law of Moses. ¶ *Contrary to the law.* In violation of the law of Moses (Le. xix. 35), "Ye shall do no unrighteousness in judgment."

4. *Revilest thou*, &c. Dost thou reproach or abuse the high-priest of God? It is remarkable that they, who knew that he was *not* the high-priest, should have offered this language. He was, however, in the place of the high-priest, and they might have pretended that respect was due to the office.

5. *Then said Paul, I wist not.* I know not; I was ignorant of the fact that he was high-priest. Interpreters have been greatly divided on the meaning of this expression. Some have supposed that Paul said it in *irony*, as if he had said, "Pardon me, brethren, I did not consider that this was the high-priest. It did not occur to me that a man who could conduct thus could be God's high-priest." Others have thought (as Grotius) that Paul used these words for the purpose of mitigating their wrath, and as an acknowledgment that he had spoken hastily, and that it was contrary to his usual habit, which was not to speak evil of the ruler of the people. As if he had said, "I acknowledge my error and my haste. I did not *consider* that I was addressing him whom God had commanded me to respect." But this interpretation is not probable, for Paul evidently did not intend to retract what he had said. Dr. Doddridge renders it, "I was not aware, brethren, that it was the high-priest," and regards it as an apology for having spoken in haste. But the obvious reply to this interpretation is, that if Ananias was the high-priest, Paul could not but be aware of it. Of so material a point it is hardly possible that he could be ignorant. Others suppose that, as Paul had been long absent from Jerusalem, and had not known the changes which had occurred there, he was a stranger to the person of the high-priest. Others suppose that Ananias did not occupy the usual seat which was appropriated to the high-priest, and that he was not clothed in the usual robes of office, and that Paul did not recognize him as the high-priest. But it is wholly improbable that on such an occasion the high-priest, who was the presiding officer in the Sanhedrim, should not be known to the accused. The true interpretation, therefore, I suppose, is that which is derived from the fact that Ananias was *not* then properly the high-priest; that there was a vacancy in the office, and that he presided by courtesy, or in virtue of his having been formerly invested with that office. The meaning then will be: "I do not regard or acknowledge him as the high-priest, or address him *as such*, since that is not his true character. Had he been truly the high-priest, even if he had thus been guilty of manifest injustice, I would not have used the language which I did. The *office*, if not the *man*, would have claimed respect. But as he is *not* truly and properly clothed with that office, and as he was guilty of manifest injustice, I did not believe that he was to be shielded in his injustice by the law which commands me to show respect to the proper ruler of the people." If this be the true interpretation, it

6 But when Paul perceived that the one part were Sadducees, and the other Pharisees, he cried out in the council, Men *and* brethren,

---

shows that Luke, in this account, accords entirely with the truth of history. The character of Ananias as given by Josephus, the facts which he has stated in regard to him, all accord with the account here given, and show that the writer of the "Acts of the Apostles" was acquainted with the history of that time, and has correctly stated it. ¶ *For it is written.* Ex. xxii. 28. Paul adduces this to show that it was his purpose to observe the law; that he would not intentionally violate it; and that, if he had known Ananias to be high-priest, he would have been restrained by his regard for the law from using the language which he did. ¶ *Of the ruler of thy people.* This passage had not any peculiar reference to the high-priest, but it inculcated the general spirit of respect for those in office, whatever that office was. As the office of high-priest was one of importance and authority, Paul declares here that he would not be guilty of showing disrespect for it, or of using reproachful language in regard to it.

6. *But when Paul perceived.* Probably by his former acquaintance with the men who composed the council. As he had been brought up in Jerusalem, and had been before acquainted with the Sanhedrim (ch. ix. 2), he would have an acquaintance, doubtless, with the character of most of those present, though he had been absent from them for fourteen years, Ga. ii. 1. ¶ *The one part,* &c. That the council was divided into two parts, Pharisees and Sadducees. This was commonly the case, though it was uncertain which had the majority. In regard to the opinions of these two sects, see Notes on Mat. iii. 7. ¶ *He cried out,* &c. The reasons why Paul resolved to take advantage of their difference of opinion were, probably, (1) That he saw that it was impossible to expect *justice* at their hands, and he therefore regarded it as prudent and proper to consult his own safety. He saw, from the conduct of Ananias, and from the spirit manifested (ver. 4), that they, like the other Jews, had prejudged the case, and were driven on by blind rage and fury. (2) His object was to show his innocence to the chief captain. To ascertain that was the purpose for which he had been arraigned. Yet that, perhaps, could be most directly and satisfactorily shown by bringing out, as he knew he could do, the real spirit which actuated the whole council, as a spirit of party strife, contention, and persecution. Knowing, therefore, how sensitive they were on the subject of the resurrection, he seems to have resolved to do what he would *not* have done had they been disposed to hear him according to the rules of justice—to abandon the *direct* argument for his defence, and to enlist a large part, perhaps a majority of the council, in his favour. Whatever may be thought of the propriety of this course, it cannot be denied that it was a master-stroke of policy, and that it evinced a profound knowledge of human nature. ¶ *I am a Pharisee.* That is, I was of that sect among the Jews. I was born a Pharisee, and I ever continued while a Jew to be of that sect. In the main he agreed with them still. He did not mean to deny that he was a Christian, but that, so far as the Pharisees differed from the Sadducees, he was with the former. He agreed with *them,* not with the Sadducees, in regard to the doctrine of the resurrection, and the existence of angels and spirits. ¶ *The son of a Pharisee.* What was the name of his father is not known. But the meaning is, simply, that he was entitled to all the immunities and privileges of a Pharisee. He had, from his birth, belonged to that sect, nor had he ever departed from the great cardinal doctrine which distinguished that sect—the doctrine of the resurrection of the dead. Comp. Phi. iii. 5. ¶ *Of the hope and resurrection of the dead.* That is, of the hope that the dead will be raised. This is the real point of the opposition to me. ¶ *I am called in question.* Greek, I am judged; that is, I am persecuted, or brought to trial. Orobio charges this upon Paul as an artful manner of declining persecution, unworthy the character of an upright and honest man. Chubb, a British Deist of the seventeenth century, charges it upon Paul as an act of gross "dissimulation, as designed to conceal the true ground of all the troubles that he had brought upon himself, and as designed to deceive and impose upon the Jews." He affirms also that "St. Paul probably

I[e] am a Pharisee, the son of a Pharisee: [f]of the hope and resurrection of the dead I am called in question.

7 And when he had so said, there arose a dissension between the Pharisees and the Sadducees; and the multitude was divided.

8 For the [g]Sadducees say that there is no resurrection, neither

e ch.26.5; Phi.3.5. f ch.24.15,21; 26.6; 28.20. g Mat.22.23; Mar.12.18; Lu.20.27.

invented this pretended charge against himself to draw over a party of the unbelieving Jews unto him." See Chubb's *Posthumous Works*, vol. ii. p. 238. Now, in reply to this, we may observe, (1) That there is not the least evidence that Paul denied that he had been, or was then, a Christian. An attempt to deny this, after all that they knew of him, would have been vain; and there is not the slightest hint that he attempted it. (2) The doctrine of the resurrection of the dead *was* the *main* and *leading* doctrine which he had insisted on, and which had been to him the cause of much of his persecution. See ch. xvii. 31, 32; 1 Co. xv.; Ac. xiii. 34; xxvi. 6, 7, 23, 25. (3) Paul defended this by an argument which he deemed invincible, and which constituted, in fact, the principal evidence of its truth —the fact that the Lord Jesus *had* been raised. That fact had *fully confirmed* the doctrine of the Pharisees that the dead would rise. As Paul had everywhere proclaimed the fact that Jesus had been raised up, and as this had been the occasion of his being opposed, it was true that he had been persecuted on account of that doctrine. (4) The real ground of the opposition which the Sadducees made to him, and of their opposition to his doctrine, was the additional zeal with which he urged this doctrine, and the additional argument which he brought for the resurrection of the dead. Perhaps the cause of the opposition of this great party among the Jews—the Sadducees—to Christianity, was the strong confirmation which the resurrection of Christ gave to the doctrine which they so much hated—the doctrine of the resurrection of the dead. It thus gave a triumph to their opponents among the Pharisees, and Paul, as a leading and zealous advocate of that doctrine, would excite their special hatred. (5) All that Paul said, therefore, was strictly true. It was because he advocated this doctrine that he was opposed. That there were *other* causes of opposition to him might be true also; but still this was the main and prominent cause of the hostility. (6) With great propriety, therefore, he might address the Pharisees and say, "Brethren, the doctrine which has distinguished you from the Sadducees is at stake. The doctrine which is at the foundation of all our hopes—the resurrection of the dead; the doctrine of our fathers, of the Scriptures, of our sect, is in danger. Of that doctrine I have been the advocate. I have never denied it. I have everywhere defended it, and have devoted myself to the work of putting it on an imperishable basis among the Jews and the Gentiles. For my zeal in that I have been opposed. I have excited the ridicule of the Gentile and the hatred of the Sadducee. I have thus been persecuted and arraigned; and for my zeal in urging the argument in defence of it which *I* have deemed most irrefragable—the resurrection of the Messiah —I have been arraigned, and now cast myself on your protection against the mad zeal of the enemies of the doctrine of our fathers." Not only, therefore, was this an act of policy and prudence in Paul, but what he affirmed was strictly *true*, and the effect was as he had anticipated.

7. *A dissension.* A dispute, or difference. ¶ *And the multitude.* The council. Comp. ch. xiv. 4. The Pharisees embraced, as he desired and expected, his side of the question, and became his advocates, in opposition to the Sadducees, who were arrayed against him.

8. *For the Sadducees say.* They believe. ¶ *No resurrection.* Of the dead. By this doctrine they also understood that there was no future state, and that the soul did not exist after death. See Notes on Mat. xxii. 23. ¶ *Neither angel.* That there are no angels. They deny the existence of good or bad angels. See Notes on Mat. iii. 7. ¶ *Nor spirit.* Nor soul. That there is nothing but matter. They were materialists, and supposed that all the operations which we ascribe to mind could be traced to some modification of matter. The Sadducees, says Josephus (*Jewish Wars*, b. ii. ch. viii. § 14), "take away the belief of the im-

angel nor spirit; but the Pharisees
confess both.
9 And there arose a great cry;
and the scribes *that were* of the
Pharisees' part arose, and strove,
saying, [h]We find no evil in this
man; but if [i]a spirit or an angel
hath spoken to him, [k]let us not
fight against God.
10 And when there arose a great
dissension, the chief captain, fearing lest Paul should have been
pulled in pieces of them, commanded the soldiers to go down,
and to take him by force from
among them, and to bring *him*
into the castle.
11 And the night following,

h ch.25.25; 26.31. *i* ch.22.17,18. *k* ch.5.39.

mortal duration of the soul, and the punishments and rewards in Hades." "The doctrine of the Sadducees is this," says he (*Antiq.*, b. xviii. ch. i. § 4), "that souls die with the bodies." The opinion that the soul is material, and that there is nothing but matter in the universe, has been held by many philosophers, ancient and modern, as well as by the Sadducees. ¶ *Confess both.* Acknowledge, or receive both as true; that is, that there is a future state, and that there are spirits distinct from matter, as angels, and the disembodied souls of men. The two points in dispute were, (1) Whether the dead would be raised and exist in a future state; and, (2) Whether mind was distinct from matter. The Sadducees denied both, and the Pharisees believed both. Their belief of the latter point was, that spirits existed in two forms—that of angels, and that of souls of men distinct from the body.

9. *A great cry.* A great clamour and tumult. ¶ *The scribes.* The learned men. They would naturally be the chief speakers. ¶ *Of the Pharisees' part.* Who were Pharisees, or who belonged to that party. The scribes were not a distinct sect, but might be either Pharisees or Sadducees. ¶ *We find no evil in this man.* No opinion which is contrary to the law of Moses; no conduct in spreading the doctrine of the resurrection which we do not approve. The importance of this doctrine, in their view, was so great as to throw into the background all the *other* doctrines that Paul might hold; and, provided this were propagated, they were willing to vindicate and sustain him. A similar testimony was offered to the innocence of the Saviour by Pilate, Jn. xix. 6. ¶ *But if a spirit or an angel*, &c. They here referred, doubtless, to what Paul had said in ch. xxii. 17, 18. He had declared that he had gone among the Gentiles in obedience to a command which he received in a vision in the temple. As the Pharisees held to the belief of spirits and angels, and to the doctrine that the will of God was often delivered to men by their agency, they were ready now to admit that he had received such a communication, and that he had gone among the Gentiles in obedience to it, to defend their great doctrine of the resurrection of the dead. We are not to suppose that the Pharisees had become the friends of Paul or of Christianity. The true solution of their conduct doubtless is, that they were so inflamed with hatred against the Sadducees that they were willing to make use of *any* argument against their doctrine. As the testimony of Paul might be turned to their account, they were willing to vindicate him. It is remarkable, too, that they *perverted* the statement of Paul in order to oppose the Sadducees. Paul had stated distinctly (ch. xxii. 17, 18) that he had been commanded to go by *the Lord*, meaning the Lord Jesus. He had said nothing of "a spirit or an angel." Yet they would unite with the Sadducees so far as to maintain that he had received no such command from the Lord Jesus. But they might easily vary his statements, and suppose that an "angel or a spirit" had spoken to him, and thus make use of his conduct as an argument against the Sadducees. Men are not always very careful about the exact correctness of their statements when they wish to humble a rival. ¶ *Let us not fight against God.* See Notes on ch. v. 39. These words are wanting in many MSS. and in some of the ancient versions. The Syriac reads it, "If a spirit or an angel have spoken to him, what is there in this?" that is, what is there unusual or wrong?

10. *A great dissension.* A great tumult, excitement, or controversy. ¶ *Into the castle.* See Notes on ch. xxi. 34.

11. *The Lord stood by him.* Evidently the Lord Jesus. See Notes on ch. i. 24.

the[l] Lord stood by him, and said,
Be of good cheer, Paul; for as
thou hast testified of me in Jerusalem, so must thou bear witness
also [m]at Rome.
12 And when it was day, [n]cer-
tain of the Jews banded together,
and bound themselves [1]under a

l Ps.46.1,7; ch.18.9; 27.23,24.
m ch.28.30,31; Ro.1.15. *n* ver.21,30; ch.25.3.
1 or, *with an oath of execration.*

curse, [o]saying that they would
neither eat nor drink till they had
killed Paul.
13 And they were more than
forty which had made this conspiracy.
14 And they came to the [p]chief
priests and elders, and said, We
have bound ourselves under a great

o Ps.31.13. *p* Ho.4.9.

Comp. ch. xxii. 18. The appearance of the Lord in this case was a proof that he approved the course which Paul had taken before the Sanhedrim. ¶ *Be of good cheer.* It would not be remarkable if Paul, by these constant persecutions, should be dejected in mind. The issue of the whole matter was as yet doubtful. In these circumstances, it must have been peculiarly consoling to him to hear these words of encouragement from the Lord Jesus, and this assurance that the object of his desires would be granted, and that he would be permitted to bear the same witness of him in Rome. Nothing else can comfort and sustain the soul in trials and persecutions but evidence of the approbation of God, and the promises of his gracious aid. ¶ *Bear witness also at Rome.* This had been the object of his earnest wish (Ro. i. 10; xv. 23, 24), and this promise of the Lord Jesus was fulfilled, ch. xxviii. 30, 31. The promise which was here made to Paul was not *directly* one of deliverance from the present persecution, but it *implied* that, and made it certain.

12. *Certain of the Jews.* Some of the Jews. They were more than forty in number, ver. 13. ¶ *Banded together.* Made an agreement or compact. They conspired to kill him. ¶ *And bound themselves under a curse.* See the margin. The Greek is, "they anathematized themselves;" that is, they bound themselves by a solemn oath. They invoked a curse on themselves, or devoted themselves to destruction, if they did not do it. Lightfoot remarks, however, that they could be absolved from this vow by the Rabbins if they were unable to execute it. Under various pretences they could easily be freed from such oaths, and it was common to take them; and if there was any difficulty in fulfilling them, they could easily apply to their religious teachers and be absolved. ¶ *That they would neither eat nor drink.* That is, that they would do it as soon as possible. This was a common form of an oath, or curse, among the Jews. Sometimes they only vowed abstinence from particular things, as from meat, or wine. But in this case, to make the oath more certain and binding, they vowed abstinence from all kinds of food and drink till they had killed him. Who these were—whether they were Sadducees or not—is not mentioned by the sacred writer. It is evident, however, that the minds of the Jews were greatly inflamed against Paul; and as they saw him in the custody of the Roman tribune, and as there was no prospect that *he* would punish him, they resolved to take the matter into their own hands. Michaelis conjectures that they were of the number of the *Sicarii*, or cutthroats, with which Judea then abounded. See Notes on ch. xxi. 38. It is needless to remark that this was a most wicked oath. It was a deliberate purpose to commit murder; and it shows the desperate state of morals among the Jews at that time, and the infuriated malice of the people against the apostle, that such an oath *could* have been taken.

13. *Which had made this conspiracy.* This oath (συνωμοσίαν), this agreement, or compact. This large number of desperate men, bound by so solemn an oath, would be likely to be successful, and the life of Paul was therefore in peculiar danger. The manner in which they purposed to accomplish their design is stated in ver. 15.

14. *And they came,* &c. Probably by a deputation. ¶ *To the chief priests and elders.* The members of the great council, or Sanhedrim. It is probable that the application was made to the party of the Sadducees, as the Pharisees had shown their determination to defend Paul. They would have had no prospect of success had they attacked the

curse, that we will eat nothing
until we have slain Paul.
15 Now therefore ye, with the
council, signify to the chief captain
that he bring him down unto you
to-morrow, as though ye would inquire something more perfectly concerning him; and we, or ever he
come near, are [q]ready to kill him.
16 And when Paul's sister's son
heard of their lying in wait, [r]he
went and entered into the castle,
and told Paul.
17 Then[s] Paul called one of the
centurions unto *him*, and said, Bring
this young man unto the chief captain; for he hath a certain thing
to tell him.
18 So he took him, and brought
him to the chief captain, and said,
[t]Paul the prisoner called me unto
him, and prayed me to bring this
young man unto thee, who hath
something to say unto thee.
19 Then the chief captain took
him by the hand, and went *with*
him aside privately, and asked *him*,
What is that thou hast to tell me?

q Ps.21.11; 37.32,33. r 2 Sa.17.17. s Pr.22.3; Mat.10.16. t ch.28.17; Ep.3.1; 4.1; Phile.9.

castle, and they therefore devised this mode of obtaining access to Paul, where they might easily despatch him. ¶ *Under a great curse.* Greek, "We have anathematized ourselves with an anathema." We have made the vow as solemn as possible.

15. *Ye, with the council.* With the concurrence or request of the Sanhedrim. It was only by such a request that they had any hope that the chief captain would remove Paul from the castle. ¶ *Signify to the chief captain.* Send a message or request to him. ¶ *That he bring him down unto you.* That he bring him from the castle to the usual place of the meeting of the Sanhedrim. As this was at some distance from the castle of Antonia, where Paul was, they supposed it would be easy to waylay him and take his life. ¶ *To-morrow.* This is wanting in the Syriac, Vulgate, and Ethiopic versions. It is, however, probably the correct reading of the text, as it would be necessary to convene the council, and make the request of the tribune, which might require the whole of one day. ¶ *As though ye would inquire,* &c. This request appeared so reasonable that they did not doubt that the tribune would grant it to the council. And though it was obviously a false and wicked pretence, yet these conspirators knew the character of the persons to whom they addressed themselves so well that they did not doubt that they would prevail on the council to make the request. Public justice must have been deeply fallen when it was known that such an iniquitous request could be made with the certain prospect of success. ¶ *Or ever he come near.* Before he comes near to the Sanhedrim. The great council will thus not be suspected of being privy to the deed. We will waylay him, and murder him *in the way.* The plan was well laid; and nothing but the interposition of Providence could have prevented its execution.

16. *Paul's sister's son.* This is all that we know of the family of Paul. Nor do we know for what purpose he was at Jerusalem. It is possible that Paul might have a sister residing there; though, as Paul himself had been sent there formerly for his education, it seems more probable that this young man was sent there for the same purpose. ¶ *Entered into the castle.* Paul had the privileges of a Roman citizen, and as no well-founded charge had been laid against him, it is probable that he was not very closely confined, and that his friends might have free access to him.

17. *Called one of the centurions.* Who might at that time have had special charge of the castle, or been on guard. Paul had the most positive divine assurance that his life would be spared, and that he would yet see Rome; but he always understood the divine promises and purposes as being consistent with his own efforts, and with all proper measures of prudence and diligence in securing his own safety. He did not rest merely on the divine promises without any effort of his own, but he took encouragement from those promises to put forth his own exertions for security and for salvation.

18. *And prayed me.* And asked me.

19. *Took him by the hand.* As an expression of kindness and civility. He

20 And he said, [u]The Jews have
agreed to desire thee that thou
wouldest bring down Paul to-morrow into the council, as though
they would inquire somewhat of
him more perfectly.
21 But[v] do not thou yield unto
them; for there lie in wait for
him of them more than forty men,
which have bound themselves with
an oath that they will neither eat
nor drink till they have killed him;
and now are they ready, looking
for a promise from thee.
22 So the chief captain *then* let
the young man depart, and charged
him, *See thou* tell no man that thou
hast showed these things to me.
23 And he called unto *him* two
centurions, saying, Make ready two
hundred soldiers to go to Cesarea,
and horsemen threescore and ten,
and spearmen two hundred, at the
third hour of the night;
24 And provide *them* beasts, that

u ver.12. *v* Ex.23.2.

did it to draw him aside from the multitude, that he might communicate his message privately.

20. *And he said*, &c. In what way this young man had received intelligence of this, we can only conjecture. It is not improbable that he was a student under some one of the Jewish teachers, and that he might have learned it of him. It is not at all probable that the purpose of the forty men would be very closely kept. Indeed, it is evident that *they* were not themselves very anxious about concealing their oath, as they mentioned it freely to the chief priests and elders, ver. 14.

21. *Looking for a promise from thee.* Waiting for your consent to bring him down to them.

23. *And he called unto* him *two centurions*, &c. Each centurion had under him one hundred men. The chief captain resolved to place Paul beyond the power of the Jews, and to protect him as became a Roman citizen. ¶ *Two hundred soldiers.* These foot soldiers were designed only to guard Paul till he was safely out of Jerusalem. The horsemen only were intended to accompany him to Cesarea. See ver. 32. ¶ *And horsemen.* These were commonly attached to foot soldiers. In this case, however, they were designed to attend Paul to Cesarea. ¶ *And spearmen*—δεξιολάβους. This word is found nowhere else in the New Testament, and occurs in no classic writer. It properly means *those who take, or apprehend by the right hand;* and might be applied to those who *apprehend prisoners*, or to those who hold a spear or dart in the right hand for the purpose of throwing it. Some have conjectured that it should be read δεξιοβόλους—those who cast or throw [a spear] with the right hand. So the Vulgate, the Syriac, and the Arabic understand it. They were probably those who were armed with spears or darts, and who attended on the tribune as a guard. ¶ *At the third hour of the night.* At nine o'clock. This was in order that it might be done with secrecy, and to elude the band of desperadoes that had resolved to murder Paul. If it should seem that this guard was very numerous for one man, it should be remembered, (1) That the number of those who had conspired against him was also large; and, (2) That they were men accustomed to scenes of blood; men of desperate characters who had solemnly sworn that they would take his life. In order, therefore, to deter them effectually from attacking the guard, it was made very numerous and strong. Nearly five hundred men were appointed to guard Paul as he left Jerusalem.

24. *And provide* them *beasts.* One for Paul, and one for each of his attendants. The word translated *beasts* (κτήνη) is of a general character, and may be applied either to horses, camels, or asses. The latter were most commonly employed in Judea. ¶ *Unto Felix the governor.* The governor of Judea. His place of residence was Cesarea, about sixty miles from Jerusalem. See Notes on ch. viii. 40. His name was Antonius Felix. He was a freedman of Antonia, the mother of the Emperor Claudius. He was high in the favour of Claudius, and was made by him governor of Judea. Josephus calls him Claudius Felix. He had married three wives in succession that were of royal families, one of whom was Drusilla, afterward mentioned in ch. xxiv. 24, who was sister to King Agrippa. Tacitus (*Hist.*, v. 9) says that he governed with all the

they may set Paul on, and bring *him* safe unto Felix the governor.

25 And he wrote a letter after this manner:

26 Claudius Lysias unto the most excellent governor Felix *sendeth* greeting.

27 This[w] man was taken of the Jews, and should have been killed of them; then came I with an army, and rescued him, having understood that he was a Roman.

28 And[x] when I would have known the cause wherefore they accused him, I brought him forth into their council:

29 Whom I perceived to be accused of [y]questions of their law, but to have [z]nothing laid to his charge worthy of death or of bonds.

w ch.21.33; 24.7. *x* ch.22.30.
y ch.18.15; 25.19. *z* ch.26.31.

30 And [a]when it was told me how that the Jews laid wait for the man, I sent straightway to thee, and [b]gave commandment to his accusers also, to say before thee what *they had* against him. Farewell.

31 Then the soldiers, as it was commanded them, took Paul, and brought *him* by night to Antipatris.

32 On the morrow they left the horsemen to go with him, and returned to the castle:

33 Who, when they came to Cesarea, and delivered [c]the epistle to the governor, presented Paul also before him.

34 And when the governor had read *the letter*, he asked of what province he was. And when he understood that *he was* [d]of Cilicia,

a ver.20,21. *b* ch.24.8; 25.6.
c ver.25-30. *d* ch.21.39.

---

authority of a king, and the baseness and insolence of a slave. "He was an unrighteous governor, a base, mercenary, and bad man" (Clarke). See his character further described in the Notes on ch. xxiv. 25.

26. *Unto the most excellent governor Felix.* The most honoured, &c. This was a mere title of office. ¶ *Greeting.* A term of salutation in an epistle wishing health, joy, and prosperity.

27. *Should have been killed of them.* Was about to be killed by them. The life of Paul had been twice endangered in this manner, ch. xxi. 30; xxiii. 10. ¶ *With an army.* With a band of soldiers, ver. 10.

29. *Questions of their law.* So he understood the whole controversy to be. ¶ *Worthy of death.* By the Roman law. He had been guilty of no crime against the Roman people. ¶ *Or of bonds.* Of chains, or of confinement.

31. *To Antipatris.* This town was anciently called Cafar-Saba. Josephus says (*Antiq.*, xiii. 23) that it was about 17 miles from Joppa. It was about 26 miles from Cesarea, and of course about 35 from Jerusalem. Herod the Great changed its name to Antipatris, in honour of his father Antipater. It was situated in a fine plain, and watered with many springs and fountains. The Rev. Eli Smith, D.D., late missionary to Palestine, who took a journey from Jerusalem to Joppa for the purpose of ascertaining Paul's route, supposes that the site of Antipatris is the present Kefr Saba. Of this village he gives the following description in the *Bibliotheca Sacra* for 1843: "It is a Muslim village of considerable size, and wholly like the most common villages of the plain, being built entirely of mud. We saw but one stone building, which was apparently a mosque, but without a minaret. No old ruins, nor the least relic of antiquity, did we anywhere discover. A well by which we stopped, a few rods east of the houses, exhibits more signs of careful workmanship than anything else. It is walled with hewn stone, and is 57 feet deep to the water. The village stands upon a slight circular eminence near the western hills, from which it is actually separated, however, by a branch of the plain."

32. *They left the horsemen.* As they were then beyond the danger of the conspirators, the soldiers who had guarded them thus far returned to Jerusalem.

34. *Of what province he was.* Greek, of what heparchy (ἐπαρχίας) he was. He knew from the letter of Lysias that he was a Roman, but he was not informed of what place or province he

35 I will hear thee, said he,
when[e] thine accusers are also come.
And he commanded him to be
kept in [f]Herod's judgment hall.

CHAPTER XXIV.

AND after five days, [a]Ananias,
the high-priest, descended
with the elders, and *with* a certain
orator *named* Tertullus, who [b]in-
formed the governor against Paul.
2 And when he was called forth,
Tertullus began to accuse *him*, saying, Seeing that by thee we enjoy
great quietness, and that [c]very
worthy deeds are done unto this
nation by thy providence,
3 We accept *it* always, and in

e ch.24.1,&c.; 25.16. f Mat.27.27. a ch.23.2; 25.2. b Ps.11.2. c Ps.12.2.

---

was. This he doubtless did in order to ascertain whether he properly belonged to his jurisdiction. Roman provinces were districts of country which were intrusted to the jurisdiction of procurators. How far the jurisdiction of Felix extended is not certainly known. It appears, however, that it included Cilicia. ¶ Was *of Cilicia*. Tarsus, the birthplace of Paul, was in this province, ch. xxi. 39.

35. *In Herod's judgment hall.* Greek, in the prætorium of Herod. The word here used denoted formerly the *tent* of the Roman prætor; and as that was the place where justice was administered, it came to be applied to halls, or courts of justice. This had been reared probably by Herod the Great as his palace, or as a place for administering justice. It is probable, also, that prisons, or places of security, would be attached to such places.

CHAPTER XXIV.

1. *And after five days.* This time was occupied, doubtless, in their receiving the command to go to Cesarea, and in making the necessary arrangements. This was the twelfth day after Paul's arrival at Jerusalem. See ver. 11. ¶ *Ananias, the high-priest.* See Notes on ch. xxiii. 2. ¶ *Descended.* Came down from Jerusalem. This was the usual language when a departure from Jerusalem was spoken of. See Notes on ch. xv. 1. ¶ With *a certain orator* named *Tertullus.* Appointed to accuse Paul. This is a Roman name, and this man was doubtless a Roman. As the Jews were, to a great extent, ignorant of the Roman laws, and of their mode of administering justice, it is not improbable that they were in the habit of employing Roman lawyers to plead their causes. ¶ *Who informed the governor against Paul.* Who acted as the accuser, or who managed their cause before the governor.

2. *And when he was called forth.* When Paul was called forth from prison. See ch. xxiii. 35. ¶ *We enjoy great quietness.* This was said in the customary style of flatterers and orators, to conciliate the favour of the judge, and is strikingly in contrast with the more honest and straightforward introduction in reply of Paul, ver. 10. Though it was said for flattery, and though Felix was in many respects an unprincipled man, yet it was true that his administration had been the means of producing much peace and order in Judea, and that he had done many things that tended to promote the welfare of the nation. In particular, he had arrested a band of robbers, with Eleazar at their head, whom he had sent to Rome to be punished (Jos. *Antiq.*, b. xx. ch. viii.); he had arrested the Egyptian false prophet who had led out four thousand men into the wilderness, and who threatened the peace of Judea (see Note, ch. xxi. 38); and he had repressed a sedition which arose between the inhabitants of Cesarea and of Syria (Jos. *Jewish Wars*, b. ii. ch. xiii. § 2). ¶ *Very worthy deeds.* Acts that tended much to promote the peace and security of the people. He referred to those which have just been mentioned as having been accomplished by Felix, particularly his success in suppressing riots and seditions; and as, in the view of the Jews, the case of Paul was another instance of a similar kind, he appealed to him with the more confidence that he would suppress that also. ¶ *By thy providence.* By thy foresight, skill, vigilance, prudence.

3. *We accept* it *always.* We *admit* that it is owing to your vigilance, and we accept your interposition to promote peace with gratitude. ¶ *Always, and in all places.* Not merely in your presence, but we always acknowledge that it is owing to your vigilance that the land is secure. "What we now do in your presence, we do also in your absence;

all places, most noble Felix, with all thankfulness.

4 Notwithstanding, that I be not further tedious unto thee, I pray thee that thou wouldest hear us of thy clemency a few words.

5 For we have found this man [d] *a* pestilent *fellow*, and a mover of sedition among all the Jews throughout the world, and a ringleader of the sect of the Nazarenes.

d Lu.23.2; ch.6.13; 16.20; 17.6; 21.28; 1 Pe.2.12,19.

6 Who also hath gone about [e] to profane the temple; whom we took, and would have [f] judged according to our law;

7 But [g] the chief captain Lysias came *upon us*, and with great violence took *him* away out of our hands,

8 Commanding [h] his accusers to come unto thee; by examining of whom, thyself mayest take know-

e ch.19.37; 21.28. *f* Jn.18.31. *g* ch.21.33. *h* ch.23.30.

we do not commend you merely when you are present" (Wetstein). ¶ *Most noble Felix.* This was the title of office. ¶ *With thankfulness.* In this there was probably sincerity, for there was no doubt that the peace of Judea was owing to Felix. But at the same time that he was an energetic and vigilant governor, it was also true that he was proud, avaricious, and cruel. Josephus charges him with injustice and cruelty in the case of Jonathan, the high-priest (*Antiq.*, b. xx. ch. viii. § 5), and Tacitus (*Hist.*, b. v. ch. ix.) and Suetonius (*Life of Claudius*, ch. xxviii.) concur in the charge.

4. *Be not further tedious unto thee.* By taking up your time with an introduction and with commendation.

5. *We have found this man* a *pestilent* fellow—λοιμὸν. This word is commonly applied to a plague or pestilence, and then to a man who corrupts the morals of others, or who is turbulent, and an exciter of sedition. Our translation somewhat weakens the force of the original expression. Tertullus did not say that he was a pestilent *fellow*, but that he was *the very pestilence itself.* In this he referred to their belief that he had been the cause of extensive disturbances everywhere among the Jews. ¶ *And a mover of sedition.* An exciter of tumult. This they pretended he did by preaching doctrines contrary to the laws and customs of Moses, and exciting the Jews to tumult and disorder. ¶ *Throughout the world.* Throughout the Roman empire, and thus leading the Jews to violate the laws, and to produce tumults, riots, and disorder. ¶ *And a ringleader*—πρωτοστάτην. This word occurs nowhere else in the New Testament. It is properly a military word, and denotes one who stands first in an army, a standard-bearer, a leader, a commander. The meaning is, that Paul had been so active, and so prominent in preaching the gospel, that he had been a leader, or the principal person in extending the sect of the Nazarenes. ¶ *Of the sect.* The original word here (αἱρέσεως) is the word from which we have derived the term *heresy.* It is, however, properly translated *sect*, or *party*, and should have been so translated in ver. 14. See Notes on ch. v. 17. ¶ *Of the Nazarenes.* This was the name usually given to Christians by way of contempt. They were so called because Jesus was of Nazareth.

6. *Who also hath gone about.* Who has endeavoured. ¶ *To profane the temple.* This was a serious, but unfounded charge. It arose from the gross calumny of the Jews, when they pretended that he had introduced Greeks into that sacred place, ch. xxi. 28. To this charge he replies in ver. 18. ¶ *And would have judged.* That is, would have condemned and punished. ¶ *According to our law.* Their law, which forbade the introduction of strangers into the temple.

7. *But the chief captain*, &c. Tertullus pretends that they would have judged Paul righteously if Lysias had not interposed; but the truth was, that, without regard to law or justice, they would have murdered him on the spot.

8. *Commanding his accusers*, &c. Ch. xxiii. 30. ¶ *By examining of whom.* That is, the Jews who were then present. Tertullus offered them as his witnesses of the truth of what he had said. It is evident that we have here only the summary or outline of the speech which he made. It is incredible that a Roman rhetorician would have on such an occasion delivered an address so brief, so meagre, and so destitute of display as this. But it is doubtless a correct summary of his ad-

ledge of all these things whereof
we accuse him.
9 And the Jews also assented,
saying that these things were so.
10 Then Paul, after that [1]the
governor had beckoned unto him
to speak, answered, Forasmuch as I
know that thou hast been of many
years a judge unto this nation, I
do the more cheerfully [i]answer for
myself:
11 Because that thou mayest

1 *Felix*, made procurator over *Judea*, A.D. 53.

i 1 Pe.3.15.

---

dress, and contains the leading points of the accusation. It is customary for the sacred writers, as for other writers, to give only the outline of discourses and arguments. Such a course was inevitable, unless the New Testament had been swelled to wholly undue proportions.

9. *And the Jews also assented.* The Jews who had accompanied Tertullus to Cesarea. They had gone as the accusers of Paul, and they bore testimony, when called upon, to the truth of all that the orator had said. Whether they were examined individually or not is not declared. In whatever way their testimony was arrived at, they confirmed unanimously the accusation which he had brought against Paul.

10. *Had beckoned unto him to speak.* Either by a nod or by the hand. ¶ *Hast been of many years.* Felix and Cumanus had been joint governors of Judea; but after Cumanus had been condemned for his bad administration of affairs, the government fell entirely into the hands of Felix. This was about seven years before Paul was arraigned, and might be called *many years*, as he had been long enough there to become acquainted with the customs and habits of the Jews; and it might also be called *long* in comparison with the short time which his immediate predecessors had held the office. See Josephus, *Antiq.*, b. xx. ch. vi. vii. ¶ *A judge.* This word is evidently used here in the sense of *magistrate*, or one appointed to administer the affairs of government. To determine litigated matters was, however, one part of his office. It is remarkable that Paul did not begin his speech, as Tertullus had done, by any flattering address, or by any of the arts of rhetoric. He founded his plea on the justice of his cause, and on the fact that Felix had had so much experience in the affairs of Judea that he was well qualified to understand the merits of the case, and to judge impartially. Paul was well acquainted with his character (see Notes on ch. xxiv. 25), and would not by flattering words declare that which was not strictly true. ¶ *I do the more cheerfully*, &c. Since you are so well acquainted with the customs and habits of the Jews, I the more readily submit the case to your disposal. This address indicated great confidence in the justice of his cause, and was the language of a man bold, fearless, and conscious of innocence.

11. *Because that thou mayest understand.* Greek, "Thou being able to know." That is, he could understand or know by taking the proper evidence. Paul does not mean to say that Felix could understand the case *because* he had been many years a judge of that nation. That fact would qualify him to judge correctly, or to understand the customs of the Jews. But the fact that he himself had been but twelve days in Jerusalem, and had been orderly and peaceable there, Felix could ascertain only by the proper testimony. The first part of Paul's defence (ver. 11–13) consists in an express denial of what they alleged against him. ¶ *Are yet but twelve days.* Beza reckons these twelve days in this manner: The first was that on which he came to Jerusalem, ch. xxi. 15. The second he spent with James and the apostles, ch. xxi. 18. Six days were spent in fulfilling his vow, ch. xxi. 21, 26. On the ninth day the tumult arose, being the seventh day of his vow, and on this day he was rescued by Lysias, ch. xxi. 27; xxii. 29. The tenth day he was before the Sanhedrim, ch. xxii. 30; xxiii. 10. On the eleventh the plot was laid to take his life, and on the same day, at evening, he was removed to Cesarea. The days on which he was confined at Cesarea are not enumerated, since his design in mentioning the number of days was to show the improbability that in that time he had been engaged in producing a tumult; and it would not be pretended that he had been so engaged while confined in a prison at Cesarea. The defence of Paul here is, that but twelve days elapsed from the time that he went to

understand that there are yet but
twelve days since [k]I went up to
Jerusalem for to worship.
12 And they [l]neither found me
in the temple disputing with any
man, neither raising up the people,
neither in the synagogues, nor in
the city.
13 Neither can they [m]prove the
things whereof they now accuse me.
14 But this I confess unto thee,
that after the way which they call

k ch.21.15. *l* ch.25.8; 28.17. *m* 1 Pe.3.16.

Jerusalem till he was put under the custody of Felix; and that during *so short a time* it was wholly improbable that he would have been able to excite sedition. ¶ *For to worship.* This farther shows that the design of Paul was not to produce sedition. He had gone up for the peaceful purpose of devotion, and not to produce riot and disorder. That this was his design in going to Jerusalem, or at least a part of his purpose, is indicated by the passage in Ac. xx. 16. It should be observed, however, that our translation conveys an idea which is not necessarily in the Greek—that this was the *design* of his going to Jerusalem. The original is, "Since I went up to Jerusalem *worshipping*" (προσκυνήσων); that is, he was actually *engaged* in devotion when the tumult arose. But his main design in going to Jerusalem was to convey to his suffering countrymen there the benefactions of the Gentile churches. See ver. 17; Ro. xv. 25, 26.

12. *And they neither found me*, &c. The first charge of Tertullus against Paul was (ver. 5) that he was "a pestilent fellow, and a mover of sedition." The charge of his being *a pest* was so general that Paul did not think it necessary to attempt to refute it. To the *specification* that he was a mover of sedition, he replies by a firm denial, and by a solemn declaration that they had not found him in any synagogue, or in the city, or in the temple, either disputing or exciting a tumult. His conduct there had been entirely peaceable, and they had no right to suppose that it had been otherwise anywhere.

13. *Neither can they prove the things*, &c. That is, that I am a mover of sedition, or a disturber of the peace of the people. This appeal he boldly makes; he challenges investigation; and as they did not offer to specify any acts of disorder or tumult excited by him, this charge falls of course.

14. *But this I confess*, &c. The next specification in the charge of Tertullus was (ver. 5) that he was "a ringleader of the sect of the Nazarenes." To this, Paul replies in this and the two following verses. Of this reply we may observe, (1) That he does not stoop to notice the contempt implied in the use of the word *Nazarenes.* He was engaged in a more important business than to contend about the *name* which they chose to give to Christians. (2) He admits that he belonged to that sect or class of people. That he was a Christian he neither denied, nor was disposed to deny. (3) He maintains that in this way he was still worshipping the God of his fathers. Of this, the fact that he was engaged in worship *in the temple* was sufficient proof. (4) He shows them that he believed only what was written in the law and the prophets; that this involved the main doctrine of their religion—the hope of the resurrection of the dead, ver. 15; and that it was his constant and earnest desire to keep a pure conscience in all things, ver. 16. These are the points of his defence to the second charge, and we shall see that they fully meet and dispose of the accusation. ¶ *After the way.* After the manner or mode of worship. ¶ *Which they call heresy.* This translation does not express to us the force of the original. We have attached to the word *heresy* an idea which is not conveyed by the Greek word, since we now commonly understand by it *error of doctrine.* In Paul's answer here, there is an explicit reference to their charge which does not appear in our version. The charge of Tertullus was, that he was the ringleader *of the sect* (τῆς αἱρέσεως) of the Nazarenes, ver. 5. To this Paul replies, "After the way which they call *sect* (αἵρεσιν, not *error of doctrine*, but after a way which they affirm is producing *division* or *schism*), so worship I the God of my fathers." Paul was not ashamed to be called a follower of that *sect* or *party* among the Jewish people. Nor should we be ashamed to worship God in a mode that is called *heresy* or *schism*, if we do it in obedience to conscience and to God. ¶ *So wor-*

heresy, [n]so worship I [o]the God of
my fathers, [p]believing all things
which are written in [q]the law and
the prophets;
15 And have [r]hope toward God,
which they themselves also allow,
that there shall be [s]a resurrection
of the dead, both of the just and
unjust.
16 And herein do I exercise
myself, [t]to have always a conscience

n Mi.4.5. *o* 2 Ti.1.3. *p* Lu.24.27; ch.26.22; 28.23. *q* Mat.22.40; Lu.16.16; Jn.1.45; ch.13.15; Ro.3.21. *r* ch.23.6,&c.; 26.6,7; 28.20,&c.

s Da.12.2; Jn.5.28,29; 1 Co.15.12-27; Re.20.6,13. *t* ch.23.1.

---

ship I. I continue to worship. I have not departed from the characteristic of the Jewish people, the proper and public acknowledgment of the God of the Jews. ¶ *The God of my fathers.* My father's God, Jehovah; the God whom my Jewish ancestors adored. There is something very touching in this, and fitted to find its way to the heart of a Jew. He had introduced no new object of worship (comp. De. xiii. 1-5); he had not become a follower of a false or foreign God; and *this* fact was really a reply to their charge that he was setting up a new *sect* in religion. The same thing Paul affirms of himself in 2 Ti. i. 3: "I thank God, whom I serve from my forefathers with a pure conscience." ¶ *Believing all things,* &c. Particularly respecting the Messiah. So he more fully explains his meaning in his speech before King Agrippa, ch. xxvi. 23. ¶ *In the law and in the prophets.* Commanded in the law of Moses, and foretold by the prophets. That Paul had ever disbelieved any of these things they could not prove; and his whole course had shown that he fully credited the sacred records. Most of his arguments in defending Christianity had been drawn from the Jewish writings.

15. *And have hope toward God.* Having a hope of the resurrection of the dead, which arises from the promises of God. ¶ *Which they themselves,* &c. That is, the Pharisees. Perhaps he designated in this remark the Pharisees who were present. He held nothing in this great cardinal point which they did not also hold. For the reasons why he introduced this point so prominently, and the success of thus introducing it, see Notes on ch. xxiii. 1-9. ¶ *Both of the just and of the unjust.* Of the righteous and the wicked; that is, of all the race. As *they* held this, they could not arraign him for holding it also.

16. *And herein.* In this, or for this purpose. ¶ *Do I exercise myself—ἀσκῶ.* I accustom or employ myself; I make it my constant aim. Paul often appeals to his conscientiousness as the leading habit of his life. Even before his conversion he endeavoured to act according to the dictates of conscience. See Ac. xxvi. 9; comp. Phi. iii. 5, 6. ¶ *To have always a conscience,* &c. To do that which is right, so that my conscience shall never reproach me. ¶ *Void of offence—ἀπρόσκοπον.* That which is inoffensive, or which does not cause one to stumble or fall. He means that he endeavoured to keep his conscience so enlightened and pure in regard to duty, and that he acted according to its dictates in such a way that his conduct should not be displeasing to God or injurious to man. To have such a conscience implies two things: (1) That it be enlightened or properly informed in regard to truth and duty; and, (2) That that which is made known to be right should be honestly and faithfully performed. Without these two things no man can have a conscience that will be inoffensive and harmless. ¶ *Toward God.* In an honest endeavour to discharge the duties of public and private worship, and to do constantly what he requires—believing all that he has spoken; doing all that he requires; and offering to him the service which he approves. ¶ Toward *men.* In endeavouring to meet all the demands of justice and mercy; to advance their knowledge, happiness, and salvation; living so that I may look back on my life with the reflection that I have done all that I *ought* to have done, and all that I *could* do to promote the welfare of the whole human family. What a noble principle of conduct was this! How elevated and how pure! How unlike the conduct of those who live to gratify debasing sensual appetites, or for gold or honour; of those who pass their lives in such a manner as to offer the grossest offence to God, and to do the most injury to man. The great and noble aim of Paul was to be pure; and no slander of his enemies, no trials, persecutions, perils, or pains of dying could take away the approving

void of offence toward God and *toward* men.

17 Now after many years [u]I came to bring alms to my nation, and offerings.

18 Whereupon certain Jews from Asia found me purified in the temple, neither with multitude, nor with tumult;

19 Who[v] ought to have been here before thee, and object, if they had aught against me.

20 Or else let these same *here* say, if they have found any evil doing in me, while I stood before the council,

21 Except it be for this one voice, that I cried standing among them,

u ch.11.29,30; 20.16; Ro.15.25.

v ch.25.16.

---

voice of conscience. Alike in his travels and in his persecutions; among friends and foes; when preaching in the synagogue, the city, or the desert; or when defending himself before governors and kings, he had this testimony of a self-approving mind. Happy they who thus frame their lives. And happy will be the end of a life where this has been the grand object of the journey through this world.

17. *Now after many years.* After many years' absence. Paul here commences a reply to the charge of Tertullus, that he had endeavoured to profane the temple, ver. 6. He begins by saying that his design in coming up to Jerusalem was to bring to his countrymen needed aid in a time of distress. It would be absurd to suppose, therefore, that his object in coming was to violate the customs of the temple, and to defile it. ¶ *I came to bring.* See ch. xi. 29, 30; comp. Notes on Ro. xv. 25, 26. ¶ *Alms.* Charities; the gift of the churches. ¶ *To my nation.* Not to *all* the nation, but to the poor saints or Christians who were in Judea, and who were suffering much by persecutions and trials. ¶ *And offerings.* The word used here properly denotes an offering or gift of any kind; but it is usually applied to an oblation or offering made to God in the temple —a thank-offering, a sacrifice. This is probably its meaning here. He came to bring aid *to his needy countrymen*, and *an offering to God;* and it was, therefore, no part of his purpose to interfere with, or to profane the worship of the temple.

18. *Certain Jews from Asia.* Ch. xxi. 27. ¶ *Found me purified in the temple.* Ch. xxi. 26, 27. They found me engaged in the sacred service of completing the observance of my vow. ¶ *Neither with multitude.* Not having introduced a multitude with me—in a quiet and peaceful manner.

19. *Who ought to have been here*, &c. They were the proper witnesses, and as they had staid away it showed that they were not prepared to undergo a strict examination. They alone could testify as to anything that occurred in the temple; and as *they* were not present, that charge ought to be dismissed.

20. *Or else.* Since they are not here to witness against me in regard to what occurred in the *temple*, let these here present bear witness against me, if they can, in regard to *any other part* of my conduct. This was a bold appeal, and it showed his full consciousness of innocence. ¶ *Let these same* here *say.* The Jews who are here present. ¶ *Any evil doing.* Any improper conduct, or any violation of the law. ¶ *While I stood before the council.* The Sanhedrim, ch. xxiii. 1–10. As they were present there, Paul admits that they were competent to bear witness to his conduct on that occasion, and calls upon them to testify, if they could, to any impropriety in his conduct.

21. *Except it be for this one voice.* For this one expression or declaration. This was what Paul had said before the council—the *main* thing on which he had insisted, and he calls on them to testify to this, and to show, if they could, that in this declaration he had been wrong. Chubb and other infidels have supposed that Paul here acknowledges that he was *wrong* in the declaration which he made when he said that he was called in question for the doctrine of the resurrection of the dead (ch. xxiii. 6), and that his conscience reproached him for appearing to be time-serving, for concealing the true cause of offence against him, and for attempting to take advantage of their divisions of sentiment, thus endeavouring to produce discord in the council. But against this supposition we may urge the following considerations: (1) Paul wished to fix their attention on the *main* thing

Touching the resurrection of the dead I am called in question by you this day.

22 And when Felix heard these things, having more perfect knowledge of *that* way, he deferred them, and said, When [w]Lysias, the chief captain, shall come down, I will know the uttermost of your matter.

23 And he commanded a centurion to keep Paul, and to [x]let *him* have liberty, and that he should forbid none of his acquaintance to minister or come unto him.

24 And after certain days, when Felix came with his wife Drusilla, which was a Jewess, he sent for Paul, and heard him concerning the faith in Christ.

w ver.7.

x ch.27.3; 28.16.

---

which he had said before the council. (2) It was true, as has been shown on the passage (xxiii. 1–10), that this was the principal doctrine which Paul had been defending. (3) If they were prepared to witness against him for holding and teaching the resurrection of the dead as a false or evil doctrine, he called on them to do it. As this had been the *only* thing which they had witnessed before the council, he calls on them to testify to what they knew only, and to show, if they could, that this was wrong. ¶ *Touching the resurrection*, &c. Respecting the resurrection, ch. xxiii. 6.

22. *Having more perfect knowledge of* that *way*. Our translation of this verse is very obscure, and critics are divided about the proper interpretation of the original. Many (Erasmus, Luther, Michaelis, Morus, &c.) render it, "Although he had a more perfect knowledge of the Christian doctrine than Paul's accusers had, yet he deferred the hearing of the cause till Lysias had come down." They observe that he might have obtained this knowledge not only from the letter of Lysias, but from public rumour, as there were doubtless Christians at Cesarea. They suppose that he deferred the cause either with the hope of receiving a bribe from Paul (comp. ver. 26), or to gratify the Jews with his being longer detained as a prisoner. Others, among whom are Beza, Grotius, Rosenmüller, and Doddridge, suppose that it should be rendered, "He deferred them, and said, after I have been more accurately informed concerning this way, when Lysias has come down, I will hear the cause." This is doubtless the true interpretation of the passage, and it is rendered more probable by the fact that Felix sent for Paul, and heard him concerning the faith of Christ (ver. 24), evidently with the design to make himself better acquainted with the charges against him, and the nature of his belief. ¶ *Of* that *way*. Of the Christian religion. This expression is repeatedly used by Luke to denote the Christian doctrine. See Notes on ch. ix. 2. ¶ *He deferred them*. He put them off; he postponed the decision of the case; he adjourned the trial. ¶ *When Lysias*, &c. Lysias had been acquainted with the excitement and its causes, and Felix regarded him as an important witness in regard to the true nature of the charges against Paul. ¶ *I will know the uttermost*, &c. I shall be fully informed, and prepared to decide the cause.

23. *And he commanded*, &c. It is evident from this verse that Felix was disposed to show Paul all the favours that were consistent with his safe keeping. He esteemed him to be a persecuted man, and doubtless regarded the charges against him as entirely malicious. What was Felix's *motive* in this cannot be certainly known. It is not improbable, however, that he detained him, (1) To gratify the Jews by keeping him in custody as if he were guilty, and, (2) That he hoped the friends of Paul would give him money to release him. Perhaps it was for this purpose that he gave orders that his friends should have free access to him, that thus Paul might be furnished with the means of purchasing his freedom.

24. *Felix came, with his wife Drusilla.* Drusilla was the daughter of Herod Agrippa the elder, and was engaged to be married to Epiphanes, the son of King Antiochus, on condition that he would embrace the Jewish religion; but as he afterward refused to do that, the contract was broken off. Afterward she was given in marriage, by her brother Agrippa the younger, to Azizus, king of Emesa, upon his consent to be circumcised. When Felix was governor

25 And as he reasoned of [y]righteousness, [z]temperance, and [a]judgment to come, [b]Felix trembled, and answered, [c]Go thy way for this time; when I have a convenient season I will call for thee.

y Pr.16.12; Je.22.15-17; Da.4.27; Jn.16.8.
z Pr.31.4,5; Da.5.1-4; Ho.7.5; 1 Pe.4.4.
a Ps.50.3,4; Da.12.2; Mat.25.31-46; 2 Co.5.10; Re. 20.12.
b Ps.99.1; Is.32.11; Hab.3.16; He.4.1,12.
c Pr.1.24-32; Mat.22.5; 25.1-10.

---

of Judea, he saw Drusilla and fell in love with her, and sent to her Simon, one of his friends, a Jew, by birth a Cyprian, who pretended to be a magician, to endeavour to persuade her to forsake her husband and to marry Felix. Accordingly, in order to avoid the envy of her sister Bernice, who treated her ill on account of her beauty, "she was prevailed on," says Josephus, "to transgress the laws of her forefathers, and to marry Felix" (Josephus, *Antiq.*, b. xx. ch. vii. § 1, 2). She was, therefore, living in adultery with him, and this was probably the reason why Paul dwelt in his discourse before Felix particularly on "temperance," or chastity. See Notes on ver. 25. ¶ *He sent for Paul, and heard him.* Perhaps he did this in order to be more fully acquainted with the case which was submitted to him. It is possible, also, that it might have been to gratify his wife, who was a Jewess, and who doubtless had a desire to be acquainted with the principles of this new sect. It is certain, also, that one object which Felix had in this was to let Paul see how dependent he was on him, and to induce him to purchase his liberty. ¶ *Concerning the faith in Christ.* Concerning the Christian religion. Faith in Christ is often used to denote the whole of Christianity, as it is the leading and characteristic feature of the religion of the gospel.

25. *And as he reasoned.* Greek, "And he discoursing"—διαλεγομένου δὲ αὐτοῦ. No argument should be drawn from the word that is used here to prove that Paul particularly appealed to *reason*, or that his discourse was *argumentative.* That it *was* so is, indeed, not improbable, from all that we know of the man, and from the topics on which he discoursed. But the word used here means simply as he *discoursed*, and is applied usually to making a public address, to preaching, &c., in whatever way it is done, Ac. xvii. 2; xviii. 4, 19; xix. 8, 9; xxiv. 12. Felix and Drusilla intended this as a matter of entertainment or amusement. Paul readily obeyed their summons, as it gave him an opportunity to preach the gospel to them; and as they desired his sentiments in regard to the faith in Christ, he selected those topics which were adapted to their condition, and stated those principles of the Christian religion which were fitted to arrest their attention, and to lead them to repentance. Paul seized every opportunity of making known the gospel; and whether a prisoner or at liberty; whether before princes, governors, kings, or common people, he was equally prepared to defend the pure and holy doctrines of the cross. His boldness in this instance is the more remarkable, as he was dependent on Felix for his release. A time-server or an impostor would have chosen such topics as would have conciliated the favour of the judge, and procured his discharge from custody. He would have flattered his vanity or palliated his vices. *But such an idea never seems to have occurred to Paul.* His aim was to defend the truth, and to save, if possible, the souls of Drusilla and of Felix. ¶ *Of righteousness*—περὶ δικαιοσύνης. Of justice. Not of the justice of God particularly, but of the nature and requirements of justice in the relations of life—the relations which we sustain to God and to man. This was a proper topic with which to introduce his discourse, as it was the office of Felix to dispense justice between man and man, and as his administration was not remarkable for the exercise of that virtue. It is evident that he could be influenced by a bribe (ver. 26), and it was proper for Paul to dwell on this, as designed to show him the guilt of his life, and his danger of meeting the justice of a Being who cannot be bribed, but who will dispense equal justice alike to the great and the mean. That Paul dwelt also on the *justice* of God, as the moral governor of the world, may also be presumed. The apprehension of *that* justice, and the remembrance of his own guilty life, tended to produce the alarm of Felix, and to make him tremble. ¶ *Temperance*—ἐγκρατείας. The word *temperance* we now use commonly to denote moderation, or restraint in regard to eating and drinking, particularly to abstinence from the use of ardent spirits. But this is

not its meaning here. There is no reason to suppose that Felix was *intemperate* in the use of intoxicating liquors. The original word here denotes a restraint of all the passions and evil inclinations, and may be applied to prudence, chastity, and moderation in general. The particular thing in the life of Felix which Paul had probably in view was the indulgence of licentious desires, or incontinence. He was living in adultery with Drusilla, and for this Paul wished doubtless to bring him to repentance. ¶ *And judgment to come.* The universal judgment that was to come on all transgressors. On this topic Paul also dwelt when he preached on Mars' Hill at Athens, Ac. xvii. 31. These topics were admirably adapted to excite the alarm of both Felix and Drusilla. It evinced great boldness and faithfulness in Paul to select them, and the result showed that he correctly judged of the kind of truth which was adapted to alarm the fears of his guilty auditor. ¶ *Felix trembled.* In view of his past sins, and in the apprehension of the judgment to come. The Greek (ἔμφοβος) does not denote that his body was agitated or shaken, but only that he was alarmed or terrified. That such fear usually shakes the frame, we know; but it is not certain that the body of Felix was thus agitated. He was alarmed and terrified, and looked with deep apprehension to the coming judgment. This was a remarkable instance of the effect of truth on the mind of a man unaccustomed to such alarms, and unused to hear such truth. It shows the power of conscience when thus, under the preaching of a *prisoner*, the judge is thrown into violent alarm. ¶ *And answered, Go thy way*, &c. How different is this answer from that of the jailer of Philippi when alarmed in a similar manner! *He* asked, "What must I do to be saved?" and was directed to him in whom he found peace from a troubled conscience, Ac. xvi. 30, 31. Felix was troubled; but instead of asking what he should do, he sent the messenger of God away. He was evidently not prepared to break off his sins and turn to God. He sought peace by sending away his reprover, and manifestly intended *then* to banish the subject from his mind. Yet, like others, he did not intend to banish it altogether. He looked forward to a time when he would be more at leisure; when the cares of office would press less heavily on his attention; or when he would be more disposed to attend to it. Thus multitudes, when they are alarmed, and see their guilt and danger, resolve to defer it to a more convenient time. One man is engaged in a career of pleasure, and it is not *now* a convenient time to attend to his soul's salvation. Another is pressed with business; with the cares of life; with a plan of gain; with the labours of office or of a profession, and it is not *now* a convenient time for him to attend to religion. Another supposes that his time of life is not the most convenient. His youth he desires to spend in pleasure, and waits for a more convenient time in middle age. His middle life he spends in business, and *this* is not a convenient time. Such a period he expects then to find in old age. But as age advances he finds an increasing disposition to defer it; he is still indisposed to attend to it; still in love with the world. Even old age is seldom found to be a convenient time to prepare for heaven; and it is deferred from one period of life to another, till death closes the scene. It has been commonly supposed and said that Felix never found that more convenient time to call for Paul. That he did not embrace the Christian religion, and forsake his sins, is probable, nay, almost certain. But it is not true that he did not take an opportunity of hearing Paul further on the subject; for it is said that he sent for him often, and communed with him. But, though Felix found this opportunity, yet, (1) We have no reason to suppose that the *main thing*—the salvation of his soul—ever again occupied his attention. There is no evidence that he was again alarmed or awakened, or that he had any further solicitude on the subject of his sins. He had passed for ever the favourable time—the golden moments when he might have secured the salvation of his soul. (2) Others have no right to suppose that their lives will be lengthened out that they may have *any* further opportunity to attend to the subject of religion. (3) When a sinner is awakened, and sees his past sins, if he rejects the appeal to his conscience *then*, and defers it to a more convenient opportunity, he has no reason to expect that his attention will ever be again called with deep interest to the subject. He may live, but he may live without the strivings of the Holy Spirit. When a man has once deliberately rejected the offers of mercy;

26 He hoped also that [d]money should have been given him of Paul, that he might loose him; wherefore he sent for him the oftener, and communed with him.

27 But after two years, Porcius Festus came into Felix' room; and

d Ex.23.8.

when he has trifled with the influences of the Spirit of God, he has no *right* or *reason* to expect that that Spirit will ever strive with him again. Such, we have too much reason to fear, was the case with Felix. Though he often saw Paul again, and "communed with him," yet there is no statement that he was again alarmed or awakened. And thus sinners often attend on the means of grace after they have grieved the Holy Spirit; they listen to the doctrines of the gospel, they hear its appeals and its warnings, but they have no feeling, no interest, and die in their sins. ¶ *A more convenient time.* Greek, "taking time." I will take a time for this. ¶ *I will call for thee.* To hear thee further on this subject. This he did, ver. 26. It is remarkable that Drusilla was not alarmed. She was as much involved in guilt as Felix; but she, being a Jewess, had been accustomed to hear of a future judgment until it caused in her mind no alarm. Perhaps also she depended on the rites and ceremonies of her religion as a sufficient expiation for her sins. She might have been resting on those false dependencies which go to free the conscience from a sense of guilt, and which thus beguile and destroy the soul.

26. *He hoped also.* He thought that by giving him access to his friends, and by often meeting him himself, and showing kindness, Paul might be induced to attempt to purchase his freedom with a bribe. ¶ *That money should have been given him of Paul.* That Paul would give him money to procure a release. This shows the character of Felix. He was desirous of procuring a bribe. Paul had proved his innocence, and should have been at once discharged. But Felix was influenced by avarice, and he therefore detained Paul in custody with the hope that, wearied with confinement, he would seek his release by a bribe. But Paul offered no bribe. He knew what was justice, and he would not be guilty, therefore, of attempting to purchase what was his due, or of gratifying a man who prostituted his high office for the purposes of gain. The Roman governors in the provinces were commonly rapacious and avaricious, like Felix. They usually took the office for its pecuniary advantage, and they consequently usually disregarded justice, and made the procuring of money their leading object. ¶ *He sent for him the oftener.* It may seem remarkable that he did not fear that he would again become alarmed. But the hope of money overcame all this. Having once resisted the reasoning of Paul, and the strivings of the Spirit of God, he seems to have had no further alarm or anxiety. He could again hear the same man, and the same truth, unaffected. When sinners have once grieved God's Spirit, they often sit with unconcern under the same truth which once alarmed them, and become entirely hardened and unconcerned. ¶ *And communed with him.* And conversed with him.

27. *But after two years.* Paul was unjustly detained during all this time. The hope of Felix seems to have been to weary his patience, and induce him to purchase his freedom. ¶ *Came into Felix' room.* As governor. ¶ *And Felix, willing to show the Jews a pleasure.* Desirous of pleasing them, even at the expense of justice. This shows the principle on which he acted. ¶ *Left Paul bound.* Left him in custody to the charge of his successor. His object in this was to conciliate the Jews; that is, to secure their favour, and to prevent them, if possible, from accusing him for the evils of his administration before the emperor. The account which Luke gives here coincides remarkably with that which Josephus has given. He says that Porcius Festus was sent as successor to Felix by Nero. He does not, indeed, mention Paul, or say that Felix sought to conciliate the favour of the Jews, but he gives such an account as to make the statement by Luke *perfectly consistent* with his character while in office. He informs us that Felix was unpopular, and that there was reason to apprehend that the Jews would accuse him before the emperor; and, *therefore,* the statement in the Acts that he would be willing to show the Jews a favour, is in perfect keeping with his character and circumstances, and is one of those *undesigned coinci-*

Felix, [e]willing to show the Jews a
pleasure, left Paul bound.

CHAPTER XXV.

NOW when Festus was come
into the province, after three
days he ascended from Cesarea to
Jerusalem.
2 Then the high-priest and the
chief of the Jews informed him
against Paul, and besought him,
3 And desired favour against
him, that he would send for him

e Mar.15.15; ch.25.9.

---

dences which show that the author of the Acts was fully acquainted with the circumstances of the time, and that his history is true. The account in Josephus is, that "when Porcius Festus was sent as successor to Felix by Nero, the principal inhabitants of Cesarea went up to Rome to accuse Felix; and he had been certainly brought to punishment unless Nero had yielded to the importunate solicitations of his brother Palias, who was at that time had in the greatest honour by him" (*Antiq.*, b. xx. ch. viii. § 9). The plan of Felix, therefore, in suppressing the enmity of the Jews, and conciliating their favour by injustice to Paul, did not succeed, and is one of those instances, so numerous in the world, where a man gains nothing by wickedness. He sought money from Paul by iniquity, and failed; he sought by injustice to obtain the favour of the Jews, and failed in that also. And the inference from the whole transaction is, that "honesty is the best policy," and that men in any office should pursue a course of firm, constant, and undeviating integrity.

CHAPTER XXV.

1. *Now when Festus was come.* See Notes on ch. xxiv. 27. ¶ *Into the province.* The province of Judea; for Judea at that time was a Roman province. ¶ *After three days.* Having remained three days at Cesarea. ¶ *He ascended.* This was the usual language in describing a journey to Jerusalem. Thus the English people speak of going up to London, because it is the capital. See Notes on ch. xv. 1. ¶ *To Jerusalem.* The governors of Judea at this time usually resided at Cesarea; but as Jerusalem had been the former capital; as it was still the seat of the religious solemnities; as the Sanhedrim held its meetings there; and as the great, and rich, and learned men, and the priests resided there, it is evident that a full knowledge of the state of the province could be obtained only there. Festus, therefore, having entered on the duties of his office, early went to Jerusalem to make himself acquainted with the affairs of the nation.

2. *Then the high-priest.* The high-priest at this time was Ismael, the son of Fabi. He had been promoted to that office by Agrippa (Josephus, *Antiq.*, b. xx. ch. viii. § 8). It is probable, however, that the person here intended was Ananias, who had been high-priest, and who would retain the name. See Notes on ch. xxiii. 2. Some MSS. read *high-priests* here in the plural number, and this reading is approved by Mill and Griesbach. There is, however, no improbability in supposing that the high-priest Ismael might have been also as much enraged against Paul as the others. ¶ *Informed him against Paul.* Informed him of the accusation against him, and doubtless endeavoured to prejudice the mind of Festus against him. They thus showed their unrelenting disposition. It might have been supposed that after two years this unjust prosecution would be abandoned and forgotten. But malice does not thus forget its object, and the spirit of persecution is not thus satisfied. It is evident that there was here every probability that injustice would be done to Paul, and that the mind of Festus would be biased against him. He was a stranger to Paul, and to the embittered feelings of the Jewish character. He would wish to conciliate their favour on entering on the duties of his office. A strong representation, therefore, made by the chief men of the nation, would be likely to prejudice him violently against Paul, and to unfit him for the exercise of impartial justice.

3. *And desired favour against him.* Desired the favour of Festus, that they might accomplish their wicked purpose on Paul. ¶ *Would send for him to Jerusalem.* Probably under a pretence that he might be tried by the Sanhedrim; or perhaps they wished Festus to hear the cause there, and to decide it while he was at Jerusalem. Their *real* motive is immediately stated. ¶ *Laying wait in*

to Jerusalem, [a]laying wait in the
way to kill him.
4 But Festus answered that Paul
should be kept at Cesarea, and that
he himself would depart shortly
thither.
5 Let them therefore, said he,
which among you are able, go down
with *me*, and accuse this man, if
there be any wickedness in him.
6 And when he had tarried
among them [1]more than ten days,
he went down unto Cesarea; and
the next day, sitting in the judgment seat, commanded Paul to be
brought.
7 And when he was come, the
Jews which came down from Jerusalem stood round about, and laid
many and grievous complaints
against Paul, [b]which they could
not prove.
8 While he answered for himself, Neither against the laws of
the Jews, neither against the temple, nor yet against Cæsar, have I
offended any thing at all.
9 But Festus, willing to do the
Jews a pleasure, answered Paul,

a ch.23.14,15.
1 or, as some copies read, *no more than eight or ten days.*

b Ps.35.11; Mat.5.11,12; ch.24.5,13.

the way to kill him. That is, they *would* lie in wait, or they would employ a band of Sicarii, or assassins, to take his life on the journey. See Notes on ch. xxi. 38; xxiii. 12. It is altogether probable that if this request had been granted, Paul would have been killed. But God had promised him that he should bear witness to the truth at Rome (ch. xxiii. 11), and his providence was remarkable in thus influencing the mind of the Roman governor, and defeating the plans of the Jewish council.

4. *But Festus answered*, &c. What induced Festus to refuse their request is not known. It is probable, however, that he was apprised that Paul was a Roman citizen, and that his case could not come before the Jewish Sanhedrim, but must be heard by himself. As Cesarea was also at that time the residence of the Roman governor, and the place of holding the courts, and as Paul was lodged there safely, there did not appear to be any sufficient reason for removing him to Jerusalem for trial. Festus, however, granted them all that they could reasonably ask, and assured them that he should have a speedy trial.

5. *Which among you are able.* Enjoy all the advantages of just trial, and exhibit your accusations with all the learning and talent in your power. This was all that they could reasonably ask at his hands.

6. *More than ten days.* See the margin. The Syriac reads it, "eight or ten." The Vulgate, "not more than eight or ten." The Coptic, "eight or ten." Griesbach supposes this to be the true reading, and has admitted it into the text. ¶ *Sitting in the judgment seat.* On the tribunal; or holding a court for the trial of Paul. ¶ *Commanded Paul to be brought.* To be brought up for trial. He had been secured, but was placed in the care of a soldier, who was commanded to let him have all the freedom that was consistent with his security.

7. *Grievous complaints.* Heavy accusations. Doubtless the same with which they had charged him before Felix, ch. xxiv. 5, 6. Comp. ch. xxv. 19. ¶ *Which they could not prove.* Ch. xxiv. 13, 19.

8. *While he answered*, &c. See this answer more at length in ch. xxiv. 10–21. As the accusations against him were the same now as then, he made to them the same reply.

9. *But Festus, willing to do the Jews a pleasure.* Desirous of securing their favour, as he had just entered on his administration. Comp. ch. xxiv. 27. In this he evinced rather a desire of popularity than an inclination to do justice. Had he been disposed to do right at once, he would have immediately discharged Paul. Festus perceived that the case was one that did not come fairly within the jurisdiction of a Roman magistrate; that it pertained solely to the customs and questions among the Jews (ver. 18–20); and he therefore proposed that the case should be tried before *him* at Jerusalem. It is remarkable, however, that he had such a sense of justice and law as not to suffer the case to go out of his own hands. He proposed still to hear the cause, but asked Paul whether he was willing that

and said, Wilt thou go up to Jerusalem, and there be judged of these things before me?
10 Then said Paul, I stand at Cæsar's judgment seat, where I ought to be judged; to the Jews have I done no wrong, as thou very well knowest.
11 For if I be an offender, or have committed any thing worthy

---

it should be tried at Jerusalem. As the question which he asked Paul was one on which he was at liberty to take his own course, and as Paul had no reason to expect that his going to Jerusalem would facilitate the cause of justice, it is not remarkable that he declined the offer, as perhaps Festus supposed he would.

10. *Then said Paul*, &c. The reasons why Paul declined the proposal to be tried at Jerusalem are obvious. He had experienced so much violent persecution from his countrymen, and their minds were so full of prejudice, misconception, and enmity, that he had neither justice nor favour to hope at their hands. He knew, too, that they had formerly plotted against his life, and that he had been removed to Cesarea for the purpose of safety. It would be madness and folly to throw himself again into their hands, or to give them another opportunity to form a plan against his life. As he was, therefore, under no obligation to return to Jerusalem, and as Festus did not propose it because it could be supposed that justice would be promoted by it, but to gratify the Jews, Paul prudently declined the proposal, and appealed to the Roman emperor. ¶ *I stand at Cæsar's judgment seat.* The Roman emperors after Julius Cæsar were all called Cæsar; thus, Augustus Cæsar, Claudius Cæsar, &c., as all the kings of Egypt were called Pharaoh, though they had each his proper name, as Pharaoh Necho, &c. The emperor at this time (A.D. 60) was Nero, one of the most cruel and impious men that ever sat on a throne. It was under him that Paul was afterward beheaded. When Paul says, "I stand at Cæsar's judgment seat," he means to say that he regarded the tribunal before which he then stood, and on which Festus sat, as really the judgment seat of Cæsar. The procurator, or governor, held his commission from the Roman emperor, and it was, in fact, his tribunal. The *reason* why Paul made this declaration may be thus expressed: "I am a Roman citizen. I have a right to justice. I am under no obligation to put myself again in the hands of the Jews. I have a right to a fair and impartial trial; and I claim the protection and privileges which all Roman citizens have before their tribunals—the right of a fair and just trial." It was, therefore, a severe rebuke of Festus for proposing to depart from the known justice of the Roman laws, and, for the sake of popularity, proposing to him to put himself in the hands of his enemies. ¶ *Where I ought to be judged.* Where I have a right to demand and expect justice. I have a right to be tried where courts are usually held, and according to all the forms of equity which are usually observed. ¶ *I have done no wrong.* I have not injured their persons, property, character, or religion. This was a bold appeal, which his consciousness of innocence and the whole course of proceedings enabled him to make without the possibility of their gainsaying it. ¶ *As thou very well knowest.* Festus knew, probably, that Paul had been tried by Felix, and that nothing was proved against him. He had now seen the spirit of the Jews, and the cause why they arraigned him. He had given Paul a trial, and had called on the Jews to adduce their "able" men to accuse him, and after all nothing had been proved against him. Festus *knew*, therefore, that he was innocent. This abundantly appears also from his own confession, ver. 18, 19. As he knew this, and as Festus was proposing to depart from the regular course of justice for the sake of popularity, it was proper for Paul to use the strong language of rebuke, and to claim what he knew Festus did not dare to deny him, the protection of the Roman laws. Conscious innocence may be bold; and Christians have a right to insist on impartial justice and the protection of the laws. Alas! how many magistrates there have been like Festus, who, when Christians have been arraigned before them, have been fully satisfied of their innocence, but who, for the sake of popularity, have departed from all the rules of law and all the claims of justice.

11. *For if I be an offender.* If I have injured the Jews so as to deserve death. If it can be proved that I have done

of death, I refuse not to die; but if there be none of these things whereof these accuse me, no man may deliver me unto them. [c]I appeal unto Cæsar.

12 Then Festus, when he had conferred with the council, answered, Hast thou appealed unto Cæsar? unto Cæsar shalt thou go.

13 And after certain days, king

c ch.26.32.

injury to anyone. ¶ *I refuse not to die.* I have no wish to escape justice. I do not wish to evade the laws, or to take advantage of any circumstances to screen me from just punishment. Paul's whole course showed that this was the noble spirit which actuated him. No true Christian wishes to escape from the laws. He will honour them, and not seek to evade them. But, like other men, he has rights; and he may and should insist that justice should be done. ¶ *No man may deliver me unto them.* No man shall be allowed to do it. This bold and confident declaration Paul could make, because he knew what the law required, and he knew that Festus would not *dare* to deliver him up contrary to the law. Boldness is not incompatible with Christianity; and innocence, when its rights are invaded, is always bold. Jesus firmly asserted his rights when on trial (Jn. xviii. 23), and no man is under obligation to submit to be trampled on by an unjust tribunal in violation of the laws. ¶ *I appeal unto Cæsar.* I appeal to the Roman emperor, and carry my cause directly before him. By the Valerian, Porcian, and Sempronian laws, it had been enacted that if any magistrate should be about to beat, or to put to death any Roman citizen, the accused could appeal to the Roman people, and this appeal carried the cause to Rome. The law was so far changed under the emperors that the cause should be carried before the emperor instead of the people. Every citizen had the right of this appeal; and when it was made, the accused was sent to Rome for trial. Thus Pliny (*Ep.* 10, 97) says that those Christians who were accused, and who, being Roman citizens, appealed to Cæsar, he sent to Rome to be tried. The reason why Paul made this appeal was that he saw that justice would not be done him by the Roman governor. He had been tried by Felix, and justice had been denied him, and he was detained a prisoner in violation of law, to gratify the Jews; he had now been tried by Festus, and saw that he was pursuing the same course; and he resolved, therefore, to assert his rights, and remove the cause far from Jerusalem, and from the prejudiced men in that city, at once to Rome. It was in this mysterious way that Paul's long-cherished desire to see the Roman church, and to preach the gospel there, was to be gratified. Comp. Notes on Ro. i. 9-11. For this he had prayed long (Ro. i. 10; xv. 23, 24), and now at length this purpose was to be fulfilled. God answers prayer, but it is often in a way which we little anticipate. He so orders the train of events; he so places us amidst a pressure of circumstances, that the desire is granted in a way which we could never have anticipated, but which shows in the best manner that he is a hearer of prayer.

12. *When he had conferred with the council.* With his associate judges, or with those who were his counsellors in the administration of justice. They were made up of the chief persons, probably military as well as civil, who were about him, and who were his assistants in the administration of the affairs of the province. ¶ *Unto Cæsar shalt thou go.* He was willing in this way to rid himself of the trial, and of the vexation attending it. He did not *dare* to deliver him to the Jews in violation of the Roman laws, and he was not willing to do justice to Paul, and thus make himself unpopular with the Jews. He was, therefore, probably rejoiced at the opportunity of thus freeing himself from all the trouble in the case in a manner against which none could object.

13. *After certain days, king Agrippa.* This Agrippa was the son of Herod Agrippa (Ac. xii. 1), and great-grandson of Herod the Great. His mother's name was Cypros (Josephus, *Jewish Wars*, b. ii. ch. xi. § 6). When his father died he was at Rome with the Emperor Claudius. Josephus says that the emperor was inclined to bestow upon him all his father's dominions, but was dissuaded by his ministers. The reason of this was, that it was thought imprudent to bestow so large a kingdom on so young a man, and one so inexperienced. Accordingly, Claudius sent Cuspius Fadus to be procurator of Judea

Agrippa and Bernice came unto
Cesarea to salute Festus.
14 And when they had been
there many days, Festus declared
Paul's cause unto the king, saying,
There is a certain man left in
bonds by Felix;
15 About whom, [d]when I was
at Jerusalem, the chief priests and
the elders of the Jews informed
me, desiring *to have* judgment
against him.
16 To whom I answered, It
is not the manner of the Romans
to deliver any man to die, before
that he which is accused have the
accusers face to face, and have

d ver.2,3.

---

and of the entire kingdom (Josephus, *Antiq.*, b. xix. ch. ix. § 2). When Herod, the brother of his father, Agrippa the Great, died in the eighth year of the reign of Claudius, his kingdom—the kingdom of Chalcis—was bestowed by Claudius on Agrippa (Josephus, *Antiq.*, b. xx. ch. v. § 2). Afterward he bestowed on him the tetrarchy of Philip and Batanea, and added to it Trachonitis with Abila (*Antiq.*, b. xx. ch. vii. § 1). After the death of Claudius, Nero, his successor, added to his dominions Julias in Perea and a part of Galilee. Agrippa had been brought up at Rome, and was strongly attached to the Romans. When the troubles commenced in Judea which ended in the destruction of Jerusalem, he did all that he could to preserve peace and order, but in vain. He afterward joined his troops with those of the Romans, and assisted them at the destruction of Jerusalem. After the captivity of that city he went to Rome with his sister Bernice, where he ended his days. He died at the age of seventy years, about A.D. 90. His manner of living with his sister gave occasion to reports respecting him very little to his advantage. ¶ *And Bernice.* She was sister of Agrippa. She had been married to Herod, king of Chalcis, her own uncle by her father's side. After his death she proposed to Polemon, king of Pontus and part of Cilicia, that if he would become circumcised she would marry him. He complied, but she did not continue long with him. After she left him she returned to her brother Agrippa, with whom she lived in a manner such as to excite scandal. Josephus directly charges her with incest with her brother Agrippa (*Antiq.*, b. xx. ch. vii. § 3). ¶ *To salute Festus.* To show him respect as the governor of Judea.

14. *Festus declared Paul's cause.* He did this, probably, because Agrippa, being a Jew, would be supposed to be interested in the case. It was natural that this trial should be a topic of conversation, and perhaps Festus might be disposed to ask what was proper to be done in such cases. ¶ *Left in bonds.* Greek, "a prisoner"—δέσμιος. He was left in custody, probably in the keeping of a soldier, ch. xxiv. 23, 27.

15. *About whom,* &c. See ver. 1–5. ¶ To have *judgment against him.* To have him condemned.

16. *It is not the manner,* &c. He here states the reasons which he gave the Jews for not delivering Paul into their hands. In ver. 4, 5, we have an account of the *fact* that he would not accede to the requests of the Jews; and he here states that the reason of his refusal was that it was contrary to the Roman law. Appian, in his *Roman History*, says, "It is not their custom to condemn men before they are heard." Philo (*De Præsi. Rom.*) says the same thing. In Tacitus (*Annales*, ii.) it is said, "A defendant is not to be prohibited from adducing all things by which his innocence may be established." It was for this that the equity of the Roman jurisprudence was celebrated throughout the world. We may remark that it is a subject of sincere gratitude to the God of our nation that this privilege is enjoyed in the highest perfection in this land. It is a right which every man has: to be heard; to know the charges against him; to be confronted with the witnesses; to make his defence; and to be tried by the *laws*, and not by the *passions* and *caprices* of men. In this respect our jurisprudence surpasses all that Rome ever enjoyed, and is not inferior to that of the most favoured nation of the earth. ¶ *To deliver.* To give him up as a favour (χαρίζεσθαι) to popular clamour and caprice. Yet our Saviour, in violation of the Roman laws, was thus given up by Pilate, Mat. xxvii. 18–25. ¶ *Have the accusers face to face.* That he may know who they are and hear their accusations. Nothing contributes

licence to answer for himself concerning the crime laid against him.

17 Therefore, [e]when they were come hither, without any delay on the morrow I sat on the judgment seat, and commanded the man to be brought forth;

18 Against whom, when the accusers stood up, they brought none accusation of such things as I supposed;

19 But[f] had certain questions against him of their own superstition, and of one Jesus, which was dead, whom Paul affirmed to be alive.

20 And because [2]I doubted of such manner of questions, I asked *him* whether he would go to Jerusalem, and there be judged of these matters.

21 But when Paul had appealed to be reserved unto the [3]hearing

e ver.6. f ch.18.15.

2 or, *I was doubtful how to inquire hereof.*
3 or, *judgment.*

---

more to justice than this. Tyrants suffer men to be accused without knowing who the accusers are, and without an opportunity of meeting the charges. It is one great principle of modern jurisprudence that the accused may know the accusers, and be permitted to confront the witnesses, and to adduce all the testimony possible in his own defence. ¶ *And have licence.* Greek, "place of apology"—may have the liberty of defending himself.

17. *Therefore when they were come hither,* &c. See ver. 6.

18. *None accusation,* &c. No charge as I expected of a breach of the peace; of a violation of the Roman law; of atrocious crime. It was natural that Festus should suppose that they would accuse Paul of some such offence. He had been arraigned before Felix; had been two years in custody; and the Jews were exceedingly violent against him. All this, Festus would presume, must have arisen from some flagrant and open violation of the laws.

19. *But had certain questions.* Certain inquiries, or litigated and disputed subjects; certain points of dispute in which they differed—ζητήματα τινα. ¶ *Of their own superstition*—δεισιδαιμονίας. This word properly denotes the worship or fear of demons; but it was applied by the Greeks and Romans to the worship of their gods. It is the same word which is used in Ac. xvii. 22, where it is used in a good sense. See Notes on that place. There are two reasons for thinking that Festus used the word here in a good sense, and not in the sense in which we use the word superstition. (1) It was the word by which the worship of the Greeks and Romans, and, therefore, of Festus himself, was denoted, and he would naturally use it in a similar sense in applying it to the Jews. He would describe their worship in such language as he was accustomed to use when speaking of religion. (2) He knew that Agrippa was a Jew. Festus would not probably speak of the religion of his royal guest as *superstition*, but would speak of it with respect. He meant, therefore, to say simply that they had certain inquiries about their own *religion*, but accused him of no crime against the Roman laws. ¶ *And of one Jesus, which was dead.* Greek, "of one dead Jesus." It is evident that Festus had no belief that Jesus had been raised up, and in this he would expect that Agrippa would concur with him. Paul had admitted that Jesus had been put to death, but he maintained that he had been raised from the dead. As Festus did not believe this, he spoke of it with the utmost contempt. "They had a dispute about one dead Jesus, whom Paul affirmed to be alive." In this manner a Roman magistrate could speak of this glorious truth of the Christian religion, and this shows the spirit with which the great mass of philosophers and statesmen regarded its doctrines.

20. *And because I doubted of such manner of questions.* See the margin. Because I hesitated about the right way of disposing of them; because I was ignorant of their nature and bearing, I proposed to go to Jerusalem, that the matter might be there more fully investigated. It is obvious, that if Paul was not found guilty of any violation of the laws, he should have been at once discharged. Some interpreters understand this as affirming that he was not satisfied about the question of Paul's innocence, or certain whether he ought to be set at liberty or not.

of Augustus, I commanded him to be kept till I might send him to Cæsar.

22 Then Agrippa said unto Festus, I would also hear the man myself. To-morrow, said he, thou shalt hear him.

23 And on the morrow, when Agrippa was come, and Bernice, with [g]great pomp, and was entered into the place of hearing, with the chief captains, and principal men of the city, at Festus' commandment [h]Paul was brought forth.

24 And Festus said, King Agrippa, and all men which are here present with us, ye see this man, about whom [i]all the multitude of the Jews have dealt with me, both at Jerusalem, and *also* here, [k]crying that he ought not to live any longer.

25 But when I found that [l]he had committed nothing worthy of death, and that [m]he himself hath appealed to Augustus, I have determined to send him.

26 Of whom I have no certain thing to write unto my lord. Wherefore I have brought him forth before you, and specially before thee, O king Agrippa, that, after examination had, I might have somewhat to write.

g Eze.7.24. *h* ch.9.15. *i* ver.3,7. *k* ch.22.22. *l* ch.23.9,29; 26.31. *m* ver.11,12.

---

21. *But when he had appealed.* Ver. 11. ¶ *To be reserved.* To be kept; not to be tried at Jerusalem, but to be sent to Rome for trial. ¶ *Unto the hearing.* Margin, "the judgment." That Augustus might hear and decide the cause. ¶ *Of Augustus.* The reigning emperor at this time was Nero. The name *Augustus* (Σεβαστός) properly denotes that which is *venerable*, or worthy of honour and reverence. It was first applied to Cæsar Octavianus, who was the Roman emperor in the time when our Saviour was born, and who is usually called Augustus Cæsar. But the title continued to be used of his successors in office, as denoting the veneration or reverence which was due to the rank of emperor.

22. *Then Agrippa said,* &c. Agrippa doubtless had heard much of the fame of Jesus, and of the new sect of Christians, and probably he was induced by mere curiosity to hear what Paul could say in explanation and defence of Christianity. This wish of Agrippa gave occasion to the noblest defence which was ever made before any tribunal, and to as splendid eloquence as can be found in any language. See ch. xxvi.

23. *With great pomp.* Greek, "with much phantasy" (φαντασίας); with much show, parade, and splendour. It was an occasion on which he could exhibit much of the splendour of royalty, and he chose to do it. ¶ *Into the place of hearing.* The court-room, or the place where the judges heard and tried causes. ¶ *With the chief captains.* Greek, the chiliarchs; the commanders of a thousand men. It means here that the military officers were assembled. ¶ *The principal men of the city.* The civil officers, or the men of reputation and influence.

24. *Have dealt with me.* Have appeared before me, desiring me to try him. They have urged me to condemn him. ¶ *Crying out,* &c. Comp. ch. xxii. 22. They had sought that he should be put to death.

26. *Of whom.* Respecting his character, opinions, and manner of life; and respecting the charges against him. ¶ *No certain thing.* Nothing definite and well established. They had not accused Paul of any crime against the Roman laws; and Festus professes himself too ignorant of the customs of the Jews to inform the emperor distinctly of the nature of the charges and the subject of trial. ¶ *Unto my lord.* To the emperor—to Cæsar. This name *Lord* the Emperors Augustus and Tiberius had rejected, and would not suffer it to be applied to them. Suetonius (*Life of Augustus,* v. 53) says "the appellation of Lord he always abhorred as abominable and execrable." See also Suetonius' *Life of Tiberius*, v. 27. The emperors that succeeded them, however, admitted the title, and suffered themselves to be called by this name. Nothing would be more satisfactory to Nero, the reigning emperor, than this title. ¶ *I might have somewhat to write.* As Agrippa was a Jew, and was acquainted with the customs and

27 For[n] it seemeth to me unreasonable to send a prisoner, and not withal to signify the crimes *laid* against him.

n Pr.18.13; Jn.7.51.

CHAPTER XXVI.

THEN Agrippa said unto Paul, Thou art permitted to speak for thyself. Then Paul stretched

---

doctrine of the Jews, Festus supposed that, after hearing Paul, he would be able to inform him of the exact nature of these charges, so that he could present the case intelligibly to the emperor.

27. *For it seemeth to me unreasonable.* Festus felt that he was placed in an embarrassing situation. He was about to send a prisoner to Rome who had been tried by himself, and who had appealed from his jurisdiction, and yet he was ignorant of the charges against him, and of the nature of his offences, if any had been committed. When prisoners were thus sent to Rome to be tried before the emperor, it would be proper that the charges should be all specified, and the evidence stated by which they were supported. Yet Festus could do neither, and it is not wonderful that he felt himself perplexed and embarrassed, and that he was glad to avail himself of the desire which Agrippa had expressed to hear Paul, that he might be able to specify the charges against him. ¶ *Withal.* Also; at the same time. ¶ *To signify.* To specify, or make them know. In concluding this chapter, we may observe:

(1) That in the case of Agrippa, we have an instance of the reasons which induce many men to hear the gospel. He had no belief in it; he had no concern for its truth or its promises; but he was led by *curiosity* to desire to hear a minister of the gospel of Christ. Curiosity thus draws multitudes to the sanctuary. In many instances they remain unaffected and unconcerned. They listen, and are unmoved, and die in their sins. In other instances, like Agrippa, they are almost persuaded to be Christians, ch. xxvi. 28. But, like him, they resist the appeals, and die uninterested in the plan of salvation. In some instances they are converted, and their curiosity, like that of Zaccheus, is made the means of their embracing the Saviour, Lu. xix. 1–9. Whatever may be the motive which induces men to desire to hear, it is the duty of the ministry cheerfully and thankfully, like Paul, to state the truth, and to defend the Christian religion.

(2) In Festus we have a specimen of the manner in which the great, and the rich, and the proud usually regard Christianity. They esteem it to be a subject in which they have no interest—a question about "one dead Jesus," whom Christians affirm to be alive. Whether he be alive or not; whether Christianity be true or false, they suppose is a question which does not pertain to them. Strange that it did not occur to Festus that if he *was* alive, his religion was true; and that it was possible that it *might* be from God. And strange that the men of this world regard the Christian religion as a subject in which *they* have no personal interest, but as one concerning which Christians *only* should inquire, and in which *they* alone should feel any concern.

(3) In Paul we have the example of a man unlike both Festus and Agrippa. He felt a deep interest in the subject—a subject which pertained as much to them as to him. He was willing not only to look at it, but to stake his life, his reputation, his all, on its truth. He was willing to defend it everywhere, and before any class of men. At the same time that he urged his rights as a Roman citizen, yet it was mainly that he might preach the gospel. At the same time that he was anxious to secure justice to himself, yet his chief anxiety was to declare the truth of God. Before any tribunal; before any class of men; in the presence of princes, nobles, and kings, of Romans and of Jews, he was ready to pour forth irresistible eloquence and argument in defence of the truth. Who would not rather be Paul than either Festus or Agrippa? Who would not rather be a *prisoner* like him, than invested with authority like Festus, or clothed in splendour like Agrippa? And who would not rather be a believer of the gospel like Paul, than, like them, to be cold contemners or neglecters of the God that made them, and of the Saviour that died and rose again?

CHAPTER XXVI.

1. *Then Paul stretched forth the hand.* See Notes on ch. xxi. 40. This was the usual posture of orators or public speakers. The ancient statues are com-

forth the hand, and answered for himself:

2 I think myself happy, king Agrippa, because I shall answer for myself this day before thee touching all the things whereof I am accused of the Jews:

3 Especially *because I know* thee to be [a]expert in all customs and questions which are among the Jews; wherefore I beseech thee [b]to hear me patiently.

4 My[c] manner of life from my

a De.17.18. *b* ch.24.4. *c* 2 Ti.3.10.

monly made in this way, with the right hand extended. The *dress* of the ancients favoured this. The long and loose robe, or outer garment, was fastened usually with a hook or clasp on the right shoulder, and thus left the arm at full liberty. ¶ *And answered for himself.* It cannot be supposed that Paul expected that his defence would be attended with a release from confinement, for he had himself appealed to the Roman emperor, ch. xxv. 11. His design in speaking before Agrippa was, doubtless, (1) To vindicate his character, and obtain Agrippa's attestation to his innocence, that thus he might allay the anger of the Jews; (2) To obtain a correct representation of the case to the emperor, as Festus had desired this in order that Agrippa might enable him to make a fair statement of the case (ch. xxv. 26, 27); and, (3) To defend his own conversion, and the truth of Christianity, and to preach the gospel in the hearing of Agrippa and his attendants, with a hope that their minds might be impressed by the truth, and that they might be converted to God.

2. *I think myself happy.* I esteem it a favour and a privilege to be permitted to make my defence before one acquainted with Jewish customs and opinions. His defence, on former occasions, had been before *Roman* magistrates, who had little acquaintance with the opinions and customs of the Jews; who were not disposed to listen to the discussion of the points of difference between him and them, and who looked upon all their controversies with contempt. See ch. xxiv. xxv. They were, therefore, little qualified to decide a question which was closely connected with the Jewish customs and doctrines; and Paul now rejoiced to know that he was before one who, from his acquaintance with the Jewish customs and belief, would be able to appreciate his arguments. Paul was not now on his trial, but he was to defend himself, or state his cause, so that Agrippa might be able to aid Festus in transmitting a true account of the case to the Roman emperor. It was his interest and duty, therefore, to defend himself as well as possible, and to put him in possession of all the facts in the case. His defence is, consequently, made up chiefly of a most eloquent statement of the *facts* just as they had occurred. ¶ *I shall answer.* I shall be permitted to make a statement, or to defend myself. ¶ *Touching*, &c. Respecting. ¶ *Whereof I am accused of the Jews.* By the Jews. The matters of the accusation were his being a mover of sedition, a ringleader of the Christians, and a profaner of the temple, ch. xxiv. 5, 6.

3. *To be expert.* To be skilled or well acquainted. ¶ *In all customs.* Rites, institutions, laws, &c. Everything pertaining to the Mosaic ritual, &c. ¶ *And questions.* Subjects of debate, and of various opinions. The inquiries which had existed between the Pharisees, Sadducees, scribes, &c. Paul could say this of Agrippa without falsehood or flattery. Agrippa was a Jew; he had passed much of his time in the kingdom over which he presided; and though he had spent the early part of his life chiefly at Rome, yet it was natural that he should make himself acquainted with the religion of his fathers. Paul did not know how to flatter men, but he was not unwilling to state the truth, and to commend men as far as truth would permit. ¶ *Wherefore.* On this account; because you are acquainted with those customs. The Romans, who regarded those customs as superstitious, and those questions as matters to be treated with contempt, could not listen to their discussion with patience. Agrippa, who knew their real importance, would be disposed to lend to all inquiries respecting them a patient attention.

4. *My manner of life.* My opinions, principles, and conduct. ¶ *From my youth.* Paul was born in Tarsus; but at an early period he had been sent to Jerusalem for the purpose of education in the school of Gamaliel, ch. xxii. 3.

youth, which was at the first among mine own nation at Jerusalem, know all the Jews;

5 Which knew me from the beginning, if they would testify, that after the most straitest sect of our religion [d]I lived a Pharisee.

d ch.22.3; Phi.3.5.

6 And [e]now I stand and am judged for the hope of [f]the promise made of God unto our fathers;

7 Unto which *promise* our twelve

e ch.23.6.
f Ge.3.15; 22.18; 49.10; De.18.15; 2 Sa.7.12; Ps.132.11; Is.4.2; 7.14; 9.6,7; Je.23.5; 33.14–16; Eze.34.23; Da.9.24; Mi.7.20; Zec.13.1,7; Mal.3.1; ch.13.32; Ga.4.4.

¶ *Which was at the first.* Which was from the beginning; the early part of which; the time when the opinions and habits are formed. ¶ *Know all the Jews.* It is not at all improbable that Paul was distinguished in the school of Gamaliel for zeal in the Jewish religion. The fact that he was early intrusted with a commission against the Christians (ch. ix.) shows that he was known. Comp. Phi. iii. 4–6. He might appeal to them, therefore, in regard to the early part of his life, and, doubtless, to the very men who had been his violent accusers.

5. *Which knew me.* Who were well acquainted with me. ¶ *From the beginning*—ἄνωθεν. Formerly; or from the very commencement of my career. Who were perfectly apprised of my whole course. ¶ *If they would testify.* If they would bear witness to what they know. ¶ *That after the most straitest.* The most rigid; the most strict, not only in regard to the written law of God, but to the traditions of the elders. Paul himself elsewhere testifies (Phi. iii. 4–6) that he had enjoyed all the advantages of birth and training in the Jewish religion, and that he had early distinguished himself by his observance of its rites and customs. ¶ *Sect.* Division or party. ¶ *I lived a Pharisee.* I lived in accordance with the rules and doctrines of the Pharisees. See Notes on Mat. iii. 7. The reasons why Paul here refers to his early life are, (1) As he had lived during the early period of his life without crime; as his principles had been settled by the instruction of the most able of their teachers, it was to be presumed that his subsequent life had been of a similar character. (2) As he, at that period of his life, evinced the utmost zeal for the laws and customs of his country, it was to be presumed that he would not be found opposing or reviling them at any subsequent period. From the strictness and conscientiousness of his past life, he supposed that Agrippa might argue favourably respecting his subsequent conduct. A virtuous and religious course in early life is usually a sure pledge of virtue and integrity in subsequent years.

6. *And now I stand.* I stand before the tribunal. I am arraigned. ¶ *And am judged.* Am tried with reference to being judged. I am undergoing a *trial* on the point in which all my nation are agreed. ¶ *For the hope.* On account of the hope; or because, in common with my countrymen, I had entertained this hope, and now believe in its fulfilment. ¶ *Of the promise,* &c. See the references in the margin. It is not quite certain whether Paul refers here to the promise of the Messiah or to the hope of the resurrection of the dead. When he stood before the Jewish Sanhedrim (ch. xxiii. 6), he said that he was called in question on account of holding the doctrine of the resurrection of the dead. But it may be observed that in his view the two things were closely united. He hoped that the Messiah would come, and he hoped *therefore* for the resurrection of the dead. He believed that he *had* come, and *had* risen, and *therefore* he believed that the dead would rise. He argued the one from the other. And as he believed that Jesus was the Messiah, and that he had risen from the dead, and that he had thus furnished a demonstration that the dead would rise, it was evident that the subject of controversy between him and the Jews involved everything that was vital to their opinions and their hopes. See ver. 8. ¶ *Made of God.* Made by God. See the marginal references. The promises had been made to the fathers of a Messiah to come, and that embraced the promise of a future state, or of the resurrection of the dead. It will help us to understand the stress which Paul and the other apostles laid on the doctrine of the resurrection of the dead to remember that it involved the whole doctrine of the separate existence of the soul and of a future state. The Sadducees denied all this; and when the Pharisees,

tribes, [g] instantly serving *God* [1] day and night, hope to come. For which hope's sake, king Agrippa, I am accused of the Jews.

8 Why[h] should it be thought a thing incredible with you that God should raise the dead?

9 I[i] verily thought with myself

g Lu.2.37; 1 Th.3.10. [1] *night and day.*

h 1 Co.15.12,20. *i* 1 Ti.1.13.

the Saviour, and the apostles opposed them, they did it by showing that there would be a future state of rewards and punishments. See the argument of the Saviour with the Sadducees explained in the Notes on Mat. xxii. 23–32. ¶ *Unto our fathers.* Our ancestors, the patriarchs, &c.

7. *Unto which* promise. To the fulfilment of which promise they hope to come; that is, they hope and believe that the promise will be fulfilled, and that they will partake of its benefits. ¶ *Our twelve tribes.* This was the name by which the Jews were designated. The ancient Jewish nation had hoped to come to that promise; it had been the hope and expectation of the nation. Long before the coming of the Messiah, ten of the twelve tribes had been carried captive to Assyria, and had not returned, leaving but the two tribes of Benjamin and Judah. But the name, "the twelve tribes," as used to designate the Jewish people, would be still retained. Comp. Ja. i. 1. Paul here says that the hope referred to had been that of the Jewish nation. Except the comparatively small portion of the nation, the Sadducees, the great mass of the nation had held to the doctrine of a future state. This Agrippa would well know. ¶ *Instantly.* Constantly; *with intensity* (ἐν ἐκτενείᾳ); with zeal. This was true, for, amidst all the sins of the nation, they observed with punctuality and zeal the outward forms of the worship of God. ¶ *Serving* God. In the ordinances and observances of the temple. As a nation they did not serve him in their hearts, but they kept up the outward forms of religious worship. ¶ *Day and night.* With unwearied zeal; with constancy and ardour, Lu. ii. 37. The ordinary Jewish services and sacrifices were in the morning and evening, and might be said to be performed day and night. Some of their services, as the Paschal supper, were prolonged usually till late at night. The main idea is, that they kept up the worship of God with constant and untiring zeal and devotion. ¶ *For which hope's sake.* On account of my cherishing this hope in common with the great mass of my countrymen. See ch. xxiii. 6. If Paul could convince Agrippa that the main point of his offence was that which had been the common belief of his countrymen, it would show to his satisfaction that he was innocent. And on this ground he put his defence—that he held only that which the mass of the nation had believed, and that he maintained this in the only consistent and defensible manner—that God had, *in fact*, raised up the Messiah, and had thus given assurance that the dead would rise.

8. *Why should it be thought*, &c. The force of this question will be better seen by an exclamation point after *why* (τί). "What! is it to be thought a thing incredible?" &c. It intimates surprise that it should be thought incredible, or implies that no reason could be given why such a doctrine should be unworthy of belief. ¶ *A thing incredible.* A doctrine which cannot be credited or believed. Why should it be regarded as absurd? ¶ *With you.* This is in the plural number, and it is evident that Paul here addressed, not Agrippa alone, but those who sat with him. There is no evidence that Agrippa doubted that the dead could be raised, but Festus, and those who were with him, probably did, and Paul, in the ardour of his speech, turned and addressed the entire assembly. It is very evident that we have only an *outline* of this argument, and there is every reason to suppose that Paul would dwell on each part of the subject at greater length than is here recorded. ¶ *That God should raise the dead.* Why should it be regarded as absurd that God—who has all power, who is the creator of all, who is the author of the human frame—should again restore man to life and continue his future existence? The resurrection is no more incredible than the original creation of the body, and it is attended with no greater difficulties. And as the perfections of God will be illustrated by his raising up the dead; as the future state is necessary to the purposes of justice in vindicating the just and punishing the unjust, and as God is a righteous moral governor, it should not be regarded as an absurdity that he will

that I ought to do many things contrary to the name of Jesus of Nazareth.

10 Which thing I also did [k]in Jerusalem; and many of the saints did I shut up in prison, [l]having received authority from the chief priests; and when they were put to death, I gave my voice against *them.*

11 And I punished them oft [m]in every synagogue, and compelled *them* to blaspheme; and being exceedingly mad against them, I persecuted *them* even unto strange cities.

k ch.8.3; Ga.1.13. *l* ch.9.14. *m* ch.22.19.

---

raise up those who have died, and bring them to judgment.

9. *I verily thought.* I *indeed* (μὲν) supposed. Paul here commences the account of his conversion, and states the evidence on which he judged that he was called of God to do what he had done. He begins by saying that it was not because he was originally disposed to be a Christian, but that he was violently and conscientiously opposed to Jesus of Nazareth, and had been converted when in the full career of opposition to him and his cause. ¶ *With myself.* I thought *to* myself; or, I myself thought. He had before stated the hopes and expectations of his countrymen, ver. 6–8. He now speaks of his own views and purposes. "For myself, I thought," &c. ¶ *That I ought to do.* That I was bound, or that it was a duty incumbent on me—δεῖν. "I thought that I owed it to my country, to my religion, and to my God, to oppose in every manner the claims of Jesus of Nazareth to be the Messiah." We here see that Paul was conscientious, and that a man may be conscientious even when engaged in enormous wickedness. It is no evidence that one is right because he is conscientious. No small part of the crimes against human laws, and almost all the cruel persecutions against Christians, have been carried on under the plea of conscience. Paul here refers to his conscientiousness in persecution to show that it was no slight matter which could have changed his course. As he was governed in persecution by conscience, it could have been only by a force of demonstration, and by the urgency of conscience equally clear and strong, that he could ever have been induced to *abandon* this course and to become a friend of that Saviour whom he had thus persecuted. ¶ *Many things.* As much as possible. He was not satisfied with a *few* things—a few words, or purposes, or arguments; but he felt bound to do as much as possible to put down the new religion. ¶ *Contrary to the name,* &c. In opposition to Jesus himself, or to his claims to be the Messiah. The name is often used to denote the person himself, ch. iii. 6.

10. *Which thing I did,* &c. Ch. viii. 3. ¶ *And many of the saints,* &c. Many Christians, ch. viii. 3. ¶ *And when they were put to death.* In the history of those transactions, there is no account of any Christian being put to death except Stephen, Ac. vii. But there is no improbability in supposing that the same thing which had happened to Stephen had occurred in other cases. Stephen was the first martyr, and as he was a prominent man his case is particularly recorded. ¶ *I gave my voice.* Paul was not a member of the Sanhedrim, and this does not mean that he *voted,* but simply that he joined in the persecution; he approved it; he assented to the putting of the saints to death. Comp. ch. xxii. 20. The Syriac renders it, "I joined with those who condemned them." It is evident, also, that Paul instigated them in this persecution, and urged them on to deeds of blood and cruelty.

11. *And I punished them oft,* &c. See ch. xxii. 19. ¶ *And compelled* them *to blaspheme.* To blaspheme the name of Jesus by denying that he was the Messiah, and by admitting that he was an impostor. This was the object which they had in view in the persecution. It was not to make them blaspheme or reproach *God,* but to deny that Jesus was the Messiah, and to reproach *him* as a deceiver and an impostor. It is not necessarily implied in the expression, "and *compelled* them to blaspheme," that he succeeded in doing it, but that he *endeavoured* to make them apostatize from the Christian religion and deny the Lord Jesus. It is certainly not impossible that a few might thus have been induced by the authority of the Sanhedrim and by the threats of Paul to do it, but it is certain

12 Whereupon [n]as I went to
Damascus with authority and commission from the chief priests,
13 At mid-day, O king, I saw
in the way a light from heaven,
above the brightness of the sun,
shining round about me, and them
which journeyed with me.
14 And when we were all fallen
to the earth, I heard a voice speaking unto me, and saying in the
Hebrew tongue, Saul, Saul, why
persecutest thou me? *it is* hard for
thee to kick against the pricks.
15 And I said, Who art thou,
Lord? And he said, I am Jesus
whom thou persecutest.
16 But rise, and stand upon thy
feet; for I have appeared unto
thee for this purpose, to make thee
a [o]minister and a [p]witness both of
these things which thou hast seen,
and of those things in the which I
will appear unto thee;
17 Delivering thee from the
people, and *from* the Gentiles, [q]unto
whom now I send thee;

n ch.9.3. *o* Ep.3.7; Col.1.23,25. *p* ch.22.15. *q* ch.22.21; Ro.11.13.

that the great mass of Christians adhered firmly to their belief that Jesus was the Messiah. ¶ *And being exceedingly mad.* Nothing could more forcibly express his violence against the Christians. He raged like a madman; he was so ignorant that he laid aside all appearance of reason; with the fury and violence of a maniac, he endeavoured to exterminate them from the earth. None but a madman will persecute men on account of their religious opinions; and all persecutions have been conducted like this, with the violence, the fury, and the ungovernable temper of maniacs. ¶ *Unto strange cities.* Unto foreign cities; cities out of Judea. The principal instance of this was his going to Damascus; but there is no evidence that he did not intend also to visit other cities out of Judea and bring the Christians there, if he found any, to Jerusalem.

12–15. See this passage explained in the Notes on ch. ix. 5, &c.

16. *But rise,* &c. The particulars mentioned in this verse and the two following are not recorded in the account of Paul's conversion in ch. ix.; but it is not improbable that many circumstances may have occurred which are not recorded. Paul dwells on them here at length in order particularly to show his authority for doing what he had done in preaching to the Gentiles. ¶ *To make thee a minister.* A minister of the gospel; a preacher of the truth. ¶ *And a witness.* See Notes on ch. xxii. 15. ¶ *Which thou hast seen.* On the road to Damascus; that is, of the Lord Jesus, and of the fact that he was risen from the dead. ¶ *And of those things,* &c. Of those further manifestations of my person, purposes, and will, which I will yet make to you. It is evident from this that the Lord Jesus promised to manifest himself to Paul in his ministry, and to make to him still further displays of his will and glory. Comp. ch. xxii. 17, 18. This was done by his rescuing him from destruction and danger; by inspiration; by the growing and expanding view which Paul was permitted to take of the character and perfections of the Lord Jesus. In this we see that it is the duty of ministers to bear witness not only to the truth of religion in general, or of that which they can demonstrate by argument, but more especially of that which they experience in their own hearts, and which they understand by having themselves been the subjects of it. No man is qualified to enter the ministry who has not a personal saving view of the glory and perfections of the Lord Jesus, and who does not go to his work as a *witness* of those things which he has felt; and no man enters the ministry with these feelings who has not, as Paul had, a promise that he shall see still brighter displays of the perfections of the Saviour, and be permitted to advance in the knowledge of him and of his work. The highest personal consolation in this work is the promise of being admitted to ever-growing and expanding views of the glory of the Lord Jesus, and of experiencing his presence, guidance, and protection.

17. *Delivering thee from the people.* From the Jewish people. This implied that he would be persecuted by them, and that the Lord Jesus would interpose to rescue him. ¶ *And from the Gentiles.* This also implied that he

18 To[r] open their eyes, *and* [s]to
turn *them* from darkness to light,
and [t]*from* the power of Satan unto
God; that they may receive [u]for-
giveness of sins, and [v]inheritance
among them [w]which are sanctified
by[x] faith that is in me.

r Is.35.5; 42.7; Ep.1.18.
s Lu.1.79; Jn.8.12; 2 Co.4.6; 1 Pe.2.9. *t* Col.1.13.
u Lu.1.77; Ep.1.7; Col.1.14.
v Ep.1.11; Col.1.12; 1 Pe.1.4.
w Jn.17.17; ch.20.32; 1 Co.1.30; Re.21.27.
x Ep.2.8; He.11.6.

19 Whereupon, O king Agrippa,
I was not disobedient unto the
heavenly vision;

20 But [y]showed first unto them
of Damascus, and at Jerusalem,
and throughout all the coasts of
Judea, and *then* to the Gentiles,
that they should repent and turn
to God, and [z]do works meet for
repentance.

y ch.9.19,&c. *z* Mat.3.8.

---

would be persecuted and opposed by them—a prospect which was verified by the whole course of his ministry. Yet in all he experienced, according to the promise, the support and the protection of the Lord Jesus. This was expressed in a summary manner in Lu. ix. 16. ¶ *Unto whom now I send thee.* Ch. xxii. 21. As the opposition of the Jews arose mainly from the fact that he had gone among the Gentiles, it was important to bring this part of his commission into full view before Agrippa, and to show that the same Saviour who had miraculously converted him had commanded him to go and preach to them.

18. *To open their eyes.* To enlighten or instruct them. Ignorance is represented by the eyes being closed, and the instruction of the gospel by the opening of the eyes. See Ep. i. 18. ¶ And *to turn* them *from darkness to light.* From the darkness of heathenism and sin to the light and purity of the gospel. Darkness is an emblem of ignorance and of sin, and the heathen nations are often represented as sitting in darkness. Comp. Notes on Mat. iv. 16; Jn. i. 4, 5. ¶ *And* from *the power of Satan.* From the dominion of Satan. Comp. Col. i. 13; 1 Pe. ii. 9. See Notes on Jn. xii. 31; xvi. 11. Satan is thus represented as the prince of this world, the ruler of the darkness of this world, the prince of the power of the air, &c. The heathen world, lying in sin and superstition, is represented as under his control; and this passage teaches, doubtless, that the great mass of the people of this world are the subjects of the kingdom of Satan, and are led captive by him at his will. ¶ *Unto God.* To the obedience of the one living and true God. ¶ *That they may receive forgiveness of sins.* Through the merits of that Saviour who died—that thus the partition wall between the Jews and the Gentiles might be broken down, and all might be admitted to the same precious privileges of the favour and mercy of God. Comp. Notes on Ac. ii. 38. ¶ *And inheritance.* An heirship, or lot (κλῆρον); that they might be entitled to the privileges and favours of the children of God. See Notes on Ac. xx. 32. ¶ *Which are sanctified.* Among the saints; the children of God. See Notes on Ac. xx. 32.

19. *Whereupon.* Whence (ὅθεν). Since the proof of his being the Messiah, of his resurrection, and of his calling me to this work, was so clear and plain, I deemed it my duty to engage without delay in the work. ¶ *I was not disobedient.* I was not incredulous or unbelieving; I yielded myself to the command, and at once obeyed. See Ac. ix. 6; comp. Ga. i. 16. ¶ *To the heavenly vision.* To the celestial appearance, or to the vision which appeared to me from heaven. I did not doubt that this splendid appearance (ver. 13) was from heaven, and I did not refuse to obey the command of him who thus appeared to me. He knew it was the command of God his Saviour, and he gave evidence of repentance by yielding obedience to it at once.

20. See ch. ix. 20–23. The 20th verse contains a *summary* of his labours in obedience to the command of the Lord Jesus. His argument is that the Lord Jesus had from heaven commanded him to do this, and that he had done no more than to obey his injunction. The word "*then*" in this verse is supplied by our translators, and is not necessary to the proper explanation of the passage. It would seem from that word that he had *not* preached "to the Gentiles" until *after* he had preached "at Jerusalem and throughout all the coasts of Judea," whereas, in fact, he had, as we have reason to believe (see Notes on ch. ix. 23), before then

21 For these causes [a]the Jews
caught me in the temple, and went
about to kill *me*.
22 Having therefore obtained
help of God, I continue unto this
day, witnessing both to small and
great, saying none other things
than those [b]which the prophets
and Moses did say should come.
23 That Christ should suffer,
and that he should be [c]the first
that should rise from the dead,
and should show light unto the
people, and to the Gentiles.

a ch.21.30. *b* Lu.24.27,46. *c* 1 Co.15.23.

"preached" to the Gentiles in Arabia. The statement here, in the original, is a *general* statement that he had preached at Damascus and at Jerusalem, and in all the coasts of Judea, *and* also *to the Gentiles*, but without specifying the exact *order* in which it was done.

21. *Caught me in the temple.* Ch. xxi. 30. ¶ *And went about*, &c. Endeavoured to put me to death.

22. *Having therefore obtained help of God.* Paul had seen and felt his danger. He had known the determined malice of the Jews, and their efforts to take his life. He had been rescued by Lysias, and had made every effort himself to avoid the danger and to save his life; and at the end of all, he traced his safety entirely to the help of God. It was not by any power of his own that he had been preserved; it was because God had interposed and rescued him. Those who have been delivered from danger, if they have just views, will delight to trace it all to God. They will recognize *his* hand, and will feel that whatever wisdom *they* may have had, or whatever may have been the kindness of their friends to them, yet that *all this also* is to be traced to the superintending providence of God. ¶ *Witnessing.* Bearing testimony to what he had seen, according to the command of Christ, ver. 16. ¶ *To small.* To those in humble life; to the poor, the ignorant, and the obscure. Like his Master, he did not despise them, but regarded it as his duty and privilege to preach the gospel to them. ¶ *And great.* The rich and noble; to kings, princes, and governors. He had thus stood on Mars' Hill at Athens; he had declared the same gospel before Felix, Festus, and now before Agrippa. He offered salvation to all. He passed by none because they were poor; and he was not deterred by the fear of the rich and the great from making known their sins and calling them to repentance. What an admirable illustration of the proper duties of a minister of the gospel! ¶ *Saying none other thing*, &c. Delivering no new doctrine, but maintaining only that the prophecies had been fulfilled. As he had done this only, there was no reason for the opposition and persecution of the Jews. ¶ *Should come.* Should come to pass, or should take place. Paul here evidently means to say that the doctrine of the atonement, and of the resurrection of Christ, is taught in the Old Testament.

23. *That Christ.* That the Messiah expected by the Jews should be a suffering Messiah. ¶ *Should suffer.* Should lead a painful life, and be put to death. See Notes on ch. xvii. 3; comp. Da. ix. 27; Is. liii. ¶ And *that he should be the first*, &c. This declaration contains two points. (1) That it was taught in the prophets that the Messiah would rise from the dead. On this, see the proof alleged in ch. ii. 24–32; xiii. 32–37. (2) That he would be the first that should rise. This cannot mean that the Messiah would be the first dead person who should be restored to life, for Elijah had raised the son of the Shunammite, and Jesus himself had raised Lazarus, and the widow's son at Nain. It does not mean that he would be the first *in the order of time* that should rise, but *first in eminence;* the most distinguished, the chief, the head of those who should rise from the dead—πρῶτος ἐξ ἀναστάσεως νεκρῶν. In accordance with this he is called (Col. i. 18) "the beginning, the first-born from the dead," having among all the dead who should be raised up the pre-eminence of primogeniture, or that which pertained to the first-born. In 1 Co. xv. 20 he is called "the first fruits of them that slept." This declaration is therefore made of him by way of eminence: (1) As being chief, a prince among those raised from the dead; (2) As being raised by his own power (Jn. x. 18); (3) As, by his rising, securing a dominion over death and the grave (1 Co. xv. 25, 26); and, (4) As bringing, by his

24 And as he thus spake for himself, Festus said with a loud voice, Paul, thou art beside thyself; much learning doth make thee [d]mad.

25 But he said, I am not mad,

d 2 Ki.9.11.

---

rising, life and immortality to light. He rose to return to death no more. And he thus secured an ascendency over death and the grave, and was thus, by way of eminence, *first* among those raised from the dead. ¶ *And should show light unto the people.* To the Jews. Would be their instructor and prophet. This Moses had predicted, De. xviii. 15. ¶ *And to the Gentiles.* This had often been foretold by the prophets, and particularly by Isaiah, Is. ix. 1, 2; comp. Mat. iv. 14–16; Is. xi. 10; xlii. 1, 6; liv. 3; lx. 3, 5, 11; lxi. 6; lxii. 2; lxvi. 12.

24. *Festus said with a loud voice.* Amazed at the zeal of Paul. Paul doubtless evinced deep interest in the subject, and great earnestness in the delivery of his defence. ¶ *Thou art beside thyself.* Thou art deranged; thou art insane. The reasons why Festus thought Paul mad were, probably, (1) His great earnestness and excitement on the subject. (2) His laying such stress on the gospel of the despised Jesus of Nazareth, as if it were a matter of infinite moment. Festus despised it; and he regarded it as proof of derangement that so much importance was attached to it. (3) Festus regarded, probably, the whole story of the vision that Paul said had appeared to him as the effect of an inflamed and excited imagination, and as a proof of delirium. This is not an uncommon charge against those who are Christians, and especially when they evince unusual zeal. Sinners regard them as under the influence of delirium and fanaticism; as terrified by imaginary and superstitious fears; or as misguided by fanatical leaders. Husbands often thus think their wives deranged, and parents their children, and wicked men the ministers of the gospel. The gay think it proof of derangement that others are serious, anxious, and prayerful; the rich, that others are willing to part with their property to do good; the ambitious and worldly, that others are willing to leave their country and home to go among the Gentiles to spend their lives in making known the unsearchable riches of Christ. The really sober and rational part of the world—they who fear God and keep his commandments; they who believe that eternity is before them, and who strive to live for it—are thus charged with insanity by those who are really deluded, and who are thus living lives of madness and folly. The tenants of a madhouse often think all others deranged but themselves; but there is no madness so great, no delirium so awful, as to neglect the eternal interest of the soul for the sake of the pleasures and honours which this life can give. ¶ *Much learning.* It is probable that Festus was acquainted with the fact that Paul was a learned man. Paul had not, while before him, manifested particularly his learning. But Festus, acquainted in some way with the fact that he was well-educated, supposed that his brain had been turned, and that the effect of it was seen by devotion to a fanatical form of religion. The tendency of long-continued and intense application to produce mental derangement is everywhere known. ¶ *Doth make thee mad.* Impels, drives, or excites thee (περιτρέπει) to madness.

25. *I am not mad.* I am not deranged. There are few more happy turns than that which Paul gives to this accusation of Festus. He might have appealed to the course of his argument; he might have dwelt on the importance of the subject, and continued to reason; but he makes an appeal at once to *Agrippa*, and brings him in for a witness that he was not deranged. This would be far more likely to make an impression on the mind of Festus than anything that Paul could say in self-defence. The same reply, "I am not mad," can be made by all Christians to the charge of derangement which the world brings against them. They have come, like the prodigal (Lu. xv. 17), to their right mind; and by beginning to act as if there were a God and Saviour, as if they were to die, as if there were a boundless eternity before them, they are conducting according to the dictates of reason. And as Paul appealed to Agrippa, who was not a Christian, for the reasonableness and soberness of his own views and conduct, so may all Christians appeal to sinners themselves as witnesses that they are acting as immortal beings *should* act. All men *know* that if there is an eternity, it is

most noble Festus, but speak forth the words of truth and soberness.

26 For the king knoweth of these things, before whom also I speak freely; for I am persuaded that none of these things are hidden from him; for this thing was not done in a corner.

27 King Agrippa, believest thou the prophets? I know that thou believest.

28 Then Agrippa said unto Paul,

---

right to prepare for it; if there is a God, it is proper to serve him; if a Saviour died for us, we should love him; if a hell, we should avoid it; if a heaven, we should seek it. And even when they charge us with folly and derangement, we may turn at once upon *them*, and appeal to their own consciences, and ask them if all our anxieties, and prayers, and efforts, and self-denials are not right? One of the best ways of convicting sinners is to appeal to them just as Paul did to Agrippa. When *so* appealed to, they will usually acknowledge the force of the appeal, and will admit that the solicitude of Christians for their salvation is according to the dictates of reason. ¶ *Most noble Festus.* This was the usual title of the Roman governor. Comp. ch. xxiv. 3. ¶ *Of truth.* In accordance with the predictions of Moses and the prophets, and the facts which have occurred in the death and resurrection of the Messiah. In proof of this he appeals to Agrippa, ver. 26, 27. Truth here stands opposed to delusion, imposture, and fraud. ¶ *And soberness.* Soberness (σωφροσύνη, *wisdom*) stands opposed here to madness or derangement, and denotes sanity of mind. The words which I speak are those of a sane man, conscious of what he is saying, and impressed with its truth. They were the words, also, of a man who, under the charge of derangement, evinced the most perfect self-possession and command of his feelings, and who uttered sentiments deep, impressive, and worthy the attention of all mankind.

26. *For the king.* King Agrippa. ¶ *Knoweth.* He had been many years in that region, and the fame of Jesus and of Paul's conversion were probably well known to him. ¶ *These things.* The things pertaining to the early persecutions of Christians; the spread of the gospel; and the remarkable conversion of Paul. Though Agrippa might not have been fully informed respecting these things, yet he had an acquaintance with Moses and the prophets; he knew the Jewish expectation respecting the Messiah; and he could not be ignorant respecting the remarkable public events in the life of Jesus of Nazareth, and of his having been put to death by order of Pontius Pilate on the cross. ¶ *I speak freely.* I speak openly—boldly. I use no disguise; and I speak the more confidently before him, because, from his situation, he must be acquainted with the truth of what I say. Truth is always bold and free, and it is an evidence of honesty when a man is willing to declare everything without reserve before those who are qualified to detect him if he is an impostor. Such evidence of truth and honesty was given by Paul. ¶ *For I am persuaded.* I am convinced; I doubt not that he is well acquainted with these things. ¶ *Are hidden from him.* That he is unacquainted with them. ¶ *For this thing.* The thing to which Paul had mainly referred in this defence, his own conversion to the Christian religion. ¶ *Was not done in a corner.* Did not occur secretly and obscurely, but was public, and was of such a character as to attract attention. The conversion of a leading persecutor, such as Paul had been, and in the manner in which that conversion had taken place, could not but attract attention and remark; and although the Jews would endeavour as much as possible to conceal it, yet Paul might presume that it could not be entirely unknown to Agrippa.

27. *King Agrippa.* This bold personal address is an instance of Paul's happy manner of appeal. He does it to bring in the testimony of Agrippa to meet the charge of Festus that he was deranged. ¶ *Believest thou the prophets?* The prophecies respecting the character, the sufferings, and the death of the Messiah. ¶ *I know that thou believest.* Agrippa was a Jew; and, as such, he of course believed the prophets. Perhaps, too, from what Paul knew of his personal character, he might confidently affirm that he professed to be a believer. Instead, therefore, of waiting for his answer, Paul anticipated it, and said that he *knew*

Almost[e] thou persuadest me to be a Christian.

e Ja.1.23,24.

29 And Paul said, [f]I would to God that not only thou, but also

f 1 Co.7.7.

that Agrippa professed to believe all these prophecies respecting the Messiah. His design is evident. It is, (1) To meet the charge of derangement, and to bring in the testimony of Agrippa, who well understood the subject, to the importance and the truth of what he was saying. (2) To press on the conscience of his royal hearer the evidence of the Christian religion, and to secure, if possible, his conversion. "Since thou believest the prophecies, and since I have shown that they are fulfilled in Jesus of Nazareth; that he corresponds in person, character, and work, with the prophets, it follows that his religion is true." Paul lost no opportunity in pressing the truth on every class of men. He had such a conviction of the truth of Christianity that he was deterred by no rank, station, or office; by no fear of the rich, the great, and the learned; but everywhere urged the evidence of that religion as indisputable. In this lay the secret of no small part of his success. A man who *really* believes the truth will be ready to defend it. A man who truly loves religion will not be ashamed of it anywhere.

28. *Then Agrippa said unto Paul.* He could not deny that he believed the prophecies in the Old Testament. He could not deny that the argument was a strong one that they had been fulfilled in Jesus of Nazareth. He could not deny that the evidence of the miraculous interposition of God in the conversion of Paul was overwhelming; and instead, therefore, of charging him, as Festus had done, with derangement, he candidly and honestly avows the impression which the proof had made on his mind. ¶ *Almost.* Except a very little—ἐν ὀλίγῳ. Thou hast nearly convinced me that Christianity is true, and persuaded me to embrace it. The arguments of Paul had been so rational; the appeal which he had made to his belief of the prophets had been so irresistible, that he had been nearly convinced of the truth of Christianity. We are to remember, (1) That Agrippa was a Jew, and that he would look on this whole subject in a different manner from the Roman Festus. (2) That he does not appear to have partaken of the violent passions and prejudices of the Jews who had accused Paul. (3) His character, as given by Josephus, is that of a mild, candid, and ingenuous man. He had no particular hostility to Christians; he knew that they were not justly charged with sedition and crime; and he saw the conclusion to which a belief of the prophets inevitably tended. Yet, as in thousands of other cases, he was not *quite* persuaded to be a Christian. What was included in the "almost;" what prevented his being *quite* persuaded, we know not. It may have been that the evidence was not so clear to his mind as he would profess to desire; or that he was not willing to give up his sins; or that he was too proud to rank himself with the followers of Jesus of Nazareth; or that, like Felix, he was willing to defer it to a more convenient season. There is every reason to believe that he was never *quite* persuaded to embrace the Lord Jesus, and that he was never nearer the kingdom of heaven than at this moment. It was the *crisis*, the turning-point in Agrippa's life, and in his eternal destiny; and, like thousands of others, he neglected or refused to allow the full conviction of the truth on his mind, and died in his sins. ¶ *Thou persuadest me.* Thou dost convince me of the truth of the Christian religion, and persuadest me to embrace it. ¶ *To be a Christian.* On the name *Christian*, see Notes on ch. xi. 26. On this deeply interesting case we may observe, (1) That there are many in the same situation as Agrippa—many who are *almost*, but not *altogether*, persuaded to be Christians. They are found among (*a*) Those who have been religiously educated; (*b*) Those who are convinced by argument of the truth of Christianity; (*c*) Those whose consciences are awakened, and who feel their guilt, and the necessity of some better portion than this world can furnish. (2) Such persons are deterred from being altogether Christians by the following, among other causes: (*a*) By the love of sin—the love of sin in general, or some particular sin which they are not willing to abandon; (*b*) By the fear of shame, persecution, or contempt, if they become Christians; (*c*) By the temptations of the world—its cares, vanities, and

all that hear me this day, were both almost, and altogether such as I am, except these bonds.

30 And when he had thus spoken, the king rose up, and the governor, and Bernice, and they that sat with them:

31 And when they were gone aside, they talked between themselves, saying, This man doeth

---

allurements—which are often presented most strongly in just this state of mind; (*d*) By the love of office, the pride of rank and power, as in the case of Agrippa; (*e*) By a disposition, like Felix, to delay to a more favourable time the work of religion, until life has wasted away, and death approaches, and it is too late, and the unhappy man dies ALMOST *a Christian.* (3) This state of mind is one of peculiar interest and peculiar danger. It is not one of safety, and it is not one that implies any certainty that the "almost Christian" will ever be saved. There is no reason to believe that Agrippa ever became *fully* persuaded to become a Christian. To be *almost* persuaded to do a thing which we ought to do, and yet *not* to do it, is the very position of guilt and danger. And it is no wonder that many are brought to *this* point—the turning-point, the *crisis* of life—and then lose their anxiety, and die in their sins. May the God of grace keep us from resting in being *almost* persuaded to be Christians! May every one who shall read this account of Agrippa be admonished by his convictions, and be alarmed by the fact that *he* then paused, and that his convictions there ended! And may every one resolve by the help of God to forsake *every* thing that prevents his becoming an *entire* believer, and without delay embrace the Son of God as his Saviour!

29. *I would to God.* I pray to God; I earnestly desire it of God. This shows, (1) Paul's intense desire that Agrippa, and all who heard him, might be saved. (2) His steady and constant belief that none but God could incline men to become altogether Christians. Paul knew well that there was nothing that would overcome the reluctance of the human heart to be an entire Christian but the grace and mercy of God. He had addressed to his hearers the convincing arguments of religion, and he now breathed forth his earnest prayer to God that those arguments might be effectual. So prays every faithful minister of the cross. ¶ *All that hear me.* Festus, and the military and civil officers who had been assembled to hear his defence, ch. xxv. 23. ¶ *Were both almost, and altogether,* &c. Paul had no higher wish for them than that they might have the faith and consolations which he himself enjoyed. He had so firm a conviction of the truth of Christianity, and had experienced so much of its supports amidst his persecutions and trials, that his highest desire for them was that they might experience the same inexpressibly pure and holy consolations. He well knew that there was neither happiness nor safety in being *almost* a Christian; and he desired, therefore, that they would give themselves, as he had done, entirely and altogether to the service of the Lord Jesus Christ. ¶ *Except these bonds.* These chains. This is an exceedingly happy and touching appeal. Probably Paul, when he said this, lifted up his arm with the chain attached to it. His wish was that in all respects they might partake of the effects of the gospel, *except those chains.* Those he did not wish them to bear. The persecutions, the unjust trials, and the imprisonments which he had been called to suffer in the cause, he did not desire them to endure. True Christians wish others to partake of the full blessings of religion. The trials which they themselves experienced from without in unjust persecutions, ridicule, and slander, they do not wish them to endure. The trials which they themselves experience from an evil heart, from corrupt passions, and from temptations, they do not wish others to experience. But even *with* these, religion confers infinitely more pure joy than the world can give; and even though others should be called to experience severe trials for their religion, still Christians wish that all should partake of the pure consolations which Christianity alone can furnish in this world and the world to come. Comp. Mar. x. 30.

31. *This man doeth nothing worthy of death.* This was the conclusion to which they had come after hearing all that the Jews had to allege against him. It was the result of the whole investigation; and we have, therefore, the concurring testimony of Claudius Lysias

nothing worthy of death or of bonds.

32 Then said Agrippa unto Festus, This man might have been set at liberty if he had not appealed unto Cæsar.

CHAPTER XXVII.

AND when it was determined that we should sail into Italy, they [a] delivered Paul and certain other prisoners unto *one* named Julius, a centurion of Augustus' band.

2 And entering into a ship of Adramyttium, we launched, meaning to sail by the coasts of Asia; *one* [b] Aristarchus, a Macedonian of Thessalonica, being with us.

a ch.25.12,25. b ch.19.29.

(ch. xxiii. 29), of Felix (ch. xxiv.), of Festus (ch. xxv. 26, 27), and of Agrippa, to the innocence of Paul. More honourable and satisfactory testimony of his innocence he could not have desired. It was a full acquittal from all the charges against him; and though he was to be sent to Rome, yet he went there with every favourable prospect of being acquitted there also.

32. *Then said Agrippa unto Festus*, &c. This is a full declaration of the conviction of Agrippa, before whom the cause had been heard, that Paul was innocent. It is an instance, also, where boldness and fidelity will be attended with happy results. Paul had concealed nothing of the truth. He had made a bold and faithful appeal (ver. 27) to Agrippa himself for the truth of what he was saying. By this appeal Agrippa had not been offended. It had only served to impress him more with the innocence of Paul. It is an instance which shows that religion may be so commended to the conscience and reason of princes, kings, and judges that they will see its truth. It is an instance which shows that the most bold and faithful appeals may be made by the ministers of religion to their hearers for the truth of what they are saying. And it is a full proof that the most faithful appeals, if respectful, may be made without offending men, and with the certainty that they will feel and admit their force. All preachers should be as faithful as Paul; and whatever may be the rank and character of their auditors, they should never doubt that they have truth and God on their side, and that their message, when most bold and faithful, will commend itself to the consciences of mankind.

CHAPTER XXVII.

1. *And when it was determined.* By Festus (ch. xxv. 12), and when the time was come when it was convenient to send him. ¶ *That we should sail.* The use of the term "we" here shows that the author of this book, Luke, was with Paul. He had been his travelling companion, and though he had not been accused, yet it was resolved that he should still accompany him. Whether he went at his own expense, or whether he was sent at the expense of the Roman government, does not appear. There is a difference of reading here in the ancient versions. The Syriac reads it, "And thus Festus determined that he [Paul] should be sent to Cæsar in Italy," &c. The Latin Vulgate and the Arabic also read "he" instead of "we." But the Greek manuscripts are uniform, and the correct reading is doubtless that which is in our version. ¶ *Into Italy.* The country still bearing the same name, of which Rome was the capital. ¶ *And certain other prisoners.* Who were probably also sent to Rome for a trial before the emperor. Dr. Lardner has proved that it was common to send prisoners from Judea and other provinces to Rome (*Credibility*, part i. ch. x. § 10, p. 248, 249). ¶ *A centurion.* A commander of a hundred men. ¶ *Of Augustus' band.* For the meaning of the word "band," see Notes on Mat. xxvii. 27; Ac. x. 1. It was a division in the Roman army consisting of from four to six hundred men. This was called "Augustus' band" in honour of the Roman emperor Augustus (see Notes on ch. xxv. 21), and was probably distinguished in some way for the care in enlisting or selecting them. The Augustine cohort or band is mentioned by Suetonius in his *Life of Nero*, 20.

2. *A ship of Adramyttium.* A maritime town of Mysia, in Asia Minor, opposite to the island of Lesbos. This was a ship which had been built there, or which sailed from that port, but which was then in the port of Cesarea. It is evident, from ver. 6, that this ship was not expected to sail to Italy, but

3 And the next *day* we touched
at Sidon. And Julius [c]courteously
entreated Paul, and gave *him* liberty
to go unto his friends to refresh
himself.
4 And when we had launched from
thence, we sailed under Cyprus, because the winds were contrary.
5 And when we had sailed over
the sea of Cilicia and Pamphylia,
we came to Myra, *a city* of Lycia.
6 And there the centurion found
a ship of Alexandria sailing into
Italy; and he put us therein.

c ch.24.23; 28.16.

---

that the centurion expected to find some other vessel into which he could put the prisoners to take them to Rome. ¶ *We launched.* We loosed from our anchorage, or we set sail. See ch. xiii. 13. ¶ *By the coasts of Asia.* Of Asia Minor. Probably the owners of the ship designed to make a coasting voyage along the southern part of Asia Minor, and to engage in traffic with the maritime towns and cities. ¶ One *Aristarchus, a Macedonian.* This man is mentioned as Paul's companion in travel in ch. xix. 29. He afterward attended him to Macedonia, and returned with him to Asia, ch. xx. 4. He now appears to have attended him, not as a prisoner, but as a voluntary companion, choosing to share with him his dangers, and to enjoy the benefit of his society and friendship. He went with him to Rome, and was a fellow-prisoner with him there (Col. iv. 10), and is mentioned (Phile. 24) as Paul's fellow-labourer. It was doubtless a great comfort to Paul to have with him two such valuable friends as Luke and Aristarchus; and it was an instance of great affection for him that they were not ashamed of his bonds, but were willing to share his dangers, and to expose themselves to peril for the sake of accompanying him to Rome.

3. *We touched at Sidon.* See Notes on Mat. xi. 21. Sidon was about 67 miles north of Cesarea, and the passage could be easily accomplished, under favourable circumstances, in twenty-four hours. It is probable that the vessel, being a "coaster," put in there for purposes of trade. Sidon is the last city on the Phœnician coast in which the presence of the apostle can be traced. ¶ *And Julius courteously entreated Paul.* Treated him kindly or humanely. ¶ *And gave* him *liberty*, &c. The same thing had been done by Felix, ch. xxiv. 23. ¶ *Unto his friends.* In Sidon. Paul had frequently travelled in that direction in going to and returning from Jerusalem, and it is not improbable, therefore, that he had friends in all the principal cities. ¶ *To refresh himself.* To enjoy the benefit of their care; to make his present situation and his voyage as comfortable as possible. It is probable that they would furnish him with many supplies which were needful for his long and perilous voyage.

4. *We sailed under Cyprus.* For an account of Cyprus, see Notes on ch. iv. 36. By sailing "*under* Cyprus" is meant that they sailed along its coasts; they kept near to it; they thus endeavoured to break off the violent winds. Instead of steering a direct course in the open sea, which would have exposed them to violent opposing winds, they kept near this large island, so that it was between them and the westerly winds. The force of the wind was thus broken, and the voyage was rendered less difficult and dangerous. They went between Cyprus and Asia Minor, leaving Cyprus to the left. A sailor would express the idea by saying that they sailed *under the lee* of Cyprus. Had it not been for the strong western winds, they would have left it on the right. ¶ *The winds were contrary.* Were from the west, or south-west, which thus prevented their pursuing a direct course. See the map.

5. *The sea of Cilicia and Pamphylia.* The sea which lies off the coast from these two regions. For their situation, see the map, and Notes on Ac. vi. 9, and xiii. 13. ¶ *We came to Myra*, a city *of Lycia.* Lycia was a province in the south-western part of Asia Minor, having Phrygia and Pisidia on the north, the Mediterranean on the south, Pamphylia on the east, and Caria on the west.

6. *A ship of Alexandria.* A ship belonging to Alexandria. Alexandria was in Egypt, and was founded by Alexander the Great. It appears from ver. 38 that the ship was laden with wheat. It is well known that great quantities of wheat were imported from Egypt to Rome, and it appears that this was one of the large ships which were employed for that purpose. Why the ship was

7 And when we had sailed slowly
many days, and scarce were come
over against Cnidus, the wind not
suffering us, we sailed under [1] Crete
over against Salmone;
8 And, hardly passing it, came
unto a place which is called The
fair havens; nigh whereunto was
the city *of* Lasea.
9 Now when much time was
spent, and when sailing was now
dangerous, because the [2] fast was
now already past, Paul admonished
them,
10 And said unto them, Sirs,
[d] I perceive that this voyage will
be with [3] hurt and much damage,
not only of the lading and ship,
but also of our lives.

1 or, *Candy*.

2 *The fast was on the* 10*th day of the* 7*th month*, Le.23.27,29.
d 2 Ki.6.9,10; Da.2.20; Am.3.7. 3 or, *injury*.

on the coast of Asia Minor is not known. But it is probable that it had been driven out of its way by adverse winds or tempests.

7. *Had sailed slowly.* By reason of the prevalence of the western winds, ver. 4. ¶ *Over against Cnidus.* This was a city standing on a promontory of the same name in Asia Minor, in the part of the province of Caria called Doris, and a little north-west of the island of Rhodes. ¶ *The wind not suffering us.* The wind repelling us in that direction; not permitting us to hold on a direct course, we were driven off near to Crete. ¶ *We sailed under Crete.* See ver. 4. We lay along near to Crete, so as to break the violence of the wind. For the situation of Crete, see Notes on ch. ii. 11. ¶ *Over against Salmone.* Near to Salmone. This was the name of the promontory which formed the eastern extremity of the island of Crete.

8. *And, hardly passing it.* Scarcely being able to pass by it without being wrecked. Being almost driven on it. They passed round the east end of the island because they had been unable to sail directly forward between the island and the mainland. ¶ *The fair havens.* This was on the south-eastern part of the island of Crete. It was probably not so much a harbour as an open *roadstead*, which afforded good anchorage for a time. It is called by Stephen, the geographer, "the fair shore." It still retains the name which it formerly had. It is called in ancient Dutch and French Sailing Directions "the beautiful bay." ¶ *Nigh whereunto was the city* of *Lasea.* There was no town or city at the "Fair Havens," but the city of Lasea seems to have been well known, and it is mentioned here to identify the place.

9. *When much time was spent.* In sailing along the coast of Asia; in contending with the contrary winds. It is evident that when they started they had hoped to reach Italy before the dangerous time of navigating the Mediterranean should arrive. But they had been detained and embarrassed contrary to their expectation, so that they were now sailing in the most dangerous and tempestuous time of the year. ¶ *Because the fast was now already past.* By the "fast" here is evidently intended the fast which occurred among the Jews on the great day of atonement. That was on the tenth of the month *Tisri*, which answers to a part of September and part of October. It was, therefore, the time of the autumnal equinox, and when the navigation of the Mediterranean was esteemed to be particularly dangerous, from the storms which usually occurred about that time. The ancients regarded this as a dangerous time to navigate the Mediterranean. See the proofs in Kuinoel on this place. ¶ *Paul admonished* them. Paul exhorted, entreated, or persuaded them. He was somewhat accustomed to the navigation of that sea, and endeavoured to persuade them not to risk the danger of sailing at that season of the year.

10. *Sirs.* Greek, Men. ¶ *I perceive.* It is not certain that Paul understood this by direct inspiration. He might have perceived it from his own knowledge of the danger of navigation at the autumnal equinox, and from what he saw of the ship as unfitted to a dangerous navigation. But there is nothing that should prevent our believing also that he was guided to this conclusion by the inspiration of the Spirit of God. Comp. ver. 23, 24. ¶ *Will be with hurt.* With injury or hazard. It is not meant that their lives would be lost, but that they would be jeoparded. ¶ *The lading.* The freight of the ship. It was

11 Nevertheless, [e]the centurion believed the master and the owner of the ship more than those things which were spoken by Paul.
12 And because the haven was not commodious to winter in, the more part advised to depart thence also, if by any means they might attain to Phenice, *and there* to winter; *which is* a haven of [f]Crete, and lieth toward the south-west and north-west.

e Pr.27.12. f ver.7.

laden with wheat, ver. 38. Paul evidently, by this, intended to suggest the propriety of remaining where they were until the time of dangerous navigation was past.

11. *The master.* The person who is here meant was the helmsman, who occupied in ancient ships a conspicuous place on the stern, and steered the ship, and gave directions to the crew. ¶ *The owner of the ship.* Probably a different person from "the master." He had the general command of the ship as his own property, but had employed "the master," or the pilot, to direct and manage it. His counsel in regard to the propriety of continuing the voyage would be likely to be followed.

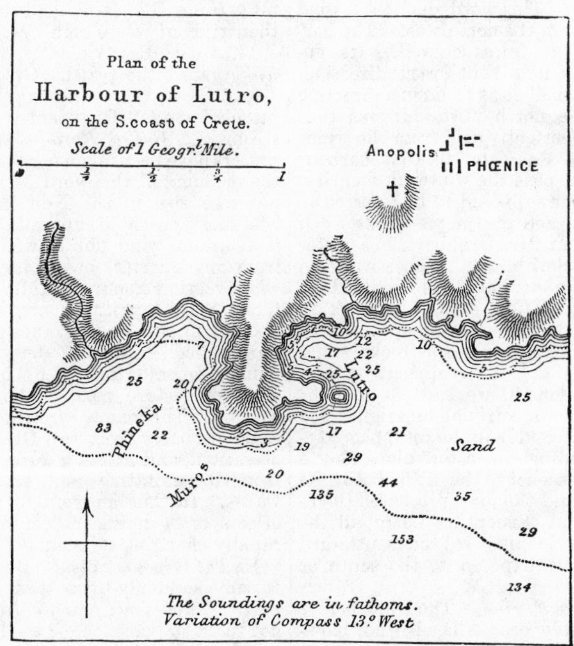

12. *The haven.* The fair havens, ver. 8. ¶ *Was not commodious to winter in.* Not safe or convenient to remain there. Probably it furnished rather a safe anchorage ground in time of a storm than a convenient place for a permanent harbour. ¶ *The more part.* The greater part of the crew. ¶ *To Phenice.* In the original this is Phœnix—Φοῖνιξ. So it is written by Strabo. The name was probably derived from the palm-trees which were common in Crete. This was a port or harbour on the south side of Crete, and west of the fair havens. It was a more convenient harbour, and was regarded as more safe. It appears, therefore, that the majority of persons on board concurred with Paul in the belief that it was not advisable to attempt the navigation of the sea until the dangers of the winter had passed by. ¶ *And lieth toward.*

13 And when the south wind blew softly, supposing that they had obtained *their* purpose, [g]loosing *thence*, they sailed close by Crete.

14 But not long after there arose[4] against it [h]a tempestuous wind, called Euroclydon.

g ver.21. [4] or, *beat.* *h* Ps.107.25.

15 And when the ship was caught, and could not bear up into the wind, we let *her* drive.

16 And running under a certain island which is called Clauda, we had much work to come by the boat;

17 Which when they had taken up, they used helps, undergirding

---

Greek, *looking* toward; that is, it was *open* in that direction. ¶ *The south-west*—κατὰ λίβα. Toward *Libya*, or *Africa.* That country was situated south-west of the mouth of the harbour. The entrance of the harbour was in a south-west direction. ¶ *And north-west*—κατὰ χῶρον. This word denotes a wind blowing from the north-west. The harbour was doubtless curved. Its entrance was in a south-west direction. It then turned so as to lie in a direction toward the north-west. It was thus rendered perfectly safe from the winds and heavy seas; and in that harbour they might pass the winter in security. The harbour supposed to be referred to is that marked on the map *Lutro.* Of this harbour Mr. Urquhart, in a letter to James Smith, Esq., whose work on this voyage of Paul has obtained so wide a reputation, says, "Lutro is an admirable harbour. You open it like a box; unexpectedly the rocks stand apart, and the town appears within. . . . We thought we had cut him off, and that we were driving him right upon the rocks. Suddenly he disappeared—and, rounding in after him, like a change of scenery, the little basin, its shipping, and the town presented themselves. . . . Excepting Lutro, all the roadsteads looking to the southward are perfectly exposed to the south or east."

13. *The south wind.* The wind before had probably been a head-wind, blowing from the west. When it veered round to the south, and when it blew gently, though not entirely favourable, yet it was so that they supposed they could sail along the coast of Crete. ¶ *Had obtained their purpose.* The object of their desire; that is, to sail safely along the coast of Crete. ¶ *Loosing* thence. Setting sail from the fair havens. ¶ *Close by Crete.* Near the shore. It is evident that they designed, if possible, to make the harbour of Phenice to winter there. They weighed anchor and passed around Cape Matala. The distance to this point is four or five miles; the bearing west by south. With a gentle southerly wind, the vessel would be able to weather the cape, and then the wind was fair to Phœnix or Phenice [Lutro], which was thirty-five miles distant from the cape, and bore from thence about west-north-west.

14. *Arose.* Beat violently. ¶ *Against it.* Against the vessel. Greek, *seizing her, and whirling her around.* ¶ *A tempestuous wind.* Turbulent—violent—strong. ¶ *Called Euroclydon.* Interpreters have been much perplexed about the meaning of this word, which occurs nowhere else in the New Testament. The most probable supposition is, that it denotes a wind not blowing steadily from any quarter, but a *hurricane*, or wind veering about to different quarters. Such hurricanes are known to abound in the Mediterranean, and are now called *Levanters*, deriving their name from blowing chiefly in the Levant, or eastern part of the Mediterranean. The name *euroclydon* is derived probably from two Greek words, εὖρος, *wind*, and κλύδων, *a wave;* so called from its agitating and exciting the waves. It thus answers to the usual effects of a hurricane, or of a wind rapidly changing its points of compass.

15. *The ship was caught.* By the wind. It came suddenly upon them as a tempest. ¶ *Could not bear up*, &c. Could not resist its violence, or the helmsman could not direct the ship. It was seized by the wind, and driven with such violence, that it became unmanageable. ¶ *We let her drive.* We suffered the ship to be borne along by the wind without attempting to control it.

16. *And running under.* Running near to an island. They ran near to it, where the violence of the wind was probably broken by the island. ¶ *Which is called Clauda.* This is a small island about twenty miles south-west of Crete. ¶ *We had much work.* Much difficulty; we

were scarcely able to do it. ¶ *To come by the boat.* This does not mean that they attempted here to land in the boat, but they had much difficulty in saving the small boat attached to the ship by lifting it into the ship. The

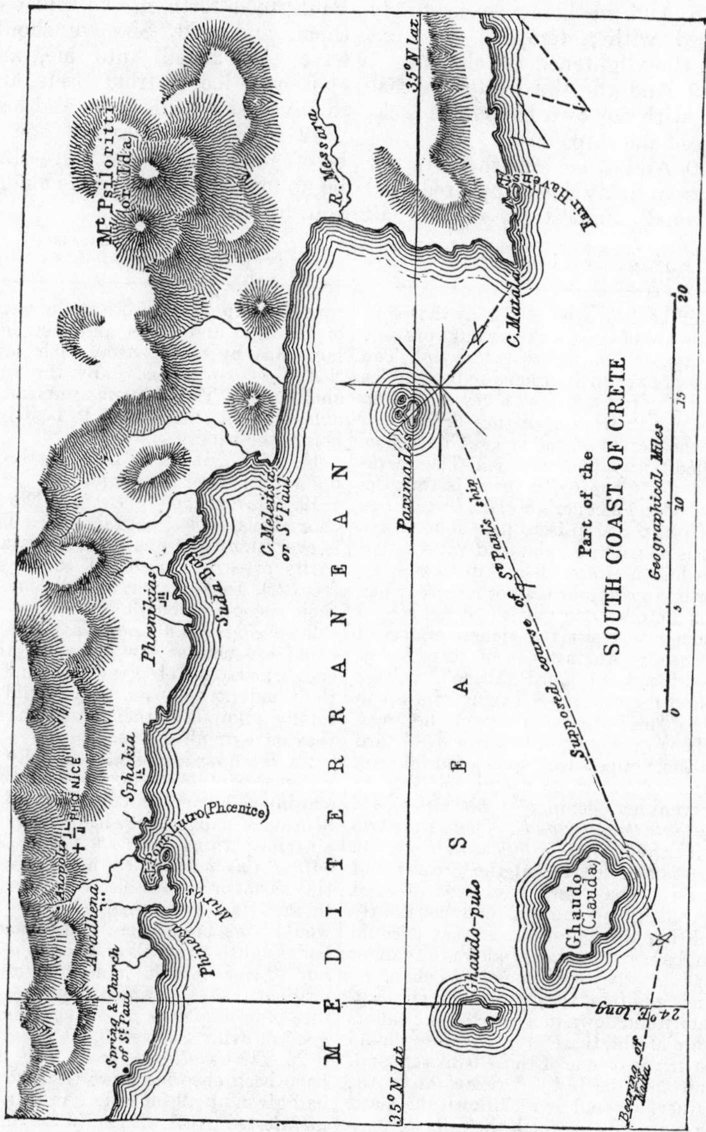

importance of securing the small boat is known by all seamen.

17. *Which when they had taken up.* When they had raised up the boat into the ship, so as to secure it. ¶ *They used helps.* They used ropes, cables, stays, or chains, for the purpose of securing the ship. The danger was that the ship

the ship; and, fearing lest they
should [i]fall into the quicksands,
strake sail, and so were driven.
18 And we being [k]exceedingly
tossed with a tempest, the next
day they lightened the ship.
19 And the third *day* [l]we cast
out with our own hands the tackling of the ship.
20 And when [m]neither sun nor
stars in many days appeared, and
no small tempest lay on *us*, [n]all
hope that we should be saved was
then taken away.
21 But after long abstinence,
Paul stood forth in the midst of
them, and said, Sirs, ye should
have [o]hearkened unto me, and
[p]not have loosed from Crete, and
to have gained this harm and loss.
22 And now [q]I exhort you to
be of good cheer; for there shall
be no loss of *any man's* life among
you, but of the ship.

i ver.41. *k* Ps.107.27. *l* Job 2.4; Jonah 1.5. *m* Ps.105.28. *n* Eze.37.11.

o ver.10. *p* ver.13. *q* Job 22.29; Ps.112.7; 2 Co.4.8,9.

---

would be destroyed, and they therefore made use of such aids as would prevent its loss. ¶ *Undergirding the ship.* The ancients were accustomed to pass cables or strong ropes around a vessel to keep the planks from springing or starting by the action of the sea. This is now called "*frapping*" a vessel. The operation of "*frapping*" a vessel is thus described in Falconer's *Marine Dictionary:* "To frap a ship is to pass four or five turns of a large cable-laid rope round the hull or frame of a ship to support her in a great storm, or otherwise, when it is apprehended that she is not strong enough to resist the violent efforts of the sea." An instance of this kind is mentioned in Lord Anson's voyage round the world. Speaking of a Spanish man-of-war in a storm, he says, "They were obliged to throw overboard all their upper-deck guns, and take six turns of the cable round the ship to prevent her opening." ¶ *Lest they should fall into the quicksands.* There were two celebrated *syrtes*, or quicksands, on the coast of Africa, called the greater and lesser. They were vast beds of sand driven up by the sea, and constantly shifting their position, so that it could not be known certainly where the danger was. As they were constantly changing their position, they could not be accurately laid down in a chart. The sailors were afraid, therefore, that they should be driven on one of those banks of sand, and thus be lost. ¶ *Strake sail.* Or, rather, lowered or took down the mast, or the yards to which the sails were attached. There has been a great variety of interpretations proposed on this passage. The most probable is that they took down the *mast*, by cutting or otherwise, as is now done in storms at sea, to save the ship. They were at the mercy of the wind and waves, and their only hope was by taking away their sails. ¶ *And so were driven.* By the wind and waves. The ship was unmanageable, and they suffered it to be driven before the wind.

18. *They lightened the ship.* By throwing out a part of the cargo.

19. *The tackling of the ship.* The anchors, sails, cables, baggage, &c. That is, everything that was not indispensable to its preservation, for it seems still (ver. 29) that they retained some of their anchors on board.

20. *Neither sun nor stars*, &c. As they could see neither sun nor stars, they could make no observations; and as they had no compass, they would be totally ignorant of their situation, and they gave up all as lost.

21. *But after long abstinence.* By the violence of the storm, by their long-continued labour, and by their apprehension of danger, they had a long time abstained from food. ¶ *And to have gained this harm.* To have *procured* this harm, or have subjected yourselves to it. Had you remained there you would have been safe. It seems to be bad English to speak of *gaining a loss*, but it is a correct translation of the original (κερδῆσαί), which expresses the idea of *acquiring* or *procuring*, whether good or evil. See ver. 9, 10.

22. *There shall be no loss.* This must have been cheering news to those who had given up all for lost. As Paul had manifested great wisdom in his former advice to them, they might be now more disposed to listen to him. The reason why he believed they would be safe, he immediately states.

23. *There stood by me.* There appeared

23 For[r] there stood by me this
night [s]the angel of God, [t]whose I
am, and [u]whom I serve.
24 Saying, Fear not, Paul; thou
must be brought before Cæsar:
and, lo, [v]God hath given thee all
them that sail with thee.
25 Wherefore, sirs, be of good
cheer; for [w]I believe God, that it
shall be even as it was told me.
26 Howbeit we must be cast
upon [x]a certain island.
27 But when the fourteenth
night was come, as we were driven
up and down in Adria, about midnight the shipmen deemed that they
drew near to some country;
28 And sounded, and found *it*
twenty fathoms; and when they
had gone a little further, they
sounded again, and found *it* fifteen
fathoms.
29 Then fearing lest we should
have fallen upon rocks, they cast
four anchors out of the stern, [y]and
wished for the day.
30 And as the shipmen were
about to flee out of the ship, when
they had let down the boat into

r ch.23.11. *s* He.1.14.
t De.32.9; Ps.135.4; Is.44.5; Mal.3.17; Jn.17.9,10; 1 Co.6.20; 1 Pe.2.9,10.
u Ps.116.16; Is.44.21; Da.3.17; 6.16; Jn.12.26; Ro. 1.9; 2 Ti.1.3. *v* Ge.19.21,29.
w Lu.1.45; Ro.4.20,21; 2 Ti.1.12. *x* ch.28.1.
y Ps.130.6.

---

to me. ¶ *The angel of God.* The messages of God were often communicated by angels. See He. i. 14. This does not mean that there was any *particular* angel, but simply *an* angel. ¶ *Whose I am.* Of the God to whom I belong. This is an expression of Paul's entire devotedness to him. ¶ *Whom I serve.* In the gospel. To whom and to whose cause I am entirely devoted.

24. *Fear not, Paul.* Do not be alarmed with the danger of the loss of life. ¶ *Thou must be brought,* &c. And therefore thy life will be spared. ¶ *God hath given thee all,* &c. That is, they shall all be preserved with thee. None of their lives shall be lost. This does not mean that they would be converted, but that their lives would be preserved. It is implied here that it was for the sake of Paul, or that the leading purpose of the divine interposition in rescuing them from danger was to save his life. The wicked often derive important benefits from being connected with Christians, and God often confers important favours on *them* in his general purpose to save his own people. The lives of the wicked are often spared because God interposes to save the righteous.

26. *Howbeit.* Nevertheless. ¶ *Upon a certain island.* Malta. See ch. xxviii. 1.

27. *The fourteenth night.* From the time when the tempest commenced. ¶ *In Adria.* In the Adriatic Sea. This sea is situated between Italy and Dalmatia, now called the Adriatic Gulf. But among the ancients the name was given not only to that gulf, but to the whole sea lying between Greece, Italy, and Africa, including the Sicilian and Ionian Sea. It is evident from the narrative that they were not in the Adriatic Gulf, but in the vicinity of Malta. See the map. ¶ *Deemed.* Judged. Probably by the appearance of the sea.

28. *And sounded.* To *sound* is to make use of a line and lead to ascertain the depth of water. ¶ *Twenty fathoms.* A fathom is six feet, or the distance from the extremity of the middle finger on one hand to the extremity of the other, when the arms are extended. The depth, therefore, was about one hundred and twenty feet. ¶ *Fifteen fathoms.* They knew, therefore, that they were drawing near to shore.

29. *They cast four anchors.* On account of the violence of the storm and waves, to make, if possible, the ship secure. ¶ *And wished for the day.* To discern more accurately their situation and danger.

30. *The shipmen.* The sailors, leaving the prisoners. ¶ *Under colour.* Under pretence. They pretended that it was necessary to get into the boat, and carry the anchors ahead of the ship so as to make it secure, but with a real intention to make for the shore. ¶ *Out of the foreship.* From the prow, so as to make the fore part of the ship secure. The reason why they did this was probably that they expected the ship would go to pieces; and as all on board could not be saved in one small boat, they resolved to escape to a place of safety as soon as possible.

the sea, under colour as though they would have cast anchors out of the foreship,

31 Paul said to the centurion and to the soldiers, Except these abide in the ship, ye cannot be saved.

32 Then the soldiers cut off the ropes of the boat, and let her fall off.

33 And while the day was coming on, Paul besought *them* all to take meat, saying, This day is the fourteenth day that ye have tarried and continued fasting, having taken nothing.

---

31. *Paul said to the centurion and the soldiers.* The centurion had, it appears, the general direction of the ship, ver. 11. Perhaps it had been pressed into the service of the government. ¶ *Except these.* These seamen. The soldiers and the centurion were unqualified to manage the ship, and the presence of the sailors was therefore indispensable to the preservation of any. ¶ *Abide in the ship.* Remain on board. ¶ *Ye cannot be saved.* You cannot be preserved from death. You will have no hope of managing the ship. It will be remembered that Paul had been informed by the angel, and had assured them (ver. 22–24) that no lives would be lost; but it was only in the use of the proper *means* that their lives would be safe. Though it had been determined, and though Paul had the assurance that their lives would be safe, yet this did not, in his view, prevent the use of the proper means to secure it. From this we may learn, (1) That the certainty of an event does not render it improper to use means to obtain it. (2) That, though the event may be determined, yet the use of means may be indispensable to secure it. The event is not more certainly ordained than the means requisite to accomplish it. (3) That the doctrine of the divine purposes or decrees, making certain future events, does not make the use of man's agency unnecessary or improper. The means are determined as well as the end, and the one will not be secured without the other. (4) The same is true in regard to the decrees respecting salvation. The end is not determined without the means; and as God has resolved that his people shall be saved, so he has also determined the means. He has ordained that they shall repent, shall believe, shall be holy, and shall *thus* be saved. (5) We have in this case a full answer to the objection that a belief in the decrees of God will make men neglect the means of salvation, and lead to licentiousness. It has just the contrary tendency. Here is a case in which Paul *certainly* believed in the purpose of God to save these men; in which he was assured that it was fully determined; and yet the effect was not to produce indolence and unconcern, but to prompt him to use strenuous efforts to accomplish the very effect which God had determined *should* take place. So it is always. A belief that God has purposes of mercy; that he designs, and has always designed, to save some, will prompt to the use of all proper means to secure it. If we had no such evidence that God had any such purpose, effort would be vain. Where we *have* such evidence, it operates, as it did in the case of Paul, to produce great and strenuous endeavours to secure the object.

32. *Cut off the ropes*, &c. It is evident that the mariners had not yet got on board the boat. They had let it down into the sea (ver. 30), and were about to go on board. By thus cutting the ropes which fastened the boat to the ship, and letting it go, all possibility of their fleeing from the ship was taken away, and they were compelled to remain on board.

33. *And while the day was coming on.* At daybreak. It was before they had sufficient light to discern what they should do. ¶ *To take meat.* Food. The word *meat* was formerly used to denote *food* of any kind. ¶ *That ye have tarried.* That you have remained or been fasting. ¶ *Having taken nothing.* No *regular* meal. It cannot mean that they had lived entirely without food, but that they had been in so much danger, were so constantly engaged, and had been so anxious about their safety, that they had taken no *regular* meal, or that what they had taken had been at irregular intervals, and had been a scanty allowance. "Appian speaks of an army which for twenty days together had neither food nor sleep; by which he must mean that they neither made full meals nor slept whole nights together,

34 Wherefore I pray you to take
some meat; for [z]this is for your
health: for [a]there shall not a hair
fall from the head of any of you.
35 And when he had thus spoken,
he took bread, and [b]gave thanks to
God in presence of them all; and
when he had broken *it*, he began
to eat.
36 Then were they all of good
cheer, and they also took *some*
meat.
37 And we were in all in the

z Mat.15.32; 1 Ti.5.23.
a 1 Ki.1.52; Mat.10.30; Lu.12.7; 21.18.
b 1 Sa.9.13; Mat.15.36; Mar.8.6; Jn.6.11,23; 1 Ti.4.3,4.

ship two hundred threescore and
sixteen souls.
38 And when they had eaten
enough, they lightened the ship,
and cast out the wheat into the sea.
39 And when it was day, they
knew not the land; but they discovered a certain creek with a
shore, into the which they were
minded, if it were possible, to
thrust in the ship.
40 And when they had [5]taken
up the anchors, they committed
themselves unto the sea, and loosed
the rudder-bands, and hoisted up

5 or, *cut the anchors, they left them in the sea*, &c.

The same interpretation must be given to this phrase" (Doddridge). The effect of this must have been that they would be exhausted, and little able to endure the fatigues which yet remained.

34. *Not a hair fall from the head*, &c. A proverbial expression, denoting that they would be preserved safe; that none of them would be lost, and that in their persons they should not experience the least damage, 1 Ki. i. 52; 1 Sa. xiv. 45.

35. *And gave thanks*, &c. This was the usual custom among the Hebrews. Notes on Mat. xiv. 19. Paul was among those who were not Christians; but he was not ashamed of the proper acknowledgment of God, and was not afraid to avow his dependence on him, and to express his gratitude for his mercy.

38. *They lightened the ship.* By casting the wheat into the sea. As they had no hope of saving the cargo, and had no further use for it, they hoped that by throwing the wheat overboard the ship would draw less water, and that thus they would be able to run the vessel on the shore.

39. *They knew not the land.* They had been driven with a tempest, without being able to make any observation, and it is probable that they were entire strangers to the coast and to the whole island. ¶ *A certain creek with a shore.* Greek, a certain *bosom* (κόλπος) or *bay.* By its having *a shore* is probably meant that it had a *level* shore, or one that was convenient for landing. It was not a high bluff of rocks, but was accessible. Kuinoel thinks that the passage should be construed, "they found a certain shore, having a bay," &c. ¶ *Were minded.* Were resolved.

40. *Had taken up the anchors.* The four anchors with which they had moored the ship, ver. 29. See the margin. The expression may mean that they slipped or cut their cables, and that thus they left the anchors in the sea. This is the most probable interpretation. ¶ *And loosed the rudder-bands.* The rudder, in navigation, is that by which a ship is steered. It is that part of the helm which consists of a piece of timber, broad at the bottom, which enters the water, and is attached by hinges to the stern-post on which it turns (Webster). But what was the precise form of the rudder among the ancients is not certainly known. Sometimes a vessel might be steered by oars. Most ships appear to have had a rudder at the prow as well as at the stern. In some instances, also, they had them on the sides. The word used here in the Greek is in the plural (τῶν πηδαλίων), and it is evident that they had in this ship more than one rudder. The *bands* mentioned here were probably the cords or fastenings by which the rudder could be made secure to the sides of the ship, or could be raised up out of the water in a violent storm, to prevent its being carried away. And as, in the tempest, the rudders had become useless (ver. 15, 17), they were probably either raised out of the water, or made fast. Now that the storm was past, and they could be used again, they were *loosed*, and they endeavoured to direct the vessel into port. ¶ *The mainsail*—ἀρτέμονα. There have been various explanations of this word. Luther translates it *the mast.* Erasmus, *the yards.* Grotius, who supposes that the main-

the mainsail to the wind, and made toward shore.

41 And falling into a place where two seas met, they ran the ship aground; and the fore part stuck fast, and remained unmovable, but the hinder part was broken with the violence of the waves.

42 And[c] the soldiers' counsel was to kill the prisoners, lest any of them should swim out and escape.

43 But[d] the centurion, willing to save Paul, kept them from *their* purpose, and commanded that they

c Ps.74.20. d 2 Co.11.25.

---

mast had been cast away (ver. 17), thinks that this must mean the foremast or bowsprit. The word usually means the *mainsail*. The Syriac and Arabic understand it of a *small sail*, that was hoisted for a temporary purpose. Mr. Smith, in his work on this voyage of Paul, supposes that it was the *foresail*. Others translate it a *jib*. "The mainsail [foresail] being hoisted showed good judgment, though the distance was so small, as it would not only enable them to steer more correctly than without it, but would press the ship farther on upon the land, and thus enable them the more easily to get to the shore" (Penrose).

41. *And falling*. Being carried by the wind and waves. ¶ *Into a place where two seas met*. Greek, into a place *of a double sea*—διθάλασσον. That is, a place which was washed on both sides by the sea. It refers properly to an isthmus, tongue of land, or a sand-bar stretching out from the mainland, and which was washed on both sides by the waves. It is evident that this was not properly an *isthmus* that was above the waves, but was probably a long sandbank that stretched far out into the sea, and which they did not perceive. In endeavouring to make the harbour, they ran on this bar or sand-bank. ¶ *They ran the ship aground*. Not designedly, but in endeavouring to reach the harbour, ver. 39. ¶ *The hinder part was broken*. The stern was broken or staved in. By this means the company was furnished with boards, &c., on which they were safely conveyed to shore, ver. 44.

42. *And the soldiers' counsel*, &c. Why they gave this advice is not known. It was probably, however, because the Roman military discipline was very strict, and if they escaped it would be charged on them that it had been done by the negligence and unfaithfulness of the soldiers. They therefore proposed to kill them, though contrary to all humanity, justice, and laws; presuming, probably, that it would be supposed that they had perished in the wreck. This is a remarkable proof that men can be cruel even when experiencing the tender mercy of God, and that the most affecting scenes of divine goodness will not mitigate the natural ferocity and cruelty of those who delight in blood.

43. *But the centurion, willing to save Paul*. He had at first been disposed to treat Paul with kindness, ver. 3. And his conduct on board the ship; the wisdom of his advice (ver. 10); the prudence of his conduct in the agitation and danger of the tempest; and not improbably the belief that he was under the divine protection and blessing, disposed him to spare his life. ¶ *Kept them from* their *purpose*. Thus, for the sake of this one righteous man, the lives of all were spared. The instance here shows, (1) That it is possible for a pious man, like Paul, so to conduct in the various trying scenes of life—the agitations, difficulties, and temptations of this world—as to conciliate the favour of the men of this world; and, (2) That important benefits often result to sinners from the righteous. Paul's being on board was the means of saving the lives of many prisoners; and God often confers important blessings on the wicked for the sake of the pious relatives, friends, and neighbours with whom they are connected. Ten righteous men would have saved Sodom (Ge. xviii. 32); and Christians are in more ways than one the salt of the earth, and the light of the world, Mat. v. 13, 14. It is a privilege to be related to the friends of God—to be the children of pious parents, or to be connected with pious partners in life. It is a privilege to be connected with the friends of God in business; or to dwell near them; or to be associated with them in the various walks and dangers of life. The streams of blessings which flow to fertilize *their* lands, flow also to bless others; the dews of heaven which descend on their habitations, descend on all around; and the God which crowns them with loving-

which could swim should cast *themselves* first *into the sea*, and get to land:

44 And the rest, some on boards, and some on *broken pieces* of the ship. And[e] so it came to pass that they escaped all safe to land.

CHAPTER XXVIII.

AND when they were escaped, then they knew that [a]the island was called Melita.

2 And the [b]barbarous people showed us no little kindness; for they kindled a fire, and [c]received us every one, because of the present rain, and because of the cold.

3 And when Paul had gathered a bundle of sticks, and laid *them* on the fire, there came a viper out of the heat, and fastened on his hand.

4 And when the barbarians saw the *venomous* beast hang on his

e Ps.107.28-30; ver.22. a ch.27.26.

b Ro.1.14; Col.3.11. c Mat.10.42; He.13.2.

---

kindness, often fills the abodes of their neighbours and friends with the blessings of peace and salvation. ¶ *And commanded.* Probably they were released from their chains.

44. *And the rest.* Those who could not swim. ¶ *They escaped all safe to land.* According to the promise which was made to Paul, ver. 22. This was done by the special providence of God. It was a remarkable instance of divine interposition to save so many through so long-continued dangers; and it shows that God can defend in any perils, and can accomplish all his purposes. On the ocean or the land we are safe in his keeping, and he can devise ways that shall fulfil all his purposes, and that can protect his people from danger.

CHAPTER XXVIII.

1. *They knew.* Either from their former acquaintance with the island, or from the information of the inhabitants. ¶ *Was called Melita.* Now called Malta. It was celebrated formerly for producing large quantities of honey, and is supposed to have been called *Melita* from the Greek word signifying honey. It is about twenty miles in length from east to west, and twelve miles in breadth from north to south, and about sixty miles in circumference. It is about sixty miles from the coast of Sicily. The island is an immense rock of white soft freestone, with a covering of earth about one foot in depth, which has been brought from the island of Sicily. There was also another island formerly called *Melita*, now called *Meleda*, in the Adriatic Sea, near the coast of Illyricum, and some have supposed that Paul was shipwrecked on that island. But tradition has uniformly said that it was on the island now called Malta. Besides, the other Melita would have been far out of the usual track in going to Italy; and it is further evident that Malta was the place, because from the place of his shipwreck he went directly to Syracuse, Rhegium, and Puteoli, thus sailing in a direct course to Rome. In sailing from the other Melita to Rhegium, Syracuse would be far out of the direct course. The island now is in the possession of the British.

2. *And the barbarous people.* See Notes on Ro. i. 14. The Greeks regarded all as barbarians who did not speak their language, and applied the name to all other nations but their own. It does not denote, as it does sometimes with us, people of savage, uncultivated, and cruel habits, but simply those whose speech was unintelligible. See 1 Co. xiv. 11. The island is supposed to have been peopled at first by the Phœcians, afterward by the Phœnicians, and afterward by a colony from Carthage. The language of the Maltese was that of Africa, and hence it was called by the Greeks the language of barbarians. It was a language which was unintelligible to the Greeks and Latins. ¶ *The rain.* The continuance of the storm. ¶ *And of the cold.* The exposure to the water in getting to the shore, and probably to the coldness of the weather. It was now in the month of October.

3. *Had gathered a bundle of sticks.* For the purpose of making a fire. ¶ *There came a viper.* A poisonous serpent. See Notes on Mat. iii. 7. The viper was doubtless in the bundle of sticks or limbs of trees which Paul had gathered, but was concealed, and was torpid. But when the bundle was laid on the fire, the viper became warmed by the heat, and ran out and fastened on the hand of Paul. ¶ *And fastened on his hand—*

hand, they said among themselves,
No[d] doubt this man is a murderer,
whom, though he hath escaped the
sea, yet vengeance suffereth not to
live.
5 And he shook off the beast
into the fire, [e]and felt no harm.

d Jn.7.24. e Mar.16.18; Lu.10.19.

6 Howbeit they looked when
he should have swollen, or fallen
down dead suddenly; but after
they had looked a great while,
and saw no harm come to him,
they changed their minds, [f]and
said that he was a god.

f ch.14.11.

καθῆψε. This word properly means to join one's self to; to touch; to adhere to. It might have been by coiling around his hand and arm, or by fastening its fangs in his hand. It is not expressly affirmed that Paul was *bitten* by the viper, yet it is evidently implied; and it is wholly incredible that a viper, unless miraculously prevented, should fasten himself to the hand without biting.

4. *The* venomous *beast.* The word *beast* we apply usually to an animal of larger size than a viper. But the original (θηρίον) is applicable to animals of any kind, and was especially applied by Greek writers to serpents. See Schleusner. ¶ *No doubt.* The fact that the viper had fastened on him; and that, as they supposed, he must now certainly die, was the proof from which they inferred his guilt. ¶ *Is a murderer.* Why they thought he was a *murderer* rather than guilty of some other crime is not known. It might have been, (1) Because they inferred that he must have been guilty of some very atrocious crime, and as murder was the highest crime that man could commit, they inferred that he had been guilty of this. Or, (2) More probably, they had an opinion that when divine vengeance overtook a man, he would be punished in a manner similar to the offence; and as murder is committed usually with the hand, and as the viper had fastened on the hand of Paul, they inferred that he had been guilty of taking life. It was supposed among the ancients that persons were often punished by divine vengeance in that part of the body which had been the instrument of the sin. ¶ *Whom, though he hath escaped the sea.* They supposed that vengeance and justice would still follow the guilty; that, though he might escape one form of punishment, yet he would be exposed to another. And this, to a certain extent, is true. These barbarians reasoned from great original principles, written on the hearts of all men by nature, that there is a God of justice, and that the guilty will be punished. They reasoned incorrectly, as many do, only because that they supposed that *every* calamity is a judgment for some particular sin. Men often draw this conclusion, and suppose that suffering is to be traced to some particular crime, and to be regarded as a direct judgment from heaven. See Notes on Jn. ix. 1–3. The general proposition that all sin will be punished at some time is true, but we are not qualified to affirm of particular calamities always that they are direct judgments for sin. In some cases we may. In the case of the drunkard, the gambler, and the profligate, we cannot doubt that the loss of property, health, and reputation is the direct result of specific crime. In the ordinary calamities of life, however, it requires a more profound acquaintance with the principles of divine government than we possess to affirm of each instance of suffering that it is a particular judgment for some crime. ¶ *That vengeance*—ἡ δίκη. *Diké*, or justice, was represented by the heathen as a goddess, the daughter of Jupiter, whose office it was to take vengeance, or to inflict punishment for crimes. ¶ *Suffereth not to live.* They regarded him as already a dead man. They supposed the effect of the bite of the viper would be so certainly fatal that they might speak of him as already in effect dead (Beza).

5. *And he shook off*, &c. In this was remarkably fulfilled the promise of the Saviour (Mar. xvi. 18): "They shall take up serpents," &c.

6. *When he should have swollen.* When they expected that he would have swollen from the bite of the viper. The poison of the viper is rapid, and they expected that he would die soon. The word rendered "swollen" (πίμπρασθαι) means properly to burn; to be inflamed, and then to be swollen from inflammation. This was what they expected here, that the poison would produce a violent inflammation. ¶ *Or fallen down dead suddenly.* As is sometimes the

7 In the same quarters were possessions of the chief man of the
island, whose name was Publius;
who received us, and lodged us
three days courteously.
8 And it came to pass, that the
father of Publius lay sick of a
fever, and of a bloody flux; [g]to
whom Paul entered in, and prayed,
and [h]laid his hands on him, and
healed him.
9 So when this was done, others
also, which had diseases in the
island, came, and were healed:
10 Who also [i]honoured us with
many honours; and when we departed, [k]they laded *us* with such
things as were necessary.
11 And after three months we
departed in a ship of Alexandria,
which had wintered in the isle,
whose sign was Castor and Pollux.
12 And landing at Syracuse, we
tarried *there* three days.
13 And from thence we fetched

g Ja.5.14,15.
h Mat.9.18; Mar.6.5; 7.32; 16.18; Lu.4.40; ch.19.11; 1 Co.12.9,28.
i 1 Th.2.6; 1 Ti.5.17.
k Mat.6.31-34; 10.8-10; 2 Co.9.5-11; Phi.4.11,12.

case from the bite of the serpent when a vital part is affected. ¶ *They changed their minds.* They saw that he was uninjured, and miraculously preserved; and they supposed that none but a god could be thus kept from death. ¶ *That he was a god.* That the Maltese were idolaters there can be no doubt; but what gods they worshipped is unknown, and conjecture would be useless. It was natural that they should attribute such a preservation to the presence of a divinity. A similar instance occurred at Lystra. See Notes on ch. xiv. 11.

7. *In the same quarters.* In that place, or that part of the island. ¶ *Possessions.* Property. His place of residence. ¶ *The chief man.* Greek, the *first* man. Probably he was the governor of the island.

8. *A bloody flux.* Greek, dysentery. ¶ *And laid his hands on him,* &c. In accordance with the promise of the Saviour, Mar. xvi. 18. This miracle was a suitable return for the hospitality of Publius, and would serve to conciliate further the kindness of the people, and prepare the way for Paul's usefulness.

10. *Who also honoured us.* As men who were favoured of heaven, and who had been the means of conferring important benefits on them in healing the sick, &c. Probably the word "honours" here means *gifts,* or marks of favour. ¶ *They laded* us. They gave us, or conferred on us. They furnished us with such things as were necessary for us on our journey.

11. *And after three months.* Probably they remained there so long because there was no favourable opportunity for them to go to Rome. If they arrived there, as is commonly supposed, in October, they left for Rome in January. ¶ *In a ship of Alexandria.* See Notes on ch. xxvii. 6. ¶ *Whose sign.* Which was ornamented with an image of Castor and Pollux. It was common to place on the prow of the ship the image of some person or god, whose name the ship bore. This custom is still observed. ¶ *Castor and Pollux.* These were two semi-deities. They were reputed to be twin brothers, sons of Jupiter and Leda, the wife of Tyndarus, king of Sparta. After their death they are fabled to have been translated to heaven, and made *constellations* under the name of *Gemini*, or the Twins. They then received divine honours, and were called the sons of Jupiter. They were supposed to preside over sailors, and to be their protectors; hence it was not uncommon to place their image on ships. Comp. Lempriere's *Dictionary.*

12. *And landing at Syracuse.* Syracuse was the capital of the island of Sicily, on the eastern coast. It was in the direct course from Malta to Rome. It contains about 18,000 inhabitants.

13. *We fetched a compass.* We coasted about; or we sailed along the eastern side of Sicily. The course can be seen on the map. ¶ *And came to Rhegium.* This was a city of Italy, in the kingdom of Naples, on the coast near the southwest extremity of Italy. It was nearly opposite to Messina, in Sicily. It is now called *Reggio.* See the map. ¶ *The south wind.* A wind favourable for their voyage. ¶ *To Puteoli.* The wells. This place was celebrated for its warm baths, and from these and its springs it is supposed to have derived its name of *The Wells.* It is now called *Pozzuoli*, and is in the campania of Naples, on the N. side of the bay, and about 8 miles

a compass, and came to Rhegium; and after one day the south wind blew, and we came the next day to Puteoli;

14 Where we found brethren, and were desired to tarry with them seven days; and so we went toward Rome.

15 And from thence, when the brethren heard of us, [l]they came to meet us as far as Appii Forum, and the Three Taverns; whom when Paul saw, he thanked God, and [m]took courage.

16 And when we came to Rome, the centurion delivered the prisoners to the captain of the guard; but [n]Paul was suffered to dwell by himself with a soldier that kept him.

17 And it came to pass, that after three days Paul called the chief of the Jews together; and when they were come together, he said unto

l ch.21.5; 3 Jn.6-8.

m Jos.1.6,7,9; 1 Sa.30.6; Ps.27.14. n ch.24.23; 27.3.

N.W. from Naples. The town contains at present about 10,000 inhabitants.

14. *Brethren.* Christian brethren. But by whom the gospel had been preached there is unknown.

15. *And from thence.* From Puteoli. ¶ *When the brethren heard of us.* The Christians who were at Rome. ¶ *As far as the Appii Forum.* This was a city about 56 miles from Rome. The remains of an ancient city are still seen there. It is on the borders of the Pontine Marshes. The city was built on the celebrated Appian Way, or the road from Rome to Capua. The road was made by Appius Claudius, and probably the city was founded by him also. It was called the *forum* or *market-place* of Appius, because it was a convenient place for travellers on the Appian Way to stop for purposes of refreshment. It was also a famous resort for peddlers and merchants. See Horace, b. i. *Sat.* 5, 3. ¶ *And the Three Taverns.* This place was about 8 or 10 miles nearer Rome than the Appii Forum (Cicero, *ad Att.*, ii. 10). It undoubtedly received its name because it was distinguished as a place of refreshment on the Appian Way. Probably the greater part of the company of Christians remained at this place while the remainder went forward to meet Paul, and to attend him on his way. The Christians at Rome had doubtless heard much of Paul. His epistle to them had been written about the year of our Lord 57, or at least five years before this time. The interest which the Roman Christians felt in the apostle was thus manifested by their coming so far to meet him, though he was a prisoner. ¶ *He thanked God.* He had long ardently desired to see the Christians of Rome, Ro. i. 9-11; xv. 23, 32. He was now grateful to God that the object of his long desire was at least granted, and that he was permitted to see them, though in bonds. ¶ *And took courage.* From their society and counsel. The presence and counsel of Christian brethren is often of inestimable value in encouraging and strengthening us in the toils and trials of life.

16. *The captain of the guard.* The commander of the Prætorian cohort, or guard. The custom was, that those who were sent from the provinces to Rome for trial were delivered to the custody of this guard. The name of the prefect or captain of the guard at this time was Burrhus Afranius (Tacit. *Ann.*, 12, 42, 1). ¶ *But Paul was suffered,* &c. Evidently by the permission of the centurion, whose favour he had so much conciliated on the voyage. See ch. xxvii. 43. ¶ *With a soldier that kept him.* That is, in the custody of a soldier to whom he was chained, and who, of course, constantly attended him. See ch. xxiv. 23; xii. 6.

17. *Paul called the chief of the Jews.* He probably had two objects in this: one was to vindicate himself from the suspicion of crime, or to convince them that the charges alleged against him were false; and the other, to explain to them the gospel of Christ. In accordance with his custom everywhere, he seized the earliest opportunity of making the gospel known to his own countrymen; and he naturally supposed that charges highly unfavourable to his character had been sent forward against him to the Jews at Rome by those in Judea. ¶ *Against the people.* Against the Jews, ch. xxiv. 12. ¶ *Or customs,* &c. The religious rites of the nation. See Notes on ch. vi. 14. ¶ *Was I delivered prisoner,* &c. By the Jews, ch. xxi. 33, &c.

them, Men *and* brethren, though [o]I
have committed nothing against the
people, or customs of our fathers,
yet was I [p]delivered prisoner from
Jerusalem into the hands of the
Romans:
18 Who,[q] when they had examined me, would have let *me* go, because there was no cause of death
in me.
19 But when the Jews spake
against *it*, I was constrained [r]to
appeal unto Cæsar; not that I had
aught to accuse my nation of.
20 For this cause, therefore, have
I called for you, to see *you*, and to
speak with *you;* because that [s]for
the hope of Israel [t]I am bound with
this chain.
21 And they said unto him,
We neither received letters out of
Judea concerning thee, neither any
of the brethren that came showed
or spake any harm of thee.
22 But we desire to hear of thee
what thou thinkest; for as concerning this sect, [u]we know that
every where it is spoken against.
23 And when they had appointed
him a day, there came many to him

o ch.24.12,13; 25.8. p ch.21.33,&c. q ch.24.10; 26.31. r ch.25.11.

s ch.26.6,7. t ch.26.29; Ep.3.1; 4.1; 6.20; 2 Ti.1.16; 2.9; Phile. 10,13. u Lu.2.34; ch.24.5,14; 1 Pe.2.12; 4.14.

18. *When they had examined me*, &c. Ch. xxiv. 10–27; xxv.; xxvi. 31, 32. ¶ *No cause of death.* No crime worthy of death.

19. *The Jews spake against* it. Against my being set at liberty. ¶ *I was constrained.* By a regard to my own safety and character. ¶ *To appeal unto Cæsar.* See Notes on ch. xxv. 11. ¶ *Not that I had aught*, &c. I did it for my own preservation and safety, not that I wished to accuse my countrymen. Paul had been unjustly accused and injured; yet, with the true spirit of the Christian religion, he here says that he cherished no unkind feelings toward those who had done him wrong.

20. *Because for the hope of Israel.* On account of the hope which the Jews cherish of the coming of the Messiah; of the resurrection; and of the future state. See this explained in the Notes on ch. xxiii. 6. ¶ *I am bound with this chain.* See Notes on ch. xxvi. 29. Probably he was attached constantly to a soldier by a chain.

21. *We neither received letters*, &c. Why the Jews in Judea had not forwarded the accusation against Paul to their brethren at Rome, that they might continue the prosecution before the emperor, is not known. It is probable that they regarded their cause as *hopeless*, and chose to abandon the prosecution. Paul had been acquitted successively by Lysias, Felix, Festus, and Agrippa; and as they had not succeeded in procuring his condemnation before them, they saw no prospect of doing it at Rome, and resolved, therefore, not to press the prosecution any farther. ¶ *Neither any of the brethren that came.* Any of the Jews. There was a very constant intercourse between Judea and Rome, but it seems that the Jews who had come before Paul had arrived had not mentioned his case, so as to prejudice them against him.

22. *What thou thinkest.* What your belief is; or what are the doctrines of Christians respecting the Messiah. ¶ *This sect.* The sect of Christians. ¶ *Spoken against.* Particularly by Jews. This was the case then, and, to a great extent, is the case still. It has been the common lot of the followers of Christ to be spoken "against." Comp. ch. xxiv. 5.

23. *Appointed him a day.* A day when they would hear him. ¶ *To his lodging.* To the house where he resided, ver. 30. ¶ *He expounded.* He explained or declared the principles of the Christian religion. ¶ *And testified the kingdom of God.* Bore witness to, or declared the principles and doctrines of the reign of the Messiah. See Notes on Mat. iii. 2. ¶ *Persuading them concerning Jesus.* Endeavouring to convince them that Jesus was the Messiah. ¶ *Both out of the law of Moses.* Endeavouring to convince them that he corresponded with the predictions respecting the Messiah in the books of Moses, and with the types which Moses had instituted to prefigure the Messiah. ¶ *And out of the prophets.* Showing that he corresponded with the predictions of the prophets. See Notes on ch. xvii. 3. ¶ *From morning until evening.* An instance of Paul's indefatigable toil in endeavour-

into *his* [v]lodging; [w]to whom he expounded and testified the kingdom of God, persuading them concerning Jesus, [x]both out of the law of Moses, and *out of* the prophets, from morning till evening.

24 And [y]some believed the things which were spoken, and some believed not.

25 And when they agreed not among themselves, they departed, after that Paul had spoken one word, Well spake the Holy Ghost by Esaias the prophet unto our fathers,

26 Saying, [z]Go unto this people, and say, Hearing ye shall hear, and shall not understand; and seeing ye shall see, and not perceive;

27 For the heart of this people is waxed gross, and their ears are dull of hearing, and their eyes have they closed, lest they should see with *their* eyes, and hear with *their* ears, and understand with *their* heart, and should be converted, and I should heal them.

28 Be it known, therefore, unto you, that [a]the salvation of God is sent unto the Gentiles, and *that* they will hear it.

29 And when he had said these words, the Jews departed, and had great reasoning among themselves.

30 And Paul dwelt two whole

v Phile.2. w Lu.24.27; ch.17.3; 19.8. x ch.26.6,22. y ch.14.1; 17.4; 19.9; Ro.3.3. z Ps.81.11,12; Is.6.9; Je.5.21; Eze.3.6,7; 12.2; Mat. 13.14,15; Ro.11.8.

a Mat.21.41; ch.13.46,47; 18.6; 22.21; 26.17,18; Ro. 11.11.

---

ing to induce his countrymen to believe in Jesus as the Messiah.

24. *And some believed*, &c. See Notes on ch. xiv. 4.

25. *Had spoken one word.* One solemn declaration, reminding them that it was the characteristic of the nation to reject the testimony of God, and that it was to be expected. It was the last warning which we know Paul to have delivered to his countrymen the Jews. ¶ *Well spake.* Or he spoke the truth; he justly described the character of the Jewish people. The passage here quoted was as applicable in the time of Paul as of Isaiah. ¶ *The Holy Ghost.* A full proof of the inspiration of Isaiah. ¶ *By Esaias.* By Isaiah, Is. vi. 9, 10.

26, 27. *Saying*, &c. See this passage explained in the Notes on Mat. xiii. 14, and Jn. xii. 39, 40.

28. *The salvation of God.* The knowledge of God's mode of saving men. ¶ *Is sent unto the Gentiles.* Since you have rejected it, it will be offered to them. See Notes on ch. xiii. 46. ¶ *And* that *they will hear it.* They will embrace it. Paul was never discouraged. If the gospel was rejected by one class of people he was ready to offer it to another. If his own countrymen despised it, he never allowed himself to suppose that Christ had died in vain, but believed that others would embrace its saving benefits. How happy would it be if all Christians had the same unwavering faith and zeal as Paul.

29. *And had great reasoning.* Great discussion or debates. That is, the part which believed that Jesus was the Messiah (ver. 24) discussed the subject warmly with those who did not believe. This whole verse is wanting in the Syriac version, and in some Greek MSS., and is supposed by Mill and Griesbach to be spurious.

30. *Paul dwelt two whole years.* Doubtless in the custody of the soldiers. Why he was not prosecuted before the emperor during this time is not known. It is evident, however (ver. 21), that the Jews were not disposed to carry the case before Nero, and the matter, during this time, was suffered quietly to sleep. There is great probability that the Jews did not dare to prosecute him before the emperor. It is clear that they had never been in favour of the appeal to Rome, and that they had no hope of gaining their cause. Probably they might remember the former treatment of their people by the emperor (see Notes on ch. xviii. 2); they might remember that they were despised at the Roman capital, and not choose to encounter the scorn and indignation of the Roman court; and as there was no prosecution, Paul was suffered to live in quietness and safety. Lardner, however, supposed (vol. v. p. 528, 529, ed. 8vo, London, 1829) that the case of Paul was soon brought before Nero and decided, and that the method of confinement was ordered by the emperor

years in his own hired house, and received all that came in unto him,
31 Preaching[b] the kingdom of God, and teaching those things which concern the Lord Jesus Christ with all confidence, no man forbidding him.

b ch.4.31; Ep.6.19.

himself. Lightfoot also supposes that Paul's "accusers, who had come from Judea to lay their charge against him, would be urgent to get their business despatched, that they might be returning to their own home again, and so would bring him to trial as soon as they could." But nothing certainly is known on the subject. It is evident, indeed, from 2 Ti. iv. 16, that he was at *some time* arraigned before the emperor; but when it was, or what was the decision, or why he was at last set at liberty, are all involved in impenetrable obscurity. ¶ *In his own hired house.* In a house which he was permitted to hire and occupy as his own. Probably in this he was assisted by the kindness of his Roman friends. ¶ *And received all*, &c. Received all hospitably and kindly who came to him to listen to his instructions. It is evident from this that he was still a prisoner, and was not permitted to go at large.

31. *Preaching the kingdom of God.* See Notes on ch. xx. 25. ¶ *With all confidence.* Openly and boldly, without anyone to hinder him. It is known also that Paul was not unsuccessful even when a prisoner at Rome. Several persons were converted by his preaching, even in the court of the emperor. The things which had happened to him, he says (Phi. i. 12–14), had fallen out rather to the furtherance of the gospel, so that his bonds in Christ were manifested in all the palace, and in all other places; and many brethren in the Lord, says he, waxing confident by my bonds, are much more bold to speak the word without fear. In this situation he was remembered with deep interest by the church at Philippi, who sent Epaphroditus to him with a contribution to supply his wants. Of their kindness he speaks in terms of the tenderest gratitude in Phi. ii. 25; iv. 18. During his confinement also, he was the means of the conversion of Onesimus, a runaway servant of Philemon, of Colosse in Phrygia (Phile. 10), whom he sent back to his master with a letter to himself, and with an epistle to the church at that place. See epistle to the Colossians, iv. 8, 9, 18. During this imprisonment, he wrote, according to Lardner, the following epistles, in the order and time mentioned, viz.:

Ephesians, April	A.D. 61
2 Timothy, May	61
Philippians, before the end of	62
Colossians	62
Philemon	62
Hebrews, spring of	63

Here closes the inspired account of the propagation of Christianity; of the organization of the Christian church, and of the toils and persecutions of the apostle Paul. Who can but be deeply affected when he comes to the conclusion of this inspired book recording the history of the spread of the Christian religion, and the labours and trials of that wonderful man, the apostle Paul? Who can help heaving a sigh of regret that the historian did not carry forward the history of Paul till his death, and that henceforward, in the history of the church, we want this faithful, inspired guide; and that, from the close of this book, everything becomes at once so involved in obscurity and uncertainty? Instead, however, of pouring forth unavailing regrets that the sacred historian has carried us no farther onward, we should rather employ the language of praise that God inspired the writer of this book to give a history of the church for thirty years after the ascension of the Saviour; that he has recorded the accounts of the first great revivals of religion; that he has presented us the examples of the early missionary zeal; that he has informed us how the early Christians endured persecution and toil; that he has conducted us from land to land, and from city to city, showing us everywhere how the gospel was propagated, until we are led to the seat of the Roman power, and see the great apostle of Christianity there proclaiming, in that mighty capital of the world, the name of Jesus as the Saviour of men. Perhaps there could be no more appropriate close to the book of the inspired history than thus to have conducted the apostle of the Gentiles to the capital of the Roman world, and to leave the principal agent in the establishment of the Christian religion in that seat of intelligence, influence, and power. It is the conducting of Christianity to the very height of its earthly victories; and having shown its power in the *provinces* of the empire, it was proper to close the account with the record of its achievements in the capital.

Why Luke closed his history here is not known. It may have been that he was not afterward the companion of Paul; or that he might have been himself removed by death. It is agreed on all hands that he did not attend Paul in his subsequent travels; and we should infer from the conclusion of this book that he did not survive the apostle, as it is almost incredible, if he did, that he did not mention his release and death. It is the uniform account of antiquity that Luke, after the transactions with which the Acts of the Apostles closes, passed over into Achaia, where he lived a year or two, and there died at the age of eighty-four years.

Everything in regard to the apostle Paul, after the account with which Luke closes this book, is involved in doubt and uncertainty. By what means he was set at liberty is not known; and there is a great contradiction of statements in regard to his subsequent travels, and even in regard to the time of his death. It is generally agreed, indeed, that he was set at liberty in the year of our Lord 63. After this some of the fathers assert that he travelled over Italy and passed into Spain. But this account is involved in great uncertainty. Lardner, who has examined all the statements with care, and than whom no one is better qualified to pronounce an opinion on these subjects, gives the following account of the subsequent life of Paul (*Works*, vol. v. p. 331-336, ed. Lond. 1829). He supposes that after his release he went from Rome to Jerusalem as soon as possible; that he then went to Ephesus, and from thence to Laodicea and Colosse; and that he returned to Rome by Troas, Philippi, and Corinth. The reason why he returned to Rome, Lardner supposes, was that he regarded that city as opening before him the widest and most important field of labour, and that, therefore, he proposed there to spend the remainder of his life.

In the year of our Lord 64, a dreadful fire happened at Rome which continued for six or seven days. It was generally supposed that the city had been set on fire by order of the Emperor Nero. In order to divert the attention of the people from this charge against himself, he accused the Christians of having been the authors of the conflagration, and excited against them a most furious and bloody persecution. In this persecution it is generally supposed that Paul and Peter suffered death, the former by being beheaded, and the latter by crucifixion. Paul is supposed to have been beheaded rather than crucified, because he was a Roman citizen, and because it was unlawful to put a Roman citizen to death on a cross. Lardner thinks that this occurred in the year 65. Where Paul was beheaded is not certainly known. It is generally supposed to have occurred at a place called the Salvian Waters, about 3 miles from Rome, and that he was buried in the Ostian Way, where a magnificent church was afterward built. But of this there is no absolute certainty.

It is far more important and interesting for us to be assured from the character which he evinced, and from the proofs of his zeal and toil in the cause of the Lord Jesus, that his spirit rested in the bosom of his Saviour and his God. Wherever he died, his spirit, we doubt not, is in heaven. And where that body rested at last, which he laboured "to keep under," and which he sought to bring "into subjection" (1 Co. ix. 27), and which was to him so much the source of conflict and of sin (Ro. vii. 5, 23), is a matter of little consequence. It will be guarded by the eye of that Saviour whom he served, and will be raised up to eternal life. In his own inimitable language, it was "sown in corruption, it shall be raised in incorruption; it was sown in dishonour, it shall be raised in glory; it was sown in weakness, it shall be raised in power; it was sown a natural body, it shall be raised a spiritual body," 1 Co. xv. 42-44. And in regard to him, and to all other saints, "when that corruptible shall have put on incorruption, and that mortal shall have put on immortality, then shall be brought to pass the saying that is written, Death is swallowed up in victory," 1 Co. xv. 54. To Paul now, what are all his sorrows, and persecutions, and toils in the cause of his Master? What but a source of thanksgiving that he was permitted thus to labour to spread the gospel through the world? So may we live—imitating his life of zeal, and self-denial, and faithfulness, that when we rise from the dead we may participate with him in the glories of the resurrection of the just.

CHRONOLOGICAL ARRANGEMENT OF THE ACTS OF THE APOSTLES.

[*From Dr. Townsend's Historical and Chronological Arrangement of the Old and New Testaments.*]

PERIOD IX.—FROM THE ASCENSION OF CHRIST TO THE TERMINATION OF THE PERIOD IN WHICH THE GOSPEL WAS PREACHED TO PROSELYTES OF RIGHTEOUSNESS, AND TO THE JEWS ONLY.

DATE.	EVENTS.	SCRIPTURES.
A.D. 29	After the Ascension of Christ, the Apostles return to Jerusalem, - - - - -	Ac. i. 1–3; and ver. 12–14.
...	Matthias by lot appointed to the Apostleship in the place of Judas, - - - - - -	Ac. i. 15, to end.
...	Descent of the Holy Spirit on the Day of Pentecost, - - - - - - - -	Ac. ii. 1–13.
...	Address of St. Peter to the Multitude, - -	Ac. ii. 14–36.
...	Effects of St. Peter's Address, - - - -	Ac. ii. 37–42.
...	Union of the first Converts in the primitive Church, - - - - - - - -	Ac. ii. 43, to end.
30	A Cripple is miraculously and publicly healed by St. Peter and St. John, - - - -	Ac. iii. 1–10.
...	St. Peter again Addresses the People, -	Ac. iii. 11, to end.
...	St. Peter and St. John are imprisoned by order of the Sanhedrim, - - - - - -	Ac. iv. 1–7.
...	St. Peter's Address to the assembled Sanhedrim,	Ac. iv. 8–22.
...	The Prayer of the Church on the liberation of St. Peter and St. John, - - - - -	Ac. iv. 23–31.
...	The Union and Munificence of the primitive Church, - - - - - - - -	Ac. iv. 32, to end.
31	Deaths of Ananias and Sapphira, - - -	Ac. v. 1–10.
...	State of the Church at this time, - - -	Ac. v. 11–16.
32	An Angel delivers the Apostles from Prison,	Ac. v. 17–20, part of ver. 21.
...	The Sanhedrim again assemble. St. Peter asserts before them the Messiahship of Christ, -	Ac. v. part of 21, 22–33.
...	By the Advice of Gamaliel the Apostles are dismissed, - - - - - - -	Ac. v. 34, to end.
...	The Appointment of the seven Deacons, - -	Ac. vi. 1–6.
33	The Church continues to increase in number, -	Ac. vi. 7.
33 or 34	St. Stephen, having boldly asserted the Messiahship of Christ, is accused of Blasphemy before the Sanhedrim, - - - - - -	Ac. vi. 8–14.

Date.	Events.	Scriptures.
A.D. 33 or 34	St. Stephen defends himself before the Sanhedrim, - - - - - - -	Ac. vi. 15; vii. 1–50.
...	Stephen, being interrupted in his Defence, reproaches the Sanhedrim as the Murderers of their Messiah, - - - - -	Ac. vii. 51–53.
...	Stephen, praying for his Murderers, is stoned to Death, - - - - - - - -	Ac. vii. 54, to end; viii. part of ver. 1, and ver. 2.
34	General Persecution of the Christians, in which Saul (afterwards St. Paul) particularly distinguishes himself, - - - - - -	Ac. viii. part of ver. 1, and ver. 3.
...	Philip the Deacon, having left Jerusalem on account of the Persecution, goes to Samaria, and preaches there, and works Miracles, -	Ac. viii. 5–13.
...	St. Peter and St. John come down from Jerusalem to Samaria, to confer the Gifts of the Holy Ghost on the new Converts, - -	Ac. viii. 14–17.
...	St. Peter reproves Simon Magus, - - - -	Ac. viii. 18–24.
...	St. Peter and St. John preach in many Villages of the Samaritans, - - - - - -	Ac. viii. 25.
...	The Treasurer of Queen Candace, a Proselyte of Righteousness, is converted and Baptized by Philip, who now preaches through the cities of Judea, - - - - -	Ac. viii. 26, to end.
...	Many of the Converts, who had fled from Jerusalem in consequence of the Persecution there, preach the Gospel to the Jews in the Provinces, - - - - - -	Ac. viii. 4.
35	Saul, on his way to Damascus, is converted to the Religion he was opposing, on hearing the Bath Col, and seeing the Shechinah, -	Ac. ix. 1–9.
...	Saul is baptized, - - - - - - -	Ac. ix. 10–19.
...	Saul preaches in the Synagogues to the Jews, -	Ac. ix. 19–30.
38 to 40	St. Peter, having preached through Judea, comes to Lydda, where he cures Æneas, and raises Dorcas from the Dead, - -	Ac. ix. 32, to end.
...	The Churches are at rest from Persecution, in consequence of the Conversion of Saul, and the conduct of Caligula, - - - -	Ac. ix. 31.

Period X.—The Gospel having now been Preached to the Jews in Jerusalem, Judea, Samaria, and the Provinces, the Time arrives for the Conversion of the Devout Gentiles, or Proselytes of the Gate.

Date.	Events.	Scriptures.
40	St. Peter sees a Vision, in which he is commanded to visit a Gentile who had been miraculously instructed to send for him, -	Ac. x. 1–16.
...	St. Peter visits Cornelius, a Roman centurion, -	Ac. x. 17–33.
...	St. Peter first declares Christ to be the Saviour of all, even of the Gentiles who believe in him,	Ac. x. 34–43.
...	Cornelius and his Friends receive the Holy Ghost, and are baptized, - - -	Ac. x. 44, to end.

Date.	Events.	Scriptures.
A.D. 40	St. Peter defends his conduct in visiting and baptizing Cornelius, - - - -	Ac. xi. 1–18.
41	The Converts who had been dispersed by the Persecution, after the Death of Stephen, having heard of the Vision of St. Peter, preach to the devout Gentiles also, - - -	Ac. xi. 19–21.
...	The Church at Jerusalem Commissions Barnabas to make Inquiries into this matter, -	Ac. xi. 22–24.
42	Barnabas goes to Tarsus for Saul, whom he takes with him to Antioch, where the Converts were preaching to the devout Gentiles,	Ac. xi. 25, 26.
43	Herod Agrippa condemns James, the Brother of John, to death, and imprisons Peter, who is miraculously released, and presents himself to the other James, who had been made Bishop of Jerusalem, - - - -	Ac. xii. 1–18, and part of ver. 19.
44	The Converts at Antioch, being forewarned by Agabus, send relief to their Brethren at Jerusalem, by the hands of Barnabas and Saul,	Ac. xi. 27, to end.
...	The Death of Herod Agrippa, - - - -	Ac. xii. part of ver. 19, and 20–23.
...	The Churches continue to increase, - - -	Ac. xii. 24.
45	Saul, having seen a Vision in the Temple, in which he is commanded to leave Jerusalem, and to preach to the Gentiles, returns with Barnabas to Antioch, - - - -	Ac. xii. 25.

Period XI.—Period for Preaching the Gospel to the Idolatrous Gentiles, and St. Paul's First Apostolical Journey.

Date.	Events.	Scriptures.
45	The Apostles having been absent from Jerusalem when Saul saw his Vision in the Temple, he and Barnabas are separated to the Apostolic Office by the Heads of the Church at Antioch, - - - - - - -	Ac. xiii. 1–3.
...	Saul, in company with Barnabas, commences his first Apostolical Journey, by going from Antioch to Seleucia, - - - - -	Ac. xiii. part of 4.
...	From Seleucia Saul and Barnabas proceed to Salamis, and Paphos, in Cyprus, where Sergius Paulus is converted; being the first known or recorded Convert of the idolatrous Gentiles,	Ac. xiii. part of 4–12.
...	From Cyprus to Perga, in Pamphylia, - -	Ac. xiii. 13.
46	From Perga to Antioch in Pisidia. St. Paul, according to his custom, first preaches to the Jews. They are driven out of Antioch,	Ac. xiii. 14–50.
...	From Antioch in Pisidia, to Iconium in Lycaonia. The people about to stone them,	Ac. xiii. 51, 52; and xiv. 1–5, and part of 6.
...	From Iconium to Lystra. The people attempt to offer them Sacrifice, and afterwards stone them,	Ac. xiv. 8–19, and part of 20.

DATE.	EVENTS.	SCRIPTURES.
A.D. 47	From Lystra to Derbe, - - - - -	Ac. xiv. last part of 20, part of 6, and 7.
...	St. Paul and Barnabas return to Lystra, Iconium, and Antioch in Pisidia, ordaining in all the Churches, - - - - - - -	Ac. xiv. 21–23.
48	They proceed through Pisidia, Perga, and Attalia, in Pamphylia, - - - -	Ac. xiv. 24, 25.
...	They return to Antioch, and submit an Account of their proceedings to the Church in that place, - - - - - - - -	Ac. xiv. 26, to end.
49	Dissensions at Antioch concerning Circumcision, before the commencement of St. Paul's second Apostolical Journey, - - - -	Ac. xv. 1, 2.
...	St. Paul and Barnabas go up to Jerusalem to consult the Apostles and Elders on the Dispute concerning Circumcision. Decree of James and of the Church therein, - -	Ac. xv. 3–29.
...	St. Paul and Barnabas return to the Church at Antioch, with the Decree of the Church at Jerusalem on the Subject of the Necessity of Circumcision, - - - - - -	Ac. xv. 30–35.

PERIOD XII.—ST. PAUL'S SECOND APOSTOLICAL JOURNEY.

DATE.	EVENTS.	SCRIPTURES.
50	After remaining some time at Antioch, St. Paul proposes to Barnabas to commence another Visitation of the Churches, - - -	Ac. xv. 36.
...	St. Paul, separating from Barnabas, proceeds from Antioch to Syria and Cilicia, - -	Ac. xv. 37, to end; xvi. 4, 5.
...	St. Paul proceeds to Derbe and Lystra in Iconium —Timothy his attendant, - - -	Ac. xvi. 1–3.
...	They proceed from Iconium to Phrygia and Galatia, - - - - - - - -	Ac. xvi. 6.
...	From Galatia to Mysia and Troas, - - -	Ac. xvi. 7–10.
...	From Troas to Samothracia, - - - -	Ac. xvi. part of 11.
...	From Samothracia to Neapolis, - - - -	Ac. xvi. part of 11.
...	From Neapolis to Philippi, where the Pythoness is dispossessed, and the Jailer converted,	Ac. xvi. 12, to end.
51	From Philippi, through Amphipolis and Appollonia, to Thessalonica, where they are opposed by the Jews, - - - - - - -	Ac. xvii. 1–9.
...	St. Paul writes his Epistle to the Galatians, to prove, in opposition to the Judaizing Teachers, that Faith in Christ, and not their imperfect Obedience to the Ceremonial Law, was the Cause of their Salvation, - - -	Epistle to the Galatians.
...	From Thessalonica to Berea. The Causes for which the Bereans are favourably disposed to receive the Gospel, - - - - -	Ac. xvii. 10–14.
...	From Berea, having left there Silas and Timothy, St. Paul proceeds to Athens, where he preaches to the Philosophers and Students, - -	Ac. xvii. 15, to end.

DATE.	EVENTS.	SCRIPTURES.
A.D. 51	From Athens St. Paul proceeds to Corinth, where he is reduced to labour for his support. Silas and Timothy join him there, - - -	Ac. xviii. 1–5.
...	St. Paul writes his First Epistle to the Thessalonians, to establish them in the Faith (when they were exposed to the Attacks of the unconverted Jews), by enforcing the Evidences of Christianity, - - - - -	First Epistle to the Thessalonians.
52	St. Paul, being rejected by the Jews, continues at Corinth, preaching to the Gentiles, -	Ac. xviii. 6–11.
...	St. Paul writes his Second Epistle to the Thessalonians, to refute an Error into which they had fallen concerning the sudden coming of the Day of Judgment. He prophesies the Rise, Prosperity, and Overthrow of a great Apostasy in the Christian Church, -	Second Epistle to the Thessalonians.
...	St. Paul, still at Corinth, is brought before the Judgment-seat of Gallio, the Proconsul, the Brother of Seneca, - - - - - -	Ac. xviii. 12–17, part of 18.
53	St. Paul, having left Corinth for Crete, is compelled, on his return, to winter at Nicopolis, from whence he writes his Epistle to Titus, whom he had left in Crete, with Power to ordain Teachers, and to Govern the Church in that Island, - - - - -	Epistle to Titus.
54	St. Paul proceeds to Cenchrea, - - - -	Ac. xviii. part of 18.
...	From Cenchrea to Ephesus, where he disputes with the Jews, - - - - - -	Ac. xviii. 19.
...	From Ephesus St. Paul proceeds to Cæsarea, and, having saluted the Church at Jerusalem, completes his Second Apostolical Journey, by returning to Antioch in Syria, - -	Ac. xviii. 20–22.

PERIOD XIII.—THE THIRD APOSTOLICAL JOURNEY OF ST. PAUL.

DATE.	EVENTS.	SCRIPTURES.
55	St. Paul again leaves Antioch, to visit the Churches of Galatia and Phrygia, - -	Ac. xviii. 23.
...	History of Apollos, who was now preaching to the Church at Ephesus, planted by St. Paul,	Ac. xviii. 24, to end.
...	St. Paul proceeds from Phrygia to Ephesus, and disputes there with the Jews, - -	Ac. xix. 1–10.
56	St. Paul continues Two Years at Ephesus. The people burn their Magical Books, - -	Ac. xix. 11–20.
...	St. Paul sends Timothy and Erastus to Macedonia and Achaia, - - - - - -	Ac. xix. 21, part of 22.
56 or 57	St. Paul writes his First Epistle to the Corinthians, to assert his Apostolic Authority, to reprove the Irregularities and Disorders of the Church, and to answer the Questions of the Converts on various points of Doctrine and Discipline, - - - - - -	First Epistle to the Corinthians.
...	St. Paul continues at Ephesus—a Mob is occasioned at that Place by Demetrius, -	Ac. xix. part of 22, to end.
...	St. Paul leaves Ephesus and goes to Macedonia,	Ac. xx. 1.

Date.	Events.	Scriptures.
A.D. 57 or 58	St. Paul writes his First Epistle to Timothy, to direct him how to proceed in the Suppression of those False Doctrines and Corruptions which the Jewish Zealots were endeavouring to establish in the Church of Ephesus, over which he was appointed to preside, - - -	First Epistle to Timothy.
...	St. Paul proceeds from Macedonia to Greece, or Achaia, and continues there Three Months,	Ac. xx. 2, part of 3.
58	St. Paul, having been informed of the reception his First Epistle had met with from the Corinthians, writes his Second Epistle from Philippi, to justify his Apostolic Conduct, and vindicate his Authority, both of which had been impugned by a False Teacher. - - -	Second Epistle to the Corinthians.
...	St. Paul returns from Achaia and Corinth to Macedonia, sending his companions forward to Troas, - - - - - -	Ac. xx. part of 3, and 4, 5.
...	St. Paul, in his way from Achaia to Macedonia, writes from Corinth his Epistle to the Gentiles and Jews of Rome—to the Gentiles, to prove to them that neither their boasted Philosophy, nor their moral Virtue, nor the Light of human Reason—and to the Jews, that neither their Knowledge of, nor Obedience to, the Law of Moses, could justify them before God; but that Faith in Christ alone was, and ever had been, the only way of Salvation to all Mankind,	Epistle to the Romans.
...	From Macedonia St. Paul proceeds to Troas, where he raises Eutychus to life, - -	Ac. xx. 6–12.
...	From Troas to Assos and Mitylene, - - -	Ac. xx. 13, 14.
...	From Mitylene to Chios, - - - - -	Ac. xx. part of 15.
...	From Chios to Samos, and Trogyllium, - -	Ac. xx. part of 15.
...	From Trogyllium to Miletus, where St. Paul meets, and takes his Farewell of, the Elders of the Church at Ephesus, - - -	Ac. xx. part of 15, to end.
...	From Miletus to Coos, and Rhodes, and Patara; whence St. Paul, together with St. Luke, the writer of the Book of the Acts of the Apostles, sails in a Phenician vessel to Syria, and lands in Tyre, - - - - - - -	Ac. xxi. 1–3.
...	St. Paul and St. Luke continue at Tyre Seven Days,	Ac. xxi. 4–6.
...	They proceed from Tyre to Ptolemais, - - -	Ac. xxi. 7.
...	From Ptolemais to Cæsarea, to the House of Philip the Evangelist. Agabus prophesies the near Imprisonment of St. Paul, - -	Ac. xxi. 8–14.
...	St. Paul and St. Luke arrive at Jerusalem, and present themselves to St. James and the Church, - - - - - - -	Ac. xxi. 15–26.
...	St. Paul is apprehended by the chief Captain of the Temple, in consequence of a Mob, occasioned by some of the Asiatic Jews, who met St. Paul in the Temple, - - - -	Ac. xxi. 27–36.
...	St. Paul makes his Defence before the Populace, - - - - - - -	Ac. xxi. 37, to end; xxii. 1–21.

DATE.	EVENTS.	SCRIPTURES.
A.D. 58	On declaring his Mission to preach to the Gentiles, the Jews clamour for his Death, -	Ac. xxii. 22.
...	St. Paul claims the Privilege of a Roman Citizen,	Ac. xxii. 23–29.
...	St. Paul is brought before the Sanhedrim, who are summoned by the Captain of the Temple,	Ac. xxii. 30; xxiii. 1–10.
...	St. Paul is encouraged by a Vision to persevere,	Ac. xxiii. 11.
...	In consequence of the Discovery of a Conspiracy to kill St. Paul, he is removed by Night from Jerusalem, through Antipatris to Cæsarea,	Ac. xxiii. 12, to end.
...	St. Paul is accused of Sedition before Felix, the Governor of Judea—His Defence, - -	Ac. xxiv. 1–21.
...	After many Conferences with Felix, St. Paul is continued in Prison till the arrival of Porcius Festus, - - - - - - -	Ac. xxiv. 22, to end.
60	Trial of St. Paul before Festus—He appeals to the Emperor, - - - - - -	Ac. xxv. 1–12.
...	Curious Account given to Agrippa by Festus, of the Accusation against St. Paul, - -	Ac. xxv. 13–22.
...	St. Paul defends his Cause before Festus and Agrippa—Their Conduct on that Occasion,	Ac. xxv. 23, to end; xxvi.
...	St. Paul, being surrendered as a Prisoner to the Centurion, is prevented from completing this Journey, by returning to Antioch, as he had usually done, - - - - - -	Ac. xxvii. 1.
	PERIOD XIV.—THE FOURTH JOURNEY OF ST. PAUL.	
60	St. Paul commences his Voyage to Rome as a Prisoner, - - - - - - -	Ac. xxvii. 2.
...	The Ship arrives at Sidon, from whence it proceeds to Cyprus, - - - - - -	Ac. xxvii. 3, 4
...	After changing their Ship at Tyre, they proceed to Cnidus, Salmone in Crete, and the City of Lasea, - - - - - - - -	Ac. xxvii. 5–8.
...	St. Paul warns the Master of the Ship of the Danger they were in. They attempt to reach Phenice in Crete, - - - - - -	Ac. xxvii. 9–13.
...	The Ship is wrecked, but the Lives of all on board are saved, as St. Paul had foretold,	Ac. xxvii. 14, to end.
...	They Land on the Island of Melita, - - -	Ac. xxviii. 1–10.
...	After Three Months they sail to Rome, - -	Ac. xxviii. 11, to part of 14.
...	St. Paul arrives at Rome, and is kindly received by the Brethren, - - - - - -	Ac. xxviii. part of to 16.
...	St. Paul summons the Jews at Rome, to explain to them the Causes of his Imprisonment,	Ac. xxviii. 17–[illegible]
61	St. Paul writes his Epistle to the Ephesians, to establish them in the Christian Faith, by describing, in the most animated language, the Mercy of God displayed in the Calling of the Gentiles through Faith in Christ, without being subjected to the Law of Moses, and to enforce upon them that Holiness and Consistency of Conduct which is required of all who have received the Knowledge of Salvation,	The [illegible]

DATE.	EVENTS.	SCRIPTURES.
A.D. 62	St. Paul writes his Epistle to the Philippians, to comfort them under the Concern they had expressed on the Subject of his Imprisonment—to exhort them to continue in union and mutual love, and to caution them against the Seductions of False Teachers, who had begun to introduce themselves among them,	The Epistle to the Philippians.
...	St. Paul writes his Epistle to the Colossians, in reply to the Message of Epaphras, to prove that the Hope of Man's Salvation is founded on the Atonement of Christ alone; and, by the Establishment of opposite Truths, to eradicate the Errors of the Judaizers, who not only preached the Mosaic Law, but also the Opinions of the Heathen, Oriental, or Essenian Philosophers, concerning the Worship of Angels, on account of their supposed Agency in human Affairs and the necessity of Abstaining from Animal Food, - -	The Epistle to the Colossians.
...	St. Paul writes his Epistle to his Friend Philemon, to intercede with him in favour of his Slave, Onesimus, who had fled from the Service of his Master to Rome; in which City he had been converted to Christianity by means of the Apostle's Ministry, - - -	The Epistle to Philemon.
...	St. James writes his Epistle to the Jewish Christians in general, to caution them against the prevalent Evils of the Day—to rectify the Errors into which many had fallen, by misinterpreting St. Paul's Doctrine of Justification, and to enforce various Duties, -	The General Epistle of St. James.
...	St. Paul remains at Rome for two years, during which time the Jews do not dare to prosecute him before the Emperor, - - -	Ac. xxviii. 30, 31.

FROM THE COMMENCEMENT OF THE FIFTH AND LAST JOURNEY OF ST. PAUL TO THE COMPLETION OF THE CANON OF THE NEW TESTAMENT.

DATE.	EVENTS.	SCRIPTURES.
62 or 63	St. Paul, while waiting in Italy for Timothy, writes the Key to the Old Testament—the Epistle to the Hebrews—to prove to the Jews, from their own Scriptures, the Humanity, Divinity, Atonement, and Intercession of Christ—the Superiority of the Gospel to the Law—and the real Object and Design of the Mosaic Institution, - - - -	The Epistle to the Hebrews.

DATE.	EVENTS.	SCRIPTURES.
A.D. 63–4	After his Liberation, St. Paul Visits Italy, Spain, Britain, and the West.	
...	He then proceeds to Jerusalem.	
65	From Jerusalem to Antioch in Syria.	
...	From Antioch to Colossé.	
...	From Colossé to Philippi.	
...	From Philippi to Corinth.	
...	From Corinth to Troas.	
...	From Troas to Miletum.	
...	From Miletum to Rome.	
...	St. Paul is imprisoned at Rome in the general Persecution by Nero.	
65 or 66	St. Paul, in the Anticipation of the near approach of Death, writes his Second Epistle to Timothy, exhorting him, as his last request, to the faithful discharge of his Duty, in all times of Apostasy, Persecution, and Dissension, - - - - - - -	The Second Epistle to Timothy.
...	St. Peter writes his First Epistle to the Jews, who, in the time of Persecution, had taken Refuge in the heathen countries mentioned in the Inscription, and also to the Gentile Converts, to encourage them to suffer cheerfully for their Religion; and to enforce upon them the Necessity of leading a Holy and Blameless Life, that they may put to shame the Calumnies of their Adversaries, - - -	The First Epistle General of St. Peter.
66	St. Peter, under the Impression of approaching Martyrdom, writes to the Jewish and Gentile Christians, dispersed in the countries of Pontus, Galatia, Cappadocia, &c., to confirm the Doctrines and Instructions of his former Letter, to Caution them against the Errors of the False Teachers, by reminding them of the Judgments of God on Apostates, and to encourage them under Persecution, by the Consideration of the happy Deliverance of those who trusted in him, and the final Dissolution both of this World and of the Jewish Dispensation, - - - - - - -	The Second Epistle General of St. Peter.
66	Jude writes his Epistle to caution the Christian Church against the dangerous Tenets of the False Teachers, who had now appeared, subverting the Doctrine of Grace to the Encouragement of Licentiousness; and to exhort them to a steadfast adherence to the Faith and Holiness, - - - - - -	The General Epistle of Jude.
...	Martyrdom of St. Peter and St. Paul.	
70	Destruction of Jerusalem.	
96	St. John writes the Apocalypse to supply the place of a continued Succession of Prophets in the Christian Church, till the second coming of Christ to Judge the World, - -	The Book of Revelation.

DATE.	EVENTS.	SCRIPTURES.
A.D. 96	St. John writes his First Epistle to confute the Errors of the False Teachers, and their different Sects—against the Docetæ, who denied the Humanity of Christ, asserting that his Body and Sufferings were not real, but imaginary—against the Cerinthians and Ebionites, who contended that he was a mere Man, and that his Divinity was only adventitious, and therefore separated from him at his Passion—and against the Nicolaitanes or Gnostics, who taught that the Knowledge of God and Christ was sufficient for Salvation; that being justified by Faith, and freed from the Restraints of the Law, they might indulge in Sin with impunity;—He cautions Christians from being seduced by these Doctrines and Practices, by condemning them in the strongest Terms—he contrasts them with the Truths and Doctrines of the Gospel, in which they had been instructed, and in which they are exhorted to continue, - - - - - - -	The First Epistle of St. John.
...	St. John writes his Second Epistle to caution a Christian Mother and her Children against the Seductions and pernicious Errors of the False Teachers, supposed to be a sect of the Gnostics, - - - - - - -	The Second Epistle of St. John.
...	St. John writes his Third Epistle to Gaius, to praise him for his steadfast faith and kindness to some Christian Brethren and strangers, and to recommend them again to his protection and benevolence—to rebuke and to caution him against the presumptuous arrogance of Diotrephes, who had denied his authority, and disobeyed his injunctions, and to recommend Demetrius to his attention, and the imitation of the Church, - - - -	The Third Epistle of St. John.
...	St. John sanctions the Books of the New Testament, and completes the Canon of Scripture, by writing his Gospel, at the request of the Church of Ephesus.	

INDEX

TO THE NOTES ON

THE ACTS OF THE APOSTLES

Notes on the New Testament

Albert Barnes

Edited by

Robert Frew

ROMANS

BAKER BOOK HOUSE

Grand Rapids, Michigan 49506

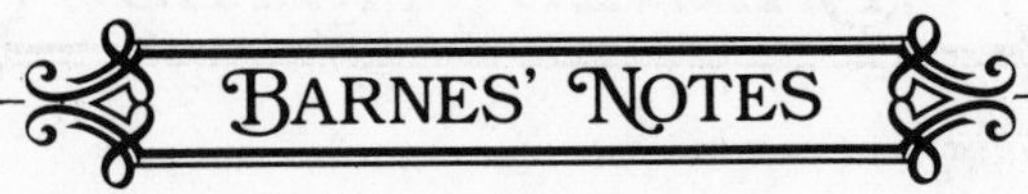

Heritage Edition

Fourteen Volumes 0834-

1. Genesis (Murphy) 0835-2
2. Exodus to Esther (Cook) 0836-0
3. Job 0837-9
4. Psalms 0838-7
5. Proverbs to Ezekiel (Cook) 0839-5
6. Isaiah 0840-9
7. Daniel 0841-7
8. Minor Prophets (Pusey) 0842-
9. The Gospels 0843-
10. Acts and Romans 0844-
11. I Corinthians to Galatians 0846-
12. Ephesians to Philemon 0847-
13. Hebrews to Jude 0848-
14. Revelation 0849-

When ordering by ISBN (International Standard Book Number), numbers listed above should be preceded by 0-8010-.

Reprinted from the 1884-85 edition published by Blackie & Son, London, edited by Robert Frew

Reprinted 1987 by Baker Book House Company

ISBN: 0-8010-0844-1

Printed and bound in the United States of America

PUBLISHERS' PREFACE

The republication, in this country, of Barnes' Notes on the Romans, will sustain and extend the author's well-earned reputation. Those who have been delighted with the perspicuity and elegance of his Notes on the Evangelists and Acts of the Apostles, will admire the same excellencies in the present volume. Regarding the meaning of certain passages in the Epistle to the Romans, many, indeed, will differ from our author. Nor is this difference of opinion surprising. The Epistle is confessedly the most difficult in the New Testament, and has given occasion to much theological controversy.

The principal point, in which Barnes is supposed to differ from orthodox divines, in this country, is the doctrine of imputation; which occupies so conspicuous a place in the opening chapters of the Romans, and is argued at great length in the fifth chapter. In some other points also, of less moment, he may be accused of using inaccurate or unguarded language. To remedy these defects, supplementary Notes have been added in several places throughout the volume; these, however, are invariably printed in a smaller type, to distinguish them from those of the author.

But whatever may be said of the author's views on imputation and other points connected with it; the most ardent lovers of orthodoxy will be unable to challenge the accuracy of his Notes on predestination and election. In his illustration of chapters viii. and ix., he maintains unconditional election against the Arminian view, and establishes the Calvinistic doctrine of the saints' perseverance, ch. viii. 29; ix. 11–15, 20.

Moreover, the excellencies of the volume are sufficient, even in the eyes of those who differ from the author, to redeem its faults. It contains a mass of varied, striking, and often original illustration; and presents, in small compass, the results of extensive reading and profound thinking. With the humble profession of writing only for Sabbath Schools and Sabbath School Teachers, Albert Barnes has furnished a commentary on the Romans, from which the lecturer in the pulpit may draw some of his richest stores.

AUTHOR'S PREFACE

The Epistle to the Romans has been usually regarded as the most difficult portion of the New Testament. It is from this cause, probably, as well as from the supposition that its somewhat abstruse discussions could not be made interesting to the young, that so few efforts have been made to introduce it into Sunday Schools and Bible Classes. It will doubtless continue to be a fact, that Sunday School instruction will be confined chiefly to the *historical* parts of the Bible. In the Sacred Scriptures there is this happy adaptedness to the circumstances of the world, that so large a portion of the volume *can* thus be made interesting to the minds of children and youth; that so much of it is occupied with historical narrative; with parables; with interesting biographies of the holy men of other times, and with the life of our blessed Lord. But still, while this is true, there is a considerable portion of the youth, in various ways under the instruction of the Bible, who may be interested in the more abstruse statements and discussions of the *doctrinal* parts of the Holy Scriptures. For such; for Sunday School teachers; for Bible Classes; and for the higher classes in Sabbath Schools, these Notes have been prepared. The humble hope has been cherished that this epistle might be introduced to this portion of the youth of the churches; and thus tend to imbue their minds with correct views of the great *doctrines* of the Christian Revelation.

This object has been kept steadily in view. The design has not been to make a *learned* commentary; nor to enter into theological discussions; nor to introduce, at length, practical reflections; nor to enter minutely into critical investigations. All these can be found in books professedly on these subjects. The design has been to state, with as much brevity and simplicity as possible, the real meaning of the sacred writer; rather the *results* of critical inquiry, as far as the author has had ability and time to pursue it, than the *process* by which those results were reached. The design has been to state what appeared to the author to be the real *meaning* of the Epistle, without *any* regard to any existing theological system; and without any deference to the opinions of others, further than the respectful deference and candid examination, which are due to the opinions of the learned, the wise, and the good, who have made this epistle their particular study. At the same time that this object has been kept in view, and the reference to the Sabbath

School teacher, and the Bible Class, has given character to the work, still it is hoped that the expositions are of such a nature as not to be uninteresting to Christians of every age and of every class. He accomplishes a service of no little moment in the cause of the church of God, and of truth, who contributes in any degree to explain the profound argument, the thorough doctrinal discussion, the elevated views, and the vigorous, manly, and masterly reasonings of the Epistle to the Romans.

Of the defects of this work, even for the purpose contemplated, no one will probably be more deeply sensible than the author. Of the time and labour necessary to prepare even such brief Notes as these, few persons, probably, are aware. This work has been prepared amidst the cares and toils of a most responsible pastoral charge. My brethren in the ministry, so far as they may have occasion to consult these Notes, will know how to appreciate the cares and anxieties amidst which they have been prepared. They will be indulgent to the faults of the book; they will not censure harshly what is well-meant for the rising generation: they will be the patrons of every purpose, however, humble, to do good.

It remains only to add, that free use has been made of all the helps within the reach of the author. The language of other writers has not been adopted without particular acknowledgment, but their ideas have been freely used where they were thought to express the sense of the text. In particular, aid has been sought and obtained from the following works: the CRITICI SACRI, CALVIN'S COMMENTARY ON THE ROMANS, DODDRIDGE, MACKNIGHT, and ROSENMULLER; and the commentaries of THOLUCK and FLATT--so far as an imperfect knowledge of the German language could render their aid available. A considerable portion was written before Professor STUART'S Commentary appeared. In the remaining portion, important aid has been freely derived from that work. The aim of this work is substantially the same as that of the "Notes on the Gospels," and on the Acts of the Apostles; and the earnest wish and prayer of the author is, that it may be one among many means of establishing the truth, and of promoting its advancement and ultimate triumph in the world.

ADVERTISEMENT TO THE FIFTH EDITION

Notwithstanding the difficulty of correcting a work which is stereotyped, the following Notes have undergone a careful revision, and several alterations have been made. The changes refer to a few phrases which did not accurately express my meaning, and to some entire paragraphs. My desire has been to make the work as little exceptionable as possible. Some expressions in the former editions have been misunderstood; some are now seen to have been ambiguous; a few that have given offence have been changed, because, without abandoning any principle of doctrine or interpretation, I could convey my ideas in language more acceptable, and less fitted to produce offence. The changes have been made with a wish to make the work more useful, and with a desire to do all that can be done, without abandoning *principle*, to promote peace and to silence the voice of alarm. On some of these passages, as is extensively known to the public, charges of inculcating dangerous doctrines have been alleged against me before the Presbytery of which I am a member. After a fair and full trial the Presbytery acquitted me; and I have taken the opportunity *after* the trial was passed and I had been acquitted, to make these changes for the sake of peace, and not to appear to have been *urged* to make them by the dread of a trial.

When the work was first published, it was not anticipated that more than two or three editions would be demanded. The fact that, within less than eight months, a *fourth* edition should be called for, is a source of gratitude, and an inducement to do all that can be done to make the work as complete as possible, that it may more perfectly accomplish the design for which it was written. Some of the alterations have been made by the suggestions of friends; some by the cry of alarm which has been raised; but, whether from the one or the other, I hold that an author should be grateful for *all* the suggestions which may go to improve his works, and should amend them accordingly.

ALBERT BARNES.

INTRODUCTION

TO THE

EPISTLE TO THE ROMANS

THIS Epistle has been, with great uniformity, attributed to the apostle Paul, and received as a part of the sacred canon. It has *never* in the church been called in question as a genuine, an inspired book, except by three of the ancient sects deemed heretical—the Ebionites, the Encratites, and Cerinthians. But they did not deny that it was written by the apostle Paul. They rejected it because they could not make its *doctrines* harmonize with their views of other parts of the Scriptures. Their rejecting it, therefore, does not militate against its genuineness. That is a question to be settled *historically,* like the genuineness of any other ancient writing. On this point the testimony of antiquity is uniform. The proof on this subject may be seen at length in Lardner's works. The *internal* evidence that this was written by Paul is stated in a most ingenious and masterly manner by Dr. Paley in his *Horæ Paulinæ.*

It is agreed by all, that this epistle was written in *Greek.* Though addressed to a people whose language was the *Latin,* yet this epistle to them, like those to other churches, was in Greek. On this point also there is no debate. The reasons why this language was chosen were probably the following. (1.) The epistle was designed doubtless to be read by other churches as well as the Roman; comp. Col. iv. 16. Yet the Greek language, being generally known and spoken, was more adapted to this design than the Latin. (2.) The Greek language was then understood at Rome, and extensively spoken. It was a part of polite education to learn it. The Roman youth were taught it; and it was the fashion of the times to study it, even so much so as to make it matter of complaint that the Latin was neglected for it by the Roman youth. Thus Cicero (Pro Arch.) says, *The Greek language is spoken in almost all nations; the Latin is confined to our comparatively narrow borders.* Tacitus (Orator 29) says, *An infant born now is committed to a Greek nurse.* Juvenal (vi. 185) speaks of its being considered as an indispensable part of polite education, to be acquainted with the Greek. (3.) It is not impossible that the Jews at Rome, who constituted a separate colony, were better acquainted with the Greek than the Latin. They had a Greek, but no Latin translation of the Scriptures, and it is very possible that they used the language in which they were accustomed to read their Scriptures, and which was extensively spoken by their brethren throughout the world. (4.) The apostle was himself probably more familiar with the Greek than the Latin. He was a native of Cilicia, where the Greek was doubtless spoken, and he not unfrequently quotes the Greek poets in his addresses and epistles. Acts xxi. 37; xvii. 28; Titus i. 12; 1 Cor. xv. 33.

This epistle is placed *first* among Paul's epistles, not because it was the first written, but because of the length and importance of the epistle itself, and the importance of the church in the imperial city. It has uniformly had this place in the sacred canon, though there is reason to believe that the Epistle to the

Galatians, the first to the Corinthians, and perhaps the two to the Thessalonians, were written before this. Of the *time* when it was written, there can be little doubt. About the year 52 or 54 the Emperor Claudius banished all Jews from Rome. In Acts xviii. 2, we have an account of the *first* acquaintance of Paul with Aquila and Priscilla, who had departed from Rome in consequence of that decree. This acquaintance was formed in Corinth; and we are told that Paul abode with them, and worked at the same occupation; Acts xviii. 3. In Romans xvi. 3, 4, he directs the church to greet Priscilla and Aquila, who had for his life laid down their own necks. This service which they rendered him must have been therefore *after* the decree of Claudius; and of course the epistle must have been written *after* the year 52.

In Acts xviii. 19, we are told that he left Aquila and Priscilla at Ephesus. Paul made a journey through the neighbouring regions, and then returned to Ephesus; Acts xix. 1. Paul remained at Ephesus at least two years (Acts xix. 8, 9, 10), and while here probably wrote the first Epistle to the Corinthians. In that epistle (xvi. 19) he sends the salutation of Priscilla and Aquila, who were of course still at Ephesus. The Epistle to the Romans, therefore, in which he sends his salutation to Aquila and Priscilla, as being then at Rome, could not be written until they had left Ephesus and returned to Rome; that is, until three years at least after the decree of Claudius in 52 or 54.

Still further. When Paul wrote this epistle, he was about to depart for Jerusalem to convey a collection which had been made for the poor saints there, by the churches in Macedonia and Achaia; Rom. xv. 25, 26. When he had done this, he intended to go to Rome; Rom. xv. 28. Now, by looking at the Acts of the Apostles, we can determine when this occurred. At this time he sent Timotheus and Erastus before him into Macedonia, while he remained in Asia for a season; Acts xix. 22. After this (Acts xx. 1, 2), Paul himself went into Macedonia, passed through Greece, and remained about three months there. In this journey it is almost certain that he went to Corinth, the capital of Achaia, at which time it is supposed this epistle was written. From this place he set out for Jerusalem, where he was made a prisoner, and after remaining a prisoner two years (Acts xxiv. 27), he was sent to Rome about A.D. 60. Allowing for the time of his travelling and his imprisonment, it must have been about *three* years from the time that he purposed to go to Jerusalem; that is, from the time that he finished the epistle (Rom. xv. 25–29) to the time when he reached Rome, and thus the epistle must have been written about A.D. 57.

It is clear also, that the epistle was written from Corinth. In chap. xvi. 1, Phebe, a member of the church at Cenchrea, is commended to the Romans. She probably had charge of the epistle, or accompanied those who had it. Cenchrea was the port of the city of Corinth, about seven or eight miles from the city. In chap. xvi. 23, Gaius is spoken of as the *host* of Paul, or he of whose hospitality Paul partook, but Gaius was baptized by Paul at Corinth, and Corinth was manifestly his place of residence; 1 Cor. i. 14. Erastus is also mentioned as the chamberlain of the city where the epistle was written; but this Erastus is mentioned as having his abode at Corinth; 2 Tim. iv. 20. From all this it is manifest that the Epistle was written at Corinth, about the year 57.

Of the state of the church at Rome at that time it is not easy to form a precise opinion. From this epistle it is evident that it was composed of Jews and Gentiles; and that one design of writing to it was to reconcile their jarring opinions, particularly about the obligation of the Jewish law; the advantage of the Jew; and the way of justification. It is probable that the two parties in the church were endeavouring to defend each their peculiar opinions, and that the apostle took this opportunity and mode to state to his converted countrymen the great doctrines of Christianity, and the relation of the law of Moses to the Christian system. The epistle itself is full proof that the church to whom it was addressed was composed of Jews and Gentiles. No small part of it is an argument expressly with the Jews; chap. ii. iii. iv. ix. x. xi. And no small part of the epistle also is designed to state the true doctrine about the character of the Gentiles and the way in which they could be justified before God.

At this time there was a large number of Jews at Rome. When Pompey the Great overran Judea, he sent a large number of Jews prisoners to Rome, to be sold as slaves. But it was not easy to control them. They persevered resolutely and obstinately in adhering to the rites of their nation; in keeping the Sabbath, &c. So that the Romans chose at last to give them their freedom, and assigned them a place in the vicinity of the city across the Tiber. Here a town was built, which was principally inhabited by Jews. Josephus mentions that 4000 Jews were banished from Rome at one time to Sardinia, and that a still greater number were punished who were unwilling to become soldiers; Ant. xviii. chap. 3, § 5. Philo (Legat. ad Caium) says, that many of the Jews at Rome had obtained their freedom; for, says he, *being made captive in war, and brought into Italy, they were set at liberty by their masters, neither were they compelled to change the rites of their fathers;* see also Josephus, Ant. xvii. chap. ii. § 1; Suetonius' Life of Tiberius, 36, and Notes on Acts vi. 9. From that large number of Jews, together with those converted from the Gentiles, the church at Rome was collected, and it is easy to see that *in* that church there would be a great diversity of sentiment, and, no doubt, warm discussions about the authority of the Mosaic law.

At what time, or by whom, the gospel was first preached at Rome has been a matter of controversy. The Roman Catholic church have maintained that it was founded by Peter, and have thence drawn an argument for their high claims and infallibility. On this subject they make a confident appeal to some of the fathers. There is strong evidence to be derived from this epistle itself, and from the Acts, that *Paul* did not regard Peter as having any such *primacy* and *ascendency* in the Roman church as are claimed for him by the Papists. (1.) In this whole epistle there is no mention of Peter at all. It is not suggested that he had been, or was then at Rome. If he had been, and the church had been founded by him, it is incredible that Paul did not make mention of that fact. This is the more striking, as it was done in *other* cases where churches had been founded by other men; see 1 Cor. i. 12–15. Especially is *Peter*, or Cephas, mentioned repeatedly by the apostle Paul in his other epistles; 1 Cor. iii. 22; ix. 5; xv. 5; Gal. ii. 9; i. 18; ii. 7, 8, 14. In these places *Peter* is mentioned in connection with the churches at Corinth and Galatia, yet never there as appealing to his authority, but in regard to the latter, expressly calling it in question. Now, it is incredible that if Peter *had been* then at Rome, and had founded the church there, and was regarded as invested with any peculiar authority over it, that Paul should never once have even suggested his name. (2.) It is clear that Peter was *not* there when Paul wrote this epistle. If he had been, he could not have failed to have sent him a salutation, amid the numbers that he saluted in the xvith chapter. (3.) In the Acts of the Apostles there is no mention of Peter's having been at Rome, but the presumption from that history is almost conclusive that he had not been. In Acts xii. 3, 4, we have an account of his having been imprisoned by Herod Agrippa near the close of his reign (comp. v. 23). This occurred about the third or fourth year of the reign of Claudius, who began to reign A.D. 41. It is altogether improbable that he had been at Rome before this. Claudius had not reigned more than three years, and all the testimony that the fathers give is, that Peter came to Rome in his reign. (4.) Peter was at Jerusalem still in the *ninth* or *tenth* year of the reign of Claudius; Acts xv. 6, &c. Nor is there any mention made then of his having been at Rome. (5.) Paul went to Rome about A.D. 60. There is no mention made then of Peter's being with him or being there. If he had been, it could hardly have failed of being recorded. Especially is this remarkable when Paul's meeting with *the brethren* is expressly mentioned (Acts xxviii. 14, 15), and when it is recorded that he met the Jews, and abode with them, and spent at Rome no less than two years. If *Peter* had been there, such a fact could not fail to have been recorded or alluded to, either in the Acts or the Epistle to the Romans. (6.) The Epistles to the Ephesians, Philippians, Colossians, to Philemon, and the second Epistle to Timothy (Lardner, vi. 235) were written from Rome during the residence of Paul as a prisoner; and the Epistle to the Hebrews probably also while he was still in Italy. In none of these epistles is there any hint that Peter was then or had been at Rome; a fact that cannot be accounted for if he was regarded as the founder of that church, and especially if he was then in that city. Yet in those epistles there are the salutations of a number to those churches. In particular, Epaphras, Luke the beloved physician (Col. iv. 12, 14), and the saints of the household of Cæsar are mentioned; Phil. iv. 22. In 2 Tim. iv. 11, Paul expressly affirms that *Luke only was with him*, a declaration utterly irreconcilable with the supposition that *Peter* was then at Rome. (7.) If Peter was ever at Rome, therefore, of which indeed there is no reason to doubt, he must have come there after Paul; at what time is unknown. That he *was* there cannot be doubted without calling in question the truth of all history.

When, or by whom, the gospel was preached first at Rome, it is not easy, perhaps not possible, to determine. In the account of the day of Pentecost (Acts ii. 10), we find, among others, that there were present *strangers of Rome*, and it is not improbable that *they* carried back the knowledge of Jesus Christ, and became the founders of the Roman church. One design and effect of that miracle was doubtless to spread the knowledge of the Saviour among all nations; see Notes on Acts ii. In the list of persons who are mentioned in Rom. xvi. it is not improbable that some of those early converts are included; and that Paul thus intended to show honour to their early conversion and zeal in the cause of Christianity. Thus, xvi. 7, he designates Andronicus and Junia his kinsmen and fellow-prisoners, who were *distinguished among the apostles*, and who had been converted before himself, *i.e.* before A.D. 34, *at least* eight years before it was ever pretended that Peter was at Rome. Other persons are mentioned also as distinguished, and it is not improbable that they were the early founders of the church at Rome, chap. xvi. 12, 13, &c.

That the church at Rome was founded early is evident from the celebrity which it had acquired. At the time when Paul wrote this epistle (A.D. 57), their faith was spoken of throughout the world, chap. i. 8. The *character* of the church at Rome cannot be clearly ascertained. Yet it is clear that it was not made up merely of the lower classes of the community. In Phil. iv. 22, it appears that the gospel had made its way to the family of Cæsar, and that a part of his household had been converted to the Christian faith. Some of the fathers affirm that *Nero* in the beginning of his reign was favourably impressed in regard to Christianity; and it is possible that this might have been through the instrumentality of his family. But little on this subject can be known. While it is probable that the great mass of believers in all the early churches was of obscure and plebeian origin, it is also certain that some who were rich, and noble, and learned, became members of the church of Christ; see 1 Tim. ii. 9; 1 Pet. iii. 3; 1 Tim. vi. 20; Col. ii. 8; 1 Cor. i. 26; Acts xvii. 34.

This epistle has been usually deemed the most difficult of interpretation of any part of the New Testament; and no small part of the controversies in the Christian church have grown out of discussions about its meaning. Early in the history of the church, even before the death of the apostles, we learn from 2 Pet. iii. 16, that the writings of Paul were some of them regarded as being hard to be understood; and that the unlearned and unstable wrested them to their own destruction. It is probable that Peter has reference here to the high and mysterious doctrines about justification and the sovereignty of God, and the doctrines of election and decrees. From the epistle of James, it would seem probable also, that already the apostle Paul's doctrine of justification by faith had been perverted and abused. It seems to have been inferred that good works were unnecessary; and here was the beginning of the cheerless and withering system of Antinomianism—than which a more destructive or pestilential heresy never found its way into the Christian church. Several reasons might be assigned for the controversies which have grown out of this epistle. (1.) The very structure of the argument, and the peculiarity of the apostle's manner of writing. He is rapid; mighty; profound; often involved; readily following a new thought; leaving the regular subject; and returning again after a considerable interval. Hence his writings abound with parentheses and with complicated paragraphs. (2.) Objections are often introduced, so that it requires close attention to determine their precise bearing. Though he employs no small part of the epistle in answering objections, yet an objector is never once formally introduced or mentioned. (3.) His *expressions* and *phrases* are many of them liable to be misunderstood, and capable of perversion. Of this class are such expressions as the righteousness of faith, the righteousness of God, &c. (4.) The doctrines themselves are high and mysterious. They are those subjects on which the profoundest minds have been in all ages exercised in vain. On them there has been, and always will be a difference of opinion. Even with the most honest intentions that men ever have, they find it difficult or impossible to approach the investigation of them without the bias of early education, or the prejudice of previous opinion. In this world it is not given to men fully to understand these great doctrines. And it is not wonderful that the discussion of them has given rise to endless controversies: and that they who have

> Reasoned high
> Of Providence, foreknowledge, will, and fate;
> Fixed fate, free will, foreknowledge absolute,
> Have found no end, in wandering mazes lost.

(5.) It cannot be denied that *one* reason why the epistles of Paul have been regarded as so difficult has been an unwillingness to admit the truth of the plain doctrines which he teaches. The heart is by nature opposed to them; and comes to believe them with great reluctance. This feeling will account for no small part of the difficulties felt in regard to this epistle. There is one great maxim in interpreting the scriptures that can never be departed from. It is, that men can never understand them aright, until they are *willing* to suffer them to speak out their fair and proper meaning. When men are determined *not* to find certain doctrines in the Bible, nothing is more natural than that they should find difficulties in it, and complain much of its great obscurity and mystery. I add, (6.) That one principal reason why so much difficulty has been felt here, has been an unwillingness to stop where the apostle does. Men have desired to advance farther, and penetrate the mysteries which the Spirit of inspiration has not disclosed. Where Paul states a simple *fact*, men often advance a *theory*. The *fact* may be clear and plain; their *theory* is obscure, involved, mysterious, or absurd. By degrees they learn to *unite* the fact and the theory:—they regard *their* explanation as the only possible one; and as the *fact* in question has the authority of divine revelation, so they insensibly come to regard their theory in the same light; and he that calls in question their speculation about the *cause*, or the *mode*, is set down as heretical, and as denying the doctrine of the apostle. A melancholy instance of this we have in the account which the apostle gives (chap. v.) about the effect of the sin of Adam. The simple *fact* is stated that that sin was followed by the sin and ruin of all his posterity. Yet he offers no explanation of the *fact*. He leaves it as indubitable; and as not demanding an explanation in his argument—perhaps as not admitting it. This is the whole of his doctrine on that subject. Yet men have not been satisfied with that. They have sought for a theory to account for it. And many suppose they have found it in the doctrine that the sin of Adam is *imputed*, or set over by an arbitrary arrangement to beings otherwise innocent, and that they are held to be responsible for a deed committed by a man thousands of years before they were born. This is the *theory;* and men insensibly forget that it *is mere theory*, and they blend that and the *fact* which the apostle states together; and deem the denial of the one, heresy as much as the denial of the other, *i.e.* they make it as impious to call in question *their philosophy*, as to doubt *the facts* stated on the authority of *the apostle Paul*. If men desire to *understand* the epistles of Paul, and avoid difficulties, they should be willing to leave it where *he* does; and this single rule would have made useless whole years and whole tomes of controversy.

Perhaps, on the whole, there is no book of the New Testament that more demands a humble, docile, and prayerful disposition in its interpretation than this epistle. Its profound doctrines; its abstruse inquiries; and the opposition of many of those doctrines to the views of the unrenewed and unsubdued heart of man, make a spirit of docility and prayer peculiarly needful in its investigation. No man ever yet understood the reasonings and views of the apostle Paul but under the influence of elevated piety. None ever found opposition to his doctrines recede, and difficulties vanish, who did not bring the mind in an humble frame to receive *all* that has been revealed; and that, in a spirit of humble prayer, did not purpose to lay aside all bias, and open the heart to the full influence of the elevated truths which he inculcates. Where there is a willingness that God should reign and do all his pleasure, this epistle may be in its general character easily understood. Where this is wanting, it will appear full of mystery and perplexity; the mind will be embarrassed, and the heart dissatisfied with its doctrines; and the unhumbled spirit will rise from its study only confused, irritated, perplexed, and dissatisfied.

ANALYSIS OF THE EPISTLE TO THE ROMANS.

SHOWING THE DESIGN AND ARGUMENT OF THE EPISTLE.

I. *Introduction to the Epistle: ch.* I. 1—15.
- Salutation to the Romans: chapter I. 1—7.
- The faith of the Roman Christians commended; and Paul's desire to see them, and his readiness to serve them, expressed: ch. I. 8—15.

II. *The subject, or main argument of the Epistle proposed:* ch. I. 16, 17.
- The main subject and design of the Epistle proposed to set forth *the distinguishing traits of the Gospel*, and *its value*. The peculiarity of the Gospel consists in the doctrine of JUSTIFICATION BY FAITH, in contradistinction from the plan of salvation by works; and IN ITS BEING ADAPTED TO ALL NATIONS: ch. I. 16, 17.

III. *The argument for the doctrine of justification by faith derived from the fact, that all other plans have failed, and that all men are guilty:* ch. I. 18—32, ch. II. III. IV.

I. IN RELATION TO THE GENTILES: ch. I. 18—32.
- (1.) God is just, and has revealed his intention to punish sinners; ch. I. 18.
- (2.) The Gentiles have the means of knowing God and his will, from the works of creation, and therefore have no excuse: ch. I. 19—21.
- (3.) They have failed to honour him; to obey his law; and are, *in fact, universally depraved;* and, therefore, *cannot* be justified by the works of the law. This account sustained by an appeal to fact: ch. I. 22—32. Compare the conclusion: ch. III. 20—26.

II. *IN* RELATION TO THE JEWS. They are equally guilty with the Gentiles. ch. II., III. 1—19.
- (1.) Their national privileges cannot screen them from guilt and punishment: ch. II. 1—4.
- (2.) They know that God is just, and impartial, and will judge all men according to their deeds: ch. II. 4—16.
- (3.) The peculiar advantages which the Jew had for knowing the will of God over the Gentiles. His obligations, therefore, to practise righteousness: ch. II. 17—20.
- (4.) His increased guilt if he fails of obedience: ch. II. 20—23.
- (5.) The actual character of the Jews: ch. II. 24.
- (6.) Their outward ceremonies avail nothing in freeing them from guilt, and are useless unless attended with purity of heart: ch. II. 25—29.
- (7.) *Answer to the objections of the Jew to the proof of his guilt:* ch. III. 1—9.
  - (*a.*) If as guilty as the Gentiles, what advantage has he? ch. III. 1. ANSWER. His advantage is great from having the Scriptures: ch. III. 2.
  - (*b.*) The unbelief of a part will not destroy the faithfulness of God: ch. III. 3. ANSWER. No such consequence follows as that God will be unfaithful and false. God is always true and right. *This is to be held as a great fixed principle:* ch. III. 4.
  - (*c.*) If God's character is illustrated, and his faithfulness and truth confirmed by means of our unbelief, will it not be unjust for him to punish us: ch. III. 5. ANSWER. The admitted fact that God will judge the world, and condemn the guilty, shows that it will be *right* to inflict punishment: ch. III. 6.
  - (*d.*) But if my lie promotes his truth, how *can* I be guilty? ch. III. 7. ANSWER. If this be a just principle, it should be carried out, and made universal, and then it will be that "we should do all the evil we can, that good may come:" ch. III. 8.
- (8.) The Jews have no pre-eminence at all in regard to moral character. Proof of their depravity from their own Scriptures. ch. III. 9—19.

III. THE CONCLUSION IN REGARD TO BOTH JEWS AND GENTILES THAT ALL ARE SINNERS, AND THAT THE PLAN OF JUSTIFICATION BY THE LAW HAS FAILED: ch. III. 20—23.

IV. THE NEW, OR CHRISTIAN PLAN OF JUSTIFICATION STATED. IT IS BY GRACE THROUGH CHRIST TO THOSE WHO BELIEVE: ch. III. 24—31.
- (1.) What it is. It is without the law. It is borne witness to by the law and the prophets. It is on all *who believe*, without distinction: ch. III. 22—24.
- (2.) It is freely by grace through the atonement. The design of the atonement: ch. III. 25, 26.
- (3.) Its effect is to humble human pride: ch. III. 27, 28.
- (4.) The Gentiles may be justified in this way as well as the Jews,—all are on a level: ch. III. 29, 30.
- (5.) It in fact goes to establish and confirm the law: ch. III. 31.

V. THE SAME DOCTRINE OF JUSTIFICATION BY FAITH TAUGHT IN THE OLD TEST. ch. IV.
- Proved, (1.) By the case of Abraham, who was justified by faith *before* he was circumcised: ch. IV. 1—5; 9—22
- Proved, (2.) By what David taught: ch. IV. 6—8.
- Inference, (3.) If Abraham was justified by faith, others may be in the same way: ch. IV. 23—25.

IV. *The benefits of the doctrine of justification by faith*: ch. V.

1. It produces peace with God, and the privilege of access to him: ch. V. 1, 2.
2. It furnishes support in affliction: ch. V. 3—5.
3. It infers the certainty of salvation from the fact that God has sent his Son to die for us: ch. V. 6—11.
4. It meets and removes all the acknowledged sins and calamities in which we were involved by the sin of Adam; it brings us more blessings than he lost; it produces mercies more wide and lasting than his transgression did woes; and thus shows that it is a plan adapted to the condition of a fallen world: ch. V. 12—21.

☞ COMPARISON OF THE EFFECT OF ADAM'S SIN WITH THE EFFECTS OF THE WORK OF CHRIST.

(1.) *Resemblance.* (*a.*) Sin entered by one man, so also of justification: ch. V. 12—18.
(*b.*) Condemnation was by the *offence* of one; so justification by the *righteousness* of one: ch. V. 18, 19.
(*c.*) The effects of the sin of the one extended to all; so of the work of the other: ch. V. 18, 19.

(2.) *Contrast.* *Christ has procured more blessings than Adam lost, and thus repairs the evils of the fall.*
(*a.*) By the crime of one many are dead; by the work of the other grace will *much* more abound: ch. V. 15.
(*b.*) In the case of Adam, *one offence* led on a train of many woes; in the case of Christ, his work led to the remission of *many offences*: ch. V. 16.
(*c.*) In regard to the effects. *Death* reigned by Adam; *life, much more* by Christ: ch. V. 17.

☞ INFERENCE FROM THE COMPARISON. GRACE SUPERABOUNDS. THE EFFECTS OF THE SIN OF ADAM ARE MET AND OVERCOME BY THE NEW PLAN OF JUSTIFICATION BY FAITH IN THE WORK OF CHRIST: ch. V. 20, 21.

V. *Justification by faith does not encourage men to sin, but frees them from it*: ch. VI. VII. 1—6.

1. Christians are *in fact* dead to sin: ch. VI. 1, 2.
2. Their baptism supposes the same thing: ch. VI. 3—7.
3. They are united to Christ, and as he rose from the dead, so should they rise from sin: ch. VI. 8—14.
4. They have yielded themselves servants to God; and should, therefore, obey him. ch. VI. 15—19.
5. They have learned by painful experience that sin produced no benefit, and they will therefore forsake it: ch. VI. 20—22.
6. The wages of sin is death; holiness produces life; and they will forsake the one, and pursue the other: ch. VI. 23.
7. Christians are dead in fact to the law, and united to Christ: ch. VII. 1—4.
8. They are freed from the law, not to *sin*, but to *obey the gospel*. ch. VII. 5, 6.

VI. *Objection that according to the previous view the law is evil.* ANSWER. *The law is itself* good; *but its effect is not to* justify, *and give* peace, *but to produce alarm and conflict*: ch. VII. 7—25.

1. *The objection stated,* that if the plan of justification be to free from the *law,* the law must be evil: ch. VII. 7.
2. *Answer to the objection,* the law is good; but it is, in all cases, the occasion of conflict and sin, not of justification and peace: ch. VII. 7.
3. The true effect of the law is not to produce peace, but strife, and sin; illustrated (1.) in the case of sinners, and (2.) of Christians.

(1.) *In regard to sinners.*
(*a.*) Produces the knowledge of sin: ch. VII. 7.
(*b.*) Is the occasion of all inordinate desire, and of sin ch. VII. 8.
(*c.*) Produces alarm and misery: ch. VII. 9—11.
☞ Yet (*d.*) the fault is not of the *law*, but is to be traced to the sin of the corrupt heart. The law itself is good, but cannot give peace: ch. VII. 12, 13.

(2.) *In regard to those who are renewed, the effect is the same to produce conflict and agitation, not peace.*
(*a.*) The law spiritual, but man, even renewed, carnal: ch. VII. 14.
(*b.*) The effect is to produce strife, and the struggles of the Christian conflict. ch. VII. 15—23.
☞ Yet (*c.*) The law is itself good, but is the occasion of agitation and strife, not of peace: ch. VII. 16.
(*d.*) The effect of the *law* is, therefore, to produce MISERY in all the conditions of life; and is consequently not adapted to produce peace. ch. VII. 24.

4. Not the law, therefore, but the Gospel can bring deliverance from sin, though the law is itself good: ch. VII. 25.

VII. *The doctrine of justification by faith frees from the penalty, and the bondage of sin*: ch. VIII. 1—17.

1. The Christian is freed from condemnation: ch. VIII. 1.
2. The coming and work of Christ has done what the law could never have done: ch. VIII. 2—4.
3. It is a fact in the experience of Christians, that they are not under the influence of a carnal mind: ch. VIII. 5—11.
4. Christians feel the obligation to lead lives of holiness: ch. VIII. 12, 13.
5. They have evidence in their own feelings that they are not under bondage, but are free from condemnation, and are the children of God: ch. VIII. 14—17.

VIII. *This doctrine not opposed by the fact that Christians suffer much. Their supports furnished by the plan in their afflictions. The provisions which are made for their certain deliverance:* ch. VIII. 18—39.

1. The afflictions of Christians not worthy to be compared with the glory before them; ch. VIII. 18.
2. They have the prospect of complete deliverance. All things in creation coincide with the expectation of the Christian: ch. VIII. 19—25. The argument. (*a.*) The *creature*, i. e. the *renewed nature*, the new creation, is waiting for future glory: ch. VIII. 19. (*b.*) The Christian is subjected to a life of vanity, affording emphatically little comfort, and much disquietude. (*c.*) This is not in accordance with the desire of his heart—"not willingly"—but is the wise appointment of God: ch. VIII. 20. (*d.*) In this condition there is hope of deliverance: ch. VIII. 21. (*e.*) This state of *subjection* is the common condition of all things: ch. VIII. 22. (*f.*) But Christians only have the prospect of deliverance. ch. VIII. 23—25.
3. God helps them in their afflictions by his Spirit: ch. VIII. 25—27.
4. It is God's purpose to save them. All things, therefore, even their afflictions, work together for their good: ch. VIII. 28—30.
5. What God has actually *done* for them shows that they will be saved from their trials: ch. VIII. 31, 32. (*a.*) God is for us, and we must be secure. (*b.*) He has sent his Son to die, and will not withhold any other blessing.
6. There is none to condemn them, and they must be safe. (*a.*) God who *justifies* them will not condemn them. (*b.*) Christ who died for them will not condemn them: ch. VIII. 33, 34.
7. Nothing *can* separate them from the love of God. They are so firmly attached to Him, *in fact*, that they *must*, and *do* adhere to Him in all these trials, and *will* persevere to the end: ch. VIII. 35—39.

IX. *God has a right to make those whom he chooses the objects of his favour. That right he has always executed*: ch. IX.

1. Paul's belief that the Gentiles would be admitted to the favour of God did not arise from any want of love to his own countrymen. His unabated love to them shown: ch. IX. 1—5.
2. It does not follow that *all* who are Jews must of necessity be saved. The *principle of election* shown by the selection of Isaac, and *proved* by that case. ch. IX. 6—8.
3. Further proved, and shown not to be according to works, in the case of Jacob and Esau. God dispenses his favours according to his good pleasure: ch. IX. 9—13.
4. Proved further, by the declaration which God made to Moses; and by the case of Pharaoh. God is not unrighteous in this: ch. IX. 14—18.
5. Answer to the objection, that if this be so, man cannot be to blame, and God cannot find fault: ch. IX. 19—24. ANSWER. (1.) God *is* a Sovereign, and has a right to do his will, as the potter has power over the clay: ch. IX. 20, 21. (2.) God does it according to the principles of *justice* and *mercy*. The doctrine of sovereignty is, of necessity, involved in the purpose of showing mercy: ch. IX. 22—24.
6. Proved by Hosea: ch. IX. 25, 26.
7. Proved by Isaiah: ch. IX. 27—29. The doctrine of election, even *among* the Jews, thus proved from their own writings.
8. Since the *principle* of election is thus established in relation *to the Jews themselves*, it may be also extended to the Gentiles: ch. IX. 30, 31.
9. The reason why any of the Jews rejected. They despised the plan of salvation: ch. IX. 32, 33.

X. *The doctrine that men are on a level before God in regard to justification, consistent with all the declarations made to the Jews:* ch. X.

1. Paul's own feelings for his countrymen. His earnest desire that they should be saved: ch. X. 1, 2.
2. Their character. The *reason* why they would be rejected. They had relied on a false method of justification, and were ignorant of God's plan ch. X. 3.
3. *Christ is the end of the law.* There is no other way of justification but by him: ch. X. 4.
4. This doctrine accords with the declaration of Moses: ch. X. 5—11. (*a.*) Moses' doctrine of salvation by works, that the man "that doeth these things, shall live by them:" ch. X. 5. (*b.*) The language of Moses has accurately described the operation of faith: ch. X. 6—8. (*c.*) *The true nature, and operation of faith:* ch. X. 9—11.
5. There is no difference, therefore, between the Jew and the Greek. All on a level. God is rich in mercy towards all: ch. X. 12, 13.
6. This doctrine was, *in fact*, made known to the Jews: ch. X. 14—21. Objection that it could not be known to all: ch. X. 14—17. ANSWER. (1.) The sound has gone unto all the earth: ch. X. 18. (2.) Moses taught this doctrine, that salvation would be made known to the Gentiles: ch. X. 19. (3.) Isaiah taught the same thing: ch. X. 20, 21.

XI. *Answer to the objection that according to the doctrine stated, that the Jews would be rejected, God had violated his promises, and cast away his own people. The true doctrine respecting the Jews stated:* ch. XI.

1. The case of Paul himself a proof that God had not violated his promises, and cast away his true people: ch. XI. 1.
2. The same thing proved in the case of Elijah. In a time of *general* corruption, when the *mass* of the people were rejected, a *few*, his true people, were saved: ch. XI. 2—7.
3. The doctrine that the mass of the nation would be rejected, proved from Isaiah (XXIX. 10.) and David (Ps. LXIX. 22, 23:) ch. XI. 7—10.
4. Yet their fall not final, but great advantages to the Gentiles will result from their fall: ch. XI. 11—14.
5. They shall be again gathered in; and greater advantages still to the Gentiles shall result from their ingathering: ch. XI. 15, 16.
6. As the Jews, the ancient covenant people of God, have been rejected for their unbelief, the Gentiles should be humble and cautious: ch. XI. 17—21.
7. That the Jews shall be again gathered in, certain; proved from the Old Testament: ch. XI. 23—32.
8. The Divine perfections illustrated by this. God's wisdom and knowledge shown. The arrangement the occasion of astonishment and praise: ch. XI. 33—36.

XII. *Practical conclusions and exhortations from the epistle*: ch. XII.—XVI.

1. EXHORTATION TO VARIOUS PERSONAL CHRISTIAN DUTIES: ch. XII.
   - (*a.*) To entire consecration to God: **ch. XII. 1.**
   - (*b.*) Against conformity to the world: **ch. XII. 2.**
   - (*c.*) Exhortation to humility. ch. XII. 3—5.
   - (*d.*) To fidelity in the discharge of our *official* duties: ch. XII. 6—8.
   - (*e.*) To fidelity in our *relative* duties as Christians—to brotherly love; mutual respect; diligence; hospitality; sympathy, &c.: ch. XII. 10—16.
   - (*f.*) To forgiveness of enemies, and kind treatment of those who injure us: ch. XII. 17—21.

2. EXHORTATION TO OBEY CIVIL MAGISTRATES; TO HOLY CONDUCT; AND TO PREPARATION FOR DEATH: ch. XIII.
   - (*a.*) Duty of *subjection* to those in authority, because it is the appointment of God: ch. XIII. 1—5.
   - (*b.*) On the same account we ought to pay tribute: ch. XIII. 6, 7.
   - (*c.*) On the same account we ought to meet *all* the claims which others have on us, and thus to fulfil the law of love. ch. XIII. 8—10.
   - (*d.*) These duties enforced from the fact that life is short; that Christians are near heaven; and that they should live as becomes such: ch. XIII. 11—14.

3. CAUTION AGAINST MAKING EXTERNAL OBSERVANCES THE OCCASION OF STRIFE AND DIVISION IN THE CHURCH: ch. XIV. XV. 1—13.
   - (*a.*) Our duty to receive and acknowledge our Christian brethren: ch. XIV. 1, 2.
   - (*b.*) Every one answerable for himself to God: ch. XIV. 3, 4.
   - (*c.*) Every man should be fully persuaded in his own mind; and though there may be a difference of opinion, yet each may desire to honour God: ch. XIV. 5—9.
   - (*d.*) We have no right to judge or despise others. Every one must answer for himself: ch. XIV. 10—12.
   - (*e.*) He ought not to put a stumbling-block in the way of a brother: ch. XIV. 13—17.
   - (*f.*) He who really *serves Christ* in these things is acceptable, and we should live with him in peace: ch. XIV. 18—23.
   - (*g.*) We ought to bear the infirmities of the weak, and thus imitate the example of Christ: ch. XV. 1—7.
   - (*h.*) The intention of God was to bring in the Gentiles according to the ancient promise, and therefore *all* Christians should live in peace: ch. XV. 8—13.

4. VARIOUS EXPRESSIONS OF PAUL'S FEELINGS TOWARDS THE ROMAN CHRISTIANS: ch. XV. 14—33.
   - (*a.*) His view of their kindness, and knowledge, and ability to regulate properly their own affairs: ch. XV. 14.
   - (*b.*) Reason why he had written this epistle, *his being a minister to the Gentiles*. Summary view of his labours and successes: ch. XV. 15—21.
   - (*c.*) His great desire to see the Roman Christians, and purpose to visit them: ch. XV. 22—29.
   - (*d.*) Their prayers asked in his behalf that he might be delivered from impending dangers, and permitted to go to Rome. ch. XV. 30—33.

5. CONCLUSION OF THE EPISTLE ch. XVI.
   - (*a.*) Various salutations: ch. XVI. 1—16.
   - (*b.*) Caution against divisions: ch. XVI. 17—20.
   - (*c.*) Other salutations: ch. XVI. 21—24.
   - (*d.*) Closing ascription of praise to God: ch. XVI. 25—27.

THE

EPISTLE TO THE ROMANS

CHAPTER I.

PAUL, a servant of [a] Jesus Christ, called [b] *to be* an apostle, separated [c] unto the gospel of God,

2 (Which he had promised afore

a Ac.27.23. *b* Ac.9.15; 1 Co.1.1. *c* Ac.13.2; Ga.1.15.

CHAPTER I.

1. *Paul.* The original name of the author of this epistle was *Saul.* Acts vi. 58; vii. 1; viii. 1, &c. This was changed to Paul (see Note, Acts xiii. 9), and by this name he is generally known in the New Testament. The reason why he assumed this name is not certainly known. It was, however, in accordance with the custom of the times; see Note, Acts xiii. 9. The name *Saul* was Hebrew; the name *Paul* was Roman. In addressing an epistle to the Romans, he would naturally make use of the name to which they were accustomed, and which would excite no prejudice among them. The ancient custom was to *begin* an epistle with the name of the writer, as Cicero to Varro, &c. *We* record the name at the end. It may be remarked, however, that the placing the *name* of the writer at the *beginning* of an epistle was always done, and is still, when the letter was one of authority, or when it conferred any peculiar privileges. Thus in the proclamation of Cyrus (Ezra i. 2), "Thus saith Cyrus, king of Persia," &c.; see also Ezra iv. 11; vii. 12. "Artaxerxes, king of kings, unto Ezra the priest," &c. Dan. iv. 1. The commencement of a letter by an apostle to a Christian church in this manner was peculiarly proper as indicating *authority.* ¶ *A servant.* This name was that which the Lord Jesus himself directed his disciples to use, as their *general* appellation; Mat. x. 25; xx. 27; Mark x. 44. And it was the customary name which they assumed; Gal. i. 10; Col iv. 12; 2 Pet. i. 1; Jude 1; Acts iv. 29; Titus i. 1; James i. 1. The *proper* meaning of this word servant, δοῦλος, is *slave,* one who is not free. It expresses the condition of one who has a master, or who is at the control of another. It is often, however, applied to *courtiers,* or the officers that serve under a king; because in an eastern monarchy the relation of an absolute king to his courtiers corresponded nearly to that of a master and a slave. Thus the word is expressive of *dignity* and *honour;* and the servants of a king denote officers of a high rank and station. It is applied to the prophets as those who were honoured by God, or peculiarly intrusted by him with office; Deut. xxxiv. 5; Josh. i. 2; Jer. xxv. 4. The name is also given to the Messiah, Isa. xlii. 1, "Behold my servant in whom my soul delighteth," &c.; liii. 11, "Shall my righteous servant justify many." The apostle uses it here evidently to denote *his* acknowledging Jesus Christ as his master; as indicating his dignity, as peculiarly appointed by him to his great work; and as showing that in this epistle he intended to assume no authority of his own, but simply to declare the will of his master, and theirs. ¶ *Called to be an apostle.* This word *called* means here not merely to be *invited,* but has the sense of *appointed.* It indicates that he had not assumed the office himself, but that he was set apart to it by the authority of Christ himself. It was important for Paul to state this, (1.) Because the other apostles had been called or chosen to this work (John xv. 16, 19; Mat. x. 1; Luke vi. 13); and (2.) Because Paul was not one of those originally appointed. It was of consequence for him therefore, to affirm

by his prophets in the holy scriptures,)

3 Concerning his Son Jesus Christ our Lord, which was made

that he had not taken this high office to himself, but that he had been *called* to it by the authority of Jesus Christ. His appointment to this office he not unfrequently takes occasion to vindicate; 1 Cor. ix. 1, &c.; Gal. i. 12—24; 2 Cor. xii. 12; 1 Tim. ii. 7; 2 Tim. i. 11; Rom. xi. 13. ¶ *An apostle.* One *sent* to execute a commission. It is applied because the apostles were *sent out* by Jesus Christ to preach his gospel, and to establish his church; Note, Mat. x. 2; Luke vi. 13. ¶ *Separated.* The word translated *separated unto,* ἀφορίζω, means to designate, to mark out by fixed limits, to bound as a field, &c. It denotes those who are *separated,* or called out from the common mass; Acts xix. 9; 2 Cor. vi. 17. The meaning here does not materially differ from the expression, *called to be an apostle,* except that perhaps this includes the notion of the *purpose* or *designation* of God to this work. Thus Paul uses the same word respecting himself; Gal. i. 15, "God, who separated me from my mother's womb, and called me by his grace," *i. e.* God designated me; marked me out; or *designed* that I should be an apostle from my infancy. In the same way Jeremiah was designated to be a prophet; Jer. i. 5. ¶ *Unto the gospel of God.* Designated or designed by God that I should make it *my business* to preach the gospel. Set apart to this, as the peculiar, great work of my life; as having no other object for which I should live. For the meaning of the word *gospel,* see Note, Mat. i. 1. It is called the gospel *of God* because it is *his* appointment; it has been originated by him, and has his authority. The office of an apostle was to preach the gospel. Paul regarded himself as *separated* to this work. It was not to live in splendour, wealth, and ease, but to devote himself to this great business of proclaiming good news, that God was reconciled to men in his Son. This is the sole business of all ministers of religion.

2. *Which he had promised afore.* Which gospel, or which doctrines, he had before announced. ¶ *By the prophets.* The word *prophets* here is used to include those who *wrote* as well as those who *spake.* It included the teachers of the ancient Jews generally. ¶ *In the holy scriptures.* In the *writings* of the Old Testament. They were called *holy* because they were inspired of the Holy Ghost, and were regarded as *separated* from all other writings, and worthy of all reverence. The apostle here declares that he was not about to advance any thing *new.* His doctrines were in accordance with the acknowledged oracles of God. Though they might *appear* to be new, yet he regarded the *gospel* as entirely consistent with all that had been declared in the Jewish dispensation; and not only consistent, but as actually promised there. He affirms, therefore, (1.) That all this was *promised,* and no small part of the epistle is employed to show this. (2.) That it was confirmed by the authority of holy and inspired men. (3.) That it depended on no vague and loose *tradition,* but was *recorded,* so that men might examine for themselves. The reason why the apostle was so anxious to show that his doctrine coincided with the Old Testament was because the church at Rome was made up in part of Jews. He wished to show them, and the remainder of his countrymen, that the Christian religion was built on the foundation of *their* prophets, and their acknowledged writings. So doing, he would disarm their prejudice, and furnish a proof of the truth of religion. It was a constant position with the apostle that he advanced nothing but what was maintained by the best and holiest men of the nation, Acts xxvi. 22, 23, "Saying none other things than those which the prophets and Moses did say should come," &c. There was a further reason here for his appealing so much to the Old Testament. He had never been at Rome. He was therefore personally a stranger, and it was proper for him then especially to show his regard for the doctrines of the pro-

phets. Hence he appeals here so often to the Old Testament; and defends every point by the authority of the Bible. The particular *passages* of the Old Testament on which he relied will come before us in the course of the epistle. See particularly chap. iii. iv. ix. x. xi. We may see here, (1.) The reverence which Paul showed for the Old Testament. He never undervalued it. He never regarded it as obsolete, or useless. He manifestly *studied* it; and never fell into the impious opinion that the Old Testament is of little value. (2.) If these things were *promised—predicted* in the Old Testament, then Christianity is true. Every passage which he adduces is therefore proof that it is from God.

3. *Concerning his Son.* This is connected with the first verse, with the word *gospel*. The gospel of God concerning his Son. The design of the gospel was to make a communication relative to his Son Jesus Christ. This is the whole of it. There is no *good news* to man respecting salvation except that which comes by Jesus Christ. ¶ *Which was made.* The word translated *was made* means usually *to be,* or *to become.* It is used, however, in the sense of *being born.* Thus, Gal. iv. 4, "God sent forth his Son *made* of a woman," born of a woman. John viii. 58, "Before Abraham *was* [*born*], I am." In this sense it seems to be used here,—who was born, or descended from the seed of David. ¶ *Of the seed of David.* Of the *posterity* or lineage of David. He was a descendant of David. David was perhaps the most illustrious of the kings of Israel. The promise to him was that there should not fail a man to sit on this throne; 1 Kings ii. 4; viii. 25; ix. 5; 2 Chron. vi. 16. This ancient promise was understood as referring to the Messiah, and hence in the New Testament he is called the descendant of David, and so much pains is taken to show that he was of his line; Luke i. 27; Mat. ix. 27; xv. 22; xii. 23; xxi. 9, 15; xxii. 42, 45; John vii. 42; 2 Tim. ii. 8. As the Jews universally believed that the Messiah would be descended from David (John vii. 42), it was of great importance for the sacred writers to make it out clearly that Jesus of Nazareth was of that line and family. Hence it happened, that though our Saviour was humble, and poor, and obscure, yet he had that on which no small part of the world have been accustomed so much to pride themselves, an illustrious ancestry. To a Jew there could be scarcely any honour so high as to be descended from the best of their kings; and it shows how little the Lord Jesus esteemed the honours of this world, that he could always evince his deep humility in circumstances where men are usually proud; and that when he spoke of the honours of this world, and told how little they were worth, he was not denouncing that which was not within his reach. ¶ *According to the flesh.* The word *flesh,* σάρξ, is used in the Scriptures in a great variety of significations. (1.) It denotes, as with us, the flesh literally of any living being; Luke xxiv. 39, "A spirit hath not flesh and bones," &c. (2.) The animal system, the body, including flesh and bones, the *visible* part of man, in distinction from the *invisible,* or the soul; Acts ii. 31, "Neither did his *flesh*" (his body) "see corruption." 1 Cor. v. 5; xv. 39. (3.) The man, the whole animated system, body and soul; Rom. viii. 3, "In the likeness of sinful *flesh.*" 1 Cor. xv. 50; Mat. xvi. 17; Luke iii. 6. (4.) *Human nature.* As a man. Thus, Acts ii. 30, "God hath sworn with an oath that of the fruit of his loins according to the flesh, *i. e.* in his human nature, he would raise up Christ to sit on his throne." Rom. ix. 5, "Whose are the fathers, and of whom, as concerning the flesh, Christ came, who is over all, God blessed for ever." The same is its meaning here. He was a descendant of David in his human nature, or as a man. This implies, of course, that he had *another* nature besides his human, or that while he was a man he was also something else; that there was a nature in which he was *not* descended from David. That this is its meaning will still further appear by the follow-

[a] of the seed of David according to the flesh;

4 And [1] declared [b] *to be* the Son of God with power, accord-

a Ps.89.36.

1 *determined.* *b* Ac.13.33,34; Re.1.18.

ing observations. (1.) The apostle *expressly* makes a contrast between his condition according to the flesh, and that according to the spirit of holiness. (2.) The expression "according to the flesh" is applied to no other one in the New Testament but to Jesus Christ. Though the word *flesh* often occurs, and is often used to denote *man*, yet the peculiar expression *according to the flesh* occurs in no other connection. In all the Scriptures it is never said of any prophet or apostle, any lawgiver or king, or any man in any capacity, that he came in the flesh, or that he was descended from certain ancestors *according to the flesh.* Nor is such an expression ever used any where else. If it were applied to a mere man, we should instantly ask in what other way *could* he come than in the flesh? Has he a higher nature? Is he an angel, or a seraph? The expression would be unmeaning. And when, therefore, it is applied to Jesus Christ, it implies, if language has any meaning, that there *was* a sense in which Jesus was not descended from David. What that was, appears in the next verse.

4. *And declared.* In the margin, *determined.* Τοῦ ὁρισθέντος. The ancient Syriac has, "And he was *known* to be the Son of God by might and by the Holy Spirit, who rose from the house of the dead." The Latin Vulgate, "Who was *predestinated* the Son of God," &c. The Arabic, "The Son of God *destined* by power peculiar to the Holy Spirit," &c. The word translated "declared to be" means properly *to bound, to fix limits to*, as to a field, to determine its proper limits or boundaries, to define, &c. Acts xvii. 26, "And *hath determined the bounds* of their habitation." Hence it means to determine, constitute, ordain, decree; *i. e.* to fix or designate the proper boundaries of a truth, or a doctrine; to distinguish its lines and marks from error; or to show, or declare a thing to be so by any action. Luke xxii. 22, "The Son of man goeth as it was *determined*," as it was fixed, purposed, defined, in the purpose of God, and declared in the prophets. Acts ii. 23, "Him being delivered by the *determinate counsel*," the definite, constituted will, or design, of God. xi. 29; Heb. iv. 7, "He *limiteth* a certain day," fixes it, defines it. In this sense it is clearly used in this place. The act of raising him from the dead *designated* him, or *constituted* him the Son of God. It was such an act *as in the circumstances of the case* showed that he was the Son of God in regard to a nature which was not "according to the flesh." The ordinary resurrection of a man, like that of Lazarus, would not show that he was the Son of God; but *in the circumstances of Jesus Christ* it did; for he had *claimed* to be so; he had taught it; and God now *attested* the truth of his teaching by raising him from the dead. ¶ *The Son of God.* The word *son* is used in a great variety of senses, denoting literally a son, then a descendant, posterity near or remote, a disciple or ward, an adopted son, or one that imitates or resembles another; see Note, Mat. i. 1. The expression *sons of God*, or son of God, is used in an almost equal latitude of signification. It is, (1.) Applied to Adam, as being immediately created by God without an earthly father; Luke iii. 38. (2.) It is applied to saints or Christians, as being *adopted* into his family, and sustaining to him the relation of children; John i. 12, 13; 1 John iii. 1, 2, &c. This name is given to them because they *resemble* him in their *moral* character; Mat. v. 45. (3.) It is given to *strong* men as resembling God in *strength;* Gen. vi. 2, "The sons of God saw the daughters of men," &c. Here these men of violence and strength are called sons of God, just as the high hills are called *hills of God*, the lofty trees of Leba-

non are called *cedars of God*, &c. (4.) Kings are sometimes called his sons, as resembling him in dominion and power, Ps. lxxxii. 6. (5.) The name is given to *angels* because they resemble God ; because he is their Creator and Father, &c., Job i. 6; ii. 1 ; Dan. iii. 25.

But the name THE *Son of God* is in the New Testament given by way of eminence to the Lord Jesus Christ. This was the common and favourite name by which the apostles designated him. The expression *Son of God* is applied to him no less than twenty-seven times in the Gospels and the Acts of the Apostles, and fifteen times in the Epistles and the Revelation. The expression *my Son*, and *his Son, thy Son*, &c. is applied to him in his peculiar relation to God, times almost without number. The other most common appellation which is given to him is *Son of man*. By this name he commonly designated himself. There can be no doubt that *that* was assumed to denote that he was a man, that he sustained a peculiar relation to man, and that he chose to speak of himself *as* a man. The first, the most obvious, impression on the use of the name *Son of man* is that he was *truly a man*, and it was used doubtless to guard against the impression that one who manifested so many *other* qualities, and did so many things like a celestial being, was *not* truly a human being. The phrase *Son of God* stands in contrast with the title *Son of man*, and as the *natural* and *obvious* import of that is that he was *a man*, so the *natural* and *obvious* import of the title *Son of God* is that he was divine; *or that he sustained relations to God designated by the name* SON OF GOD, *corresponding to the relations which he sustained to man designated by the name* SON OF MAN. The natural idea of the term Son of God therefore is, that he sustained a relation to God in his nature which implied more than was human or angelic; which implied *equality* with God Accordingly, this idea was naturally suggested to the Jews by his calling God his Father; John v. 18, "But said also that God was his Father, *making himself equal with God*." This idea Jesus immediately proceeded to confirm; see Note, John v. 19—30. The same idea is also suggested in John x. 29—31, 33, 36, "Say ye of him whom the Father hath sanctified, and sent into the world, Thou blasphemest: *because I said I am the Son of God?*" There is in these places the fullest proof that the title suggested *naturally* the idea of equality with God; or the idea of his sustaining a relation to God corresponding to the relation of equality to man suggested by the title Son of man. This view is still further sustained in the first chapter of the epistle to the Hebrews, ver. 1, 2, "God hath spoken unto us BY HIS SON." He is *the brightness of his glory*, and the *express image of his person*, ver. 3. He is higher than the angels, and they are required to worship him, ver. 4—6. He is called *God*, and his throne is for ever and ever, ver. 8. He is *the Creator of the heavens and the earth*, and is IMMUTABLY THE SAME, ver. 10—12. Thus the rank or title of *the Son of God* suggests the ideas and attributes of the Divinity. This idea is sustained throughout the New Testament. See John xiv. 9, "He that hath seen me hath seen the Father;" ver. 23, "That all men shall honour the Son even as they honour the Father;" Col. i. 19, "It hath pleased the Father that in him should all fulness dwell;" ii. 9, "For in him dwelleth all the fulness of the Godhead bodily:" Phil. ii. 2—11; Rev. v. 13, 14; ii. 23. It is not affirmed that this title was given to the second person of the Trinity *before* he became *incarnate;* or to suggest the idea of any *derivation* or *extraction* before he was made flesh. There is no instance in which the appellation is not conferred to express his relation *after* he assumed human flesh. Of any *derivation* from God, or emanation from him in eternity, the Scriptures are silent. The title is conferred on him, it is supposed, with reference to his condition in this world, as the Messiah. And it is conferred, it is believed, for the following reasons, or to denote the following things, viz. (1.) To designate his peculiar relation to God, as equal with him, (John i. 14,

18; Mat. xi. 27; Luke x. 22; iii. 22; 2 Pet. i. 17), or as sustaining a most intimate and close connection with him, such as neither man nor angels could do, an acquaintance with his nature (Mat. xi. 27), plans, and counsels, such as no being but one who was *equal* with God *could* possess. In this sense, I regard it as conferred on him in the passage under consideration. (2.) It designates him as the anointed king, or the Messiah. In this sense it accords with the use of the word in Ps. lxxxii. 6. See Mat. xvi. 16, "Thou art *the Christ, the Son of the living God.*" Mat. xxvi. 63, "I adjure thee by the living God, that thou tell us whether thou *be the Christ, the Son of God.*" Mark xiv. 61; Luke xxii. 70; John i. 34; Acts ix. 20, "He preached *Christ* in the synagogues, that *he is the Son of God.*" (3.) It was conferred on him to denote his miraculous conception in the womb of the Virgin Mary. Luke i. 35, "The Holy Ghost shall come upon thee, THEREFORE (διὸ) also that holy thing which shall be born of thee shall be called *the Son of God.*"

[It is readily admitted, that on the subject of the *eternal Sonship* very much has been said of an unintelligible kind. Terms applicable only to the relation as it exists among men have been freely applied to this mystery. But whatever may be thought of such language as "the eternal generation," "the eternal procession," and "the subordination" of the Son; the doctrine itself, which this mode of speaking was invented to illustrate, and has perhaps served to obscure, is in no way affected. The question is not, Have the friends of the doctrine at all times employed judicious illustration? but, What is the *Scripture evidence* on the point? If the eternal Sonship is to be discarded on such grounds, we fear the doctrine of the Trinity must share a similar fate. Yet, those who maintain the divinity of Christ, and notwithstanding deny the eternal Sonship, seem generally to found their objections on these incomprehensible illustrations, and from thence leap to the conclusion that the doctrine itself is false.

That the title Son of God, when applied to Jesus, denotes a *natural* and not merely an *official* Sonship, a *real* and not a *figurative* relation; in other words, that it takes origin from the divine nature, is the view which the Catholic Church has all along maintained on this subject: no explanation which falls short of divinity will exhaust the meaning of the title. Christ is indeed called the Son of God on account of his miraculous conception; "That holy thing," said the angel to the Virgin, "which shall be born of thee, shall be called *the Son of the Highest.*" But the creation of Adam, by the immediate power of God, without father or mother, would constitute *him* the Son of God, in a sense *equally* or even *more exalted* than that in which the title is applied to Jesus, if the miraculous conception were allowed to exhaust its meaning. Nor will an appeal to the *resurrection of Christ* serve the purpose of those who deny the divine origin of the title, since *that* is assigned as the *evidence only*, and not the *ground* of it. The Redeemer was not *constituted*, but "*declared*" or *evidenced to be*, "the Son of God with power by the resurrection from the dead." In the search for a solution short of divine Sonship, recourse is next had to the office of Christ as Mediator. Yet though the appellation in question be frequently given in connection with the official character of Jesus, a careful examination of some of these passages will lead to the conclusion, that *though the Son of God hold the office, yet the office does not furnish the reason or ground of the title.* The name is given to distinguish Jesus from all others who have held office, and *in such a way as to convince us that the office is rendered honourable by the exalted personage discharging its duties, and not that the person merits the designation in virtue of the office.* "When the fulness of the time was come, God sent forth *his Son*, made of a woman," &c. "God so loved the world that he gave *his only begotten Son*," &c. Now the glory of the mission in the first of these passages, and the greatness of the gift in the second, is founded on the *original dignity* of the person sent and given. But if the person derive his title from the office only, there would seem to be comparatively little grandeur in the mission, and small favour in the gift. The passages quoted would more readily prove that God had bestowed favour on Jesus, by giving *him* an office from which he derived so much personal dignity!

The following are some of the passages in which the appellation "Son of God" is found connected with the office of Christ. "These are written that ye might believe that Jesus is the Christ, (an official term signifying anointed Saviour,) the Son of God;" "He answered and said, I believe that Jesus Christ (the official designation) is the Son of God;" "Whom say ye that I am? And Simon Peter answered and said, Thou art the Christ, the Son of the living God." Now it is reasonable to suppose, that these declarations and confessions concerning the person of Christ, contain not only an acknowledgment of his official character, but also of his personal dignity. "Thou art Jesus the Christ," is the acknowledgment of his office, and "thou art the Son of God," is an acknowledgment of his natural dignity. The confession of the Ethiopian eunuch, and of Peter, would be incomplete on any other supposition. It should be borne in mind also, that the question of Christ to Peter was not, What office do ye suppose I hold? but, "Whom say ye that *I am?*" *See Haldane on* Rom. i. 4.

If, then. the miraculous conception, the resurrection, and the office of Christ, do not all of them together exhaust the meaning of the appellation, we must seek for its origin higher still—we must ascend to the divine nature. We may indeed take one step more upwards before we reach the divine nature, and suppose, with Professor Stuart and others, that the name denotes "the complex person of the Saviour," as God and man, or in one word, Mediator. *Comment on Heb. Exe.* 2. But this is just the old resolution of it into official character, and is therefore liable to all the objections stated above. For while it is admitted by those who hold this view, that Christ is divine, it is distinctly implied, that the title Son of God would not have been his *but for his office*.

In the end therefore we must resolve the name into the divine nature. That it implies *equality* with God is clearly proved in this commentary. So the Jews understood it, and the Saviour tacitly admitted that their construction was right. And as there is no equality with God without divinity, the title clearly points to such a *distinction* in the Godhead as is implied in the relative terms, Father and Son. Indeed it is not easy to understand how the doctrine of the Trinity can be maintained apart from that of the eternal Sonship. If there be in the Godhead a distinction of persons, does not that distinction belong to the *nature* of the Godhead, independent of any *official* relations. Or will it be maintained, that the distinction of Father, Son, and Holy Ghost, arises entirely from the scheme of redemption, and did not exist from eternity? We may find fault with Dr Owen, and others, who speak of a "hypostatical subordination of persons in the Godhead." *Prof. Stuart, Com. Heb. Exe.* 1. Yet, *the distinction* itself, though we cannot explain it, *must* be allowed to exist.

The remaining evidence of the eternal Sonship may be thus stated.

1. Christ is called God's "own Son," his "beloved," and "well beloved," and "only begotten Son.' So strong and peculiar adjuncts seem intended to prevent any *such* idea as that of *figurative* Sonship. If these do not express the *natural* relationship, it is beyond the power of language to do it. Moreover, correct criticism binds us to adopt the natural and ordinary signification of words, unless in such cases as plainly refuse it.

2. In a passage already quoted, God is said "to have sent *forth His Son* to redeem us," &c. And there are many passages to the same effect, in which is revealed, not only the pre-existence of Christ, but the *capacity in which* he *originally moved*, and the *rank* which he held in heaven. "God sent *forth* his Son," implies that he held that title *prior* to his mission. This at least is the most obvious sense of the passage, and the sense which an ordinary reader would doubtless affix to it. The following objection, however, has been supposed fatal to this argument: "The name Son of God is indeed used, when speaking of him previous to his having assumed human nature, but so are the names of Jesus and the Christ, which yet we know properly to belong to him, only as united to humanity." It is readily allowed that the *simple fact* of the name being given *prior* to the incarnation proves nothing of itself. But the case is altered when this fact is viewed in connection with the difficulty or impossibility of resolving the Sonship into an official relation. No such difficulty exists in regard to the terms "Jesus" and "Christ," for they are *plainly* official names, signifying "anointed Saviour."

3. Rom. i. 3, 4. If in this passage we understand the apostle to declare, that Christ was *of the* seed of David, *according to his human nature*, the rule of antithesis demands, that we understand him next to assert what he was *according to his divine nature*, viz. the Son of God.

The views given in this Note are those adopted by the most eminent orthodox divines. The language of the Westminster divines is well known; "The only Redeemer of the covenant of grace is the Lord Jesus Christ, who *being the eternal Son of God*, of one substance &c." *Larger Catechism.* Mr Scott "is decidedly of opinion, that Christ is called the only Son of God *in respect of his divine nature.*" *Comment. Heb.* i. 3, 4. The late Principal Hill, in his Theological System, having exposed what he deemed erroneous views on this subject, adds, "there is a more ancient and a more exalted title to this name, (Son of God,) which is inseparable from the *nature* of Christ." *3d edit. vol. i., page* 363.]

¶ *With power,* ἐν δυνάμει. By some, this expression has been supposed to mean *in* power or authority, *after* his resurrection from the dead. It is said, that he was before a man of sorrows; now he was clothed with power and authority. But I have seen no instance in which the expression *in power* denotes *office*, or authority. It denotes *physical* energy and might, and this was bestowed on Jesus *before* his resurrection as well as after; Acts x. 38, "God anointed Jesus of Nazareth with the Holy Ghost, and *with power;*" Rom. xv. 19; 1 Cor. xv. 43. With *such* power Jesus will come to judgment; Mat. xxiv. 30. If there is any passage in which the word *power* means authority, office, &c., it is Mat. xxviii. 18, "All power in heaven and earth is given unto me." But this is not a power which was given unto him *after* his resurrection, or which he did not possess before. The same authority to commission his disciples he had exercised *before* this on the same ground, Mat. x. 7, 8. I am inclined to believe, therefore, that the expression means *powerfully, efficiently;* he was with great power, or conclusiveness, shown to be the Son of God by his resurrection from the dead. Thus the phrase *in power* is used to qualify a verb in Col. i. 29, "Which worketh in me *mightily,*" *Greek,* in power, *i. e.* operating in me effectually, or powerfully. The ancient versions seem to have understood it in the same way. *Syriac,* "He was known to be the Son of God by power, and by the Holy Ghost." *Æthiopic,* "Whom he declared to be the Son of God by his own power, and by his Holy Spirit," &c. *Arabic,* "Designated the Son of God by power appropriate to the Holy Spirit." ¶ *According to the spirit of holiness,* Κατὰ πνεῦμα ἁγιωσύνης. This expression has been variously understood. We may arrive at its meaning by the following considerations. (1.) It is not the third person in the Trinity that is referred to here. The designation of that person is *always* in a different form. It is *the Holy Spirit,* the Holy Ghost, πνεῦμα ἅγιον, or τὸ πνεῦμα τὸ ἅγιον; never *the spirit of holiness.* (2.) It stands in contrast with *the flesh*; ver. 3, "According to the flesh, the seed of David: according to the spirit of holiness, the Son of God." As the former refers doubtless to his human nature, so this must refer to the nature designated by the title Son of God, that is, to his superior or divine nature. (3.) The expression is altogether peculiar to the Lord Jesus Christ. No where in the Scriptures, or in any other writings, is there an affirmation like this. What would be meant by it if affirmed of a mere man? (4.) It cannot mean that the Holy Spirit, the third person in the Trinity, showed that Jesus was the Son of God by raising him from the dead, because that act is no where attributed to him. It is uniformly ascribed either to God, *as God* (Acts ii. 24, 32; iii. 15, 26; iv. 10; v. 30; x. 40; xiii. 30, 33, 34; xvii. 31; Rom. x. 9; Eph. i. 20), or to the Father (Rom. vi. 4), or to Jesus himself (John x. 18). In no instance is this act ascribed to the Holy Ghost. (5.) It indicates a state far more elevated than any human dignity, or honour. In regard to his earthly descent, he was of a royal race; in regard to the Spirit of holiness, much more than that, he was the Son of God. (6.) The word *Spirit* is used often to designate God, the holy God, as distinguished from all the *material* forms of idol worship, John iv. 24. (7.) The word Spirit is applied to the Messiah, in his more elevated or divine nature. 1 Cor. xv. 45, "The last Adam was made a quickening Spirit." 2 Cor. iii. 17, "Now the Lord (Jesus) is that Spirit." Heb. ix. 14, Christ is said to have offered himself *through the eternal Spirit.*" 1 Pet. iii. 18, he is said to have been "put to death in the flesh, but quickened by the Spirit." 1 Tim. iii. 16, he is said to have been "justified in the Spirit." In most of these passages there is the same contrast noticed between *his flesh,* his human nature, and his other state, which occurs in Rom. i. 3, 4. In all these instances, the design is, doubtless, to speak of him *as a man,* and as something more than a man: he was one thing as a man; he was another thing in his other nature. In the one, he was of David; was put to death, &c. In the other, he was of God, he was manifested to be such, he was restored to the elevation which he had sustained before his incarnation and death, John xvii. 1—5; Phil. ii. 2—11. The expression, *according to the Spirit of holiness,* does not indeed of itself imply divinity. It denotes that *holy* and more *exalted nature* which he possessed as distinguished from the human. What that is, is to be learned from other declarations. *This expression implies simply that it was such as to make proper the appellation, the Son of God.* Other places, as we have seen, show that *that* designation naturally implied divinity. And that this was the true idea couched under the expression, *according to the Spirit of holiness,* appears from those numerous texts of scripture which explicitly assert his divinity; see John i. 1, &c., and the Note on that place. ¶ *By the resurrection from the dead.* This has been also variously understood. Some have maintained that the word *by,* ἐξ, denotes AFTER. He was declared to be the Son of God *in* power *after* he rose from the dead; that is, he was solemnly invested with the dignity that became the Son of God after he had been so long in a state of voluntary humiliation. But to this view there are some insuperable objections. (1.) It is not the natural and usual meaning of the word *by.* (2.) It is not the object of the apostle to state the *time* when the thing was done, or the *order,* but evidently to declare the *fact,* and the evidence of the fact. If such had been his design, he would have said that *previous* to his death he was *shown* to be of the seed of David, but *afterwards* that he was invested with power. (3.) Though it must be admitted that the preposition *by,* ἐξ, sometimes means AFTER (Mat. xix. 20; Luke viii. 27; xxiii. 8, &c.), yet its proper and usual meaning is to denote the efficient cause, or the agent, or origin of a thing, Mat. i. 3, 18; xxi. 25; John iii. 5; Rom. v. 16; xi. 36, "OF him are all things." 1 Cor. viii. 6, "One God, the Father, OF whom are all things," &c. In this sense, I suppose it is used here; and that the apostle means to affirm that he was *clearly* or *decisively* shown to be the Son of God *by* his resurrection from the dead. But here will it be asked, *how* did his *resurrection* show this? Was not Lazarus raised from the dead? And did not many saints rise also after Jesus? And were not the dead raised by the apostles; by Elijah, by the bones of Elisha, and by Christ himself? And did *their* being raised prove that they were the sons of God? I answer that the mere fact of the *resurrection* of the body proves nothing *in itself* about the character and rank of the being that is raised. But *in the circumstances* in which Jesus was placed it might show it conclusively. When Lazarus was raised, it was not in attestation of any thing which he had taught or done. It was a mere display of the power and benevolence of Christ. But in regard to the resurrection of Jesus, let the following circumstances be taken into the account. (1.) He came as the Messiah. (2.) He uniformly taught that he was the Son of God. (3.) He maintained that God was his Father in such a sense as to imply equality with him, John v. 17—30; x. 36. (4.) He claimed authority to abolish the laws of the Jews, to change their customs, and to be himself absolved from the observance of those laws, even as his Father was, John v. 1—17; Mark ii. 28. (5.) When God raised *him* up therefore, it was not an ordinary event. It was *a public attestation, in the face of the universe, of the truth of his claims to be the Son of God.* God would not sanction the doings and doctrines of an impostor. And when, therefore he raised up Jesus, he, by this act, showed the truth of his claims, that he was the Son of God. Further, in the view of the apostles, the *resurrection* was intimately connected with the *ascension* and *exaltation* of Jesus. The one made the other certain. And it is not improbable that when they spoke of his resurrection, they meant to include, not merely that single act, but the entire series of doings of which that was the *first,* and which was the *pledge* of the elevation and majesty of the Son of God. Hence, when they had proved his *resurrection,* they *assumed* that all the others would follow. That involved and supposed all. And the *series,* of which that was the first, *proved* that he was the Son of God; see Acts xvii. 31, "He will judge the world in righteousness, by that man whom he hath ordained, whereof he hath given ASSURANCE to all men, *in that he hath raised him from the dead.*" The one involves the other; see Acts i. 6. Thus Peter (Acts ii. 22—32) having proved that

ing to the spirit [a] of holiness, by the resurrection from the dead:

5 By whom we have received grace and apostleship, [1] for obedience [b] to the faith among all nations, for his name:

a Heb.9.14.

1 or, *to the obedience of faith.* b Ac.6.7; chap.16.26.

Jesus was raised up, adds, ver. 33, "THEREFORE, being by the right hand exalted, he hath shed forth this," &c.; and ver. 36, "THEREFORE, let all the house of Israel KNOW ASSUREDLY that God hath made that same Jesus whom ye have crucified, BOTH LORD AND CHRIST."

This verse is a remarkable instance of the apostle Paul's manner of writing. Having mentioned a subject, his mind seems to catch fire; he presents it in new forms, and amplifies it, until he seems to forget for a time the subject on which he was writing. It is from this cause that his writings abound so with parentheses, and that there is so much difficulty in following and understanding him.

5. *By whom.* The apostle here returns to the subject of the salutation of the Romans, and states to them his authority to address them. That authority he had derived from the Lord Jesus, and not from man. On this fact, that he had received his apostolic commission, not from man, but by the direct authority of Jesus Christ, Paul not unfrequently insisted. Gal. i. 12, "For I neither received it of man, neither was I taught it, but by revelation of Jesus Christ;" 1 Cor. xv. 1—8; Eph. iii. 1—3. ¶ *We.* The plural here is probably put for the singular; see Col. iv. 3; comp. Eph. vi. 19, 20. It was usual for those who were clothed with authority to express themselves in this manner. Perhaps here, however, he refers to the general nature of the apostolic office, as being derived from Jesus Christ, and designs to assure the Romans that *he* had received the apostolic commission as the others had. '*We*, the apostles, have received the appointment from Jesus Christ.' ¶ *Grace and apostleship.* Many suppose that this is a figure of speech, *hendiadys*, by which one thing is expressed by two words, meaning the grace or favour of the apostolic office. Such a figure of speech is often used. But it may mean, as it does probably here, the two things, *grace*, or the favour of God to his own soul, as a personal matter; and the apostolic office as a distinct thing. He often, however, speaks of the office of the apostleship as a matter of special favour, Rom. xv. 15, 16; Gal. ii. 9; Eph. iii. 7—9. ¶ *For obedience to the faith.* In order to produce, or promote obedience to the faith; that is, to induce them to render that obedience to God which *faith* produces. There are two things therefore implied. (1.) That the design of the gospel and of the apostleship is to induce men to *obey* God. (2.) That the tendency of *faith* is to produce obedience. There is no true faith which does not produce that. This is constantly affirmed in the New Testament, Rom. xv. 18; xvi. 19; 2 Cor vii. 15; Jam. ii. ¶ *Among all nations.* This was the original commission which Jesus gave to his apostles, Mark xvi. 15, 16; Mat. xxviii. 18, 19. This was the special commission which Paul received when he was converted, Acts ix. 15. It was important to show that the commission extended thus far, as he was now addressing a distant church which he had not seen. ¶ *For his name.* This means probably *on his account*, that is, on account of Christ, John xiv. 13, 14; xvi. 23, 24. The design of the apostleship was to produce obedience to the gospel among all nations, that *thus* the name of Jesus might be honoured. Their work was not one in which they were seeking to honour themselves, but it was solely for the honour and glory of Jesus Christ. For him they toiled, they encountered perils, they laid down their lives, because by so doing they might bring men to obey the gospel, and thus Jesus Christ might wear a brighter

6 Among whom are ye also the called of Jesus Christ:

7 To all that be in Rome, beloved of God, called [a] *to be* saints: Grace [b] to you, and peace, from God our Father, and the Lord Jesus Christ.

8 First, I thank my God through

a 1 Cor.1.2; 1 Th.4.7. *b* 1 Cor.1.3,&c.; 2 Pe.1.2.

crown, and be attended by a longer and more splendid train of worshippers in the kingdom of his glory.

6. *Among whom.* That is, among the Gentiles who had become obedient to the Christian faith in accordance with the design of the gospel, ver. 8. This proves that the church at Rome was made up *partly* at least, if not mainly, of Gentiles or pagans. This is fully proved in the xvith. chapter by the *names* of the persons whom Paul salutes. ¶ *The called of Jesus Christ.* Those whom Jesus Christ has called to be his followers. The word *called* (see ver. 1) denotes not merely an external invitation to a privilege, but it also denotes the *internal* or *effectual* call which secures conformity to the will of him who calls, and is thus synonymous with the name Christians, or believers. That true Christians are contemplated by this address, is clear from the whole scope of the epistle; see particularly chap. viii.; comp. Phil. iii. 14; Heb. iii. 1.

7. *To all that be in Rome.* That is, to all who bear the Christian name. Perhaps he here included not only *the church* at Rome, but all who might have been there from abroad. Rome was a place of vast concourse for foreigners; and Paul probably addressed all who happened to be there. ¶ *Beloved of God.* Whom God loves. This is the privilege of all Christians. And this proves that the persons whom Paul addressed were *not* those merely who had been invited to the external privileges of the gospel. The importance of this observation will appear in the progress of these Notes. ¶ *Called to be saints.* So called, or influenced by God who had called them, as to become saints. The word *saints,* ἅγιοι, means those who are holy, or those who are devoted or consecrated to God. The radical idea of the word is that which is separated from a common to a sacred use, and answers to the Hebrew word, קדוש, *kadosh.* It is applied to any thing that is set apart to the service of God, to the temple, to the sacrifices, to the utensils about the temple, to the garments, &c. of the priests, and to the priests themselves. It was applied to the Jews as a people *separated* from other nations, and devoted or consecrated to God, while other nations were devoted to the service of idols. It is also applied to Christians, as being a people devoted or set apart to the service of God. The *radical* idea then, as applied to Christians, is, that *they are separated from other men, and other objects and pursuits, and consecrated to the service of God.* This is the peculiar characteristic of the *saints.* And this characteristic the Roman Christians had shown. For the use of the word, as stated above, see the following passages of scripture; Luke ii. 23; Ex. xiii. 2, Rom. xi. 16; Mat. vii. 6; 1 Pet. i. 16; Acts ix. 13; 1 Pet. ii. 5; Acts iii. 21, Eph. iii. 5; 1 Pet. ii. 9; Phil. ii. 15; 1 John iii. 1, 2. ¶ *Grace.* This word properly means *favour.* It is very often used in the New Testament, and is employed in the sense of benignity or benevolence; felicity, or a prosperous state of affairs; the Christian religion, as the highest expression of the benevolence or favour of God; the happiness which Christianity confers on its friends in this and the future life; the apostolic office; charity, or alms; thanksgiving; joy, or pleasure; and the benefits produced on the Christian's heart and life by religion—the grace of meekness, patience, charity, &c., *Schleusner.* In this place, and in similar places in the beginning of the apostolic epistles, it seems to be a word including *all* those blessings that are applicable to Christians in common; denoting an ardent wish that *all* the mercies and favours of God for time

Jesus Christ for you all, that your
faith [a] is spoken of throughout the
whole world.

9 For God is my witness, whom
[b] I serve with [1] my spirit in the gospel of his Son, that without ceas-

a chap.16.19. *b* Ac.27.23. 1 or, *in*.

and eternity, *blended* under the general name *grace*, may be conferred on them. It is to be understood as connected with a word implying invocation. I *pray*, or I desire, that *grace*, &c. may be conferred on you. It is the customary form of salutation in nearly all the apostolic epistles; 1 Cor. i. 3; 2 Cor. i. 2; Gal. i. 3; Eph. i. 2; Phil. i. 2; Col. i. 2; 1 Thess. i. 1; 2 Thess. i. 2; Philem. 3. ¶ *And peace. Peace* is the state of freedom from war. As war conveys the idea of discord and numberless calamities and dangers, so peace is the opposite, and conveys the idea of concord, safety, and prosperity. Thus, to wish one *peace* was the same as to wish him all safety and prosperity. This form of salutation was common among the Hebrews. Gen. xliii. 23, "Peace to you! fear not;" Judg. vi. 23; xix. 20; Luke xxiv. 36. But the word *peace* is also used in contrast with that state of agitation and conflict which a sinner has with his conscience, and with God. The sinner is like the troubled sea, which cannot rest, Isa. lvii. 20. The Christian is at peace with God through the Lord Jesus Christ, Rom. v. 1. By this word, denoting reconciliation with God, the blessings of the Christian religion are often described in the scriptures, Rom. viii. 6; xiv. 17; xv. 13; Gal. v. 22; Phil. iv. 7. A prayer for peace, therefore, in the epistles, is not a mere formal salutation, but has a special reference to those *spiritual* blessings which result from reconciliation with God through the Lord Jesus Christ. ¶ *From God our Father.* The Father of all Christians. He is the Father of all his creatures, as they are his offspring, Acts xvii. 28, 29. He is especially the Father of all Christians, as they have been "begotten by him to a lively hope," have been adopted into his family, and are like him; Mat. v. 45; 1 Pet. i. 3; 1 John v. 1; iii. 1, 2. The expression here is equivalent to a *prayer* that God the Father *would* bestow grace and peace on the Romans. It implies that these blessings proceed from God, and are to be expected from him. ¶ *And the Lord Jesus Christ. From* him. The Lord Jesus Christ is especially regarded in the New Testament as the source of *peace*, and the procurer of it; see Luke ii. 14; xix. 38, 42; John xiv. 27; xvi. 33; Acts x. 36; Rom. v. 1; Eph. ii. 17. Each of these places will show with what propriety *peace* was invoked from the Lord Jesus. From thus connecting the Lord Jesus with the Father in this place, we may see, (1.) That the apostle regarded *him* as the source of grace and peace as *really* as he did the Father. (2.) He introduced them in the same connection, and with reference to the bestowment of the same blessings. (3.) If the mention of the Father in this connection implies a *prayer* to him, or an act of worship, the mention of the Lord Jesus implies the same thing, and was an act of homage to him. (4.) All this shows that *his* mind was *familiarized* to the idea that he was divine. No man would introduce his name in such connections if he did not believe that he was equal with God; comp. Phil. ii. 2—11. It is from this *incidental* and *unstudied* manner of expression, that we have one of the most striking proofs of the manner in which the sacred writers regarded the Lord Jesus Christ.

These seven verses are one sentence. They are a striking instance of the manner of Paul. The subject is simply a salutation to the Roman church. But at the mention of some single words, the mind of Paul seems to catch fire, and to burn and blaze with signal intensity. He leaves the immediate subject before him, and advances some vast thought that awes us, and fixes us in contemplation, and

ing *a* I make mention of you always in my prayers;

10 Making request if by any means now at length I might have

a 1 Thess.3.10.

involves us in difficulty about his meaning, and then returns to his subject. This is the characteristic of his great mind; and it is this, among other things, that makes it so difficult to interpret his writings.

8. *First.* In the first place, not in point of importance, but before speaking of other things, or before proceeding to the main design of the epistle. ¶ *I thank my God.* The God whom I worship and serve. The expression of thanks to God for his mercy to them was fitted to conciliate their feelings, and to prepare them for the truths which he was about to communicate to them. It showed the deep interest which he had in their welfare; and the happiness it would give him to do them good. It is proper to give thanks to God for his mercies to others as well as to ourselves. We are members of one great family, and we should make it a subject of thanksgiving that he confers any blessings, and especially the blessing of salvation, on any mortals. ¶ *Through Jesus Christ.* The duty of presenting our thanks to God *through* Christ is often enjoined in the New Testament, Eph. v. 20; Heb. xiii. 15; comp. John xiv. 14. Christ is the *mediator* between God and men, or the *medium* by which we are to present our prayers and also our thanksgivings. We are not to approach God *directly,* but *through* a mediator at all times, depending on him to present our cause before the mercy-seat; to plead for us there; and to offer the desires of our souls to God. It is no less proper to present *thanks* in his name, or through him, than it is *prayer.* He has made the way to God accessible to us, whether it be by prayer or praise; and it is owing to *his* mercy and grace that *any* of our services are acceptable to God. ¶ *For you all.* On account of you all, *i. e.* of the entire Roman church. This is one evidence that that church then was remarkably pure. How few churches have there been of whom a similar commendation could be expressed. ¶ *That your faith. Faith* is put here for the whole of religion, and means the same as your piety. Faith is one of the principal things of religion; one of its first requirements; and hence it signifies religion itself. The readiness with which the Romans had embraced the gospel, the firmness with which they adhered to it, was so remarkable, that it was known and celebrated every where. The same thing is affirmed of them in chap. xvi. 19, "For your obedience is come abroad unto all men." ¶ *Is spoken of.* Is celebrated, or known. They were in the capital of the Roman empire; in a city remarkable for its wickedness; and in a city whose influence extended every where. It was natural, therefore, that their remarkable conversion to God should be celebrated every where. The religious or irreligious influence of a great city will be felt far and wide, and this is one reason why the apostles preached the gospel so much in such places. ¶ *Throughout the whole world.* As we say, every where; or throughout the Roman empire. The term *world* is often thus limited in the scriptures; and here it denotes those parts of the Roman empire where the Christian church was established. All the churches would hear of the work of God in the capital, and would rejoice in it; comp. Col. i. 6, 23; John xii. 19. It is not improper to *commend* Christians, and to remind them of their influence; and especially to call to their mind the great power which they may have on other churches and people. Nor is it improper that great displays of divine mercy should be celebrated every where, and excite in the churches praise to God.

9. *For God is my witness.* The reason of this strong appeal to God is, to show to the Romans the deep interest which he felt in their welfare

a prosperous journey by [a] the will
of God to come unto you.

a Jam.4.15.

11 For I long to see you, that
[c] I may impart unto you some

b chap.15.23,32. c chap.15.29.

This interest was manifested in his prayers, and in his earnest desires to see them. A deep interest shown in this way was well fitted to prepare them to receive what he had to say to them. ¶ *Whom I serve;* see ver. 1; comp. Acts xvii. 23. The expression denotes that he was devoted to God in this manner; that he obeyed him; and had given himself to do his will in making known his gospel. ¶ *With my spirit.* Greek, ἐν, *in* my spirit, *i. e.* with my *heart.* It is not an external service merely; it is internal, real, sincere. He was really and sincerely devoted to the service of God. ¶ *In the gospel of his Son.* In making known the gospel, or as a minister of the gospel. ¶ *That without ceasing.* ἀδιαλείπτως. This word means constantly, always, without intermission. It was not only *once,* but repeatedly. It had been the burden of his prayers. The same thing he also mentions in regard to other churches, 1 Thess. i. 3; ii. 13. ¶ *I make mention.* I call you to remembrance, and present your case before God. This evinced his remarkable interest in a church which he had never seen, and it shows that Paul was a man of prayer; praying not for his friends and kindred only, but for those whom he had never seen. If with the same intensity of prayer all Christians, and Christian ministers, would remember the churches, what a different aspect would the Christian church soon assume! ¶ *Always.* This word should be connected with the following verse, "Always making request," &c.

10. *Making request.* It was his earnest desire to see them, and he presented the subject before God. ¶ *If by any means.* This shows the earnest desire which he had to see them, and implies that he had designed it, and had been hindered; see ver. 13. ¶ *Now at length.* He had purposed it a long time, but had been hindered. He doubtless cherished this purpose for years. The expressions in the Greek imply an earnest wish that this long-cherished purpose might be accomplished before long. ¶ *A prosperous journey.* A safe, pleasant journey. It is right to regard all success in travelling as depending on God, and to pray for success and safety from danger. Yet all such prayers are not answered according to the *letter* of the petition. The prayer of Paul that he might see the Romans was granted, but in a remarkable way. He was persecuted by the Jews, and arraigned before king Agrippa. He appealed to the Roman emperor, and was taken there in chains as a prisoner. Yet the journey *might* in this way have a more deep effect on the Romans, than if he had gone in any other way. In so mysterious a manner does God often hear the prayers of his people; and though their prayers *are* answered, yet it is in his own time and way; see the last chapters of the Acts. ¶ *By the will of God.* If God shall grant it; if God will by his mercy grant me the great favour of my coming to you. This is a proper model of a prayer; and is in accordance with the direction of the Bible; see Jam. iv. 14, 15.

11. *For I long to see you.* I earnestly desire to see you; comp. chap. xv. 23, 32. ¶ *That I may impart.* That I may *give,* or communicate to you. ¶ *Some spiritual gift.* Some have understood this as referring to *miraculous gifts,* which it was supposed the apostles had the power of conferring on others. But this interpretation is forced and unnatural. There is no instance where this expression denotes the power of working miracles. Besides, the apostle in the next verse explains his meaning, "That I may be comforted together *by the mutual faith,*" &c. From this it appears that he desired to be among them to exercise the office of the ministry, to establish them in the gospel,

spiritual gift, to the end you may be established:

12 That is, that I may be comforted together with [1] you by the mutual [a] faith both of you and me.

13 Now I would not have you ignorant, brethren, that oftentimes I purposed to come unto you, (but was let hitherto,) that I might have some fruit [2] among

1 or, *in*. a 2 Pet.1.1.

2 or, *in*.

and to confirm their hopes. He expected that the preaching of the gospel would be the means of confirming them in the faith; and he desired to be the means of doing it. It was a wish of benevolence, and accords with what he says respecting his intended visit in chap. xv. 29, "And I am sure that when I come, I shall come in the fullness of the blessing of the gospel of Christ." To make known to them more fully the blessings of the gospel, and *thus* to impart spiritual gifts, was the design he had in view. ¶ *To the end*, &c. With the design, or purpose. ¶ *Ye may be established*. That is, that they might be *confirmed* in the truths of the gospel. This was one design of the ministry, that Christians may be established, or strengthened, Eph. iv. 13. It is not to have dominion over their faith, but to be "helpers of their joy," 2 Cor. i. 24. Paul did not doubt that this part of his office might be fulfilled among the Romans, and he was desirous there also of making full proof of his ministry. His wish was to preach not simply where he *must*, but where he *might*. This is the nature of this work.

12. *That I may be comforted*, &c. It was not merely to confirm *them* that Paul wished to come. He sought the communion of saints; he expected to be *himself* edified and strengthened: and to be comforted by seeing their strength of faith, and their rapid growth in grace. We may remark here, (1.) That one effect of religion is to produce the desire of the communion of saints. It is the nature of Christianity to seek the society of those who are the friends of Christ. (2.) Nothing is better fitted to produce growth in grace than such communion. Every Christian should have one or more Christian friends to whom he may unbosom himself. No small part of the difficulties which young Christians experience would vanish, if they should communicate their feelings and views to others. Feelings which *they* suppose no Christians ever had, which greatly distress them, they will find are common among those who are experienced in the Christian life. (3.) There is nothing better fitted to excite the feelings, and confirm the hopes of Christian ministers, than the firm faith of young converts, of those just commencing the Christian life, 3 John 4. (4.) The apostle did not disdain to be taught by the humblest Christians. He expected to be strengthened himself by the faith of those just beginning the Christian life. "There is none so poor in the church of Christ, that he cannot make some addition of importance to our stores," *Calvin*.

13. *That oftentimes I purposed;* see ver. 10. How often he had purposed this we have no means of ascertaining. The fact, however, that he had done it, showed his strong desire to see them, and to witness the displays of the grace of God in the capital of the Roman world; comp. chap. xv. 23, 24. One *instance* of his having purposed to go to Rome is recorded in Acts xix. 21, "After these things were ended (viz. at Ephesus), Paul purposed in the spirit, when he had passed through Macedonia and Achaia to go to Jerusalem; saying, After I have been there, I must also see Rome." This purpose expressed in this manner in the *epistle*, and the *Acts* of the Apostles, has been shown by Dr. Paley (Horæ Paulinæ on Rom. i. 13) to be one of those *undesigned coincidences* which strongly show that both books are genuine; comp. Rom. xv. 23, 24, with Acts xix. 21. A forger of these books would not have *thought* of such a contrivance

you also, even as among other Gentiles.

14 I am debtor [a] both to the Greeks and to the Barbarians, both to the wise and to the unwise.

15 So, as much as in me is, I

[a] 1 Cor.9.16.

as to *feign* such a purpose to go to Rome at that time, and to have mentioned it in that manner. Such coincidences are among the best proofs that can be demanded, that the writers did not intend to impose on the world; see Paley. ¶ *But was let hitherto.* The word "let" means to *hinder*, or to *obstruct*. In what way this was done we do not know, but it is probable that he refers to the various openings for the preaching of the gospel where he had been, and to the obstructions of various kinds from the enemies of the gospel to the fulfilment of his purposes. ¶ *That I might have some fruit among you.* That I might be the means of the conversion of sinners and of the edification of the church in the capital of the Roman empire. It was not curiosity to see the splendid capital of the world that prompted this desire; it was not the love of travel, and of roaming from clime to clime; it was the specific purpose of doing good to the souls of men. To *have fruit* means to obtain success in bringing men to the knowledge of Christ. Thus the Saviour said (John xv. 16), "I have chosen you, and ordained you that you should bring forth fruit, and that your fruit should remain."

14, 15. *I am debtor.* This does not mean that *they* had conferred any favour on *him*, which bound him to make this return, but that he was under *obligation* to preach the gospel to all to whom it was possible. This *obligation* arose from the favour that God had shown him in appointing him to this work. He was specially chosen as a vessel to bear the gospel to the Gentiles (Acts ix. 15; Rom. xi. 13), and he did not feel that he had discharged the obligation until he had made the gospel known as far as possible among all the nations of the earth. ¶ *To the Greeks.* This term properly denotes those who dwelt in Greece. But as the Greeks were the most polished people of antiquity, the term came to be synonymous with the polished, the refined, the wise, as opposed to barbarians. In this place it doubtless means the same as "the wise," and includes the Romans also, as it cannot be supposed that Paul would designate the Romans as barbarians. Besides, the Romans claimed an origin from Greece, and Dionysius Halicarnassus (book i.) shows that the Italian and Roman people were of Greek descent. ¶ *Barbarians.* All who were not included under the general name of Greeks. Thus Ammonius says that "all who were not Greeks were barbarians." This term *barbarian*, βάρβαρος, properly denotes one who speaks a foreign language, a foreigner, and the Greeks applied it to all who did not use their tongue; comp. 1 Cor. xiv. 11, "I shall be unto him that speaketh, *a barbarian*," &c. *i. e.* I shall speak a language which he cannot understand. The word did not, therefore, of necessity denote any rusticity of manners, or any want of refinement. ¶ *To the wise.* To those who esteemed themselves to be wise, or who boasted of their wisdom. The term is synonymous with "the Greeks," who prided themselves much in their wisdom. 1 Cor. i. 22, "The Greeks seek after wisdom;" comp. 1 Cor. i. 19; iii. 18, 19; iv. 10; 2 Cor. xi. 19. ¶ *Unwise.* Those who were regarded as the ignorant and unpolished part of mankind. The expression is equivalent to ours, 'to the learned and the unlearned.' It was an evidence of the proper spirit to be willing to preach the gospel to either. The gospel claims to have power to instruct all mankind, and they who are called to preach it, should be *able* to instruct those who esteem themselves to be wise, and who are endowed with science, learning, and talent; and they should be *willing* to labour to enlighten the most obscure, ignorant, and degraded portions of the race. This is the true spirit of the Christian ministry.

am ready to preach the gospel to you that are at Rome also.

16 For I am not ashamed [a] of the gospel of Christ: for it is

a Mark 8.38; 2 Tim.1.8.

15. *So, as much as in me is.* As far as opportunity may be offered, and according to my ability. ¶ *I am ready, &c.* I am prepared to preach among you, and to show the power of the gospel, even in the splendid metropolis of the world. He was not deterred by any fear; nor was he indifferent to their welfare; but he was under the direction of God, and as far as *he* gave him opportunity, he was ready to make known to them the gospel, as he had done at Antioch, Ephesus, Athens, and Corinth.

This closes the *introduction* or *preface* to the epistle. Having shown his deep interest in their welfare, he proceeds in the next verse to state to them the great doctrines of that gospel which he was desirous of proclaiming to them.

16. *For I am not ashamed, &c.* The Jews had cast him off, and regarded him as an apostate; and by the *wise* among the Gentiles he had been persecuted, and despised, and driven from place to place, and regarded as the filth of the world, and the offscouring of all things (1 Cor. iv. 13), but still he was not ashamed of the gospel. He had so firm a conviction of its value and its truth; he had experienced so much of its consolations; and had seen so much of its efficacy; that he was so far from being ashamed of it that he gloried in it as the power of God unto salvation. Men should be ashamed of crime and folly. They are ashamed of their own offences, and of the follies of their conduct, when they come to reflect on it. But they are not ashamed of that which they feel to be right, and of that which they know will contribute to their welfare, and to the benefit of their fellow-men. Such were the views of Paul about the gospel; and it is one of his favourite doctrines that they who believe on Christ shall not be ashamed, Rom. x. 11; v. 5; 2 Cor. vii. 14; 2 Tim. i. 12; Phil. i. 20; Rom. ix. 33; 2 Tim. i. 8; comp. Mark viii. 38; 1 Pet. iv. 16; 1 John ii. 28.

¶ *Of the gospel.* This word means the *good news*, or the glad intelligence; see Note, Mark i. 1. It is so called because it contains the glad annunciation that sin may be pardoned, and the soul saved. ¶ *Of Christ.* The good news respecting the Messiah; or which the Messiah has brought. The expression probably refers to the former, the good news which relates *to* the Messiah, to his character, advent, preaching, death, resurrection, and ascension. Though this was "to the Jews a stumbling-block, and to the Greeks foolishness," yet he regarded it as the only hope of salvation, and was ready to preach it even in the rich and splendid capital of the world. ¶ *The power of God.* This expression means that it is the way in which God exerts his power in the salvation of men. It is the efficacious or mighty plan, by which power goes forth to save, and by which all the obstacles of man's redemption are taken away. This expression implies, (1.) That it is God's plan, or *his* appointment. It is not the device of man. (2.) It is adapted to the end. It is fitted to overcome the obstacles in the way. It is not *merely* the instrument by which God exerts his power, but it has an inherent adaptedness to the end, it is *fitted* to accomplish salvation to man so that it may be denominated *power*. (3.) It is mighty, hence it is called power, and the power of God. It is not a feeble and ineffectual instrumentality, but it is "mighty to the pulling down of strong holds," 2 Cor x. 4, 5. It has shown its power as applicable to every degree of sin, to every combination of wickedness. It has gone against the sins of the world, and evinced its power to save sinners of all grades, and to overcome and subdue every mighty form of iniquity, comp. Jer. xxiii. 29, "Is not my word like as a fire? saith the Lord; and like a hammer *that* breaketh the rock in pieces?" 1 Cor. i. 18, "The preaching of the cross is to them that

the power [a] of God unto salvation, to every one that believeth; [b] to the Jew first, and also to the Greek.

17 For therein [a] is the righteousness of God revealed from faith to faith: as it is written, [b] The just shall live by faith.

a Jer.23.29; 1 Cor.1.18. *b* Mark 16.16. *c* Acts 3.26.

a chap.3.21,25. *b* Hab.2.4.

perish, foolishness, but unto us which are saved, it is the power of God." ¶ *Unto salvation.* This word means complete deliverance from sin and death, and all the foes and dangers that beset man. It cannot imply any thing less than eternal life. If a man should believe and then fall away, he could in no correct sense be said *to be saved.* And hence when the apostle declares that it is the power of God unto salvation "to *every one* that believeth," it implies that *all* who become believers "shall be kept by the power of God through faith unto salvation" (see 1 Pet. i. 5), and that none shall ever fall away and be lost. The apostle thus *commences* his discussion with one of the important doctrines of the Christian religion, the final preservation of the saints. He is not defending the gospel for any *temporary* object, or with any temporary hope. He looks *through* the system, and sees in it a plan for the complete and eternal recovery of *all* those who believe in the Lord Jesus Christ. When he says it is the power of God *unto* salvation, he means that it is the power of God for the *attainment* of salvation. This is the *end,* or the design of this exertion of power. ¶ *To every one that believeth.* Comp. Mark xvi. 16, 17. This expresses the condition, or the terms, on which salvation is conferred through the gospel. It is not indiscriminately to *all* men, whatever may be their character. It is only to those who confide or trust in it; and it *is* conferred on all who receive it in this manner. If this qualification is possessed, it bestows its blessings freely and fully. All men know what *faith* is. It is exercised when we confide in a parent, a friend, a benefactor. It is such a reception of a promise, a truth, or a threatening, as to suffer it to make its *appropriate* impression on the mind, and such as to lead us to act under its influence, or to act as we *should* on the supposition that it is true. Thus a sinner credits the threatenings of God, and fears. This is faith. He credits his promises, and hopes. This is faith. He feels that he is lost, and relies on Jesus Christ for mercy. This is faith. And, in general, faith is such an impression on the mind made by truth as to lead us to feel and act as if it were *true;* to have the *appropriate* feelings, and views, and conduct under the commands, and promises, and threatenings of God; see Note, Mark xvi. 16. ¶ *To the Jew first.* First *in order of time.* Not that the gospel was any more adapted to Jews than to others; but to them had been committed the oracles of God; the Messiah had come through them; they had had the law, the temple, and the service of God, and it was natural that the gospel should be proclaimed to them before it was to the Gentiles. This was the order in which the gospel was *actually* preached to the world, first to the Jews, and then to the Gentiles. Comp. Acts ii. and x; Mat. x. 6; Luke xxiv. 49; Acts xiii. 46, "It was necessary that the word of God should first have been spoken to you; but seeing ye put it from you, and judge yourselves unworthy of everlasting life, lo, we turn to the Gentiles." Comp. Mat. xxi. 43. ¶ *And also to the Greek.* To all who were not Jews, that is, to all the world. It was not confined in its intention or efficacy to any class or nation of men. It was *adapted* to all, and was designed to be extended to all.

17. *For.* This word implies that he is now about to give a *reason* for that which he had just said, a reason why he was not ashamed of the gospel of Christ. That reason is stated in

this verse. It embodies the *substance* of all that is contained in the epistle. It is the *doctrine* which he seeks to establish; and there is not perhaps a more important passage in the Bible than this verse; or one more difficult to be understood. ¶ *Therein.* In it, ἐν οὕτῳ, *i. e.* in the gospel. ¶ *Is the righteousness of God,* δικαιοσύνη Θεοῦ. There is not a more important expression to be found in the epistle than this. It is capable of only the following interpretations. (1.) Some have said that it means that the *attribute* of God which is denominated *righteousness* or *justice,* is here displayed. It has been supposed that this was the design of the gospel to make this known; or to evince his *justice* in his way of saving men. There is an important sense in which this is true (chap. iii. 26). But this does not seem to be the meaning in the passage before us. For, (*a*) The leading design of the gospel is not to evince the *justice* of God, or the attribute of *justice,* but the *love* of God; see John iii. 16; Eph. ii. 4; 2 Thess. ii. 16; 1 John iv. 8. (*b*) The attribute of *justice* is not that which is principally evinced in the gospel. It is rather mercy, *or mercy in a manner consistent with justice,* or that does not interfere with justice. (*c*) The passage, therefore, is not designed to teach simply that the righteousness of God, *as an attribute,* is brought forth in the gospel, or that the main idea is to reveal his justice.

(2.) A second interpretation which has been affixed to it is, to make it the same as *goodness,* the *benevolence* of God is revealed, &c. But to this there are still stronger objections. For (*a*) It does not comport with the design of the apostle's argument. (*b*) It is a departure from the established meaning of the word *justice,* and the phrase "the righteousness of God." (*c*) If this had been the design, it is remarkable that the usual words expressive of *goodness* or mercy had not been used. Another meaning, therefore, is to be sought as expressing the sense of the phrase.

(3.) The phrase *righteousness of God* is equivalent to *God's plan of justifying men; his scheme of declaring them just in the sight of the law; or of acquitting them from punishment, and admitting them to favour.* In this sense it stands opposed to *man's* plan of justification, *i. e.* by his own works: God's plan is by faith. The *way* in which that is done is revealed in the gospel. The object contemplated to be done is to treat men as if they were righteous. Man attempted to accomplish this by obedience to the law. The plan of God was to arrive at it by *faith.* Here the two schemes differ; and the great design of this epistle is to show that man cannot be justified on his own plan, to wit, by works; and that the plan of God is the only way, and a wise and glorious way of making man just in the eye of the law. No small part of the perplexity usually attending this subject will be avoided if it is remembered that the discussion in this epistle pertains to the question, "how can mortal man be just with God?" The apostle shows that it *cannot* be by works; and that it *can be* by faith. This *latter* is what he calls the *righteousness of God* which is revealed in the gospel.

To see that this is the meaning, it is needful only to look at the connection; and at the usual meaning of the words. The word to *justify,* δικαιόω, means properly *to be just, to be innocent, to be righteous.* It then means to *declare,* or treat as righteous; as when a man is charged with an offence, and is acquitted. If the crime alleged is not *proved* against him, he is declared by the law *to be innocent.* It then means to *treat as if innocent,* to *regard as innocent;* that is, to pardon, to forgive, and consequently to treat *as if* the offence had not occurred. It does not mean that the man *did not* commit the offence; or that the law might not have held him *answerable* for it; but that the offence is forgiven; and it is consistent to receive the offender into favour, and treat him *as if* he had not committed it. *In what way* this may be done rests with him who has the pardoning power. And in regard to the salvation of man, it rests solely with God, and must be done in that way only which he appoints and approves. The design of Paul in this epistle is to show *how* this is done, or to show that it *is* done by faith. It may be remarked here that the expression before us does not imply any particular *manner* in which it is done; it does not touch the question whether it is by imputed righteousness or not; it does not say that it is on legal principles; it simply affirms *that the gospel contains God's plan of justifying men by faith.*

The primary meaning of the word is, therefore, *to be innocent, pure,* &c. and hence the name means *righteousness* in general. For this use of the word, see Mat. iii. 15; v. 6, 10, 20; xxi. 32; Luke i. 75; Acts x. 35; xiii. 10; Rom. ii. 26; viii. 4, &c.

In the sense of pardoning sin, or of treating men as if they were innocent, on the condition of faith, it is used often, and especially in this epistle; see Rom. iii. 24, 26, 28, 30; iv. 5; v. 1; viii. 30; Gal. ii. 16; iii. 8, 24; Rom. iii. 21, 22, 25; iv. 3, 6, 13; ix. 30, &c.

It is called *God's* righteousness, because it is God's plan, in distinction from all the plans set up by men. It was originated by him; it differs from all others; and it claims him as its author, and tends to his glory. It is called his *righteousness,* as it is the way by which he receives and treats men *as* righteous. The same plan was foretold in various places where the word *righteousness* is nearly synonymous with *salvation;* Isa. lvi. 5, "My righteousness is near, my salvation is gone forth;" 6, "My salvation shall be for ever, and my righteousness shall not be abolished;" Isa. lvi. 1, "My salvation is near to come, and my righteousness to be revealed;" Dan. ix. 24, "To make reconciliation for iniquity, and to bring in everlasting righteousness."

[There is yet another sense lying on the very surface of the passage, and adopted by nearly all the evangelical expositors, according to which "the righteousness of God" is that righteousness, which Christ wrought out in his active and passive obedience. This is a righteousness which GOD hath devised, procured, and accepted. It is therefore eminently HIS. It is imputed to believers, and *on account of it* they are held righteous in the sight of God. It is of the highest importance that the true meaning of this leading expression be preserved; for if it be explained away, the doctrine of imputed righteousness is materially affected, as will appear in a subsequent Note.

That the phrase is to be understood of the righteousness which Christ has procured by his obedience and death, appears from the general sense of the original term δικαιοσύνη. Mr. Haldane in a long and elaborate comment on Rom. iii. 21, has satisfactorily shown that it signifies "righteousness in the abstract, and also conformity to law," and that "WHEREVER it refers to the subject of man's salvation, and is not merely a personal attribute of Deity, it signifies that righteousness which, in conformity with his justice, God has appointed and provided."

Besides, if the expression be understood of "God's plan of justifying men," we shall have great difficulty in explaining the parallel passages. They will not bend to any such principle of interpretation. In chap. v. 17, this righteousness is spoken of as a "gift" which we "receive," and in the 18th and 19th verses, the "righteousness of one" and "the obedience of one," are used as convertible terms. Now it is easy to understand how the righteousness which Christ has procured by his obedience, becomes "a gift," but "a plan of justification" is appropriately said to be declared, or promulgated. It cannot be spoken of in the light of a *gift received.* The same observation applies with still greater force to the passage in 2 Cor. v. 21, "For he hath made him to be sin for us who knew no sin, that we might be made *the righteousness of God* in him." How would this passage appear, if "plan of justification" were substituted for righteousness of God?

In Phil. iii. 9, Paul desires to be found in Christ, "not having his own righteousness, which is of the law, but that which is through the faith of Christ, the righteousness which is of God by faith." Is not his own righteousness that which he could attain to by his works or obedience, and is not the righteousness of Christ that which Jesus had procured by *his* obedience?

Lastly, in Rom. x, 3, the righteousness of God is thus opposed to the righteousness of man, "they being ignorant of *God's righteousness,* and going about to establish *their own righteousness,* have not submitted themselves to the righteousness of God." Now what is that righteousness which natural men seek to establish, and which is peculiarly called "their own?" Doubtless it is a righteousness founded on *their own works,* and therefore that which is here properly opposed to it is a righteousness founded on the *work of God. See Haldane, Hodge, Scott, Guyse,* &c. This meaning of the term furnishes a key to unlock *all* the passages in which it is used in connection with the sinner's justification, whereas any other sense, however it may suit a few places, will be found generally inapplicable.]

In regard to this plan it may be observed; (1.) That it is not to declare that men *are* innocent and pure. That would not be true. The truth is just the reverse; and God does not esteem men to be different from what they are. (2.) It is not to *take part* with the sinner, and to mitigate his offences. It admits them to their full extent; and makes *him* feel them also. (3.) It is not that we become partakers of the essential righteousness of God. That is impossible. (4.) It is not that *his* righteousness becomes *ours*. This is not true; and there is no intelligible sense in which that can be understood.

[It is true indeed that the righteousness of Christ cannot be called *ours* in the sense of our having *actually* accomplished it *in our own persons*. This is a view of imputation easily held up to ridicule, yet *there is a sense* in which the righteousness of Christ may be *ours*. Though we have not achieved it, yet it may be so placed to our account that we shall be *held righteous, and treated as such*. I have said, first, we shall be *held* righteous, and then *treated* as such; for God treats none as righteous who in some sense or other are not really so. *See the Note on* chap. iv. 3.]

But it is God's plan for *pardoning* sin, and for *treating us* as if we had not committed it; that is, adopting us as his children, and admitting us to heaven on the ground of what the Lord Jesus has done in our stead. This is God's plan. Men seek to save themselves by their own works. God's plan is to save them by the merits of Jesus Christ. ¶ *Revealed*. Made known, and communicated. The gospel states the *fact* that God *has* such a plan of justification; and shows the *way* or *manner* in which it might be done. The *fact* seems to have been understood by Abraham, and the patriarchs (Heb. xi.), but the full mode or manner in which it was to be accomplished, was not revealed until it was done in the gospel of Christ And *because* this great and glorious truth was thus made known, Paul was not ashamed of the gospel. Nor should *we* be. ¶ *From faith*, ἐκ πίστεως. This phrase I take to be connected with the expression, "the righteousness of God." Thus, the righteousness of God, or God's plan of justifying men *by faith*, is revealed in the gospel. Here the great truth of the gospel is brought out, that men are justified *by faith*, and not by the deeds of the law. The common interpretation of the passage has been, that the righteousness of God in this is revealed *from one degree of faith to another*. But to this interpretation there are many objections. (1.) It is not true. The gospel was not *designed* for this. It did not *suppose* that men had a certain *degree* of faith by nature which needed only to be *strengthened* in order that they might be saved. (2.) It does not make good sense. To say that the righteousness of God, meaning, as is commonly understood, his *essential justice*, is *revealed* from one degree of faith to another, is to use words without any meaning. (3.) The connection of the passage does not admit of this interpretation. The design of the passage is evidently to set forth the doctrine of justification as the grand theme of remark, and it does not comport with that design to introduce here the advance from one degree of faith to another, as the main topic. (4.) The epistle is intended clearly to establish the fact that men are justified *by faith*. This is the grand idea which is kept up; and to show *how* this may be done is the main purpose before the apostle; see chap. iii. 22, 30; ix. 30; ix. 32; x. 6, &c. (5.) The passage which he immediately quotes shows that he did not speak of different *degrees* of faith, but of the doctrine that men are to be justified *by* faith. ¶ *To faith*. Unto those who believe (comp. chap. iii. 22); or to every one that believeth, ver. 16. The abstract is here put for the concrete. It is designed to express the idea, *that God's plan of justifying men is revealed in the gospel, which plan is by faith, and the benefits of which plan shall be extended to all that have faith, or that believe*. ¶ *As it is written*. See Hab. ii. 4. ¶ *The just shall live by faith*. The LXX

18 For the wrath [c] of God is revealed from heaven against all

c Eph. 5. 6.

translate the passage in Habakkuk, 'If any man shall draw back, my soul shall have no pleasure in him, but the just by my faith," or by faith in me, 'shall live." The very words are used by them which are employed by the apostle, except they add the word "my, μου," *my* faith. The Syriac renders it in a similar manner, "The just by faith shall live." The meaning of the Hebrew in Habakkuk is the same. It does not refer originally to the doctrine of justification by faith; but its meaning is this, "The just man, or the righteous man, shall live by his confidence in God." The prophet is speaking of the woes attending the Babylonish captivity. The Chaldeans were to come upon the land and destroy it, and remove the nation, chap. i. 6—10. But this was not to be perpetual. It should have an end (chap. ii. 3), and they who had confidence in God should live (ver. 4); that is, should be restored to their country, should be blessed and made happy. Their *confidence in God* should sustain them, and preserve them. This did not refer primarily to the doctrine of justification by faith, nor did the apostle so quote it, but it expressed a *general principle* that those who had confidence in God should be happy, and be preserved and blessed. This would *express* the doctrine which Paul was defending. It was not by relying on his own *merit* that the Israelite would be delivered, but it was by confidence in God, by *his* strength and mercy. On the same *principle* would men be saved under the gospel. It was not by reliance on their own works or merit; it was by *confidence* in God, by *faith*, that they were to live. ¶ *Shall live.* In Habakkuk this means to be made happy, or blessed; shall find comfort, and support, and deliverance. So in the gospel the blessings of salvation are represented as *life*, eternal life. Sin is represented as death, and man by nature is represented as dead in trespasses and sins, Eph. ii. 1. The gospel restores to *life* and salvation, John iii. 36; v. 29, 40; vi. 33, 51, 53; xx. 31; Acts ii. 28; Rom. v. 18; viii. 6.—This expression, therefore, does not mean, as it is sometimes supposed, the *justified by faith* shall live; but it is expressive of a *general principle* in relation to men, that they shall be defended, preserved, made happy, not by their own merits, or strength, but by *confidence* in God. This *principle* is exactly applicable to the gospel plan of salvation. Those who rely on God the Saviour shall be justified, and saved.

18. *For.* This word denotes that the apostle is about to give a *reason* for what he had just said. This verse commences the argument of the epistle, an argument designed to establish the proposition advanced in ver. 17. The proposition is, that God's plan of justification is revealed in the gospel. To show this, it was necessary to show that all other plans had failed; and that there was need of some *new* plan or scheme to save men. To this he devotes this and the two following chapters. The design of this argument is, to show that men were sinners. And in order to make this out, it was necessary to show that they were under law. This was clear in regard to the Jews. They had the Scriptures; and the apostle in *this* chapter shows that it was equally clear in regard to the Gentiles, and *then* proceeds to show that *both* had failed of obeying the law. To see this clearly it is necessary to add only, that there can be but *two* ways of justification conceived of; one by obedience to law, and the other by grace. The former was the one by which Jews and Gentiles had sought to be justified; and if it could be shown that in this they had failed, the way was clear to show that there was need of some other plan. ¶ *The wrath of God,* ὀργὴ Θεοῦ. The word rendered *wrath* properly denotes that earnest appetite or desire by which we seek any thing, or an intense effort to obtain it. And it is particularly applied to the desire which a man has to take vengeance who is injured, and who is enraged.

It is thus synonymous with revenge. Eph. iv. 31, "Let all bitterness, and *wrath*," &c; Col. iii. 8, "Anger, *wrath*, malice," &c; 1 Tim. ii. 8; James i. 19. But it is also often applied to God; and it is clear that when we think of the word as applicable to him, it must be divested of every thing like human passion, and especially of the passion of *revenge*. As he cannot be *injured* by the sins of men (Job xxv. 6—8), he has no motive for vengeance properly so called, and it is one of the most obvious rules of interpretation that we are not to apply to God passions and feelings which, among us, have their origin in evil. In making a revelation, it was indispensable to use words which men used; but it does not follow that when applied to *God* they mean *precisely* what they do when applied to *man*. When the Saviour is said (Mark iii. 5.) to have looked on his disciples with *anger* (Greek, *wrath*, the same word is here), it is not to be supposed that he had the feelings of an implacable *man* seeking vengeance. The nature of the feeling is to be judged of by the character of the person. So, in this place, the word denotes the *divine displeasure* or *indignation* against sin; the divine purpose to *inflict punishment*. *It is the opposition of the divine character against sin;* and the determination of the divine mind to *express* that opposition in a proper way, by excluding the offender from the favours which he bestows on the righteous. It is not an unamiable, or arbitrary principle of conduct. We all admire the character of a father who is *opposed* to disorder, and vice, and disobedience in his family, and who *expresses* his opposition in a proper way. We admire the character of a ruler who is *opposed* to all crime in the community, and who *expresses* those feelings in the laws. And the more he is *opposed* to vice and crime, the more we admire his character and his laws; and why shall we be not equally pleased with God, who is opposed to *all* crime in all parts of the universe, and who determines to *express* it in the proper way for the sake of preserving order and promoting peace? The word divine *displeasure* or *indignation*, therefore, expresses the meaning of this phrase; see Mat. iii. 7; Luke iii. 7; xxi. 23; John iii. 36; Rom. ii. 5, 8; iii. 5; iv. 15; v. 9; ix. 22; xii. 19; xiii. 4, 5; Eph. ii. 3; v. 6; 1 Thess. i. 10; ii. 16, &c. The word occurs thirty-five times in the New Testament. ¶ *Is revealed.* That is, revealed to the Jews by their law; and to the Gentiles in their reason, and conscience, as the apostle proceeds to show. ¶ *From heaven.* This expression I take to mean simply that the divine displeasure against sin is made known by a divine appointment; by an arrangement of events, communications, and arguments, which evince that they have had their origin in heaven; or are divine. How this is, Paul proceeds to state, in the works of creation, and in the law which the Hebrews had. A variety of meanings have been given to this expression, but this seems the most satisfactory. It does not mean that the wrath *will be sent* from heaven; or that the heavens *declare* his wrath; or that the heavenly bodies are proofs of his wrath against sin; or that Christ, the executioner of wrath, will be manifest from heaven (Origen, Cyril, Beza, &c.); or that it is from God *who is in heaven;* but that it is by an arrangement which shows that it had its origin in heaven, or has proofs that it is divine. ¶ *Against all ungodliness.* This word properly means *impiety* towards God, or neglect of the worship and honour due to him. ἀσέβειαν. It refers to the fact that men had failed to honour the true God, and had paid to idols the homage which was due to him. Multitudes also in every age refuse to honour him, and neglect his worship, though they are not idolaters. Many men suppose that if they do not neglect their duty to their fellow-men, if they are honest and upright in their dealings, they are not guilty, even though they are not righteous, or do not do their duty to God; as though it were a less crime to dishonour God than man; and as though it were innocence to neglect and disobey our Maker and Redeemer. The apostle here shows that the wrath of God is as really revealed against the *neglect* of God as it is against positive iniquity; and that this is an offence of so much consequence as to be placed *first*, and as deserving the divine indignation more than the neglect of our duties towards men; comp. Rom. xi. 26; 2 Tim. ii. 16; Titus ii. 12; Jude 15, 18. The word does not elsewhere occur in the New Testament. ¶ *Unrighteousness of men.* Unrighteousness, or iniquity *towards* men. All offences against our neighbour, our parents, our country, &c. The word *ungodliness* includes all crimes against God; this, all crimes against our fellow-men. The two words express that which comprehends the violation of all the commands of God; "Thou shalt love the Lord thy God, &c. and thy neighbour as thyself," Mat. xxii. 37—40. The wrath of God is thus revealed against *all* human wickedness. ¶ *Who hold the truth.* Who *keep back*, or *restrain* the truth. The word translated *hold* here, sometimes means to *maintain*, to *keep*, to *observe* (1 Cor. vii. 30; 2 Cor. vi. 12); but it also means *to hold back, to detain, to hinder.* Luke iv. 42, "The people sought him (Jesus), and came to him, and *stayed* him." (Greek, the same as here.) Philemon 13, "Whom I would have *retained* with me," &c.; 2 Thess. ii. 6, "And now ye know what *withholdeth*," &c. In this place it means also that they *held back*, or *restrained* the truth, by their wickedness. ¶ *The truth.* The truth of God, in whatever way made known, and particularly, as the apostle goes on to say, that which is made known by the light of nature. The truth pertaining to his perfections, his law, &c. They *hold it back*, or restrain its influence. ¶ *In unrighteousness.* Or rather, *by* their iniquity. Their *wickedness* is the cause why *the truth* had had so little progress among them, and had exerted so little influence. This was done by their yielding to corrupt passions and propensities, and by their being therefore unwilling to retain the knowledge of a pure and holy God, who is opposed to such deeds, and who will punish them. As they were determined to *practise* iniquity, they chose to exclude the knowledge of a pure God, and to worship impure idols, by which they might give a sanction to their lusts. Their vice and tendency to iniquity was, therefore, the reason why they had so little knowledge of a holy God; and by the love of this, they *held back* the truth from making progress, and becoming diffused among them.

The same thing is substantially true now. Men hold back or resist the truth of the gospel by their sins in the following ways. (1.) Men of influence and wealth employ both, in directly opposing the gospel. (2.) Men directly resist the *doctrines* of religion, since they know they could not hold to those doctrines without abandoning their sins. (3.) Men who resolve to live in sin, of course, resist the gospel, and endeavour to prevent its influence. (4.) Pride, and vanity, and the love of the world also resist the gospel, and oppose its advances. (5.) Unlawful business—business that begins in evil, and progresses, and ends in evil—has this tendency to hold back the gospel. Such is the effect of the traffic in ardent spirits, in the slave-trade, &c. They begin in the love of money, the root of all evil (1 Tim. vi. 10); they progress in the tears and sorrows of the widow, the orphan, the wife, the sister, or the child; and they end in the deep damnation of multitudes in the world to come. Perhaps there has been nothing that has so much *held back* the influence of truth, and of the gospel, as indulgence in the vice of intemperance, and traffic in liquid fire. (6.) Indulgence in vice, or wickedness of *any kind*, holds back the truth of God. Men who are resolved to indulge their passions *will not* yield themselves to this truth. And hence all the wicked, the proud, and vain, and worldly are responsible, not only for their own sins directly, but for hindering, by their example and their crimes, the effect of religion on others. They are answerable for standing in the way of God and his truth; and for *opposing* him in the

ungodliness, and unrighteousness
of men, who hold the truth in unrighteousness:
19 Because that which may
be known of God is manifest in [1]
them; for [a] God hath showed *it*
unto them.
20 For the invisible things of

1 or, *to*.

a John 1.9.

benevolent design of doing good to all men. There is nothing that prevents the universal spread and influence of truth but sin. And men of wickedness are answerable for all the ignorance and wo which are spread over the community, and which have extended themselves over the world.

19. *Because.* The apostle proceeds to show *how* it was that the heathen hindered the truth by their iniquity. This he does by showing that the truth *might* be known by the works of creation; and that nothing but their iniquity prevented it. ¶ *That which may be known of God.* That which is *knowable* concerning God. The expression implies that there may be many things concerning God which cannot be known. But there are also many things which may be ascertained. Such are his existence, and many of his attributes, his power, and wisdom, and justice, &c. The object of the apostle was not to say that *every thing* pertaining to God could be known by them, or that they could have as clear a view of him as if they had possessed a revelation. We must interpret the expression according to the object which he had in view. That was to show that so much might be known of God as to prove that they had *no excuse* for their crimes; or that God would be just in punishing them for their deeds. For this, it was needful only that his existence and his justice, or his determination to punish sin, should be known; and this, the apostle affirms, *was* known among them, and had been from the creation of the world. This expression, therefore, is not to be pressed as implying that they knew *all* that *could* be known about God, or that they knew as much as they who had a revelation; but that they knew enough to prove that they had no excuse for their sins. ¶ *Is manifest.* Is known; is understood. ¶ *In them. Among* them. So the preposition *in* is often used. It means that they *had* this knowledge; or it had been communicated to them. The great mass of the heathen world was indeed ignorant of the true God; but their leaders, or their philosophers, *had* this knowledge; see Note on ver. 21. But this was not true of the mass, or body of the people. Still it was true that this knowledge was in the possession of man, or was *among* the pagan world, and would have spread, had it not been for the love of sin. ¶ *God hath showed it to them.* Comp. John i. 9. He had endowed them with reason and conscience (chap. ii. 14, 15); he had made them capable of seeing and investigating his works; he had spread before them the proofs of his wisdom, and goodness, and power, and had thus given them the *means* of learning his perfections and will.

20. *For the invisible things of him.* The expression "his invisible things" refers to those things which cannot be perceived by the senses. It does not imply that there *are* any things pertaining to the divine character which *may* be seen by the eye; but that there are things which may be known of him, though not discoverable by the eye. We judge of the objects around us by the senses, the sight, the touch, the ear, &c. Paul affirms, that though we cannot judge thus of God, yet there *is* a way by which we may come to the knowledge of him. What he means by the *invisible* things of God he specifies at the close of the verse, *his eternal power and Godhead.* The affirmation extends only to that; and the argument implies that that was enough to leave them without any excuse for their sins. ¶ *From the creation of the world.* The word *creation* may either mean the *act* of creating, or more commonly it means *the thing created,* the world, the universe. In this sense it is commonly

him from the creation of the world are clearly seen, being understood by the things [a] that are made, *even* his eternal power and Godhead: [1] so that they are without excuse.

a Ps.19.1,&c.

1 or, *that they may be.*

used in the New Testament; comp. Mark x. 6; xiii. 19; xvi. 5; Rom. i. 25; 2 Cor. v. 17; Gal. vi. 15; Col. i. 15, 23; Heb. iv. 13; ix. 11; 1 Pet. ii. 13; 2 Pet. iii. 4; Rev. iii. 14. The word "from" may mean *since,* or it may denote *by means of.* And the expression here may denote that, as an historical fact, God *has been* known *since* the act of creation; or it may denote that he is known *by means of* the material universe which he has formed. The latter is doubtless the true meaning. For, (1.) This is the common meaning of the word *creation;* and, (2.) This accords with the design of the argument. It is not to state an *historical fact,* but to show that they had the means of knowing their duty within their reach, and were without excuse. Those means were in the wisdom, power, and glory of the universe, by which they were surrounded. ¶ *Are clearly seen.* Are made manifest; or may be perceived. The word used here does not occur elsewhere in the New Testament. ¶ *Being understood.* His perfections may be investigated, and comprehended by means of his works. They are the *evidences* submitted to our intellects, by which we may arrive at the true knowledge of God. ¶ *Things that are made.* By his works; comp. Heb. xi. 3. This means, not by the original *act* of creation, but by the continual operations of God in his Providence, by his *doings,* ποιήμασι, by what he is continually producing and accomplishing in the displays of his power and goodness in the heavens and the earth. What they were capable of understanding, he immediately adds, and shows that he did not intend to affirm that *every* thing could be known of God by his works; but so much as to free them from excuse for their sins. ¶ *His eternal power.* Here are two things implied. (1.) That the universe contains an exhibition of his *power,* or a display of that attribute which we call *omnipotence;* and, (2.) That this power has existed from eternity, and of course implies an eternal existence in God. It does not mean that this power has been exerted or put forth *from eternity,* for the very idea of *creation* supposes that it had not, but that there is proof, in the works of creation, of power which must have *existed* from eternity, or have belonged to an eternal being. The proof of this was clear, even to the heathen, with their imperfect views of creation and of astronomy; comp. Ps. xix. The majesty and grandeur of the heavens would strike their eye, and be full demonstration that they were the work of an infinitely great and glorious God. But to us, under the full blaze of modern science, with our knowledge of the magnitude, and distances, and revolutions of the heavenly bodies, the proof of this *power* is much more grand and impressive. *We* may apply the remark of the apostle to the present state of the science, and his language will cover all the ground, and the proof to human view is continually rising of the amazing power of God, by every new discovery in science, and especially in astronomy. Those who wish to see this object presented in a most impressive view, may find it done in Chalmer's Astronomical Discourses, and in Dick's Christian Philosopher. Equally clear is the proof that this power must have been *eternal.* If it had not *always* existed, it could in no way have been produced. But it is not to be supposed that it was *always exerted,* any more than it is that God *now* puts forth *all* the power that he *can,* or than that *we* constantly put forth all the power which we possess. God's power was *called forth* at the creation. He *showed* his omnipotence; and gave, by that one great act, eternal demonstration that he was almighty; and we may survey the *proof* of that, as clearly as if we had *seen* the operation of his hand there. The proof is not weakened

21 Because that, when they knew God, they glorified *him* not as God, neither were thankful, but became vain [a] in their

a Je.2.5: Ep.4.17,18.

because we do not see the process of creation constantly going on. It is rather augmented by the fact that he *sustains* all things, and controls continually the vast masses of matter in the material worlds. ¶ *Godhead.* His deity; divinity; divine nature, or essence. The word is not elsewhere used in the New Testament. Its meaning cannot therefore be fixed by any parallel passages. It proves the truth that the *supremacy*, or supreme divinity of God, was exhibited in the works of creation, or that he was exalted above all creatures and things. It would not be proper, however, to *press* this word as implying that all that we know of God by revelation was known to the heathen; but that so much was known as to show his supremacy; his right to their homage; and of course the folly and wickedness of idolatry. This is all that the argument of the apostle demands, and, of course, on this principle the expression is to be interpreted. ¶ *So that they are without excuse.* God has given them so clear evidence of his existence and claims, that they have no excuse for their idolatry, and for hindering the truth by their iniquity. It is implied here that in order that men should be responsible, they should have the means of knowledge; and that he does not judge them when their ignorance is involuntary, and the means of knowing the truth have not been communicated. But where men *have* these means within their reach, and will not avail themselves of them, all excuse is taken away. This was the case with the Gentile world. They *had* the means of knowing *so much* of God, as to show the folly of worshipping dumb idols; comp. Isa. xliv. 8—20. They had also *traditions* respecting his perfections; and they could not plead for their crimes and folly that they had no means of knowing him. If this was true of the pagan world then, how much more is it true of the world now? And especially how true and fearful is this, respecting that great multitude in Christian lands who have the Bible, and who never read it; who are within the reach of the sanctuary, and never enter it; who are admonished by friends, and by the providences of God, and who regard it not; and who look upon the heavens, and *even yet* see no proof of the eternal power and Godhead of him who made them all! Nay, there are those who are apprized of the discoveries of modern astronomy, and who yet do not seem to reflect that all these glories are proof of the existence of an eternal God; and who live in ignorance of religion as really as the heathen, and in crimes as decided and malignant as disgraced the darkest ages of the world. For such there is no excuse, or shadow of excuse, to be offered in the day of doom. And there is no fact more melancholy in our history, and no one thing that more proves the stupidity of men, than this sad forgetfulness of Him that made the heavens, even amid all the wonders and glories that have come fresh from the hand of God, and that every where speak his praise.

21. *Because that.* The apostle here is showing that it was right to condemn men for their sins. To do this it was needful to show them that they *had* the knowledge of God, and the means of knowing what was right; and that the true source of their sins and idolatries was a corrupt and evil heart. ¶ *When they knew God.* Greek, *knowing God.* That is, they had an acquaintance with the existence and many of the perfections of one God. That many of the philosophers of Greece and Rome had a knowledge of one God, there can be no doubt. This was undoubtedly the case with Pythagoras, who had travelled extensively in Egypt, and even in Palestine; and also with Plato and his disciples. This point is clearly shown by Cudworth in his Intellectual System, and by Bishop Warburton in the Divine Legation of Moses. Yet the knowledge of this great truth was not

communicated to the people. It was confined to the philosophers; and not improbably one design of the *mysteries* celebrated throughout Greece was to keep up the knowledge of the one true God. Gibbon has remarked that "the philosophers regarded all the popular superstitions as equally false: the common people as equally true; and the politicians as equally useful." This was probably a correct account of the prevalent feelings among the ancients. A single extract from Cicero (de Natura Deorum, lib. ii. c. 6) will show that they *had* the knowledge of one God. "There is something in the nature of things, which the mind of man, which reason, which human power cannot effect; and certainly that which produces this must be better than man. What can this be called but *God?*" Again (c. 2), "What can be so plain and manifest, when we look at heaven, and contemplate heavenly things, as that there is some divinity of most excellent mind, by which these things are governed?" ¶ *They glorified* him *not as God.* They did not *honour* him as God. This was the true source of their abominations. To glorify him *as God* is to regard with proper reverence all his perfections and laws; to venerate his name, his power, his holiness, and presence, &c. As they were not *inclined* to do this, so they were given over to their own vain and wicked desires. Sinners are not willing to give honour to God, *as God.* They are not pleased with his perfections; and therefore the mind becomes fixed on other objects, and the heart gives free indulgence to its own sinful desires. A willingness to honour God as God—to reverence, love, and obey him, would effectually restrain men from sin. ¶ *Neither were thankful.* The obligation to be *thankful* to God for his mercies, for the goodness which we experience, is plain and obvious. Thus we judge of favours received of our fellow-men. The apostle here clearly regards this unwillingness to render *gratitude* to God for his mercies as one of the causes of their subsequent corruption and idolatry. The reasons of this are the following. (1.) The effect of *ingratitude* is to render the heart hard and insensible. (2.) Men seek to *forget* the Being to whom they are unwilling to exercise gratitude. (3.) To do this, they fix their affections on other things; and hence the heathen expressed their gratitude not to God, but to the sun, and moon, and stars, &c., the *mediums* by which God bestows his favours on men. And we may here learn that an unwillingness to thank *God* for his mercies is one of the most certain causes of alienation and hardness of heart. ¶ *But became vain.* To *become vain,* with us, means to be elated, or to be self-conceited, or to seek praise from others. The meaning here seems to be, they became foolish, frivolous in their thoughts and reasonings. They acted foolishly; they employed themselves in useless and frivolous questions, the effect of which was to lead the mind farther and farther from the truth respecting God. ¶ *Imaginations.* This word means properly *thoughts,* then *reasonings,* and also *disputations.* Perhaps our word, *speculations,* would convey its meaning here. It implies that they were unwilling to honour God, and *being* unwilling to honour him, they *commenced those speculations* which resulted in all their vain and foolish opinions about idols, and the various rites of idolatrous worship. Many of the speculations and inquiries of the ancients were among the most vain and senseless which the mind can conceive. ¶ *And their foolish heart.* The word *heart* is not unfrequently used to denote the *mind,* or the *understanding.* We apply it to denote the *affections.* But such was not its common use among the Hebrews. We speak of the *head* when we refer to the understanding, but this was not the case with the Hebrews. They spoke of the *heart* in this manner, and in this sense it is clearly used in this place; see Eph. i. 18; Rom. ii. 15; 2 Cor. iv. 6; 2 Pet. i. 19. The word *foolish* means literally that which is without *understanding*; Mat. xv. 16. ¶ *Was darkened.* Was rendered

imaginations, and their foolish heart was darkened:
22 Professing themselves to be wise, they [a] became fools.
23 And changed the glory of the uncorruptible God into an image [b] like to corruptible man, and to birds, and four-footed beasts, and creeping things.
24 Wherefore God also gave [c]

a Jer.8.8,9. b Isa.40.18,26; Ezek.8.10. c Ps.81.12; 2 Thess.2.11.

obscure, so that they did not perceive and comprehend the truth. The process which is stated in this verse is, (1.) That men had the knowledge of God. (2.) That they refused to *honour* him when they knew him, and were *opposed* to his character and government. (3.) That they were ungrateful. (4.) That they then began to doubt, to reason, to speculate, and wandered far into darkness. This is substantially the process by which men wander away from God now. They *have* the knowledge of God, but they do not love him; and being dissatisfied with his character and government, they begin to speculate, fall into error, and then "find no end in wandering mazes lost," and sink into the depths of heresy and of sin.

22. *Professing themselves to be wise.* This was the common boast of the *philosophers* of antiquity. The very word by which they chose to be called, *philosophers*, means literally *lovers of wisdom.* That it was their *boast* that they were wise, is well known; comp. chap. i. 14; 1 Cor. i. 19, 20—22; iii. 19; 2 Cor. xi. 19. ¶ *They became fools;* comp. Jer. viii. 8, 9. They became really foolish in their opinions and conduct. There is something particularly pungent and cutting in this remark, and as true as it is pungent. In what way they *evinced* their folly, Paul proceeds immediately to state. Sinners of all kinds are frequently spoken of as fools in the Scriptures. In the sense in which it is thus used, the word is applied to them as void of understanding or moral sense; as idolaters, and as wicked; Ps. xiv. 1; Prov. xxvi. 4; i. 17, 22; xiv. 8, 9. The senses in which this word here is applied to the heathen are, (1.) That their speculations and doctrines were senseless; and (2.) That their conduct was corrupt.

23. *And changed.* This does not mean that they literally *transmuted* God himself; but that in their views they exchanged him; or they changed him *as an object of worship* for idols. They produced, of course, no *real* change in the glory of the infinite God, but the *change* was in themselves. They *forsook* him of whom they had knowledge (ver. 21), and offered the homage which was due to him, to idols. ¶ *The glory.* The majesty, the honour, &c. This word stands opposed here to the *degrading* nature of their worship. Instead of adoring a Being clothed with *majesty* and *honour*, they bowed down to reptiles, &c. They exchanged a *glorious* object of worship for that which was degrading and humiliating. The *glory* of God, in such places as this, means his essential *honour*, his *majesty*, the concentration and expression of his perfections, as the *glory of the sun*, (1 Cor. xv. 41) means his shining, or his splendour; comp. Jer. ii. 11; Ps. cvi. 20. ¶ *The uncorruptible God.* The word *uncorruptible* is here applied to God in opposition to *man.* God is unchanging, indestructible, immortal. The word conveys also the idea that God is eternal. As he is incorruptible, he is the proper object of worship. In all the changes of life, man may come to him, assured that he is the same. When man decays by age or infirmities, he may come to God, assured that *he* undergoes no such change, but is the same yesterday, to-day, and for ever; comp. 1 Tim. i. 17. ¶ *Into an image.* An image is a representation or likeness of any thing, whether made by painting, or from wood, stone, &c. Thus the word is applied to *idols*, as being *images* or *representations* of heavenly objects; 2 Chron. xxxiii. 7; Dan. iii. 1; Rev. xi. 4, &c. See instances of this among the

hem up to uncleanness through the lusts of their own hearts, to dishonour their own bodies between themselves:

Jews described in Isa. xl. 18—26, and Ezek. viii. 10. ¶ *To corruptible man.* This stands opposed to the *incorruptible* God. Many of the images or idols of the ancients were in the forms of men and women. Many of their gods were heroes and benefactors, who were *deified,* and to whom temples, altars, and statues were erected. Such were Jupiter, and Hercules, and Romulus, &c. The worship of these *heroes* thus constituted no small part of their idolatry, and their *images* would be of course representations of them in human form. It was proof of great degradation, that they thus adored *men* with like passions as themselves; and attempted to *displace* the true God from the throne, and to substitute in his place an idol in the likeness of men. ¶ *And to birds.* The *ibis* was adored with peculiar reverence among the Egyptians, on account of the great benefits resulting from its destroying the *serpents* which, but for this, would have overrun the country. The *hawk* was also adored in Egypt, and the *eagle* at Rome. As one great principle of pagan idolatry was to adore all objects from which important benefits were derived, it is probable that all *birds* would come in for a share of pagan worship, that rendered service in the destruction of noxious animals. ¶ *And four-footed beasts.* Thus the ox, under the name *apis,* was adored in Egypt; and even the dog and the monkey. In imitation of the Egyptian ox, the children of Israel made their golden calf, Ex. xxii. 4 At this day, two of the most sacred objects of worship in Hindostan are the cow and the *monkey.* ¶ *And creeping things.* Reptiles. "Animals that have no feet, or such short ones that they seem to creep or crawl on the ground." (*Calmet.*) Lizards, serpents, &c. come under this description. The *crocodile* in Egypt was an object of adoration, and even the serpent so late as the second century of the Christian era, there was a sect in Egypt, called *Ophites* from their worshipping a serpent, and who even claimed to be Christians, (Murdock's Mosheim, vol. i. p. 180, 181) There was scarcely an object, animal or vegetable, which the Egyptians did not adore. Thus the *leek,* the *onion,* &c. were objects of worship, and men bowed down and paid adoration to the sun and moon, to animals, to vegetables, and to reptiles. Egypt was the source of the views of religion that pervaded other nations, and hence their worship partook of the same wretched and degrading character. (See *Leland's* "Advantage and Necessity of Revelation.")

24. *Wherefore.* That is, because they were unwilling to retain him in their knowledge, and chose to worship idols. Here is traced the practical tendency of heathenism; not as an *innocent* and *harmless* system, but as resulting in the most gross and shameless acts of depravity. ¶ *God gave them up.* He abandoned them, or he ceased to restrain them, and suffered them to *act out* their sentiments, and to manifest them in their life. This does not imply that he exerted any *positive* influence in inducing them to sin, any more than it would if we should seek, by argument and entreaty, to restrain a headstrong youth, and when neither would prevail, should *leave him to act out* his propensities, and to go as he chose to ruin. It is implied in this, (1.) That the tendency of *man* was to these sins; (2.) That the tendency of *idolatry* was to promote them; and (3.) That all that was needful, in order that men should commit them, was for God to leave him to follow the devices and desires of his own heart; comp. Ps. lxxxi. 12; 2 Thess. ii. 10, 12. ¶ *To uncleanness.* To impurity, or moral defilement; particularly to those impurities which he proceeds to specify, ver. 26, &c. ¶ *Through the lusts of their own hearts.* Or, in consequence of their own evil and depraved passions and desires. He left them to act out, or manifest, their depraved affections and

25 Who changed the truth of God [a] into a lie, and worshipped and served the creature more [1] than the Creator, who is blessed for ever. Amen.

26 For this cause God gave them

a Amos 2.4.

1 or, *rather*.

inclinations. ¶ *To dishonour.* To disgrace; ver. 26, 27. ¶ *Between themselves.* Among themselves; or mutually. They did it by unlawful and impure connections with one another.

25. *Who changed the truth of God.* This is a repetition of the declaration in ver. 23, in another form. The phrase, "the truth of God" is a Hebrew phrase, meaning *the true God.* In such a case, where two nouns come together, one is employed as an adjective to qualify the other. Most commonly the latter of two nouns is used as the adjective, but sometimes it is the former, as in this case. God is called the *true God* in opposition to idols, which are called false gods. There is but one *real* or *true* God, and all others are false. ¶ *Into a lie.* Into *idols,* or false gods. Idols are not unfrequently called *falsehood* and *lies,* because they are not true representations of God; Jer. xiii. 25; Isa. xxviii. 15; Jer. x. 14; Ps. xl. 4. ¶ *The creature.* Created things, as the sun, moon, animals, &c. ¶ *Who is blessed for ever.* It was not uncommon to add a *doxology,* or ascription of praise to God, when his name was mentioned; see Rom. ix. 5; 2 Cor. xi. 31; Gal. i. 5. The Jews also usually did it. In this way they preserved veneration for the name of God, and accustomed themselves to speak of him with reverence. "The Mahometans also borrowed this custom from the Jews, and practise it to a great extent. Tholuck mentions an Arabic manuscript in the library at Berlin which contains an account of heresies in respect to Islamism, and as often as the writer has occasion to mention the name of a new heretical sect, he adds, 'God be exalted above all which they say.'" (*Stuart.*) ¶ *Amen.* This is a Hebrew word denoting strong affirmation. So let it be. It implies here the solemn assent of the writer to what was just said; or his strong wish that what he had said might be—that the name of God might be esteemed and be blessed for ever. The mention of the degrading idolatry of the heathens was strongly calculated to impress on his mind the superior excellency and glory of the one living God. It is mentioned respecting the honourable Robert Boyle, that he never *mentioned* the name of God without a solemn pause, denoting his profound reverence. Such a practice would tend eminently to prevent an unholy familiarity and irreverence in regard to the sacred name of the Most High; comp. Ex. xx. 7.

26. *For this cause.* On account of what had just been specified; to wit, that they did not glorify him as God, that they were unthankful, that they became polytheists and idolaters. In the previous verses he had stated their *speculative belief.* He now proceeds to show its practical influences on their conduct. ¶ *Vile affections.* Disgraceful passions or desires. That is, to those which are immediately specified. The great object of the apostle here, it will be remembered, is to shew the state of the heathen world, and to prove that they had need of some other way of justification than the law of nature. For this purpose, it was necessary for him to enter into a detail of their sins. The sins which he proceeds to specify are the most indelicate, vile, and degrading which can be charged on man. But this is not the fault of the apostle. If they *existed,* it was necessary for him to charge them on the pagan world. His argument would not be complete without it. The shame is not in *specifying* them, but in *their existence;* not in the apostle, but in those who practised them, and imposed on him the necessity of accusing them of these enormous offences. It may be further remarked, that the *mere fact* of his charging them with these sins is strong

up unto vile [a] affections: for even their women did change the natural use into that which is against nature:

27 And likewise also the men, leaving the natural use of the women, burned in their lust one toward another; men with men working that which is unseemly, and receiving in themselves that

a Eph.5.12; Jude 10.

presumptive proof of their being practised. If they did *not* exist, it would be easy for them to *deny it,* and *put him to the proof of it.* No man would venture charges like these without evidence; and the presumption is, that these things were known and practised without shame. But this is not all. There is still abundant proof on record in the writings of the heathen themselves, that these crimes were known and extensively practised. ¶ *For even their women,* &c. Evidence of the shameful and disgraceful fact here charged on the women is abundant in the Greek and Roman writers. Proof may be seen, which it would not be proper to specify, in the lexicons, under the words τριβὰς, ὄλισβον, and ἑταιρίστης. See also Seneca, epis. 95; Martial, epis. i. 90. Tholuck on the State of the heathen World, in the Biblical Repository, vol. ii.; Lucian, Dial. Meretric. v.; and Tertullian de Pallio.

27. *And likewise the men,* &c. The sin which is here specified is that which was the shameful sin of Sodom, and which from that has been called *sodomy.* It would scarcely be credible that man had been guilty of a crime so base and so degrading, unless there was ample and full testimony to it. Perhaps there is no sin which so deeply shows the depravity of man as this; none which would so much induce one "to hang his head, and *blush* to think himself a man." And yet the evidence that the apostle did not bring a *railing accusation* against the heathen world; that he did not advance a charge which was unfounded, is too painfully clear. It has been indeed a matter of controversy whether *pæderastry,* or the love of boys, among the ancients was not a pure and harmless love, but the evidence is against it. (See this discussed in Dr. Leland's Advantage and Necessity of Revelation, vol. i. 49—56.) The crime with which the apostle charges the Gentiles here was by no means confined to the *lower* classes of the people. It doubtless pervaded *all* classes, and we have distinct specifications of its existence in a great number of cases. Even Virgil speaks of the attachment of Corydon to Alexis, without seeming to feel the necessity of a blush for it. Maximus Tyrius (Diss. 10) says that in the time of Socrates, this vice was common among the Greeks; and is at pains to vindicate *Socrates* from it as almost a solitary exception. Cicero (Tuscul. Ques. iv. 34) says, that "Dicearchus had accused *Plato* of it, and probably not *unjustly.*" He also says (Tuscul. Q. iv. 33), that the practice was common among the Greeks, and that their poets and great men, and even their learned men and philosophers, not only practised, but gloried in it. And he adds, that it was the custom, not of particular cities only, but of Greece in general. (Tuscul. Ques. v. 20.) Xenophon says, that "the unnatural love of boys is so common, that in many places it is established by the public laws." He particularly alludes to Sparta. (See Leland's Advantage, &c. i. 56.) Plato says that the *Cretans* practised this crime, and justified themselves by the example of Jupiter and Ganymede. (Book of Laws, i.) And Aristotle says, that among the Cretans there was a law encouraging that sort of unnatural love. (Arist. Politic. b. ii. chap. 10.) Plutarch says, that this was practised at Thebes, and at Elis. He further says, that *Solon,* the great lawgiver of Athens, "was not proof against beautiful boys, and had not courage to resist the force of love." (Life of Solon.) Diogenes Laertius says that this vice was practised by the Stoic Zeno. Among the Romans, to whom Paul was writing, this vice

recompense of their error which was meet.

28 And even as they did not like [1] to retain God in *their* knowledge, God gave them over to [2] a reprobate mind, to do

1 or, *to acknowledge.*

2 or, *a mind void of judgment.*

was no less common. Cicero introduces, without any mark of disapprobation, *Cotta*, a man of the first rank and genius, freely and familiarly owning to other Romans of the same quality, that this worse than beastly vice was practised by himself, and quoting the authority of ancient philosophers in vindication of it. (De Natura Deorum, b. i. chap. 28.) It appears from what Seneca says (epis. 95) that in his time it was practised openly at Rome, and without shame. He speaks of flocks and troops of boys, distinguished by their colours and nations; and says that great care was taken to train them up for this detestable employment. Those who may wish to see a further account of the *morality* in the pagan world may find it detailed in Tholuck's "Nature and moral Influence of Heathenism," in the Biblical Repository, vol. ii., and in Leland's Advantage and Necessity of the Christian Revelation. There is not the least evidence that this abominable vice was *confined* to Greece and Rome. If so common there, if it had the sanction even of their philosophers, it may be presumed that it was practised elsewhere, and that the sin against nature was a common crime throughout the heathen world. Navaratte, in his account of the empire of China (book ii. chap. 6), says that it is extremely common among the Chinese. And there is every reason to believe, that both in the old world and the new, this abominable crime is still practised. If such was the state of the pagan world, then surely the argument of the apostle is well sustained, that there was need of some other plan of salvation than was taught by the light of nature. ¶ *That which is unseemly.* That which is shameful, or disgraceful. ¶ *And receiving in themselves,* &c. The meaning of this doubtless is, that the effect of such base and unnatural passions was, to enfeeble the body, to produce premature old age, disease, decay, and an early death. That this is the effect of the indulgence of licentious passions, is amply proved by the history of man. The despots who practise polygamy, and keep harems in the East, are commonly superannuated at forty years of age; and it is well known, even in Christian countries, that the effect of licentious indulgence is to break down and destroy the constitution. How much more might this be expected to follow the practice of the vice specified in the verse under examination! God has marked the indulgence of licentious passions with his frown. Since the time of the Romans and the Greeks, as if there had not been sufficient restraints before, he has originated a new disease, which is one of the most loathsome and distressing which has ever afflicted man, and which has swept off millions of victims. But the effect on the body was not all. It tended to debase the mind; to sink man below the level of the brute; to destroy the sensibility; and to "sear the conscience as with a hot iron." The last remnant of reason and conscience, it would seem, must be extinguished it those who would indulge in this unnatural and degrading vice. See Suetonius' Life of Nero, 28.

28. *And even as they did not like,* &c. This was the true source of their crimes. They did not *choose* to acknowledge God. It was not because they *could not,* but because they were *displeased* with God, and chose to forsake him, and follow their own passions and lusts. ¶ *To retain God,* &c. To think of him, or to serve and adore him. This was the *first step* in their sin. It was not that God *compelled* them; or that he did not give them knowledge; nor even is it said that he arbitrarily abandoned them as the first step; but they forsook *him,* and as a consequence he gave them up to a reprobate mind. ¶ *To a reprobate mind.* A mind destitute of judgment.

those things which are not convenient;

29 Being filled with all unrighteousness, fornication, wickedness, covetousness, maliciousness; full of envy, murder, de-

In the Greek the same word is used here, which, in another form, occurs in the previous part of the verse, and which is translated "like." The apostle meant doubtless to retain a reference to that in this place. "As they did not *approve*, ἐδοκίμασαν, or choose to retain God, &c. he gave them up to a mind *disapproved, rejected*, reprobate," ἀδόκιμον, and he means that the state of their minds was such that God could not *approve* it. It does not mean that they were *reprobate* by any arbitrary decree; but that *as a consequence* of their headstrong passions, their determination to *forget* him, he left them to a state of mind which was *evil*, and which he could not *approve*. ¶ *Which are not convenient.* Which are not fit or proper; which are disgraceful and shameful; to wit, those things which he proceeds to state in the remainder of the chapter.

29. *Being filled.* That is, the things which he specifies were *common* or *abounded* among them. This is a strong phrase, denoting that these things were so often practised as that it might be said they were *full of them*. We have a phrase like this still, when we say of one that he is *full of mischief*, &c. ¶ *Unrighteousness*, ἀδικία. This is a word denoting *injustice*, or iniquity in general. The particular specifications of the iniquity follow. ¶ *Fornication.* This was a common and almost universal sin among the ancients, as it is among the moderns. The word denotes *all illicit intercourse*. That this was a common crime among the ancient heathen, it would be easy to show, were it proper, even in relation to their wisest and most learned men. They who wish to see ample evidence of this charge may find it in Tholuck's "Nature and Moral Influence of Heathenism," in the Biblical Repository, vol. ii. p. 441—464. ¶ *Wickedness.* The word used here denotes *a desire of injuring others;* or, as we should express it, *malice*. It is that depravity and obliquity of mind which strives to produce injury on others. *(Calvin.)* ¶ *Covetousness.* Avarice, or the desire of obtaining that which belongs to others. This vice is common in the world; but it would be particularly so where the other vices enumerated here abounded, and men were desirous of luxury, and the gratification of their senses. Rome was particularly desirous of the wealth of other nations, and hence its extended wars, and the various evils of rapine and conquest. ¶ *Licentiousness*, κακία. This word denotes evil in general; rather the *act* of doing wrong than the *desire* which was expressed before by the word *wickedness*. ¶ *Full of envy.* "Pain, uneasiness, mortification, or discontent, excited by another's prosperity, accompanied with some degree of hatred or malignity, and often with a desire or an effort to depreciate the person, and with pleasure in seeing him depressed." *(Webster.)* This passion is so common still, that it is not necessary to attempt to prove that it was common among the ancients. It seems to be natural to the human heart. It is one of the most common manifestations of wickedness, and shows clearly the deep depravity of man. Benevolence rejoices at the happiness of others, and seeks to promote it. But envy exists almost everywhere, and in almost every human bosom:

> "All human virtue, to its latest breath,
> Finds *envy* never conquered but by death."
> *Pope.*

¶ *Murder.* "The taking of human life with premeditated malice by a person of a sane mind." This is necessary to constitute murder now, but the word used here denotes all manslaughter, or taking human life, except that which occurs as the punishment of crime. It is scarcely necessary to show that this was common among the Gentiles. It has prevailed in all communities, but it was particularly prevalent in Rome. It is necessary only to refer the reader to the combate, deceit, malignity; whisperers,

30 Backbiters, haters of God, despiteful; proud, boasters, inventors of evil things, disobedient to parents,

mon events in the Roman history of assassinations, deaths by poison, and the destruction of slaves. But in a special manner the charge was properly alleged against them, on account of the inhuman contests of the gladiators in the amphitheatres. These were common at Rome, and constituted a favourite amusement with the people. Originally captives, slaves, and criminals were trained up for combat; but it afterwards became common for even Roman citizens to engage in these bloody combats, and Nero at one show exhibited no less than four hundred senators and six hundred knights as gladiators. The fondness for this bloody spectacle continued till the reign of Constantine the Great, *the first Christian emperor*, by whom they were abolished about six hundred years after the original institution. "Several hundred, perhaps several thousand, victims were annually slaughtered in the great cities of the empire." Gibbon's Decline and Fall, chap. xxx. A. D. 404. As an instance of what *might* occur in this inhuman spectacle, we may refer to what took place on such an occasion in the reign of Probus (A. D. 281.) During his triumph, near *seven hundred* gladiators were reserved to shed each other's blood for the amusement of the Roman people. But "disdaining to shed their blood for the amusement of the populace, they killed their keepers, broke from their place of confinement, and filled the streets of Rome with blood and confusion." Gibbon's Decline and Fall, chap. 12. With such views and with such spectacles before them, it is not wonderful that *murder* was regarded as a matter of little consequence, and hence *this* crime prevailed throughout the world. ¶ *Debate.* Our word *debate* does not commonly imply evil. It denotes commonly *discussion* for elucidating truth; or for maintaining a proposition, as the *debates* in Parliament, &c. But the word in the original meant also *contention, strife,* altercation, connected with anger and heated zeal; Rom. xiii. 13; 1 Cor. i. 11; iii. 3; 2 Cor. xii. 20; Gal. v. 20: Phil. i. 15; 1 Tim. vi. 4; Tit. iii. 9. This contention and strife would, of course, follow from malice and covetousness, &c. ¶ *Deceit.* This denotes *fraud, falsehood,* &c. That this was common is also plain. The *Cretans* are testified by one of the Greek poets to have been always liars. (Tit. i. 12.) Juvenal charges the same thing on the Romans. (Sat. iii. 41.) "What," says he, "should I do at Rome? *I cannot lie.*" Intimating that if he were there, it would follow, of course, that he would be expected to be false. The same thing is still true. Writers on India tell us that the word of a Hindoo even under oath is not to be regarded; and the same thing occurs in most pagan countries. ¶ *Malignity.* This word signifies here, not malignity in general, but that particular species of it which consists in misinterpreting the words or actions of others, or putting the worst construction on their conduct. ¶ *Whisperers.* Those who secretly, and in a sly manner, by hints and inuendoes, detract from others, or excite suspicion of them. It does not mean those who *openly calumniate*, but that more dangerous class who give *hints* of evil in others, who affect great knowledge, and communicate the evil report under an injunction of secrecy, knowing that it will be divulged. This class of people abounds every where, and there is scarcely any one more dangerous to the peace or happiness of society.

30. *Backbiters.* Those who calumniate, slander, or speak ill of those who are absent. Whisperers declare secretly, and with great reserve, the supposed faults of others. Backbiters proclaim them publicly and avowedly. ¶ *Haters of God.* There is no charge which can be brought against men more severe than this. It is the highest possible crime; yet it is a charge which the conduct of men will abundantly justify, and the truth of which all those experience who are brought

to see their true character. To an awakened sinner there is often nothing more plain and painful than that he is a hater of God. His heart rises up against Him, and his law, and his plan of saving men; and he deeply feels that nothing can subdue this but the mighty power of the Holy One. This is a charge which is not unfrequently brought against men in the Bible; see John vii. 7; xv. 18, 24, 25; iii. 19, 20. Surely, if this be the native character of man, then it is "far gone from original righteousness." No more striking proof of depravity could be given; and in no creed or confession of faith is there a more painful and humiliating representation given of human wickedness, than in this declaration of an inspired apostle, that men are by nature HATERS OF GOD. ¶ *Despiteful.* This word denotes those who abuse, or treat with unkindness or disdain, *those who are present. Whisperers* and *backbiters* are those who calumniate those who are *absent.* ¶ *Proud.* Pride is well understood. It is an inordinate self-esteem; an unreasonable conceit of one's superiority in talents, beauty, wealth, accomplishments, &c. (*Webster.*) Of the existence of this every where, there is abundant proof. And it was particularly striking among the ancients. The sect of the *Stoics* was distinguished for it, and this was the general character of their philosophers. Men will be proud where they suppose none are superior; and it is only the religion that reveals a great and infinite God, and that teaches that *all* blessings are *his* gift, and that *he* has given us the station which we occupy, that will produce true humility. We may add, that the system of heathenism did not disclose the wickedness of the heart, and that this was a main reason why they were elevated in self-esteem. ¶ *Boasters.* Those who arrogate to themselves that which they do not possess, and glory on it. This is closely connected with *pride.* A man who has an inordinate self-conceit, will not be slow to proclaim his own merits to those around him. ¶ *Inventors of evil things.* This doubtless refers to their seeking to find out new arts or plans to practise evil; new devices to gratify their lusts and passions; new forms of luxury, and vice, &c. So intent were they on practising evil, so resolved to gratify their passions, that the mind was excited to discover new modes of gratification. In cities of luxury and vice, this has always been done. Vices change their form, men become satiated, and they are obliged to resort to some new form. The passions cease to be gratified with old forms of indulgence, and consequently men are obliged to resort to new devices to pamper their appetites, and to rekindle their dying passions to a flame. This was eminently true of ancient Rome; a place where all the arts of luxury, all the devices of passion, all the designs of splendid gratification, were called forth to excite and pamper the evil passions of men. Their splendid entertainments, their games, their theatres, their sports—cruel and bloody—were little else than new and ever-varying inventions of evil things to gratify the desires of lust and of pride. ¶ *Disobedient to parents.* This expresses the idea that they did not show to parents that honour, respect, and attention which was due. This has been a crime of paganism in every age; and though among the Romans the duty of honouring parents was enjoined by the laws, yet it is not improbable that the duty was often violated, and that parents were treated with great neglect and even contempt. "Disobedience to parents was punished by the Jewish law with death, and with the Hindoos it is attended with the loss of the child's inheritance. The ancient Greeks considered the neglect of it to be extremely impious, and attended with the most certain effects of divine vengeance. Solon ordered all persons who refused to make due provision for their parents to be punished with infamy, and the same penalty was incurred for personal violence towards them." *Kent's* Commentaries on American Law, vol. ii. p. 207; comp. Virg. Æniad, ix. 283. The feelings of pride and haughtiness would lead to disregard of parents. It might also

31 Without understanding, covenant-breakers, without [1] natural affection, implacable, unmerciful:

1 or, *unsociable*.

be felt that to provide for them when aged and infirm was a burden; and hence there would arise disregard for their wants, and probably open opposition to their wishes, as being the demands of petulance and age. It has been one characteristic of heathenism every where, that it leaves children to treat their parents with neglect. Among the Sandwich islanders it was customary, when a parent was old, infirm, and sick beyond the hope of recovery, for his own children to bury him alive; and it has been the common custom in India for children to leave their aged parents to perish on the banks of the Ganges.

31. *Without understanding*. Inconsiderate, or foolish; see ver. 21, 22. ¶ *Covenant breakers*. Perfidious; false to their contracts. ¶ *Without natural affection*. This expression denotes the want of affectionate regard towards their children. The attachment of parents to children is one of the strongest in nature, and nothing can overcome it but the most confirmed and established wickedness. And yet the apostle charges on the heathen generally the want of this affection. He doubtless refers here to the practice so common among heathens of *exposing* their children, or putting them to death. This crime, so abhorrent to all the feelings of humanity, was common among the heathen, and is still. The Canaanites, we are told (Ps. cvi. 37, 38), "sacrificed their sons and their daughters unto devils, and shed innocent blood, even the blood of their sons and their daughters, whom they sacrificed unto the idols of Canaan." Manasseh among the Jews imitated their example, and introduced the horrid custom of sacrificing children to Moloch, and set the example by offering his own; 2 Chron. xxxiii. 6. Among the ancient Persians it was a common custom to bury children alive. In most of the Grecian states, infanticide was not merely permitted, but actually enforced by law. The Spartan lawgiver expressly ordained that every child that was born should be examined by the ancient men of the tribe, and that if found weak or deformed, should be thrown into a deep cavern at the foot of Mount Taygetus. Aristotle, in his work on government, enjoins the exposure of children that are naturally feeble and deformed, in order to prevent an excess of population. But among all the nations of antiquity, the Romans were the most unrelenting in their treatment of infants. Romulus obliged the citizens to bring up *all* their male children, and the *eldest* of the females, proof that the others were to be destroyed. The Roman father had an absolute right over the life of his child, and we have abundant proof that that right was often exercised. Romulus expressly authorized the destruction of all children that were deformed, only requiring the parents to exhibit them to their five nearest neighbours, and to obtain their consent to their death. The law of the Twelve Tables enacted in the 301st year of Rome, sanctioned the same barbarous practice. Minucius Felix thus describes the barbarity of the Romans in this respect: "I see you exposing your infants to wild beasts and birds, or strangling them after the most miserable manner." (chap. xxx.) Pliny the elder defends the right of parents to destroy their children, upon the ground of its being necessary in order to preserve the population within proper bounds. Tertullian, in his apology, expresses himself boldly on this subject. "How many of you (addressing himself to the Roman people, and to the governors of cities and provinces) might I deservedly charge with infant murder; and not only so, but among the different kinds of death, for choosing some of the cruelest for their own children, such as drowning, or starving with cold or hunger, or exposing to the mercy of

32 Who knowing the judgment of God, that they which commit such things are worthy of death, not only do the same, but [1] have pleasure in them that do them.

1 or, *consent with them.*

dogs; dying by the sword being too sweet a death for children." Nor was this practice arrested in the Roman government until the time of Constantine, the first Christian prince. The Phenicians and Carthaginians were in the habit of sacrificing infants to the gods. It may be added that the crime is no less common among modern pagan nations. No less than 9000 children are exposed in Pekin in China annually. Persons are employed by the police to go through the city with carts every morning to pick up all the children that may have been thrown out during the night. The bodies are carried to a common pit without the walls of the city, into which all, whether *dead or living*, are promiscuously thrown. (*Barrow's* Travels in China, p. 113, Am. ed.) Among the Hindoos the practice is perhaps still more common. In the provinces of Cutch and Guzerat alone the number of infantile murders amounted, according to the lowest calculation in 1807, to 3000 annually; according to another calculation, to 30,000. Females are almost the only victims. (*Buchanan's* Researches in Asia, Eng. ed. p. 49. *Ward's* View of the Hindoos.) In Otaheite, previously to the conversion of the people to Christianity, it was estimated that at least *two-thirds* of the children were destroyed. (*Turnbull's* Voyage round the World in 1800, 2, 3, and 4.) The natives of New South Wales were in the habit of burying the child with its mother, if she should happen to die. (*Collins'* Account of the Colony of New South Wales, p. 124, 125.) Among the Hottentots, infanticide is a common crime. "The altars of the *Mexicans* were continually drenched in the blood of infants." In Peru, no less than two hundred infants were sacrificed on occasion of the coronation of the Inca. The authority for these melancholy statements may be seen in *Beck's* Medical Jurisprudence, vol. i. 184—197, ed. 1823; see also *Robertson's* History of America, p. 221, ed. 1821. This is a *specimen* of the views and feelings of the heathen world; and the painful narrative might be continued to almost any length. After this statement, it cannot surely be deemed a groundless charge when the apostle accused them of being destitute *of natural affection.* ¶ *Implacable.* This word properly denotes those who will not be reconciled where there is a quarrel; or who pursue the offender with unyielding revenge. It denotes an unforgiving temper; and was doubtless common among the ancients, as it is among all heathen people. The aborigines of America have given the most striking manifestation of this that the world has known. It is well known that among them, neither time nor distance will obliterate the memory of an offence; and that the avenger will pursue the offender over hills and streams, and through heat or snow, happy if he may at last, though at the expiration of years, bury the tomahawk in the head of his victim, though it may be at the expense of his own life. See *Robertson's* America, book iv. § lxiii.—lxxxi. ¶ *Unmerciful.* Destitute of compassion. As a proof of this, we may remark that no provisions for the poor or the infirm were made among the heathen. The sick and the infirm were cast out, and doomed to depend on the stinted charity of individuals. Pure religion, only, opens the heart to the appeals of want; and nothing but Christianity has yet expanded the hearts of men to make public provisions for the poor, the ignorant, and the afflicted.

32. *Who knowing.* That the Gentiles had a *moral sense,* or were capable of knowing the will of God in this case, is clear from chap. ii. 14, 15. The means which they had of arriving at the knowledge of God were, their own reason, their conscience, and an observation of the *effects*

of depravity. ¶ *The judgment of God.* The word *judgment* here denotes the declared *sentiment* of God that such things deserved death. It does not mean his *inflictions*, or his *statutes* or *precepts;* but it means that God *thought* or *judged* that they which did such things ought to die. As they were aware of this, it showed their guilt in still persevering in the face of his judgments, and his solemn purpose to inflict punishment. ¶ *Were worthy of death.* The word *death* in the Scriptures is often used to denote punishment. But it does not mean here that these deserved capital punishment from the civil magistrate, but that they knew they were *evil*, and offensive to God, and deserving of punishment from his hand; see John viii. 51 ; Rom. v. 12—19. ¶ *Have pleasure*, &c. They delight in those who commit sin; and hence encourage them in it, and excite them to it. This was a grievous aggravation of the offence. It greatly heightens guilt when we excite others to do it, and seduce them from the ways of innocence. That this was the case with the heathen there can be no doubt. Men do not commit sin often alone. They need the countenance of others. They "join hand in hand," and become confederate in iniquity. *All* social sins are of this class; and most of those which the apostle mentioned were sins of this character.

If this revolting and melancholy picture of the pagan world was a true representation, then it was clear that there was need of some other plan of religion. And that it was true has already in part been seen. In the conclusion of this chapter we may make a few additional observations.

1. The charges which the apostle makes here were evidently those which were well known. He does not even appeal to their writings, as he does on some other occasions, for proof; comp. Titus i. 12 So well known were they, that there was no need of proof. A writer would not advance charges in this manner unless he was *confident* that they were well-founded, and could not be denied.

2. They are abundantly sustained by the heathen writers themselves. This we have in part seen In addition we may adduce the testimony of two Roman writers respecting the state of things at Rome in the time of the apostle. Livy says of the age of Augustus, in some respects the brightest period of the Roman history, "Rome has increased by her virtues until now, *when we can neither bear our vices nor their remedy.*" Preface to his History. Seneca, one of the purest moralists of Rome, who died A. D. 65, says of his own time, "All is full of criminality and vice ; indeed much more of these is committed than can be remedied by force. A monstrous contest of abandoned wickedness is carried on. The lust of sin increases daily ; and shame is daily more and more extinguished. Discarding respect for all that is good and sacred, lust rushes on wherever it will. Vice no longer hides itself. It stalks forth before all eyes. So public has abandoned wickedness become, and so openly does it flame up in the minds of all, that innocence is no longer *seldom*, but has wholly ceased to exist." Seneca de Ira, ii. 8. Further authorities of this kind could be easily given, but these will show that the apostle Paul did not speak at random when he charged them with these enormous crimes.

3. If this was the state of things, then it was clear that there was need of another plan of saving men. It will be remembered that, in these charges, the apostle speaks of the most enlightened and refined nations of antiquity ; and especially that he speaks of the Romans at the very height of their power, intelligence, and splendour. The experiment whether man could save himself by his own works, had been fairly made. After all that their greatest philosophers could do, this was the result, and it is clear that there was need of some better plan than this. More profound and laborious philosophers than had arisen, the pagan world could not hope to see ; more refinement and civilization than then ex-

CHAPTER II.

THEREFORE thou art inexcusable, O man, whosoever thou art that judgest: for [a] wherein thou judgest another, thou condemnest thyself; for thou that judgest, doest the same things.

a 2 Sam.12.6,7.

---

isted, the world could not expect to behold under heathenism. At this time, when the experiment had been made for four thousand years, and when the inefficacy of all human means, even under the most favourable circumstances, to reform mankind, had been tried, *the gospel* was preached to men. It disclosed *another* plan; and its effects were seen at once throughout the most abandoned states and cities of the ancient world.

4. If this was the state of things in the ancient heathen world, the same may be expected to be the state of heathenism still. And it is so. The account given here of ancient heathens would apply substantially still to the pagan world. The same things have been again and again witnessed in China, and Hindostan, and Africa, the Sandwich islands, and in aboriginal America. It would be easy to multiply proofs almost without end of this; and to this day the heathen world is exhibiting substantially the same characteristics that it was in the time of Paul.

5. There was need of some better religion than the pagan. After all that infidels and deists have said of the sufficiency of natural religion, yet here is the sad result. This shows what man can do, and these facts will demonstrate for ever that there was need of some other religion than that furnished by the light of nature.

6. The account in this chapter shows the propriety of missionary exertions. So Paul judged; and so we should judge still. If *this* be the state of the world, and if Christianity, as all Christians believe, contains the remedy for all these evils, then it is wisdom and benevolence to send it to them. And it is not *wisdom* or *benevolence* to withhold it from them. Believing as they do, Christians are bound to send the gospel to the heathen world. It is on this principle that modern missions to the heathen are established; and if the toils of the apostles were demanded to spread the gospel, then are the labours of Christians now. If it was right, and wise, and proper for *them* to go to other lands to proclaim "the unsearchable riches of Christ," then it is equally proper and wise to do it now. If there was danger that the heathen world *then* would perish without the gospel, there is equal danger that the heathen world will perish now.

7. If it should be said that many of these things are practised now in nations which are called *Christian*, and that, therefore, the charge of the apostle that this was the effect of heathenism could not be well-founded, we may reply, (1.) That this is true, too true. But this very fact shows the deep and dreadful depravity of human nature. If such things exist in lands that have a *revelation*, what must have been the state of those countries that had none of its restraints and influences? But, (2.) These things do *not* exist where religion exerts its influence. They are *not* in the bosom of the Christian church. They are not practised by Christians. And the effect of the Christian religion, so far as it has influence, is to call off men from such vices, and to make them holy and pure in their life. Let religion exert its *full influence* on any nominally Christian nation, and these things would cease. Let it send its influence into other lands, and the world, the now polluted world, would become pure before God.

CHAPTER II.

1. *Therefore.* Διὸ. The force of this word here has been the subject of much discussion. The design of this and the following chapter is to show that the *Jews* were no less guilty than

the Gentiles, and that *they* needed the benefit of the same salvation. This the apostle does by showing that they had *greater light* than the Gentiles; and yet that they did the same things. Still they were in the habit of accusing and condemning the Gentiles as wicked and abandoned; while they *excused* themselves on the ground that they possessed the *law* and *oracles* of God, and were his favourite people. The apostle here affirms that they were *inexcuseable* in their sins, that *they* must be condemned in the sight of God, *on the same ground* on which they condemned the Gentiles; to wit, that they had light and yet committed wickedness. If the *Gentiles* were without excuse (chap. i. 20.) in *their* sins, much more would the Jew, who condemned them, be without excuse on the same ground. The word *therefore*, I suppose, refers not to any particular word in the previous chapter, or to any particular verse, but to the general considerations which were suggested by a view of the whole case. And its sense might be thus expressed. "Since you Jews condemn the Gentiles for their sins, on the ground that they *have* the means of knowing their duty, THEREFORE, you who are far more favoured than they, are entirely without an excuse for the same things." ¶ *Thou art inexcusable.* This does not mean that they were inexcusable for *judging others;* but that they had no excuse for their *sins* before God; or that they were under condemnation for their crimes, and needed the benefits of another plan of justification. As the *Gentiles* whom they judged were *condemned*, and were without excuse (i. 20), so were the *Jews* who condemned them without excuse on the same principle; and in a still greater degree. ¶ *O man.* This address is *general* to *any* man who should do this. But it is plain, from the connection, that he means especially the Jews. The use of this word is an instance of the apostle's skill in argument. If he had openly named the Jews here, it would have been likely to have excited opposition from them. He therefore approaches the subject gradually, affirms it of man in general, and then makes a particular application to the Jews. This he does not do, however, until he has advanced so far in the *general principles* of his argument that it would be impossible for them to evade his conclusions; and then he does it in the most tender, and kind, as well as convincing manner, ver. 17, &c. ¶ *Whosoever thou art that judgest.* The word *judgest* (κρίνεις) here is used in the sense of *condemning.* It is not a word of equal strength with that which is rendered "*condemnest*" (κατακρίνεις). It implies, however, that they were accustomed to express themselves freely and severely of the character and doom of the Gentiles. And from the New Testament, as well as from their own writings, there can be no doubt that such was the fact; that they regarded the entire Gentile world with abhorrence, considered them as shut out from the favour of God, and applied to them terms expressive of the utmost contempt. Comp. Mat. xv. 27. ¶ *For wherein.* For in the *same thing.* This implies that substantially the same crimes which were committed among the heathen were also committed among the Jews. ¶ *Thou judgest another.* The meaning of this clearly is, "for the same thing for which you condemn *the heathen*, you condemn yourselves." ¶ *Thou that judgest.* You Jews who condemn other nations. ¶ *Doest the same things.* It is clearly implied here, that they were guilty of offences similar to those practised by the Gentiles. It would not be a just principle of interpretation *to press* this declaration as implying that *precisely* the same offences, and *to the same extent*, were chargeable on them. Thus they were not guilty, in the time of the apostle, of *idolatry;* but of the other crimes enumerated in the first chapter, the Jews might be guilty. The character of the nation, as given in the New Testament, is that they were "an evil and adulterous generation" (Mat. xii. 39; comp. John viii. 7); that they were a "generation of vipers" (Mat. iii. 7; xii. 34); that they were wicked (Mat.

2 But we are sure that the judgment of God is according to truth, against them which commit such things.

xii. 45); that they were sinful (Mark viii. 38); that they were proud, haughty, hypocritical, &c.; (Mat. xxiii.) If such was the character of the Jewish nation *in general*, there is no improbability in supposing that they practised most of the crimes specified in chap. i. On this verse we may remark, (1.) That men are prone to be severe judges of others. (2.) This is often, perhaps commonly, done when the accusers themselves are guilty of the same offences. It often happens, too, that men are remarkably zealous in opposing those offences which they themselves secretly practise. A remarkable instance of this occurs in John viii. 1, &c. Thus David readily condemned the supposed act of injustice mentioned by Nathan; 2 Sam. xii. 1—6. Thus also kings and emperors have enacted severe laws against the very crimes which they have constantly committed themselves. Nero executed the laws of the Roman empire against the very crimes which he was constantly committing; and it was a common practice for Roman *masters* to commit offences which they punished with death in their slaves. (See instances in Grotius on this place.) (3.) Remarkable zeal against sin may be no proof of innocence; compare Mat. vii. 3. The zeal of persecutors, and often of pretended reformers, may be far from proof that *they* are free from the very offences which they are condemning in others. It may all be the work of the hypocrite to conceal some base design; or of the man who seeks to show his hostility to one kind of sin, in order to be a salvo to his conscience for committing some other. (4.) The heart is deceitful. When we judge others we should make it a rule to examine ourselves *on that very point.* Such an examination might greatly *mitigate the severity of our judgment;* or might turn the whole of our indignation against ourselves.

2. *But we are sure.* Greek, "We know." That is, it is the common and admitted sentiment of mankind. It is known and believed by men generally that God will punish such crimes. It is *implied* in this declaration that this was known to the Jews, and it was particularly to the purpose of the apostle so to express himself as to *include* the Jews. *They* knew it because it was every where taught in the Old Testament, and it was the acknowledged doctrine of the nation. The design of the apostle here, says Calvin, is to take away the subterfuges of the hypocrite, lest he should pride himself if he obtained the praise of men, for a far more important trial awaited him at the bar of God. Outwardly he might appear well to men; but *God* searched the heart, and saw the secret as well as the open deeds of men, and they who practised *secretly* what they condemned openly, could not expect to escape the righteous judgment of God. God, without respect of persons would punish wickedness, whether it was *open,* as among the Gentiles, or whether it was concealed under the guise of great regard for religion, as among the Jews. ¶ *The judgment of God.* That God condemns it, and will punish it. He regards those who do these things as guilty, and will treat them accordingly. ¶ *According to truth.* This expression is capable of two meanings. The Hebrews sometimes use it to denote *truly* or *certainly.* God will *certainly* judge and punish such deeds. Another meaning, which is probably the correct one here, is that God will judge those who are guilty of such things, not according *to appearance,* but in *integrity,* and with *righteousness.* He will judge men according to the *real nature* of their conduct, and *not* as their conduct may appear unto men. The secret, as well as the open sinner therefore; the hypocrite, as well as the abandoned profligate, must expect to be judged according to their true character. This meaning comports with the design of the apostle, which is to show that the *Jew,* who *secretly* and *hypocritically* did the very things which he condemned in

3 And thinkest thou this, O man, that judgest them which do such things, and doest the same, that thou shalt escape the judgment of God?

4 Or despisest thou the riches [a]

[a] chap.9.23.

the Gentile, could not escape the righteous judgment of God. ¶ *Against him.* That is, against *every man*, no matter of what age or nation. ¶ *Which commit such things.* The crimes enumerated in chap. i. The apostle is not to be understood as affirming that each and every individual among the Jews was guilty of the specific crimes charged on the heathen, but that they were *as a people* inclined to the same things. Even where they might be *externally* moral, they might be guilty of cherishing evil desires in their hearts, and thus be guilty of the offence, Mat. v. 28. When men *desire* to do evil, and are prevented by the providence of God, it is right to punish them for their evil intentions. The fact that *God*, prevents them from carrying their evil purposes into execution, does not constitute a difference between their *real* character and the character of those who are suffered to *act out* their wicked designs.

3. *And thinkest thou*, &c. This is an appeal to their common sense, to their deep and instinctive conviction of what was *right*. If *they* condemned those who practised these things; if, imperfect and obscure as their sense of justice was; if, unholy as they were, they yet condemned those who were guilty of these offences, would not a holy and just God be far more likely to pronounce judgment? And could *they* escape who had themselves delivered a similar sentence? God is of "purer eyes than to behold evil, and cannot look upon iniquity," (Hab. i. 13.) And if *men* condemned their fellow-men, *how much more* would a pure and holy God condemn iniquity. This appeal is evidently directed against the *Jew*. It was doubtless a prevalent sentiment among them, that provided they adhered to the rites of their religion, and observed the ceremonial law, God would not judge them with the same severity as he would the abandoned and idolatrous Gentiles; compare Mat. iii. 9; John viii. 33. The apostle shows them *that crime is crime*, wherever committed: that sin does not lose its essential character by being committed in the midst of religious privileges; and that those who professed to be the *people of God* have no peculiar *license* to sin. Antinomians in all ages, like the Jews, have supposed that *they*, being the friends of God, have a right to do many things which would not be proper in others; that what *would be* sin in others, *they* may commit with impunity; and that God will not be strict to mark the offences of his people. Against all this Paul is directly opposed, and the Bible uniformly teaches that the most aggravated sins among men are those committed by the professed people of God; comp. Isa. i. 11—17; lxv. 2—5; Rev. iii. 16.

4. *Or despisest.* This word properly means to *contemn*, or to treat with neglect. It does not mean here that they *professedly* treated God's goodness with neglect or contempt; but that they *perverted* and *abused* it; they did not make a proper use of it; they did not regard it as fitted to lead them to repentance; but they derived a *practical impression*, that because God *had* not come forth in judgment and cut them off, but had continued to follow them with blessings, that *therefore* he did not regard them as *sinners*, or they inferred that they were innocent and safe. This argument the Jews were accustomed to use (comp. Luke xiii. 1—5; John ix. 2); and thus sinners still continue to abuse the goodness and mercy of God. ¶ *The riches of his goodness.* This is a Hebrew mode of speaking, for "his rich goodness," *i. e.* for his *abundant* or *great* goodness. *Riches* denote superfluity, or that which *abounds*, or which *exceeds* a man's present wants; and hence the word in the New Testament is used to denote *abundance;* or that which is very great and valuable; see Note, chap. ix. 23; compare chap. xi. 12, 33; 2 Cor. viii. 2:

of his goodness and forbearance [a] and long-suffering, [b] not knowing that the goodness of God leadeth [c] thee to repentance?

a Isa.30.18. *b* John 4.2. *c* Isa. 30. 18.

Eph. i. 7, 18; iii. 8, 16; Col. i. 27; Eph. ii. 4. The word is used here to qualify *each* of the words which follow it, his *rich* goodness, and forbearance, and long-suffering. ¶ *Goodness.* Kindness, benignity. ¶ *Forbearance,* ἀνοχῆς. Literally his *holding-in* or *restraining* his indignation; or forbearing to manifest his displeasure against sin. ¶ *Long-suffering.* This word denotes his slowness to anger; or his suffering them to commit sins *long* without punishing them. It does not differ essentially from forbearance. This is shown by his not coming forth, at the moment that sin is committed, to punish it. He might do it justly, but he spares men from day to day, and year to year, to give them opportunity to repent, and be saved. The way in which men *despise* or *abuse* the goodness of God is to *infer* that He does not intend to punish sin; that they may do it safely; and instead of turning from it, to go on in committing it more constantly, as if they were safe. "Because sentence against an evil work is not executed speedily, therefore the heart of the sons of men is fully set in them to do evil," Eccl. viii. 11. The same thing was true in the time of Peter; 2 Pet. iii. 3, 4. And the same thing is true of wicked men in every age; nor is there a more decisive proof of the wickedness of the human heart, than this disposition to abuse the goodness of God, and because *he* shows kindness and forbearance, to take occasion to plunge deeper into sin, to forget his mercy, and to provoke him to anger. ¶ *Not knowing.* Not *considering.* The word used here, ἀγνοῶν, means not merely *to be ignorant of,* but it denotes such a degree of inattention as to result in ignorance. Comp. Hos. ii. 8. In this sense it denotes a *voluntary*, and therefore a *criminal* ignorance. ¶ *Leadeth thee,* &c. Or the tendency, the design of the goodness of God is to induce men to repent of their sins, and not to lead them to deeper and more aggravated iniquity. The same sentiment is expressed in 2 Pet. iii. 9, "The Lord is long-suffering to us-ward, not willing that any should perish, but that all should come to repentance." See also Isa. xxx. 18, "And therefore will the Lord wait, that he may be gracious unto you;" Hos. v. 15; Ezek. xviii. 23, 32. ¶ *Repentance.* Change of mind, and purpose, and life. The word here evidently means, not merely sorrow, but a forsaking of sin, and turning from it. The tendency of God's goodness and forbearance to lead men to repentance, is manifest in the following ways. (1.) It shows the *evil* of transgression when it is seen to be committed against so kind and merciful a Being. (2.) It is fitted to melt and soften the heart. Judgments often harden the sinner's heart, and make him obstinate. But if while *he* does evil God is as constantly doing him good; if the patience of God is seen from year to year, while the man is rebellious, it is adapted to melt and subdue the heart. (3.) The *great* mercy of God in this often appears to men to be overwhelming; and so it would to all, if they saw it as it is. God bears with men from childhood to youth; from youth to manhood; from manhood to old age; often while *they* violate every law, contemn his mercy, profane his name, and disgrace their species; and still, notwithstanding all this, his anger is turned away, and the sinner lives, and "riots in the beneficence of God." If there is any thing that can affect the heart of man, it is this; and when he is brought to see it, and contemplate it, it rushes over the soul and overwhelms it with bitter sorrow. (4.) The mercy and forbearance of God are constant. The manifestations of his goodness come in every form; in the sun, and light, and air; in the rain, the stream, the dew-drop; in food, and raiment, and home; in friends, and liberty, and protection; in health, and peace; and in the gospel of Christ, and the offers of life; and in all these ways God is appealing to his creatures each moment.

5 But, after thy hardness and impenitent heart, treasurest [a] up unto thyself wrath, against the day of wrath, and [b] revelation of the righteous judgment of God;

a Deut.32.34. b Eccl.12.14.

and setting before them the evils of ingratitude, and beseeching them to turn and live.

And from this passage, we cannot but remark, (1.) That the most effectual preaching is that which sets before men most of the goodness of God. (2.) Every man is under obligation to forsake his sins, and turn to God. There is no man who has not seen repeated proofs of his mercy and love. (3.) Sin is a stubborn and an amazing evil. Where it can resist all the appeals of God's mercy; where the sinner can make his way down to hell through *all* the proofs of God's goodness; where he can refuse to hear God speaking to him each day, and each hour, it shows an amazing extent of depravity to resist all this, and still remain a sinner. Yet there are thousands and millions who do it; and who can be won by no exhibition of love or mercy to forsake their sins, and turn to God. Happy is the man who is melted into contrition by the goodness of God, and who sees and mourns over the evil of sinning against so good a Being as is the Creator and Parent of all.

5. *But after thy hardness.* The word "after" here (κατὰ) means *in respect to,* or you act according *to the direct tendency* of a hard heart in treasuring up wrath. The word *hardness* is used to denote *insensibility* of mind. It properly means that which is insensible to the *touch,* or on which no *impression* is made by contact, as a stone, &c. Hence it is applied to the *mind,* to denote a state where no motives make an impression; which is *insensible* to all the appeals made to it; see Mat. xxv. 24; xix. 8; Acts xix. 9. And here it expresses a state of mind where the *goodness* and *forbearance* of God have no effect. The man still remains *obdurate,* to use a word which has precisely the meaning of the Greek in this place. It is implied in this expression that the *direct tendency,* or the *inevitable result,* of that state of mind was to treasure up wrath, &c. ¶ *Impenitent heart.* A heart which is not affected with sorrow for sin, in view of the mercy and goodness of God. This is an *explanation* of what he meant by *hardness.* ¶ *Treasurest up.* To *treasure up,* or to *lay up treasure,* commonly denotes a laying by in a place of security of property that may be of use to us at some future period. In this place it is used, however, in a more general sense, to *accumulate,* to *increase.* It still has the idea of *hoarding up,* carries the thought beautifully and impressively *onward* to future times. *Wrath,* like wealth treasured up, is not exhausted at present, and hence the sinner becomes bolder in sin. But it exists, *for future use;* it is *kept in store* (comp. 2 Pet. iii. 7) against future times; and the man who commits sin is only *increasing* this by every act of transgression. The same sentiment is taught in a most solemn manner in Deut. xxxii. 34, 35. —It may be remarked here, that most men have an *immense treasure* of this kind in store, which eternal ages of pain will not exhaust or diminish! Stores of wrath are thus reserved for a guilty world, and in due time it "will come upon man *to the uttermost,*" 1 Thess. ii. 16. ¶ *Unto thyself.* For thyself, and not for another; to be exhausted on *thee,* and not on your fellow-man. This is the case with every sinner, as really and as certainly as though he were the only solitàry mortal in existence. ¶ *Wrath.* Note, chap. i. 18. ¶ *Day of wrath.* The day when God shall show or execute his wrath against sinners; comp. Rev. vi. 17; 1 Thess. i. 10; John iii. 36; Eph. v. 6. ¶ *And revelation.* On the day when the righteous judgment of God will be *revealed,* or made known. Here we learn, (1.) That the punishment of the wicked will be *just.* It will not be a judgment of *caprice* or *tyranny,* but a *righteous* judgment, that is, such a judgment as it will be

6 Who [a] will render to every man according to his deeds;

7 To them, who, by patient continuance in well doing, seek

a Prov.24.12; Mat.16.27; Rev.20.12.

right to render, or as *ought* to be rendered, and THEREFORE such as God *will* render, for he will do right; 2 Thess. i. 6. (2.) The punishment of the wicked is *future*. It is *not* exhausted in this life. It is *treasured* up for a future day, and that day is a day of wrath. How contrary to this text are the pretences of those who maintain that *all* punishment is executed in this life. (3.) How foolish as well as wicked is it to lay up *such* a treasure for the future; to have the *only* inheritance in the eternal world, an inheritance of *wrath* and *wo!*

6. *Who will render.* That is, who will make *retribution* as a righteous Judge; or who will *give* to every man as he deserves. ¶ *To every man.* To each one. This is a general principle, and it is clear that in this respect God would deal with the Jew as he does with the Gentile. This *general principle* the apostle is establishing, that he may bring it to bear on the *Jew*, and to show that *he* cannot escape *simply because he is a Jew*. ¶ *According to his deeds.* That is, *as he deserves;* or God will be just, and will treat every man as he *ought* to be treated, or according to his character. The word *deeds* (ἔϱγα) is sometimes applied to the *external conduct.* But it is plain that this is not its meaning here. It denotes every thing connected with conduct, including the *acts* of the mind, the motives, the principles, as well as the mere external act. Our word *character* more aptly expresses it than any single word. It is not true that God will treat men according to their *external* conduct; but the whole language of the Bible implies that he will judge men according to the *whole* of their conduct, including their thoughts, and principles, and motives; *i. e.*, as they deserve. The doctrine of this place is elsewhere abundantly taught in the Bible, Prov. xxiv. 12; Matt. xvi. 27; Rev. xx. 12; Jer. xxxii. 19. It is to be observed here that the apostle does not say that men will be rewarded *for* their deeds, (comp. Luke xvii. 10,) but *according to* (κατὰ) their deeds. Christians will be saved *on account of* the merits of the Lord Jesus Christ, (Titus iii. 5,) but still the rewards of heaven will be *according to* their works; that is, they who have laboured most, and been most faithful, shall receive the highest reward, or their fidelity in their Master's service shall be the measure or rule according to which the rewards of heaven shall be distributed, Matt. xxv. 14—29. Thus the ground or reason *why* they are saved shall be the merits of the Lord Jesus. The measure of their happiness shall be according to their *character and deeds.* On what principle God will distribute his rewards the apostle proceeds immediately to state.

7. *To them.* Whoever they may be. ¶ *Patient continuance.* Who by *perseverance* in well doing, or in a good work. It means that they who so continue, or persevere, in good works as to evince that they are disposed to obey the law of God. It does not mean those who perform one *single act*, but those who so live as to show that this is their *character* to obey God. It is the uniform doctrine of the Bible that none will be saved but those who *persevere* in a life of holiness, Rev. ii. 10; Matt. x. 22; Heb. x. 38, 39. No other conduct gives evidence of piety but that which *continues* in the ways of righteousness. Nor has God ever promised eternal life to men unless they so *persevere* in a life of holiness as to show that this is their *character*, their settled and firm rule of action. The words *well doing* here denote such conduct as shall be conformed to the law of God; not merely *external* conduct, but that which proceeds from a heart attached to God and his cause. ¶ *Seek for.* This word properly denotes the act of endeavouring to find any thing that is lost, Matt. xviii. 12; Luke ii. 48, 49. But it also denotes the act when one

for glory and honour and immortality, eternal life:

8 But unto them that are [a] contentious, and [b] do not obey the

a 1 Tim. 6. 3. 4. b 2 Thess. 1. 8.

earnestly strives, or desires to obtain any thing; when he puts forth his efforts to accomplish it. Thus, Matt. vi. 33, " Seek ye first the kingdom of God," &c. Acts xvi. 10; 1 Cor. x. 24; Luke xiii. 24. In this place it denotes an earnest and intense desire to obtain eternal life. It does not mean simply the desire of a sinner *to be happy*, or the efforts of those who are *not willing* to forsake their sins and yield to God, but the intense effort of those who are willing to forsake all their crimes, and submit to God and obey his laws. ¶ *Glory and honour and immortality.* The three words used here, denote the happiness of the heavenly world. They vary somewhat in their meaning, and are *each* descriptive of *something* in heaven, that renders it an object of intense desire. The expressions are *cumulative*, or they are designed to express the happiness of heaven in the highest possible degree. The word *glory* (δόξαν) denotes properly *praise, celebrity*, or any thing distinguished for beauty, ornament, majesty, splendour, as of the sun, &c.; and then it is used to denote the highest happiness or felicity, as expressing every thing that shall be splendid, rich, and grand. It denotes that there will be an absence of every thing *mean, grovelling, obscure.* The word *honour* (τιμὴν) implies rather the idea of *reward*, or just retribution—the honour and reward which shall be conferred in heaven on the friends of God. It stands opposed to contempt, poverty, and want among men. Here they are *despised* by men; there, they shall be *honoured* by God. ¶ *Immortality.* That which is not corruptible or subject to decay. It is applied to heaven as a state where there shall be no *decay* or *death*, in strong contrast with our present condition, where all things are corruptible, and soon vanish away. These expressions are undoubtedly descriptive of a state of things *beyond the grave.* They are never applied in the Scriptures to any condition of things *on the earth.* This consideration proves, therefore, that the expressions in the next verse, *indignation*, &c. apply to the punishment of the wicked *beyond the grave.* ¶ *Eternal life.* That is, God will "*render*" eternal life to those who seek it in this manner. This is a great principle; and this shows that the apostle means by "*their deeds*" (ver. 6,) not merely their *external conduct*, but their inward thoughts, and efforts *evinced by* their *seeking* for glory, &c. For the meaning of the expression "eternal life," see Note, John v. 24.

8. *Who are contentious.* This expression usually denotes those who are of a quarrelsome or litigious disposition; and generally has reference to controversies *among men.* But here it evidently denotes a disposition *towards God*, and is of the same signification as *rebellious*, or as *opposing God.* They who contend with the Almighty; who resist his claims, who rebel against his laws, and refuse to submit to his requirements, however made known. The LXX. use the verb to translate the Hebrew word מרה, *marah*, in Deut. xxi. 20. One striking characteristic of the sinner is, that he *contends* with God, *i. e.*, that he opposes and resists his claims. This is the case with *all* sinners; and it was particularly so with the Jews, and hence the apostle used the expression here to characterize them particularly. His argument he intended to apply to the Jews, and hence he used such an expression as would *exactly* describe them. This character of being a *rebellious people* was one which was *often* charged on the Jewish nation, Deut. ix. 7, 24; xxxi. 27; Isa. i. 2; xxx. 9; lxv. 2; Jer. v. 23; Ezek. ii. 3, 5. ¶ *Do not obey the truth.* Comp. chap. i. 18. The *truth* here denotes the divine will, which is alone the light of truth. *(Calvin.)* It means true doctrine in opposition to false opinions; and to refuse to *obey it* is to regard it as false, and to resist its influence.

truth, but obey unrighteousness; indignation and wrath,

9 Tribulation and anguish, upon every soul of man that doeth evil,

---

The *truth* here means all the correct representations which had been made of God, and his perfections, and law, and claims, whether by the light of nature or by revelation. The description thus included Gentiles and Jews, but particularly the *latter*, as they had been more signally favoured with the light of truth. It had been an eminent characteristic of the Jews that they had refused to obey the commands of the *true* God, Josh. v. 6; Judg. ii. 2; vi. 10; 2 Kings xviii. 12; Jer. iii. 13, 25; xlii. 21; xliii. 4, 7; ix. 13. ¶ *But obey unrighteousness.* The expression means that they yielded themselves to iniquity, and thus became *the servants of sin,* Rom. vi. 13, 16, 17, 19. Iniquity thus may be said to *reign* over men, as they follow the dictates of evil, make no resistance to it, and implicitly obey all its hard requirements. ¶ *Indignation and wrath.* That is, these *shall be rendered* to those who are contentious, &c. The difference between indignation and wrath, says Ammonius, is that the former is of *short duration,* but the latter is a long continued remembrance of evil. The one is *temporary*, the other denotes *continued* expressions of hatred of evil. Eustathius says that the word *indignation* denotes the *internal* emotion, but *wrath* the *external* manifestation of indignation. (*Tholuck.*) Both words refer to the opposition which God will cherish and express against sin in the world of punishment.

9. *Tribulation.* This word commonly denotes *affliction*, or the situation of being *pressed down* by a burden, as of trials, calamities, &c.; and hence to be *pressed down* by punishment or pain inflicted for sins. As applied to future punishment, it denotes the pressure of the calamities that will come upon the soul as the just reward of sin. ¶ *And anguish,* στενοχωρία. This noun is used in but three other places in the New Testament; Rom. viii. 35; 2 Cor. vi. 4; xii. 10. The *verb* is used in 2 Cor. iv. 8; vi. 12. It means literally *narrowness of place, want of room,* and then the anxiety and distress of mind which a man experiences who is pressed *on every side* by afflictions, and trials, and want, or by punishment, and who does not know where he may turn himself to find relief. (*Schleusner.*) It is thus expressive of the punishment of the wicked. It means that they shall be *compressed* with the manifestations of God's displeasure, so as to be in deep distress, and so as not to know where to find relief. These words *affliction and anguish* are often connected; Rom. viii. 35. ¶ *Upon every soul of man.* Upon *all* men. In Hebrew the word *soul* often denotes the man himself. But still, the apostles, by the use of this word here, meant perhaps to signify that the punishment should not be *corporeal*, but afflicting the *soul.* It should be a *spiritual* punishment, a punishment of *mind.* (*Ambrose.* See *Tholuck.*) ¶ *Of the Jew first.* Having stated the *general principle* of the divine administration, he comes now to make the application. To the *principle* there could be no objection. And the apostle now shows that it was applicable to the Jew as well as the Greek, and to the Jew pre-eminently. It was applicable *first*, or in an *eminent degree,* to the Jew, because, (1.) He had been peculiarly favoured with light and knowledge on all these subjects. (2.) These principles were fully stated in his own law, and were in strict accordance with all the teaching of the prophets; see Note on ver. 6; also Ps. vii. 11; ix. 17; cxxxix. 19; Prov. xiv. 32. ¶ *Of the Gentile.* That is, of all who were not Jews. On what principles God will inflict punishment on them, he states in ver. 12—16. It is clear that this refers to the *future* punishment of the wicked, for, (1.) It stands in contrast with the *eternal life* of those who seek for glory (ver. 7). If this description of the effect of sin refers to *this life*, then the effects spoken of in relation to the righteous refer to this life also. But in no place in the Scriptures is it said that men experience *all* the blessings of *eternal* life

of the Jew first, and also of the [1] Gentile.

10 But glory, [a] honour, and peace, to every man that worketh good, to the Jew first, and also to the [1] Gentile:

11 For [b] there is no respect of persons with God.

1 or, *Greek.* a 1 Pet.1.7. b Deut.10.17; 2Chron.19.7; Gal.6.7,8; 1 Pet.1.17

in this world; and the very supposition is absurd. (2.) It is not *true* that there is a just and complete retribution to every man, according to his deeds, in this life. Many of the wicked are prospered in *life,* and "there are no bands in their death, but their strength is firm;" Ps. lxxiii. 4. Many of the righteous pine in poverty and want and affliction, and die in the flames of persecution. Nothing is more clear than there is *not* in this life a full and equitable distribution of rewards and punishments; and as the *proposition* of the apostle here is, that *God* WILL *render to every man* ACCORDING *to his deeds* (ver. 6), it follows that this must be accomplished in another world. (3.) The Scriptures uniformly affirm, that for *the very things* specified here, God will consign men to eternal death; 2 Thess. i. 8, "In flaming fire, taking vengeance on them that know not God, and that OBEY NOT the gospel of our Lord Jesus Christ, who shall be punished with everlasting destruction," &c.; 1 Pet. iv. 17. We may remark also, that there could be no more alarming description of future suffering than is specified in this passage. It is *indignation;* it is *wrath;* it is *tribulation;* it is *anguish* which the sinner is to endure for ever. Truly men exposed to this awful doom should be alarmed, and should give diligence to escape from the woe which is to come.

11. *For.* This particle is used here to *confirm* what is said before, particularly that this punishment should be experienced by the *Jew* as well as the *Gentile.* For God would deal with both on the principles of justice. ¶ *Respect of persons.* The word thus rendered means *partiality,* in pronouncing judgment, in favouring one party or individual more than another, not because his cause is more just, but on account of something personal—on account of his wealth, or rank, or office, or influence, or by personal friendship, or by the fear of him. It has special reference to a *judge* who pronounces judgment between parties at law. The exercise of such partiality was strictly and often forbidden to the Jewish magistrates; Lev. xix. 15; Deut. i. 17; Prov. xxiv. 23; James ii. 1, 3, 9. In his capacity as a *Judge,* it is applied often to God. It means that he will not be influenced in awarding the retributions of eternity, in *actually* pronouncing and executing sentence, by any partiality, or by regard to the wealth, office, rank, or appearance of men. He will judge righteous judgment; he will judge men as they *ought* to be judged; according to their *character* and deserts; and not contrary to their character, or by partiality. The *connection* here demands that this affirmation should be limited *solely to his dealing with men* AS THEIR JUDGE. And in this sense, and this only, this is affirmed often of God in the Scriptures; Deut. x. 17; 2 Chron. xix. 7; Eph. vi. 9; Col. iii. 25; Gal. vi. 7, 8; 1 Pet. i. 17; Acts x. 34. It does not affirm that he *must* make all his creatures *equal* in talent, health, wealth, or privilege; it does not imply that, as a sovereign, he may not make a difference in their endowments, their beauty, strength, or graces; it does not imply that he may not bestow his favours where he pleases where *all* are undeserving, or that he may not make a difference in the *characters* of men by his providence, and by the agency of his Spirit. All these are *actually* done, done not out of any respect to their *persons,* to their rank, office, or wealth, but according to his own sovereign good pleasure; Eph. i. To deny that this *is* done, would be to deny the manifest arrangement of things every where on the earth. To deny that God had a *right* to do it, would be, (1.) To maintain that sin-

12 For as many as have sinned without law, shall also perish

ners had a *claim* on his favours. (2.) That he might not do what he willed with his own; or, (3.) To affirm that God was under obligation to make all men with just the same talents and privileges, *i. e.* that all creatures *must be*, in all respects, *just alike*. This passage, therefore, is very improperly brought to *disprove* the doctrine of decrees, or election, or sovereignty. It has respect to a different thing, to the *actual exercise* of the office of *the Judge of the world;* and whatever may be the truth about God's decrees, or his electing love, *this* passage teaches nothing in relation to either. It may be added that this passage contains a most alarming truth for guilty men. It is that God will not be influenced by *partiality*, but will treat them *just as they deserve*. He will not be won or awed by their rank or office; by their wealth or endowments; by their numbers, their power, or their robes of royalty and splendour. Every man should tremble at the prospect of falling into the hands of a *just God*, who will treat him just as he deserves, and should without delay seek a refuge in the Saviour and Advocate provided for the guilty; 1 John ii. 1, 2.

12. *For*. This is used to give a *reason* for what he had just said, or to show on what principles God would treat man, so as not to be a respecter of persons. ¶ *As many*. *Whosoever*. This includes *all* who have done it, and evidently has respect to the Gentile world. It is of the more importance to remark this, because he does not say that it is applicable to a *few* only, or to great and incorrigible instances of pagan wickedness, but it is a universal, sweeping declaration, obviously including *all*. ¶ *Have sinned* Have been guilty of crimes of any kind toward God or man. Sin is the transgression of a rule of conduct, however made known to mankind. ¶ *Without law*, ἀνόμως. This expression evidently means without *revealed* or *written* law, as the apostle immediately says that they *had* a law of nature, (ver. 14, 15). The word law, νόμος, is often used to denote the revealed law of God, the Scriptures, or revelation in general; Mat. xii. 5; Luke ii. 23, 24; x. 26; John viii. 5, 17. ¶ *Shall also perish*, ἀπολοῦνται. The Greek word used here occurs frequently in the New Testament. It means to *destroy*, to *lose*, or to *corrupt*, and is applied to *life*, (Mat. x. 39); to a *reward* of labour, (Mat. x. 42); to *wisdom* (1 Cor. i. 19); to *bottles*, (Mat. ix. 17). It is also used to denote future punishment, or the destruction of soul and body in hell, (Mat. x. 28; xviii. 14; John iii. 15), where it is *opposed to eternal life*, and therefore denotes *eternal death;* Rom. xiv. 15; John xvii. 12. In this sense the word is evidently used in this verse. The connection demands that the reference should be to a future judgment to be passed on the heathen. It will be remarked here that the apostle does not say they shall *be saved* without law. He does not give even an intimation respecting their salvation. The strain of the argument, as well as this express declaration, shows that they who had *sinned*—and in the first chapter he had proved that *all* the heathen were sinners—would be punished. If any of the heathen are saved, it will be, therefore, an exception to the *general rule* in regard to them. The apostles evidently believed that the great mass of them would be destroyed. *On this ground* they evinced such zeal to save them; on this ground the Lord Jesus commanded the gospel to be preached to them; and on this ground Christians are now engaged in the effort to bring them to the knowledge of the Lord Jesus. It may be added here, that all modern investigations have gone to confirm the position that the heathen are as degraded now as they were in the time of Paul. ¶ *Without law*. That is, they shall not be judged by a law which they have not. They shall not be tried and condemned by the *revelation* which the Jews had. They shall be condemned only according to the knowledge and the law which they actually possess. This is the equit-

without law: and as many as have sinned in the law shall be judged by the law;

13 (For [a] not the hearers of the law *are* just before God, but the doers of the law shall be justified.

a James 1.22,25.

able rule on which God will judge the world. According to this, it is not to be apprehended that they will suffer *as much* as those who have the revealed will of God; comp. Mat. x. 15; xi. 24; Luke x. 12. ¶ *Have sinned in the law.* Have sinned *having* the revealed will of God, or endowed with greater light and privileges than the heathen world. The apostle here has undoubted reference to the *Jews*, who had the law of God, and who prided themselves much on its possession. ¶ *Shall be judged by the law.* This is an equitable and just rule; and to this the Jews could make no objection. Yet the admission of this would have led directly to the point to which Paul was conducting his argument, to show that *they* also were under condemnation, and needed a Saviour. It will be observed here, that the apostle uses a different expression in regard to the Jews from what he does of the Gentiles. He says of the former, that they "*shall be judged;*" of the latter, that they "*shall perish.*" It is not certainly known why he varied this expression. But if conjecture may be allowed, it may have been for the following reasons. (1.) If he had affirmed of the Jews that they should *perish*, it would at once have excited their prejudice, and have armed them against the conclusion to which he was about to come. Yet they could bear the word to be applied to *the heathen*, for it was in accordance with their own views and their own mode of speaking, and was strictly true. (2.) The word "judged" is *apparently* more *mild*, and yet *really* more *severe*. It would arouse no prejudice to say that they would be judged by their law. It was indeed paying a sort of tribute or regard to that on which they prided themselves so much, the possession of the law of God. Still, it was a word, *implying* all that he wished to say, and *involving* the idea that *they* would be punished and destroyed. If it was admitted that the heathen would perish; and if God was to judge the Jews by an unerring rule, that is, according to their privileges and light; then it would follow that they would also be condemned, and *their own minds* would come at once to the conclusion. The change of words here may indicate, therefore, a nice *tact*, or delicate address in argument, urging home to the conscience an offensive truth rather by the deduction of the mind of the opponent *himself* than by a harsh and severe charge of the writer. In instances of this, the Scriptures abound; and it was this especially that so eminently characterized the arguments of our Saviour.

13. *For not the hearers*, &c. The same sentiment is implied in James i. 22; Mat. vii. 21, 24; Luke vi. 47. The apostle here doubtless designed to meet an objection of the Jews; to wit, that they had the law, that they manifested great deference for it, that they heard it read with attention, and professed a willingness to yield themselves to it. To meet this, he states a very plain and obvious principle, that this was insufficient to justify them before God, unless they rendered actual obedience. ¶ *Are just.* Are justified before God, or are personally holy. Or, in other words, simply *hearing* the law is not meeting all its requirements, and making men holy. If they expected to be saved by the *law*, it required something more than merely to *hear it*. It demanded *perfect obedience*. ¶ *But the doers of the law.* They who comply entirely with its demands; or who yield to it perfect and perpetual obedience. This was the plain and obvious demand, not only of common sense, but of the Jewish law itself; Deut. iv. 1; Lev. xviii. 5; comp. Rom. x. 9. ¶ *Shall be justified.* This expression is evidently synonymous with that in Lev. xviii. 5, where it is said that "he shall live in

14 For when the Gentiles, which
have not the law, do by nature the
things contained in the law, these
having not the law, are a law [a]
unto themselves.
15 Which show the work of the

[a] 1 Cor.11.14.

them." The meaning is, that it is a *maxim* or *principle* of the law of God, that if a creature will keep it, and obey it entirely, he shall not be *condemned*, but shall be *approved* and *live for ever*. This does not affirm that any one ever *has* thus lived in this world, but it is an affirmation of a great general principle of law, that if a creature is justified BY *the law*, the obedience must be entire and perpetual. If such *were* the case, as there would be no ground of condemnation, man would be saved by the law. If the Jews, therefore, expected to be saved by their law, it must be, not by *hearing* the law, nor by being called a Jew, but by perfect and unqualified obedience to all its requirements. This passage is designed, doubtless, to meet a very common and pernicious sentiment of the Jewish teachers, that *all* who became hearers and listeners to the law would be saved. The *inference* from the passage is, that no man can be saved by his *external* privileges, or by an *outward* respectful deference to the truths and ordinances of religion.

14. *For when.* The apostle, in ver. 13, had stated a general principle, that the *doers of the law* only can be justified, if justification is attempted by the law. In this verse and the next, he proceeds to show that the same *principle* is applicable to the heathen; that though they have not the *written* law of God, yet that they have sufficient knowledge of his will to take away every excuse for sin, and consequently that the course of reasoning by which he had come to the conclusion that they were guilty, is well founded. This verse is not to be understood as affirming, as an *historical fact*, that any of the heathen ever *did* perfectly obey the law which they had, any more than the previous verse affirms it of the Jews. The main point in the argument is, that if men are justified by the *law*, their obedience must be *entire* and *perfect;* that this is not to be external only, or to consist in *hearing* or in acknowledging the justice of the law; and that the Gentiles had an opportunity of illustrating this principle as well as the Jews, since they also had a law among themselves. The word *when* (ὅταν) does not imply that the thing *shall certainly* take place, but is one form of introducing a supposition; or of stating the connection of one thing with another, Matt. v. 11; vi. 2, 5, 6, 16; x. 19. It is, however, true that the main things contained in this verse, and the next, actually occurred, that the Gentiles did *many* things which the law of God required. ¶ *The Gentiles.* All who were not Jews. ¶ *Which have not the law.* Who have not a revelation, or the written word of God. In the Greek the article is omitted, "who have not law," *i. e.* any revealed law. ¶ *By nature.* By some, this phrase has been supposed to belong to the previous member of the sentence, "who have not the law *by nature.*" But our translation is the more natural and usual construction. The expression means clearly by the light of conscience and reason, and whatever other helps they may have *without* revelation. It denotes simply, *in that state which is without the revealed will of God.* In that condition they had many helps of tradition, conscience, reason, and the observation of the dealings of divine Providence, so that to a considerable extent they knew what was right and what was wrong. ¶ *Do the things.* Should they not merely *understand* and *approve*, but actually *perform* the things required in the law. ¶ *Contained in the law.* Literally the things *of* the law, *i. e.* the things which the law *requires.* Many of those things might be done by the heathen, as, *e. g.* respect to parents, truth, justice, honesty, chastity. *So far* as they *did* any of those things, so far they showed that they *had* a law among themselves. And wherein they *failed* in these things they showed

law written in their hearts, their [1] conscience also bearing witness, and *their* thoughts the [2] mean while accusing or else excusing one another.)

16 In the day when God shall

1 or, *the conscience witnessing with them.*

2 or, *between themselves.*

that they were justly condemned. ¶ *Are a law unto themselves.* This is explained in the following verse. It means that their own reason and conscience constituted, *in these things*, a law, or prescribed that for them which the revealed law did to the Jews.

15. *Which show.* Who thus evince or show. ¶ *The work of the law.* The design, purpose, or object which is contemplated by the revealed law; that is, to make known to man his duty, and to *enforce* the obligation to perform it. This does not mean, by any means, that they had *all* the knowledge which the law would impart, for then there would have been no need of a revelation, but that, *as far as it went*, as far as they had a knowledge of right and wrong, they *coincided* with the revealed will of God. In other words, the will of God, whether made known by reason or revelation, will be *the same* so far as reason goes. The difference is that revelation *goes farther* than reason; sheds light on new duties and doctrines; as the information given by the naked eye and the telescope is the same, except that the telescope carries the sight *forward*, and reveals new worlds to the sight of man. ¶ *Written in their hearts.* The revealed law of God was written on tables of stone, and then recorded in the books of the Old Testament. This law the Gentiles did not possess, but, to a certain extent, the same requirements were written on their hearts. Though not *revealed* to them as to the Jews, yet they had obtained the knowledge of them by the light of nature. The word *hearts* here denotes the *mind itself*, as it does also frequently in the sacred Scriptures; not the heart, as the seat of the affections. It does not mean that they loved or even approved of the law, but that they had knowledge of it; and that that knowledge was deeply engraven on their minds. ¶ *Their conscience.* This word properly means the judgment of the mind respecting right and wrong; or the judgment which the mind passes on the morality or immorality of its own actions, when it instantly approves or condemns them. It has usually been termed the *moral sense*, and is a very important principle in a moral government. Its design is to answer the purposes of an *ever attendant witness* of a man's conduct; to compel him to pronounce on his own doings, and thus to excite him to virtuous deeds, to give comfort and peace when he does right, to deter from evil actions by making him, whether he will or no, *his own executioner*; see John viii. 9; Acts xxiii. 1; xxiv. 16; Rom. ix. 1; 1 Tim. i. 5. By nature every man thus approves or condemns his own acts; and there is not a profounder principle of the Divine administration, than thus compelling every man to pronounce on the moral character of his own conduct. Conscience may be enlightened or unenlightened; and its use may be greatly perverted by false opinions. Its province is not to communicate any *new truth*, it is simply to express *judgment*, and to impart pleasure or inflict pain for a man's own good or evil conduct. The apostle's argument does not require him to say that conscience *revealed* any truth, or any knowledge of duty, to the Gentiles, but that *its actual exercise* proved that they *had* a knowledge of the law of God. Thus it was a *witness* simply of that fact. ¶ *Bearing witness.* To bear witness is to furnish testimony, or proof. And the exercise of the conscience here showed or proved that they *had* a knowledge of the law. The expression does not mean that the exercise of *their* conscience bore witness of any thing to *them*, but that its exercise may be alleged as a proof that they were not without some knowledge of the law. ¶ *And their thoughts.* The word thoughts (λογισμῶν) means properly *reasonings*, or *opinions*, sen-

judge the secrets [a] of men, by Jesus Christ, according to my [b] gospel.

a Luke 8.17. b Rom.16.25.

timents, &c. Its meaning here may be expressed by the word *reflections.* Their reflections on their own conduct would be attended with pain or pleasure. It differs from *conscience,* inasmuch as the decisions of conscience are *instantaneous,* and without any process of reasoning. This supposes subsequent reflection, and it means that such reflections would only deepen and confirm the decisions of conscience. ¶ *The mean while.* Margin, "Between themselves." The rendering in the margin is more in accordance with the Greek. The expression sometimes means, in the mean time, or at the same time; and sometimes *afterward,* or *subsequently.* The Syriac and Latin Vulgate render this *mutually.* They seem to have understood this as affirming that the heathen among themselves, by their writings, accused or acquitted one another. ¶ *Accusing.* If the actions were evil. ¶ *Excusing.* That is, if their actions were good. ¶ *One another.* The margin renders this expression in connection with the adverb, translated "in the mean while," "between themselves." This view is also taken by many commentators, and this is its probable meaning. If so, it denotes the fact that in their *reflections,* or their *reasonings,* or *discussions,* they accused each other of crime, or acquitted one another; they showed that they *had* a law; that they acted on the supposition that they had. To show this was the design of the apostle; and there was no further proof of it needed than that which he here adduced. (1.) They had a *conscience,* pronouncing on their *own* acts; and, (2.) Their *reasonings, based on the supposition of some such common and acknowledged standard* of accusing or acquitting, supposed the same thing. If, therefore, they condemned or acquitted *themselves;* if in these reasonings and reflections, they proceeded on the principle that they *had* some rule of right and wrong, *then* the proposition of the apostle was made out that it was right for God to judge them, and to destroy them; ver. 8—12.

16. *In the day.* This verse is doubtless to be connected with verse 12, and the intermediate verses are a parenthesis, and it implies that the heathen world, as well as the Jews, will be arraigned at the bar of judgment. At that time God will judge all in righteousness, the Jew by the law which *he* had, and the heathen by the law which *he* had. ¶ *When God shall judge.* God is often represented as the Judge of mankind; Deut. xxxii. 36; Ps. l. 4; 1 Sam. ii. 10; Eccl. iii. 17; Rom. iii. 6; Heb. xiii. 4. But this does not militate against the fact that he will do it *by* Jesus Christ. God has appointed his Son to administer judgment; and it will be not by God *directly,* but by Jesus Christ that it will be administered. ¶ *The secrets of men.* See Luke viii. 17; Eccl. xii. 14, "For God shall bring every work into judgment, *with every secret thing,*" &c., Matt. x. 26; 1 Cor. iv. 5. The expression denotes the hidden desires, lusts, passions, and motives of men; the thoughts of the heart, as well as the outward actions of the life. It will be a characteristic of the day of judgment, that all these will be brought out, and receive their appropriate reward. The propriety of this is apparent, for, (1.) It is by these that the *character* is really determined. The *motives* and *principles* of a man constitute his character, and to judge him impartially, these must be known. (2.) They are not judged or rewarded in this life. The external conduct only can be seen by men, and of course that only can be rewarded or punished here. (3.) Men of pure motives and pure hearts are often here basely aspersed and calumniated. They are persecuted, traduced, and often overwhelmed with ignominy. It is proper that the *secret* motives of their conduct should be brought out and approved. On the other hand, men of base motives, men of unprincipled character, and who are corrupt at the heart, are often lauded, flattered, and exalted into pub-

17 Behold, thou [a] art called a Jew, and restest in the law, and makest thy boast of God.

[a] ver. 28.

lic estimation. It is proper that their secret principles should be detected, and that they should take their proper place in the government of God. In regard to this expression, we may further remark, (1.) That the fact that *all* secret thoughts and purposes will be brought into judgment, invests the judgment with an awful character. Who should not tremble at the idea that the secret plans and desires of his soul, which he has so long and so studiously concealed, should be brought out into noon-day in the judgment? All his artifices of concealment shall be then at an end. He will be able to practise disguise no longer. He will be seen as he is; and he will receive the doom he deserves. There will be *one* place, at least, where the sinner shall be treated as he ought. (2.) To execute this judgment implies the power of searching the heart; of knowing the thoughts; and of developing and unfolding all the purposes and plans of the soul. Yet this is intrusted to Jesus Christ, and the fact that *he* will exercise this, shows that he is divine. ¶ *Of men.* Of all men, whether Jew or Gentile, infidel or Christian. The day of judgment, therefore, may be regarded as a day of universal development of all the plans and purposes that have ever been entertained in this world. ¶ *By Jesus Christ.* The fact that Jesus Christ is appointed to judge the world is abundantly taught in the Bible, Acts xvii. 31; 2 Tim. iv. 1; 1 Pet. iv. 5; John v. 22, 27; 1 Thess. iv. 16—18; Matt. xxv. 31—46. ¶ *According to my gospel.* According to the gospel which *I preach.* Comp. Acts xvii. 31; 2 Tim. iv. 8. This does not mean that the gospel which he preached would be the *rule* by which God would judge all mankind, for he had just said that the heathen world would be judged by a different rule, ver. 12. But it means that he was intrusted with the gospel to make it known; and that one of the great and prime articles of that gospel was, that God would judge the world by Jesus Christ. To make *this* known he was appointed; and it could be called *his* gospel only as being a part of the important message with which he was intrusted.

17. *Behold.* Having thus stated the *general principles* on which God would judge the world; having shown how they condemned the Gentiles; and having removed all objections to them, he now proceeds to *another* part of his argument, to show how they applied to the *Jews.* By the use of the word *behold,* he calls their attention to it, as to an important subject; and with great skill and address, he states their privileges, before he shows them how those privileges might enhance their condemnation. He admits all their claims to pre-eminence in privileges, and then with great faithfulness proceeds to show how, if abused, these might deepen their final destruction. It should be observed, however, that the word rendered *behold* is in many MSS. written in two words, εἰ δὲ, instead of ἴδε. If this, as is probable, is the correct reading there, it should be rendered, "if now thou art," &c. Thus the Syriac, Latin, and Arabic read it. ¶ *Thou art called.* Thou art *named* Jew, implying that this name was one of very high honour. This is the *first* thing mentioned on which the Jew would be likely to pride himself. ¶ *A Jew.* This was the name by which the Hebrews were at that time generally known; and it is clear that they regarded it as a name of honour, and valued themselves much on it; see Gal. ii. 15; Rev. ii. 9. Its origin is not certainly known. They were called the children of Israel until the time of Rehoboam. When the *ten* tribes were carried into captivity, but two remained, the tribes of *Judah* and Benjamin. The name *Jews* was evidently given to denote those of the tribe of *Judah.* The reasons why the name of *Benjamin* was lost in that of *Judah,* were probably, (1.) Because the tribe of Benjamin was small, and

18 And knowest *a* his will, and
[1] approvest *b* the things that are
more excellent, being instructed
out of the law;

a Ps.147.19,20. 1 or, *triest the things that differ.* *b* Phil.1.10.

comparatively without influence or importance. (2.) The *Messiah* was to be of the tribe of *Judah* (Gen. xlix. 10;) and that tribe would therefore possess a consequence proportioned to their expectation of that event. The name of *Jews* would therefore be one that would suggest the facts that they were preserved from captivity, that they had received remarkably the protection of God, and that the Messiah was to be sent to that people. Hence it is not wonderful that they should regard it as a special favour to be a *Jew*, and particularly when they added to this the idea of *all* the other favours connected with their being the peculiar people of God. The name *Jew* came thus to denote all the peculiarities and special favours of their religion. ¶ *And restest in the law.* The word *rest* here is evidently used in the sense of *trusting to*, or *leaning upon.* The Jew *leaned on*, or *relied* on the law for acceptance or favour; on the fact that he *had* the law, and on his obedience to it. It does not mean that he relied on his own works, though that was true, but that he leaned on *the fact* that he had the law, and was thus distinguished above others. The *law* here means the entire Mosaic economy; or all the rules and regulations which Moses had given. Perhaps also it includes, as it sometimes does, the whole of the Old Testament. ¶ *Makest thy boast in God.* Thou dost boast, or glory, that thou hast the knowledge of the true God, while other nations are in darkness. On this account the Jew felt himself far elevated above all other people, and despised them. It was true that they only had the true knowledge of God, and that he had declared himself to be their God, (Deut. iv. 7; Ps. cxlvii. 19, 20;) but this was not a ground for *boasting*, but for *gratitude.* This passage shows us that it is much more common to *boast* of privileges than to be *thankful* for them, and that it is no evidence of piety for a man to *boast* of his knowledge of God. An humble, ardent thankfulness that we *have* that knowledge—a thankfulness which leads us not to *despise* others, but to desire that *they* may have the same privilege—*is* an evidence of piety.

18. *And knowest his will.* The will or commands of God. This knowledge they obtained from the Scriptures; and of course in this they were distinguished from other nations. ¶ *And approvest.* The word used here is capable of two interpretations. It may mean either to *distinguish*, or *to approve.* The word is properly and usually applied to the process of testing or trying metals by fire. Hence it comes to be used in a general sense to *try* or to *distinguish* any thing; to ascertain its nature, quality, &c.; Luke xii. 56. This is probably its meaning here, referring rather to the *intellectual* process of discriminating, than to the *moral* process of approving. It could not, perhaps, be said with propriety, at least the scope of the passage does not properly suppose this, that the Jew *approved* or *loved* the things of God; but the scope of the passage is, that the Jew valued himself on his *knowledge* of that which was conformable to the will of God; see Notes on chap. xiv. ¶ *The things that are more excellent.* The word here translated *more excellent* denotes properly the things that *differ* from others, and then also the things that *excel.* It has an ambiguity similar to the word translated "approved." If the interpretation of that word above given is correct, then this word here means those things that differ from others. The reference is to the rites and customs, to the distinctions of meats and days, &c., prescribed by the law of Moses. The Jew would pride himself on the fact that he had been taught by the law to make these distinctions, while all the heathen world had been left in ignorance of them. This was one of the advantages on which he valued himself and his reli-

19 And art confident that thou thyself art a guide of the blind, a light of them which are in darkness,

20 An instructor of the foolish, a teacher of babes, which hast the form [a] of knowledge and of the truth in the law

a 2 Tim.1.13; 3.5.

gion. ¶ *Being instructed*, &c. That is, in regard to the one God, his will, and the distinguishing rites of his worship.

19. *And art confident.* This expression denotes the full assurance of the Jew that he was superior in knowledge to all other people. It is a remarkable fact that the Jews put the fullest confidence in their religion. Though proud, wicked, and hypocritical, yet they were not speculative infidels. It was one of their characteristics, evinced through all their history, that they had the fullest assurance that God was the author of their institutions, and that their religion was his appointment. ¶ *A guide of the blind.* A guide of the blind is a figurative expression to denote an instructor of the ignorant. The *blind* here properly refers to the *Gentiles*, who were thus regarded by the Jews. The meaning is, that they esteemed themselves qualified to instruct the heathen world; Mat. xv. 14; xxiii. 15. ¶ *A light.* Another figurative expression to denote a *teacher*; comp. Isa. xlix. 6; John i. 4, 5, 8, 9. ¶ *In darkness.* A common expression to denote the *ignorance* of the Gentile world; see Note, Mat. iv. 16.

20. *Of the foolish.* The word *foolish* is used in the Scriptures in two significations: to denote those who are void of understanding, and to denote the wicked. Here it is clearly used in the former sense, signifying that the Jew esteemed himself qualified to instruct those without knowledge. ¶ *Of babes.* This is the *literal* meaning of the original word. The expression is figurative, and denotes those who were as *ignorant as children*—an expression which they would be likely to apply to all the Gentiles. It is evident that the character here given by Paul to the Jews is one which they claimed, and of which they were proud. They are often mentioned as arrogating this prerogative to themselves, of being qualified to be guides and teachers of others; Mat. xv. 14; xxiii. 2, 16, 24. It will be remembered, also, that the Jews considered themselves to be qualified to teach all the world, and hence evinced great zeal to make proselytes. And it is not improbable (*Tholuck*) that their Rabbies were accustomed to give the names "foolish" and "babes" to the ignorant proselytes which they had made from the heathen. ¶ *Which hast the form of knowledge.* The word here translated *form* properly denotes a *delineation* or *picturing* of a thing. It is commonly used to denote also the *appearance* of any object; that which we see, without reference to its internal character; the external figure. It sometimes denotes the external appearance *as distinguished* from that which is internal; or a hypocritical profession of religion without its reality; 2 Tim. iii. 5. "Having the form of godliness, but denying its power." It is sometimes used in a good, and sometimes in a bad sense. Here it denotes that in their teaching they retained the *semblance*, *sketch*, or *outline* of the true doctrines of the Old Testament. They had in the Scriptures a correct *delineation* of the truth. Truth is the representation of things as they are; and the doctrines which the Jews had in the Old Testament were a correct representation or delineation of the objects of knowledge; comp. 2 Tim. i. 13. ¶ *In the law.* In the Scriptures of the Old Testament. In these verses the apostle concedes to the Jews all that they would claim. Having made this concession of their superior knowledge, he is prepared with the more fidelity and force to convict them of their deep and dreadful depravity in sinning against the superior light and privileges which God had conferred on them.

21. *Thou therefore*, &c. He who

21 Thou *a* therefore which teachest another, teachest thou not thyself? thou that preachest a man should not steal, dost thou steal?

22 Thou that sayest a man should not commit adultery, dost thou commit adultery? thou that abhorrest idols, dost thou commit sacrilege?

23 Thou that makest thy boast of the law, through breaking the law dishonourest thou God?

24 For the name of God is

a Mat.23.3,&c.

is a teacher of others may be expected to be learned himself. They *ought* to be found to be possessed of superior knowledge; and by this question the apostle *impliedly* reproves them for their ignorance. The form of a *question* is chosen because it conveys the truth with greater force. He puts the question as if it were undeniable that they were grossly ignorant; comp. Mat. xxiii. 3, "They say, and do not," &c. ¶ *That preachest.* This word means to *proclaim* in any manner, whether in the synagogue, or in any place of public teaching. ¶ *Dost thou steal?* It cannot be proved, perhaps, that the Jews were extensively guilty of this crime. It is introduced partly, no doubt, to make the inconsistency of their conduct more apparent. We expect a man to set an example of what he means by his public instruction.

22. *Dost thou commit adultery?* There is no doubt that this was a crime very common among the Jews; see Notes, Mat. xii. 39; John viii. 1—11. The Jewish Talmud accuses some of the most celebrated of their Rabbies, by name, of this vice. (*Grotius.*) Josephus also gives the same account of the nation. ¶ *Thou that abhorrest idols.* It was one of the doctrines of their religion to abhor idolatry. This they were every where taught in the Old Testament; and this they doubtless inculcated in their teaching. It was impossible that they could recommend idolatry. ¶ *Dost thou commit sacrilege?* Sacrilege is the crime of violating or profaning sacred things; or of appropriating to common purposes what has been devoted to the service of religion. In this question, the apostle shows remarkable tact and skill. He could not accuse them of *idolatry*, for the Jews, after the Babylonish captivity, had never fallen into it. But then, though they had not the *form*, they might have the *spirit* of idolatry. That spirit consisted in withholding from the true God that which was his due, and bestowing the affections upon something else. This the Jews did by perverting from their proper use the offerings which were designed for his honour; by withholding that which he demanded of tithes and offerings; and by devoting to other uses that which was devoted to him, and which properly belonged to his service. That this was a common crime among them is apparent from Mal. i. 8, 12—14; iii. 8, 9. It is also evident from the New Testament that the temple was in many ways desecrated and profaned in the time of our Saviour; Notes, Mat. xxi. 12, 13.

23. *Makest thy boast,* &c. To boast in the law implied their conviction of its excellence and obligation, as a man does not boast of that which he esteems to be of no value. ¶ *Dishonourest thou God.* By boasting of the law, they proclaimed their conviction that it was from God. By breaking it, they denied it. And as actions are a true test of man's real opinions, their breaking the law did it more dishonour than their boasting of it did it honour. This is always the case. It matters little what a man's speculative opinions may be; his practice may do far more to disgrace religion than his profession does to honour it. It is the life and conduct, and not merely the profession of the lips, that does real honour to the true religion. Alas, with what pertinency and force may this question be put to many who call themselves Christians!

24. *The name of God.* The name and character of the true God. ¶ *Is blasphemed.* Note, Mat. ix. 3. That is, your conduct is such as to lead the

blasphemed among the Gentiles through you, as it is written.[a]

25 For circumcision verily profiteth, if thou keep the law: but

[a] Ezek.36.20,23.

heathen world to blaspheme and reproach both your religion and its Author. By your hypocrisy and crimes the pagan world is led to despise a religion which is observed to have no effect in purifying and restraining its professors; and of course the reproach will terminate on the Author of your religion—that is, the true God. A life of purity would tend to honour religion and its Author; a life of impurity does the reverse. There is no doubt that this was actually the effect of the deportment of the Jews. They were scattered every where; every where they were corrupt and wicked; and every where they and their religion were despised. ¶ *Among the Gentiles.* In the midst of whom many Jews lived. ¶ *Through you.* By means of you, or as the result of your conduct. It *may* mean, that you Jews do it, or profane the name of God; but the connection seems rather to require the former sense. ¶ *As it is written.* To what place the apostle has reference, cannot be certainly determined. There are two passages in the Old Testament which will bear on the case, and perhaps he had them both in his view; Isa. lii. 5; Ezek. xxxvi. 22, 23. The meaning is not that the passages in the Old Testament, referred to by the phrase, "as it is written," had any particular reference to the conduct of the Jews in the time of Paul, but that this had been the *character of the people,* and the effect of their conduct *as a nation,* instances of which had been before observed and recorded by the prophets. The same thing has occurred to a most melancholy extent in regard to professed Christian nations. For purposes of commerce, and science, and war, and traffic, men from nations nominally Christian have gone into almost every part of the heathen world. But they have not often been real Christians. They have been intent on gain; and have to a melancholy extent been profane, and unprincipled, and profligate men. Yet the heathen have regarded them as *Christians;* as fair specimens of the effect of the religion of Christ. They have learned therefore, to abuse the name of Christian, and the Author of the Christian religion, as encouraging and promoting profligacy of life. Hence *one* reason, among thousands, of the importance of Christian missions to the heathen. It is well to disabuse the pagan world of their erroneous opinions of the tendency of Christianity. It is well to teach them that we do not regard these men as Christians. As we have sent to them the *worst part* of our population, it is well to send them holy men, who shall exhibit to them the true nature of Christianity, and raise our character in their eyes as a Christian people. And were there no other result of Christian missions, it would be worth all the expense and toil attending them, *to raise the national character* in the view of the pagan world.

25. *For circumcision.* Note, John vii. 22; Acts vii. 8. This was the peculiar rite by which the relation to the covenant of Abraham was recognised; or by which the right to all the privileges of a member of the Jewish commonwealth was acknowledged. The Jews of course affixed a high importance to the rite. ¶ *Verily profiteth.* Is truly a benefit; or is an advantage. The meaning is, that their being recognised as members of the Jewish commonwealth, and introduced to the privileges of the Jew, was an advantage; see chap. iii. 1, 2. The apostle was not disposed to deny that they possessed this advantage, but he tells them *why* it was a benefit, and how it might fail of conferring any favour. ¶ *If thou keep the law.* The mere *sign* can be of no value. The mere fact of being a Jew is not what God requires. It may be a favour to *have* his law, but the mere possession of the law cannot entitle to the favour of God. So it is a privilege to be born in a Christian land; to have had pious

[a] if thou be a breaker of the law,
thy circumcision is made uncircumcision.
26 Therefore if [b] the uncircumcision keep the righteousness of
the law, shall not his uncircumcision be counted for circumcision?
27 And shall not uncircumcision which is by nature, if it fulfil
the law, [c] judge thee, who by the

a Gal.5.3. b Acts 10.34,35. c Mat.12.41,42.

parents; to be amidst the ordinances of religion; to be trained in Sunday-schools; and to be devoted to God in baptism: for all these are favourable circumstances for salvation. But none of them entitle to the favour of God; and unless they are improved as they should be, they may be only the means of increasing our condemnation; 2 Cor. ii. 16. ¶ *Thy circumcision is made uncircumcision.* Thy circumcision, or thy being called a Jew, is of no value. It will not distinguish you from those who are *not* circumcised. You will be treated as a heathen. No external advantages, no name, or rite, or ceremony will save you. God requires the obedience of the heart and of the life. Where there is a disposition to render that, there *is* an advantage in possessing the external means of grace. Where that is wanting, no rite or profession can save. This applies with as much force to those who have been baptized in infancy, and to those who have made a profession of religion in a Christian church, as to the Jew.

26. *Therefore, if the uncircumcision.* If those who are not circumcised, *i. e.* the heathen. ¶ *Keep the righteousness of the law.* Keep that which the law of Moses commands. It could not be supposed that a heathen would understand the requirements of the *ceremonial* law; but reference is had here to the *moral* law. The apostle does not expressly affirm that this was ever done; but he supposes the case, to show the true nature and value of the rites of the Jews. ¶ *Shall not his uncircumcision.* Or, shall the fact that he is uncircumcised stand in the way of the acceptance of his services? Or, shall he not as certainly and as readily be accepted by God as if he were a Jew? Or in other words, the apostle teaches the doctrine that acceptance with God does not depend on a man's external privileges, but on the state of the heart and life. ¶ *Be counted for circumcision.* Shall he not be *treated* as if he were circumcised? Shall his being uncircumcised be any barrier in the way of his acceptance with God? The word rendered "be counted," is that which is commonly rendered *to reckon*, TO IMPUTE; and its use here shows that the Scripture use of the word is not to *transfer*, or to charge with that which is not deserved, or not true. It means simply that a man shall be treated as if it were so; that this want of circumcision shall be no bar to acceptance. There is nothing set over to his account; nothing transferred; nothing reckoned different from what it is. God judges things as they are; and as the man, though uncircumcised, who keeps the law, *ought* to be treated *as if* he had been circumcised, so he who believes in Christ agreeably to the divine promise, *and trusts to his merits alone for salvation*, ought to be treated *as if* he were himself righteous. God judges the thing as *it is*, and treats men as it is proper to treat them, *as being* pardoned and accepted through his Son.

27. *Which is by nature.* Which is the natural state of man; his condition before he is admitted to any of the peculiar rites of the Jewish religion. ¶ *If it fulfil the law.* If they who are uncircumcised keep the law. ¶ *Judge thee.* Condemn thee as guilty. As we say, the conduct of such a man condemns us. He acts so much more consistently and uprightly than we do, that we see our guilt. For a similar mode of expression, see Mat. xii. 41, 42. ¶ *Who by the letter*, &c. The translation here is certainly not happily expressed. It is difficult to ascertain its meaning. The evident meaning of the original is, "Shall not a heathen man who has none of your external

letter and circumcision dost transgress the law?
28 For he [a] is not a Jew which
is one outwardly; neither *is that*
circumcision which is outward in
the flesh:

29 But he *is* a Jew, which is
one inwardly; and circumcision
is that of the heart, [b] in the spirit,
and not in the letter; whose
praise [c] *is* not of men, but of
God.

a Mat.3.9; John 8.39; chap.9.6,7; Gal.6.15; Rev.2.9.

b Deut.10.16; 30.6; Jer.4.4; Phil.3.3; Col.2.11. *c* 2 Cor.10.18.

privileges, if he keeps the law, condemn you who are Jews; who, *although* you have the letter and circumcision, are nevertheless transgressors of the law?' ¶ *The letter.* The word *letter* properly means the mark or character from which syllables and words are formed. It is also used in the sense of *writing* of any kind (Luke xvi. 6, 7; Acts xxviii. 21; Gal. vi. 11), particularly the writings of Moses, denoting, by way of eminence, *the letter,* or *the writing;* Rom. vii. 6; 2 Tim. iii. 15.

28. *For he is not a Jew,* &c. He who is merely descended from Abraham, and is circumcised, and externally conforms to the law only, does not possess the true character, and manifest the true spirit, contemplated by the separation of the Jewish people. Their separation required much more. ¶ *Neither is that circumcision,* &c. Neither does it meet the full design of the rite of circumcision, that it is externally performed. It contemplated much more; see ver. 29.

29. *But he is a Jew.* He comes up to the design of the Jewish institution; he manifests truly what it is to be a Jew. ¶ *Which is one inwardly.* Who is *in heart* a Jew. Who has the true spirit, and fulfils the design of their being separated as a peculiar people. This passage proves that the *design* of separating them was not merely to perform certain external rites, or to conform to external observances, but to be a people holy in heart and in life. It cannot be denied that this design was not generally understood in the time of the apostles; but it was abundantly declared in the Old Testament; Deut. vi. 5; x. 12, 13, 20; xxx. 14; Isa. i. 11—20; Mic. vi. 8; Ps. li. 16, 17; l. 7—23. ¶ *And circumcision is that of the heart.* That is, that circumcision which acceptable to God, and which meets the design of the institution, is that which is attended with holiness of heart; with the cutting off of sins; and with a pure life. The design of circumcision was to be a sign of separation from the heathen world, and of consecration to the holy God. And this design implied the renunciation and forsaking of all sins; or the cutting off of every thing that was offensive to God. This was a work peculiarly of the heart. This design was often stated and enforced in the writings of the Old Testament; Deut. x. 16, "Circumcise, therefore, the foreskin of your heart, and be no more stiff-necked;" Jer. iv. 4; Deut. xxx. 6. ¶ *In the spirit.* This is an expression explaining further what he had just said. It does not mean *by the Holy Spirit,* but that the work was to take place *in* the soul, and not in the body only. It was to be an internal, spiritual work, and not merely an external service. ¶ *And not in the letter.* That is, not only according to the literal, external command. ¶ *Whose praise,* &c. Whose object is not to secure the praise of men. One of the main characteristics of the Jews in the time of Christ was, a desire to secure honour among men, as being exactly scrupulous in the performance of all the duties of their religion. They prided themselves on their descent from Abraham, and on their regular conformity to the precepts of the law of Moses; Mat. iii. 9; vi. 2, 5; Luke xviii. 10, 11, 12; Mat. xxiii. 23. ¶ *But of God.* "Man looketh on the outward appearance, but the Lord looketh on the heart;" 1 Sam. xvi. 7. The praise of God can be bestowed only on those who conform *really,* and not externally only, to his requirements.

The remarks which are made here respecting the Jews, are also strictly

CHAPTER III.

WHAT advantage then hath the
Jew? or what profit *is there*
of circumcision?

2 Much every way: chiefly, because that unto them [a] were committed the oracles of God.
3 For what if some [b] did not be-

[a] Deut.4.7,8.

[b] chap.10.16; Heb. 4.2.

applicable to professing Christians, and we may learn,

1. That the external rites of religion are of much less importance than the state of the heart.

2. That the only value of those rites is to promote holiness of heart and life.

3. That the mere fact that we are born of pious ancestors will not save us.

4. That the fact that we were dedicated to God in baptism will not save us.

5. That a mere profession of religion, however orthodox may be our creed, will not save us.

6. That the estimate which men may put on our piety is not the proper measure of our true character and standing.

7. It is an inexpressible privilege to be in possession of the word of God, and to know our duty. It may, if improved, conduce to our elevation in holiness and happiness here, and to our eternal felicity hereafter.

8. It is also a fearful thing to neglect the privileges which we enjoy. We shall be judged according to the light which we have; and it will be an awful event to go to eternity from a Christian land unprepared.

9. Whatever may be the destiny of the heathen, it is *our* duty to make preparation to meet God. The most wicked of the heathen may meet a far milder doom than many who are externally moral, or who profess religion in Christian lands. Instead, therefore, of speculating on what may be their destiny, it is the duty of every individual to be at peace himself with God, and to flee from the wrath to come.

CHAPTER III.

1. *What advantage*, &c. The design of the first part of this chapter is to answer some of the objections which might be offered by a Jew to the statements in the last chapter. The *first* objection is stated in this verse. A Jew would naturally ask, if the view which the apostle had given were correct, what *peculiar* benefit could the Jew derive from his religion? The objection would arise particularly from the position advanced (chap. ii. 25, 26), that if a heathen should do the things required by the law, he would be treated *as if* he had been circumcised. Hence the question, "what profit is there of circumcision?"

2. *Much every way*. Or, in every respect. This is the answer of the apostle to the objection in ver. 1. ¶ *Chiefly*. That is, this is the *principal* advantage, and one including all others. The *main* benefit of being a Jew is, to possess the sacred Scriptures and their instructions. ¶ *Unto them were committed*. Or were intrusted, were *confided*. The word translated "were committed," is that which is commonly employed to express *faith* or *confidence*, and it implied *confidence* in them on the part of God in intrusting his oracles to them; a confidence which was not misplaced, for no people ever guarded a sacred trust or deposit with more fidelity, than the Jews did the sacred Scriptures. ¶ *The oracles*. The word *oracle* among the heathen meant properly the answer or response of a god, or of some priest supposed to be inspired, to an inquiry of importance, usually expressed in a brief sententious way, and often with great ambiguity. The *place* from which such a response was usually obtained was also called *an oracle*, as *the oracle at Delphi*, &c. These oracles were frequent among the heathen, and affairs of great importance were usually submitted to them. The word rendered *oracles* occurs in the New Testament but four times, Acts vii. 38; Heb. v. 12; 1 Pet. iv. 11; Rom. iii. 2. It is evidently here used to denote the Scriptures, as being that which was

lieve? Shall their unbelief make the faith of God without effect?

4 God forbid: yea, let God be true, but every man a liar; as

---

spoken by God, and particularly perhaps the divine promises. To possess these was of course an eminent privilege, and included all others, as they instructed them in their duty, and were their guide in every thing that pertained to them in this life and the life to come. They contained, besides, many precious promises respecting the future dignity of the nation in reference to the Messiah. No higher favour can be conferred on a people than to be put in possession of the sacred Scriptures. And this fact should excite us to gratitude, and lead us to endeavour to extend them also to other nations; comp. Deut. iv. 7, 8; Ps. cxlvii. 19, 20.

3. *For what if some did not believe?* This is to be regarded as another objection of a Jew. "What then? or what follows? if it be admitted that some of the nation did not believe, does it not follow that the faithfulness of God in his promises will fail?" The points of the objection are these: (1.) The apostle had maintained that the nation was sinful (chap. ii); that is, that they had not obeyed or believed God. (2.) This, the objector for the time admits or supposes in relation to *some* of them. But, (3.) He asks whether this does not involve a consequence which is not admissible, that God is unfaithful. Did not the fact that God chose them as his people, and entered into covenant with them, imply that the Jews *should* be kept from perdition? It was evidently their belief that *all* Jews would be saved, and this belief they grounded on his covenant with their fathers. The doctrine of the apostle (chap. ii.) would seem to imply that in certain respects they were on a level with the Gentile nations; that if they sinned, they would be treated just like the heathen; and hence they asked of what value was the promise of God? Had it not become vain and nugatory? ¶ *Make the faith.* The word *faith* here evidently means the *faithfulness* or *fidelity of God to his promises.* Comp. Matt. xiii. 23; 2 Tim. iii. 10; Hos. ii. 20. ¶ *Of none effect.* Destroy it; or prevent him from fulfilling his promises. The meaning of the objection is, that the fact supposed, that the Jews would become unfaithful and be lost, would imply that God had *failed* to keep his promises to the nation; or that he had made promises which the result showed he was not able to perform.

4. *God forbid.* Greek. Let not this be. The sense is, *let not this by any means be supposed.* This is the answer of the apostle, showing that no such consequence followed from his doctrines; and that *if* any such consequence should follow, the doctrine should be at once abandoned, and that every *man*, no matter who, should be rather esteemed false than God. *The veracity of God was a great first principle*, which was to be held, whatever might be the consequence. This implies that the apostle believed that the fidelity of God could be maintained in strict consistency with the fact that any number of the Jews might be found to be unfaithful, and be cast off. The apostle has not entered into an explanation of this, or shown how it could be, but it is not difficult to understand how it was. The promise made to Abraham, and the fathers, was not unconditional and absolute, that *all* the Jews should be saved. It was *implied* that they were to be obedient; and that if they were not, they would be cast off; Gen. xviii. 19. Though the apostle has not stated it here, yet he has considered it at length in another part of this epistle, and showed that it was not only *consistent* with the original promise that a part of the Jews should be found unfaithful, and be cast off, but that it had *actually occurred* according to the prophets; chap. x. 16—21; xi. Thus the *fidelity* of God was preserved; at the same time that it was a matter of fact that no small part of the nation was rejected and lost. ¶ *Let God be true.* Let God be esteemed true and faithful, whatever

it is written, [a] That thou mightest be justified in thy sayings, and mightest overcome when thou art judged.

a chap.10.16.

consequence may follow. This was a first principle, and should be now, that God should be believed to be *a God of truth*, whatever consequence it might involve. How happy would it be, if *all* men would regard this as a fixed principle, a matter not to be questioned in their hearts, or debated about, that God is true to his word! How much doubt and anxiety would it save professing Christians; and how much error would it save among sinners! Amidst all the agitations of the world, all conflicts, debates, and trials, it would be a fixed position where every man might find rest, and which would do more than all other things to allay the tempests and smooth the agitated waves of human life. ¶ *But every man a liar*. Though every man and every other opinion should be found to be false. Of course this included the apostle and his reasoning; and the expression is one of those which show his magnanimity and greatness of soul. It implies that every opinion which he and all others held; every doctrine which had been defended; should be at once abandoned, if it implied that God was false. It was to be assumed as a *first principle* in all religion and all reasoning, that if a doctrine implied that God was not faithful, it was of course a false doctrine. This showed *his* firm conviction that the doctrine which he advanced was strictly in accordance with the veracity of the divine promise. What a noble principle is this! How strikingly illustrative of the humility of true piety, and of the confidence which true piety places in God above all the deductions of human reason! And if all men were willing to sacrifice their opinions when they appeared to impinge on the veracity of God; if they started back with instinctive shuddering at the very supposition of such a want of fidelity in him; how soon would it put an end to the boastings of error, to the pride of philosophy, to lofty dictation in religion! No man with this feeling could be for a moment a universalist; and none could be an infidel. ¶ *As it is written;* Ps. li. 4. To confirm the sentiment which he had just advanced and to show that it accorded with the spirit of religion as expressed in the Jewish writings, the apostle appeals to the language of David, uttered in a state of deep penitence for past transgressions. Of all quotations ever made, this is one of the most beautiful and most happy. David was overwhelmed with grief; he saw his crime to be awful; he feared the displeasure of God, and trembled before him. Yet *he held it as a fixed, indisputable principle that* GOD WAS RIGHT. This he never once thought of calling in question. He had sinned against God, God only; and he did not once think of calling in question the fact that God was just altogether in reproving him for his sin, and in pronouncing against him the sentence of condemnation. ¶ *That thou mightest be justified.* That thou mightest *be regarded as just or right,* or, that it may appear that God is not unjust. This does not mean that David had sinned against God *for the purpose* of justifying him, but that he now clearly saw that his sin had been so *directly* against him, and so aggravated, that God was right in his sentence of condemnation. ¶ *In thy sayings.* In what thou hast spoken; that is, in thy sentence of condemnation; in thy words in relation to this offence. It may help us to understand this, to remember that the psalm was written immediately after Nathan, at the command of God, had gone to reprove David for his crime; (see the title of the psalm.) God, by the mouth of Nathan, had *expressly* condemned David for his crime. To this expression of condemnation David doubtless refers by the expression "in thy sayings;" see 2 Sam. xii. 7—13 ¶ *And mightest overcome.* In the Hebrew, "*mightest be pure,*" or mightest be esteemed pure, or just.

5 But if our unrighteousness commend the righteousness of God, what shall we say? *Is* God unrighteous, who taketh vengeance? (I speak as a man.)

The word which the LXX. and the apostle have used, "mightest *overcome*," is sometimes used with reference to litigations or trials in a court of justice. He that was accused and acquitted, or who was adjudged to be innocent, might be said to *overcome*, or to gain the cause. The expression is thus used here. As if there were a *trial* between David and God, God would overcome; that is, would be esteemed pure and righteous in his sentence condemning the crime of David. ¶ *When thou art judged.* The Hebrew is, *when thou judgest;* that is, in thy judgment pronounced on this crime. The Greek *may* also be in the middle voice as well as the passive, and may correspond, therefore, in meaning precisely with the Hebrew. So the Arabic renders it. The Syriac renders it, "*when they* (*i. e. men*) *shall judge thee.*" The meaning, as expressed by David, is, that God is to be esteemed right and just in condemning men for their sins, and that a true penitent, *i. e.* a man placed in the best circumstances to form a proper estimate of God, will see this, though it should condemn himself. The meaning of the expression in the connection in which Paul uses it, is, that it is to be held as a fixed, unwavering principle, that God is right and true, whatever consequences it may involve; whatever doctrine it may overthrow; or whatever man it may prove to be a liar.

5. *But if our unrighteousness.* If our *sin.* The *particular* sin which had been specified (ver. 3) was *unbelief.* But the apostle here gives the objection a general form. This is to be regarded as an *objection* which a Jew might make. The force of it is this: (1.) It had been conceded that some had not believed; that is, had sinned. (2.) But God was true to his promises. Notwithstanding *their* sin, God's character was the same. Nay, (3.) *In the very midst of sin,* and as one of the *results* of it, tbe character of God, as a just Being, shone out illustriously. The question then was, (4.) If his glory resulted from it; if the effect of all was to *show* that his character was pure; how could he *punish* that sin from which his own glory resulted? And this is a question which is often asked by sinners. ¶ *Commend.* Recommend; show forth; render illustrious. ¶ *The righteousness of God.* His just and holy character. This was the effect on David's mind, that he saw more clearly the justice of God in his threatenings against sin, in consequence of his own transgression. And if *this* effect followed, if honour was thus done to God, the question was, how he could consistently *punish* that which tended to promote his own glory? ¶ *What shall we say?* What follows? or, what is the inference? This is a mode of speech as if the objector *hesitated* about expressing an inference which would seem to follow, but which was horrible in its character. ¶ *Is God unrighteous?* The meaning of this would be better expressed thus: "Is *not* God unrighteous in punishing? Does it not follow that if God is honoured by sin, that it would be wrong for him to inflict punishment?" ¶ *Who taketh vengeance.* The meaning of this is simply, *who inflicts punishment.* The idea of *vengeance* is not necessarily in the original (ὀργήν). It is commonly rendered *wrath*, but it often means simply *punishment*, without any reference to the state of the mind of him who inflicts it, Matt. iii. 7; Luke iii. 7; xxi. 23; John iii. 36. Note, Rom. i. 18; iv. 15. ¶ *I speak as a man.* I speak after the manner of men. I speak as appears to be the case to human view; or as would strike the human mind. It does not mean that the language was such as *wicked men* were accustomed to use; but that the objector expressed a sentiment which to human view would seem to follow from what had been said. This I regard as the language

6 God forbid: for then how [a] shall God judge the world?

7 For if the truth of God hath more abounded through my lie

a Job 8.3.

of an objector. It implies a degree of reverence for the character of God, and a seeming unwillingness to *state* an objection which seemed to be dishonourable to God, but which nevertheless pressed itself so strong on the mind as to appear irresistible. No way of stating the objection could have been more artful or impressive.

6. *God forbid.* Note, ver. 4. ¶ *For then.* If it be admitted that it would be unjust for God to inflict punishment. ¶ *How shall God,* &c. How will it be *right* or consistent for him to judge the world. ¶ *Judge.* To *judge* implies the possibility and the correctness of *condemning* the guilty; for if it were not right to condemn them, judgment would be a farce. This does not mean that God would condemn all the world; but that the fact of *judging* men implied the possibility and propriety of condemning those who were guilty. It is remarkable that the apostle does not attempt to explain *how* it could be that God could take occasion from the sins of men to promote his glory; nor does he even admit the fact; but he meets *directly* the objection. To understand the force of his answer, it must be remembered that it was *an admitted fact,* a fact which *no one* among the Jews would call in question, that God would judge the world. This fact was fully taught in their own writings, Gen. xviii. 25; Eccl. xii. 14; xi. 9. It was besides an admitted point with them that God would *condemn the heathen world;* and perhaps the term "world" here refers particularly to them. But how could this be if it *were not right* for God to inflict punishment at all? The inference of the objector, therefore, *could not* be true; though the apostle does not tell us *how* it was consistent to inflict punishment for offences from which God took occasion to promote his glory. It may be remarked, however, that God will judge offences, not from what *he* may do in *overruling* them, but from the nature of the crime itself. The question is not, what good God may bring out of it, but what does the crime itself deserve? what is the character of the offender? what was his intention? It is not what God may do to overrule the offence when it *is* committed. The just punishment of the murderer is to be determined by the law, and by his own desert; and not from any reputation for integrity and uprightness which the *judge* may manifest on his trial; or from any honour which may accrue to the police for detecting him; or any security which may result to the commonwealth from his execution; or from any honour which the *law* may gain as a just law by his condemnation. Nor should any of these facts and advantages which may result from his execution, be pleaded in bar of his condemnation. So it is with the sinner under the divine administration. It is indeed a truth (Ps. lxxvi. 10) that the wrath of man shall praise God, and that he will take *occasion* from men's wickedness to glorify himself as a just judge and moral governor; but this will be no ground of acquittal for the sinner.

7. *For if,* &c. This is an objection similar to the former. It is indeed but another form of the same. ¶ *The truth of God.* His truth or faithfulness in adhering to his threatenings. God threatened to punish the guilty. By their guilt he will take *occasion* to show his own truth; or their crime will furnish occasion for such an exhibition. ¶ *Hath more abounded.* Has been more striking, or more manifest. His *truth* will be shown by the fulfilment of all his promises to his people, and of all his predictions. But it will also be shown by fulfilling his threatenings on the guilty. It will, therefore, *more abound* by their condemnation; that is, their condemnation will furnish new and striking *instances* of his truth. Every lost sinner will be, therefore, an eternal monument of the truth of God. ¶ *Through my lie.* By means of my lie, or as one of the results of my falsehood. The word *lie* here

unto his glory, why yet am I also judged as a sinner?

8 And not *rather* (as we be slanderously reported, and as some

means falsehood, deceitfulness, *unfaithfulness.* If by the unfaithfulness of the Jewish people to the covenant, occasion should be given to God to glorify himself, how could they be condemned for it? ¶ *Unto his glory.* To his praise, or so as to show his character in such a way as to excite the praise and admiration of his intelligent creation. ¶ *Why yet am I*, &c. How *can* that act be regarded as evil, which tends to promote the glory of God? The fault in the reasoning of the objector is this, that he takes for granted that the *direct* tendency of his conduct is to promote God's glory, whereas it is just the reverse; and it is by God's *reversing* that tendency, or overruling it, that he obtains his glory. The *tendency* of murder is not to honour the law, or to promote the security of society, but just the reverse. Still, his execution shall avert the *direct* tendency of his crime, and do honour to the law and the judge, and promote the peace and security of the community by restraining others.

8. *And not rather.* This is the answer of the apostle. He meets the objection by showing its tendency if *carried out*, and if it were made a principle of conduct. The meaning is, "If the glory of God is to be promoted by sin, and if a man is not therefore to be condemned, or held guilty for it; if this fact absolves man from crime, *why not carry the doctrine out, and make it a principle of conduct, and* DO ALL THE EVIL WE CAN, *in order to promote his glory.*" This was the fair consequence of the objection. And yet this was a result so shocking and monstrous, that all that was necessary in order to answer the objection was merely to state this consequence. Every man's moral feelings would revolt at the doctrine; every man would *know* that it could not be true; and every man, therefore, could see that the objection was not valid. ¶ *As we.* This refers, doubtless, to the apostles, and to Christians generally. It is unquestionable, that this accusation was often brought against them. ¶ *Slanderously reported.* Greek, As we are *blasphemed.* This is the legitimate and proper use of the word *blaspheme,* to speak of one in a reproachful and calumnious manner. ¶ *As some affirm,* &c. Doubtless Jews. Why they should affirm this, is not known. It was doubtless, however, some *perversion* of the doctrines that the apostles preached. The doctrines which were thus misrepresented and abused, were probably these: the apostles taught that the *sins* of men were the occasion of promoting God's glory in the plan of salvation. That "where sin abounded, grace did much more abound;" chap. v. 20. That God, in the salvation of men, would be glorified just in proportion to the depth and pollution of the guilt which was forgiven. This was true; but how easy was it to misrepresent this as teaching that men *ought* to sin in order to promote God's glory! and instead of stating it as an *inference* which THEY drew from the doctrine, to state it as what the apostles *actually taught.* This is the common mode in which charges are brought against others. Men draw an *inference* themselves, or suppose that the doctrine *leads* to such an inference, and then *charge* it on others as what they actually *hold* and *teach.* There is one maxim which should never be departed from: *That a man is not to be held responsible for the inferences which* WE *may draw from his doctrine; and that he is never to be represented as holding and teaching that which* WE *suppose follows from his doctrine.* He is answerable only for what he avows. ¶ *Let us do evil.* That is, since sin is to promote the glory of God, let us commit as much as possible. ¶ *That good may come.* That God may take occasion by it to promote his glory. ¶ *Whose damnation is just.* Whose *condemnation*; see Note, chap. xiv. 23. This does not necessarily refer to future punishment, but it means that the conduct of those who thus slanderously perverted the doctrines of the Christian religion, and

affirm that we say), Let [a] us do
evil, that good may come? whose
damnation is just.

9 What then? are we better *than they?* No, in no wise: for we have before proved [1] both Jews and Gentiles, that they are all under sin:

10 As it is written, [a] There is none righteous, no, not one.

a chap.6.1,15.

1 charged. a Ps.xiv.liii.

accused the apostles of teaching this doctrine, was deserving of condemnation or punishment. Thus he expressly disavows, in strong language, the doctrine charged on Christians. Thus he silences the objection. And thus he teaches, as a great fundamental law, *that evil is not to be done that good may come.* This is a universal rule. And this is *in no case* to be departed from. Whatever is evil is not to be done under any pretence. Any imaginable good which we may think will result from it; any advantage to ourselves or to our cause; or any glory which we may think may result to God, will not sanction or justify the deed. Strict, uncompromising integrity and honesty is to be the maxim of our lives; and in *such* a life only can we hope for success, or for the blessing of God.

9. *What then?* This is another remark supposed to be made by a Jewish objector. "What follows? or are we to infer that we are better than others? ¶ *Are we better than they?* Are we Jews better than the Gentiles? Or rather, have we any *preference,* or advantage as to character and prospects, over the Gentiles? These questions refer only *to the great point in debate,* to wit, about justification before God. The apostle had admitted (ver. 2) that the Jews *had* important advantages *in some respects,* but he now affirms that those advantages did not make a difference between them and the Gentiles about justification. ¶ *No, in no wise.* Not at all. That is, the Jews have no preference or advantage over the Gentiles in regard to the subject of justification before God. They have failed to keep the law; they are sinners; and if they are justified, it must be in the same way as the rest of the world. ¶ *We have before proved,* &c. chap. i. 21—32; chap. ii. ¶ *Under sin.* Sinners. Under the power and dominion of sin.

10. *As it is written.* The apostle is reasoning with Jews; and he proceeds to show from their own Scriptures, that what he had affirmed was true. The point to be proved was, that the Jews, in the matter of justification, had no advantage or preference over the Gentiles; that the Jew had failed to keep the law which had been given *him,* as the Gentile had failed to keep the law which had been given *him;* and that both, therefore, were equally dependent on the mercy of God, incapable of being justified and saved by their works. To show this, the apostle adduces texts to show what was *the character of the Jewish people;* or to show that according to their own Scriptures, they were sinners no less than the Gentiles. The point, then, is to prove the depravity of *the Jews,* not that of *universal* depravity. The interpretation should be confined to the bearing of the passages on the Jews, and the quotations should not be adduced as *directly* proving the doctrine of universal depravity. In a certain sense, which will be stated soon, they may be adduced as bearing on that subject. But their direct reference is to the Jewish nation. The passages which follow, are taken from various parts of the Old Testament. The design of this is to show, that this characteristic of sin was not confined to any particular period of the Jewish history, but pertained to them *as a people;* that it had characterised them *throughout* their existence as a nation. Most of the passages are quoted in the language of the Septuagint. The quotation in ver. 10—12, is from Ps. xiv. 1, 2, 3; and from Ps. liii. 1—3. The 53d psalm is the same as the 14th, with some slight variations.

[Yet if we consult Ps. xiv. and liii., from which the quotations in verses 10—12 are taken, we shall be constrained to admit that their original application is nothing short of universal. The Lord is represented as looking down from heaven, (not upon the Jewish people only, but upon the "children of men" at large, "to see if there were *any* that did understand and seek God);" and declaring, as the result of his unerring scrutiny, "there is *none* that doeth good, no, not one."

That the apostle applies the passages to the case of the Jews is admitted, yet it is evident more is contained in them than the single proof of Jewish depravity. They go all the length of proving the depravity of mankind, and are cited expressly with this view. "We have before proved both Jews and Gentiles," says Paul in the 9th verse, "that they are all under sin." Immediately on this, the quotations in question are introduced with the usual formula, "as it is written," &c. Now since the apostle adduces his Scripture proofs, to establish the doctrine that "*both* Jews and Gentiles are *all* under sin," we cannot reasonably decide against him by confining their application to the Jews only.

In the 19th verse Paul brings his argument to bear *directly* on the Jews. That they might not elude his aim, by interpreting the universal expressions he had introduced, of all the heathen only, leaving themselves favourably excepted; he reminds them that "whatsoever things the law saith, it saith to them that were under it." Not contented with having placed them alongside of the Gentiles in the 9th verse; by this second application of the general doctrine of human depravity, to their particular case, he renders escape or evasion impossible. The scope of the whole passage then, is, that all men are depraved, and that the Jews form no exception. This view is farther strengthened by the apostle's conclusion in the 20th verse. "Therefore, by the deeds of the law there shall *no flesh* be justified in his (God's) sight."

"If the words," says President Edwards, "which the apostle uses, do not most fully and determinately signify an universality, no words ever used in the Bible are sufficient to do it. I might challenge any man to produce any one paragraph in the scriptures, from the beginning to the end, where there is such a repetition and accumulation of terms, so strongly, and emphatically, and carefully, to express the most perfect and absolute universality, or any place to be compared to it."—*Edwards on Original Sin,—Haldane's Commentary*

¶ *There is none righteous.* The Hebrew (Ps. xiv. 1) is, there is none that doeth good. The Septuagint has the same. The apostle quotes according to the *sense* of the passage. The design of the apostle is to show that none could be *justified* by the law. He uses an expression, therefore, which is exactly conformable to his argument, and which accords in meaning with the Hebrew, *there is none just*, δίκαιος. ¶ *No, not one.* This is not in the Hebrew, but is in the Septuagint. It is a strong universal expression, denoting the state of almost universal corruption which existed in the time of the psalmist. The expression should not be interpreted to mean that there was not literally *one pious man* in the nation; but that the characteristic of the nation was, at that time, that it was exceedingly corrupt. Instead of being righteous, as the Jew claimed, *because* they were Jews, the testimony of their own Scriptures was, that they were universally wicked.

[The design of the apostle, however, is not to prove that there were few or none pious. He is treating of the impossibility of justification by works, and alleges in proof that, according to the judgment of God in the 14th Psalm, there were none righteous, &c., in regard to their natural estate, or the condition in which man is, previous to his being justified. In this condition, all are deficient in righteousness, and have nothing to commend them to the Divine favour. What men may afterwards become by grace is another question, on which the apostle does not, in this place, enter. Whatever number of pious men, therefore, there might be in various places of the world, the argument of the apostle is not in the least affected. It will hold good even in the millennium!]

11. *There is none that understandeth.* In the Hebrew (Ps. xiv. 2), God is represented as looking down from heaven *to see*, that is, to make investigation, whether there were any that understood or sought after him. This circumstance gives not only high poetic beauty to the passage, but deep solemnity and awfulness. God, the searcher of hearts, is represented as making investigation *on this very point.* He looks down from heaven for this very purpose, to ascertain whether there were any righteous. In the Hebrew it is not asserted, though it is clearly and strongly implied, that *none such were found.* That fact the apostle *states.* If, as the result of

11 There is none that understandeth, there is none that seeketh after God.

12 They are all gone out of the way, they are together become unprofitable; there is none that doeth good, no, not one.

13 Their [a] throat *is* an open

a Ps.5.9.

such an investigation, none were found; if God did not specify that there *were* any such; then it follows that there were none. For none could escape the notice of his eye; and if there *had* been any, the benevolence of his heart would have led him to record it. To *understand* is used in the sense of being wise; or of having such a state of moral feeling as to dispose them to serve and obey God. The word is often used in the Bible, not to denote a mere *intellectual* operation of the mind, but the state of the heart *inclining the mind* to obey and worship God; Ps. cvii. 43; cxix. 27, 100; Prov. v. 5; Isa. vi. 10; "Lest they should understand with their heart," &c. ¶ *That seeketh after God.* That endeavours to know and do his will, and to be acquainted with his character. A disposition *not* to seek after God, that is, to neglect and forget him, is one of the most decided proofs of depravity. A righteous man counts it his highest privilege and honour to know God, and to understand his will. A man can indulge in wickedness only by forgetting God. Hence a disposition *not* to seek God is full proof of depravity.

12. *They have all gone out of the way.* They have *declined* from the true path of piety and virtue. ¶ *They are together.* They have *at the same time;* or *they have equally* become unprofitable. They are *as one;* they are joined, or *united* in this declension. The expression denotes *union,* or *similarity.* ¶ *Become unprofitable.* This word in Hebrew means to become *putrid* and *offensive,* like fruit that is spoiled. In Arabic, it is applied to *milk* that becomes sour. Applied to moral subjects, it means to become corrupt and useless. They are of *no value* in regard to works of righteousness. ¶ *There is none,* &c. This is taken literally from the Hebrew.

13. *Their throat,* &c. This expression is taken from Ps. v. 9, literally from the Septuagint. The design of the psalm is to reprove those who were false, traitorous, slanderous, &c. (Ps. v. 6.) The psalmist has the sin of deceit, and falsehood, and slander particularly in his eye. The expressions here are to be interpreted in accordance with that. The sentiment here may be, as the grave is ever open to receive all into it, that is, into destruction, so the mouth or the throat of the slanderer is ever open to swallow up the peace and happiness of all. Or it may mean, as from an open sepulchre there proceeds an offensive and pestilential vapour, so from the mouths of slanderous persons there proceed noisome and ruinous words. (*Stuart.*) I think the connection demands the former interpretation. ¶ *With their tongues,* &c. In their conversation, their promises, &c., they have been false, treacherous, and unfaithful. ¶ *The poison of asps.* This is taken literally from the Septuagint of Ps. cxl. 3. The *asp,* or adder, is a species of serpent whose poison is of such active operation that it kills almost the instant that it penetrates, and that without remedy. It is small, and commonly lies concealed, often in the *sand* in a road, and strikes the traveller before he sees it. It is found chiefly in Egypt and Lybia. It is said by ancient writers that the celebrated Cleopatra, rather than be carried a captive to Rome by Augustus, suffered an asp to bite her in the arm, by which she soon died. The precise species of serpent which is here meant by the psalmist, however, cannot be ascertained. All that is necessary to understand the passage is, that it refers to a serpent whose bite was deadly, and rapid in its execution. ¶ *Is under their lips.* The poison of the serpent is contained in a small bag which is concealed at the root of the tooth. When the tooth is

sepulchre; with their tongues they have used deceit; the poison [a] of asps *is* under their lips.

14 Whose mouth [b] *is* full of cursing and bitterness.

15 Their feet [c] *are* swift to shed blood:

16 Destruction and misery *are* in their ways:

17 And the way of peace have they not known:

18 There [d] is no fear of God before their eyes.

19 Now we know, that what

a Ps.140.3. *b* Ps.10.7. *c* Isa.59.7,8. *d* Ps.36.1.

struck into the flesh, the poison is pressed out, through a small hole in the tooth, into the wound. Whether the psalmist was acquainted with that fact, or referred to it, cannot be known: his words do not of necessity imply it. The sentiment is, that as the poison of the asp is rapid, certain, spreading quickly through the system, and producing death; so the words of the slanderer are deadly, pestiferous, quickly destroying the reputation and happiness of man. They are as subtle, as insinuating, and as deadly to the reputation, as the poison of the adder is to the body. Wicked men in the Bible are often compared to serpents; Mat. xxiii. 33; Gen. xlix. 17.

14. *Whose mouth;* Ps. x. 7. The apostle has not quoted this literally, but has given the sense. David in the psalm is describing his bitter enemies. ¶ *Cursing.* Reproachful and opprobrious language, such as Shimei used in relation to David; 2 Sam. xvi. 5, 7, 8. ¶ *Bitterness.* In the psalm, *deceits.* The word *bitterness* is used to denote severity, harshness, cruelty; reproachful and malicious words.

15. *Their feet,* &c. The quotation in this and the two following verses, is abridged or condensed from Isa. lix. 7, 8. The expressions occur in the midst of a description of the character of the nation in the time of the prophet. The apostle has selected a few expressions out of many, rather making a reference to the entire passage, than a formal quotation. The expression, "their feet are swift," &c., denotes the eagerness of the nation to commit crime, particularly deeds of injustice and cruelty. They thirsted for the blood of innocence, and *hasted* to shed it, to gratify their malice, or to satisfy their vengeance.

16. *Destruction.* That is, they *cause* the destruction or the ruin of the reputation, happiness, and peace of others. ¶ *Misery.* Calamity, ruin. ¶ *In their ways.* Wherever they go. This is a striking description not only of the wicked *then,* but of all times. The tendency of their conduct is to destroy the virtue, happiness, and peace of all with whom they come in contact.

17. *And the way of peace,* &c. What tends to promote their own happiness, or that of others, they do not regard. Intent on their plans of evil, they do not know or regard that which is fitted to promote the welfare of themselves or others. This is the case with all who are selfish, and who seek to gain their own purposes of crime and ambition.

18. *There is no fear of God,* Ps. xxxvi. 1. The word *fear* here denotes *reverence, awe, veneration.* There is no such regard or reverence for the character, authority, and honour of God as to restrain them from crime. Their conduct shows that they are not withheld from the commission of iniquity by any regard to the fear or favour of God. The only thing that will be effectual in restraining men from sin, will be a regard to the honour and law of God.

In regard to these quotations from the Old Testament, we may make the following remarks. (1.) They fully establish the position of the apostle, that the nation, as such, was far from being righteous, or that they could be justified by their own works. By quotations from no less than six distinct places in their own writings, referring to different periods of their history, he shows what the character of the nation was. And as this was the characteristic of *those* times, it followed that a

things soever the law saith, it saith to them who are under the law; that every [a] mouth may be stopped, and all the world may become [1] guilty before God.

20 Therefore [b] by the deeds

a Ps.107.42.

1 or, *subject to the judgment of God.*
b Ps.143.2.

Jew could not hope to be saved simply *because he was a Jew*. He needed, as much as the Gentile, the benefit of some other plan of salvation. (2.) These passages show us how to use the Old Testament, and the facts of ancient history. They are to be adduced not as showing *directly* what the character of man is, *now*, but to show what *human nature* is. They demonstrate what man is when under the most favourable circumstances; in different situations; and at different periods of the world. The concurrence of *past* facts shows what the race is. And as past facts are uniform; as man thus far, in the most favourable circumstances, has been sinful; it follows that this is the characteristic of man every where. It is settled by the *facts* of the world, just as any other characteristic of man is settled by the uniform occurrence of facts in all circumstances and times. Ancient facts, and quotations of Scripture, therefore, are to be adduced as proofs of *the tendency of human nature*. So Paul used them, and so it is lawful for us to use them. (3.) It may be observed further, that the apostle has given a view of human depravity which is very striking. He does not confine it to one faculty of the mind, or to one set of actions; he *specifies* each member and each faculty as being perverse, and inclined to evil. The depravity extends to all the departments of action. The *tongue*, the *mouth*, the *feet*, the *lips*, are all involved in it; all are perverted, and all become the occasion of the commission of sin. The *entire man* is corrupt; and the painful description extends to every department of action. (4.) If such was the character of the Jewish nation under all its advantages, what must have been the character of the heathen? We are prepared thus to credit all that is said in chap. i., and elsewhere, of the sad state of the pagan world. (5.) What a melancholy view we have thus of human nature. From whatever quarter we contemplate it, we come to the same conclusion. Whatever record we examine; whatever history we read; whatever time or period we contemplate; we find the same facts, and are forced to the same conclusion. All are involved in sin, and are polluted, and ruined, and helpless. Over these ruins we should sit down and weep, and lift our eyes with gratitude to the God of mercy, that he has pitied us in our low estate, and has devised a plan by which "these ruins may be built again," and lost, fallen man be raised up to forfeited "glory, honour, and immortality."

19. *Now we know.* We all admit. It is a conceded plain point. ¶ *What things soever.* Whether given as precepts, or recorded as historical facts. Whatever things are found *in* the law. ¶ *The law saith.* This means here evidently the Old Testament. From that the apostle had been drawing his arguments, and his train of thought requires us here to understand the whole of the Old Testament by this. The same principle applies, however, to all law, that it speaks only to those to whom it is expressly given. ¶ *It saith to them,* &c. It speaks to them for whom it was expressly intended; to them for whom the law was made. The apostle makes this remark in order to prevent the Jew from evading the force of his conclusion. He had brought proofs from their *own* acknowledged laws, from writings given expressly *for* them, and which recorded their own history, and which they admitted to be divinely inspired. These proofs, therefore, they could not evade. ¶ *That every mouth may be stopped.* This is perhaps, a proverbial expression, Job v. 15; Ps. cvii. 42. It denotes that they would be thoroughly convinced; that the argument would be so conclusive as that they would have nothing to reply; that all objections would be

of the law there shall no flesh be justified in his sight: for by the law *is* the knowledge of sin.

---

silenced. Here it denotes that the argument for the depravity of the Jews from the Old Testament was so clear and satisfactory, that nothing could be alleged in reply. This may be regarded as the *conclusion* of his whole argument, and the expressions may refer not to the Jews only, but to all the world. Its meaning may, perhaps, be thus expressed, "The Gentiles are proved guilty by their own deeds, and by a violation of the laws of nature. *They* sin against their own conscience; and have thus been shown to be guilty before God (chap. i.) The Jews have also been shown to be guilty; all their objections have been silenced by an independent train of remark; by appeals to *their own law;* by arguments drawn from the authority which *they* admit. Thus the mouths of both are stopped. Thus the whole world becomes guilty before God." I regard, therefore, the word "*that*" here (ἵνα) as referring, not particularly to the argument from the *law* of the Jews, but to *the whole previous train of argument,* embracing both Jews and Gentiles. His conclusion is thus *general* or *universal,* drawn from arguments adapted to the two great divisions of mankind. ¶ *And all the world.* Both Jews and Gentiles, for so the strain of the argument shows. That is, all by nature; all who are out of Christ; all who are not pardoned. All are guilty where there is not some scheme contemplating forgiveness, and which is not applied to purify them. The apostle in all this argument speaks of what man is, and ever would be, without some plan of justification appointed by God. ¶ *May become.* May *be.* They are not *made* guilty by the law; but the argument *from* the law, and from fact, *proves* that they *are* guilty. ¶ *Guilty before God.* ὑπόδικος τῷ Θεῷ. Margin, *subject to the judgment of God.* The phrase is taken from courts of justice. It is applied to a man who has not vindicated or defended himself; against whom therefore the charge or the indictment is found true; and who is in consequence subject to punishment. The idea is that of subjection to *punishment;* but *always* because the man personally *deserves* it, and because being unable to vindicate himself, he *ought* to be punished. It is never used to denote simply an obligation to punishment, but with reference to the fact that the punishment is personally *deserved.* This word, rendered *guilty,* is not elsewhere used in the New Testament, nor is it found in the Septuagint. The *argument* of the apostle here shows, (1.) That in order to guilt, there must be a *law,* either that of nature or by revelation (chap. i. ii. iii.); and, (2.) That in order to *guilt,* there must be a violation of that law which may be charged on them as individuals, and for which they are to be held personally responsible.

20. *By the deeds of the law.* By works; or by such deeds as the law requires. The word *law* has, in the Scriptures, a great variety of significations. Its strict and proper meaning is, a *rule* of conduct prescribed by superior authority. The course of reasoning in these chapters shows the sense in which the apostle uses it here. He intends evidently to apply it to those *rules* or laws by which the Jews and Gentiles pretended to frame their lives; and to affirm that men could be justified by no conformity to those laws. He had shown (chap. i.) that *the heathen, the entire Gentile world,* had violated the laws of nature; the rules of virtue made known to them by reason, tradition, and conscience. He had shown the same (chap. ii. iii.) in respect to the Jews. They had equally failed in rendering obedience to *their* law. In both these cases the reference was, not to *ceremonial* or *ritual* laws, but to the moral law; whether that law was made known by reason or by revelation. The apostle had not been discussing the question whether they had yielded obedience to their ceremonial law, but whether they had been found

21 But now the righteousness of God without the law is manifested,

holy, i. e. whether they had obeyed the *moral* law. The conclusion was, that in all this they had failed, and that therefore they could not be justified by that law. That the apostle did not intend to speak of *external* works only is apparent; for he all along charges them with a want of conformity of the heart no less than with a want of conformity of the life; see chap. i. 26, 29—31; ii. 28, 29. The conclusion is therefore a general one, that by no law, made known either by reason, conscience, tradition, or revelation, could man be justified; that there was no form of *obedience* which could be rendered, that would justify men in the sight of a holy God. ¶ *There shall no flesh.* No man; no human being, either among the Jews or the Gentiles. It is a strong expression, denoting the absolute universality of his conclusion; see Note on chap. i. 3. ¶ *Be justified.* Be regarded and treated as righteous. None shall be esteemed as having *kept* the law, and as being entitled to the rewards of obedience; see Note, chap. i. 17. ¶ *In his sight.* Before him. God sits as a Judge to determine the characters of men, and he shall not adjudge any to have kept the law. ¶ *For by the law.* That is, by *all* law. The connection shows that this is the sense. Law is a rule of action. The effect of *applying* a rule to our conduct is to show us what sin is. The meaning of the apostle clearly is, that the application of a law to try our conduct, instead of being a ground of justification, will be merely to show us our own sinfulness and departures from duty. A man may esteem himself to be very right and correct, until he compares himself with a rule, or law; so whether the Gentiles compared their conduct with *their* laws of reason and conscience, or the Jew his with his *written* law, the effect would be to show them how far they had departed. The more closely and faithfully it should be applied, the more they would see it. So far from being justified by it, they would be more and more condemned; comp. Rom. vii. 7—10. The same is the case now. This is the way in which a sinner is converted; and the more closely and faithfully the law is preached, the more will it condemn him, and show him that he needs some other plan of salvation.

21. *But now.* The apostle, having shown the entire failure of all attempts to be justified by the *law*, whether among Jews or Gentiles, proceeds to state fully the plan of justification by Jesus Christ in the gospel. To do this, was the main design of the epistle, chap. i. 17. He makes, therefore, in the close of this chapter, an explicit statement of the nature of the doctrine; and in the following parts of the epistle he fully proves it, and illustrates its effects. ¶ *The righteousness of God.* God's plan of justifying men; see Note, chap. i. 17. ¶ *Without the law.* In a way different from personal obedience to the law. It does not mean that God *abandoned* his law; or that Jesus Christ did not *regard* the law, for he came to "magnify" it (Isa. xlii. 21); or that sinners *after* they are justified have no regard to the law; but it means simply what the apostle had been endeavouring to show, that justification could not be accomplished by *personal* obedience to any law of Jew or Gentile, and that it must be accomplished in some other way. ¶ *Being witnessed.* Being borne witness to. It was not a *new* doctrine; it was found in the Old Testament. The apostle makes this observation with special reference to the *Jews.* He does not declare any *new* thing, but that which was fully declared in their own sacred writings. ¶ *By the law.* This expression here evidently denotes, as it did commonly among the Jews, the five books of Moses. And the apostle means to say that this doctrine was found in *those books;* not that it was in the ten commandments, or in the *law,* strictly so called. It is not a part of *law* to declare justification except by strict and perfect obedience. That it was

being witnessed by the law [a] and the prophets;

22 Even the righteousness of God, *which is* by faith [b] of Jesus

a Acts 26.22. b chap.5.1,&c.

found *in* those books, the apostle shows by the case of Abraham; chap. iv.; see also his reasoning on Lev. xviii. 5; Deut. xxx. 12—14, in Rom. x. 5—11; comp. Ex. xxxiv. 6, 7. ¶ *And the prophets.* Generally, the remainder of the Old Testament. The phrase "the law and the prophets" comprehended the whole of the Old Testament; Mat. v. 17; xi. 13; xxii. 40; Acts xiii. 15; xxviii. 23. That this doctrine was contained in *the prophets,* the apostle showed by the passage quoted from Hab. ii. 4, in chap. i. 17, "The just shall live by faith." The same thing he showed in chap. x. 11, from Isa. xxviii. 16; xlix. 23; chap. iv. 6—8, from Ps. xxxii. The same thing is fully taught in Isa. liii. 11; Dan. ix. 24. Indeed, the general tenor of the Old Testament —the appointment of sacrifices, &c. taught that man was a sinner, and that he could not be justified by obedience to the moral law.

22. *Even the righteousness of God.* The apostle, having stated that the design of the gospel was to reveal a new plan of becoming just in the sight of God, proceeds here more fully to explain it. The explanation which he offers, makes it plain that the phrase so often used by him, "righteousness of God," does not refer to an *attribute* of God, but to his plan of making men righteous. Here he says that it is by faith in Jesus Christ; but surely an *attribute* of God is not produced by faith in Jesus Christ. It means God's mode of regarding men as righteous through their belief in Jesus Christ.

[That the "righteousness of God" cannot be explained of the attribute of justice, is obvious enough. It cannot be said of divine justice, that *it* is "unto and upon all them that believe." But we are not reduced to the alternative of explaining the phrase, either of God's justice, or God's plan of justifying men. Why may we not understand it of that righteousness which Jehovah devised, Jesus executed, and the Spirit applies; and which is therefore justly denominated the righteousness of GOD? It consists in that conformity to law which Jesus manifested in his atoning death, and meritorious obedience. His death, by reason of his divine nature, was of infinite value. And when he *voluntarily* submitted to yield a life that was forfeited by no transgression of his own, the law, in its *penal* part, was more magnified than if every descendant of Adam had sunk under the weight of its vengeance. Nor was the *preceptive* part of the law less honoured, in the spotless obedience of Christ. He abstained from every sin, fulfilled every duty, and exemplified every virtue. Neither God nor man could accuse him of failure in duty. To God he gave his piety, to man his glowing love, to friends his heart, to foes his pity and his pardon. And by the obedience of the Creator in human form, the precept of the law was more honoured than if the highest angels had come down to do reverence to it, in presence of men. Here then is a righteousness worthy of the name, divine, spotless, broad, lasting—beyond the power of language to characterize. It is that everlasting righteousness which Daniel predicted the Messiah should bring in. Adam's righteousness failed and passed away. That of once happy angels perished too, but this shall endure. "The heavens, "says Jehovah," shall vanish away like smoke, and the earth shall wax old like a garment, and they that dwell therein shall die in like manner, but *my salvation* shall be for ever, and *my righteousness* shall not be abolished." This righteousness is broad enough to cover every sinner and every sin. It is pure enough to meet the eye of God himself. It is therefore the sinner's only shield. See Note, chap. i. 17, for the true meaning of the expression "righteousness of God."]

¶ *By faith of Jesus Christ.* That is, by faith *in* Jesus Christ. Thus the expression, Mark xi. 22, "Have the faith of God" (*margin*), means, have faith *in* God. So Acts iii. 16, the "faith of his name" (*Greek*), means, faith *in* his name. So Gal. ii. 20, the "faith of the Son of God" means, faith *in* the Son of God. This cannot mean that faith is the meritorious cause of salvation, but that it is the instrument or means by which we become justified. It is *the state of mind,* or *condition of the heart,* to which God has been pleased to promise justification. (On the nature of faith see Note, Mark xvi. 16.) God

Christ, unto all and upon all them that believe: for there is no difference:

23 For all [a] have sinned, and come short of the glory of God;

24 Being justified freely by his

a Ec.7.20.

has promised that they who believe in Christ shall be pardoned and saved. This is *his* plan in distinction from the plan of those who seek to be justified by works. ¶ *Unto all and upon all.* It is evident that these expressions are designed to be emphatic, but why both are used is not very apparent. Many have supposed that there was no essential difference in the meaning. If there be a difference, it is probably this: the first expression, "unto all" (εἰς πάντας), may denote that this plan of justification has come (*Luther*) *unto* all men, to Jews and Gentiles; *i. e.* that it has been provided for them, and offered to them without distinction. The plan was ample for all, was fitted for all, was equally necessary for all, and was offered to all. The second phrase, "upon all" (ἐπὶ παντας), may be designed to guard against the supposition that *all* therefore would be benefited by it, or be saved by the mere fact that the announcement had come to all. The apostle adds therefore, that the benefits of this plan must actually come *upon* all, or must be *applied to* all, if they would be justified. They could not be justified merely by the fact that the plan was provided, and that the knowledge of it had come to all, but by their actually coming *under* this plan, and availing themselves of it. Perhaps there is reference in the last expression, "upon all," to a robe, or garment, that is placed upon one to hide his nakedness, or sin; comp. Isa. lxiv. 6, also Phil. iii. 9. ¶ *For there is no difference.* That is, there is no difference *in regard to the matter under discussion.* The apostle does not mean to say that there is no difference in regard to the talents, dispositions, education, and property of men; but there is no distinction in regard to the way in which they must be justified. All must be saved, if saved at all, in the same mode, whether Jews or Gentiles, bond or free, rich or poor, learned or ignorant. None can be saved by works; and all are therefore dependent on the mercy of God in Jesus Christ.

23. *For all have sinned.* This was the point which he had fully established in the discussion in these chapters. ¶ *Have come short.* Greek, *Are deficient in regard to;* are wanting, &c. Here it means, that they had *failed to obtain,* or were destitute of. ¶ *The glory of God.* The praise or approbation of God. They had sought to be justified, or *approved, by God;* but all had failed. Their works of the law had not secured his approbation; and they were therefore under condemnation. The word *glory* (δόξα) is often used in the sense of *praise,* or *approbation,* John v. 41, 44; vii. 18; viii. 50, 54; xii. 43.

24. *Being justified.* Being treated as if righteous; that is, being regarded and treated as if they had kept the law. The apostle has shown that they *could not* be so regarded and treated by any merit of their own, or by personal obedience to the law. He now affirms that if they were so treated, it must be by mere favour, and as a matter not of right, but of gift. This is the essence of the gospel. And to show this, and the way in which it is done, is the main design of this epistle. The expression here is to be understood as referring to *all* who are justified; ver. 22. The righteousness of God by faith in Jesus Christ, is "upon all who believe," who are all "justified freely by his grace." ¶ *Freely* (δωρεὰν). This word stands opposed to that which is purchased, or which is obtained by labour, or which is a matter of claim. It is a free, undeserved gift, not merited by our obedience to the law, and not that to which we have any claim. The apostle uses the word here in reference to those who are justified. To *them* it is a mere undeserved gift. It does not mean that it has been obtained, however, without any price or merit from any

grace through the redemption that is in Christ Jesus.

25 Whom God hath [1] set forth *to be* a propitiation through faith in his blood, to declare his righteousness for the [2] remission of sins that are past, through the forbearance of God;

1 or, *fore-ordained.*

2 or, *passing over.*

one, for the Lord Jesus has purchased it with his own blood, and *to him* it becomes a matter of justice that those who were given to him should be justified, 1 Cor. vi. 20; vii. 23; 2 Pet. ii. 1; 1 Pet. ii. 9. (*Greek*). Acts xx. 28; Isa. liii. 11. *We* have no offering to bring, and no claim. To us, therefore, it is entirely a matter of gift. ¶ *By his grace.* By his favour; by his mere undeserved mercy; see Note, chap. i. 7. ¶ *Through the redemption* (διὰ τῆς ἀπολυτρώσεως). The word used here occurs but ten times in the New Testament, Luke xxi. 28; Rom. iii. 24; viii. 23; 1 Cor. i. 30; Eph. i. 7, 14; iv. 30; Col. i. 14; Heb. ix. 15; xi. 35. Its root (λύτρον, *lutron*) properly denotes the price which is paid for a prisoner of war; the ransom, or stipulated purchase-money, which being paid, the captive is set free. The word here used is then employed to denote liberation from bondage, captivity, or evil of any kind, usually keeping up the idea of a *price,* or a *ransom paid,* in consequence of which the delivery is effected. It is sometimes used in a large sense, to denote simple deliverance *by any means,* without reference to a price paid, as in Luke xxi. 28; Rom. viii. 23; Eph. i. 14. That this is *not* the sense here, however, is apparent. For the apostle in the next verse proceeds to specify the *price* which has been paid, or the means by which this redemption has been effected. The word *here* denotes that *deliverance from sin, and from the evil consequences of sin,* which has been effected by the offering of Jesus Christ as a propitiation; ver. 25. ¶ *That is in Christ Jesus.* Or, that has been effected by Christ Jesus; that of which he is the author and procurer; comp. John iii. 16.

25. *Whom God hath set forth.* Margin, *Fore-ordained* (προέθετο). The word properly means, *to place in public view;* to exhibit in a conspicuous situation, as goods are exhibited or exposed for sale, or as premiums or rewards of victory were exhibited to public view in the games of the Greeks. It *sometimes* has the meaning of decreeing, purposing, or constituting, as in the margin (comp. Rom. i. 13; Eph. i. 9); and many have supposed that this is its meaning here. But the connection seems to require the usual signification of the word; and it means that God has *publicly exhibited Jesus Christ* as a propitiatory sacrifice for the sins of men. This public exhibition was made by his being offered on the cross, in the face of angels and of men. It was not concealed; it was done openly. He was put to open shame; and *so* put to death as to attract towards the scene the eyes of angels, and of the inhabitants of all worlds. ¶ To be *a propitiation* (ἱλαστήριον). This word occurs but in one other place in the New Testament, Heb. ix. 5, "And over it (the ark) the cherubim of glory shadowing *the mercy-seat.*" It is used here to denote the lid or cover of the ark of the covenant. It was made of gold, and over it were the cherubim. In this sense it is often used by the LXX. Ex. xxv. 17, "And thou shalt make a propitiatory (ἱλαστήριον) of gold," 18, 19, 20, 22; xxx. 6; xxxi. 7; xxxv. 11; xxxvii. 6–9; xl. 18; Lev. xvi. 2, 13. The Hebrew name for this was *capphoreth,* from the verb *caphar,* to cover, or conceal. It was from *this* place that God was represented as speaking to the children of Israel. Ex. xxv. 22, "And I will speak to thee from above the *Hilasterion,*" the propitiatory, the mercy-seat. Lev. xvi. 2, "For I will appear in the cloud upon the mercy-seat." This seat, or cover, was covered with the smoke of the *incense,* when the high-priest entered the most holy place, Lev. xvi. 13. And the blood of the bullock offered on the great day of atonement, was to be sprinkled "upon the mercy-

seat," and "before the mercy-seat," "seven times," Lev. xvi. 14, 15. This sprinkling or offering of blood was called making "an atonement for the holy place because of the uncleanness of the children of Israel," &c. Lev. xvi. 16. It was from this mercy-seat that God pronounced pardon, or expressed himself as *reconciled* to his people. The atonement was made, the blood was sprinkled, and the reconciliation thus effected. The *name* was thus given to that cover of the ark, because it was the place from which God declared himself reconciled to his people. Still the inquiry is, why is this name given to Jesus Christ? In what sense is *he* declared to be a propitiation? It is evident that it cannot be applied to him in any *literal* sense. Between the golden cover of the ark of the covenant and the Lord Jesus, the analogy *must* be *very* slight, if *any* such analogy can be perceived. We may observe, however, (1.) That the *main idea*, in regard to the cover of the ark called the mercy-seat, was that of God's being *reconciled* to his people; and that this is the main idea in regard to the Lord Jesus whom "God hath set forth." (2.) This reconciliation was effected *then* by the sprinkling of blood on the mercy-seat, Lev. xvi. 15, 16. The same is true of the Lord Jesus—by blood. (3.) In the former case it was by the blood of atonement; the offering of the bullock on the great day of atonement, that the reconciliation was effected, Lev. xvi. 17, 18. In the case of the Lord Jesus it was also by blood; by the blood of atonement. But it was by his *own* blood. This the apostle distinctly states in this verse. (4.) In the former case there was a *sacrifice*, or *expiatory* offering; and so it is in reconciliation by the Lord Jesus. In the former, the mercy-seat was the visible, declared place where God would express his reconciliation with his people. So in the latter, the offering of the Lord Jesus is the manifest and open way by which God will be reconciled to men. (5.) In the former, there was joined the idea of a *sacrifice* for sin, Lev. xvi. So in the latter. And hence the *main idea* of the apostle here is to convey the idea of *a sacrifice for sin;* or to set forth the Lord Jesus as such a sacrifice. Hence the word "propitiation" in the original may express the idea of a *propitiatory sacrifice*, as well as the cover to the ark. The word is an *adjective*, and may be joined to the noun *sacrifice*, as well as to denote the mercy-seat of the ark. This meaning accords also with its classic meaning to denote *a propitiatory offering*, or an offering to produce reconciliation. Christ is thus represented, not *as a mercy-seat*, which would be unintelligible; but as the medium, the offering, the expiation, by which reconciliation is produced between God and man. ¶ *Through faith.* Or by means of faith. The offering will be of no avail without *faith.* The offering has been made; but it will not be applied, except where there is faith. He has made an offering which may be efficacious in putting away sin; but it produces no reconciliation, no pardon, except where it is accepted by faith. ¶ *In his blood.* Or in his death—his bloody death. Among the Jews, *the blood* was regarded as the seat of life, or vitality. Lev. xvii. 11, "The life of the flesh is in the blood." Hence they were commanded not to eat blood. Gen. ix. 4, "But flesh with the life thereof, which is the blood thereof, shall ye not eat." Lev. xix. 26; Deut. xii. 23; 1 Sam. xiv. 34. This doctrine is contained uniformly in the sacred Scriptures. And it has been also the opinion of not a few celebrated physiologists, as well in modern as in ancient times. The same was the opinion of the ancient Parsees and Hindoos. Homer thus often speaks of *blood* as the seat of life, as in the expression πορφυρεος θανατος, or *purple death.* And Virgil speaks of *purple life,*

> Purpuream vomit ille animam.
> *Æniad*, ix. 349.

Empedocles and Critias among the Greek philosophers, also embraced this opinion. Among the moderns, Harvey, to whom we are indebted for a knowledge of the circulation of the blood, fully believed it. Hoffman and Huxham believed it. Dr John Hunter has fully adopted the belief, and sustained it, as he supposed, by a great variety of considerations. See Good's Book of Nature, pp. 102, 108, Ed. New York, 1828. This was undoubtedly the doctrine of the Hebrews; and hence with them to shed the blood was a phrase signifying to kill; hence the efficacy of their sacrifices was supposed to consist in *the blood,* that is, in the *life* of the victim. Hence it was unlawful to *eat* it, as it were the *life,* the seat of vitality; the more immediate and direct gift of God. When, therefore, *the blood of Christ* is spoken of in the New Testament, it means *the offering of his life as a sacrifice,* or his *death* as an expiation. *His* life was given to make atonement. See the word *blood* thus used in Rom. v. 9; Eph. i. 7; Col. i. 14; Heb. ix. 12, 14; xiii. 12; Rev. i. 5; 1 Pet. i. 19; 1 John i. 7. By faith in his death as a sacrifice for sin; by believing that he took *our* sins; that he died in *our* place; by thus, in some sense, making his offering ours; by *approving* it, loving it, embracing it, trusting it, our sins become pardoned, and our souls made pure. ¶ *To declare* (εἰς ἔνδειξιν). *For the purpose* of showing, or exhibiting; to present it to man. The meaning is, that the plan was adopted; the Saviour was given; he suffered and died: and the scheme is proposed to men, *for the purpose* of making a full manifestation of *his* plan, in contradistinction from all the plans of men. ¶ *His righteousness.* His plan of justification. The method or scheme which *he* has adopted, in distinction from that of man; and which he now exhibits, or proffers to sinners. There is great variety in the explanation of the word here rendered *righteousness.* Some explain it as meaning *veracity;* others as *holiness;* others as *goodness;* others as *essential justice.* Most interpreters, perhaps, have explained it as referring to an attribute of God. But the whole connection requires us to understand it here as in chap. i. 17, not of an *attribute* of God, but of his *plan* of justifying sinners. He has adopted and proposed a plan by which men may become *just* by faith in Jesus Christ, and not by their own works. His acquitting men from sin; his regarding them and treating them as just, is set forth in the gospel by the offering of Jesus Christ as a sacrifice on the cross. [For the true meaning of this phrase, see Note, chap. i. 17; iii. 22.] ¶ *For the remission of sins.* Margin, *Passing over.* The word here used (πάρεσιν) occurs no where else in the New Testament, nor in the Septuagint. It means *passing by,* as not noticing, and hence forgiving. A similar idea occurs in 2 Sam. xxiv. 10, and Micah vii. 18. "Who is a God like unto thee, that passeth by the transgression of the remnant of his inheritance?" In Romans it means for the *pardoning,* or in order to pardon past transgression. ¶ *That are past.* That have been committed; or that have existed before. This has been commonly understood to refer to past generations, as affirming that sins under all dispensations of the world are to be forgiven in this manner, through the sacrifice of Christ. And it has been supposed that all who have been justified, have received pardon by the merits of the sacrifice of Christ. This may be true; but there is no reason to think that this is the idea in *this* passage. For, (1.) The scope of the passage does not require it. The argument is not to show how men *had* been justified, but how they *might* be. It is not to discuss an historical *fact,* but to state the way in which sin was to be forgiven under the gospel. (2.) The language has no immediate or necessary reference to past generations. It evidently refers to the past lives of the *individuals* who are justified, and not to the sins of former times. All that the passage means, therefore, is, that the plan of pardon is such as completely to remove all the former sins of *the life,* not of all former generations. If it referred to the sins of former times, it would not be easy to avoid the doctrine of universal salvation.

[The design of the apostle is to show the alone ground of a sinner's justification. That ground is "the righteousness of God." To manifest this righteousness, Christ had been set forth in the beginning of the gospel age as a propitiatory sacrifice. But though at this time *manifested* or declared, it had in reality

26 To declare, *I say*, at this time, his righteousness: that [a] he might be just, and the justifier of him which believeth in Jesus.

a Acts 13.38,39.

been the ground of justification *all along*. Believers in every past dispensation, looking forward to the period of its revelation, had built their hopes on it, and been admitted into glory.

The idea of *manifestation* in gospel times, seems most intimately connected with the fact that, in past ages, the ground of pardon had been *hidden*, or at best but dimly seen through type and ceremony. There seems little doubt that these two things were associated in the apostle's mind. Though the ground of God's procedure in remitting the sins of his people, during the former economy, had long been concealed, it was now gloriously displayed before the eyes of the universe. Paul has the very same idea in Heb. ix. 15, "And for this cause he is the Mediator of the New Testament, that by means of death, *for the redemption of the transgressions that were under the first testament*, they which are called might receive the promise of eternal inheritance." It may be noticed also that the expression in the 20th verse, "at this time," *i. e.* in the gospel age, requires us to understand the other clause, "sins that are past," as pointing to sin committed under former dispensations. Nor is there any fear of lending support to the doctrine of universal salvation, if we espouse this view, the sins remitted in past ages being obviously those of *believers only*. The very same objection might be urged against the parallel passage in Heb. ix. 15.]

¶ *Through the forbearance of God.* Through his patience, his long-suffering. That is, he did not come forth in judgment *when* the sin was committed; he spared us, though deserving of punishment; and now he comes forth completely to *pardon* those sins concerning which he has so long and so graciously exercised forbearance. This expression obviously refers not to the *remission* of sins, but to the fact that they were *committed* while he evinced such long-suffering; comp. Acts xvii. 30. I do not know better how to show the practical value and bearing of this important passage of Scripture, than by transcribing a part of the affecting experience of the poet *Cowper*. It is well known that *before* his conversion he was oppressed by a long and dreadful melancholy; that this was finally heightened to despair; and that he was then subjected to the kind treatment of Dr. Cotton in St. Alban's, as a melancholy case of derangement. His leading thought was that he was doomed to inevitable destruction, and that there was no hope. From this he was roused only by the kindness of his brother, and by the promises of the gospel; (see Taylor's Life of Cowper). The account of his conversion I shall now give in his own words. "The happy period, which was to shake off my fetters, and afford me a clear discovery of the free mercy of God in Christ Jesus, was now arrived. I flung myself into a chair near the window, and seeing a Bible there, ventured once more to apply to it for comfort and instruction. The first verse I saw was the 25th of the 3d of Romans; *Whom God hath set forth*, &c. Immediately I received strength to believe, and the full beam of the Sun of righteousness shone upon me. I saw the sufficiency of the atonement he had made for my pardon and justification. In a moment I believed, and received the peace of the gospel. Unless the Almighty arm had been under me, I think I should have been overwhelmed with gratitude and joy. My eyes filled with tears, and my voice choked with transport. I could only look up to heaven in silent fear, overwhelmed with love and wonder. How glad should I now have been to have spent every moment in prayer and thanksgiving. I lost no opportunity of repairing to a throne of grace; but flew to it with an earnestness irresistible, and never to be satisfied."

26. *At this time.* The time now since the Saviour has come, now is the time when he manifests it. ¶ *That he might be just.* This verse contains the substance of the gospel. The word "just" here does not mean benevolent, or merciful, though it *may* sometimes have that meaning; see Note, Mat. i. 19, also John xvii. 25. But it refers to the fact that God had retained the integrity of his character as a moral

27 Where *is* boasting then? It is excluded. By what law? of works? Nay; but by the law of faith.

governor; that he had shown a due regard to his law, and to the penalty of the law by his plan of salvation. Should he forgive sinners without an atonement, *justice* would be sacrificed and abandoned. The law would cease to have any terrors for the guilty, and its penalty would be a nullity. In the plan of salvation, therefore, he has shown a regard to the law by appointing his Son to be *a substitute* in the place of sinners; not to endure its precise penalty, for his sufferings were not eternal, nor were they attended with remorse of conscience, or by despair, which are the proper *penalty* of the law; but he endured so much as to accomplish the same ends as if those who shall be saved by him had been doomed to eternal death. That is, he showed that the law could not be violated without introducing suffering; and that it could not be broken with impunity. He showed that he had so great a regard for it, that he would not pardon *one sinner* without an atonement. And *thus* he secured the proper honour to his character as a lover of his law, a hater of sin, and a just God. He has shown that if sinners do not avail themselves of the offer of pardon by Jesus Christ, *they* must experience in their own souls for ever the pains which this substitute for sinners endured in behalf of men on the cross. Thus, no principle of justice has been abandoned; no threatening has been modified; no claim of his law has been let down; no disposition has been evinced to do *injustice* to the universe by suffering the guilty to escape. He is, in all this great transaction, a just moral governor, as *just* to his law, to himself, to his Son, to the universe, when he *pardons*, as he is when he sends the incorrigible sinner down to hell. A full compensation, an equivalent, has been provided by the sufferings of the Saviour in the sinner's stead, and the sinner may be pardoned. ¶ *And the justifier of him*, &c. Greek, *Even justifying him that believeth*, &c. This is the peculiarity and the wonder of the gospel. *Even while* pardoning, and treating the ill-deserving *as if* they were innocent, he can retain his pure and holy character. His treating the guilty with favour does not show that he loves guilt and pollution, for he has expressed his abhorrence of it in the atonement. His admitting them to friendship and heaven does not show that he *approves* their past conduct and character, for he showed how much he hated even *their* sins by giving his Son to a shameful death *for* them. When an executive pardons offenders, there is an abandonment of the principles of justice and law. The sentence is *set aside;* the threatenings of the law are departed from; and it is done without compensation. It is declared that in certain cases the law *may be* violated, and its penalty *not* be inflicted. But not so with God. He shows no less regard to his law in pardoning than in punishing. This is the grand, glorious, peculiar feature of the gospel plan of salvation. ¶ *Him which believeth in Jesus.* Greek, *Him who is of the faith of Jesus;* in contradistinction from him who is of the works of the law; that is, who depends on his own works for salvation.

27. *Where is boasting then?* Where is there ground or occasion of boasting or pride? Since all have sinned, and since all have failed of being able to justify themselves by obeying the law, and since all are alike dependent on the mere mercy of God in Christ, all ground of boasting is of course taken away. This refers particularly to the Jews, who were much addicted to *boasting* of their peculiar privileges; See Note, chap. iii. 1, &c. ¶ *By what law?* The word *law* here is used in the sense of *arrangement, rule,* or *economy.* By what arrangement, or by the operation of what *rule*, is boasting excluded? *(Stuart).* See Gal. iii. 21; Acts xxi. 20. ¶ *Of works.* The law which commands works, and on which the Jews relied. If this were complied with, and they were thereby justified, they would have had ground of self-confidence, or boasting, as

28 Therefore we conclude that [a] a man is justified by faith without the deeds of the law.

29 *Is he* the God of the Jews only? *is he* not also of the Gentiles? Yes, of the Gentiles also:

30 Seeing *it is* one God, which [a] shall justify the circumcision by faith, and uncircumcision through faith.

31 Do we then make void the law through [b] faith? God forbid: yea, we establish the law.

a ver.20-22. chap.8.3; Gal.2.16.

a Gal.3.8,28. *b* Heb.10.15,16.

being justified by their own merits. But a plan which led to this, which ended in boasting, and self-satisfaction, and pride, could not be true. ¶ *Nay.* No. ¶ *The law of faith.* The rule, or arrangement which proclaims that we have no merit; that we are lost sinners; and that we are to be justified *only* by faith.

28. *Therefore.* As the result of the previous train of argument. ¶ *That a man.* That *all* who are justified; that is, that there is no other way. ¶ *Is justified by faith.* Is regarded and treated as righteous, by believing in the Lord Jesus Christ. ¶ *Without the deeds of the law.* Without works as a meritorious ground of justification. The apostle, of course, does not mean that Christianity does not *produce* good works, or that they who are justified will not obey the law, and be holy; but that no righteousness of their own will be the ground of their justification. They are sinners; and as such can have no claim to be treated as righteous. God has devised a plan by which they may be pardoned and saved; and that is by faith alone. This is the grand peculiarity of the Christian religion. This was the peculiar point in the reformation from popery. Luther often called this doctrine of justification by faith, the article on which the church stood or fell—*articulus stantis, vel cadentis ecclesiæ*—and it is so. If this doctrine is held entire, all others will be held with it. If this is abandoned, all others will fall also. It may be remarked here, however, that this doctrine by no means interferes with the doctrine that good works are to be performed by Christians. Paul urges this as much as any other writer in the New Testament. His doctrine is, that they are not to be relied on as a *ground* of justification; but that he did not mean to teach that they are not to be performed by Christians is apparent from the connection, and from the following places in his epistles: Rom. ii. 7; 2 Cor. ix. 8; Eph. ii. 10; 1 Tim. ii. 10; v. 10, 25; vi. 18; 2 Tim. iii. 17; Tit. ii. 7, 14; iii. 8; Heb. x. 24. That we are not *justified* by our works is a doctrine which he has urged and repeated with great power and frequency. See Rom. iv. 2, 6; ix. 11, 32; xi. 6; Gal. ii. 16; iii. 2, 5, 10; Eph. ii. 9; 2 Tim. i. 9.

29, 30. *Is he the God,* &c. The Jews supposed that he was the God of their nation only, that *they* only were to be admitted to his favour. In these verses Paul showed that as all had alike sinned, Jews and Gentiles; and as the plan of salvation by faith was adapted *to sinners,* without any special reference to *Jews;* so God could show favours to all, and all might be admitted on the same terms to the benefits of the plan of salvation.

30. *It is one God.* The same God, there is but one, and his plan is equally fitted to Jews and Gentiles. ¶ *The circumcision.* Those who are circumcised—the *Jews.* ¶ *The uncircumcision.* Gentiles; all who were not Jews. ¶ *By faith...through faith.* There is no difference in the meaning of these expressions. Both denote that faith is the instrumental cause of justification, or acceptance with God.

31. *Do we then make void the law.* Do we render it vain and useless; do we destroy its moral obligation; and do we prevent obedience to it, by the doctrine of justification by faith? This was an *objection* which would naturally be made; and which has thousands of times been since made, that the doctrine of justification by faith tends to licentiousness. The

word *law* here, I understand as referring to the *moral law*, and not merely to the Old Testament. This is evident from ver. 20, 21, where the apostle shows that no man could be justified by *deeds of law*, by conformity with the moral law. See Note. ¶ *God forbid.* By no means. Note, ver. 4. This is an explicit denial of any such tendency. ¶ *Yea, we establish the law.* That is, by the doctrine of justification by faith; by this scheme of treating men as righteous, the moral law is confirmed, its obligation is enforced, obedience to it is secured. This is done in the following manner: (1.) God showed respect to it, in being unwilling to pardon sinners without an atonement. He showed that it could not be violated with impunity; that he was resolved to fulfil its threatenings. (2.) Jesus Christ came to magnify it, and to make it honourable. He showed respect to it in his life; and he died to show that God was determined to inflict its penalty. (3.) The plan of justification by faith leads to an observance of the law. The sinner sees the evil of transgression. He sees the respect which God has shown to the law. He gives his heart to God, and yields himself to obey his law. All the sentiments that arise from the conviction of sin; that flow from gratitude for mercies; that spring from love to God; all his views of the sacredness of the law, prompt him to yield obedience to it. The fact that Christ endured such sufferings to show the evil of violating the law, is one of the strongest motives prompting to obedience. We do not easily and readily repeat that which overwhelms our best friends in calamity; and we are brought to *hate* that which inflicted such woes on the Saviour's soul. The sentiment recorded by Watts is as true as it is beautiful:—

"'Twas for my sins my dearest Lord
Hung on the cursed tree.
And groan'd away his dying life,
For thee, my soul, for thee.

"O how I hate those lusts of mine
That crucified my Lord;
Those sins that pierc'd and nail'd his flesh
Fast to the fatal wood.

"Yes, my Redeemer, they shall die,
My heart hath so decreed;
Nor will I spare the guilty things
That made my Saviour bleed."

This is an advantage in moral influence which no cold, abstract law ever has over the human mind. And one of the chief glories of the plan of salvation is, that while it justifies the sinner, it brings a new set of influences from heaven, more tender and mighty than can be drawn from any other source, to produce obedience to the law of God.

[This is indeed a beautiful and just view of the moral influence of the gospel, and especially of the doctrine of justification by faith alone. It may be questioned, however, whether the apostle in this place refers chiefly, or even at all, to the sanctifying tendency of his doctrine. *This* he does very fully in the 6th chap.; and therefore, if another and consistent sense can be found, we need not resort to the supposition that he now anticipates what he intended, in a subsequent part of his epistle, more fully to discuss. In what other way, then, does the apostle's doctrine establish the law? How does he vindicate himself from the charge of making it void? In the preceding chapter he had pointed out the true ground of pardon in the "righteousness of God." He had explained that *none* could be justified but they who had by faith received it. "Do we THEN," he asks in conclusion, "make void the law by maintaining thus, that no sinner can be accepted who does not receive a righteousness commensurate with all its demands?." "Yea, we establish the law," is the obvious answer. Jesus has died to satisfy its claims, and lives to honour its precepts. Thus he hath brought in "righteousness," which, being imputed to them that believe, forms such a ground of pardon and acceptance, as the law CANNOT CHALLENGE.

Calvin, in his commentary on the passage, though he does not exclude the idea of sanctification, yet gives prominence to the view now stated. "When," says he, "we come to Christ, *the exact righteousness of the law* is FIRST found in him, which also becomes ours by imputation; in the next place sanctification is acquired," &c.]

CHAPTER IV.

THE main object of this chapter is to show that the doctrine of justification by faith, which the apostle was defending, was found in the Old Testament. The argument is to be regarded as addressed particularly to *a Jew*, to show him that no *new* doctrine was advanced. The argument is derived,

CHAPTER IV.

WHAT shall we say, then, that Abraham, our father [a] as pertaining to the flesh, hath found?

2 For if Abraham were justified by works, he hath *whereof* to glory: but not [b] before God.

3 For what saith the Scripture? [c]

a Mat. 3. 9. *b* chap.3.27. *c* Gen.15.6.

first, from the fact that Abraham was so justified, (ver. 1—5); Secondly, from the fact that the same thing is declared by David (ver. 6—8).

A question might still be asked, whether this justification was not in consequence of their being circumcised, and thus grew out of conformity to the law? To answer this, the apostle shows (ver. 9—12) that Abraham was justified by faith *before* he was circumcised, and that even his circumcision was *in consequence* of his being justified by faith, and a public seal or attestation of that fact.

Still further, the apostle shows that if men were to be justified by works, faith would be of no use; and the promises of God would have no effect. The law works wrath (ver. 13, 14), but the conferring of the favour by faith is demonstration of the highest favour of God (ver. 16). Abraham, moreover, had evinced a strong faith; he had shown what it was; he was an example to all who should follow. And he had thus shown that as *he* was justified *before* circumcision, and *before* the giving of the law, so the same thing might occur in regard to those who had never been circumcised. In chap. ii. and iii., the apostle had shown that all had failed of keeping the law, and that there was no other way of justification but by faith. To the salvation of the heathen, the Jew would have strong objections. He supposed that none could be saved but those who had been circumcised, and who were Jews. This objection the apostle meets in this chapter by showing that Abraham was justified in the very way in which he maintained the heathen *might be;* that Abraham was justified by faith *without* being circumcised. If the father of the faithful, the ancestor on whom the Jews so much prided themselves, was thus justified, then Paul was advancing no new doctrine in maintaining that the same thing might occur now. He was keeping strictly within the spirit of their religion in maintaining that the Gentile world might also be justified by faith. This is the outline of the reasoning in this chapter. The reasoning is such as a serious Jew must feel and acknowledge. And keeping in mind the main object which the apostle had in it, there will be found little difficulty in its interpretation.

1. *What shall we say then?* See chap. iii. 1. This is rather the objection of a Jew. "How does your doctrine of justification by faith agree with what the Scriptures say of Abraham? Was the law set aside in his case? Did he derive no advantage in justification from the rite of circumcision, and from the covenant which God made with him." The object of the apostle now is to answer this inquiry. ¶ *That Abraham our father.* Our ancestor; the father and founder of the nation; see Note, Matt. iii. 9 The Jews valued themselves much on the fact that he was their father; and an argument, drawn from his example or conduct, therefore, would be peculiarly forcible. ¶ *As pertaining to the flesh.* This expression is one that has been much controverted. In the original, it may refer either to Abraham as their father "according to the flesh," that is, their natural father, or from whom they were descended; or it may be connected with "hath found." "What shall we say that Abraham our father hath found in respect to the flesh?" κατὰ σάρκα. The latter is doubtless the proper connection. Some refer the word *flesh* to external privileges and advantages; others to his own strength or power (*Calvin* and *Grotius*); and others make it refer to circumcision. This latter I take to be the correct interpretation. It agrees best with the connection, and equally well with the usual meaning of the word. The idea is, "If men are justified by *faith;* if works are to have no place; if, therefore, all rites

and ceremonies, all legal observances, are useless in justification; what is the advantage of circumcision? What benefit did Abraham derive from it? Why was it appointed? And why is such an importance attached to it in the history of his life?" A similar question was asked in chap. iii. 1. ¶ *Hath found.* Hath obtained. What advantage has he derived from it?

2. *For if Abraham,* &c. This is the answer of the apostle. If Abraham was justified on the ground of his own merits, he would have reason to boast, or to claim praise. He might regard himself as the author of it, and take the praise to himself; see ver. 4. The inquiry, therefore, was, whether in the account of the justification of Abraham, there was to be found any such statement of a reason for self-confidence and boasting. ¶ *But not before God.* In the sight of God. That is, in his recorded judgment, he had no ground of boasting on account of works. To show this, the apostle appeals at once to the Scriptures, to show that there was no such record as that Abraham could boast that he was justified by his works. As God judges right in all cases, so it follows that Abraham had no just ground of boasting, and of course that he was not justified by his own works. The sense of this verse is well expressed by Calvin. "If Abraham was justified by his works, he might boast of his own merits. But he has no ground of boasting before God. Therefore he was not justified by works."

3. *For what saith the Scripture?* The inspired account of Abraham's justification. This account was final, and was to settle the question. This account is found in Gen. xv. 6. ¶ *Abraham believed God.* In the Hebrew, "Abraham believed *Jehovah.*" The sense is substantially the same, as the argument turns on the *act* of believing. The faith which Abraham exercised was, that his posterity should be like the stars of heaven in number. This promise was made to him when he had no child, and of course when he had no prospect of such a posterity. See the strength and nature of this faith further illustrated in ver. 16—21. The *reason* why it was counted to him for righteousness was, that it was such a strong, direct, and unwavering act of confidence in the promise of God. ¶ *And it.* The word "it" here evidently refers to the *act* of believing It does not refer to the righteousness of another—of God, or of the Messiah; but the discussion is solely of the ***strong act*** of Abraham's faith, which ***in** some sense* was counted to him for righteousness. In what sense this was, is explained directly after. All that is material to remark here is, that *the act* of Abraham, the strong confidence of his mind in the promises of God, his unwavering assurance that what God had promised he would perform, was reckoned for righteousness. The same thing is more fully expressed in ver. 18—22. When therefore it is said that the righteousness of Christ is accounted or imputed to us; when it is said that his merits are transferred and reckoned as ours; whatever may be the truth of the doctrine, it cannot be defended by *this* passage of Scripture.

[Dr. Doddridge in a Note on the clause, "faith was reckoned to Abraham for righteousness," seems to give the true meaning of the apostle. "Nothing," says he, "can be easier than to understand how this may be said, in full consistence with our being justified by the imputation of the righteousness of Christ, that is, our being treated by God as righteous, for the sake of what he has done and suffered; for though this be the meritorious cause of our acceptance with God, yet faith may be said to be imputed to us, εις δικαιοσυνην *in order to our being justified,* or becoming righteous; that is, as we are charged as debtors in the book of God's account, what Christ has done in fulfilling all righteousness for us, is charged as the grand balance of the account; but that it may appear that we are, according to the tenor of the gospel, entitled to the benefit of this, it is also entered in the book of God's remembrance that we are believers, and this appearing, we are graciously discharged, yea, and rewarded, as if we ourselves had been perfectly innocent and obedient."

This view, it will be noticed, turns upon the force of the preposition εις before δικαιοσυνην That it should be translated *unto,* and not *for,* is evident from the sense it bears in such passages as Rom. vi. 3; x. 1, 10, where εις τον θανατον, εις σωτηριαν, and εις δικαιοσυνην, clearly signify *unto* "death," *unto* "salvation," (Eng. Trans. *that* "they might be saved," *i. e.* Israel), and *unto* "righteousness." Faith therefore, is not counted *as* righteousness, or accepted *in any way instead of it;* but is counted only *unto, i. e.* in order to the reception of righteousness. Instead of faith itself being the righteousness that justifies, the apostle repeatedly tells us, that it is "revealed *to* faith, received "*by*" and "*through* faith," that faith indeed is only the instrument of reception, and can therefore no more be confounded with the righteousness in question, than the beggar's hand with the money that relieves his indigence, or the robe that covers his nakedness, Rom. i. 17; iii. 22; Phil iii. 3, 9.]

Faith is uniformly an act of the mind. It is not a created essence which is placed within the mind. It is not a substance created independently of the soul, and placed within it by almighty power. It is not a *principle,* for the expression *a principle of faith,* is as unmeaning as a principle of joy, or a principle of sorrow, or a principle of remorse. God promises; the man believes; and this is the whole of it.

[A principle is the "element or original cause," out of which certain consequences arise, and to which they may be traced. And if faith be the *root* of all acceptable obedience, then certainly, in this sense, it *is* a principle. But whatever faith be, it is not here asserted that it is imputed *for,* or *instead of,* righteousness.—*See the Note above.*]

While the word *faith* is sometimes used to denote *religious doctrine,* or the system that is to be believed (Acts vi. 7; xv. 9; Rom. i. 5; x. 8; xvi. 26; Eph. iii. 17; iv. 5; 1 Tim. ii. 7, &c.); yet, when it is used to denote that which is required of men, it *always* denotes *an acting of the mind* exercised in relation to some object, or some promise, or threatening, or declaration of some other being; see the Note, Mark xvi. 16. ¶ *Was counted* (ἐλογίσθη). The same word in ver. 22, is is rendered "it was imputed." The word occurs frequently in the Scriptures. In the Old Testament, the verb חָשַׁב (*hashab*), which which is translated by the word λογίζομαι, means literally, *to think, tc intend,* or *purpose; to imagine, invent,* or *devise; to reckon,* or *account; to esteem; to impute,* i. e. to impute to a man what belongs to himself, or what *ought* to be imputed to him. It occurs only in the following places: 1 Sam. xviii. 25; Esth. viii. 3; ix. 24, 25; Isa. xxxiii 8; Jer. xlix. 20; l. 45; Lam. ii. 8; 2 Sam. xiv. 14; Jer. xlix. 30; Gen. l. 20; Job xxxv. 2; 2 Sam. xiv. 13; Ezek. xxxviii. 10; Jer. xviii. 8; Ps. xxi. 12; cxl. 3, 5; Jer. xi. 19; xlviii. 2; Amos vi. 5; Ps. x. 2; Isa. liii. 3, 4; Jer. xxvi. 3; Micah ii. 3; Nah. i. 11; Jer. xviii. 11; Job xiii. 34; xli. 19, 24; Ps. xxxii. 2; xxxv. 5; Isa. x. 7; Job xix. 11; xxxiii. 10; Gen. xvi. 6; xxxviii. 15; 1 Sam. i. 13; Ps. lii. 4; Jer. xviii. 18; Zech. vii. 10; Job vi. 40; xix. 16; Isa. xiii. 17; 1 Kings x. 21; Num. xviii. 27, 30; Ps. lxxxviii. 4; Isa. xl. 17; Lam. iv. 2; Isa. xl. 15; Gen. xxxi. 16. I have examined *all* the passages, and as the result of my examination have come to the conclusion, that there is not *one* in which the word is used in the sense of *reckoning* or *imputing* to a man that which does not strictly *belong* to him; or of charging on him that which *ought* not to be charged on him as a matter of personal right. The word is never used to denote *imputing* in the sense of *transferring,* or of charging that on one which does not properly belong to him. The same is the case in the New Testament. The word occurs about forty times (see *Schmidius' Concord*), and in a similar signification. No doctrine of *transferring,* or of setting over to a man what does not properly belong to him, be it sin or holiness, can be derived, therefore, from this word. Whatever is meant by it here, it evidently is declared that the act of believing is that which is intended, both by Moses and by Paul.

[The above list of passages, in which the original word חָשַׁב occurs, cannot be reckoned altogether complete. Gesenius, in his Hebrew Lexicon, cites under the word two passages from Leviticus, *viz.* vii. 18; xvii. 4, in both of which it is employed; and in one of them, plainly with the sense of reckoning *that* to a man, which *did not, and could not personally or actually belong to him,* and yet neither of these passages have obtained a place in the author's catalogue. In the last mentioned passage it is declared, that whosoever bringeth not his victim "unto the door of the tabernacle of the congregation, to offer an offering unto the Lord, before the tabernacle of the Lord, דָּם יֵחָשֵׁב *blood shall be imputed* unto that man; he hath shed blood, and that man shall be cut off from among his people." Now it is manifest that the transgression alluded to in the text involved no actual murder, and yet *that* crime is imputed to the individual. God declares that he shall hold him guilty of it, and visit him with consequent punishment.

Nor can it be proved that the Greek λογίζομαι, which corresponds to the Hebrew word חָשַׁב, is *always* used in the sense of imputing to a man that which does strictly or personally belong to him. Philem. ver. 18, 19, forms an exception, in which Paul begs that a wrong might be placed to his account, though he had no hand in committing it. He says to Philemon, in regard to his slave Onesimus, "if he hath wronged thee, or oweth thee ought, *put that on mine account*, τοῦτο ἐμοὶ ἐλλόγει. I Paul have written it with mine own hand, I will repay it." We are entitled also to assert, till the contrary be established, that the passages in this very chapter of the Epistle to the Romans, in which "righteousness," is said to be "imputed *without works*," are exceptions exactly to the point. Surely that righteousness which is "WITHOUT WORKS," is altogether different from the actual or personal righteousness of men, which cannot be but BY WORKS.

The doctrine of the imputation of Christ's righteousness has indeed been assailed by numerous objections. Generally, however, these originate in a misconception or misstatement of the doctrine itself. It is readily admitted that the righteousness of Christ cannot be made ours, *in the same sense that it is his*. It can never be ours in the sense of having actually accomplished it. Yet the doctrine, time after time, is represented as if it involved this absurd conclusion, and then gravely condemned. This is "to fight without an antagonist, and triumph without a victory." Nor does the doctrine involve any transference of moral character. "It never was the doctrine of the Reformation," says Professor Hodge, "or of the Lutheran and Calvinistic divines, that the imputation of righteousness affected the moral character of those concerned. It is true, whom God justifies he also sanctifies; but justification is not sanctification, and the imputation of righteousness is not the infusion of it." Here then is another false view of the subject, on which a second class of objections is seriously founded. Indeed, to these two sources, may be traced *almost every objection* that at any time has been raised against this doctrine. It would, therefore, greatly simplify the subject, if it were once for all distinctly understood, that the friends of imputed righteousness fully admit all that their brethren on the opposite side of the question allege, in regard to the two points noticed above. *On these there is no dispute*. What then? That while we make these admissions, we yet hold the doctrine in its integrity, and cannot allow it to be explained away as intimating only "that God treats us as righteous." This is true. It is, however, a part of the truth only, and not the whole, for the judgment of God proceeds upon just principles, and he *can and will treat none as righteous*, whom he does not in some sense *esteem to be really such*. Nor is it less evasive to allege that only "the results or benefits of Christ's death" are imputed. "To *talk* of their imputation, I think, is an affront to sound sense, as I am sure to be *put off* with their imputation, would be a fatal disappointment of our hopes; all these benefits are not imputed, but imparted. They are not reckoned to us, but are really enjoyed by us. Ours they are, not barely in the divine estimation, but by proper and personal possession."—*Hervey, Ther. and Asp. Dial*. x.

We may quarrel with the term imputation, but will find it difficult to get quit of the thing that is intimated by it. When the righteousness of Christ is said to be imputed to us, the meaning is, that God so places it to our account, that in the eyes of law we are *held* righteous, and therefore *treated* accordingly. And what is there so unreasonable in all this? Were not our sins laid to the charge of Christ, when he who knew no sin *was made sin for us?* Is not Adam's sin imputed to his posterity? The fact that we do suffer on account of it, cannot be denied, even on the principles of those who deny imputed sin, and allow only the transmission of depravity. For the question recurs, Why have we been visited with this impurity of nature, this disorganization both of physical and mental powers? Why *this, antecedent* to all personal transgression? One answer only can be given. *It is the punishment of the first sin*, which, as it was not personally ours, must have been imputed to us, unless we adopt the other side of the alternative, and maintain that God can punish where there is no guilt. Many, moreover, who can be charged with no personal sin are subjected to the pain of dying; and the agonies of tender infants, who have scarce opened their eyes on the light, irresistibly prove the imputation of the first sin. But if we allow the imputation of our sins to Christ, and of Adam's guilt to his posterity, the imputation of the Redeemer's righteousness cannot consistently be denied. These doctrines stand or fall together. Christ is the representative of his people, as Adam is the representative of mankind; and the apostle in the next chapter runs a parallel between them, which concludes with these words: "Therefore, as by the *offence of one*, judgment came upon all men to condemnation, even so by *the righteousness of one*, the free gift came upon all men unto justification. For as by *one man's disobedience*, many were *made sinners*, so by the *obedience of one*, shall many be *made righteous*."[1]

Abraham believed God, and it was counted unto him for righteousness.

4 Now to him that worketh [a] is the reward not reckoned of grace, but of debt.

a chap.11.6.

¶ *For righteousness.* In order to justification; or to regard and treat him in connection with this *as a* righteous man; as one who was admitted to the favour and friendship of God. In reference to this we may remark, (1.) That it is evidently not intended that the act of believing, on the part of Abraham, was the *meritorious* ground of acceptance; for then it would have been a work. Faith was as much his own act, as any act of obedience to the law. (2.) The design of the apostle was to show that by the *law,* or by *works,* man could not be justified; chap. iii. 28; iv. 2. (3.) *Faith* was not that which the law required. It demanded complete and perfect obedience; and if a man was justified by *faith,* it was *in some other way* than by the law. (4.) As the law did not demand this; and as faith was something different from the demand of the law; so if a man were justified by that, it was *on a principle* altogether different from justification by works. It was not by personal merit. It was not by complying with the law. It was in a mode entirely different. (5.) In being justified by faith, it is meant, therefore, that we are treated as righteous; that we are forgiven; that we are admitted to the favour of God, and treated as his friends. (6.) In this act, *faith* is a mere instrument, an antecedent, a *sine qua non,* that which God has been pleased to appoint as a condition on which men may be treated as righteous. It expresses a state of mind which is demonstrative of love to God; of affection for his cause and character; of reconciliation and friendship; and is therefore that state to which he has been graciously pleased to promise pardon and acceptance. (7.) As this is not a matter of law; as the law could not be said to *demand* it; as it is on a different principle; and as the acceptance of faith, or of a believer, cannot be a matter of merit or claim, so justification is of grace, or mere favour. It is in no sense a matter of merit on our part, and thus stands distinguished entirely from justification by works, or by conformity to the law. From beginning to end, it is, so far as *we* are concerned, a matter of grace. The *merit* by which all this is obtained, is the work of the Lord Jesus Christ, through whom this plan is proposed, and by whose atonement alone God can consistently pardon and treat as righteous those who are in themselves ungodly; see ver. 5. In this place we have also evidence that *faith* is always substantially of the same character. In the case of Abraham it was confidence in God and his promises. All faith has the same nature, whether it be confidence in the Messiah, or in any of the divine promises or truths. As this *confidence* evinces the same state of mind, so it was as consistent to justify Abraham by it, as it is to justify him who believes in the Lord Jesus Christ under the gospel; see Heb. xi.

4. *Now to him that worketh,* &c. This passage is not to be understood as affirming that any actually *have* worked out their salvation by conformity to the law so as to be saved by their own merits; but it expresses a general truth in regard to works. *On that plan,* if a man were justified by his works, it would be a matter *due* to him. It is a general principle in regard to contracts and obligations, that where a man fulfils them he is entitled to the reward as that which is *due* to him, and which he can claim. This is well understood in all the transactions among men. Where a man has fulfilled the terms of a contract, to pay him is not a matter of *favour;* he has *earned* it; and we are *bound* to pay him. So says the apostle, it *would* be, if a man were justified by his works. He would have a *claim* on God. It would be wrong *not* to justify him. And this is an additional reason why the doctrine cannot be true; comp. Rom. xi. 6. ¶ *The reward.* The pay, or wages. The word

5 But to him that worketh not, but believeth on him that justifieth the ungodly, his faith *a* is counted for righteousness.

a Hab.2.4.

6 Even as David also describeth the blessedness of the man unto whom God imputeth righteousness without works.

is commonly applied to the pay of soldiers, day-labourers, &c; Matt. xx. 8; Luke x. 7; 1 Tim. v. 18; James. v. 4. It has a similar meaning here. ¶ *Reckoned.* Greek, Imputed. The same word which, in ver. 3, is rendered *counted*, and in ver. 22, *imputed*. It is here used in its strict and proper sense, to *reckon* that as belonging to a man which is his own, or which is due to him; see the Note on verse 3. ¶ *Of grace.* Of favour; as a gift. ¶ *Of debt.* As due; as a claim; as a fair compensation according to the contract.

5. *But to him that worketh not.* Who does not rely on his conformity to the law for his justification; who does not depend on his works; who seeks to be justified in some other way. The reference here is to the Christian plan of justification. ¶ *But believeth*; Note, chap. iii. 26. ¶ *On him.* On God. Thus the connection requires; for the discussion has immediate reference to Abraham, whose faith was in the promise of God. ¶ *That justifieth the ungodly.* This is a very important expression. It implies, (1.) That men are sinners, or are ungodly. (2.) That God regards them as such when they are justified. He does not justify them *because* he sees them to be, or regards them to be righteous; but knowing that they are *in fact* polluted. He does not *first esteem* them, contrary to fact, to be pure; but knowing that they *are* polluted, and that they deserve no favour, he resolves to forgive them, and to treat them as his friends. (3.) In themselves they are equally undeserving, whether they are justified or not. Their souls have been defiled by sin; and that is known when they are pardoned. God judges things as they are; and sinners who are justified, he judges *not* as if they were pure, or as if they had a claim; but he regards them *as united by faith to the Lord Jesus; and* IN THIS RELATION *he judges that they* SHOULD *be treated as his friends, though they have been, are, and always will be, personally undeserving.* It is not meant that the righteousness of Christ is *transferred* to them, so as to become personally theirs—for moral character cannot be transferred;—nor that it is *infused* into them, making them personally meritorious—for then they could not be spoken of as ungodly; but that Christ died in their stead, to atone for their sins, and is regarded and esteemed by God to have died; and that the results or benefits of his death are so reckoned or imputed to believers as to make it proper for God to regard and treat them as if they had themselves obeyed the law; that is, as righteous in his sight; see the Note on verse 3.

6. *Even as David.* The apostle having adduced the example of Abraham to show that the doctrine which he was defending was not new, and contrary to the Old Testament, proceeds to adduce the case of David also; and to show that he understood the same doctrine of justification without works. ¶ *Describeth.* Speaks of. ¶ *The blessedness.* The happiness; or the desirable state or condition. ¶ *Unto whom God imputeth righteousness.* Whom God treats as righteous, or as entitled to his favour in a way different from his conformity to the law. This is found in Ps. xxxii. And the whole scope and design of the psalm is to show the blessedness of the man who is *forgiven*, and whose sins are not charged on him, but who is freed from the punishment due to his sins. Being thus pardoned, he is treated as a righteous man. And it is evidently in this sense that the apostle uses the expression "imputeth righteousness," *i. e.* he does *not* impute, or charge on the man his sins; he reckons and treats him as a pardoned and righteous man; Ps. xxxii. 2. See the Note on verse 3. He regards him as one who is forgiven

7 *Saying*, [a] Blessed *are* they
whose iniquities are forgiven, and
whose sins are covered.
8 Blessed *is* the man to whom
the Lord will not impute sin.
9 *Cometh* this blessedness then
upon the circumcision *only*, or upon
the uncircumcision also? for we say
that faith was reckoned to Abraham for righteousness.
10 How was it then reckoned?
when he was in circumcision, or in

a Ps.32.1.2.

---

and admitted to his favour, and who is to be treated henceforward as though he had not sinned. That is, he partakes of the benefits of Christ's atonement, so as not henceforward to be treated as a sinner, but as a friend of God.

7. *Blessed*. Happy are they: they are highly favoured; see Note, Mat. v. 3. ¶ *Whose sins are covered*. Are concealed; or hidden from the view. On which God will no more look, and which he will no more remember. "By these words," says Calvin (in loco), "we are taught that justification with Paul is nothing else but pardon of sin." The word *cover* here has not reference to the atonement, but is expressive of *hiding*, or *concealing* *i. e.* of forgiving sin.

8. *Will not impute sin*. On whom the Lord will not charge his sins; or who shall not be *reckoned* or regarded as guilty. This shows clearly what the apostle meant by imputing faith without works. It is to pardon sin, and to treat with favour; *not* to reckon or charge a man's sin to him; but to treat him, though personally undeserving and ungodly (ver. 5), as though the sin had not been committed. The word "impute" here is used in its natural and appropriate sense, as denoting to charge on man that which properly belongs to him. See the Note on verse 3.

9. *Cometh*, &c. The apostle has now prepared the way for an examination of the inquiry whether this came *in consequence* of obedience to the law? or whether it was *without* obedience to the law? Having shown that Abraham was justified by faith in accordance with the doctrine which he was defending, the only remaining inquiry was whether it was *after* he was circumcised or before; whether *in consequence* of his circumcision or not. If it was *after* his circumcision, the Jew might still maintain that it was by complying with the works of the law; but if it was *before*, the point of the apostle would be established, that it was without the works of the law. Still further, if he was justified by faith *before* he was circumcised, then here was an instance of justification and acceptance without conformity to the Jewish law; and if the father of the Jewish nation was so justified, and reckoned as a friend of God, *without* being circumcised, *i. e.* in the condition in which the heathen world then was, then it would follow that the Gentiles might be justified in a similar way now. It would not be departing, therefore, from the spirit of the Old Testament itself, to maintain, as the apostle had done (chap. iii.), that the Gentiles who had not been circumcised might obtain the favour of God as well as the Jew; that is, that it was *independent* of circumcision, and might be extended to all. ¶ *This blessedness*. This happy state or condition. This state of being justified by God, and of being regarded as his friends. This is the sum of all blessedness; the only state that can be truly pronounced happy. ¶ *Upon the circumcision only*. The *Jews* alone, as *they* pretended. ¶ *Or upon the uncircumcision also*. The *Gentiles* who believed, as the *apostle* maintained. ¶ *For we say*. We all admit. It is a conceded point. It was the doctrine of the apostle, as well as of the Jews; and as much theirs as his. With this, then, as a conceded point, what is the fair inference to be drawn from it?

10. *How*. In what circumstances, or time. ¶ *When he was in circumcision*, &c. Before or after he was circumcised? This was the very point of the inquiry. For if he was justified

uncircumcision? Not in circumcision, but in uncircumcision.

11 And [a] he received the sign of circumcision; a seal of the righteousness of the faith which *he had*, *yet* being uncircumcised; that he might be the father [b] of all them that believe, though they be not circumcised; that righteousness might be imputed unto them also:

12 And the father of circumcision to them who are not of the circum-

a Gen.17.10,11.

b Luke 19. 9.

---

by faith *after* he was circumcised, the Jew might pretend that it was in virtue of his circumcision; that even his *faith* was acceptable, *because* he was circumcised. But if it was *before* he was circumcised, this plea could not be set up; and the argument of the apostle was confirmed by the case of Abraham, the great father and model of the Jewish people, that circumcision and the deeds of the law did not conduce to justification; and that as Abraham was justified *without* those works, so might others be, and the heathen, therefore, might be admitted to similar privileges. ¶ *Not in circumcision.* Not *being* circumcised, or *after* he was circumcised, but before. This was the record in the case; Gen. xv. 6; Comp. Gen. xvii. 10.

11. *And he received the sign*, &c. A *sign* is that by which any thing is *shown*, or *represented*. And circumcision thus *showed* that there was a *covenant* between Abraham and God; Gen. xvii. 1—10. It became the public mark or token of the relation which he sustained to God. ¶ *A seal.* See Note, John iii. 33. A *seal* is that mark of wax or other substance, which is attached to an instrument of writing, as a deed, &c., to confirm, ratify it, or to make it binding. Sometimes instruments were sealed, or made authentic by *stamping* on them some word, letter, or device, which had been engraved on silver, or on precious stones. The *seal* or *stamp* was often worn as an ornament on the finger; Esth. viii. 8; Gen. xli. 42; xxxviii. 18; Ex. xxviii. 11, 36; xxix. 6 To *affix* the seal, whether of wax, or otherwise, was to confirm a contract or an engagement. In allusion to this, circumcision is called a *seal* of the covenant which God had made with Abraham. That is, he appointed this as a public attestation to the fact that he had previously approved of Abraham, and had made important promises to him. ¶ *Which he had, yet being circumcised.* He believed (Gen. xv. 5); was accepted, or justified; was admitted to the favour of God, and favoured with clear and remarkable promises (Gen. xv. 18—21; xvii. 1—9,) *before* he was circumcised. Circumcision, therefore, could have contributed neither to his justification, nor to the promises made to him by God. ¶ *That he might be the father*, &c. All this was done that Abraham might be held up as an example, or a model, of the very doctrine which the apostle was defending. The word *father* here is used evidently in a spiritual sense, as denoting that he was the ancestor of all true believers; that he was their model, and example. They are regarded as his *children* because they are possessed of his spirit; are justified in the same way, and are imitators of his example; see Note, Mat. i. 1. In this sense the expression occurs in Luke xix. 9; John viii. 33; Gal. iii. 7, 29. ¶ *Though they be not circumcised.* This was stated in opposition to the opinion of the Jews that all *ought* to be circumcised. As the apostle had shown that *Abraham* enjoyed the favour of God previous to his being circumcised, *i. e. without* circumcision; so it followed that others might on the same principle also. This instance settles the point; and there is nothing which a Jew can reply to this. ¶ *That righteousness*, &c. That is, in the same way, by faith without works: that they might be accepted, and treated as righteous.

12. *And the father of circumcision.* The father, *i. e.* the ancestor, exemplar, or model of those who are circumcised, and who possess the same faith that he did. Not only the father of all believers (ver. 11), but in a

cision only, but also walk in the steps of the faith of our father Abraham, which *he had*, being *yet* uncircumcised.

13 For the promise that [a] he should be the heir of the world, *was* not to Abraham, or to his seed, through the law, but through the righteousness of faith.

14 For if [b] they which are of the law be heirs, faith is made void, and the promise made of none effect;

a Gen. 17. 4, &c.

b Gal. 3. 18.

special sense the father of the Jewish people. In this, the apostle intimates that though *all* who believed would be saved as he was, yet the Jews had a special *proprietorship* in Abraham; they had special favours and privileges from the fact that he was their ancestor. ¶ *Not of the circumcision only.* Who are not merely circumcised, but who possess his spirit and his faith. Mere circumcision would not avail; but circumcision connected with faith like his, showed that they were peculiarly his descendants; see Note, chap. ii. 25. ¶ *Who walk in the steps,* &c. Who imitate his example; who imbibe his spirit; who have his faith. ¶ *Being* yet *uncircumcised.* Before he was circumcised. Comp. Gen. xv. 6, with Gen. xvii.

13. *For the promise,* &c. To show that the faith of Abraham, on which his justification depended, was not by the law, the apostle proceeds to show that the promise concerning which his faith was so remarkably evinced was *before* the law was given. If this was so, then it was an additional important consideration in opposition to the Jew, showing that acceptance with God depended on faith, and not on works. ¶ *That he should be heir of the world.* An *heir* is one who succeeds, or is to succeed to an estate. In this passage, *the world,* or the entire earth, is regarded as the *estate* to which reference is made, and the promise is that the posterity of Abraham should succeed to that, or should possess it as their inheritance. The precise expression here used, "heir of the world," is not found in the promises made to Abraham Those promises were that God would make of him a great nation (Gen. xii. 2); that in him all the families of the earth should be blessed (ver. 3); that his posterity should be as the stars for multitude (Gen. xv. 5); and that he should be a father of many nations (Gen. xvii. 5). As this latter promise is one to which the apostle particularly refers (see ver. 17), it is probable that he had this in his eye. This promise had, at first, respect to his numerous natural descendants, and to their possessing the land of Canaan. But it is also regarded in the New Testament as extending to the Messiah (Gal. iii. 16) as his descendant, and to all his followers as the spiritual seed of the father of the faithful. When the apostle calls him "the heir of the world," he sums up in this comprehensive expression all the promises made to Abraham, intimating that his spiritual descendants, *i. e.* those who possess his faith, shall yet be so numerous as to possess all lands. ¶ *Or to his seed.* To his posterity, or descendants. ¶ *Through the law.* By the observance of the law; or made in consequence of observing the law; or depending on the condition that he should observe the law. The covenant was made *before* the law of circumcision was given; and long before the law of Moses (comp. Gal. iii. 16, 17, 18), and was independent of both. ¶ *But through,* &c. In consequence of or in connection with the strong confidence which he showed in the promises of God, Gen. xv. 6.

14. *For if they which are of the law.* Who seek for justification and acceptance by the law. ¶ *Faith is made void.* Faith would have no place in the scheme; and consequently the strong commendations bestowed on the faith of Abraham, would be bestowed without any just cause. If men are justified by the *law,* they cannot be by faith, and faith would be useless in this work. ¶ *And the promise,* &c. A *promise* looks to the future. Its design and tendency is to

15 Because the law [a] worketh wrath: for where no [b] law is, *there is* no transgression.
16 Therefore *it is* of faith, that *it might be* by grace; to the end the promise might be sure to all the seed; not to that only which is of the law, but to that also which is

a chap.5.20. *b* 1 John3.4.

excite trust and confidence in him who makes it. All the promises of God have this design and tendency; and consequently, as God has given *many* promises, the object is to call forth the lively and constant *faith* of men, all going to show that in the divine estimation, *faith* is of inestimable value. But if men are justified by the *law;* if they are rendered acceptable by conformity to the institutions of Moses; then they cannot depend for acceptance on any *promise* made to Abraham, or his seed. They cut themselves off from that promise, and stand independent of it. That promise, like all other promises, was made to excite faith. If, therefore, the Jews depended on the *law* for justification, they were cut off from all the *promises* made to Abraham; and if they *could* be justified by the law, the promise was useless. This is as true now as it was then. If men seek to be justified by their morality or their forms of religion, they cannot depend on any *promise* of God; for he has *made* no promise to any such attempt. They stand independently of any promise, covenant, or compact, and are depending on a scheme of their *own;* a scheme which would render his plan vain and useless; which would render his promises, and the atonement of Christ, and the work of the Spirit of no value. It is clear, therefore, that *such* an attempt at salvation cannot be successful.

15. *Because the law.* All law. It is the tendency of law. ¶ *Worketh wrath.* Produces or causes wrath. While man is fallen, and a sinner, its tendency, so far from *justifying* him, and producing peace, is just the reverse. It condemns, denounces wrath, and produces suffering. The word *wrath* here is to be taken in the sense of *punishment.* chap. ii. 8. And the meaning is, that the law of God, demanding perfect purity, and denouncing every sin. condemns the sinner, and consigns him to punishment. As the apostle had proved (chap. i. ii. iii.) that *all* were sinners, so it followed that if any attempted to be justified by the *law,* they would be involved only in condemnation and wrath. ¶ *For where no law is,* &c. This is a general principle; a maxim of common justice and of common sense. Law is a *rule* of conduct. If no such rule is given and known, there can be no crime. Law expresses what may be done, and what may not be done. If there is no command to pursue a certain course, no injunction to forbid certain conduct, actions will be innocent. The connection in which this declaration is made here, seems to imply that as the Jews had a multitude of clear laws, and as the Gentiles had the laws of nature, there could be no hope of escape from the charge of their violation. Since human nature was depraved, and men were prone to sin, the more just and reasonable the laws, the less hope was there of being justified *by* the law, and the more certainty was there that the law would produce wrath and condemnation.

16. *Therefore.* In view of the course of reasoning which has been pursued. We have come to this conclusion. ¶ It is *of faith.* Justification is by faith; or the plan which God has devised of saving men is by faith, chap. iii. 26. ¶ *That* it might be *by grace.* As a matter of mere undeserved mercy. If men were justified by *law,* it would be by their own merits; now it is of mere unmerited favour. ¶ *To the end.* For the purpose, or design. ¶ *The promise,* &c. ver. 13. ¶ *Might be sure.* Might be firm, or established. On any other ground, it could not be established. If it had depended on entire conformity to the *law,* the promise would never have been established, for none would have yielded such obedience. But

of the faith of Abraham, who is the father of us all.

17 (As it is written, [a] I have made thee a father of many nations,) [1] before him whom he believed, *even* God, who quickeneth [b] the dead, and calleth those [c] things which be not as though they were.

18 Who against hope believed in hope, that he might become the father of many nations, according to that which was spoken, [d] So shall thy seed be.

19 And being not weak in faith, he considered not his own body now dead, when he was about an

a Gen.17.4. 1 or, *like unto*. *b* Eph.2.1,5. *c* 1Cor.1.28; 1Pet.2.10. *d* Gen.15.5.

now it may be secured to all the posterity of Abraham. ¶ *To all the seed*, ver. 13. ¶ *Not to that only.* Not to that part of his descendants alone who were *Jews*, or who had the law. ¶ *But to that*, &c. To *all* who should possess the same faith as Abraham. ¶ *The father of us all.* Of all who believe, whether they be Jews or Gentiles.

17. *As it is written.* Gen. xvii. 5. ¶ *I have made thee.* The word here used in the Hebrew (Gen. xvii. 5) means literally, *to give, to grant;* and also, to set, or constitute. This is also the meaning of the Greek word used both by the LXX. and the apostle. The quotation is taken literally from the Septuagint. The argument of the apostle is founded in part on the fact that the *past* tense is used—I *have* made thee—and that God spoke of a thing as already *done*, which he had promised or purposed to do. The sense is, he had, *in his mind* or *purpose*, constituted him the father of many nations; and so certain was the fulfilment of the divine purposes, that he spoke of it as already accomplished. ¶ *Of many nations.* The apostle evidently understands this promise as referring, not to his *natural* descendants only, but to the great multitude who should believe as he did. ¶ *Before him.* In his view, or sight; *i. e.* God regarded him as such a father. ¶ *Whom he believed.* Whose *promise* he believed; or in whom he trusted. ¶ *Who quickeneth the dead.* Who gives *life* to the dead, Eph. ii. 1, 5. This expresses the power of God to give life. But why it is used here has been a subject of debate. I regard it as having reference to the strong natural improbability of the fulfilment of the prophecy when it was given, arising from the age of Abraham and Sarah, ver. 19. Abraham exercised power in the God who gives life, and who gives it as he pleases. It is one of his prerogatives to give life to the dead (νεκροὺς), to raise up those who are in their graves; and a power *similar* to that, or strongly *reminding* of that, was manifested in fulfilling the promise to Abraham. The giving of this promise, and its fulfilment, were such as strongly to remind us that God has power to give life to the dead. ¶ *And calleth*, &c. That is, those things which he foretels and promises are so certain, that he may speak of them as already in existence. Thus in relation to Abraham, God, instead of simply *promising* that he *would* make him the father of many nations, speaks of it as already done, "I *have* made thee," &c. In his own mind, or purpose, he had so constituted him, and it was so certain that it *would* take place, that he might speak of it as *already* done.

18. *Who against hope.* Who against all apparent or usual ground of hope. He refers here to the prospect of a posterity; see ver. 19—21. ¶ *Believed in hope.* Believed in that which was promised to excite his hope. Hope here is put for the object of his hope —that which was promised. ¶ *According to that which was spoken;* Gen. xv. 5. ¶ *So shall thy seed be.* That is, as the stars in heaven for multitude. Thy posterity shall be very numerous.

19. *And being not weak in faith.* That is, having strong faith. ¶ *He considered not.* He did not regard the fact that his body was now dead, as any obstacle to the fulfilment of the promise. He did not suffer that fact to influence him, or to produce any doubt about the fulfilment. Faith looks to the strength of God, not to second

hundred years old, neither yet
the deadness [a] of Sarah's womb:
20 He staggered not at the promise of God through unbelief; but
was strong in faith, giving glory to
God;
21 And being fully persuaded
that what he had promised, he was
able [b] also to perform.
22 And therefore it was imputed to him for righteousness.
23 Now [c] it was not written for
his sake alone, that it was imputed
to him;
24 But for us [d] also, to whom it
shall be imputed, if we believe [e] on
him that raised up Jesus our Lord
from the dead;

a Heb.11.11. b Gen.18.14; Lu.1.37,45; Heb.11.19.

c chap.15.4; 1 Cor.10.11. d Acts 2.39. e Mark 16.16; John 3.14-16.

causes, or to difficulties that may appear formidable to man. ¶ *Now dead.* Aged; dead as to the purpose under consideration; comp. Heb. xi. 12, "As good as dead." That is, he was now at an age when it was highly improbable that he would have any children; comp. Gen. xvii. 17. ¶ *Deadness,* &c; Heb. xi. 11, "When she was past age;" comp. Gen. xviii. 11.

20. *He staggered not.* He was not moved, or agitated; he steadily and firmly believed the promise. ¶ *Giving glory to God.* Giving honour to God by the firmness with which he believed his promises. His conduct was such as to honour God; that is, to show Abraham's conviction that he was worthy of implicit confidence and trust. In this way *all* who believe in the promises of God do honour to him. They bear testimony to him that he is worthy of confidence. They become so many witnesses in his favour; and furnish to their fellow-men evidence that God has a claim on the credence and trust of mankind.

21. *And being fully persuaded.* Thoroughly or entirely convinced; Luke i. 1; Rom. xiv. 5; 2 Tim. iv. 5, 17. ¶ *He was able;* comp. Gen. xviii. 14. This was not the *only* time in which Abraham evinced this confidence. His faith was equally implicit and strong when he was commanded to sacrifice his promised son; Heb. xi. 19.

22. *And therefore.* His faith was so implicit, and so unwavering, that it was a demonstration that he was the firm friend of God. He was tried, and he had such confidence in God that he showed that he was supremely attached to him, and would obey and serve him. This was reckoned as a full proof of friendship; and he was recognised and treated as righteous; *i. e.* as the friend of God. [The true sense of faith being imputed for righteousness is given in a Note at the beginning of the chapter.] See Note on ver. 3, 5.

23. *Now it was not written.* The record of this extraordinary faith was not made on his account only; but it was made to show the way in which men may be regarded and treated as righteous by God. If Abraham was so regarded and treated, then, on the same principle, all others may be. God has but one mode of justifying men. ¶ *Imputed.* Reckoned; accounted. He was regarded and treated as the friend of God.

24. *But for us also.* For our use; (comp. chap. xv. 4; 1 Cor. x. 11), that we might have an example of the way in which men may be accepted of God. It is recorded for our encouragement and imitation, to show that *we* may in a similar manner be accepted and saved. ¶ *If we believe on him,* &c. Abraham showed his faith in God by believing *just what God revealed to him.* This was *his* faith, and it might be as *strong* and *implicit* as could be exercised under the fullest revelation. Faith, now, is belief in God *just so far as he has revealed his will to us.* It is therefore the same *in principle,* though it may have reference to different objects. It is confidence in the same God, according to what we know of his will. Abraham showed *his* faith mainly in confiding in the promises of God respecting a numerous posterity. This was the leading truth made known to *him,* and this he believed.

25 Who was delivered [a] for our offences, and was raised [b] again for our justification.

a Isa.53.5,6; 2 Cor.5.21; Heb.9.28; 1 Pet.2.24; Rev.1.5. *b* 1 Cor.15.17; 1 Pet.1.21.

CHAPTER V.

THEREFORE [c] being justified by faith, we have peace with

c Isa.32.17; Eph.2.14; Col.1.20.

[The promise made to Abraham was, "in thy seed shall all nations of the earth be blessed," on which we have the following inspired commentary: "And the scriptures foreseeing that God would justify the heathen through faith, preached before *the gospel* unto Abraham, saying, In thee shall all nations be blessed," Gal. iii. 8. It would seem, then, that this promise, like that made immediately after the fall, contained the very germ and principles of the gospel. So that after all there is not so great difference between the object of Abraham's faith, and that of ours. Indeed the object in both cases is manifestly the same.]

The main or leading truths that God has made known to *us* are, that he has given his Son to die; that he has raised him up; and that through him he is ready to pardon. To put confidence in these truths is to believe now. Doing this, we believe in the same God that Abraham did; we evince the same spirit; and thus show that we are the friends of the same God, and may be treated in the same manner. This is *faith* under the gospel (comp. Notes, Mark xvi. 16), and shows that the faith of Abraham and of all true believers is substantially the same, and is varied only by the difference of the truths made known.

25. *Who was delivered.* To death; comp. Notes, Acts ii. 23. ¶ *For our offences.* On account of our crimes. He was delivered up to death in order to make expiation for our sins. ¶ *And was raised again.* From the dead. ¶ *For our justification.* On account of our justification. In order that we may be justified. The word *justification* here seems to be used in a large sense, to denote acceptance with God; including not merely the formal act by which God pardons sins, and by which we become reconciled to him, but also the *completion* of the work—the treatment of us as righteous, and raising us up to a state of glory. By the *death* of Christ an atonement is made for sin. If it be asked how his *resurrection* contributes to our acceptance with God, we may answer, (1.) It rendered *his* work complete. His *death* would have been unavailing, his work would have been imperfect, if he had not been raised up from the dead. He submitted to death as a sacrifice, and it was needful that he should rise, and thus conquer death and subdue our enemies, that the work which he had undertaken might be complete. (2.) His resurrection was a proof that his work was *accepted* by the Father. What he had done, in order that sinners might be saved, was approved. Our justification, therefore, became sure, as it was *for* this that he had given himself up to death. (3.) His resurrection is the main-spring of all our hopes, and of all our efforts to be saved. Life and immortality are thus brought to light, 2 Tim. i. 10. God "hath begotten us again to a lively hope (a living, active, real hope), by the resurrection of Jesus Christ from the dead," 1 Pet. i. 3. Thus the fact that *he* was raised becomes the ground of hope that *we* shall be raised and accepted of God. The fact that *he* was raised, and that all who love him shall be raised also, becomes one of the most efficient motives to *us* to seek to be justified and saved. There is no higher motive that can be presented to induce man to seek salvation than the fact that he may be raised up from death and the grave, and made immortal. There is no satisfactory proof that man *can* be thus raised up, but the resurrection of Jesus Christ. In that resurrection we have a pledge that all his people will rise. "For if we believe that Jesus died and rose again, even so them also which sleep in Jesus will God bring with him," 1 Thess. iv. 14. "Because I live," said the Redeemer, "ye shall live also," John xiv. 19; comp. 1 Pet. i. 21.

CHAPTER V.

THE design of this chapter, which has usually been considered as one of the most difficult portions of the New Testament, especially ver. 12—21, is evidently to show the *results* or *benefits* of the doctrine of justification by faith. That doctrine the apostle had now fully established. He had shown in the previous chapters, (1.) That men were under condemnation for sin; (2.) That this extended alike to the Jews and the Gentiles; (3.) That there was no way of escape now but by the doctrine of pardon, not by personal merit, but by grace; (4.) That this plan was fully made known by the gospel of Christ; and (5.) That this was no *new* doctrine, but was in fact substantially the same by which Abraham and David had been accepted before God.

Having thus stated and vindicated the doctrine, it was natural to follow up the demonstration, by stating its bearing and its practical influence. This he does by showing that its *immediate* effect is to produce *peace,* ver. 1. It gives us the privilege of access to the favour of God, ver. 2. But not only this, we are in a world of affliction. Christians, like others, are surrounded with trials; and a very important question was, whether this doctrine would have an influence in supporting the soul in those trials. This question the apostle discusses in ver. 3—11. He shows that *in fact* Christians glory in tribulation, and that the reasons why they do so are, (1.) That the natural effect of tribulations under the gospel was to lead to *hope,* ver. 3, 4. (2.) That the *cause* of this was, that the love of God was shed abroad in the heart by the Holy Ghost. This doctrine he further confirms by showing the consolation which would be furnished by the fact that Christ had died for them. This involved a security that they would be sustained in their trials, and that a victory would be given them. For, (1.) It was the highest expression of love that he should die for enemies, ver. 6, 7, 8. (2.) It followed that if he was given for them when *they* were enemies, it was much more probable, it was *certain,* that all needful grace would be furnished to them now that they were reconciled, ver. 9, 10, 11.

But there was another very material inquiry. Men were not only exposed to affliction, but they were in the midst of *a wreck of things—of a fallen world—of the proofs and memorials of sin every where.* The first man had sinned, and the *race* was subject to sin and death. The monuments of death and sin were every where. It was to be expected that a remedy from God would have reference to this universal state of sin and woe; and that it would tend to meet and repair these painful and wide spread ruins. The apostle then proceeds to discuss the question, how the plan of salvation which involved justification by faith was adapted to meet these universal and distressing evils, ver. 12—21. The design of this part of the chapter is to show that the blessings procured by the redemption through Christ, and the plan of justification through him, greatly exceed all the evils which had come upon the world in consequence of the apostacy of Adam. And if this was the case, the scheme of justification by faith was complete. It was adapted to the condition of fallen and ruined man; and was worthy of his affection and confidence. A particular examination of this argument of the apostle will occur in the Notes on ver. 12—21.

1. *Therefore* (οὖν.) Since we are thus justified, or as a consequence of being justified, we have peace. ¶ *Being justified by faith;* see Notes, chap. i. 17; iii. 24; iv. 5. ¶ *We.* That is, all who *are* justified. The apostle is evidently speaking of true Christians. ¶ *Have peace with God;* see Note, John xiv. 27. True religion is often represented as *peace* with God; see Acts x. 36; Rom. viii. 6; x. 15; xiv. 17; Gal. v. 22; see also Isa. xxxii. 17.

"And the work of righteousness shall be peace,
And the effect of righteousness
Quietness and assurance for ever."

This is called *peace,* because, (1.) The sinner is represented as the enemy of God, Rom. viii. 7; Eph. ii. 16; James iv. 4; John xv. 18, 24; xvii. 14; Rom. i. 30. (2.) The state of a sinner's mind is far from peace. He is often agitated, alarmed, trembling. He feels that he is alienated from God. For

God through our Lord Jesus Christ;

2 By whom [a] also we have access by faith into this grace wherein we stand, and rejoice [b] in hope of the glory of God.

a John 14.6. b Heb.3.6.

"The wicked are like the troubled sea.
For it never can be at rest;
Whose waters cast up mire and dirt."
Isa. lvii. 20.

The sinner in this state regards God as his enemy. He trembles when he thinks of his law; fears his judgments; is alarmed when he thinks of hell. His bosom is a stranger to peace. This has been felt in all lands, alike under the thunders of the law of Sinai among the Jews; in the pagan world; and in lands where the gospel is preached. It is the effect of an alarmed and troubled conscience. (3.) The plan of salvation by Christ reveals God as willing to be reconciled. He is ready to pardon, and to be at peace. If the sinner repents and believes, God can now consistently forgive him, and admit him to favour. It is therefore a plan by which the mind of God and of the sinner can become reconciled, or united in feeling and in purpose. The obstacles on the part of God to reconciliation, arising from his justice and law, have been removed, and he is now willing to be at peace. The obstacles on the part of man, arising from his sin, his rebellion, and his conscious guilt, may be taken away, and he can now regard God as his friend. (4.) The *effect* of this plan, when the sinner embraces it, is to produce *peace* in his own mind. He *experiences* peace; a peace which the world gives not, and which the world cannot take away, Phil. iv. 7; 1 Pet. i. 8; John xvi. 22. Usually in the work of conversion to God, this *peace* is the first evidence that is felt of the change of heart. Before, the sinner was agitated and troubled. But often suddenly, a peace and calmness is felt, which is before unknown. The alarm subsides; the heart is calm; the fears die away, like the waves of the ocean after a storm. A sweet tranquillity visits the heart—a pure shining light, like the sunbeams that break through the opening clouds after a tempest. The views, the feelings, the desires are changed; and the bosom that was just before filled with agitation and alarm, that regarded God as its enemy, is now at peace with him, and with all the world. ¶ *Through our Lord Jesus Christ.* By means of the atonement of the Lord Jesus. It is *his* mediation that has procured it.

2. *We have access;* see Note, John xiv. 6, "I am the way," &c. Doddridge renders it, "by whom we have *been introduced*," &c. It means, *by whom we have the privilege of obtaining the favour of God which we enjoy when we are justified.* The word rendered "access" occurs but in two other places in the New Testament, Eph. ii. 18; iii. 12. By Jesus Christ the way is opened for us to obtain the favour of God. ¶ *By faith.* By means of faith, chap. i. 17. ¶ *Into this grace.* Into this *favour* of reconciliation with God. ¶ *Wherein we stand.* In which we now are in consequence of being justified. ¶ *And rejoice.* Religion is often represented as producing joy, Isa. xii. 3; xxxv. 10; lii. 9; lxi. 3, 7; lxv. 14, 18; John xvi. 22, 24; Acts xiii. 52; Rom. xiv. 17; Gal. v. 22; 1 Pet. i. 8. The sources or *steps* of this joy are these: (1.) We are justified, or regarded by God as righteous. (2.) We are admitted into his favour, and abide there. (3.) We have the prospect of still higher and richer blessings in the fulness of his glory when we are admitted to heaven. ¶ *In hope.* In the earnest desire and expectation of obtaining that glory. *Hope* is a complex emotion made up of a *desire* for an object; and an *expectation* of obtaining it. Where either of these is wanting, there is not *hope.* Where they are mingled in improper proportions, there is not peace. But where the *desire* of obtaining an object is attended with an *expectation* of obtaining it, in proportion to that desire, there exists that peaceful, happy state

3 And not only *so*, but we glory [a] in tribulations also: knowing that tribulation worketh patience;

a Matt.5.11,12; James 1.2,12.

of mind which we denominate *hope*. And the apostle here implies that the Christian *has* an earnest *desire* for that glory; and that he has a confident *expectation* of obtaining it. The result of that he immediately states to be, that we are by it sustained in our afflictions. ¶ *The glory of God*. The glory that God will bestow on us. The word *glory* usually means splendour, magnificence, honour; and the apostle here refers to that honour and dignity which will be conferred on the redeemed when they are raised up to the full honours of redemption; when they shall triumph in the completion of the work; and be freed from sin, and pain, and tears, and permitted to participate in the full splendours that shall encompass the throne of God in the heavens; see Note, Luke ii. 9; comp. Rev. xxi. 22—24; xxii. 5; Isa. lx. 19, 20.

3. *And not only so*. We not only rejoice in times of prosperity, and of health. Paul proceeds to show that this plan is not less adapted to produce support in trials. ¶ *But we glory*. The word used here is the same that is in ver. 2, translated, "we rejoice" (καυχώμεθα). It should have been so rendered here. The meaning is, that we rejoice not only *in hope;* not only in the *direct* results of justification, in the immediate effect which religion itself produces; but we carry our joy and triumph even into the midst of trials. In accordance with this, our Saviour directed his followers to rejoice in persecutions, Matt. v. 11, 12. Comp. James i. 2, 12. ¶ *In tribulations*. In afflictions. The word used here refers to *all kinds* of trials which men are called to endure; though it is possible that Paul referred particularly to the various persecutions and trials which they were called to endure *as Christians*. ¶ *Knowing*. Being assured of this. Paul's assurance might have arisen from reasoning on the nature of religion, and its tendency to produce comfort; or it is more probable that he was speaking here the language of his own experience. He had found it to be so. This was written near the close of his life, and it states the personal experience of a man who endured, perhaps, as much as any one ever did, in attempting to spread the gospel; and *far more* than commonly falls to the lot of mankind. Yet he, like all other Christians, could leave his deliberate testimony to the fact that Christianity was sufficient to sustain the soul in its severest trials; see 2 Cor. i. 3—6; xi. 24—29; xii. 9, 10. ¶ *Worketh*. Produces; the effect of afflictions on the minds of Christians is to make them patient. Sinners are irritated and troubled by them; they murmur, and become more and more obstinate and rebellious. They have no sources of consolation; they deem God a hard master; and they become fretful and rebellious just in proportion to the depth and continuance of their trials. But in the mind of a Christian, who regards his Father's hand in it; who sees that he deserves no mercy; who has confidence in the wisdom and goodness of God; who feels that it is necessary for his own good to be afflicted; and who experiences its happy, subduing, and mild effect in restraining his sinful passions, and in weaning him from the world—the effect is to produce *patience*. Accordingly it will usually be found that those Christians who are longest and most severely afflicted are the most patient. Year after year of suffering produces increased peace and calmness of soul; and at the end of his course the Christian is more willing to be afflicted, and bears his afflictions more calmly, than at the beginning. He who on earth was most afflicted was the most patient of all sufferers; and not less patient when he was "led as a lamb to the slaughter," than when he experienced the first trial in his great work. ¶ *Patience*. "A calm temper, which suffers evils without murmuring or discontent." (*Webster*.)

4. *And patience, experience*. Patient endurance of trial produces

4 And patience, experience; and experience, hope;
5 And hope [a] maketh not ashamed; because the love of God is shed abroad in our hearts by the Holy Ghost, [b] which is given unto us.
6 For when we were yet with-

a Phil.1.20.
b Eph.1.13,14.

---

experience. The word rendered experience (δοκιμὴν) means *trial, testing,* or that thorough examination by which we ascertain the quality or nature of a thing, as when we test a metal by fire, or in any other way, to ascertain that it is genuine. It also means *approbation,* or the *result* of such a trial; the being approved, and accepted as the effect of a trying process. The meaning is, that long afflictions borne patiently show a Christian what he is; they test his religion, and prove that it is genuine. Afflictions are often sent for this purpose, and patience in the midst of them shows that the religion which can sustain them is from God. ¶ *And experience, hope.* The result of such long trial is to produce *hope.* They show that religion is genuine; that it is from God; and not only so, but they direct the mind *onward* to another world; and sustain the soul by the prospect of a glorious immortality there. The various steps and stages of the benefits of afflictions are thus beautifully delineated by the apostle in a manner which accords with the experience of all the children of God.

5. *And hope maketh not ashamed.* That is, this hope will not disappoint, or deceive. When we hope for an object which we do not obtain, we are conscious of disappointment; perhaps sometimes of a feeling of shame. But the apostle says that the Christian hope is such that it will be fulfilled; it will not disappoint; what we hope for we shall certainly obtain; see Phil. i. 20. The expression used here is probably taken from Ps. xxii. 4, 5.

'Our fathers trusted in thee;
They trusted; and thou didst deliver them.
They cried unto thee,
And were delivered;
They trusted in thee,
And were not confounded" [ashamed].'

¶ *Because the love of God.* Love toward God. There is produced an abundant, an overflowing love to God. ¶ *Is shed abroad.* Is diffused; is poured out; is abundantly produced (ἐκκέχυται). This word is properly applied to *water,* or to any other liquid that is poured out, or diffused. It is used also to denote imparting, or communicating freely or abundantly, and is thus expressive of the influence of the Holy Spirit *poured down,* or abundantly imparted to men; Acts x. 45. Here it means that love towards God is copiously or abundantly given to a Christian; his heart is conscious of high and abundant love to God, and by this he is sustained in his afflictions. ¶ *By the Holy Ghost.* It is produced by the influence of the Holy Spirit. All Christian graces are traced to his influence; Gal. v. 22, "But the fruit of the Spirit is *love,* joy," &c. ¶ *Which is given unto us.* Which *Spirit* is given or imparted to us. The Holy Spirit is thus represented as dwelling in the hearts of believers; 1 Cor. vi. 19; iii. 16; 2 Cor. vi. 16. In all these places it is meant that Christians are under his sanctifying influence; that he produces in their hearts the Christian graces; and fills their minds with peace, and love, and joy.

6. *For when,* &c. This opens a new view of the subject, or it is a new argument to show that our hope will not make ashamed, or will not disappoint us. The first argument he had stated in the previous verse, that the Holy Ghost was given to us. The next, which he now states, is, that God had given the most ample proof that he would save us by giving his Son when we were sinners; and that he who had done so much for us when we were *enemies,* would not now fail us when we are his friends; ver. 6—10. He has performed the more *difficult* part of the work by reconciling us when we were enemies; and he will not now forsake us, but will carry forward and *complete* what he

out strength, [1] in due [a] time Christ died for the ungodly.

7 For scarcely for a righteous man will one die; yet peradventure for a good man some would even dare to die.

1 or, *according to the time.*

a Gal.4.4.

has begun. ¶ *We were yet without strength.* The word here used (ασθενῶν) is usually applied to those who are sick and feeble, deprived of strength by disease; Mat. xxv. 38; Luke x. 9; Acts iv. 9; v. 15. But it is also used in a *moral* sense, to denote inability or feebleness with regard to any undertaking or duty. Here it means that we were without strength *in regard to the case which the apostle was considering;* that is, we had no power to devise a scheme of justification, to make an atonement, or to put away the wrath of God, &c. While all hope of man's being saved by any plan of his own was thus taken away; while he was thus lying exposed to divine justice, and dependent on the mere mercy of God; God provided a plan which met the case, and secured his salvation. The remark of the apostle here has reference *only* to the condition of the race *before* an atonement is made. It does not pertain to the question whether man has strength to repent and to believe after an atonement *is* made, which is a very different inquiry. ¶ *In due time.* Margin *According to the time* (κατὰ καιρὸν). In a *timely* manner; at the proper time; Gal. iv. 4, "But when the fulness of time was come," &c. This may mean, (1.) That it was a *fit* or *proper* time. All experiments had failed to save men. For four thousand years the trial had been made under the law among the Jews; and by the aid of the most enlightened reason in Greece and Rome; and still it was in vain. No scheme had been devised to meet the maladies of the world, and to save men from death. It was then *time* that a better plan should be presented to men. (2.) It was the time *fixed* and appointed by God for the Messiah to come; the time which had been designated by the prophets; Gen. xlix. 10; Dan. ix. 24—27; see John xiii. 1; xvii. 1. (3.) It was a most *favourable* time for the spread of the gospel. The world was expecting such an event; was at peace; and was subjected mainly to the Roman power; and furnished facilities never before experienced for introducing the gospel rapidly into every land; see Notes, Mat. ii. 1, 2. ¶ *For the ungodly.* Those who do not worship God. It here means *sinners* in general, and does not differ materially from what is meant by the word translated "without strength;" see Note, chap. iv. 5.

7. *For scarcely,* &c. The design of this verse and the following is, to illustrate the great love of God by comparing it with what *man* was willing to do. "It is an unusual occurrence, an event which is all that we can hope for from the highest human benevolence and the purest friendship, that one would be willing to die for *a good man.* There are none who would be willing to die for a man who was seeking to do us injury, to calumniate our character, to destroy our happiness or our property. But Christ was willing to die for bitter foes." ¶ *Scarcely.* With difficulty. It is an event which cannot be expected to occur often. There would scarcely be found an instance in which it would happen. ¶ *A righteous man.* A just man; a man distinguished simply for *integrity* of conduct; one who has no remarkable claims for amiableness of character, for benevolence, or for personal friendship. Much as we may *admire* such a man, and applaud him, yet he has not the characteristics which would appeal to our hearts to induce us to lay down our lives for him. Accordingly, it is not known that any instance has occurred where for *such* a man one would be willing to die. ¶ *For a righteous man.* That is, in his place, or in his stead. A man would scarcely lay down his own life to save that of a righteous man. ¶ *Will one die.* Would one be will-

8 But God commendeth his love towards us, in that while [a] we were yet sinners, Christ died for us.

9 Much more then, being now justified by his blood, [b] we shall be saved from [c] wrath through him.

10 For if, when we were enemies, we were reconciled to God

a John 15.13; 1Pet.3.18; 1 John 3.16. b Heb.9.14,22. c 1 Thess.1.10.

ing to die. ¶ *Yet peradventure.* Perhaps; implying that this was an event which might be expected to occur. ¶ *For a good man.* That is, not merely a man who is coldly just; but a man whose characteristic is that of kindness, amiableness, tenderness. It is evident that the case of such a man would be much more likely to appeal to our feelings, than that of one who is merely a man of integrity. Such a man is susceptible of tender friendship; and probably the apostle intended to refer to such a case—a case where we would be willing to expose life for a kind, tender, faithful friend. ¶ *Some would even dare to die.* Some would have courage to give his life. Instances of this kind, though not many, have occurred. The affecting case of Damon and Pythias is one. Damon had been condemned to death by the tyrant Dionysius of Sicily, and obtained leave to go and settle his domestic affairs on promise of returning at a stated hour to the place of execution. Pythias pledged himself to undergo the punishment if Damon should not return in time, and deliver himself into the hands of the tyrant. Damon returned at the appointed moment, just as the sentence was about to be executed on Pythias; and Dionysius was so struck with the fidelity of the two friends, that he remitted their punishment, and entreated them to permit him to share their friendship; (Val. Max. 4. 7.) This case stands almost alone. Our Saviour says that it is the highest expression of love among men. "Greater love hath no man than this, that a man lay down his life for his friends;" John xv. 13. The friendship of David and Jonathan seems also to have been of this character, that one would have been willing to lay down his life for the other.

8. *But God commendeth,* &c. God has exhibited or showed his love in this unusual and remarkable manner. ¶ *His love.* His kind feeling; his beneficence; his willingness to submit to sacrifice to do good to others. ¶ *While we were yet sinners.* And of course his enemies. In this, his love surpasses all that has ever been manifested among men. ¶ *Christ died for us.* In our stead; to save us from death. He took our place; and by dying himself on the cross, saved us from dying eternally in hell.

9. *Much more, then.* It is much more reasonable to expect it. There are fewer obstacles in the way. If, when we were enemies, he overcame all that was in the way of our salvation; much more have we reason to expect that he will afford us protection now that we are his friends. This is one ground of the hope expressed in ver. 5. ¶ *Being now justified.* Pardoned; accepted as his friends. ¶ *By his blood.* By his death; Note, chap. iii. 25. The fact that we are purchased by his blood, and sanctified by it, renders us *sacred* in the eye of God; bestows a value on us proportionate to the worth of the price of our redemption; and is a pledge that he will *keep* that which has been so dearly bought. ¶ *Saved from wrath.* From hell; from the punishment due to sin; Note, chap ii. 8.

10. *For if.* The idea in this verse is simply a repetition and enlargement of that in ver. 9. The apostle dwells on the thought, and places it in a new light, furnishing thus a strong confirmation of his position. ¶ *When we were enemies.* The work was undertaken while we were enemies. From being enemies we were changed to friends by that work. Thus it was commenced by God; its foundation was laid while we were still hostile to it; it evinced, therefore, a determined purpose on the

by the death of his Son, much [a] more, being reconciled, we shall be saved by [b] his life.

a chap.8.32. b John 14.9.

11 And not only *so*, but we also joy [c] in God, through our Lord Jesus Christ, by whom we

c Hab.3.18.

part of God to perform it; and he has thus given a pledge that it shall be perfected. ¶ *We were reconciled;* Note, Mat. v. 24. We are brought to an *agreement; to a state of friendship and union.* We became his friends, laid aside our opposition, and embraced him as our friend and portion. To effect this is the great design of the plan of salvation; 2 Cor. v. 1—20; Col. i. 21; Eph. ii. 16. It means that there were *obstacles* existing on both sides to a reconciliation; and that these have been removed by the death of Christ; and that a union has thus been effected. This has been done in removing the obstacles on the part of God—by maintaining the honour of his law; showing his hatred of sin; upholding his justice, and maintaining his truth, at the same time that he pardons; Note, chap. iii. 26. And on the part of man, by removing his *unwillingness* to be reconciled; by subduing, changing, and sanctifying his heart; by overcoming his hatred of God, and of his law; and bringing him into submission to the government of God. So that the Christian is in fact reconciled to God; he is his friend; he is pleased with his law, his character, and his plan of salvation. And all this has been accomplished by the sacrifice of the Lord Jesus as an offering in our place. ¶ *Much more.* It is much more to be expected; there are still stronger and more striking considerations to show it. ¶ *By his life.* We were reconciled by his death. *Death* may include possibly his low, humble, and suffering condition. Death has the appearance of great feebleness; the death of Christ had the appearance of the *defeat* of his plans. His enemies triumphed and rejoiced over him on the cross, and in the tomb. Yet the effect of this feeble, low, and humiliating state was to reconcile us to God. If in *this* state, when humble, despised, dying, *dead,* he had power to accomplish so great a work as to reconcile us to God, how much more may we expect that he will be able to keep us now that he is a living, exalted, and triumphant Redeemer. If his fainting powers in *dying* were such as to reconcile us, how much more shall his full, vigorous powers as an exalted Redeemer, be sufficient to keep and save us. This argument is but an expansion of what the Saviour himself said; John xiv. 19, "Because I live, ye shall live also."

11. *And not only so.* The apostle states *another* effect of justification. ¶ *We also joy in God.* In ver. 2, he had said that we rejoice in tribulations, and in hope of the glory of God. But he here adds that we rejoice *in God himself;* in his existence; his attributes; his justice, holiness, mercy, truth, love. The Christian rejoices that God is such a being as he is; and glories that the universe is under his administration. The sinner is opposed to him; he finds no pleasure in him; he fears or hates him; and deems him unqualified for universal empire. But it is one characteristic of true piety, one evidence that we are truly reconciled to God, that we rejoice in him *as he is;* and find pleasure in the contemplation of his perfections as they are revealed in the Scriptures. ¶ *Through our Lord,* &c. By the mediation of our Lord Jesus, who has revealed the true character of God, and by whom we have been reconciled to him. ¶ *The atonement.* Margin, or *reconciliation.* This is the only instance in which our translators have used the word *atonement* in the New Testament. The word frequently occurs in the Old, Ex. xxix. 33, 36, 37; xxx. 10, 15, 16, &c. As it is now used by us, it commonly means *the ransom,* or *the sacrifice* by means of which reconciliation is effected between God and man. But in this place it has a different sense. It means the *reconciliation itself* between God and man; not the *means* by

which reconciliation is effected. It denotes not that we have received a *ransom*, or an offering by which reconciliation *might* be effected; but that *in fact we have become reconciled through him*. This was the ancient meaning of the English word *atonement*—AT ONE MENT—being *at one*, or reconciled.

> ——He seeks to make *atonement*
> Between the duke of Glo'ster and your brothers.—*Shakspeare.*

The Greek word which denotes the expiatory offering by which a reconciliation is effected, is different from the one here; see Note, chap. iii. 25. The word used here (καταλλαγὴ) is never used to denote such an offering, but denotes the *reconciliation itself*.

12—21. This passage has been usually regarded as the most difficult part of the New Testament. It is not the design of these Notes to enter into a minute criticism of contested points like this. They who wish to see a full discussion of the passage, may find it in the professedly critical commentaries; and especially in the commentaries of Tholuck and of Professor Stuart on the Romans. The meaning of the passage in its *general* bearing is not difficult; and probably the whole passage would have been found *far less* difficult if it had not been attached to a *philosophical theory* on the subject of man's sin, and if a strenuous and indefatigable effort had not been made to prove that it teaches what it was never designed to teach. The plain and obvious design of the passage is this, *to show one of the benefits of the doctrine of justification by faith*. The apostle had shown, (1.) That that doctrine produced peace, ver. 1. (2.) That it produces joy in the prospect of future glory, ver. 2. (3.) That it sustained the soul in afflictions; (*a*) by the regular *tendency* of afflictions under the gospel, ver. 3, 4; and (*b*) by the fact that the Holy Ghost was imparted to the believer. (4.) That this doctrine rendered it certain that we should be saved, because Christ had died for us, ver. 6; because this was the highest expression of love, ver. 7, 8; and because if we had been *reconciled* when thus alienated, we should be saved now that we are the friends of God, ver. 9, 10. (5.) That it led us to rejoice *in God himself;* produced joy in his presence, and in all his attributes. He now proceeds to show the bearing on that great mass of evil which had been introduced into the world by sin, and to prove that the benefits of the atonement were far greater than the evils which had been introduced by the acknowledged effects of the sin of Adam. "The design is to exalt our views of the work of Christ, and of the plan of justification through him, by comparing them with the evil consequences of the sin of our first father, and by showing that the blessings in question not only extend to the removal of these evils, but far beyond this, so that the grace of the gospel has not only abounded, but *superabounded*." *(Prof. Stuart.)* In doing this, the apostle admits, as an undoubted and well-understood fact,—

1. That sin came into the world by one man, and death as the consequence. ver. 12.

2. That death had passed on all; even on those who had not the light of revelation, and the express commands of God, ver. 13, 14.

3. That Adam was the figure, the type of him that was to come; that there was some sort of analogy or resemblance between the results of his act and the results of the work of Christ. That analogy consisted in the fact that the effects of his doings did not terminate on himself, but extended to numberless other persons, and that it was thus with the work of Christ, ver. 14. But he shows,

4. That there were very material and important differences in the two cases. There was not a perfect paralelism. The effects of the work of Christ were far more than simply to counteract the evil introduced by the sin of Adam. The *differences* between the effect of his act and the work of Christ are these. (1.) The sin of Adam led to condemnation. The work of Christ has an opposite tendency, ver. 15. (2.) The condemnation which came from the sin of Adam was the result of one offence. The work of

have now received the [1] atonement.

12 Wherefore, as[a] by one man sin entered into the world, and death by sin; and so death passed upon all men, [2] for that all have sinned.

1 or, *reconciliation.* a Gen.3.6,19. 2 or, *in whom.*

Christ was to deliver from *many* offences, ver. 16. (3.) The work of Christ was far more abundant and overflowing in its influence. It extended deeper and farther. It was more than a compensation for the evils of the fall, ver. 17.

5. As the act of Adam threw its influence over all men to secure their condemnation, so the work of Christ was fitted to affect all men, Jews and Gentiles, in bringing them into a state by which they might be delivered from the fall, and restored to the favour of God. It was *in itself* adapted to produce far more and greater benefits than the crime of Adam had done evil; and was thus a glorious plan, just fitted to meet the actual condition of a world of sin; and to repair the evils which apostacy had introduced. It had thus the evidence that it originated in the benevolence of God, and that it was adapted to the human condition, ver. 18—21.

[The learned author denies the doctrine of imputed sin, and labours to prove that it is not contained in Rom. v. 12, 19. The following introductory Note is intended to exhibit the orthodox view of the subject, and meet the objections which the reader will find in the Commentary. The very first question that demands our attention is, What character did Adam sustain under the covenant of works, that of a single and independent individual, or that of the representative of the human kind?

This is one of the most important questions in Theology, and according to the answer we may be prepared to give, in the affirmative or negative, will be almost the entire complexion of our religious views. If the question be resolved in the affirmative, then what Adam did must be held *as* done by us, and the imputation of his guilt would seem to follow as a necessary consequence.

1. That Adam sustained the character of representative of the human race; in other words, that he was *the federal as well as natural head* of his descendants, is obvious from the circumstances of the history in the book of Genesis. It has been said indeed, that in the record of the threatening no mention is made of the posterity of Adam, and that on this account, all idea of federal headship or representation must be abandoned, as a mere theological figment, having no foundation in Scripture. But if God regarded Adam only in his individual capacity, when he said unto him "in the day thou eatest thereof thou shalt surely die," then, the other addresses of God to Adam, which form part of the same history, must be construed in the same way. And was it to Adam only, and not to the human kind at large, viewed in him, that God said, "be fruitful, and multiply, and replenish the earth?" Was it to Adam in his individual capacity, that God gave the grant of the earth, with all its rich and varied productions? Or was it to mankind at large? Was it to Adam alone that God said, "in the sweat of thy face shalt thou eat bread, till thou return unto the ground," &c.? The universal infliction of the penalty shows, that the threatening was addressed to Adam as the federal head of the race. All toil, and sweat, and die. Indeed, the entire history favours the conclusion, that God was dealing with Adam, not in his individual, but representative capacity; nor can its consistency be preserved on any other principle.

2. Moreover, there are certain facts connected with the moral history of mankind, which present insuperable difficulties, if we deny the doctrines of representation and imputed sin. *How shall we on any other principle account for the universality of death, or rather of penal evil?* It can be traced back beyond all *personal* guilt. Its origin is higher. *Antecedent* to all actual transgression, man is visited with penal evil. He *comes into the world* under a necessity of dying. His whole constitution is disordered. His body and his mind bear on them the marks of a blighting curse. It is impossible on any theory to deny this. And why is man thus visited? Can the righteous God punish where there is no guilt? We *must* take one side or other of the alternative, that God inflicts punishment without guilt, or that Adam's sin is imputed to his posterity. If we take the latter branch of the alternative, we are furnished with the ground of the divine procedure, and freed from many difficulties that press upon the opposite view.

It may be noticed in this place also, that the death of infants is a striking proof of the infliction of penal evil, *prior* to personal or actual sin. Their tender bodies are assailed in a multitude of instances by acute and violent diseases, that call for our sympathy the more that the sufferers cannot disclose or communicate the source of their agony. They labour with death and struggle hard in his hands, till they resign the gift of life they had retained for so short a while. It is said, indeed, that the case of infants is not introduced in Scripture in connection with this subject, and our author tells us, that they are not at all referred to in any part of this disputed passage, nor included in the clause, "death reigned, *even* over them that had not sinned after the similitude of Adam's transgression." On this, some observations will be found in the proper place. Meanwhile, there is *the fact itself*, and with it we are concerned now. *Why do infants die?* Perhaps it will be said that though they have committed no actual sin, yet they have a depraved nature; but this cedes the whole question, for that depraved nature is just a part of the penal evil, formerly noticed. Why are innocent infants visited with that which entails death on them? One answer only can be given, and no ingenuity can evade the conclusion,—"in Adam all die." The wonder is, that this doctrine should ever have been denied. On the human family at large, on man and woman, on infant child, and hoary sire, on earth and sky, are traced the dismal effects of the first sin.

3. The parallelism between Adam and Christ is another branch of evidence on this subject. That they bear a striking resemblance to each other is allowed on all hands. Hence Christ is styled, in the 15th of 1st Corinthians, "the last Adam," and "the second man," and in this very passage, Adam is expressly called a type, or "figure of him that was to come." Now in what does this resemblance consist? Between these two persons there are very many points of dissimilarity, or contrast. The first man is earthy, the second is the Lord from heaven. From the one come guilt, and condemnation, and death; and from the other, righteousness, justification, and life. Where then is the similarity? "They are alike," says Beza, "in this, that each of them shares what he has with his." Both are covenant or representative heads, and communicate their respective influences to those whom they represent. Here then, is one great leading point of similarity, nor is it possible in any other view to preserve the parallel. For suppose we disturb the parallel as now adjusted, and argue that Adam was not a federal head, that we are therefore neither held guilty of Adam's sin, nor condemned and punished on account of it; where shall we find the counterpart of this in Christ? Must we also maintain that he does not represent his people, that they are neither esteemed righteous on account of his work, nor justified and saved by it? Such is the legitimate consequence of the opposite views. If we hold that from Adam we receive only a corrupt nature, in consequence of which we sin personally, and *then* become guilty, and are in consequence condemned; we must also argue that we receive from Christ only a pure or renewed nature, in consequence of which we become personally righteous, and are *then and therefore* justified and saved. But such a scheme would undermine the whole gospel. Though the derivation of holiness from Christ be a true and valuable doctrine, we are not justified on account of that derived holiness. On the contrary, we are justified on account of something *without* us—something that has no dependence whatever on our personal holiness, viz. the righteousness of Christ. Nay, according to the doctrine of Paul, justification in order *of* nature, is before sanctification, and the cause of it.

It is but justice to state, that the commentator maintains that a resemblance between Adam and Christ lies not at all *in the mode* in which sin and righteousness, life and death, have been respectively introduced by them; but is found in the *simple fact* that "the effect of their doings did not terminate on themselves, but extended to numberless other persons." pp. 117, 118, 128. Indeed, he repeatedly affirms, that in regard to the introduction of sin by Adam, nothing whatever is said in this passage in regard to *the mode* of it. The fact alone is announced. If this were true, it is allowed that the arguments we have now employed would be much weakened. But the assertion cannot be substantiated. If the analogy do not lie in *the mode,* but in the simple fact, that the effects of their doings do not terminate on themselves; what greater resemblance is there between Adam and Christ, than between any two persons that might be named? David and Ahab might be compared in the same way; the good deeds of the one, and the evil deeds of the other, not terminating with themselves. Besides, Paul certainly does state in the previous chapter, *the mode* in which the righteousness of Christ becomes available for salvation. He states plainly that "God imputeth it without works." When then in the 5th chapter he looks back upon this subject, and introduces his parallel with "WHEREFORE AS by one man," &c. are we to believe that he intends no similarity in the mode? Shall we make the apostle explain *the manner* in which the righteousness becomes available, and say nothing of *the way* in which its opposite is introduced, at the very time he is professedly comparing the two?

Such is a brief outline of the evidence on which the doctrine of imputed sin is based. The principal arguments are those derived from the universality of penal evil, and the parallel between Adam and Christ. And these are the very topics handled by the apostle in this much vexed passage. Our author, indeed, in his opening remarks maintains, that nothing is said by the apostle of original sin in this place. "The apostle here is not discussing the doctrine of original sin;" and "his design is to show one of the benefits of the doctrine of justification." But the design of Paul is to *illustrate* the doctrine of justification, and not simply to show one of its benefits. For in the former part of this chapter (ver. 1-11,) the apostle had fully enlarged on these benefits, and there is no evidence that verses 12, 19, are a continuation of the same theme. On the contrary, there is obviously a break in the discourse at ver. 12, where the apostle, recalling the discussion, introduces a new illustration of his principal point, viz. justification through the righteousness of Christ. On this the apostle had discoursed largely in the 3d and 4th chapters. And lest any should think it anomalous and irrational to justify men, on account of a work they themselves had no hand in accomplishing, he now appeals to the "great analogous fact in the history of the world." This seems the most natural construction. No wonder," says President Edwards, "when the apostle is treating so fully and largely of our restoration, righteousness, and life by Christ, that he is led by it to consider our fall, sin, death, and ruin by Adam."—*Orig. Sin.* p. 303. The following analysis will assist the reader in understanding the whole passage: "As the point to be illustrated is the justification of sinners, on the ground of the righteousness of Christ, and the source of illustration is the fall of all men in Adam; the passage begins with a statement of this latter truth. 'As on account of one man death has passed on all men; so on account of one,' &c. ver. 12. Before, however, carrying out the comparison, the apostle stops to establish his position, that all men are regarded, and treated as sinners on account of Adam. His proof is this. The infliction of a penalty implies the transgression of a law, since sin is not imputed where there is no law, ver. 13. All mankind are subject to death or penal evils, therefore all men are regarded as transgressors of a law, ver. 13. The law or covenant which brings death on all men, is not the law of Moses, because multitudes died before that law was given, ver. 14. Nor is it the law of nature, since multitudes die who have never violated even that law, ver. 14. Therefore, we must conclude, that men are subject to death on account of Adam; that is, it is for the offence of one that many die, ver. 13, 14. Adam is, therefore, a type of Christ. Yet the cases are not completely parallel. There are certain points of dissimilarity, ver. 15, 17. Having thus limited and illustrated the analogy, the apostle resumes, and carries the comparison fully out in ver. 18, 19. "Therefore as on account of one man," &c. *Prof. Hodge.*]

12. *Wherefore,* (διὰ τοῦτο). On this account. This is not an *inference* from what has gone before, but a *continuance* of the design of the apostle to show the advantages of the plan of justification by faith; as if he had said, "The advantages of that plan have been seen in our comfort and peace, and in its sustaining power in afflictions. Further, the advantages of the plan are seen in regard to this, that it is applicable to the condition of man in a world where the sin of one man has produced so much wo and death. *On this account* also it is a matter of joy. It meets the ills of a fallen race; and it is therefore a plan adapted to man." Thus understood, the connection and design of the passage is easily explained. *In respect to the state of things* into which man is fallen, the benefits of this plan may be seen, as adapted to heal the maladies, and to be commensurate with the evils which the apostasy of one man brought upon the world. This explanation is not that which is usually given to this place, but it is that which seems to me to be demanded by the strain of the apostle's reasoning. The passage is *elliptical,* and there is a necessity of supplying something to make out the sense. ¶ *As* (ὥσπερ). This is the form of a *comparison.* But the other part of the comparison is deferred to ver. 18. The connection evidently requires us to understand the other part of the comparison of the work of Christ. In the rapid train of ideas in the mind of the apostle, this was deferred to make room for explanations (ver. 13—17). "As by one man sin entered into the world, &c., *so* by the work of Christ a remedy has been provided, commensurate with the evils. As the sin of one man had such an influence, *so* the work of the Redeemer has an influence to meet and to counteract those evils." The passage in ver. 13—17 is therefore to be regarded as a parenthesis thrown in for the purpose of making explanations, and to show how the cases of Adam and of Christ *differed* from each other. ¶ *By one man,* &c. By means of one man; by the crime of one man. His act was the occasion of the introduction of all sin into all the world. The apostle here refers to the well known historical fact (Gen. iii. 6, 7), without any explanation of the *mode* or *cause* of this. He adduced it as a fact that was well known; and evidently meant

to speak of it not for the purpose of *explaining* the mode, or even of making this the leading or prominent topic in the discussion. His *main* design is not to speak of the manner of the introduction of sin, but to show that the work of Christ meets and removes well-known and extensive evils. His explanations, therefore, are chiefly confined to the work of Christ. He speaks of the introduction, the spread, and the effects of sin, not as having any *theory* to defend on that subject, not as designing to enter into a minute description of the case, but as it was manifest *on the face of things*, as it stood on the historical record, and as it was understood and admitted by mankind. Great perplexity has been introduced by forgetting the *scope* of the apostle's argument here, and by supposing that he was defending a peculiar *theory* on the subject of the introduction of sin; whereas, nothing is more foreign to his design. He is showing how the plan of justification *meets well understood and acknowledged universal evils.* Those evils he refers to just as they were seen, and admitted to exist. All men see them, and feel them, and practically understand them. The truth is, that the doctrine of the fall of man, and the prevalence of sin and death, do not belong peculiarly to Christianity any more than the introduction and spread of disease does to the science of the *healing art.* Christianity did not introduce sin; nor is it responsible for it The existence of sin and wo belongs to the *race;* appertains equally to all systems of religion, and is a part of the melancholy history of man, whether Christianity be true or false. The existence and extent of sin and death are not affected if the infidel could show that Christianity was an imposition. They would still remain. The Christian religion is just *one mode of proposing a remedy for well-known and desolating evils;* just as the science of medicine proposes a remedy for diseases which it did not introduce, and which could not be stayed in their desolations, or modified, if it could be shown that the whole science of healing was pretension and quackery. Keeping this design of the apostle in view, therefore, and remembering that he is not defending or stating a theory about the introduction of sin, but that he is explaining the way in which the work of Christ delivers *from* a deep-felt universal evil, we shall find the explanation of this passage disencumbered of many of the difficulties with which it has been thought usually to be invested. ¶ *By one man.* By *Adam;* see ver. 14. It is true that sin was literally introduced by *Eve,* who was first in the transgression; Gen. iii. 6; 1 Tim. ii. 14. But the apostle evidently is not explaining the precise *mode* in which sin was introduced, or making this his *leading* point. He therefore speaks of the introduction of sin in a *popular* sense, as it was generally understood. The following reasons may be suggested why the *man* is mentioned rather than the woman as the cause of the introduction of sin: (1.) It was the natural and usual way of expressing such an event. We say that *man* sinned, that *man* is redeemed, *man* dies, &c. We do not pause to indicate the sex in such expressions. So in this, he undoubtedly meant to say that it was introduced by the *parentage* of the human race. (2.) The name *Adam* in Scripture was given to the *created pair,* the parents of the human family, a name designating their earthly origin; Gen. v. 1, 2, "In the day that God created man, in the likeness of God made he him; male and female created he them, and blessed them, and called THEIR *name Adam.*" The name *Adam,* therefore, used in this connection (ver. 14), would suggest the *united parentage* of the human family. (3.) In transactions where man and woman are mutually concerned, it is usual to speak of the man first, on account of his being constituted superior in rank and authority. (4.) The comparison on the one side, in the apostle's argument, is of the *man* Christ Jesus; and to secure *the fitness, the congruity* (*Stuart*) of the comparison, he speaks of the *man* only in the previous transaction. (5.) The sin of the woman was not complete in its effects without the concurrence of the man. It was their *uniting* in it which was the cause of the evil. Hence *the man* is especially mentioned as having *rendered the offence what it was;* as having completed it, and entailed its curses on the race. From these remarks it is clear that the apostle does not refer to the *man* here from any idea that there was any particular covenant transaction with *him*, but that he means to speak of it in the usual, popular sense; referring to him as being the fountain of all the woes that sin has introduced into the world.

["In the day thou eatest thereof thou shalt surely die," Gen. ii. 17. This is an account of the first great covenant transaction between God and man. It carries us back to the origin of mankind, and discloses the source of evil, about which so much has been written and spoken in vain. That God entered into covenant with Adam in innocence, is a doctrine, with which the Shorter Catechism has made us familiar from our infant years. Nor is it without higher authority. It would be improper, indeed, to apply to this transaction every thing that may be supposed essential to a human compact or bargain. Whenever divine things are represented by things analogous among men, care must be taken to exclude every idea that is inconsistent with the dignity of the subject. If the analogy be pressed beyond due bounds, the subject is not illustrated, but degraded. For example, in the present case, we must not suppose that because in human covenants, the consent of parties is essential, and both are at full liberty to receive or reject the proposed terms as they shall see fit; the same thing holds true in the case of Adam. He indeed freely gave his consent to the terms of the covenant, as a holy being could not fail to do, but he was not at liberty to withhold that consent. He was a creature entirely at the divine disposal, whose duty from the moment of his being was implicit obedience. He had no power either to dictate or reject terms. The relation of parties in this covenant, renders the idea of power to withhold consent, inadmissible.

But, because the analogy cannot be pressed beyond certain limits, must we therefore entirely abandon it? Proceeding on this principle, we should speedily find it impossible to retain any term or figure, that had ever been employed about religious subjects. *The leading essentials of a covenant are found in this great transaction*, and no more is necessary to justify the appellation which orthodox divines have applied to it. "A covenant is a contract, or agreement, between two or more parties, on certain terms." It is commonly supposed to imply the existence of parties, a promise, and a condition. All these constituent parts of a covenant meet in the case under review. The parties are God and man, God and the first parent of the human race; the promise is life, which though not expressly stated, is yet distinctly implied in the penalty; and the condition is obedience to the supreme will of God. In human covenants no greater penalty is incurred than the forfeiture of the promised blessing, and therefore the idea of penalty is not supposed essential to a covenant. In every case of forfeited promise, however, there is the infliction of penalty, to the exact amount of the value of the blessing lost. We cannot think of Adam losing life without the corresponding idea of suffering death. So that, in fact, the loss of the promise, and the infliction of the penalty, are nearly the same thing.

It is no valid objection to this view, that "the word covenant," as our author tells us, (p. 137,) "is not applied in the transaction in the Bible," for there are many terms, the accuracy of which is never disputed, that are no more to be found in the Scriptures than this. Where do we find such terms as "the fall," and "the Trinity," and many others that might be mentioned? The mere name, indeed, is not a matter of very great importance, and if we allow that in the transaction itself, there were parties, and a promise, and a condition, (which cannot easily be denied,) it is of less moment whether we call it a covenant, or with our author and others, "a divine constitution." It is obvious to remark, however, that this latter title is just as little to be found "applied in the transaction in the Bible," as the former, and besides is more "liable to be misunderstood;" being vague and indefinite, intimating only, that Adam was under a divine law, or constitution; whereas the word covenant distinctly expresses *the kind or form of law*, and gives definite character to the whole transaction.

But although the doctrine of the covenant of works is independent of the occurrence of the name in the Scriptures, even this narrow ground of objection is not so easily maintained as some imagine. In Hos. vi. 7, it is said (according to the marginal reading, which is in strict accordance with the original Hebrew,) they *like Adam* כְּאָדָם have transgressed the covenant. And in that celebrated passage in the epistle to the Galatians, ch. iv. 24, when Paul speaks of "the two covenants," he alludes, in the opinion of some of the highest authorities, to the covenant of works and the covenant of grace. This opinion is espoused, and defended with great ability by the late Mr. Bell of Glasgow, one of the most distinguished theologians of his times, in a learned dissertation on the subject: *Bell on the Covenants*, p. 85. Scripture authority, then, would seem not to be entirely awanting, *even* for the name.

This doctrine of the covenant is intimately connected with that of imputed sin, for if there were no covenant, there could be no covenant or representative head; and if there were no covenant head, there could be no imputation of sin. Hence the dislike to the name.]

¶ *Sin entered into the world.* He was the first sinner of the race. The word *sin* here evidently means the violation of the law of God. He was the first sinner among men, and in consequence all others became sinners. The apostle does not here refer to Satan, the tempter, though he was the *suggester* of evil; for his *design* was to discuss the effect of the plan of salvation in meeting the sins and calamities of *our race.* This design, therefore, did not require him to introduce the sin of *another order* of beings. He says, therefore, that Adam was the first sinner of the race, and that death was the consequence. ¶ *Into the world.* Among mankind; John i. 10; iii. 16, 17. The term *world* is often thus used to denote human beings, the race, the human family. The apostle here evidently is not discussing the doctrine of *original* sin, but he is stating a simple fact, intelligible to all: "The first man violated the law of God, and in this way sin was introduced among men." In this fact—this general, simple declaration—there is no mystery. ¶ *And death by sin.* Death was the consequence of sin; or was introduced *because* man sinned. This is a simple statement of an obvious and well-known fact. It is repeating simply what is said in Gen. iii. 19, "In the sweat of thy face shalt thou eat bread, till thou return into the ground; for out of it wast thou taken; for dust thou art, and unto dust shalt thou return." The threatening was (Gen. ii. 17), "Of the tree of the knowledge of good and evil, thou shalt not eat of it, for in the day that thou eatest thereof, thou shalt surely die." If an inquiry be made here, how *Adam* would understand this; I reply, that we have no reason to think he would understand it as referring to any thing more than the loss of life as an expression of the displeasure of God. Moses does not intimate that he was learned in the nature of laws and penalties; and his narrative would lead us to suppose that this was *all* that would occur to Adam. And indeed, there is the highest evidence that the case admits of, that this *was* his understanding of it. For in the account of the *infliction* of the penalty *after* the law was violated; in God's own interpretation of it, in Gen. iii. 19, there is still *no* reference to any thing further. "Dust thou art, and unto dust shalt thou return." Now it is incredible that Adam should have understood this as referring to what has been called "spiritual death," and to "eternal death," when neither in the threatening, nor in the account of the infliction of the sentence, is there the slightest recorded reference to it. Men have done great injury in the cause of correct interpretation by carrying *their* notions of doctrinal subjects to the explanation of words and phrases in the Old Testament. They have usually described Adam as endowed with all the refinement, and possessed of all the knowledge, and adorned with all the metaphysical acumen and subtility of a modern theologian. They have deemed him qualified, in the very infancy of the world, to understand and discuss questions, which, under all the light of the Christian revelation, still perplex and embarrass the human mind. After these accounts of the endowments of Adam, which occupy so large a space in books of theology, one is surprised, on opening the Bible, to find how unlike all this, is the simple statement in Genesis. And the wonder cannot be suppressed that men should describe the obvious *infancy* of the race as superior to its highest advancement; or that the *first* man, just looking upon a world of wonders, imperfectly acquainted with law, and moral relations, and the effects of transgression, should be represented as endowed with knowledge which four thousand vears afterwards *it* required the advent of the Son of God to communicate!

[Yet it may be fairly questioned whether this singular account of the endowments of Adam, is itself very consistent with "the simple statement in Genesis." It certainly appears as like "a philosophical theory," as a Scripture doctrine. Adam was created *in the image of God*, Gen. i. 27. On this we have an inspired commentary in Col. iii. 10, and Eph. iv. 24, where the divine image is made to consist in KNOWLEDGE, righteousness, and true holiness. Now, as none will deny that the *holiness* of Adam in innocence was of a perfect kind, what authority have we for depreciating his knowledge? The capacity of knowing, like the other powers of the soul, must have been perfect from the hands of God. No dark shades of sin could then obscure the intellectual vision. There is no authority in Scripture for speaking of Adam in innocence, as if he possessed *less* "knowledge and refinement than modern theologians," and "were imperfectly acquainted with law and moral relations!" And though the question, *how* Adam would understand the threatening, does not determine its meaning, yet it would seem strange indeed, that God should threaten Adam with a penalty, which it was impossible for him to understand, except in so limited a way, as leaves more than half its meaning undisclosed.]

The account in Moses is simple. Created man was told not to violate a simple law, on pain of death. He did it; and God announced to him that the sentence would be inflicted, and that he should return to the dust whence he was taken. What else this *might* involve, what *other* consequences sin might introduce, might be the subject of future developments and revelations. It is absurd to suppose that *all* the consequences of the violation of a law can be foreseen, or must *necessarily* be foreseen, in order to make the law and the penalty just. It is sufficient that the law be known; that its violation be forbidden; and what the consequences of that violation will be, must be left in great part to future developments. Even we, yet know not *half* the results of violating the law of God. The murderer knows not the results fully of taking a man's life. He breaks a just law, and exposes himself to the numberless unseen woes which may flow from it.

We may ask, therefore, what light subsequent revelations have cast on the character and result of the first sin? and whether the apostle here meant to state that the consequences of sin were *in fact* as limited as they must have appeared to the mind of Adam? or had subsequent developments and revelations, through four thousand years, greatly extended the right understanding of the penalty of the law? This can be answered only by inquiring in what sense the apostle Paul here uses the word *death*. The passage before us shows in what sense he intended here to use the word. In his argument it stands opposed to "the grace of God, and the gift by grace," (ver. 15); to "justification," by the forgiveness of "many offences," (ver. 16); to the reign of the redeemed in eternal life, (ver. 17); and to "justification of life," (ver. 18). To all these, the words "death" (ver. 12, 17) and "judgment" (ver. 16, 18) stand opposed. These are the benefits which result from the work of Christ; and these *benefits* stand opposed to the *evils* which sin has introduced; and as it cannot be supposed that these benefits relate to *temporal life*, or solely to the resurrection of the body, so it cannot be that the evils involved in the words "death," "judgment," &c., relate simply to temporal death. The evident meaning is, that the word "death," as here used by the apostle, refers to *the train of evils* which have been introduced by sin. It does not mean simply temporal death; but that group and collection of woes, including temporal death, condemnation, and exposure to eternal death, which is the consequence of transgression. The apostle often uses the word *death*, and *to die*, in this wide sense, Rom. i. 32; vi. 16, 31; vii. 5, 10, 13, 24; viii. 2, 6, 13; 2 Cor. ii. 16; vii. 10; Heb. ii. 14. In the same sense the word is often used elsewhere, John viii. 51; xi. 26; 1 John v. 16, 17; Rev. ii. 11; xx. 6, &c. &c. In contrasting with this the results of the work of Christ, he describes not the resurrection merely, nor deliverance from temporal death, but *eternal* life in heaven; and it therefore follows that he here intends by death that gloomy and sad train of woes which sin has introduced into the world. The consequences of sin are, besides, elsewhere specified to be far more than temporal death, Ezek. xviii. 4; Rom. ii. 8, 9, 12. Though therefore Adam might not have foreseen all the evils which were to come upon the race as the consequence of his sin, yet these evils might nevertheless follow. And the apostle, four thousand years after the reign of sin had commenced, and under the guidance of inspiration, had full opportunity to see and describe that *train of woes* which he comprehends under the name of death. That train included evidently temporal death, condemnation for sin, remorse of conscience, and exposure to eternal death, as the penalty of transgression. ¶ *And so.* Thus. In this way it is to be accounted for that death has passed upon all men, *to wit,* because all men have sinned. As death followed sin in the first transgression, so it has in all; for all have sinned. There is a connection between death and sin which existed in the case of Adam, and which subsists in regard to all who sin. And as all have sinned, so death has passed on all men. ¶ *Death passed upon* (διῆλθεν). Passed through; pervaded; spread over the whole race, as pestilence passes through, or pervades a nation. Thus death, with its train of woes, with its withering and blighting influence, has passed through the world, laying prostrate all before it. ¶ *Upon all men.* Upon the race; all die. ¶ *For that* (ἐφ' ᾧ). This expression has been greatly controverted; and has been very variously translated. Elsner renders it, "on account of whom." Doddridge, "unto which all have sinned." The Latin Vulgate renders it, "in whom [Adam] all have sinned." The same rendering has been given by Augustine, Beza, &c. But it has never yet been shown that our translators have rendered the expression improperly. The old Syriac and the Arabic agree with the English translation in this interpretation. With this agree Calvin, Vatablus, Erasmus, &c. And this rendering is sustained also by many other considerations. (1.) If ᾧ be a relative pronoun here, it would refer naturally to *death,* as its antecedent, and not to *man.* But this would not make sense. (2.) If this had been its meaning, the preposition ἐν would have been used; see Note of Erasmus on the place. (3.) It comports with the apostle's argument to state a cause *why* all died, and not to state that men sinned *in* Adam. He was inquiring into the cause *why* death was in the world; and it would not account *for that* to say that all sinned *in* Adam. It would require an *additional* statement to see how *that* could be a cause. (4.) As his posterity had not then an existence, they could not commit actual transgression. Sin is the transgression of the law by a moral agent; and as the interpretation "*because* all have sinned" meets the argument of the apostle, and as the Greek favours that certainly *as much* as it does the other, it is to be preferred. ¶ *All have sinned.* To sin is to transgress the law of God; to do wrong. The apostle in this expression does not *say* that all have sinned in Adam, or that their nature has become corrupt, which is true, but which is not affirmed here; nor that the sin of Adam is imputed to them; but simply affirms that all men have sinned. He speaks evidently of the great universal fact that all men are sinners. He is not settling a metaphysical difficulty; nor does he speak of the condition of man as he comes into the world. He speaks as other men would; he addresses himself to the common sense of the world; and is discoursing of universal, well-known facts. *Here is the fact—that all men experience calamity, condemnation, death.* How is this to be accounted for? The answer is, "All have sinned." This is a sufficient answer; it meets the case. And as his design cannot be shown to be to discuss a metaphysical question about the *nature* of man, or about the character of infants, the passage should be interpreted according to his design, and should not be pressed to bear on that of which he says nothing, and to which the passage evidently has no reference. I understand it, therefore, as referring to the fact that men sin *in their own persons, sin themselves*—as, indeed, how *can* they *sin* in any other way?—and that *therefore* they die. If men maintain that it refers to any metaphysical properties of the nature of man, or to infants, they should not *infer* or *suppose* this, but should show distinctly that it is in the text. Where is there evidence of any such reference?

[The following Note on ver. 12, is intended to exhibit its just connection and force. It is the first member of a comparison between Adam and Christ, which is completed in ver. 18, 19. "*As* by one man," &c. The first point which demands our attention, is the meaning of the words, "By one man *sin entered* into the world." Our author has rendered them, "He was the first sinner;" and in this he follows Prof. Stewart and Dr. Taylor; the former of whom gives this explanation of the clause; that Adam "began transgression," and the latter interprets it by the word "commence." It is, however, no great discovery, that sin commenced with one man, or that Adam was the first sinner. If sin commenced at all, it must have commenced with some one. And if Adam sinned at all, while yet he stood alone in the world, he must have been the first sinner of the race! President Edwards, in his reply to Dr. Taylor of Norwich, has the following animadversions on this view: "That the world was full of sin, and full of death, were too great and notorious, deeply affecting the interests of mankind; and they seemed very wonderful facts, drawing the attention of the more thinking part of mankind everywhere, who often asked this question, 'whence comes this evil,' moral and natural evil? (the latter chiefly visible in death.) It is manifest the apostle here means to tell us how these came into the world, and prevail in it as they do. But all that is meant, according to Dr Taylor's interpretation, is 'he began transgression,' as if all the apostle meant, was to tell us who happened to sin first, not how such a malady came upon the world, or how any one in the world, besides Adam himself, came by such a distemper."—*Orig. Sin.* p. 270.

The next thing that calls for remark in this verse, is the force of the connecting words "and so" (καὶ οὕτως). They are justly rendered "in this way," "in this manner," "in consequence of which." And therefore, the meaning of the first three clauses of the first verse is, that by one man sin entered into the world, and death by sin, in consequence of which sin of this one man, death passed upon all men.

It will not do to render "and so" by "in like manner," as Prof. Stewart does, and then explain with our author, "there is a connection between death and sin, which existed in the case of Adam, and which subsists in regard to all who sin." This is quite contrary to the acknowledged force of καὶ οὕτως, and besides, entirely destroys the connection which the apostle wishes to establish between the sin of the one man, and the penal evil, or death, that is in the world. It, in effect, says there is no connection whatever between those things although the language may seem to imply it and so large a portion of Christian readers in every age have understood it in this way. Adam sinned and he died, other men have sinned and they died! And yet this verse is allowed to be the first member of a comparison between Adam and Christ! Shall we supply then the other branch of the comparison, thus: Christ was righteous and lived, other men are righteous and they live? If we destroy the connection in the one case, how do we maintain it in the other? *See the supplementary Note at page* 115.

The last clause "for that all have sinned," is to be regarded as explanatory of the sentiment, that death passed on all, in consequence of the sin of the one man. Some have translated ἐφ' ᾧ, in whom; and this, indeed, would assign the only just reason, why all are visited with penal evil on account of Adam's sin. All die through him, because in him all have sinned. But the translation is objectionable, on account of the distance of the antecedent. However, the common rendering gives precisely the same sense, "for that," or "because that" all have sinned, *i. e.* according to an explanation in Bloomfield's Greek Testament, "are considered guilty in the sight of God on account of Adam's fall. Thus, the expression may be considered equivalent to ἁμαρτωλοὶ κατεστάθησαν at ver. 19." There can be no doubt that ἥμαρτον *does* bear this sense, Gen. xliv. 32; xliii. 9. Moreover, the other rendering "because all have sinned personally," is inconsistent with fact. Infants have not sinned in this way, therefore, according to this view, their death is left unaccounted for, and so is all that evil comprehended in the term "death," that comes upon us *antecedent* to actual sin. *See the supplementary Note at page* 115.

Lastly, this interpretation would render the reasoning of the apostle inconclusive. "If," observes Witsius, "we must understand this of some personal sin of each, the reasoning would not have been just, or worthy of the apostle. For his argument would be thus: that by the one sin of one, all were become guilty of death, because each in particular had besides this one and first sin, his own personal sin, which is inconsequential." That men are punished for personal or actual transgression is true. But it is not the particular truth Paul seeks here to establish, any more than he seeks

13 (For until the law, sin was in the world: but sin is not [a] imputed when there is no law.

a chap.4.15; 1 John 3.4.

to prove in the previous part of his epistle, that men are justified on account of *personal* holiness, which is clearly no part of his design.]

13. *For until the law*, &c. This verse, with the following verses to the 17th, is usually regarded as a parenthesis. The *law* here evidently means the law given by Moses. "Until the commencement of that administration, or state of things under the law." To see the reason why he referred to this period *between* Adam and the law, we should recall the design of the apostle, which is, to show the exceeding grace of God in the gospel, abounding, and superabounding, as a complete remedy for all the evils introduced by sin. For this purpose he introduces *three* leading conditions, or states, where men sinned, and where the effects of sin were seen; in regard to *each* and *all* of which the grace of the gospel superabounded. The *first* was that of Adam, with its attendant train of ills (ver. 12,) which ills were all met by the death of Christ, ver. 15—18. The *second* period or condition was that long interval in which men had only the light of nature, that period occurring *between* Adam and Moses. This was a fair representation of the condition of the world without revelation, and without law, ver. 13, 14. Sin *then* reigned—reigned everywhere where there was no law. But the grace of the gospel abounded over the evils of *this* state of man. The *third* was *under* the law, ver. 20. The law entered, and sin was increased, and its evils abounded. But the gospel of Christ abounded even over this, and grace triumphantly reigned. So that the plan of justification met *all* the evils of sin, and was adapted to remove them; sin and its consequences as flowing from Adam; sin and its consequences when there was no written revelation; and sin and its consequences under the light and terrors of the law. ¶ *Sin was in the world.* Men sinned. They did that which was evil. ¶ *But sin is not imputed.* Is not charged on men, or they are not held guilty of it where there is no law. This is a self-evident proposition, for sin is a violation of law; and if there is no law, there can be no wrong. Assuming this as a self-evident proposition, the connection is, that there must have been a law of some kind; a "law written on their hearts," since sin was in the world, and men could not be charged with sin, or treated as sinners, unless there was *some* law. The passage here states a great and important principle, that men will not be held to be guilty unless there is a law which binds them of which they are apprized, and which they voluntarily transgress; see Note, chap. iv. 15. This verse, therefore, meets an objection that might be started from what had been said in chap. iv. 15. The apostle had affirmed that "where no law is there is no transgression." He here stated that all were sinners. It might be objected, that as during this long period of time they had no law, they could not be sinners. To meet this, he says that men were then *in fact* sinners, and were treated as such, which showed that there must have been a law.

14. *Nevertheless.* Notwithstanding that sin is not imputed where there is no law, yet death reigned. ¶ *Death reigned.* Men died; they were under the dominion of death in its various melancholy influences. The expression "death reigned" is one that is very striking. It is a representation of death as a monarch; having dominion over all that period, and over all those generations. Under his dark and withering reign men sank down to the grave. We have a similar expression when we represent death as "the king of terrors." It is a striking and affecting personification, for (1.) His reign is absolute. He strikes down whom he pleases, and when he pleases. (2.) There is no escape. All must bow to his sceptre, and be humbled beneath his hand. (3.) It is universal. Old and young alike are the subjects of his gloomy empire

14 Nevertheless death reigned [a] from Adam to Moses, even over them that had not sinned after the similitude of Adam's transgression, who is the [b] figure of him that was to come.

a Heb.9.27. b 1 Cor.15.22,45.

(4.) It would be an eternal reign if it were not for the gospel. It would shed unmitigated woes upon the earth; and the silent tread of this terrific king would produce only desolation and tears for ever. ¶ *From Adam to Moses.* From the time when God gave one revealed law to Adam, to the time when another revealed law was given to Moses. This was a period of 2500 years; no inconsiderable portion of the history of the world. Whether men were regarded and treated as sinners then, was a very material inquiry in the argument of the apostle. The fact that they *died* is alleged by him as full proof that they were sinners; and that sin had therefore scattered extensive and appalling woes among men. ¶ *Even over them.* Over all those generations. The *point* or *emphasis* of the remark here is, that it reigned over those that had sinned under a different economy from that of Adam. This was that which rendered it so remarkable; and which showed that the withering curse of sin had been felt in all dispensations, and in all times. ¶ *After the similitude, &c.* In the same way; in like manner. The expression "after the similitude" is an Hebraism, denoting in like manner, or *as.* The difference between their case and that of Adam was plainly that Adam had a revealed and positive law. They had not. They had only the law of nature, or of tradition. The giving of a law to Adam, and again to the world by Moses, were two great *epochs* between which no such event had occurred. The race wandered without revelation. The difference contemplated is not that Adam was an *actual* sinner, and that *they* had sinned only by *imputation.* For, (1.) The expression "to sin by imputation" is unintelligible, and conveys no idea. (2.) The apostle makes no such distinction, and conveys no such idea. (3.) His very object is different. It is to show that they *were actual sinners;* that they transgressed law; and the proof of this is that they died. (4.) It is utterly absurd to suppose that men from the time of Adam to Moses were sinners *only by imputation.* All history is against it; nor is there the slightest ground of plausibility in such a supposition. ¶ *Of Adam's transgression.* When he broke a plain, positive revealed law. This transgression was the open violation of a positive precept; theirs the violation of the laws communicated in a different way; by tradition, reason, conscience, &c. Many commentators have supposed that *infants* are particularly referred to here. Augustine first suggested this, and he has been followed by many others. But probably in the whole compass of the expositions of the Bible, there is not to be found a more unnatural and forced construction than this. For, (1.) The apostle makes no mention of infants. He does not in the remotest form allude to them by name, or give any intimation that he had reference to them. (2.) The scope of his argument is against it. Did infants only die? Were they the only persons that lived in this long period? His argument is complete without supposing that he referred to them. The question in regard to this long interval was, whether men were sinners? Yes, says the apostle. *They died.* Death reigned; and this proves that they were sinners. If it should be said that the death of *infants* would prove that *they* were sinners also, I answer, (*a*) That this was an inference which the *apostle* does not draw, and for which he is not responsible. It is not affirmed by him. (*b*) If it did refer to infants, what would it prove? Not that the sin of Adam was imputed, but that they were *personally* guilty, and transgressors. For this is the only point to which the argument tends. The apostle here says not *one word* about imputation. He does not even refer to infants by name; nor does he here introduce at all the doctrine of imputation. All this is mere philosophy introduced to explain difficulties; but whether true or false, whether the theory explains or embarrasses the subject, it is not needful here to inquire. (3.) *The very expression* here is against the supposition that infants are intended. One form of the doctrine of imputation as held by Edwards, Stapfer, &c. has been that there was a constituted oneness or personal identity between Adam and his posterity; and that his sin was regarded as truly and properly theirs; and they as personally blameworthy or ill-deserving for it, in the same manner as a man at 40 is answerable for his crime committed at 20. If this doctrine be true, then it is certain that they not only *had* "sinned after the similitude of Adam's transgression," but had *committed the very identical sin*, and that they were answerable for it as their own. But this doctrine is now abandoned by all or nearly all who profess to be Calvinists; and as the apostle expressly says that they had *not* sinned after the similitude of Adam's transgression, it cannot be intended here. (4.) The same explanation of the passage is given by interpreters who nevertheless held to the doctrine of imputation. Thus CALVIN says on this passage, "Although this passage is understood commonly of infants, who, being guilty of no actual sin, perish by original depravity, yet I prefer that it should be interpreted generally of those who have not the law. For this sentiment is connected with the preceding words, where it is said that sin is not imputed where there is no law. For they had not sinned according to the similitude of Adam's transgression, because they had not as he had the will of God revealed. For the Lord forbid Adam to touch the fruit [of the tree] of the knowledge of good and evil; but to them he gave no command but the testimony of conscience." Calvin, however, supposes that infants are included in the "universal catalogue" here referred to. Turretine also remarks that the discussion here pertains to all the *adults* between Adam and Moses. Indeed, it is perfectly manifest that the apostle here has no particular reference to infants; nor would it have ever been supposed, but for the purpose of giving support to the mere *philosophy* of a theological system.

[According to our author, the disputed clause in ver. 14, "even over them," &c., is to be understood of those who had not sinned against "a revealed or positive law." Many eminent critics have explained the phrase in the same way, and yet arrived at a very different conclusion from that stated in the commentary, viz. that men die simply on account of actual or personal sin.—*Bloomfield Crit. Dig.* vol. v. p. 520. There are, however, very strong objections against this interpretation. 1. It is not consistent with the scope of the passage. The apostle had asserted in ver. 12, that all die in consequence of the sin of the one man (see Supplem. Note). And in the 13th and 14th verses proceeds to prove his position thus:—Men universally die; they must, therefore, have transgressed some law; not the law of Moses, for men died before *that* was in being. Death absolutely reigned between Adam and Moses, even over them who had not broken a revealed law. THEREFORE men have died, in consequence of the sin of the one man. But in this chain of reasoning there is a link awanting. The conclusion does not follow; for though the persons in question had not broken a positive law, they had yet broken the law of nature, written on the heart, and might, therefore, have been condemned on account of a breach of it, Rom. ii. 12. But if we explain the clause under discussion, of infants who have not *personally* sinned *like* Adam against any law whatever, we ascend at once to the conclusion, that all die on account of Adam's sin.

2. The particle "even," (καὶ) seems to intimate, that a new class different from that before mentioned, or at all events a subdivision of it, is now to be introduced. None of all the multitudes that lived between Adam and Moses, had sinned against a positive or revealed law. To avoid an unmeaning tautology therefore, some other sense must be attached to the clause. It is vain to affirm that the particle "even" simply lays "emphasis" on the fact, that they die who had not sinned against a positive law, since were we to admit this forced construction, we should still ask, to what purpose is the emphasis? The fact to which it is supposed to draw attention, as has been noticed already, falls short of proving the apostle's point.

3. Moreover, since "the similitude," &c. is quite a general expression containing no particular intimation in itself, as to that, in which

the likeness consists, we are just as much at liberty to find the resemblance in *personal* transgression, as others, in transgression against revealed laws. To sin personally *is* to sin *like* Adam. Nay, the resemblance in this case is complete; in the other view it is imperfect, scarcely deserving to be called a resemblance at all. For *they who have no revealed law, may yet be said to sin like Adam in some very important respects.* They sin wilfully and presumptuously against the law written in their hearts, in spite of the remonstrances of conscience, &c. The only difference, in fact, lies in the *mode* or *manner* of revelation. But if we suppose the likeness to lie in *personal* sin, we can find a class who have not sinned like Adam *in any way whatever.* And why this class should be supposed omitted, in an argument to prove that all men die in consequence of Adam's sin, it is difficult to conceive.

What though infants are not "alluded to by name?" No one has ever asserted it. Had this been the case, there could have been no dispute on the point. To say, however, that the apostle "does not give any intimation that he had reference to infants," is just a begging of the question, a taking for granted what requires to be proved. Perhaps, as Edwards suggests, "such might be the state of language among Jews and Christians at that day, that the apostle might have no phrase more aptly to express this meaning. The manner in which the epithets personal and actual, are used and applied now in this case, is probably of later date, and more modern use," p. 312, *Orig. Sin.*

The learned author of this commentary objects farther, to the opinion that infants who have not sinned personally are embraced in the clause under discussion; that "to sin by imputation is unintelligible, and conveys no idea." It is his own language, and he alone is responsible for it. He tells us also, that "it is utterly absurd, to suppose that men, from the time of Adam to Moses, were sinners *only by imputation.*" No one ever supposed so, nor does the view, to which he objects, at all involve any such consequence. Again he affirms, "that the scope of the apostle's argument is against the application of the clause to infants;" and asks, for what purpose we cannot divine: "Did infants only die?" The answer is obvious. No! Death reigned over all who lived from Adam to Moses, *even* over that class who had not sinned personally. As to the true scope of the passage, and the view that is most consonant to it, enough has been said already.]

¶ *Who is the figure* (τύπος). *Type.* This word occurs sixteen times in the New Testament, John xx. 25 (twice); Acts vii. 43, 44; xxiii. 25; Rom. v. 14; vi. 17; 1 Cor. x. 6, 11; Phil. iii. 17; 1 Thess. i. 7; 2 Thess. iii. 9; 1 Tim. iv. 12; Titus ii. 7; Heb. viii. 5; 1 Pet. v. 3. It properly means, (1.) Any *impression, note,* or *mark,* which is made by percussion, or in any way, John xx. 25, "the print *(type)* of the nails." (2.) An effigy or image which is made or formed by any rule; a *model,* pattern. Acts vii. 43, "Ye took up the tabernacle of Moloch, and the star of your god Remphan, figures *(types)* which ye had made." 44, "That he should make it [the tabernacle] according to the fashion *(type)* which he had seen," Heb. viii. 5 (3.) A brief argument, or summary, Acts xxiii. 25. (4.) A rule of doctrine, or a law or *form* of doctrine, Rom. vi. 17. (5.) An *example* or model to be imitated; an example of what we ought to be, (Phil. iii. 17; 1 Thess. i. 7; 2 Thess. iii. 9; 1 Tim. iv. 12; Titus ii. 7; 1 Pet. v. 3); or an example which is to be *avoided,* an example to *warn us,* 1 Cor. x. 6, 11. In this place it is evidently applied to the Messiah. The expression "he who was to come" is often used to denote the Messiah. As applied to him, it means that there was in some respects a *similarity* between the results of the conduct of Adam and the effects of the work of Christ. It does not mean that Adam was constituted or appointed *a type* of Christ, which would convey no intelligible idea; but that a *resemblance* may be traced between the *effects* of Adam's conduct and the work of Christ. It does not mean that *the person* of Adam was typical of Christ; but that between the results of his conduct and the work of Christ, *there may be instituted a comparison,* there may be traced some resemblance. What that is, is stated in the following verses. It is mainly by way of *contrast* that the comparison is instituted, and may be stated as consisting in the following points of resemblance or contrast. (1.) *Contrast.* *(a)* By the crime of one, many are dead; by the work of the other, grace will *much more* abound, ver. 15. *(b)* In regard to the *acts* of the two. In the case of Adam, one offence led on the train of

15 But not as the offence, so also *is* the free gift. For if through the offence of one many be dead; much more the grace *a* of God, and the gift by grace, *which is* by one man, Jesus Christ, hath abounded unto many.[b]

a Eph.2.8.

b Isa.53.11; Mat.20.28; 26.28; 1John2.2.

woes; in the case of Christ, his work led to the remission of *many offences*, ver. 16. *(c)* In regard to the effects. *Death* reigned by the one; but life *much more* over the other. (2.) *Resemblance.* By the disobedience of one, many were made sinners; by the obedience of the other, many shall be made righteous, ver. 18, 19. It is clear, therefore, that the comparison which is instituted is rather by way of *antithesis* or *contrast*, than by direct resemblance. *The main design is to show that greater benefits have resulted from the work of Christ, than evils from the fall of Adam.* A comparison is also instituted between Adam and Christ in 1 Cor. xv. 22, 45. The reason is, that Adam was the first of the race; he was the fountain, the head, the father; and the consequences of that first act could be seen everywhere. By a divine constitution the race was so connected with him, that it was made certain that, if he fell, all would come into the world with a nature depraved, and subject to calamity and death, and would be treated as if fallen, and his sin would thus spread crime, and woe, and death everywhere. The evil effects of the apostacy were everywhere seen; and the object of the apostle was to show that the plan of salvation was adapted to meet and more than countervail the evil effects of the fall. He argued on great and acknowledged facts—that Adam was the first sinner, and that from him, as a fountain, sin and death had flowed through the world. Since the consequences of that sin had been so disastrous and wide-spread, his design is to show that from the Messiah effects had flowed more beneficent than the former were ruinous.

"In him the tribes of Adam boast
More blessings than their father lost."
WATTS.

15. *But not as the offence.* This is the first point of *contrast* between the effect of the sin of Adam and of the work of Christ. The word *offence* means properly *a fall*, where we *stumble* over any thing lying in our way. It then means *sin* in general, or crime, Mat. vi. 14, 15; xviii. 35. Here it means the fall, or first sin of Adam. We use the word *fall* as applied to Adam, to denote his first offence, as being that act by which he *fell* from an elevated state of obedience and happiness into one of sin and condemnation. ¶ *So also.* The gift is *not* in its nature and effects like the offence. ¶ *The free gift.* The favour, benefit, or good bestowed gratuitously on us. It refers to the favours bestowed in the gospel by Christ. These are *free, i. e.* without merit on our part, and bestowed on the undeserving. ¶ *For if,* &c. The apostle does not labour *to prove* that this *is* so. This is not the point of his *argument.* He assumes that as what was seen and known every where. His *main point* is to show that greater benefits have resulted from the work of the Messiah than evils from the fall of Adam. ¶ *Through the offence of one.* By the fall of one. This simply *concedes the fact* that it is so. The apostle does not attempt an explanation of the *mode* or *manner* in which it happened. He neither says that it is by *imputation*, nor by *inherent depravity*, nor by *imitation.* Whichever of these modes may be the proper one of accounting for the fact, it is certain that the apostle *states* neither. His object was, not to *explain* the manner in which it was done, but to argue from the acknowledged existence of the fact. All that is certainly established from *this* passage is, that as a certain fact resulting from the transgression of Adam, "many" were "dead." This simple fact is all that can be proved from this passage. Whether it is to be explained by the doctrine of imputation, is to be a subject of inquiry independent of this passage. Nor

have we a right to *assume* that this teaches the doctrine of the imputation of the sin of Adam to his posterity. For, (1.) The apostle says nothing of it. (2.) That doctrine is nothing but an effort to explain the *manner* of an event which the apostle Paul did not think it proper to attempt to explain. (3.) That doctrine is in fact no explanation. It is introducing an additional difficulty. For to say that I am blameworthy, or ill-deserving for a sin in which I had no agency, is no *explanation*, but is involving me in an additional difficulty still more perplexing, to ascertain how such a doctrine can possibly be just. The way of wisdom would be, doubtless, to rest satisfied with the simple statement of a fact which the apostle has assumed, without attempting to explain it by a philosophical theory. Calvin accords with the above interpretation. "For we do not so perish by his [Adam's] crime, as if we were ourselves innocent; but Paul ascribes our ruin to him *because his sin is* THE CAUSE *of our sin*."

[This is not a fair quotation from Calvin. It leaves us to infer, that the Reformer affirmed, that Adam's sin is the cause of *actual* sin in us, on account of which last *only* we are condemned. Now under the twelfth verse Calvin says, "The inference is plain, that the apostle *does not treat of actual sin, for if every person was the cause of his own guilt*, why should Paul compare Adam with Christ?" If our author had not stopt short in his quotation, he would have found immediately subjoined, as an explanation: "I call that our sin, which is inbred, and with which we are born." Our being born with this sin is a proof of our guilt in Adam. But whatever opinion may be formed of Calvin's general views on this subject, nothing is more certain, than that he did not suppose the apostle treated of actual sin in these passages.

Notwithstanding of the efforts that are made to exclude the doctrine of imputation from this chapter, *the full and varied manner* in which the apostle expresses it, cannot be evaded. "Through the offence of one many be dead"—"the judgment was by one to condemnation"—"By one man's offence death reigned by one"—"By the offence of one, judgment came upon all men to condemnation"—"By one man's disobedience, many were made sinners," &c.

It is vain to tell us, as our author does under each of these clauses respectively, that the apostle simply *states the fact*, that the sin of Adam has involved the race in condemnation, without adverting to the *manner;* for Paul does more than state the fact. He intimates that we are involved in condemnation in a way that bears a certain analogy to the *manner in which we become righteous*. And on this last, he is, without doubt, sufficiently explicit. *See a former supplem. Note at p.* 115.

In the 18th and 19th verses the apostle seems plainly to affirm the *manner* of the fact "AS by the offence of one," &c., "EVEN so," &c. "As by one man's disobedience," &c., "so," &c. There is a resemblance in the manner of the two things compared. If we wish to know *how* guilt and condemnation come by Adam, we have only to inquire, how righteousness and justification come by Christ. "*So*," *i. e.* in *this* way, not in *like* manner. It is not in a manner that has merely some likeness, but it is in the very same manner, for although there is a contrast in the things, the one being disobedience, and the other obedience, yet there is a perfect identity in the manner.—*Haldane*.

It is somewhat remarkable, that while our author so frequently affirms, that the apostle states the *fact* only, he himself should throughout assume the *manner*. He will not allow the apostle to explain the manner, nor any one who has a different view of it from himself. Yet he tells us, it is *not* by imputation that we become involved in Adam's guilt; that men "sin in their own persons, and that *therefore* they die." This he affirms to be the apostle's meaning. And is this not an explanation of the manner. Are we not left to conclude, that from Adam we simply derive a corrupt nature, in consequence of which we sin personally, and therefore die?]

¶ *Many*. Greek, *The many*. Evidently meaning *all;* the whole race; Jews and Gentiles. That it means *all* here is proved in ver. 18. If the inquiry be, why the apostle used the word "*many*" rather than *all*, we may reply, that the design was to express an *antithesis*, or contrast to the cause —one offence. *One* stands opposed to *many*, rather than to *all*. ¶ *Be dead*; see Note on the word *death*, ver. 12. The race is under the dark and gloomy reign of death. This is a simple fact which the apostle assumes, and which no man can deny. ¶ *Much more*. The reason of this "much more" is to be found in the abounding mercy and goodness of God. If a wise, merciful, and good Being has suffered such a train of woes to be introduced by the offence of one, have we not much more reason to expect that his grace will superabound? ¶ *The grace of God.* The favour or kindness of God We have reason to expect under the administration of God more extensive benefits, than we have ills, flowing from a constitution of things which is the result of his appointment. ¶ *And the gift by grace.* The gracious gift; the benefits flowing from that grace. This refers to the blessings of salvation. ¶ Which is *by one man.* Standing in contrast with Adam. His appointment was the result of grace; and as he was constituted to bestow favours, we have reason to expect that they will superabound. ¶ *Hath abounded.* Has been abundant, or ample; will be more than a counterbalance for the ills which have been introduced by the sin of Adam. ¶ *Unto many.* Greek, Unto the many. The obvious interpretation of this is, that it is as unlimited as "the many" who are dead. Some have supposed that Adam represented *the whole* of the human race, and Christ a part, and that "the many" in the two members of the verse refer to the *whole* of those who were thus represented. But this is to do violence to the passage; and to introduce a theological doctrine to meet a supposed difficulty in the text. The obvious meaning is—one from which we cannot depart without doing violence to the proper laws of interpretation—that "the many" in the two cases are co-extensive; and that as the sin of Adam has involved the race—the many—in death; so the grace of Christ has abounded *in reference to* the many, to the race. If asked how this can be possible, since all have not been, and will not be savingly benefitted by the work of Christ, we may reply, (1.) That it *cannot* mean that the benefits of the work of Christ should be *literally* co-extensive with the results of Adam's sin, since it is a fact that men *have* suffered, and *do* suffer, from the effects of that fall. In order that the Universalist may draw an argument from this, he must show that it was the design of Christ to destroy ALL the effects of the sin of Adam. But this has *not* been in fact. Though the favours of that work have abounded, yet men have suffered and died. And though it may still abound to *the many,* yet some may suffer here, and suffer on the same principle for ever. (2.) Though men are indubitably affected by the sin of Adam, as *e. g.* by being born with a corrupt disposition; with loss of righteousness, with subjection to pain and woe; and with exposure to eternal death; yet there is reason to believe that all those who die in infancy are, through the merits of the Lord Jesus, and by an influence which we cannot explain, changed and prepared for heaven. As nearly half the race die in infancy, therefore there is reason to think that, in regard to this large portion of the human family, the work of Christ has more than repaired the evils of the fall, and introduced them into heaven, and that his grace has *thus* abounded unto many. In regard to those who live to the period of moral agency, a scheme has been introduced by which the offers of salvation may be made to them, and by which they may be renewed, and pardoned, and saved. The work of Christ, therefore, may have introduced advantages adapted to meet the evils of the fall as man comes into the world; and the original applicability of the one be as extensive as the other. In this way the work of Christ was *in its nature* fitted to abound unto the many. (3.) The intervention of the plan of atonement by the Messiah, prevented the immediate execution of the penalty of the law, and produced *all* the benefits to *all* the race, resulting from the sparing mercy of God. In this respect it was co-extensive with the fall. (4.) He died for all the race, Heb. ii. 9; 2 Cor. v. 14, 15; 1 John ii. 2. Thus his death, in its adaptation to a great and glorious result, was as extensive as the ruins of the fall. (5.) The *offer* of salvation is made to all, Rev. xxii. 17; John vii. 37; Mat. xi. 28, 29; Mark xvi. 15. Thus his grace has extended unto the many—to all the race. Provision has been made to meet the evils of the fall; a provision as extensive in its applicability as was the ruin. (6.) More *will* probably be actually saved by the work of Christ, than will be finally ruined by the fall of Adam. The number of those who shall be saved from all the human race, it is to be believed, will yet be many more than those who shall be lost. The gospel is to spread throughout the world. It is to be evangelized. The millennial glory is to rise upon the earth; and the Saviour is to reign with undivided empire. Taking the race as a whole, there is no reason to think that the number of those who shall be lost, compared with the immense multitudes that shall be saved by the work of Christ, will be more than are the *prisoners* in a community now, compared with the number of peaceful and virtuous citizens. A medicine may be discovered that shall be said to *triumph* over disease, though it may have been the fact that thousands *have* died since its discovery, and thousands yet *will not* avail themselves of it; yet the medicine shall have the properties of universal triumph; it is adapted to the many; it might be applied by the many; where it *is* applied, it completely answers the end. Vaccination is adapted to meet the evils of the small-pox every where; and *when* applied, saves men from the ravages of this terrible disease, though thousands may die to whom it is not applied. It is a *triumphant* remedy. So of the plan of salvation. Thus, though all shall not be saved, yet the sin of Adam shall be counteracted; and grace abounds unto the many. All this fulness of grace the apostle says we have reason to expect from the abounding mercy of God.

[The "many" in the latter clause of this verse, cannot be regarded as co-extensive with the "many" that are said to be dead through the offence of Adam. Very much is affirmed of the "many to whom grace abounds," that cannot, "without doing violence to the whole passage," be applied to *all* mankind. They are said to "*receive* the gift of righteousness," and to "reign in life." They are actually "constituted righteous," (ver. 19) and these things cannot be said of all men *in any sense whatever*. The only way of explaining the passage, therefore, is to adopt that view which our author has introduced only to condemn, viz. "that Adam represented the whole of the human race, and Christ a part, and that 'the many in the two members of the verse, refers to the whole of those who were thus represented."

The same principle of interpretation must be adopted in the parallel passage, "As in Adam all die, so in Christ shall all be made alive." It would be preposterous to affirm, that "the all" in the latter clause is co-extensive with "the all" in the former. The sense plainly is, that all whom Christ represented should be made alive in him, even as all mankind, or all represented by Adam, had died in him.

It is true indeed that all mankind are i some sense benefitted on account of the atonement of Christ: and our author has enlarged on several things of this nature, which yet fall short of "saving benefit." But will it be maintained, that the apostle in reality affirms no more than that the many to whom grace abounds, participate in certain benefits, short of salvation? If so, what becomes of the comparison between Adam and Christ? If "the many" in the one branch of the comparison are only benefitted by Christ in a way that falls short of saving benefit, then "the many" in the other branch must be affected by the fall of Adam only in the same limited way, whereas the apostle affirms that in consequence of it they are *really* "dead."

"The principal thing," says Mr. Scott, "which renders the expositions generally given of these verses perplexed and unsatisfactory, arises from an evident misconception of the apostle's reasoning, in supposing that Adam and Christ represented exactly the same company; whereas Adam was the surety of the whole human species, as his posterity; Christ, only of that chosen remnant, which has been, or shall be one with him by faith, who alone 'are counted to him for a generation.' If we exclusively consider the benefits which believers derive from Christ as compared with the loss sustained in Adam by the human race, we shall then see the passage open most perspicuously and gloriously to our view."—*Commentary*, ch. v. 15, 19.

But our author does not interpret this passage upon any consistent principle. For "the many" in the 15th verse, to whom "grace abounded" are obviously the same with those in the 17th verse, who are said to receive abundance of grace, &c., and yet he interprets the one of all mankind, and the other of believers only. What is asserted in the 17th verse, he says, "is particularly true of the redeemed, of whom the apostle in this verse is speaking."]

16. *And not,* &c. This is the *second* point in which the effects of the work of Christ differ from the sin of Adam.

16 And not as *it was* by one
that sinned, *so is* the gift: for
the judgment *was* by one to
condemnation; but the free gift
is of many [a] offences unto justification.
17 For if [1] by one man's offence
death reigned by one; much more

a Is. 1. 18.

1 or, *by one offence*.

The *first* part (ver. 15) was, that the evil consequences flowed from the sin of *one* MAN, Adam; and that the benefits flowed from the work of *one* MAN, Jesus Christ. The point in this verse is, that the evil consequences flowed from *one* CRIME, one act of guilt; but that the favours had respect to MANY ACTS of guilt. The effects of Adam's sin, whatever they were, pertained to the *one sin;* the effects of the work of Christ, to *many sins.* ¶ *By one that sinned* (δι' ἑνὸς ἁμαρτήσαντος). By means of *one* [*man*] *sinning;* evidently meaning by *one offence,* or by one act of sin. So the Vulgate, and many MSS. And the connection shows that this is the sense. ¶ *The gift.* The benefits resulting from the work of Christ. ¶ *The judgment.* The sentence; the declared penalty. The word expresses properly the *sentence* which is passed by a judge. Here it means the *sentence* which God passed, as a judge, on Adam for the one offence, involving himself and his posterity in ruin, Gen. ii. 17; iii. 17—19. ¶ *Was by one.* By one offence; or one act of sin. ¶ *Unto condemnation.* Producing condemnation; or involving in condemnation. It is proved by this, that the effect of the sin of Adam was to involve the race in condemnation, or to secure this as a result that all mankind would be under the condemning sentence of the law, and be transgressors. But *in what way* it would have this effect, the apostle does not state. He does not intimate that his sin would be imputed to them; or that they would be held to be personally guilty for it. He speaks of a broad, every where perceptible fact, that the effect of that sin had been somehow to whelm the race in condemnation. In what *mode* this was done is a fair subject of inquiry; but the apostle does not attempt to explain it. ¶ *The free gift.* The unmerited favour, by the work of Christ. ¶ *Is of many offences.* In *relation* to many sins. It differs thus from the condemnation. That had respect to one offence; this has respect to many crimes. Grace therefore abounds. ¶ *Unto justification;* Note, chap. iii. 24. The work of Christ is designed to have reference to many offences, so as to produce pardon or justification in regard to them all. But the apostle here does not intimate *how* this is done. He simply states the fact, without attempting in this place to explain it; and as we know that that work does not produce its effect to *justify* without some act on the part of the individual, are we not hence led to conclude the same respecting the condemnation for the sin of Adam? As the work of Christ does not benefit the race unless it is embraced, so does not the reasoning of the apostle imply, that the deed of Adam does not involve in criminality and ill-desert unless there be some voluntary act on the part of each individual? However this may be, it is certain that the apostle has in neither case here explained the *mode* in which it is done. He has simply stated the *fact,* a fact which he did not seem to consider himself called on to explain. Neither has he affirmed that in the two cases the *mode* is the same. On the contrary, it is strongly implied that it is *not* the same, for the leading object here is to present, not an entire *resemblance,* but a strong contrast between the effects of the sin of Adam and the work of Christ.

17. *For if.* This verse contains the same idea as before presented, but in a varied form. It is *condensing* the whole subject, and presenting it in a single view. ¶ *By one man's offence.* Or, by one offence. Margin. The reading of the text is the more correct. "If, under the administration of a just and merciful Being, it has occurred, that by the offence of one,

they which receive abundance [a] of grace, and of the gift [b] of righteousness shall reign in life by one, Jesus Christ:)

18 Therefore, as [1] by the offence of one *judgment came* upon all men to condemnation; even so [2] by the righteousness of one *the*

a John10.10. *b* chap.6.23. 1 or, *by one offence.* 2 or, *by one righteousness.*

death hath exerted so wide a dominion; we have reason much more to expect under that administration, that they who are brought under his plan of saving mercy shall be brought under a dispensation of life." ¶ *Death reigned;* Note, ver. 14. ¶ *By one.* By means of one man. ¶ *Much more.* We have much more reason to expect it. It evidently accords much more with the administration of a Being of infinite goodness. ¶ *They which receive abundance of grace.* The *abundant favour;* the mercy that shall counterbalance and surpass the evils introduced by the sin of Adam. That favour shall be more than sufficient to counterbalance all those evils. This is particularly true of the redeemed, of whom the apostle in this verse is speaking. The evils which *they* suffer in consequence of the sin of Adam bear no comparison with the mercies of eternal life that shall flow to them from the work of the Saviour. ¶ *The gift of righteousness.* This stands opposed to the evils introduced by Adam. As the effect of his sin was to produce condemnation, so here the gift of righteousness refers to the opposite, to pardon, to justification, to acceptance with God. To show that men were thus justified by the gospel, was the leading design of the apostle; and the argument here is, that if by one man's sin, death reigned over those who were under condemnation in consequence of it, we have much more reason to suppose that they who are delivered from sin by the death of Christ, and accepted of God, shall reign with him in life. ¶ *Shall reign.* The word *reign* is often applied to the condition of saints in heaven, 2 Tim. ii. 12, "If we suffer, we shall also reign with him;" Rev. v. 10; xx. 6; xxii. 5. It means that they shall be exalted to a glorious state of happiness in heaven; that they shall be triumphant over all their enemies; shall gain an ultimate victory; and shall partake with the Captain of their salvation in the splendours of his dominion above, Rev. iii. 21; Luke xxii. 30. ¶ *In life.* This stands opposed to the *death* that reigned as the consequence of the sin of Adam. It denotes complete freedom from condemnation; from temporal death; from sickness, pain, and sin. It is the usual expression to denote the complete bliss of the saints in glory; Note, John iii. 36. ¶ *By one, Jesus Christ.* As the consequence of his work. The apostle here does not state the *mode* or manner in which this was done; nor does he say that it was perfectly parallel in the mode with the effects of the sin of Adam. He is comparing the *results* or *consequences* of the sin of the one and of the work of the other. There is a similarity in the consequences. The way in which the work of Christ had contributed to this he had stated in chap. iii. 24, 28.

18. *Therefore.* Wherefore (Ἄρα οὖν). This is properly a *summing up,* a recapitulation of what had been stated in the previous verses. The apostle resumes the statement or proposition made in ver. 12, and after the intermediate explanation in the parenthesis (ver. 13—17), in this verse and the following, sums up the whole subject. The explanation, therefore, of the previous verses is designed to convey the real meaning of ver. 18, 19. ¶ *As by the offence of one.* Admitting this as an undisputed and every where apparent fact, a fact which no one can call in question. ¶ *Judgment came.* This is not in the Greek, but it is evidently implied, and is stated in ver. 16. The meaning is, that all have been brought under the reign of death by one man. ¶ *Upon all men.* The whole race. This explains what is meant by "the many" in ver. 15. ¶ *To condemna-*

free gift came upon all [a] men unto justification of life.

19 For as by one man's disobedience many were made sinners, so by the obedience of one shall many be made righteous.

a John 12.32.

tion; ver. 16. ¶ *Even so.* In the manner explained in the previous verses. With the same certainty, and to the same extent. The apostle does not explain the *mode* in which it was done, but simply states the *fact.* ¶ *By the righteousness of one.* This stands opposed to the *one offence* of Adam, and must mean, therefore, the holiness, obedience, purity of the Redeemer. The *sin* of one man involved men in ruin; the *obedience unto death* of the other (Phil. ii. 8) restored them to the favour of God. ¶ *Came upon all men* (εἰς πάντας ἀνθρώπους). Was with reference to all men; had a bearing upon all men; was *originally adapted* to the race. As the sin of Adam was of such a nature in the relation in which he stood as to affect all the race, so the work of Christ in the relation in which he stood was adapted also to all the race. As the tendency of the one was to involve the race in condemnation, so the tendency of the other was to restore them to acceptance with God. There was an *original applicability* in the work of Christ to all men—a richness, a fulness of the atonement fitted to meet the sins of the entire world, and restore the race to favour. ¶ *Unto justification of life.* With reference to that justification which is connected with eternal life. That is, his work is *adapted* to produce acceptance with God, to the same extent as the crime of Adam has affected the race by involving them in sin and misery The apostle does not affirm that in fact as many *will be* affected by the one as by the other; but that it is fitted to meet all the consequences of the fall; to be as wide-spread in its effects; and to be as salutary as that had been ruinous. This is all that the argument requires. Perhaps there could not be found a more striking declaration any where, that the work of Christ had *an original applicability* to all men; or that it is in its own nature fitted to save all. The course of argument here leads inevitably to this; nor is it possible to avoid it without doing violence to the obvious and fair course of the discussion. It does not prove that all will in fact be saved, but that the plan is *fitted* to meet all the evils of the fall. A certain kind of medicine may have an original applicability to heal all persons under the same disease; and may be abundant and certain, and yet *in fact* be applied to few. The sun is fitted to give light to all, yet many may be blind, or may voluntarily close their eyes. Water is adapted to the wants of all men, and the supply may be ample for the human family, yet *in fact,* from various causes, many may be deprived of it. So of the provisions of the plan of redemption. They are adapted to all; they are ample, and yet *in fact,* from causes which this is not the place to explain, the benefits, like those of medicine, water, science, &c. may never be enjoyed by all the race. *Calvin* concurs in this interpretation, and thus shows that it is one which commends itself even to the most strenuous advocates of the system which is called by his name. He says, "He [the apostle] makes the grace common to all, because it is offered to all, not because it is in fact applied to all. *For although Christ suffered for the sins* OF THE WHOLE WORLD (nam etsi passus est Christus pro peccatis totius mundi),and it is offered to all without distinction (indifferenter), yet all do not embrace it." See Cal. Comm. on this place.*

19. *For,* &c.. This verse is not a *mere* repetition of the former, but it is an explanation. By the former statements it might perhaps be inferred that men were condemned without any guilt or blame of theirs. The apostle in this verse guards against this, and affirms that they are *in fact sinners.* He affirms that

*** See the opposite view stated in a supplementary Note at page 131.**

those who are sinners are condemned, and that the sufferings brought in on account of the sin of Adam, are introduced because many were made *sinners*. *Calvin* says, " Lest any one should arrogate to himself innocence, [the apostle] adds, that *each one is condemned because he is a sinner*."

[The same objection which was stated against a previous quotation from Calvin, applies here. The reformer does not mean that each is condemned because he is *actually* a sinner. He affirms that the *ground* of condemnation lies in something with which we are born, which belongs to us *antecedent* to actual transgression.]

¶ *By one man's disobedience*. By means of the sin of Adam. This affirms simply the fact that such a result followed from the sin of Adam. The word *by* (δια) is used in the Scriptures as it is in all books and in all languages. It may denote the efficient cause; the instrumental cause; the principal cause; the meritorious cause; or the chief occasion by which a thing occurred. (See *Schleusner*.) It does not express one mode, and one only, in which a thing is done; but that one thing is the result of another. When we say that a young man is ruined in his character *by* another, we do not express the *mode*, but the *fact*. When we say that thousands have been made infidels *by* the writings of Paine and Voltaire, we make no affirmation about the mode, but about the fact. In each of these, and in all other cases, we should deem it most inconclusive reasoning to attempt to determine the mode by the preposition *by;* and still more absurd if it were argued from the use of that preposition that the sins of the seducer were *imputed* to the young man; or the opinions of Paine and Voltaire *imputed* to infidels.

[What is here said of the various significations of δια is true. Yet it will not be denied, that in a multitude of instances it points to the *real* cause or ground of a thing. The sense is to be determined by the connection. "We have in this single passage no less than three cases, ver. 12, 18, 19, in which this preposition with the genitive indicates the *ground or reason* on account of which something is given or performed. All this is surely sufficient to prove that it may, in the case before us, express the ground why the sentence of condemnation has passed upon all men." To draw an illustration from the injury inflicted by Voltaire and Paine, will not serve the author's purpose, till he can prove, that *they* stand in a relation, to those whom they have injured, similar to that which Adam bears to the human family. When we say that thousands have been ruined by Voltaire, it is true we can have no idea of imputation; yet we *may* fairly entertain such an idea when it is said, "all mankind have been ruined *by* Adam."]

¶ *Many*. Greek, *The many*, ver. 15. ¶ *Were made* (κατεσταθησαν). The verb here used, occurs in the New Testament in the following places: Mat. xxiv. 45, 47; xxv. 21, 23; Luke xii. 14, 42, 44; Acts vi. 3; vii. 10, 27, 35; xvii. 15; Rom. v. 19; Titus i. 5; Heb. ii. 7; v. 1; vii. 28; viii. 3; James iii. 6; iv. 4; 2 Pet. i. 8. It usually means to constitute, set, or appoint. In the New Testament it has *two* leading significations. (1.) To appoint to an office, to set over others (Mat. xxiv. 45, 47; Luke xii. 42, &c.); and (2.) It means to *become*, to be in fact, &c.; James iii. 6, "So *is* the tongue among our members," &c. That is, it *becomes* such; James iv. 4, "The friendship of the world *is* enmity with God; it becomes such; it is *in fact* thus, and is thus to be regarded. The word is *in no instance* used to express the idea of *imputing that to one which belongs to another*. It here either means that this was *by a constitution of divine appointment* that they in fact became *sinners*, or simply declares that they *were* so in fact. There is not the slightest intimation that it was by imputation. The whole scope of the argument is, moreover, against this; for the object of the apostle is not to show that they were charged with the sin of another, but that they were in fact *sinners* themselves. If it means that they were condemned for *his* act, without any concurrence of their own will, then the correspondent part will be true, that all are constituted righteous in the same way; and thus the doctrine of universal salvation will be inevitable. But as none are constituted righteous who do not voluntarily avail themselves of the provisions of mercy, so it follows that those who are condemned, are not condemned for the sin of another without their own concurrence, nor unless they personally deserve it.

[Does not the word κατεσταθησαν, in the last clause of this verse intimate that we are *really and directly* made righteous, by the obedience of Christ, *without the intervention of any obedience of our own?* Why then may not the same word in the first clause, intimate that we are made sinners by the disobedience of Adam, without the intervention of any disobedience of our own? It is impossible otherwise to explain the analogy between Adam and Christ.

That we are involved in Adam's guilt "without (rather before) any concurrence of our own will" is true, and capable of proof from the author's own admission, that we *come into the world* with a depraved nature. But that our will is not concerned in the reception of righteousness, does not follow. To this, except in the case of infants, *faith* is essential, chap. i. 17; iii. 22. It is not a little surprising, that the commentator should, in one place, deny that there is any resemblance between the *manner* in which sin and righteousness are respectively communicated, and, in another, gravely argue upon the analogy, and that too, after having stretched it beyond its legitimate bounds!

"This whole reasoning of the apostle," says Principal Hill in his concluding observation on these verses, "favours the notion of an imputation of Adam's sin. The phrase, indeed, does not occur, but the thing meant by the phrase appears to be the natural meaning of the passage; and I know no better way in which you can satisfy yourselves that it is the true meaning, than by comparing the interpretation now given, with the forced paraphrases, to which those are obliged to have recourse, who wish to show that the fourth opinion (of imputation) does not receive any countenance from the authority of Paul."—*Hill's Lectures*, vol. 2. p. 28, 3d. edit.]

¶ *Sinners.* Transgressors; those who deserve to be punished. It does not mean those who are condemned for the sin of another; but those who are violators of the law of God. All who are condemned are *sinners.* They are not *innocent* persons condemned for the crime of another. Men may be involved in the *consequences* of the sins of others without being to blame. The consequences of the crimes of a murderer, a drunkard, a pirate may pass over from them, and affect thousands, and whelm them in ruin. But this does not prove that they are blameworthy. In the divine administration none are *regarded* as guilty who are not guilty; none are condemned who do not *deserve* to be condemned. All who sink to hell are *sinners.* ¶ *By the obedience of one.* Of Christ. This stands opposed to the *disobedience* of Adam, and evidently includes the entire work of the Redeemer which has a bearing on the salvation of men; Phil. ii. 8, "He... became *obedient* unto death." *Shall many.* Greek, *The many;* corresponding to the term in the former part of the verse, and evidently commensurate with it; for there is no reason for limiting it to *a part* in this member, any more than there is in the former. ¶ *Be made.* The same Greek word as before—be appointed, or *become.* The apostle has explained the mode in which this is done; chap. i. 17; iii. 24—26; iv. 1—5. That explanation is to limit the meaning here. No more are considered righteous than become so *in that way.* And as *all* do *not* become righteous thus, the passage cannot be adduced to prove the doctrine of universal salvation.

The following remarks may express the doctrines which are established by this much-contested and difficult passage. (1.) Adam was created holy; capable of obeying law; yet free to fall. (2.) A law was given him, adapted to his condition—simple, plain, easy to be obeyed, and fitted to give human nature a trial in circumstances as favourable as possible. (3.) Its violation exposed him to the threatened penalty as he had understood it, and to all the collateral woes which it might carry in its train—involving, as subsequent developments showed, the loss of God's favour; his displeasure evinced in man's toil, and sweat, and sickness, and death; in hereditary depravity, and the curse, and the pains of hell for ever. (4.) Adam was the head of the race; he was the fountain of being; and human nature was so far tried in him, that it may be said he was on trial not for himself alone, but for his posterity, inasmuch as his fall would involve them in ruin. Many nave chosen to call this a covenant, and to speak of him as a federal head; and if the above account is the idea involved in these terms, the explanation is not exceptionable. As the word covenant, however, is not applied in the transaction in the Bible, and as it is liable to be misunderstood, others prefer to speak of it as a *law* given to Adam, and as *a divine constitution*, under which he was placed. (5.) *His posterity are, in consequence of his sin, subjected to the same train of ills as if they had been personally the transgressors.* Not that they are regarded as personally ill-deserving, or criminal for his sin,* God reckons things as they are, and not falsely, (see Note, chap. iv. 3,) and his imputations are all according to truth. He regarded Adam as standing at the head of the race; and regards and treats all his posterity as coming into the world subject to pain, and death, and depravity, as a consequence of his sin; see Note, p. 128. This is the Scripture idea of imputation; and this is what has been commonly meant when it has been said that "the GUILT of his first sin"—*not the sin itself*—"is imputed to his posterity." (6.) There is *something* antecedent to the moral action of his posterity, and growing out of the relation which they sustain to him, which makes it certain that they will sin as soon as they begin to act as moral agents. What this is, we may not be able to say; but we may be certain that it is not physical depravity, or any created essence of the soul, or any thing which prevents the first act of sin from being voluntary. This hereditary tendency to sin has been usually called "original sin;" and this the apostle evidently teaches. (7.) As an infant comes into the world with a certainty that he will sin as soon as he becomes a moral agent here, there is the same certainty that, if he were removed to eternity, he would sin there also, unless he were changed. There is, therefore, need of the blood of the atonement and of the agency of the Holy Ghost, that an infant may be saved. (8.) The *facts* here stated accord with all the analogy in the moral government of God. The drunkard secures as a result commonly, that his family will be reduced to beggary, want, and woe. A pirate, or a traitor, will whelm not himself only, but his family in ruin. Such is the great law or constitution on which society is now organized; and we are not to be surprised that the same *principle* occurred in the *primary organization* of human affairs. (9.) As this is the *fact* every where, the analogy disarms all objections which have been made against the scriptural statements of the effects of the sin of Adam. If just *now*, it was just *then*. If it exists *now*, it existed *then*. (10.) The doctrine should be left, therefore, simply as it is in the Scriptures. It is there the simple statement of *a fact*, without any attempt at explanation. That fact accords with all that we see and feel. It is a great principle in the constitution of things, that the conduct of one man may pass over in its effects on others, and have an influence on their happiness. The simple fact in regard to Adam is, that he sinned; and that such is the organization of the great society of which he was the head and father, that his sin has secured as a certain result that all the race will be sinners also. *How* this is, the Bible has not explained. It is a part of a great system of things. That it is *unjust* no man can prove, for none can show that any sinner suffers more than he deserves. That it is *wise* is apparent, for it is attended with numberless blessings. It is connected with all the advantages that grow out of the social organization. The race *might* have been composed of *independent individuals*, where the conduct of an individual, good or evil, might have affected no one but himself. But then *society* would have been impossible. All the benefits of organization into families, and communities, and nations would have been unknown. Man would have lived alone; wept alone; rejoiced alone; died alone. There would have been no sympathy; no compassion; no mutual aid. God has therefore *grouped* the race into

* See the foregoing Supplementary Notes.

20 Moreover,[a] the law entered, that the offence might abound.

a John 15.22; chap.7.8-13; Gal.3.19.

separate communities. He has organized society. He has constituted families, tribes, clans, nations; and though on the general principle the conduct of one *may* whelm another in misery, yet the union, the grouping, the constitution, is the source of most of the blessings which man enjoys in this life, and may be of numberless mercies in regard to that which is to come. If it was the organization on which the race might be plunged into sin, it is also the organization on which it may be raised to life eternal. If, on the one hand, it may be abused to produce misery, it may, on the other, be improved to the advancement of peace, sympathy, friendship, prosperity, salvation. At all events, such *is* the organization in common life and in religion, and it becomes man not to murmur, but to *act* on it, and to endeavour, by the tender mercy of God, to turn it to his welfare here and hereafter. As by this organization, through Adam, he has been plunged into sin, so by the same organization, he shall, through "the second Adam," rise to life, and ascend to the skies.

20. *Moreover.* But. What is said in this verse and the following, seems designed to meet the Jew, who might pretend that the law of Moses was intended to meet the evils of sin introduced by Adam, and therefore that the scheme defended by the apostle was unnecessary. He therefore shows them that the *effect* of the law of Moses was to *increase* rather than to *diminish* the sins which had been introduced into the world. And if *such* was the fact, it could not be pled that it was adapted to overcome the acknowledged evils of the apostacy. ¶ *The law.* The Mosaic laws and institutions. The word seems to be used here to denote *all* the laws which were given in the Old Testament. ¶ *Entered.* This word usually means *to enter secretly* or *surreptitiously*. But it appears to be used here simply in the sense that the law came in, or was given. It came in addition to, or it supervened the state before Moses, when men were living without a revelation. ¶ *That sin,* &c. The word "that" (ἵνα) in this place does not mean that it was the *design* of giving the law that sin might abound or be increased, but that such was *in fact* the effect. It had this tendency, not to restrain or subdue sin, but to excite and increase it. That the word has this sense may be seen in the lexicons. The way in which the law produces this effect is stated more fully by the apostle in chap. vii. 7—11. The law expresses the duty of man; it is spiritual and holy; it is opposed to the guilty passions and pleasures of the world; and it thus excites opposition, provokes to anger, and is the occasion by which sin is called into exercise, and shows itself in the heart. All law, where there is a *disposition* to do wrong, has this tendency. A command given to a child that is *disposed* to indulge his passions, only tends to excite anger and opposition. If the heart was holy, and there was a disposition to do right, law would have no such tendency. See this subject further illustrated in the Notes on chap. vii. 7—11. ¶ *The offence.* The offence which had been introduced by Adam, *i. e.* sin. Compare ver. 15. ¶ *Might abound.* Might increase; that is, would be more apparent, more violent, more extensive. The introduction of the Mosaic law, instead of diminishing the sins of men, only increases them. ¶ *But where sin abounded.* Alike in all dispensations —before the law, and under the law. In all conditions of the human family before the gospel, it was the characteristic that sin was prevalent. ¶ *Grace.* Favour; mercy. ¶ *Did much more abound.* Superabounded. The word is used no where else in the New Testament, except in 2 Cor. vii. 4. It means that the pardoning mercy of the gospel greatly triumphed over sin, even over the sins of the Jews, though those sins were greatly aggravated by the light which they enjoyed under the advantages of divine revelation.

21. *That as sin hath reigned;* Note,

But where sin abounded, grace did much more [a] abound;
21 That as sin hath reigned unto death, even so might grace [b] reign through righteousness, unto eternal life, by Jesus Christ our Lord.

[a] John 10.10; 1 Ti.1.14. [b] John 1.17.

ver. 14. ¶ *Unto death.* Producing or causing death. ¶ *Even so.* In like manner, also. The provisions of redemption are in themselves ample to meet all the ruins of the fall. ¶ *Might grace reign.* Might mercy be triumphant; see John i. 17, "Grace and truth came by Jesus Christ." ¶ *Through righteousness.* Through, or by means of, God's plan of justification; Note, chap. i. 17. ¶ *Unto eternal life.* This stands opposed to "death" in the former part of the verse, and shows that there the apostle had reference to *eternal* death. The result of God's plan of justification shall be to produce *eternal life.* The triumphs of the gospel here celebrated cannot refer to the *number* of the subjects, for it has not actually freed all men from the dominion of sin. But the apostle refers to the fact that the gospel is able to overcome sin of the most malignant form, of the most aggravated character, of the longest duration. Sin in all dispensations and states of things can be thus overcome; and the gospel is more than sufficient to meet *all* the evils of the apostacy, and to raise up the race to heaven.

This chapter is a most precious portion of divine revelation. It brings into view the amazing evils which have resulted from the apostacy. The apostle does not attempt to deny or palliate those evils; he admits them fully; admits them in their deepest, widest, most melancholy extent; just as the physician *admits* the extent and ravages of the disease which he hopes to cure. At the same time, Christianity is not responsible for those evils. It did not introduce them. It finds them in existence, as a matter of sober and melancholy fact, pertaining to all the race. Christianity is no more answerable for the introduction and extent of sin, than the science of medicine is responsible for the introduction and extent of disease. Like that science, it *finds* a state of wide-spread evils in existence; and like that science, it is strictly *a remedial* system. And whether true or false, still the evils of sin exist, just as the evils of disease exist, whether the science of medicine be well-founded or not. Nor does it make any difference in the existence of these evils, whether Christianity be true or false. If the Bible could be proved to be an imposition, it would not prove that men are not sinners. If the whole work of Christ could be shown to be imposture, still it would annihilate no sin, nor would it prove that man has not fallen. The fact would still remain—a fact certainly quite as universal, and quite as melancholy, as it is under the admitted truth of the Christian revelation—and a fact which the infidel is just as much concerned to account for as is the Christian. Christianity proposes a remedy; and it is permitted to the Christian to rejoice that that remedy is ample to meet all the evils; that it is just fitted to recover our alienated world; and that it is destined yet to raise the race up to life, and peace, and heaven. In the provisions of that scheme we may and should triumph; and on the same principle as we may rejoice in the triumph of medicine over disease, so may we triumph in the ascendancy of the Christian plan over all the evils of the fall. And while Christians thus rejoice, the infidel, the deist, the pagan, and the scoffer shall contend with these evils which their systems cannot alleviate or remove, and sink under the chilly reign of sin and death; just as men pant, and struggle, and expire under the visitations of disease, because they *will* not apply the proper remedies of medicine, but choose rather to leave themselves to its unchecked ravages, or to use all the nostrums of quackery in a vain attempt to arrest evils which are coming upon them.

CHAPTER VI.

THE argument commenced in this chapter is continued through the two following. The general design is the

CHAPTER VI.

WHAT shall we say then? Shall [a] we continue in sin, that grace may abound?

2 God forbid, How shall we that are dead [b] to sin, live any longer therein?

3 Know ye not, that so many of us

a chap.3.8.

b ver.16,11; Col.3.3; 1Pe.2.24.

same—*to show that the scheme of justification which God had adopted does not lead men to sin, but on the contrary to holiness.* This is introduced by answering an objection, chap. vi. 1. The apostle pursues this subject by various arguments and illustrations, all tending to show that the design and bearing of the scheme of justification was to produce the hatred of sin, and the love and practice of holiness. In this chapter, the argument is mainly drawn from the following sources: (1.) From the *baptism* of Christians, by which they have professed to be dead to sin, and to be bound to live to God, ver. 2—13. (2.) From the fact that they were now the *servants* of God, and under obligation, by the laws of servitude, to obey him, ver. 15—20. (3.) From their former *experience* of the evil of sin, from its tendency to produce misery and death, and from the fact that by the gospel they had been made ashamed of those things, and had now given themselves to the pure service of God. By these various considerations, he repels the charge that the tendency of the doctrine was to produce licentiousness, but affirms that it was a system of purity and peace. The argument is continued in the two following chapters, showing still farther the purifying tendency of the gospel.

1. *What shall we say then?* This is a mode of presenting an objection. The objection refers to what the apostle had said in chap. v. 20. What shall we say to such a sentiment as that where sin abounded grace did much more abound? ¶ *Shall we continue in sin?* &c. If sin has been the occasion of grace and favour, ought we not to continue in it, and commit as much as possible, in order that grace might abound? This objection the apostle proceeds to answer. He shows that the consequence does not follow; and proves that the doctrine of justification does not lead to it.

2. *God forbid.* By no means. Greek, It may not be; Note, chap. iii. 4. The expression is a strong *denial* of what is implied in the objection in ver. 1. ¶ *How shall we?* &c. This contains a *reason* of the implied statement of the apostle, that we should not continue in sin. The reason is drawn from the fact that we are dead in fact to sin. It is impossible for those who are *dead* to act as if they were alive. It is just as absurd to suppose that a Christian should desire to live in sin as that a dead man should put forth the actions of life. ¶ *That are dead to sin.* That is, all Christians. To be *dead* to a thing is a strong expression denoting that it has no influence over us. A man that is dead is uninfluenced and unaffected by the affairs of this life. He is insensible to sounds, and tastes, and pleasures; to the hum of business, to the voice of friendship, and to all the scenes of commerce, gaiety, and ambition. When it is said, therefore, that a Christian is *dead to sin*, the sense is, that it has lost its influence over him; he is not subject to it; he is in regard to that, as the man in the grave is to the busy scenes and cares of this life. The expression is not infrequent in the New Testament; Gal. ii. 19, "For I...am dead to the law;" Col. iii. 3, "For ye are dead, and your life is hid with Christ in God;" 1 Pet. ii. 24, "Who...bare our sins...that we, being dead to sin," &c. The apostle does not here attempt to prove that Christians are thus dead, nor to state in what way they become so. He assumes the fact without argument. All Christians are thus in fact dead to sin. They do not live *to* sin; nor has sin dominion over them. The expression used here by the apostle is common in all languages. We familiarly speak of a man's being dead to sensual pleasures, to ambition, &c., to denote that they have lost their influence over him. ¶ *Live any longer*

as were [1] baptized into Jesus Christ were baptized into [a] his death?

1 or, *are*.

a 1 Co.15.29.

---

therein. How shall we, who have become sensible of the evil of sin, and who have renounced it by solemn profession, continue to practise it? It is therefore abhorrent to the very nature of the Christian profession. It is remarkable that the apostle did not attempt to argue the question on metaphysical principles. He did not attempt to show by abstruse argument that this consequence did not follow; but he appeals at once to Christian *feeling*, and shows that the supposition is abhorrent to that. To convince the great mass of men, such an appeal is far better than laboured metaphysical argumentation. All Christians can understand that; but few would comprehend an abstruse speculation. The best way to silence objections is, sometimes, to show that they violate the feelings of all Christians, and that therefore the objection must be wrong.

[Considerable difficulty exists in regard to the meaning of the expression "dead to sin." Certainly the most obvious interpretation is that given above in the Commentary, viz. that Christians are insensible to sin, as dead persons to the charms and pleasures of life. It has, however, been objected to this view, that it is inconsistent with fact, since Christians, so far from being insensible to sin, are represented in the next chapter as carrying on a perpetual struggle with it. The corrupt nature, though weakened, is not eradicated, and too frequently occasions such mournful falls, as leave little doubt concerning its existence and power. Mr. Scott seems to have felt this difficulty, for, having explained the phrase of "separation from iniquity, as a dead man ceases from the actions of life," he immediately adds, "not only *ought* this to be the believer's character, but in a measure it actually is so." It is not probable, however, that the apostle meant by the strong expression under discussion, that believers were not *altogether* "dead to sin," but only *in a measure*.

Perhaps we shall arrive at a more satisfactory meaning of the words by looking at the analogous expression in the context, used in reference to Christ himself. He also, in the 10th verse, is said to have "died unto sin," and the believer, in virtue of union with Christ, is regarded as "dead *with* him," ver. 8; and, in consequence of this death with Christ, is moreover freed, or rather justified, (δεδίκαιωται) from sin, ver. 7. Now it cannot be said of Christ that he died unto sin, in the sense of *becoming* dead to its charms, for it was never otherwise with him. The believer, therefore, cannot be dead *with* Christ in this way; nor *on this ground*, can he be *justified* from sin, since justification proceeds upon something very different from our insensibility to sinful pleasures. What then is the meaning of the language when applied to Christ? Sin is here supposed to be possessed of certain power. That power or strength the apostle elsewhere tells us, is derived from the law. "The strength of sin is the law," which demands satisfaction to its injured honour, and insists on the infliction of its penalty. Though then Jesus had no sin of his own, yet when he voluntarily stood in the room of sinners, sin, or its strength, viz. the law, had power over him, *until* he died, and thus paid the penalty. His death cancelled every obligation. Henceforth sin had no more power to exact any thing at his hands.

Now Christians are *one* with Christ. When he died unto sin, they are regarded as having died unto it also, and are therefore, equally with their covenant head, justified from it. Sin, or its strength, the law, has from the moment of the saint's union with Christ, no more power to condemn him, than human laws have to condemn one over again who had *already* died to answer the demands of justice. "The law has dominion over a man so long only as he liveth." On the whole, then, the expression "dead to sin," is to be regarded as entirely parallel with that other expression in the seventh chapter, "dead to the law," that is, *completely* delivered from its authority as a covenant of works, and more especially from its power to condemn.

This view exercises a decided influence on the believer's sanctification. "How shall we that are dead to sin, live any longer therein?" The two things are incompatible. If in virtue of union with Christ, we are dead with him, and freed from the penalty of sin, shall not the same union secure our deliverance from its dominion? "If we be dead *with* Christ, we believe that we shall also live *with* him."

The whole argument, from the 1st to the 11th verse, proceeds upon the fact of the saint's union with Christ.]

3. *Know ye not.* This is a farther appeal to the Christian profession, and the principles involved in it, in answer to the objection. The simple argument in this verse and the two

4 Therefore we are buried[a] with him by baptism into death; that like[b] as Christ was raised up from the dead by[c] the glory of the Father, even so we also should walk in newness[d] of life.

a Col.2.12; 1Pet.3.21. b ch.8.11; 2Cor.13.4. c Mat.28.2,3. d Gal.6.15; Eph.4.22-24; 1John 2.6.

following is, that by our very profession made in baptism, we have renounced sin, and have pledged ourselves to live to God. ¶ *So many of us*, &c. All who were baptized; *i. e.* all professed Christians. As this renunciation of sin had been thus made by all who professed religion, so the objection could not have reference to Christianity in any manner. ¶ *Were baptized.* The act of baptism denotes dedication to the service of him in whose name we are baptized. One of its designs is to dedicate or consecrate us to the service of Christ. Thus (1 Cor. x. 2,) the Israelites are said to have been "baptized unto Moses in the cloud and in the sea;" *i. e.* they became consecrated, or dedicated, or bound *to* him as their leader and lawgiver. In the place before us, the argument of the apostle is evidently drawn from the supposition that we have been solemnly consecrated by baptism to the service of Christ; and that to sin is therefore a violation of the very nature of our Christian profession. ¶ *Into* (εἰς). This is the word which is used in Mat. xxviii. 19, "Teach all nations, baptizing them *into* (εἰς) the name of the Father," &c. It means, being baptized *unto* his service; receiving him as the Saviour and guide, devoting all *unto* him and his cause. ¶ *Were baptized unto his death.* We were baptized with special reference to his death. Our baptism had a strong resemblance to his death. By that he became insensible to the things of the world; by baptism we in like manner become dead to sin. Farther, we are baptized with particular reference to the *design* of his death, the great leading feature and purpose of his work. That was, to expiate sin; to free men from its power; to make them pure. We have professed our devotion to the same cause; and have solemnly consecrated ourselves to the same design —to put a period to the dominion of iniquity.

4. *Therefore we are buried*, &c. It is altogether probable that the apostle in this place had allusion to the custom of baptizing by immersion. This cannot, indeed, be *proved*, so as to be liable to no objection; but I presume that this is the idea which would strike the great mass of unprejudiced readers. But while this is admitted, it is also certain that his main scope and intention was not to describe the *mode* of baptism; nor to affirm that that mode was to be universal. The design was very different. It was to show *that by the solemn profession made at our baptism, we had become dead to sin, as Christ was dead to the living world around him when he was buried;* and that as he was raised up to life, so *we* should also rise to a new life. A similar expression occurs in Col. ii. 12, "Buried with him in baptism," &c. ¶ *Into death* (εἰς). Unto death; *i. e.* with a solemn purpose *to be dead* to sin and to the world. Grotius and Doddridge, however, understand this as referring to the death of Christ—in order to represent the death of Christ—or to bring us into a kind of fellowship with his death. ¶ *That like as.* In a similar manner. Christ rose from death in the sepulchre; and so we are bound by our vows at baptism to rise to a holy life. ¶ *By the glory of the Father.* Perhaps this means, amidst the glory, the majesty and wonders evinced by the Father when he raised him up; Mat. xxviii. 2, 3. Or possibly the word *glory* is here used to denote simply his *power*, as the resurrection was a signal and glorious display of his *omnipotence*. ¶ *Even so.* As he rose to new life, so should we. As he rose from *death*, so we, being made *dead* to sin and the world by that religion whose profession is expressed by baptism, should rise to a new life, a life of holiness. ¶ *Should walk.* Should live, or conduct. The word *walk* is often used to express the course of a man's life, or the tenor of his conduct; Note, chap

5 For if [a] we have been planted together in the likeness of his death, we shall be also *in the likeness* of *his* resurrection:

a Phil.3.10.

iv. 12; viii. 1; 1 Cor. v. 7; x. 3; Eph. ii. 10; iv. 1, &c. ¶ *In newness of life.* This is a Hebraism to denote *new life.* We should rise with Christ to a new life; and having been made dead to sin, as he was dead in the grave, so should we rise to a holy life, as he rose from the grave. The argument in this verse is, therefore, drawn from the nature of the Christian profession. By our very baptism, by our very profession, we have become dead to sin, as Christ became dead; and being devoted to him by that baptism, we are bound to rise, as he did, to a new life.

While it is admitted that the allusion here was probably to the custom of immersion in baptism, yet the passage cannot be adduced as an argument that that is the only mode, or that it is binding on all Christians in all places and ages, for the following reasons: (1.) The scope or design of the apostle is not to discuss the mode of baptism, or to state any doctrine on the subject. It is an incidental allusion in the course of an argument, without stating or implying that this was the universal mode even then, still less that it was the only possible mode. His *main design* was to state the obligation of Christians to be holy, from the nature of their profession at baptism—an obligation just as impressive, and as forcible, from the application of water in any other mode as by immersion. It arises from the *fact* of baptism, not from the mode. It is just as true that they who are baptized by affusion, or by sprinkling, are baptised into his death; become professedly dead to sin and the world, and under obligations to live to God, as those who are immersed. It results from the *nature* of the ordinance, not from the *mode.* (2.) If this was the mode commonly, it does not follow that it was the *only* mode, nor that it was to be universally observed. *There is no command that this should be the only mode.* And the simple fact that it was usually practised in a warm climate, where ablutions were common, does not prove that it is to be observed amidst polar snows and ice, and in infancy, and age, and feebleness, and sickness; see Note on Acts viii. 38, 39. (3.) If this is to be pressed *literally* as a matter of obligation, why should not also the following expression, "If we have been *planted together*," &c., be pressed literally, and it be demanded that Christians should somehow be "planted" as well as "buried?" Such an interpretation only shows the absurdity of insisting on a *literal* interpretation of the Scriptures in cases of simple allusion, or where the main scope is illustration by figurative language.

5. *For if we have been planted together.* The word here used (σύμφυτος), does not elsewhere occur in the New Testament. It properly means sown or planted at the same time; that which sprouts or springs up together; and is applied to plants and trees that are planted at the same time, and that sprout and grow together. Thus the name would be given to a field of grain that was sown at the same time, and where the grain sprung up and grew *simultaneously.* Hence it means *intimately connected,* or *joined together.* And here it denotes that Christians and the Saviour have been united intimately in regard to death; as he died and was laid in the grave, so have they by profession died to sin. And it is therefore natural to expect, that, like grain sown at the same time, they should grow up in a similar manner, and resemble each other. ¶ *We shall be also.* We shall be also *fellow-plants; i. e.* we shall resemble him in regard to the resurrection. As he rose from the grave, so shall we rise from sin. As he lived a *new life,* being raised up, so shall we *live* a new life. The propriety of this figure is drawn from the doctrine often referred to in the New Testament, of a union between

6 Knowing this, that our old man is crucified with *him*, that the body [a] of sin might be destroyed, that henceforth we should not serve sin.

a Col.2.11.

Christ and his people. See this explained in the Notes on John xv. 1—10. The sentiment here inferred is but an illustration of what was said by the Saviour (John xiv. 19.), "Because I live, ye shall live also." There is perhaps not to be found a more beautiful illustration than that employed here by the apostle—of seed sown together in the earth, sprouting together, growing together, and ripening together for the harvest. Thus the Saviour and his people are united together in his death, start up to life together in his resurrection, and are preparing together for the same harvest of glory in the heavens. ¶ In the likeness *of* his *resurrection*. This does not mean that we shall resemble him when we are raised up at the last day—which may be, however, true—but that our rising from sin will resemble his resurrection from the grave. As he rose from the tomb and lived, so shall we rise from sin and live a new life.

6. *Knowing this*. We all knowing this. All Christians are supposed to know this. This is a new illustration drawn from the fact that by his crucifixion our corrupt nature has been crucified also, or put to death; and that thus we should be free from the servitude of sin. ¶ *Our old man*. This expression occurs also in Eph. iv. 22, "That ye put off . . . . the old man which is corrupt according to the deceitful lusts." Col. iii. 9, "Lie not to one another, seeing that ye have put off the old man with his deeds." From these passages it is evident that Paul uses the expression to denote our sinful and corrupt nature; the passions and evil propensities that exist before the heart is renewed. It refers to the love of sin, the indulgence of sinful propensities, in opposition to the new disposition which exists after the soul is converted, and which is called "the new man." ¶ *Is crucified*. Is put to death, as if on a cross. In this expression there is a *personification* of the corrupt propensities of our nature represented as "our old man," our native disposition, &c. The figure is here carried out, and this old man, this corrupt nature, is represented as having been put to death in an agonizing and torturing manner. The pains of crucifixion were perhaps the most torturing of any that the human frame could bear. Death in this manner was most lingering and distressing. And the apostle here by the expression "is crucified" doubtless refers to the painful and protracted struggle which every one goes through when his evil propensities are subdued; when his corrupt nature is slain; and when, a converted sinner, he gives himself up to God. Sin *dies* within him, and he becomes *dead* to the world, and to sin; "for as by the cross death is most lingering and severe, so that corrupt nature is not subdued but by anguish." (*Grotius.*) All who have been born again can enter into this description. They remember "the wormwood and the gall." They remember the anguish of conviction; the struggle of corrupt passion for the ascendency; the dying convulsions of sin in the heart; the long and lingering conflict before it was subdued, and the soul became submissive to God. Nothing will better express this than the lingering agony of crucifixion: and the argument of the apostle is, that as sin has produced *such* an effect, and as the Christian is now free from its embrace and its power, he will live to God. ¶ *With him*. The word "with" (συν) here is joined to the verb "is crucified" and means "is crucified *as* he was." ¶ *That the body of sin*. This expression doubtless means the same as that which he had just used, "our old man." But why the term *body* is used, has been a subject in which interpreters have not been agreed. Some say that it is a Hebraism, denoting mere *intensity* or *emphasis*. Some that it means the same as *flesh, i. e.*, denoting our sinful propensities and lusts. Grotius thinks that the term "body" is elegantly attributed to *sin*,

7 For [a] he that is dead is [1] freed from sin.
8 Now if we be dead with Christ, we believe that we shall also live with him:
9 Knowing that Christ, [b] be-

a 1Pet.4.1. 1 *justified.* b Rev.1.18.

because the body of man is made up of many members joined together *compactly,* and sin also consists of numerous vices and evil propensities joined compactly, as it were, in one *body.* But the expression is evidently merely another form of conveying the idea contained in the phrase "our old man" —a personification of sin as if it had a living form, and as if it had been put to death on a cross. It refers to the *moral* destruction of the power of sin in the heart by the gospel, and not to any *physical* change in the nature or faculties of the soul; comp. Col. ii. 11. ¶ *Might be destroyed.* Might be put to death; might become inoperative and powerless. Sin becomes *enervated, weakened,* and finally annihilated, by the work of the cross. ¶ *We should not serve.* Should not *be the slave* of sin (δουλεύειν). That we should not be subject to its control. The sense is, that before this we were *slaves* of sin (comp. ver. 17,) but that now we are made free from this bondage, because the *moral death* of sin has freed us from it. ¶ *Sin.* Sin is here personified as a *master* that had dominion over us, but is now dead.

7. *For he that is dead.* This is evidently an expression having a proverbial aspect, designed to illustrate the sentiment just expressed. The Rabbins had an expression similar to this, "When one is dead he is free from commands." *(Grotius.)* So says Paul, when a man dies he is exempt from the power and dominion of his master, of him who reigned over him. The Christian *had* been subject to sin before his conversion. But he has now become *dead* to it. And as when a servant dies, he ceases to be subject to the control of his master, so the Christian being now dead to sin, on the same principle, is released from the control of his former master, sin. The idea is connected with ver. 6, where it is said that we should not be the *slaves* of sin any more. The reason of this is assigned here, where it is said that we are freed from it as a slave is freed when he dies. Of course, the apostle here is saying nothing of the *future world.* His whole argument has respect to the state of the Christian here; to his being freed from the bondage of sin. It is evident that he who is not freed from this bondage here, will not be in the future world. But the argument of the apostle has no bearing on that point. ¶ *Is freed.* Greek, *Is justified.* The word here is used clearly in the sense of *setting at liberty,* or *destroying the power or dominion.* The word is often used in this sense; comp. Acts xiii. 38, 39; comp. a similar expression in 1 Pet. iv. 1, "He that hath suffered in the flesh hath ceased from sin." The design of the apostle is not to say that the Christian is *perfect,* but that sin has ceased to have *dominion* over him, as a master ceases to have power over a slave when he is dead. That dominion may be broken, so that the Christian may not be a *slave* to sin, and yet he may be conscious of many failings and of much imperfection; see chap. vii.

8—11. This passage is a confirmation and illustration of what the apostle had said before, ver. 5—7. The argument is, that as Christ was once dead but now lives to God, and will no more die, so we, being dead to sin, but living unto God, should not obey sin, but should live only to God.

8. *Now if we be dead with Christ.* If we be dead in a manner similar to what he was; if we are made dead to sin by his work, as he was dead in the grave; see Note, ver. 4. ¶ *We believe.* All Christians. It is *an article of our faith.* This does not refer to the future world so much as to the present. It becomes an article of our belief that we are to live with Christ. ¶ *That we shall also live with him.* This does not refer primarily to the resurrection, and to the future

ing raised from the dead, dieth no
more; death hath no more dominion over him.
10 For in that he died, he died
[a] unto sin once: but in that he
liveth, he liveth unto God.
11 Likewise reckon ye also yourselves to be dead [b] indeed unto sin,
but alive [c] unto God through Christ
Jesus our Lord.
12 Let [d] not sin therefore
reign in your mortal body, that
ye should obey it in the lusts
thereof.

a Heb.9.28. b ver.2. c Gal.2. 19. d Ps.19.13; 119.133

state, but to the present. *We hold it as an article of our faith, that we shall be alive with Christ.* As he was raised up from death, so we shall be raised from the death of sin. As he *lives*, so we shall live in holiness. We *are* in fact raised up here, and, as it were, made *alive* to him. This is not *confined*, however, to the present life, but as Christ lives for ever, so the apostle goes on to show that *we* shall.

9. *Knowing.* As we all know. This is assumed as an undoubted article of belief. ¶ *Dieth no more.* Will never die again. He will have occasion to make no other atonement for sin; for that which he has made is sufficient for all. He is beyond the dominion of death, and will live for ever, Rev. i. 18, "I am he that liveth and was dead, and behold I am alive for evermore." This is not only a *consolation* to the Christian, but it is an *argument* why he should be holy. ¶ *No more dominion.* No rule; no lordship; no power. He is free from its influence; and the king of terrors cannot reach his throne; comp. Heb. ix. 25—28; x. 12.

10. *For in that he died.* For in respect to the design of his death. ¶ *He died unto sin.* His death had *respect to sin.* The design of his death was to destroy sin; to make an atonement for it, and thus to put it away. As his death was designed to effect this, so it follows that Christians being baptized into his death, and having it as their object to destroy sin, should not indulge in it. The whole force of the motive, therefore, drawn from the death of Christ, is to induce Christians to forsake sin; comp. 2 Cor. v. 15, "And that he died for all, that they which live should not henceforth live unto themselves, but unto him which died for them and rose again." ¶ *Once* (ἐφάπαξ). Once only; once for all. This is an adverb denying a repetition (*Schleusner*), and implies that it will not be done again; comp. Heb. vii. 27; ix. 12; x. 10. The argument of the apostle rests much on this, that his death was once for all; that it would not be repeated. ¶ *In that he liveth.* The object, the design of his living. He aims with his living power to promote the glory of God. ¶ *Unto God.* He seeks to promote his glory. The argument of Paul is this: Christians by their profession are united to him. They are bound to imitate him. As *he* now lives only to advance the glory of God; as all his mighty power, now that he is raised from the dead, and elevated to his throne in heaven, is exerted to promote *his* glory; so should *their* powers, being raised from the death of sin, be exerted to promote the glory of God.

11. *Likewise.* In like manner. This is an exhortation drawn from the argument in the previous verses. It shows the design and tendency of the Christian scheme. ¶ *Reckon ye yourselves.* Judge, or esteem yourselves. ¶ *To be dead indeed unto sin.* So that sin shall have no influence or control over you, any more than the objects of this world have over the dead in their graves; see Note, ver. 2. ¶ *But alive unto God.* Bound to live to promote his glory; to make this the great and sole object of your living. ¶ *Through Jesus Christ.* By means of the death, and resurrection, and example of Jesus Christ. The apostle regards all our disposition to live to God as resulting from the work of the Lord Jesus Christ.

12. *Let not sin therefore.* This is a conclusion drawn from the previous train of reasoning. The result of all

13 Neither yield ye your members [a] *as* instruments [1] of unrighteousness unto sin: but yield [b] yourselves unto God, as those that are alive from the dead, and your members *as* instruments of righteousness unto God.

14 For sin shall not have [c] dominion over you: for ye are not under the law, but under grace.

a Col.3.5. 1 *arms, or, weapons.* b chap.12.1. c Mic.7.19.

these considerations is, that sin should *not* be suffered to reign in us. ¶ *Reign.* Have dominion; obtain the ascendency, or rule. ¶ *In your mortal body.* In you. The apostle uses the word "mortal" here, perhaps, for these reasons, (1.) To remind them of the tendency of the flesh to sin and corruption, as equivalent to "fleshly," since the *flesh* is often used to denote evil passions and desires (comp. chap. vii. 5, 23; viii. 3, 6); and (2.) To remind them of their *weakness,* as the body was mortal, was soon to decay, and was therefore liable to be overcome by temptation. Perhaps, also, he had his eye on the *folly* of suffering the "*mortal* body" to overcome the immortal mind, and to bring it into subjection to sin and corruption. ¶ *That ye should obey it.* That sin should get such an ascendency as to rule entirely over you, and make you the slave. ¶ *In the lusts thereof.* In its *desires,* or propensities.

13. *Neither yield ye your members.* Do not give up, or devote, or employ your members, &c. The word *members* here refers to the *members of the body*—the hands, feet, tongue, &c. It is a specification of what in ver. 12. is included under the general term "body;" see chap. vii. 5, 23; 1 Cor. vi. 15; xii. 12, 18, 20. ¶ *As instruments.* This word (ὅπλα) properly signifies *arms,* or implements of war; but it also denotes an instrument of any kind which we use for defence or aid. Here it means that we should not devote our members—our hands, tongue, &c., as if under the direction of sinful passions and corrupt desires, to accomplish purposes of iniquity. We should not make the members of our bodies the slaves of sin reigning within us. ¶ *Unto sin.* In the service of sin; to work iniquity. ¶ *But yield yourselves,* &c. Give or devote yourselves to God. ¶ *That are alive,* ver. 11. ¶ *And your members,* &c. Christians should devote every member of the body to God and to his service. Their *tongue* should be consecrated to his praise, and to the office of truth, and kindness, and benevolence; their *hands* should be employed in useful labour for him and his cause; their *feet* should be swift in his service, and should not go in the paths of iniquity; their *eyes* should contemplate his works to excite thanksgiving and praise; their *ears* should not be employed to listen to words of deceit, or songs of dangerous and licentious tendency, or to persuasion that would lead astray, but should be open to catch the voice of God as he utters his will in the Book of truth, or as he speaks in the gale, the zephyr, the rolling thunder, the ocean, or in the great events of his providence. He speaks to us every day, and we should hear him; he spreads his glories before us, and we should survey them to praise him; he commands, and our hands, and heart, and feet should obey.

14. *For sin,* &c. The propensity or inclination to sin. ¶ *Shall not have dominion.* Shall not reign, chap. v. 12; vi. 6. This implies that sin *ought* not to have this dominion; and it also expresses the conviction of the apostle that it *would* not have this rule over Christians. ¶ *For we are not under law.* We who are Christians are not subject to that law where sin is excited, and where it rages unsubdued. But it may be asked here, What is meant by this declaration? Does it mean that Christians are absolved from all the obligations of the law? I answer, (1.) The apostle does not affirm that Christians are not bound to *obey the moral law.* The whole scope of his reasoning shows that he maintains that they *are.* The whole structure of Chris-

15 What then? Shall we sin, because we are not under the law, but under grace? God forbid.

16 Know ye not, that to whom ye *d* yield yourselves servants to obey, his servants ye are to whom

d John 8.34; 2 Pet.2.19.

tianity supposes the same thing; comp. Mat. v. 17—19. (2.) The apostle means to say that Christians are not under the law as *legalists,* or as attempting to be justified by it. They seek a different plan of justification altogether: and they do not attempt to be justified by their own obedience. The Jews did; they do not. (3.) It is *implied* here that the effect of an attempt to be justified *by the law* was, not to *subdue* sins, but to excite them, and to lead to indulgence in them. Justification by works would destroy no sin, would check no evil propensity, but would leave a man to all the ravages and riotings of unsubdued passion. If, therefore, the apostle had maintained that men were justified by *works,* he could not have consistently exhorted them to abandon their sins. He would have had no powerful motives by which to urge it; for the scheme would not lead to it. But he here says that the Christian was seeking justification on a plan which *contemplated* and which *accomplished* the destruction of sin; and he therefore infers that sin should not have dominion over them. ¶ *But under grace.* Under a scheme of mercy, the design and tendency of which is to subdue sin, and destroy it. In what way the system of grace removes and destroys sin, the apostle states in the following verses.

15. *What then? shall we sin,* &c. The apostle proceeds to notice an objection which might be suggested. "If Christians are not under the law, which *forbids* all sin, but are under grace, which *pardons* sin, will it not follow that they will feel themselves released from obligation to be holy? Will they not commit sin freely, since the system of grace is one which contemplates pardon, and which will lead them to believe that they may be forgiven to any extent?" This consequence has been drawn by many professing Christians; and it was well therefore, for the apostle to guard against it. ¶ *God forbid;* Note, chap. iii. 4.

16. *Know ye not,* &c. The objection noticed in ver. 15, the apostle answers by a reference to the known laws of servitude or slavery, (ver. 16—20), and by showing that Christians, who had been the slaves of sin, have now become the servants of righteousness, and were therefore bound by the proper laws of servitude to obey their new master: as if he had said, "I assume that you know: you are acquainted with the laws of servitude; you know what is required in such cases." This would be known to all who had been either masters or slaves, or who had observed the usual laws and obligations of servitude. ¶ *To whom ye yield yourselves.* To whom ye give up yourselves for servitude or obedience. The apostle here refers to voluntary servitude; but where this existed, the power of the master over the time and services of the servant was absolute. The argument of the apostle is, that Christians had become the *voluntary servants* of God, and were therefore bound to obey him entirely. Servitude among the ancients, whether voluntary or involuntary, was rigid, and gave the master an absolute right over his slave, Luke xvii. 9; John viii. 34; xv. 15. ¶ *To obey.* To be obedient; or for the purpose of obeying his commands. ¶ *To whom ye obey.* To whom ye come under subjection. That is, you are bound to obey his requirements. ¶ *Whether of sin.* The general law of servitude the apostle now applies to the case before him. If men became the servants of sin, if they gave themselves to its indulgence, they would obey it, let the consequences be what they might. Even with death, and ruin, and condemnation before them, they would obey sin. They give indulgence to their evil passions and desires, and follow them as obedient servants even if they lead them down to hell. Whatever be the consequences of sin.

ye obey; whether of sin unto
death, or of obedience unto righteousness?
17 But God be thanked, that ye
were the servants of sin; but ye
have obeyed from the heart that
form [a] of [1] doctrine which was
delivered you.

a 2 Tim.1.13.

1 whereto ye were delivered.

yet he who yields to it must abide by them, even if it leads him down to death and eternal woe. ¶ *Or of obedience,* &c. The same law exists in regard to holiness or obedience. The man who becomes the servant of holiness will feel himself bound by the law of servitude to obey, and to pursue it to its regular consequences. ¶ *Unto righteousness.* Unto justification; that is, unto eternal life. The expression stands contrasted with "death," and doubtless means that he who thus becomes the voluntary servant of holiness, will feel himself bound to obey it, unto complete and eternal justification and life; comp. ver. 21, 22. The argument is drawn from what the Christian would *feel* of the nature of obligation. He *would* obey him to whom he had devoted himself.

[This would seem to imply that justification is the effect of obedience. Δικαιοσυνη, however, does not signify justification, but righteousness, *i. e.* in this case, personal holiness. The sense is, that while the service of sin leads to death, that of obedience issues in holiness or righteousness. It is no objection to this view that it does not preserve the antithesis, since "justification" is not the opposite of "death," any more than holiness. "There is no need," says Mr. Haldane, "that there should be such an exact correspondence in the parts of the antithesis, as is supposed. And there is a most obvious reason why it could not be so. Death is the wages of sin, but life is not the wages of obedience."]

17. *But God be thanked.* The argument in this verse is drawn from a direct appeal to the feelings of the Roman Christians themselves. From *their experience,* Paul was able to draw a demonstration to his purpose, and this was with him a ground of gratitude to God. ¶ *That ye were,* &c. The *sense* of this passage is plain. The *ground* of the thanksgiving was not that they had been the slaves of sin; but it is, that notwithstanding this, or although they had been thus, yet that they were now obedient. To give thanks to God that men were sinners, would contradict the whole spirit of this argument, and of the Bible. But to give thanks that *although* men had been sinners, yet that now they had become obedient; that is, *that great sinners had become converted,* is in entire accordance with the spirit of the Bible, and with propriety. The word *although* or *whereas,* understood here, expresses the sense, "But thanks unto God, that *whereas* ye were the servants of sin," &c. Christians should thank God that they themselves, though once great sinners, have become converted; and when others who are great sinners are converted, they should praise him. ¶ *The servants of sin.* This is a strong expression implying that they had been in *bondage* to sin; that they had been completely its slaves. ¶ *From the heart.* Not in external form only; but as a cordial, sincere, and entire service. No other obedience is genuine. ¶ *That form of doctrine.* Greek, *type;* see Note, chap. v. 14. The form or type of doctrine means that shape or model of instruction which was communicated. It does not differ materially from *the doctrine itself,* "you have obeyed that doctrine," &c. You have yielded obedience to the instructions, the rules, the tenor of the Christian revelation. The word *doctrine* does not refer to an abstract dogma, but means *instruction, that which is taught.* And the meaning of the whole expression is simply, that they had yielded a cheerful and hearty obedience to that which had been communicated to them by the teachers of the Christian religion; comp. chap. i. 8. ¶ *Which was delivered you.* Marg. "Whereto ye were delivered." This is a literal translation of the Greek; and the sense is simply in which you have been instructed.

18. *Being then made free from sin.* That is, as a *master.* You are not

18 Being then made free [a] from sin, ye became the servants of righteousness.

19 I speak after the manner of men, because of the infirmity of your flesh: for as ye have yielded your members servants to uncleanness, and to iniquity unto iniquity; even so now yield your members servants to righteousness, unto holiness.

20 For when ye were the servants [b] of sin, ye were free [1] from righteousness.

[a] John 8.32. [b] ver.16. [1] *to.*

under its dominion; you are no longer its slaves. They were made free, as a servant is who is set at liberty, and who is, therefore, no longer under obligation to obey. ¶ *Ye became the servants,* &c. You became voluntarily under the dominion of righteousness; you yielded yourselves to it; and are therefore bound to be holy; comp. Note, John viii. 32.

19. *I speak after the manner of men.* I speak as men usually speak; or I draw an illustration from common life, in order to make myself better understood. ¶ *Because of the infirmity of your flesh.* The word *infirmity* means weakness, feebleness; and is opposed to vigour and strength. The word *flesh* is used often to denote the corrupt passions of men; but it may refer here to their intellect, or understanding; "Because of your imperfection of spiritual knowledge; or incapacity to discern arguments and illustrations that would be more strictly *spiritual* in their character." This dimness or feebleness had been caused by long indulgence in sinful passions, and by the blinding influence which such passions have on the mind. The sense here is, "I use an illustration drawn from common affairs, from the well-known relations of master and slave, because you will better see the force of such an illustration with which you have been familiar, than you would one that would be more abstract, and more strictly spiritual." It is a kind of apology for drawing an illustration from the relation of master and slave. ¶ *For as ye have yielded;* Note, ver. 13. *Servants to uncleanness.* Have been in bondage to impurity. The word *uncleanness* here refers to impurity of life in any form; to the degraded passions that were common among the heathen; see chap. i. ¶ *And to iniquity.* Transgression of law. ¶ *Unto iniquity.* For the purpose of committing iniquity. It implies that they had done it in an excessive degree. It is well for Christians to be reminded of their former lives, to awaken repentance, to excite gratitude, to produce humility and a firmer purpose to live to the honour of God. This is the use which the apostle here makes of it. ¶ *Unto holiness.* In order to practise holiness. Let the surrender of your members to holiness be as sincere and as unqualified as the surrender was to sin. This is all that is required of Christians. Before conversion they were *wholly* given to sin; after conversion they should be *wholly* given to God. If all Christians would employ the same energies in advancing the kingdom of God that they have in promoting the kingdom of Satan, the church would rise with dignity and grandeur, and every continent and island would soon feel the movement. No require ment is more reasonable than this; and it should be a source of lamentation and mourning with Christians that it is not so; that they have employed so mighty energies in the cause of Satan, and do so little in the service of God. This argument for *energy* in the divine life, the apostle proceeds further to illustrate by comparing the *rewards* obtained in the two kinds of servitude, that of the world, and of God.

20. *Ye were free from righteousness.* That is, in your former state, you were not at all under the influence of righteousness. You were entirely devoted to sin; a strong expression of total depravity. It settles the question; and proves that they had no native goodness. The argument which is *implied* here rather than expressed

21 What fruit [a] had ye then
in those things whereof ye are
now ashamed? for the end [b] of
those things *is* death.
22 But now being made free from
sin, and become servants to God,
ye have your fruit unto holiness;
and the end, everlasting life.
23 For [c] the wages of sin *is*
death; but the gift [d] of God *is*
eternal life, [e] through Jesus Christ
our Lord.

a chap.7.5. *b* chap.1.32; James1.15. *c* Gen.2.17. *d* chap.5.17,21. *e* 1Pet.1.4.

---

is, that now they *ought* to be equally free from sin, since they had become released from their former bondage, and had become the servants of another master.

21. *What fruit, then,* &c. What reward, or what advantage. This is an argument drawn from the experience of Christians respecting the indulgence of sinful passions. The question discussed throughout this chapter is, whether the gospel plan of justification by faith leads to indulgence in sin? The argument here is drawn from the past experience which Christians have had in the ways of transgression. They have tried it; they know its effects; they have tasted its bitterness; they have reaped its fruits. It is *implied* here that having *once* experienced these effects, and *knowing* the tendency of sin, they will not indulge in it now; comp. chap. vii. 5. ¶ *Whereof ye are now ashamed.* Having seen their nature and tendency, you are now ashamed of them; comp. chap. i. Eph. v. 12, "For it is a shame to speak of those things which are done of them in secret," 2 Cor. iv. 2; Jude 13; Phil. iii. 19. ¶ *For the end.* The tendency; the result. Those things lead to death. ¶ *Is death;* Note, ver. 22.

22. *But now.* Under the Christian plan of justification. ¶ *Being made free from sin.* Being delivered from its dominion, and from bondage; in the same manner as before conversion they were free from righteousness, ver. 20. ¶ *Ye have your fruit unto holiness.* The fruit or result is holiness. *This* service produces holiness, as the other did sin. It is *implied* here, though not expressly affirmed, that in this service which leads to holiness, they received important benefits, as in the service of sin they had experienced many evils. ¶ *And the end.* The final result—the ultimate consequence will be. *At present* this service produces holiness; hereafter it will terminate in everlasting life. By this consideration the apostle states the tendency of the plan of justification, and urges on them the duty of striving after holiness. ¶ *Everlasting life;* Note, John iii. 36. This stands in contrast with the word *death* in ver. 21, and shows its meaning. *One is just as long in duration as the other;* and if the one is limited, the other is. If those who *obey* shall be blessed with life for ever, those who disobey will be cursed with death for ever. Never was there an antithesis more manifest and more clear. And there could not be a stronger proof that the word *death* in ver. 21, refers not to temporal death, but to eternal punishment. For what force would there be in the argument on the supposition that temporal death only is meant? The argument would stand thus: "The end of those sins is to produce *temporal death;* the end of holiness is to produce *eternal life!*" Will not temporal death be inflicted, it would be immediately asked, at any rate? Are Christians exempt from it? And do not men suffer this, whether they become Christians or not? How then could this be an argument bearing on the tenor of the apostle's reasoning? But admit the fair and obvious construction of the passage to be the true one, and it becomes plain. They were pursuing a course tending to everlasting ruin; they are now in a path that shall terminate in eternal life. By this weighty consideration, therefore, they are urged to be holy.

23. *For the wages of sin.* The word here translated *wages* (ὀψώνια) properly denotes what is purchased to be eaten with bread, as fish, flesh, vegetables, &c. (*Schleusner*); and thence it means

CHAPTER VII.

KNOW ye not, brethren, (for I speak to them that know the law,) how that the law hath dominion over a man as long as he liveth.

the pay of the Roman soldier, because formerly it was the custom to pay the soldier in these things. It means hence that which a man earns or deserves; that which is his proper pay, or what he merits. As applied to sin, it means that death is what sin deserves; that which will be its proper reward. Death is thus called the wages of sin, not because it is an arbitrary, undeserved appointment, but (1.) Because it is its proper *desert*. Not a pain will be inflicted on the sinner which he does not deserve. Not a sinner will die who ought not to die. *Sinners even in hell will be treated just as they deserve to be treated;* and there is not to man a more fearful and terrible consideration than this. No man can conceive a more dreadful doom than for himself to be treated for ever just as he deserves to be. But, (2.) This is the wages of sin, because, like the pay of the soldier, it is just what was threatened, Ezek. xviii. 4, "The soul that sinneth, it shall die." God will not inflict any thing more than was threatened, and therefore it is just. ¶ *Is death.* This stands opposed here to eternal life, and proves that one is just as enduring as the other. ¶ *But the gift of God.* Not the wages of man; not that which is due to him; but the mere gift and mercy of God. The apostle is careful to distinguish, and to specify that this is not what man deserves, but that which is gratuitously conferred on him; Note, ver. 15. ¶ *Eternal life.* The same words which in ver. 22 are rendered "everlasting life." The phrase is opposed to death; and proves incontestably that that means eternal death. We may remark, therefore, (1.) That the one will be as long as the other. (2.) As there is no doubt about the duration of *life,* so there can be none about the duration of death. The one will be rich, blessed, everlasting; the other sad, gloomy, lingering, awful, eternal. (3.) If the sinner is lost, he will deserve to die. He will have his reward. He will suffer only what shall be the *just due* of sin. He will not be a *martyr* in the cause of injured innocence. He will not have the compassion of the universe in his favour. He will have no one to take his part against God. He will suffer just as much, and just as long, as he *ought* to suffer. He will suffer as the culprit pines in the dungeon, or as the murderer dies on the gibbet, because this is *the proper reward of sin.* (4.) They who are saved will be raised to heaven, not because they merit it, but by the rich and sovereign grace of God. All their salvation will be ascribed to him; and they will celebrate his mercy and grace for ever. (5.) It becomes us, therefore, to flee from the wrath to come. No man is so foolish and so wicked as he who is willing to reap the proper wages of sin. None so blessed as he who has part in the mercy of God, and who lays hold on eternal life.

CHAPTER VII.

FEW chapters in the bible have been the subject of more decidedly different interpretations than this. And after all that has been written on it by the learned, it is still made a matter of discussion, whether the apostle has reference in the main scope of the chapter to his own experience *before* he became a Christian; or to the conflicts in the mind of a man who is renewed. Which of these opinions is the correct one I shall endeavour to state in the Notes on the particular verses in the chapter. The main design of the chapter is not very difficult to understand. It is, evidently, to show the insufficiency of the law to produce peace of mind to a troubled sinner. In the previous chapters he had shown that it was incapable of producing *justification,* chap. i—iii. He had shown the way in which men were justified by faith; chap. iii. 21—31; iv. He had shown how that plan produced peace, and met the evils introduced by the fall of Adam; chap. v. He had shown that Christians were freed from the law as a

2 For [a] the woman which hath an husband is bound by the law to *her* husband, so long as he liveth; but if the husband be

a 1 Cor. 7. 39.

matter of obligation, and yet that this freedom did not lead to a licentious life; chap. vi. And he now proceeds *still further* to illustrate the tendency of the law on a man both in a state of nature and of grace; to show that *its uniform effect* in the present condition of man, whether impenitent and under conviction, or in a state of grace under the gospel, so far from promoting peace, as the Jew maintained, was to excite the mind to conflict, and anxiety, and distress. Nearly all the peculiar opinions of the Jews the apostle had overthrown in the previous argument. He here gives the finishing stroke, and shows that the tendency of the law, as a practical matter, was every where the same. It was not *in fact* to produce peace, but agitation, conflict, distress. Yet this was not the fault of the *law*, which was in itself good, but of sin, ver. 7—24. I regard this chapter as not referring *exclusively* to Paul in a state of nature, or of grace. The discussion is conducted without particular reference to that point. It is rather designed to group together the actions of a man's life, whether in a state of conviction for sin, or in a state of grace, and to show that the effect of the law is every where substantially the same. *It equally fails every where in producing peace and sanctification.* The argument of the Jew respecting the efficacy of the law, and its sufficiency for the condition of man, is thus overthrown by a succession of proofs relating to justification, to pardon, to peace, to the evils of sin, and to the agitated and conflicting moral elements in man's bosom. The effect is every where the same. The deficiency is apparent in regard to ALL the great interests of man. And having shown this, the apostle and the reader are prepared for the language of triumph and gratitude, that deliverance from all these evils is to be traced to the gospel of Jesus Christ the Lord; chap. vii. 25; viii.

1. *Know ye not.* This is an appeal to their own observation respecting the relation between husband and wife. The illustration (ver. 2, 3) is designed simply to show that as when a man dies, and the connection between him and his wife is dissolved, his law ceases to be binding on her, so also a separation has taken place between Christians and the law, in which *they* have become dead *to it*, and they are not now to attempt to draw their life and peace from it, but from that *new* source with which they are connected by the gospel, ver. 4. ¶ *For I speak to them,* &c. Probably the apostle refers here more particularly to the Jewish members of the Roman church, who were qualified particularly to understand the nature of the law, and to appreciate the argument. That there were many Jews in the church at Rome has been shown (see Introduction); but the illustration has no exclusive reference to them. The law to which he appeals is sufficiently general to make the illustration intelligible to all men. ¶ *That the law.* The immediate reference here is probably to the Mosaic law. But what is here affirmed is equally true of all laws. ¶ *Hath dominion.* Greek, Rules; exercises lordship. The law is here personified, and represented as setting up a lordship over a man, and exacting obedience. ¶ *Over a man.* Over the man who is under it. ¶ *As long as he liveth.* The Greek here may mean either "as HE liveth," or "as IT liveth," *i. e.* the law. But our translation has evidently expressed the sense. The sense is, that death releases a man from the laws by which he was bound in life. It is a general principle, relating to the laws of the land, the law of a parent, the law of a contract, &c. This general principle the apostle proceeds to apply in regard to the law of God.

2. *For the woman.* This verse is a *specific* illustration of the general principle in ver. 1, that death dissolves

dead, she is loosed from the law of her husband.

3 So then, if, while [a] *her* husband liveth, she be married to another man, she shall be called an adulteress: but if her husband be dead, she is free from that law; so that she is no adulteress, though she be married to another man.

4 Wherefore, my brethren, ye also are become dead to the law [b] by the body of Christ; that ye should be married to another, *even*

a Matt.5.32.

b Gal.5.18.

those connections and relations which make law binding in life. It is a simple illustration; and if this had been kept in mind, it would have saved much of the perplexity which has been felt by many commentators, and much of their wild vagaries in endeavouring to show that "men are the wife, the law the former husband, and Christ the new one;" or that "the old man is the wife, sinful desires the husband, sins the children." *Beza.* (See Stuart.) Such expositions are sufficient to humble us, and to make us mourn over the puerile and fanciful interpretations which even wise and good men often give to the Bible. ¶ *Is bound by the law,* &c. See the same sentiment in 1 Cor. vii. 39. ¶ *To her husband.* She is united to him; and is under his authority as the head of the household. To *him* is particularly committed the headship of the family, and the wife is subject to his law, in the Lord, Eph. v. 23, 33. ¶ *She is loosed,* &c. The husband has no more authority. The connection from which obligation resulted is dissolved.

3. *So then if,* &c.; comp. Matt. v. 32. ¶ *She shall be called.* She will be. The word used here (χρηματίσει) is often used to denote being called by an oracle or by divine revelation. But it is here employed in the simple sense of being commonly called, or of being so regarded.

4. *Wherefore.* This verse contains an application of the illustration in the two preceding. The idea there is, that *death dissolves a connection from which obligation resulted.* This is the single point of the illustration, and consequently there is no need of inquiring whether by the wife the apostle meant to denote the old man, or the Christian, &c. The meaning is, as death dissolves the connection between a wife and her husband, and of course the obligation of the law resulting from that connection, so the death of the Christian to the law dissolves *that* connection, so far as the scope of the argument here is concerned, and prepares the way for another union, a union with Christ, from which a new and more efficient obligation results. The design is to show that the *new* connection would accomplish more important effects than the old. ¶ *Ye also are become dead to the law;* Notes, chap. vi. 3, 4, 8. The connection between us and the law is dissolved, so far as the scope of the apostle's argument is concerned. He does not say that we are dead to it, or released from it as a rule of duty, or as a matter of obligation to obey it; for there neither is, nor can be, any such release, but we are dead to it as a way of justification and sanctification. In the great matter of acceptance with God, we have ceased to rely on the law, having become dead to it, and having embraced another plan. ¶ *By the body of Christ.* That is, by his body crucified; or in other words, by his death; comp. Eph. ii. 15, "Having abolished *in his flesh* the enmity," &c. *i. e.* by his death. Col. i. 22, "In the body of his flesh through death," &c. ii. 14; 1 Pet. ii. 24, "Who bare our sins in his own body on the tree." The sense, is, therefore, that by the death of Christ as an atoning sacrifice; by his suffering for us that which would be sufficient to meet the demands of the law; by his taking our place, he has released us from the law as a way of justification; freed us from its penalty; and saved us from its curse. Thus released, we are at liberty to be united to the law of him who has thus bought

to him who is raised from the dead, that we should bring forth fruit [a] unto God.

5 For when we were in [b] the flesh, the motions [1] of sins, which were by the law, did work in our members, to bring forth fruit [c] unto death.

6 But now we are delivered from the law, [1] that being dead

a Gal.5.22. *b* chap.8.8,9. 1 *passions.* *c* chap.6.21. 1 or, *being dead to that.*

us with his blood. ¶ *That ye should be married to another.* That you might be united to another, and come under his law. This is the completion of the illustration in ver. 2, 3. As the woman that is freed from the law of her husband by his death, when married again comes under the authority of another, so we who are made free from the law and its curse by the death of Christ, are brought under the new law of fidelity and obedience to him with whom we are thus united. The union of Christ and his people is not unfrequently illustrated by the most tender of all earthly connections, that of a husband and wife, Eph. v. 23—30; Rev. xxi. 9. "I will show thee the bride, the Lamb's wife," xix. 7. ¶ *Even to him who is raised,* &c. See the force of this explained, chap. vi. 8. ¶ *That we should bring forth fruit unto God.* That we should live a holy life. This is the point and scope of all this illustration. The new connection is such as will make us holy. It is also implied that the tendency of the law was only to bring forth fruit unto death (ver. 5,) and that the tendency of the gospel is to make man holy and pure; comp. Gal. v. 22, 23.

5. *For when,* &c. The illustration in this verse and the following is designed to show more at length the effect of the law, whenever and wherever applied; whether in a state of nature or of grace. It was *always* the same. It was the occasion of agitation and conflict in a man's own mind. This was true when a sinner was under conviction; and it was true when a man was a Christian. In all circumstances where the law was applied to the corrupt mind of man, it produced this agitation and conflict. Even in the Christian's mind it produced this agitation (ver. 14—24), as it had done and would do in the mind of a sinner under conviction (ver. 7—12), and consequently there was *no* hope of release but in the delivering and sanctifying power of the gospel (ver. 25; chap. viii. 1—3). ¶ *In the flesh.* Unconverted; subject to the controlling passions and propensities of a corrupt nature; comp. chap. viii. 8, 9. The connection shows that this must be the meaning here, and the design of this illustration is to show the effect of the law *before* a man is converted, (ver. 5—12). This is the obvious meaning, and all the laws of interpretation require us so to understand it. ¶ *The motions of sins* (τὰ παθήματα.) This translation is unhappy. The expression "motions of sins" conveys no idea. The original means simply *the passions, the evil affections, the corrupt desires;* see the margin. The expression, *passions of sins,* is a Hebraism meaning *sinful passions,* and refers here to the corrupt propensities and inclinations of the unrenewed heart. ¶ *Which were by the law.* Not that they were originated or created by the law; for a law does not *originate* evil propensities, and a holy law would not cause sinful passions; but they were *excited,* called up, inflamed by the law, which forbids their indulgence. ¶ *Did work in our members.* In our body; that is, in us. Those sinful propensities made use of our members as instruments, to secure gratification; Note, chap. vi. 12, 13; comp. ver. 23. ¶ *To bring forth fruit unto death.* To produce crime, agitation, conflict, distress, and to lead to death. We were brought under the dominion of death; and the consequence of the indulgence of those passions would be fatal; comp. Note, chap. vi. 21.

6. *But now.* Under the gospel. This verse states the consequences of the gospel, in distinction from the effects of the law. The way in which

wherein we were held; that we should serve in newness of spirit, and not *in* the oldness of the letter.

this is accomplished, the apostle illustrates more at length in chap. viii. with which this verse is properly connected. The remainder of chap. vii. is occupied in illustrating the statement in ver. 5, of the effects of *the law;* and after having shown that its effects *always* were to increase crime and distress, he is prepared in chap. viii. to take up the proposition in this verse, and to show the superiority of the gospel in producing peace. ¶ *We are delivered.* We who are Christians. Delivered from it as a means of justification, as a source of sanctification, as a bondage to which we were subjected, and which tended to produce pain and death. It does not mean that Christians are freed from it as a rule of duty.

[Believers "are delivered from the law" as a covenant of works. In the language of the Confession, they are "not under it to be thereby justified or condemned." This seems to be the *whole* import of the apostle's language. To say that Christians are delivered from the law "as a source of sanctification," is to affirm, that *once* they were under it in this sense, otherwise there could be no deliverance in the case. But when, or to whom, was the law ever proposed as the source of sanctification? The *rule* of sanctification, it always has been, the *source* never. This explanation is similar to that of Prof. Stuart, who renders "no longer placing our reliance on it as a means of subduing and sanctifying our sinful natures," on which Mr. Haldane justly remarks, that "to cease to rely on the law, for such a purpose, was not, in any sense, to be delivered from it. The law never proposed such a thing, and therefore to cease to look for such an effect, is not a deliverance from the law."]

¶ *That being dead.* Margin, "Being dead to that." There is a variation here in the MSS. Some read it, as in the text, as if the *law* was dead; others, as in the margin, as if we were dead. The majority is in favour of the reading as in the margin; and the connection requires us to understand it in this sense. So the Syriac, the Arabic, the Vulgate, Æthiopic. The sentiment here, that we are dead to the law, is that which is expressed in ver. 4. ¶ *Wherein we were held.* That is, as captives, or as slaves. We were held in bondage to it; ver. 1. ¶ *That we should serve.* That we may now serve or obey *God.* ¶ *In newness of spirit.* In a new spirit; or in a new and spiritual manner. This is a form of expression implying, (1.) That their service under the gospel was to be of a *new* kind, differing from that under the former dispensation. (2.) That it was to be of a *spiritual* nature, as distinguished from that practised by the Jews; comp. 2 Cor. iii. 6; Note, Rom. ii. 28, 29. The worship required under the gospel is uniformly described as that of the spirit and the heart, rather than that of form and ceremony; John iv. 23, "The true worshippers shall worship the Father in spirit and in truth; Phil. iii. 3. ¶ *And not in the oldness of the letter.* Not in the old letter. It is implied here in this, (1.) That the form of worship here described pertained to an *old* dispensation that had now passed away; and (2.) That that was a worship that was in the *letter.* To understand this, it is necessary to remember that the *law* which prescribed the forms of worship among the Jews, was regarded by the apostle as destitute of that efficacy and power in renewing the heart which he attributed to the gospel. It was a service consisting in external forms and ceremonies; in the offering of sacrifices and of incense, according to the literal requirements of the law rather than the sincere offering of the heart; 2 Cor. iii. 6, "The letter killeth; the spirit giveth life;" John vi. 63; Heb. x. 1—4; ix. 9, 10. It is not to be denied that there were many holy persons under the law, and that there were many spiritual offerings presented, but it is at the same time true that the great mass of the people rested in the mere form; and that the service offered was the mere service of the letter, and not of the heart. The main idea is, that the services under the gospel are purely

7 What shall we say then? *Is* the law sin? God forbid. Nay, I had not [a] known sin, but by the law: for I had not known lust, [1] except the law had said, [b] Thou shalt not covet.

a chap.3.20.

1 or, *concupiscence.* b Ex.20.17.

and entirely spiritual, the offering of the *heart,* and not the service rendered by external forms and rites.

[But the contrast here is not between services required under the legal and gospel dispensations respectively, but between services yielded in the opposite states of nature and grace. In the former state, we are "under the law" though we live in gospel times, and in the latter, we are "delivered from the law" as a covenant of works. or of life, just as pious Jews might be though they lived under the dispensation of Moses. The design of God in delivering us from the law, is, that we might 'serve him in newness of spirit, and not in the oldness of the letter," *i. e.* in such a spiritual way as the new state requires, and from such spiritual motives and aids as it furnishes; and not in the manner we were wont to do, under our old condition of subjection to the law, in which we could yield only an external and forced obedience. "It is evident," says Prof. Hodge that the clause "in the oldness of the letter' is substituted by the apostle, for 'under the law' and 'in the flesh;' all which he uses to describe the legal and corrupt condition of men, prior to the believing reception of the gospel."]

7. *What shall we say then?* The objection which is here urged is one that would very naturally rise, and which we may suppose would be urged with no slight indignation. The Jew would ask, "Are we then to suppose that the holy law of God is not only insufficient to sanctify us, but that it is the mere occasion of increased sin? Is its tendency to produce sinful passions, and to make men worse than they were before?" To this objection the apostle replies with great wisdom, by showing that the evil was not in *the law,* but *in man;* that though these effects often followed, yet that the law itself was good and pure. ¶ *Is the law sin?* Is it sinful? Is it evil? For if, as it is said in ver. 5, the sinful passions were "*by* the law," it might naturally be asked whether the law itself was not an evil thing? ¶ *God forbid;* Note, chap. iii. 4. ¶ *Nay, I had not known sin.* The word translated *nay* (ἀλλὰ) means more properly *but;* and this would have more correctly expressed the sense, "I deny that the law is sin. My doctrine does not lead to that; nor do I affirm that it is evil. I strongly repel the charge; BUT, notwithstanding this, I still maintain that it *had* an effect in exciting sins, yet so as that *I* perceived that the law itself was good;" ver. 8—12. At the same time, therefore, that the law must be admitted to be the occasion of exciting sinful feelings, by crossing the inclinations of the mind, yet the fault was not to be traced to the law. The apostle in these verses refers, doubtless, to the state of his mind *before* he found that peace which the gospel furnishes by the pardon of sins. ¶ *But by the law;* chap. iii. 20. By the *law* here, the apostle has evidently in his eye *every* law of God, however made known. He means to say that the effect which he describes attends *all* law, and this effect he illustrates by a single instance drawn from the tenth commandment. When he says that he should not have known sin, he evidently means to affirm, that he had not understood that certain things were sinful, unless they had been forbidden; and having stated this, he proceeds to *another* thing, to show the *effect* of their being thus forbidden on his mind. He was not merely acquainted abstractly with the nature and existence of sin, with what constituted crime because it was forbidden, but he was conscious of a certain effect on his mind resulting from this knowledge, and from the effect of strong, raging desires when thus restrained, ver. 8, 9. ¶ *For I had not known lust.* I should not have been acquainted with the nature of the sin of *covetousness.* The desire might have existed, but he would not have known it to be sinful, and he would not have experienced that raging, impetuous, and ungoverned propensity which he did when he found it to be forbidden. Man without law might have the strong feelings of desire.

8 But sin, taking occasion by the commandment, wrought in me all manner of concupiscence. For without the law, sin *was* dead.

He might covet that which others possessed. He might take property, or be disobedient to parents; but he would not *know* it to be evil. The *law* fixes bounds to his desires, and teaches him what is right and what is wrong. It teaches him where lawful indulgence ends, and where sin begins. The word "lust" here is not limited as it is with us. It refers to *all* covetous desires; to all wishes for that which is forbidden us. ¶ *Except the law had said.* In the tenth commandment; Exod. xx. 17. ¶ *Thou shalt not covet.* This is the beginning of the command, and all the rest is implied. The apostle knew that it would be understood without repeating the whole. This particular commandment he selected because it was more pertinent than the others to his purpose. The others referred particularly to external actions. But his object was to show the effect of sin on the mind and conscience. He therefore chose one that referred particularly to the desires of the heart.

8. *But sin.* To illustrate the *effect* of the law on the mind, the apostle in this verse depicts its influence in exciting to evil desires and purposes. Perhaps no where has he evinced more consummate knowledge of the human heart than here. He brings an illustration that might have escaped most persons, but which goes directly to establish his position that the law is insufficient to promote the salvation of man. *Sin* here is personified. It means not a real *entity;* not a physical subsistence; not something independent of the mind, having a separate existence, and lodged *in* the soul, but it means the corrupt passions, inclinations, and desires *of the mind itself.* Thus we say that lust burns, and ambition rages, and envy corrodes the mind, without meaning that lust, ambition, or envy are any independent physical subsistences, but meaning that the *mind* that is ambitious, or envious, is thus excited. ¶ *Taking occasion.* The word *occasion* (ἀφορμὴν) properly denotes any material, or preparation for accomplishing any thing; then any opportunity, occasion, &c. of doing it. Here it means that *the law* was the exciting cause of sin; or was that which called the sinful principle of the heart into exercise. *But for this,* the effect here described would not have existed. Thus we say that a tempting object of desire presented is the exciting cause of covetousness. Thus an object of ambition is the exciting cause of the principle of ambition. Thus the presentation of wealth, or of advantages possessed by others which we have not, may excite covetousness or envy. Thus the fruit presented to Eve was the exciting cause of sin; the wedge of gold to Achan excited his covetousness. Had not these objects been presented, the evil principles of the heart might have slumbered, and never have been called forth. And hence no men understand the full force of their native propensities until some object is presented that calls them forth into decided action. The *occasion* which called these forth in the mind of Paul was the law *crossing his path,* and irritating and exciting the native strong inclinations of the mind. ¶ *By the commandment.* By all law appointed to restrain and control the mind. ¶ *Wrought in me.* Produced or worked in me. The word used here means often to operate in a powerful and efficacious manner. *(Doddridge.)* ¶ *All manner of.* Greek, "All desire." Every species of unlawful desire. It was not confined to one single desire, but extended to every thing which the law declared to be wrong. ¶ *Concupiscence.* Unlawful or irregular desire. Inclination for unlawful enjoyments. The word is the same which in ver. 7 is rendered lust. If it be asked in what way the law led to this, we may reply, that the main idea here is, that opposition by law to the desires and passions of wicked men only tends to inflame and exasperate them. This is the case with regard to sin in every form. An attempt to restrain it by

9 For I was alive without the law once: but when the commandment came, sin revived, and I died.

force; to denounce it by laws and penalties; to cross the path of wickedness; only tends to irritate, and to excite into living energy, that which otherwise would be dormant in the bosom. This it does, because, (1.) It crosses the path of the sinner, and opposes his intention, and the current of his feelings and his life. (2.) The law acts the part of a *detector*, and lays open to view that which was in the bosom, but was concealed. (3.) Such is the depth and obstinacy of sin in man, that the very *attempt* to restrain often only serves to exasperate, and to urge to greater deeds of wickedness. Restraint by law rouses the mad passions; urges to greater deeds of depravity; makes the sinner stubborn, obstinate, and more desperate. The very attempt to set up authority over him throws him into a posture of resistance, and makes him a party, and excites all the feelings of party rage. Any one may have witnessed this effect often on the mind of a wicked and obstinate child. (4.) This is particularly true in regard to a sinner. He is calm often, and apparently tranquil. But let the law of God be brought home to his conscience, and he becomes maddened and enraged. He spurns its authority, yet his conscience tells him it is right; he attempts to throw it off, yet trembles at its power; and to show his independence, or his purpose to sin, he plunges into iniquity, and becomes a more dreadful and obstinate sinner. It becomes a struggle for victory; and in the controversy with God he resolves *not* to be overcome. It accordingly happens that many a man is more profane, blasphemous, and desperate when under conviction for sin than at other times. In revivals of religion it often happens that men evince violence, and rage, and cursing, which they do not in a state of spiritual death in the church; and it is often a very certain indication that a man is under conviction for sin when he becomes particularly violent, and abusive, and outrageous in his opposition to God. (5.) The effect here noticed by the apostle is one that has been observed at all times, and by all classes of writers. Thus Cato says (Livy, xxxiv. 4,) "Do not think, Romans, that it will be hereafter as it was before the law was enacted. It is more safe that a bad man should not be accused, than that he should be absolved; and luxury not excited would be more tolerable than it will be now, by the very chains irritated and excited as a wild beast." Thus Seneca says (de Clementia, i. 23,) "Parricides began with the law." Thus Horace (Odes, i. 3,) "The human race, bold to endure all things, rushes through forbidden crime." Thus Ovid (Amor. iii. 4,) "We always endeavour to obtain that which is forbidden, and desire that which is denied." (These passages are quoted from Tholuck.) See also Prov. ix. 17, "Stolen waters are sweet, and bread eaten in secret is pleasant." If such be the effect of the law, then the inference of the apostle is unavoidable, that it is not adapted to save and sanctify man. ¶ *For without the law.* Before it was given; or where it was not applied to the mind. ¶ *Sin was dead.* It was inoperative, inactive, unexcited. This is evidently in a comparative sense. The connection requires us to understand it only so far as it was excited by the law. Men's passions would exist; but without law they would not be known to be evil, and they would not be excited into wild and tumultuous raging.

9. *For I.* There seems to be no doubt that the apostle here refers to his own past experience. Yet in this he speaks the sentiment of all who are unconverted, and who are depending on their own righteousness. ¶ *Was alive.* This is opposed to what he immediately adds respecting *another* state, in which he was when he *died.* It must mean, therefore, that he had a certain kind of peace; he deemed himself secure; he was free from the convictions of conscience and the agitations of alarm. The state to which

10 And the commandment, which *was ordained* to life, [a] I found *to be* unto death.

a Ezek.20.11.&c.

he refers here must be doubtless that to which he himself elsewhere alludes, when he deemed himself to be righteous, depending on his own works, and esteeming himself to be blameless, Phil. iii. 4—6; Acts xxiii. 1; xxvi. 4, 5. It means that he was then free from those agitations and alarms which he afterwards experienced when he was brought under conviction for sin. At that time, though he had the law, and was attempting to obey it, yet he was unacquainted with its spiritual and holy nature. He aimed at *external* conformity. Its claims on the heart were unfelt. This is the condition of every self-confident sinner, and of every one who is unawakened. ¶ *Without the law.* Not that Paul was ever really without the law, that is, without the law of Moses; but he means before the law was applied to his heart in its spiritual meaning, and with power. ¶ *But when the commandment came.* When it was applied to the heart and conscience. This is the only intelligible sense of the expression; for it *cannot* refer to the time when the law was given. *When* this was, the apostle does not say. But the expression denotes *whenever* it was so applied; when it was urged with power and efficacy on his conscience, to control, restrain, and threaten him, it produced this effect. We are unacquainted with the early operations of his mind, and with his struggles against conscience and duty. We know enough of him before conversion, however, to be assured that he was proud, impetuous, and unwilling to be restrained; see Acts viii. ix. In the state of his self-confident righteousness and impetuosity of feeling, we may easily suppose that the holy law of God, which is designed to restrain the passions, to humble the heart, and to rebuke pride, would produce only irritation, and impatience of restraint, and revolt. ¶ *Sin revived.* Lived again. This means that it was before dormant (ver. 8,) but was now quickened into new life. The word is usually applied to a renewal of life, (Rom. xiv. 19; Luke xv. 24, 32,) but here it means substantially the same as the expression in ver. 8, "Sin.... wrought in me all manner of concupiscence." The power of sin, which was before dormant, became quickened and active. ¶ *I died.* That is, I was by it involved in additional guilt and misery. It stands opposed to "I was alive," and must mean the opposite of that; and evidently denotes that the effect of the commandment was to bring him under what he calls *death*, (comp. chap. v. 12, 14, 15;) that is, sin reigned, and raged, and produced its withering and condemning effects; it led to aggravated guilt and misery. It may also include this idea,—that before, he was self-confident and secure, but that by the commandment he was stricken down and humbled, his self-confidence was blasted, and his hopes were prostrated in the dust. Perhaps no words would better express the humble, subdued, melancholy, and helpless state of a converted sinner than the expressive phrase "*I died.*" The essential idea here is, that the law did not answer the purpose which the Jew would claim for it, to sanctify the soul and to give comfort, but that *all* its influence on the heart was to produce aggravated, unpardoned guilt and woe.

10. *And the commandment.* The law to which he had referred before. ¶ *Which was ordained to life.* Which was intended to produce life, or happiness. *Life* here stands opposed to *death*, and means felicity, peace, eternal bliss; Note, John iii. 36. When the apostle says that it was ordained to life, he probably has reference to the numerous passages in the Old Testament which speak of the law in this manner, Lev. xviii. 5, "Ye shall keep my statutes and my judgments; which if a man do, he shall live in them," Ezek. xx. 11, 13, 21; xviii. 9, 21. The meaning of these passages, in connection with this declaration of Paul, may be thus expressed: (1.) The law is good; it has no evil, and is itself fitted to produce no evil. (2.)

11 For sin, taking occasion by the commandment, deceived me, and by it slew *me*.
12 Wherefore the law [a] *is* holy; and the commandment holy, and just, and good.
13 Was then that which is good made death unto me? God forbid.

a Ps.19.7-9.

If man was pure, and it was obeyed perfectly, it would produce life and happiness only. On those who have obeyed it in heaven, it has produced only happiness. (3.) For this it was ordained; it is adapted to it; and when perfectly obeyed, it produces no other effect. But, (4.) Man is a sinner; he has *not* obeyed it; and in such a case the law threatens woe. It crosses the inclination of man, and instead of producing peace and life, as it would on a being perfectly holy, it produces only woe and crime. The law of a parent may be good, and may be appointed to promote the happiness of his children; it may be admirably fitted to it if all were obedient; yet *in* the family there may be one obstinate, self-willed, and stubborn child, resolved to indulge his evil passions, and the results to him would be woe and despair. The commandment, which was ordained for the good of the family, and which would be adapted to promote their welfare, *he* alone, of all the number, would find to be unto death. ¶ *I found.* It was to me. It produced this effect. ¶ *Unto death.* Producing aggravated guilt and condemnation, ver. 9.

11. *For sin.* This verse is a repetition, with a little variation of the sentiment in ver. 8. ¶ *Deceived me.* The word here used properly means to lead or seduce from the right way; and then to deceive, solicit to sin, cause to err from the way of virtue, Rom. xvi. 18; 1 Cor. iii. 18; 2 Cor. xi. 3, "The serpent *beguiled* Eve through his subtilty," 2 Thess. ii. 3. The meaning here seems to be, that his corrupt and rebellious propensities, excited by the law, led him astray; caused him more and more to sin; practised a species of deception on him by urging him on headlong, and without deliberation, into aggravated transgression. In this sense, all sinners are deceived. Their passions urge them on, deluding them, and leading them farther and farther from happiness, and involving them, before they are aware, in crime and death. No being in the universe is more deluded than a sinner in the indulgence of evil passions. The description of Solomon in a particular case will apply to all, Prov. vii. 21—23.

> "With much fair speech she caused him to yield,
> With the flattering of her lips she forced him.
> He goeth after her straightway,
> As an ox goeth to the slaughter,
> Or as a fool to the correction of the stocks;
> Till a dart strike through his liver,
> As a bird hasteth to the snare."

¶ *By it.* By the law, ver. 8. ¶ *Slew me.* Meaning the same as "I died," ver. 8.

12. *Wherefore.* So that. The conclusion to which we come is, that the law is not to be blamed, though these are its effects under existing circumstances. The source of all this is not the law, but the corrupt nature of man. The law is good; and yet the position of the apostle is true, that it is not adapted to purify the heart of fallen man. Its tendency is to excite increased guilt, conflict, alarm, and despair. This verse contains an answer to the question in ver. 7, "Is the law sin?" ¶ *Is holy.* Is not sin; comp. ver. 7. It is pure in its nature. ¶ *And the commandment.* The word commandment is here synonymous with the law. It properly means that which is enjoined. ¶ *Holy.* Pure. ¶ *Just.* Righteous in its claims and penalties. It is not unequal in its exactions. ¶ *Good.* In itself good; and in its own nature tending to produce happiness. The sin and condemnation of the guilty is not the fault of the law. If obeyed, it would produce happiness every where. See a most beautiful description of the law of God in Ps. xix. 7—11.

13. *Was then that which is good,* &c. This is another objection which the apostle proceeds to answer. The objection is this, "Can it be possible that that which is admitted to be good

But sin, that it might appear sin, worketh death in me by that which is good; that sin by the commandment might become exceeding sinful.

14 For we know that the law

---

and pure, should be changed into evil? Can that which tends to life, be made death to a man?" In answer to this, the apostle repeats that the fault was not in the *law*, but was in himself, and in his sinful propensities. ¶ *Made death,* ver. 8, 10. ¶ *God forbid;* Note, chap. iii. 4. ¶ *But sin.* This is a personification of sin as in ver. 8. ¶ *That it might appear sin.* That it might develope its true nature, and no longer be dormant in the mind. The law of God is often applied to a man's conscience, that he may see how deep and desperate is his depravity. No man knows his own heart until the law thus crosses his path, and shows him what he is. ¶ *By the commandment;* Note, ver. 8. ¶ *Might become exceeding sinful.* In the original this is a very strong expression, and is one of those used by Paul to express strong emphasis, or intensity (καθ' ὑπερβολὴν) by hyperboles. In an excessive degree; to the utmost possible extent, 1 Cor. xii. 31; 2 Cor. i. 8; iv. 7; xii. 7; Gal. i. 13. The phrase occurs in each of these places. The sense here is, that by the giving of the command, and its application to the mind, sin was completely developed; it was excited, inflamed, aggravated, and showed to be excessively malignant and deadly. It was not a dormant, slumbering principle; but it was awfully opposed to God and his law. Calvin has well expressed the sense: "It was proper that the enormity of sin should be revealed by the law; because unless sin should break forth by some dreadful and enormous excess (as they say,) it would not be known to be sin. This excess exhibits itself the more violently, while it turns life into death." The sentiment of the whole is, that the tendency of the law is to excite the dormant sin of the bosom into active existence, and to reveal its true nature. It is desirable that that should be done, and as that is all that the law accomplishes, it is not adapted to sanctify the soul. To show that this was the design of the apostle, it is *desirable* that sin should be thus seen in its true nature, because, (1.) Man should be acquainted with his true character. He should not deceive himself. (2.) Because it is one part of God's plan to develope the secret feelings of the heart, and to show to all creatures what they are. (3.) Because only by knowing this, will the sinner be induced to take a remedy, and strive to be saved. God often thus *suffers* men to plunge into sin; to act out their nature, that they may see themselves, and be alarmed at the consequences of their own crimes.

14. The remainder of this chapter has been the subject of no small degree of controversy. The question has been whether it describes the state of Paul before his conversion, or afterwards. It is not the purpose of these Notes to enter into controversy, or into extended discussion. But after all the attention which I have been able to give to this passage, I regard it as describing the state of a man under the gospel, as descriptive of the operations of the mind of Paul subsequent to his conversion. This interpretation is adopted for the following reasons: (1.) Because it seems to me to be the most obvious. It is that which will strike plain men as being the natural meaning; men who have not a theory to support, and who understand language in its usual sense. (2.) Because it agrees with the design of the apostle, which is to show that the law is not adapted to produce sanctification and peace. This he had done in regard to a man *before* he was converted. If this relates to the same period, then it is a useless discussion of a point already discussed. If it relates to that period also, then there is a large field of action, including the whole period after a man's conversion to Christianity, in which the question might still be unsettled, whether the law *there* might not be adapted to

sanctify. The apostle therefore makes thorough work with the argument, and shows that the operation of the law is every where the same. (3.) Because the expressions which occur are such as cannot be understood of an impenitent sinner; see Notes on ver. 15, 32. (4.) Because it accords with parallel expressions in regard to the state of the conflict in a Christian's mind. (5.) Because there is a change made here from the past tense to the present. In ver. 7, &c. he had used the past tense, evidently describing some former state. In ver. 14 there is a change to the present, a change inexplicable, except on the supposition that he meant to describe some state different from that before described. That could be no other than to carry his illustration forward in showing the inefficacy of the law on a man in his renewed state; or to show that such was the remaining depravity of the man, that it produced substantially the same effects as in the former condition. (6.) Because it accords with the experience of Christians, and not with sinners. It is just such language as plain Christians, who are acquainted with their own hearts, use to express their feelings. I admit that this last consideration is not by itself conclusive; but if the language did *not* accord with the experience of the Christian world, it would be a strong circumstance *against* any proposed interpretation. The view which is here expressed of this chapter, as supposing that the previous part (ver. 7—13) refers to a man in his unregenerate state, and that the remainder describes the effect of the law on the mind of a renewed man, was adopted by studying the chapter itself, without aid from any writer. I am happy, however, to find that the views thus expressed are in accordance with those of the late Rev. Dr. J. P. Wilson, than whom, perhaps, no man was ever better qualified to interpret the Scriptures. He says, "In the fourth verse, he (Paul) changes to the first person plural, because he intended to speak of the former experience of Christians, who had been Jews. In the seventh verse, he uses the first person singular, but speaks in the past tense, because he describes his own experience when he was an unconverted Pharisee. In the fourteenth verse, and unto the end of the chapter, he uses the first person singular, and the present tense, because he exhibits his own experience since he became a Christian and an apostle." ¶ *We know.* We admit. It is a conceded, well understood point. ¶ *That the law is spiritual.* This does not mean that the law is designed to control the spirit, in contradistinction from the body, but it is a declaration showing that the evils of which he was speaking were not the fault of the law. That was not, in its nature, sensual, corrupt, earthly, carnal; but was pure and spiritual. The *effect* described was not the fault of the law, but of the man, who was sold under sin. The word spiritual is often thus used to denote that which is pure and holy, in opposition to that which is fleshly or carnal; chap. viii. 5, 6; Gal. v. 16—23. The *flesh* is described as the source of evil passions and desires: the *spirit* as the source of purity; or as that which is agreeable to the proper influences of the Holy Spirit. ¶ *But I am.* The present tense shows that he is describing himself as he was at the time of writing. This is the natural and obvious construction, and if this be not the meaning, it is impossible to account for his having changed the past tense (ver. 7) to the present. ¶ *Carnal.* Fleshly; sensual; opposed to spiritual. This word is used because in the Scriptures the *flesh* is spoken of as the source of sensual passions and propensities, Gal. v. 19—21. The sense is, that these corrupt passions still retained a strong and withering and distressing influence over the mind. The renewed man is exposed to temptations from his strong native appetites; and the power of these passions, strengthened by long habit before he was converted, has travelled over into religion, and they continue still to influence and distress him. It does not mean that he is *wholly* under their influence: but that the tendency of his natural inclinations is to indulgence. ¶ *Sold under sin.* This expression is often adduced

is spiritual, but I am carnal, sold *a* under sin.
15 For that which I do, I allow [1] not: for what I would, that do I not; but what I hate, that do I.

a 2Kings 17.17.

1 know.

to show that it cannot be of a renewed man that the apostle is speaking. The argument is, that it cannot be affirmed of a Christian that he is sold under sin. A sufficient answer to this might be, that IN FACT, this is the very language which Christians often now adopt to express the strength of that native depravity against which they struggle, and that no language would *better* express it. It does not mean that they choose or prefer sins. It strongly implies that the *prevailing bent* of their mind is against it, but that such is its strength that it brings them into slavery to it. The expression here used, "*sold* under sin," is "borrowed from the practice of selling captives taken in war, as slaves." *(Stuart.)* It hence means to deliver into the power of any one, so that he shall be dependent on his will and control. *(Schleusner.)* The emphasis is not on the word *sold*, as if any *act* of selling had taken place, but the *effect* was as if he had been sold; *i. e.* he was subject to it, and under its control, and it means that sin, contrary to the prevailing inclination of his mind (ver. 15—17), had such an influence over him as to lead him to commit it, and thus to produce a state of conflict and grief; ver. 19—24. The verses which follow this are an explanation of the sense, and of the manner in which he was "sold under sin."

15. *For that which I do.* That is, the evil which I do, the sin of which I am conscious, and which troubles me. ¶ *I allow not.* I do not approve; I do not wish it; the prevailing bent of my inclinations and purposes is against it. Greek, "I *know* not;" see the margin. The word *know*, however, is sometimes used in the sense of approving, Prov. ii. 24, "Which have not *known* [approved] the depths of Satan;" compare Ps. ci. 4, I will not *know* a wicked person." Jer. i. 5. ¶ *For what I would.* That which I approve; and which is my prevailing and established desire. What I would wish *always* to do. ¶ *But what I hate.* What I disapprove of: what is contrary to my judgment; my prevailing inclination; my established principles of conduct. ¶ *That do I.* Under the influence of sinful propensities, and carnal inclinations and desires. This represents the strong native propensity to sin; and even the power of corrupt propensity under the restraining influence of the gospel. On this remarkable and important passage we may observe, (1.) That the prevailing propensity; the habitual fixed inclination of the mind of the Christian, is to do right. The evil course is hated, the right course is loved. This is the characteristic of a pious mind. It distinguishes a holy man from a sinner. (2.) The evil which is done is disapproved; is a source of grief; and the habitual desire of the mind is to avoid it, and be pure. This also distinguishes the Christian from the sinner. (3.) There is no need of being embarrassed here with any metaphysical difficulties or inquiries *how* this can be; for (*a*) it is *in fact* the experience of all Christians. The habitual, fixed inclination and desire of their minds is to serve God. They have a fixed abhorrence of sin; and yet they are conscious of imperfection, and error, and sin, that is the source of uneasiness and trouble. The strength of natural passion may in an unguarded moment overcome them. The power of long habits of previous thoughts may annoy them. A man who was an infidel before his conversion, and whose mind was filled with scepticism, and cavils, and blasphemy, will find the effect of his former habits of thinking lingering in his mind, and annoying his peace for years. These thoughts will start up with the rapidity of lightning. Thus it is with every vice and every opinion. It is one of the effects of *habit*. "The very passage of an impure thought through

16 If then I do that which I would not, I consent unto the law, that *it is* good.

17 Now then it is no more I that do it, but sin that dwelleth in me.

---

the mind leaves pollution behind it," and where sin has been long indulged, it leaves its withering, desolating effect on the soul long after conversion, and produces that state of conflict with which every Christian is familiar. (*b*) An effect *somewhat* similar is felt by all men. All are conscious of doing that, under the excitement of passion and prejudice, which their conscience and better judgment disapprove. A conflict thus exists, which is attended with as much metaphysical difficulty as the struggle in the Christian's mind referred to here. (*c*) The same thing was observed and described in the writings of the heathen. Thus Xenophon (Cyrop. vi. 1), Araspes, the Persian, says, in order to excuse his treasonable designs, "Certainly I must have two souls; for plainly it is not one and the same which is both evil and good; and at the same time wishes to do a thing and not to do it. Plainly then, there are two souls; and when the good one prevails, then it does good; and when the evil one predominates, then it does evil." So also Epictetus (Enchixid. ii. 26) says, "He that sins does not do what he would, but what he would not, that he does." With this passage it would almost seem that Paul was familiar, and had his eye on it when he wrote. So also the well-known passage from Ovid, Meta. vii. 9.

Aliudque Cupido,
Mens aliud suadet. Video meliora, proboque,
Deteriora sequor.

"Desire prompts to one thing, but the mind persuades to another. I see the good, and approve it, and yet pursue the wrong."—See other passages of similar import quoted in Grotius and Tholuck.

16. *I consent unto the law.* The very struggle with evil shows that it is not loved, or approved, but that the law which condemns it is really loved. Christians may here find a test of their piety. The fact of struggling against evil,—the desire to be free from it, and to overcome it, the anxiety and grief which it causes,—is an evidence that we do not love it, and that therefore we are the friends of God. Perhaps nothing can be a more decisive test of piety than a long-continued and painful struggle against evil passions and desires in every form, and a panting of the soul to be delivered from the power and dominion of sin.

17. *It is no more I that do it.* This is evidently figurative language, for it is really the man that sins when evil is committed. But the apostle makes a distinction between *sin* and that which he intends by the pronoun *I*. By the former he evidently means his corrupt nature. By the latter he refers to his renewed nature, his Christian principles. He means to say that he does not approve or love it in his present state, but that it is the result of his native propensities and passions. In his heart, and conscience, and habitual feeling, he did not choose to commit sin, but abhorred it. Thus every Christian can say that *he* does not choose to do evil, but would wish to be perfect; that he hates sin, and yet that his corrupt passions lead him astray. ¶ *But sin.* My corrupt passions and native propensities. ¶ *That dwelleth in me.* Dwelling in me as its home. This is a strong expression, denoting that sin had taken up its habitation in the mind, and abode there. It had not been yet wholly dislodged. This expression stands in contrast with another that occurs, where it is said that "the Spirit of God dwells" in the Christian, Rom. viii. 9; 1 Cor. iii. 16. The sense is, that he is strongly *influenced* by sin on the one hand, and by the Spirit on the other. From this expression has arisen the phrase so common among Christians, *in-dwelling sin*.

18. *For I know.* This is designed as an illustration of what he had just said, that sin dwelt in him. ¶ *That is, in my flesh.* In my unrenewed nature; in my propensities and incli-

18 For I know that in me (that is, in my flesh) dwelleth no [a] good thing: for to will is present with me; but *how* to perform that which is good I find not.

a Gen.6.5.

19 For [b] the good that I would, I do not: but the evil which I would not, that I do.

20 Now if I do that I would not, it is no more I that do it, but sin that dwelleth in me.

b Gal.5.17.

nations before conversion. Does not this qualifying expression show that in this discussion he was speaking of himself as a renewed man? Hence he is careful to imply that there was at that time in him something that was right or acceptable with God, but that that did not pertain to him by nature. ¶ *Dwelleth.* His soul was wholly *occupied* by that which was evil. It had taken entire possession. ¶ *No good thing.* There could not be possibly a stronger expression of belief of the doctrine of *total depravity.* It is Paul's own representation of himself. It proves that his heart was wholly evil. And if this was true of him, it is true of all others. It is a good way to examine ourselves, to inquire whether *we* have such a view of our own native character as to say that we *know* that in our flesh there dwelleth no good thing. The sense here is, that so far as the flesh was concerned, that is, in regard to his natural inclinations and desires, there was nothing good; all was evil. This was true in his entire conduct before conversion, where the desires of the flesh reigned and rioted without control; and it was true *after* conversion, so far as the natural inclinations and propensities of the flesh were concerned. All those operations in every state were evil, and not the less evil because they are experienced under the light and amidst the influences of the gospel. ¶ *To will.* To purpose or intend to do good. ¶ *Is present with me.* I can do that. It is possible; it is in my power. The expression may also imply that it was *near* to him (παϱάκειται), that is, it was constantly before him; it was now his habitual inclination and purpose of mind. It is the uniform, regular, habitual purpose of the Christian's mind to do *right.* ¶ *But how.* The sense would have been better retained here if the translators had not introduced the word *how.* The difficulty was not in the *mode* of performing it, but to do the *thing itself.* ¶ *I find not.* I do not find it in my power; or I find strong, constant obstacles, so that I fail of doing it. The obstacles are not natural, but such as arise from long indulgence in sin; the strong native propensity to evil.

19. *For the good,* &c. This is substantially a repetition of what is said in ver. 15. The repetition shows how full the mind of the apostle was of the subject; and how much inclined he was to dwell upon it, and to place it in every variety of form. It is not uncommon for Paul thus to express his intense interest in a subject, by placing it in a great variety of aspects, even at the hazard of much repetition.

20. *Now if I do,* &c. This verse is also a repetition of what was said in ver. 16, 17.

21. *I find then a law.* There is a law whose operation I experience whenever I attempt to do good. There have been various opinions about the meaning of the word *law* in this place. It is evident that it is used here in a sense somewhat unusual. But it retains the notion which commonly attaches to it of that which *binds,* or *controls.* And though this to which he refers differs from a *law,* inasmuch as it is not imposed by a superior, which is the usual idea of a law, yet it has so far the sense of law that it binds, controls, influences, or is that to which he was subject. There can be no doubt that he refers here to his carnal and corrupt nature; to the evil propensities and dispositions which were leading him astray. His representing this as a *law* is in accordance with all that he says of it, that it is *servitude,* that he is in bondage to it, and that it impedes his efforts to be holy and pure. The meaning is this,

21 I find then a law, that when I would do good, evil is present [a] with me.

22 For I delight [b] in the law of God after the inward [c] man.

23 But I see another law in [d]

a Ps.65.3. b Ps.1.2. c 2Cor.4.16; 1Pet.3.4. d chap.6.13,19.

"I find a habit, a propensity, an influence of corrupt passions and desires, which, when I would do right, impedes my progress, and prevents my accomplishing what I would." Comp. Gal. v. 17. Every Christian is as much acquainted with this as was the apostle Paul. ¶ *Do good.* Do right. Be perfect. ¶ *Evil.* Some corrupt desire, or improper feeling, or evil propensity. ¶ *Is present with me.* Is near; is at hand. It starts up unbidden, and undesired. It is in the path, and never leaves us, but is always ready to impede our going, and to turn us from our good designs; comp. Ps. lxv. 3, "Iniquities *prevail* against me.' The sense is, that to do evil is agreable to our strong natural inclinations and passions.

22. *For I delight.* The word used here (Συνήδομαι), occurs no where else in the New Testament. It properly means to rejoice with any one; and expresses not only *approbation* of the understanding, as the expression, "I *consent* unto the law," in ver. 16, but more than that it denotes sensible pleasure in the heart. It indicates not only *intellectual* assent, but *emotion*, an emotion of pleasure in the contemplation of the law. And this shows that the apostle is not speaking of an unrenewed man. Of such a man it might be said that his conscience approved the law; that his understanding was convinced that the law was good; but never yet did it occur that an impenitent sinner found emotions of pleasure in the contemplation of the pure and spiritual law of God. If this expression can be applied to an unrenewed man, there is, perhaps, not a single mark of a pious mind which may not with equal propriety be so applied. It is the natural, obvious, and usual mode of denoting the feelings of piety, an assent to the divine law followed with emotions of sensible delight in the contemplation. Comp. Ps. cxix. 97, "O how love I thy law; it is my meditation all the day." Ps. i. 2, "But his delight is in the law of the Lord." Ps. xix. 7—11; Job xxiii. 12. ¶ *In the law of God.* The word *law* here is used in a large sense, to denote all the communications which God had made to control man. The sense is, that the apostle was pleased with the whole. One mark of genuine piety is to be pleased with the whole of the divine requirements. ¶ *After the inward man.* In respect to the inward man. The expression "the inward man" is used sometimes to denote the rational part of man as opposed to the sensual; sometimes the mind as opposed to the body (comp. 2 Cor. iv. 16; 1 Pet. iii. 4). It is thus used by the Greek classic writers. Here it is used evidently in opposition to a carnal and corrupt nature; to the evil passions and desires of the soul in an unrenewed state; to what is called elsewhere "the old man which is corrupt according to the deceitful lusts." Eph. iv. 22. The "inward man" is elsewhere called "the *new* man" (Eph. iv. 24); and denotes not the mere intellect, or conscience, but is a personification of the principles of action by which a Christian is governed; the new nature; the holy disposition; the inclination of the heart that is renewed.

23. *But I see another law;* Note, ver. 21. ¶ *In my members.* In my body; in my flesh; in my corrupt and sinful propensities; Note, chap. vi. 13; comp. 1 Cor. vi. 15; Col. iii. 5. The body is composed of many members; and as the flesh is regarded as the source of sin (ver. 18), the law of sin is said to be in the members, *i. e.* in the body itself. ¶ *Warring against.* Fighting against; or resisting. ¶ *The law of my mind.* This stands opposed to the prevailing inclinations of a corrupt nature. It means the same as was expressed by the phrase "the inward man," and denotes the desires and purposes of a renewed heart. ¶ *And bringing me into captivity.* Making me a prisoner,

my members, warring against the law of my mind, and bringing me into captivity [a] to the law of sin which is in my members.

24 O [b] wretched man that I am! who shall deliver me from [1] the body of this death? [a]

25 I [b] thank God, through Jesus Christ our Lord. So then, with

a Ps.142.7. *b* Ps.38.2,10; 77.3—9.

1 or, *this body of death.* *a* Ps.88.5. *b* 1Cor.15.57.

or a captive. This is the completion of the figure respecting the warfare. A captive taken in war was at the disposal of the victor. So the apostle represents himself as engaged in a warfare; and as being overcome, and made an unwilling captive to the evil inclinations of the heart. The expression is strong; and denotes strong corrupt propensities. But though strong, it is believed it is language which all sincere Christians can adopt of themselves, as expressive of that painful and often disastrous conflict in their bosoms when they contend against the native propensities of their hearts.

24. *O wretched man that I am!* The feeling implied by this lamentation is the result of this painful conflict; and this frequent subjection to sinful propensities. The effect of this conflict is, (1.) To produce pain and distress. It is often an agonizing struggle between good and evil; a struggle which annoys the peace, and renders life wretched. (2.) It tends to produce humility. It is humbling to man to be thus under the influence of evil passions. It is degrading to his nature; a stain on his glory; and it tends to bring him into the dust, that he is under the control of *such* propensities, and so often gives indulgence to them. In such circumstances, the mind is overwhelmed with wretchedness, and instinctively sighs for relief. Can the law aid? Can man aid? Can any native strength of conscience or of reason aid? In vain all these are tried, and the Christian then calmly and thankfully acquiesces in the consolations of the apostle, that aid can be obtained only through Jesus Christ. ¶ *Who shall deliver me.* Who shall rescue me; the condition of a mind in deep distress, and conscious of its own weakness, and looking for aid. ¶ *The body of this death.* Marg. *This body of death.* The word *body* here is probably used as equivalent to *flesh,* denoting the corrupt and evil propensities of the soul; Note, ver. 18. It is thus used to denote the law of sin in the members, as being that with which the apostle was struggling, and from which he desired to be delivered. The expression "body of this death" is a Hebraism, denoting a body deadly in its tendency; and the whole expression may mean the corrupt principles of man; the carnal, evil affections that lead to death or to condemnation. The expression is one of vast strength, and strongly characteristic of the apostle Paul. It indicates, (1.) That it was near him, attending him, and was distressing in its nature. (2.) An earnest wish to be delivered from it. Some have supposed that he refers to a custom practised by ancient tyrants, of binding a dead body to a captive as a punishment, and compelling him to drag the cumbersome and offensive burden with him wherever he went. I do not see any evidence that the apostle had this in view. But such a fact may be used as a striking and perhaps not improper illustration of the meaning of the apostle here. No strength of words could express deeper feeling; none more feelingly indicate the necessity of the grace of God to accomplish that to which the unaided human powers are incompetent.

25. *I thank God.* That is, I thank God for effecting a deliverance to which I am myself incompetent. There *is* a way of rescue, and I trace it altogether to his mercy in the Lord Jesus Christ. What conscience could not do, what the law could not do, what unaided human strength could not do, has been accomplished by the plan of the gospel; and complete deliverance can be expected there, and there alone. This is the point to which all his reasoning had tended; and having thus

the mind I myself serve the law of God, but with the flesh the law of sin.

CHAPTER VIII.

THERE *is*, therefore, now no [a] condemnation to them which

a John3.18.

shown that the law was insufficient to effect this deliverance, he is now prepared to utter the language of Christian thankfulness that it can be effected by the gospel. The superiority of the gospel to the law in overcoming all the evils under which man labours, is thus triumphantly established; comp. 1 Cor. xv. 57. ¶ *So then.* As the result of the whole inquiry we have come to this conclusion. ¶ *With the mind.* With the understanding, the conscience, the purposes, or intentions of the soul. This is a characteristic of the renewed nature. Of no impenitent sinner could it be ever affirmed that with his mind he served the law of God. ¶ *I myself.* It is still the same person, though acting in this apparently contradictory manner. ¶ *Serve the law of God.* Do honour to it as a just and holy law (ver. 12, 16,) and am inclined to obey it, ver. 22, 24. ¶ *But with the flesh.* The corrupt propensities and lusts, ver. 18. ¶ *The law of sin.* That is, in the members. The flesh throughout, in all its native propensities and passions, leads to sin; it has no tendency to holiness; and its corruptions can be overcome only by the grace of God. We have thus, (1.) A view of the sad and painful conflict between sin and God. They are opposed in all things. (2.) We see the raging, withering effect of sin on the soul. In all circumstances it tends to death and woe. (3.) We see the feebleness of the law and of conscience to overcome this. The tendency of both is to produce conflict and woe. And, (4.) We see that the gospel only can overcome sin. To us it should be a subject of ever-increasing thankfulness, that what could not be accomplished by the law, can be thus effected by the gospel; and that God has devised a plan that thus effects complete deliverance, and which gives to the captive in sin an everlasting triumph.

CHAPTER VIII.

THIS chapter is one of the most interesting and precious portions of the sacred Scriptures. Some parts of it are attended with great difficulties; but its main scope and design is apparent to all. It is a continuation of the subject discussed in the previous chapter, and is intended mainly to show that the gospel could effect what the law was incapable of doing. In that chapter the apostle had shown that the law was incapable of producing sanctification or peace of mind. He had traced its influence on the mind in different conditions, and shown that equally before regeneration and afterwards, it was incapable of producing peace and holiness. Such was man, such were his propensities, that the application of *law* only tended to excite, to irritate, to produce conflict. The conscience, indeed, testified to the law that it was good; but still it had shown that it was not adapted to produce holiness of heart and peace, but agitation, conflict, and a state of excited sin. In opposition to this, he proceeds to show in this chapter the power of the gospel to produce that which the law could not. In doing this, he illustrates the subject by several considerations. (1.) The gospel does what the law could not do in giving life, and delivering from condemnation, ver. 1—13. (2.) It produces a spirit of *adoption*, and all the blessings which result from the filial confidence with which we can address God as our Father, in opposition to the law which produced only terror and alarm, ver. 14—17. (3.) It sustains the soul amidst its captivity to sin, and its trials, with the hope of a future deliverance—a complete and final redemption, of the body from all the evils of this life, ver. 18—25. (4.) It furnishes the aid of the Holy Spirit to sustain us in our trials and infirmities, ver. 26, 27. (5.) It gives the assurance that all things shall work together for good, since all things are connected with the purpose of God, and all that can occur to a Christian

are in Christ Jesus, who walk not [a]
after the flesh, but after the Spirit.
2 For the law of the Spirit of life
[b] in Christ Jesus hath made me free
[c] from the law of sin and death.
3 For what the law could not [d]

a Gal.5.16. b 2 Cor.3.6. c Gal.2.19; 5.1. d Acts 12.39; Heb.7.18,19.

---

comes in as a part of the *plan* of him who has resolved to save him, ver. 28—30. (6.) It ministers consolation from the fact that every thing that can affect the happiness of man is *on the side* of the Christian, and will cooperate in his favour; as, *e. g.* (*a*) *God*, in giving his Son, and in justifying the believer, ver. 31—33. (*b*) *Christ*, in dying, and rising, and interceding for Christians, ver. 34. (*c*) The love of a Christian to the Saviour is in itself so strong, that nothing can separate him from it, ver. 35—39. By all these considerations the superiority of the gospel to the law is shown, and assurance is given to the believer of his final salvation. By this interesting and conclusive train of reasoning, the apostle is prepared for the triumphant language of exultation with which he closes this most precious portion of the word of God.

1. There is, *therefore, now.* This is connected with the closing verses of chap. vii. The apostle had there shown that the law could not effect deliverance from sin, but that such deliverance was to be traced to the gospel alone; chap. vii. 23—25. It is implied here that there *was* condemnation under the law, and would be still, but for the intervention of the gospel. ¶ *No condemnation.* This does not mean that sin in believers is not to be condemned as much as any where, for the contrary is every where taught in the Scriptures; but it means, (1.) That the gospel does not pronounce condemnation like the law. Its office is to pardon; the office of the law, to condemn. The one never affords deliverance, but always condemns; the object of the other is to free from condemnation, and to set the soul at liberty. (2.) There is no *final* condemnation under the gospel. The office, design, and tendency of the gospel is to free from the condemning sentence of law. This is its first and its glorious announcement, that it frees lost and ruined men from a most fearful and terrible condemnation.

[The first verse of this chapter seems to be an inference from the whole preceding discussion. The apostle having established the doctrine of justification, and answered the objections commonly urged against it, now asserts his triumphant conclusion, "There is therefore, &c.; that is to say, it follows from all that has been said concerning the believer's justification by the righteousness of Christ, and his complete deliverance from the law as a covenant, that to him there can be no condemnation. The design of Paul is not so much to assert the different offices of the law and the gospel, as simply to state the fact in regard to the condition of a certain class, viz., those who are in Christ. To them there is *no* condemnation whatever; not only no *final* condemnation, but no condemnation *now*, from the moment of their union to Christ, and deliverance from the curse of the law. The reason is this: that Christ hath endured the penalty, and obeyed the precept of the law in their stead.

"Here," says Mr. Haldane on the passage, "it is often remarked that the apostle does not say, that there is in them (believers) neither matter of accusation, nor cause of condemnation; and yet this is all included in what he does say. And afterwards, in express terms, he denies that they can be either accused or condemned, which they might be, were there any ground for either. All that was condemnable in them, which was sin, has been condemned in their Surety, as is shown in the third verse."]

¶ *Which are in Christ Jesus.* Who are united to Christ. To be *in* him is an expression not seldom used in the New Testament, denoting close and intimate union. Phil. i. 1; iii. 9. 2 Cor. v. 17; Rom. xvi. 7—11. The *union* between Christ and his people is compared to that between the vine and its branches (John xv. 1—6), and hence believers are said to be *in* him in a similar sense, as deriving their support from him, and as united in feeling, in purpose, and destiny. (See the Supplem. Note on ver. 10.) *Who walk.* Who conduct, or live. Note, chap. iv. 12. *Not after the flesh.* Who do not live to gratify the corrupt desires and

do in that it was weak through the flesh, God, sending his own Son [b] in the likeness of sinful flesh, and [1] for sin, condemned sin in the flesh.

b Gal.3.13.

1 or, *by a sacrifice for sin.*

passions of the flesh; Note, chap. vii. 18. This is a characteristic of a Christian. What it is to walk after the flesh may be seen in Gal. v. 19—21. It follows that a man whose purpose of life is to gratify his corrupt desires, cannot be a Christian. Unless he lives not to gratify his flesh, he can have no evidence of piety. This is a test which is easily applied; and if every professor of religion were honest, there could be no danger of mistake, and there need be no doubts about his true character. ¶ *But after the Spirit.* As the Holy Spirit would lead or prompt. What the Spirit produces may be seen in Gal. v. 22, 23. If a man has these fruits of the Spirit, he is a Christian; if not, he is a stranger to religion, whatever else he may possess. And *this* test also is easily applied.

2. *For the law.* The word *law* here means that *rule, command,* or *influence* which "the Spirit of life" produces. That exerts a *control* which is here called *a law,* for a law often means any thing by which we are ruled or governed; see Notes, chap. vii. 21, 23. *Of the Spirit.* I see no reason to doubt here that this refers to the Holy Spirit. Evidently, at the close of ver. 1, the word has this reference. The phrase "the Spirit of life" then means the Holy Spirit producing or giving life; *i. e.* giving peace, joy, activity, salvation; in opposition to the law spoken of in chap. vii. that produced death and condemnation. ¶ *In Christ Jesus.* Under the Christian religion; or sent by Christ to apply his work to men. John xvi. 7—14. The Spirit is sent by Christ; his influence is a part of the Christian scheme; and his power accomplishes that which the law could not do. ¶ *Hath made me free.* That is, has delivered me from the predominating influence and control of sin. He cannot mean that he was perfect, for the whole tenor of his reasoning is opposed to that. But the design, the tendency, and the spirit of the gospel was to produce this freedom from what the law could not deliver; and he was now brought under the general power of this scheme. In the former state he was under a most bitter and galling bondage; chap. vii. 7—11. Now, he was brought under the influence of a scheme which contemplated freedom, and which produced it. ¶ *The law of sin and death.* The controlling influence of sin, leading to death and condemnation; chap. vii. 5—11.

[The law of sin and death may be explained of the moral law, which, though good in itself, has, ever since the fall, been the *occasion* both of sin and death. On the other hand, the law of the Spirit of life in Christ Jesus, may be explained of the gospel, which is ministered by the life-giving Spirit of Christ. He reveals and applies it. Now the gospel covenant sets free from the law of sin and death, and, therefore, this sense gives a good reason why there is no condemnation to them that are in Christ Jesus. But if we understand the apostle in the second verse, to speak of the opposite principles of grace and corruption, and to affirm, that the law, or influence of the former, hath made him free from the influence of the latter, we make him assert what is not consistent with the experience of the people of God, and assign as a reason of the assertion in the first verse, what is not a reason, since the *sanctification* of believers cannot be regarded as the ground of their deliverance from condemnation. The apostle must not be made to say, "there is no condemnation," &c., for we are sanctified, or freed from the law of corruption; but there is no condemnation, for the gospel hath delivered us from the condemning sentence of the law. This view likewise accords best with the continuation of the subject in the third verse, which assigns the reason of the assertion in verse second.]

3. *For what the law could not do.* The law of God, the moral law. It could not free from sin and condemnation. This the apostle had fully shown in chap. vii. ¶ *In that.* Because. ¶ *It was weak.* It was feeble and inefficacious. It could not accomplish it. ¶ *Through the flesh.* In consequence of the strength of sin, and of the evil and corrupt desires of the unrenewed heart. The fault was not in the law, which was good (chap. vii. 12), but it was owing to the strength

4 That the righteousness of the law might be fulfilled in us, who walk [a] not after the flesh, but after the Spirit.

a ver.1.

of the natural passions and the sinfulness of the unrenewed heart; see chap. vii. 7—11, where this influence is fully explained. ¶ *God, sending his own Son.* That is, God *did*, or *accomplished*, that, by sending his Son, which the law could not do. The word *did*, or *accomplished*, it is necessary to understand here, in order to complete the sense. ¶ *In the likeness of sinful flesh.* That is, he so far resembled sinful flesh that he partook of flesh, or the nature of man, but without any of its sinful propensities or desires. It was not human nature; not, as the Docetæ taught, human nature in appearance only; but it was human nature without any of its corruptions. ¶ *And for sin.* Margin, "By a sacrifice for sin." The expression evidently means, by an offering for sin, or that he was given as a sacrifice on account of sin. His being given had respect to sin. ¶ *Condemned sin in the flesh.* The *flesh* is regarded as the source of sin; Note, chap. vii. 18. The flesh being the seat and origin of transgression, the atoning sacrifice was made in the likeness of sinful flesh, that thus he might meet sin, as it were, on its own ground, and destroy it. He may be said to have *condemned* sin in this manner, (1.) Because the fact that he was given for it, and died on its account, was a condemnation of it. If sin had been approved by God he would not have made an atonement to secure its destruction. The depth and intensity of the woes of Christ on its account show the degree of abhorrence with which it is regarded by God. (2.) The word *condemn* may be used in the sense of *destroying*, *overcoming*, or *subduing*; 2 Pet. ii. 6, "And turning the cities of Sodom and Gomorrah into ashes, *condemned* them with an overthrow." In this sense the sacrifice of Christ has not only *condemned* sin as being evil, but has weakened its power and destroyed its influence, and will finally annihilate its existence in all who are saved by that death.

[By the sacrifice of Christ, God indeed showed his abhorrence of sin, and secured its final overthrow. It is not, however, of the *sanctifying influence* of this sacrifice, that the apostle seems here to speak, but of its *justifying power*. The sense, therefore, is that God passed a judicial sentence on sin, in the person of Christ, on account of which, *that* has been effected which the law could not effect, (justification namely). Sin being condemned in the human nature of Christ, cannot be condemned and punished in the persons of those represented by him. They *must* be justified.

This view gives consistency to the whole passage, from the first verse to the fourth inclusive. The apostle clearly *begins* with the subject of justification, when, in the first verse, he affirms, that to them who are in Christ Jesus, there is no condemnation. If the question be put, Why is this? the second verse gives for answer, that believers are delivered from the law as a covenant of works. (See the foregoing Supplementary Note). If the question again be put, Whence this deliverance? the third verse points to the sacrifice of Christ, which, the fourth verse assures us, was offered with the very design "that the righteousness of the law might be fulfilled in us." This clause, according to the principle of interpretation laid down above, does not relate to the believer's obedience to the righteous requirements of the law. The apostle has in view a more immediate design of the sacrifice of Christ. The right or demand of the law, (δικαιωμα) was satisfaction to its injured honour. Its penalty must be borne, as well as its precept obeyed. The sacrifice of Christ answered every claim. And as believers are *one* with him, the righteousness of the law has been "fulfilled in them."

The whole passage is thus consistently explained of justification.]

4. *That the righteousness of the law.* That we might be conformed to the law, or be obedient to its requirements, and no longer under the influence of the flesh and its corrupt desires. ¶ *Might be fulfilled.* That we might be obedient, or comply with its demands. ¶ *Who walk.* Note, ver. 1.

5. *For they that are after the flesh.* They that are under the influence of the corrupt and sinful desires of the flesh; Gal. v. 19—21. Those who are unrenewed. ¶ *Do mind the things of the flesh.* They are supremely devoted to the gratification of their cor-

5 For they that are after the flesh, [a] do mind the things of the flesh; but they that are after the Spirit, the things [b] of the Spirit.

6 For [1] to be carnally minded *is* death; [c] but [2] to be spiritually minded *is* life and peace:

7 Because the carnal mind is

a John.3.6; 1Cor.15.48. *b* 1Cor.2.14. 1 *the minding of the flesh.* *c* Gal.6.8. 2 *the minding of the Spirit.*

rupt desires. ¶ *But they that are after the Spirit.* Who are under its influence; who are led by the Spirit. ¶ *The things of the Spirit.* Those things which the Spirit produces, or which he effects in the mind, Gal. v. 21—23. This verse is for the purpose of illustration, and is designed to show that the tendency of religion is to produce as entire a devotedness to the service of God as men had before rendered to sin; that is, that they would be fully engaged in that to which they had devoted themselves. As the Christian, therefore, had devoted himself to the service of the Spirit, and had been brought under his influence, it was to be expected that he would make it his great and only object to cherish and cultivate the graces which that Spirit would produce.

6. *For to be carnally minded.* Margin, "The minding of the flesh." The sense is, that to follow the inclinations of the flesh, or the corrupt propensities of our nature, leads us to condemnation and death. The expression is one of great energy, and shows that it not only *leads* to death, or leads to misery, but that it is death itself; there is woe and condemnation in the *very act and purpose* of being supremely devoted to the corrupt passions. Its only tendency is condemnation and despair. ¶ Is *death.* The penalty of transgression; condemnation and eternal ruin; Note, chap. v. 12. ¶ *But to be spiritually minded.* Margin, "The minding of the Spirit." That is, making it the object of the mind, the end and aim of the actions, to cultivate the graces of the Spirit, and to submit to his influence. To be spiritually minded is to seek those feelings and views which the Holy Spirit produces, and to follow his leadings. ¶ Is *life.* This is opposed to *death* in ver. 5. It tends to life, and is in fact real life. For to possess and cultivate the graces of the spirit, to be led where he would guide us, is the design of our existence, and is the only path of happiness. ¶ *And peace.* Note, chap. vi.

7. *Because.* This is given as a reason for what is said in ver. 6. In that verse the apostle had affirmed that to be carnally minded *was* death, but he had not stated *why* it was. He now explains it by saying that it is enmity against God, and thus involves a sinner in conflict with him, and exposes to his condemnation. ¶ *The carnal mind.* This is the same expression as occurs in ver. 6 (τὸ φρόνημα τῆς σαρκός). It does not mean the mind itself, the intellect, or the will; it does not suppose that the mind or soul is *physically* depraved, or opposed to God; but it means that *the minding of the things of the flesh*, giving to them supreme attention, is hostility against God; and involves the sinner in a controversy with him, and hence leads to death and woe. This passage should not be alleged in proof that the *soul is physically depraved*, but merely that where there is a supreme regard to the flesh there is hostility to God. It does not directly prove the doctrine of universal depravity; but it proves only that where such attention exists to the corrupt desires of the soul, *there* is hostility to God. It is indeed *implied* that that supreme regard to the flesh exists every where by nature, but this is not expressly affirmed. For the object of the apostle here is not to teach the doctrine of depravity, but to show that where such depravity in fact exists, it involves the sinner in a fearful controversy with God. ¶ *Is enmity.* Hostility; hatred. It means that such a regard to the flesh is in fact hostility to God, because it is opposed to his law, and to his plan for purifying the soul; comp. James iv. 4; 1 John ii. 15. The minding of the things of the flesh also leads to the hatred of *God himself*, because he is opposed to it, and has expressed his

enmity against God; for it is not
subject to the law of God, neither
indeed can be.
8 So then they that are in the
flesh cannot please God.
9 But ye are not in the flesh, but

---

abhorrence of it. ¶ *Against God.* Towards God; or in regard to him. It supposes hostility to him. ¶ *For it.* The word "*it*" here refers to the minding of the things of the flesh. It does not mean that the *soul itself* is not subject to his law, but that the *minding* of those things is hostile to his law. The apostle does not express any opinion about the metaphysical ability of man, or discuss that question at all. The amount of his affirmation is simply, that the *minding of the flesh,* the supreme attention to its dictates and desires, is not and cannot be subject to the law of God. They are wholly contradictory and irreconcilable, just as much as the love of falsehood is inconsistent with the laws of truth; as intemperance is inconsistent with the law of temperance; and as adultery is a violation of the seventh commandment. But whether the *man himself* might not obey the law,—whether *he* has, or has not, ability to do it,— is a question which the apostle does not touch, and on which this passage should not be adduced. For whether the law of a particular sin is utterly irreconcilable with an opposite virtue, and whether the sinner is able to abandon that sin and pursue a different path, are very different inquiries. ¶ *Is not subject.* It is not in *subjection to* the command of God. The minding of the flesh is opposed to that law, and thus shows that it is hostile to God. ¶ *Neither indeed can be.* This is absolute and certain. It is impossible that it should be. There is the utmost inability in regard to it. The things are utterly irreconcilable. But the affirmation does not mean that the *heart* of the sinner might not be subject to God; or that his *soul* is so physically depraved that he cannot obey, or that *he* might not obey the law. On that, the apostle here expresses no opinion. That is not the subject of the discussion. It is simply that the supreme regard to the flesh, the minding of that, is *utterly irreconcilable* with the law of God. They are different things, and *can never* be made to harmonize; just as adultery *cannot* be chastity; falsehood *cannot* be truth; dishonesty *cannot* be honesty; hatred *cannot* be love. This passage, therefore, should not be adduced to prove the doctrine of man's inability to love God, for it does not refer to that, but it proves merely that a supreme regard to the things of the flesh is utterly inconsistent with the law of God; can never be reconciled with it; and involves the sinner in hostility with his Creator.

[Calvinists have been loudly accused of "taking an unfair advantage of this language, for the support of their favourite doctrine of the utter impotency of the unregenerate man, in appreciating, much less conforming to the divine injunctions." It is alleged that φρονημα της σαρκος refers to the disposition of the mind, and is properly translated, "the minding of the flesh." Therefore, it is this *disposition or affection*, and not the *mind itself*, that is enmity against God. But the meaning of the passage is not affected by this change in the translation. For the apostle affirms that this minding of the flesh is the uniform and prevailing disposition of unregenerate men. "They that are after the flesh," *i. e.*, unregenerate men, "*do mind* the things of the flesh." This is their character without exception. Now, if the natural mind be uniformly under the influence of this depraved disposition, is IT not enmity to God. Thus, in point of fact, there is no difference between the received and the amended translation. To affirm that the mind itself is not hostile to God, and that its disposition alone is so, is little better than metaphysical trifling, and deserves no more regard than the plea which any wicked man might easily establish, by declaring that his disposition only, and not himself, was hostile to the laws of religion and morals. On the whole, it is not easy to conceive how the apostle could more forcibly have affirmed the enmity of the natural mind against God. He first describes unrenewed men by their character or bent, and then asserts that this bent is the very essence of enmity against God—enmity in the abstract.

To any one ignorant of the subtleties of theological controversy, the doctrine of *moral inability* would seem a plain consequence from this view of the natural mind. "It is," says Mr Scott, on the passage "*morally* unable to do any thing but revolt against the divine law, and refuse obedience to it." We are told, however, that the passage under conin the Spirit, if so be that the Spirit of God dwell [a] in you. Now if any

a 1 Cor.8.19; Gal.4.6.

sideration affirms only, that unregenerate men, *while they continue in that state*, cannot please God, or yield obedience to his law, and leaves untouched the other question, concerning the power of the carnal mind to throw off the disposition of enmity, and return to subjection. But if it be not expressly affirmed by the apostle here, that *the carnal mind has not this power*, it would seem at least to be a plain enough *inference* from his doctrine. For if the disposition of the unregenerate man be enmity against God, whence is the motive to arise that shall make him dislike that disposition, and throw it aside, and assume a better in its stead? From *within* it cannot come, because, according to the supposition, *there* is enmity only; and love cannot arise out of hatred. If it come from without, from the aids and influences of the Spirit, the question is ceded, and the dispute at an end.

A very common way of casting discredit on the view which Calvinists entertain of the doctrine of man's inability, is to represent it as involving some *natural* or *physical* disqualification. Nothing can be more unfair. There is a wide difference between natural and moral inability. The one arises from "some defect or obstacle *extrinsic to the will*, either in the understanding, constitution of the body, or external objects:" the other from "the want of inclination, or the strength of a contrary inclination." Now the Scriptures no where assert, nor have rational Calvinists ever maintained, that there is any physical incapacity of this kind, apart from the corrupt bias and inclination of the will, on account of which, the natural man cannot be subject to the law of God. But on the other hand, the Scriptures are full of evidence on the subject of moral inability. Even were we to abandon this passage, the *general* doctrine of revelation is, that unregenerate men are *dead* in trespasses and in sins; and the entire change that takes place in regeneration and sanctification, is uniformly ascribed not to the "man himself," but to the power of the Spirit of God. Not only is the change carried on and perfected, but *begun* by him.

8. *So then*. It follows; it leads to this conclusion. ¶ *They that are in the flesh.* They who are unrenewed sinners; who are following supremely the desires of the flesh; chap. vii. 18. Those are meant here who follow fleshly appetites and desires, and who are not led by the Spirit of God. ¶ *Cannot please God*. That is, while they are thus in the flesh; while they thus pursue the desires of their corrupt nature, they cannot please God. But this affirms nothing respecting their ability to turn from this course, and to pursue a different mode of life. That is a different question. A child may be obstinate, proud, and disobedient; and *while in this state*, it may be affirmed of him that he cannot please his parent. But whether he might not *cease* to be obstinate, and become obedient, is a very different inquiry; and the two subjects should never be be confounded. It follows from this, (1.) That those who are unrenewed are *totally* depraved, since in this state they cannot please God. (2.) That none of their actions while in this state can be acceptable to him, since he is pleased only with those who are spiritually minded. (3.) That those who are in this state should turn from it without delay; as it is desirable that every man *should* please God. (4.) That if the sinner does not turn from his course, he will be ruined. With his present character he can never please him; neither in health nor sickness; neither in life nor death; neither on earth nor in hell. He is engaged in hostility against God; and if he does not himself forsake it, it will be endless, and involve his soul in all the evils of a personal, and direct, and eternal warfare with the Lord Almighty.

9. *But ye*. You who are Christians. This is the opposite character to that which he had been describing, and shows the power of the gospel. ¶ *Not in the flesh.* Not under the full influence of corrupt desires and passions. ¶ *But in the Spirit.* That is, you are spiritually minded; you are under the direction and influence of the Holy Spirit. ¶ *The Spirit of God.* The Holy Ghost. ¶ *Dwell in you.* The Holy Spirit is often represented as dwelling in the hearts of Christians (comp. 1 Cor. ii. 16, 17; vi. 19; 2 Cor. vi. 16; Eph. ii. 21, 22; Gal. iv. 6); and the meaning is not that there is a *personal* or *physical* indwelling of the Holy Ghost, but that he influences, directs, and guides Christians, producing meekness, love, joy, peace, long-

man have not the Spirit of Christ, he is none of his.

10 And if Christ *be* in you, the body *is* dead because of sin; but the Spirit *is* life because of righteousness.

suffering, gentleness, goodness, &c. Gal. v. 22, 23. The expression, *to dwell in* one, denotes intimacy of connection, and means that those things which are the fruits of the Spirit are produced in the heart. (See the Supplem. Note on ver. 10.) ¶ *Have not the Spirit of Christ.* The word *Spirit* is used in a great variety of significations in the Scriptures. It most commonly in the New Testament refers to the third person of the Trinity, the Holy Ghost. But the expression "the Spirit *of Christ*" is not, I believe, any where applied to him, except it may be 1 Pet. i. 11. He is called often the Spirit of God (Matt. iii. 16; xii. 28; 1 Cor. ii. 11, 14; iii. 16; vi. 11; Eph. iv. 30), but not the Spirit of the Father. The word spirit is often used to denote the temper, disposition; thus we say, a man of a generous *spirit*, or of a revengeful *spirit*, &c. It may possibly have this meaning here, and denotes that he who has not the temper or disposition of Christ is not his, or has no evidence of piety. But the connection seems to demand that it should be understood in a sense similar to the expression "the Spirit of God," and "the Spirit of him that raised up Jesus" (ver. 11); and if so, it means the Spirit which Christ imparts, or sends to accomplish his work (John xiv. 26), the Holy Spirit, sent to make us like Christ, and to sanctify our hearts. And in this sense it evidently denotes the Spirit which Christ would send to produce in us the views and feelings which he came to establish, and which shall assimilate us to himself. If this refers to the Holy Spirit, then we see the manner in which the apostle spoke of the Saviour. He regarded "the Spirit" as equally the Spirit of God and of Christ, as proceeding from both; and thus evidently believed that there is a union of nature between the Father and the Son. Such language could never be used except on the supposition that the Father and Son are one; that is. that Christ is divine. ¶ *Is none of his.* Is not a Christian. This is a test of piety that is easily applied; and this settles the question. If a man is not influenced by the meek, pure, and holy spirit of the Lord Jesus, if he is not conformed to his image, if his life does not resemble that of the Saviour, he is a stranger to religion. No test could be more easily applied, and none is more decisive. It matters not what else he may have. He may be loud in his professions, amiable in his temper, bold in his zeal, or active in promoting the interests of his own party or denomination in the church; but if he has not the temper of the Saviour, and does not manifest his Spirit, it is as sounding brass or a tinkling cymbal. May all who read this, honestly examine themselves; and may they have that which is the source of the purest felicity, the spirit and temper of the Lord Jesus.

10. *And if Christ* be *in you.* This is evidently a figurative expression, where the word "Christ" is used to denote his spirit, his principles; that is, he influences the man. Literally, he cannot be *in* a Christian; but the close connexion between him and Christians, and the fact that they are entirely under his influence, is expressed by this strong figurative language. It is language which is not unfrequently used; comp. Gal. ii. 20; Col. i. 27.

[The union between Christ and his people is sometimes explained of a merely *relative* in opposition to a *real* union. The union which subsists between a substitute, or surety, and the persons in whose room he has placed himself, is frequently offered in explanation of the Scripture language on the subject. In this view, Christ is regarded as *legally* one with his people, inasmuch, as what he has done or obtained, is held *as* done and obtained by them. Another relative union, employed to illustrate that which subsists between Christ and believers, is the union of a chief and his followers, which is simply a union of design, interest, sentiment, affection, destiny, &c. Now these representations are true *so far as they go*, and furnish much interesting and profitable illustration. They fall short, however, of the full sense of Scripture on the point. That there is a *real* or vital union between Christ and his people, appears from the *language* of the inspired writers in regard to it. The peculiar phraseology which they employ, cannot well be explained of any relative union At all events, it is as strong as they could have employed, on the supposition, that they had wished to convey the idea of the *most intimate possible connection.* Christ is said to be "*in them,*" and they are represented as "*in him.*" He "*abides* in them, and they in him." They "*dwell*" in each other; John xiv. 20; xv. 4; 1 John iii. 24; iv.12. Moreover, the Scripture *illustrations* of the subject furnish evidence to the same effect. The mystical union, as it has been called, is compared to the union of stones in a building, branches in a vine, members in a human body, and even to that which subsists between the Father and the Son; 1 Pet. ii. 4; Eph. ii. 20, 22; John xv. 1—8; 1 Cor. xii. 12—31; John xvii. 20—23. Now if all these are *real* unions, is not this union *real* also? If not, where is the propriety or justice of the comparisons? Instead of leading us to form accurate notions on the subject, they would seem calculated to mislead.

This real and vital union is formed by the one Spirit of Christ, the Holy Ghost pervading the Head and the members of the mystical body; 1 Cor. vi. 17; xii. 13; 1 John iii. 24; iv. 13. It is true, indeed, that the *essential* presence of Christ's Spirit is every where, but he is present in Christ's members, in a peculiar way, as the fountain of spiritual influence. This spiritual presence, which is the bond of union, is manifested immediately upon a man's reception of Christ by faith. From that hour he is one with Christ, because the same Spirit lives in both. Indeed this union is the *foundation* of all the relative unions which have been employed to illustrate the subject; without it, we could have no saving relation to Christ whatever. That it is mysterious cannot be denied. The apostle himself affirms as much, Eph. v. 32; Col. i. 27. Although we know the *fact,* we cannot explain the *manner* of it, but must not on this account reject it, any more than we would the doctrine of the Spirit's essential presence, because we do not understand *it.*]

¶ *The body* is *dead.* This passage has been interpreted in very different ways. Some understand it to mean that the body is dead *in respect to sin;* that is, that sin has no more power to excite evil passions and desires; others, that the body must die on account of sin but that the spiritual part shall live, and even the body shall live also in the resurrection. Thus Calvin, Beza, and Augustine. Doddridge understands it thus:—Though the body is to die on account of the first sin that entered into the world, yet the spirit is life, and shall continue to live on for ever, through that righteousness which the second Adam has introduced." To each of these interpretations there are serious objections, which it is not necessary to urge. I understand the passage in the following manner: The *body* refers to that of which the apostle had said so much in the previous chapters—the flesh, the man before conversion. It is subject to corrupt passions and desires, and may be said thus to be *dead,* as it has none of the elements of spiritual life. It is under the reign of sin and death. The word *μὲν, indeed,* or *truly,* has been omitted in our translation, and the omission has obscured the sense. The expression is an *admission* of the apostle, or a summary statement of what had before been shown. "It is to be admitted, indeed, or it is true, that the unrenewed nature, the man before conversion, under the influence of the flesh, is spiritually dead. Sin has its seat in the fleshly appetites; and the whole body may be admitted thus to be dead or corrupt." ¶ *Because of sin. Through* sin (δι' ἁμαρτίαν); by means of sinful passions and appetites. ¶ *But the spirit.* This stands opposed to the body; and it means that the soul, the immortal part, the renovated man, was alive, or was under the influence of living principles. It was imbued with the life which the gospel imparts, and had become active in the service of God. The word "spirit" here does not refer to the Holy Ghost, but to the spirit of man, the immortal part, recovered, renewed, and imbued with life under the gospel. ¶ *Because of righteousness.* Through righteousness (διὰ δικαιοσύνην). This is commonly interpreted to mean, with reference to righteousness, or that it may become righteous. But I understand the expression to be used in the sense in which the word is so frequently used in this epistle, as denoting *God's plan of justification*; see Note, chap. i. 17. "The spirit of man has been recovered and made alive through his plan of

11 But if the Spirit of him
that raised up Jesus from the
dead dwell in you, he [a] that raised
up Christ from the dead shall
also quicken your mortal bodies
[1] by his Spirit that dwelleth in
you.
12 Therefore, brethren, we are
debtors, not[b] to the flesh, to live
after the flesh.

a 2Cor.4.14.

1 or, *because of*. b Ps.116.16.

justification. It communicates life, and recovers man from his death in sin to life."

The "body" in this passage has generally been understood in the literal sense, which, doubtless, ought not to be rejected without some valid reason. There is nothing in the connection that demands the figurative sense. The apostle admits that, notwithstanding of the indwelling of the Spirit, the body *must* die. "It *indeed* (μὲν) is dead because of sin." The believer is not delivered from temporal death. Yet there are two things which may well reconcile him to the idea of laying aside for a while the clay tabernacle. The "mortal body," though it now die, is not destined to remain for ever under the dominion of death, but shall be raised again incorruptible and glorious, by the power of the same Spirit that raised up Jesus from the dead. Meanwhile, "the spirit, or soul, is life, because of righteousness." In consequence of that immaculate righteousness, of which Paul had had said so much in the previous part of this epistle, the souls of believers, even now, enjoy spiritual life, which shall issue in eternal life and glory.

Those who understand σῶμα figuratively in the 10th verse, insist, indeed, that the resurrection in the 11th, is figurative also. But "the best commentators" says Bloomfield, "both ancient and modern, with reason prefer the literal view, especially on account of the phrase θνητὰ σώματα which seems to confine it to this sense."]

11. *But if the Spirit of him*, &c. The Holy Spirit, ver. 9. ¶ *He that raised up Christ*, &c. He that had *power* to restore him to life, has power to give life to you. He that did, *in fact*, restore him to life, will also restore you. The argument here seems to be founded, first, on the power of God; and, secondly, on the connection between Christ and his people; comp. John xiv. 19, "Because I live, ye shall live also." ¶ *Shall also quicken*. Shall make alive. ¶ *Your mortal bodies*. That this does not refer to the resurrection of the dead seems to be apparent, because that is not attributed to the Holy Spirit. I understand it as referring to the body, subject to carnal desires and propensities; by nature under the reign of death, and therefore mortal; *i. e.* subject to death. The sense is, that under the gospel, by the influence of the Spirit, the entire man will be made alive in the service of God. Even the corrupt, carnal, and mortal body, so long under the dominion of sin, shall be made alive and recovered to the service of God. This will be done by the Spirit that dwells in us, because that Spirit has restored life to our souls, abides with us with his purifying influence, and because the design and tendency of his indwelling is to purify the entire man, and restore all to God. Christians thus in their bodies and their spirits become sacred. For even their body, the seat of evil passions and desires, shall become alive in the service of God.

12. *We are debtors*. We owe it as a matter of solemn obligation. This obligation arises, (1.) From the fact that the Spirit dwells in us; (2.) Because the design of his indwelling is to purify us; (3.) Because we are thus recovered from the death of sin to the life of religion; and he who has imparted life, has a right to require that it be spent in his service. ¶ *To the flesh*. To the corrupt propensities and passions. We are not bound to indulge them because the end of such indulgence is death and ruin; chap. vii. 21, 22. But we are bound to live to God, and to follow the leadings of his Spirit, for the end is life and peace; chap. vii. 22, 23. The reason for this is stated in the following verse.

13. *For if you live*, &c. If you live to indulge your carnal propensities, you will sink to eternal death; chap. vii. 23. ¶ *Through the Spirit*. By the aid of the Spirit; by cherishing and cultivating his influences. What is here required can be accomplished

13 For if ye live after the flesh, ye shall die: but if ye through the Spirit do mortify [a] the deeds of the body, ye shall live.

14 For as many as are led [b] by the Spirit of God, they are the sons of God.

15 For ye have not received the

a Col. 3.5. b Gal.5.18.

only by the aid of the Holy Ghost. ¶ *Do mortify.* Do put to death; do destroy. Sin is mortified when its power is destroyed, and it ceases to be active. ¶ *The deeds of the body.* The corrupt inclinations and passions; called deeds of *the body,* because they are supposed to have their origin in the fleshly appetites. ¶ *Ye shall live.* You shall be happy and saved. Either your sins must die, or you must. If they are suffered to live, you will die. If they are put to death, you will be saved. No man can be saved in his sins. This closes the argument of the apostle for the superiority of the gospel to the law in promoting the purity of man. By this train of reasoning, he has shown that the gospel has accomplished what the law could not do—the sanctification of the soul, the destruction of the corrupt passions of our nature, and the recovery of man to God.

14. *For as many.* Whosoever; all who are thus led. This introduces a new topic, illustrating the benefits of the gospel, to wit, that it produces a spirit of *adoption,* ver. 14—17. ¶ *As are led.* As submit to his influence and control. The Spirit is represented as influencing, suggesting, and controlling. One evidence of piety is, a willingness to *yield* to that influence, and submit to him. One decided evidence of the want of piety is, where there is an unwillingness to submit to that influence, but where the Holy Spirit is grieved and resisted. All Christians submit to his influence; all sinners decidedly reject it and oppose it. The influence of the Spirit, if followed, would lead every man to heaven. But when neglected, rejected, or despised, man goes down to hell. The glory belongs to the conducting Spirit when man is saved; the fault is man's when he is lost. The apostle here does not agitate the question *how* it is that the people of God are led by the Spirit, or why they yield to it when others resist it. His design is simply to state the fact, that they who *are* thus led are the sons of God, or have evidence of piety. ¶ *Are the sons of God.* Are adopted into his family, and are his children. This is a name of endearment, meaning that they sustain to him this relation; that they are his friends, disciples, and imitators; that they are parts of the great family of the redeemed, of whom he is the Father and Protector. It is often applied to Christians in the Bible; Job i. 6; John i. 12; Phil. ii. 15; 1 John iii. 1, 2; Mat. v. 9, 45; Luke vi. 35. This is a test of piety which is easily applied. (1.) Are we conscious that an influence from above has been drawing us away from the corrupting passions and vanities of this world? This is the work of the Spirit. (2.) Are we conscious of a desire to *yield* to that influence, and to be conducted in the path of purity and life? This is an evidence that we are the sons of God. (3.) Do we offer no resistance; do we follow cheerfully, and obey this pure influence, leading us to mortify pride, subdue passion, destroy lust, humble ambition, and annihilate the love of wealth and of the world? If so, we are his children. God will not lead us astray; and our peace and happiness consists only in *yielding* ourselves to this influence entirely, and in being willing to be conducted by this unseen hand "beside the still waters of salvation."

15. *The spirit of bondage.* The spirit that binds you; or the spirit of a slave, that produces only fear. The slave is under constant fear and alarm. But the spirit of religion is that of freedom and of confidence; the spirit of children, and not of slaves; compare Note, John viii. 32—36. ¶ *Again to fear.* That you should again be afraid, or be subjected to servile fear. This implies that in their former state

spirit of bondage [a] again, to fear;
but [b] ye have received the Spirit
of adoption, [c] whereby we cry,
Abba, Father.
16 The Spirit itself beareth witness [d] with our spirit, that we are
the children of God:
17 And if children, then heirs;
[e] heirs of God, and joint-heirs with
Christ; [f] if so be that we suffer

a 2Tim.1.7. *b* 1Cor.2.12. *c* Jer.3.19;Gal.4.5 6. *d* 2Cor.1.22;1John4.13. *e* Acts26.18;1Pet.1.4. *f* 2Tim.2.11,12.

under the law, they were in a state of servitude, and that the tendency of it was merely to produce alarm. Every sinner is subject to such fear. He has every thing of which to be alarmed. God is angry with him; his conscience will trouble him; and he has every thing to apprehend in death and in eternity. But it is not so with the Christian; comp. 2 Tim. i. 7. ¶ *The spirit of adoption.* The feeling of affection, love, and confidence which pertains to children; not the servile, trembling spirit of slaves, but the temper and affectionate regard of sons. Adoption is the taking and treating a stranger as one's own child. It is applied to Christians because God treats them as his children; he receives them into this relation, though they were by nature strangers and enemies. It implies, (1.) That we by nature had no claim on him; (2.) That therefore, the act is one of mere kindness—of pure, sovereign love; (3.) That we are now under his protection and care; and, (4.) That we are bound to manifest towards him the spirit of children, and yield to him obedience. See Note, John i. 12; comp. Gal. iv. 5; Eph. i. 5. It is for this that Christians are so often called the sons of God. ¶ *Whereby we cry.* As children who need protection and help. This evinces the habitual spirit of a child of God; a disposition, (1.) To express towards him the feelings due to a father; (2.) To call upon him; to address him in the language of affection and endearing confidence; (3.) To seek his protection and aid. ¶ *Abba.* This word is Chaldee (אבא), and means *father*. Why the apostle *repeats* the word in a different language, is not known. The Syriac reads it, "By which we call the Father our Father." It is probable that the repetition here denotes merely *intensity*, and is designed to denote the *interest* with which a Christian dwells on the name, in the spirit of an affectionate, tender child. It is not unusual to repeat such terms of affection; comp. Mat. vii. 22; Ps. viii. 1. This is an evidence of piety that is easily applied. He that can in sincerity, and with ardent affection apply this term to God, addressing him with a filial spirit as his Father, has the spirit of a Christian. Every child of God has this spirit; and he that has it not is a stranger to piety.

16. *The Spirit.* The Holy Spirit. That the Holy Spirit here is intended, is evident, (1.) Because this is the natural meaning of the expression; (2.) Because it is of the Holy Spirit that the apostle is mainly treating here; (3.) Because it would be an unnatural and forced construction to say of the *temper of adoption* that *it* bore witness. ¶ *Beareth witness.* Testifies, gives evidence. ¶ *With our spirit.* To our minds. This pertains to the adoption; and it means that the Holy Spirit furnishes evidence to our minds that we are adopted into the family of God. This effect is not unfrequently attributed to the Holy Spirit, 2 Cor. i. 22; 1 John v. 10, 11; 1 Cor. ii. 12. If it be asked *how* this is done, I answer, it is not by any revelation of new truth; it is not by inspiration; it is not always by assurance; it is not by a mere persuasion that we are elected to eternal life; but it is by *producing in us the appropriate effects of his influence.* It is his to renew the heart; to sanctify the soul; to produce "love, joy, peace, long-suffering, gentleness, goodness, faith, meekness, temperance," Gal. v. 22, 23. If a man has *these*, he has evidence of the witnessing of the Spirit with *his* spirit. If not, he has no such evidence. And the way, therefore, to ascertain whether we have this witnessing of the Spirit, is by an honest and prayerful inquiry whether these *fruits* of the Spirit

with *him*, that we may be also glorified together.

18 For I reckon [a] that the sufferings of this present time *are* not

a Cor.4.17.

actually exist in our minds. If they do, the evidence is clear. If not, all vain confidence of good estate; all visions, and raptures, and fancied revelations, will be mere delusions. It may be added, that the *effect* of these fruits of the Spirit on the mind is to produce a calm and heavenly frame; and in that frame, when attended with the appropriate fruits of the Spirit in a holy life, we may rejoice as an evidence of piety. ¶ *That we are the children of God.* That we are adopted into his family.

17. *And if children.* If adopted into his family. ¶ *Then heirs.* That is, he will treat us as sons. An *heir* is one who succeeds to an estate. The meaning here is, that if we sustain the relation of sons to God, that we shall be treated as such, and admitted to share his favours. An adopted son comes in for a part of the inheritance, Num. xxvii. ¶ *Heirs of God.* This expression means that we shall be partakers of that inheritance which God confers on his people. That inheritance is his favour here, and eternal life hereafter. This is an honour infinitely higher than to be heir to the most princely earthly inheritance; or than to be the adopted son of the most magnificent earthly monarch. ¶ *And joint heirs with Christ.* Christ is by eminence THE *Son of God.* As such, he is heir to the full honours and glory of heaven. Christians are united to him; they are his friends; and they are thus represented as destined to partake with him of his glory. They are the sons of God in a different sense from what he is; *he* by his nature and high relation, *they* by adoption; but still the idea of *sonship* exists in both; and hence both will partake in the glories of the eternal inheritance; compare Phil. ii. 8, 9; Heb. ii. 9, 10. The connection between Christ and Christians is often referred to in the New Testament. The fact that they are united here is often alleged as a reason why they will be in glory, John xiv. 19, "Because I live, ye shall live also," 2 Tim. ii. 11, 12; "For if we be dead with him, we shall also live with him; if we suffer, we shall also reign with him, Rev. iii. 21; "To him that overcometh will I grant to sit with me in my throne," &c., John xvii. 22—24. ¶ *If so be.* If this condition exist. We shall not be treated as co-heirs with him, unless we here give evidence that we are united to him. ¶ *That we suffer with* him. Greek, "If we suffer together, that we may also be glorified together." If we suffer in his cause; bear afflictions as he did; are persecuted and tried for the same thing; and thus show that we are united to him. It does not mean that we suffer to the same *extent* that he did, but we may *imitate* him in the kind of our sufferings, and in the spirit with which they are borne; and thus show that *we are* united to him. ¶ *That we may be also glorified together.* If united in the same kind of sufferings, there is propriety in being united in destiny beyond the scenes of all suffering, the kingdom of blessedness and love.

18. *For I reckon.* I think; I judge. This verse commences a new division of the subject, which is continued to ver. 25. Its design is to show the power of the gospel in sustaining the soul in trials; a very important and material part of the scheme. This had been partially noticed before (chap. v. 3—5), but its full power to support the soul in the prospect of a glorious immortality had not been fully discussed. This topic seems here to have been suggested by what is said of *adoption.* The mind of the apostle instantly adverted to the effects or benefits of that adoption; and one of the most material of those benefits was the sustaining grace which the gospel imparted in the midst of afflictions. It should be borne in mind that the early Christians were comparatively few and feeble, and exposed to many trials, and that *this* topic would be often, therefore, introduced into the discus-

worthy *to be compared* with the glory which shall be revealed in us.

19 For the earnest expectation of the creature waiteth for the manifestation of the sons of God.

---

sions about their privileges and condition. ¶ *The sufferings.* The afflictions; the persecutions, sicknesses, &c. The expression evidently includes not only the *peculiar* trials of Christians at that time, but all that believers are ever called to endure. ¶ *Of this present time.* Probably the apostle had *particular* reference to the various calamities *then* endured. But the expression is equally applicable to afflictions of all times and in all places. ¶ Are *not worthy* to be compared. Are nothing in comparison; the one is far more than an equivalent, in compensation for the other. ¶ *With the glory.* The happiness; the honour in heaven. ¶ *Which shall be revealed in us.* That shall be disclosed to us; or of which we shall be the partakers in heaven. The usual representation of heaven is that of glory, splendour, magnificence, or light; comp. Rev. xxi. 10, 23, 24; xxii. 5. By this, therefore, Christians may be sustained. Their sufferings may seem great; but they should remember that they are nothing in comparison with future glory. They are nothing *in degree.* For these are light compared with that "eternal weight of glory" which they shall "work out." 2 Cor. iv. 17. They are nothing *in duration.* For these sufferings are but for a moment; but the glory shall be eternal. These will soon pass away; but that glory shall never become dim or diminished; it will increase and expand for ever and ever. ¶ *In us.* Unto us (εἰς ἡμᾶς).

19. *For the earnest expectation.* (ἀποκαραδοκία). This word occurs only here and in Phil. i. 20, "According to my *earnest expectation* and my hope," &c. It properly denotes a state of earnest desire to see any object when the head is thrust forward; an intense anxiety; an ardent wish; and is thus well employed to denote the intense interest with which a Christian looks to his future inheritance. ¶ *Of the creature* (τῆς κτίσεως). Perhaps there is not a passage in the New Testament that has been deemed more difficult of interpretation than this (ver. 19—23); and after all the labours bestowed on it by critics, still there is no explanation proposed which is perfectly satisfactory, or in which commentators concur. The object here will be to give what appears to the writer the true meaning, without attempting to controvert the opinions of critics. The *main design* of the passage is, to *show the sustaining power of the gospel in the midst of trials, by the prospect of the future deliverance and inheritance of the sons of God.* This scope of the passage is to guide us in the interpretation. The following are, I suppose, the leading points in the illustration. (1.) The word *creature* refers to the renewed nature of the Christian, or to the Christian as renewed. (2.) He is waiting for his future glory; *i. e.* desirous of obtaining the full development of the honours that await him as the child of God; ver. 19. (3.) He is subjected to a state of trial and vanity, affording comparatively little comfort and much disquietude. (4.) This is not in accordance with the desire of his heart, "not willingly," but is the wise appointment of God; ver. 20. (5.) In this state there is the hope of deliverance into glorious liberty; ver. 21. (6.) This condition of things does not exist merely in regard to the Christian, but is the common condition of the world. It all groans, and is in trial, as much as the Christian. He therefore should not deem his condition as peculiarly trying. It is the common lot of all things here; ver. 22. But, (7.) Christians only have the prospect of deliverance. To them is held out the hope of final rescue, and of an eternal inheritance beyond all these sufferings. They wait, therefore, for the full benefits of the adoption; the complete recovery even of the body from the effects of sin, and the toils and trials of this live; and thus they are sustained by hope, which is the argument which the apostle has in view; ver. 23, 24. With this view of

the general scope of the passage, we may examine the particular phrases.

[The opinion which is perhaps most generally adopted of this difficult passage, is that which explains κτίσις of the whole irrational creation. According to this view, the apostle, having adverted to the glory that awaited the Christian, as a ground of joy and comfort under present sufferings, exalts our idea of it still higher by representing the external world as participating in, and waiting for it. "This interpretation is suitable to the design of the apostle. Paul's object is not to confirm the certainty of a future state, but to produce a strong impression of its glorious character. Nothing could be better adapted to this object, than the grand and beautiful figure of the whole creation waiting and longing for the glorious revelation of the Son of God, and the consummation of his kingdom." *Hodge.* In the original it is the same word that is rendered alternately "creature" and "creation." And the meaning of the passage depends, in great measure, on the sense of this single word. Generally speaking, it signifies any thing created. The particular kind of creation is determined by the context alone. Of course, whatever sense we may attach to it, must be continued throughout the whole passage, as we cannot suppose the apostle uses the same word in two different senses, in one place, without any intimation of the change. To what then does κτίσις refer? It is maintained by those who adopt the view noticed above, that it cannot refer to angels, either elect or fallen, since the former have never been subject to the bondage of corruption, and the latter are not waiting for the manifestation of the sons of God; that it cannot allude to wicked men, for neither do they anxiously look out for this manifestation; that it can no more refer to saints or renewed men, since these are expressly distinguished as a separate class in the 23d verse; and that, therefore, it must be understood of the whole inanimate and irrational creation. It is further argued, that every part of the context may be explained consistently with this view. The passage is supposed to present a very bold and beautiful instance of the figure called prosopopoeia, by which things inanimate are invested with life and feeling, a figure which is indeed very common in Scripture, and which we need not be surprised to find in this place, amid so much that is grand and elevating; Joel i. 10, 20; Jer. xii. 4; Is. xxiv. 4, 7. According to this interpretation of κτίσις then, the general sense of the apostle may be thus given. The whole irrational creation is interested in the future glory of the sons of God, and is anxiously waiting for it. For then the curse will be removed from the very ground, and the lower animals relieved from oppression and cruelty. The very creation, on account of the sin of man, has been subjected to the curse, and has become "vain" or useless in regard to the original design of it, having been made subservient to the evil purposes and passions of man. This state of subjection to vanity is not willing, but by restraint. Violence is imposed, as it were, on external nature. But this shall not continue. There is hope in the heart of the subject world, that (ὅτι) it shall be delivered from this bondage, and participate in the liberty of the children of God. This representation may seem strange and unusual, but "we know" certainly, adds the apostle, that it is so; that "the *whole* creation πᾶσα ἡ κτίσις, groaneth and travaileth in pain throughout every part. Even we, who are saints of God, and have been favoured with the earnests of future bliss, feel the general oppression, and groan within ourselves, while we wait for the period of deliverance, in which the very body shall be ransomed from the grave and fashioned like unto Christ's glorious body.]

¶ *Of the creature.* The word here rendered creature (κτίσις), occurs in the New Testament nineteen times, and is used in the following senses: (1.) Creation; the act of creating; Rom. i. 20. (2.) The creature; that which is created or formed; the universe; Mark x. 6; xiii. 19; 2 Pet. iii. 4; Rom. i. 25; viii. 39. (3.) The rational creation; man as a rational being; the world of mankind; Mark xvi. 15; Col. i. 23; 1 Pet. ii. 13. (4.) Perhaps the church, the new creation of God taken collectively; Col. i. 15; Rev. iii. 14. (5.) The *Christian*, the new creation, regarded individually; the work of the Holy Spirit on the renewed heart; the new man.—After all the attention which I can give to this passage, I regard this to be the meaning here, for the following reasons, viz. (1.) Because this alone seems to me to suit the connection, and to make sense in the argument. If the word refers, as has been supposed by different interpreters, either to angels, or to the bodies of men, or to the material creation, or to the rational creation—to men, or mankind; it is difficult to see what connection either would have with the argument. The apostle is discoursing of the benefits of the gospel to *Christians* in time of trial; and the bearing of the argument requires us to under-

20 For the creature was made subject to vanity, not willingly,

stand this illustration of them, unless we are compelled *not* to understand it thus by the proper laws of interpreting words. (2.) The word *creature* is used in a similar sense by the same apostle. Thus 2 Cor. v. 17, "If any man be in Christ, he is a *new creature*" (καινὴ κτίσις). Gal. vi. 15, "For in Christ Jesus neither circumcision availeth any thing, nor uncircumcision, but a *new creature*." (3.) The verb *create* is thus used. Thus Eph. ii. 10, "For we are his workmanship, *created* in Christ Jesus unto good works." Ver. 15, "Having abolished in his flesh the enmity....for to make in himself of twain one new man:" Greek, "That he might *create* (κτίσῃ) the two into one new man." iv. 24, "The new man, which *is created* in righteousness," &c. (4.) Nothing was more natural than for the sacred writers thus to speak of a Christian as a new creation, a new creature. The great power of God involved in his conversion, and the strong resemblance between the creation and imparting spiritual life, led naturally to this use of the language. (5.) Language similar to this occurs in the Old Testament, and it was natural to transfer it to the New. The Jewish people were represented as *made* or created by God for his service, and the phrase, therefore, might come to designate those who were thus formed by him to his service. Deut. xxxii. 6, "Hath he not *made thee*, and established thee?" Isaiah xliii. 7, "....Every one that is called by my name; for I have *created* him for my glory, I have formed him; yea, I have made him." 21, "This people have I *formed* for myself." From all which reasons, it seems to me that the expression here is used to denote Christians, renewed men. Its meaning, however, is varied in ver. 22. ¶ *Waiteth for*. Expects; is not in a state of possession, but is looking for it with interest. ¶ *The manifestation of the sons of God*. The full development of the benefits of the sons of God; the time when they shall be acknowledged, and received into the full privileges of sons. Here Christians have *some* evidence of their adoption. But they are in a world of sin; they are exposed to trials; they are subject to many calamities; and though they have evidence *here* that they are the sons of God, yet they wait for that period when they shall be fully delivered from all these trials, and be admitted to the enjoyment of all the privileges of the children of the Most High. The time when this shall take place will be at the day of judgment, when they shall be fully acknowledged in the presence of an assembled universe as his children. All Christians are represented as in this posture of *waiting* for the full possession of their privileges as the children of God. 1 Cor. i. 7, "Waiting for the coming of our Lord Jesus Christ." 2 Thess. iii. 5; Gal. v. 5, "For we through the Spirit wait for the hope of righteousness by faith." 1 Thess. i. 10.

20. *For the creature*. The renewed creature; the Christian mind. This is given as a reason for its *aspiring* to the full privileges of adoption, that the present state is not one of choice, or one which is preferred, but one to which it has been subjected for wise reasons by God. ¶ *Subject to vanity*. The word "subject to" means placed in such a state; subjected to it by the appointment of another, as a soldier has his rank and place assigned him in an army. The word *vanity* here (ματαιότης) is descriptive of the present condition of the Christian, as frail and dying; as exposed to trials, temptations, and cares; as in the midst of conflicts, and of a world which may be emphatically pronounced *vanity*. More or less, the Christian is brought under this influence; his joys are marred; his peace is discomposed; his affections wander; his life is a life of vanity and vexation. ¶ *Not willingly*. Not voluntarily. It is not a matter of choice. It is not that which is congenial to his renewed nature. That would aspire to perfect holiness and peace. But this subjection is one that is contrary to it, and from which he desires to be delivered. This describes substantially the same con-

but by reason of him who hath subjected *the same* in hope;

21 Because [a] the creature itself also shall be delivered from the

a 2Pet.3.13.

dition as chap. vii. 15—24. ¶ *But by reason. By* him (διὰ). It is the appointment of God, who has chosen to place his people in this condition; and who for wise purposes retains them in it. ¶ *Who hath subjected* the same. Who has appointed his people to this condition. It is his wise arrangement. Here we may observe, (1.) That the instinctive feelings of Christians lead them to desire a purer and a happier world, Phil. i. 23. (2.) That it is not what they desire, to be subjected to the toils of this life, and to the temptations and vanities of this world. They sigh for deliverance. (3.) Their lot in life; their being subjected to this state of vanity, is the arrangement of God. *Why* it is, he has not seen fit to inform us fully. He *might* have taken his people at once to heaven as soon as they are converted. But though we know not *all* the reasons why they are continued here in this state of *vanity*, we can see some of them: (*a*) Christians are subjected to this state *to do good* to their fellow sinners. They remain on earth for this purpose: and this should be their leading aim. (*b*) By their remaining here the power of the gospel is shown in overcoming their sin; in meeting their temptations; in sustaining them in trial; and in thus furnishing living evidence to the world of the power and excellency of that gospel. This could not be attained if they were removed at once to heaven. (*c*) It furnishes occasion for some interesting exhibitions of character—for hope, and faith, and love, and for increasing and progressive excellence. (*d*) It is a proper *training* for heaven. It brings out the Christian character, and *fits it* for the skies. There may be inestimable advantages, all of which we may not see, in subjecting the Christian to a process of *training* in overcoming his sins, and in producing confidence in God, before he is admitted to his state of final rest. (*e*) It is fit and proper that he should engage here in the service of Him who has redeemed him. He has been ransomed by the blood of Christ, and God has the highest claim on him in all the conflicts and toils, in all the labours and services to which he may be subjected in this life. ¶ *In hope;* see Note, chap. v. 4. Hope has reference to the future; and in this state of the Christian, he sighs for deliverance, and expects it.

21. *Because.* This is the ground of his hope, and this sustains him now. It is the purpose of God that deliverance shall be granted, and this supports the Christian amidst the trials to which he is subjected here. The hope is, that this same renewed man shall be delivered from all the toils, and cares, and sins of this state. ¶ *The creature itself.* The very soul that is renewed; the ransomed man without essential change. It will be the same being, though purified; the same man, possessed of the same body and soul, though freed from all the corruptions of humanity, and elevated above all the degradations of the present condition. The idea is every where presented, that the identical person shall be admitted to heaven without essential change, 1 Cor. xv. 35—38, 42—44. That this is the hope of all Christians, see 2 Pet. iii. 13. ¶ *From the bondage of corruption.* This does not differ materially from "vanity," ver. 20. It implies that this state is not a *willing* state, or not a condition of choice, but is one of *bondage* or *servitude* (see chap. vii. 15—24); and that it is a *corrupt*, imperfect, perishing condition. It is one that leads to sin, and temptation, and conflict and anxiety. It is a condition often which destroys the peace, mars the happiness, dims the hope, enfeebles the faith, and weakens the love of Christians, and this is called the *bondage* of corruption. It is also one in which temporal death has dominion, and in the bondage of which, believers as well as unbelivers shall be held. Yet from *all* this bondage the children of God

bondage of corruption into the glorious liberty of the children of God.

22 For we know that the whole creation groaneth and travaileth in pain together until now.

1 or, *every creature.*

shall be delivered. ¶ *The glorious liberty.* Greek, The freedom of the glory of the children of God. This is, (1.) *Liberty.* It is freedom from the bondage under which the Christian groans. It will be freedom from sin; from corruption; from evil desires; from calamity; from death. The highest *freedom* in the universe is that which is enjoyed in heaven, where the redeemed are under the sovereignty and government of their king, but where they do that, and that only, which they desire. All is slavery but the service of God; all is bondage but that law which accords with the supreme wish of the soul, and where commands accord with the perfect desires of the heart. (2.) This is *glorious* liberty. It is encompassed with majesty; attended with honour; crowned with splendour. The heavenly world is often described as a state of glory; Note, chap. ii. 10. ¶ *Of the children of God.* That the children of God shall enjoy.

22. *For we know.* The sentiment of this verse is designed as an illustration of what had just been said. ¶ *That the whole creation.* Margin, "*every creature.*" This expression has been commonly understood as meaning the same as "the creature" in ver. 20, 21. But I understand it as having a different signification; and as being used in the natural and usual signification of the word creature, or creation. It refers, as I suppose, to the whole animate creation; to all living beings; to the state of all created things here, as in a condition of pain and disorder, and groaning and death. Every thing which we see; every creature which lives, is thus subjected to a state of servitude, pain, vanity, and death. The reasons for supposing that this is the true interpretation, are, (1.) That the apostle expressly speaks of "the *whole* creation," of every creature, qualifying the phrase by the expression "we know," as if he was drawing an illustration from a well-understood, universal fact. (2.) This interpretation makes consistent sense, and makes the verse have a direct bearing on the argument. *It is just an argument from analogy.* He had (ver. 20, 21) said that the condition of a Christian was one of bondage and servitude. It was an imperfect, humiliating state; one attended with pain, sorrow, and death. This might be regarded as a melancholy description, and the question might arise, why was not the Christian at once delivered from this? The answer is in this verse. *It is just the condition of every thing.* It is the manifest principle on which God governs the world. *The whole creation is in just this condition;* and we are not to be surprised, therefore, if it is the condition of the believer. It is a part of the universal system of things; it accords with every thing we see; and we are not to be surprised that the church exists on the same principle of administration; in a state of bondage, imperfection, sorrow, and sighing for deliverance. ¶ *Groaneth.* Greek, Groans together. All is united in a condition of sorrow. The expression denotes mutual and universal grief. It is one wide and loud lamentation, in which a dying world unites; and in which it has united "until now." ¶ *And travaileth in pain together.* This expression properly denotes the extreme pain of parturition. It also denotes any intense agony, or extreme suffering; and it means here that the condition of all things has been that of intense, united, and continued suffering; in other words, that we are in a world of misery and death. This has been *united;* all have partaken of it: it has been *intense;* all endure much: it has been *unremitted;* every age has experienced the repetition of the same thing. ¶ *Until now.* Till the time when the apostle wrote. It is equally true of the time since he wrote. It

23 And not only *they*, but ourselves also, which have the first-fruits [a] of the Spirit, even we ourselves groan [b] within ourselves, waiting for the adoption, *to wit*, the redemption [c] of our body.

a Eph.1.14. b 2Cor.5.2,4. c Luke 21.28.

has been the characteristic of every age. It is remarkable that the apostle does not here say of "the whole creation," that it had any hope of deliverance; an additional consideration that shows that the interpretation above suggested is correct, ver. 20, 21, 23. Of the sighing and suffering universe, he says nothing with respect to its future state. He does not say that the suffering brutal creation shall be compensated, or shall be restored or raised up. He simply adverts to the fact that it suffers, as an illustration that the condition of the Christian is not singular and peculiar. The Scriptures say nothing of the future condition of the brutal creation.

23. *And not only* they. Not only the creation in general. ¶ *But ourselves also.* Christians. ¶ *Which have the first-fruits of the Spirit.* The word used (ἀπαρχὴ) denotes properly the first-fruits of the harvest, the portion that was first collected and consecrated to God as an offering of gratitude, Deut. xxvi. 2; Ex. xxiii. 19; Num. xviii. 13. Hence the word means that which is *first in order of time.* Here it means, as I suppose, that the Christians of whom Paul was speaking had partaken of the *first* influences of the Spirit, or had been among the first partakers of his influences in converting sinners. The Spirit had been sent down to attend the preaching of the gospel, and they were among the first who had partaken of those influences. Some, however, have understood the word to mean a pledge, or earnest, or foretaste of joys to come. This idea has been attached to the word because the first-fruits of the harvest were a pledge of the harvest, an evidence that it was ripe, &c. But the word does not seem to be used in this sense in the New Testament. The only places where it occurs are the following; Rom. viii. 23; xi. 16; xvi. 5; 1 Cor. xv. 20, 23; xvi. 15; James i. 18; Rev. xiv. 4. ¶ *Groan within ourselves.* We sigh for deliverance. The expression denotes strong internal desire; the deep anguish of spirit when the heart is oppressed with anguish, and earnestly wishes for succour. ¶ *Waiting for the adoption.* Waiting for the full blessings of the adoption. Christians are adopted when they are converted (ver. 15), but they have not been yet admitted to the full privileges of their adoption into the family of God. Their adoption when they are converted is secret, and may at the time be unknown to the world. The fulness of the adoption, their complete admission to the privileges of the sons of God, shall be in the day of judgment, in the presence of the universe, and amidst the glories of the final consummation of all things. This adoption is not different from the first, but is the *completion* of the act of grace when a sinner is received into the family of God. ¶ *The redemption of the body.* The complete recovery of the body from death and corruption. The particular and striking act of the adoption in the day of judgment will be the raising up of the body from the grave, and rendering it immortal and eternally blessed. The particular effects of the adoption in this world are on *the soul.* The completion of it on the last day will be seen particularly in *the body;* and thus *the entire man* shall be admitted into the favour of God, and restored from all his sins and all the evil consequences of the fall. The apostle here speaks the language of every Christian. The Christian has joys which the world does not know; but he has also sorrows; he sighs over his corruption; he is in the midst of calamity; he is going to the grave; and he looks forward to that complete deliverance, and to that elevated state, when, in the presence of an assembled universe, he shall be acknowledged as a child of God. This elevated privilege gives to Christianity its high value; and the hope of being acknowledged in the presence of the

24 For we are saved by hope: but hope that is seen, is not hope; for what a man seeth, why doth he yet hope [a] for?

25 But if we hope for that we see not, *then* do we with patience wait for *it*.

26 Likewise the Spirit also help-

a 2Cor.5.7.

universe as the child of God—the hope of the poorest and the humblest believer—is of infinitely more value than the prospect of the most princely inheritance, or of the brightest crown that a monarch ever wore.

24. *For we are saved by hope.* It cannot be said that *hope* is the instrument or condition of salvation. Most commentators have understood this as meaning that we have as yet attained salvation only *in* hope; that we have arrived only to a condition in which we hope for *future* glory; and that we are in an attitude of waiting for the future state of adoption. But perhaps the word *saved* may mean here simply, we are *kept, preserved, sustained* in our trials, by hope. Our trials are so great that nothing but the prospect of future deliverance would uphold us; and the prospect is sufficient to enable us to bear them with patience. This is the proper meaning of the word *save;* and it is often thus used in the New Testament; see Matt. viii. 25; xvi. 25; Mark iii. 4; viii. 35. The Syriac renders this, "For by hope we live." The Arabic, "We are preserved by hope." Hope thus sustains the soul in the midst of trials, and enables it to bear them without a murmur. ¶ *But hope that is seen. Hope* is a complex emotion, made up of an earnest desire, and an expectation of obtaining an object. It has reference, therefore, to that which is at present unseen. But when the object is seen, and is in our possession, it cannot be said to be an object of hope. The word *hope* here means the *object* of hope, the thing hoped for. ¶ *What a man seeth.* The word *seeth* is used here in the sense of possessing, or enjoying. What a man already possesses, he cannot be said to hope for. ¶ *Why.* How. What a man actually possesses, *how* can he look forward to it with anticipation?

25. *But if we hope,* &c. The effect here stated is one which exists everywhere. Where there is a *strong desire* for an object, and a *corresponding expectation* of obtaining it—which constitutes true hope—then we can wait for it with patience. Where there is a strong desire without a corresponding expectation of obtaining it, there is *impatience.* As the Christian has a strong desire of future glory, and as he has an expectation of obtaining it just in proportion to that desire, it follows that he may bear trials and persecutions patiently in the hope of his future deliverance. Compared with our future glory, our present sufferings are light, and but for a moment; 2 Cor. iv. 17. In the hope of that blessed eternity which is before him, the Christian can endure the severest trial, and bear the intensest pain without a murmur.

26. *Likewise the Spirit.* This introduces a new source of consolation and support, that which is derived from the Spirit. It is a continuation of the argument of the apostle, to show the sustaining power of the Christian religion. The "Spirit" here undoubtedly refers to the Holy Spirit, who dwells in us, and who strengthens us. ¶ *Helpeth.* This word properly means, to sustain *with* us; to aid us in supporting. It is applied usually to those who *unite* in supporting or carrying a burden. The meaning may be thus expressed: "he greatly assists or aids us." ¶ *Our infirmities.* Assists us in our infirmities, or aids us to bear them. The word *infirmities* refers to the weaknesses to which we are subject, and to our various trials in this life. The Spirit helps us in this, (1.) By giving us strength to bear them; (2.) By exciting us to make efforts to sustain them; (3.) By ministering to us consolations, and truths, and views of our Christian privileges, that enable us to endure our trials. ¶ *For we know not,* &c. This is a *specification* of the aid which the Holy Spirit renders us. The reasons why Christians do not know

eth our infirmities: for we know not what we should pray for as we ought; but [a] the Spirit itself maketh intercession for us with groanings which cannot be uttered.

a Zech.12.10.

27 And he [b] that searcheth the hearts knoweth what *is* the mind of the Spirit because [1] he maketh intercession for the saints according [c] *to the will of* God.

b Jer.17.10; Rev.2.23. 1 or, *that*. c 1John 5.14.

---

what to pray for may be, (1.) That they do not know what would be really best for them. (2.) They do not know what God might be willing to grant them. (3.) They are to a great extent ignorant of the character of God, the reason of his dealings, the principles of his government, and their own real wants. (4.) They are often in real, deep perplexity. They are encompassed with trials, exposed to temptations, feeble by disease, and subject to calamities. In these circumstances, if left alone, they would neither be able to bear their trials, nor know what to ask at the hand of God. ¶ *But the Spirit itself.* The Holy Spirit; ver. 9—11. ¶ *Maketh intercession.* The word here used (ὑπερεντυγχάνει), occurs no where else in the New Testament. The word ἐντυγχάνω, however, is used several times. It means properly to be present with any one for the purpose of aiding, as an advocate does in a court of justice; hence to intercede for any one, or to aid or assist in any manner. In this place it simply means that the Holy Spirit *greatly assists* or *aids* us; not by praying for us, but in our prayers and infirmities. ¶ *With groanings.* With *sighs*, or that deep feeling and intense anxiety which exists in the oppressed and burdened heart of the Christian. ¶ *Which cannot be uttered.* Or rather, perhaps, which is *not* uttered; those emotions which are too deep for utterance, or for expression in articulate language. This does not mean that the Spirit *produces* these groanings; but that *in* these deep-felt emotions, when the soul is oppressed and overwhelmed, he lends us his assistance and sustains us. The phrase may be thus translated: "The Spirit greatly aids or supports us in those deep emotions, those intense feelings, those inward sighs which cannot be expressed in language, but which he enables us to bear, and which are understood by Him that searcheth the hearts."

27. *And he that searcheth the hearts.* God. To search the heart is one of his attributes which cannot be communicated to a creature; Jer. xvii. 10. ¶ *Knoweth what is the mind of the Spirit.* Knows the desires which the Holy Spirit excites and produces in the heart. He does not need that those deep emotions should be expressed in words; he does not need the eloquence of language to induce him to hear; but he sees the anxious feelings of the soul, and is ready to aid and to bless. ¶ *Maketh intercession for the saints.* Aids and directs Christians. ¶ *According to the will of God.* Greek, "According to God." It is according to his will in the following respects: (1.) The Spirit is given according to his will. It is his gracious purpose to grant his aid to all who truly love him. (2.) The desires which he excites in the heart of the Christian are those which are according to his will; they are such as God wishes to exist; the contrite, humble, and penitent pleading of sinners for mercy. (3.) He superintends and guards Christians in their prayers. It is not meant that they are infallible, or that they *never* make an improper petition, or have an improper desire; but that he has a *general* superintendence over their minds, and that so far as they will yield themselves to his direction, they shall not be led into error. That man is most safe who yields himself most entirely to the influence of the Holy Spirit. And the doctrine here stated is one that is full of consolation to the Christian. We are poor, and needy, and ignorant, and blind; we are the creatures of a day, and are crushed before the moth. But in the midst of our feebleness we may look to God for the aid of his Spirit, and rejoice in his presence, and

28 And we know [a] that all things work together for good to them that love God, to them who are the called according to *his* purpose.

a Ps.46.1,2, Heb.12.6-12.

---

in his power to sustain us in our sighings, and to guide us in our wanderings.

28. *And we know.* This verse introduces another source of consolation and support, drawn from the fact that all things are under the direction of an infinitely wise Being, who has purposed the salvation of the Christian, and who has so appointed all things that they shall contribute to it. ¶ *All things.* All our afflictions and trials; all the persecutions and calamities to which we are exposed. Though they are numerous and long-continued, yet they are among the means that are appointed for our welfare. ¶ *Work together for good.* They shall co-operate; they shall mutually contribute to our good. They take off our affections from this world; they teach us the truth about our frail, transitory, and lying condition; they lead us to look to God for support, and to heaven for a final home; and they produce a subdued spirit, a humble temper, a patient, tender, and kind disposition. This has been the experience of all saints; and at the end of life they have been able to say it was good for them to be afflicted; Ps. cxix. 67, 71; Jer. xxxi. 18, 19; Heb. xii. 11. ¶ *For good.* For our real welfare; for the promotion of true piety, peace, and happiness in our hearts. ¶ *To them that love God.* This is a characteristic of true piety. To them, afflictions are a blessing. To others, they often prove otherwise. On others they are sent as chastisements; and they produce murmuring, instead of peace; rebellion, instead of submission; and anger, impatience, and hatred, instead of calmness, patience, and love. The Christian is made a better man by receiving afflictions as they should be received, and by desiring that they should accomplish the purpose for which they are sent; the sinner is made more hardened by resisting them, and refusing to submit to their obvious intention and design. ¶ *To them who are the called.* Christians are often represented as *called* of God. The word (κλητὸς) is sometimes used to denote an external invitation, offer, or calling; Matt. xx. 16; xxii. 14. But excepting in these places, it is used in the New Testament to denote those who had *accepted* the call, and were true Christians; Rom. i. 6, 7; 1 Cor. i. 2, 24; Rev. xvii. 14. It is evidently used in this sense here—to denote those who were true Christians. The connection as well as the usual meaning of the word, requires us thus to understand it. Christians are said to be *called* because God has invited them to be saved, and has sent into their heart such an influence as to make the call effectual to their salvation.[a] In this way their salvation is to be traced entirely to God. ¶ *According to his purpose.* The word here rendered *purpose* (πρόθεσις) means properly a *proposition,* or a laying down any thing in view of others; and is thus applied to the *bread* that was laid on the table of *show-bread;* Matt. xii. 4; Mark ii. 26; Luke vi. 4. Hence it means, when applied to the mind, a *plan* or *purpose* of mind. It implies that God had a plan, purpose, or intention, in regard to all who became Christians. They are not saved by chance or hap-hazard. God does not convert men without design; and his designs are not new, but are eternal. What he does, he always meant to do. What it is *right* for him to do, it was right always to *intend* to do. What God always meant to do, is his purpose or plan. That he *has* such a purpose in regard to the salvation of his people, is often affirmed; Rom. ix. 11; Eph. i. 11; iii. 11; 2 Tim. i. 9; Jer. li. 29. This *purpose* of saving his people is, (1.) One over which a creature can have no control; it is according to the counsel of his own will; Eph. i. 11. (2.) It is without any merit on the part of the sinner—a purpose to save him by grace; 2 Tim. i. 9. (3.) It is eternal; Eph. iii. 11. (4.) It is such as should excite lively gratitude in all who have been inclined by the grace

29 For whom he did foreknow, [a] he also did predestinate *to be* conformed to the image of his Son, that he might be the first-born among many brethren.

30 Moreover whom he did pre-

a 1Pet.1.2.

of God to accept the offers of eternal life. They owe it to the mere mercy of God, and they should acknowledge *him* as the fountain and source of all their hopes of heaven.

29. *For whom he did foreknow.* The word used here (προέγνω) has been the subject of almost endless disputes in regard to its meaning in this place. The *literal* meaning of the word cannot be a matter of dispute. It denotes properly to *know beforehand;* to be acquainted with future events. But whether it means here simply to know that certain persons *would* become Christians ; or to ordain, and constitute them to be Christians, and to be saved, has been a subject of almost endless discussion. Without entering at large into an investigation of the word, perhaps the following remarks may throw light on it. (1.) It does not here have reference to *all* the human family ; for all are not, and have not, been conformed to the image of his Son. It has reference therefore only to those who would become Christians, and be saved. (2.) It implies *certain knowledge.* It was certainly foreseen, in some way, that they would believe, and be saved. There is nothing, therefore, in regard to them that is *contingent,* or subject to doubt in the divine Mind, since it was certainly foreknown. (3.) The event which was thus foreknown must have been, for some cause, *certain* and *fixed ;* since an uncertain event could not be possibly foreknown. To talk of a foreknowing a contingent event, that is, of foreknowing an event as certain which may or may not exist, is an absurdity. (4.) In what way such an event became certain is not determined by the use of this word. But it must have been somehow in connection with a divine appointment or arrangement, since in no other way can it be conceived to be certain. While the *word* used here, therefore, does not of necessity mean to decree, yet its use supposes that there *was* a purpose or plan; and the phrase is an explanation of what the apostle had just said, that it was *according to the purpose* of God that they were called. This passage does not affirm *why,* or *how,* or, *on what grounds* God foreknew that some of the human family would be saved. It simply affirms the fact ; and the mode in which those who will believe were designated, must be determined from other sources. This passage simply teaches that he knew them ; that his eye was fixed on them ; that he regarded them as to be conformed to his Son ; and that, thus knowing them, he designated them to eternal life. The Syriac renders it in accordance with this interpretation : " And from the beginning he knew them, and sealed them with the image of his Son," &c. As, however, none *would* believe but by the influences of his Spirit, it follows that they were not foreknown on account of any faith which they would themselves exercise, or any good works which they would themselves perform, but according to the purpose or plan of God himself. ¶ *He also did predestinate.* See the meaning of the original of this word explained in Notes on chap. i. 4 ; see also Note on Acts iv. 28 ; and 1 Cor. ii. 7. In these places the word evidently means to determine, purpose, or decree beforehand ; and it *must* have this meaning here. No other idea could be consistent with the proper meaning of the word, or be intelligible. It is clear also that it does not refer to *external* privileges, but to real conversion and piety ; since that to which they were predestinated was not the external privilege of the gospel, but conformity to his Son, and salvation ; see ver. 30. No passage could possibly teach in stronger language that it was God's purpose to save those who will be saved. Eph. i. 5, " Having predestinated us unto the adoption of children by Jesus Christ unto himself." ver. 11, Being

destinate, them he also called: [a]
and whom he called, them he also
justified: [b] and whom he justified,
them he also glorified. [c]

31 What shall we then say to
these things? If [d] God *be* for us,
who *can be* against us?
32 He [e] that spared not his own

a Heb.9.15. b 1Cor.6.11. c John17.22. d Ps.118.6. e chap.5.6-10.

predestinated according to the purpose of Him who worketh all things after the counsel of his own will." ¶ *To be conformed to the image of his Son.* To resemble his Son; to be of like form with the image of his Son. We may learn here, (1.) That God does not determine to save men, whatever their character may be. The decree is not to save them in their sins, or whether they be sinful or holy. But it has primary respect to their character. It is that they *should be* holy; and, as a *consequence* of this, that they should be saved. (2.) The only evidence which we can have that we are the subjects of his gracious purpose is, that we are *in fact* conformed to the Lord Jesus Christ. For this was the design of the decree. This is the only satisfactory proof of piety; and by this alone can we determine that we are interested in his gracious plan of saving men. ¶ *That he might be the first-born.* The *first-born* among the Hebrews had many peculiar privileges. The idea here is, (1.) That Christ might be pre-eminent as the model and exemplar; that he might be clothed with peculiar honours, and be so regarded in his church; and yet, (2.) That he might still sustain a fraternal relation to them; that he might be one in the same great family of God where *all* are sons; comp. Heb. ii. 12—14. ¶ *Many brethren.* Not a few. The purpose of God is that *many* of the human family shall be saved.

30. *Moreover,* &c. In this verse, in order to show to Christians the true consolation to be derived from the fact that they are predestinated, the apostle states the connection between that predestination and their certain salvation. The one implied the other. ¶ *Whom he did predestinate.* All whom he did predestinate. ¶ *Them he also called.* Called by his Spirit to become Christians. He called, not merely by an *external* invitation, but in such a way as that they *in fact* were justified. This cannot refer simply to an *external* call of the gospel, since those who are here said to be called are said also to be justified and glorified. The meaning is, that there is a certain connection between the predestination and the call, which will be manifested in due time. The connection is so certain that the one infallibly secures the other. ¶ *He justified*; see Note, chap. iii. 24. Not that he justified them *from eternity,* for this was not true; and *if* it were, it would also follow that he *glorified* them from eternity, which would be an absurdity. It means that there is a regular *sequence* of events—the predestination precedes and secures the calling; and the calling precedes and secures the justification. The one is connected in the purpose of God with the other; and the one, *in fact,* does not take place without the other. The purpose was *in eternity.* The calling and justifying *in time.* ¶ *Them he also glorified.* This refers probably to heaven. It means that there is a connection between justification and glory. The one does not exist without the other in its own proper time; as the calling does not subsist without the act of justification. This *proves,* therefore, the doctrine of the perseverance of the saints. There is a connection infallible and ever existing between the predestination and the final salvation. They who are subjects of the one are partakers of the other. That this is the sense is clear, (1.) Because it is the natural and obvious meaning of the passage. (2.) Because this only would meet the design of the argument of the apostle. For how would it be a source of consolation to say to them that whom God foreknew he predestinated, and whom he predestinated he called, and whom he called he justified, and whom he justified *might fall away and be lost for ever?*

31. *What shall we then say,* &c.

Son, but delivered him up for us all, how shall he not with him also freely give us all things?

33 Who [a] shall lay any thing to the charge of God's elect? It [b] *is* God that justifieth.

a Isa.50.8,9. *b* Rev.12.10,11.

What fairly follows from the facts stated? or what conclusion shall we draw in regard to the power of the Christian religion to support us in our trials from the considerations which have been stated? What the influence *is* he proceeds to state. ¶ *If God be for us.* Be on our side, or is our friend, as he has shown himself to be by adopting us (ver. 15), by granting to us his Spirit (ver. 16, 17, 26, 27), and by his gracious purpose to save us, ver. 29, 30). ¶ *Who can be against us?* Who can injure or destroy us? Sinners may be against us, and so may the great enemy of our souls, but their power to destroy us is taken away. God is more mighty than all our foes; and he can defend and save us; see Ps. cxviii. 6. "The Lord is on my side; I will not fear what man can do unto me." The proposition advanced in this verse, Paul proceeds to illustrate by various specifications, which continue to the end of the chapter.

32. *He that spared not.* Who did not retain, or keep from suffering and death. ¶ *His own Son.* Who thus gave the *highest* proof of love that a father could give, and the highest demonstration of his willingness to do good to those for whom he gave him. ¶ *But delivered him up.* Gave him into the hands of men, and to a cruel death; Note, Acts ii. 23. ¶ *For us all.* For all Christians. The connection requires that this expression should be understood here with this limitation. The argument for the security of *all* Christians is here derived from the fact, that God had shown them equal love in giving his Son for them. It was not merely for the apostles; not only for the rich, and the great; but for the most humble and obscure of the flock of Christ. For them he endured as severe pangs, and expressed as much love, as for the rich and the great that shall be redeemed. The most humble and obscure believer may derive consolation from the fact that Christ died for *him*, and that God has expressed the highest love for him which we can conceive to be possible. ¶ *How shall he not.* His giving his Son is a proof that he *will* give to us all things that we need. The argument is from the greater to the less. He that has given the greater gift will not withhold the less. ¶ *All things.* All things that may be needful for our welfare. These things he will give *freely;* without money and without price. His first great gift, that of his Son, was a free gift; and all others that we may need will be given in a similar manner. It is not by money, nor by our merit, but it is by the mere mercy of God; so that from the beginning to the end of the work it is all of grace. We see here, (1.) The privilege of being a Christian. He has the friendship of God; has been favoured with the highest proofs of divine love; and has assurance that he shall receive all that he needs. (2.) He has evidence that God will continue to be his friend. He that has given *his Son* to die for his people will not withdraw the lesser mercies that may be necessary to secure their salvation. The argument of the apostle here, therefore, is one that strongly shows that God will not forsake his children, but will keep them to eternal life.

33. *Who shall lay any thing to the charge.* This expression is taken from courts of law, and means, who shall accuse, or condemn, or so charge with crime before the tribunal of God as to cause their condemnation? ¶ *God's elect.* His chosen people. Those who have been chosen according to his eternal purpose; Note, ver. 28. As they are the chosen of God, they are dear to him; and as he purposed to save them, he will do it in such a way as that none can bring against them a charge that would condemn them. ¶ *It is God that justifieth.* That is, who has pardoned them, and admitted them to his favour; and pronounced them *just* in his sight; Note, chap. is

34 Who *is* he that condemneth? *It is* Christ that died, yea rather, that is risen again, who is even at the right hand of God, who also maketh intercession for us.

35 Who shall separate us from

17; iii. 24. It would be absurd to suppose that *he* would again condemn them. The fact that he has justified them is, therefore, a strong proof that they will be saved. This may be read with more force as a question, "Who shall lay any thing to the charge of God's elect? Shall God who justifieth?" The Greek will bear either mode of rendering. The passage implies that there would be a high degree of absurdity in supposing that the same Being would both justify and condemn the same individual. The Christian, therefore, is secure.

34. *Who is he that condemneth?* Who shall pass sentence of condemnation, and consign to perdition? The office of passing sentence of condemnation on men shall pertain to Christ, the judge of quick and dead, and the apostle proceeds to say that it was certain that *he* would not condemn the elect of God. They were therefore secure. ¶ It is *Christ that died.* Or as it may be rendered, "Shall Christ who has died, condemn them?" The argument here is, that as Christ died *to save* them, and not to destroy them, he will not condemn them. His death *for* them is a security that he will not condemn them. As he died to save them, and as they have actually *embraced* his salvation, there is the highest security that *he* will not condemn them. This is the *first* argument for their security from the death of Christ. ¶ *Yea rather, that is risen again.* This is a *second* consideration for their security from his work. *He rose for their justification* (Note, chap. iv. 25); and as this was the object which he had in view, it follows that he will not condemn them. ¶ *Who is even at the right hand of God.* Invested with power, and dignity, and authority in heaven. This is a *third* consideration to show that Christ will not condemn us, and that Christians are secure. He is clothed with power; he is exalted to honour; he is placed at the head of all things. And this solemn enthronement and investiture with power over the universe, is with express reference to the salvation of his church and people; Matt. xxviii. 18, 19; John xvii. 2; Eph. i. 20—23. The Christian is, therefore, under the *protection* of Christ, and is secure from being condemned by him. ¶ *Who also maketh intercession for us;* Note, ver. 26. Who pleads our cause; who aids and assists us; who presents our interests before the mercy-seat in the heavens. For this purpose he ascended to heaven; Heb. vii. 25. This is the *fourth* consideration which the apostle urges for the security of Christians drawn from the work of Christ. By all these, he argues their complete security from being subject to condemnation by him who shall pronounce the doom of all mankind, and therefore their complete safety in the day of judgment. Having the Judge of all for our friend, we are safe.

35. *Who shall separate us.* That is, finally or entirely separate us. This is a new argument of the apostle, showing his strong confidence in the safety of the Christian. ¶ *From the love of Christ.* This expression is ambiguous; and may mean either our love *to* Christ or *his* love to us. I understand it in the former sense, and suppose it means, "Who shall cause us to cease to love the saviour?" In other words, the love which Christians have for their Redeemer is so strong, that it will surmount and survive all opposition and all trials. The reason for so understanding the expression is, that it is not conceivable how afflictions, &c. should have any tendency to alienate Christ's love *from us;* but their supposed tendency to alienate *our love* from him might be very strong. They are endured in his cause. They are caused, in a good degree, by professed attachment to him. The persecutions and trials to which Christians are exposed on account of their professed attachment to him, might be supposed to make them weary of a service that

the love of Christ? *Shall* tribulation, or distress, or persecution, or famine, or nakedness, or peril, or sword?
36 As it is written,[a] For thy sake we are killed all the day long;
we are accounted as sheep for the slaughter.
37 Nay, in [b] all these things we are more than conquerors, through him [c] that loved us.
38 For I am persuaded, that [d]

a Ps.44,22;1Cor.15.30,31. *b* 1Cor.15.57. *c* Jude24. *d* John10.28.

involved so many trials. But no, says the apostle. Our love for him is so strong that we are willing to bear all; and nothing that these foes of our peace can do, can alienate us from him and from his cause. The argument, therefore, is drawn from the strong love of a Christian to his Saviour; and from the assurance that nothing would be able to separate him from that love.

[On the other hand, it is alleged that "the object of the apostle is to assure us, not so immediately of our love to God, as of his love to us, by directing our attention to his predestinating, calling, justifying, and glorifying us, and not sparing his own Son, but delivering him up for us; that in addition to this it contributes more to our consolation, to have our minds fixed upon God's love to us, than upon our love to him, which is subject to so many failings and infirmities." *Haldane.*

Indeed the whole of this passage proceeds, in its triumphing strain, on the ground of what God and Christ have done *for us*, and not on the ground of any thing belonging *to us*. It is therefore improbable, that the apostle, in the midst of such a strain, should introduce the love of the creature to God, as a just reason for such unparalleled confidence. It is more natural to the Christian to triumph in the love of Christ to him, than in any return he can make. He can glory in the strength of the former, while he mourns over the weakness of the latter. As to the objection that afflictions can have no tendency to alienate Christ's love, these are the *very things* that alienate men from us. There are persons who are called "summer friends" because they desert us in the winter of adversity. But the love of Christ is greatly exalted by the fact, that none of all possible adverse circumstances, of which the apostle enumerates not a few, shall ever change his love.

¶ *Shall tribulation* (θλίψις); Note, chap. ii. 9. The word properly refers to *pressure* from without; affliction arising from external causes. It means, however, not unfrequently, trial of any kind. ¶ *Or distress* (στενοχωρία). This word properly means *narrowness of place;* and then, great anxiety and distress of mind, such as arises when a man does not know where to turn himself or what to do for relief. It refers, therefore, to distress or anxiety *of mind*, such as the early Christians were often subject to from their trials and persecutions; 2 Cor. vii. 5, "Without were fightings, *within were fears;*" see Note, Rom. ii. 9. ¶ *Or persecutions;* Note, Matt. v. 11. To these the early Christians were constantly exposed. ¶ *Or famine.* To this they were also exposed as the natural result of being driven from home, and of being often compelled to wander amidst strangers, and in deserts and desolate places. ¶ *Or peril.* Danger of any kind. ¶ *Or sword.* The sword of persecution; the danger of their lives to which they were constantly exposed. As all these things happened to them in consequence of their professed attachment to Christ, it might be supposed that they would tend to alienate their minds from him. But the apostle was assured that they had not this power, but that their love to the Saviour was so strong as to overcome all, and to bind them unalterably to his cause in the midst of the deepest trials. The *fact* is, that the more painful the trials to which they are exposed on his account, the more strong and unwavering is their love to him, and their confidence in his ability to save.

36. *As it is written;* Ps. xliv. 22. This passage the apostle quotes not as having originally reference to Christians, but as *aptly descriptive* of their condition. The condition of saints in the time of the psalmist was similar to that of Christians in the time of Paul. The same language would express both. ¶ *For thy sake.* In thy cause; or on account of attachment to thee. ¶ *We are killed.* We are

neither death, nor life, nor angels, nor principalities, nor powers, nor things present, nor things to come,

subject to, or exposed to death. We endure sufferings equivalent to dying; comp. 1 Cor. iv. 9, "God hath set forth us the apostles last, *as it were appointed to death.*" ¶ *All the day long.* Continually; constantly. There is no intermission to our danger, and to our exposure to death. ¶ *We are accounted.* We are reckoned; we are regarded, or dealt with. That is, our enemies judge that we ought to die, and deem us the appropriate subjects of slaughter, with as little concern or remorse as the lives of sheep are taken.

37. *Nay.* But. Notwithstanding our severe pressures and trials. ¶ *In all these things.* In the very midst of them; while we are enduring them we are able to triumph; comp. 1 Cor. xv. 57. ¶ *We are more than conquerors.* We gain the victory. That is, they have not power to subdue us; to alienate our love and confidence; to produce apostacy. *We* are the victors, not *they*. Our faith is not destroyed; our love is not diminished; our hope is not blasted. But it is not simple victory; it is not *mere* life, and continuance of what we had before; it is *more* than simple triumph; it augments our faith, increases our strength, expands our love to Christ. The word used here is a strong, emphatic expression, such as the apostle Paul often employs (comp. 2 Cor. iv. 17), and which is used with great force and appropriateness here. ¶ *Through him,* &c. Not by their own strength or power. It was by the might of the Saviour, and by his power pledged to them, and confirmed by the love evinced when he gave himself for them; comp. Phil. iv. 13, "I can do all things through Christ who strengtheneth me."

38. *For I am persuaded.* I have a strong and unwavering confidence. Latin Vulgate, "*I am certain.*" The expression here implies unwavering certainty. ¶ *Neither death.* Neither the fear of death, nor all the pains and tortures of the dying scene, even in the most painful trials of persecution; death in no form. ¶ *Nor life.* Nor the hope of life; the love of life; the offer of life made to us by our persecutors, on condition of abjuring our Christian faith. The words evidently refer to times of persecution; and it was not uncommon for persecutors to offer life to Christians, on condition of their renouncing attachment to the Saviour, and offering sacrifice to idols. All that was demanded in the times of persecution under the Roman emperors was, that they should throw a few grains of incense on the altar of a heathen god, as expressive of homage to the idol. But even this they would not do. The hope of life on so very easy terms would not, could not alienate them from the love of Christ. ¶ *Nor angels.* It seems to be apparent that *good angels* cannot be intended here. The apostle was saying that nothing would separate Christians from the love of Christ. Of course, it would be implied that the things which he specifies might be supposed to have some power or tendency to do it. But it is not conceivable that good angels, who are "sent forth to minister for them who shall be heirs of salvation" (Heb. i. 14), should seek to alienate the minds of Christians from the Saviour, or that their influence should have any such tendency. It seems to be clear, therefore, that he refers to the designs and temptations of evil spirits. The word *angels* is applied to evil spirits in Matt. xxv. 41; 1 Cor. vi. 3. ¶ *Nor principalities* (ἀρχαὶ). This word usually refers to magistrates and civil rulers. But it is also applied to evil angels, as having dominion over men; Eph. vi. 12, "For we wrestle against....*principalities*;" Col. ii. 15, "And having spoiled principalities:" 1 Cor. xv. 24, "When he shall have put down all *rule*;" Greek, ἀρχήν. Some have supposed that it refers here to magistrates and those in authority who persecuted Christians; but the connection of the word with *angels* seems to require us to understand it of evil spirits. ¶ *Nor powers.* This word (δυνάμεις) is often applied to magistrates; but it is also applied to evil spirits that have dominion over men;

39 Nor height, nor depth, nor any other creature, shall be able to separate us from the love of God, which is in Christ Jesus our Lord.

1 Cor. xv. 24. The ancient Rabbins also give the name *powers* to evil angels. (*Schleusner.*) There can be no doubt that the Jews were accustomed to divide the angels of heaven into various ranks and orders, traces of which custom we find often in the Scriptures. And there is also reason to suppose that they made such a division with reference to evil angels, regarding Satan as their leader, and other evil spirits, divided into various ranks, as subordinate to him; see Matt. xxv. 41; Eph. vi. 12; Col. ii. 15. To such a division there is probably reference here; and the meaning is, that no order of evil angels, however powerful, artful, or numerous, would be able to alienate the hearts of Christians from their Redeemer. ¶ *Nor things present.* Calamities and persecutions to which we are now subject. ¶ *Nor things to come.* Trials to which we may be yet exposed. It evinced strong confidence to say that no possible trials should be sufficient to destroy their love for Christ.

39. *Nor height.* This has been variously understood. Some have regarded it as referring to evil spirits in the air; others, to high and lofty speculation in doctrine; others, to heaven—to all that is in heaven. I regard it here as a synonymous with prosperity, honour, elevation in this life. The meaning is, that *no possible circumstances* in which Christians could be placed, though surrounded with wealth, honour, splendour, and though elevated to rank and office, could alienate them from the love of Christ. The tendency of these things to alienate the mind, to engross the affections, and to occupy the time, all know; but the apostle says that even these would not be sufficient to withdraw their strong love from the Lord Jesus Christ. ¶ *Nor depth.* Nor the lowest circumstances of depression, poverty, contempt, and want; the very lowest rank of life. ¶ *Nor any other creature.* Nor any other created thing; any other thing in the universe; any thing that can occur. This expresses the most unwavering confidence that all who were Christians would certainly continue to love the Lord Jesus, and be saved. ¶ *Shall be able.* Shall have *power* to do it. The love to Christ is stronger than any influence which they *can* exert on the mind. ¶ *The love of God.* The love which we have to God. ¶ *Which is in Christ Jesus.* Which is produced and secured by his work. Of which he is the bond, the connecting link. It was caused by his mediation; it is secured by his influence; it is *in* and through him, and him alone, that men love God. There is no true love of God which is not produced by the work of Christ. There is no man who truly loves the Father, who does not do it in, and by the Son.

Perhaps there is no chapter in the Bible on the whole so interesting and consoling to the Christian as this; and there certainly is not to be found any where a specimen of more elevated, animated, and lofty eloquence and argumentation. We may remark in view of it, (1.) That it is the highest honour that can be conferred on mortal man to be a Christian. (2.) Our trials in this life are scarcely worth regarding in comparison with our future glory. (3.) Calamities should be borne without a murmur; nay, without a sigh. (4.) The Christian has every possible security for his safety. The purposes of God, the work of Christ, the aid of the Holy Ghost, and the tendency of all events under the direction of his Father and Friend, conspire to secure his welfare and salvation. (5.) With what thankfulness, then, should we approach the God of mercy. In the gospel, we have a blessed and cheering hope which nothing else can produce, and which nothing can destroy. Safe in the hands of God our Redeemer, we may commit our way to him, whether it lead through persecutions, or trials, or sickness, or a martyr's grave; and triumphantly we may wait until the day of our complete adoption, the entire redemption of soul and body, shall fully come.

CHAPTER IX.

I SAY the truth in Christ, I lie not, my conscience also bearing me witness in the Holy Ghost,

2 That I have great heaviness

CHAPTER IX.

This chapter opens in some degree a new train of thought and argumentation. Its main design probably was to meet objections which would be alleged against the positions advanced and defended in the previous parts of the epistle. In the previous chapters, Paul had defended the position that the barrier between the Jews and Gentiles had been removed; that the Jews could not be saved by any external advantages which they possessed; that all were alike guilty before God; and that there was but one way for Jews and Gentiles of salvation—by faith in Jesus Christ; chap. i. ii. iii. He had stated the benefits of this plan (chap. v.), and showed its bearing in accomplishing what the law of Moses could not effect in overcoming sin; chap. vi. vii. In chap. viii. he had stated also on what principles this was done; that it was according to the purpose of God—the principle of electing mercy applied indiscriminately to the *mass* of guilty Jews and Gentiles. To this statement two objections might arise: first, that it was unjust; and second, that the whole argument involved a departure from the promises made to the Jewish nation. It might further be supposed that the apostle had ceased to feel an interest in his countrymen, and had become the exclusive advocate of the Gentiles. To meet these objections and feelings, seems to have been the design of this chapter. He shows them, (1.) His unabated love for his countrymen, and regard for their welfare; ver. 1—5. (2.) He shows them from their own writings that the principle of *election* had existed in former times—in the case of Isaac (ver. 7—13); in the writings of Moses (ver. 15); in the case of Pharaoh (ver. 17); and in the prophecies of Hosea and Isaiah (ver. 25—29.) (3.) He takes occasion throughout the chapter to vindicate this principle of the divine administration; to answer objections; and to show that, on the acknowledged principles of the Old Testament, *a part* of the Jewish nation might be rejected; and that it was the purpose of God to call others to the privileges of the people of God; ver. 16, 19—23, 25, 26, 29—33. The chapter, therefore, has not reference to national election, or to choice to external privileges, but has direct reference to the doctrine of the election to salvation which had been stated in chap. viii. To suppose that it refers merely to *external* privileges and *national* distinctions, makes the whole discussion unconnected, unmeaning, and unnecessary.

1. *I say the truth.* In what I am about to affirm respecting my attachment to the nation and people. ¶ *In Christ.* Most interpreters regard this as a form of an oath, as equivalent to calling Christ to witness. It is certainly to be regarded, in its obvious sense, as an appeal *to* Christ as the searcher of the heart, and as the judge of falsehood. Thus the word translated "in" (ἐν) is used in the form of an oath in Mat. v. 34—36; Rev. x. 6, *Greek.* We are to remember that the apostle was addressing those who had been Jews; and the expression has all the force of an oath *by the Messiah.* This shows that it is *right* on great and solemn occasions, and in a solemn manner, AND THUS ONLY, to appeal to Christ for the sincerity of our motives, and for the truth of what we say. And it shows further, that it is *right* to regard the Lord Jesus Christ as present with us, as searching the heart, as capable of detecting insincerity, hypocrisy, and perjury, and as therefore divine. ¶ *My conscience.* Conscience is that act or judgment of the mind by which we decide on the lawfulness or unlawfulness of our actions, and by which we instantly approve or condemn them. It exists in every man, and is a strong witness to our integrity or to our guilt. ¶ *Bearing me witness.* Testifying to the truth of what I say. ¶ *In the Holy Ghost.* He does not say that he speaks the truth by or in the Holy Ghost, as

and continual sorrow in my heart.

3 For I [a] could wish that myself were accursed [1] from Christ for my brethren my kinsmen according to the flesh:

a Ex.32.32.

1 or, *separated*.

he had said of Christ; but that the conscience pronounced its concurring testimony *by* the Holy Ghost; that is, conscience as enlightened and influenced by the Holy Ghost. It was not simply natural conscience, but it was conscience under the full influence of the Enlightener of the mind and Sanctifier of the heart. The reasons of this solemn asseveration are probably the following: (1.) His conduct and his doctrines had led some to believe that he was an apostate, and had lost his love for his countrymen. He had forsaken their institutions, and devoted himself to the salvation of the Gentiles. He here shows them that it was from no want of love to them. (2.) The doctrines which he was about to state and defend were of a similar character; he was about to maintain that no small part of his own countrymen, notwithstanding their privileges, would be rejected and lost. In this solemn manner, therefore, he assures them that this doctrine had not been embraced because he did not love them, but because it was solemn, though most painful truth. He proceeds to enumerate their privileges as a people, and to show to them the strength and tenderness of his love.

2. *Great heaviness*. Great grief. ¶ *Continual sorrow*. The word rendered *continual* here must be taken in a popular sense. Not that he was literally all the time pressed down with this sorrow, but that whenever he thought on this subject, he had great grief; as we say of a painful subject, it is a source of constant pain. The cause of this grief, Paul does not *expressly* mention, though it is implied in what he immediately says. It was the fact that so large a part of the nation would be rejected, and cast off.

3. *For I could wish*, &c. This passage has been greatly controverted. Some have proposed to translate it, "I *did* wish," as referring to a former state, when he renounced Christ, and sought to advance the interests of the nation by opposing and defying him. But to this interpretation there are insuperable objections. (1.) The object of the apostle is not to state his *former* feelings, but his *present* attachment to his countrymen, and willingness to suffer for them. (2.) The proper grammatical construction of the word used here is not I *did* wish, but I *could* desire; that is, if the thing were possible. It is not I *do* wish, or *did* wish, but I *could* desire ('Ηυχόμην), implying that he was willing now to endure it; that his present love for them was so strong, that he would, if practicable, save them from the threatened ruin and apostacy. (3.) It is not *true* that Paul ever *did* wish before his conversion to be accursed by Christ, *i. e.* by the Messiah. He opposed Jesus of Nazareth; but he did not believe that he was the Messiah. At no time would he have wished to be devoted to destruction *by the Messiah*, or *by Christ*. Nothing would have been more terrible to a Jew; and Saul of Tarsus never doubted that he was the friend of the promised Messiah, and was advancing the true interests of his cause, and defending the hopes of his nation against an impostor. The word, therefore, expresses a feeling which the apostle had, when writing this epistle, in regard to the condition and prospects of the nation. ¶ *Were accursed from Christ*. Might be anathema by Christ (ἀνάθεμα εἶναι ἀπὸ τοῦ Χριστοῦ). This passage has been much controverted. The word rendered *accursed* (anathema) properly means, (1.) Any thing that was *set up*, or set apart, or consecrated to the gods in the temples, as spoils of war, images, statues, &c. This is its classical Greek meaning. It has a similar meaning among the Hebrews, It denoted that which was set apart or consecrated to the service of God, as sacrifices or offerings of any kind. In this respect it is used to express the sense of the Hebrew word חרם, *any thing devoted to Jehovah*,

4 Who are Israelites; to whom
pertaineth the adoption,[a] and the
glory,[b] and the [1] covenants,[c] and
the giving of the law,[d] and the [e] service *of God*, and the promises;[f]
5 Whose *are* the fathers,[g] and

a Deut.7.6. b Ps.90.16; Isa.60.19. 1 or, *testaments*. c Gen.17.2; Deut.29.14; Jer.31.33. d Ps.147.19; chap.3.2. e Ex.12.25. f Eph.2.12. g chap.11.28.

without the possibility of redemption. Lev. xxvii. 21; xxviii. 29; Num. xviii. 14; Deut. vii. 26; Josh. vi. 17, 18; vii. 1; 1 Sam. xv. 21; Ezek. xliv. 29. (2.) As that which was thus dedicated to Jehovah was alienated from the use of him who devoted it, and was either burnt or slain and devoted to destruction as an offering, the word came to signify a devotion of any thing to destruction, or to complete ruin. And as whatever is devoted to destruction may be said to be subject to a *curse*, or to be *accursed*, the word comes to have this signification; 1 Kings xx. 42; Isa. xxxiv. 5. But in none of these cases does it denote eternal death. The idea, therefore, in these places is simply, "I could be willing to be destroyed, or devoted, to death, for the sake of my countrymen." And the apostle evidently means to say that he would be willing to suffer the bitterest evils, to forego all pleasure, to endure any privation and toil, nay, to offer his *life*, so that he might be wholly devoted to sufferings, as an offering, if he might be the means of benefiting and saving the nation. For a similar case, see Ex. xxxii. 32. This does *not* mean that Paul would be willing to be damned for ever. For, (1.) The words do not imply that, and will not bear it. (2.) *Such* a destruction could in no conceivable way benefit the Jews. (3.) Such a willingness is not and cannot be required. And, (4.) It would be impious and absurd. No man has a right to be willing to be the *eternal enemy* of God; and no man ever yet was, or could be willing to endure everlasting torments. ¶ *From Christ.* By Christ. Grotius thinks it means from the church of Christ. Others think it means "after the example of Christ;" and others, *from* Christ for ever. But it evidently means that he was willing to be devoted by Christ; *i. e.* to be regarded *by* him, and appointed *by* him, to suffering and death, if by that means he could save his countrymen. It was thus the highest expression of true patriotism and benevolence. It was an example for all Christians and Christian ministers. *They* should be willing to be devoted to pain, privation, toil, and death, if by that they could save others from ruin. ¶ *My kinsmen*, &c. My countrymen; all of whom he regarded as his kinsmen, or relations, as descended from the same ancestors. ¶ *According to the flesh.* By birth. They were of the same blood and parentage, though not now of the same religious belief.

4. *Who are Israelites;* Descended from Israel, or Jacob; honoured by having such an ancestor, and by bearing a name so distinguished as that of his descendants. It was formerly the honourable appellation of the people of God. ¶ *To whom* pertaineth. To whom it belongs. It was their elevated external privilege. ¶ *The adoption.* Of the nation into the family of God, or to be regarded as his peculiar people; Deut. vii. 6. ¶ *And the glory.* The symbol of the divine presence that attended them from Egypt, and that finally rested over the ark in the first temple—*the Shechinah;* Ex. xiii. 21, 22; xxv. 22. ¶ *And the covenants.* The various compacts or promises which had been made from time to time with Abraham, Isaac, and Jacob, and with the nation; the pledges of the divine protection. ¶ *The giving of the law.* On Mount Sinai; Ex. xx; comp. Ps. cxlvii. 19. ¶ *And the service of God.* The temple service; regarded by them as the pride and ornament of their nation. ¶ *And the promises.* Of the Messiah; and of the spread of the true religion from them as a nation.

5. *Whose* are *the fathers.* Who have been honoured with so illustrious an ancestry. Who are descended from Abraham, Isaac, &c. On this they highly valued themselves, and in a certain sense not unjustly; comp. Matt. iii. 9. ¶ *Of whom.* Of whose

of whom, [a] as concerning the flesh, Christ *came*, who is [b] over all, God blessed for ever. Amen.

6 Not as though the word of God hath taken [c] none effect. For [d] they *are* not all Israel which are of Israel.

7 Neither, because they are the seed of Abraham, *are they* all children: but in [e] Isaac shall thy seed be called.

8 That is, they which are the children of the flesh, these *are* not the children of God: but the chil-

a Luke 3.23, &c. b John 1.1. c Isa.55.11. d chap.2.28,29. e Gen.21.12,

nation. This is placed as the crowning and most exalted privilege, that their nation had given birth to the long-expected Messiah, the hope of the world. ¶ *As concerning the flesh.* So far as his human nature was concerned. The use of this language supposes that there was a *higher* nature in respect to which he was *not* of their nation; see Note, chap. i. 3. ¶ *Christ* came. He had already *come;* and it was their high honour that he was one of their nation. ¶ *Who is over all.* This is an appellation that belongs only to the true God. It implies supreme divinity; and is full proof that the Messiah is divine. Much effort has been made to show that this is not the true rendering, but without success. There are no various readings in the Greek MSS. of any consequence; and the connection here evidently requires us to understand this of a nature that is not "according to the flesh," *i. e.* as the apostle here shows, of the divine nature. ¶ *God blessed for ever.* This is evidently applied to the Lord Jesus; and it *proves* that he is divine. If the translation is fairly made,—and it has never been proved to be erroneous,—it demonstrates that he is God as well as man. The doxology "blessed for ever" was usually added by the Jewish writers after the mention of the name God, as an expression of reverence. (See the various interpretations that have been proposed on this passage examined in Prof. Stuart's Notes on this verse.)

6. *Not as though,* &c. Not as though the promise of God had entirely failed. Though I grieve thus (ver. 2, 3), though I am deeply apprehensive for the nation, yet I do not affirm that *all* the nation is to be destroyed. The promise of God will not entirely fail. ¶ *Not all Israel.* Not all the descendants of Jacob have the true spirit of Israelites, or are Jews in the scriptural sense of the term; see Note, chap. ii. 28, 29.

7. Are they *all children.* Adopted into the true family of God. Many of the descendants of Abraham were rejected. ¶ *But in Isaac.* This was the promise; Gen. xxi. 12. ¶ *Shall thy seed,* &c. Thy true people. This implied a selection, or choice; and therefore the doctrine of *election* was illustrated in the very commencement of the history of the nation; and as God had *then* made such a distinction, he might still do it. As he had then rejected a part of the natural descendants of Abraham, so he might still do it. This is the argument which the apostle is pursuing.

8. *They which are the children of the flesh.* The natural descendants. ¶ *These* are *not the children of God.* Are not of necessity the adopted children of God; or are not so in virtue of their descent merely. This was in opposition to one of the most settled and deeply cherished opinions of the Jews. They supposed that the mere fact of being a Jew, entitled a man to the blessings of the covenant, and to be regarded as a child of God. But the apostle shows them that it was not by their natural descent that these spiritual privileges were granted; that they were not conferred on men simply from the fact that they were Jews; and that consequently those who were not Jews might become interested in those spiritual blessings. ¶ *But the children of the promise.* The descendants of Abraham on whom the promised blessings would be bestowed. The sense is, that God at first contemplated a distinction among the descendants of Abraham, and intended to confine his blessings to such as he chose; that is, to those to whom the promise particularly appertained, to

dren [a] of the promise are counted for the seed.

9 For this *is* the word of promise. At [b] this time will I come, and Sarah shall have a son.

10 And not only *this;* but when Rebecca [c] also had conceived by one, *even* by our father Isaac;

11 (For *the children* being not yet born, neither having done any good

a Gal.4.28. b Gen.18.10,14. c Gen.25.21,23.

the descendants of Isaac. The argument of the apostle is, that *the principle* was thus established that a distinction might be made among those who were Jews; and as that distinction had been made in former times, so it might be under the Messiah. ¶ *Are counted.* Are regarded, or reckoned. God reckons things as they are; and therefore designed that they should be his true children. ¶ *As the seed.* The spiritual children of God; the partakers of his mercy and salvation. This refers, doubtless, to spiritual privileges and to salvation; and therefore has relation not to nations as such, but to individuals.

9. *For this* is *the word of promise.* This is the promise made to Abraham. The design of the apostle, in introducing this, is doubtless to show to whom the promise appertained; and by specifying this, he shows that it had not reference to Ishmael, but to Isaac. ¶ *At this time.* Greek, According to this time; see Gen. xviii. 10, 14. Probably it means at the exact time promised; I will fulfil the prediction at the very time; comp. 2 Kings iv. 16.

10. *And not only* this. Not only is the *principle* of making a distinction among the natural descendants of Abraham thus settled by the promise, but it is still further seen and illustrated in the birth of the two sons of Isaac. He had shown that the principle of thus making a distinction among the posterity of Abraham was recognised in the original promise, thus proving that *all* the descendants of Abraham were not of course to be saved; and he now proceeds to show that the principle was recognised in the case of his posterity in the family of Isaac. And he shows that it is not according to any natural principles that the selection was made; that he not only made a distinction between Jacob and Esau, but that he did it according to his good pleasure, choosing the younger to be the object of his favour, and rejecting the older, who, according to the custom of the times, was supposed to be entitled to peculiar honour and rights. And in order to prove that this was done according to his own pleasure, he shows that the distinction was made before they were born; before they had formed any character; and, consequently, in such a way that it could not be pretended that it was in consequence of any works which they had performed. ¶ *But when Rebecca.* The wife of Isaac; see Gen. xxv. 21, 23.

11. *For* the children *being not yet born.* It was not, therefore, by any works of theirs. It was not because they had formed a character and manifested qualities which made this distinction proper. It was laid *back* of any such character, and therefore had its foundation in the purpose or plan of God. ¶ *Neither having done any good or evil.* That is, when the declaration (ver. 12) was made to Rebecca. This is a very important passage in regard to the question about the purposes of God. (1.) They had *done* nothing good or bad; and when that is the case, there can be, properly speaking, no moral character, for "a *character* is not formed when the person has not acquired stable and distinctive qualities." *Webster.* (2.) That the period of moral agency had not yet commenced; comp. Gen. xxv. 22, 23. *When* that agency commences, we do not know; but here is a case of which it is affirmed that it had not commenced. (3.) The purpose of God is antecedent to the formation of character, or the performance of any actions, good or bad. (4.) It is not a purpose formed *because* he sees any thing in the individuals as a ground for his choice, but for some reason which he has not explained, and which in the Scripture is

or evil, that the purpose of God, according to election, might stand, not of works, but of him that calleth;)

12 It was said unto her, the [1] elder shall serve the [2] younger.
13 As it is written, [a] Jacob

1 or, *greater*. 2 or, *lesser*. *a* Mal.1.2,3.

simply called *purpose* and *good pleasure*; Eph. i. 5. (5.) If it existed in this case, it does in others. If it was right then, it is now. And if God then dispensed his favours on this principle, he will now. But, (6.) This affirmation respecting Jacob and Esau does not prove that they had not a nature inclined to evil; or a corrupt and sensual propensity; or that they would not sin as soon as they became moral agents. It proves merely that they had not yet committed *actual* sin. That they, as well as all others, *would* certainly sin as soon as they committed moral acts at all, is proved every where in the sacred Scriptures. ¶ *The purpose of God;* Note, chap. viii. 28. ¶ *According to election.* To dispense his favours according to his sovereign will and pleasure. Those favours were not conferred in consequence of the *merits* of the individuals; but according to a wise plan *lying back* of the formation of their characters, and before they had done good or evil. The favours were thus conferred according to his choice, or election. ¶ *Might stand.* Might be confirmed; or might be proved to be true. The case shows that God dispenses his favours as a sovereign. The purpose of God was thus proved to have been formed without respect to the merits of either. ¶ *Not of works.* Not by any thing which they had done either to merit his favour or to forfeit it. It was formed on other principles than a reference to their works. So it is in relation to all who shall be saved. God has good reasons for saving those who shall be saved. What the reasons are for choosing some to life, he has not revealed; but he *has* revealed to us that it is *not* on account of their works, either performed or foreseen. ¶ *But of him that calleth.* According to the will and purpose of him that chooses to dispense those favours in this manner. It is not by the merit of man, but it is by a purpose having its origin with God, and formed and executed according to his good pleasure. It is also implied here that it is formed in such a way as to secure *his* glory as the primary consideration.

12. *It was said unto her.* By Jehovah; see Gen. xxv. 23. ¶ *The elder.* The eldest son, which was Esau. By the law of primogeniture among the Hebrews, he would have been entitled to peculiar honours and privileges. But it was said that in his case this custom should be reversed, and that he should take the rank of the younger. ¶ *Should serve.* Shall be subject to; shall not have the authority and priority, but should be inferior to. The passage in Genesis (xxv. 23) shows that this had reference particularly to the posterity of Esau, and not to him as an individual. The sense is, that the descendants of Esau, who were Edomites, should be inferior to, and subject to the descendants of Jacob. Jacob was to have the priority; the promised land; the promises; and the honour of being regarded as the chosen of God. There was reference here, therefore, to the whole train of temporal and spiritual blessings which were to be connected with the two races of people. If it be asked how this bears on the argument of the apostle, we may reply, (1.) That it settles *the principle* that God might make a distinction among men, in the same nation, and the same family, without reference to their works or character. (2.) That he might confer his blessings on such as he pleased. (3.) If this is done in regard to nations, it may be in regard to individuals. The principle is the same, and the justice the same. If it be supposed to be unjust in God to make such a distinction in regard to individuals, it is surely not less so to make a distinction in nations. The fact that numbers are thus favoured, does not make it the more proper, or remove any difficulty. (4.) If this

have I loved, but Esau have I hated.

14 What shall we say then? *Is*[a] *there* unrighteousness with God? God forbid.

15 For he saith to Moses, I[b] will

a Deut.32.4. b Ex.33.19.

distinction may be made in regard to *temporal* things, why not in regard to *spiritual* things? The *principle* must still be the same. If unjust in one case, it would be in the other. The fact that it is done in one case proves also that it will be in the other; for the same great principle will run through all the dealings of the divine government. And as men do not and cannot complain that God makes a distinction among them in regard to talents, health, beauty, prosperity, and rank, neither can they complain if he acts also as a sovereign in the distribution of his spiritual favours. They, therefore, who regard this as referring only to temporal and national privileges, gain no relief in respect to the real difficulty in the case, for the unanswerable question would still be asked, why has not God made all men equal in every thing? Why has he made any distinction among men? The *only* reply to all such inquiries is, "Even so, Father, for so it seemeth good in thy sight;" Matt. xi. 26.

13. *As it is written*; Mal. i. 2, 3. That is, the distribution of favours is on the principle advanced by the prophet, and is in accordance with the declaration that God had in fact loved the one and hated the other. ¶ *Jacob.* This refers, doubtless, to the posterity of Jacob. ¶ *Have I loved.* I have shown affection for that people; I have bestowed on them great privileges and blessings, as proofs of attachment. I have preferred Jacob to Esau. ¶ *Esau.* The descendants of Esau, the Edomites; see Mal. i. 4. ¶ *Have I hated.* This does not mean any *positive* hatred; but that he had preferred Jacob, and had *withheld* from Esau those privileges and blessings which he had conferred on the posterity of Jacob. This is explained in Mal. i. 3, "And I hated Esau, and laid his mountains and heritage waste for the dragons of the wilderness;" comp. Jer. xlix. 17, 18; Ezek. xxxv. 6. It was common among the Hebrews to use the terms *love* and *hatred* in this comparative sense, where the former implied strong *positive* attachment, and the latter, not positive hatred, but merely a less love, or the withholding of the expressions of affection; comp. Gen. xxix. 30, 31; Prov. xiii. 24, "He that spareth his rod *hateth* his son; but he that *loveth* him chasteneth him betimes;" Matt. vi. 24, "No man can serve two masters, for either he will *hate* the one and *love* the other," &c; Luke xiv. 26, "If any man come to me, and *hate* not his father and mother," &c.

14. *What shall we say then?* What conclusion shall we draw from these acknowledged facts, and from these positive declarations of Scripture. ¶ Is there *unrighteousness with God?* Does God do injustice or wrong? This charge has often been brought against the doctrine here advanced. But this charge the apostle strongly repels. He meets it by further showing that it is the doctrine explicitly taught in the Old Testament (ver. 15, 17), and that it is founded on the principles of equity, and on just views of the sovereignty of God; ver. 19—23. ¶ *God forbid;* Note, chap. iii. 4.

15. *For he saith to Moses.* Ex. xxxiii. 19. ¶ *I will have mercy.* This is said by God when he declared expressly that he would make all his *goodness* pass before Moses (Ex. xxxiii. 19), and when, therefore, it was regarded, not as a proof of stern and inexorable justice, but as *the very proof of his benevolence,* and the highest which he thought proper to exhibit. When men, therefore, under the influence of an unrenewed and hostile heart, charge this as an unjust and arbitrary proceeding, they are resisting and perverting that which God regards as the very demonstration of his benevolence. The sense of the passage clearly is, that he would choose the objects of his favour, and bestow his mercies as he chose. None of the human race deserved his favour; and

have mercy on whom I will have mercy, and I will have compassion on whom I will have compassion.

16 So then *it is* not of him that willeth, nor of him that runneth, but of God that showeth mercy.

he had a right to pardon whom he pleased, and to save men on his own terms, and according to his sovereign will and pleasure. ¶ *On whom I will have mercy.* On whom I *choose* to bestow mercy. The *mode* he does not explain. But there could not be a more positive declaration of these truths, (1.) That he does it as a sovereign, without giving an account of the reason of his choice to any. (2.) That he does it without regard to any claim on the part of man; or that man is regarded as destitute of merit, and as having no right to his mercy. (3.) That he will do it to any extent which he pleases, and in whatever time and manner may best accord with his own good pleasure. (4.) That he has regard to a definite number; and that on that number he intends to bestow eternal life; and, (5.) That no one has a right to complain. It is proof of his benevolence that *any* are saved; and where none have a claim, where all are justly condemned, he has a right to pardon whom he pleases. The executive of a country may select any number of criminals whom he may see fit to pardon, or who may be forgiven in consistency with the supremacy of the laws and the welfare of the community and none has a right to murmur, but every good citizen should rejoice that *any* may be pardoned with safety. So in the moral world, and under the administration of its holy Sovereign, it should be a matter of joy that *any* can be pardoned and saved; and not a subject of murmuring and complaint that those who shall finally deserve to die shall be consigned to woe.

16. *So then.* It follows as a consequence from this statement of God to Moses. Or it is a doctrine established by that statement. ¶ *Not of him that willeth.* This does not mean that he that becomes a Christian, and is saved, does not *choose* eternal life; or is not made willing; or that he is *compelled* to enter heaven against his own choice. It is true that men by nature have no desire of holiness, and do not choose eternal life. But the effect of the influences of God's Spirit on the heart is to make it "willing in the day of his power;" Ps. cx. 3. The meaning here is evidently, that eternal life is not bestowed because man had any original willingness or disposition to be saved; it is not because *he* commences the work, and is himself disposed to it; but it is because God inclines him to it, and disposes him to seek for mercy, and then confers it in his own way. The word *willeth* here denotes *wish* or *desire.* ¶ *Nor of him that runneth.* This denotes *strenuous, intense effort,* as when a man is anxious to obtain an object, or hastens from danger. The meaning is not that the sinner does not make an effort to be saved; nor that all who become Christians do not *in fact* strive to enter into the kingdom, or earnestly desire salvation, for the Scriptures teach the contrary; Luke xvi. 16; xiii. 24. There is no effort more intense and persevering, no struggle more arduous or agonizing, than when a sinner seeks eternal life. Nor does it mean that they who strive in a proper way, and with proper effort, shall not obtain eternal life; Matt. vii. 7. But the sense is, (1.) That the sinner would not put forth any effort himself. If left to his own course, he would never seek to be saved. (2.) That he is pardoned, not *on account* of his effort; not *because* he makes an exertion; but because God chooses to pardon him. There is no merit in his anxiety, and prayers, and agony, on account of which God would forgive him; but he is still dependent on the mere mercy of God to save or destroy him at his will. The sinner, however anxious he may be, and however much or long he may strive, does not bring God under an obligation to pardon him any more than the condemned criminal, trembling with the fear of execution, and the consciousness of crime, lays the judge or the jury under an obliga-

17 For the Scripture saith [a] unto Pharaoh, Even for this same purpose have I raised thee up, that I might show my power in thee, and that my name might be declared throughout all the earth.

a Ex.9.16.

---

tion to accquit him. This fact, it is of great importance for an awakened sinner to know. Deeply anxious he should be, but there is no *merit* in his distress. Pray he should, but there is no merit in his prayers. Weep and strive he may, but in this there is no ground of claim on God for pardon; and, after all, he is dependent on his mere sovereign mercy, as a lost, ruined, and helpless sinner, to be saved or lost at his will. ¶ *But of God that showeth mercy.* Salvation in its beginning, its progress, and its close, is of him. He has a right, therefore, to bestow it when and where he pleases. All our mercies flow from his mere love and compassion, and not from our deserts. The essential idea here is, that *God* is the original fountain of all the blessings of salvation.

17. *For the Scripture saith;* Ex. ix. 16. That is, God saith to Pharaoh *in* the Scriptures; Gal. iii. 8. 22. This passage is designed to illustrate the doctrine that God shows mercy according to his sovereign pleasure by a reference to one of the most extraordinary cases of hardness of heart which has ever occurred. The design is to show that God has a right to pass by those to whom he does not choose to show mercy; and to place them in circumstances where they shall develope their true character, and where in fact they shall become more hardened and be destroyed; ver. 18. ¶ *Unto Pharaoh.* The haughty and oppressive king of Egypt; thus showing that the most mighty and wicked monarchs are at his control; comp. Isa. x. 5—7. ¶ *For this same purpose.* For the design, or with the intent that is immediately specified. This was the leading purpose or design of his sustaining him. ¶ *Have I raised thee up.* Margin in Ex. ix. 16, "made thee stand," *i. e.* sustained thee. The Greek word used by the apostle (ἐξήγειρα), means properly, *I have excited, roused,* or *stirred* thee up. But it may also have the meaning, "I have sustained or supported thee." That is, I have kept thee from death; I have preserved thee from ruin; I have ministered strength to thee, so that thy full character has been developed. It does not mean that God had infused into his mind any positive evil, or that by any direct influence he had excited any evil feelings, but that he had kept him in circumstances which were fitted to develope his true character. The meaning of the word and the truth of the case may be expressed in the following particulars: (1.) God meant to accomplish some great purposes by his existence and conduct. (2.) He kept him, or sustained him, with reference to that. (3.) He had control over the haughty and wicked monarch. He could take his life, or he could continue him on earth. As he had control over all things that could affect the pride, the feelings, and the happiness of the monarch, so he had control over the monarch himself. (4.) *He placed him in circumstances just fitted to develope his character.* He kept him amidst those circumstances until his character was fully developed. (5.) He did not exert a positive evil influence on the mind of Pharaoh; for, (6.) In all this the monarch acted freely. He did that which he chose to do. He pursued his own course. He was voluntary in his schemes of oppressing the Israelites. He was voluntary in his opposition to God. He was voluntary when he pursued the Israelites to the Red sea. In all his doings he acted as he *chose* to do, and with a determined *choice of evil,* from which neither warning nor judgment would turn him away. Thus he is said to have hardened his own heart; Ex. viii. 15. (7.) Neither Pharaoh nor any sinner can justly blame God for placing them in circumstances where they shall develope their own character, and show what they are. It is not the fault of God, but their own fault. The sinner is not compelled to sin; nor is

18 Therefore hath he mercy on whom he will *have mercy*, and whom he will he hardeneth.

19 Thou wilt say then unto me, Why doth he yet find fault? for who [a] hath resisted his will?

a 2 Ch.20.6; Dan.4.35.

God under obligation to save him contrary to the prevalent desires and wishes of the sinner himself. ¶ *My power in thee.* Or by means of thee. By the judgments exerted in delivering an entire oppressed people from thy grasp. God's most signal acts of *power* were thus shown in consequence of his disobedience and rebellion. ¶ *My name.* The name of Jehovah, as the only true God, and the deliverer of his people. ¶ *Throughout all the earth.* Or throughout all the land of Egypt; Note, Luke ii. 1. We may learn here, (1.) That a leading design of God in the government of the world is to make his power, and name, and character known. (2.) That this is often accomplished in a most signal manner by the destruction of the wicked. (3.) That wicked men should be alarmed, since *their* arm cannot contend with God, and since his enemies shall be destroyed. (4.) It is right that the incorrigibly wicked should be cut off. When a man's character is fully developed; when he is fairly tried; when in all circumstances, he has shown that he *will* not obey God, neither justice nor mercy hinders the Almighty from cutting him down and consigning him to death.

18. *Therefore hath he mercy,* &c. This is a conclusion stated by the apostle as the result of all the argument. ¶ *Whom he will he hardeneth.* This is not stated in what the Scripture said to Pharaoh, but is a conclusion to which the apostle had arrived, in view of the case of Pharaoh. The word *hardeneth* means only to harden in the manner specified in the case of Pharaoh. It does not mean to exert a positive influence, but to leave a sinner to his own course, and to place him in circumstances where the character will be more and more developed; see Note, John xii. 40. It implies, however, an act of sovereignty on the part of God in thus *leaving* him to his chosen course, and in not putting forth that influence by which he could be saved from death. *Why* this is, the apostle does not state. We should, however, not dispute a fact every where prevalent; and should have sufficient confidence in God to believe that it is in accordance with infinite wisdom and rectitude.

19. *Thou wilt say then unto me.* The apostle here refers to an objection that might be made to his argument. If the position which he had been endeavouring to establish were true; if God had a purpose in all his dealings with men; if all the revolutions among men happened according to his decree, so that he was not disappointed, or his plan frustrated; and if his own glory was secured in all this, why could he blame men? ¶ *Why doth he yet find fault?* Why does he *blame* men, since their conduct is in accordance with his purpose, and since he bestows mercy according to his sovereign will? This objection has been made by sinners in all ages. It is the standing objection against the doctrines of grace. The objection is founded, (1.) On the difficulty of reconciling the purposes of God with the free agency of man. (2.) It *assumes,* what cannot be proved, that a plan or purpose of God *must* destroy the freedom of man. (3.) It is said that if the *plan* of God is accomplished, then that which is best to be done is done, and, of course, man cannot be blamed. These objections are met by the apostle in the following argument. ¶ *Who hath resisted his will?* That is, who has *successfully opposed* his will, or frustrated his plan? The word translated *resist* is commonly used to denote the resistance offered by soldiers or armed men. Thus, Eph. vi. 13, "Take unto you the whole armour of God, that ye may be able to *withstand* (*resist* or successfully oppose) in the evil day;" see Luke xxi. 15, "I will give you a mouth and wisdom which all your adversaries shall not be

20 Nay but, O man, who art thou that repliest [1] against God? Shall [a] the thing formed say to him that formed *it*, Why hast thou made me thus?
21 Hath not the potter [b] power

1 or, *answerest again*; or, *disputest with God.*

a Is.29.16. b Isa.64.8.

able to gainsay or *resist*;" see also Acts vii. 10; xiii. 8, "But Elymas... *withstood* them," &c. The same Greek word, Rom. xiii. 2; Gal. ii. 11. This does not mean that no one has offered resistance or opposition to God, but that no one has done it successfully. God had accomplished his purposes *in spite of* their opposition. This was an established point in the sacred writings, and one of the admitted doctrines of the Jews. To establish it had even been a part of the apostle's design; and the difficulty now was to see how, *this* being admitted, men could be held chargeable with crime. That it was the doctrine of the Scriptures, see 2 Chron. xx. 6, "In thine hand *is there not* power and might, so that none is able to withstand thee?" Dan. iv. 35, "He doeth according to his will in the army of heaven, and *among* the inhabitants of the earth, and none can stay his hand, or say unto him, What doest thou?" See also the case of Joseph and his brethren, Gen. l. 20, "As for you, ye thought evil against me, *but* God meant it unto good."

20. *Nay but, O man,* &c. To this objection the apostle replies in *two* ways; first, by asserting the sovereignty of God, and affirming that he had a *right* to do it (ver. 20, 21); and secondly, by showing that he did it according to the principles of justice and mercy, or that it was *involved* of necessity in his dispensing *justice* and *mercy* to mankind; ver. 22, 23, 24. ¶ *Who art thou,* &c. Paul here strongly reproves the impiety and wickedness of arraigning God. This impiety appears, (1.) Because man is a *creature* of God, and it is improper that he should arraign his Maker. (2.) He is *unqualified* to understand the subject. "Who art thou?" What qualifications has a creature of a day,—a being just in the *infancy* of his existence; of so limited faculties; so perverse, blinded, and interested as man,—to sit in judgment on the doings of the Infinite Mind? Who gave him the authority, or invested him with the prerogatives of a *judge* over his Maker's doings? (3.) Even if man *were* qualified to investigate those subjects, what right has he to *reply* against God, to arraign him, or to follow out a train of argument tending to involve his Creator in shame and disgrace? No where is there to be found a more cutting or humbling reply to the pride of man than this. And on no subject was it more needed. The experience of every age has shown that this has been a prominent topic of objection against the government of God; and that there has been no point in the Christian theology to which the human heart has been so ready to make objections as to the doctrine of the sovereignty of God. ¶ *Repliest against God.* Margin, "Answerest again; or, disputest with God." The passage conveys the idea of *answering* again; or of arguing to the dishonour of God. It implies that when God declares his will, man should be still. God has his own plans of infinite wisdom, and it is not ours to reply against him, or to arraign him of injustice, when we cannot see the reason of his doings. ¶ *Shall the thing formed,* &c. This sentiment is found in Isa. xxix. 16; see also Isa. xlv. 9. It was peculiarly proper to adduce this to a *Jew*. The objection is one which is supposed to be made by a Jew, and it was proper to reply to him by a quotation from his own Scriptures. Any being has a right to fashion his work according to his own views of what is best; and as this right is not denied to *men*, we ought not to blame the infinitely wise God for acting in a similar way. They who have received every blessing they enjoy from him, ought not to blame him for not making them different.

21. *Hath not the potter,* &c. This same sovereign right of God the apostle proceeds to urge from another illustration, and another passage from

over the clay, of the same lump to make one vessel unto honour, and another unto dishonour?
22 *What* [a] if God, willing to shew *his* wrath, and to make his power known, endured with much long-suffering the vessels [b] of wrath [1] fitted to destruction;

a Pro.16.4. b 2 Tim.2.20. 1 or, *made up*.

the Old Testament; Isa. lxiv. 8, "But now, O Lord, thou art our Father; we are the clay, and thou our potter; and we all are the work of thy hand." This passage is preceded in Isaiah by one declaring *the depravity of man;* Isa. lxiv. 6, "We are all as an unclean thing, and all our righteousnesses are as filthy rags; and we all do fade as a leaf; and our iniquities, like the wind, have taken us away." As they were polluted with sin, as they had transgressed the law of God, and had *no claim* and *no merit,* God might bestow his favours as he pleased, and mould them as the potter did the clay. He would do no injury to those who were left, and *who had no claim to his mercy,* if he bestowed favours on others, any more than the potter would do injustice to one part of the mass, if he put it to an ignoble use, and moulded another part into a vessel of honour. This is still the condition of sinful men. God does no injustice to a man if he leaves him to take his own course to ruin, and makes another, equally undeserving, the recipient of his mercy. He violated none of my rights by not conferring on me the talents of Newton or of Bacon; or by not placing me in circumstances like those of Peter and Paul. Where *all* are undeserving, the utmost that can be demanded is that he should not treat them with *injustice.* And this is secured even in the case of the lost. No man will suffer more than he deserves; nor will any man go to perdition feeling that he has *a claim* to better treatment than he receives. The same sentiment is found in Jer. xviii. 6, "O house of Israel, cannot I do with you as this potter? saith the Lord. Behold, as the clay is in the potter's hand, so are ye in my hand, O house of Israel. At what instant I shall speak concerning a nation," &c. The passage in Isaiah proves that God has the right of a sovereign over guilty *individuals;* that in Jeremiah, that he has the same right over *nations;* thus meeting the whole case as it was in the mind of the apostle. These passages, however, assert only the *right* of God to do it, without affirming any thing about the *manner* in which it is done. In fact, God bestows his favours in a *mode* very different from that in which a potter moulds his clay. God does not create holiness by a mere act of power, but he produces it in a manner consistent with the moral agency of men; and bestows his favours not to *compel* men, but to incline them to be *willing* to receive them; Ps. cx. 3, "Thy people shall be willing in the day of thy power." It should be further remarked, that the argument of the apostle here does not refer to *the original creation* of men, as if God had then made them one for honour and another for dishonour. He refers to man *as* fallen and lost. His argument is this: "Man is in ruins; he is fallen; he has no claim on God; all deserve to die; on this *mass,* where none have any claim, he may bestow life on whom he pleases, without injury to others; he may exercise the right of a sovereign to pardon whom he pleases; or of a potter to mould any part of the useless mass to purposes of utility and beauty." ¶ *Potter.* One whose occupation it is to make earthen vessels. ¶ *Power.* This word denotes here not merely *physical power,* but authority, right; see Matt. vii. 29, translated "authority;" xxi. 23; 2 Thess. iii. 9; Mark ii. 10; Luke v. 24, "The Son of man hath *power* on earth to forgive sins," &c. ¶ *Lump.* Mass. It denotes any thing that is reduced to a fine consistency, and mixed, and made soft by water; either clay, as in this place, or the *mass* produced of grain pounded and mixed with water; Rom. xi. 16, "If the first-fruit be holy, the *lump* is also holy;" 1 Cor. v. 6, "Know ye not that a little leaven leaveneth the whole *lump?*" ¶ *One vessel.* A cup, or other utensil, made of clay. ¶ *Unto honour.* Fitted to an honourable use, or designed for a more useful and refined purpose. ¶ *Unto dishonour.* To a meaner service, or more common use. This is a common mode of expression among the Hebrews. The *lump* here denotes the mass of men, sinners, having no claim on God. The potter illustrates God's right over that mass, to dispose of it as seems good in his sight. The doctrine of the passage is, that men have no right to complain if God bestows his blessings where and when he chooses.

22, 23. *What if God,* &c. If God does what the apostle supposes, what then? Is it not right? This is the second point in the answer to the objection in ver. 19. The answer has respect to the *two classes* of men which actually exist on the earth—the righteous and the wicked. And the question is, whether *in regard to these two classes God does* IN FACT *do wrong?* If he does not, then the doctrine of the apostle is established, and the objection is not valid. It is assumed here, as it must be, that the world is *in fact* divided into two classes—saints and sinners. The apostle considers the case of sinners in ver. 22. ¶ *Willing.* Being disposed; having an inclination to. It denotes an inclination of mind towards the thing proposed. If the thing itself was right; if it was *proper to "show* his wrath," then it was proper to be WILLING to do it. If it is right *to do* a thing, it is right to *purpose* or *intend* to do it. ¶ *His wrath* (τὴν ὀργὴν). This word occurs *thirty-five* times in the New Testament. Its meaning is derived from the idea of earnestly desiring or reaching for an object, and properly denotes, in its general sense, a vehement desire of attaining any thing. Hence it comes to denote an earnest desire of revenge, or of inflicting suffering on those who have injured us; Eph. iv. 31, "Let all bitterness and wrath," &c. Col. iii. 8; 1 Tim. ii. 8. Hence it denotes *indignation* in general, which is *not* joined with a desire of revenge; Mark iii. 5, "He looked round about on them with *anger.*" It also denotes punishment for sin; the anger or displeasure of God against transgression; Note, Rom. i. 18; Luke iii. 7; xxi. 23, &c. In this place it is evidently used to denote *severe displeasure against sin.* As sin is an evil of so great magnitude, *it is right* for God to be *willing* to evince his displeasure against it; and just in proportion to the extent of the evil. This displeasure, or wrath, it is proper that God should *always* be willing to show; nay, it would not be right for him *not* to show it, for that would be the same thing as to be *indifferent* to it, or to *approve* it. In this place, however, it is *not* affirmed, (1.) That God has any pleasure in sin, or its punishment; nor, (2.) That he exerted any agency to *compel* man to sin. It affirms only that God is willing to show his hatred of incorrigible and long-continued wickedness when it *actually* exists. ¶ *To make his power known.* This *language* is the same as that which was used in relation to Pharaoh; ver. 17; Ex. ix. 16. But it is not probable that the apostle intended to confine it to the Egyptians only. In the following verse he speaks of "the vessels of mercy prepared *unto glory;*" which cannot be supposed to be language adapted to the *temporal* deliverance of the Jews. The case of Pharaoh was *one instance,* or *illustration* of the general principle on which God would deal with men. His government is conducted on great and uniform principles; and the case of Pharaoh was a development of the great laws on which he governs the universe. ¶ *Endured.* Bore with; was patient, or forbearing; Rev. ii. 3. "And hast borne, and hast patience," &c. 1 Cor. xiii. 7, "Charity, (love) beareth all things." Luke xviii. 7, "Will not God avenge his elect, though he *bear long* with them?" ¶ *With much long-suffering.* With much patience. He suffered them to live while they deserved to die. God bears with all sinners with much patience; he spares them amid all their provocations, to give them opportunity of repentance; and though they are fitted for destruction, yet he prolongs their lives, and offers them pardon, and loads them with benefits. This fact is a complete vindication of the government of God from the aspersions of all his enemies. ¶ *Vessels of wrath.* The word *vessel* means a cup, &c. made of earth. As the human body is frail, easily broken and destroyed, it comes to signify also the body. 2 Cor. iv. 7; "We have this treasure in earthen vessels." 1 Thess. iv. 4, "That every one of you should know how to possess his *vessel* in sanctification and honour"—that every one should keep *his body* from the indulgence of unlawful passions; comp. ver. 3. Hence also it means *the man himself.* Acts ix. 15, "He is a chosen *vessel* unto me," &c. comp. Isa. xiii. 5. In this place there is doubtless, allusion to what he had just said of clay in the hands of the potter. The phrase "vessels of wrath" denotes wicked men against whom it is *fit* or proper that wrath should be shown; as Judas is called "the son of perdition," see Note on John xvii. 12. This does not mean that men by their very *creation*, or their physical nature, are thus denominated; but men who, from long continuance in iniquity, *deserve* to experience wrath; as Judas was not called "son of perdition" by any arbitrary appointment, or as an *original* designation, but because in consequence of his avarice and treason this was the name which *in fact* actually described him, or fitted his case. ¶ *Fitted* (κατηρτισμένα). This word properly means to *restore; to place in order; to render complete; to supply a defect; to fit to, or adapt to, or prepare for;* see Mat. iv. 21, "Were *mending* their nets." Gal. vi. 1, "*Restore* such an one," &c. In this place it is a *participle*, and means those who *are* fitted for or *adapted to* destruction; those whose characters are such as to *deserve* destruction, or as to make destruction proper. See the same use of the word in Heb. xi. 3, "Through faith we understand that the worlds were *framed*"—beautifully fitted up in proper proportions, one part adapted to another—"by the word of God." Heb. x. 5, "A body hast thou *prepared* for me;" fitted, or adapted to me; comp. Ps. lxviii. 10; lxxiv. 16. In this place there is not the semblance of a declaration that God *had* PREPARED *them, or* FITTED *them for destruction.* It is a simple declaration that they were IN FACT fitted for it, without making an affirmation about the manner in which they became so. A reader of the English Bible may, perhaps, sometimes draw the impression that God had fitted them for this. But this is not affirmed; and there is an evident design in *not* affirming it, and a distinction made between them and the vessels of mercy which ought to be regarded. In relation to the latter it is expressly *affirmed* that *God* fitted or *prepared* them for glory; see ver. 23, "Which HE had afore prepared unto glory." The same distinction is remarkably striking in the account of the last judgment in Mat. xxv. 34, 41. To the righteous, Christ will say, "Come, ye blessed of my Father, inherit the kingdom prepared FOR YOU," &c. To the wicked, "Depart from me, ye cursed, into everlasting fire, prepared FOR THE DEVIL AND HIS ANGELS;" not said to have been originally prepared *for them.* It is clear, therefore, that God intends to keep the great truth in view, that *he* prepares his people *by direct agency* for heaven; but that he exerts *no such agency* in preparing the wicked for destruction. ¶ *For destruction* (εἰς ἀπώλειαν). This word occurs in the New Testament no less than twenty times; Mat. vii. 13, "Which leadeth to destruction." John xvii. 12, "Son of *perdition.*" Acts viii. 20, "Thy money *perish* with thee;" Greek, be for *destruction* with thee, xxv. 16; Phil. i. 28, "Token of perdition." iii. 19, "Whose end is destruction." 2 Thess. ii. 3, "The son of perdition." 1 Tim. v. 9, "Which drown men in destruction and perdition." Heb. x. 39, "Which draw back into perdition; see also 2 Pet. ii. 1, 3; iii. 7, 16, &c. In these places it is clear that the reference is to the future punishment of wicked men, and in *no instance* to national calamities. No such use of the word is to be found in the New Testament; and this is further clear

23 And that he might make known the riches [a] of his glory on the vessels of mercy, which [b] he had afore prepared unto glory.

a Eph.1.18. b 1 Thess.5.9.

from the contrast with the word "glory" in the next verse. We may remark here, that if men are *fitted* or prepared for destruction; if future torment is adapted to them, and they to it; if it is fit that they should be subjected to it; then God will do what is *fit* or *right* to be done, and, unless they repent, they must perish. Nor would it be right for God to take them to heaven as they are; to a place for which they are not *fitted*, and which is not adapted to their feelings, their character, or their conduct.

23. *And that he might make known.* That he might manifest or display. The apostle had shown (in ver. 22) that the dealings of God towards the wicked were not liable to the objection made in ver. 19. In this verse he proceeds to show that the objection could not lie against his dealings with the *other* class of men—the righteous. If his dealings towards *neither* were liable to the objection, then he has *met the whole case*, and the divine government is vindicated. This he proves by showing that for God to show the riches of his glory towards those whom he has prepared for it, cannot be regarded as unjust. ¶ *The riches of his glory.* This is a form of expression common among the Hebrews, meaning the same as *his rich* or *his abundant glory.* The same expression occurs in Eph. i. 18. ¶ *On the vessels of mercy.* Men towards whom his mercy was to be displayed (see ver. 22); that is, on those towards whom he has purposed to display his mercy. ¶ *Mercy.* Favour, or pity shown to the *miserable.* Grace is favour to the *undeserving;* mercy, favour to those in distress. This distinction is not, however, always strictly observed by the sacred writers. ¶ *Which he had afore prepared.* We are here brought to a remarkable difference between God's mode of dealing with them and with the wicked. Here it is expressly affirmed that God himself had prepared them for glory. In regard to the wicked, it is simply affirmed that they *were fitted* for destruction, without affirming any thing of the *agency* by which it was done. That *God* prepares his people for glory—commences and continues the work of their redemption—is abundantly taught in the Scriptures; 1 Thess. v. 9, "God hath appointed us, to obtain salvation by our Lord Jesus Christ." 2 Tim. i. 9, "Who hath saved us and called us with an holy calling, not according to our works, but according to his own purpose and grace, which was given us in Christ Jesus before the world began." See also Eph. i. 4, 5, 11; Rom. viii. 28, 29, 30; Acts xiii. 48; John i. 13. As the renewing of the heart and the sanctifying of the soul is an act of goodness, it is worthy of God, and of course no objection could lie against it. No man could complain of a course of dealings designed to make men *better;* and as this is the sole design of the electing love of God, his dealings with *this* class of men are easily vindicated. No Christian can complain that God has chosen him, renewed him, and made him pure and happy. And as this was an important part of the plan of God, it is easily defended from the objection in ver. 19. ¶ *Unto glory.* To happiness; and especially to the happiness of heaven Heb. ii. 10, "It became him, in bringing many sons unto glory," &c. Rom. v. 2, "We rejoice in hope of the glory of God." 2 Cor. iv. 17, "Our light affliction worketh for us a far more exceeding and eternal weight of glory," 2 Thess. ii. 14; 2 Tim. ii. 10; 1 Pet. v. 4. This eternal state is called "glory," because it blends together every thing that constitutes honour, dignity, purity, love, and happiness. All these significations are in various places attached to this word, and all mingle in the eternal state of the righteous. We may remark here, (1.) That this word

24 Even us, whom he hath called, not of the Jews only, but also of the Gentiles?

25 As he saith also in Osee, [a] I will call them my people, which were not my people; and her beloved, which was not beloved.

26 And [b] it shall come to pass,

a Hos.2.23.

b Hos.1.10.

"glory" is not used in the Scriptures to denote any *external national privileges;* or to describe any external call of the gospel. No such instance is to be found. Of course the apostle here by vessels of mercy meant *individuals* destined to eternal life, and not *nations* externally called to the gospel. No instance can be found where God speaks of nations called to external privileges, and speaks of them as "prepared unto glory." (2.) As this word refers to the future state of individuals, it shows what is meant by the word "destruction" in ver. 22. That term stands contrasted with glory; and describes, therefore, the future condition of individual wicked men. This is also its uniform meaning in the New Testament. On this vindication of the apostle we may observe, (1.) That all men will be treated as they *ought* to be treated. Men will be dealt with according to their characters at the end of life. (2.) If men will suffer no injustice, then this is the same as saying that they will be treated justly. But what is this? That the wicked shall be treated as they deserve. What they *deserve* God has told us in the Scriptures. "These shall go away into everlasting punishment." (3.) God has a right to bestow his blessings as he chooses. Where *all* are undeserving, where none have any claim, he may confer his favours on whom he pleases. (4.) He actually *does* deal with men in this way. The apostle takes this for granted. He does not deny it. He most evidently believes it, and labours to show that it is *right* to do so. If *he* did not believe it, and meant to teach it, he would have said so. It would have met the objection at once, and saved all argument. He reasons as if he *did* believe it; and this settles the question that the doctrine is true.

24. *Even us,* &c.; see chap. i. 16; ii. 10; iii. 29, 30. To prove that the *Gentiles* might be called as well as the Jews, was a leading design of the epistle. ¶ *Us.* Christians, selected from both Jews and Gentiles. This proves that he did not refer to *nations* primarily, but to *individuals* chosen *out of* nations. Two things are established here. (1.) That the grace of God was not confined to the Jewish people, as they supposed, so that it could be conferred on no others. (2.) That God was not bound to confer grace on *all* the descendants of Abraham, as he bestowed it on those selected *from* the mass, according to his own will, and not of necessity *on the mass* itself.

25. *As he saith also.* The doctrine which he had established, he proceeds now to confirm by quotations from the writings of *Jews,* that he might remove *every* objection. The doctrine was, (1.) That God intended to call his people from the Gentiles as well as the Jews. (2.) That he was bound by no promise and no principle of obligation to bestow salvation on *all* the Jews. (3.) That, therefore, it was right for him to reject any or all of the Jews, if he chose, and cut them off from their privileges as a people and from salvation. ¶ *In Osee.* This is the Greek form of writing the Hebrew word *Hosea.* It means in the book of Hosea, as *in David* means in the book of David, or by David, Heb. iv. 7. The passage is found in Hosea ii. 23. This quotation is not made according to the *letter,* but the *sense* of the prophet is preserved. The meaning is the same in Hosea and in this place, that God would bring those into a covenant relation to himself, who were before deemed outcasts and strangers. Thus he supports his main position that God would choose his people from among the Gentiles as well as the Jews, or would exercise towards both his right as a sovereign, bestowing or withholding his blessings as he pleases.

26. *And it shall come to pass.* It shall happen, or take place. This is a continuation of the quotation from

that in the place where it was said unto them, Ye *are* not my people; there shall they be called the children of the living God.

27 Esaias also [a] crieth concerning Israel, Though the number of the children of Israel be as the sand of the sea, a remnant shall be saved.

[a] Is.10.22,23.

---

the prophet Hosea (chap. i. 10), designed to confirm the doctrine which he was establishing. Both these quotations have the same design, and are introduced for the same end. In Hosea they did not refer to the calling of the Gentiles, but to the recalling the rejected Jews. God says, after the Jews had been rejected and scattered for their idolatry; after they had forfeited his favour, and been cast off as if they were not his people; he would *recall* them, and bestow on them again the appellation of sons. The apostle does not quote this as having original reference to the Gentiles, but for the following purposes:—(1.) If God formerly purposed to recall to himself a people whom he had rejected; if he bestowed favours on his own people *after* they had forfeited his favour, and ceased to be entitled to the name of "his people:" then the same thing was not to be regarded as absurd if he dealt in a similar manner with the Gentiles—also a part of his original great family, the family of man, but long since rejected and deemed strangers. (2.) The dealings of God towards the Jews in the time of Hosea settled *a general principle of government.* His treatment of them in this manner was a *part* of his great plan of governing the world. On the same plan he now admitted the Gentiles to favour. And as this *general principle* was established; as the history of the Jews themselves was a *precedent* in the case, it ought not to be objected in the time of Paul that the *same principle* should be carried out to meet the case also of the Gentiles. ¶ *In the place.* The place where they may be scattered, or where they may dwell. Or rather, perhaps, in those nations which were not regarded as the people of God, *there* shall be a people to whom this shall apply. ¶ *Where it was said unto them.* Where the proper appellation of the people was, that they were not the people of God; where they were idolatrous, sinful, aliens, strangers; so that they had none of the marks of the children of God. ¶ *Ye are not my people.* People in covenant with God; under his protection, as *their* Sovereign, and keeping his laws. ¶ *There shall they be called.* That is, there they *shall be.* The verb *to call* in the Hebrew writings means often the same as *to be.* It denotes that this shall be the appellation which properly expresses their character. It is a figure perhaps almost peculiar to the Hebrews; and it gives additional interest to the case. Instead of saying coldly and abstractedly, "they *are* such," it introduces also the idea that such is the *favourable judgment* of God in the case; see Mat. v. 9, "Peace-makers...shall be called the children of God;" see the Note on that place; also ver. 19; Mat. xxi. 13, "My house shall *be called* the house of prayer;" Mark xi. 17; Luke i. 32, 35, 76; Isa. lvi. 7. ¶ *The children of,* &c. Greek, *Sons;* see Note, Mat. i. 1. ¶ *Living God.* Called *living* God in opposition to dead idols; see Note, Mat. xvi. 16; also xxvi. 63; John vi. 69; Acts xiv. 15; 1 Thes. i. 9; "Turn from idols to serve the *living* and true God," Jer. x. 10. This is a most honourable and distinguished appellation. No higher favour can be conferred on mortals than *to be* the sons of the living God; members of his family; entitled to his protection; and secure of his watch and care. This was an object of the highest desire with the saints of old; see Psal. xlii. 2; lxxxiv. 2, "My soul thirsteth for God, the *living* God;" "My heart and my flesh cry out for the *living* God."

27, 28. *Esaias.* The Greek way of writing the word *Isaiah.* ¶ *Crieth;* Isa. x. 22, 23. Exclaims, or speaks aloud or openly: compare John i. 15. Isaiah brings forth the doctrine fully, and without any concealment or disguise. This doctrine related to the rejection of the Jews; a far more diffi-

28 For he will finish [1] the work, and cut *it* short in righteousness:

1 Or, *the account.*

cult point to establish than was that of the calling of the Gentiles. It was needful, therefore, to fortify it by some explicit passage of the Scriptures. ¶ *Concerning Israel.* Concerning *the Jews.* It is probable that Isaiah had reference primarily to the Jews of his own time; to that wicked generation that God was about to punish, by sending them captive into other lands. The case was one, however, which settled a *general principle of the Jewish government;* and, therefore, it was applicable to the case before the apostle. If the thing for which he was contending—that the Jews might be rejected—existed in the time of Isaiah, and was settled then as a precedent, it might exist also in his time, and under the gospel. ¶ *As the sand of the sea.* This expression is used to denote an indefinite or an innumerable multitude. It often occurs in the sacred writings. In the infancy of society, before the art of numbering was carried to a great extent, men were obliged to express themselves very much in this manner, Gen. xxii. 17, "I will multiply thy seed...as the sand which is upon the sea-shore;" xxxii. 12, Isaiah doubtless had reference to this promise; "Though all that was promised to Abraham shall be fulfilled, and his seed shall be as numerous as God declared, yet a remnant only," &c. The apostle thus shows that his doctrine does not conflict at all with the *utmost* expectation of the Jews drawn from the promises of God; see a similar use of the term *sand* in Judg. vii. 12; 1 Sam. xiii. 5; 2 Sam. xvii. 11, &c. In the same manner great numbers were denoted by the *stars of heaven,* Gen. xxii. 17; xv. 5. ¶ *A remnant shall be saved.* Meaning a remnant *only.* This implies that great multitudes of them would be *cast off,* and *be not saved.* If only a *remnant* was to be saved, many must be lost; and this was just the point which the apostle was endeavouring to establish. The word remnant means *that which is left,* particularly what may remain after a battle or a great calamity, 2 Ki. xix. 31; x. 11; Judg. v. 11; Isa. xiv. 22. In this place, however, it means a small part or portion. Out of the great multitude there shall be so few left as to make it proper to say that it was a mere remnant. This implies, of course, that the great mass should be cast away or rejected. And this was the use which the apostle intended to make of it; compare the Wisdom of Sirach, xliv. 17, "Noah ...was left unto the earth as *a remnant* when the flood came." ¶ *Shall be saved.* Shall be preserved or kept from destruction. As Isaiah had reference to the captivity of Babylon, this means that only a remnant should return to their native land. The great mass should be rejected and cast off. This was the case with the ten tribes, and also with many others who chose to remain in the land of their captivity The use which the apostle makes of it is this: In the history of the Jews, by the testimony of Isaiah, a large part of the Jews of that time were rejected, and cast off from being the peculiar people of God. It is clear, therefore, that God has brought himself under no obligation to save *all* the descendants of Abraham. This case settles the principle. If God did it *then,* it was equally consistent for him to do it in the time of Paul, under the gospel. The conclusion, therefore, to which the apostle came, that it was the intention of God to reject and cast off the Jews as a people, was in strict accordance with their own history and the prophecies. It was still true that a remnant was to be saved, while the great mass of the people was rejected. The apostle is not to be understood here as affirming that the passage in Isaiah had reference to the gospel, but only that *it settled one great principle of the divine administration in regard to the Jews, and that their rejection under the gospel was strictly in accordance with that principle.*

28. *He will finish the work.* This is taken from the Septuagint translation of Isa. x. 23. The Hebrew is, "The Lord God of hosts shall make

because [a] a short work will the Lord make upon the earth.

a Isa.22.32.

29 And as Esaias said before, [b] Except the Lord of Sabaoth had

b Isa.1.9; Lam.3.22.

a consumption, even determined, in the midst of all the land." Or, as it may be rendered, "Destruction is decreed which shall make justice overflow; yea, destruction is verily determined on; the Lord Jehovah will execute it in the midst of all the land." (*Stuart.*) The Septuagint and the apostle adhere to *the sense* of the passage, but do not follow the *words.* The phrase, *will finish the work,* means *he will bring the thing to an end,* or will accomplish it. It is an expression applicable to a firm purpose to accomplish an object. It refers here to his *threat* of cutting off the people; and means that he will fulfil it. ¶ *Cut it short.* This word here means to *execute it speedily.* The destruction shall not be delayed. ¶ *In righteousness.* So as to manifest his own *justice.* The work, though apparently severe, yet shall be a *just* expression of God's abhorrence of the sins of the people. ¶ *Because a short work.* The word here rendered "short" means properly that which is *determined on* or *decreed.* This is the sense of the Hebrew; and the phrase here denotes *the purpose which was determined on* in relation to the Jews. ¶ *Upon the earth.* Upon the *land* of Israel; see Notes on Matt. v. 4; iv. 8. The design for which the apostle introduces this passage is to show that God of old destroyed many of the Jews for their sin; and that, therefore, the doctrine of the apostle was no new thing, that *the Jews* might be excluded from the peculiar privileges of the children of God.

29. *And as Esaias said;* Isa. chap. i. 9. ¶ *Before.* The apostle had just cited one prediction from the tenth chapter of Isaiah. He now says that Isaiah had affirmed the same thing in a previous part of his prophecy. ¶ *Except the Lord of Sabaoth.* In Isaiah, the Lord of Hosts. The word *Sabaoth* is the Hebrew word rendered *hosts.* It properly denotes *armies* or military hosts organized for war. Hence it denotes *the hosts of heaven,* and means, (1.) The *angels* who are represented as *marshalled* or arranged into military orders; Eph. i. 21; iii. 10; vi. 12; Col. i. 16; ii. 15; Jude 6; 1 Kings xxii. 19, "I saw the Lord sitting on his throne, and all the host of heaven standing by him;" Psalm ciii. 21; cxlviii. 2. (2.) The stars; Jer. xxxiii. 22, "As the host of heaven cannot be numbered," &c. Isa. xl. 26; Deut. iv. 19, &c. God is called the Lord of hosts, as being at the head of all these armies; their King and their Commander. It is a phrase properly expressive of his majesty and power, and is appropriately introduced here, as the act of saving "the seed" was a signal *act of power* in the midst of great surrounding wickedness. ¶ *Had left.* Had *preserved,* or kept from destruction. Here their preservation is ascribed to God, and it is affirmed that if God had not interposed, *the whole nation* would have been cut off. This fully establishes the doctrine of the apostle, that God *might* cast off the Jews, and extend the blessings to the Gentiles. ¶ *A seed.* The Hebrew in Isaiah means *one surviving* or *escaping,* corresponding with the word *remnant.* The word *seed* commonly means in the Scriptures *descendants, posterity.* In this place it means *a part, a small portion; a remnant,* like the small portion of the harvest which is reserved for sowing. ¶ *We had been as Sodoma.* The nation was so wicked, that unless God had preserved a small number who were pious from the general corruption of the people, they would have been swept off by judgment, like Sodom and Gomorrah. We are told that ten righteous men would have saved Sodom; Gen. xviii. 32. Among the Israelites, in a time of great general depravity, a small number of holy men were found who preserved the nation. The design of the apostle here was the same as in the previous verses—to show that it was settled in the Jewish history that God *might* cast off the people, and reject them from enjoying the

left us a seed, we [a] had been as Sodoma, and been made like unto Gomorrha.

30. What shall we say then? that [b] the Gentiles, which followed not after righteousness, have attained to righteousness, even the righteousness [c] which is of faith.

a Gen.19.24,25; Isa.13.19. *b* chap.10.20. *c* chap.1.17; Philem. 3,9.

peculiar privileges of his friends. It is true that in Isaiah he has reference to the *temporal* punishments of the Jews. But it settles *a great principle*, for which Paul was contending, that God *might* cast off the nation consistently with his promises and his plans.—We may learn here, (1.) That the existence of religion among a people is owing to the love of God. "Except the Lord *had left us*," &c. (2.) It is owing to his mercy that *any men* are kept from sin, and any nation from destruction. (3.) We see the value of religion and of pious men in a nation. Ten such would have saved Sodom; and a few such saved Judea; comp. Mat. v. 13, 14. (4.) God has a right to withdraw his mercies from any other people, however exalted their privileges, and leave them to ruin; and we should not be high-minded, but fear; Rom. x. 20.

30. *What shall we say then?* What conclusion shall we draw from the previous train of remarks? To what results have we come by the passages adduced from the Old Testament? This question is asked preparatory to his summing up the argument; and he had so stated the argument that the conclusion which he was about to draw was inevitable. ¶ *The Gentiles.* That *many* of the Gentiles; or that the way was open for them, and many of them *had actually* embraced the righteousness of faith. This epistle was written as late as the year 57 (see Introduction), and at that time multitudes of heathens *had* embraced the Christian religion. ¶ *Which followed not after righteousness.* The apostle does not mean that none of the pagans had any solicitude about right and wrong, or that there were no anxious inquiries among them; but he intends particularly to place them in contrast with the Jew. They had not made it their main object to justify themselves; they were not filled with prejudice and pride as the Jews were, who supposed that they *had* complied with the law, and who felt no need of any other justification; they were sinners, and they felt it, and had no such mighty obstacle in a system of self-righteousness to overcome as the Jew had. Still it was true that they were excessively wicked, and that the prevailing characteristic among them was that they did not follow after righteousness; see chap. i. The word "followed" here often denotes to pursue with intense energy, as a hunter pursues his game, or a man pursues a flying enemy. The Jews had sought righteousness in that way; the Gentiles had not. The word *righteousness* here means the same as *justification.* The Gentiles, which sought not justification, have obtained justification. ¶ *Have attained to righteousness.* Have become justified. This was a matter of fact; and this was what the prophet had predicted. The apostle does not say that the sins of the Gentiles, or their indifference to the subject, was any *reason* why God justified them, or that men would be as safe in sin as in attempting to seek for salvation. He establishes the doctrine, indeed, that God is a sovereign; but still it is implied that the gospel had not the *peculiar* obstacle to contend with among the Gentiles that it had among the Jews. There was less pride, obstinacy, self-confidence; and men were more easily brought *to see* that they were sinners, and to feel their need of a Saviour. Though God dispenses his favours as a sovereign, and though *all* are opposed by nature to the gospel, yet it is always true that the gospel finds *more* obstacles among some men than among others. This was a most cutting and humbling doctrine to the pride of a Jew; and it is no wonder, therefore, that the apostle guarded it as he did. ¶ *Which is of faith.* Justification by faith in Christ; see Note, chap. i. 17.

31. *But Israel.* The Jews. The apostle does not mean to affirm that

31 But Israel, which [a] followed after the law of righteousness, hath not attained to the law of righteousness.

32 Wherefore? Because *they sought it* not by faith, but as it were by the works of the law: for they stumbled at that stumbling-stone;

a chap.10.2; 11.7.

none of the Jews had obtained mercy, but that *as a people,* or acting according to the prevalent principles of the nation to work out their own righteousness, they had not obtained it. ¶ *Which followed after the law of righteousness.* The phrase, "the law of righteousness," means the law of justice, or *the just law.* That law demands perfect purity; and even its external observance demanded holiness. The Jews supposed that they rendered such *obedience* to that law as to constitute a *meritorious* ground of justification. This they had *followed after,* that is, pursued zealously and unremittingly. The reason why they did not obtain justification in that way is fully stated in chap. i—iii. where it is shown that the law demands perfect compliance with its precepts; and that Jews, as well as Gentiles, had altogether failed in rendering such compliance. ¶ *Hath not attained to the law of righteousness.* They have not come to yield *true* obedience to the law, even though imperfect; not such obedience as to give *evidence* that they have been justified. We may remark here, (1.) That no conclusion could have been more humbling to a Jew than this. It constituted the whole of the prevalent religion, and was the object of their incessant toils. (2.) As they made the experiment fully, and failed: as they had the best advantages for it, and did not succeed, but reared only a miserable and delusive system of self-righteousness (Phil. iii. 4—9;) it follows, that all similar experiments must fail, and that none now can be justified by the law. (3.) Thousands fail in the same attempt. They seek to justify themselves before God. They attempt to weave a righteousness of their own. The moral man does this. The immoral man attempts it as much as the moral man, and is as confident in his own righteousness. The troubled sinner does this; and this it is which keeps him so long from the cross of Christ. All this must be renounced; and man must come as a poor, lost, ruined sinner, and throw himself upon the mere mercy of God in Christ for justification and life.

32. *Wherefore?* Why? The apostle proceeds to state the reason why so uniform and remarkable a result happened. *They sought it not by faith,* &c. They depended on their own righteousness, and not on the mercy of God to be obtained by faith. ¶ *By the works of the law.* By complying with *all* the demands of the law so that they might *merit* salvation. Their attempted obedience included their prayers, fastings, sacrifices, &c., as well as compliance with the demands of the moral law. It may be asked here, perhaps, how the Jews could know any better than this? how should *they* know any thing about justification by faith? To this I answer, (1.) That the doctrine was stated in the Old Testament; see Hab. ii. 4; comp. Rom. i. 17; Ps. xxxii. cxxx. xiv. comp. Rom. iii. Job. ix. 2. (2.) The sacrifices had reference to a future state of things, and were doubtless so understood; see the epistle to the Hebrews. (3.) The *principle* of justification, and of living by faith, had been *fully* brought out in the lives and experience of the saints of old; see Rom. iv. and Heb. xi. ¶ *They stumbled.* They fell; or failed; or *this was the cause* why they did not obtain it. ¶ *At that stumbling-stone.* To wit, at that which he specifies in the following verse. A *stumbling-stone* is a stone or impediment in the path over which men may fall. Here it means *that obstacle which prevented their attaining the righteousness of faith; and which was the occasion of their fall, rejection, and ruin.* That was the rejection and the crucifixion of their own Messiah; their unwillingness to be saved by him; their contempt of him and his message. For

33 As it is written, [a] Behold, I lay in Sion a stumbling-stone and rock of offence; and whosoever believeth on him shall not be [1] ashamed.

a Ps.118.22; Isa.8.14.

1 or, *confounded.*

this God withheld from them the blessings of justification, and was about to cast them off as a people. This also the apostle proceeds to prove was foretold by the prophets.

33. *As it is written;* see Isa. viii. 14; xxviii. 16. The quotation here is made up of both these passages, and contains the substance of both; comp. also Ps. cxviii. 22; 1 Pet. ii. 6. ¶ *Behold I lay in Sion.* Mount Sion was the hill or eminence in Jerusalem, over-against Mount Moriah, on which the temple was built. On this was the palace of David, and this was the residence of the court; 1 Chron. xi. 5—8. Hence the whole city was often called by that name; Ps. xlviii. 12; lxix. 35; lxxxvii. 2. Hence also it came to signify the capital, the glory of the people of God, the place of solemnities; and hence also the church itself; Ps. ii. 6; li. 18; cii. 13; cxxxvii. 3; Isa. i. 27; lii. 1; lix. 20, &c. In this place it means the church. God will place or establish in the midst of that church. ¶ *A stumbling-stone and rock of offence.* Something over which men shall fall; see Note, Matt. v. 29. This is by Paul referred to the Messiah. He is called *rock of stumbling,* not because it was the *design* of sending him that men *should* fall, but because such *would* be the result. The application of the term *rock* to the Messiah is derived from the custom of *building,* as he is the *corner-stone* or the *immovable foundation* on which the church is to be built. It is not on human merits, but by the righteousness of the Saviour, that the church is to be reared; see 1 Pet. ii. 4, "I lay in Sion a *chief corner-stone;*" Ps. cxviii. 22, "The stone which the builders rejected, is become the head stone of the corner;" Eph. ii. 20, "Jesus Christ himself being the chief corner-stone." This rock, *designed* as a corner stone to the church, became, by the wickedness of the Jews, the block over which they fall into ruin; 1 Pet. ii. 8. ¶ *Shall not be ashamed.* This is taken substantially from the Septuagint translation of Isa, xxviii. 16, though with some variation. The Hebrew is, "shall not make haste," as it is in our English version. This is the literal meaning of the Hebrew word; but it means also *to be afraid;* as one who makes haste often is; to be agitated with fear or fright; and hence it has a signification nearly similar to that of shame. It expresses the substance of the same thing, viz. *failure of obtaining expected success and happiness.* The meaning here is, that the man who believes shall not be agitated, or thrown into commotion, by fear of want or success; shall not be disappointed in his hopes; and, of course, he shall never be ashamed that he became a Christian. They who do *not* believe in Christ shall be agitated, fall, and sink into eternal shame and contempt. Dan. xii. 2. They who *do* believe shall be confident; shall not be deceived, but shall obtain the object of their desires. It is clear that Paul regarded the passage in Isaiah as referring to the Messiah. The same also is the case with the other sacred writers who have quoted it; 1 Pet. ii. 5—8; see also Matt. xxi. 42; Luke xx. 17, 18; ii. 34. The ancient Targum of Jonathan translates the passage, Isa. xxviii. 16, "Lo, I will place in Zion a king, a king strong, mighty and terrible;" referring doubtless to the Messiah. Other Jewish writings also show that this interpretation was formerly given by the Jews to the passage in Isaiah.

In view of this argument of the apostle, we may remark, (1.) That God is a sovereign, and has a right to dispose of men as he pleases. (2.) The doctrine of election was manifest in the case of the Jews as an established principle of the divine government, and is therefore true. (3.) It argues great want of proper feeling to be opposed to this doctrine. It is saying, in other words, that we have not confidence in God; or that we do not believe that he is qualified to direct the affairs of his own universe as well as

CHAPTER X.

BRETHREN, my heart's desire
and prayer to God for Israel is,
that they might be saved.

2 For I bear them record, that
they have a zeal [a] of God, but not
according to knowledge.

3 For they being ignorant [b] of

a Acts 21.20.

b chap.9.30.

we. (4.) The doctrine of election is a doctrine which is not *arbitrary;* but which will yet be seen to be wise, just, and good. It is the source of all the blessings that any mortals enjoy; and in the case before us, it can be *seen* to be benevolent as well as just. It is *better* that God should cast off a part of the small nation of the Jews, and extend these blessings to the Gentiles, than that they should always have been confined to Jews. The world is better for it, and more good has come out of it. (5.) The fact that the gospel has been extended to all nations, is proof that it is from heaven. To a Jew there was no motive to attempt to break down all the existing institutions of his nation, and make the blessings of religion common to all nations, unless he knew that the gospel system was true. Yet the apostles were Jews; educated with all the prejudices of the Jewish people. (6.) The interests of Christians are safe. They shall not be ashamed or disappointed. God will keep them, and bring them to his kingdom. (7.) Men still are offended at the cross of Christ. They contemn and despise him. He is to them as a root out of dry ground, and they reject him, and fall into ruin. This is the cause why sinners perish; and this only. Thus as the ancient Jews brought ruin on themselves and their country, so do sinners bring condemnation and woe on their souls. And as the ancient despisers and crucifiers of the Lord Jesus perished, so will all those who work iniquity and despise him now.

CHAPTER X.

1. *Brethren.* This expression seems intended particularly for the Jews, his ancient friends, fellow-worshippers, and kinsmen, but who had embraced the Christian faith. It is an expression of tenderness and affection, denoting his deep interest in their welfare. ¶ *My heart's desire.* The word "desire" (εὐδοκία) means benevolence, and the expression, *my heart's desire,* means my earnest and sincere wish. ¶ *Prayer to God.* He not only cherished this feeling, but he expressed it in a desire to God. He had no desire that his kinsmen should be destroyed; no pleasure in the appalling doctrine which he had been defending. He still wished their welfare; and could still pray for them that they might return to God. Ministers have no pleasure in proclaiming the truth that men must be lost. Even when they declare the truths of the Bible that some *will* be lost; when they are constrained by the unbelief and wickedness of men to proclaim it of *them,* they still can sincerely say that they seek their salvation. ¶ *For Israel.* For the Jewish nation. ¶ *That they might be saved.* This clearly refers to salvation from the sin of unbelief; and the consequences of sin in hell. It does not refer to the temporal calamities which were coming upon them, but to preservation from the eternal anger of God; comp. chap. xi. 26; 1 Tim. ii. 4. The reasons why the apostle commences this chapter in this tender manner are the following. (1.) Because he had stated and defended one of the most offensive doctrines that could be preached to a Jew; and he was desirous to show them that it was not from any want of affection for them, but that he was urged to it by the pressure of truth. (2.) He was regarded by them as an apostate. He had abandoned them when bearing their commission, and while on his way to execute their favourite purposes, and had preached the doctrine which they had sent him to destroy; comp. Acts ix. He had opposed them every where; had proclaimed their pride, self-righteousness, and crime in crucifying their Messiah; had forsaken all that they valued; their pomp of worship, their city, and their temple; and had gone to other lands to bear the message of mercy to the nations that

they despised. He was willing to show them that this proceeded from no want of affection for them, but that he still retained towards them the feelings of a Jew, and could give them credit for much that they valued themselves on, ver. 2. (3.) He was aware of the deep and dreadful condemnation that was coming on them. In view of that he expressed his tender regard for their welfare, and his earnest prayer to God for their salvation. And we see here the proper feelings of a minister of the gospel when declaring the most terrible of the truths of the Bible. Paul was tender, affectionate, kind; convincing by cool argument, and not harshly denouncing; stating the appalling truth, and then pouring out his earnest desires to God that he would avert the impending doom. So should the awful doctrines of religion be preached by all the ambassadors of God.

2. *For I bear them record.* To bear record means to be a witness; to give evidence. This, Paul was well qualified to do. He had been a Jew of the strictest order (Acts xxvi. 5; Phil. iii. 5), and he well knew the extraordinary exertions which they put forth to obey the commands of the law. ¶ *A zeal of God.* A zeal *for* God. Thus John ii. 17, "The zeal of thine house hath eaten me up;" an earnest desire *for* the honour of the sanctuary has wholly absorbed my attention; comp. Ps. lxix. 9; Acts xxi. 20, "Thou seest, brother, how many thousands of Jews there are which believe, and they are all zealous of the law;" xxii. 3, "And was zealous toward God as ye all are this day." Zeal for God here means passionate ardour in the things pertaining to God, or in the things of religion. In this they were, doubtless, many of them sincere; but sincerity does not of itself constitute true piety; John xvi. 2, "The time cometh that whosoever killeth you will think that he doeth God service." This would be an instance of extraordinary zeal, and in this they would be sincere; but persecution to death of apostles cannot be true religion; see also Matt. xxiii. 15; Acts xxvi. 9, "I thought that *I ought* to do," &c. So many persons suppose that, provided they are *sincere* and *zealous*, they must of course be accepted of God. But the zeal which is acceptable is that which aims at the glory of God, and which is founded on true benevolence to the universe; and which does not aim primarily to establish a system of self-righteousness, as did the Jew, or to build up *our own sect*, as many others do. We may remark here, that Paul was not insensible to what the Jews did, and was not unwilling to give them credit for it. A minister of the gospel should not be blind to the amiable qualities of men or to their zeal; and should be willing to speak of it tenderly, even when he is proclaiming the doctrine of depravity, or denouncing the just judgments of God. ¶ *Not according to knowledge.* Not an enlightened, discerning, and intelligent zeal. Not that which was founded on correct views of God and of religious truth. Such zeal is enthusiasm, and often becomes persecuting. Knowledge without zeal becomes cold, abstract, calculating, formal; and may be possessed by devils as well as men. It is the union of the two—the action of the man called forth to intense effort by just *views* of truth and by right *feeling*—that constitutes true religion. This was the zeal of the Saviour and of the apostles.

3. *For they being ignorant.* The ignorance of the Jews was voluntarily, and therefore criminal. The apostle does not affirm that they could not have known what the plan of God was; for he says (ver. 18—21) that they had full opportunity of knowing. An attentive study of their own Scriptures would have led them to the true knowledge of the Messiah and his righteousness; see John v. 39; comp. Isa. liii. &c. Yet the fact that they were ignorant, though not an excuse, is introduced here, doubtless, as a mild and mitigating circumstance, that should take off the severity of what he might appear to them to be saying; 1 Tim. i. 13, "But I obtained mercy because I did it ignorantly, in unbelief;" Luke xxiii. 34, "Then said Jesus, Father, forgive them, for they know not what

God's righteousness, and going about to establish their own righteousness, have not submitted themselves unto the righteousness of God.

4 For Christ *is* the end [a] of the law for righteousness to every one that believeth.

5 For Moses describeth [b] the

a Heb.10.14. *b* Lev.18.5.

---

they do;" Acts vii. 60. Involuntary ignorance excuses from guilt; but ignorance produced by our sin or our indolence is no excuse for crime. ¶ *Of God's righteousness.* Not of the personal holiness of God, but *of God's plan of justifying men, or of declaring them righteous by faith in his Son;* see Note, chap. i. 17. Here God's plan stands opposed to their efforts to make themselves righteous by their own works. ¶ *And seeking to establish,* &c. Endeavouring to *confirm* or *make valid* their own righteousness; to render it such as to constitute a ground of justification before God; or to make good their own claims to eternal life by their merits. This stands opposed to the justification by grace, or to God's plan. And they must *ever* be opposed. This was the constant effort of the Jews; and in this they supposed they had succeeded. see Paul's experience in Phil. iii. 4—6; Acts xxvi. 5. Instances of their belief on this subject occur in all the gospels, where our Saviour combats their notions of their own righteousness. See particularly their views and evasions exposed in Matt. xxiii; comp. Matt. v. 20, &c.; vi. 2—5. It was this which mainly opposed the Lord Jesus and his apostles; and it is this confidence in their own righteousness, which still stands in the way of the progress of the gospel among men. ¶ *Have not submitted themselves.* Confident in their own righteousness, they have not yielded their hearts to a plan which requires them to come confessing that they have *no* merit, and to be saved by the merit of another. No obstacle to salvation by grace is so great as the self-righteousness of the sinner. ¶ *Righteousness of God.* His plan or scheme of justifying men.

4. *For Christ.* This expression implies *faith* in Christ. This is the design of the discussion, to show that justification cannot be obtained by our own righteousness, but by faith in Christ. As no direct benefit results to men from Christ unless they believe on him, faith in him is implied where the word occurs in this connection. ¶ *Is the end of the law.* The word translated "end" means that which *completes* a thing, or renders it perfect; also the boundary, issue, or termination of any thing, as the end of life, the result of a prophecy, &c.; John xiii. 1; Luke xxii. 37. It also means the *design* or *object* which is had in view; the principal purpose for which it was undertaken; 1 Tim. i. 5, "The *end* of the commandment is charity;" the main design or purpose of the command is to produce love; 1 Pet. i. 9, "The end of your faith, the salvation of your souls;" the main design or purpose of faith is to secure salvation; Rom. xiv. 9, "To this end Christ both died," &c. For this design or purpose. This is doubtless its meaning here. *The main design or object which the perfect obedience of the law would accomplish, is accomplished by faith in Christ.* That is, perfect obedience to the law would accomplish justification before God, secure his favour and eternal life. The same end is now accomplished by faith in Christ. The great design of both is the same; and the same great end is finally gained. This was the subject of discussion between the apostle and the Jews; and this is all that is necessary to understand in the case. Some have supposed that the word *end* refers to the ceremonial law; that Christ fulfilled it, and brought it to an end. Others, that he perfectly fulfilled the moral law. And others, that the law *in the end* leads us to Christ, or that its design is to point us to him. All this is true, but not the truth taught in this passage. That is simple and plain, that by faith in Christ the same end is accomplished in regard to our justification, that

righteousness which is of the law, That the man which doeth those things shall live by them.

6 But the righteousness which is of faith speaketh on this wise, Say [a] not in thine heart, Who

a Deut.30.12-14.

would be by perfect obedience to the moral law. ¶ *For righteousness.* Unto justification with God. ¶ *To every*, &c. see Note, chap. i. 17.

5. *For Moses describeth*, &c. This is found in Lev. xviii. 5, "Ye shall therefore keep my statutes and my judgments, which if a man do he shall live in them." This appeal is made to Moses, both in regard to the righteousness of the law and that of faith, in accordance with the usual manner of Paul to sustain all his positions by the Old Testament, and to show that he was introducing no new doctrine. He was only affirming that which had been long before taught in the writings of the Jews themselves. The word *describeth* is literally *writes* (γράφει), a word often used in this sense. ¶ *The righteousness*, &c. The righteousness which a perfect obedience to the law of God would produce. That consisted in perfectly *doing* all that the law required. ¶ *The man which doeth these things.* The man who shall perform or obey what was declared in the previous statutes. Moses here had reference to all the commandments which God had given, moral and ceremonial. And the doctrine of Moses is that which pertains to all laws, that he who shall render *perfect* and continued compliance with *all* the statutes made known, shall receive the reward which the law promises. This is a first principle of *all* law; for all law holds a man to be innocent, and, of course, entitled to whatever immunities and rewards it has to confer, until he is *proved* to be guilty. In this case, however, Moses did not affirm that *in fact* any one either had yielded or would yield perfect obedience to the law of God. The Scriptures elsewhere abundantly teach that it never *has* been done. ¶ *Doeth.* Obeys, or yields obedience. So also Mat. v. 19, "Shall *do* and teach them." vii. 24, 26, "Whosoever heareth these sayings....and *doeth* them." xxiii. 3; Mark iii. 35; vi. 20; Luke vi. 46, 47, 49. ¶ *Shall live.* Shall obtain felicity. Obedience shall render him happy, and entitled to the rewards of the obedient. Moses doubtless referred here to *all* the results which would follow obedience. The *effect* would be to produce happiness in this life and in the life to come. The *principle* on which happiness would be conferred, would be the same whether in this world or the next. The tendency and result of obedience would be to promote order, health, purity, benevolence; to advance the welfare of man, and the honour of God, and thus *must* confer happiness. The idea of happiness is often in the Scriptures represented by the word *life;* see Note, John v. 24. It is evident moreover that the Jews understood Moses here as referring to more than temporal blessings. The ancient Targum of Onkelos renders the passage in Leviticus thus—"The man who does these things shall live in them to eternal life." So the Arabic version is, "The retribution of him who works these things is that he shall live an eternal life." ¶ *By them* (ἐν αὐτοῖς). In them. *In* their observance he shall find happiness. Not simply as a *result*, or *reward*, but *the very act of obeying* shall carry its own reward. This is the case with all true religion. This declaration of Moses is still true. If perfect obedience were rendered, it would, from the nature of the case, confer happiness and life as long as the obedience was rendered. God would not punish the innocent. But in this world it never has been rendered, except in the case of the Lord Jesus; and the consequence is, that the course of man has been attended with pain, sorrow, and death.

6. *But the righteousness which is of faith.* It is observable here that Paul does not affirm that *Moses* describes any where the righteousness by faith, or the effect of the scheme of justification by faith. His object was different, to give the law, and state its demands and rewards. Yet though he had not *formally* described the plan of

shall ascend into heaven? (that is, to bring Christ down *from above:*)

7 Or, who shall descend into the deep? (that is, to bring up Christ again from the dead.)

justification by faith, yet he had used language which would *fitly express* that plan. The scheme of justification by faith is here *personified*, as if it were living and describing its own effects and nature. One describing it would say, Or the plan itself speaks in this manner. The words here quoted are taken from Deut. xxx. 11—14. The original meaning of the passage is this: Moses, near the end of his life, having given his commandments to the Israelites exhorts them to obedience. To do this, he assures them that his commands are reasonable, plain, intelligible, and accessible. They did not require deep research, long journeys, or painful toil. There was no need of crossing seas, and going to other lands, of looking into the profound mysteries of the high heavens, or the deep abyss; but they were near them, had been plainly set before them, and were easily understood. To see the excellency of this characteristic of the divine law, it may be observed, that among the ancients, it was not uncommon for legislators and philosophers to travel to distant countries in pursuit of knowledge. They left their country, encountered dangers on the sea and land, to go to distant regions that had the reputation of wisdom. Egypt was peculiarly a land of such celebrity; and in subsequent times Pythagoras, and the principal philosophers of Greece, travelled into that country to converse with their priests, and to bear the fruits of their wisdom to benefit their native land. And it is not improbable that this had been done to some extent even in or before the time of Moses. Moses says that *his* precepts were to be obtained by no such painful and dangerous journeys. They were near them, plain, and intelligible. This is the general meaning of this passage Moses dwells on the thought, and places it in a variety of forms by the questions, "who shall go up to heaven for us," &c.; and Paul regards this as *appropriately* describing the language of Christian faith; but without affirming that Moses himself had any reference in the passage to the faith of the gospel. ¶ *On this wise.* In this manner. ¶ *Say not in thine heart.* The expression *to say in the heart* is the same as *to think*. Do not *think*, or suppose, that the doctrine is so difficult to be understood, that one must ascend to heaven in order to understand it. ¶ *Who shall ascend into heaven?* This expression was used among the Jews to denote any difficult undertaking. To say that it was high as heaven, or that it was necessary to ascend to heaven to understand it, was to express the highest difficulty. Thus Job xi. 7, "Canst thou by searching find out God? It is high as heaven, what canst thou do?" &c. Moses says it was not so with his doctrine. It was not impossible to be understood, but was plain and intelligible. ¶ *That is, to bring Christ,* &c. Paul does not here affirm that it was the original design of *Moses* to affirm this of Christ. His words related to his own doctrine. Paul makes this use of the words because, (1.) They appropriately *expressed* the language of faith. (2.) If this might be affirmed of the doctrines of Moses, much more might it of the Christian religion. Religion had no such difficult work to do as to ascend to heaven to bring down a Messiah. That work was already accomplished when God gave his Son to become a man, and to die. To save man it was indeed indispensable that Christ should have come down from heaven. But the language of faith was that this *had* already been done. Probably the word *Christ* here includes all the *benefits* mentioned in ver. 4 as resulting from the work of Christ.

7. *Or who shall descend into the deep?* These words are also a part of the address of Moses, Deut. xxx. 13. But it is not literally quoted. The Hebrew is, "Neither is it beyond the sea, that thou shouldst say, Who shall go over the sea for us," &c. The *words* of the quotation are changed, but not the sense; and it is to be

8 But what saith it? The word is nigh thee, *even* in thy mouth, and in thy heart: that is, the word of faith, which we preach;

remembered that Paul is not professing to quote the *words* of Moses, but to *express the language of faith;* and this he does mainly by words which Moses had used, which also expressed *his* meaning. The words as used by Moses refer to that which is *remote,* and therefore difficult to be obtained. To cross the sea in the early times of navigation involved the highest difficulty, danger, and toil. The *sea* which was in view was doubtless the Mediterranean, but the crossing of that was an enterprise of the greatest difficulty, and the regions *beyond* that were regarded as being at a vast distance. Hence it is spoken of as being the *widest* object with which they were acquainted, and the fairest illustration of infinity, Job xi. 9. In the same sense Paul uses the word deep, *ἄβυσσον*—*the abyss.* This word is applied to any thing the depth or bottom of which is not known. It is applied to the ocean (in the Septuagint), Job xli. 31, "He maketh the deep to boil as a pot." Isa. xliv. 27, "That saith to the deep, Be dry," &c. Gen. vii. 11; viii. 2; to a broad place (Job xxxvi. 16); and to the *abyss* before the world was formed, Gen. i. 2. In the New Testament it is not applied to *the ocean,* unless in the passage Luke viii. 31 (see Note on that place), but to the abode of departed spirits; and particularly to the dark, deep, and bottomless pit, where the wicked are to dwell for ever. Rev. ix. 1, 2, "And to him was given the key of the bottomless pit. And he opened the bottomless pit;" Greek, *The pit of the abyss.* Rev. xi. 7; xvii. 8; xx. 1, 3. In these places the word means the deep, awful regions of the nether world. The word stands opposed to heaven; as deep as that is high; as dark as that is light; while the one is as vast as the other. In the place before us it is opposed to heaven; and to descend there to bring up one, is supposed to be as impossible as to ascend to heaven to bring one down. Paul does not affirm that Christ descended to those regions; but he says that there is no such difficulty in religion *as if one were required* to descend into those profound regions to call back a departed spirit. That work was *in fact* done, when Jesus was recalled from the dead, and now the work of salvation is easy. The word *abyss* here, therefore, answers to *hades,* or the dark regions of departed spirits. ¶ *That is, to bring up Christ,* &c. Justification by faith had no such difficult and impossible work to perform as would be an attempt for man to raise the dead. That would be impossible; but the work of religion is easy. *Christ, the ground of hope, is not by* OUR EFFORTS *to be brought down from heaven to save us, for that is done; nor* BY OUR EFFORTS *to be raised from the dead, for that is done; and what remains for us, that is* TO BELIEVE, *is easy, and is near us.* This is the meaning of the whole passage.

8. *But what saith it?* That is, what is the language of the doctrine of justification by faith? Or what is *to be done* according to that doctrine? ¶ *The word is nigh thee.* This is still a use of the language of Moses. Deut. xxx. 14. The meaning is, the doctrine is not difficult to be understood and embraced. What is *nigh us* may be easily obtained. What is remote, with difficulty. The doctrine of Moses and of the gospel was *nigh;* that is, it was easily obtained, embraced, and understood. ¶ *In thy mouth.* This is taken from the Septuagint. Deut. xxx. 14. The meaning is, that the doctrine was already so familiar, and so well understood, that it was actually in their mouth, that is, their language, their common conversation. Moses had so often inculcated it, that it was understood and talked about by the people, so that there was no need to search in distant climes to obtain it. The same was true of the gospel. The facts were so well known by the preaching of the apostles, that they might be said to be *in every man's mouth.* ¶ *In thy heart.* The word *heart* is very variously used in the sacred Scriptures. As used by Moses

9 That if *a* thou shalt confess
with thy mouth the Lord Jesus,
and shalt believe in thine heart *b*
that God hath raised him from
the dead, thou shalt be saved.
10 For with the heart man

a 1 John 4.2. *b* Acts 8.37.

in this place, it evidently means that his doctrines were in their *mind*, or were a subject of meditation and reflection. They already possessed them, and talked and thought about them: so that there was no need of going to distant places to learn them. The same was true of the doctrine requiring faith in Christ. It was already among them by the preaching of the apostles, and was a subject of conversation and of thought. ¶ *That is.* This is the use which the apostle makes of it; not that Moses referred to the gospel. His *language* conveys the main idea which Paul wished to do, that the doctrine was plain and intelligible. ¶ *The word of faith.* The doctrine which requires faith, *i.e.* the gospel; comp. 1 Tim. iv. 6. The gospel is called the *word* of faith, the word of God, as being that which was *spoken*, or communicated by God to man, ver. 17; Heb. vi. 5; xi. 3. ¶ *Which we preach.* Which is proclaimed by the apostles, and made known to Jews and Gentiles. As this was now made known to all, as the apostles preached it every where, it could be said to be nigh them; there was no need of searching other lands for it, or regarding it as a hidden mystery, for it was plain and manifest to all. Its simplicity and plainness he proceeds immediately to state.

9. *That if thou shalt confess.* The word here rendered *confess* (ὁμολογέω) is often rendered *profess;* Mat. vii. 23, "Then will I profess to them, I never knew you;" Titus i. 16; iii. 14; Rom. i. 22; 1 Tim. ii. 10; vi. 12, 13, 21; Heb. iii. 1, &c. It properly means *to speak that which agrees with something which others speak or maintain.* Thus confession or profession expresses our *agreement or concord with what* GOD *holds to be true, and what he declares to be true.* It denotes a public declaration or assent to that, here expressed by the words "with thy mouth." A profession of religion then denotes a public declaration of our agreement with what God has declared, and extends to *all* his declarations about our lost estate, our sin, and need of a Saviour; to his doctrines about his own nature, holiness, and law; about the Saviour and the Holy Spirit; about the necessity of a change of heart and holiness of life; and about the grave and the judgment; about heaven and hell. As the doctrine respecting a Redeemer is the main and leading doctrine, it is put here by way of eminence, as *in fact* involving all others; and publicly to express our assent to this, is to declare our agreement with God on all kindred truths. ¶ *With thy mouth.* To profess a thing *with the mouth* is to speak of it; to declare it; to do it openly and publicly. ¶ *The Lord Jesus.* Shalt openly acknowledge attachment to Jesus Christ. The meaning of it may be expressed by regarding the phrase "the Lord" as the *predicate;* or the thing to be confessed is, that *he is Lord;* comp. Acts ii. 36; Phil. ii. 11, "And that every tongue should confess that Jesus Christ is Lord." Here it means to acknowledge him as Lord, *i. e.* as having a right to rule over the soul. ¶ *Shalt believe in thy heart.* Shalt *sincerely* and *truly* believe this, so that the external profession shall correspond with the real, internal feelings. Where this is *not* the case, it would be hypocrisy; where this *is* the case, there would be the highest sincerity, and this religion requires. ¶ *That God hath raised him.* This fact, or article of Christian belief, is mentioned here because of its great importance, and its bearing on the Christian system. If this be true, then *all* is true. Then it is true that he came forth from God; that he died for sin; and that God approved and accepted his work. Then it is true that he ascended to heaven, and is exalted to dominion over the universe, and that he will return to judge the quick and the dead. For all this was

believeth unto righteousness; and with the mouth confession is made unto salvation.

11 For the Scripture saith, *a* Whosoever believeth on him shall not be ashamed.

a Isa.28. 6; 49.23.

professed and taught; and all this was regarded as depending on the truth of his having been raised from the dead; see Phil. ii. 8—11; Eph. i. 21; Acts ii. 24, 32, 33; xvii. 31; 2 Cor. iv. 14; 1 Cor. xv. 13—20. To profess this doctrine was, therefore, virtually to profess *all* the truths of the Christian religion. No man could believe this who did not also believe *all* the truths dependent on it. Hence the apostles regarded this doctrine as so important, and made it so prominent in their preaching; See Note on Acts i. 3. ¶ *Thou shalt be saved:* From sin and hell. This is the doctrine of the gospel throughout; and all this shows that salvation by the gospel was easy.

10. *For with the heart.* Not with the understanding merely, but with such a faith as shall be sincere, and shall influence the life. There *can be* no other genuine faith than that which influences the *whole mind.* ¶ *Believeth unto righteousness.* Believes so that justification is obtained.* (*Stuart.*) In God's plan of justifying men, this is the way by which we may be declared just or righteous in his sight. The moment a sinner believes, therefore, he is justified; his sins are pardoned; and he is introduced into the favour of God. No man can be justified without this; for this is God's plan, and he will not depart from it. ¶ *With the mouth confession is made,* &c. That is, confession or profession is so made as to obtain salvation. He who in all appropriate ways professes his attachment to Christ shall be saved. This profession is to be made in all the proper ways of religious duty; by an avowal of our sentiments; by declaring on all proper occasions our belief of the truth; and by an unwavering adherence to them in all persecutions, oppositions, and trials. He who *declares* his belief makes a profession. He who associates with Christian people does it. He who acts with them in the prayer meeting, in the sanctuary, and in deeds of benevolence, does it. He who is baptized, and commemorates the death of the Lord Jesus, does it. And he who leads an humble, prayerful, spiritual life, does it. He shows his regard to the precepts and example of Christ Jesus; his regard for them more than for the pride, and pomp, and allurements of the world. All these are included in a profession of religion. In whatever way we can manifest attachment to it, it must be done. The reason why this is made so important is, that there *can be* no true attachment to Christ which will not manifest itself in the life. A city that is set on a hill cannot be hid. It is impossible that there should be true belief in the heart of man, unless it should show itself in the life and conversation. This is the only test of its existence and its power; and hence it is made so important in the business of religion. And we may here learn, (1.) That *a profession* of religion is, by Paul, made *as really* indispensable to salvation *as believing.* According to him it is connected with salvation as really as faith is with justification; and this accords with all the declarations of the Lord Jesus; Mat. x. 32; xxv. 34—46; Luke xii. 8. (2.) There can be no religion where there is not a willingness to confess the Lord Jesus. There is no true repentance where we are not willing to *confess* our faults. There is no true attachment to a father or mother or friend, unless we are willing on all proper occasions to avow it. And so there can be no true religion where there is too much pride, or vanity, or love of the world, or fear of shame to confess it. (3.) Those who never profess any religion have none; and they are not safe. To deny God the Saviour before men is not safe. They who do

* See supplementary Notes; chap. i. 17, iii. 21.

12 For [a] there is no difference between the Jew and the Greek: for [b] the same Lord over all is rich unto all that call upon him.

a Acts 15.9; Gal.3.28. *b* 1 Tim.2.5.

not profess religion, profess the opposite. The *real* feelings of the heart will be expressed in the life. And they who profess by their lives that they have no regard for God and Christ, for heaven and glory, must expect to be met in the last day, as those who deny the Lord that bought them, and who bring upon themselves quick destruction; 2 Pet. i. 2.

11. *For the Scripture saith*, &c.; Isa. xxviii. 16. This was the uniform doctrine of the Scripture, that he who holds an opinion on the subject of religion *will not* be ashamed to avow it. This is the nature of religion, and without this there can be none; see this passage explained in Rom. ix. 33.

12. *For there is no difference.* In the previous verse Paul had quoted a passage from Isa. xxviii. 16, which says that *every one* (Greek, πᾶς) that believeth shall not be ashamed; that is, every one of every nation and kindred. This implies that it was not to be confined to the *Jews.* This thought he now *further* illustrates and confirms by expressly declaring that there is no difference between the Jew and the Greek. This doctrine it was one main design of the epistle to establish, and it is fully proved in the course of the argument in chap. i—iv. See particularly chap. iii. 26—30. When the apostle says there is *no difference* between them, he means in regard to the subject under discussion. In many respects there might be a difference; but not in *the way of justification before God.* There *all* had sinned; all had failed of obeying the law; and all must be justified in the same way, by faith in the Lord Jesus Christ. The word *difference* (διαστολὴ) means *distinction, diversity.* It also means *eminence, excellence, advantage.* There is no eminence or *advantage* which the Jew has over the Greek in regard to justification before God. ¶ *The Jew.* That portion of mankind which professed to yield obedience to the law of Moses. ¶ *The Greek.* Literally, those who dwelt in Greece, or those who spoke the Greek language. As the Jews, however, were acquainted chiefly with the Greeks, and knew little of other nations, the name *Greek* among them came to denote all who were not Jews; that is, the same as the Gentiles. The terms "Jew and Greek," therefore, include all mankind. There is no difference among men about the terms of salvation; they are the same to all. This truth is frequently taught. It was a most important doctrine, especially in a scheme of religion that was to be preached to all men. It was very offensive to the Jews, who had always regarded themselves as a peculiarly favoured people. Against this, all their prejudices were roused, as it completely overthrew all their own views of national eminence and pride, and admitted despised Gentiles to the same privileges with the long favoured and chosen people of God. The apostles, therefore, were at great pains fully to establish it; see Acts x. 9; Gal. iii. 28. ¶ *For the same Lord over all*, &c. For there is the same Lord of all; that is, the Jews and Gentiles have one common Lord; comp. Rom. iii. 29, 30. The same God had formed them, and ruled them; and God now opened the same path to life. See this fully presented in Paul's address to the people of Athens, in Acts xvii. 26—30; see also 1 Tim. ii. 5. As there was but *one* God; as all, Jews and Gentiles, were his creatures; as one law was applicable to all; as all had sinned; and as all were exposed to wrath; so it was reasonable that there should be *the same way* of return—through the mere mercy of God. Against this the Jew ought not to object; and in this he and the Greek should rejoice. ¶ *Is rich unto all* (πλουτῶν εἰς πάντας). The word *rich* means to *have abundance*, to have in store much more than is needful for present or personal use. It is commonly applied to wealth. But applied to God, it means that he *abounds* in mercy or

13 For [a] whosoever shall call [b] upon the name of the Lord shall be saved.

14 How then shall they call on him in whom they have not believed? and how shall they

a Joel 2.32. b 1 Cor.1.2.

goodness towards others. Thus Eph. ii. 4, "God, who is *rich in mercy*," &c.; 1 Tim. vi. 17, 18, "Charge them that are rich in this world......that they *be rich in good works.*" James ii. 5, "God hath chosen the poor...*rich in faith;*" *i. e. abounding* in faith and good works, &c. Thus God is said to be *rich* towards all, as he abounds in mercy and goodness towards them in the plan of salvation. ¶ *That call upon him.* This expression means properly *to supplicate, to invoke,* as in prayer. As prayer constitutes no small part of religion; and as it is a *distinguishing characteristic* of those who are true Christians (Acts xi. 11, "Behold he prayeth;") to call on the name of the Lord is put for religion itself, and is descriptive of acts of devotion towards God; 1 Pet. i. 17, "And if ye call on the Father," &c.; Acts ii. 21; ix. 14, "He hath authority...to bind all *that call on thy name;*" Acts vii. 59; xxii. 16; Gen. iv. 26, "Then began men to call on the name of the Lord."

13. *For whosoever shall call,* &c. This sentiment is found substantially in Joel ii. 32, "And it shall come to pass, that whosoever shall call on the name of the Lord shall be delivered." This is expressly applied to the times of the gospel, by Peter, in Acts ii. 21; see Note on that place. To call on *the name* of the Lord is the same as to call on the Lord himself. The word *name* is often used in this manner. "The *name* of the Lord is a strong tower," &c.; Prov. xviii. 10. "The name of the God of Jacob defend thee;" Ps. xx. 1. That is, *God himself* is a strong tower, &c. It is clear from what follows, that the apostle applies this to Jesus Christ; and this is one of the numerous instances in which the writers of the New Testament apply to him expressions which in the Old Testament are applicable to God; see 1 Cor. i. 2. ¶ *Shall be saved.* This is the uniform promise; see Acts ii. 21; xxii. 16, "Arise, and be baptized, and wash away thy sins, *calling on the name of the Lord.*" This is proper and indispensable, because, (1.) We have sinned against God, and it is right that we should confess it. (2.) Because he only can pardon us, and it is fit, that if we obtain pardon, we should ask it of God. (3.) To call upon him is to acknowledge him as our Sovereign, our Father, and our Friend; and it is right that we render him our homage. It is *implied* in this, that we call upon him with right feelings; that is, with a humble sense of our sinfulness and our need of pardon, and with a willingness to receive eternal life as it is offered us in the gospel. And if this be done, this passage teaches us that *all* may be saved who will do it. He will cast none away who come in this manner. The invitation and the assurance extend to all nations and to men of all times.

14. *How then shall they call,* &c. The apostle here adverts to an objection which might be urged to his argument. His doctrine was, that faith in Christ was essential to justification and salvation; and that this was needful for all; and that, without this, man must perish. The objection was, that they could not call on him in whom they had not believed; that they could not believe in him of whom they had not heard; and that this was *arranged by God himself,* so that a large part of the world was destitute of the gospel, and *in fact* did not believe; ver. 16, 17. The objection had *particular* reference to the Jews; and the ground of injustice which a Jew would complain of, would be, that the plan made salvation dependent on *faith,* when a large part of the nation had not heard the gospel, and had had no opportunity to know it. This objection the apostle meets, so far as it was of importance to his argument, in ver. 18—21. The first part of the objection is, that they could "not call on him in whom they had not believed." That is, how could they call on one in

believe in him of whom they have not heard? and how shall they hear without a preacher?

15 And how shall they preach, except they be sent? as it is written, [a] How beautiful are the

a Isa.52.7; Nah.1.15.

whose existence, ability, and willingness to help, they did not believe? The objection is, that in order to our calling on one for help, we must be satisfied that there *is* such a being, and that he is able to aid us. This remark is just, and every man feels it. But the point of the objection is, that *sufficient evidence of the divine mission and claims of Jesus Christ had not been given to authorize the doctrine that eternal salvation depended on belief in him, or that it would be right to suspend the eternal happiness of Jew and Gentile on this.* ¶ *How shall they believe in him,* &c. This position is equally undeniable, that men could not believe in a being of whom they had not heard. And the implied objection was, that men could not be expected to believe in one of whose existence they knew nothing, and, of course, that they could not be blamed for not doing it. It was not right, therefore, to make eternal life depend, both among Jews and Gentiles, on faith in Christ. ¶ *And how shall they hear,* &c. How *can* men hear, unless some one *proclaim* to them, or preach to them that which is to be heard and believed? This is also true. The *objection* thence derived is, that it is not right to condemn men for not believing what has never been proclaimed to them; and, of course, that the doctrine that eternal life is suspended on faith cannot be just and right.

15. *And how shall they preach.* In what way shall there *be preachers,* unless they are commissioned by God? The word "*how*" does not refer to the *manner* of preaching, but to the fact that there would be no preachers *at all* unless they were sent forth. To *preach* means to proclaim in a public manner, as a *crier* does. In the Scriptures it means to *proclaim* the gospel to men. ¶ *Except they be sent.* That is, except they are divinely commissioned, and sent forth by God. This was an admitted doctrine among the Jews, that a proclamation of a divine message must be made by one who was commissioned by God for that purpose; Jer. xxiii. 21; i. 7; xiv. 14, 15; vii. 25. He who sends a message to men can alone designate the proper persons to bear it. The point of the objection, therefore, was this: Men could not believe unless the message was sent to them; yet God had *not* actually sent it to all men: it could not, therefore, be *just* to make eternal life depend on so impracticable a thing as *faith,* since men had not the means of believing. ¶ *As it is written.* In Isa. lii. 7. ¶ *How beautiful,* &c. The reason why this passage is introduced here is, that it confirms what had just been advanced in the objection—the *importance* and *necessity* of there being messengers of salvation. That importance is seen in the high encomium which is passed on them in the sacred Scriptures. They are regarded as objects peculiarly attractive; their necessity is fully recognised; and a distinguished rank is given to them in the oracles of God. *How beautiful.* How attractive, how lovely. This is taken from the Hebrew, with a slight variation. In the Hebrew, the words "upon the mountains" occur, which makes the passage more picturesque, though the sense is retained by Paul. The image in Isaiah is that of a herald seen at first leaping or running on a distant hill, when he first comes in sight, with tidings of joy from a field of battle, or from a distant land. Thus, the appearance of such a man to those who were in captivity, would be an image full of gladness and joy. ¶ *Are the feet.* Many have supposed that the meaning of this expression is this: The *feet* of a herald, naked and dusty from travelling, would be *naturally* objects of disgust. But that which would be naturally disagreeable is thus made pleasant by the joy of the message. But this explanation is far fetched, and wants parallel instances. Besides,

feet of them that preach the gospel of peace, and bring glad tidings of good things!

16 But [a] they have not all obeyed the gospel. For Esaias saith, [b] Lord, who hath believed [1] our [2] report.

17 So then faith *cometh* by

a Acts 28.24; Heb.4.2. b Isa.53.1; John 12.38. 1 *the hearing of us.* 2 or, *preaching.*

it is a violation of the image which the apostle had used. That was a *distant* object—a herald running on the distant hills; and it supposes a picture too remote to observe distinctly the *feet*, whether attractive or not. The meaning of it is clearly this: "how beautiful is the *coming* or the *running* of such a herald." The feet are emblematic of his coming. Their rapid motion would be seen; and their rapidity would be beautiful from the desire to hear the message which he brought. The whole meaning of the passage, then, as applied to ministers of the gospel, is, that their *coming* is an attractive object, regarded with deep interest, and productive of joy—an honoured and a delightful employment. ¶ *That preach,* &c. Literally, "that evangelize peace." That proclaim *the good news* of peace; or bring the glad message of peace. ¶ *And bring glad tidings,* &c. Literally, "and evangelize good things;" or that bring the glad message of good things. *Peace* here is put for good of any kind; and as the apostle uses it, for the news of reconciliation with God by the gospel. *Peace,* at the end of the conflicts, distresses, and woes of war, is an image of all blessings. Thus it is put to denote the blessings when a sinner ceases to be the enemy of God, obtains pardon, and is admitted to the joys of those who are his children and friends. The coming of those messengers who proclaim it is joyful to the world. It fills the bosom of the anxious sinner with peace; and they and their message will be regarded with deep interest, as sent by God, and producing joy in an agitated bosom, and peace to the world. This is an illustration of the proper feeling with which we should regard the ministers of religion. This passage in Isaiah is referred by the Jews themselves to the times of the gospel. (*Rosenmüller.*)

16. *But they have not all obeyed the gospel.* It is not easy to see the connection of this; and it has been made a question whether this is to be regarded as a *continuation* of the objection of the Jew, or as a part of the answer of the apostle. After all the attention which I have been able to give it, I am inclined to regard it as an *admission* of the apostle; as if he had said, "It must be *admitted* that all have not obeyed the gospel. So far as the objection of the Jew arises from *that fact,* and so far as that fact can bear on the case, it is to be conceded that *all* have not yielded obedience to the gospel. For this was clearly declared even by the prophet;" comp. Acts xxviii. 24; Heb. iv. 2. ¶ *For Esaias saith;* Isa. liii. 1. ¶ *Who hath believed our report?* That is, Isaiah complains that his declarations respecting the Messiah had been rejected by his countrymen. The form of expression, "Who hath believed?" is a mode of saying *emphatically* that few or none had done it. The great mass of his countrymen had rejected it. This was an example to the purpose of the apostle. In the time of Isaiah this fact existed; and it was not a new thing that it existed in the time of the gospel. *Our report.* Our message; or that which is delivered to be heard and believed. It originally means the doctrine which Isaiah delivered about the Messiah; and implies that the same thing would occur when the Messiah should actually come. Hence in the fifty-third chapter he proceeds to give the reasons why the report would not be credited, and why the Messiah would be rejected. It would be because he was a root out of a dry ground; because he was a man of sorrows, &c. And this actually took place. Because he did not come with splendour and pomp, as a temporal prince, he was rejected, and put to death. On substantially the same grounds he is even

hearing, and hearing by the word of God.

18 But I say, Have they not heard? Yes, verily, their [d] sound

d Ps.19.4; Mat.28.19; Col.1.6,23.

---

yet rejected by thousands. The force of this verse, perhaps, may be best seen by including it in a parenthesis, "How beautiful are the feet," &c. how important is the gospel ministry —(*although* it must be admitted, that all have not obeyed, for this was predicted also by Isaiah, &c.)

17. *So then faith cometh*, &c. This I take to be clearly the language of the objector. As if he had said, by the very quotation which you have made from Isaiah, it appears that *a report* was necessary. He did not condemn men for not believing what they had not *heard;* but he complains of those who did not believe a message actually delivered to them. Even by this passage, therefore, it seems that a message was necessary, that faith comes by *hearing*, and hearing by the divine message. It could not be right, therefore, to condemn those who had not *obeyed* the gospel because they had not *heard* it; and hence not right to make salvation dependent on a condition which was, by the arrangement of God, put beyond their power. The very quotation from Isaiah, therefore, goes to confirm the objection in the 14th and 15th verses. ¶ *By hearing.* Our translation has varied the expression here, which is the same in two places in the Greek: "Isaiah said, Who hath believed our report (τῇ ἀκοῇ)? So then, you must admit that faith comes *by that report* (ἐξ ἀκοῆς), and therefore this *report* or message is necessary." When it is said that faith cometh *by hearing*, it is not meant that all who hear actually believe, for that is not true; but that faith does not exist unless there is a message, or report, to be heard or believed. It cannot come otherwise than *by* such a message; in other words, unless there is something *made known to be believed.* And this shows us at once the importance of the message, and the fact that men are converted by the instrumentality of truth, and of truth only. ¶ *And hearing.* And the *report*, or the message (ἡ ἀκοὴ), is by the word of God; that is, the message is sent by the *command* of God. It is *his* word, sent by his direction, and therefore if withheld *by* him, those who did not believe could not be blamed. The argument of the objector is, that God could not justly condemn men for not believing the gospel.

18. *But I say.* But to this objection, I, the apostle, reply. The objection had been carried through the previous verses. The apostle comes now to reply to it. In doing this, he does not deny the *principle* contained in it, that the gospel should be *preached* in order that men might be justly condemned for not believing it; not that the messengers must be sent by God, not that faith comes by hearing. All this he fully admits. But he proceeds to show, by an ample quotation from the Old Testament, that this *had been actually furnished* to the Jews and to the Gentiles, and that they *were actually* in possession of the message, and could not plead that they had never heard it. This is the substance of his answer. ¶ *Have they not heard?* A question is often, as it is here, an emphatic way of affirming a thing. The apostle means to *affirm* strongly that they *had* heard. The word "they," in this place, I take to refer to the *Gentiles.* What was the fact in regard to *Israel*, or the Jew, he shows in the next verses. One main design was to show that the *same* scheme of salvation extended to both Jews and Gentiles. The objection was, that it had not been made known to either, and that therefore it could not be maintained to be just to condemn those who rejected it. To this the apostle replies that *then* it was extensively known to *both;* and *if so*, then the objection in ver. 14, 15, was not well founded, for *in fact* the thing existed which the objector maintained to be necessary, to wit, that they *had* heard, and that preachers *had* been sent to them. ¶ *Yes, verily.* In the original, a single word, μενοῦνγε, compounded of μεν and ουν and γε. An

went into all the earth, and their words unto the ends of the world.

19 But I say, Did not Israel know? First Moses saith, [a] I

a Deut.32.21.

---

intense expression, denoting strong affirmation. ¶ *Their sound went,* &c. These *words* are taken in substance from Psalm xix. 4. The psalmist employs them to show that the *works* of God, the heavens and the earth, proclaim his existence every where. By using them here, the apostle does not affirm that David had reference to the gospel in them, but *he uses them to express his own meaning;* he makes an affirmation about the gospel in language used by David on another occasion, but without intimating or implying that David had such a reference. In this way we often quote the language of others as expressing in a happy way our own thoughts, but without supposing that the author had any such reference. The meaning here is, that that may be affirmed *in fact* of the gospel which David affirmed of the works of God, that their sound had gone into all the earth. ¶ *Their sound.* Literally the sound or tone which is made by a stringed instrument (φθόγγος). Also a *voice,* a report. It means here they *have spoken,* or declared truth. As applied to the heavens, it would mean that they speak, or proclaim, the wisdom or power of God. As used by Paul, it means that the message of the gospel had been *spoken,* or proclaimed, far and wide. The Hebrew, is "their *line,*" &c. The Septuagint translation is the same as that of the apostle —their voice (ὁ φθόγγος αὐτῶν). The Hebrew word may denote the *string* of an instrument, of a harp, &c. and then the *tone* or sound produced by it; and thus was understood by the Septuagint. The apostle, however, does not affirm that this was the *meaning* of the Hebrew; but he conveyed *his* doctrine in language which aptly expressed it. ¶ *Into all the earth.* In the psalm, this is to be taken in its utmost signification. The works of God *literally* proclaim his wisdom to *all* lands and to all people. As applied to the gospel, it means that it was spread far and wide, that it had been extensively preached in all lands. ¶ *Their words.* In the psalm, the heavens are represented as *speaking,* and teaching men the knowledge of the true God. But the meaning of the apostle is, that the message of the gospel *had* sounded forth; and he referred doubtless to the labours of the apostles in proclaiming it to the heathen nations. This epistle was written about the year 57. During the time which had elapsed after the ascension of Christ, the gospel had been preached extensively in all the known nations; so that it might be said that it was proclaimed in those regions designated in the Scripture as the uttermost parts of the earth. Thus it had been proclaimed in Jerusalem, Syria, Asia Minor, Greece, Rome, Arabia, and in the islands of the Mediterranean. Paul, reasoning before Agrippa, says, that *he* could not be ignorant of those things, for they had not been done in a corner; Acts xxvi. 26. In Col. i. 23, Paul says that the gospel had been preached to every creature which is under heaven; see Col. i. 6. Thus the great facts and doctrines of the gospel had *in fact* been made known; and the objection of the Jew was met. It would be *sufficiently* met by the declaration of the psalmist that the true God was made known by his works, and that therefore they were without excuse (comp. Rom. i. 20); but *in fact* the *gospel* had been preached, and its great doctrine and duties had been proclaimed to all nations far and near.

19. *But I say,* &c. Still further to meet the objection, he shows that the doctrine which he was maintaining was *actually* taught in the Old Testament. ¶ *Did not Israel know?* Did not the *Jews* understand. Is it not recorded in their books, &c. that they had full opportunity to be acquainted with this truth? This *question* is an emphatic way of affirming that they *did* know. But Paul does not here state *what* it was that they knew.

will provoke you to jealousy by *them that are* no people, *and* by a foolish [a] nation I will anger you.

a Tit.3.3.

That is to be gathered from what he proceeds to say. From that it appears that he referred to the fact that the gospel was to be preached to the *Gentiles,* and that the *Jews* were to be cast off. This doctrine followed from what he had already maintained in ver. 12, 13, that there was no difference in regard to the terms of salvation, and that the Jew had no particular privileges. If so, then the barrier was broken down; and if the Jews did not believe in Jesus Christ, they must be rejected. Against this was the objection in ver. 14, 15, that they could not believe; that they had not heard; and that a preacher had not been sent to them. If, now, the apostle could show that it was an *ancient* doctrine of the Jewish prophets that the Gentiles *should* believe, and that the Jews *would not* believe, the whole force of the objection would vanish. Accordingly he proceeds to show that this doctrine was distinctly taught in the Old Testament. ¶ *First.* First in order; as we say, *in the first place.* ¶ *I will provoke you.* These words are taken from Deut. xxxii. 21. In that place the declaration refers to the idolatrous and wicked conduct of the Jews. God says that they had *provoked* him, or excited his indignation, by worshipping that which was not God, that is, by *idols;* and *he,* in turn, would excite *their* envy and indignation by showing favours to those who were not regarded as a people; that is, to the Gentiles. *They* had shown *favour,* or affection, for that which was not God, and by so doing had provoked him to anger; and *he* also would show favour to those whom *they* regarded as no people, and would thus excite *their* anger. Thus he would illustrate the great principle of his government in 2 Sam. xxii. 26, 27, "With the merciful thou wilt show thyself merciful; with the pure, thou wilt show thyself pure; and with the froward thou wilt show thyself unsavory," *i. e.* froward. Ps. xviii. 26. In this passage the great doctrine which Paul was defending is abundantly established—that the Gentiles were to be brought into the favour of God; and the *cause* also is suggested to be the obstinacy and rebellion of the Jews. It is not clear that Moses had particularly in view the times of the gospel; but he affirms *a great principle* which is applicable to those times—that if the Jews should be rebellious, and prove themselves unworthy of his favour, that favour would be withdrawn, and conferred on other nations. The effect of this would be, of course, to excite their indignation. This *principle* the apostle applies to his own times; and affirms that it ought to have been understood by the Jews themselves. ¶ *That are no people.* That is, those whom you regard as unworthy the name of a people. Those who have no government, laws, or regular organization; who wander in tribes and clans, and who are under no settled form of society. This was the case with most barbarians; and the Jews, evidently regarded all ancient nations in this light, *as unworthy the name of a people.* ¶ *A foolish nation.* The word *fool* means one void of understanding. But it also means one who is *wicked,* or *idolatrous;* one who contemns God. Ps. xiv. 1, "The *fool* hath said in his heart, there is no God." Prov. i. 7, "Fools despise wisdom and instruction." Here it means a nation who had *no understanding* of the true God (ἀσυνέτῳ). ¶ *I will anger.* My bestowing favours on them will excite your anger. We may remark here, (1.) That God is a sovereign, and has a right to bestow his favours on whom he pleases. (2.) That when men abuse his mercies, become proud, or cold, or dead in his service, he often takes away their privileges, and bestows them on others. (3.) That the *effect* of his sovereignty is to excite men to anger. Proud and wicked men are always enraged that he bestows his favours on others; and the effect of his sovereign dealings is,

20 But Esaias is very bold, and saith, [a] I was found of them that sought me not; I was made manifest unto them that asked not after me.

21 But to Israel he saith, All day long I have stretched forth my hands unto a disobedient and gainsaying people.

a Isa.65.1,2.

to provoke to anger the very men who by their sins have rejected his mercy. Hence there is no doctrine that proud man hates so cordially as he does the doctrine of divine sovereignty; and none that will so much *test* the character of the wicked.

20. *But Esaias;* Isaiah lxv. 1, 2. ¶ *Is very bold.* Expresses the doctrine openly, boldly, without any reserve. The word ἀποτολμάω means *to dare,* to be venturesome, to be bold. It means here that however unpopular the doctrine might be, or however dangerous it was to avow that the Jews were extremely wicked, and that God for their wickedness would cast them off, yet that Isaiah had long since done it. This was the point which Paul was establishing; and against this, the objection was urged, and all the Jewish prejudices excited. This is the reason why he so much insists on it, and is so anxious to defend every part by the writings of acknowledged authority among the Jews—the Old Testament. The quotation is made from the Septuagint, with only a slight change in the *order* of the phrases. The meaning is, that God was found, or the true knowledge of him was obtained, by those who had not sought after him; that is, by the Gentiles, who had worshipped idols, and who had not sought for the true God. This does not mean that *we* are to expect to find God if we do not seek for him; or that *in fact* any become Christians who do not *seek* for it, and make an effort. The contrary is abundantly taught in the Scriptures; Heb. xi. 6; 1 Chron. xxviii. 8, 9; Mat. vi. 33; vii. 7; Luke xi. 9. But it means that the *Gentiles,* whose characteristic was *not* that they sought God, would have the gospel sent to them, and would embrace it. The phrase, "I *was* found," in the *past* tense here, is in the *present* in the Hebrew, intimating that the time would come when God would say this of himself; that is, that the time would come when the Gentiles would be brought to the knowledge of the true God. This doctrine was one which Isaiah had constantly in his eye, and which he did not fear to bring openly before the Jews.

21. *But to Israel he saith.* The preceding quotation established the doctrine that the Gentiles were to be called. But there was still an important part of his argument remaining—that the Jews were to be rejected. This he proceeds to establish; and he here, in the language of Isaiah (lxv. 2), says that while the *Gentiles* would be obedient, the character of the Jews was, that they were a disobedient and rebellious people. ¶ *All day long.* Continually, without intermission; implying that their acts of rebellion were not momentary; but that this was the *established* character of the people. ¶ *I have stretched forth my hands.* This denotes an attitude of entreaty; a willingness and earnest desire to receive them to favour; to invite and entreat; Prov. i. 24. ¶ *A disobedient.* In the Hebrew, *rebellious, contumacious.* The Greek answers substantially to that; *disbelieving,* not confiding or obeying. ¶ *Gainsaying. Speaking against;* resisting, opposing. This is not in the Hebrew, but the substance of it was implied. The prophet Isaiah proceeds to *specify* in what this rebellion consisted, and to show that this was their character; Isa. lxv. 2—7. The argument of the apostle is this; viz. the ancient character of the people was that of wickedness; God is represented as stretching out his hands in vain; they rejected him, and he was sought and found by others. It was *implied,* therefore, that the rebellious Jews would be rejected; and, of course, the apostle was advancing and defending no doctrine which was not found in the writ-

CHAPTER XI.

I SAY then, Hath *a* God cast away his people? God forbid. For I also am an Israelite, of the seed of Abraham, *of* the tribe of Benjamin.

a 1 Sam.12,22; Ps.77,7,8; 89.31-37.

ings of the Jews themselves. And thus, by a different course of reasoning, he came to the same conclusion which he had arrived at in the first four chapters of the epistle, that the Gentiles and Jews were on the same level in regard to justification before God.

In the closing part of this chapter, the great doctrine is brought forth and defended that the way of salvation is open for all the world. This, in the time of Paul, was regarded as a novel doctrine. Hence he is at so much pains to illustrate and defend it. And hence, with so much zeal and self-denial, the apostles of the Lord Jesus went and proclaimed it to the nations. This doctrine is not the less important now. And from this discussion we may learn the following truths: (1.) The heathen world is *in danger* without the gospel. They are sinful, polluted, wretched. The testimony of all who visit pagan nations accords most strikingly with that of the apostles in their times. Nor is there *any* evidence that the great mass of heathen population has changed for the better. (2.) The provisions of the gospel are ample for them—for all. Its power has been tried on many nations; and its mild and happy influence is seen in meliorated laws, customs, habits; in purer institutions; in intelligence and order; and in the various blessings conferred by a pure religion. The same gospel is fitted to produce on the wildest and most wretched population, the same comforts which are now experienced in the happiest part of our own land. (3.) The command of Jesus Christ remains still the same, *to preach the gospel to every creature.* That command has never been repealed or changed. The apostles met the injunction, and performed what they could. It remains for the church to act as they did, to feel as they did, and put forth their efforts as they did, in obeying one of the most plain and positive laws of Jesus Christ. (4.) If the gospel is to be proclaimed every where, men must be sent forth into the vast field. Every nation must have an opportunity to say, "How beautiful are the feet of him that preaches the gospel of peace." Young men, strong and vigorous in the Christian course, must give themselves to this work, and devote their lives in an enterprise which the apostles regarded as honourable to them; and which infinite Wisdom did not regard as unworthy the toils, and tears, and self-denials of the Son of God. (5.) The church, in training young men for the ministry, in fitting her sons for these toils, is performing a noble and glorious work; a work which contemplates the triumph of the gospel among all nations. Happy will it be when the church shall feel the full pressure of this great truth, that the gospel MAY BE preached to every son and daughter of Adam; and when every man who enters the ministry shall count it, not self-denial, but a glorious privilege to be permitted to tell dying pagan men that a Saviour bled for ALL sinners. And happy that day when it can be said with literal truth that their sound has gone out into all the earth; and that as far as the sun in his daily course sheds his beams, so far the Sun of righteousness sheds also his pure and lovely rays into the abodes of men. And we may learn, also, from this, (6.) That God will withdraw his favours from those nations that are disobedient and rebellious. Thus he rejected the ancient Jews; and thus also he will forsake all who abuse his mercies; who become proud, luxurious, effeminate and wicked. In this respect it becomes the people of this favoured land to remember the God of their fathers; and not to forget, too, that national sin provokes God to withdraw, and that a nation that forgets God must be punished.

CHAPTER XI.

1. *I say then.* This expression is to be regarded as conveying the sense

of an objection. Paul, in the previous chapters, had declared the doctrine that all the Jews were to be rejected. To this a Jew might naturally reply, Is it to be believed, that God would cast off his people whom he had once chosen; to whom pertained the adoption, and the promises, and the covenant, and the numerous blessings conferred on a favourite people? It was natural for a Jew to make such objections. And it was important for the apostle to show that *his* doctrine was consistent with all the promises which God had made to his people. The objection, as will be seen by the answer which Paul makes, is formed on the supposition that God had rejected *all his people,* or *cast them off entirely.* This objection he answers by showing, (1.) That God had saved *him,* a Jew, and therefore that he could not mean that God had cast off *all* Jews (ver. 1); (2.) That now, as in former times of great declension, God *had* reserved a remnant (ver. 2—5); (3.) That it accorded with the Scriptures that *a part* should be hardened (ver. 6—10); (4.) That the design of the rejection was not *final,* but was to admit the Gentiles to the privileges of Christianity (ver. 11—24); (5.) That the Jews should yet return to God, and be reinstated in his favour: so that it could not be objected that God had *finally* and *totally* cast off his people, or that he had violated his promises. At the same time, however, the doctrine which Paul had maintained was true, that God had taken away their *exclusive* and *peculiar* privileges, and had rejected a large part of the nation. ¶ *Cast away.* Rejected, or put off. Has God so renounced them that they *cannot* be any longer his people? ¶ *His people.* Those who have been long in the covenant relation to him; that is, the Jews. ¶ *God forbid.* Literally, *it may not* or *cannot be.* This is an expression strongly denying that this could take place; and means that Paul did not intend to advance such a doctrine; Luke xx. 16; Rom. iii. 4, 6, 31; vi. 2, 15; vii. 7, 13. ¶ *For I am also an Israelite.* To show them that he did not mean to affirm that *all Jews* must of necessity be cast off, he adduces his own case. He was a Jew; and yet he looked for the favour of God, and for eternal life. That favour he hoped now to obtain by being a Christian; and if *he* might obtain it, others might also. "If I should say that *all* Jews must be excluded from the favour of God, then *I* also must be without hope of salvation, for I am a Jew." ¶ *Of the seed of Abraham.* Descended from Abraham. The apostle mentions this to show that he was a Jew in every respect; that he had a title to all the privileges of a Jew, and must be exposed to all their liabilities and dangers. If the seed of Abraham must of necessity be cut off, he must be himself rejected. The Jews valued themselves much on having been descended from so illustrious an ancestor as Abraham (Mat. iii. 9); and Paul shows them that *he* was entitled to all the privileges of such a descent; comp. Phil. iii. 4, 5. ¶ *Of the tribe of Benjamin.* This tribe was one that was originally located near Jerusalem. The temple was built on the line that divided the tribes of Judah and Benjamin. It is not improbable that it was regarded as a peculiar honour to have belonged to one of those tribes. Paul mentions it here in accordance with their custom; for they regarded it as of great importance to preserve their genealogy, and to be able to state not only that they were *Jews,* but to designate the tribe and family to which they belonged.

2. *God hath not cast away.* This is an explicit denial of the objection. ¶ *Which he foreknew.* The word *foreknew* is expressive not merely of *foreseeing* a thing, but implies in this place a previous purpose or plan; see Note, chap. viii. 29. The meaning of the passage is simply, God has not cast off those whom he had before purposed or designed to be his people. It is the declaration of a great principle of divine government that God is not changeable; and that he would not reject those whom he had purposed should be his people. Though the mass of the nation, therefore, should be cast off, yet it would not

2 God hath not cast away his
people which he foreknew.[a] Wot
ye not what the Scripture saith [1]
of Elias? how he maketh intercession to God against Israel, [b]
saying,
3 Lord, they have killed thy
prophets, and digged down thine

[a] chap.8.29. [1] or, *in*. [b] 1 Kings 19.10-18.

follow that God had violated any promise or compact; or that he had rejected *any* whom he had foreknown as his true people. God makes no covenant of salvation with those who are in their sins; and if the unbelieving and the wicked, however many external privileges they may have enjoyed, are rejected, it does not follow that he has been unfaithful to *one* whom he had foreknown or designated as an heir of salvation. It follows from this, also, that it is one principle of the divine government that God *will not* reject those who are foreknown or designated as his friends. It is a part of the plan, therefore, that those who are truly renewed shall persevere, and obtain eternal life. ¶ *Wot ye not. Know* ye not. ¶ *What the Scripture saith?* The passage here quoted is found in 1 Kings xix. 10—18. ¶ *Of Elias.* Of *Elijah.* Greek, "*In* Elijah" (εν Ηλιᾳ). This does not mean that it was said *about* Elijah, or *concerning* him; but the reference is to the usual manner of quoting the Scriptures among the Jews. The division into chapters and verses was to them unknown. (See the Introduction to the Notes on Matthew.) Hence the Old Testament was divided into portions designated by *subjects.* Thus Luke xx. 37; Mark xii. 26, "At the bush," means the passage which contains the account of the burning bush; (see Notes on those places.) Here it means, in that passage or portion of Scripture which gives an account of Elijah. ¶ *He maketh intercession to God against Israel.* The word translated *maketh intercession* (ἐντυγχάνει) means properly to come to the aid of any one; to transact the business of any one; especially to discharge the office of an advocate, or to plead one's cause in a court of justice. In a sense similar to this it is applied to Christ in his office of making intercession for us in heaven; Heb. vii. 25; Isa. liii. 12. In the English language, the word is constantly used in a good sense, to plead *for* one; never, to plead *against* one; but the Greek word may imply either. It expresses the office of one who manages the business of another; and hence one who manages the business of the state *against* a criminal; and when followed by the preposition *for*, means to intercede or plead *for* a person; when followed by *against* (κατα), it means to *accuse* or *arraign.* This is its meaning here. He accuses or arraigns the nation of the Jews before God; he charges them with crime; the crime is specified immediately.

3. *Lord, they have killed,* &c. This is taken from 1 Kings xix. 10. The quotation is not literally made, but the sense is preserved. This was a charge which Elijah brought against the whole nation; and the act of killing the prophets he regarded as expressive of the character of the people, or that they were *universally* given to wickedness. The *fact* was true that they had killed the prophets, &c.; (1 Kings xviii. 4, 13); but the *inference* which Elijah seems to have drawn from it, that there were no pious men in the nation, was not well founded. ¶ *And digged down.* Altars, by the law of Moses, were required to be made of earth or unhewn stones; Exod. xx. 24, 25. Hence the expression *to dig* them down means completely to demolish or destroy them. ¶ *Thine altars.* There was one great altar in the front of the tabernacle and the temple, on which the daily sacrifices of the Jews were to be made. But they were not forbidden to make altars also elsewhere; Exod. xx. 25. And hence they are mentioned as existing in other places; 1 Sam. vii. 17; xvi. 2, 3; 1 Kings xviii. 30, 32. These were the altars of which Elijah complained as having been thrown down by the Jews; an act which was regarded as

**altars; and I am left alone, and
they seek my life.
4 But what saith the answer of
God unto him? I have reserved
to myself seven thousand men,
who have not bowed the knee to
the image of Baal.
5 Even so [a] then at this present**

a chap.9.27.

expressive of signal impiety. ¶ *I am left alone.* I am the only prophet which is left alive. We are told that when Jezebel cut off the prophets of the Lord, Obadiah took a hundred of them and hid them in a cave; 1 Kings xviii. 4. But it is not improbable that they had been discovered and put to death by Ahab. The account which Obadiah gave Elijah when he met him (1 Kings xviii. 13) seems to favour such a supposition. ¶ *Seek my life.* That is, Ahab and Jezebel seek to kill me. This they did because he had overcome and slain the prophets of Baal; 1 Kings xix. 1, 2. There could scarcely be conceived a time of greater distress and declension in religion than this. It has not often happened that so many things that were disheartening have occurred to the church at the same period of time. The prophets of God were slain; but one lonely man appeared to have zeal for true religion; the nation was running to idolatry; the civil rulers were criminally wicked, and were the leaders in the universal apostasy; and all the influences of wealth and power were setting in against the true religion to destroy it. It was natural that the solitary man of God should feel disheartened and lonely in this universal guilt; and should realize that *he* had no power to resist this tide of crime and calamities.

4. *The answer of God* (ὁ χρηματισμός). This word is used no where else in the New Testament. It means *an oracle*, a divine response. It does not indicate the *manner* in which it was done, but implies only that it was an oracle, or answer made to his complaint by God. Such an answer, at such a time, would be full of comfort, and silence every murmur. The way in which this answer was *in fact* given, was not in a storm, or an earthquake, but in a still, small voice; 1 Kings xix. 11, 12. ¶ *I have reserved.* The Hebrew is, "I have caused *to remain*," or to be reserved. This shows that it was of God that this was done. Amidst the general corruption and idolatry *he* had restrained a part, though it was a remnant. The honour of having done it he claims for himself, and does not trace it to any goodness or virtue in them. So in the case of all those who are saved from sin and ruin, the honour belongs not to man, but to God. ¶ *To myself.* For my own service and glory. I have kept them steadfast in my worship, and have not suffered them to become idolaters. ¶ *Seven thousand men. Seven* is often used in the Scriptures to denote an indefinite or round number. Perhaps it may be so here, to intimate that there was a considerable number remaining. This should lead us to hope that even in the darkest times in the church, there may be many more friends of God than we suppose. Elijah supposed he was alone; and yet at that moment there were thousands who were the true friends of God; a *small* number, indeed, compared with the multitude of idolaters; but *large* when compared with what was supposed to be remaining by the dejected and disheartened prophet. ¶ *Who have not bowed the knee.* To *bow* or *bend* the knee is an expression denoting worship; Phil. ii. 10; Eph. iii. 14; Isa. xlv. 23. ¶ *To Baal.* The word *Baal* in Hebrew means Lord, or Master. This was the name of an idol of the Phenicians and Canaanites, and was worshipped also by the Assyrians and Babylonians under the name of *Bel;* (comp. the Book of *Bel* in the Apocrypha.) This god was represented under the image of a *bull*, or a *calf;* the one denoting the Sun, the other the Moon. The prevalent worship in the time of Elijah was that of this idol.

5. *At this present time.* In the time when the apostle wrote. Though the

time also there is a remnant according to the election of grace.

6 And if by grace, [a] then *is it* no more of works: otherwise grace is no more grace. But if *it be* of works, then is it no more grace: otherwise work is no more work.

a chap.4.5; Gal.5.4; Eph.2.8.

mass of the nation was to be rejected, yet it did not follow that *all* were to be excluded from the favour of God. As in the time of Elijah, when all appeared to be dark, and *all* the nation, except one, seemed to have become apostate, yet there was a considerable number of the true friends of God; so in the time of Paul, though the nation had rejected their Messiah,—though, as a consequence, *they* were to be rejected as a people; and though they were eminently wicked and corrupt,—yet it did not follow that *all* were cast off, or that *any* were excluded on whom God had purposed to bestow salvation. ¶ *A remnant.* That which is *left* or reserved; chap. ix. 27. He refers here doubtless, to that part of the nation which was truly *pious,* or which had embraced the Messiah. ¶ *According to the election of grace.* By a gracious or merciful *choosing,* or election; and not by any merit of their own. As in the time of Elijah, it was because *God had reserved them unto himself* that any were saved from idolatry, so now it was by the same gracious sovereignty that *any* were saved from the prevalent unbelief. The apostle here does not specify the number, but there can be no doubt that a multitude of Jews had been saved by becoming Christians, though compared with the *nation*—the *multitude* who rejected the Messiah—it was but a remnant.

The apostle thus shows that neither *all* the ancient people of God were cast way, nor that *any* whom *he foreknew* were rejected. And though he had proved that a large part of the Jews were to be rejected, and though infidelity was prevalent, yet still there were some who had been Jews who were truly pious, and entitled to the favour of God. Nor should they deem this state of things remarkable, for a parallel case was recorded in their own Scriptures. We may learn from this narrative, (1.) That it is no unparalleled thing for the love of many to wax cold, and for iniquity to abound. (2.) The tendency of this is to produce deep feeling and solicitude among the true friends of God. Thus David says, "Rivers of waters run down mine eyes because they keep not thy law;" Ps. cxix. 136; comp. Jer. ix. 1; Luke xix. 41. (3.) That in these darkest times we should not be discouraged. There *may be* much more true piety in the world than in our despondency we may suppose. We should take courage in God, and believe that he will not forsake any that are his true friends, or on whom he has purposed to bestow eternal life. (4.) It is of God that *all* are not corrupt and lost. It is owing only to the election of grace, to his merciful choosing, that *any* are saved. And as in the darkest times he has reserved a people to himself, so we should believe that he will still meet abounding evil, and save those whom he has chosen from eternal death.

6. *And if grace,* &c. If the fact that any are reserved be by grace, or favour, then it cannot be as a reward of merit. Paul thus takes occasion *incidentally* to combat a favourite notion of the Jews, that we are justified by obedience to the law. He reminds them that in the time of Elijah it was because God had *reserved* them; that the same was the case now; and therefore their doctrine of *merit* could not be true; see chap. iv. 4, 5; Gal. v. 4; Eph. ii. 8, 9. ¶ *Otherwise grace,* &c. If men are justified by their *works,* it could not be a matter of *favour,* but was a *debt.* If it could be that the doctrine of justification by grace could be held, and yet at the same time that the Jewish doctrine of *merit* was true, then it would follow that *grace* had changed its nature, or was a different thing from what the word properly signified. The idea of being saved by *merit* contradicts the very idea of

7 What then? Israel [a] hath not obtained that which he seeketh for; but the election hath obtained it, and the rest were [1] blinded.

8 (According as it is written, God hath given them the spirit of [2] slumber, [b] eyes [c] that they should not see, and ears that they should not hear) unto this day.

a chap.9.31 1 hardened. 2 or, *remorse.* b Isa.29.10. c Deut.29.4.

grace. If a man *owes* me a *debt,* and pays it, it cannot be said to be done by *favour,* or *by grace.* I have a *claim* on him for it, and there is no *favour* in his paying his just dues. ¶ *But if it be of works,* &c. *Works* here mean conformity to the law; and to be saved *by works* would be to be saved *by* such conformity as the *meritorious* cause. Of course there could be no *grace* or *favour* in giving what was *due:* if there was favour, or grace, then *works* would lose their essential characteristic, and cease to be the meritorious cause of procuring the blessings. What is paid as a *debt* is not conferred as a *favour.*

And from this it follows that salvation cannot be *partly* by grace and *partly* by works. It is not because men can advance *any* claims to the favour of God; but from his mere unmerited grace. He that is not willing to obtain eternal life in that way, cannot obtain it at all. The doctrines of *election,* and of salvation by mere grace, cannot be more explicitly stated than they are in this passage.

7. *What then?* What is the proper conclusion from this argument? ¶ *Israel hath not obtained.* That is, the Jews as a people have not obtained that which they sought. They sought the favour of God by their own merit; and as it was impossible to obtain it in that manner, they have, *as a people,* failed of obtaining his favour at all, and will be rejected. ¶ *That which he seeketh for.* To wit, salvation by their own obedience to the law. ¶ *The election hath.* The *purpose of choosing* on the part of God has obtained, or secured, that which the *seeking* on the part of the Jews could not secure. Or the abstract here may be put for the concrete, and the word "election" may mean the same as *the elect.* The *elect,* the *reserved,* the chosen part of the people, have obtained the favour of God. ¶ *Hath obtained it.* That is, the favour, or mercy, of God. ¶ *The rest.* The great mass of the people who remained in unbelief, and had rejected the Messiah. ¶ *Were blinded.* The word in the original means also *were hardened* (ἐπωρώθησαν). It comes from a word which signifies properly to become *hard,* as bones do which are broken and are then united; or as the joints sometimes do when they become callous or stiff. It was probably applied also to the formation of a hard substance in the eye, a cataract; and then means the same as to be blinded. Hence, applied to the mind, it means that which is *hard, obdurate, insensible, stupid.* Thus it is applied to the Jews, and means that they were blind and obstinate; see Mark vi. 52, "Their heart was hardened;" ch. viii. 17; John xii. 40. The word does not occur in any other place in the New Testament. This verse affirms simply that "the rest *were* hardened," but it does not affirm any thing about the *mode* by which it was done. In regard to "the election," it is affirmed that it was *of God;* ver. 4. Of the remainder, *the fact* of their blindness is simply mentioned, without affirming any thing of the cause; see ver. 8.

8. *According as it is written.* That is, they are blinded in accordance with what is written. The *fact* and the *manner* accord with the ancient declaration. This is recorded in Isa. xxix. 10, and in Deut. xxix. 4. The same sentiment is found also substantially in Isa. vi. 9, 10. The principal place referred to here, however, is doubtless Isa. xxix. 10, "For the Lord hath poured out upon you the spirit of deep sleep, and hath closed your eyes; the prophets and your rulers hath he covered." The quotation is not how-

9 And David saith, Let [a] their table be made a snare, and a trap, and a stumbling-block, and a recompense unto them.

[a] Ps.69.22,23.

ever *literally* made either from the Hebrew or the Septuagint; but *the sense* is preserved. The phrase "according as" means *upon the same principle,* or in the same manner. ¶ *God hath given.* Expressions like this are common in the Scriptures, where *God* is represented as having an agency in producing the wickedness and stupidity of sinners; see chap. ix. 17, 18; see Note, Mat. xiii. 15; Mark iv. 11, 12; see also 2 Thess. ii. 11. This quotation is not made literally. The Hebrew in Isaiah is, God has *poured upon* them the spirit of slumber. The sense, however, is retained. ¶ *The spirit of slumber.* The *spirit* of slumber is not different from slumber itself. The word *spirit* is often used thus. The word *slumber* here is a literal translation of the Hebrew. The Greek word, however (κατανύξεως), implies also the notion of *compunction,* and hence in the margin it is rendered *remorse.* It means any emotion, or *any* influence whatever, that shall *benumb* the faculties, and make them insensible. Hence it here means simply insensibility. ¶ *Eyes that they should not see,* &c. This expression is not taken literally from any *single* place in the Old Testament; but expresses the general sense of several passages; Isa. vi. 10; Deut. xxix. 4. It denotes a state of mind not different from a spirit of slumber. When we sleep, the eyes are insensible to surrounding objects, and the ear to sounds. Though in themselves the organs may be perfect, yet the mind is as though they were not; and we have eyes which then do not see, and ears which do not hear. Thus with the Jews. Though they had all the proper faculties for understanding and receiving the gospel, yet they rejected it. They were stupid and insensible to its claims and its truths. ¶ *Unto this day.* Until the day that Paul wrote. The characteristic of the Jews that existed in the time of Isaiah, existed also in the time of Paul. It was a trait of the people; and their insensibility to the demands of the gospel developed nothing new in them.

9, 10. *And David saith,* &c. This quotation is made from Ps. lxix. 22. 23. This Psalm is repeatedly quoted as having reference to the events recorded in the New Testament. (See Note on Acts i. 2.) This quotation is introduced *immediately* after one that undoubtedly refers to the Lord Jesus. Ver. 21, "They gave me also gall for my meat, and in my thirst they gave me vinegar to drink." The passage here quoted immediately follows as an *imprecation* of vengeance for their sins. "Let their table," &c. The quotation is not made, however, either literally from the Hebrew or from the Septuagint, but the *sense* only is retained. The Hebrew is, "Let their table before them be for a snare, and for those at peace, let it be for a gin." The Septuagint is, "Let their table before them be for a snare, and for a stumbling-block, and for an offence." The ancient Targum is, "Let their table which they had prepared before me be for a snare, and *their sacrifices* be for an offence." The meaning is this. The word *table* denotes food. In this they expected pleasure and support. David prays that even this, where they expected joy and refreshment, might prove to them the means of punishment and righteous retribution. A *snare* is that by which birds or wild beasts were taken. They are decoyed into it, or walk or fly carelessly into it, and it is sprung suddenly on them. So of the Jews. The petition is, that *while they* were seeking refreshment and joy, and anticipating at their table no danger, it might be made the means of their ruin. The only way in which this could be done would be, that their *temporal* enjoyments would lead them away from God, and produce stupidity and indifference to their spiritual interests. This is often the result of the pleasures of the *table,* or of seeking sensual gratifications. The apos-

10 Let their eyes be darkened, that they may not see, and bow down their back alway.

tle does not say whether this prayer was right or wrong. The use which he seems to make of it is this, that David's imprecation was to be regarded in *the light of a prophecy;* that what he prayed for would come to pass; and that this *had actually* occurred in the time of the apostle; that their very enjoyments, their national and private privileges, had been the means of alienating them from God; had been a snare to them; and was the cause of their blindness and infidelity. This also is introduced in the psalm as a *punishment* for giving him vinegar to drink; and their treatment of the Messiah was the immediate cause why all this blindness had come upon the Jews. ¶ *A trap.* This properly means any thing by which *wild beasts* are taken in hunting. The word *snare* more properly refers to birds. ¶ *And a stumbling-block.* Any thing over which one stumbles or falls. Hence any thing which occasions us to sin, or to ruin ourselves. ¶ *And a recompense.* The Hebrew word translated "*that which should have been* for *their* welfare," is capable of this meaning, and may denote *their recompense,* or that which is appropriately rendered to them. It means here that their ordinary comforts and enjoyments, instead of promoting their permanent welfare, may be the occasion of their guilt and ruin. This is often the effect of earthly comforts. They *might* lead us to God, and *should* excite our gratitude and praise; but they are often abused to our spiritual slumber and guilt, and made the occasion of our ruin. The rich are thus often most forgetful of God; and the very abundance of their blessings made the means of darkness of mind, ingratitude, prayerlessness, and ruin. Satisfied with them, they forget the Giver; and while they enjoy many earthly blessings, God sends barrenness into their souls. This was the guilt of Sodom, "pride, and fulness of bread, and abundance of idleness," (Ezek. xvi. 49); and against this Moses solemnly warned the Jews; Deut. vi. 11, 12; viii. 10—12. This same caution might be extended to the people of this land, and especially to those who are rich, and are blessed with all that their hearts have wished. From the use which the apostle makes of this passage in the Psalms, it is clear that he regarded it rather *as a prophetic denunciation* for their sins—a prediction of what *would be*—than as *a prayer.* In his time it had been fulfilled; and the very national privileges of the Jews, on which they so much prided themselves, and which *might* have been so great blessings, were the occasion of their greater sin in rejecting the Messiah, and of their greater condemnation. Thus their table was made a trap, &c.

10. *Let their eyes be darkened.* This is taken literally from the psalm, and was evidently the *main* part of the passage which the apostle had in his eye. This was fulfilled in the insensibility and blindness of the Jews. And the apostle shows them that it was long ago predicted, or *invoked,* as a punishment on them for giving the Messiah vinegar to drink; Ps. lix. 21, 23. ¶ *And bow down their back alway.* The Hebrew (Ps. lix. 23) is, "Let their loins *totter* or shake," *i. e.* as one does when he has on him a heavy burden. The apostle has retained this sense. It means, let them be called to bear heavy and oppressive burdens; let them be subjected to toil or servitude, as a reward for their sins. That this had come upon the Jews in the time of Paul is clear; and it is further clear that it came upon them, as it was implied in the psalm, in consequence of their treatment of the Messiah. Much difficulty has been felt in reconciling the petitions in the psalms for calamities on enemies, with the spirit of the New Testament. Perhaps they cannot all be thus reconciled; and it is not at all improbable that many of those imprecations were wrong. David was not a perfect man; and the Spirit of inspiration is not responsible for his imperfections. Every *doctrine*

11 I say then, Have they stumbled that they should fall? God forbid: but *rather* through their fall salvation *is come* unto

delivered by the sacred writers is true; every fact recorded is recorded as it was. But it does not follow that all the *men* who wrote, or about whom a narrative was given, were perfect. The reverse is the fact. And it does not militate against the inspiration of the Scriptures that we have a *record* of the failings and imperfections of those men. When they uttered improper sentiments, when they manifested improper feelings, when they performed wicked actions, it is no argument against the inspiration of the Scriptures that they were recorded. All that is done in such a case, and all that inspiration demands, is that they be recorded *as they are.* We wish to see human nature as it is; and one design of making the record of such failings is to show what *man* is, even under the influence of religion; not as a *perfect* being, for that would not be true; but as he actually exists mingled with imperfection. Thus many of the wishes of the ancient saints, imperfect as they were, are *condemned* as sinful by the spirit of the Christian religion. They were never *commended* or *approved,* but they are *recorded* just to show us what was *in fact* the character of man, even partially under the influence of religion. Of this nature probably, were many of the petitions in the Psalms; and the Spirit of God is no more answerable for the feeling because it is recorded, than he is for the feelings of the Edomites when they said, "Rase it, rase it to the foundation" Ps. cxxxvii. 7. Many of those prayers, however, were imprecations on his enemies as a public man, as the magistrate of the land. As it is *right* and *desirable* that the robber and the pirate should be detected and punished; as all good men seek it, and it is indispensable for the welfare of the community, where is the impropriety of *praying* that it may be done? Is it not right to pray that the laws may be executed; that justice may be maintained; and that restraint should be imposed on the guilty? Assuredly this may be done with a very different spirit from that of *revenge.* It may be the prayer of the *magistrate* that God will help him in that which he is *appointed* to do, and in what *ought* to be done. Besides, many of these imprecations were regarded as simply *predictions* of what *would be* the effect of sin; or of what God *would* do to the guilty. Such was the case we are now considering, as understood by the apostle. But in a *prediction* there can be nothing wrong.

11. *Have they stumbled that they should fall?* This is to be regarded as an objection, which the apostle proceeds to answer. The meaning is, is it the design of God that the Jews should totally and irrecoverably be cast off? Even admitting that they are now unbelieving, that they have rejected the Messiah, that they have stumbled, is it the purpose of God finally to exclude them from mercy? The expression to *stumble* is introduced because he had just mentioned a *stumbling-stone.* It does not mean to fall down to the ground, or to fall so that a man may not recover himself; but to strike the foot against an obstacle, to be arrested in going, and to be in danger of falling. Hence it means to *err,* to *sin,* to be in danger. To *fall* expresses the state when a man pitches over an obstacle so that he cannot recover himself, but falls to the ground. Hence to err, to sin, or to be cast off irrecoverably. The apostle shows that this last was not the way in which the Jews had fallen that they were not to be cast off for ever, but that occasion was taken *by* their fall to introduce the Gentiles to the privileges of the gospel, and then they should be restored. ¶ *God forbid.* By no means; see ver. 1. ¶ *But rather through their fall.* By means of their fall. The word *fall* here refers to all their conduct and doom at the coming of the Messiah, and in the breaking up of their establishment as a nation. Their rejection of the Messiah; the destruction of their city and temple; the ceasing of their ceremonial rites; and the rejection and

the Gentiles, [a] for to provoke them to jealousy.

a Acts 13.46; 28.24-28; chap.10.19.

12 Now if the fall of them *be* the riches of the world, and the [1] diminishing of them the riches of the Gentiles; how much more their fulness?

1 or, *decay*, or, *loss*.

dispersion of their nation by the Romans, all enter into the meaning of the word *fall* here, and were all the occasion of introducing salvation to the Gentiles. ¶ *Salvation.* The Christian religion, with all its saving benefits. It does not mean that all the Gentiles were to *be saved*, but that the way was open; they might have access to God, and obtain his favour through the Messiah. ¶ *The Gentiles.* All the world that were not Jews. The rejection and fall of the Jews contributed to the introduction of the Gentiles in the following manner: (1.) It broke down the barrier which had long subsisted between them. (2.) It made it consistent and proper, as *they* had rejected the Messiah, to send the knowledge of him to others. (3.) It was connected with the destruction of the temple, and the rites of the Mosaic law; and taught *them*, and all others, that the worship of God was not to be confined to any single place. (4.) The calamities that came upon the Jewish nation scattered the inhabitants of Judea, and with the Jews also those who had become Christians, and thus the gospel was carried to other lands. (5.) These calamities, and the conduct of the Jews, and the close of the Jewish economy, were the means of giving to apostles and other Christians right views of the true design of the Mosaic institutions. If the temple had remained; if the nation had continued to flourish; it would have been long before they would have been effectually detached from those rites. Experience showed even as it was, that they were slow in learning that the Jewish ceremonies were to cease. Some of the most agitating questions in the early church pertained to this; and if the temple had not been destroyed, the contest would have been much longer and more difficult. ¶ *For to provoke them to jealousy.* According to the prediction of Moses; Deut. xxxii. 21; see Rom. x. 19.

12. *If the fall of them.* If their lapse, or falling. If their *temporal* rejection and being cast off for a time has already accomplished so much. ¶ *Be the riches of the world.* The word *riches* means *wealth, abundance* of property; more than is *necessary* to the supply of our wants. Hence it means also any thing that may *promote* our comfort or happiness, as wealth is the *means* of securing our welfare. The gospel is called *riches*, as it is the means of our highest enjoyment, and eternal welfare. It is the means of conferring numberless spiritual blessings on the *Gentile* world; and as this was done by the fall of the Jews, so it could be said that *their* fall was the riches of the world. It was the *occasion* or *means* without which the blessings of the gospel could not be conferred on the world. ¶ *The diminishing of them.* Margin, *Decay.* *Loss* (ἥττημα). This word means *diminution, defect, that which is lacked or wanting.* Hence also judgment, condemnation. Here it means their degradation; the withdrawing of their special privileges; their rejection. It stands opposed to "their fulness." ¶ *The riches of the Gentiles.* The means of conferring important blessings on the Gentiles. ¶ *How much more their fulness.* The word *fulness* (πλήρωμα) means that which *fills up*, or completes any thing. Thus it is applied to that which fills a vessel or cup; also to the piece of cloth which is put in to *fill up* the rent in a garment; Mat. ix. 16. To the fragments which were left when Christ had fed the five thousand; Mark viii. 20; Rom. xiii. 10. "Love is the fulfilling of the law," *i. e.* it is the *filling up* of the law, or that which renders the obedience complete; see Gal. v. 14. Here it stands opposed to their *fall*, and their *diminution*, and evidently means their complete restoration to the favour of God; their recovery from unbelief and apostasy. That there *will* be such a recovery, the apostle proceeds to show. The sentiment of the passage then is, If

ishing of them the riches of the Gentiles, how much more their fulness?

13 For I speak to you Gentiles, inasmuch as I [a] am the apostle

a Acts 9.15; Gal.1.16; Eph.3.8.

their rejection and punishment; their being cut off from the favour of God, an event apparently so unlikely to promote the spread of true religion, if their being *withrawn* from all active influence in spreading the true knowledge of God, be yet the occasion of so many blessings to mankind as have attended the spread of the gospel in consequence of it; how much more shall we expect when they shall be restored; when the energy and zeal of the Jewish nation shall *unite* with the efforts of others in spreading the knowledge of the true Messiah. In what way, or when, this shall be, we know not. But it is easy to see, that if the Jewish people should be converted to the Christian faith, they would have facilities for spreading the truth, which the church has never had without them. (1.) They are scattered in all nations, and have access to all people. (2.) Their conversion, after so long unbelief, would have all the power and influence of *a miracle* performed in view of all nations. It would be seen *why* they had been preserved, and their conversion would be a most striking fulfilment of the prophecies. (3.) They are familiar with the languages of the world, and their conversion would *at once* establish many Christian missionaries in *the heart* of all the kingdoms of the world. It would be kindling at once a thousand lights in all the dark parts of the earth. (4.) The *Jews* have shown that they are eminently fitted to spread the true religion. It was by *Jews* converted to Christianity, that the gospel was first spread. Each of the apostles was a Jew; and they have lost none of the ardour, enterprise, and zeal that always characterized their nation. Their conversion would be, therefore, to give to the church a host of missionaries prepared for their work, familiar with all customs, languages, and climes, and already in the heart of all kingdoms, and with facilities for their work *in advance*, which others must gain only by the slow toil of many years.

13. *For I speak to you Gentiles.* What I am saying respecting the Jews, I say with reference to you who are Gentiles, to show you in what manner you have been admitted to the privileges of the people of God; to excite your gratitude; to warn you against abusing those mercies, &c. As Paul also was *appointed* to preach to them, he had a right to speak to them with authority. ¶ *I am the apostle of the Gentiles.* The apostle of the Gentiles, not because *other* apostles did not preach to Gentiles, for they all did, except perhaps James; nor because Paul did not himself preach occasionally among the Jews; but because he was especially called to carry the gospel to the Gentiles, and that this was his original commission (Acts ix. 15); because he was principally employed in collecting and organizing churches in heathen lands; and because the charge of the Gentile churches was especially intrusted to him, while that of the Jewish churches was especially intrusted to Peter; see Gal. i. 16; Eph. iii. 8; Gal. ii. 7, 8. As Paul was especially appointed to this office, he claimed special authority to address those who were gathered into the Christian church from heathen lands. ¶ *I magnify mine office.* I honour (δοξάζω) my ministry. I esteem it of great importance; and by thus showing that the gospel is to be preached to the Gentiles, that the barrier between them and the Jews is to be broken down, that the gospel may be preached to all men, I show that the office which *proclaims* this is one of signal honour. A minister may not magnify *himself*, but he may magnify *his office*. He may esteem *himself* as less than the least of all saints, and unworthy to be called a servant of God (Eph. iii. 8), yet he may feel that he is an ambassador of Christ, intrusted with a message of salvation, entitled to the respect due to an ambassador, and to the honour which is appropriate to a messenger of God. To unite these two things constitutes

of the Gentiles, I magnify mine office;

14 If by any means I may provoke to emulation *them which are* my flesh, and might save [a] some of them.

15 For if the casting away of them *be* the reconciling of the

a 1Cor.7.16.

the dignity of the Christian ministry.

14. *If by any means.* If even by stating unpleasant truths, if by bringing out all the counsel of God, even that which threatens their destruction, I may arrest their attention, and save them. ¶ *I may provoke to emulation.* I may awaken up to zeal, or to an earnest desire to obtain the like blessings. This was in accordance with the prediction of Moses, that the calling in of the Gentiles would excite their attention, and provoke them to deep feeling; Note, chap. x. 19. The apostle expected to do this by calling their attention to the ancient prophecies; by alarming their fears about their own danger; and by showing them the great privileges which *Gentiles* might enjoy under the gospel; thus appealing to them by every principle of benevolence, by all their regard for God and man, to excite them to seek the same blessings. ¶ *My flesh.* My countrymen. My kinsmen. Those belonging to the same family or nation; chap. ix. 3; Gen. xxix. 14; Judg. ix. 2; 2 Sam. v. 1; Isa. lviii. 7. ¶ *And save some of them.* This desire the apostle often expressed; (see chap. ix. 2, 3; x. 1, 2.) We may see here, (1.) That it is the earnest wish of the ministry to save the souls of men. (2.) That they should urge every argument and appeal with reference to this. (3.) That even the most awful and humbling truths *may* have this tendency. No truth could be more likely to irritate and offend than that the Jews would be cast off; and yet the apostle used this so faithfully, and yet so tenderly, that he expected and desired it might be the means of saving the souls of his countrymen. Truth often irritates, enrages, and thus excites the attention. Thought or inquiry, *however* it may be excited, may result in conversion. And thus, even restlessness, and vexation, and anger, *may* be the means of leading a sinner to Jesus Christ. It should be no part of a minister's object, however, to *produce* anger. It is a bad emotion; in itself it is evil; and if men can be won to embrace the Saviour *without* anger, it is better. No wise man would excite a storm and tempest that might require infinite power to subdue, when the same object could be gained with comparative peace, and under the mild influence of love. (4.) It is right to use all the means in our power, not absolutely wicked, to save men. Paul was full of devices; and much of the success of the ministry will depend on a wise use of plans, that may, by the divine blessing, arrest and save the souls of men.

15. *For if the casting away of them.* If their rejection as the *peculiar* people of God—their exclusion from their national privileges, on account of their unbelief. It is the same as "the *fall* of them;" ver. 12. ¶ *Be the reconciling of the world.* The word reconciliation (καταλλαγὴ) denotes commonly a *pacification* of contending parties; a removing the occasion of difference, so as again to be united; 1 Cor. vii. 11, "Let her remain unmarried, or be *reconciled* to her husband." It is commonly applied to the *reconciliation*, or pacification, produced between man and God by the gospel. They are brought to union, to friendship, to peace, by the intervention of the Lord Jesus Christ; Rom. v. 10; 2 Cor. v. 18, 19, "God was in Christ reconciling the world unto himself." Hence the ministry is called the "ministry of reconciliation;" 2 Cor. v. 18. And hence this word is used to express the *atonement;* Rom. v. 11, "By whom we have now received the *atonement*" (*the reconciliation*). In this place it means that many of the Gentiles—the world—had become reconciled to God as the *result* of the casting off of the Jews. By *their* unbelief, the way had been opened to preach the gospel

world, what *shall* the receiving *of*
them be, but life from the dead?
16 For if [a] the first-fruit *be*
holy, the lump *is* also *holy:*
and if the root *be* holy, so *are* the
branches.

a Lev.23.10; Num.15.18-21.

---

to the Gentiles; it was *the occasion* by which God sent it to the nations of the earth; comp. Acts xiii. 46. ¶ *The receiving of* them. The same as was denoted (ver. 12) by *their fulness.* If the casting them off, an event so little likely, apparently, to produce any good effect, was nevertheless *overruled* so as to produce important benefits in the spread of the gospel, how much more may we expect will be accomplished by their conversion and return; an event *fitted in itself* to produce an important influence on mankind. One would have *supposed* that *their* rejection of the Messiah would have been an important obstacle *in the way* of the gospel. It was overruled, however, to promote its increase. Their *return* will have a *direct* tendency to spread it. How much more, therefore, may we expect to be accomplished by that? ¶ *But life from the dead.* This is an instance of the peculiar, glowing, and vigorous manner of the apostle Paul. His mind catches at the thought of what *may be* produced by the recovery of the Jews, and no ordinary language would convey his idea. He had already exhausted the usual forms of speech by saying that even their rejection had *reconciled* the world, and that it was the *riches* of the Gentiles. To say that their *recovery*—a striking and momentous event; an event so much better fitted to produce important results—would be attended by the conversion of the world, would be insipid and tame. He uses, therefore, a most bold and striking figure. The *resurrection of the dead* was an image of the most vast and wonderful event that could take place. This image, therefore, in the apostle's mind, was a striking illustration of the great change and reformation which should take place when the Jews should be restored, and the effect should be felt in the conversion also of the Gentile world. Some have supposed that the apostle here refers to a *literal* resurrection of the dead, as the conversion of the Jews. But there is not the slightest evidence of this. He refers to the recovery of the nations from the *death of sin* which shall take place when the Jews shall be converted to the Christian faith. The prophet Ezekiel (chap. xxxvii. 1—14) has also used the same image of the resurrection of the dead to denote a great moral change among a people. It is clear here that the apostle fixed his eye on a future conversion of the Jews to the gospel, and expected that their conversion would *precede* the universal conversion of the Gentiles to the Christian faith. There could be no event that would make so immediate and decided an impression on the pagan world as the conversion of the Jews. They are scattered every where; they have access to all people; they understand all languages; and their conversion would be like kindling up thousands of lights at once in the darkness of the pagan world.

16. *For if the first-fruit be holy.* The word *first-fruit* (ἀπαρχὴ) used here denotes the *firstling* of fruit or grain which was separated from the mass and presented as an offering to God. The Jews were required to present such a portion of their harvest to God, as an expression of gratitude and of their sense of dependence; Num. xv. 19—21. Till this was done, it was not lawful to partake of the harvest. The offering of this was regarded as rendering the mass *holy, i. e.* it was lawful then to partake of it. The first-fruits were regarded as among the best portions of the harvest; and it was their duty to devote to God that which would be the best expression of their thanksgiving. This was the general practice in relation to all that the land produced. The expression here, however, has reference to the small portion of *dough* or *kneaded meal* that was offered to God; and then the mass or *lump* (φύραμα) was

17 And if some of the branches [a] be broken off, and thou, [b] being a wild olive-tree, wert graffed in [1] among them, and with them partakest of the root and fatness of the olive-tree;

a Jer.11.16. b Eph.2.12,13. 1 or *for*.

left for the use of him who made the offering; Num. xv. 20. ¶ *Be holy.* Be set apart, or consecrated to God, as he commanded. ¶ *The lump.* The *mass.* It refers here properly to the *dough* of which a part had been offered. The same was true also in relation to the harvest, after the *waive-sheaf* had been offered; of the flock, after the first male had been offered, &c. ¶ *Is also holy.* It is lawful then for the owner to partake of it. The offering of *a part* has consecrated the whole. By this illustration Paul doubtless means to say that the *Jewish nation,* as a people, were set apart to the service of God, and were so regarded by him. Some have supposed that by the *first-fruit* here the apostle intends to refer to the early converts made to the Christian faith in the first preaching of the gospel. But it is more probable that he refers to the *patriarchs,* the pious men of old, as the *first-fruits* of the Jewish nation; see ver. 28. By *their* piety the nation was, in a manner, sanctified, or set apart to the service of God; implying that yet the great mass of them would be reclaimed and saved. ¶ *If the root be holy.* This figure expresses the same thing as is denoted in the first part of the verse. The *root* of a tree is the source of nutritious juices necessary for its growth, and gives its character to the tree. If that be sound, pure, vigorous, we expect the same of the branches. A root bears a similar relation to the tree that the first-fruit does to the mass of bread. Perhaps there is allusion here to Jer. xi. 16, where the Jewish nation is represented under the image of "a green olive-tree, fair, and of goodly fruit." In this place the reference is doubtless to Abraham and the patriarchs, as the *root* or founders of the Jewish nation. If they were holy, it is to be expected that the distant branches, or descendants, would also be so regarded. The mention of the *root* and *branches* of a tree gives the apostle occasion for an illustration of the relation at that time of the Jews and Gentiles to the church of Christ.

17. *If some of the branches.* The illustration here is taken from the practice of those who ingraft trees. The useless branches, or those which bear poor fruit, are cut off, and a better kind inserted. "If some of the natural descendants of Abraham, the holy root, are cast off because they are unfruitful, *i. e.* because of unbelief and sin." ¶ *And thou.* The word *thou* here is used to denote the *Gentile,* whom Paul was then particularly addressing. ¶ *Being a wild olive-tree.* From this passage it would seem that the *olive-tree* was sometimes cultivated, and that cultivation was necessary in order to render it fruitful. The cultivated olive-tree is "of the a moderate height, its trunk knotty, its bark smooth and ash-coloured, its wood is solid and yellowish, the leaves are oblong, and almost like those of the willow, of a green colour, &c. The wild olive is smaller in all its parts." (*Calmet.*) The wild olive was unfruitful, or its fruit very imperfect and useless. The ancient writers explain this word by "unfruitful, barren." (*Schleusner.*) This was used, therefore, as the emblem of unfruitfulness and barrenness, while the cultivated olive produced much fruit. The meaning here is, that the Gentiles had been like the wild olive, unfruitful in holiness; that they had been uncultivated by the institutions of the true religion, and consequently had grown up in the wildness and sin of nature. The Jews had been like a cultivated olive, long under the training and blessing of God. ¶ *Wert graffed in.* The process of grafting consists in inserting a scion or a young shoot into another tree. To do this, a useless limb is removed; and the ingrafted limb producesfruit according to its new nature or kind, and not according to

18 Boast [a] not against the branches. But if thou boast thou bearest not the root, but the root thee.

19 Thou wilt say then, The branches were broken off, that I might be graffed in.

20 Well; because of unbelief

a 1 Cor.10.12.

the tree in which it is inserted. In this way a tree which bears no fruit, or whose branches are decaying, may be recovered, and become valuable. The figure of the apostle is a very vivid and beautiful one. The ancient root or stock, that of Abraham, &c. was good. The branches—the Jews in the time of the apostle—had become decayed and unfruitful, and broken off. The Gentiles had been graffed into this stock, and had restored the decayed vigour of the ancient people of God; and a fruitless church had become vigorous and flourishing. But the apostle soon proceeds to keep the Gentiles from exaltation on account of this. ¶ *Among them.* Among the branches, so as to partake *with* them of the juices of the root. ¶ *Partakest of the root.* The ingrafted limb would derive nourishment from the root as much as though it were a natural branch of the tree. The Gentiles derived now the benefit of Abraham's faith and holy labours, and of the promises made to him and to his seed. ¶ *Fatness of the olive-tree.* The word *fatness* here means *fertility, fruitfulness*—the rich juices of the olive producing fruit; see Judg. ix. 9.

18. *Boast not,* &c. The tendency of men is to triumph over one that is fallen and rejected. The danger of pride and boasting on account of privileges is not less in the church than elsewhere. Paul saw that some of the Gentiles *might* be in danger of exultation over the fallen Jews, and therefore cautions them against it. The ingrafted shoot, deriving all its vigour and fruitfulness from the stock of another tree, ought not to boast against the branches. ¶ *But if thou boast.* If thou art so inconsiderate and wicked, so devoid of humility, and lifted up with pride, as to boast, yet know that there is no occasion for it. If there *were* occasion for boasting, it would rather be in the root or stock which sustains the branches; least of all can it be in those which were graffed in, having been before wholly unfruitful. ¶ *Thou bearest not the root.* The source of all your blessings is in the ancient stock. It is clear from this, that the apostle regarded the church as one; and that the Christian economy was only a prolongation of the ancient dispensation. The tree, even with a part of the branches removed, and others ingrafted, retains its identity, and is never regarded as a different tree.

19. *Thou wilt say then.* Thou who art a Gentile. ¶ *The branches were broken off,* &c. The Jews were rejected in order that the gospel might be preached to the Gentiles. This would seem to follow from what the apostle had said in ver. 11, 12. Perhaps it might be said that there was some ground of exultation from the fact that God had rejected his ancient people for the sake of making a way open to admit the Gentiles to the church. The objection is, that the branches were broken off *in order that* others might be graffed in. To this Paul replies in the next verse, that this was not the *reason* why they were rejected, but their *unbelief* was the cause.

20. *Well.* True. It is true they were broken off; but in order to show that there was no occasion for boasting, he adds that they were not rejected *in order* to admit others, but because of their unbelief, and that *their* fate should have a salutary impression on those who had no occasion for boasting, but who might be rejected for the same cause. This is an instance of remarkable *tact* and delicacy in an argument, admitting the *main* force of the remark, but giving it a slight change in accordance with the truth, so as to parry its force, and give it a practical bearing on the very point which he wished to enforce. ¶ *Thou standest by faith.*

they were broken off; and thou
standest by faith. Be not high-
minded, but fear: [a]
21 For if God spared not the
natural branches, *take heed* lest he
spare not thee.
22 Behold therefore the goodness and severity of God; on

a Phil.2.12.

The continuance of these mercies to you depends on your fidelity. If you are faithful, they will be preserved; if, like the Jews, you become unbelieving and unfruitful, like them you will be also rejected. This fact should repress boasting, and excite to anxiety and caution. ¶ *Be not high-minded.* Do not be elated in the conception of your privileges, so as to produce vain self-confidence and boasting. ¶ *But fear.* This *fear* stands opposed to the spirit of boasting and self-confidence, against which he was exhorting them. It does not mean *terror* or *horror*, but it denotes humility, watchfulness, and solicitude to abide in the faith. Do not be haughty and high-minded against the Jew, who has been cast off, but "demean yourself as a humble believer, and one who has need to be continually on his guard, and to fear lest he may fall through unbelief, and be cast off." (*Stuart.*) We may here learn, (1.) That there is danger lest those who are raised to eminent privileges should become unduly exalted in their own estimation, and despise others. (2.) The tendency of *faith* is to promote humility and a sense of our dependence on God. (3.) The system of salvation by faith produces that solicitude, and careful guarding, and watchfulness, which is necessary to preserve us from apostasy and ruin.

21. *For if God*, &c. If God did not refrain from rejecting the Jews who became unbelievers, assuredly he will not refrain from rejecting you in the same circumstances. It may be supposed that he will be quite as ready to reject the *ingrafted* branches, as to cast off those which belonged to *the parent stock.* The situation of the Gentiles is not such as to give them any security over the condition of the rejected Jew.

22. *Behold, therefore,* &c. Regard, or contemplate, for purposes of your own improvement and benefit, the dealings of God. We should look on *all* his dispensations of judgment or of mercy, and derive lessons from all to promote our own steadfast adherence to the faith of the gospel. ¶ *The goodness.* The benevolence or mercy of God towards you in admitting you to his favour. This calls for gratitude, love, confidence. It demands expressions of thanksgiving. It should be highly prized, in order that it may excite to diligence to secure its continuance. ¶ *The severity of God.* That is, towards the Jews. The word *severity* now suggests sometimes the idea of *harshness*, or even of *cruelty.* (*Webster.*) But nothing of this kind is conveyed in the original word here. It properly denotes *cutting off*, ἀποτομίαν, from ἀποτέμνω, to cut off; and is commonly applied to the act of the gardener or vine-dresser in trimming trees or vines, and cutting off the decayed or useless branches. Here it refers to the act of God in *cutting off* or rejecting the Jews as useless branches; and conveys no idea of injustice, cruelty, or harshness. It was a just act, and consistent with all the perfections of God. It indicated a purpose to do that which was *right*, though the inflictions might *seem* to be severe, and though they *must* involve them in many heavy calamities. ¶ *On them which fell, severity.* On the Jews, who had been rejected because of their unbelief. ¶ *But towards thee, goodness.* Towards the Gentile world, benevolence. The word *goodness* properly denotes *benignity* or *benevolence.* Here it signifies the kindness of God in bestowing these favours on the Gentiles. ¶ *If thou continue in his goodness.* The word "his" is not in the original. And the word goodness may denote *integrity, probity, uprightness,* as well as favour; Rom. iii. 12, "There is none that doeth *good.*" The Septuagint often thus uses the word; Ps.

them which fell, severity; but towards thee, goodness; if [a] thou continue in *his* goodness: otherwise thou [b] also shalt be cut off.

23 And they also, if [c] they bide not still in unbelief, shall be graffed in: for God is able to graft them in again.

24 For if thou wert cut out of the olive-tree which is wild by nature, and wert graffed contrary to nature into a good olive-tree;

a Heb.3.6,14; 10.23,38. b John 15.2. c 2 Cor.3.16.

xiii. 1, 3, &c. This is probably the meaning here; though it may mean "if thou dost continue in a state of favour;" that is, if your faith and good conduct shall be such as to make it proper for God to continue his kindness towards you. Christians do not *merit* the favour of God by their faith and good works; but their obedience is an indispensable condition on which that favour is to be continued. It is thus that the grace of God is magnified, at the same time that the highest good is done to man himself. ¶ *Otherwise thou also shalt be cut off;* comp. John xv. 2. The word *thou* refers here to the Gentile churches. In relation to them the favour of God was dependent on their fidelity. If they became disobedient and unbelieving, then the same *principle* which led him to withdraw his mercy from the Jewish people would lead also to their rejection and exclusion. And on this principle, God has acted in numberless cases. Thus his favour was withdrawn from the seven churches of Asia (Rev. i—iii.), from Corinth, from Antioch, from Philippi, and even from Rome itself.

23. *And they also.* The Jews. ¶ *If they bide not,* &c. If they do not continue in wilful obstinacy and rejection of the Messiah. As their unbelief was the sole cause of their rejection, so if that be removed, they may be again restored to the divine favour. ¶ *For God is able,* &c. He has, (1.) *Power* to restore them, to bring them back and replace them in his favour. (2.) He has not *bound* himself *utterly* to reject them, and for ever to exclude them. In this way the apostle reaches his purpose, which was to show them that God had not cast away his people or finally rejected the Jewish nation; ver. 1, 2. That God has this power, the apostle proceeds to show in the next verse.

24. *For if thou.* If you who are Gentiles. ¶ *Wert cut out of.* Or, if thou wert of the cutting of the wild olive-tree. ¶ *Which is wild by nature.* Which is uncultivated and unfruitful. That is, if you were introduced into a state of favour with God from a condition which was one of enmity and hostility to him. The argument here is, that it was in itself as difficult a thing to *reclaim* them, and change them from opposition to God to friendship, as it would seem difficult or impossible to reclaim and make fruitful the wild olive-tree. ¶ *And were graffed contrary to nature.* Contrary to your natural habits, thoughts, and practices. There was among the Gentiles no inclination or tendency towards God. This does not mean that they were *physically* depraved, or that their disposition was *literally* like the wild olive; but it is used, for the sake of illustration, to show that their moral character and habits were unlike those of the friends of God. ¶ *How much more,* &c. The meaning of this whole verse may be thus expressed; "If God had mercy on the Gentiles, who were outcasts from his favour, shall he not much rather on those who were so long his people, to whom had been given the promises, and the covenants, and the law, whose ancestors had been so many of them his friends, and among whom the Messiah was born?" In some respects, there are facilities among the Jews for their conversion, which had not existed among the Gentiles. They worship one God; they admit the authority of revelation; they have the Scriptures of the Old Testament; they expect a Messiah; and they have a *habit* of professed reverence for the will of God.

25. *Ignorant of this mystery.* The word *mystery* means properly that which is *concealed, hidden,* or *un-*

how much more shall these, which be the natural *branches*, be graffed into their own olive-tree?

25 For I would not, brethren, that ye should be ignorant of this mystery, lest ye should be wise in your own conceits, that blindness [1] in part [a] is happened to Israel, until the fulness [b] of the Gentiles be come in.

1 or, *hardness*. a ver.7; 2Cor.3.11. b Luke 21.24.

known. And it especially refers, in the New Testament, to the truths or doctrines which God had reserved to himself, or had not before communicated. It does not mean, as with us often, that there was any thing *unintelligible* or *inscrutible* in the nature of the doctrine itself, for it was commonly perfectly plain when it was made known. Thus the doctrine, that the division between the Jews and the Gentiles was to be broken down, is called a *mystery*, because it had been, to the times of the apostles, concealed, and was then revealed fully for the first time; Rom. xvi. 25; Col. i. 26, 27; comp. 1 Cor. xv. 51; Mark iv. 11; Eph. i. 9; iii. 3. Thus the doctrine which the apostle was stating was one that until then had been concealed, or had not been made known. It does not mean that there was any thing unintelligible or incomprehensive in it, but until then it had not been made known. ¶ *Lest ye should be wise in your own conceits.* Paul communicated the truth in regard to this, lest they should attempt to inquire into it; should speculate about the reason why God had rejected the Jews; and should be elated with the belief that they had, by their own skill and genius, ascertained the cause. Rather than leave them to vain speculations and self-gratulation, he chose to cut short all inquiry, by stating the truth about their present and future state. ¶ *Blindness.* Or hardness; see ver. 7. ¶ *In part.* Not *totally*, or entirely. They are not absolutely or completely blinded. This is a qualifying expression; but it does not denote *what* part or portion, or for what time it is to continue. It means that the blindness in respect to the whole nation was only partial. Some were then enlightened, and had become Christians; and many more *would* be. ¶ *To Israel.* To the Jews. ¶ *Until the fulness of the Gentiles,* &c. The word *fulness* in relation to the Jews is used in ver. 12. It means until the abundance or the great multitude of the Gentiles shall be converted. The word is not elsewhere used in respect to the Gentiles; and it is difficult to fix its meaning definitely. It doubtless refers to the future spread of the Gospel among the nations; to the time when it may be said that the *great mass*, the abundance of the nations, shall be converted to God. At present, they are, as they were in the times of the apostle, idolators, so that the *mass* of mankind are far from God. But the Scriptures have spoken of a time when the gospel shall spread and prevail among the nations of the earth; and to this the apostle refers. He does not say, however, that the Jews may not be converted until *all* the Gentiles become Christians; for he expressly supposes (ver. 12—15) that the conversion of the Jews will have an important influence in extending the gospel among the Gentiles. Probably the meaning is, that this blindness is to continue until *great numbers* of the Gentiles shall be converted; until the gospel shall be extensively spread; and *then* the conversion of the Jews will be *a part* of the rapid spread of the gospel, and will be among the most efficient and important aids in completing the work. If this is the case, then Christians may labour still for their conversion. They may *seek* that in connection with the effort to convert the heathen; and they may toil with the expectation that the conversion of the Jews and Gentiles will not be separate, independent, and distinct events; but will be intermingled, and will be perhaps simultaneous. The word *fulness* may denote such a *general* turning to God, without affirming that each individual shall be thus converted to the Christian faith.

26 And so all Israel shall be
saved: as it is written, [a] There shall
come out of Sion the Deliverer,
and shall turn away ungodliness
from Jacob:
27 For [b] this *is* my covenant

a Isa.59.20.

b Jer.31.31,&c.; Heb.10.16.

26. *And so.* That is, in this manner; or when the great abundance of the Gentiles shall be converted, then all Israel shall be saved. ¶ *All Israel.* All the Jews. It was a maxim among the Jews that "every Israelite should have part in the future age." (*Grotius.*) The apostle applies that maxim to his own purpose; and declares the sense in which it would be true. He does not mean to say that *every* Jew of every age would be saved; for he had proved that a large portion of them would be, in his time, rejected and lost. But the time would come when, *as a people,* they would be recovered; when the *nation* would turn to God; and when it could be said of them that, *as a nation,* they were restored to the divine favour. It is not clear that he means that even then every *individual* of them would be saved, but the *body* of them; the great *mass* of the nation would be. Nor is it said *when* this would be. This is one of the things which "the Father hath put in his own power;" Acts i. 7. He has given us the assurance that it *shall* be done to encourage us in our efforts to save them; and he has concealed the *time* when it shall be, lest we should relax our efforts, or feel that no exertions were needed to accomplish what *must* take place at a fixed time. ¶ *Shall be saved.* Shall be recovered from their rejection; be restored to the divine favour; become followers of the Messiah, and thus be saved as all other Christians are. ¶ *As it is written;* Isa. lix. 20. The quotation is not *literally* made, but the *sense* of the passage is preserved. The Hebrew is, "There shall come to Zion a Redeemer, and for those who turn from ungodliness in Jacob." There can be no doubt that Isaiah refers here to the times of the gospel. ¶ *Out of Zion. Zion* was one of the hills of Jerusalem. On this was built the city of David. It came thus to denote, in general, the church, or people of God. And when it is said that the Redeemer should come *out of Zion,* it means that he should arise among that people, be descended from themselves, or should not be a foreigner. The LXX. however render it, "the Redeemer shall come *on account of* Zion." So the Chaldee paraphrase, and the Latin Vulgate. ¶ *And shall turn away,* &c. The Hebrew is, "to those forsaking ungodliness in Jacob." The Septuagint has rendered it in the same manner as the apostle.

27. *For this is my covenant,* &c. This expression is found immediately following the other in Isa. lix. 21. But the apostle connects with it a part of *another* promise taken from Jer. xxxi. 33, 34; or rather he *abridges* that promise, and expresses *its substance,* by adding "when I shall take away their sins." It is clear that he intended to express the *general sense* of the promises, as they were well known to the Jews, and as it was a point concerning which he did not need to argue or reason with them, that God had made a covenant with them, and intended to restore them if they were cast off, and should then repent and turn to him. The time and manner in which this shall be, is not revealed. It may be remarked, however, that that passage does *not* mean that the Redeemer shall come *personally* and preach to them, or re-appear for the purpose of recalling them to himself; nor does it mean that they will be restored to the land of their fathers. Neither of these ideas is contained in the passage. God will doubtless convert the Jews, as he does the Gentiles, by human means, and in connection with the prayers of his people; so that the Gentiles shall yet *repay* the toil and care of the ancient Jews in preserving the Scriptures, and preparing the way for the Messiah; and *both* shall

unto them, when I shall take away their sins.

28 As concerning the gospel, *they are* enemies for your sakes: but as touching the election, *they are* beloved [a] for the fathers' sakes.

29 For the gifts and calling of God *are* without [b] repentance.

[a] Deut. 10.15. [b] Num.23.19.

rejoice that they were made helps in spreading the knowledge of the Messiah.

28. *As concerning the gospel.* So far as the gospel is concerned; or, in order to promote its extension and spread through the earth. ¶ *They are enemies.* The word *enemies* here stands opposed to "beloved;" and as in *one* respect, to wit, on account of "election," they were still beloved, *i. e.* beloved *by God*, so in another respect they were his enemies, *i. e.* opposed to him, or cast off from him. The enemies of God denote all who are not his true friends; Col. i. 21; Rom. v. 10; comp. ver. 8. The word here is applied to the Jews because they had rejected the Messiah; had become opposed to God; and were therefore rejected by him. ¶ *For your sakes.* For your advantage. Their rejection has become the occasion by which the gospel has been preached to you; comp. ver. 11, 19, 20. ¶ *As touching the election.* So far as the purpose of election is concerned. That is, the election of their fathers and of the nation to be the peculiar people of God. ¶ *They are beloved.* God still regards them with interest; has purposes of mercy towards them; intends still to do them good. This does not mean that he *approved* of their conduct or character, or that he had for them the same kind of affection which he would have had if they had been obedient. God does not love a sinful character; but he may have still purposes of mercy, and regard men with deep interest on whom he intends yet to bestow mercy. ¶ *For the fathers' sakes;* comp. Deut. x. 15. He had chosen their fathers to be his peculiar people. He had made many promises to Abraham respecting his seed, and extended these promises to his remotest posterity. Though salvation is by grace, and not from human merit, yet God has respect to his covenant made with the fathers, and will not forget his promises. It is not on account of any *merit* of the fathers or of ancient saints, but solely because God had made a covenant with them; and this purpose of *election* would be manifest to their children in the latest times. As those contemplated in the covenant made with Abraham, God retained for them feelings of peculiar interest; and designed their recovery to himself. It is clear here that the word *election* does not refer to *external* privileges; for Paul is not teaching the doctrine that they shall be restored to the external privileges of Jews, but that they shall be truly converted to God. Yet this should not be abused by others to lead them to security in sin. No man has any security of happiness, and of the favour of God, but he who complies with the terms of his mercy. His commands are explicit to repent and believe, nor can there be safety except in entire compliance with the terms on which he is willing to bestow eternal life.

29. *For the gifts.* The favours or benefits which God bestows on men. The word χαρίσμα properly denotes any benefit which is conferred on another as a mere matter of *favour*, and not of *reward;* see Rom. v. 15, 16; vi. 23. Such are *all* the favours which God bestows on sinners including pardon, peace, joy, sanctification, and eternal life. ¶ *And calling of God.* The word *calling* (κλῆσις) here denotes that act of God by which he extends an *invitation* to men to come and partake of his favours, whether it be by a personal revelation as to the patriarchs, or by the promises of the gospel, or by the influences of his Spirit. All such invitations or callings imply a pledge that he will bestow

30 For as ye in times [a] past have not believed [1] God, yet have now obtained mercy through their unbelief:

31 Even so have these also now not believed, [1] that through your mercy they also may obtain mercy.

a Eph.2.2.

1 or, *obeyed.*

the favour, and will not *repent*, or turn from it. God never draws or invites sinners to himself without being willing to bestow pardon and eternal life. The word *calling* here, therefore, has not respect to external privileges, but to that *choosing* of a sinner, and influencing him to come to God, which is connected with eternal life. ¶ *Without repentance.* This does not refer to *man*, but to *God*. It does not mean that God confers his favours on man without his exercising repentance, but that *God* does not repent, or change, in his purposes of bestowing his gifts on man. What he promises he will fulfil; what he purposes to do, he will not change from or repent of. As he made promises to the fathers, he will not repent of them, and will not depart from them; they shall all be fulfilled; and thus it was certain that the ancient people of God, though many of them had become rebellious, and had been cast off, should not be forgotten and abandoned. This is a *general* proposition respecting God, and one repeatedly made of him in the Scriptures; see Num. xxiii. 19, "God is not a man, that he should lie; neither the son of man, that he should repent: hath he not said, and shall he not do it? hath he spoken, and shall he not make it good?" Ezek. xxiv. 14; 1 Sam. xv. 29; Ps. lxxxix. 35, 36; Tit. i. 2; Heb. vi. 18; James i. 17. It follows from this, (1.) That all the promises made to the people of God shall be fulfilled. (2.) That his people need not be discouraged or desponding, in times of persecution and trial. (3.) That none who become his true friends will be forsaken, or cast off. God does not bestow the gift of repentance and faith, of pardon and peace, on men, for a temporary purpose; nor does he capriciously withdraw them, and leave the soul to ruin. When he renews a soul, it is with reference to his own glory; and to withdraw those favours, and leave such a soul once renewed to go down to hell, would be as much a violation of all the principles of his nature as it would be to all the promises of the Scripture. (4.) For God to forsake such a soul, and leave it to ruin, would imply that he *did* repent. It would suppose a *change* of purpose and of feeling. It would be the character of a capricious being, with no settled plan or principles of action; no confidence could be reposed in him, and his government would be unworthy the affections and trust of his intelligent creation.

30. *For as ye.* You who were Gentiles. ¶ *In times past.* Before the gospel was preached. This refers to the former idolatrous and sinful state of the heathen world; comp. Eph. ii. 2; Acts xiv. 16. ¶ *Have not believed God.* Or have not *obeyed* God. This was the character of all the heathen nations. ¶ *Yet have now obtained mercy.* Have been pardoned and admitted to the favour of God. ¶ *Through their unbelief.* By means of the unbelief and rejection of the Jews; see Note on ver. 11.

31. *Even so have these*, &c. That is, the Jews. ¶ *That through your mercy*, &c. The *immediate* effect of the unbelief of the Jews was to confer salvation on the Gentiles, or to open the way for the preaching of the gospel to them. But its *remote* effect would be to secure the preaching of the gospel again to the Jews. Through the *mercy*, that is, the *compassion* or deep feeling of the converted Gentiles; through the deep and tender pity which they would feel for the blinded and degraded Jews; the gospel should be again carried to them, and they should be recalled to the long lost favour of God. Each party should thus cause salvation to come to the other—the Jews to the Gentiles by their *unbelief;* but the Gentiles, in

32 For God [a] hath [1] concluded
them all in unbelief, that he might
have mercy upon all.
33 O [b] the depth of the riches
both of the wisdom and knowledge
of God! How unsearchable [c] *are*
his judgments, and his ways past
finding out!

a chap.3.33; Gal.3.22. 1 or, *shut them all up together*. *b* Ps.107.8,&c. *c* Job 11.7; Ps.92.5.

their turn, to the Jews by their *belief*. We may here learn, (1.) That the Jews are to be converted by the instrumentality of the Gentiles. It is not to be by miracle, but by the regular and common way in which God blesses men. (2.) That this is to be done by the *mercy*, or *compassion* of the Gentiles; by their taking pity on the lost and wretched condition of the Jewish people. (3.) It is to be when the *abundance* of the Gentiles—that is, when great numbers of the Gentiles—shall be called in. It may be asked here whether the time is not approaching for the Gentiles to make efforts to bring the Jews to the knowledge of the Messiah. Hitherto those efforts have been unsuccessful; but it will not always be so; the time is coming when the promises of God in regard to them shall be fulfilled. Christians shall be moved with deep compassion for the degraded and forsaken Jews, and they shall be called into the kingdom of God, and made efficient agents in extending the gospel through the whole world. May the time soon come when they shall feel as they *should*, for the rejected and forsaken children of Abraham, and when their labours for their conversion shall be attended with success.

32. *For God hath concluded*, &c. The word here translated "concluded" (συνέκλεισε), is rendered in the margin "shut them all up together." It is properly used in reference to those who are shut up in prison, or to those in a city who are shut up by a besieging army; 1 Mac. v. 5; vi. 18; xi. 65; xv. 25; Josh. vi. 6; Isa. xlv. 1. It is used in the New Testament of *fish* taken in a net; Luke v. 6, "They *enclosed* a great multitude of fishes;" Gal. iii. 22, "But the Scripture hath *concluded* all under sin, that the promise," &c. In this place the Scripture is declared to have *shut them up* under sin, *i. e.* *declared* them to be sinners; gave no hope of rescue by any works of their own; and thus *kept them* (ver. 23) "*shut up* unto the faith which should afterwards be revealed." All are represented, therefore, as in *prison*, enclosed or confined by God, and to be liberated only in his own way and time. In regard to the *agency* of God in this, we may remark, (1.) That the word does not mean that God *compelled* them to disbelieve the gospel. When, in Gal. iii. 22, the Scripture is said to have *included* all under sin, it is not meant that the Scripture *compelled* them not to believe. (2.) The word does not imply that the sin and unbelief for which they were shut up were not voluntary. Even when a man is committed to prison, the crime which brought him there is voluntary, and for it he is responsible. (3.) The keeper of a prison does no wrong in confining a criminal; or the judge in condemning him; or the executioner in fulfilling the sentence of the law. So of God. What he does is not to *compel* men to remain under unbelief, but to *declare* that they are so; so to encompass them with the proof of it that they shall realize that there is no escape from the evidence of it, and thus to *press* on them the evidence of their need of a Saviour. This he does in relation to all sinners who ever become converted. (4.) Yet God permitted this; suffered Jews and Gentiles to fall into unbelief, and to be concluded under it, because he had a special purpose to answer in leaving man to the power of sin and unbelief. One of those purposes was, doubtless, to manifest the power of his grace and mercy in the plan of redemption. (5.) In all this, and in all other sin. man is voluntary. He chooses his course of evil; and God is under no obligation to *compel* him to do otherwise. Being *under* unbelief, God declares the *fact*,

and avails himself of it, in the plan of salvation by grace. ¶ *Them all.* Both Jews and Gentiles. ¶ *In unbelief* (εἰς). *Unto* unbelief. He has delivered them over *unto* unbelief, as a man is delivered over into prison. This is the literal meaning of the expression. ¶ *That he might have mercy upon all. Mercy* is favour shown to the undeserving. It could not have been shown to the Jews and the Gentiles unless it was before proved that they were guilty. For this purpose proof was furnished that they were all in unbelief. It was clear, therefore, that if favour was shown to either, it must be on the same ground, that of mere undeserved *mercy.* Thus all men were on a level; and thus all might be admitted to heaven without any invidious distinctions, or any dealings that were not in accordance with mercy and love. "The emphasis in this verse is on the word MERCY. It signifies that God is under obligation to no one, and therefore that all are saved by grace, because all are equally ruined." (*Calvin.*) It does not prove that all men will be saved; but that those who *are* saved shall be alike saved by the mercy of God; and that He intends to confer salvation on Jews and Gentiles on the same terms. This is properly the close of the argument of this epistle. By several independent trains of reasoning, the apostle had come to the same conclusion, that the Jews had no peculiar privileges in regard to religion, that all men were on a level, and that there was no hope of salvation for any but in the mercy of a sovereign God. This conclusion, and the wonderful train of events which had led to this state of things, give rise to the exclamations and ascriptions of praise with which the chapter closes.

33. *O the depth,* &c. This passage should have been translated "O the depth of the riches, *and* of the wisdom, and of the knowledge of God." The apostle has *three* subjects of admiration. Our translation, by the word "both" introduced here, confines it to two. The apostle wishes to express his admiration of the riches *and* the wisdom, and the knowledge of God. So the Syriac, Arabic, &c. Our translation has followed the Latin Vulgate. The word *depth* is applied in the Scriptures to any thing vast and incomprehensible. As the *abyss* or the *ocean* is unfathomable, so the word comes to denote that which words cannot express, or that which we cannot comprehend; Ps. xxxvi. 6, "Thy judgments are a great deep;" 1 Cor. ii. 10, "The Spirit searcheth ...the deep things of God;" Rev. ii. 24, "The *depths* of Satan"—the deep, profound, cunning, and wicked plans of Satan. ¶ *Riches;* see Note, ver. 12. The word denotes the abundant blessings and mercies which had been conferred on sinful men by the gospel. These were vast and wonderful. The pardon of sin; the atonement; the hope of heaven; the peace of the gospel; all bestowed on the sinful, the poor, the wretched, and the dying; all bespeak the great mercy and *rich* grace of God. So every pardoned sinner may still exclaim. The grace of God which pardons him is felt to be indeed wonderful, and past comprehension. It is beyond the power of language to express; and all that the Christian can do, is to follow the example of the apostle, and sit down in profound admiration of the rich grace of God. The expression "the depth of the riches" is a Hebraism, meaning the deep or profound riches. ¶ *The wisdom.* Wisdom is the choice of the best means to accomplish the best ends. The end or design which God had in view was to bestow mercy on all; *i. e.* to save men by *grace,* and not by their own works; ver. 32. He intended to establish a glorious system that should present his *mercy* as the prominent attribute, standing out in living colours in all the scheme of salvation. This was to be alike shown in relation to Jews and Gentiles. The wonderful wisdom with which this was done, is the object of the apostle's profound admiration. This wisdom was seen, (1.) In adapting the plan to the condition of man. All were sinners. The apostle in this epistle has fully shown that all had come short of the glory of God. Man had no power to save himself by his

own wisdom. The Jews and Gentiles in different ways had sought to justify themselves, and had both failed. God had suffered both to make the experiment in the most favourable circumstances. He had left the world for four thousand years to make the trial, and then introduced the plan of divine wisdom, just so as to meet the manifest wants and woes of men. (2.) This was shown in his making the *Jews* the occasion of spreading the system among the Gentiles. They were cast off, and rejected; but the God of wisdom had made even this an occasion of spreading his truth. (3.) The same wisdom was yet to be seen in his appointing the Gentiles to carry the gospel back to the Jews. Thus they were to be mutual aids; until all their interests should be blended, and the entire race should be united in the love of the same gospel, and the service of the same God and Saviour. When, therefore, this profound and wonderful plan is contemplated, and its history traced from the commencement to the end of time, no wonder that the apostle was fixed in admiration at the amazing wisdom of him who devised it, and who has made all events subservient to its establishment and spread among men. ¶ *And knowledge.* That is, foreknowledge, or omniscience. This *knowledge* was manifest, (1.) In the profound view of man, and acquaintance with all his wants and woes. (2.) In a view of the precise scheme that would be fitted to recover and save. (3.) In a view of the time and circumstances in which it would be best to introduce the scheme. (4.) In a discernment of the effect of the rejection of the Jews, and of the preaching of the gospel among the Gentiles. Who but God could see that such effects would follow the rejection of the Jews? Who but he could *know* that the gospel should yet prevail among all the nations? We have only to think of the changes in human affairs; the obstacles to the gospel; the difficulties to be surmounted; and the vast work yet to be done, to be amazed at the knowledge which can adapt such a scheme to men, and which can certainly predict its complete and final spread among all the families of man. ¶ *How unsearchable.* The word *unsearchable* means that which cannot be investigated or fully understood. ¶ *His judgments.* This word in this place evidently means his *arrangement*, his *plan*, or *proceeding.* It sometimes refers to laws; at other times to the decision or determination of God; at others to the inflictions of his justice. In this last sense it is now commonly used. But in the case before us, it means his arrangements for conferring the gospel on men. comp. Ps. xxxvi. 7, "His *judgments* are a great deep." ¶ *His ways.* The word rendered *ways* properly denotes a *path*, or *road* on which one travels. Hence it comes also to denote the *course* or manner of life in which one moves; or his principles, or morals; his doctrine, or teaching, &c. Applied to God, it denotes his mode or manner of doing things; the order, &c. of his divine Providence; his movements, in his great plans, through the universe; Acts xiii. 10, "Wilt thou not cease to pervert the *right ways* of the Lord?" to oppose, or to render vain, his plan of guiding and saving man; Heb. iii. 10, "They have not known my ways;" Ps. lxxvii. 19, "Thy way is in the sea, thy footsteps are not known." Here it refers particularly to his *way* or plan of bringing all nations within the reach of his mercy in the gospel. ¶ *Past finding out.* Literally, which cannot be *tracked* or *traced* out. The footsteps cannot be followed. As if his path were in the sea (Ps. lxvii. 19), and the waves closed immediately, leaving no *track*, it cannot be followed or sought out. It is known that he has passed, but there is no way of tracing his goings. This is a beautiful and striking figure. It denotes that God's plans are deep, and beyond our comprehension. We can see the proofs that he is every where; but *how* it is, we cannot comprehend. We are permitted to see the vast movements around us; but the invisible hand we cannot see, nor trace the footsteps of that mighty God who performs his wonders on the ocean and on the land.

34 For [a] who hath known the mind of the Lord? or who hath been his counsellor?

a Isa.40.13; Jer.23.18.

35 Or [b] who hath first given to him, and it shall be recompensed unto him again?

b Job 41.11.

34. *For who hath known?* &c. This verse is a quotation, with a slight change, from Isa. xl. 13, "Who hath directed the Spirit of the Lord, or being his counsellor hath taught him?" It is designed to express the *infinite* wisdom and knowledge of God, by affirming that no being could teach him, or counsel him. Earthly monarchs have counsellors of state, whom they may consult in times of perplexity or danger. But God has no such council. He sits alone; nor does he call in any or all of his creatures to advise him. All created beings are not qualified to contribute *any* thing to enlighten or to direct him. It is also designed to silence all opposition to his plans, and to hush all murmurings. The apostle had proved that this *was* the plan of God. However mysterious and inscrutable it might appear to the Jew or the Gentile, yet it was his duty to submit to God, and to confide in his wisdom, though he was not able to trace the reason of his doings.

35. *Or who hath,* &c. The sentiment in this verse is found substantially in Job xli. 11, "Who hath prevented me, that I should repay him." The Hebrew word "prevented" means to *anticipate*, to *go before;* and God asks "who has *anticipated* me; who has conferred favours on me before I have on him; who has thus laid me under *obligation* to him." This is the sense in which the apostle uses the word here. Who has, by his services, laid God under obligation to recompense or pay him again? It is added in Job, "Whatsoever is under the whole heaven is mine." Thus Paul, contrary to the prevailing doctrine of the Jews, shows that no one could plead his own merits, or advance with a *claim* on God. All the favours of salvation must be bestowed by mercy or grace. God owned them all; and he had a right to bestow them when and where he pleased. The same claim to *all* things is repeatedly made by God; Ex. xix. 5; Deut. x. 14; Ps. xxiv. 1; l. 12. ¶ *Shall be recompensed.* Repaid as a matter of debt. None of God's mercies can be conferred in that way; if they could, man could bring God under obligation, and destroy the freeness and benevolence of his favours.

36. *For of him* (ἐξ αὐτοῦ); comp. 1 Cor. i. 30; viii. 6. This expression doubtless means that he is the original source and fountain of all blessings. He is the Creator of all, the rich "fountain from which all streams of existence take their rise." The design of this verse is to show that no creature has any *claim* on God. Jews and Gentiles must alike receive salvation on the ground of his *mercy.* So far from having a *claim* on God, the apostle here affirms that *all* things have come from him, and therefore all must be derived to us. Nothing has been produced by chance, or haphazard; nothing by created skill or might. All has been formed by God; and therefore he has a right to dispose of all. ¶ *And through him* (δι' αὐτοῦ.) That is, by his immediate operating agency. The former expression, "of him," affirmed that he was the *original* source of all things; this declares that all are *by* him, or through him, as their *immediate* cause. It is not merely by his plan or purpose; it is by his agency, by the direct exertion of his power in their creation and bestowment. By his power they are still directed and controlled. Human agency, therefore, could not lay him under any obligation. He does not *need* the aid of man; and he did not call in that aid in the creation and government of the world. He is the independent Creator and Lord, and on him none can have a claim. ¶ *To him* (εἰς αὐτὸν). This expression denotes the *final cause,* the reason or end for which all things were formed. It is to promote *his* honour and glory. It is to manifest his praise, or to give a proper putting forth of the glorious attributes of God; that the exceeding

36 For [a] of him, and through him, and to him, *are* all things: to [1] whom *be* glory for ever. Amen.

a 1 Cor.8.6; Col.1.16.

1 *Him.*

greatness, and goodness, and grandeur of his character might be evinced. It is not to promote his *happiness,* for he was eternally happy; not to *add* any thing to him, for he is infinite; but that he might act *as God,* and have the honour and praise that is due to God. As this was the design of all things, so it followed that the bestowment of his favours must be in accordance with this—in such a way as to promote *his* glory; and not so as to consult the feelings or views of either Jews or Gentiles. ¶ *All things.* The universe; the creation, or still more particularly, the things of which the apostle is discoursing. He does not affirm that he is the author of sin or of sinful thoughts; not that he creates evil, or that evil is designed to promote his glory. The apostle is not discoursing of these, but of his method of bestowing his favours; and he says that *these* are to be conferred in such a way as to promote *his* honour, and to declare the praise of him who is the original source, the creator, and the proprietor of all things. ¶ *To whom be glory.* This ascription of praise is the appropriate close of the *argumentative* part of the epistle, as well as appropriate to the train of remarks into which the apostle had fallen. It expresses his hearty *amen* in concurrence with this view; the deep desire of a pious man that all *might* be to God's glory and honour. He had not merely come to it by *reasoning,* but it was the sincere desire of his soul that it *might* be so. The Christian does not merely *admit* this doctrine; he is not merely *driven* to it by argument, but it finds a hearty response in his bosom. He rejoices in it; and sincerely desires that all may be to the honour of God. Sinners are often *compelled* by argument to *admit* it, but they do not love it. They would rejoice were it otherwise, and be glad if they were permitted rather to seek their own glory than that of the living God. ¶ *Glory.* Praise, honour. ¶ *For ever.* Not merely amid transitory events now, but ever onward to eternity. This will be the case. There never will be a time when the affairs of the universe shall not be conducted with reference to the glory of God. That honour and glory shall shine brighter and brighter, and all worlds shall be perfectly adapted to show his praise, and to evince his greatness, goodness, power, and love for ever and ever. Thus let it be, is the language of every one that truly loves him.

This closes the argumentative part of the epistle. From the close of this chapter we may make the following observations.

1. God is infinitely wise, and just, and good. This is seen in all his plans and doings, and especially in the glorious plan of saving men.

2. It becomes man to be *humble.* He can see but few of the reasons of the doings of an infinite God. He is not qualified to sit in judgment on his plans. He is not fitted to arraign him. There is nothing more absurd than for a man to contend with God, or to find fault with his plans; and yet there is nothing more common. Man speaks, and thinks, and reasons on the great things pertaining to the divine mind and plan, as if he were qualified to counsel the being of infinite wisdom, and to arraign at the bar of his own reason the being of infinite goodness.

3. It is our duty to be *submissive* to God. His plans may often require him to cross the path of our pleasures, or to remove some of our enjoyments. He tries us by requiring us to put confidence in him where we cannot *see* the reason of his doings, and to *believe* that he is qualified for universal empire. In all such cases it is our duty to submit to his will. He is seeking a grander and nobler object than our private good. He is seeking the welfare of a vast universe; and he best knows in what way that can be promoted.

4. God is the creator and proprietor of all things. It would be possible to

CHAPTER XII.

I BESEECH you therefore, brethren, by the mercies of God, that ye present your bodies [a] a living sacrifice, holy, acceptable unto God, *which is* your reasonable service.

a 1 Cor.6.15-20.

prove this from his works. But his word unequivocally asserts it. He has formed, and he upholds, and he directs all things for his glory. He who formed all has a right to all. He who is the source of life has the right to direct it, or to withdraw the gift. He on whom all depend has a right to homage and praise.

5. He has formed a universe that is eminently adapted to declare his glory. It evinces infinite power in its creation; and it is fitted to fill the mind with ever-growing wonder and gladness in its contemplation. The sacred writers were filled with rapture when they contemplated it; and all the discoveries of astronomy, and geology, and science in general, in modern times, are fitted to carry forward the wonder, and fill the lips with new expressions of praise. The universe is vast and grand enough to occupy the thoughts for ever. How little do we know of the wonders of his creation, even pertaining to this little world; to our own bodies and souls; to the earth, the ocean, the beast and the reptile, the bird and the insect; how much less of that amazing view of worlds and systems which modern astronomy has opened to our view,—the vast starry frame which the eye can penetrate for millions and millions of miles, and where it finds world piled on world, and system rising above system, in wonderful order and grandeur, and where the utmost power of the telescope can as yet find no bounds.

6. Equally true is this in his moral government. The system is such as to excite our wonder and praise. The creation and control of free, and active, and mighty minds is as wonderful as the creation and control of matter, even the vast masses of the planetary systems. Creation is filled with minds. God has peopled the worlds with conscious, free, and active intelligences. The wonderful wisdom by which he controls them; the amazing moral power by which he guards and binds them to himself, by which he restrains and awes the rebellious; and the complete subjection by which he will bring all yet at his feet, is as much replete with wonder as the wisdom and skill by which he framed the heavens. To govern *mind* requires more wisdom and skill than to govern matter. To control angels and men evinces more glory than to roll the streams or the ocean, or than to propel and guide the planets. And especially is this true of the plan of salvation. That wondrous scheme is adapted to call forth eternal praise, and to show *for ever* the wisdom and mercy of God. Without *such* a plan, we cannot see how the Divinity could be fully manifested; *with* that, we see God as God, vast, grand, mighty, infinite; but still seeking to do good, and having power to enter any vast mass of iniquity, and to diffuse purity and peace over the face of an alienated and dying world.

7. The salvation of sinners is not to promote their own glory primarily, but that of God. "He is first, and he last; he is midst, and without end," in their salvation. God seeks his own honour, and seeks it by their return and their obedience. But if they *will not* promote his glory in that way, they must be made to promote it in their ruin.

8. It is the duty of men to seek the honour of this infinitely wise and holy God. It commends itself to every man's conscience. God has formed us all; and man *can* have no higher destiny and honour than to be permitted to promote and spread abroad through all the universe the knowledge of a Being whose character is infinitely lovely, whose government is right, and whose presence and favour will diffuse blessings of salvation and eternal peace on all the wide creation that will be obedient to his will.

CHAPTER XII.

1. *I beseech you.* The apostle, having finished the *argument* of this

epistle, proceeds now to close it with a *practical* or *hortatory* application, showing its bearing on the duties of life, and the practical influence of religion. None of the doctrines of the gospel are designed to be cold and barren speculations. They bear on the hearts and lives of men; and the apostle therefore calls on those to whom he wrote to dedicate themselves without reserve unto God. ¶ *Therefore.* As the effect or result of the argument or doctrine. In other words, the whole argument of the eleven first chapters is fitted to show the obligation on us to devote ourselves to God. From expressions like these, it is clear that the apostle never supposed that the tendency of the doctrines of grace was to lead to licentiousness. Many have affirmed that such was the tendency of the doctrines of justification by faith, of election and decrees, and of the perseverance of the saints. But it is plain that Paul had no such apprehensions. After having fully stated and established those doctrines, he concludes that we ought *therefore* to lead holy lives, and on the ground of them he exhorts men to do it. ¶ *By the mercies of God.* The word *by* (διὰ) denotes here the *reason* why they should do it, or the *ground of appeal.* So great had been the mercy of God, that this constituted a *reason why* they should present their bodies, &c. see 1 Cor. i. 10; Rom. xv. 30. The word *mercies* here denotes favour shown to the undeserving, or kindness, compassion, &c. The plural is used in imitation of the Hebrew word for mercy, which has no singular. The word is not often used in the New Testament; see 2 Cor. i. 3, where God is called "the Father of mercies;" Phil. ii. 1; Col. iii. 12; Heb. x. 28. The particular mercy to which the apostle here refers, is that shown to those whom he was addressing. He had proved that all were by nature under sin; that they had no claim on God; and that he had showed great compassion in giving his Son to die for them in this state, and in pardoning their sins. This was a ground or reason why *they* should devote themselves to God. ¶ *That ye present.* The word used here commonly denotes the action of bringing and presenting an animal or other sacrifice before an altar. It implies that the action was a free and voluntary offering. Religion is free; and the act of devoting ourselves to God is one of the most free that we ever perform. ¶ *Your bodies.* The *bodies* of animals were offered in sacrifice. The apostle specifies their *bodies* particularly in reference to that fact. Still the entire animal was devoted; and Paul evidently meant here the same as to say, *present* YOURSELVES, your entire person, to the service of God; comp. 1 Cor. vi. 16; James iii. 6. It was not customary or proper to speak of a sacrifice as an offering of a soul or spirit, in the common language of the Jews; and hence the apostle applied their customary language of sacrifice to the offering which Christians were to make of themselves to God. ¶ *A living sacrifice.* A *sacrifice* is an offering made to God as an atonement for sin; or *any* offering made to him and his service as an expression of thanksgiving or homage. It implies that he who offers it presents it *entirely*, releases all claim or right to it, and leaves it to be disposed of for the honour of God. In the case of an *animal*, it was slain, and the blood offered; in the case of any other offering, as the first-fruits, &c., it was set apart to the service of God; and he who offered it released all claim on it, and submitted it to God, to be disposed of at his will. This is the offering which the apostle entreats the Romans to make: to devote themselves to God, as if they had no longer any *claim* on themselves; to be disposed of by him; to suffer and bear all that he might appoint; and to promote *his* honour in any way which *he* might command. This is the nature of true religion. ¶ *Living* (ζῶσαν). The expression probably means that they were to devote the vigorous, active powers of their bodies and souls to the service of God. The Jew offered his victim, slew it, and presented it *dead.* It could not be presented again. In opposition to this, we are to present ourselves with all our living, vital energies. Christianity does not require a service of death or inactivity. It demands vigorous and active powers in the service of God the Saviour. There is something very affecting in the view of such a sacrifice; in regarding life, with all its energies, its intellectual, and moral, and physical powers, as one long *sacrifice;* one continued offering unto God. An immortal being *presented* to him; presented voluntarily, with all his energies, from day to day, until life shall close, so that it may be said that he has lived and died an offering made freely unto God. This is religion. ¶ *Holy.* This means properly without blemish or defect. No other sacrifice could be made to God. The Jews were expressly forbid to offer that which was lame, or blind, or in any way deformed; Deut. xv. 21; Lev. i. 3, 10; iii. 1; xxii. 20; Deut. xvii. 1; comp. Mal. i. 8. If offered without any of these defects, it was regarded as *holy, i. e.* appropriately set apart, or consecrated to God. In like manner we are to consecrate to God our *best* faculties; the vigour of our minds, and talents, and time. Not the feebleness of sickness merely; not old age alone; not time which we cannot otherwise employ, but the first vigour and energies of the mind and body; our youth, and health, and strength. Our sacrifice to God is to be not divided, separate; but it is to be entire and complete. Many are expecting to be Christians in sickness; many in old age; thus purposing to offer unto him the blind and the lame. The sacrifice is to be free from sin. It is not to be a divided, and broken, and polluted service. It is to be with the best affections of our hearts and lives. ¶ *Acceptable unto God.* They are exhorted to offer such a sacrifice as *will be* acceptable to God; that is, such a one as he had just specified, one that was living and holy. No sacrifice should be made which is not acceptable to God. The offerings of the heathen; the pilgrimages of the Mahometans; the self-inflicted penalties of the Roman Catholics, uncommanded by God, cannot be acceptable to him. Those services will be acceptable to God, and those only, which he appoints; comp. Col. ii. 20—23. Men are not to *invent* services; or to *make* crosses; or to *seek* persecutions and trials; or to *provoke* opposition. They are to do just what God requires of them, and that will be acceptable to God. And this fact, that what we do is acceptable to God, is the highest recompense we can have. It matters little what *men* think of us, if *God* approves what we do. To please *him* should be our highest aim; the fact that we *do* please him is our highest reward. ¶ *Which is your reasonable service.* The word rendered *service* (λατρείαν) properly denotes *worship,* or the *homage* rendered to God. The word *reasonable* with us means that which is "governed by reason; thinking, speaking, or acting conformably to the dictates of reason" (*Webster*)*;* or that which can be shown to be rational or proper. This does not express the meaning of the original. That word (λογικὴν) denotes that which pertains to the mind, and a reasonable service means that which is mental, or pertaining to reason. It stands opposed, not to that which is foolish or unreasonable, but to the *external* service of the Jews, and such as they relied on for salvation. The worship of the Christian is that which pertains to the *mind,* or is spiritual; that of the Jew was *external.* Chrysostom renders this phrase "your spiritual ministry." The Syriac, "That ye present your bodies, &c., *by a rational ministry.*"

We may learn from this verse, (1.) That the proper worship of God is the free homage of the mind. It is not forced or constrained. The offering of ourselves should be voluntary. No other can be a true offering, and none other can be acceptable. (2.) We are to offer our entire selves, all that we have and are, to God. No other offering can be such as he will approve. (3.) The character of God is such as should lead us to that. It is a character of mercy; of long-continued and patient forbearance, and it should influence us to devote ourselves to him. (4.) It should be done without delay. God is as *worthy* of such service *now*

2 And [a] be not conformed to this world: but be ye transformed by the renewing of your mind, that ye may prove [b] what *is* that good, and acceptable, and perfect will of God.

a 1 John 2.15. b Eph.5.10,17.

---

as he ever *will* or *can* be. He has every possible *claim* on our affections and our hearts.

2. *And be not conformed*, &c. The word rendered *conformed* properly means to put on the *form, fashion*, or *appearance* of another. It may refer to *any* thing pertaining to the habit, manner, dress, style of living, &c., of others. ¶ *Of this world* (τῷ αἰῶνι τούτῳ). The word which is commonly rendered *world*, when applied to the material universe, is κόσμος, *cosmos*. The word used here properly denotes an *age*, or *generation* of men. It may denote a *particular* generation, or it may be applied to the race. It is sometimes used in each of these senses. Thus here it may mean that Christians should not conform to the maxims, habits, feelings, &c., of a wicked, luxurious, and idolatrous age, but should be conformed solely to the precepts and laws of the gospel; or the same principle may be extended to *every age*, and the direction may be, that Christians should not conform to the prevailing habits, style, and manners of the world, the people who know not God. They are to be governed by the laws of the Bible; to fashion their lives after the example of Christ; and to form themselves by principles different from those which prevail in the world. In the *application* of this rule there is much difficulty. Many may think that *they* are not conformed to the world, while they can easily perceive that their neighbour is. They indulge in many things which others may think to be conformity to the world, and are opposed to many things which others think innocent. The design of this passage is doubtless to produce a spirit that should not find *pleasure* in the pomp and vanity of the world; and which will regard all vain amusements and gayeties with disgust, and lead the mind to find pleasure in better things. ¶ *Be ye transformed.* The word from which the expression here is derived means *form, habit* (μόρφη). The direction is, "put on another *form*, change the *form* of the world for that of Christianity." This word would properly refer to the *external appearance*, but the expression which the apostle immediately uses, "renewing of the mind," shows that he did not intend to use it with reference to that only, but to the change of the whole man. The meaning is, do not cherish a spirit devoted to the world, following its vain fashions and pleasures, but cultivate a spirit attached to God, and his kingdom and cause. ¶ *By the renewing.* By the *making new;* the changing into *new* views and feelings. The Christian is often represented as a *new creature;* 2 Cor. v. 17; Gal. vi. 15; Eph. iv. 24; 1 Pet. ii. 2. ¶ *Your mind.* The word translated *mind* properly denotes *intellect*, as distinguished from the will and affections. But here it seems to be used as applicable *to the whole spirit* as distinguished from the *body*, including the understanding, will, and affections. As if he had said, Let not this change appertain to the *body* only, but to the *soul.* Let it not be a mere *external* conformity, but let it have its seat in the spirit. All external changes, if the mind was not changed, would be useless, or would be hypocrisy. Christianity seeks to reign in the *soul;* and having its seat there, the external conduct and habits will be regulated accordingly. ¶ *That ye may prove.* The word used here (δοκιμάζω) is commonly applied to *metals*, to the operation of testing, or trying them by the severity of fire, &c. Hence it also means to explore, investigate, ascertain. This is its meaning here. The sense is, that such a *renewed* mind is essential to a successful inquiry after the will of God. Having a *disposition* to obey him, the mind will be prepared to understand his precepts. There will be a *correspondence* between the feelings of the heart and his will; a nice *tact* or taste, which will admit

3 For I say, through the grace
given unto me, to every man
that is among you, not to think
of himself more [a] highly than he
ought to think; but to [1] think
soberly, according as God hath

a chap.11.20. [1] to sobriety.

his laws, and see the propriety and beauty of his commands. A renewed heart is the best preparation for studying Christianity; as a man who is *temperate* is the best fitted to understand the arguments for temperance; the man who is chaste, has most clearly and forcibly the arguments for chastity, &c. A heart in love with the fashions and follies of the world is ill-fitted to appreciate the arguments for humility, prayer, &c. "If any man will do his will, he shall know of the doctrine whether it be of God," John vii. 17. The *reason why* the heart is renewed is that we may do the will of God: the heart that *is* renewed is best fitted to appreciate and understand his will. ¶ *That good*, &c. This part of the verse might be rendered, that ye may investigate the will of God, or ascertain the will of God, that which is good, and perfect, and acceptable. The *will of God* relates to his commands in regard to our conduct, his doctrines in regard to our belief, his providential dealings in relation to our external circumstances. It means what God demands of us, in whatever way it may be made known. They do not err from his ways who seek his guidance, and who, not confiding in their own wisdom, but in God, commit their way to him. "The meek will he guide in judgment, and the meek will he teach his way," Ps. xxv. 9. The word *good* here is not an *adjective* agreeing with "will," but a *noun*. "That ye may find the will of God, that which is good and acceptable." It implies that that thing which is *good is* his will; or that we may find his will by finding that which is good and perfect. That is good which promotes the honour of God and the interests of his universe. ¶ *Perfect*. Free from defect, stain, or injury. That which has all its parts complete, or which is not disproportionate. Applied to religion, it means that which is *consistent*, which is *carried out;* which is evinced in all the circumstances and reations of life. ¶ *Acceptable*. That which will be pleasing to God, or which he will approve. There is scarcely a more difficult text in the Bible than this, or one that is more full of meaning. It involves the main *duty* of religion to be separated from the world; and expresses the *way* in which that duty may be performed, and in which we may live so as to ascertain and do the will of God. If all Christians would obey this, religion would be every where honoured. If all would separate from the vices and follies, the amusements and gayeties of the world, Christ would be glorified. If all were truly renewed in their minds, they would lose their relish for such things, and seeking only to do the will of God, they would not be slow to find it.

3. *For I say*. The word "for" shows that the apostle is about to introduce some additional considerations to enforce what he had just said, or to show how we may evince a mind that is not conformed to the world. ¶ *Through the grace*. Through the *favour*, or in virtue of the favour of the apostolic office. By the *authority* that is conferred on me to declare the will of God as an apostle; see Note, chap. i. 5; see also Gal. i. 6, 15; ii. 9; Eph. iii. 8; 1 Tim. i. 14. ¶ *Not to think*, &c. Not to *over-estimate* himself, or to think more of himself than he ought to. What is the true standard by which we *ought* to estimate ourselves he immediately adds. This is a caution against *pride;* and an exhortation not to judge of ourselves by our talents, wealth, or office, but to form another standard of judging of ourselves, by our Christian character. The Romans would probably be in much danger from this quarter. The prevailing habit of judging among them was according to rank, or wealth, or eloquence, or office. While this habit of judging prevailed in the world around them, there was danger that it might also prevail in the church. And

dealt to every man the measure [a] of faith.

4 For as we have many [b] members in one body, and all

a Eph.4.7,&c.

b 1 Cor.12.4,12.

the exhortation was that they should not judge of their own characters by the usual modes among men, but by their Christian attainments. There is no sin to which men are more prone than an inordinate self-valuation and pride. Instead of judging by that which constitutes true excellence of character, they pride themselves on that which is of no intrinsic value; on rank, and titles, and external accomplishments; or on talents, learning, or wealth. The only true standard of character pertains to the principles of action, or to that which constitutes the *moral* nature of the man; and to that the apostle calls the Roman people. ¶ *But to think soberly.* Literally, "to think so as to act soberly or wisely." So to estimate ourselves as to act or demean ourselves wisely, prudently, modestly. Those who over-estimate themselves are proud, haughty, foolish in their deportment. Those who think of themselves as they ought, are modest, sober, prudent. There is no way to maintain a wise and proper conduct so certain, as to form a humble and modest estimate of our own character. ¶ *According as God hath dealt.* As God has *measured* to each one, or apportioned to each one. In this place *the faith* which Christians have, is traced to God as its giver. This *fact*, that *God* has given it, will be itself one of the most effectual promoters of humility and right feeling. Men commonly regard the objects on which they pride themselves as things of their own creation, or as depending on themselves. But let an object be regarded as the gift of God, and it ceases to excite *pride*, and the feeling is at once changed into *gratitude*. He, therefore, who regards *God* as the source of all blessings, and he only, will be an humble man. ¶ *The measure of faith.* The word *faith* here is evidently put for *religion*, or Christianity. Faith is a main thing in religion. It constitutes its *first* demand, and the Christian religion, therefore, is characterized by its *faith*, or its *confidence* in God; see Mark xvi. 17; comp. Heb. xi.; Rom. iv. We are not, therefore, to be elated in our view of ourselves; we are not to judge of our own characters by wealth, or talent, or learning, but by our attachment to God, and by the influence of faith on our minds. The meaning is, judge yourselves, or estimate yourselves, by your *piety*. The propriety of this rule is apparent, (1.) Because no other standard is a correct one, or one of value. Our talent, learning, rank, or wealth, is a very improper rule by which to estimate ourselves. All may be wholly unconnected with moral worth; and the worst as well as the best men may possess them. (2.) God will judge us in the day of judgment by our attachment to Christ and his cause (Mat. xxv.); and that is the true standard by which to estimate ourselves here. (3.) Nothing else will secure and promote humility but this. All other things may produce or promote pride, but this will effectually secure humility. The fact that *God* has given all that we have; the fact that the poor and obscure may have as true an elevation of character as ourselves; the consciousness of our own imperfections and short-comings in the Christian faith; and the certainty that we are soon to be arraigned to try this great question, whether we have evidence that we are the friends of God; will all tend to promote humbleness of mind, and to bring down our usual inordinate self-estimation. If all Christians judged themselves in this way, it would remove at once no small part of the pride of station and of life from the world, and would produce deep attachment for those who are blessed with the faith of the gospel, though they may be unadorned by any of the wealth or trappings which now promote pride and distinctions among men.

4. *For.* This word here denotes a further *illustration* or proof of what he had just before said. The duty to which he was exhorting the Romans was, not

members have not the same office;

5 So we, *being* many, are one body [a] in Christ, and every one members one of another.

6 Having then gifts differing [b]

a Eph.1.23.

b 1 Pet.4.10,11.

to be unduly exalted or elevated in their own estimation. In order to produce proper humility, he shows them that God has appointed certain orders or grades in the church; that all are useful in their proper place; that we should seek to discharge our duty in our appropriate sphere; and *thus* that due subordination and order would be observed. To show this, he introduces a beautiful comparison drawn from the human body. There are various members in the human frame; all useful and honourable in their proper place; and all designed to promote the order, and beauty, and harmony of the whole. So the church is one body, consisting of many members, and each is fitted to be useful and comely in its proper place. The same comparison he uses with great beauty and force in 1 Cor. xii. 4—31; also Eph. iv. 25; v. 30. In that chapter the comparison is carried out to much greater length, and its influence shown with great force. ¶ *Many members.* Limbs, or parts; feet, hands, eyes, ears, &c.; 1 Cor. xii. 14, 15. ¶ *In one body.* Constituting one body; or united in one, and making one person. Essential to the existence, beauty, and happiness of the one body or person. ¶ *The same office.* The same use or design; not all appointed for the same thing; one is to see, another to hear, a third to walk with, &c.; 1 Cor. xii. 14—23.

5. *So we, being many.* We who are Christians, and who are numerous as individuals. ¶ *Are one body.* Are united together, constituting one society, or one people, mutually dependent, and having the same great interests at heart, though to be promoted by us according to our peculiar talents and opportunities. As the welfare of the same body is to be promoted in one manner by the feet, in another by the eye, &c.; so the welfare of the body of Christ is to be promoted by discharging our duties in our appropriate sphere, as God has appointed us. ¶ *In Christ.* One body, *joined to* Christ, or connected *with* him as the head; Eph. i. 22, 23, "And gave him to be *head* over all things to the church, which is his *body;*" comp. John xv. 1—7. This does not mean that there is any *physical* or *literal* union, or any destruction of personal identity, or any thing particularly mysterious or unintelligible. Christians acknowledge him as their *head, i. e.* their lawgiver; their counsellor, guide, and Redeemer. They are bound to him by peculiarly tender ties of affection, gratitude, and friendship; they are united *in him, i. e.* in acknowledging him as their common Lord and Saviour. Any other union than this is impossible; and the sacred writers never intended that expressions like these should be explained *literally.* The union of Christians to Christ is the most tender and interesting of any in this world, but no more mysterious than that which binds friend to friend, children to parents, or husbands to their wives; comp. Eph. v. 23—33. [See Supp. Note on chap. VIII. verse 17.] ¶ *And every one members one of another;* comp. 1 Cor. xii. 25, 26. That is, we are so united as to be mutually dependent; each one is of service to the other; and the existence and office of the one is necessary to the usefulness of the other. Thus the members of the body may be said to be members one of another; as the feet could not, for example, perform their functions or be of use if it were not for the eye; the ear, the hand, the teeth, &c., would be useless if it were not for the other members, which go to make up the entire person. Thus in the church, every individual is not only necessary in his place as an individual, but is needful to the proper symmetry and action of the whole. And we may learn here, (1.) That no member of the church of Christ should esteem himself to be of no importance. In his own place he may be of as much consequence as the man of learning,

according to the grace that is given to us, whether prophecy, *let us prophesy* according to the proportion of faith.

---

wealth, and talent may be in his. (2.) God designed that there should be differences of endowments of nature and of grace in the church; just as it was needful that there should be differences in the members of the human body. (3.) No one should despise or lightly esteem another. All are necessary. We can no more spare the foot or the hand than we can the eye; though the latter may be much more curious and striking as a proof of divine skill. We do not despise the hand or the foot any more than we do the eye; and in all we should acknowledge the goodness and wisdom of God. See these thoughts carried out in 1 Cor. xii. 21—25.

6. *Having then gifts.* All the endowments which Christians have are regarded by the apostle as *gifts.* God has conferred them; and this fact, when properly felt, tends much to prevent our thinking of ourselves more highly than we ought to think, ver. 3. For the use of the word rendered *gifts,* see chap. i. 11; v. 15, 16; vi. 23; xi. 29; 1 Cor. vii. 7; xii. 4, 9, 28, &c. It may refer to natural endowments as well as to the favours of grace; though in this place it refers doubtless to the distinctions conferred on Christians in the churches. ¶ *Differing.* It was never designed that all Christians should be equal. God designed that men should have different endowments. The very nature of society supposes this. There never was a state of perfect equality in any thing; and it would be impossible that there should be, and yet preserve society. In this, God exercises a sovereignty, and bestows his favours as he pleases, injuring no one by conferring favours on others; and holding *me* responsible for the right use of what *I* have, and not for what may be conferred on my neighbour. ¶ *According to the grace.* That is, the *favour,* the *mercy* that is bestowed on us. As all that we have is a matter of *grace,* it should keep us from pride; and it should make us willing to occupy our appropriate place in the church. True honour consists not in splendid endowments, or great wealth and office. It consists in rightly discharging the duties which God requires of us in our appropriate sphere. If all men held their talents as the gift of God; if all would find and occupy in society the place for which God designed them, it would prevent no small part of the uneasiness, the restlessness, the ambition, and misery of the world. ¶ *Whether prophecy.* The apostle now proceeds to *specify* the different classes of gifts or endowments which Christians have, and to exhort them to discharge aright the duty which results from the rank or office which they held in the church. The first is *prophecy.* This word properly means to predict *future events,* but it also means to declare the divine will; to interpret the purposes of God; or to make known in any way the truth of God, which is designed to influence men. Its *first* meaning is to *predict* or *foretell* future events; but as those who did this were messengers of God, and as they commonly connected with such *predictions,* instructions, and exhortations in regard to the sins, and dangers, and duties of men, the word came to denote *any* who warned, or threatened, or in any way communicated the will of God; and even those who uttered devotional sentiments or praise. The name in the New Testament is commonly connected with *teachers;* Acts xiii. 1, "There were in the church at Antioch certain *prophets,* and teachers, as Barnabas," &c.; xv. 32, "And Judas and Silas, being *prophets* themselves," &c.; xxi. 10, "A certain prophet named Agabus." In 1 Cor. xii. 28, 29, *prophets* are mentioned as a class of teachers immediately *after* apostles, "And God hath set some in the church; first apostles, secondly *prophets;* thirdly teachers," &c. The same class of persons is again mentioned in 1 Cor. xiv. 29—32, 39. In this place they are spoken of as being under the influence of *revelation,* "Let the prophets speak two or three, and let the other judge. If any thing be *revealed* to another that sitteth by,

let the first hold his peace. And the spirits of the prophets are subject to the prophets;" ver. 39, "Covet to *prophesy*, and forbid not to speak with tongues." In this place endowments are mentioned under the name of *prophecy* evidently in advance even of the power of speaking with tongues. Yet all these were to be subject to the authority of the apostle. 1 Cor. xiv. 37. In Eph. iv. 11, they are mentioned again in the same order; "And he gave some apostles; and some prophets; and some evangelists; and some pastors, and teachers," &c. From these passages the following things seem clear in relation to this class of persons. (1.) They were an order of teachers distinct from the apostles, and *next* to them in authority and rank. (2.) They were under the influence of revelation, or inspiration in a certain sense. (3.) They had power of *controlling* themselves, and of speaking or keeping silence as they chose. They had the power of *using* their prophetic gifts as *we* have the ordinary faculties of our minds; and of course of *abusing* them also. This abuse was apparent also in the case of those who had the power of speaking with tongues, 1 Cor. xiv. 2, 4, 6, 11, &c. (4.) They were subject to the apostles. (5.) They were *superior* to the other teachers and pastors in the church. (6.) The office or the endowment was *temporary*, designed for the settlement and establishment of the church; and then, like the apostolic office, having accomplished its purpose, to be disused, and to cease. From these remarks, also, will be seen the propriety of *regulating* this office by apostolic authority; or stating, as the apostle does here, the *manner* or *rule* by which this gift was to be exercised. ¶ *According to the proportion.* This word (ἀναλογίαν) is no where else used in the New Testament. The word properly applies to mathematics (*Schleusner*), and means the ratio or proportion which results from comparison of one number or magnitude with another. In a large sense, therefore, as applied to other subjects, it denotes *the measure* of any thing. With us it means *analogy*, or the congruity or resemblance discovered between one thing and another, as we say there is an *analogy* or *resemblance* between the truths taught by reason and revelation. (See Butler's *Analogy*.) But this is not its meaning here. It means the *measure*, the *amount* of faith bestowed on them, for he was exhorting them to (ver. 3.) "Think soberly, according as God hath dealt to every man *the measure of faith*." The word *faith* here means evidently, not the truths of the Bible elsewhere revealed; nor their *confidence* in God; nor their personal piety; but the *extraordinary endowment* bestowed on them by the gifts of prophecy. They were to *confine* themselves strictly to that; they were not to *usurp* the apostolic authority, or to attempt to exercise *their* peculiar office; but they were to *confine* themselves *strictly* to the functions of their office according to the measure of their faith, *i. e.* the extraordinary endowment conferred on them. The word *faith* is thus used often to denote that extraordinary confidence in God which attended the working of miracles, &c., Matt. xvii. 26; xxi. 21; Luke xvii. 6. If this be the fair interpretation of the passage, then it is clear that the interpretation which applies it *to systems of theology*, and which demands that we should interpret the Bible so as to accord with the system, is one that is wholly unwarranted. It is to be referred solely to this class of religious teachers, without reference to any system of doctrine, or to any thing which had been revealed to any other class of men; or without affirming that there is any resemblance between one truth and another. All that may be true, but it is not the truth taught in this passage. And it is equally clear that the passage is not to be applied to teachers now, except as an illustration of the *general principle* that even those endowed with great and splendid talents are not to over-estimate them, but to regard them as the gift of God; to exercise them in subordination to his appointment; and to seek to employ them in the manner, the place, and to the purpose that shall be according to his will. *They are to employ them in*

7 Or ministry, *let us wait* on *our* ministering; or he that teacheth, on teaching;

8 Or he that exhorteth, on exhortation: he that [1] giveth, *let him do it* [2] with simplicity; he [a]

1 or, *imparteth.* 2 or, *liberally.* *a* Ps.ci.

the purpose for which God gave them; AND FOR NO OTHER.

7. *Or ministry* (διακονίαν). This word properly means *service* of any kind; Luke x. 40. It is used in religion to denote the *service* which is rendered to Christ as the *Master.* It is applied to *all* classes of ministers in the New Testament, as denoting their being the *servants* of Christ; and it is used particularly to denote that class who from this word were called *deacons, i. e.* those who had the care of the poor, who provided for the sick, and who watched over the *external* matters of the church. In the following places it is used to denote the *ministry,* or *service,* which Paul and the other apostles rendered in their public work; Acts i. 17, 25; vi. 4; xii. 25; xx. 24; xxi. 19; Rom. xi. 13; xv. 31; 2 Cor. v. 18; vi. 3; Eph. iv. 12; 1 Tim. i. 12. In a few places this word is used to denote the office which the *deacons* fulfilled; Acts vi. 1; Acts xi. 29; 1 Cor. xvi. 15; 2 Cor. xi. 8. In this sense the word *deacon* (διάκονος) is most commonly used, as denoting the office which was performed in providing for the poor and administering the alms of the church. It is not easy to say in what sense it is used here. I am inclined to the opinion that he did *not* refer to those who were appropriately called *deacons,* but to those engaged in the office of the *ministry of the word;* whose business it was to preach, and thus to serve the churches. In this sense the word is often used in the New Testament, and the connection seems to demand the same interpretation here. ¶ *On our ministering.* Let us be wholly and diligently occupied in this. Let this be our great business, and let us give entire attention to it. Particularly the connection requires us to understand this as directing those who *ministered* not to aspire to the office and honours of those who prophesied. Let them not think of themselves more highly than they ought, but be engaged entirely in their own appropriate work. ¶ *He that teacheth.* This word denotes those who *instruct,* or communicate knowledge. It is clear that it is used to denote a class of persons different, in some respects, from those who *prophesied* and from those who *exhorted.* But in what this difference consisted, is not clear. *Teachers* are mentioned in the New Testament in the grade next to the *prophets;* Acts xiii. 1; 1 Cor. xii. 28, 29; Eph. iv. 11. *Perhaps* the difference between the *prophets,* the *ministers,* the *teachers,* and the *exhorters* was this, that the first spake by inspiration; the second engaged in all the functions of the ministry properly so called, including the administration of the sacraments; the teachers were employed in communicating instruction simply, teaching the *doctrines* of religion, but without assuming the office of ministers; and the fourth *exhorted,* or entreated Christians to lead a holy life, without making it a particular subject to *teach,* and without pretending to administer the ordinances of religion. The fact that *teachers* are so often mentioned in the New Testament, shows that they were a class by themselves. It may be worthy of remark that the churches in New England had, at first, a class of men who were called *teachers.* One was appointed to this office in every church, distinct from the pastor, whose proper business it was to *instruct* the congregation in the *doctrines* of religion. The same thing exists substantially now in most churches, in the appointment of Sunday school *teachers,* whose main business it is to instruct the children in the doctrines of the Christian religion. It is an office of great importance to the church; and the exhortation of the apostle may be applied to them: that they should be assiduous, constant, diligent in their teaching; that they should confine themselves to their appropri-

that ruleth, with diligence; he that sheweth mercy, with cheerfulness. [a]

9 *Let* love be without dissimulation. [b] Abhor [c] that which is evil; cleave to that which is good.

a 2 Cor.9.7. b 1 Pet.1.22. c Ps.34.14.

ate place; and should feel that their office is of great importance in the church of God; and remember that this is *his* arrangement, designed to promote the edification of his people.

8. *He that exhorteth.* This word properly denotes one who urges to the *practical duties* of religion, in distinction from one who teaches its *doctrines.* One who presents the *warnings* and the *promises* of God to excite men to the discharge of their duty. It is clear that there were persons who were recognised as engaging especially in this duty, and who were known by this appellation, as distinguished from prophets and teachers. How long this was continued, there is no means of ascertaining; but it cannot be doubted that it may still be expedient, in many times and places, to have persons designated to this work. In most churches this duty is now blended with the other offices of the ministry. ¶ *He that giveth.* Margin, "*imparteth.*" The word denotes the person whose office it was to distribute; and probably designates him who distributed the *alms* of the church, or him who was the *deacon* of the congregation. The *connection* requires that this meaning should be given to the passage; and the word rendered *giveth* may denote one who imparts or distributes that which has been *committed to him for that purpose,* as well as one who gives out of his private property. As the apostle is speaking here of *offices* in the church, the former is evidently that which is intended. It was deemed an important matter among the early Christians to impart *liberally* of their substance to support the poor, and provide for the needy; Acts ii. 44—47; iv. 34—37; v. 1—11; Gal. ii. 10; Rom. xv. 26; 2 Cor. viii. 8; ix. 2, 12. Hence it became necessary to appoint persons over these contributions, who should be especially charged with the management of them, and who would see that they were properly distributed; Acts vi. 1—6. *These* were the persons who were denominated *deacons;* Phil. i. 1; 1 Tim. iii. 8, 12. ¶ *With simplicity;* see Mat. vi. 22, "If thine eye be *single,*" &c.; Luke xi. 34. The word *simplicity* (ἁπλοτής) is used in a similar sense to denote *singleness,* honesty of aim, purity, integrity, without any mixture of a base, selfish, or sinister end. It requires the bestowment of a favour without seeking any *personal* or selfish ends; without partiality; but actuated only by the desire to bestow them in the best possible manner to promote the object for which they were given; 2 Cor. viii. 2; ix. 11, 13; i. 12; Eph. vi. 5; Col. iii. 22. It is plain that when *property* was intrusted to them, there would be danger that they might be tempted to employ it for selfish and sinister ends, to promote their influence and prosperity; and hence the apostle exhorted them to do it with a *single aim* to the object for which it was given. Well did he know that there was nothing more tempting than the possession of wealth, though given to be appropriated to others. And this exhortation is applicable not only to the deacons of the churches, but to all who in this day of Christian benevolence are intrusted with money to advance the kingdom of the Lord Jesus Christ. ¶ *He that ruleth.* This word properly designates one who is *set over* others, or who *presides* or rules, or one who attends with diligence and care to a thing. In 1 Thess. v. 12, it is used in relation to ministers in general: "And we beseech you, brethren, to know them which labour among you, and *are over you* in the Lord;" 1 Tim. iii. 4, 5, 12, it is applied to the head of a family, or one who diligently and faithfully performs the duty of a father: "One that ruleth well his own house;" 1 Tim. v. 17, it is applied to "*elders*" in the church: "Let the elders that rule well," &c. It is not elsewhere used except in Titus iii. 8, 14, in a differ-

ent sense, where it is translated "*to maintain* good works." The prevailing sense of the word, therefore, is to *rule*, to *preside over*, or to have the management of. But to what class of persons reference is had here, and what was precisely their duty, has been made a matter of controversy, and it is not easy to determine. Whether this refers to a *permanent* office in the church, or to an *occasional* presiding in their assemblies convened for business, &c. is not settled by the use of the word. It has the idea of *ruling*, as in a family, or of *presiding*, as in a deliberate assembly; and either of these ideas would convey all that is implied in the original word; comp. 1 Cor. xii. 28. ¶ *With diligence*. This word properly means *haste* (Mark vi. 25; Luke i. 39); but it also denotes *industry, attention, care;* 2 Cor. vii. 11, "What *carefulness* it wrought in you;" 12, "That our *care* for you in the sight of God," &c.; viii. 7, 8, (Gr.) Heb. vi. 11. It means here that they should be *attentive* to the duties of their vocation, and engage with *ardour* in that which was committed to them to do. ¶ *He that showeth mercy*. It is probable, says Calvin, that this refers to those who had the care of the sick and infirm, the aged and the needy; not so much to *provide* for them by charity, as to attend on them in their affliction, and to take care of them. To the *deacons* was committed the duty of distributing alms, but to others that of *personal* attendance. This can hardly be called an *office*, in the technical sense; and yet it is not improbable that they were designated to this by the church, and requested to perform it. There were no hospitals and no almshouses. Christians felt it their duty to show personal attention to the infirm and the sick; and so important was their office, that it was deemed worthy of notice in a general direction to the church. ¶ *With cheerfulness*. The direction given to those who distributed alms was to do it *with simplicity*, with an honest aim to meet the purpose for which it was intrusted to them. The direction here varies according to the duty to be performed. It is to be done with cheerfulness, pleasantness, joy; with a kind, benign, and happy temper. The importance of this direction to those in this situation is apparent. Nothing tends so much to enhance the value of personal attendance on the sick and afflicted, as a kind and cheerful temper. If any where a mild, amiable, cheerful, and patient disposition is needed, it is near a sick bed, and when administering to the wants of those who are in affliction. And whenever we may be called to such a service, we should remember that this is indispensable. If moroseness, or impatience, or fretfulness is discovered in us, it will pain those whom we seek to benefit, embitter their feelings, and render our services of comparatively little value. The needy and infirm, the feeble and the aged, have enough to bear without the impatience and harshness of professed friends. It may be added that the example of the Lord Jesus Christ is the brightest which the world has furnished of this temper. Though constantly encompassed by the infirm and the afflicted, yet he was always kind, and gentle, and mild, and has left before us *exactly* what the apostle meant when he said, "he that showeth mercy with cheerfulness." The example of the good Samaritan is also another instance of what is intended by this direction; comp. 2 Cor. ix. 7. This direction is particularly applicable to a physician.

We have here an account of the establishment, the order, and the duties of the different members of the Christian church. The amount of it all is, that we should discharge with fidelity the duties which belong to us in the sphere of life in which we are placed; and not despise the rank which God has assigned us; not to think of ourselves more highly than we ought; but to act well our part, according to the station where we are placed, and the talents with which we are endowed. If this were done, it would put an end to discontent, ambition, and strife, and would produce the blessings of universal peace and order.

10 *Be* kindly [a] affectioned one to another [1] with brotherly love; in honour preferring [b] one another.

a 1 Pet.2.17. 1 or, *in the love of the brethren.* b 1 Pet.5.5.

9. Let *love.* The apostle proceeds to specify the duties of Christians in general, that they might secure the beauty and order of the church. The first which he specifies is *love.* This word here evidently refers to *benevolence,* or to good-will toward all mankind. In ver. 10 he specifies the duty of brotherly love; and there can be no doubt that he here refers to the benevolence which we ought to cherish towards all men. A similar distinction is found in 2 Pet. i. 7, "And to brotherly-kindness add *charity,*" *i. e.* benevolence, or good will, and kind feelings to others. ¶ *Without dissimulation.* Without *hypocrisy.* Let it be sincere and unfeigned. Let it not consist in words or professions only, but let it be manifested in acts of kindness and in deeds of charity; 1 John iii. 18; comp. 1 Pet. i. 22. Genuine benevolence is not that which merely *professes* attachment, but which is evinced by acts of kindness and affection. ¶ *Abhor that which is evil.* The word *abhor* means to hate; to turn from; to avoid. The word *evil* here has reference to *malice,* or *unkindness,* rather than to evil in general. The apostle is exhorting to *love,* or kindness; and *between* the direction to love all men, and the particular direction about brotherly love, he places this general direction to abhor that which is evil; that which is evil in relation *to the subject under discussion,* that is, *malice* or *unkindness.* The word *evil* is not unfrequently used in this limited sense to denote some particular or special evil; Mat. v. 37, 39, &c.; comp. Ps. xxxiv. 14; 2 Tim. ii. 19; Ps. xcvii. 10; 1 Thess. v. 22. ¶ *Cleave to that which is good.* The word rendered *cleave to* denotes properly the act of *gluing,* or uniting firmly by glue. It is then used to denote a very firm *adherence* to an object; to be firmly united to it. Here it means that Christians should be *firmly attached* to that which is good, and not *separate* or *part* from it. The *good* here referred to is particularly that which pertains to *benevolence*—to all men, and especially to Christians. It should not be *occasional only,* or irregular; but it should be constant, active, decided.

10. Be *kindly affectioned.* The word here used occurs no where else in the New Testament. It properly denotes tender affection, such as that which subsists between parents and children; and it means that Christians should have similar feelings towards each other, as belonging to the same family, and as united in the same principles and interests. The Syriac renders this, "Love your brethren, and love one another;" comp. 1 Pet. ii. 17. ¶ *With brotherly love.* Or in love to the brethren. The word denotes the affection which subsists between *brethren.* The duty is one which is often presented in the New Testament, and which our Saviour intended should be regarded as a badge of discipleship; see Note, John xiii. 34, 35, "By this shall all men know that ye are my disciples, if ye have love one to another; John xv. 12, 17; Eph. v. 2; 1 Thess. iv. 9; 1 Pet. i. 22; 1 John ii. 7, 8; iii. 11, 23; iv. 20, 21. The apostle Paul in this place manifests his peculiar manner of writing. He does not simply enjoin brotherly love, but he adds that it should be *kindly affectioned.* It should be with the *tenderness* which characterizes the most endearing natural relationship. This he expresses by a word which is made for the occasion (φιλόστοργοι), blending love with natural affection, and suffering it to be manifest in your intercourse with one another. ¶ *In honour.* In *showing* or *manifesting* respect or honour. Not in *seeking* honour, or striving after respect, but in showing it to one another. ¶ *Preferring one another.* The word *preferring* means going before, leading, setting an example. Thus in showing mutual respect and honour, they were to strive to excel; not to see which could *obtain* most honour, but which could *confer* most,

11 Not slothful in business; [a] [b] fervent in spirit; serving the [c] Lord.

12 Rejoicing [d] in hope; patient [e] in tribulation; continuing [f] instant in prayer;

a Acts 20.34,35. *b* Col.4.12. *c* Heb.12.28.

d chap.5.2,3. *e* James1.4. *f* Luke18.1.

or manifest most respect; comp. 1 Pet. i. 5; Eph. v. 21. Thus they were to be studious to show to each other all the respect which was due in the various relations of life; children to show proper respect to parents, parents to children, servants to their masters, &c.; and *all* to strive by mutual kindness to promote the happiness of the Christian community. How different this from the spirit of the world; the spirit which seeks, not to confer honour, but to obtain it; which aims, not to diffuse respect, but to attract all others to give honour to us. If this single direction were to be obeyed in society, it would put an end at once to no small part of the envy, and ambition, and heart-burning, and dissatisfaction of the world. It would produce contentment, harmony, love, and order in the community; and stay the progress of crime, and annihilate the evils of strife, and discord, and malice. And especially, it would give order and beauty to the church. It would humble the ambition of those who, like Diotrephes, love to have the pre-eminence (3 John 9), and make every man willing to occupy the place for which God has designed him, and rejoice that his brethren may be exalted to higher posts of responsibility and honour.

11. *Not slothful.* The word rendered *slothful* refers to those who are slow, idle, destitute of promptness of mind and activity; comp. Matt. xxv. 16. ¶ *In business* (τῇ σπουδῇ). This is the same word which in ver. 8 is rendered *diligence.* It properly denotes *haste, intensity, ardour of mind;* and hence also it denotes *industry, labour.* The direction means that we should be diligently occupied in our proper employment. It does not refer to any *particular* occupation, but is used in a *general sense* to denote *all* the labour which we may have to do; or is a direction to be faithful and industrious in the discharge of all our appropriate duties; comp. Eccl. ix. 10. The tendency of the Christian religion is to promote *industry.* (1.) It teaches the value of time. (2.) Presents numerous and important things to be done. (3.) It inclines men to be conscientious in the improvement of each moment. (4.) And it takes away the mind from those pleasures and pursuits which generate and promote indolence. The Lord Jesus was constantly employed in filling up the great duties of his life, and the effect of his religion has been to promote industry wherever it has spread both among nations and individuals. An *idle man* and a *Christian* are names which do not harmonize. Every Christian has enough to do to occupy *all* his time; and he whose life is spent in ease and in doing nothing, should doubt altogether his religion. God has assigned us much to accomplish; and he will hold us answerable for the faithful performance of it; comp. John v. 17; ix. 4; 1 Thess. iv. 11; 2 Thess. iii. 10, 12. All that would be needful to transform the idle, and vicious, and wretched, into sober and useful men, would be to give to them the spirit of the Christian religion; see the example of Paul, Acts xx. 34, 35. ¶ *Fervent.* This word is usually applied to water, or to metals so *heated* as to bubble, or boil. It hence is used to denote *ardour, intensity,* or as we express it, a *glow,*—meaning intense zeal, Acts xviii. 25. ¶ *In Spirit.* In your mind or heart. The expression is used to denote a mind filled with intense ardour in whatever it is engaged. It is supposed that Christians would first find appropriate objects for their labour, and then engage in them with intense ardour and zeal. ¶ *Serving* Regarding yourselves as the servants of the Lord. This direction is to be understood as connected with the preceding, and as growing out of it. They were to be diligent and fervid, and in *doing*

so were to regard themselves as *serving* the Lord, or to do it in obedience to the command of God, and to promote his glory. The propriety of this caution may easily be seen. (1.) The tendency of worldly employments is to take off the affections from God. (2.) Men are prone to forget God when deeply engaged in their worldly employments. It is proper to recall their attention to him. (3.) The right discharge of our duties in the various employments of life is to be regarded as serving God. He has arranged the order of things in this life to promote employment. He has made industry essential to happiness and success; and hence to be industrious from proper motives is to be regarded as acceptable service of God. (4.) He has *required* that all such employments should be conducted with reference to his will and to his honour, 1 Cor. x. 31; Eph. vi. 5; Col. iii. 17, 22—24; 1 Pet. iv. 11. The meaning of the whole verse is, that Christians should be *industrious,* should be ardently engaged in some lawful employment, and that they should pursue it with reference to the will of God, in obedience to his commands, and to his glory.

12. *Rejoicing in hope.* That is, in the hope of eternal life and glory which the gospel produces; see Notes on chap. v. 2, 3. ¶ *Patient in tribulation.* In affliction patiently enduring all that may be appointed. Christians may be enabled to do this by the sustaining influence of their *hope* of future glory; of being admitted to that world where there shall be no more death, and where all tears shall be wiped away from their eyes, Rev. xxi. 4; vii. 17; comp. James i. 4. See the influence of *hope* in sustaining us in affliction more fully considered in the Notes on chap. viii. 18—28. ¶ *Continuing instant in prayer.* That is, *be persevering* in prayer; see Col. iv. 2; see Notes, Luke xviii. 1. The meaning of this direction is, that in order to discharge aright the duties of the Christian life, and especially to maintain a joyful hope, and to be sustained in the midst of afflictions, it is necessary to cherish a spirit of prayer, and to live near to God. How *often* a Christian should pray, the Scriptures do not inform us. Of David we are told that he prayed seven times a-day (Ps. cxix. 164); of Daniel, that he was accustomed to pray three times a day (Dan. vi. 10); of our Saviour we have repeated instances of his praying mentioned; and the same of the apostles. The following rules, perhaps, may guide us in this. (1.) Every Christian should have some *time* allotted for this service, and some *place* where he may be alone with God. (2.) It is not easy, perhaps not possible, to maintain a life of piety without *regular* habits of secret devotion. (3.) *The morning,* when we have experienced God's protecting care, when the mind is fresh, and the thoughts are as yet clear and unoccupied with the world, when we go forth to the duties, trials, and temptations of the day; and *the evening,* when we have again experienced his goodness, and are about to commit ourselves to his protecting care, and when we need his pardoning mercy for the errors and follies of the day, seem to be times which commend themselves to all as appropriate seasons for private devotion. (4.) Every person will also find other times when private prayer will be needful, and when he will be inclined to it. In affliction, in perplexity, in moments of despondency, in danger, and want, and disappointment, and in the loss of friends, we shall feel the propriety of drawing near to God, and of pouring out the heart before him. (5.) Besides this, every Christian is probably conscious of times when he feels *peculiarly inclined* to pray; *he feels just like praying;* he has a spirit of supplication; and nothing *but* prayer will meet the instinctive desires of his bosom. We are often conscious of an earnest desire to see and converse with an absent friend, to have communion with those we love; and we value such fellowship as among the happiest moments of life. So with the Christian. He may have an earnest desire to have communion with God; his heart pants for it; and he cannot resist the propensity to seek him, and pour out his desires before him. Compare the feelings ex-

13 Distributing[a] to the necessity of saints; given to hospitality.[b]

14 Bless[c] them which persecute you: bless, and curse not.

a Ps.41.1; Heb.13.16. b Heb.13.2; 1 Pet.4.9. c Matt.5.44.

pressed by David in Ps. xlii. 1, 2, "As the hart panteth after the water-brooks, so panteth my soul after thee, O God. My soul thirsteth for God, for the living God; when shall I come and appear before God;" comp. Ps. lxiii. 1. Such seasons should be improved; they are the "spring times" of our piety; and we should expand every sail, that we may be "filled with all the fullness of God." They are happy, blessed moments of our life; and *then* devotion is sweetest and most pure; and then the soul knows what it is to have *fellowship* with the Father and with his Son Jesus Christ, 1 John i. 3. (6.) In addition to all this, Christians may be in the habit of praying to God without the formality of retirement. God looks upon the heart; and the *heart* may pour forth its secret desires to Him even when in business, when conversing with a friend, when walking, when alone, and when in society. Thus the Christian may live a life of prayer; and it shall be one of the characteristics of his life that *he prays!* By this he shall be known; and in this he shall learn the way to possess peace in religion.

"In every joy that crowns my days,
In every pain I bear.
My heart shall find delight in praise,
Or seek relief in prayer.

"When gladness wings my favour'd hour,
Thy love my thoughts shall fill,
Resign'd when storms of sorrow lower,
My soul shall meet thy will,

"My lifted eye, without a tear
The gathering storm shall see
My steadfast heart shall know no fear,
That heart shall rest on thee."

13. *Distributing.* The word used here denotes having things in *common* (κοινωνοῦντες). It means that they should be *communicative,* or should regard their property as so far *common* as to supply the wants of others. In the earliest times of the church, Christians had all things in common (Notes, Acts ii. 44), and felt themselves bound to meet all the wants of their brethren. One of the most striking effects of Christianity was to loosen their grasp on *property,* and dispose them to impart liberally to those who had need. The direction here does not mean that they should *literally* have all things *in common;* that is, to go back to a state of *savage barbarity;* but that they should be liberal, should *partake* of their good things with those who were needy; comp. Gal. vi. 6; Rom. xv. 27; Phil. iv. 15; 1 Tim. vi. 18. ¶ *To the necessity.* To the *wants.* That is, distribute to them such things as they *need,* food, raiment, &c. This command, of course, has reference to the *poor.* ¶ *Of saints.* Of Christians, or the friends of God. They are called *saints* as being holy (ἅγιοι), or consecrated to God. This duty of rendering aid to *Christians* especially, does not interfere with the general love of mankind. The law of the New Testament is (Gal. vi. 10), "As we have opportunity, let us do good to all men, especially to them who are of the household of faith." The Christian is indeed to love all mankind, and to do them good as far as may be in his power, Matt. v. 43, 44; Titus iii. 8; 1 Tim. vi. 18; Heb. xiii. 16. But he is to show *particular* interest in the welfare of his brethren, and to see that the poor members of the church are provided for; for, (1.) They are our brethren; they are of the same family; they are attached to the same Lord; and to do good to them is to evince love to Christ, Matt. xxv. 40; Mark ix. 41. (2.) They are left especially to the care of the church; and if the church neglects them, we may be sure the world will also, Matt. xxvi. 11. Christians, especially in the time of the apostles, had reason to expect little compassion from the men of the world. They were persecuted and oppressed; they would be embarrassed in their business, perhaps thrown out of occupation by the opposition of their enemies; and it was therefore

peculiarly incumbent on their brethren to aid them. To a certain extent it is always true, that the world is reluctant to aid the friends of God; and hence the poor followers of Christ are in a peculiar manner thrown on the benefactions of the church. (3.) It is not improbable that there might be a peculiar reason at that time for enjoining this on the attention of the Romans. It was a time of persecution, and perhaps of extensive distress. In the days of Claudius (about A. D. 50), there was a famine in Judea which produced great distress, and many of the poor and oppressed might flee to the capital for aid. We know, from other parts of the New Testament, that at that time the apostle was deeply interested in procuring aid for the poor brethren in Judea, Rom. xv. 25, 26; comp. Acts xix. 21; 2 Cor. viii. 1—7; ix. 2—4. But the same reasons for aiding the *poor* followers of Christ will exist substantially in every age; and one of the most precious *privileges* conferred on men is to be permitted to assist those who are the friends of God, Ps. xli. 1—3; Pr. xiv. 21. ¶ *Given to hospitality.* This expression means that they should *readily* and *cheerfully* entertain strangers. This is a duty which is frequently enjoined in the Scriptures, Heb. xiii. 2, "Be not forgetful to entertain strangers, for thereby many have entertained angels unawares;" 1 Pet. iv. 9, "Use hospitality one to another without grudging." Paul makes this especially the duty of a Christian bishop; 1 Tim. iii. 2, "A bishop then must...be given to hospitality;" Titus i. 8. Hospitality is especially enjoined by the Saviour, and its exercise commanded; Matt. x. 40, 42, "He that receiveth you receiveth me," &c. The *want* of hospitality is one of the charges which the Judge of mankind will allege against the wicked, and on which he will condemn them; Matt. xxv. 43, "I was a stranger, and ye took me not in." It is especially commended to us by the example of Abraham (Gen. xviii. 1—8), and of Lot (Gen. xix. 1, 2), who thus received angels unawares. It was one of the virtues on which *Job* particularly commended himself, and which he had not failed to practise; Job xxxi. 16, 17, "If I have withheld the poor from their desire, or have caused the eyes of the widow to fail; or *have eaten my morsel myself alone, and the fatherless hath* not eaten thereof," &c. In the time of our Saviour it was evidently practised in the most open and frank manner; Luke x. 7, "And in the same house remain, eating and drinking such things as they give." A remarkable instance is also mentioned in Luke xi. 5. This virtue is no less common in eastern nations at present than it was in the time of Christ. It is *eminently* the virtue of oriental nations, of their ardent and open temperament. It springs up naturally in countries thinly settled, where the sight of a stranger would be therefore peculiarly pleasant; in countries too, where the occupation was chiefly to attend flocks, and where there was much leisure for conversation; and where the population was too sparse, and the travellers too infrequent, to justify *inn-keeping* as *a business.* From all these causes, it has happened that there are, properly speaking, no *inns* or *taverns* in the regions around Palestine. It was customary, indeed, to erect places for lodging and shelter at suitable distances, or by the side of springs or watering places, for travellers to lodge in. But they are built at the public expense, and are unfurnished. Each traveller carries his own bed and clothes and cooking utensils, and such places are merely designed as a *shelter* for caravans; (see *Robinson's Calmet,* art. Caravanserai.) It is still so; and hence it becomes, in their view, a virtue of high order to entertain, at their own tables, and in their families, such *strangers* as may be travelling. Niebuhr says, that "the hospitality of the Arabs has always been the subject of praise; and I believe that those of the present day exercise this virtue no less than the ancients did. There are, in the villages of Tehama, houses which are public, where travellers may lodge and be entertained some days *gratis,* if they will be content with the fare; and they are much frequented. When

15 Rejoice [a] with them that do rejoice, and weep with them that weep.

16 *Be* [b] of the same mind one toward another. Mind [c] not high things, but condescend [1] to men of

a 1Cor.12.26. b 1Pet.3.8. c Jer.45.5. 1 or, *be contented with mean things.*

the Arabs are at table, they invite those who happen to come to eat with them, whether they be Christians or Mahometans, gentle or simple."—"The primitive Christians," says Calmet, "considered one principal part of their duty to consist in showing hospitality to strangers. They were in fact so ready in discharging this duty, that the very heathen admired them for it. They were hospitable to all strangers, but especially to those who were of the household of faith. Believers scarcely ever travelled without letters of communion, which testified the purity of their faith, and procured for them a favourable reception wherever the name of Jesus Christ was known;" (*Calmet,* Dict.) Calmet is also of opinion that the two minor epistles of John may be such letters of recommendation and communion; comp. 2 John 10. It may be added that it would be particularly expected of Christians that they should show hospitality to the ministers of religion. They were commonly poor; they received no fixed salary; they travelled from place to place; and they would be dependent for support on the kindness of those who loved the Lord Jesus Christ. This was particularly intended by our Saviour's instructions on the subject, Matt. x. 11—13, 40—42. The duty of *hospitality* is still binding on Christians and all men. The law of Christ is not repealed. The customs of society are indeed changed; and one evidence of advancement in commerce and in security, is furnished in the fact that *inns* are now provided and patronized for the traveller in all Christian lands. Still this does not lessen the obligations to show hospitality. It is demanded by the very genius of the Christian religion; it evinces proper love towards mankind; it shows that there is a feeling of *brotherhood* and kindness towards others, when such hospitality is shown. It unites society, creates new bonds of interest and affection, to show kindness to the stranger and to the poor. To what *extent* this is to be done, is one of those questions which are to be left to every man's conscience and views of duty. No *rule* can be given on the subject. Many men have not the means to be extensively hospitable; and many are not placed in situations that require it. No rules *could* be given that should be applicable to *all* cases; and hence the Bible has left the *general* direction, has furnished examples where it was exercised, has recommended it to mankind, and then has left every man to act on the rule, as he will answer it to God; see Matt. xxv. 34—46.

14. *Bless them,* &c; see Note, Mat. v. 44; comp. Luke vi. 28. ¶ *Bless, and curse not.* Bless only; or continue to bless, however long or aggravated may be the injury. Do not be provoked to anger, or to cursing, by any injury, persecution, or reviling. This is one of the most severe and difficult duties of the Christian religion; and it is a duty which nothing else *but* religion will enable men to perform. To *curse* denotes properly to *devote to destruction.* Where there is power to do it, it implies the destruction of the object. Thus the fig-tree that was cursed by the Saviour soon withered away; Mark xi. 21. Thus those whom *God* curses will be certainly destroyed; Mat. xxv. 41. Where there is not *power* to do it, *to curse* implies the invoking of the aid of God to devote to destruction. Hence it means to imprecate; to implore a curse from God to rest on others; to pray that God would destroy them. In a larger sense still, it means to abuse by reproachful words; to calumniate; or to express one's self in a violent, profane, and outrageous manner. In this passage it seems to have especial reference to this.

15. *Rejoice with them,* &c. This command grows out of the doctrine stated in ver. 4, 5, that the church is

low estate. [a] Be not wise in your own conceits.

17 Recompense [b] to no man evil for evil. Provide [c] things

a Isa.5.21.

b Mat.5.39; 1 Pet.3.9. c 2 Cor.8.21.

---

one; that it has one interest; and therefore that there should be common sympathy in its joys and sorrows. Or, enter into the welfare of your fellow-Christians, and show your attachment to them by rejoicing that *they* are made happy; comp. 1 Cor. xii. 26, "And whether....one member be honoured, all the members rejoice with it." In this way happiness diffuses and multiplies itself. It becomes expanded over the face of the whole society; and the *union* of the Christian body tends to enlarge the sphere of happiness and to prolong the joy conferred by religion. God has bound the family of man together by these sympathies, and it is one of the happiest of all devices to perpetuate and extend human enjoyments. ¶ *Weep,* &c.; see Note on John xi. 35. At the grave of Lazarus our Saviour evinced this in a most tender and affecting manner. The design of this direction is to produce mutual kindness and affection, and to divide our sorrows by the sympathies of friends. Nothing is so well fitted to do this as the sympathy of those we love. All who are afflicted know how much it diminishes their sorrow to see others sympathizing with them, and especially those who evince in their sympathies the Christian spirit. How sad would be a suffering world if there were none who regarded our griefs with interest or with tears! if every sufferer were left to bear his sorrows unpitied and alone! and if all the ties of human sympathy were rudely cut at once, and men were left to suffer in solitude and unbefriended! It may be added that it is the special duty of Christians to sympathize in each other's griefs, (1.) Because their Saviour set them the example; (2.) Because they belong to the same family; (3.) Because they are subject to similar trials and afflictions; and, (4.) Because they cannot expect the sympathy of a cold and unfeeling world.

16. Be *of the same mind,* &c. This passage has been variously interpreted. "Enter into each other's circumstances in order to see how you would yourself feel." *Chrysostom.*—"Be agreed in your opinions and views." *Stuart.*—"Be united or agreed with each other." *Flatt*; comp. Phil. ii. 2; 2 Cor. xiii. 11. A literal translation of the Greek will give somewhat a different sense, but one evidently correct. "Think of, *i. e.* regard, or seek after the same thing for each other; *i. e.* what you regard or seek for *yourself,* seek also for your brethren. Do not have divided interests; do not be pursuing different ends and aims; do not indulge counter plans and purposes; and do not seek honours, offices, for yourself which you do not seek for your brethren, so that you may still regard yourselves as brethren on a level, and aim at the same object." The Syriac has well rendered the passage: "And what you think concerning yourselves, the same also think concerning your brethren; neither think with an elevated or ambitious mind, but accommodate yourselves to those who are of humbler condition;" comp. 1 Pet. iii. 8. ¶ *Mind not high things.* Greek, Not thinking of high things. That is, not seeking them, or aspiring after them. The connection shows that the apostle had in view those things which pertained to worldly offices and honours; wealth, and state, and grandeur. They were not to seek them for themselves; nor were they to court the society or the honours of the men in an elevated rank in life. Christians were commonly of the poorer ranks, and they were to seek their companions and joys there, and not to aspire to the society of the great and the rich; comp. Jer. xlv. 5, "And seekest thou great things for thyself? Seek them not;" Luke xii. 15. ¶ *Condescend* (συναπαγομενοι). Literally, "*being led away by, or being conducted by.*" It does not properly mean to *condescend,* but denotes a *yielding,* or being guided and led in the thoughts, feelings, plans, by humble objects. Margin, "*Be contented with mean things.*" ¶ *To men of low estate.* In the Greek the word

honest in the sight of all men.

18 If it be possible, as much as lieth in you, live peaceably [a] with all men.

19 Dearly beloved, avenge [b] not

[a] Ps.34.14; Heb.12.14. [b] Lev.19.18.

here is an adjective (ταπεινοῖς), and may refer either to *men* or to *things*, either in the masculine or neuter gender. The sentiment is not materially changed whichever interpretation is adopted. It means that Christians should seek the objects of interest and companionship, not among the great, the rich, and the noble, but among the humble and the obscure. They should do it because their Master did it before them; because his friends are most commonly found among those in humble life; because Christianity prompts to benevolence rather than to a fondness for pride and display; and because of the influence on the mind produced by an attempt to imitate the great, to seek the society of the rich, and to mingle with the scenes of gaiety, folly, and ambition. ¶ *Be not wise*, &c; comp. Isa. v. 21, " Wo unto them that are wise in their own eyes, and prudent in their own sight." See Note chap. xi. 25. The meaning is, do not trust in the conceit of your own superior skill and understanding, and refuse to hearken to the counsel of others. ¶ *In your own conceits.* Greek, *Among yourselves.* Syriac, " In your own opinion." The direction here accords with that just given, and means that they should not be elated with pride above their brethren; or be headstrong and self-confident. The tendency of religion is to produce a low estimate of our own importance and attainments.

17. *Recompense.* Render, give, or return; see Note, Mat. v. 39. This is probably one of the most difficult precepts of Christianity; but the law of Christ on the subject is unyielding. It is a solemn demand made on all his followers, and it *must* be obeyed. ¶ *Provide.* The word rendered *provide* means properly to *think* or *meditate beforehand.* Make it a matter of *previous thought*, of *settled plan*, of *design.* This direction would make it a matter of *principle* and fixed purpose to do that which is right; and not to leave it to the fluctuations of feeling, or to the influence of excitement. The same direction is given in 2 Cor. viii. 21. ¶ *Things honest.* Literally things *beautiful*, or *comely.* The expression here does not refer to *property*, or to *provision* made for a family, &c. The connexion requires us to understand it respecting *conduct*, and especially our conduct towards those who injure us. It requires us to evince a spirit, and to manifest a deportment in such cases, that shall be *lovely* and *comely* in the view of others; such as all men will approve and admire. And the apostle wisely cautions us to *provide* for this, *i. e.* to think of it beforehand, to make it a matter of fixed principle and purpose, so that we shall not be overtaken and excited by passion. If left to the time when the offence shall be given, we may be excited and off our guard, and may therefore evince an improper temper. All persons who have ever been provoked by injury (and who has not been?) will see the profound wisdom of this caution to *discipline* and *guard* the temper by previous purpose, that we may not evince an improper spirit. ¶ *In the sight of all men.* Such as all must approve; such that no man can blame; and, therefore, such as shall do no discredit to religion. This expression is taken from Prov. iii. 4. The passage shows that men may be expected to approve a mild, kind, and patient temper in the reception of injuries; and facts show that this is the case. The Christian spirit is one that the world *must* approve, however little it is disposed to act on it.

18. *If it be possible.* If it can be done. This expression implies that it could not always be done. Still it should be an object of desire; and we should endeavour to obtain it. ¶ *As much as lieth in you.* This implies two things: (1.) We are to do our utmost endeavours to preserve peace, and to appease the anger and malice of others. (2.) We are not to *begin* or to *originate* a quarrel. So far as *we*

yourselves; but *rather* give place unto wrath; for it is written, [a] Vengeance *is* mine; I will repay, saith the Lord.

a Deut.32.35.

are concerned, we are to seek peace. But then it does not always depend on us. Others may oppose and persecute us; they will hate religion, and may slander, revile, and otherwise injure us; or they may commence an assault on our persons or property. For *their* assaults we are not answerable; but we *are* answerable for our conduct towards them; and on no occasion are we to commence a warfare with them. It may not be *possible* to prevent their injuring and opposing us; but it is possible not to begin a contention with them; and *when they* have commenced a strife, to seek peace, and to evince a Christian spirit. This command doubtless extends to every thing connected with strife; and means that we are not to *provoke* them to controversy, or to prolong it when it is commenced; see Ps. xxxiv. 14; Mat. v. 9, 39, 40, 41; Heb. xii. 14. If all Christians would follow this command, if they would never *provoke* to controversy, if they would injure no man by slander or by unfair dealing, if they would compel none to prosecute them in law by want of punctuality in payment of debts or honesty in business, if they would do nothing to irritate, or to prolong a controversy when it is commenced, it would put an end to no small part of the strife that exists in the world.

19. *Dearly beloved.* This expression of tenderness was peculiarly appropriate in an exhortation to peace. It reminded them of the affection and friendship which ought to subsist among them as brethren. ¶ *Avenge not yourselves.* To *avenge* is to take satisfaction for an injury by inflicting punishment on the offender. To take such satisfaction for injuries done to society, is lawful and proper for a magistrate; chap. xiii. 4. And to take satisfaction for injuries done by sin to the universe, is the province of God. But the apostle here is addressing private individual Christians. And the command is, to avoid a spirit and purpose of revenge. But this command is not to be so understood that we may not seek for *justice* in a regular and proper way before civil tribunals. If our character is assaulted, if we are robbed and plundered, if we are oppressed contrary to the law of the land, religion does not require us to submit to such oppression and injury without seeking our rights in an orderly and regular manner. If it did, it would be to give a premium to iniquity, to countenance wickedness, and require a man, by becoming a Christian, to abandon his rights. Besides, the magistrate is appointed for the praise of those who do well, and to punish evil-doers; 1 Pet. ii. 14. Further, our Lord Jesus did not surrender his rights (John xviii. 23); and Paul demanded that he himself should be treated according to the rights and privileges of a Roman citizen; Acts xvi. 37. The command here *not to avenge ourselves* means, that we are not to take it out of the hands of God, or the hands of the law, and to inflict it ourselves. It is well known that where there are no laws, the business of vengeance is pursued by individuals in a barbarous and unrelenting manner. In a state of savage society, vengeance is *immediately* taken, if possible, or it is pursued for years, and the offended man is never satisfied until he has imbrued his hands in the blood of the offender. Such was eminently the case among the Indians of this country (America). But Christianity seeks the ascendancy of the laws; and in cases which do not admit or require the interference of the laws, in private assaults and quarrels, it demands that we bear injury with patience, and commit our cause unto God; see Lev. xix. 18. ¶ *But rather give place unto wrath.* This expression has been interpreted in a great variety of ways. Its obvious design is to induce us not to attempt to avenge ourselves, but to leave it with God. To *give place*, then, is to leave it for God to come in and execute wrath or vengeance on the enemy. Do not execute wrath; leave it to God; commit

20 Therefore, if [a] thine enemy hunger, feed him; if he thirst, give

a Prov.25.21,22; Mat.5.44.

all to him; leave yourself and your enemy in his hands, assured that he will vindicate you and punish him. ¶ *For it is written.* Deut. xxxii. 35. ¶ *Vengeance is mine.* That is, it belongs to me to inflict revenge. This expression implies that it is *improper* for men to interfere with that which properly belongs to God. When we are angry, and attempt to avenge ourselves, we should remember, therefore, that we are infringing on the prerogatives of the Almighty. ¶ *I will repay,* &c. This is said in substance, though not in so many words, in Deut. xxxii. 35, 36. Its design is to assure us that those who deserve to be punished, shall be; and that, therefore, the business of revenge may be safely left in the hands of God. Though *we* should not do it, yet if it ought to be done, it will be done. This assurance will sustain us, not in the *desire* that our enemy shall be punished, but in the belief that *God* will take the matter into his own hands; that he can administer it better than we can; and that if our enemy *ought* to be punished, he will be. *We,* therefore, should leave it all with God. That God will vindicate his people, is clearly and abundantly proved in 2 Thess. i. 6—10; Rev. vi. 9—11; Deut. xxxii. 40—43.

20. *Therefore, if thine enemy hunger,* &c. This verse is taken almost literally from Prov. xxv. 21, 22. Hunger and thirst here are put for want in general. If thine enemy is needy in any way, do him good, and supply his wants. This is, in spirit, the same as the command of the Lord Jesus (Mat. v. 44), "Do good to them that hate you," &c. ¶ *In so doing.* It does not mean that we are to do this *for the sake* of heaping coals of fire on him, but that this *will be* the result. ¶ *Thou shalt heap,* &c. Coals of fire are doubtless emblematical of *pain.* But the idea here is not that in so doing we shall call down divine vengeance on the man; but the apostle is speaking of the natural effect or result of showing him kindness. Burning coals heaped on a man's head would be expressive of intense agony. So the apostle says that the *effect* of doing good to an enemy would be to produce pain. But the pain will result from shame, remorse of conscience, a conviction of the evil of his conduct, and an apprehension of divine displeasure that may lead to repentance. To do this, is not only perfectly right, but it is desirable. If a man can be brought to reflection and true repentance, it should be done. In regard to this passage we may remark, (1.) That the way to promote *peace* is to do good even to enemies. (2.) The way to bring a man to repentance is to do him good. On this principle God is acting continually. He does good to all, even to the rebellious; and he designs that his goodness should lead men to repentance; Rom. ii. 4. Men will resist wrath, anger, and power; but *goodness* they cannot resist; it finds its way to the heart; and the conscience does its work, and the sinner is overwhelmed at the remembrance of his crimes. (3.) If men would act on the principles of the gospel, the world would soon be at peace. No man would suffer himself many times to be overwhelmed in this way with coals of fire. It is not human nature, bad as it is; and if Christians would meet all unkindness with kindness, all malice with benevolence, and all wrong with right, peace would soon pervade the community, and even opposition to the gospel might soon die away.

21. *Be not overcome of evil.* Be not *vanquished* or *subdued* by injury received from others. Do not suffer your temper to be excited; your Christian principles to be abandoned; your mild, amiable, kind, and benevolent temper to be ruffled by any opposition or injury which you may experience. Maintain your Christian principles amidst all opposition, and thus show the power of the gospel. They are overcome by evil who suffer their temper to be excited, who become enraged and revengeful, and who engage in contention with those

him drink: for in so doing thou shalt heap coals of fire on his head.

21 Be [a] not overcome of evil, but overcome evil with good.

a Prov.16.32.

who injure them; Prov. xvi. 22. ¶ *But overcome evil with good.* That is, subdue or vanquish evil by doing good to others. Show them the loveliness of a better spirit; the power of kindness and benevolence; the value of an amiable, Christian deportment. So doing, you may disarm them of their rage, and be the means of bringing them to better minds.

This is the noble and grand sentiment of the Christian religion. Nothing like this is to be found in the heathen classics; and nothing like it ever existed among pagan nations. Christianity alone has brought forth this lovely and mighty principle; and one design of it is to advance the welfare of man by promoting peace, harmony, and love. The idea of *overcoming evil with good* never occurred to men until the gospel was preached. It never has been acted on except under the influences of the gospel. On this principle God shows kindness; on this principle the Saviour came, and bled, and died; and on this principle all Christians should act in treating their enemies, and in bringing a world to the knowledge of the Lord Jesus. If Christians will show benevolence, if they will send forth proofs of love to the ends of the earth, the evils of the world will be overcome. Nor can the nations be converted until Christians act on this great and most important principle of their religion, *on the largest scale possible,* TO "OVERCOME EVIL WITH GOOD."

CHAPTER XIII.

1. *Let every soul.* Every person. In the seven first verses of this chapter, the apostle discusses the subject of the duty which Christians owe to civil government; a subject which is extremely important, and at the same time exceedingly difficult. There is no doubt that he had express reference to the peculiar situation of the Christians at Rome; but the subject was of so much importance that he gives it a *general* bearing, and states the great principles on which all Christians are to act. The circumstances which made this discussion proper and important were the following: (1.) The Christian religion was designed to extend throughout the world. Yet it contemplated the rearing of a kingdom amid other kingdoms, an empire amid other empires. Christians professed supreme allegiance to the Lord Jesus Christ; he was their lawgiver, their sovereign, their judge. It became, therefore, a question of great importance and difficulty, *what kind* of allegiance they were to render to earthly magistrates. (2.) The kingdoms of the world were then *pagan* kingdoms. The laws were made by pagans, and were adapted to the prevalence of heathenism. Those kingdoms had been generally founded in conquest, and blood, and oppression. Many of the monarchs were blood-stained warriors; were unprincipled men; and were polluted in their private, and oppressive in their public character. Whether Christians were to acknowledge the laws of such kingdoms and of such men, was a serious question, and one which could not but occur very early. It would occur also very soon, in circumstances that would be very affecting and trying. Soon the hands of these magistrates were to be raised against Christians in the fiery scenes of persecution; and the duty and extent of submission to them became a matter of very serious inquiry. (3.) Many of the early Christians were composed of Jewish converts. Yet the Jews had long been under Roman oppression, and had borne the foreign yoke with great uneasiness. The whole heathen magistracy they regarded as founded in a system of idolatry; as opposed to God and his kingdom; and as abomination in his sight. With these feelings they had become Christians; and it was natural that their former sentiments should exert an influence on them after their conversion. How

CHAPTER XIII.

LET every soul be subject [a] unto the higher powers. For there [b] is no power but of God: the powers that be are [1] ordained of God.

a 1 Pet.2.13. *b* Dan.2.21. 1 or, *ordered.*

far they should submit, if at all, to heathen magistrates, was a question of deep interest; and there was danger that the *Jewish* converts might prove to be disorderly and rebellious citizens of the empire. (4.) Nor was the case much different with the *Gentile* converts. They would naturally look with abhorrence on the system of idolatry which they had just forsaken. They would regard all as opposed to God. They would denounce the *religion* of the pagans as abomination; and as that religion was interwoven with the civil institutions, there was danger also that they might denounce the government altogether, and be regarded as opposed to the laws of the land. (5.) There *were* cases where it was right to *resist* the laws. This the Christian religion clearly taught; and in cases like these, it was indispensable for Christians to take a stand. When the laws interfered with the rights of conscience; when they commanded the worship of idols, or any moral wrong, then it was their duty to refuse submission. Yet in what cases this was to be done, where the line was to be drawn, was a question of deep importance, and one which was not easily settled. It is quite probable, however, that the main danger was, that the early Christians would err in *refusing* submission, even when it was proper, rather than in undue conformity to idolatrous rites and ceremonies. (6.) In the *changes* which were to occur in human governments, it would be an inquiry of deep interest, what part Christians should take, and what submission they should yield to the various laws which might spring up among the nations. The *principles* on which Christians should act are settled in this chapter. ¶ *Be subject.* Submit. The word denotes that kind of submission which soldiers render to their officers. It implies *subordination;* a willingness to occupy our proper place, to yield to the authority of those over us. The word used here does not designate the *extent* of the submission, but merely enjoins it in general. The general principle will be seen to be, that we are to obey in all things which are not contrary to the law of God. ¶ *The higher powers.* The magistracy; the supreme government. It undoubtedly here refers to the Roman magistracy, and has relation not so much to the *rulers* as to the supreme *authority* which was established as the constitution of government; comp. Mat. x. 1; xxviii. 18. ¶ *For.* The apostle gives a *reason* why Christians should be subject; and that reason is, that magistrates have received their appointment from God. As Christians, therefore, are to be subject to God, so they are to honour *God* by honouring the arrangement which he has instituted for the government of mankind. Doubtless, he here intends also to repress the vain curiosity and agitation with which men are prone to inquire into the *titles* of their rulers; to guard them from the agitation and conflicts of party, and of contentions to establish a favourite on the throne. It might be that those in power had not a proper title to their office; that they had secured it, not according to justice, but by oppression; but into that question Christians were not to enter. The government was established, and they were not to seek to overturn it. ¶ *No power.* No office; no magistracy; no civil rule. ¶ *But of God.* By God's permission, or appointment; by the arrangements of his providence, by which those in office had obtained their power. God often claims and asserts that *He* sets up one, and puts down another; Ps. lxxv. 7; Dan. ii. 21; iv. 17, 25, 34, 35. ¶ *The powers that be.* That is, all the civil magistracies that exist; those who have the *rule* over nations, by whatever means they may have obtained it. This is equally true at all times, that the powers that exist, exist by the permission and providence of God.

2 Whosoever therefore resisteth the power, resisteth the ordinance of God: and they that resist shall receive to themselves damnation.

¶ *Are ordained of God.* This word *ordained* denotes the *ordering* or *arrangement* which subsists in a *military* company, or army. God sets them *in order,* assigns them their location, changes and directs them as he pleases. This does not mean that he *originates* or causes the evil dispositions of rulers, but that he *directs* and *controls* their appointment. By this, we are not to infer, (1.) That he approves their conduct; nor, (2.) That what they do is always right; nor, (3.) That it is our duty *always* to submit to them. Their requirements *may be* opposed to the law of God, and then we are to obey God rather than man; Acts iv. 19; v. 29. But it is meant that the power is intrusted to them by God; and that he has the authority to remove them when he pleases. If they abuse their power, however, they do it at their peril; and *when* so abused, the obligation to obey them ceases. That this is the case, is apparent further from the nature of the *question* which would be likely to arise among the early Christians. It *could not be* and *never was* a question, whether they should obey a magistrate when he commanded a thing that was plainly contrary to the law of God. But the question was, whether they should obey a heathen magistrate *at all.* This question the apostle answers in the affirmative, because *God* had made government necessary, and because it was arranged and ordered by his providence. Probably also the apostle had another object in view. At the time in which he wrote this epistle, the Roman empire was agitated with civil dissensions. One emperor followed another in rapid succession. The throne was often seized, not by right, but by crime. Different claimants would rise, and their claims would excite controversy. The object of the apostle was to prevent Christians from entering into those disputes, and from taking an active part in a political controversy. Besides, the throne had been *usurped* by the reigning emperors, and there was a prevalent disposition to rebel against a tyrannical government. Claudius had been put to death by poison; Caligula in a violent manner; Nero was a tyrant; and amidst these agitations, and crimes, and revolutions, the apostle wished to guard Christians from taking an active part in political affairs.

2. *Whosoever therefore resisteth,* &c. That is, they who rise up against *government itself;* who seek anarchy and confusion; and who oppose the regular execution of the laws. It is implied, however, that those laws shall not be such as to violate the rights of conscience, or oppose the laws of God. ¶ *Resisteth the ordinance of God.* What God has ordained, or appointed. This means clearly that we are to regard *government* as instituted by God, and as agreeable to his will. *When* established, we are not to be agitated about the *titles* of the rulers; not to enter into angry contentions, or to refuse to submit to them, because we are apprehensive of a defect in their *title,* or because they may have obtained it by oppression. If the government is established, and if its decisions are not a manifest violation of the laws of God, we are to submit to them. ¶ *Shall receive to themselves damnation.* The word *damnation* we apply now exclusively to the punishment of hell; to future torments. But this is not necessarily the meaning of the word which is here used (κρίμα). It often simply denotes *punishment;* Rom. iii. 8; 1 Cor. xi. 29; Gal. v. 10. In this place the word implies *guilt* or *criminality* in resisting the ordinance of God, and affirms that the man that does it shall be punished. Whether the apostle means that he shall be punished by *God,* or by the *magistrate,* is not quite clear. Probably the *latter,* however, is intended; comp. ver. 4. It is also true that such resistance shall be attended with the displeasure of God, and be punished by him.

3 For rulers are not a terror to good works, but to the evil. Wilt thou then not be afraid of the power? do [a] that which is good, and thou shalt have praise of the same:

4 For he is the minister of God to thee for good. But if thou do that which is evil, be afraid: for he beareth not the sword in vain: for he is the minister of God, a revenger of God to *execute* wrath upon him that doeth evil.

a 1 Pet.2.14.

3. *For rulers.* The apostle here speaks of rulers *in general.* It may not be *universally* true that they are not a terror to good works, for many of them have *persecuted* the good; but it is generally true that they who are virtuous have nothing to fear from the laws. It is *universally* true that the design of their appointment by God was, not to injure and oppress the good, but to detect and punish the evil. Magistrates, *as such,* are not a terror to good works. ¶ *Are not a terror,* &c. Are not appointed to *punish the good.* Their appointment is not to inspire terror in those who are virtuous and peaceable citizens; comp. 1 Tim. i. 9. ¶ *But to the evil.* Appointed to detect and punish evil-doers; and therefore an object of terror to them. The design of the apostle here is evidently to reconcile Christians to submission to the government, from its *utility.* It is appointed to protect the good against the evil; to restrain oppression, injustice, and fraud; to bring offenders to justice, and thus promote the peace and harmony of the community. As it is designed to promote order and happiness, it should be submitted to; and so long as *this* object is pursued, and obtained, government should receive the countenance and support of Christians. But if it departs from this principle, and becomes the protector of the evil and the oppressor of the good, the case is reversed, and the obligation to its support must cease. ¶ *Wilt thou not,* &c. If you do evil by resisting the laws, and in any other manner, will you not fear the power of the government? Fear is *one* of the means by which men are restrained from crime in a community. On many minds it operates with much more power than any other motive. And it is one which a magistrate must make use of to restrain men from evil. ¶ *Do that which is good.* Be a virtuous and peaceable citizen; abstain from crime, and yield obedience to all the just laws of the land. ¶ *And thou shalt have praise of the same;* comp. 1 Pet. ii. 14, 15. You shall be unmolested and uninjured, and shall receive the commendation of being peaceable and upright citizens. The prospect of that protection, and even of that reputation, is not an unworthy motive to yield obedience to the laws. Every Christian should desire the reputation of being a man seeking the welfare of his country, and the just execution of the laws.

4. *The minister of God.* The *servant* of God he is appointed by God to do his will, and to execute his purposes. ¶ *To thee.* For your benefit. ¶ *For good.* That is, to protect you in your rights; to vindicate your name, person, or property; and to guard your liberty, and secure to you the results of your industry. The magistrate is not appointed directly to *reward* men, but they *practically* furnish a reward by protecting and defending them, and securing to them the interests of justice. ¶ *If thou do that,* &c. That is, if any citizen should do evil. ¶ *Be afraid.* Fear the just vengeance of the laws. ¶ *For he beareth not the sword in vain.* The *sword* is an instrument of punishment, as well as an emblem of war. Princes were accustomed to wear a sword as an emblem of their authority; and the *sword* was often used for the purpose of *beheading,* or otherwise punishing the guilty. The meaning of the apostle is, that he does not wear this badge of authority as an unmeaning show, but that it will be used to execute the laws. As this

5 Wherefore [a] ye must needs be subject, not only for wrath, but also for conscience' sake.
6 For, for this cause pay ye tribute also: for they are God's ministers, attending continually upon this very thing.
7 Render therefore to all [b] their

a Eccl.8.2. b Mat.22.21.

is the design of the power intrusted to him, and as he will *exercise* his authority, men should be influenced *by fear* to keep the law, even if there were no better motive. ¶ *A revenger*, &c. In chap. xii. 19, vengeance is said to belong to God. Yet he *executes* his vengeance by means of subordinate agents. It belongs to him to take vengeance by direct judgments, by the plague, famine, sickness, or earthquakes; by the appointment of magistrates; or by letting loose the passions of men to prey upon each other. When a magistrate inflicts punishment on the guilty, it is to be regarded as the act of God taking vengeance *by him;* and on this principle only is it right for a judge to condemn a man to death. It is not because one man has by nature any right over the life of another, or because *society* has any right collectively which it has not as individuals; but because *God* gave life, and because he has chosen to take it away when crime is committed by the appointment of magistrates, and not by coming forth himself visibly to execute the laws. Where *human* laws fail, however, he often takes vengeance into his own hands, and by the plague, or some signal judgments, sweeps the guilty into eternity. ¶ *To execute wrath.* For an explanation of the word *wrath*, see Notes on chap. i. 18. It denotes here *punishment*, or the just execution of the laws. It may be remarked that this verse is an *incidental* proof of the propriety of *capital punishment.* The *sword* was undoubtedly an instrument for this purpose, and the apostle mentions its use without any remark of *disapprobation.* He enjoins subjection to those who *wear the sword*, that is, to those who execute the laws *by that;* and evidently intends to speak of the magistrate *with the sword*, or in inflicting capital punishment, as having received the appointment of God. The tendency of society now is *not* to too sanguinary laws. It is rather to forget that God has doomed the murderer to death; and though humanity should be consulted in the execution of the laws, yet there is no humanity in suffering the murderer to live to infest society, and endanger many lives, in the place of his own, which was forfeited to justice. Far better that one murderer should die, than that he should be suffered to live, to imbrue his hands perhaps in the blood of many who are innocent. But the authority of God has settled this question (Gen. ix. 5, 6), and it is neither right nor safe for a community to disregard his solemn decisions; see *Blackstone's Commentaries*, vol. iv. p. 8, [9.]

5. *Wherefore* (διὸ). The *reasons* why we should be subject, which the apostle had given, were two, (1.) That government was appointed by God. (2.) That violation of the laws would necessarily expose to punishment. ¶ *Ye must needs be.* It is *necessary* (ἀνάγκη) to be. This is a word stronger than that which implies mere *fitness* or propriety. It means that it is a matter of high obligation and of *necessity* to be subject to the civil ruler. ¶ *Not only for wrath.* Not only on account of the *fear of punishment;* or the fact that wrath will be executed on evil doers. ¶ *For conscience' sake.* As a matter of conscience, or of *duty to God*, because *he* has appointed it, and made it necessary and proper. A good citizen yields obedience because it is the will of God; and a Christian makes it a part of his religion to maintain and obey the just laws of the land; see Mat. xxii. 21; comp. Eccl. viii. 2, "I counsel them to keep the king's commandments, and *that in regard of the oath of God.*"

6. *For this cause.* Because they are appointed by God; for the sake of conscience, and in order to secure the execution of the laws. As they

dues; tribute to whom tribute *is due;* custom to whom custom; fear to whom fear; honour to whom honour.

---

are appointed by God, the tribute which is needful for their support becomes an act of homage to God, an act performed in obedience to his will, and acceptable to him. ¶ *Tribute also.* Not only be subject (ver. 5), but pay what may be necessary to support the government. *Tribute* properly denotes the *tax,* or annual compensation, which was paid by one province or nation to a superior, as the price of protection, or as an acknowledgment of subjection. The Romans made all conquered provinces pay this *tribute;* and it would become a question whether it was *right* to acknowledge this claim, and submit to it. Especially would this question be agitated by the Jews and by Jewish Christians. But on the principle which the apostle had laid down (ver. 1, 2), it was right to do it, and was demanded by the very purposes of government. In a larger sense, the word *tribute* means any tax paid on land or personal estate for the support of the government. ¶ *For they are God's ministers.* His servants; or they are appointed by him. As the government is *his* appointment, we should contribute to its support as a matter of conscience, because we thus do honour to the arrangement of God. It may be observed here, also, that the fact that civil rulers are the ministers of God, invests their character with great sacredness, and should impress upon *them* the duty of seeking to do his will, as well as on others the duty of submitting to them. ¶ *Attending continually.* As they attend to this, and devote their time and talents to it, it is proper that they should receive a suitable support. It becomes then a duty for the people to contribute cheerfully to the necessary expenses of the government. If those taxes should be unjust and oppressive, yet, like other evils, they are to be submitted to, until a remedy can be found in a proper way.

7. *Render therefore,* &c. This injunction is often repeated in the Bible; see Notes on Mat. xxii. 21; see also Mat. xvii. 25—27; 1 Pet. ii. 13—17; Prov. xxiv. 21. It is one of the most lovely and obvious of the duties of religion. Christianity is not designed to break in upon the proper order of society, but rather to establish and confirm that order. It does not rudely assail existing institutions; but it comes to put them on a proper footing, to diffuse a mild and pure influence over all, and to secure *such* an influence in all the relations of life as shall tend best to promote the happiness of man and the welfare of the community. ¶ *Is due.* To whom it properly belongs by the law of the land, and according to the ordinance of God. It is represented here as a matter of *debt,* as something which is *due* to the ruler; a fair *compensation* to him for the service which he renders us by devoting his time and talents to advance *our* interests, and the welfare of the community. As taxes are a *debt,* a matter of strict and just obligation, they should be paid as conscientiously and as cheerfully as any other just debts, however contracted. ¶ *Custom* (τέλος). The word rendered *tribute* means, as has been remarked, the tax which is paid by a *tributary* prince or dependent people; also the tax imposed on land or real estate. The word here translated *custom* means properly the revenue which is collected on *merchandise,* either imported or exported. ¶ *Fear.* See ver. 4. We should stand in awe of those who wear the sword, and who are appointed to execute the laws of the land. As the execution of their office is fitted to excite *fear,* we should render to them that reverence which is appropriate to the execution of their office. It means a solicitous anxiety lest we do any thing to offend them. ¶ *Honour.* The difference between this and *fear* is, that this rather denotes *reverence, veneration, respect* for their names, offices, rank, &c. The former is the *fear* which arises from the dread of punishment. Religion gives to men all their just titles, recognises their rank and office, and seeks to promote due subordina-

8 Owe no man any thing, but to love one another: for [a] he that

a James 2.8.

tion in a community. It was no part of the work of our Saviour, or of his apostles, to quarrel with the mere *titles* of men, or to withhold from them the customary tribute of respect and homage; comp. Acts xxiv. 3; xxvi. 25; Luke i. 3; 1 Pet. ii. 17. In this verse there is summed up the duty which is owed to magistrates. It consists in rendering to them proper honour; contributing cheerfully and conscientiously to the necessary expenses of the government; and in yielding obedience to the laws. These are made a part of the duty which we owe to God, and should be considered as enjoined by our religion.

On the subject discussed in these seven verses, the following *principles* seem to be settled by the authority of the Bible, and are now understood, (1.) That government is essential; and its necessity is recognised by God, and it is arranged by his providence. God has never been the patron of anarchy and disorder. (2.) Civil rulers are dependent on God. He has the entire control over them, and can set them up or put them down when he pleases. (3.) The authority of God is superior to that of civil rulers. They have no right to make enactments which interfere with *his* authority. (4.) It is not the business of civil rulers to regulate or control religion. That is a distinct department, with which they have no concern, except to protect it. (5.) The rights of all men are to be preserved. Men are to be allowed to worship God according to the dictates of their own conscience, and to be protected in those rights, provided they do not violate the peace and order of the community. (6.) Civil rulers have no right to persecute Christians, or to attempt to secure conformity to their views by force. The conscience cannot be compelled; and in the affairs of religion man must be free.

In view of this subject we may remark, (1.) That the doctrines respecting the rights of civil rulers, and the line which is to be drawn between their powers and the rights of conscience, have been slow to be understood. The struggle has been long; and a thousand persecutions have shown the anxiety of the magistrate to rule the conscience, and to control religion. In pagan countries it has been conceded that the civil ruler had a right to control the *religion* of the people: church and state there have been one. The same thing was attempted under Christianity. The magistrate still claimed this right, and attempted to enforce it. Christianity resisted the claim, and asserted the independent and original rights of conscience. A conflict ensued, of course, and the magistrate resorted to persecutions, to *subdue* by force the claims of the new religion and the rights of conscience. Hence the ten fiery and bloody persecutions of the primitive church. The blood of the early Christians flowed like water; thousands and tens of thousands went to the stake, until Christianity triumphed, and the right of religion to a free exercise was acknowledged throughout the empire. (2.) It is matter of devout thanksgiving that the subject is now settled, and the principle is now understood. In our own land (America) there exists the happy and bright illustration of the true principle on this great subject. The rights of conscience are regarded, and the laws peacefully obeyed. The civil ruler understands his province; and Christians yield a cheerful and cordial obedience to the laws. The church and state move on in their own spheres, united only in the purpose to make men happy and good; and divided only as they relate to different departments, and contemplate, the one, the rights of civil society, the other, the interests of eternity. Here, every man worships God according to his own views of duty; and at the same time, here is rendered the most cordial and peaceful obedience to the laws of the land. Thanks should be rendered without ceasing to the God of our fathers for the wondrous train of events by which this contest has

loveth another hath fulfilled the law.

9 For this, Thou [a] shalt not commit adultery, Thou shalt not kill, Thou shalt not steal, Thou shalt not bear false witness, Thou shalt not covet; and if *there be* any other commandment, it is briefly comprehended in this saying, namely, [b] Thou shalt love thy neighbour as thyself.

[a] Ex.20.13,&c.

[b] Lev.19.18; Mat.22.39,40.

been conducted to its issue; and for the clear and full understanding which we now have of the different departments pertaining to the church and the state.

8. *Owe no man any thing.* Be not *in debt* to any one. In the previous verse the apostle had been discoursing of the duty which we owe to magistrates. He had particularly enjoined on Christians to pay to *them* their just dues. From this command to discharge fully this obligation, the transition was natural to the subject of debts *in general*, and to an injunction not to be indebted to *any one.* This law is enjoined in this place, (1.) Because it is a part of our duty as good citizens; and, (2.) Because it is a part of that law which teaches us to love our neighbour, and to *do no injury to him*, ver. 10. The interpretation of this command is to be taken with this limitation, that we are not to be indebted to him so as to *injure* him, or to work *ill* to him.

This rule, together with the other rules of Christianity, would propose a remedy for all the evils of bad debts in the following manner. (1.) It would teach men to be *industrious*, and this would commonly prevent the *necessity* of contracting debts. (2.) It would make them *frugal, economical*, and *humble* in their views and manner of life. (3.) It would teach them to bring up their families in habits of industry. The Bible often enjoins that; see Note, chap. xii. 11; comp. Phil. iv. 8; Prov. xxiv. 30—34; 1 Thess. iv. 11; 2 Thess. iii. 10; Eph. iv. 25. (4.) Religion would produce sober, chastened views of the end of life, of the great design of living; and would take off the affections from the splendour, gayety, and extravagances which lead often to the contraction of debts; 1 Thess. v. 6, 8; 1 Pet. i. 13; iv. 7; Tit. ii. 12; 1 Pet. iii. 3, 5; 1 Tim. ii. 9. (5.) Religion would put a period to the *vices* and unlawful desires which now prompt men to contract debts. (6.) It would make them *honest* in paying them. It would make them conscientious, prompt, friends of truth, and disposed to keep their promises.

¶ *But to love one another.* Love is a debt which *can* never be discharged. We should feel that we *owe* this to all men, and though by acts of kindness we may be constantly discharging it, yet we should feel that it can *never* be fully met while there is opportunity to do good. ¶ *For he that loveth*, &c. In what way this is done is stated in ver. 10. The law in relation to our neighbour is there said to be simply that we do no *ill* to him. Love to him would prompt to no injury. It would seek to do him good, and would thus fulfil all the purposes of justice and truth which we owe to him. In order to illustrate this, the apostle, in the next verse, runs over the laws of the ten commandments in relation to our neighbour, and shows that all those laws proceed on the principle that we are to *love* him, and that love would prompt to them all.

9. *For this. This* which follows is the sum of the laws. *This* is to regulate us in our conduct towards our neighbour. The word *this* here stands opposed to "*that*" in ver. 11. *This* law of love would prompt us to seek our neighbour's good; *that* fact, that our salvation is near, would prompt us to be active and faithful in the discharge of all the duties we owe to him. ¶ *Thou shalt not commit adultery.* All the commands which follow are designed as an illustration of the duty of loving our neighbour; see these commands considered in the Notes on Mat. xix. 18, 19. The apostle has not enumerated *all* the commands of the second table. He has shown generally

10 Love worketh no ill to his
neighbour: therefore love *is* the
fulfilling of the law.

11 And that, knowing the time,
that now *it is* high time to awake
[a] out of sleep; for now *is* our sal-

a 1 Thess.5,5-8.

---

what they required. The command to honour our parents he has omitted. The reason might have been that it was not so immediately to his purpose when discoursing of love to a *neighbour* —a word which does not immediately suggest the idea of near relatives. The expression, "Thou shalt not bear false witness," is rejected by the best critics as of doubtful authority, but it does not materially affect the spirit of the passage. It is wanting in many MSS. and in the Syriac version. ¶ *If there be any other commandment.* The law respecting parents; or if there be any duty which does not seem to be *specified* by these laws, it is implied in the command to love our neighbour as ourselves. ¶ *It is briefly comprehended.* Greek, It may be reduced to *this head;* or it is summed up in this. ¶ *In this saying.* This word, or command. ¶ *Thou shalt love,* &c. This is found in Lev. xix. 18. See it considered in the Notes on Mat. xix. 19. If this command were fulfilled, it would prevent all fraud, injustice, oppression, falsehood, adultery, murder, theft, and covetousness. It is the same as our Saviour's golden rule. And if every man would do to others as he would wish them to do to him, all the design of the law would be at once fulfilled.

10. *Love worketh no ill,* &c. Love would seek to do him good; of course it would prevent all dishonesty and crime towards others. It would prompt to justice, truth, and benevolence. If this law were engraven on every man's heart, and practised in his life, what a change would it immediately produce in society! If all men would at once *abandon* that which is fitted to *work ill* to others, what an influence would it have on the business and commercial affairs of men. How many plans of fraud and dishonesty would it at once arrest. How many schemes would it crush. It would silence the voice of the slanderer; it would stay the plans of the seducer and the adulterer; it would put an end to cheating, and fraud, and all schemes of dishonest gain. The gambler desires the property of his neighbour without any compensation, and thus works *ill* to him. The dealer in *lotteries* desires property for which he has never toiled, and which must be obtained at the expense and loss of others. And there are many *employments* all whose tendency is to work *ill* to a neighbour. This is pre-eminently true of the traffic in *ardent spirits.* It cannot do him good, and the almost uniform result is to deprive him of his property, health, reputation, peace, and domestic comfort. He that sells his neighbour liquid fire, knowing what *must* be the result of it, is not pursuing a business which works no *ill* to him; and love to that neighbour would prompt him to abandon the traffic; see Hab. ii. 15, "Wo unto him that giveth his neighbour drink, that puttest thy bottle to him, and makest him drink also, that thou mayest look on their nakedness." ¶ *Therefore,* &c. *Because* love does no harm to another, it is *therefore* the fulfilling of the law, implying that all that the law requires is to *love* others. ¶ *Is the fulfilling.* Is the *completion,* or meets the requirements of the law. The law of God on this *head,* or in regard to our duty to our neighbour, requires us to do justice towards him, to observe truth, &c. *All* this will be met by *love;* and if men truly *loved* others, all the demands of the law would be satisfied. ¶ *Of the law.* Of the law of Moses, but particularly the ten commandments.

11. *And that.* The word "that," in this place, is connected in signification with the word "this" in ver. 9. The meaning may be thus expressed: All the requirements of the law towards our neighbour may be met by two things: one is (ver. 9, 10) by love; the other is (ver. 11—14) by remembering that we are near to eternity; keeping a deep sense of *this* truth before the mind. *This* will prompt to a life of

vation nearer than when we believed.

12 The night is far spent, the day is at hand: let us [a] therefore cast off the works of darkness, and let us put [b] on the armour of light.

a Eph.5.11. *b* Eph.6.13,&c.

honesty, truth, and peace, and contentment. ver. 13. The doctrine in these verses (11—14), therefore, is, *that a deep conviction of the nearness of eternity will prompt to an upright life in the intercourse of man with man.* ¶ *Knowing the time.* Taking a proper *estimate* of the time. Taking just views of the shortness and the value of time; of the design for which it was given, and of the fact that it is, in regard to us, rapidly coming to a close. And still further considering, that the time in which you live is the time of the gospel, a period of light and truth, when you are particularly called on to lead holy lives, and thus to do justly to all. The *previous* time had been a period of ignorance and darkness, when oppression, and falsehood, and sin abounded. This, the time of the *gospel*, when God had *made known* to men his will that they should be pure. ¶ *High time.* Greek, "*the hour.*" *To awake,* &c. This is a beautiful figure. The dawn of day, the approaching light of the morning, is the time to arouse from slumber. In the darkness of night, men sleep. So says the apostle. The world has been sunk in the *night* of heathenism and sin. At that time it was to be expected that they would sleep the sleep of spiritual death. But now the morning light of the gospel dawns. The Sun of righteousness has arisen. It is *time,* therefore, for men to cast off the deeds of darkness, and rise to life, and purity, and action; comp. Acts xvii. 30, 31. The same idea is beautifully presented in 1 Thess. v. 5—8. The meaning is, "Hitherto we have walked in darkness and in sin. Now we walk in the light of the gospel. We know our duty. We are sure that the God of light is around us, and is a witness of all we do. We are going soon to meet him, and it becomes us to rouse, and to do those deeds, and those only, which will bear the bright shining of the light of truth, and the scrutiny of him who is "light, and in whom is no darkness at all;" 1 John i. 5. ¶ *Sleep.* Inactivity; insensibility to the doctrines and duties of religion. Men, by nature, are active only in deeds of wickedness. In regard to religion they are insensible, and the slumbers of night are on their eyelids. Sleep is "the kinsman of death," and it is the emblem of the insensibility and stupidity of sinners. The deeper the ignorance and sin, the greater is this insensibility to spiritual things, and to the duties which we owe to God and man. ¶ *For now is our salvation.* The word *salvation* has been here variously interpreted. Some suppose that by it the apostle refers to the personal reign of Christ on the earth. (Tholuck, and the Germans generally.) Others suppose it refers to deliverance from *persecutions.* Others, to increased *light* and knowledge of the gospel, so that they could more clearly discern their duty than when they became believers. (*Rosenmüller.*) It probably, however, has its usual meaning here, denoting that deliverance from sin and danger which awaits Christians in heaven; and is thus equivalent to the expression, "You are advancing nearer to heaven. You are hastening to the world of glory. Daily we are approaching the kingdom of light; and in prospect of that state, we ought to lay aside every sin, and live more and more in preparation for a world of light and glory." ¶ *Than when we believed.* Than when we *began* to believe. Every day brings us nearer to a world of perfect light.

12. *The night.* The word *night,* in the New Testament, is used to denote *night* literally (Mat. ii. 14, &c.); the starry heavens (Rev. viii. 12); and then it denotes a state of *ignorance* and *crime,* and is synonymous with the word darkness, as such deeds are committed commonly in the night; 1 Thess. v. 5. In this place it seems to denote our present imperfect and obscure condition in this world as contrasted with the pure light of heaven.

13 Let us walk [1] honestly, [a] as in the day; not in rioting [b] and drunkenness, not in chambering [c] and wantonness, not in strife and envying.

14 But put [d] ye on the Lord Jesus

1 or, *decently*. a Phil.4.8;1Pet.2.12. b 1Pet.4.3. c 1Cor.6.9,10. d Gal.3.27.

The *night*, the time of comparative obscurity and sin in which we live even under the gospel, is far gone in relation to us, and the pure splendours of heaven are at hand. ¶ *Is far spent.* Literally, "is cut off." It is becoming *short;* it is hastening to a close. ¶ *The day.* The full splendours and glory of redemption in heaven. Heaven is often thus represented as a place of pure and splendid day; Rev. xxi. 23, 25; xxii. 5. The times of the *gospel* are represented as times of *light* (Isa. lx. 1, 2; 19, 20, &c.); but the reference here seems to be rather to the still brighter glory and splendour of heaven, as the place of pure, unclouded, and eternal day. ¶ *Is at hand.* Is near; or is drawing near. This is true respecting all Christians. The day is near, or the time when they shall be admitted to heaven is not remote. This is the uniform representation of the New Testament; Heb. x. 25; 1 Pet. iv. 7; James v. 8; Rev. xii. 20; 1 Thess. v. 2—6; Phil. iv. 5. That the apostle did not mean, however, that the end of the world was near, or that the day of judgment would come soon, is clear from his own explanations; see 1 Thess. v. 2—6; comp. 2 Thess. ii. ¶ *Let us therefore.* As we are about to enter on the glories of that eternal day, we should be pure and holy. The *expectation* of it will teach us to *seek* purity; and a pure life alone will fit us to enter there; Heb. xii. 14. ¶ *Cast off.* Lay aside, or put away. ¶ *The works of darkness.* Dark, wicked deeds, such as are specified in the next verse. They are called *works of darkness,* because darkness in the Scriptures is an emblem of crime, as well as of ignorance, and because such deeds are commonly committed in the night; 1 Thess. v. 7, "They that be drunken, are drunken *in the night;*" comp. John iii. 20; Eph. v. 11—13. ¶ *Let us put on.* Let us clothe ourselves with. ¶ *The armour of light.* The word *armour* (ὅπλα) properly means *arms,* or instruments of war, including the helmet, sword, shield, &c. Eph. vi. 11—17. It is used in the New Testament to denote the *aids* which the Christian has, or the *means of defence* in his warfare, where he is represented as a soldier contending with his foes, and includes truth, righteousness, faith, hope, &c. as the instruments by which he is to gain his victories. In 2 Cor. vi. 7, it is called "the armour of righteousness on the right hand and on the left." It is called armour of *light,* because it is not to accomplish any deeds of darkness or of crime; it is appropriate to one who is pure, and who is seeking a pure and noble object. Christians are represented as the *children of light;* 1 Thess. v. 5; Note, Luke xvi. 8. By the armour of light, therefore, the apostle means those graces which stand opposed to the deeds of darkness (ver. 13); those graces of faith, hope, humility, &c. which shall be appropriate to those who are the children of the day, and which shall be their defence in their struggles with their spiritual foes. see the description in full in Eph. vii. 11—17.

13. *Let us walk.* To *walk* is an expression denoting *to live;* let us *live,* or *conduct,* &c. ¶ *Honestly.* The word here used means rather in a *decent* or *becoming* manner; in a manner *appropriate* to those who are the children of light. ¶ *As in the day.* As if all our actions were seen and known. Men by day, or in open light, live decently; their foul and wicked deeds are done in the night. The apostle exhorts Christians to live as if all their conduct were seen, and they had nothing which they wished to conceal. ¶ *In rioting.* Revelling; denoting the licentious conduct, the noisy and obstreperous mirth, the scenes of disorder and sensuality, which attend luxurious living. ¶ *Drunkenness.* Rioting and drunkenness con-

Christ, and make [a] not provision for the flesh, to *fulfil* the lusts *thereof*.

CHAPTER XIV.

HIM that is weak in the faith receive ye, *but* [1] not to doubtful disputations.

a Gal.5.16.1. [1] or, *not to judge his doubtful thoughts.*

stitute the *first* class of sins from which he would keep them. It is scarcely necessary to add that these were common crimes among the heathen. ¶ *In chambering.* "Lewd, immodest behaviour." (*Webster.*) The Greek word includes illicit indulgences of all kinds, adultery, &c. The words chambering and wantonness constitute the *second* class of crimes from which the apostle exhorts Christians to abstain. That these were common crimes among the heathen, it is not necessary to say; see Notes to Rom. i.; also Eph. v. 12. It is not possible, nor would it be proper, to describe the scenes of licentious indulgence of which all pagans are guilty. As Christians were to be a peculiar people, therefore the apostle enjoins on them purity and holiness of life. ¶ *Not in strife.* Strife and envying are the *third* class of sins from which the apostle exhorts them. The word *strife* means *contention, disputes, litigations.* The exhortation is that they should live in peace. ¶ *Envying.* Greek, Zeal. It denotes any intense, vehement, *fervid* passion. It is not improperly rendered here by envying. These vices are properly introduced in connection with the others. They usually accompany each other. Quarrels and contentions come out of scenes of drunkenness and debauchery. But for such scenes, there would be little contention, and the world would be comparatively at peace.

14. *But put ye on;* comp. Gal. iii. 17. The word rendered "put ye on" is the same used in ver. 12, and is commonly employed in reference to *clothing* or *apparel*. The phrase *to put on* a person, which seems a harsh expression in our language, was one not unfrequently used by Greek writers, and means to imbibe his principles, to imitate his example, to copy his spirit, to become like him. Thus in Dionysius Halicarnassus the expression occurs, "having *put on* or clothed themselves with Tarquin;" *i. e.* they imitated the example and morals of Tarquin. So Lucian says, "having *put on* Pythagoras;" having received him as a teacher and guide. So the Greek writers speak of putting on Plato, Socrates, &c. meaning to take them as instructors, to follow them as disciples. (See *Schleusner.*) Thus to put on the Lord Jesus means to take him as a pattern and guide, to imitate his example, to obey his precepts, to become like him, &c. In *all* respects the Lord Jesus was unlike what had been specified in the previous verse. He was temperate, chaste, pure, peaceable, and meek; and to *put him on* was to imitate him in these respects; Heb. iv. 15; vii. 26; 1 Pet. ii. 22; Isa. liii. 9; 1 John iii. 5. ¶ *And make not provision.* The word *provision* here is that which is used to denote *provident care,* or preparation for future wants. It means that we should not make it an object to gratify our lusts, or study to do this by laying up any thing beforehand with reference to this design. ¶ *For the flesh.* The word *flesh* is used here evidently to denote the corrupt propensities of the body, or those which he had specified in ver. 13. ¶ *To* fulfil *the lusts* thereof. With reference to its corrupt desires. The gratification of the flesh was the main object among the Romans. Living in luxury and licentiousness, they made it their great object of study to multiply and prolong the means of licentious indulgence. In respect to this, Christians were to be a separate people, and to show that they were influenced by a higher and purer desire than this grovelling propensity to minister to sensual gratification. It is right, it is a Christian duty, to labour to make provision for all the *real* wants of life. But the real wants are few; and with a heart disposed to be pure and temperate, the necessary wants of life are easily satis-

2 For one believeth that he may eat all things: another, who is weak, eateth herbs.

3 Let not him that eateth despise him that eateth not; and let not him which eateth not judge him that eateth; for God hath received him.

---

fied; and the mind may be devoted to higher and purer purposes.

CHAPTER XIV.

THE XIVth chapter is designed to settle some difficult and delicate questions that could not but arise between the Jews and Gentiles respecting food and the observance of particular days, rites, &c. The *occasions* of these questions were these: The converts to Christianity were from both Jews and Gentiles. There were many Jews in Rome; and it is probable that no small part of the church was composed of them. The New Testament every where shows that they were disposed to bind the Gentile converts to their own customs, and to insist on the observance of the peculiar laws of Moses; see Acts xv. 1, 2, &c; Gal. ii. 3, 4. The *subjects* on which questions of this kind would be agitated were, circumcision, days of fasting, the distinction of meats, &c. A part of these only are discussed in this chapter. The views of the apostle in regard to *circumcision* had been stated in chap. iii. and iv. In *this* chapter he notices the disputes which would be likely to arise on the following subjects; (1.) The use of *meat,* evidently referring to the question whether it was lawful to eat the meat that was offered in sacrifice to idols; ver. 2. (2.) The distinctions and observances of the days of Jewish fastings, &c. ver. 5, 6. (3.) The laws observed by the Jews in relation to animals as *clean* or *unclean*; ver. 14. It is probable that these are mere *specimens* adduced by the apostle to settle *principles* of conduct in regard to the Gentiles, and to show to each party how they ought to act in *all* such questions.

The apostle's design here is to allay all these contentions by producing peace, kindness, charity. This he does by the following considerations, viz. (1.) That we have no right to *judge* another man in this case, for he is the servant of God; ver. 3, 4. (2.) That whatever course is taken in these questions, it is done conscientiously, and with a desire to glorify God. In such a case there should be kindness and charity; ver. 6, &c. (3.) That we must stand at the judgment-seat of Christ, and give an account *there*; and that *we,* therefore, should not usurp the office of judging; ver. 10—13. (4.) That there is really nothing unclean of itself; ver. 14. (5.) That religion consisted in more important matters than *such* questions; ver. 17, 18. (6.) That we should follow after the things of peace, &c.; ver. 19—23. The principles of this chapter are applicable to all *similar* cases of difference of opinion about rites and ceremonies, and unessential doctrines of religion; and we shall see that if they were honestly applied, they would settle no small part of the controversies in the religious world.

1. *Him that is weak.* The design here is to induce Christians to receive to their fellowship those who had scruples about the propriety of certain things, or that might have peculiar prejudices and feelings as the result of education or former habits of belief. The apostle, therefore, begins by admitting that such an one may be *weak, i. e.* not fully established, or not with so clear and enlarged views about Christian liberty as others might have. ¶ *In the faith.* In believing. This does not refer to *saving faith* in Christ, for he might have that; but to belief in regard *to the things which the apostle specifies,* or which would come into controversy. Young converts have often a peculiar delicacy or sensitiveness about the lawfulness of many things in relation to which older Christians may be more fully established. To produce peace, there must be kindness, tenderness, and faithful teaching; not denunciation, or harshness, on one side or the other. ¶ *Receive ye.* Admit to your society or fellowship: receive him kindly, not meet with a cold and harsh repulse; comp. chap. xv. 7. ¶ *Not to doubtful disputations.* The plain meaning of this is, "Do not admit

him to your society for the purpose of debating the matter in an angry and harsh manner; of repelling him by denunciation; and thus, *by the natural reaction of such a course*, confirming him in his doubts." Or, "do not deal with him in such a manner as shall have a tendency to increase his scruples about meats, days, &c." *(Stuart.)* The *leading* idea here—which all Christians should remember—is, that a harsh and angry denunciation of a man in relation to things not morally wrong, but where he may have honest scruples, will only tend to confirm him more and more in his doubts. To denounce and abuse him will be to confirm him. To receive him affectionately, to admit him to fellowship with us, to talk freely and kindly with him, to do him good, will have a far greater tendency to overcome his scruples. In questions which now occur about modes of *dress*, about *measures* and means of promoting revivals, and about rites and ceremonies, this is by far the wisest course, if we wish to overcome the scruples of a brother, and to induce him to think as we do.—Greek, "Unto doubts or fluctuations of opinions or reasonings." Various senses have been given to the words, but the above probably expresses the true meaning.

2. *For one believeth.* This was the case with the Gentiles in general, who had none of the scruples of the Jew about the propriety of eating certain kinds of meat. Many of the converts who had been Jews might also have had the same view as the apostle Paul evidently had while the great mass of Jewish converts might have cherished these scruples. ¶ *May eat all things.* That is, he will not be restrained by any scruples about the lawfulness of certain meats, &c. ¶ *Another who is weak.* There is reference here, doubtless, to the Jewish convert. The apostle admits that he was *weak, i. e.* not fully established in the views of Christian liberty. The question with the Jew doubtless was, whether it was lawful to eat the meat which was offered in sacrifice to idols. In those sacrifices a part only of the animal was offered, and the remainder was eaten by the worshippers, or offered for sale in the market like other meat. It became an inquiry whether it was lawful to eat this meat; and the question in the mind of a Jew would arise from the express command of his law; Ex. xxxiv. 15. This question the apostle discussed and settled in 1 Cor. x. 20—32, which see. In that place the general principle is laid down, that it was lawful to partake of that meat as a man would of any other, *unless it was expressly pointed out to him as having been sacrificed to idols, and unless his partaking of it would be considered as countenancing the idolators in their worship*; ver. 28. But with this principle many Jewish converts might not have been acquainted; or what is quite as probable, they might not have been disposed to admit its propriety. ¶ *Eateth herbs.* Herbs or *vegetables* only; does not partake of meat at all, for *fear* of eating that, inadvertently, which had been offered to idols. The Romans abounded in sacrifices to idols; and it would not be easy to be certain that meat which was offered in the market, or on the table of a friend, had *not* been offered in this manner. To avoid the possibility of partaking of it, even *ignorantly*, they chose to eat no meat at all. The scruples of the Jews on the subject might have arisen in part from the fact that sins of *ignorance* among them subjected them to certain penalties; Lev. iv. 2, 3, &c.; v. 15; Num. xv. 24, 27—29. Josephus says (Life, § 3) that in his time there were certain priests of his acquaintance who "supported themselves with figs and nuts." These priests had been sent to Rome to be tried on some charge before Cæsar; and it is probable that they abstained from meat because it might have been offered to idols. It is expressly declared of Daniel when in Babylon, that he lived on pulse and water, that he might not "defile himself with the portion of the king's meat, nor with the wine which he drank;" Dan. i. 8—16.

3. *Let not him that eateth.* That is, he who has no scruples about eating *meat*, &c., who is not restrained by the law of the Jews respecting the clean and unclean, or by the fact that

4 Who [a] art thou that judgest another man's servant? to his own master he standeth or falleth. Yea, he shall be holden up: for God [b] is able to make him stand.

a James 4.12.

b Isa.40.29.

meat *may* have been offered to idols. ¶ *Despise him.* Hold him in contempt, as being unnecessarily scrupulous, &c. The word *despise* here is happily chosen. The Gentile would be very likely to *despise* the Jew as being restrained by foolish scruples and mere distinctions in matters of no importance. ¶ *Him that eateth not.* Him that is restrained by scruples of conscience, and that will eat only *vegetables;* ver. 2. The reference here is doubtless to the *Jew.* ¶ *Judge him.* To *judge* here has the force of *condemn.* This word also is very happily chosen. The Jew would not be so likely to *despise* the Gentile for what he did as to *judge* or condemn him. He would deem it too serious a matter for contempt. He would regard it as a violation of the law of God, and would be likely to assume the right of *judging* his brother, and pronouncing him guilty. The apostle here has happily met the whole case in all disputes about rites, and dress, and scruples in religious matters that are not essential. One party commonly *despises* the other as being needlessly and foolishly scrupulous; and the other makes it a matter of *conscience,* too serious for ridicule and contempt; and a matter, to neglect which, is, in their view, deserving of condemnation. The true direction to be given in such a case is, *to the one party,* not to treat the scruples of the other with derision and contempt, but with tenderness and indulgence. Let him have his way in it. If he can be *reasoned* out of it, it is well; but to attempt to *laugh* him out of it is unkind, and will tend only to confirm him in his views. And *to the other party,* it should be said they have no *right* to judge or condemn another. If I cannot see that the Bible requires a particular cut to my coat, or makes it my duty to observe a particular festival, he has no right to judge me harshly, or to suppose that I am to be rejected and condemned for it. He has a right to *his* opinion; and while I do not *despise* him, he has no right to *judge* me. This is the foundation of true charity; and if this simple rule had been followed, how much strife, and even bloodshed, would it have spared in the church. Most of the contentions among Christians have been on subjects of this nature. Agreeing substantially in the *doctrines* of the Bible, they have been split up into sects on subjects just about as important as those which the apostle discusses in this chapter. ¶ *For God hath received him.* This is the same word that is translated "receive" in ver. 1. It means here that God hath received him kindly; or has acknowledged him as his own friend; or he is a true Christian. These scruples, on the one side or the other, are not inconsistent with true piety; and as *God* has acknowledged him as *his,* notwithstanding his opinions on these subjects, so *we* also ought to recognise him as a Christian brother. Other denominations, though they may differ from us on some subjects, may give evidence that they are recognised by God as his, and where there is this evidence, we should neither despise nor judge them.

4. *Who art thou,* &c. That is, who gave you this right to sit in judgment on others; comp. Luke xii. 14. There is reference here particularly to the *Jew,* who on account of his ancient privileges, and because he had the law of God, would assume the prerogative of *judging* in the case, and insist on conformity to his own views; see Acts xv. The doctrine of this epistle is uniformly, that the Jew had no such privilege, but that in regard to salvation he was on the same level with the Gentile. ¶ *That judgest,* &c.; comp. James iv. 12. This is a principle of common sense and common propriety. It is not ours to sit in judgment on the servant of another man. He has the control over him; and if *he* chooses to forbid his doing any

5 One [a] man esteemeth one day above another: another esteemeth every day *alike*. Let every man be fully [1] persuaded in his own mind.

a Col.2.16.

1 or, *assured*.

thing, or to allow him to do any thing, it pertains to *his* affairs not ours. To attempt to control him, is to intermeddle improperly, and to become a "busy-body in other men's matters;" 1 Pet. iv. 15. Thus Christians are the servants of God; they are answerable to him; and *we* have no right to usurp *his* place, and to act as if we were "lords over his heritage;" 1 Pet. v. 3. ¶ *To his own master.* The servant is responsible to his master only. So it is with the Christian in regard to God. ¶ *He standeth or falleth.* He shall be approved or condemned. If his conduct is such as pleases his master, he shall be approved; if not, he will be condemned. ¶ *Yea, he shall be holden up.* This is spoken of the Christian only. In relation to the servant, he might stand or fall; he might be approved or condemned. The master had no power to keep him in a way of obedience, except by the hope of reward, or the fear of punishment. But it was not so in regard to the Christian. The Jew who was disposed to *condemn* the Gentile might say, that he admitted the general principle which the apostle had stated about the servant; that it was just what he was saying, that he might *fall*, and be condemned. But no, says the apostle, this does not follow, in relation to the Christian. He shall not fall. God has power to make him stand; to hold him; to keep him from error, and from condemnation, and *he shall be holden up*. He shall not be suffered to fall into condemnation, for it is the *purpose* of God to keep him; comp. Ps. i. 5. This is one of the incidental but striking evidences that the apostle believed that all Christians should be kept by the power of God through faith unto salvation. ¶ *Is able;* see John x. 29. Though a master cannot exert such an influence over a servant as to *secure* his obedience, yet *God* has this power over his people, and will preserve them in a path of obedience.

5. *One man esteemeth.* Gr. *judgeth* (κρίνει). The word is here properly translated *esteemeth;* comp. Acts xiii. 46; xvi. 15. The word originally has the idea of *separating*, and then *discerning*, in the act of judging. The expression means that one would set a higher value on one day than on another, or would regard it as more sacred than others. This was the case with the *Jews* uniformly, who regarded the days of their festivals, and fasts, and Sabbaths as peculiarly sacred, and who would retain, to no inconsiderable degree, their former views, even after they became converted to Christianity. ¶ *Another esteemeth.* That is, the *Gentile* Christian. Not having been brought up amidst the Jewish customs, and not having imbibed their opinions and prejudices, they would not regard these days as having any special sacredness. The appointment of those days had a special reference *to the Jews.* They were designed to keep them as a separate people, and to prepare the nation for the *reality*, of which their rites were but the shadow. When the Messiah came, the passover, the feast of tabernacles, and the other peculiar festivals of the Jews, of course vanished, and it is perfectly clear that the apostles never intended to inculcate their observance on the Gentile converts. See this subject discussed in the second chapter of the epistle to the Galatians. ¶ *Every day* alike. The word "alike" is not in the original, and it may convey an idea which the apostle did not design. The passage means that he regards *every day* as consecrated to the Lord; ver. 6. The question has been agitated whether the apostle intends in this to include the Christian Sabbath. Does he mean to say that it is a matter of *indifference* whether this day be observed, or whether it be devoted to ordinary business or amusements? This is a very important question in regard to the Lord's day. That the apostle did *not* mean to say that it

6 He that [1] regardeth the day, regardeth *it* unto the Lord and he that regardeth not the day, to the Lord he doth not regard *it*. He that eateth, eateth to the Lord; for he giveth God thanks: and he that eateth not, to the Lord he eateth not; and giveth God thanks.

1 or, *observeth*.

was a matter of indifference whether it should be kept as holy, or devoted to business or amusement, is plain from the following considerations. (1.) The discussion had reference only to the peculiar customs of the *Jews*, to the rites and practices which *they* would attempt to impose on the Gentiles, and not to any questions which might arise among Christians *as Christians*. The inquiry pertained to *meats*, and festival observances among the Jews, and to their scruples about partaking of the food offered to idols, &c.; and there is no more propriety in supposing that the subject of the Lord's day is introduced here than that he advances principles respecting *baptism* and *the Lord's supper*. (2.) The *Lord's day* was doubtless observed by *all* Christians, whether converted from Jews or Gentiles; see 1 Cor. xvi. 2; Acts xx. 7; Rev. i. 10; comp. Notes on John xx. 26. The propriety of observing *that day* does not appear to have been a matter of controversy. The only inquiry was, whether it was proper to *add* to that the observance of the Jewish Sabbaths, and days of festivals and fasts. (3.) It is expressly said that those who did not regard the day regarded it as not to God, or to honour God; ver. 6. They did it as a matter of respect to him and his institutions, to promote his glory, and to advance his kingdom. Was this ever done by those who disregard the Christian Sabbath? Is their design ever to promote his honour, and to advance in the knowledge of him, by *neglecting* his holy day? Who knows not that the Christian Sabbath has *never* been neglected or profaned by any design to glorify the Lord Jesus, or to promote his kingdom? It is for purposes of business, gain, war, amusement, dissipation, visiting, crime. Let the heart be filled with a sincere desire to *honour the Lord Jesus*, and the Christian Sabbath will be reverenced, and devoted to the purposes of piety. And if any man is disposed to plead *this passage* as an excuse for violating the Sabbath, and devoting it to pleasure or gain, let him quote it *just as it is, i. e.* let *him neglect the Sabbath from a conscientious desire to honour Jesus Christ*. Unless *this* is his motive, the passage cannot avail him. But this motive never yet influenced a Sabbath-breaker. ¶ *Let every man*, &c. That is, subjects of this kind are not to be pressed as matters of conscience. Every man is to examine them for himself, and act accordingly. This direction pertains to the subject under discussion, and not to any other. It does not refer to subjects that were *morally* wrong, but to ceremonial observances. If the *Jew* esteemed it wrong to eat meat, he was to abstain from it; if the Gentile esteemed it right, he was to act accordingly. The word "*be fully persuaded*" denotes the highest conviction, not a matter of opinion or prejudice, but a matter on which the mind is made up by examination; see Rom. iv. 21; 2 Tim. iv. 5. This is the general principle on which Christians are called to act in relation to festival days and fasts in the church. If some Christians deem them to be for edification, and suppose that their piety will be promoted by observing the days which commemorate the birth, and death, and temptations of the Lord Jesus, they are not to be reproached or opposed in their celebration. Nor are they to attempt to impose them on others as a matter of conscience, or to reproach others because they do not observe them.

6. *He that regardeth*. Greek, *Thinketh of;* or pays attention to; that is, he that *observes* it as a festival, or as holy time. ¶ *The day*. Any of the days under discussion; the days that the Jews kept as reli-

7 For [a] none of us liveth to himself, and no man dieth to himself.

8 For whether we live, we live unto the Lord: and whether we die, we die unto the Lord; whether

a 1 Pet.4.2.

---

gious occasions. ¶ *Regardeth it unto the Lord.* Regards it as *holy*, or as set apart to the service of God. He believes that he is *required* by God to keep it, *i. e.* that the laws of Moses in regard to such days are binding on him. ¶ *He that regardeth not the day.* Or who does not observe such distinctions of days as are demanded in the laws of Moses. ¶ *To the Lord*, &c. That is, he does not believe that God *requires* such an observance. ¶ *He that eateth.* The Gentile Christian, who freely eats all kinds of meat; ver. 2. ¶ *Eateth to the Lord.* Because he believes that God does not forbid it; and because he desires, in doing it, to glorify God; 1 Cor. x. 31. *To eat to the Lord*, in this case, is to do it believing that such is his will. In all other cases, it is to do it feeling that we receive our food from him; rendering thanks for his goodness, and desirous of being strengthened that we may do his commands. ¶ *He giveth God thanks.* This is an incidental proof that it is our duty to give God thanks at our meals for our food. It shows that it was the *practice* of the early Christians, and has the commendation of the apostle. It was, also, uniformly done by the Jews, and by the Lord Jesus; Mat. xiv. 19; xxvi. 26; Mark vi. 41; xiv. 22; Luke ix. 16; xxiv. 30. ¶ *To the Lord he eateth not.* He abstains from eating because he believes that God requires him to do it, and with a desire to obey and honour him. ¶ *And giveth God thanks.* That is, the Jew thanked God for the law, and for the favour he had bestowed on him in giving him more light than he had the Gentiles. For this privilege they valued themselves highly, and this feeling, no doubt, the converted Jews would continue to retain; deeming themselves as spepecially favoured in having a *peculiar* acquaintance with the law of God.

7. *For none of us*, &c. Whether by nature Jews or Gentiles. In the great principles of religion we are now united. Where there was evidence of a sincere desire to do the will of God there should be charitable feeling, though there was difference of opinion and judgment in many smaller matters. The meaning of the expression is, that no Christian lives to gratify his own inclinations or appetites. He makes it his great aim to do the will of God; to subordinate all his desires to his law and gospel; and though, therefore, one should eat flesh, and should feel at liberty to devote to common employments time that another deemed sacred, yet it should not be uncharitably set down as a desire to indulge his sensual appetites, or to become rich. Another motive *may be* supposed, and where there is not positive *proof* to the contrary, *should be* supposed; see the beautiful illustration of this in 1 Cor. xiii. 4—8. To live *to ourselves* is to make it the great object to become rich or honoured, or to indulge in the ease, comfort, and pleasures of life. These are the aim of all men but Christians; and in nothing else do Christians more differ from the world than in this; see 1 Pet. iv. 1, 2; 2 Cor. v. 15; 1 Cor. vi. 19, 20; Mat. x. 38; xvi. 24; Mark viii. 34; x. 21; Luke ix. 23. On no point does it become Christians more to examine themselves than on this. To *live to ourselves* is an evidence that we are strangers to piety. And if it be the great motive of our lives to live at ease (Amos vi. 1)—to gratify the flesh, to gain property, or to be distinguished in places of fashion and amusement—it is evidence that we know nothing of the power of that gospel which teaches us *to deny ourselves, and take up our cross daily.* ¶ *No man.* No *one*, the same Greek word (οὐδεὶς) which is used in the former part of the verse. The word is used only in reference to *Christians* here, and makes no affirmation about other men. ¶ *Dieth to himself;* see ver. 8. This expression is

we live therefore, or die, we are the Lord's.

9 For [a] to this end Christ both died, and rose, and revived, that he might be Lord both of the dead and living.

a Phil.2.9-11.

used to denote the *universality* or the *totality* with which Christians belong to God. Every thing is done and suffered with reference to his will. In our conduct, in our property, in our trials, in our death, we are *his;* to be disposed of as he shall please. In the grave, and in the future world, we shall be equally his. As this is the great principle on which *all* Christians live and act, we should be kind and tender towards them, though in some respects they differ from us.

8. *For whether we live.* As long as we live. ¶ *We live unto the Lord.* We live to do his will, and to promote his glory. This is the grand purpose of the life of the Christian. Other men live to gratify themselves; the Christian to do those things which the Lord requires. By *the Lord* here the apostle evidently intends the Lord Jesus, as it is evident from ver. 9; and the truth taught here is, that it is the leading and grand purpose of the Christian to do honour to the Saviour. It is this which constitutes his peculiar character, and which distinguishes him from other men. ¶ *Whether we die.* In the dying state, or in the state of the dead; in the future world. We are *no where* our own. In all conditions we are *his,* and bound to do his will. The connection of this declaration with the argument is this:—Since we belong to another in every state, and are bound to do his will, we have no right to assume the prerogative of sitting in judgment on another. *We* are subjects, and are bound to do the will of Christ. All other Christians are subjects in like manner, and are answerable, not to us, but directly to the Lord Jesus, and should have the same liberty of conscience that we have. The passage proves also that the soul does not cease to be conscious at death. We are still the Lord's; his even when the body is in the grave; and his in all the future world; see ver. 9.

9. *For to this end.* For this purpose or design. The apostle does not say that this was the *only* design of his death, but that it was a main purpose, or an object which he had distinctly in view. This declaration is introduced in order to confirm what he had said in the previous verse, that in all circumstances we are the Lord's. This he shows by the fact that Jesus died *in order* that we *might* be his. ¶ *And rose.* This expression is rejected by most modern critics. It is wanting in many manuscripts, and has been probably introduced in the text from the margin. ¶ *And revived.* There is also a variation in the Greek in this place, but not so great as to change the sense materially. It refers to his *resurrection,* and means that he was *restored to life* in order that he might exercise dominion over the dead and the living. ¶ *That he might be Lord.* Greek. That he might *rule over.* The Greek word used here implies the idea of his being *proprietor* or *owner* as well as *ruler.* It means that he might exercise entire dominion over all, as the sovereign Lawgiver and Lord. ¶ *Both of the dead.* That is, of those who *are* deceased, or who have gone to another state of existence. This passage proves that those who die are not annihilated; that they do not cease to be conscious; and that they still are under the dominion of the Mediator. Though their bodies moulder in the grave, yet the spirit lives, and is under his control. And though the body dies and returns to its native dust, yet the Lord Jesus is still its Sovereign, and shall raise it up again.

> "God our Redeemer lives,
> And often from the skies
> Looks down and watches all our dust,
> Till he shall bid it rise."

It gives an additional sacredness to the grave when we reflect that the tomb is under the watchful care of the Redeemer. Safe in his hands, the body may sink to its native dust with the assurance that in his own time he

10 But why dost thou judge thy brother? or why dost thou set at nought thy brother? for we shall all stand before the judgment-seat of Christ.

11 For it is written, [a] *As* I live,

[a] Isa.45.23.

will again call it forth, with renovated and immortal powers, to be for ever subject to his will. With this view, we can leave our friends with confidence in his hands when they die, and yield our own bodies cheerfully to the dust when he shall call our spirits hence. But it is not only over the *body* that his dominion is established. This passage proves that the departed souls of the saints are still subject to him; comp. Mat. xxii. 32; Mark xii. 27. He not only has *dominion* over those spirits, but he is their protector and Lord. They are safe under his universal dominion. And it does much to alleviate the pains of separation from pious, beloved friends, to reflect that they depart still to love and serve the same Saviour in perfect purity, and unvexed by infirmity and sin. Why should we wish to recall them from his perfect love in the heavens to the poor and imperfect service which they would render if in the land of the living? ¶ *And living.* To the redeemed, while they remain in this life. He died to *purchase* them to himself, that they might become his obedient subjects; and they are bound to yield obedience by all the sacredness and value of the price which he paid, even his own precious blood; comp. 1 Cor. vi. 20, "For ye are bought with a price; therefore glorify God in your body and in your spirit, which are God's;" vii. 23; Rev. xiv. 4 (Greek, *bought*): 1 Pet. ii. 9, (Greek, *purchased*). If it be asked how this *dominion over the dead and the living* is connected with the death and resurrection of the Lord Jesus, we may reply, (1.) That it is secured over Christians from the fact that they are *purchased* or *ransomed* by his precious blood; and that they are bound by this sacred consideration to live to him. This obligation every Christian feels (1 Pet. i. 18), and its force is continually resting on him. It was by the love of Christ that he was ever brought to love God at all; and his deepest and tenderest obligations to live to him arise from this source; 2 Cor. v. 14, 15. (2.) Jesus, by his death and resurrection, established a dominion over the grave. He destroyed him that had the power of death, (Heb. ii. 14), and triumphed over him; Col. ii. 15. Satan is a humbled foe; and his sceptre over the grave is wrested from his hands. When Jesus rose, in spite of all the power of Satan and of men, he burst the bands of death, and made an invasion on the dominions of the dead, and showed that he had power to control all. (3.) This dominion of the Lord Jesus is felt by the spirits on high. They are subject to him *because* he redeemed them; Rev. v. 9. (4.) It is often revealed in the Scriptures that *dominion* was to be given to the Lord Jesus as the reward of his sufferings and death; see Note to John xvii. 2, 4, 5; v. 26—29; Phil. ii. 5—11; Eph. i. 20, 21; Heb. ii. 9, 10; xii. 2. The *extent* of his dominion as mediator is affirmed, in this place, only to be over the dead and the living; that is, over the human race. Other passages of the Scripture, however, seem to imply that it extends over all worlds.

10. *But why,* &c. Since we are all subjects and servants alike, and must all stand at the same tribunal, what right have we to sit in judgment on others? ¶ *Thou judge.* Thou who art a *Jewish* convert, why dost thou attempt to arraign the *Gentile* disciple, as if he had violated a law of God? comp. ver. 3. ¶ *Thy brother.* God has recognised him as his friend (ver. 3), and he should be regarded by thee as *a brother* in the same family. ¶ *Or why dost thou set at nought.* Despise (ver. 3); why dost thou, who art a *Gentile* convert, despise the *Jewish* disciple as being unnecessarily scrupulous and superstitious? ¶ *Thy brother.* The Jewish convert is now a brother; and all the contempt which you Gentiles once cherished for the Jew should

saith the Lord, every knee shall bow to me, and every tongue shall confess to God.

12 So then every one of us shall give account of himself to God.

---

cease, from the fact that *he* is now *a Christian.* Nothing will do so much, on the one hand, to prevent a censorious disposition, and on the other, to prevent contempt for those who are in a different rank in life, as to remember that they are *Christians*, bought with the same blood, and going to the same heaven as ourselves. ¶ *We must all stand*, &c. That is, we must all be tried alike at the same tribunal; we must answer for our conduct, not to our-fellow men, but to Christ; and it does not become us to sit in judgment on each other.

11. *For it is written.* This passage is recorded in Isa. xlv. 23. It is not quoted literally, but the sense is preserved. In Isaiah there can be no doubt that it refers to Jehovah. The speaker expressly calls himself JEHOVAH, the name which is appropriate to God alone, and which is never applied to a creature; ver. 18, 21, 24, 25. In the place before us, the words are applied by Paul expressly to Christ; comp. ver. 10. This mode of quotation is a strong incidental proof that the apostle regarded the Lord Jesus as divine. On no other principle could he have made these quotations. ¶ *As I live.* The Hebrew is, "I have sworn by myself." One expression is equivalent to the other. An *oath* of God is often expressed by the phrase "as I live;" Num. xiv. 21; Isa. xlix. 18; Ezek. v. 11; xiv. 16, &c. ¶ *Saith the Lord.* These words are not in the Hebrew text, but are added by the apostle to show that the passage quoted was spoken by the Lord, the Messiah; comp. Isa. xlv. 18, 22. ¶ *Every knee shall bow to me.* To *bow the knee* is an act expressing homage, submission, or adoration. It means that every person shall acknowledge him as God, and admit his right to universal dominion. The passage in Isaiah refers particularly to the homage which *his own people* should render to him; or rather, it means that all who are saved shall acknowledge *him* as their God and Saviour. The original reference was not to *all men*, but only to those who should be saved; Isa. xlv. 17, 21, 22, 24. In this sense the apostle uses it; not as denoting that *all men* should confess to God, but that all *Christians*, whether Jewish or Gentile converts, should alike give account to Him. *They* should all bow before their common God, and acknowledge *his* dominion over them. The passage originally did not refer particularly to the day of judgment, but expressed the truth that all believers should acknowledge his dominion. It is as applicable, however, to the judgment, as to any other act of homage which his people will render. ¶ *Every tongue shall confess to God.* In the Hebrew, "Every tongue shall swear." Not swear *by God*, but *to him;* that is, pay to him our vows, or *answer to him on oath* for our conduct; and this is the same as *confessing* to him, or acknowledging him as our Judge.

12. *So then.* Wherefore; or according to the doctrine of the Old Testament. ¶ *Every one of us.* That is, every Christian; for the connection requires us to understand the argument only of Christians. At the same time it is a truth abundantly revealed elsewhere, that *all men* shall give account of their conduct to God; 2 Cor. v. 10; Mat. xxv; Eccl. xii. 14. ¶ *Give account of himself.* That is, of his character and conduct; his words and actions; his plans and purposes. In the fearful arraignment of that day every work and purpose shall be brought forth, and tried by the unerring standard of justice. As we shall be called to so fearful an account with God, we should not be engaged in condemning our brethren, but should examine whether we are prepared to give up our account with joy, and not with grief. ¶ *To God.* The judgment will be conducted by the Lord Jesus; Mat. xxv. 31—46; Acts xvii. 31. All judgment is committed to the Son; John v. 22, 27. Still we may be said to give account to God, (1.) Because He *appointed* the Messiah to be the Judge

13 Let us not therefore judge one another any more: but judge this rather, that no man put a stumbling-block or an occasion to fall in *his* brother's way.

14 I know, and am persuaded

(Acts xvii. 31); and, (2,) Because the Judge himself is divine. The Lord Jesus being God as well as man, the account will be rendered directly to the Creator as well as the Redeemer of the world. In this passage there are *two* incidental proofs of the divinity of the Lord Jesus Christ. *First,* the fact that the apostle applies to him language which in the prophecy is expressly spoken by *Jehovah;* and, *Secondly,* the fact that Jesus is declared to be the Judge of all. No being that is not *omniscient* can be qualified to judge the secrets of all men. None who has not *seen* human purposes at all times, and in all places; who has not been a witness of the conduct by day and by night; who has not been present with all the race at all times, and who in the great day cannot discern the true character of the soul, can be qualified to conduct the general judgment. Yet none can possess these qualifications but God. The Lord Jesus, "the judge of quick and dead" (2 Tim. iv. 1), is therefore divine.

13. *Let us not therefore judge,* &c. Since we are to give account of ourselves at the same tribunal; since we must be there on the same *level,* let us not suppose that we have a right here to sit in judgment on our fellow-Christians. ¶ *But judge this rather.* If disposed to *judge,* let us be employed in a better kind of judging; let us come *to a determination* not to injure the cause of Christ. This is an instance of the happy *turn* which the apostle would give to a discussion. Some men have an irresistible propensity to sit in judgment, to pronounce opinions. Let them make good use of that. It will be well to exercise it on that which can do no injury, and which may turn to good account. Instead of forming a judgment about *others,* let the man form a determination about his own conduct. ¶ *That no man,* &c. A *stumbling-block* literally means any thing laid in a man's path, over which he may fall. In the Scriptures, however, the word is used commonly in a figurative sense to denote any thing which shall cause him to *sin,* as sin is often represented by *falling;* see Note, Mat. v. 29. And the passage means that we should resolve to act so as not *by any means* to be the occasion of leading our brethren into sin, either by our example, or by a severe and harsh judgment, provoking them to anger, or exciting jealousies, and envyings, and suspicions. No better rule than this could be given to promote peace. If every Christian, instead of judging his brethren severely, would resolve that *he* would so live as to promote peace, and so as not to lead others into sin, it would tend more, perhaps, than any other thing to advance the harmony and purity of the church of Christ.

14. *I know.* This is an admission made to the *Gentile* convert, who believed that it was lawful to partake of food of every kind. This the apostle concedes; and says he is fully apprized of this. But though he knew this, yet he goes on to say (ver. 15), that it would be well to regard the conscientious scruples of others on the subject. It may be remarked here that the apostle Paul had formerly quite as many scruples as any of his brethren had then. But his views had been changed. ¶ *And am persuaded.* Am convinced. ¶ *By the Lord Jesus.* This does not mean by any *personal* instruction received from the Lord Jesus, but by all the knowledge which he had received by inspiration of the nature of the Christian religion. The *gospel* of Jesus had taught him that the rites of the Mosaic economy had been abolished, and among those rites were the rules respecting clean and unclean beasts, &c. ¶ *There is nothing unclean.* Gr. *common.* This word was used by the Jews to denote that which was *unclean,* because, in their apprehension, whatever was partaken by the multitude, or all men, must be impure. Hence the words *common* and *impure* are often used as expressing the same

by the Lord Jesus, that *there is* nothing [1] unclean of itself: but to him that esteemeth any thing to be [2] unclean, to him *it is* unclean.

15 But if thy brother be grieved

1 *common.*

2 *common.*

thing. It denotes that which was forbidden by the laws of Moses. ¶ *To him that esteemeth*, &c. He makes it a matter of conscience. He regards certain meats as forbidden by God; and while he so regards them, it would be wrong for him to partake of them. Man may be in error, but it would not be proper for him to act in violation of what he *supposes* God requires.

15. *But if thy brother*, &c. This address is to the *Gentile* convert. In the previous verse, Paul admitted that the prejudice of the Jew was not well-founded. But admitting that still the question was, *how* he should be treated while he had that prejudice. The apostle here shows the Gentile that *he* ought not so to act as unnecessarily to wound his feelings, or to grieve him. ¶ *Be grieved.* Be pained; as a conscientious man always is, when he sees another, and especially a Christian brother, do any thing which *he* esteems to be wrong. The *pain* would be real, though the *opinion* from which it arose might not be well founded. ¶ *With* thy *meat.* Greek, On account of meat, or food; that is, because *you* eat that which he regards as unclean. ¶ *Now walkest.* To *walk*, in the sacred Scriptures, often denotes to act, or to do a thing; Mark vii. 5; Acts xxi. 21; Rom. vi. 4; viii. 1, 4. Here it means that *if* the Gentile convert persevered in the use of such food, notwithstanding the conscientious scruples of the Jew, he violated the law of love. ¶ *Charitably.* Greek, According to charity, or love; that is, he would violate that law which required him to sacrifice his own comfort to promote the happiness of his brother; 1 Cor. xiii. 5; x. 24, 28, 29; Phil. ii. 4, 21. ¶ *Destroy not him.* The word *destroy* here refers, doubtless, to the ruin of the soul in hell. It properly denotes ruin or destruction, and is applied to the *ruin* or *corruption* of various things, in the New Testament. To *life* (Mat. x. 39); to a reward, in the sense of *losing* it (Mark x. 41; Luke xv. 4); to food (John vi. 27); to the Israelites represented as *lost* or wandering (Mat. x. 6); to *wisdom* that is rendered vain (1 Cor. i. 9); to *bottles*, rendered useless (Mat. ix. 17), &c. But it is also frequently applied to destruction in hell, to the everlasting ruin of the soul; Mat. x. 28, "Who is able to destroy both soul and body in *hell;*" Mat. xviii. 14; John iii. 15; Rom. ii. 12. That *this* is its meaning here is apparent from the parallel place in 1 Cor. viii. 11, "And through thy knowledge shall thy weak brother *perish.*" If it be asked how the eating of meat by the Gentile convert could be connected with the perdition of the Jew, I reply, that the apostle supposes that in this way an occasion of stumbling would be afforded to him, and he would come into condemnation. He might be led by example to partake against his own conscience, or he might be excited to anger, disgust, and apostasy from the Christian faith. Though the apostle believed that all who were true Christians would be saved, Rom. viii. 30—39, yet he believed that it would be brought about by the use of means, and that nothing should be done that would tend to hinder or endanger their salvation; Heb. vi. 4—9; ii. 1. God does not bring his people to heaven without the use of *means adapted to the end*, and one of those means is that employed here to warn professing Christians against such conduct as might jeopard the salvation of their brethren. ¶ *For whom Christ died.* The apostle speaks here of the possibility of endangering the salvation of those for whom Christ died, just as he does respecting the salvation of those who are in fact Christians. By those for whom Christ died, he undoubtedly refers here to *true Christians*, for the whole discussion relates to them, and them only; comp. ver. 3, 4, 7, 8. This passage should not be brought, therefore, to prove that Christ died for all men,

with *thy* meat, now walkest thou not [1]charitably. Destroy [a] not him with thy meat, for whom Christ died.

16 Let not then your good be evil spoken of.

17 For [b] the kingdom of God is not meat and drink; but righteous-

1 *According to charity.* a 1 Cor.8.11. b Matt.6.33.

or for any who shall finally perish. Such a doctrine is undoubtedly true [in this sense; that there is in the death of Christ a *sufficiency for all,* and that the *offer* is *to* all.] (comp. 2 Cor. v. 14, 15; 1 John ii. 2; 2 Pet. ii. 1), but it is not the truth which is taught here. The design is to show the criminality of a course that would tend to the ruin of a brother. For these weak brethren, Christ laid down his precious life. He loved them; and shall we, to gratify our appetites, pursue a course which will tend to defeat the work of Christ, and ruin the souls redeemed by his blood?

16. *Let not then your good,* &c. That which you esteem to be right, and which may be right in itself. You are not bound by the ceremonial law. You are free from the yoke of bondage. This freedom you esteem to be *a good* —a favour—a high privilege. And so it is; but you should not make such a use of it as to do injury to others. ¶ *Be evil spoken of.* Greek, Be blasphemed. Do not so use your Christian liberty as to give occasion for railing and unkind remarks from your brethren, so as to produce contention and strife, and thus to give rise to evil reports among the wicked about the tendency of the Christian religion, as if it were adapted only to promote controversy. How much strife would have been avoided if all Christians had regarded this plain rule. In relation to dress, and rites, and ceremonies in the church, we may be conscious that we are right; but an obstinate adherence to them may only give rise to contention and angry discussions, and to evil reports among men, of the tendency of religion. In such a case we should yield our private, unimportant personal indulgence to the good of the cause of religion and of peace.

17. *For the kingdom of God.* For an explanation of this phrase, see Note, Mat. iii. 2. Here it means that the *peculiarities* of the kingdom of God, or of the Church of Christ on earth, do not consist in observing the distinctions between meats and drinks. It was true that by these things the Jews had been particularly characterized, but the Christian church was to be distinguished in a different manner. ¶ *Is not.* Does not consist in, or is not distinguished by. ¶ *Meat and drink.* In observing distinctions between different kinds of food, or making such observances a matter of conscience as the Jews did. Moses did not prescribe any particular drink or prohibit any, but the Nazarites abstained from wine and all kinds of strong liquors; and it is not improbable that the Jews had invented some distinctions on this subject which they judged to be of importance. Hence it is said in Col. ii. 16, "Let no man judge you in meat or *in drink;*" comp. 1 Cor. viii. 8; iv. 20. ¶ *But righteousness.* This word here means *virtue, integrity,* a faithful discharge of all the duties which we owe to God or to our fellow-men. It means that the Christian must so live as to be appropriately denominated a righteous man, and not a man whose whole attention is absorbed by the mere ceremonies and outward forms of religion. To produce this, we are told, was the main design, and the principal teaching of the gospel; Tit. ii. 12; Comp. Rom. viii. 13; 1 Pet. ii. 11. Thus it is said (1 John ii. 29), "Every one that doeth righteousness is born of God;" iii. 10, "Whosoever doeth not righteousness is not of God;" comp. 1 John iii. 7; 1 Cor. xv. 34; 2 Cor. iii. 9; vi. 7, 14; Eph. v. 9; vi. 14; 1 Tim. vi. 11; 1 Pet. ii. 24; Eph. iv. 24. He that is a righteous man, whose characteristic it is to lead a holy life, is a Christian. If his great aim is to do the will of God, and if he seeks to discharge with fidelity all his duties to God and man, he is renewed. On that righteousness he will not *depend* for sal-

ness, [a] and peace, [b] and joy [c] in the Holy Ghost,

18 For he that in these things serveth Christ, *is* acceptable to God, and approved of men.

19 Let [d] us therefore follow after

a Phil.3.9. *b* John 16.33; chap.5.1; Phil.4.7. *c* chap.15.13. *d* Ps.34.14; He.12.14.

vation (Phil. iii. 8, 9), but he will regard this character and this disposition as evidence that he is a Christian, and that the Lord Jesus is made unto him "wisdom, and righteousness, and sanctification, and redemption;" 1 Cor. i. 30. ¶ *And peace.* This word, in this place, does not refer to the internal *peace* and happiness which the Christian has in his own mind (comp. Notes on chap. v. 1); but to peace or concord in opposition to *contention* among brethren. The tendency and design of the kingdom of God is to produce concord and love, and to put an end to alienation and strife. Even though, therefore, there might be ground for the opinions which some cherished in regard to rites, yet it was of more importance to maintain peace than obstinately to press those matters at the expense of strife and contention. That the tendency of the gospel is to promote peace, and to induce men to lay aside all causes of contention and bitter strife, is apparent from the following passages of the New Testament; 1 Cor. vii. 15; xiv. 33; Gal. v. 22; Eph. iv. 3; 1 Thess. v. 13; 2 Tim. ii. 22; James iii. 18; Mat. v. 9; Eph. iv. 31, 32; Col. iii. 8; John xiii. 34, 35; xvii. 21—23. This is the second evidence of piety on which Christians should examine their hearts—a disposition to promote the peace of Jerusalem; Ps. cxxii. 6; xxxvii. 11. A contentious, quarrelsome spirit; a disposition to magnify trifles; to make the Shibboleth of party an occasion of alienation, and heart-burning, and discord; to sow dissensions on account of unimportant points of doctrine or of discipline, is full proof that there is no attachment to Him who is the Prince of peace. Such a disposition does infinite dishonour to the cause of religion, and perhaps has done more to retard its progress than all other causes put together. Contentions commonly arise from some small matter in doctrine, in dress, in ceremonies; and often the smaller the matter the more fierce the controversy, till the spirit of religion disappears, and desolation comes over the face of Zion.

> "The Spirit, like a peaceful dove,
> Flies from the realms of noise and strife."

¶ *And joy.* This refers, doubtless, to the *personal* happiness produced in the mind by the influence of the gospel; see Notes, chap. v. 1—5. ¶ *In the Holy Ghost.* Produced *by* the Holy Ghost; chap. v. 5; comp. Gal. v. 22, 23.

18. *In these things.* In righteousness, peace, and joy. ¶ *Serveth Christ.* Or obeys Christ, who has commanded them. He receives Christ as his *master* or *teacher* and does *his* will in regard to them. To do these things is to do honour to Christ, and to show the excellency of his religion. ¶ *Is acceptable to God.* Whether he be converted from the Jews or the Gentiles. ¶ *And approved of men.* That is, men will *approve* of such conduct; they will esteem it to be right, and to be in accordance with the spirit of Christianity. He does not say that the wicked world will *love* such a life, but it will commend itself to them as such a life as men *ought* to lead.

19. *Let us therefore follow,* &c. The object of this verse is to persuade the church at Rome to lay aside their causes of contention, and to live in harmony. This exhortation is founded on the considerations which the apostle had presented, and may be regarded as the conclusion to which the argument had conducted him. ¶ *The things which make for peace.* The high purposes and objects of the Christian religion, and not those smaller matters which produce strife. If men aim at the great objects proposed by the Christian religion, they will live in peace. If they seek to promote their private ends, to follow their own passions and prejudices, they will be involved in strife and contention.

the things which make for peace, and [a] things wherewith one may edify another.

20 For meat destroy not the work of God. All things indeed *are* pure; [b] but *it is* [c] evil for that man who eateth with offence.

a 1 Co.14.12. b Titus 1.15. c 1 Cor.8.10-13.

There *are* great common objects before *all* Christians in which they can unite, and in the pursuit of which they will cultivate a spirit of peace. Let them all strive for holiness; let them seek to spread the gospel; let them engage in circulating the Bible, or in doing good in any way to others, and their smaller matters of difference will sink into comparative unimportance, and they will unite in one grand purpose of saving the world. Christians have more things in which they *agree* than in which they differ. The points in which they are agreed are of infinite importance; the points on which they differ are commonly some minor matters in which they may "agree to differ," and still cherish love for all who bear the image of Christ. ¶ *And things wherewith,* &c. That is, those things by which we may render *aid* to our brethren; the doctrines, exhortations, counsels, and other helps which may benefit them in their Christian life. ¶ *May edify.* The word *edify* means properly to *build,* as a house; then to *rebuild* or *reconstruct;* then to adorn or ornament; then to do any thing that will confer favour or advantage, or which will further an object. Applied to the church, it means to do any thing by teaching, counsel, advice, &c. which will tend to promote its great object; to aid Christians, to enable them to surmount difficulties, to remove their ignorance, &c.; Acts ix. 31; 1 Cor. viii. 1; xiv. 4. In these expressions the idea of a *building* is retained, reared on a firm, tried corner-stone, the Lord Jesus Christ; Eph. ii. 20; Isa. xxviii. 16. Compare Rom. ix. 33. Christians are thus regarded, according to Paul's noble idea (Eph. ii. 20—22), as one great temple erected for the glory of God, having no separate interest, but as united for one object, and therefore bound to do all that is possible, that each other may be fitted to their appropriate place, and perform their appropriate function in perfecting and adorning this temple of God.

20. *For meat.* By your obstinate, pertinacious attachment to your own opinions about the distinctions of meat and drinks, do not pursue such a course as to lead a brother into sin, and ruin his soul. Here is a new argument presented why Christians should pursue a course of charity—that the opposite would tend to the ruin of the brother's soul. ¶ *Destroy not.* The word here is that which properly is applied to pulling down an edifice; and the apostle continues the figure which he used in the previous verse. Do not pull down or destroy the *temple* which God is rearing. ¶ *The work of God.* The work of God is that which God *does,* and here especially refers to his work in rearing *his church.* The *Christian* is regarded peculiarly as the work of God, as God renews his heart and makes him what he is. Hence he is called God's "building" (1 Cor. iii. 9), and his "workmanship, created in Christ Jesus unto good works" (Eph. ii. 10), and is denominated "a new creature;" 2 Cor. v. 17. The meaning is, "Do not so conduct yourself, in regard to the distinction of meats into clean and unclean, as to cause your brother to sin, and to impair or ruin the work of religion which God is carrying on in his soul." The expression does not refer to *man* as being the work of God, but to the *piety* of the Christian; to that which God, by his Spirit, is producing in the heart of the believer. ¶ *All things are indeed pure;* comp. ver. 14. This is a concession to those whom he was exhorting to peace. All things under the Christian dispensation are lawful to be eaten. The distinctions of the Levitical law are not binding on Christians. ¶ *But it is evil.* Though pure in itself, yet it may become an occasion of sin, if another is grieved by it. It is evil to the man who pursues a course that

21 *It is* good neither to eat flesh, nor to drink wine, nor *any thing* whereby thy brother stumbleth, or is offended, or is made weak.

22 Hast thou faith? have *it*

will give offence to a brother; that will pain him, or tend to drive him off from the church, or lead him any way into sin. ¶ *With offence.* So as to offend a brother, such as *he* esteems to be sin, and by which he will be grieved.

21. *It is good.* It is right; or it is better. This verse is an explanation or enlarged specification of the meaning of the former. ¶ *To eat flesh.* That is, such flesh as the *Jewish* convert regarded as unclean; ver. 2. ¶ *Nor to drink wine.* Wine was a common drink among the Jews, and usually esteemed lawful. But the Nazarites were not allowed to drink it (Numb. vi. 3), and the Rechabites (Jer. xxxv.) drank no wine, and it is possible that some of the early converts regarded it as unlawful for Christians to drink it. Wine was moreover used in libations in heathen worship, and perhaps the Jewish coverts might be scrupulous about its use from this cause. The caution here shows us what should be done *now* in regard to the use of wine. It may not be possible to prove that wine is absolutely unlawful, but still many friends of *temperance* regard it as such, and are grieved at its use. They esteem the habit of using it as tending to intemperance, and as encouraging those who cannot afford expensive liquors. Besides, the wines which are now used are different from those which were common among the ancients. That was the pure juice of the grape. That which is now in common use is mingled with alcohol, and with other intoxicating ingredients. Little or none of the wine which comes to this country is pure. And in this state of the case, does not the command of the apostle here require the friends of temperance to abstain even from the use of wine? ¶ *Nor any thing.* Any article of food or drink, or any course of conduct. So valuable is peace, and so desirable is it not to offend a brother, that we should rather deny ourselves to any extent, than to be the occasion of offences and scandals in the church. ¶ *Stumbleth.* For the difference between this word and the word *offended,* see Note, Rom. xi. 11. It means here that by eating, a Jewish convert might be led to eat also, contrary to his own conviction of what was right, and thus be led into sin. ¶ *Or is made weak.* That is, shaken, or rendered less stable in his opinion or conduct. By being led to imitate the Gentile convert, he would become less firm and established; he would violate his own conscience; his course would be attended with regrets and with doubts about its propriety, and thus he would be made *weak.* In this verse we have an eminent instance of the charity of the apostle, and of his spirit of concession and kindness. If this were regarded by all Christians, it would save no small amount of strife, and heart-burnings, and contention. Let a man begin to act on the principle that peace is to be promoted, that other Christians are not to be offended, and what a change would it at once produce in the churches, and what an influence would it exert over the life!

22. *Hast thou faith?* The word *faith* here refers only to the subject under discussion—to the subject of meats, drinks, &c. Do you believe that it is right to eat all kinds of food, &c. The apostle had admitted that this was the true doctrine; but he maintains that it should be so held as not to give offence. ¶ *Have it to thyself.* Do not obtrude your faith or opinion on others. Be satisfied with cherishing the opinion, and acting on it in private, without bringing it forward to produce disturbance in the church. ¶ *Before God.* Where God only is the witness. God sees your sincerity, and will approve your opinion. That opinion cherish and act on, yet so as not to give offence, and to produce disturbance in the church. God sees your sincerity; he sees that you are right; and you will not offend him. Your brethren do *not* see that you are right, and *they* will be offended. ¶ *Happy is he,* &c. This state of

to thyself before God. Happy [a] *is* he that condemneth not himself in that thing which he alloweth.

23 And he that [1] doubteth is damned if he eat, because *he eateth* not of faith: for whatsoever [a] is not of faith is sin.

a 1John 3.21.

1 or, *discerneth and putteth a difference between meats.* a Heb.11.6.

mind, the apostle says, is one that is attended with peace and happiness; and this is a *further* reason why they should indulge their opinion in private, without obtruding it on others. They were conscious of doing right, and that consciousness was attended with peace. This fact he states in the form of a universal proposition, as applicable not only to *this* case, but to *all* cases; comp. 1 John iii. 21. ¶ *Condemneth not himself.* Whose conscience does not reprove him. ¶ *In that which he alloweth.* Which he *approves,* or which he *does.* Who has a clear conscience in his opinions and conduct. Many men indulge in practices which their consciences condemn, many in practices of which they are in doubt. But the way to be happy is to have a *clear conscience* in what we do; or in other words, if we have *doubts* about a course of conduct, it is not safe to indulge in that course, but it should be at once abandoned. Many men are engaged in *business* about which they have many doubts; many Christians are in doubt about certain courses of life. But they can have *no doubt* about the propriety of abstaining from them. They who are engaged in the slave-trade; or they who are engaged in the manufacture or sale of ardent spirits; or they who frequent the theatre or the ball-room, or who run the round of fashionable amusements, if professing Christians, MUST often be troubled with *many* doubts about the propriety of their manner of life. But they can have no doubt about the propriety of an *opposite* course. Perhaps a single inquiry would settle all debate in regard to these things: *Did any one ever become a slave-dealer, or a dealer in ardent spirits, or go to the theatre, or engage in scenes of splendid amusements, with any belief that he was imitating the Lord Jesus Christ, or with any desire to honour him or his religion?* But one answer would be given to this question; and in view of it, how striking is the remark of Paul, "Happy is he that condemneth not himself in that which he alloweth."

23. *He that doubteth.* He that is not fully satisfied in his mind; who does not do it with a clear conscience. The margin has it rendered correctly, "He that discerneth and putteth a difference between meats." He that conscientiously believes, as the Jew did, that the Levitical law respecting the difference between meats was binding on Christians. ¶ *Is damned.* We apply this word almost exclusively to the future punishment of the wicked in hell. But it is of importance to remember, in reading the Bible, that this is not of necessity its meaning. It means properly *to condemn;* and here it means only that the person who should thus violate the dictates of his conscience would incur guilt, and would be blameworthy in doing it. But it does not affirm that he would inevitably sink to hell. The same construction is to be put on the expression in 1 Cor. xi. 29, "He that eateth and drinketh unworthily, eateth and drinketh damnation to himself." ¶ *For whatsoever, &c. Whatever is not done with a full conviction that it is right, is sinful; whatever is done when a man doubts whether it is right, is sin.* This is evidently the fair interpretation of this place. Such the connection requires. It does not affirm that all or any of the actions of impenitent and unbelieving men are sinful, which is true, but not the truth taught here; nor does it affirm that all acts which are not performed by those who have faith in the Lord Jesus, are sinful; but the discussion pertains to Christians; and the whole scope of the passage requires us to understand the apostle as simply say-

CHAPTER XV.

WE then that are strong ought to [a] bear the infirmities of the weak, and not to please ourselves.

2 Let every one of us please

a chap.14.1; Gal.6.2.

ing that a man should not do a thing doubting its correctness; that he should have a strong conviction that what he does is right; and that if he has *not* this conviction, it is sinful. The rule is of universal application. In all cases, if a man does a thing which he does not *believe* to be right, it is a sin, and his conscience will condemn him for it. It may be proper, however, to observe that the converse of this is not always true, that if a man believes a thing to be right, that therefore it is not sin. For many of the persecutors were conscientious (John xvi. 2; Acts xxvi. 9); and the murderers of the Son of God did it ignorantly (Acts iii. 17; 1 Cor. ii. 8); and yet were adjudged as guilty of enormous crimes; comp. Luke xi. 50, 51; Acts ii. 23, 37.

In this chapter we have a remarkably fine discussion of the nature of Christian charity. Differences of *opinion* will arise, and men will be divided into various sects; but if the rules which are laid down in this chapter were followed, the contentions, and altercations, and strifes among Christians would cease. Had these rules been applied to the controversies about rites, and forms, and festivals, that have arisen, peace might have been preserved. Amid all such differences, the great question is, whether there is true love to the Lord Jesus. If there is, the apostle teaches us that we have no right to judge a brother, or despise him, or contend harshly with him. Our object should be to promote peace, to aid him in his efforts to become holy, and to seek to build him up in holy faith.

CHAPTER XV.

It may be of importance to state that between the last verse of the preceding chapter and the first verse of this, the Arabic version, some MSS. and many of the Greek fathers, as Chrysostom, Theodoret, Theophylact, &c. have introduced ver. 25—27 of chap. xvi. of this epistle. Why this was done, has been a matter of controversy. The discussion, however, is of no practical importance, and most critics concur in the opinion that the present arrangement of the Greek text is genuine.

1. *We then that are strong.* The apostle resumes the subject of the preceding chapter; and continues the exhortation to brotherly love and mutual kindness and forbearance. By the *strong* here he means the strong *in faith* in respect to the matters under discussion; those whose minds were free from doubts and perplexities. His own mind was free from doubt, and there were many others, particularly of the Gentile converts, that had the same views. But many also, particularly of the *Jewish* converts, had many doubts and scruples. ¶ *Ought to bear.* This word *bear* properly means to *lift up*, to *bear away*, to *remove.* But here it is used in a larger sense; *to bear with, to be indulgent to, to endure patiently, not to contend with;* Gal. vi. 2; Rev. ii. 2, "Thou canst not bear them that are evil." ¶ *And not to please ourselves.* Not to make it our main object to gratify our own wills. We should be willing to deny ourselves, if by it we may promote the happiness of others. This refers particularly to *opinions* about meats and drinks; but it may be applied to Christian conduct generally, as denoting that we are not to make our own happiness or gratification the standard of our conduct, but are to seek the welfare of others; see the example of Paul, 1 Cor. ix. 19, 22; see also Phil. ii. 4; 1 Cor. xiii. 5, "Love seeketh not her own;" x. 24, "Let no man seek his own, but every man another's wealth; also Mat. xvi. 24.

2. *Please his neighbour.* That is, all other persons, but especially the friends of the Redeemer. The word *neighbour* here has special reference to the members of the church. It is often used, however, in a much larger

his neighbour [a] for *his* good to edification.

3 For even Christ [b] pleased not himself; but, as it is written, [c] The reproaches of them that reproached thee fell on me.

a 1 Cor.9.19; Phil.2.4,5. b John 6.38. c Ps.69.9.

sense; see Luke x. 36. ¶ *For his good.* Not seek to secure for him indulgence in those things which would be injurious to him, but in all those things whereby his welfare would be promoted. ¶ *To edification;* see Note, chap. xiv. 19.

3. *For even Christ.* The apostle proceeds, in his usual manner, to illustrate what he had said by the example of the Saviour. To a Christian, the example of the Lord Jesus will furnish the most ready, certain, and happy illustration of the nature and extent of his duty. ¶ *Pleased not himself.* This is not to be understood as if the Lord Jesus did not voluntarily and cheerfully engage in his great work. He was not *compelled* to come and suffer. Nor is it to be understood as if he did not *approve* the work, or see its propriety and fitness. If he had not, he would never have engaged in its sacrifices and self-denials. But the meaning may be expressed in the following particulars: (1.) He came to do the will or desire of God in *undertaking* the work of salvation. It was the will of God; it was agreeable to the divine purposes, and the Mediator did not consult his own happiness and honour in heaven, but cheerfully came to *do the will* of God; Ps. xl. 7, 8; comp. Heb. x. 4—10; Phil. ii. 6; John xvii. 5. (2.) Christ when on earth, made it his great object to do the will of God, to finish the work which God had given him to do, and not to seek his own comfort and enjoyment. This he expressly affirms; John vi. 38; v. 30. (3.) He was willing for this to endure whatever trials and pains the will of God might demand, not seeking to avoid them or to shrink from them. See particularly his prayer in the garden; Luke xxii. 42. (4.) In his life, he did not seek personal comfort, wealth, or friends, or honours. He denied himself to promote the welfare of others; he was poor that they might be rich; he was in lonely places that he might seek out the needy and provide for them. Nay, he did not seek to preserve his own life when the appointed time came to die, but gave himself up for all. (5.) There may be another idea which the apostle had here. He bore with patience the ignorance, blindness, erroneous views, and ambitious projects of his disciples. He evinced kindness to them when in error; and was not harsh, censorious, or unkind, when they were filled with vain projects of ambition, or perverted his words, or were dull of apprehension. So says the apostle, *we* ought to do in relation to our brethren. ¶ *But as it is written;* Ps. lxix. 9. This psalm, and the former part of this verse, is referred to the Messiah; comp. ver. 21, with Mat. xxvii. 34, 48. ¶ *The reproaches.* The calumnies, censures, harsh, opprobrious speeches. ¶ *Of them that reproached thee.* Of the wicked, who vilified and abused the law and government of God. ¶ *Fell on me.* In other words, Christ was willing to suffer reproach and contempt in order to do good to others. He endured calumny and contempt all his life, from those who by their lips and lives calumniated God, or reproached their Maker. We may learn here, (1.) That the contempt of Jesus Christ is contempt of him who appointed him. (2.) We may see the kindness of the Lord Jesus in being willing thus to *throw himself* between the sinner and God; to *intercept,* as it were, our sins, and to bear the effects of them in his own person. He stood between *us* and God; and both the reproaches and the divine displeasure due to them, *met* on his sacred person, and produced the sorrows of the atonement—his bitter agony in the garden and on the cross. Jesus thus showed his love of God in being willing to bear the reproaches aimed at him; and his love to *men* in

4 For whatsoever [a] things were written aforetime were written for our learning, that we through patience and comfort of the Scriptures might have hope.

5 Now the God of patience and consolation grant you to be like-minded [b] one toward another, [1] according to Christ Jesus;

6 That ye may with one [c] mind

a 1 Cor.10.11; 2 Tim.3.16,17.

b 1 Cor.1.10. 1 or, *after the example of.* c Acts 4.24,32.

being willing to endure the sufferings necessary to atone for these very sins. (3.) If Jesus thus bore reproaches, *we* should be willing also to endure them. We suffer in the cause where he has gone before us, and where he has set us the example; and as *he* was abused and vilified, we should be willing to be so also.

4. *For whatsoever things,* &c. This is a *general* observation which struck the mind of the apostle, from the particular case which he had just specified. He had just made use of a striking passage in the Psalms to his purpose. The thought seems suddenly to have occurred to him that *all* the Old Testament was admirably adapted to express Christian duties and doctrine, and he therefore turned aside from his direct argument to express this sentiment. It should be read as a parenthesis. ¶ *Were written aforetime.* That is, in ancient times; in the Old Testament. ¶ *For our learning.* For our *teaching* or instruction. Not that this was the *only* purpose of the writings of the Old Testament, to instruct Christians; but that all the Old Testament might be useful *now* in illustrating and enforcing the doctrines and duties of piety towards God and man. ¶ *Through patience.* This does not mean, as our translation might seem to suppose, patience *of the Scriptures,* but it means that by patiently enduring sufferings, in connection with the consolation which the Scriptures furnish, we might have hope. The *tendency* of patience, the apostle tells us (Rom. v. 4), is to produce *hope;* see Notes on this place. ¶ *And comfort of the Scriptures.* By means of the consolation which the writings of the Old Testament furnish. The word rendered *comfort* means also *exhortation* or *admonition.* If this is its meaning here, it refers to the admonitions which the Scriptures suggest, instructions which they impart, and the exhortations to patience in trials. If it means *comfort,* then the reference is to the examples of the saints in affliction; to their recorded expressions of confidence in God in their trials, as of Job, Daniel, David, &c. Which is the precise meaning of the word here, it is not easy to determine. ¶ *Might have hope;* Note, chap. v. 4. We may learn here, (1.) That afflictions may prove to be a great blessing. (2.) That their proper tendency is to produce *hope.* (3.) That the way to find support in afflictions is to go to the Bible. By the example of the ancient saints, by the expression of their confidence in God, by their patience, *we* may learn to suffer, and may not only be *instructed,* but may find *comfort* in all our trials; see the example of Paul himself in 2 Cor. i. 2—11.

5. *Now the God of patience.* The God who is *himself* long-suffering, who bears patiently with the errors and faults of his children, and who can *give* patience, may he give you of his Spirit, that you may bear patiently the infirmities and errors of each other. The example of God here, who bears long with his children, and is not angry soon at their offences, is a strong argument why Christians should bear with each other. If God bears long and patiently with *our* infirmities, *we* ought to bear with each other. ¶ *And consolation.* Who gives or imparts consolation. ¶ *To be like-minded,* &c. Gr. To think the same thing; that is, to be united, to keep from divisions and strifes. ¶ *According to Christ Jesus.* According to the example and spirit of Christ; his was a spirit of peace. Or, according to what his religion requires. The name of Christ is sometimes thus put for his religion; 2 Cor.

and one mouth glorify God, even the Father of our Lord Jesus Christ.

7 Wherefore receive ye one another, as Christ also received [a] us, to the glory of God.

8 Now I say that Jesus Christ was a minister of the circumci-

a Eph.1.6.

xi. 4; Eph. iv. 20. If all Christians would imitate the example of Christ, and follow his instructions, there would be no contentions among them. He earnestly sought in his parting prayer their unity and peace; John xvii. 21—23.

6. *That ye may with one mind.* The word here used is translated "with one accord;" Acts i. 14; ii. 1; iv. 24. It means unitedly, with one purpose, without contentions, and strifes, and jars. ¶ *And one mouth.* This refers, doubtless, to their prayers and praises. That they might join without contention and unkind feeling, in the worship of God. Divisions, strife, and contention in the church prevent union in worship. Though the *body* may be there, and the church *professedly* engaged in public worship, yet it is a *divided* service; and the prayers of strife and contention are not heard; Isa. lviii. 4. ¶ *Glorify God.* Praise or honour God. This would be done by their union, peace, and harmony; thus showing the tendency of the gospel to overcome the sources of strife and contention among men, and to bring them to peace. ¶ *Even the Father,* &c. This is an addition designed to produce love. (1.) He is *a Father;* we then, his children, should regard him as pleased with the union and peace of his family. (2.) He is the Father of OUR LORD; our *common* Lord; our Lord who has commanded us to be united, and to love one another. By the desire of honouring *such* a Father, we should lay aside contentions, and be united in the bands of love.

7. *Wherefore.* In view of all the considerations tending to produce unity and love, which have been presented. He refers to the various arguments in this and the preceding chapter. ¶ *Receive ye one another.* Acknowledge one another as Christians, and treat one another as such, though you may differ in opinion about many smaller matters; see chap. xiv. 3. ¶ *As Christ also received us.* That is, received us as his friends and followers; see chap. xiv. 3. ¶ *To the glory of God.* In order to promote his glory. He has redeemed us, and renewed us, in order to promote the honour of God; comp. Eph. i. 6. As Christ has received us in order to promote the glory of God, so ought we to treat each other in a similar manner for a similar purpose. The exhortation in this verse is to those who had been divided on various points pertaining to rites and ceremonies; to those who had been converted from among *Gentiles* and *Jews;* and the apostle here says that Christ had received *both.* In order to enforce this, and especially to show the *Jewish* converts that they ought to receive and acknowledge their *Gentile* brethren, he proceeds to show, in the following verses, that Christ had reference to *both* in his work. He shows this in reference to the *Jews* (ver. 8), and to the *Gentiles* (ver. 9—12). Thus he draws all his arguments from the work of Christ.

8. *Now I say.* I affirm, or maintain. I, a *Jew,* admit that his work had reference to the Jews; I affirm also that it had reference to the Gentiles. ¶ *That Jesus Christ.* That *the Messiah.* The force of the apostle's reasoning would often be more striking if he would retain the word *Messiah,* and not regard the word *Christ* as a mere surname. It is the name of his *office;* and to *a Jew* the name *Messiah* would convey much more than the idea of a mere proper name. ¶ *Was a minister of the circumcision.* Exercised his office—the office of the Messiah—among the Jews, or with respect *to* the Jews, for the purposes which he immediately specifies. He was born a Jew; was circumcised; came *to* that nation; and died in their midst, without hav-

sion for the truth of God, to confirm *a* the promises *made* unto the fathers.

9 And that the Gentiles might glorify God for *his* mercy; as it is written, *b* For this cause I will confess to thee among the Gentiles, and sing unto thy name.

10 And again he saith, *c* Rejoice, ye Gentiles, with his people.

11 And again, *d* Praise the Lord, all ye Gentiles; and laud him, all ye people.

12 And again Esaias saith, *e* There shall be a root *f* of Jesse,

a Acts 3.25,26. *b* Ps.18.49. *c* Deut.32.43. *d* Ps.117.1. *e* Isa.11.1,10. *f* Rev.5.5, 22,16.

ing gone himself to any other people. ¶ *For the truth of God.* To confirm or establish the truth of the promises of God. He remained among them in the exercise of his ministry, to show that God was *true*, who had said that the Messiah should come to them. ¶ *To confirm the promises,* &c. To *establish*, or to show that the promises were true; see Note, Acts iii. 25, 26. The *promises* referred to here, are those particularly which related to the coming of the Messiah. By thus admitting that the Messiah was the minister of the circumcision, the apostle conceded all that the Jew could ask, that he was to be peculiarly *their* Messiah; see Note, Luke xxiv. 47.

9. *And that the Gentiles,* &c. The benefits of the gospel were not to be confined to *the Jews;* and as God *designed* that those benefits should be extended to the *Gentiles*, so the Jewish converts ought to be willing to admit them and treat them as brethren. That God *did* design this, the apostle proceeds to show. ¶ *Might glorify God.* Might *praise*, or give thanks to God. This implies that the favour shown to them was a *great* favour. ¶ *For* his *mercy*. Greek, On account of the mercy shown to them. ¶ *As it is written;* Ps. xviii. 49. The expression there is one of David's. He says that he will praise God for his mercies *among* the heathen, or when surrounded *by* the heathen; or that he would confess and acknowledge the mercies of God to him, as we should say, *to all the world.* The apostle, however, uses it in this sense, that the *Gentiles* would *participate* with the Jew in offering praise to God, or that they would be united. This does not appear to have been the original design of David in the psalm, but the *words* express the idea of the apostle. ¶ *And sing,* &c. Celebrate thy praise. This supposes that *benefits* would be conferred on them, for which they would celebrate his goodness.

10. *And again,* &c.; Deut. xxxii. 43. In this place the *nations* or Gentiles are called on to rejoice with the Jews, for the interposition of God in their behalf. The design of the quotation is to show that the Old Testament speaks of the Gentiles as called on to celebrate the praises of God; of course, the apostle infers that they are to be introduced to the same privileges as his people.

11. *And again;* Ps. cxvii. 1. The object in this quotation is the same as before. The apostle accumulates quotations to show that it was the common language of the Old Testament, and that he was not depending on a single expression for the truth of his doctrine. ¶ *All ye Gentiles.* In the psalm, "all ye *nations;*" but the original is the same. ¶ *And laud him. Praise* him. The psalm is directly in point. It is a call on *all* nations to praise God; the very point in the discussion of the apostle.

12. *Esaias saith;* Isaiah chap. xi. 1, 10. ¶ *There shall be a root.* A descendant, or one that should proceed from him when he was dead. When a tree dies, and falls, there may remain a *root* which shall retain life, and which shall send up a sprout of a similar kind. So Job says (chap. xiv. 7), "For there is hope of a tree, if it be cut down, that it will sprout again, and that the tender branch thereof will not cease." So in relation to Jesse. Though *he* should fall, like an aged tree, yet his name and family

and he that shall rise to reign over
the Gentiles; in him shall the
Gentiles trust.
13 Now the God of hope fill
you with all [a] joy and peace in
believing, that ye may abound in
hope, through the power of the
Holy Ghost.
14 And I myself also am per
suaded [b] of you, my brethren, that

a chap.14.17.

b Heb.6.9; 2 Pet.1.12.

should not be extinct. There should be a descendant who should rise, and reign over the Gentiles. The Lord Jesus is thus called also the "root and the offspring of David;" Rev. xxii. 16; v. 5. ¶ *Of Jesse.* The father of David; 1 Sam. xvii. 58. The Messiah was thus descended from Jesse. ¶ *He that shall rise.* That is, as a sprout springs up from a decayed or fallen tree. Jesus thus *rose* from the family of David, that had fallen into poverty and humble life in the time of Mary. ¶ *To reign over the Gentiles.* This is quoted from the LXX. of Isa. xi. 10. The Hebrew is, "Which shall stand up for an ensign of the people;" that is, a standard to which they shall flock. Either the Septuagint or the Hebrew would express the idea of the apostle. The *substantial* sense is retained, though it is not literally quoted. The idea of his *reigning* over the Gentiles is one that is fully expressed in the second psalm. ¶ *In him,* &c. Hebrew, "To it shall the Gentiles seek." The sense, however, is the same. The design of this quotation is the same as the preceding, to show that it was predicted in the Old Testament that the Gentiles should be made partakers of the privileges of the gospel. The argument of the apostle is, that if this was designed, then converts to Christianity from among the *Jews* should lay aside their prejudices, and *receive* them as their brethren, entitled to the same privileges of the gospel as themselves. The *fact* that the Gentiles would be admitted to these privileges, the apostle had more fully discussed in chap. x. xi.

13. *Now the God of hope.* The God who *inspires,* or *produces* the Christian hope. ¶ *All joy and peace;* chap. xiv. 17. If they were filled with this, there would be no strife and contention. ¶ *In believing.* The effect of believing is to produce this joy and peace. ¶ *That ye may abound,* &c. That your hope may be steadfast and strong. ¶ *Through the power,* &c. By means of the powerful operation of the Holy Spirit. It is by his power alone that the Christian has the hope of eternal life; see Eph. i. 13, 14; Rom. viii. 24.

14. *And I myself also.* The apostle here proceeds to show them why he had written this epistle, and to state his confidence in them. He had exhorted them to peace; he had opposed some of their strongest prejudices; and in order to secure their obedience to his injunctions, he now shows them the deep interest which he had in their welfare, though he had never seen them. ¶ *Am persuaded.* He had never seen them (chap. i. 10—13), but he had full confidence in them. This confidence he had expressed more fully in the first chapter. ¶ *Of you.* Concerning you. I have full confidence in you. ¶ *My brethren.* An address of affection; showing that he was not disposed to assume undue authority, or to lord it over their faith. ¶ *Are full of goodness.* Filled with *kindness* or *benevolence.* That is, they were *disposed* to obey any just commands; and that consequently any errors in their opinions and conduct had not been the effect of obstinacy or perverseness. There was indeed danger in the city of Rome of pride and haughtiness; and among the Gentile converts there might have been some reluctance to receive instruction from a foreign Jew. But the apostle was persuaded that all this was overcome by the mild and humbling spirit of religion, and that they were disposed to obey any just commands. He made this observation, therefore, to conciliate respect to his authority as an apostle. ¶ *Filled with all knowledge.* That is,

ye also are full of goodness, filled
with all knowledge, [a] able also to
admonish one another.

15 Nevertheless, brethren, I
have written the more boldly unto
you in some sort, as putting you in
mind, because [b] of the grace that is
given to me of God.

16 That I should be the minister of Jesus Christ to the Gen-

a 1 Cor.8.1,7,10.

b Eph.3.7,8.

---

instructed in the doctrines and duties of the Christian religion. This was true; but there might be still some comparatively unimportant and non-essential points, on which they might not be entirely clear. On these, the apostle had written; and written, not professedly to communicate *new* ideas, but to *remind* them of the great principles on which they were before instructed, ver. 15. ¶ *Able also*, &c. That is, you are so fully instructed in Christian principles, as to be able to give advice and counsel, if it is needed. From this verse we may learn, (1.) That when it is our duty to give instruction, admonition, or advice, it should be in a kind, conciliating manner; not with harshness, or with the severity of authority. Even *an apostle* did not assume harshness or severity in his instructions. (2.) There is no impropriety in speaking of the good qualities of Christians in their presence; or even of *commending* and *praising* them when they deserve it. The apostle Paul was as far as possible from always dwelling on the faults of Christians. When it was necessary to reprove them, he did it, but did it with tenderness and tears. When he *could* commend, he preferred it; and never hesitated to give them credit to the utmost extent to which it could be rendered. He did not *flatter*, but he told the truth; he did not commend to excite pride and vanity, but to encourage, and to prompt to still more active efforts. The minister who always censures and condemns, whose ministry is made up of complaints and lamentations, who never speaks of Christians but in a strain of fault-finding, is unlike the example of the Saviour and of Paul, and may expect little success in his work; comp. Rom. i. 8; xvi. 19; 1 Cor. i. 5; 2 Cor. viii. 7; ix. 2; Phil. i. 3—7; Heb. vi. 9; 2 Pet. i. 12.

15. *Nevertheless.* Notwithstanding my full persuasion of your knowledge and your purpose to do right. Perhaps he refers also to the fact that he was a stranger to them. ¶ *The more boldly.* More boldly than might have been expected from a stranger. The reason why he showed this boldness in declaring his sentiments, he immediately states—that he had been specially called to the office of instructing the Gentiles. ¶ *In some sort* (ἀπὸ μέρους). In part. Some have supposed that he referred to a *party* at Rome—the Gentile party. (*Whitby.*) Some refer it to different *parts* of his epistle—on some subjects. (*Stuart.*) Probably the expression is designed to qualify the phrase *more boldly.* The phrase, says Grotius, *diminishes* that of which it is spoken, as 1 Cor. xiii. 9, 12; 2 Cor. i. 14; ii. 5; and means the same as "somewhat more freely;" that is, I have been induced to write the more freely, *partly* because I am appointed to this very office. I write somewhat more freely to a church among the Gentiles than I even should to one among the Jews, *because* I am appointed to this very office. ¶ *As putting you in mind.* Greek, Calling to your *remembrance*, or *reminding* you; comp. 2 Pet. i. 12, 13. This was a delicate way of communicating instruction. The apostles presumed that all Christians were acquainted with the great doctrines of religion; but they did not command, enjoin, or assume a spirit of dictation. How happy would it be if all teachers would imitate the example of the *apostles* in this, and be as modest and humble *as they were.* ¶ *Because of the grace*, &c. Because God has conferred the *favour* on me of appointing me to this office; see Note, chap. i. 5.

16. *The minister* (λειτουργὸν). This is not the word which is commonly translated *minister* (διάκονος). This word is properly appropriated to those

tiles, ministering the gospel of God, that the [1] offering [a] up of the Gentiles might be acceptable, being sanctified [b] by the Holy Ghost.

1 or, *sacrificing*. a Isa.66.20. b Acts 20.32.

who minister in public offices or the affairs of the state. In the New Testament it is applied mainly to the Levitical priesthood, who ministered and served at the altar; Heb. xi. 11. It is however applied to the ministers of the New Testament, as discharging *substantially* the same offices towards the church which were discharged by the Levitical priesthood; *i. e.* as engaged in promoting the welfare of the church, occupied in holy things, &c.; Acts xiii. 2, "As they *ministered* to the Lord and fasted," &c. It is used in a larger sense still in Rom. xv. 27; 2 Cor. ix. 12. ¶ *To the Gentiles;* comp. chap. i. 5; Acts ix. 15. ¶ *Ministering* (ἱερουργοῦντα). Performing the office of a priest in respect to the gospel of God. The office of a *priest* was to offer sacrifice. Paul here retains the *language*, though without affirming or implying that the ministers of the New Testament were literally *priests* to offer sacrifice. The word used here occurs no where else in the New Testament. Its meaning here is to be determined from the connection. The question is, What is the *sacrifice* of which he speaks? It is the *offering up*—the sacrifice of the Gentiles. The Jewish sacrifices were abolished. The Messiah had fulfilled the design of their appointment, and they were to be done away. (See the epistle to the Hebrews.) There was to be no further *literal* sacrifice. But now the *offerings* of the Gentiles were to be as acceptable as had been the offerings of the Jews. God made no distinction; and in speaking of these offerings, Paul used *figurative* language drawn from the Jewish rites. But assuredly he did not mean that the offerings of the Gentiles were *literal* sacrifices to expiate sins; nor did he mean that there was to be an order of men who were to be called *priests* under the New Testament. If this passage *did* prove that, it would prove that it should be confined to the *apostles*, for it is of them only that he uses it. The meaning is this: "Acting in the Christian church substantially as the priests did among the Jews; that is, endeavouring to secure the acceptableness of the offerings which the Gentiles make to God." ¶ *That the offering up.* The word here rendered *offering up* (προσφορὰ) commonly means *a sacrifice* or an *expiatory* offering, and is applied to Jewish sacrifices; Acts xxi. 26; xxiv. 17. It is also applied to the sacrifice which was made by our Lord Jesus Christ when he offered himself on the cross for the sins of men; Eph. v. 2; Heb. x. 10. It does not always mean *bloody* sacrifices, but is used to denote *any* offering to God; Heb. x. 5, 8, 14, 18. Hence it is used in this large sense to denote the *offering* which the Gentiles who were converted to Christianity made of themselves; their *devoting* or dedicating themselves to God. The *language* is derived from the customs of the Jews; and the apostle represents himself *figuratively* as *a priest* presenting this offering to God. ¶ *Might be acceptable.* Or, approved by God. This was in accordance with the prediction in Isa. lxvi. 20, "They shall bring all your brethren for an offering unto the Lord out of all nations," &c. This does not mean that it was by any *merit* of the apostle that this offering was to be rendered acceptable; but that he was appointed to prepare the way, so that *their* offering, as well as that of the *Jews*, might come up before God. ¶ *Being sanctified.* That is, *the offering* being sanctified, or made holy. The sacrifice was *prepared* or made fit *to be* an offering, among the Jews, by salt, oil, or frankincense, according to the nature of the sacrifice; Lev. vi. 14, &c. In allusion to this, the apostle says that the offering of the Gentiles was rendered holy, or fit to be offered, by the converting and purifying influences of the Holy Spirit. They were prepared, not by salt and frankincense, but by the cleansing influences of God's Spirit. The same idea, substantially,

17 I have therefore whereof I may glory [a] through Jesus Christ in those things [b] which pertain to God.

18 For I will not dare to speak of any of those things which Christ hath not wrought by me, to make [c] the Gentiles obedient, by word and deed.

19 Through mighty signs [d] and wonders, by the power of the Spirit of God; so that from Jerusalem,

a 2 Cor.12.1,&c. b Heb.5.1. c Gal.2.8. d Acts 19.11.

is expressed by the apostle Peter in Acts x. 46; xi. 17.

17. *I have therefore,* &c. I have cause of glorying. I have cause of rejoicing that God has made me a minister to the Gentiles, and that he has given me such success among them. The ground of this he states in ver. 18—22. ¶ *Glory.* Of *boasting* (καύχησιν, the word usually rendered *boasting*); James iv. 16; Rom. iii. 27; 2 Cor. vii. 14; viii. 24; ix. 3, 4; x. 15; xi. 10, 17. It means also *praise, thanksgiving,* and *joy*; 1 Cor. xv. 31; 2 Cor. i. 12; vii. 4; viii. 24; 1 Thess. ii. 19. This is its meaning here, that the apostle had great cause of *rejoicing* or *praise* that he had been so highly honoured in the appointment *to* this office, and in his success *in* it. ¶ *Through Jesus Christ.* By the assistance of Jesus Christ; ascribing his success among the Gentiles to the *aid* which Jesus Christ had rendered him. ¶ *In those things which pertain to God*; comp. Heb. v. 1. The things of religion; the things which God has commanded, and which pertain to his honour and glory. They were not things which pertained to *Paul,* but to *God:* not wrought *by* Paul, but *by* Jesus Christ; yet he might rejoice that he had been the means of diffusing so far those blessings. The success of a minister is not for *his own* praises, but for the honour of God; not by *his* skill or power, but by the aid of Jesus Christ; yet he may rejoice that *through* him such blessings are conferred on men.

18. *For I will not dare to speak.* I should be restrained; I should be afraid to speak, if the thing were not as I have stated. I should be afraid to set up a claim beyond that which is strictly in accordance with the truth. ¶ *Which Christ hath not wrought by me.* I confine myself *strictly* to what I have done. I do not arrogate to myself what Christ has done by others. I do not exaggerate my own success, or claim what others have accomplished. ¶ *To make the Gentiles obedient.* To bring them to obey God in the gospel. ¶ *By word and deed.* By *preaching,* and by all other means; by miracle, by example, &c. The *deeds,* that is, the *lives* of Christian ministers are often as efficacious in bringing men to Christ as their public ministry.

19. *Through mighty signs and wonders.* By stupendous and striking miracles; see Note, Acts ii. 43. Paul here refers, doubtless, to the miracles which he had himself wrought; see Acts xix. 11, 12, "And God wrought special miracles by the hands of Paul," &c. ¶ *By the power of the Spirit of God.* This may either be connected with *signs and wonders,* and then it will mean that those miracles were performed by the power of the Holy Spirit; or it may constitute a new subject, and refer to the gift of prophecy, the power of speaking other languages. Which is its true meaning cannot, perhaps, be ascertained. The interpretations *agree* in this, that he traced his success in *all* things to the aid of the Holy Spirit. ¶ *So that from Jerusalem.* Jerusalem, as a *centre* of his work; the centre of all religious operations and preaching under the gospel. This was not the place where *Paul* began to preach (Gal. i. 17, 18), but it was the place where the *gospel* was first preached, and the apostles began to reckon their success from that as a point; comp. Note, Luke xxiv. 49. ¶ *And round about* (καὶ κύκλῳ). In a circle. That is, taking Jerusalem as a centre, he had fully preached round that centre until you come to Illyricum. ¶ *Unto Illyricum.* Illyricum was a province lying to the northwest of Macedonia, bounded north by a part of

and round about unto Illyricum,
I [a] have fully preached the gospel
of Christ.
20 Yea, so have I strived to
preach the gospel, not where Christ
was named, [b] lest I should build
upon another man's foundation:
21 But, as it is written, [c] To
whom he was not spoken of they
shall see: and they that have not
heard shall understand.
22 For which cause also I have
been much [1] hindered [d] from coming
to you;
23 But now having no more
places in these parts, and having

a chap. 1.14-16. *b* 2Cor. 10.13-16. *c* Isa. 52.15.

1 or, *many ways*, or, *oftentimes*. *d* 1Thess.2.18.

Italy and Germany, east by Macedonia, south by the Adriatic, west by Istria. It comprehended the modern Croatia and Dalmatia. So that taking Jerusalem as a centre, Paul preached not only in Damascus and Arabia, but in Syria, in Asia Minor, in all Greece, in the Grecian Islands, and in Thessaly and Macedonia. This comprehended no small part of the then known world; *all* of which had heard the gospel by the labours of one indefatigable man. There is no where in the *Acts* express mention of Paul's going *into* Illyricum; nor does the expression imply that he preached the gospel *within* it, but only *unto* its borders. It may have been, however, that when in Macedonia, he crossed over into that country; and this is rendered somewhat probable from the fact that *Titus* is mentioned as having gone into *Dalmatia* (2 Tim. iv. 10), which was a part of Illyricum. ¶ *I have fully preached.* The word here used means properly *to fill up* (πεπληρωκέναι), *to complete*, and here is used in the sense of *diffusing abroad*, or of *filling up* all that region with the gospel; comp. 2 Tim. iv. 17. It means that he had faithfully diffused the knowledge of the gospel in all that immense country.

20. *Yea, so have I strived.* The word used here (φιλοτιμούμενον) means properly *to be ambitious, to be studious of honour;* and then to *desire* earnestly. In that sense it is used here. He earnestly desired; he made it a point for which he struggled, to penetrate into regions which had not heard the gospel. ¶ *Not where Christ was named.* Where the gospel had not been before preached. ¶ *Lest I should build*, &c. That is, he desired to found churches himself; he regarded himself as particularly called to this. Others might be called to edify the church, but he regarded it as *his* office to make known the name of the Saviour where it was not before known. This work was particularly adapted to the ardour, zeal, energy, and bravery of such a man as Paul. Every man has his proper gift; and there are some particularly fitted to *found* and establish churches; others to edify and comfort them; comp. 2 Cor. x. 13—16. The apostle chose the higher honour, involving most danger and responsibility; but still *any* office in building up the church is honourable.

21. *But as it is written.* Isa. lii. 15. This is not literally quoted, but the sense is retained. The design of quoting it is to justify the principle on which the apostle acted. It was revealed that the gospel should be preached to the Gentiles; and he regarded it as a high honour to be the instrument of carrying this prediction into effect.

22. *For which cause.* I have been so entirely occupied in this leading purpose of my life, that I have not been able to come to you. ¶ *Much hindered.* Many ways; not many times. I had so frequent and urgent demands on my time elsewhere, that I could not come to you. ¶ *From coming to you.* Where the gospel *has been* preached. I have desired to come, but have been unable to leave the vast region where I might preach the gospel to those who had never heard it.

23. *But now*, &c. Having no further opportunity in these regions to preach to those who have never heard the gospel. ¶ *In these parts.* In the regions before specified. He had gone over them, had established churches, had left them in the care of elders

a great desire these many years to
come unto you ;
24 Whensoever I take my journey into Spain, I will come to you:
for I trust to see you in my journey,
and to be [a] brought on my way
thitherward by you, if first I be
somewhat filled [1] with your *company.*
25 But now I go [b] unto Jerusalem, to minister unto the saints.
26 For it hath pleased them of

a Acts 15.3; 3John 6.

1 *with you.* *b* Acts 19.21.

(Acts xx. 17), and was now prepared to penetrate into some new region, and lay the foundation of other churches. ¶ *And having a great desire,* &c. see chap. i. 9—13.

24. *Whensoever I take my journey into Spain.* Ancient Spain comprehended the modern kingdoms of Spain and Portugal, or the whole of the Spanish peninsula. It was then subject to the Romans. It is remarkable, even here, that the apostle does not say that his principal object was to visit the church at Rome, much as he desired that, but only to *take it in his way* in the fulfilment of his higher purpose to preach the gospel in regions where Christ was not named. Whether he ever fulfilled his purpose of visiting *Spain* is a matter of doubt. Some of the fathers, Theodoret (on Phil. i. 25 ; 2 Tim. iv. 17) among others, say that after he was released from his captivity when he was brought before Nero, he passed two years in Spain. If he was imprisoned a *second* time at Rome, such a visit is not improbable as having taken place *between* the two imprisonments. But there is no certain evidence of this. Paul probably projected *many* journeys which were never accomplished. ¶ *To be brought on my way,* &c. To be assisted by you in regard to this journey; or to be accompanied by you. This was the custom of the churches ; Acts xv. 3 ; xvii. 14, 15; xx. 38; xxi. 5; 1 Cor. xvi. 6, 11 ; 3 John 6. ¶ *If first,* &c. If on my journey, before I go into Spain. ¶ *Somewhat.* Greek, *In part.* As though he could not be *fully* satisfied with their company, or could not hope to enjoy their society as fully and as long as he could desire. This is a very tender and delicate expression. ¶ *Filled.* This is a strong expression, meaning to be *satisfied,* to enjoy. To be *filled* with a thing is to have great satisfaction and joy in it. ¶ *With your* company. Greek, With *you ;* meaning in your society. The expression *to be filled* with one, in the sense of being *gratified,* is sometimes used in the classic writers. (See *Clarke* on this verse.)

25. *But now I go,* &c. I am about to go now. The mention of this intended journey to Jerusalem is introduced in several other places, and is so mentioned that Dr. Paley has derived from it a very strong argument for the genuineness of this epistle.* This intended journey is mentioned in Acts xix. 21, " Paul purposed in the spirit, when he had passed through Macedonia and Achaia, *to go to Jerusalem, saying after I have been there, I must also see Rome ;*" see also Acts xx. 2, 3. That he *went* to Jerusalem according to his purpose is recorded in his defence before Felix (Acts xxiv. 17), " Now after many years, I came to bring alms to my nation and offerings." ¶ *To minister to the saints.* To supply their necessities by bearing the contribution which the churches have made for them.

26. *For it hath pleased them of Macedonia.* That is, they have done it *cheerfully* and *voluntarily.* See their liberality and cheerfulness commended by the apostle in 2 Cor. viii. 1—6; ix. 2. Paul had been at much pains to obtain this collection, but still they did it freely ; see 2 Cor. ix. 4—7. It was with reference to *this* collection that he directed them to lay by for this purpose as God had prospered them on the first day of the week ; 1 Cor. xvi. 1. ¶ *Of Macedonia.* That is, the Christians in Macedonia—those who had been Gentiles, and who had been converted to the Christian religion ; ver. 27. Macedonia was a country of Greece, bounded north by Thrace,

* Paley's Horæ Paulinæ, chap. ii. no. 1.

Macedonia [a] and Achaia to make a certain contribution for the poor saints which are at Jerusalem.

27 It hath pleased them, verily; and their debtors they are. For if the Gentiles have been made partakers of their spiritual things, their duty [b] is also to minister unto them in carnal things.

28 When, therefore, I have performed this, and have sealed to them this fruit, [c] I will come by you into Spain.

29 And I am sure that, when [d]

a 2Cor. 8.1; 9.2,12. b 1 Cor.9.11. c Phil.4.17. d chap.1.11,12.

south by Thessaly, west by Epirus, and east by the Ægean sea. It was an extensive region, and was the kingdom of Philip, and his son Alexander the Great. Its capital was Philippi, at which place Paul planted a church. A church was also established at Thessalonica, another city of that country; Acts xvi. 9, &c.; comp. xviii. 5; xix. 21; 2 Cor. vii. 5; 1 Thess. i. 1, 7, 8; iv. 10. ¶ *And Achaia.* Achaia in the largest sense comprenended *all* ancient Greece. Achaia Proper, however, was a province of Greece embracing the western part of the Peloponnesus, of which Corinth was the capital; see Note, Acts xviii. 12. This place is mentioned as having been concerned in this collection in 2 Cor. ix. 2. ¶ *The poor saints,* &c. The Christians who were in Judea were exposed to peculiar trials. They were condemned by the sanhedrim, opposed by the rulers, and persecuted by the people; see Acts viii. 1, &c.; xii. 1, &c. Paul sought not only to relieve them by this contribution, but also to promote fellow-feeling between them and the Gentile Christians. And *this* circumstance would tend much to enforce what he had been urging in chap. xiv. xv. on the duty of kind feeling between the Jewish and Gentile converts to Christianity. Nothing tends so much to wear off prejudice, and to prevent unkind feeling in regard to others, as to set about some purpose *to do them* good, or to unite *with* them in doing good.

27. *Their debtors.* The reason he immediately states; comp. Rom. i. 14. ¶ *Of their spiritual things.* Have received the gospel by the instrumentality of those who had been Jews; and were admitted now to the same privileges with them. ¶ *Carnal things.* Things pertaining to the flesh; that is, to this life. On this ground the apostle puts the obligation to support the ministers of the gospel; 1 Cor. ix. 11. It becomes a matter of *debt* where the hearer of the gospel *receives,* in spiritual blessings, far more than he confers by supporting the ministry. Every man who contributes his due proportion to support the gospel may receive far more, in return, in his own peace, edification, and in the order and happiness of his family, than his money could purchase in any other way. The *gain* is on his side, and the money is not lost. The minister is not a beggar; and that which is necessary to his support is not almsgiving. He has an equitable claim—as much as a physician, or a lawyer, or a teacher of youth has—on the necessaries and comforts of life.

28. *Have sealed to them.* That is, have *secured it* to them. To seal an instrument of writing, a contract, deed, &c. is to *authenticate it,* to make it *sure.* In this sense it is used here. Paul was going himself to see that it was placed *securely* in their hands. ¶ *This fruit.* This result of the liberality of the Gentile churches—the fruit which their benevolence had produced. ¶ *I will come,* &c. This was Paul's full purpose; but it is not clear that he ever accomplished it; Note, ver. 24. ¶ *By you.* Taking Rome in my way.

29. *I am sure.* Greek, I know; expressing the fullest confidence, a confidence that was greatly confirmed by the success of his labours elsewhere. ¶ *In the fulness of the blessings,* &c. This is a Hebrew mode of expression, where one noun performs the purpose of an adjective, and means *with a full or abundant blessing.* This confidence he expressed in other language in chap. i. 11, 12; see Notes. ¶ *Of the*

I come unto you, I shall come in the fulness of the blessing of the gospel of Christ.

30 Now I beseech you, brethren, for the Lord Jesus Christ's sake, and for the [a] love of the Spirit, that ye strive [b] together with me in *your* prayers to God for me.

31 That [c] I may be delivered from them that [1] do not believe in

a Phil.2.1. b Col.4.12. c 2Thess.3.2. 1 or, *are disobedient.*

gospel of Christ. Which the gospel of Christ is fitted to impart. Thus every minister of the gospel should wish to go. This should be his ever-burning desire in preaching. Paul went to Rome; but he went in bonds; Acts xxvii. xxviii. But though he went in this manner, he was permitted there to preach the gospel for at least two years, nor can we doubt that his ministry was attended with the anticipated success; Acts xxviii. 30, 31. God may disappoint us in regard to the *mode* in which we purpose to do good; but if we really desire it, he will enable us to do it in *his own way.* It *may* be better to preach the gospel in *bonds* than at liberty; it *is* better to do it even in a prison, than not at all. Bunyan wrote the Pilgrim's Progress to amuse his heavy hours during a twelve years' cruel imprisonment. If he had been at liberty, he probably would not have written it at all. The great desire of his heart was accomplished, but a *prison* was the place in which to do it. Paul preached; but preached in chains.

30. *For the Lord Jesus Christ's sake.* Greek, By or through (διὰ) our Lord Jesus Christ. It means probably out of love and regard to him; in order to promote his honour and glory, and to extend his kingdom among men. Paul desired to be delivered from the hands of the Jews, that he might promote the honour of Jesus Christ among the Gentiles. ¶ *And for the love of the Spirit* (διὰ). By the mutual love and sympathy which the Spirit of God produces in the minds of all who are the friends of God. I beseech you now to manifest that love by praying earnestly for me. ¶ *That ye strive together with me.* That you unite with me in earnest prayer. The word *strive* denotes intense *agony* or effort, such as was used by the wrestlers in the Greek games; and then the *agony,* or strong effort, which a man makes in prayer, who is earnestly desirous to be heard. The use of the word here denotes Paul's earnest desire that they should make an *intense* effort in their prayers that he might be delivered. Christians, though at a distance from each other, may unite their prayers for a common object. Christians everywhere *should* wrestle in prayer for the ministers of the gospel, that they may be kept from temptations; and especially for those who are engaged, as the apostle was, in arduous efforts among the heathen, that they may be kept from the many dangers to which they are exposed in their journeyings in pagan lands.

31. *That I may be,* &c. The unbelieving Jews in Judea had been opposed to Paul's conversion. They could not forget that he had borne letters of commission from them to persecute the Christians at Damascus. They regarded him as an apostate. They had heard of his success among the Gentiles; and they had been informed that he "taught all the Jews among the Gentiles to forsake the laws of Moses;" Acts xxi. 21. Hence the apostle could not but be aware that in returning to Judea, he exposed himself to peculiar dangers. His fears, as the result showed, were well founded. They evinced all the opposition to him which he had ever anticipated; Acts xxi. ¶ *And that my service.* My ministry; or the act of service which I am going to perform for them; referring to the contribution which he was bearing for the poor saints at Jerusalem. ¶ *For Jerusalem.* For the poor Christians in Jerusalem. ¶ *May be accepted of the saints.* That the poor Christians there may be willing to receive it. The grounds of *doubt* and *hesitation* whether they would be willing to receive this, seem to have been two.

Judea; and that my service which *I have* for Jerusalem may be accepted of the saints;

32 That I may come unto you with joy by the will of God, and may with you be refreshed.

33 Now the God of peace [a] *be* with you all. Amen.

CHAPTER XVI.

I COMMEND unto you Phebe our sister, which is a servant of the church which is at Cenchrea.

a 1 Cor.14.33; Heb.13.20.

(1.) Many, even among Christians, might have had their minds filled with prejudice against the apostle, from the reports constantly in circulation among the Jews, that he was opposing and denouncing the customs of Moses. Hence, in order to satisfy them, when he went up to Jerusalem, he actually performed a *vow,* in accordance with the law of Moses, to show that he did not intend to treat his laws with contempt; Acts xxi. 22, 23, 26, 27. (2.) Many of the converts from Judaism might be indisposed to receive an offering made by *Gentiles.* They might have retained many of their former feelings—that the Gentiles were polluted, and that they ought to have no fellowship with them. Early opinions and prejudices wear off by slow degrees. Christians retain former notions long after their conversion; and often many years are required to teach them enlarged views of Christian charity. It is not wonderful that the Christians in Judea should have been slow to learn all the ennobling lessons of Christian benevolence, surrounded as they were by the institutions of the Jewish religion, and having been themselves educated in the strictest regard for those institutions.

32. *That I may come to you.* That I may not be impeded in my intended journey by opposition in Judea. ¶ *With joy.* Joy to myself in being permitted to come; and producing joy to you by my presence. ¶ *By the will of God.* If God will; if God permit. After all his desires, and all their prayers, it still depended on the will of God; and to that the apostle was desirous to submit. This should be the end of our most ardent desires, and this the object of all our prayers, that the will of God should be done; comp. James. iv. 14, 15. Paul *did* go by the will of God; but he went in bonds. ¶ *And be refreshed.* Greek, May find *rest* or *solace* with you.

33. *Now the God of peace.* God, the author or promoter of peace and union. In ver. 13, he is called the God of hope. Here the apostle desires that the God who gives peace would impart to them union of sentiment and feeling, particularly between the Jewish and Gentile Christians—the great object for which he laboured in his journey to Judea, and which he had been endeavouring to promote throughout this epistle; see 1 Cor. xiv. 33; Heb. xiii. 20.

This is the close of the doctrinal and hortatory parts of this epistle. The remainder is made up chiefly of salutations. In the verses concluding this chapter, Paul expressed his earnest desire to visit Rome. He besought his brethren to pray that he might be delivered from the unbelievers among the Jews. His main desire was granted. He was permitted to visit Rome; yet the very thing from which he sought to be delivered, the very opposition of the Jews, made it necessary for him to appeal to Cæsar, and this was the means of his accomplishing his desire. (See the closing chapters of the Acts of the Apostles.) God thus often grants our *main* desire; he hears our prayer; but he may make use of that from which we pray to be delivered as the *means* of fulfilling our own requests. The Christian prays that he may be sanctified; yet at the same time he may pray to be delivered from affliction. God will hear his *main* desire, to be made holy; will convert that which he fears into a blessing, and make it the means of accomplising the great end. It is right to express our *desires—all* our desires—to God; but it should be with a willingness that he should choose his own means to accomplish

2 That ye receive [a] her in the Lord, as becometh saints, and that

a Phil.2.29.

the object of our wishes. Provided the *God of peace* is with us, all is well.

CHAPTER XVI.

THE epistle concludes with various salutations. The *names* which occur in this chapter are chiefly *Greek;* and the persons designated had been probably inhabitants of Greece, but had removed to Rome for purposes of commerce, &c. Possibly some of them had been converted under the ministry of the apostle himself during his preaching in Corinth and other parts of Greece. It is remarkable that the name of *Peter* does not occur in this catalogue; which is conclusive evidence, contrary to the Papists, that Peter was not then known by Paul to be in Rome.

1. *I commend.* It was common then, as now, to bear letters of introduction to strangers, commending the person thus introduced to the favourable regards and attentions of those to whom the letters were addressed; 2 Cor. iii. 1; Acts xviii. 27. This epistle, with the apostle's commendation, was designed thus to introduce its bearer to the Roman Christians. The mention of Phebe in this manner leaves it beyond a doubt that she was either the bearer of this epistle, or accompanied those who bore it to Rome. The epistle was therefore written, probably, at Corinth. (See Introduction.) ¶ *Our sister.* A member of the Christian church. ¶ *Which is a servant.* Greek, "Who is a *deaconess.*" It is clear from the New Testament that there was an order of women in the church known as *deaconesses.* Reference is made to a class of females whose duty it was to *teach* other females, and to take the general superintendence of that part of the church, in various places in the New Testament; and their existence is expressly affirmed in early ecclesiastical history. They appear to have been commonly aged and experienced widows, sustaining a fair reputation, and fitted to guide and instruct those who were young and inexperienced; comp. 1 Tim. v. 3, 9—11; Tit. ii. 4. The Apostolical Constitutions, book iii. say, "Ordain a deaconess who is faithful and holy, for the ministries toward the women." Pliny in his celebrated letter to Trajan, says, when speaking of the efforts which he made to obtain information respecting the opinions and practices of Christians, "I deemed it necessary to put two maidservants who are called *ministræ* [that is *deaconesses*] to the torture, in order to ascertain what is the truth." The reasons of their appointment among the Gentiles were these: (1.) The females were usually separate from the men. They were kept secluded, for the most part, and not permitted to mingle in society with men as is the custom now. (2.) It became necessary, therefore, to appoint aged and experienced females to instruct the young, to visit the sick, to provide for them, and to perform for them the services which male deacons performed for the whole church. It is evident, however, that they were confined to these offices, and that they were never regarded as an order of ministers, or suffered *to preach* to congregations; 1 Tim. ii. 12; 1 Cor. xiv. 34. ¶ *Of the church,* &c. This is the only mention which occurs of a church at that place. It was probably collected by the labours of Paul. ¶ *At Cenchrea.* This was the *sea-port* of Corinth. Corinth was situated on the middle of the isthmus, and had *two* harbours, or ports: *Cenchrea* on the east, about eight or nine miles from the city; and *Lechæum* on the west. Cenchrea opened into the Ægean sea, and was the principal port. It was on this *isthmus,* between these two ports, that the *Isthmian* games were celebrated, to which the apostle refers so often in his epistles.

2. *That ye receive her,* &c. That you acknowledge her as being in the Lord, or as being a servant of the Lord; that is, as a Christian; comp. chap. xiv. 3; Phil. ii. 29. ¶ *As becometh saints.* As it is proper that Christians should treat their brethren. ¶ *She hath been a succourer of many.*

ye assist her in whatsoever business she hath need of you: for she hath been a succourer of many, and of myself also.

3 Greet Priscilla [a] and Aquila, my helpers in Christ Jesus:

4 Who have for my life laid down their own necks; unto whom not only I give thanks, but also all the churches of the Gentiles.

5 Likewise *greet* the church that is in their house. [b] Salute

a Acts 18.2, &c.

b 1 Cor.16.19.

The word used here (προστάτις), means properly *a patron, a help*, and was applied by the Greeks to one who *presided* over an assembly; to one who became *a patron* of others; who aided or defended them in their cause; and especially to one who undertook to manage the cause of *strangers* and foreigners before the courts. It was, therefore, an honourable appellation. Applied to Phebe, it means probably that she had shown great kindness in various ways to the apostle, and to other Christians; probably by receiving them into her house; by administering to the sick, &c. Such persons have a claim on the respect and Christian attentions of others.

3. *Greet Priscilla and Aquila.* Salute; implying the apostle's kind remembrance of them, and his wishes for their welfare. ¶ *Priscilla.* Priscilla was the wife of Aquila. They are mentioned in Acts xviii. 2, 26; 1 Cor. xvi. 19. Paul at first found them at Corinth. Aquila was a Jew, born in Pontus, who had resided at Rome, and who had left Rome, and come to Corinth, when Claudius expelled the Jews from Rome; see Notes, Acts xviii. 2. It is probable that they were converted under the preaching of Paul. Paul lived with them, and they had the advantage of his private instruction; Acts xviii. 3; comp. 26. At the death of Claudius, or whenever the decree for the expulsion of the Jews was repealed, it is probable that they returned to Rome. ¶ *My helpers.* My fellow-workers. They had aided him in his work. A particular instance is mentioned in Acts xviii. 26. They are mentioned as having been with Paul when he wrote the first epistle to the Corinthians; 1 Cor. xvi. 19. ¶ *In Christ Jesus.* In the Christian cause.

4. *Who have for my life.* In order to save my life. ¶ *Laid down their own necks.* To *lay down the neck* is to lay the head on a block to be cut off with the axe; or to bow down the head as when the neck was exposed to be cut off by the sword of the executioner. The meaning is, that they had hazarded their lives, had exposed themselves to imminent danger, to save the life of Paul. On what occasion this was done, is not known, as it is not elsewhere referred to in the New Testament. As Paul, however, lived with them (Acts xviii. 3), and as he was often persecuted by the Jews, it is probable that he refers to some such period when he was persecuted, when Aquila and Priscilla took him into their house at the imminent hazard of their lives. ¶ *All the churches of the Gentiles.* All the churches that had been founded by the apostles. They *felt* their deep obligation to them for having saved the life of him who had been their founder, and who was their spiritual father.

5. *The church that is in their house.* Aquila and Priscilla are mentioned (Acts xviii. 26) as having received *Apollos* into their family, to instruct him more perfectly. The church in their house is also mentioned 1 Cor. xvi. 19. This may mean either the church that was accustomed to assemble for worship at their hospitable mansion; or it may mean their own family with their guests, regarded as a *church*. In those times Christians had no houses erected for public worship, and were therefore compelled to meet in their private dwellings. ¶ *Salute.* The same word before translated "*greet.*" ¶ *Who is the first-fruits.* One who first embraced Christianity under my preaching in Achaia. The *first-fruits* were a small part of the harvest, which was first gathered and offered to the Lord; Ex.

my well-beloved Epenetus, who is the first-fruits of Achaia unto Christ.

6 Greet Mary: who bestowed much labour on us.

7 Salute Andronicus and Junia, my kinsmen and my fellow-prisoners, who are of note among the apostles; who also were in [a] Christ before me.

8 Greet Amplias, my beloved in the Lord.

9 Salute Urbane, our helper in Christ; and Stachys my beloved.

10 Salute Appelles, approved in Christ. Salute them which are of Aristobulus's *household.* [1]

11 Salute Herodian my kinsman. Greet them that be of the [1] *household* of Narcissus, which are in the Lord.

12 Salute Tryphena and Tryphosa, who labour in the Lord.

a Gal.1.22.

1 or, *friends.*

xxii. 29; xxiii. 16; Lev. ii. 12; Deut. xviii. 4. In allusion to this, Paul calls Epenetus the first-fruits of the great spiritual harvest which had been gathered in Achaia. ¶ *Achaia.* See Note, chap. xv. 26. This name and those which follow are chiefly *Greek,* but we know little of the persons mentioned, except what is here recorded.

6. *Who bestowed much labour on us.* Who laboured much for us. Nothing more is known of her but this honourable mention of her name. It is probable that these persons were formerly residents in Greece, and that the apostle had there become acquainted with them, but that they had now removed to Rome.

7. *My kinsmen.* In Rom. ix. 3, the apostle calls *all* the Jews *his kinsmen,* and it has been doubted whether he means any thing more here than that they were *fellow Jews.* But as many others who were Jews are mentioned here without this appellation, and as he especially designates these persons, and Herodian (ver. 11), it seems probable that they were remote relatives of the apostle. ¶ *My fellow-prisoners.* Paul was often in prison; and it is probable that on some of those occasions they had been confined with him; comp. 2 Cor. xi. 23, "In prisons more frequent." ¶ *Who are of note.* The word translated *of note* (ἐπίσημοι), denotes properly those who are *marked,* designated, or distinguished in any way, used either in a good or bad sense; comp. Mat. xxvii. 16. Here it is used in a good sense. ¶ *Among the apostles.* This does not mean that they *were* apostles, as has been sometimes supposed. For, (1.) There is no account of their having been appointed as such. (2.) The expression is not one which would have been used if they *had* been. It would have been "who were distinguished *apostles;*" comp. Rom. i. 1; 1 Cor. i. 1; 2 Cor. i. 1; Phil. i. 1. (3.) It by no means implies that they were apostles All that the expression fairly implies is, that they were known to the other apostles; that they were regarded by them as worthy of their affection and confidence; that they had been known by them, as Paul immediately adds, before *he* was himself converted. They had been converted *before* he was, and were distinguished in Jerusalem among the early Christians, and honoured with the friendship of the other apostles. (4.) The design of the office of *apostles* was to bear *witness* to the life, death, resurrection, doctrines, and miracles of Christ; comp. Mat. x; Acts i. 21, 22; xxii. 15. As there is no evidence that they had been *witnesses* of these things, or appointed to it, it is improbable that they were set apart to the apostolic office. (5.) The word *apostles* is used sometimes to designate *messengers* of churches; or those who were *sent* from one church to another on some important business, and *if* this expression meant that they *were* apostles, it could only be in some such sense as having obtained deserved credit and eminence in that business; see Phil. ii. 25; 2 Cor. viii. 23. ¶ *Who were in Christ,* &c. Who were *converted* before I was. The meaning is clear. The expression, *in Christ,*

Salute the beloved Persis, which laboured much in the Lord.

13 Salute Rufus, chosen [a] in the Lord; and his mother and mine.

14 Salute Asyncritus, Phlegon, Hermas, Patrobas, Hermes, and the brethren which are with them.

15 Salute Philologus, and Julia, Nereus, and his sister, and Olympas, and all the saints which are with them.

16 Salute one another with an holy kiss. [b] The churches of Christ salute you.

17 Now I beseech you, brethren, mark them which cause divisions [c] and offences contrary to the doc-

a Eph.1.4; 2 John 1. b 1 Cor.16.20; 1 Pet.5.14. c 1 Tim 6.3-5.

means to be united to him, to be interested in his religion, to be Christians.

10. *Approved in Christ.* An approved or tried Christian; approved and beloved by Christ.

12. *Tryphena and Tryphosa.* These names, with the participle rendered "who labour," are in the feminine gender, and these were probably two holy women, who performed the office of deaconesses, or who ministered to the sick, and who with Persis, thus by example, and perhaps by instruction, laboured to promote the spread of Christianity. Pious females, then, as now, were able to do much in their proper sphere to extend the truths and blessings of the gospel.

13. *Chosen in the Lord. Elect* in the Lord; that is, a chosen follower of Christ. ¶ *And his mother and mine.* "His mother in a literal sense, and mine in a figurative one." An instance of the delicacy and tenderness of Paul; of his love for this disciple and his mother, as if he were of the same family. Religion binds the hearts of all who embrace it tenderly together. It makes them feel that they are one great family, united by tender ties, and joined by peculiar attachments. See what the Lord Jesus declared in Mat. xii. 47—50, and his tender address to John when he was on the cross; John xix. 26, 27.

16. *Salute one another.* Greet one another in an affectionate manner; that is, treat each other with kindness and love, and evince all proper marks of affection. ¶ *With an holy kiss.* This mode of salutation has been practised at all times; and particularly in eastern nations. It was even practised by *men;* see Note, Luke xxii. 47, 48. The use of the word *holy* here serves to denote that Paul intended it as an expression of *Christian* affection; and to guard against all improper familiarity and scandal. It was common, according to Justin Martyr (Apology), for the early Christians to practise it in their religious assemblies. ¶ *The churches of Christ.* That is, the churches in the vicinity of the place where the apostle wrote this epistle; probably the churches particularly in Achaia.

17. *Now I beseech you.* One great object of this epistle had been to promote *peace* between the Jewish and Gentile converts. So much did this subject press upon the mind of the apostle, that he seems unwilling to leave it. He returns to it again and again; and even after the epistle is apparently concluded, he returns to it, to give them a new charge on the subject. ¶ *Mark them.* Observe attentively, cautiously, and faithfully (Phil. iii. 17); be on your guard against them. Ascertain *who are* the real causes of the divisions that spring up, and avoid them. ¶ *Which cause.* Who make. Probably he refers here to *Jewish* teachers, or those who insisted strenuously on the observance of the rites of Moses, and who set up a claim for greater purity and orthodoxy than those possessed who received the Gentile converts as Christian brethren. The Jews were perpetually thus recalling the Christian converts to the law of Moses; insisting on the observance of those rites; troubling the churches, and producing dissensions and strifes; Gal. iii. 1; v. 1—8; Acts xv. 1, 24. ¶ *Divisions.*

trine which ye have learned; and
avoid [a] them.
18 For they that are such serve
not our Lord Jesus Christ, but
their own belly; [b] and by good
words [c] and fair speeches deceive
the hearts of the simple.
19 For your obedience is come
[d] abroad unto all *men*. I am glad
therefore on your behalf, but yet I

a Mat.18.17; 1Cor.5.11; 2 Thess.3.6,14. *b* Phil. 3.19.

c Col.2.4; 2 Pet.2.3. *d* chap.1.8.

Dissensions; parties; factions; 1 Cor. iii. 3; Gal. v. 20. The very *attempt* to form such parties was evil, no matter what the pretence. They who attempt to form parties in the churches are commonly actuated by some evil or ambitious design. ¶ *And offences.* Scandals; or that give occasion for others to fall into sin. These two things are different. The first means parties; the other denotes such a course of life as would lead others into sin. The *Jew* would form parties, on the pretence of superior holiness; the Gentiles, or some bold Gentile convert might deride the scrupulous feelings of the Jew, and might thus lead him into *sin* in regard to what his conscience really forbade; see chap. xiv. 15. These persons on both sides were to be avoided, and they were to refuse to follow them, and to cultivate the spirit of unity and peace. ¶ *Contrary to the doctrine.* To the *teaching* which you have received in this epistle and elsewhere; the teaching that these divisions should cease; that the Jewish ceremonies are not binding; that all should lay aside their causes of former difference, and be united in one family; see chap. xiv. xv. ¶ *And avoid them.* Give them no countenance or approbation. Do not follow them; comp. 1 Tim. vi. 3, 4, 5; 2 John 10; Gal. i. 8, 9. That is, avoid them *as teachers;* do not follow them. It does not mean that they were to be treated harshly; but that they were to be avoided in their *instructions.* They were to disregard all that they could say tending to produce alienation and strife; and resolve to cultivate the spirit of peace and union. This would be an admirable rule if always followed. Let men make *peace* their prime object; resolve to love all who *are* Christians, and it will be an infallible guage by which to measure the arguments of those who seek to promote alienations and contentions.

18. *Serve not.* Obey not. Though they are professedly, yet they are not his real friends and followers. ¶ *But their own belly.* Their own *lusts;* their own private interests; they do this to obtain support. The authors of parties and divisions, in church and state, have this usually in view. It is for the indulgence of some earthly appetite; to obtain office or property; or to gratify the love of dominion. ¶ *And by good words.* Mild, fair, plausible speeches; with an appearance of great sincerity, and regard for the truth; comp. Col. ii. 4; 2 Pet. iii. 3. Men who cause divisions commonly make great pretensions to peculiar love of truth and orthodoxy; and put on the appearance of great sincerity, sanctity, and humility. ¶ *And fair speeches.* Greek (εὐλογίας), eulogy, praise, flattery. This is another very common art. *Flattery* is one of the most powerful means of forming parties in the church; and *a little special attention,* or promise of an office, or commendation for talents or acquirements, will secure *many* to the purposes of party whom no regard for truth or orthodoxy could influence a moment. ¶ *Deceive the hearts of the simple.* The minds of the unsuspecting, or those who are without guile (τῶν ἀκάκων). The apostle means to designate those who are simple-hearted, without any disposition to deceive others themselves, and of course without any suspicions of the *designs* of others. He has thus drawn the art of making parties with the hand of a master. First, there are smooth, plausible pretences, as of great love for truth. Then, an artful mingling of attentions and flatteries; and all

would have you wise [a] unto that
which is good and [1] simple concerning evil.
20 And the [b] God of peace shall
[2] bruise [c] Satan under your feet
shortly. [d] The [e] grace of our Lord
Jesus Christ *be* with you. Amen.
21 Timotheus my work-fellow
and Lucius, and Jason, and Sosipater, my kinsmen, salute you.
22 I Tertius, who wrote *this*
epistle, salute you in the Lord.
23 Gaius [f] mine host, and of the
whole church, saluteth you. Eras-

a Mat.10.16. 1 or, *harmless.* *b* chap.15.33. 2 or, *tread.* *c* Gen.3.15. *d* Rev.12.10.
e 1Cor.16.23,&c.; Rev.22.21. *f* 1Cor.1.14; 3John1.

this practised on the minds of the unsuspecting, drawing their *hearts* and *affections* towards themselves. Happy would it have been if the art had been confined to his own times.

19. *For your obedience,* &c. chap. i. 8. Your mild, obedient disposition to learn, and to obey the precepts of the teachers of religion. ¶ *I am glad,* &c. I rejoice that you evince such a disposition. But he immediately adds, that *this* was just the temper to be imposed upon, and cautions them against that danger. ¶ *Wise unto that which is good.* Evince understanding of that which is adapted to promote good and worthy ends. ¶ *Simple concerning evil.* Greek, *harmless.* Not disposed to do wrong; having no plan and yielding to none of the allurements of evil. You have shown your wisdom in *obeying* the gospel. I would have you still evince wisdom towards *every good* design; but to be unacquainted with *any* plan of evil. Do not yield to those plans, or follow those who would lead you into them.

20. *And the God of peace.* The God who promotes peace; chap. xv. 33. ¶ *Will bruise.* The *language* here refers to the prediction in Gen. iii. 15. It here means to *subdue, to gain the victory over.* It denotes Paul's confidence that they *would* gain the victory, and would be able to overcome all the arts of those who were endeavouring to sow discord and contention among them. ¶ *Satan.* The word *Satan* is Hebrew, meaning originally *an accuser, a calumniator,* and then *an enemy.* It is given to the prince of evil spirits from his enmity to God and men. He is here regarded as the *author* of all attempts to promote discord in the church, by whomsoever those attempts were made. Hence they who attempt to produce divisions are called "his ministers;" 2 Cor. xi. 15. God would disappoint their malignant purposes, and promote the prevalence of peace. ¶ *The grace.* The favour; the mercy, &c. The Lord Jesus is the Prince of peace (Isa. ix. 6; comp. Luke ii. 14; John xiv. 27), and this expression is *a prayer* to him, or an earnest wish expressed, that the design of his coming might be accomplished in promoting the prevalence of order and peace; comp. 1 Cor. xvi. 23; Rev. xxii. 21.

21. *Timotheus.* Timothy; to whom the epistles which bear his name were written. He was long the companion of Paul in his labours; Acts xvi. 1; 1 Cor. xvi. 10; 2 Cor. i. 1, 19; Phil. ii. 29; 1 Thess. iii. 2; 1 Tim. i. 2; Heb. xiii. 23. ¶ *And Lucius.* He is mentioned in Acts xiii. 1, as a prophet and teacher, a native of Cyrene. Nothing more is known of him. ¶ *My kinsmen,* ver. 7.

22. *I Tertius.* Of Tertius nothing more is known than is mentioned here. ¶ *Who wrote this.* It is evident that Paul employed an amanuensis to write this epistle, and perhaps he commonly did it. Tertius, who thus wrote it, joins with the apostle in affectionate salutations to the brethren at Rome. To the epistle, Paul signed his own name, and added a salutation in his own hand-writing. Col. iv. 18, "The salutation by the hand of me Paul;" and in 2 Thess. iii. 17, he says that this was done in every epistle. 1 Cor. xvi. 21. ¶ *In the Lord.* As Christian brethren.

23. *Gaius mine host.* Who has receïved me into his house, and shown

tus [a] the chamberlain of the city
saluteth you, and Quartus a brother.
24 The [b] grace of our Lord Jesus Christ *be* with you all. Amen.
25 Now [c] to him that is of
power to establish you according to my gospel and the preaching of Jesus Christ, (according to the revelation [d] of the mystery, which was kept secret since the world began.

a Acts19.22. *b* ver.20. *c* Eph. 3.20; Jude 24. *d* Eph.1.9; Col.1.26,27.

me hospitality. The word *host* means one who entertains another at his own house without reward. ¶ *And of the whole church.* Who has opened his house to entertain *all* Christians; or to show hospitality to them all. He was baptized by Paul himself at Corinth (1 Cor. i. 14); and was so highly esteemed by the church that John wrote an epistle to him; 3 John 1. He was probably a wealthy citizen of Corinth, who freely opened his house to entertain Christians, and for the purpose of religious worship. ¶ *Erastus.* Erastus is mentioned (Acts xix. 22) as having been sent by Paul with Timothy into Macedonia. He is also mentioned (2 Tim. iv. 20) as having resided at Corinth. ¶ *The chamberlain.* A *chamberlain* is properly an officer who has charge of a chamber, or of chambers. In England, the lord chamberlain is the sixth officer of the crown, and has charge of the king's lodgings, and wardrobe, &c. He has also an important rank on days of public solemnities, as the coronation day, &c. The word used here is commonly in the New Testament translated *steward.* It properly means one who has charge of domestic affairs, to provide for a family, to pay the servants, &c. In this place it means one who presided over the pecuniary affairs of the *city*, and should have been translated *the treasurer; the city treasurer;* an office of trust and of some importance, showing that *all* who were converted at Corinth were not of the lowest rank. This is implied in 1 Cor i. 26, "Not *many* wise men, not *many* mighty, not *many* noble, are called," implying that there were *some* such. ¶ *Quartus a brother.* A fellow-Christian.

25. *Now to him.* This and the two following verses are found in many manuscripts at the close of the xivth chapter. Its proper place, however, is here; and the apostle thus concludes the whole epistle with an ascription of praise. ¶ *To him,* &c. To God; be glory; ver. 20. ¶ *Is of power.* Greek, Is able; who has power; Eph. iii. 20; Jude 24, "Now unto him that is able to keep you from falling," &c. God only can keep Christians in the path of salvation; and it was well to bring that truth prominently into view at the close of the epistle. ¶ *To establish you.* To strengthen and confirm you. ¶ *According to my gospel.* According to the gospel which I preach; the doctrines which I have been defending in this epistle. It is called *his* gospel, not because he was the author of it, or because others did not preach it also, but because he had been *particularly* defending it in this epistle. The doctrines which he had advanced were just those which were fitted to strengthen and confirm them,—the doctrine of justification, of election, of perseverance, and of the protection and favour of God to both Jews and Gentiles. These were the doctrines which he had defended; and it might easily be shown that *these* are the doctrines that give stability to the Christian faith, hope, and love. ¶ *And the preaching of Jesus Christ.* Not his *personal* preaching; but according to that preaching of which Christ is the author and the subject; and particularly, as the following clause shows, to the doctrines by which the partition between the Jews and the Gentiles was broken down, and by which they were admitted to the same privileges and hopes. ¶ *According to the revelation.* According to the communication of that which has been so long concealed, but which is now made manifest. The word *revelation* refers to the *publication* of the plan by the gospel. ¶ *Of the mystery.* The word

26 But now is made manifest, and by the scriptures of the prophets, according to the commandment of the everlasting God, made known to all [a] nations for the obedience of faith;)

27 To God [b] only wise, *be* glory, through Jesus Christ, for ever. Amen.

Written to the Romans from Corinthus, *and sent* by Phebe, servant of the church at Cenchrea.

a Mat. 28.19.

b 1 Tim.1.17; Jude 25.

---

mystery means properly that which *is hidden* or *concealed*, and is thus applied to any doctrine which was not before known. It does not mean necessarily that which is *unintelligible;* but that which had not been before revealed; see Note to Mat. xiii. 11. The word here seems to refer to the principal doctrines of the gospel; its main truths, which had been concealed, especially from the entire Gentile world, but which were now made known. ¶ *Which was kept secret.* Which were kept in *silence* (Greek, σεσιγημένου), were not divulged or proclaimed. ¶ *Since the world began.* In all past times. This refers particularly to the Gentiles. The Jews had some obscure intimations of these truths, but they were now made known to all the world. The phrase "since the world began" is in Greek, "in eternal times;" that is, in *all* past times; or, as we should say, they have been *always* concealed.

26. *But now is made manifest.* Is revealed, or made known; that which was so long concealed is now divulged, *i. e.* God's plan of saving men is now made known to all nations. ¶ *And by the Scriptures,* &c. By the *writings* of the prophets. The prophetic writings contained the doctrines, obscurely indeed, but so as to be an important means of disseminating and confirming the truth that the Gentiles should be made acquainted with the gospel. To those writings the apostle had repeatedly appealed in his defence of the proposition that the gospel was to be preached to the Gentile word; chap. x. xi. xv. The prophetic writings, moreover, were extensively scattered among the Gentile nations, and thus were readily appealed to in defence of this position. Their writings being thus translated, and read, were an important means of propagating the truths of the Christian religion. ¶ *According to the commandment,* &c. By his command through Jesus Christ; made known in the gospel of his Son. ¶ *The everlasting God.* God who is *eternal,* and therefore unchanged. He who has indeed *concealed* this truth, but who has always *intended* that it should be revealed. ¶ *To all nations.* Mat. xxviii. 19; comp. Col. i. 23. ¶ *For the obedience of faith.* To produce obedience to the requirements of the gospel; see Note, chap. i. 5.

27. *To God only wise.* The apostle here resumes the doxology which had been interrupted by the parenthesis. The attribute of *wisdom* is here brought into view, because it had been particularly displayed in this plan which was now revealed. It evinced, in an eminent degree, the *wisdom* of God. That wisdom was evinced in devising the plan; in adapting it to the renewing of the heart; the justification of the sinner; his preservation, guidance, and sanctification; and in the manner in which the divine attributes had all been seen to harmonize. All this the apostle had illustrated in the previous parts of the epistle; and now, full of the convictions of this wisdom, he desires that all the praise and honour should be to God. The *tendency* of the plan is to promote his glory. The *obligation* on all who are benefitted by it is to give him praise. ¶ Be *glory.* Praise; honour. ¶ *Through Jesus Christ.* By means of the work which Jesus Christ has performed; through him now as mediator and intercessor in the heavens

The subscription, "written to the Romans," &c. is evidently added by some other hand, but by whom is unknown. Paul assuredly would not write this to inform the Romans that it was sent by Phebe, whom he had just commended to their kindness. It has been shown, moreover, that no reliance is to be placed on any of the subscriptions to the epistles. Some of them are known to be false. By whom they were added is unknown. In this case, however, the fact which it states is correct, that it was written from Corinth, and sent by Phebe.

APPENDIX

ROME.

ANCIENT ROME was situated nearly on the site of the modern city, in Latium, on several hills (whence the poetical appellation of the *seven-hilled city*), on both sides of the river Tiber, not far from the Mediterranean Sea; but the principal part of the city lay upon the eastern side of the river. Here is situated the Pincian Mount, and nearer the river the Campus Martius (the site of most of the modern city), the Capitoline Hill, the Roman Forum, and Mount Aventine. The Quirinal, Palatine, and Cœlian Hills form a second range, eastward of the preceding, extending from north to south; the Viminal and Esquiline, a third. On the western side of the Tiber are the Vatican mount and Janiculum.—(*See our Plan of Ancient Rome.*)

Different epochs are assigned for the foundation of Rome, but the date generally adopted is 753 years before Christ. The founding of the city commenced with ceremonies borrowed from the Etrurians. Romulus traced a square furrow round the Palatine hill with a plough drawn by two white cattle, and caused a wall of earth to be thrown up in the direction of the furrow. The interior was filled with huts.

The history of Rome is divided into three periods, in the first of which Rome was a kingdom, in the second a republic, and in the third an empire.

Our design here is simply to present such a view of the monuments of Rome, as may serve to make our illustrations more intelligible and interesting, and give the reader some idea of the imperial city in the days of Paul, and of the changes that have passed over it since his martyred body was interred by friendly hands near the Via Ostiensis. Wherever it is practicable, our description shall be inwoven with the personal history of the apostle, in so far as the more reliable traditions may enable us to trace it.

The following contrasted condition of Ancient and Modern Rome is abridged from an able article in the *Bibliotheca Sacra* for 1854:—"Through what vicissitudes has the city of the Cæsars passed! Of the Regal period (244 years), nought but the old Tullian wall,[1] the Italian prison overhanging the Forum, now the 'Mammertine,'[2] and the Cloaca Maxima show remains. Of the Republican period (461 years), some bridges, military ways, as the Appian, along which the apostle travelled, and aqueducts, are traceable. Of the Imperial (507 years), more meets the delighted eye of the antiquarian. The Pantheon (A.D. 27), the Colosseum (A.D. 80), the columns of Trajan and Antoninus, the arches of Titus, Septimius Severus, and Constantine, the mausoleum of Hadrian, (*Castel di St. Angelo*), and other structures, show something of their former grandeur. But yet how changed! Let the visitor, as he enters Rome, take his stand upon the tower of the Capitol, and turn his face to the north-west, towards the high dome of St. Peter's. Modern Rome lies mostly before him, covering the sloping sides of the Quirinal and Pincian Hills, the ancient Campus Martius, and the Vatican Hill, with the sides of the Janiculum west of the Tiber. The seven hills of ancient Rome, except the Capitoline, on which he stands, are mainly behind him, strewed with ruins of towers and walls, temples and theatres, circuses and baths, palaces and senate-houses, triumphal arches and columns. Let him first survey the Capitoline Hill. He cannot identify the spot on which the Asylum, 'the place of refuge,' stood, nor that of the Capitolium of Tarquinius, the strong citadel of Rome, whose gates were of brass, and whose gilded dome shone from afar. The Capitol now standing, with its museum and palaces, though built from the designs of Michael Angelo, only mocks the man who would see the great sanctuary and citadel of Rome; where the senate had, during kings, consuls, and emperors, held their deliberations in times of danger; where Cicero thundered against Catiline, and whither Pompey, Cæsar, and other generals were led along the Via Sacra, and up from the Forum in proud triumph.

"Let him now turn his back upon St. Peter's and the Vatican, and face the Colosseum. Ancient Rome lies before him. He looks down on the Forum (*see our larger Engraving*),[3] instituted by Romulus, decorated and enlarged by subsequent rulers; a

---

[1] See the inner circle of walls, built by Servius Tullius, traced in our plan. The outer circle was erected in part by Aurelian, and is therefore called the Aurelian wall.

[2] The scene, according to Baronius, of the imprisonment both of Peter and of Paul.

[3] The larger ruin (eight columns), on the lower side of the Clivus Capitolinus, is supposed to be the temple of Vespasian. The lesser ruin, of like kind (three columns), is the temple of Saturn. The building on the extreme left of our view is St. Peter's, or the prison: it is built over the Mammertine, the traditional scene of our apostle's imprisonment. More to the right is seen the dome of St. Martin's. In the middle towards the foreground is the arch of Septimius Severus.

place for the assemblies of the people, and the administration of justice, surrounded by the Capitol, temples, porticos, and palaces; having within the tribunal of justice, the statue of Marsyas, and the Rostra, adorned with trophies from the seas and statues of distinguished men, from which the Roman orators addressed the people. But he looks in vain for such a forum as this. The very pavement on which the bustling millions of old Rome here trod lies buried with twenty feet of rubbish from falling columns, pillars, and arches, which have been crumbling for centuries He next looks over the Forum, at the Palatine Hill, but he sees nothing of Augustus' imperial palace, set with rows of oak, and fronting the Via Sacra; nothing of the rich library, or of the marble temple of the Palatine Apollo, or even of the 'golden house' of Nero, vast in its extent, reaching the Esquiline, and richly adorned with gold and silver, and precious stones, and statues, and paintings, and other costly ornaments; nay, on the spot where at an earlier date could have been seen the elegant mansions of the Gracchi, of Crassus, Hortensius, and Cicero, the visitor can see little but the Farnese gardens, or other miserable places, to mock the genius of the past. He need look no farther to feel that the Rome he is now looking at is not ROME. The 'Lux orbis Terrarum,' the 'Arx omnium Gentium,' the 'Queen city of the world,' is no longer found upon her seven hills."[1]

Of existing remains, which the visitor of Rome, standing on the Capitol, and looking southward, may see lying before him, some of the most important are the column of Phocas; the three pillars of the Comitium, models of the Corinthian order of architecture; the ruins of the palace of the Cæsars, on Mount Palatine; and the arch of Titus, erected to commemorate the conquest of Jerusalem, and with that view representing the triumphal procession of the conqueror, the captive Jews, and the spoils of the Holy Place. (*See our Plan.*) The Capitol is now surmounted by a square of palaces built by Paul III., from designs by Michael Angelo. Further, towards the south and east, is the Colosseum, the glory of Rome, and the wonder of the world. Our illustrations will give the reader a good idea of the present state of this structure, as well as of the palace on the Palatine. These two monuments of ancient Rome, though not existing till several years after the death of Paul, may yet be taken as fair specimens of the architecture of the city in his time. The palace particularly must have been modelled on that which Paul had often visited, and within which he had gathered fruits of his ministry.

Shortly after the burning of Rome, Nero built his magnificent golden house or palace, to which allusion has already been made. This structure was burned to the ground, and again rebuilt in the reign of Commodus, and the ruins which are now seen by our travellers, and represented by our artists, are those of this latter building. As already noticed, it may be taken as a fair approximation to the palace of Paul's time, and the eye of the Christian, therefore, rests with the deepest interest on "its mouldering vestiges of imperial splendour, matted together and overgrown with the cypress and the vine." There were saints in Cæsar's household (Phil. iv. 22). Under the shadow of the palace and the throne Paul won his converts.

The Colosseum was a gigantic building erected by Vespasian, and has been regarded by many as a greater wonder than the Pyramids of Egypt. It was built in one year, by the compulsory labour of 12,000 Jews and Christians. The traveller, it is said, after having viewed the Colosseum by daylight, should return to gaze again by the light of the moon, to have a just idea of its solemn and stupendous grandeur. "It was a building of an elliptic figure, 564 feet in length, and 467 in breadth, founded on fourscore arches, and rising, with four successive orders of architecture, to the height of 140 feet. The outside of the edifice was incrusted with marble, and decorated with statues. The slopes of the vast concave, which formed the inside, were filled and surrounded with sixty or eighty rows of seats, of marble likewise, covered with cushions, and capable of seating with ease above fourscore thousand spectators. Sixty-four vomitories or doors poured forth the immense multitude. An ample canopy protected from the sun and rain. The air was continually refreshed by the playing of fountains, profusely impregnated with the grateful scent of aromatics. In the centre of the edifice the arena or stage was strewed with the finest sand, and successively assumed the most different forms. At one moment it seemed to rise out of the earth like the garden of the Hesperides, and was afterwards broken into the rocks and caverns of Thrace. The subterranean pipes conveyed an inexhaustible supply of water, and what had just before appeared a level plain, might be suddenly converted into a wide lake, covered with armed vessels, and replenished with the monsters of the deep."[2]

Beyond the temple of Vespasian the column of Phocas rises in the distance, with the temple of Antoninus and Faustina, and the temple of Peace.

[1] Prof. Spear, in *Bibliotheca Sacra*, July, 1854, pp. 559-561.

[2] *Antiquities of Rome.*

The Colosseum and the circus were the scenes of gladiatorial combats, which were witnessed not only by the populace, but by the most refined classes, and by the gentler sex. Bartlett says in his own happiest manner: "Few, we should think, can stand within this area, once slippery with human gore, and repeople the mouldering seats of the amphitheatre, tier above tier to the very sky, not only with the populace, but with all that was great and beautiful in ancient Rome; with the most refined patrician, and even with woman, gazing with one feeling of eager delight, not only on the skill, but on the very blood of their victims, without a shudder. But 'Time, the beautifier,' has thrown over the scene a solemn charm; feeding 'like dull fire upon a hoary brand,' on the stupendous ruin; in which now, worn with the rents and weather-stains of ages, the huge broken vaults and buttresses are all overgrown by a wild garland of ivy, and bird-haunted foliage—it has half obliterated the dark page of history, and withdraws the mind from its past purpose to its present beauty."[1]

Leaving the Capitol and the stupendous monuments of the power and greatness of ancient Rome, we request the reader to cast his eye again on the plan of the city, and accompany us north-west to where the Yellow Tiber takes a strong bend under the base of the Janiculum. The region on the opposite side, to which there was access by many bridges, was the abode of the Jews, the ancient "Ghetto." The feet of Paul must often have traversed these bridges. With this part of the city he must have grown familiar, as we may suppose him almost daily to have passed and repassed between his Gentile converts in the palace, and his Jewish countrymen on the other side of the river. Farther to the north still, is the Vatican and church of St. Peter's, where, in despite of Paul, Popery has established a power in many respects greater and more terrible than that whose representatives dwelt on Mount Palatine. In this quarter, by the river-side, stands the castle of St. Angelo, as it is now called, built by the Emperor Hadrian about A.D. 130 as his own mausoleum. Here were deposited his remains, as well as those of succeeding emperors, down to the time of Septimius Severus. It was early diverted from its original purpose and turned into a fortress, and was long a stronghold of the papal power. It is a massive circular tower 987 feet in circumference, standing on a square basement, each side of which is 247 feet long. It derives its present name from a bronze statue of the Archangel Michael on the summit. The splendid bridge of St Angelo was built by Hadrian as a means of communication with his mausoleum, and was originally called the Ælian Bridge, from one of the emperor's names.

Let us now turn for a moment to the closing scenes of our apostle's life. We have already seen him enter Rome a prisoner. A graphic and picturesque pen,[2] to which we have already professed our obligations, and to which we shall again be indebted for not a little of the information embodied in the subsequent portion of this article, has thus reproduced Paul's first walk amid the glories of Rome. "Entering within the city by the Porta Capena (*see the Plan*), Julius and his prisoners moved on with the Aventine on their left, close round the base of the Cœlian, and through the hollow ground which lay between this hill and the Palatine; thence over the low ridge called Velia, where afterwards was built the arch of Titus, and then descending by the *Sacra Via* into that space which was the centre of imperial power and magnificence—the Forum of Rome. All around were the stately buildings which were raised in the closing years of the republic, and by the earlier emperors. In front was the Capitoline Hill. Close on the left, covering that hill (the Palatine) whose name is associated in every modern European language with the notion of imperial splendour, were the vast ranges of the palace, the house of Cæsar. And here (unless indeed it was in the great Prætorian camp, outside the city wall), Julius gave up his prisoner to Burrus the Prætorian præfect." What were the thoughts of the apostle as he passed through the Forum of Rome, and found himself under the walls of the imperial palace, with the statues of Rome's illustrious citizens, and the temples of her gods around him? History is silent. But we may rest assured that, as amid the glories of Athens, his spirit was here also stirred within him when he saw the city wholly given to idolatry.

Our apostle is now, after a considerable interval, in the presence of Nero. The knowledge we have of the manner in which cases of appeal to the emperor were conducted in those times, enables us, with probable accuracy, to depict the scene. "Nero, after the example of Augustus, heard these causes in the imperial palace. Here, at one end of a splendid hall, lined with the precious marbles of Egypt and of Libya, we must imagine the Cæsar seated in the midst of his assessors. These counsellors, twenty in number, were men of the highest rank. Among them were the two consuls, and selected representatives of each of the other great magistracies of Rome. The remainder consisted of senators chosen by lot." Over

[1] *Footsteps of our Lord and his Apostles*, p. 235.

[2] Howson's

this bench of distinguished judges presided the blood-stained adulterer Nero, who already, at the early age of twenty-five, had murdered mother, and wife, and brother. Contrary, however, to what might have been expected at such a tribunal, Paul was on this occasion set at liberty, through what influence is unknown. Possibly the emperor disdained to intermeddle in questions which might appear to him in no way to affect the wellbeing of the state. In one short year from this period, as we shall immediately see, the Christian cause came to be viewed in a very different light. But in the meantime the fires of persecution had not been kindled, and the emperor had not yet that motive which subsequently impelled him to practise incredible cruelties on the unoffending Christians. On his liberation, Paul is supposed to have visited many of the scenes of his former labours in Asia and Greece, to have visited Spain, and probably Crete and Dalmatia. Arrested at Nicopolis in mid-winter of A.D. 68, he was hurried to Rome, and executed there in the summer of the same year.[1] The fact of a second imprisonment has, however, been much disputed. But the weight of evidence is in its favour, and it is now very generally admitted.[2] The testimony of the early church is decisive on the point.

On occasion of our apostle's second trial, the forms would be somewhat different from those observed on his first trial. It was now an ordinary criminal case, and not a case of appeal to the emperor, and would, therefore, according to the custom of the times, come on before the præfect of the city. The scene, in all likelihood, was in one of the great basilicas of the Forum. "From specimens which still exist, as well as from the descriptions of Vetruvius, we have an accurate knowledge of the character of those halls of justice. They were rectangular buildings, consisting of a central nave and two aisles, separated from the nave by rows of columns. At the end of the nave was the tribune, in the centre of which was placed the magistrate's curule chair of ivory, elevated on a platform called the tribunal. Here also sat the assessors of the præfect. On the sides were seats for distinguished persons; in front, the prisoner, accusers, and advocates. The public was admitted into the remainder of the nave and aisles; and, at any trial of importance, a vast multitude of spectators was usually present." In such a scene we may imagine Paul. Fearlessly he defended himself. No advocate or friend appeared for him. At his first answer no man stood by him. For a time he was remanded to prison.[3] He seems, however, to have had no hope of deliverance from the very first.[4] The great fire, which Nero himself was suspected to have kindled, and in which so large a part of Rome was consumed, had taken place in the interval, between Paul's first and second imprisonment (A.D. 64). The emperor blamed the Christians. The result was a fierce persecution. In these circumstances, so conspicuous a Christian as Paul, became a mark for the rage of the heathen. He understood the circumstances, and prepared himself at once to die. He was again dragged before the tribunal, and condemned. His beloved Timotheus was far away; and although, in obedience to the command of Paul, he may have hastened to Rome, it is doubtful if he arrived in time for the closing scene. His Roman citizenship secured for the apostle the privilege of decapitation. The scene of his execution was the Ostian Road (Via Ostiensis, *see the Plan*). "As he issued forth from the gate, his eyes must have rested for a moment on that sepulchral pyramid which stood beside the road, and still stands unshattered amid the wreck of so many centuries upon the same spot. The mausoleum of Caius Cestius rises conspicuously amongst humbler graves, and marks the site where Papal Rome suffers her Protestant sojourners to bury their dead. It is the only surviving monument of the martyrdom of Paul, a monument unconsciously erected by a pagan to the memory of a martyr." A small troop of soldiers conduct the prisoner—Paul the aged—through the busy crowd that thronged the road between the metropolis and its harbour. Arrived at the place of execution, the headsman's sword[5] terminated the earthly career of the apostle. His remains were laid by friends in the Catacombs,[6] which furnished to the Christian community in these times a refuge for the living, and a grave for the dead. Other accounts place the grave of the apostle on or near the spot where he died.[7] The noble concluding reflections of Mr. Barnes, in the last paragraph of his commentary on Acts, will fall in with the reader's state of mind, as he returns now in contemplative mood from the grave of him who was, perhaps, the best and greatest of mortals.

[1] The dates of Lardner and others are slightly different; the date of Paul's death being A.D. 66.

[2] See an able article in Kitto's *Bib. Cyclopedia*—Timothy, Epistles to; also Horne's *Introduction.*

[3] 2 Tim. iv. 17, 21.

[4] 2 Tim. iv. 6–8.

[5] So Clement, contemporary with Paul; Caius, the Roman presbyter, A.D. 200; and Jerome.

[6] Eusebius.

[7] Jerome.